LAROUSSE'S FRENCH-ENGLISH
ENGLISH-FRENCH DICTIONARY

Newly edited by the foremost authorities in the field of French-language reference books, this dictionary is concise and authentic. It is an indispensable guide, and the user will appreciate its value each day.

DICTIONNAIRE LAROUSSE
ANGLAIS-FRANÇAIS
FRANÇAIS-ANGLAIS

Rédigé tout récemment par les plus éminents spécialistes en matière de lexicologie française, il est à la fois concis et précis. C'est un guide indispensable, dont l'utilisateur mesurera chaque jour la valeur.

Dictionnaire

FRANÇAIS-ANGLAIS
ANGLAIS-FRANÇAIS

Larousse

Deux volumes en un seul

par

Marguerite-Marie Dubois
Docteur ès lettres, Professeur à la Sorbonne

Denis J. Keen
M. A. (Cantab.). Assistant à la Sorbonne,
Directeur de la Section de français
à l'Institut britannique des Universités
de Paris et de Londres

Barbara Shuey
M. A.
University of California

avec la collaboration de

Jean-Claude Corbeil
Professeur adjoint à l'Université de
Montréal, Membre du Conseil
international de la langue française

Lester G. Crocker
Dean of Humanities
Case Western Reserve
University (Cleveland)

Édition revue et augmentée

PUBLISHED BY POCKET BOOKS NEW YORK

Larousse's

FRENCH-ENGLISH
ENGLISH-FRENCH

Dictionary

Two volumes in one

by

MARGUERITE-MARIE DUBOIS

Docteur ès lettres, Professeur à la Sorbonne

DENIS J. KEEN

M. A. (Cantab). Assistant à la Sorbonne,
Directeur de la Section de français
à l'Institut britannique des Universités
de Paris et de Londres

BARBARA SHUEY

M. A.
University of California

with the assistance of

JEAN-CLAUDE CORBEIL

Professeur adjoint à l'Université de
Montréal, Membre du Conseil
international de la langue française

LESTER G. CROCKER

Dean of Humanities
Case Western Reserve
University (Cleveland)

Revised and enlarged

PUBLISHED BY POCKET BOOKS NEW YORK

POCKET BOOKS, a Simon & Schuster division of
GULF & WESTERN CORPORATION
1230 Avenue of the Americas, New York, N.Y. 10020

First edition copyright © 1955 by Librairie Larousse,
Paris, France; revised and enlarged edition copyright
© 1971 by Librairie Larousse, Paris, France

Published by arrangement with Librairie Larousse

ISBN: 0-671-83461-4

First Pocket Books printing (revised and enlarged edition)
May, 1971

39 38 37 36 35 34 33 32

Trademarks registered in the United States and other countries.

Printed in the U.S.A.

PREFACE

The present work is the first handy-sized French-English, English-French dictionary to treat the American language with the same importance as the English language. Intended for a wide public, this book aims at satisfying the requirements not only of tourists, but also of students, teachers, technicians, business people, manufacturers and even those who have just a general interest in matters of language.

More than 35,000 words, arranged in their alphabetical order, make possible a ready translation of the most varied ideas. Difficult turns of phrase are clearly explained and illustrated by examples. rules and idiomatic expressions; careful discrimination is made between Americanisms and Anglicisms; Canadianisms are pointed out; the latest neologisms and even present-day slang enrich the standard vocabulary; the usual abbreviations add to the accuracy of the text; and a perfectly clear type enables the root-word to be distinguished at a glance from the compound word or the colloquial phrase deriving from it.

Words of the same family have, for reasons of greater etymological accuracy, been grouped together in paragraphs; and to avoid possible misinterpretations, we have clarified the meaning or the implication of certain words by the use of explanatory terms placed between square brackets.

The spelling used throughout the work invariably follows American usage, brackets indicating where necessary the English forms. E.g.: hono(u)r; travel(l)ed, etc.

A summary of English and French grammar enables the reader to refer to irregular forms, marked by asterisks, without difficulty, and to use the fundamental rules indispensable for correct speaking or writing.

The phonetic pronunciation used is both simple to understand and scientifically accurate. The transcription adopted reproduces textually, by means of familiar letters, the symbols of the International Phonetic Alphabet. In the English-French section, we have given preference to the American pronunciation as recorded in the dictionary of J. S. Kenyon and Th. A. Knott; in the French-English section, we have followed the method of A. Barbeau and E. Rohde.

Finally, conversion tables for money, weights and measures will prove of real service to travelers spending some time in one or another of our countries.

PRÉFACE

Voici le premier dictionnaire bilingue français-anglais, anglais-français qui, dans un format réduit, donne à la langue américaine autant d'importance qu'à la langue anglaise. Destiné à un vaste public, ce livre s'adresse aussi bien aux touristes qu'aux étudiants et aux professeurs, aux techniciens, commerçants ou industriels comme aux simples curieux amateurs de linguistique.

Plus de 35 000 mots, présentés dans l'ordre alphabétique, permettent de traduire sans peine les idées les plus variées Des exemples, des règles, des expressions idiomatiques précisent les emplois difficiles : les américanismes et les anglicismes différenciés avec soin, les canadianismes, les néologismes les plus récents l'argot courant lui-même enrichissent le vocabulaire de base; les abréviations usuelles. aisément comprises dans les deux langues, ajoutent à la précision du texte ; enfin, une typographie parfaitement claire permet de distinguer au premier coup d'œil le mot souche du mot composé ou de l'expression familière qui en découlent.

Les mots de la même famille ont été groupés en paragraphes — une plus grande précision étymologique en résulte - et, pour éviter des confusions de sens, nous avons placé entre crochets quelques termes explicatifs qui précisent la signification ou la portée de certains vocables.

L'orthographe donnée dans le cours de l'ouvrage reproduit toujours l'usage américain, des parenthèses indiquant au besoin la graphie anglaise. Ex. : hono(u)r ; travel(l)ed, etc.

Un précis grammatical de l'anglais et du français permet de retrouver sans peine les formes irrégulières, signalées par un astérisque, et d'utiliser les notions indispensables pour parler ou écrire correctement.

La prononciation figurée est présentée selon un système clair et scientifiquement exact. Les notations adoptées reproduisent textuellement, au moyen de graphies commodes, les symboles de l'alphabet phonétique international. Dans la partie anglais-français, nous avons donné de préférence la prononciation américaine d'après le dictionnaire de J. S. Kenyon et Th. A. Knott; dans la partie français-anglais, nous avons suivi la méthode de A. Barbeau et E. Rohde.

Enfin, des tables de monnaies et de mesures rendront de réels services aux voyageurs et aux touristes qui séjournent dans l'un ou l'autre de nos pays.

ABBREVIATIONS

abbrev.	abbreviation	abréviation	jur.	jurisdiction	juridiction
adj.	adjective	adjectif	lit.	literature	littérature
adv.	adverb	adverbe	*m.*	masculine	masculin
agr.	agriculture	agriculture	math.	mathematics	mathématiques
Am.	American	américain	mech.	mechanics	mécanique
anat.	anatomy	anatomie	med.	medicine	médecine
arch.	architecture	architecture	metall.	metallurgy	métallurgie
art.	article	article	meteor	meteorology	météorologie
artill.	artillery	artillerie	mil.	military	militaire
astr.	astrology	astrologie	min.	mineralogy	minéralogie
aux.	auxiliary	auxiliaire	mus.	music	musique
aviat.	aviation	aviation	naut.	nautical	marine
bot.	botany	botanique	*pers.*	personal	personnel
Br.	British	anglais	pharm	pharmacy	pharmacie
©	Canadianism	canadianisme	phot.	photography	photographie
caval.	cavalry	cavalerie	phys.	physics	physique
chem.	chemistry	chimie	*pl.*	plural	pluriel
colloq.	colloquial	familier	poet.	poetry	poésie
comm.	commerce	commerce	pol.	politics	politique
comp.	comparative	comparatif	pop.	popular	populaire
conj.	conjunction	conjonction	*poss.*	possessive	possessif
constr.	construction	construction	*p. p.*	past participle	participe passé
culin.	culinary	culinaire			
def.	definite	défini	*pref.*	prefix	préfixe
defect.	defective	défectif	*prep.*	preposition	préposition
demonstr.	demonstrative	démonstratif	*pret.*	preterit	prétérit
eccles.	ecclesiastical	ecclésiastique	*pron.*	pronoun	pronom
econ.	economics	économie	*prop.*	proper	propre
educ.	educational	éducatif	*pr. p.*	present participle	participe présent
electr.	electricity	électricité			
ent.	entomology	entomologie	psych.	psychology	psychologie
f.	feminine	féminin	railw.	railway	chemin de fer
fam.	familiar	familier	*refl.*	reflexive	réfléchi
fig.	figuratively	figuré	*rel.*	relative	relatif
fin.	finances	finances	relig.	religion	religion
Fr. Can.	(French) Canadianism	canadianisme (français)	*s.*	substantive	substantif
			sup.	superlative	superlatif
geogr.	geography	géographie	surg.	surgery	chirurgie
geol.	geology	géologie	techn	technical	technique
geom.	geometry	géométrie	telegr	telegraphy	télégraphie
gramm.	grammar	grammaire	teleph	telephony	téléphonie
hist.	history	histoire	text.	textile	textile
hort.	horticulture	horticulture	theat.	theater	théâtre
hyg.	hygiene	hygiène	theol.	theology	théologie
impers.	impersonal	impersonnel	topogr.	topography	topographie
ind.	industry	industrie	typogr.	typography	typographie
indef.	indefinite	indéfini	univ.	university	université
interj.	interjection	interjection	*v.*	verb	verbe
interrog.	interrogation	interrogation	vet.	veterinary	vétérinaire
inv.	invariable	invariable	zool.	zoology	zoologie

* See grammatical part for irregular forms marked by asteriks.	* voir la partie grammaticale pour les formes irrégulières signalées par un astérisque.

PART ONE

FRENCH-ENGLISH

THE ESSENTIALS OF FRENCH GRAMMAR

SENTENCE-BUILDING

Interrogation.

When the subject is a pronoun, place it after the verb, and, in compound tenses, between the auxiliary and the verb. Ex. : *Do you speak?* PARLEZ-VOUS? *Did you speak?* AVEZ-VOUS PARLÉ?

With verbs ending in a vowel, put an euphonic t before a third person pronoun. Ex. : *Did he speak?* A-T-IL PARLÉ? *Does he speak?* PARLE-T-IL?

When the subject is a noun, add a pronoun. Ex. : *Does Paul speak?* PAUL PARLE-T-IL?

A handy way of putting questions is merely to place EST-CE QUE before the positive sentence. Ex. : *Does he write?* EST-CE QU'IL ÉCRIT?

Objective pronouns.

They are placed after the verb only in the imperative of reflexive verbs : *sit down*, ASSEYEZ-VOUS. They come before the verb even in compound tenses : *he had said it to me*, IL ME L'AVAIT DIT. The verb should be separated from its auxiliary only by an adverb, or by a pronoun subject in an interrogative sentence. Ex. : IL A BIEN FAIT; AVEZ-VOUS MANGÉ?

THE ARTICLE

Definite article.

The definite article is LE (m.), LA (f.), LES (m. f. pl.). Ex. : *the dog*, LE CHIEN; *the girl*, LA FILLE; *the cats*, LES CHATS. LE, LA are shortened to L' before a vowel or a mute *h*. Ex. : *the man*, L'HOMME; *the soul*, L'ÂME (but LE HÉROS).

Indefinite article.

The indefinite article is UN, UNE. Ex. : *a boy*, UN GARÇON; *a woman*, UNE FEMME.

The plural DES is generally translated by *some : some books*, DES LIVRES.

Partitive article.

The partitive article DU (m.), DE LA (f.) is used in sentences like : *take some bread*, PRENEZ DU PAIN; *to have a temperature*, AVOIR DE LA FIÈVRE.

THE NOUN

Plural.

- The plural is generally formed in *s*, as in English.
- Nouns in s, x and z do not change in the plural.
- Nouns in **au, eau** and **eu** (except BLEU) and some in **ou** (CHOU, BIJOU, GENOU, CAILLOU, HIBOU, JOUJOU, POU) form their plural in x. Ex. : CHOU *(cabbage)*, CHOUX; JEU *(game)*, JEUX.

- Nouns in **al** form generally their plural in **aux**. Ex. : CHEVAL, CHEVAUX. A few nouns form their plural in **als** : BAL, CAL, CARNAVAL, CHACAL, FESTIVAL, PAL, RÉCITAL, RÉGAL.

- A few nouns in **ail** form their plural in **aux** : BAIL, CORAIL, ÉMAIL, SOUPIRAIL, TRAVAIL, VITRAIL.

- AÏEUL, CIEL and ŒIL become AÏEUX, CIEUX, YEUX in the ordinary meaning.

Gender of nouns.

- There are no neuter nouns in French. Nearly all nouns ending in a mute *e* are feminine, except those in **isme**, **age** (but IMAGE, NAGE, RAGE are f.), and **iste** (the latter being often either m. or f.).

- Nearly all nouns ending in a consonant or a vowel other than a mute *e* are masculine, except nouns in **ion** and **té** (but ÉTÉ, PÂTÉ are m.).

Feminine.

- The feminine is generally formed by adding **e** to the masculine. Ex. : PARENT *(relative)*, PARENTE ; AMI *(friend)*, AMIE.

- Nouns in **er** form their feminine in **ère**. Ex. : LAITIER *(milkman)*, LAITIÈRE.

- Nouns in **en, on** form their feminine in **enne, onne**. Ex. : CHIEN, CHIENNE ; LION, LIONNE.

- Nouns in **eur** form their feminine in **euse**, except those in **teur**, which give **trice**. Ex. : DANSEUR, DANSEUSE ; ADMIRATEUR, ADMIRATRICE. (Exceptions : ACHETEUR, ACHETEUSE ; CHANTEUR, CHANTEUSE ; MENTEUR, MENTEUSE.)

- Nouns in **x** change *x* into **se**. Ex. : ÉPOUX, ÉPOUSE.

- A few words in **e** form their feminine in **esse**. Ex. : MAÎTRE, MAÎTRESSE ; ÂNE, ÂNESSE.

THE ADJECTIVE

Plural.

- The plural is generally formed by adding **s** to the masculine (m. pl.) or feminine form (f. pl.).

- The masculine of adjectives in **s** or **x** do not change in the plural.

- Adjectives in **al** form their plural in **aux** (m.), **ales** (f.). Ex. : PRINCIPAL, PRINCIPAUX (m. pl.), PRINCIPALES (f. pl.). But BANCAL, GLACIAL, NATAL, NAVAL form their plural in **als, ales**.

Feminine.

- The feminine is generally formed by adding **e** to the masculine form. Ex. : ÉLÉGANT, ÉLÉGANTE ; POLI, POLIE.

- Adjectives in **f** change *f* into **ve**. Ex. : VIF, VIVE. Those in **x** change *x* into **se**. Ex. : HEUREUX, HEUREUSE. (Exceptions : DOUX, DOUCE ; FAUX, FAUSSE ; ROUX, ROUSSE and VIEUX, VIEILLE.)

- Adjectives in **er** form their feminine in **ère**. Ex. : AMER, AMÈRE.

- Adjectives in **gu** form their feminine in **guë**, which is pronounced [gü]. Ex. : AIGU, AIGUË.

- Adjectives in **el, eil, en, et, on** double the final consonant before adding *e*. Ex. : BEL, BELLE; BON, BONNE; ANCIEN, ANCIENNE. (Exceptions : COMPLET, INCOMPLET, CONCRET, DÉSUET, DISCRET, INDISCRET, INQUIET, REPLET, SECRET, which change **et** in **ète**.)

- Some adjectives in **c** change *c* into **qu** (CADUC, CADUQUE; LAÏC, LAÏQUE; PUBLIC, PUBLIQUE; TURC, TURQUE) or **ch** (BLANC, BLANCHE; FRANC, FRANCHE). The feminine of GREC is GRECQUE.

- A few adjectives in **s** double *s* before adding *e* : BAS, GRAS, LAS, ÉPAIS, MÉTIS, GROS.

- BOULOT, PÂLOT, SOT, VIEILLOT double *t* (BOULOTTE, PÂLOTTE, etc.).

- Adjectives in **eur** form generally their feminine in **euse**, except those in **teur**, which give **trice**. Ex. : MOQUEUR, MOQUEUSE; PROTECTEUR, PROTECTRICE (but MENTEUR, MENTEUSE). A few adjectives in **eur** form their feminine in **eure** : ANTÉRIEUR, POSTÉRIEUR, ULTÉRIEUR, EXTÉRIEUR, INTÉRIEUR, MAJEUR, MINEUR, SUPÉRIEUR, INFÉRIEUR, MEILLEUR.

Comparative.

- *More* or the ending *er* of adjectives should be translated by PLUS; *less* by MOINS, and *than* by QUE. Ex. : *more sincere*, PLUS SINCÈRE; *stronger*, PLUS FORT; *less good than*, MOINS BON QUE, MOINS BONNE QUE.

- *As... as* should be translated by AUSSI... QUE; *as much... as* and *as many... as* by AUTANT... QUE; *not so... as* by PAS SI... QUE, *not so much (many)... as* by PAS TANT... QUE.

Superlative.

- *The most* or the ending *est* should be translated by LE PLUS. Ex. : *the poorest*, LE PLUS PAUVRE; *the most charming*, LE PLUS CHARMANT.

- *Most* is in French TRÈS. Ex. : *most happy*, TRÈS HEUREUX.

Comparative and superlative : irregular forms.

- *Better*, MEILLEUR; *the best*, LE MEILLEUR; *smaller*, MOINDRE; *the least*, LE MOINDRE; *worse*, PIRE; *the worst*, LE PIRE.

Cardinal numbers.

- UN, DEUX, TROIS, QUATRE, CINQ, SIX, SEPT, HUIT, NEUF, DIX, ONZE, DOUZE, TREIZE, QUATORZE, QUINZE, SEIZE, DIX-SEPT, DIX-HUIT, DIX-NEUF, VINGT, VINGT ET UN, VINGT-DEUX...; TRENTE; QUARANTE; CINQUANTE; SOIXANTE; SOIXANTE-DIX; QUATRE-VINGTS; QUATRE-VINGT-DIX; CENT, CENT UN, CENT DEUX...; DEUX CENTS; TROIS CENTS...; MILLE; UN MILLION; UN MILLIARD.

- **Vingt** and **cent** are invariable when immediately followed by another number. Ex. : QUATRE-VINGT-TROIS ANS; DEUX CENT DOUZE FRANCS (but MILLE QUATRE-VINGTS FRANCS, MILLE DEUX CENTS FRANCS).

- **Mille** is invariable (in dates, it is written MIL).

Ordinal numbers.

- PREMIER, DEUXIÈME, TROISIÈME, QUATRIÈME, CINQUIÈME, SIXIÈME, SEPTIÈME, HUITIÈME, NEUVIÈME, DIXIÈME, ONZIÈME, DOUZIÈME, TREIZIÈME, QUATORZIÈME, QUINZIÈME, SEIZIÈME, DIX-SEPTIÈME...; VINGTIÈME, VINGT ET UNIÈME, VINGT-DEUXIÈME...; TRENTIÈME; QUARANTIÈME...; CENTIÈME, CENT UNIÈME, CENT DEUXIÈME...; DEUX CENTIÈME...; MILLIÈME...; MILLIONIÈME...

Demonstrative adjectives.

- *This* and *that* are generally translated by CE, CET (m.), CETTE (f.), CES (pl.) [CE before a masc. noun beginning with a consonant or an aspirate *h*; CET before a masc. word beginning with a vowel or a mute *h*]. The opposition between *this* and *that* may be emphasized by adding -CI or -LÀ. Ex. : *this book,* CE LIVRE-CI ; *those men,* CES HOMMES-LÀ.

- *That of* should be translated by CELUI (f. CELLE, pl. CEUX, CELLES) DE, *he who, the one which, those* or *they who* by CELUI (CELLE, CEUX, CELLES) QUI.

Possessive adjectives.

My is in French MON (m.), MA (f.), MES (pl.) ; *your* (for *thy*) is TON, TA, TES ; *his, her, its* are SON, SA, SES (agreeing with the following noun) ; *our* is NOTRE (m. f.), NOS (pl.) ; *your* is VOTRE, VOS ; *their* is LEUR (m. f.), LEURS (pl.). Ex. : *his king,* SON ROI ; *his sister,* SA SŒUR, *his books,* SES LIVRES ; *her father,* SON PÈRE ; *her mother,* SA MÈRE.

THE PRONOUN

Personal pronouns (subject).

- JE, TU, IL, ELLE (f.) ; pl. NOUS, VOUS, ILS, ELLES (f.). Ex. : *you speak,* TU PARLES [VOUS PARLEZ] ; *she says,* ELLE DIT.

- The second person singular (TU, TE, TOI, TON, TA, TES, LE TIEN, etc.), indicating intimacy, is used between members of the same family, at school, between soldiers and close friends.

Personal pronouns (direct object).

ME, TE, LE, LA (f.) ; pl. NOUS, VOUS, LES. Ex. : *I see her,* JE LA VOIS; *I see him* (or *it*), JE LE VOIS (the same pr. is used for masculine and neuter in most cases).

Personal pronouns (indirect object; dative).

ME, TE, LUI (m. f.) ; pl. NOUS, VOUS, LEUR. Ex. : *he speaks to her,* IL LUI PARLE.

Personal pronouns (after a preposition).

MOI, TOI, LUI, ELLE (f.) ; pl. NOUS, VOUS, EUX. They are also used emphatically : *I think,* MOI, JE PENSE.

Reflexive pronouns.

- ME, TE, SE ; pl. NOUS, VOUS, SE. Ex. : *they flatter themselves,* ILS SE FLATTENT ; *he spoke to himself,* IL SE PARLAIT.

- The same pronoun is used to translate *each other* and *one another.* Ex. : *they flatter each other,* ILS SE FLATTENT.

Possessive pronouns.

LE MIEN (f. LA MIENNE, pl. LES MIENS, LES MIENNES) ; LE TIEN (f. LA TIENNE, pl. LES TIENS, LES TIENNES) ; LE SIEN (f. LA SIENNE, pl. LES SIENS, LES SIENNES) ; LE NÔTRE (f. LA NÔTRE, pl. LES NÔTRES) ; LE VÔTRE (f. LA VÔTRE, pl. LES VÔTRES) ; LE LEUR (f. LA LEUR, pl. LES LEURS). Ex. : *I have lost my watch, lend me yours,* J'AI PERDU MA MONTRE, PRÊTEZ-MOI LA VÔTRE.

Note. — *This book is mine, yours, his, hers...* CE LIVRE EST À MOI, À TOI (À VOUS), À LUI, À ELLE... See *Personal pronouns (after a preposition).*

Relative pronouns.

Who is translated by QUI, *whom* by QUE (QUI after a preposition), *whose* by DONT, *which* by QUI (subject) or QUE (object). Ex. : *the man who comes,* L'HOMME QUI VIENT; *the girl whom I see,* LA FILLE QUE JE VOIS; *the author whose book I read,* L'AUTEUR DONT JE LIS LE LIVRE; *the books which (that) I read,* LES LIVRES QUE JE LIS.

Note. — After a preposition, *which* should be translated by LEQUEL (m.), LAQUELLE (f.), LESQUELS (m. pl.), LESQUELLES (f. pl.); *of which* by DUQUEL, DE LAQUELLE, DESQUELS, DESQUELLES; *to which* by AUQUEL, À LAQUELLE, AUXQUELS, AUXQUELLES.

Interrogative pronouns.

Who, whom are translated by QUI; *what* by QUE (object). *What* when an adjective should be translated by QUEL, QUELLE, QUELS, QUELLES, when a subject by QU'EST-CE QUI. Ex. : *Who came?* QUI EST VENU? *What do you say?* QUE DIS-TU? *What time is it?* QUELLE HEURE EST-IL? *What happened?* QU'EST-CE QUI EST ARRIVÉ?

THE ADVERB

Adverbs of manner.

● Most French adverbs of manner are formed by adding *ment* to the **feminine** form of the corresponding adjective. Ex. : *happily,* HEUREUSEMENT.

● Adjectives in **ant** form their adverbs in **amment**, and those in **ent** in **emment**. Ex. : *abundantly,* ABONDAMMENT; *patiently,* PATIEMMENT.

Negative adverbs and pronouns.

● *Not* should be translated by NE... PAS, *never* by NE... JAMAIS, *nobody* by NE... PERSONNE, *nothing* by NE... RIEN, *nowhere* by NE... NULLE PART. Ex. : *I do not speak,* JE NE PARLE PAS; *he never comes,* IL NE VIENT JAMAIS.

● *Nobody,* when subject, should be translated by PERSONNE NE, and *nothing,* by RIEN NE. Ex. : *nobody laughs,* PERSONNE NE RIT; *nothing stirred,* RIEN N'A BOUGÉ.

THE VERB

Note. — French regular verbs are generally grouped in four classes or conjugations ending in **er, ir, oir** and **re.**

Compound tenses.

Compound tenses are conjugated with the auxiliary AVOIR and the **past participle,** except reflexive verbs and the most usual intransitive verbs (like ALLER, ARRIVER, DEVENIR, PARTIR, RESTER, RETOURNER, SORTIR, TOMBER, VENIR, etc.), which are conjugated with ÊTRE. Ex. : *he spoke,* IL A PARLÉ; *he came,* IL EST VENU.

The French past participle.

● It always agrees with the noun to which it is either an attribute or an adjective. Ex. : *the woman was punished,* LA FEMME FUT PUNIE; *the broken tables,* LES TABLES BRISÉES.

● It agrees with the object of a verb conjugated with AVOIR **only** when the object comes before it. Ex. : *he broke the plates,* IL A CASSÉ LES ASSIETTES; *the plates he broke,* LES ASSIETTES QU'IL A CASSÉES.

First conjugation — AIMER (to love)

INDICATIVE	SUBJUNCTIVE

Present | **Present**
- J'aime — Que j'aime
- Tu aimes — Que tu aimes
- Il aime — Qu'il aime
- Nous aimons — Que n. aimions
- Vous aimez — Que v. aimiez
- Ils aiment — Qu'ils aiment

Imperfect | **Imperfect**
- J'aimais — Que j'aimasse
- Tu aimais — Que tu aimasses
- Il aimait — Qu'il aimât
- Nous aimions — Que n. aimassions
- Vous aimiez — Que v. aimassiez
- Ils aimaient — Qu'ils aimassent

Past tense | **CONDITIONAL**
- J'aimai — J'aimerais
- Tu aimas — Tu aimerais
- Il aima — Il aimerait
- Nous aimâmes — Nous aimerions
- Vous aimâtes — Vous aimeriez
- Ils aimèrent — Ils aimeraient

Future | **IMPERATIVE**
- J'aimerai
- Tu aimeras — Aime   Aimons   Aimez
- Il aimera
- Nous aimerons — **PARTICIPLE**
- Vous aimerez — Present — Past
- Ils aimeront — Aimant — Aimé, ée, és, ées

Second conjugation — FINIR (to end)

INDICATIVE	SUBJUNCTIVE

Present | **Present**
- Je finis — Que je finisse
- Tu finis — Que tu finisses
- Il finit — Qu'il finisse
- Nous finissons — Que n. finissions
- Vous finissez — Que v. finissiez
- Ils finissent — Qu'ils finissent

Imperfect | **Imperfect**
- Je finissais — Que je finisse
- Tu finissais — Que tu finisses
- Il finissait — Qu'il finît
- Nous finissions — Que n. finissions
- Vous finissiez — Que v. finissiez
- Ils finissaient — Qu'ils finissent

Past tense | **CONDITIONAL**
- Je finis — Je finirais
- Tu finis — Tu finirais
- Il finit — Il finirait
- Nous finîmes — Nous finirions
- Vous finîtes — Vous finiriez
- Ils finirent — Ils finiraient

Future | **IMPERATIVE**
- Je finirai
- Tu finiras — Finis   Finissons   Finissez
- Il finira
- Nous finirons — **PARTICIPLE**
- Vous finirez — Present — Past
- Ils finiront — Finissant — Fini, ie, is, ies

Third conjugation   RECEVOIR (to receive)

INDICATIVE	SUBJUNCTIVE

Present

Je reçois	Que je reçoive
Tu reçois	Que tu reçoives
Il reçoit	Qu'il reçoive
Nous recevons	Que n. recevions
Vous recevez	Que v. receviez
Ils reçoivent	Qu'ils reçoivent

Imperfect

Je recevais	Que je reçusse
Tu recevais	Que tu reçusses
Il recevait	Qu'il reçût
Nous recevions	Que n. reçussions
Vous receviez	Que v. reçussiez
Ils recevaient	Qu'ils reçussent

Past tense

CONDITIONAL

Je reçus	Je recevrais
Tu reçus	Tu recevrais
Il reçut	Il recevrait
Nous reçûmes	Nous recevrions
Vous reçûtes	Vous recevriez
Ils reçurent	Ils recevraient

Future

IMPERATIVE

Je recevrai		
Tu recevras	Reçois Recevons Recevez	
Il recevra		
Nous recevrons	PARTICIPLE	
Vous recevrez	*Past* *Present*	
Ils recevront	Recevant Reçu, ue, us, ues	

Fourth conjugation   VENDRE (to sell)

INDICATIVE	SUBJUNCTIVE

Present

Je vends	Que je vende
Tu vends	Que tu vendes
Il vend	Qu'il vende
Nous vendons	Que n. vendions
Vous vendez	Que v. vendiez
Ils vendent	Qu'ils vendent

Imperfect

Je vendais	Que je vendisse
Tu vendais	Que tu vendisses
Il vendait	Qu'il vendît
Nous vendions	Que n. vendissions
Vous vendiez	Que v. vendissiez
Ils vendaient	Qu'ils vendissent

Past tense

CONDITIONAL

Je vendis	Je vendrais
Tu vendis	Tu vendrais
Il vendit	Il vendrait
Nous vendîmes	Nous vendrions
Vous vendîtes	Vous vendriez
Ils vendirent	Ils vendraient

Future

IMPERATIVE

Je vendrai		
Tu vendras	Vends Vendons Vendez	
Il vendra		
Nous vendrons	PARTICIPLE	
Vous vendrez	*Present* *Past*	
Ils vendront	Vendant Vendu, ue, us, ues	

FRENCH IRREGULAR VERBS[1]

FIRST CONJUGATION

Aller. *Pr. ind.* : vais, vas, va, vont. *Fut.* : irai, iras, etc. *Imper.* : va (vas-y). *Pr. subj.* : aille, ailles, aille, allions, alliez, aillent.

Envoyer, Renvoyer. *Fut.* : (r)enverrai, etc.

Verbs in **cer** take **ç** before **a** and **o**. Ex. : *percer*, je perçais, nous perçons.

Verbs in **ger** add **e** before endings in **a** and **o**. Ex. : *manger*, je mangeais, nous mangeons.

Verbs in **eler, eter** double the **l** or **t** before a mute **e**. Ex. · *appeler*, j'appelle ; *jeter*, je jette. (*Acheter, celer, ciseler, congeler, crocheter, déceler, dégeler, démanteler, écarteler, fureter, geler, haleter, marteler, modeler, peler, racheter, receler* only take **è**. Ex. : *geler*, gèle ; *acheter*, achète.)

Verbs having a mute **e** in the last syllable but one change **e** into **è** when the ending begins with a mute **e**. Ex. : *peser*, je pèse.

Verbs having an acute **é** in the last syllable but one change it for a grave **è** when the ending begins with a mute **e** (except in the future and cond.). Ex. : *protéger*, je protège.

Verbs in **yer** change **y** into **i** before a mute **e**. Ex. : *ployer*, je ploie.

Verbs in **ayer** keep the **y**.

SECOND CONJUGATION

Acquérir. *Pr. ind.* : acquiers, acquiers, acquiert, acquérons, acquérez, acquièrent. *Imp.* : acquérais, etc. *Past tense* : acquis, etc. *Fut.* : acquerrai, etc. *Pr. subj.* : acquière, acquières, acquière, acquérions, acquériez, acquièrent. *Pr. part.* : acquérant. *Past part.* : acquis.

Assaillir. *Pr. ind.* : assaille, etc. (1). *Pr. subj.* : assaille, etc. (1). *Pr. part.* : assaillant.

Bénir. *Past part.* : béni, ie ; bénit, bénite [consecrated].

Bouillir. *Pr. ind.* : bous, bous, bout, bouillons, bouillez, bouillent. *Imp.* : bouillais, etc. (1). *Pr. subj.* : bouille (1). *Pr. part.* : bouillant.

Conquérir. See *Acquérir.*

Courir. *Pr. ind.* : cours, cours, court, courons, courez, courent. *Imp.* : courais, etc. (1). *Past tense* : courus (3). *Fut.* : courrai, etc. *Pr. subj.* : coure, etc. (1). *Imp. subj.* : courusse (3). *Pr. part.* : courant.

Couvrir. See *Ouvrir.*

Cueillir. *Pr. ind.* : cueille, etc. (1). *Imp.* : cueillais, etc. (1). *Fut.* : cueilleral, etc. (1). *Pr. subj.* : cueille (1). *Pr. part.* : cueillant.

Découvrir. See *Ouvrir.*

Défaillir. See *Assaillir.*

Démentir. See *Mentir.*

Départir. See *Mentir.*

Desservir. See *Servir.*

Détenir, Devenir. See *Tenir.*

Dormir. *Pr. ind.* : dors, dors, dort, dormons, dormez, dorment. *Imp.* : dormais, etc. (1). *Pr. subj.* : dorme (1). *Pr. part.* : dormant.

Encourir. See *Courir.*

Endormir. See *Dormir.*

Enfuir (s'). See *Fuir.*

Faillir. *Pr. ind.* : faux, faux, faut, faillons, faillez, faillent. *Imp.* : faillais (1). *Pr. part.* : faillant.

Fleurir. *Has a form in the imperfect* florissais, etc., *and for pr. part.* : florissant, *in the meaning of* « prospering ».

Fuir. *Pr. ind.* : fuis, fuis, fuit, fuyons, fuyez, fuient. *Imp.* : fuyais, etc. (1). *Pr. subj.* : fuie, fuies, fuie, fuyions, fuyiez, fuient. *Pr. part.* : fuyant. *Past part.* : fui, fuie.

Gésir. *Used only in pr. ind.* : gis, gis, gît, gisons, gisez, gisent ; *imp.* : gisais, etc. (1); *pr. part.* : gisant.

Haïr. *Regular except in singular of present ind. and imper.* : je hais, tu hais, il hait ; hais, haïssons, haïssez.

Intervenir. See *Tenir.*

Maintenir. See *Tenir.*

Mentir. *Pr. ind.* : mens, mens, ment, mentons, mentez, mentent. *Imp.* : mentais (1). *Pr. subj.* : mente, etc.

Mourir. *Pr. ind.* : meurs, meurs, meurt, mourons, mourez, meurent. *Imp.* : mourais, etc. (1). *Past tense* : mourus, etc. (3). *Fut.* : mourrai, etc. *Pr. subj.* : meure, meures, meure, mourions, mouriez, meurent. *Pr. part.* : mourant. *Past part.* : mort, morte.

Obtenir. See *Tenir.*

Offrir. *Pr. ind.* : offre, etc. (1). *Imp.* : offrais, etc. (1). *Pr. part.* : offrant. *Past part.* : offert, offerte.

Ouvrir. *Pr. ind.* : ouvre, etc. (1). *Imp.* : ouvrais, etc. (1). *Pr. part.* : ouvrant. *Past part.* : ouvert, ouverte.

---

1. In this list numbers (1), (2), (3) indicate whether the foregoing tense should be conjugated like the corresponding tense of the first, second or third conjugation.

Parcourir. See *Courir.*
Partir. See *Mentir.*
Parvenir. See *Tenir.*
Recourir. See *Courir.*
Recueillir. See *Cueillir.*
Repentir. See *Mentir.*
Requérir. See *Acquérir.*
Ressentir. See *Sentir.*
Ressortir. See *Sortir.*
Ressortir à is conjugated like FINIR (3).
Retenir, Revenir. See *Tenir.*
Revêtir. See *Vêtir.*
Saillir (meaning « to gush »). *Pr. ind.* : saille, saillent. *Imp.* : saillait. *Fut.* : saillera. *Pr. subj.* : saille. *Pr. part.* : saillant. *Past part.* : sailli, ie.
Secourir. See *Courir.*
Sentir. See *Mentir.*

Servir. *Pr. ind.* : sers, sers, sert, servons, servez, servent. *Imp.* : servais, etc. (1). *Pr. subj.* : serve, etc. (1). *Pr. part.* : servant.
Sortir. See *Mentir.*
Souffrir. See *Offrir.*
Soutenir, Souvenir, Subvenir, Survenir. See *Tenir.*
Tenir. *Pr. ind.* : tiens, tiens, tient, tenons, tenez, tiennent. *Imp.* : tenais, etc. (1). *Past tense* : tins, tins, tint, tînmes, tîntes, tinrent. *Fut.* : tiendrai, etc. *Pr. subj.* : tienne. *Pr. part.* : tenant. *Past part.* : tenu, ue.
Tressaillir. See *Assaillir.*
Venir. See *Tenir.*
Vêtir. *Pr. ind.* : vêts, vêts, vêt, vêtons, vêtez, vêtent. *Imp.* : vêtais, etc. (1). *Pr. subj.* : vête, etc. (1). *Pr. part.* : vêtant. *Past part.* : vêtu, ue.

THIRD CONJUGATION

Asseoir. *Pr. ind.* : assieds, assieds, assied, asseyons, asseyez, asseyent. *Imp.* : asseyais, etc. *Past tense* : assis, etc. (2). *Fut.* : assiérai, etc. *or* asseyerai, etc. *Pr. subj.* : asseye, etc. *Pr. part.* : asseyant. *Past part.* : assis, assise.
Avoir. *Pr. ind.* : ai, as, a, avons, avez, ont. *Past tense* : eus, eus, eut, eûmes, eûtes, eurent. *Fut.* : aurai, etc. *Pr. subj.* : aie, aies, ait, ayons, ayez, aient. *Imp. subj.* : eusse, eusses, eût, eussions, eussiez, eussent. *Imper.* : aie, ayons, ayez. *Pr. part.* : ayant. *Past part.* : eu, eue.
Choir. *Past part.* : chu, chue.
Déchoir. *Pr. ind.* : déchois, déchois, déchoit, déchoyons, déchoyez, déchoient. *Imp.* : déchoyais, etc. *Fut.* : décherrai, etc. *Pr. subj.* : déchoie, déchoies, déchoie, déchoyions, déchoyiez, déchoient. *Pr. part.* : none. *Past part.* : déchu, ue.
Devoir. *Pr. ind.* : dois, dois, doit, devons, devez, doivent. *Imp.* : devais, etc. *Past tense* : dus, etc. *Fut.* : devrai, etc. *Pr. subj.* : doive, etc. *Pr. part.* : devant. *Past part.* : dû, due.
Echoir. *Pr. ind.* : échoit. *Imp.* : échéait. *Past tense* : échus, etc. *Fut.* : écherrai, etc. *Pr. part.* : échéant. *Past part.* : échu, ue.
Emouvoir. See *Mouvoir.*
Entrevoir. See *Voir.*
Falloir. *Pr. ind.* : il faut. *Imp.* : il fallait. *Past tense* : il fallut. *Fut.* : il faudra. *Pr. subj.* : il faille. *Past part.* : fallu.
Mouvoir. *Pr. ind.* : meus, meus, meut, mouvons, mouvez, meuvent. *Imp.* : mouvais. *Past tense* : mus, etc. *Fut.* : mouvrai, etc. *Pr. subj.* : meuve, etc. *Pr. part.* : mouvant. *Past part.* : mû, ue.
Pleuvoir. *Pr. ind.* : pleut, pleuvent. *Imp.* : pleuvait. *Past tense* : plut.

Fut. : pleuvra. *Pr. subj.* : pleuve. *Pr. part.* : pleuvant. *Past part.* : plu.
Pourvoir. *Like* VOIR, *except in the past tense* : pourvus, etc. *Fut.* : pourvoirai.
Pouvoir. *Pr. ind.* : puis *or* peux, peux, peut, pouvons, pouvez, peuvent. *Past tense* : pus, etc. *Fut.* : pourrai, etc. *Pr. subj.* : puisse, puisses, puisse. *Pr. part.* : pouvant. *Past part.* : pu.
Prévaloir. *Like* VALOIR, *except in pr. subj.* : prévale, etc.
Prévoir. See *Voir.*
Promouvoir. *Like* MOUVOIR, *but used only in compound tenses.*
Revoir. See *Voir.*
Savoir. *Pr. ind.* : sais, sais, sait, savons, savez, savent. *Past tense* : sus, etc. *Fut.* : saurai, etc. *Imper.* : sache, sachons, sachez. *Pr. subj.* : sache. *Pr. part.* : sachant. *Past part.* : su, sue.
Seoir. *Pr. ind.* : sieds, sieds, sied, seyons, seyez, siéent. *Imp.* : seyait, seyaient. *Fut.* : siéra, siéront. *Pr. subj.* : siée, siéent. *Pr. part.* : séant.
Surseoir. See *Asseoir.*
Valoir. *Pr. ind.* : vaux, vaux, vaut, valons, valez, valent. *Imp.* : valais, etc. *Past tense* : valus, etc. *Fut.* : vaudrai, etc. *Pr. subj.* : vaille. *Part.* : valant (pr.), valu, ue (past).
Voir. *Pr. ind.* : vois, vois, voit, voyons, voyez, voient. *Imp.* : voyais, etc. *Past tense* : vis, etc. (2). *Fut.* : verrai, etc. *Pr. subj.* : voie, voies, voie, voyions, voyiez, voient. *Pr. part.* : voyant. *Past part* : vu, vue.
Vouloir. *Pr. ind.* : veux, veux, veut, voulons, voulez, veulent. *Imp.* : voulais, etc. *Past tense* : voulus, etc. *Fut.* : voudrai, etc. *Imper.* : veux *or* veuille, veuillons, veuillez. *Pr. subj.* : veuille, etc. *Pr. part.* : voulant. *Past part.* : voulu, ue.

FOURTH CONJUGATION

Absoudre. *Pr. ind. :* absous, absous, absout, absolvons, absolvez, absolvent. *Imp. :* absolvais, etc. *Fut. :* absoudrai, etc. *Pr. subj. :* absolve, etc. *Pr. part. :* absolvant. *Past part. :* absous, absoute.

Atteindre. See *Peindre.*

Battre. *Pr. ind. :* bats, bats, bat, battons, battez, battent. *The other tenses like* VENDRE (4).

Boire. *Pr. ind. :* bois, bois, boit, buvons, buvez, boivent. *Imp. :* buvais, etc. *Past tense :* bus, bus, but, bûmes, bûtes, burent. *Fut. :* boirai, etc. *Pr. subj. :* boive, boives, boive, buvions, buviez, boivent. *Imp. subj. :* busse, etc. (3). *Pr. part. :* buvant. *Past part. :* bu, bue.

Braire. *Pr. ind. :* brait. *Imp. :* brayait. *Cond. :* brairait.

Ceindre. See *Peindre.*

Circonscrire. See *Ecrire.*

Clore. *Pr. ind. :* clos, clos, clôt. *Pr. subj. :* close. *Past part. :* clos, close.

Combattre. See *Battre.*

Commettre. See *Mettre.*

Comparaître. See *Paraître.*

Complaire. See *Plaire.*

Comprendre. See *Prendre.*

Conclure. *Pr. ind. :* conclus, conclus, conclut, concluons, concluez, concluent. *Imp. :* concluais. *Past tense :* conclus, etc. (3). *Pr. subj. :* conclue, conclues, conclue, concluions, concluiez, concluent. *Imp. subj. :* conclusse, etc. *Pr. part. :* concluant. *Past part. :* conclu, ue.

Conduire. See *Déduire.*

Confire. See *Interdire.*

Connaître. See *Paraître.*

Construire. See *Déduire.*

Contraindre. See *Craindre.*

Contredire. *Pr. ind. :* contredis, contredisez, contredisent. *The other tenses like* DIRE.

Convaincre. See *Vaincre.*

Coudre. *Pr. ind. :* couds, couds, coud, cousons, cousez, cousent. *Imp. :* cousais, etc. *Past tense :* cousis, etc. *Pr. subj. :* couse, etc. *Pr. part. :* cousant. *Past part. :* cousu, ue.

Craindre. *Pr. ind. :* crains, crains, craint, craignons, craignez, craignent. *Imp. :* craignais, etc. *Past tense :* craignis, etc. *Pr. subj. :* craigne, etc. *Pr. part. :* craignant. *Past part. :* craint, crainte.

Croire. *Pr. ind. :* crois, crois, croit, croyons, croyez, croient. *Imp. :* croyais, etc. *Fut. :* croirai, etc. *Past tense :* crus, crus, crut, crûmes, crûtes, crurent. *Pr. subj. :* croie, croies, croie, croyions, croyiez, croient. *Imp. subj. :* crusse, etc. *Pr. part. :* croyant. *Past part. :* cru, crue.

Croître. *Pr. ind. :* croîs, croîs, croît, croissons, croissez, croissent. *Imp. :* croissais, etc. *Past tense :* crûs, crûs, crût, crûmes, crûtes, crûrent. *Pr. subj. :* croisse, etc. *Imp. subj. :* crûsse, etc. *Pr. part. :* croissant. *Past part. :* crû, crue.

Débattre. See *Battre.*

Décrire. See *Ecrire.*

Décroître. See *Croître.*

Déduire. *Pr. ind. :* déduis, déduis, déduit, déduisons, déduisez, déduisent. *Imp. :* déduisais, etc. *Past tense :* déduisis, etc. *Fut. :* déduirai, etc. *Pr. subj. :* déduise, etc. *Pr. part. :* déduisant. *Past part. :* déduit, déduite.

Défaire. See *Faire.*

Démettre. See *Mettre.*

Dépeindre. See *Peindre.*

Déplaire. See *Plaire.*

Déteindre. See *Peindre.*

Détruire. See *Déduire.*

Dire. *Pr. ind. :* dis, dis, dit, disons, dites, disent. *Imp. :* disais, etc. *Past tense :* dis, dis, dit, dîmes, dîtes, dirent. *Fut. :* dirai, etc. *Pr. subj. :* dise, etc. *Pr. part. :* disant. *Past part. :* dit, dite.

Disparaître. See *Paraître.*

Dissoudre. See *Absoudre.*

Ecrire. *Pr. ind. :* écris, écris, écrit, écrivons, écrivez, écrivent. *Imp. :* écrivais, etc. *Past tense :* écrivis, etc. *Fut. :* écrirai, etc. *Pr. subj. :* écrive, etc. *Pr. part. :* écrivant. *Past part. :* écrit, écrite.

Elire. See *Lire.*

Enclore. See *Clore.*

Enduire. See *Déduire.*

Enfreindre. See *Peindre.*

Entreprendre. See *Prendre.*

Eteindre. See *Peindre.*

Etre. *Pr. ind. :* suis, es, est, sommes, êtes, sont. *Imp. :* étais, etc. *Past tense :* fus, fus, fut, fûmes, fûtes, furent. *Fut. :* serai, seras, etc. *Imper. :* sois, soyons, soyez. *Pr. subj. :* sois, sois, soit, soyons, soyez, soient. *Pr. part. :* étant. *Past part. :* été.

Etreindre. See *Peindre.*

Exclure. See *Conclure.*

Faire. *Pr. ind. :* fais, fais, fait, faisons, faites, font. *Imp. :* faisais, etc. *Past tense :* fis, fit, etc. *Fut. :* ferai, etc. *Pr. subj. :* fasse, etc. *Pr. part. :* faisant. *Past part. :* fait, faite.

Feindre. See *Peindre.*

Frire. *Pr. ind.* : fris, fris, frit. *Fut.* : frirai. *Past part.* : frit, frite. *No other tenses.*

Inclure. See *Conclure.*

Induire. See *Déduire.*

Instruire. See *Déduire.*

Interdire. Like DIRE. 2ⁿᵈ *pers. pl. pr. ind. and imper.* : interdisez.

Joindre. *Pr. ind.* : joins, joins, joint, joignons, joignez, joignent. *Imp.* : joignais, etc. *Fut.* : joindrai, etc. *Past tense* : joignis, etc. *Pr. subj.* : joigne, etc. *Pr. part.* : joignant. *Past part.* : joint, jointe.

Lire. *Pr. ind.* : lis, lis, lit, lisons, lisez, lisent. *Imp.* : lisais, etc. *Past tense* : lus, etc. *Fut.* : lirai, etc. *Pr. subj.* : lise, etc. *Pr. part.* : lisant. *Past part.* : lu, lue.

Luire. See *Déduire.*

Maudire. *Pr. ind.* : maudis, etc. (2). The other tenses like DIRE.

Médire. See *Interdire.*

Mettre. *Pr. ind.* : mets, mets, met, mettons, mettez, mettent. *Imp.* : mettais, etc. *Past tense* : mis, etc. *Pr. subj.* : mette, etc. *Past part.* : mis, mise.

Moudre. *Pr. ind.* : mouds, mouds, moud, moulons, moulez, moulent. *Imp.* : moulais, etc. *Past tense* : moulus, etc. (3). *Pr. subj.* : moule, etc. *Pr. part.* : moulant. *Past part.* : moulu, ue.

Naître. *Pr. ind.* : nais, nais, naît, naissons, naissez, naissent. *Imp.* : naissais, etc. *Past tense* : naquis, etc. *Pr. subj.* : naisse, naisses, naisse. *Pr. part.* : naissant. *Past part.* : né, née.

Nuire. Like DÉDUIRE (except past part. : nui).

Oindre. See *Joindre.*

Omettre. See *Mettre.*

Paître. Like PARAÎTRE. *No past tense.*

Paraître. *Pr. ind.* : parais, parais, paraît, paraissons, paraissez, paraissent. *Imp.* : paraissais, etc. *Past tense* : parus, etc. *Pr. subj.* : paraisse, etc. *Pr. part.* : paraissant. *Past part.* : paru, ue.

Peindre. *Pr. ind.* : peins, peins, peint, peignons, peignez, peignent. *Imp.* : peignais, etc. *Past tense* : peignis. *Pr. subj.* : peigne, etc. *Pr. part.* : peignant. *Past part.* : peint, peinte.

Permettre. See *Mettre.*

Plaindre. See *Craindre.*

Plaire. *Pr. ind.* : plais, plais, plaît, plaisons, plaisez, plaisent. *Imp.* : plaisais, etc. *Past tense* : plus, etc. *Pr. subj.* : plaise, etc. *Pr. part.* : plaisant. *Past part.* : plu, plue.

Poindre. See *Joindre.*

Poursuivre. See *Suivre.*

Prédire. See *Contredire.*

Prendre. *Pr. ind.* : prends, prends, prend, prenons, prenez, prennent. *Imp.* : prenais, etc. *Past tense* : pris, etc. *Pr. subj.* : prenne, etc. *Pr. part.* : prenant. *Past part.* : pris, prise.

Produire. See *Déduire.*

Reconduire. See *Déduire.*

Reconnaître. See *Paraître.*

Reconstruire. See *Déduire.*

Redire. See *Dire.*

Réduire. See *Déduire.*

Rejoindre. See *Joindre.*

Reluire. See *Déduire.*

Remettre. See *Mettre.*

Repaître. See *Paraître.*

Reprendre. See *Prendre.*

Reproduire. See *Déduire.*

Résoudre. Like ABSOUDRE. *Past tense* : résolus, etc. (3).

Restreindre. See *Peindre.*

Rire. *Pr. ind.* : ris, etc. (2). *Imp.* : riais, riais, riait, riions, riiez, riaient. *Past tense* : ris, etc. *Fut.* : rirai, etc. *Pr. subj.* : rie, etc. *Pr. part.* : riant. *Past part.* : ri.

Rompre. *Pr. ind.* : il rompt. The other tenses like VENDRE (4).

Séduire. See *Déduire.*

Soumettre. See *Mettre.*

Sourire. See *Rire.*

Souscrire. See *Ecrire.*

Soustraire. See *Traire.*

Suffire. See *Déduire.*

Suivre. *Pr. ind.* : suis, suis, suit, suivons, suivez, suivent. *Imp.* : suivais, etc. *Past tense* : suivis, etc. *Pr. subj.* : suive, etc. *Pr. part.* : suivant. *Past part.* : suivi, ie.

Surfaire. See *Faire.*

Surprendre. See *Prendre.*

Survivre. See *Vivre.*

Taire. See *Plaire.*

Teindre. See *Peindre.*

Traduire. See *Déduire.*

Traire. *Pr. ind.* : trais, trais, trait, trayons, trayez, traient. *Imp.* : trayais, etc. *No past tense.* *Pr. subj.* : traie, etc. *Pr. part.* : trayant. *Past part.* : trait, traite.

Transcrire. See *Ecrire.*

Transmettre. See *Mettre.*

Transparaître. See *Paraître.*

Vaincre. *Pr. ind.* : vaincs, vaincs, vainc, vainquons, vainquez, vainquent. *Imp.* : vainquais, etc. *Past tense* : vainquis, etc. *Pr. subj.* : vainque. *Pr. part.* : vainquant. *Past part.* : vaincu, ue.

Vivre. *Pr. ind.* : vis, vis, vit, vivons, vivez, vivent. *Past tense* : vécus, etc. (3). *Pr. subj.* : vive. *Pr. part.* : vivant. *Past part.* : vécu, ue.

FRENCH CURRENCY, WEIGHTS AND MEASURES

CURRENCY

(when the rate of exchange is £ 1 : 13.00 F and 1 $: 5.50 F)

1 centime	1/4 penny.	1/5 cent.
1 franc (100 centimes).	1 shilling and 6 pence.	18 cents.

Coins : 1 centime, 2 centimes, 5 centimes, 10 centimes, 20 centimes, 1 F, 5 F, 10 F.

Banknotes : 5 F, 10 F, 50 F, 100 F, 500 F.

METRIC WEIGHTS

Milligramme	1 thousandth of a gram.	0.015 grain.
Centigramme	1 hundredth of a gram.	0.154 grain.
Décigramme	1 tenth of a gram.	1.543 grain.
Gramme	1 cub. centim. of pure water.	15.432 grains.
Décagramme	10 grams.	6.43 pennyweights.
Hectogramme	100 grams.	3.527 oz. avoir.
Kilogramme	1 000 grams.	2.204 pounds.
Quintal métrique ..	100 kilograms.	220.46 pounds.
Tonne	1 000 kilograms.	19 cwts 2 grs 23 lbs.

METRIC LINEAL MEASURES

Millimètre	1 thousandth of a meter.	0.039 inch.
Centimètre	1 hundredth of a meter.	0.393 inch.
Décimètre	1 tenth of a meter.	3.937 inch.
Mètre		1.0936 yard.
Décamètre	10 meters.	32.7 ft., 10.9 yards.
Hectomètre	100 meters.	109.3 yards.
Kilomètre	1 000 meters.	1,093 yards.

METRIC SQUARE AND CUBIC MEASURES

Centiare	1 square meter.	1.196 square yard.
Are	100 square meters.	about 4 poles.
Hectare	100 ares.	about 2 1/2 acres.
Stère	1 cubic meter.	35 cubic feet.
Décastère	10 cubic meters.	13.1 cubic yards.

METRIC FLUID AND CORN MEASURES

Centilitre	1 hundredth of a liter.	0.017 pint.
Décilitre	1 tenth of a liter.	0.176 pint.
Litre		1.76 pint.
Décalitre	10 liters.	2.2 gallons.
Hectolitre	100 liters.	22.01 gallons.

THERMOMETER

0° Celsius *of* Réaumur = 32° Fahrenheit. — 100° Celsius = 212° Fahrenheit = 80° Réaumur.

To convert Fahrenheit degrees into Celsius, deduct 32, multiply by 5 and divide by 9.

Pour convertir les degrés Celsius en degrés Fahrenheit, multiplier par 9, diviser par 5 et ajouter 32.

THE FRENCH SOUNDS
EXPLAINED TO ENGLISH-SPEAKING PEOPLE

SIGN	FRENCH TYPE	NEAREST ENGLISH SOUND	EXPLANATION
î	bise	bees	Shorter than English *ee*.
ì	vif	beef	Same sound but shorter.
é	clé	clay	The French sound is closer and without the final *i*.
è	bec	beck	French sound more open.
•	re(gain)	a(gain)	*a* as short as possible. Cf. the *a* in *abed* and *China*.
ë	eux	ear(th)	French sound closer, with the lips well rounded.
œ	œuf	up	The *u* sound of *up*, but closer.
à	bague	bag	Between *bag* and *bug*.
â	pâme	palm	
ò	bosse	boss	The French sound is closer.
ô	seau	so	Without the final *u* of *so*.
au	lau(re)	law	
û	poule	pool	
ü	du		There is no such sound in English : round your lips as if to whistle and try to pronounce the *e* sound of *he* (German *ü*).
aⁿ iⁿ oⁿ uⁿ			These four nasal sounds are best described as the sounds of *â*, *é*, *ò*, *œ*, uttered while keeping the passage between throat and nose closely shut, but it has been thought advisable to note them with their usual French spelling (a smaller ⁿ being used to emphasize the nasal sound).
t, d			In French are placed next to the teeth.
l			French *l* is much lighter and clearer than in English, especially when final.
r			Though usually uvular in French, is quite correctly pronounced as a slightly rolled English *r*.
ñ			Is spelt *gn* in French. It is found in the *ni* of *lenient*.
y			Like *y* in *yes*, even at the end of a word (*fille* : fìy).
j			Is never *dj* but always like *ge* in *rouge*.
g, g			Is never *dj*. Before *a*, *o*, *u*, French *g* has the English sound; before *e*, *i*, *y*, it has the value of French *j*. In figurative pronunciation *g* (before *e*, *i*) has the value of *g* in *give*.
h, '			Is never sounded in French. When it is said to be « aspiré » (in which case we print a (') before the word), it merely means that no *liaison* should be made.

Stress. — It falls on the last sounded syllable (printed in italics).

Liaison. — In most cases, when a word begins with a vowel (or a mute *h*), it is joined with the last consonant of the preceding word, even when the consonant is followed by a mute *e*. Ex. : *sept heures* (sètœr), *cette âme* (sètâm). In such cases, final *c* and *g* are pronounced as *k* [*avec elle* (avèkèl)]; final *s* and *x* as *z* : [*six années* (sìzàné)]; final *d* as *t* [*grand homme* (graⁿtòm)].

The *liaison* only occurs when the two words are intimately connected and pronounced in one breath.

FRANÇAIS-ANGLAIS

A

a [à], *see* **avoir.**

à [à] *prep.* at, in; to; from; of; on; for; by; with; *à la française,* French style; *tasse à thé.* teacup; *machine à coudre* sewing-machine; *à la barbe grise,* grey-bearded; *au, aux = à + le, les*

abaissement [àbèsmaⁿ] *m.* dip, drop, fall; humiliation; subsidence. ‖ *abaisser* [-é] *v.* to lower, to drop; to reduce, to bring down; to humble; *s'abaisser,* to subside; to sink; to humble oneself; to stoop.

abandon [àbaⁿdoⁿ] *m.* surrender; waiver, abandonment; neglect; unreserve. ‖ *abandonner* [-òné] *v.* to give up, to forsake, to abandon; *s'abandonner à,* to give oneself up to, to indulge in, to give way to.

abasourdir [àbàzûrdîr] *v.* to dumbfound, to amaze. ‖ *abasourdissement* [-îsmaⁿ] *m* stupefaction.

abâtardir [àbâtàrdîr] *v.* to debase; to mar, *s'abâtardir,* to degenerate.

abat-jour [àbàjûr] *m.* lamp-shade; eye-shade, sun-blind.

abats [àbà] *m. pl.* offal; giblets.

abattage [àbàtaj] *m.* felling [arbres]; slaughtering [animaux].

abattis [àbàtî] *m.* felling [arbres]; slaughter [gibier]; *pl.* giblets. ‖ *abattoir* [-wàr] *m.* slaughter-house. ‖ *abattre* [àbàtr] *v* to pull down; to fell; to demolish; to dishearten; to kill; to slaughter, *s'abattre,* to fall down; to subside, to crash. ‖ *abattu* [-ü] *adj* felled; prostrate; dejected; dispirited downcast; *p. p. of abattre.*

abbaye [àbéí] *f.* abbey. ‖ *abbé* [-é] *m.* abbot, priest; curate. ‖ *abbesse* [-ès] *f.* abbess.

A. B. C. [âbésé] *m.* rudiments.

abcès [àbsè] *m.* abscess.

abdication [àbdìkàsyoⁿ] *f.* abdication. ‖ *abdiquer* [àbdìké] *v.* to abdicate.

abdomen [àbdòmèn] *m.* abdomen.

abeille [àbèy] *f.* bee.

aberrant [àbèraⁿ] *adj.* aberrant; deviating. ‖ *aberration* [àbèr(r)àsyoⁿ] *f.* aberration, error.

abêtir [àbètîr] *v.* to dull; to make stupid, to besot.

abhorrer [àbòré] *v.* to abhor.

abîme [àbîm] *m.* abyss. ‖ *abîmer* [-îmé] *v.* to spoil, to damage; *s'abi-*

mer, to sink; to be submerged, plunged in [pensée chagrin]; to get spoiled.

abject [àbjèkt] *adj* abject, base. ‖ *abjection* [àbjèksyoⁿ] *f.* abjection, abjectnes abasement

abjurer [àbjüré] *v.* to abjure; to forswear to renounce; to recant.

ablation [àblàsyoⁿ] *f.* ablation; removal excision

abnégation [abnégàsyoⁿ] *f.* abnegation; self-sacrifice

aboi [àbwà], **aboiement** [-maⁿ] *m.* bark(ing), *aux abois,* at bay; with one's back to the wall

abolir [àbòlîr] - to abolish, to suppress. *abolition* [àbòlìsyoⁿ] *f.* abolition. *abolitionnisme* [-syònìsm] *m.* abolitionism *abolitionniste* [-nìst] *m.* abolitionist. free-trader

abominable [àbòmìnàbl] *adj.* abominable horrible [temps]. ‖ *abomination* [-nàsyoⁿ] *f.* abomination; detestation; filthy stuff

abondamment [aboⁿdàmaⁿ] *adv.* abundantly plentifully. ‖ *abondance* [-aⁿs] *f* abundance plenty; copiousness. ‖ *abondant* [-aⁿ] *adj.* abundant; plentiful copious ‖ *abonder* [-é] *v.* to abound. to be plentiful; to teem.

abonné [àbòné] *m* subscriber; consumer commuter [train]. ‖ *abonnement* [-maⁿ] *m.* subscription; *carte d'abonnement Br* season-ticket, *Am.* commutation ticket, commute-book. ‖ *abonner* [-é] ‸ to take out a subscription (à, to), *s'abonner,* to subscribe; to contract; to commute.

abord [àbòr] *m.* approach; access; *pl.* approaches, surroundings, outskirts; *d'un abord facile,* easy to approach; *d'abord,* at first; *tout d'abord,* first of all. ‖ *abordable* [-dàbl] *adj.* accessible. ‖ *abordage* [-dàj] *m* collision, boarding (naut.); coming alongside [quai]. ‖ *aborder* [-dé] ‸ to land, to approach; to board (naut.); to attack; to engage; to embark upon.

aborigène [àbòrìjèn] *m.* native.

aboucher [àbûshé] *v.* to join together; to connect (techn.); *s'aboucher,* to parley.

about [àbû] *m.* butt-end (techn.). *abouter* [àbûté] *v.* to join end to end; to butt, to bend.

aboutir [àbûtîr] *v.* to lead, to come (à, to); to end at; to result in; to succeed; *ne pas aboutir*, to fail. ‖ **aboutissement** [-ìsmaⁿ] *m.* issue, outcome; result; effect; upshot; materialization [projets].

aboyer [àbwàyé] *v.* to bark; to bay. ‖ **aboyeur** [àbwàyœr] *m.* barker; dun; carper; tout.

abracadabrant [àbràkàdàbraⁿ] *adj.* staggering, astounding, amazing.

abrégé [àbréjé] *m.* summary; abridgment; digest. ‖ **abréger** [-é] *v.* to abridge; to shorten; to cut short.

abreuver [àbrœvé] *v.* to water [bétail]; to prime [pompe]; to soak; to steep; **s'abreuver** *v.* to drink. ‖ **abreuvoir** [-wàr] *m.* watering place; watering-trough.

abréviation [àbrévyàsyoⁿ] *f.* abbreviation; contraction; curtailment.

abri [àbrî] *m.* shelter; cover; refuge; dugout; *à l'abri*, sheltered, protected, under cover; *à l'abri du besoin*, secure from want; *abri blindé*, bombproof shelter.

abricot [àbrìkô] *m.* apricot. ‖ **abricotier** [-tyé] *m.* apricot-tree.

abriter [àbrìté] *v.* to shelter; to protect; to shield; to hide; to shadow; **s'abriter**, to take shelter; to take cover.

abroger [àbròjé] *v.* to rescind; to abrogate; to repeal.

abrupt [àbrüpt] *adj.* steep; abrupt; blunt [parole].

abruti [àbrütî] *m.* dolt, dullard; sot; clod; boor.

abrutir [àbrütîr] *v.* to brutalize; to daze; to stupefy; to besot.

abscisse [àbsîs] *f.* abscissa; co-ordinate.

absence [àbsaⁿs] *f.* absence; *absence d'esprit*, absent-mindedness, abstraction. ‖ **absent** [àbsaⁿ] *adj.* absent, missing, away; *m.* absentee. ‖ **s'absenter** [sàbsaⁿté] *v.* to leave; to be absent; to be away.

abside [àbsîd] *f.* apse.

absinthe [àbsîⁿt] *f.* wormwood (bot.); absinth [boisson].

absolu [àbsòlü] *adj.* absolute, complete, total; peremptory; positive.

absolution [àbsòlüsyoⁿ] *f.* acquittal, discharge (jur.); absolution. ‖ **absolvant,** *pr. p. of* absoudre.

absorbant [àbsòrbaⁿ] *adj.* absorbent; absorptive; absorbing. ‖ **absorber** [-é] *v.* to absorb; to soak up; to imbibe; to consume; to interest; **s'absorber dans**, to be swallowed up by; to become engrossed in. ‖ **absorption** [àbsòrpsyoⁿ] *f.* absorption.

absoudre [àbsûdr] *v.** to absolve; to exonerate. ‖ **absous, -te** [àbsû, -t] *p. p.*

of absoudre. ‖ **absoute** [àbsût] *f.* absolution.

abstenir (s') [sàbstⁿîr] *v.* to abstain, to refrain. ‖ **abstention** [àbstaⁿsyoⁿ] *f.* abstention.

abstinence [àbstìnaⁿs] *f.* abstinence; abstemiousness.

abstinent [àbstìnaⁿ] *m.* teetotaller.

abstraction [àbstràksyoⁿ] *f.* abstraction; *abstraction faite de*, leaving... out of account. ‖ **abstraire** [àbstrèr] *v.* to abstract; to separate; **s'abstraire,** to withdraw oneself. ‖ **abstrus** [àbstrü] *adj.* abstruse, recondite.

absurde [àbsürd] *adj.* absurd, preposterous; senseless; *par l'absurde*, ad absurdum. ‖ **absurdité** [-ìté] *f.* absurdity; nonsense.

abus [àbü] *m.* abuse, misuse; error; breach; excess. ‖ **abuser** [-zé] *v.* to abuse; to take unfair advantage (*de*, of); to impose (*de*, upon); to deceive; to delude (*quelqu'un*, someone); to indulge in; to seduce; **s'abuser,** to deceive oneself. ‖ **abusif** [zîf] *adj.** improper, wrong; excessive; unauthorized.

acabit [àkàbî] *m.* stamp; *du même acabit*, of the same kidney.

acacia [àkàsyà] *m.* acacia.

académicien [àkàdémìsyⁿ] *m.* academician. ‖ **académie** [-î] *f.* academy; University; nude. ‖ **académique** [-ìk] *adj.* academic.

acajou [àkàjû] *m.* mahogany; *adj.* dark auburn.

acariâtre [àkàryâtr] *adj.* cantankerous; shrewish.

accablant [àkàblaⁿ] *adj.* overwhelming [preuve]; crushing [désastre]; overpowering [chaleur]. ‖ **accablement** [àkàblⁿmaⁿ] *m.* pressure [travail]; dejection; prostration. ‖ **accabler** [àkàblé] *v.* to crush; to overthrow; to overpower; to overcome; to overwhelm (fig.).

accalmie [àkàlmî] *f.* lull; calm.

accaparement [àkàpàrmaⁿ] *m.* monopolizing; cornering. ‖ **accaparer** [-é] *v.* to monopolize; to corner; to hoard. ‖ **accapareur** [-œr] *m.* monopolist.

accéder [àksédé] *v.* to have access (*à*, to); to comply (*à*, with).

accélérateur [àkséléràtœr] *m.* accelerator. ‖ **accélération** [-àsyoⁿ] *f.* acceleration; hastening; speeding up. ‖ **accélérer** [àkséléré] *v.* to accelerate; to quicken; to hasten; *pas accéléré*, quick march.

accent [àksaⁿ] *m.* accent; stress; tone; pronunciation; strains. ‖ **accentuation** [-tüàsyoⁿ] *f.* accentuation;

emphasis. ‖ **accentuer** [-tüé] *v.* to stress; to emphasize; to accentuate; *s'accentuer,* to increase, to grow stronger.

acceptable [àksèptàbl] *adj.* acceptable; agreeable; welcome; fair; decent. ‖ **acceptation** [àksèptàsyon] *f.* acceptance. ‖ **accepter** [-é] *v.* to accept; to admit, to agree to; to acquiesce. ‖ **acception** [àksèpsyon] *f.* acceptation; meaning.

accès [àksè] *m.* access; approach, admission; fit, attack (med.); outburst [colère]. ‖ **accessible** [-sìbl] *adj.* accessible; approachable. **accessoire** [-swàr] *adj.* accessory, additional; secondary; *m.* accessory, fitting; *pl.* appliances; accessories, properties (theat.). ‖ **accessoiriste** [-swàrìst] *m.* property man (theat.).

accident [àksidan] *m.* accident; mishap, wreck, casualty; fold, feature [terrain]; *sans accident,* safely ‖ **accidenté** [-té] *adj.* hilly, uneven rough, broken (topogr.); checkered [carrière]; eventful; *m.* victim, casualty, *pl.* injured. ‖ **accidentel** [-tèl] *adj.*° accidental; adventitious, haphazard. ‖ **accidenter** [-té] *v.* to render uneven; to vary, to cause an accident to.

acclamation [àklàmàsyon] *f.* cheering; acclamation; applause. ‖ **acclamer** [-é] *v.* to acclaim; to cheer; to applaud; to hail.

acclimatation [àklìmàtàsyon] *f.* acclimatization; *jardin d'acclimatation,* zoo. ‖ **acclimater** [-é] *v.* to acclimatize; *s'acclimater,* to become acclimatized; to get used.

accointance [àkwintans] *f.* intimacy; *pl.* dealings; relations.

accolade [àkòlàd] *f.* accolade; embrace; brace (typogr.). ‖ **accoler** [-é] *v.* to couple; to bracket.

accommodant [àkòmòdan] *adj.* easygoing, accommodating; good-natured. ‖ **accommodation** [-àsyon] *f.* adaptation; conversion. ‖ **accommodement** [-man] *m.* compromise; settlement; arrangement. ‖ **accommoder** [-é] *v.* to suit; to season; to accommodate; to arrange; to adapt; to dress [repas]; *s'accommoder à,* to adapt oneself to; *s'accommoder de,* to put up with, to make the best of.

accompagnateur [àkonpañàtœr] *m.* accompanist. ‖ **accompagnement** [-man] *m.* accompaniment; escorting. ‖ **accompagner** [-é] *v.* to accompany; to convoy; to escort.

accompli [àkonpli] *adj.* accomplished; finished; perfect; thorough. ‖ **accomplir** [-ìr] *v.* to accomplish; to do; to perform; to fulfil(l); to achieve, to carry out, to finish; *s'accomplir,* to

happen; to take place. ‖ **accomplissement** [-ìsman] *m.* accomplishment; completion; performance; fulfil(l)ment.

accord [àkòr] *m.* accord, agreement; settlement; harmony, concord; chord, tune, strains (mus.); tuning [radio]; *d'accord,* agreed; *mettre d'accord,* to reconcile; *se mettre d'accord,* to come to an agreement. ‖ **accordailles** [-dày] *f. pl.* betrothal. ‖ **accordéon** [-déon] *m.* accordion; *en accordéon,* pleated, crumpled up. ‖ **accorder** [-dé] *v.* to reconcile; to grant, to concede, to give; to admit; to harmonize; to award (jur.); to tune [piano]; *s'accorder,* to agree; to come to terms; to harmonize (avec, with). ‖ **accordeur** [-dœr] *m.* tuner.

accorte [àkòrt] *adj. f.* sprightly, trim.

accoster [àkòsté] *v.* to come alongside, to accost, to approach.

accotement [àkòtman] *m.* side-path.

accouchée [àkûshé] *f.* woman in childbed. ‖ **accouchement** [àkûshman] *m.* delivery, child-birth; confinement. ‖ **accoucher** [-é] *v.* to be delivered; to deliver (med.). ‖ **accoucheur** [-œr] *m.* obstetrician. ‖ **accoucheuse** [-ëz] *f.* midwife.

accouder (s') [àkûdé] *v.* to lean on one's elbows. ‖ **accoudoir** [àkûdwàr] *m.* elbow-rest.

accouplement [àkûplman] *m.* coupling, joining; linking; pairing; mating; connection (mech.); copulation (med.). ‖ **accoupler** [-é] *v.* to couple; to connect; to mate, to pair; to yoke; *s'accoupler,* to pair, to mate, to copulate.

accourir [àkûrìr] *v.* to run up.

accoutrement [àkûtreman] *m.* costume, « get-up » (fam.).

accoutumance [àkûtümans] *f.* habit, usage. ‖ **accoutumer** [àkûtümé] *v.* to accustom; to inure; to familiarize; *s'accoutumer à,* to get used to; *à l'accoutumée,* usually.

accréditer [àkrédìté] *v.* to accredit; to confirm; to authorize; to open a credit to; *s'accréditer,* to gain credence. ‖ **accréditif** [-ìf] *m.* credential.

accroc [àkrô] *m.* tear; rent; hindrance, hitch, snag (fam.). ‖ **accrochage** [-òshàj] *m.* hooking, catching, fouling; clinch; engagement (mil.); coupling (techn.); collision. ‖ **accroche-cœur** [-òshkœr] *m. inv.* kiss-curl. ‖ **accrocher** [-òshé] *v.* to hook; to hang up [tableau]; to catch on a nail; to engage (mil.); to ram (naut.); to clinch [affaire]; *accrocher quelqu'un,* to buttonhole someone; *s'accrocher,* to get caught [obstacle]; to cling [à, to]; to have a set-to.

accroissement [àkrwàsmaⁿ] *m.* growth, increase ‖ **accroître** [àkrwâtr] *v.** to increase, to augment; to enlarge; to add to; **s'accroître,** to grow, to increase

accroupir (s') [sàkrûpîr] *v.* to squat; to crouch, to cower.

accueil [àkœy] *m.* reception; greeting; welcome. ‖ **accueillir** [-îr] *v.* to greet, to welcome, to receive; to give ear to, to credit.

acculer [àkülé] *v.* to drive back; to corner, to bring to bay.

accumulateur [àkümülàtœr] *m.* accumulator (electr.); storage battery; *adj.** acquisitive. ‖ **accumulation** [-àsyoⁿ] *f.* accumulation. ‖ **accumuler** [àkümülé] *v.* to accumulate; to amass; to hoard.

accusateur [àküzatœr] *m.* accuser; prosecutor, indicter (jur.); *adj.** accusing. ‖ **accusation** [-àsyoⁿ] *f.* charge; accusation, indictment; prosecution. ‖ **accuser** [àküzé] *v.* to accuse; to charge; to indict; to impute; to show up; to bring out; to indicate; to acknowledge [réception]; **s'accuser,** to accuse oneself; to stand out, to be marked.

acerbe [àsèrb] *adj.* sour, bitter; biting, sharp.

acéré [àséré] *adj.* sharp, keen, cutting; stinging. ‖ **acérer** [-é] *v.* to steel; to sharpen; to edge.

achalandage [àshàlaⁿdàj] *m.* custom, trade, connection; goodwill. ‖ **achalander** [-é] *v.* to bring custom to.

acharné [àshàrné] *adj.* eager in pursuit; inveterate, keen [joueur]; fierce, bitter [haine], stubborn, strenuous [lutte, travail]. ‖ **acharnement** [àshàrnᵉmaⁿ] *m.* relentlessness; determination; stubbornness ‖ **acharner** [-é] *v.* to flesh [chien]; **s'acharner à,** to go for; to work away at, to slog at.

achat [àshà] *m.* buying; purchase.

acheminement [àshmìnmaⁿ] *m.* way; course, progress, forwarding; routing [marchandises]. ‖ **acheminer** [-é] *v.* to direct, to forward, to route; **s'acheminer,** to proceed, to move.

acheter [àshté] *v.* to buy; to purchase; to bribe. ‖ **acheteur, -teuse** [-œr, -èz] *m., f.* buyer.

achèvement [àshèvmaⁿ] *m.* completion, termination; conclusion. ‖ **achever** [àshvé] *v.* to finish, to terminate; to complete; to dispatch, to finish off (fam.).

achigan [àshìgaⁿ] *m.* © bass [fish].

achopper [àshòpé] *v.* to stumble.

acide [àsìd] *m.* acid; *adj.* acid, tart, sour. ‖ **acidité** [àsìdìté] *f.* acidity. ‖

acidulé [-ülé] *adj.* acidulated; *bonbons acidulés* acid drops.

acier [àsyé] *m.* steel. ‖ **aciérie** [-rî] *f.* steelworks

acompte [àkoⁿt] *m.* instalment; payment on account; margin.

à-côté [àkôté] *m.* aside. ‖ *pl.* byways, side-lights; side-issues; extras, kick-back

acoustique [àkûstìk] *adj.* acoustic; *f.* acoustics

acquéreur [àkérœr] *m.* acquirer; buyer **acquérir** [-îr] *v.** to buy; to acquire to obtain ‖ **acquêts** [âkè] *m. pl* acquisition; acquests

acquiescement [àkyèsmaⁿ] *m.* acquiescence acceptance. ‖ **acquiescer** [àkyèsé] v to consent; to comply; to agree, to assent.

acquis [àkì] *adj.* devoted; acquired; *mal acquts* ill-gotten, *m.* experience. ‖ **acquisition** [-zìsyoⁿ] *f.* acquisition; purchase *pl* attainments

acquit [àkì] *m* discharge; receipt. ‖ **acquittement** [-tmaⁿ] *m.* acquittal; discharge payment. ‖ **acquitter** [-té] *v.* to acquit, to discharge; to receipt [note]; **s'acquitter de,** to fulfil(l); to discharge; to carry out.

acre [àkr] *f.* acre.

âcre [àkr] *adj.* acrid; pungent; sharp, bitter ‖ **acrimonieux** [àkrìmònyë] *adj ** acrimonious.

acrobate [àkròbàt] *m. f.* acrobat. ‖ **acrobaties** [-basî] *f. pl.* acrobatics, stunts *faire des acrobaties,* to stunt.

acte [àkt] *m.* action; act; deed; document, certificate; record; instrument, writ (jur.), *acte de décès,* death certificate *acte de naissance,* birth certificate *acte notarié,* notarial deed; *prendre acte de,* to take note of. ‖ **acteur, -trice** [-œr, -tris] *m., f.* actor, actress player. ‖ **actif, -ẏf** *adj.** active, busy, agile; *m.* assets; credit [compte] *armée active,* regular army. ‖ **action** [àksyoⁿ] *f.* action; deed; operation engagement (mil.); share (comm.) stock, suit (jur.); plot (theat.) *entrer en action,* to come into action, *action de grâces,* thanksgiving ‖ **actionnaire** [-yònèr] *m. f.* stockholder, ‖ **actionner** [-yòné] *v.* to set in motion (mech.); to sue (jur.); to stimulate.

activer [àktìvé] *v.* to stir up; to quicken to activate; to push on. ‖ **activisme** [-ìsm] *m.* activism. ‖ **activiste** [-ìst] *m.* activist. ‖ **activité** [ìté] *f.* activity; action; briskness; active service.

actualité [àktüàlìté] *f.* actuality; reality; *d'actualité,* of topical interest; *pl.* current events; news. ‖ **actuel**

[àktüèl] *adj.** real; current; present; actual. ‖ **actuellement** [-maⁿ] *adv.* now; at the present time.

acuité [àküité] *f.* sharpness, acuteness, keenness.

adage [àdàj] *m.* saying, adage.

adaptation [àdàptàsyoⁿ] *f.* adaptation; adjustment; *faculté d'adaptation,* adaptability. ‖ **adapter** [-é] *v.* to adapt; to adjust; *s'adapter,* to adapt oneself; to suit.

addition [àdìsyoⁿ] *f.* addition; bill, check [restaurant]. ‖ **additionner** [-yòné] *v.* to add up; to tot up.

adepte [àdèpt] *m.*, *f.* adept.

adéquat [àdékwà] *adj.* adequate.

adhérent [àdéraⁿ] *adj.* adhesive; *m.* adherent. ‖ **adhérer** [-é] *v.* to adhere, to cling; to join [parti]. ‖ **adhésion** [àdézyoⁿ] *f.* adherence; membership; accession.

adieu [àdyë] *m.* farewell; good-bye; leave-taking.

adipeux [àdìpë] *adj.** adipose.

adjacent [àdjàsaⁿ] *adj.* adjacent; adjoining; neighbo(u)ring.

adjectif [àdjèktìf] *m.* adjective.

adjoindre [àdjwⁿdr] *v.** to unite; to associate; to enroll. ‖ **adjoint** [àdjwⁿ] *m.* associate; assistant; *adjoint au maire,* deputy mayor.

adjudant [àdjüdaⁿ] *m.* warrant officer, battery Serjeant-Major.

adjudication [àdjüdìkàsyoⁿ] *f.* auction; allocation, award; *Br.* tender. ‖ **adjuger** [àdjüjé] *v.* to award; to knock down [enchères].

adjurer [àdjüré] *v.* to entreat, to exorcise.

admettre [àdmètr] *v.** to admit; to allow; to let in; to permit; to grant; to assume [supposition].

administrateur [àdmìnìstràtœr] *m.* administrator; director; guardian; manager; trustee. ‖ **administration** [-àsyoⁿ] *f.* administration; management; direction; trusteeship; *conseil d'administration,* board of directors. ‖ **administrer** [-é] *v.* to administer; to direct; to govern; to manage; to control.

admirable [àdmìràbl] *adj.* admirable, wonderful; excellent. ‖ **admirateur, -trice** [-àtœr, -trìs] *m.*, *f.* admirer; fan. ‖ **admiration** [-àsyoⁿ] *f.* admiration. ‖ **admirer** [-é] *v.* to admire; to wonder at.

admis [àdmì] *adj.* admitted; accepted; conventional. ‖ **admissible** [-sìbl] *adj.* admissible; eligible; allowable. ‖ **admission** [-syoⁿ] *f.* admission; intake; entry [douane].

admonestation [àdmònèstàsyoⁿ] *f.* admonition, admonishment. ‖ **admonester** [àdmònèsté] *v.* to admonish; to reprimand.

adolescence [àdòlèsaⁿs] *f.* adolescence; youth. ‖ **adolescent** [àdòlèsaⁿ] *m.* adolescent, teenager.

adonner (s') [sàdòné] *v.* to devote oneself; to become addicted [à, to].

adopter [àdòpté] *v.* to adopt; to take up; to espouse [cause]; to pass [projet de loi]. ‖ **adoption** [àdòpsyoⁿ] *f.* adoption.

adorateur [àdòràtœr] *m.* adorer; worshipper. ‖ **adoration** [-àsyoⁿ] *f.* adoration; worship. ‖ **adorer** [àdòré] *v.* to adore; to worship; to dote upon; to idolize.

adosser [àdòsé] *v.* to back against; *s'adosser à,* to lean [à, on].

adoucir [àdûsîr] *v.* to soften; to mellow; to smooth; to tone down; to sweeten. ‖ *s'adoucir,* to become mild. ‖ **adoucissement** [-ìsmaⁿ] *m.* softening; mollifying; appeasement; mitigation.

adresse [àdrès] *f.* address; cleverness; skill. ‖ **adresser** [-é] *v.* to address, to direct; to recommend; *s'adresser à,* to apply to, to appeal to, to be meant for.

adroit [àdrwà] *adj.* skil(l)ful; deft; clever, crafty; shrewd.

adulateur [àdülàtœr] *adj.** adulatory, fawning; *m.* adulator; toady. ‖ **adulation** [-syoⁿ] *f.* adulation. ‖ **aduler** [àdülé] *v.* to adulate; to flatter; to fawn upon.

adulte [àdült] *m.*, *adj.* adult; grown-up.

adultère [àdültèr] *m.* adultery; adulterer; *f.* adulteress.

advenir [àdv•nîr] *v.** to happen; to occur, to turn out; *advienne que pourra,* come what may.

adverbe [àdvèrb] *m.* adverb.

adversaire [àdvèrsèr] *m.* adversary; opponent; enemy; antagonist. ‖ **adverse** [àdvèrs] *adj.* opposing; hostile; adverse. ‖ **adversité** [-ìté] *f.* adversity.

aération [àéràsyoⁿ] *f.* airing; ventilation ‖ **aérer** [àéré] *v.* to aerate; to air; to ventilate. ‖ **aérien** [-yⁿ] *adj.* aerial, elevated; airy. ‖ **aérodrome** [-òdròm] *m.* aerodrome; *Am.* airdrome ‖ **aérodynamique,** aerodynamic; streamlined (auto). ‖ **aérogare** [-ògar] *f* air terminal. ‖ **aéronautique** [-ònôtìk] *f.* aeronautics; aerial navigation. ‖ **aéronef** [-ònèf] *m.* airship; aircraft ‖ **aéroplane** [-òplàn] *m.* airplane. ‖ **aéroport** [-òpòr] *m.* airport.

affabilité [àfàbìlìté] *f.* affability. ‖ **affable** [àfàbl] *adj.* affable.

affadir [àfàdîr] *v.* to make insipid, dull; *s'affadir*, to lose flavor, to become dull.

affaiblir [àfèblîr] *v.* to weaken. || **affaiblissement** [-ìsmaⁿ] *m.* weakening; attenuation.

affaire [àfèr] *f.* affair, business; matter; engagement (mil.); case, lawsuit (jur.); duel; *pl.* things, belongings; dealings, business; *dans les affaires*, in business; *avoir affaire à*, to deal with; *avoir affaire avec*, to have business with; *cela fera l'affaire*, that will do it; *son affaire est faite*, he's done for; *chiffre d'affaires*, turnover; *affaire en instance*, pending matter. || **affairé** [-é] *adj.* busy. || *s'affairer* *v.* to be busy; to fuss; to bustle about.

affaissement [àfèsmaⁿ] *m.* subsidence; depression; prostration (med.); collapse. || **affaisser** [-é] *v.* to weigh down; to overwhelm; *s'affaisser*, to sink; to sag; to give way; to become depressed; to flop.

affaler [àfàlé] *v.* to haul down; *s'affaler*, to drop, to slouch.

affamé [àfàmé] *adj.* hungry; starving; famished. || **affamer** [-é] *v.* to starve.

affectation [àfèktàsyoⁿ] *f.* affectation; appropriation; mannerism, affectedness; *Am.* assignment (mil.); *Br.* posting (mil.). || **affecter** [-é] *v.* to affect; to allot; to pretend; to feign; to hurt, to harm; *Am.* to assign (mil.); *Br.* to post (mil.).

affectif [àfèktîf] *adj.* emotional. || **affection** [-syoⁿ] *f.* affection; ailment, disease (med.). || **affectueux** [-tüé] *adj.* affectionate.

afférent [àféraⁿ] *adj.* relevant, applicable, pertaining.

affermer [àfèrmé] *v.* to rent; to lease; to farm out; to let.

affermir [àfèrmîr] *v.* to strengthen; to steady; to consolidate; *s'affermir*, to harden; to take root.

affichage [àfishàj] *m.* bill-posting; flaunting (fig.). || **affiche** [àfish] *f.* bill, poster, placard. || **afficher** [-é] *v.* to post up; to placard; to bill; to display; to flaunt; *s'afficher*, to attract notice.

affiler [àfìlé] *v.* to sharpen; to whet.

affiliation [àfìlyàsyoⁿ] *f.* affiliation. || **affilier** [-yé] *v.* to affiliate.

affiner [àfìné] *v.* to refine; to improve; *s'affiner*, to mature.

affirmatif [àfìrmàtîf] *adj.* affirmative; positive. || **affirmation** [-àsyoⁿ] *f.* assertion. || **affirmative** [-àtìv] *f.* affirmative. || **affirmer** [àfìrmé] *v.* to affirm; to assert; *s'affirmer*, to assert oneself.

affleurer [àflœré] *v.* to level; to make flush; to crop out [mine].

affliction [àflìksyoⁿ] *f.* affliction. || **affliger** [-jé] *v.* to afflict, to distress; *s'affliger*, to grieve.

affluence [àflüaⁿs] *f.* flow, flood; affluence, abundance; crowd; *heures d'affluence*, peak, rush hours. || **affluent** [-üaⁿ] *m.* tributary [rivière]. || **affluer** [-üé] *v.* to flow; to abound; to flock, to crowd.

affolement [àfôlmaⁿ] *m.* distraction; panic. || **affoler** [-é] *v.* to madden; to drive crazy, to disturb (mech.); *s'affoler*, to fall into a panic; to get crazy (*de*, about); to spin [boussole]; to race [moteur].

affranchir [àfraⁿshîr] *v.* to free; to emancipate, to exempt; to prepay; to stamp [lettre]. || **affranchissement** [-ìsmaⁿ] *m.* liberation; emancipation; postage, mailing; stamping.

affres [àfr] *f.* throes, pangs.

affrètement [àfrètmaⁿ] *m.* chartering; freighting. || **affréter** [àfrété] *v.* to charter. || **affréteur** [-œr] *m.* charterer; freighter.

affreux [àfrë] *adj.* horrible; frightful; hideous; dreadful; shocking.

affrioler [àfrìyòlé] *v.* to entice; to allure.

affront [àfroⁿ] *m.* affront; insult; snub. || **affronter** [-té] *v.* to confront; to face; to encounter; to brave.

affût [àfü] *m.* gun carriage; mount (mil.), hiding-place; *à l'affût de*, on the lookout for. || **affûter** [-té] *v.* to set; to sharpen [outil]; to grind.

afin [àfîⁿ] *adv.* *afin de*, in order to; *afin que*, in order that.

africain [àfrìkⁿ] *m.*, *adj.* African.

agaçant [àgàsaⁿ] *adj.* aggravating, provoking, annoying. || **agacement** [-maⁿ] *m.* irritation; annoyance. || **agacer** [-é] *v.* to irritate; tͦ entice; to lead on; *s'agacer*, to get annoyed.

âge [âj] *m.* age; period; epoch; *âge de raison*, years of discretion; *bas âge*, infancy; early childhood; *jeune âge*, childhood; *Moyen Age*, Middle Ages; *entre deux âges*, middle-aged; *hors d'âge*, over age; *d'un certain âge*, elderly; *quel âge a-t-il*? how old is he? || **âgé** [-é] *adj.* aged; old; *plus âgé*, older; *le plus âgé*, the eldest.

agence [àjaⁿs] *f.* agency; bureau; branch office; *agence immobilière*, real-estate agency. || **agencements** [àjaⁿsmaⁿ] *m. pl.* fittings, fixtures. || **agencer** [-é] *v.* to arrange; to dispose; to set up; to fit up; to adjust.

agenda [àjìⁿdà] *m.* memorandum-book; agenda; diary.

agenouiller (s') [sàjnûyé] *v.* to kneel down.

agent [àjaⁿ] *m.* agent; representative; medium; *agent de police,* policeman; *agent de change,* stockbroker; *agent de liàison,* liaison agent; **agent voyer,** road surveyor.

agglomération [àglòméràsyoⁿ] *f.* agglomeration; mass; aggregation; built-up area; caking. || **aggloméré** [-é] *m.* compressed fuel; conglomerate. || **agglomérer** [-é] *v.* to agglomerate; **s'agglomérer,** to agglomerate; to cake; to mass.

aggraver [àgràvé] *v.* to aggravate; to make worse; to increase [taxation]; **s'aggraver,** to grow worse.

agile [àjîl] *adj.* agile, nimble, light-footed; prompt. || **agilité** [-îté] *f.* nimbleness, agility, quickness.

agioter [àjyòté] *v.* to speculate; to gamble; to play the market.

agir [àjîr] *v.* to act; to take action; to operate; to proceed; to work; to carry on; to behave; **s'agir de,** to be a question of; to concern; *de quoi s'agit-il?,* what is it about? || **agissant** [-ìsaⁿ] *adj.* active, effective; drastic (med.). || **agissements** [-ìsmaⁿ] *m. pl.* doings; goings-on, machinations.

agitateur [àjìtàtœr] *m.* agitator. || **agitation** [-ìtàsyoⁿ] *f.* agitation; shaking; tossing; waving; perturbation; excitement; restlessness; roughness [mer]. || **agiter** [-ìté] *v.* to agitate; to shake; to wave; to disturb; to excite; to discuss; **s'agiter,** to be restless, to bustle.

agneau [àñô] *m.** lamb.

agonie [àgònî] *f.* death-throes. || **agoniser** [-ìzé] *v.* to be dying; to be at one's last gasp.

agrafe [àgràf] *f.* clasp; buckle; fastening; clip; clamp; staple. || **agrafer** [-é] *v.* to clasp; to buckle. || **agrafeuse** [-fëz] *f.* stapler.

agraire [àgrèr] *adj.* agrarian.

agrandir [àgraⁿdîr] *v.* to enlarge; to increase; to augment; to elevate; **s'agrandir,** to expand, to grow, to extend. || **agrandissement** [-ìsmaⁿ] *m.* enlargement, expansion.

agréable [àgréàbl] *adj.* agreeable; pleasing; pleasant. || **agréer** [àgréé] *v.* to accept; to recognize; to approve; to suit; to please.

agrégat [àgrégà] *m.* aggregate. || **agrégation** [-syoⁿ] *f.* aggregation; conglomeration; binding; competitive university examination.

agrément [àgrémaⁿ] *m.* assent, approval; pleasure; amusement; charm, gracefulness; *pl.* accomplishments [arts]; ornaments.

agrès [àgrè] *m. pl.* rigging, tackle (naut.); apparatus (gymnastique).

agresseur [àgrèsœr] *m.* aggressor; assailant. || **agression** [-yoⁿ] *f.* aggression; attack; assault.

agricole [àgrìkòl] *adj.* agricultural, farming. || **agriculteur** [-ûltœr] *m.* farmer; agriculturist. || **agriculture** [-ûltûr] *f.* agriculture; husbandry; tillage; farming.

agripper [àgrìpé] *v.* to clutch, to grab, to snatch.

aguerri [àgèrî] *adj.* seasoned; hardened; inured. || **aguerrir** [-îr] *v.* to season, to harden; to inure.

aguets [àgè] *m. pl.* watch, watching; *aux aguets,* on the lookout.

aguicher [àgìshé] *v.* to allure, to ogle; *Am.* to give the come-on to.

ahurir [àürîr] *v.* to dumbfound; to daze; to bewilder; to flabbergast. || **ahurissement** [-ìsmaⁿ] *m.* stupefaction, bewilderment.

aide [èd] *f.* aid; help; assistance; rescue; *m.* aide, assistant; helper. || **aider** [-é] *v.* to aid; to help; to assist; to relieve [pauvres]; **s'aider de,** to make use of.

aïeul, aïeule [àyœl] (*pl.* **aïeux** [àyë]) *m.* grandfather, *f.* grandmother; *pl.* ancestors; forefathers.

aigle [ègl] *m.* eagle; genius (fig.); *f.* standard, banner.

aigre [ègr] *adj.* sour, bitter; harsh, acid, tart; *aigre-doux,* bitter-sweet. || **aigrefin** [-efⁱⁿ] *m.* sharper. || **aigreur** [-œr] *f.* sourness; bitterness; tartness; acidity; ranco(u)r. || **aigrir** [-îr] *v.* to embitter; to make sour; **s'aigrir,** to turn sour; to become embittered.

aigrette [ègrèt] *f.* aigrette, egret; tuft, crest.

aigu [ègü] *adj.** sharp; acute; pointed; keen, shrill; piercing; critical. || **aiguille** [ègüiy] *f.* needle; hand [pendule], point [obélisque]; *Am.* switch, *Br.* point (railw.); needle (med.); *travaux d'aiguille,* needlework. || **aiguiller** [-é] *v.* to shunt; to switch (railw.). || **aiguilleur** [-œr] *m.* switchman; *Br.* pointsman. || **aiguillette** [-èt] *f.* aiguillette; shoulder-knot (mil.); strip of flesh [viande]. || **aiguillon** [-oⁿ] *m.* goad; spur; stimulus; sting [guêpe]; prickle (bot.). || **aiguillonner** [-òné] *v.* to spur; to stimulate; to urge on. || **aiguiser** [ègüizé] *v.* to sharpen; to whet; to point; to stimulate [appétit].

ail [ày] (*pl.* **aulx** [ô]) *m.* garlic; *gousse d'ail,* clove of garlic; **ailloli,** garlic mayonnaise.

aile [èl] *f.* wing; pinion; sail; whip [moulin]; blade [hélice]; aisle [église]; brim [chapeau]; fluke [ancre]; *Am.*

fender, *Br.* wing [auto]; vane (mech.); *rogner les ailes à,* to clip the wings of; *voler de ses propres ailes,* to stand on one's own feet. ‖ **aileron** [-roⁿ] *m.* aileron; wing flap (aviat.); pinion [oiseau]; flipper [pingouin]; fin [requin]. ‖ **ailier** [-lyé] *m.* winger.

ailleurs [àyœr] *adv.* elsewhere; *d'ailleurs,* besides; moreover; furthermore; *par ailleurs,* incidentally, otherwise, besides.

aimable [èmàbl] *adj.* kind, amiable, pleasant, nice. ‖ **aimant** [èmaⁿ] *m.* magnet, lodestone; *adj.* loving. ‖ **aimanter** [-té] *v.* to magnetize. ‖ **aimer** [èmé] *v.* to love; to like; to fancy; to be fond of; to care for; to enjoy; *aimer mieux,* to prefer.

aine [èn] *f.* groin.

aîné [èné] *m.* elder; eldest; senior. ‖ **aînesse** [ènès] *f.* primogeniture; *droit d'aînesse,* birth-right.

ainsi [ĩsi] *adv.* thus, so; hence; therefore; thus, as well as; *ainsi de suite,* and so on; *s'il en est ainsi,* if so; *pour ainsi dire,* so to speak; *ainsi soit-il,* amen.

air [èr] *m.* air; wind; appearance; look; tune; *avoir l'air,* to look, to seem; *donner de l'air,* to air; *courant d'air,* draft; *air de famille,* family likeness; *se donner des airs,* to put on airs.

airain [èrĩ] *m.* brass; bronze.

aire [èr] *f.* area, space; surface; threshing floor; eyrie [aigle].

airelle [èrèl] *f.* huckleberry, blueberry.

aisance [èzaⁿs] *f.* ease; comfort; sufficiency; freedom [mouvement]. ‖ **aise** [èz] *f.* ease; comfort; convenience; content; *adj.* glad; well-pleased; *à votre aise,* as you like; *comblé d'aise,* overjoyed; *mal à l'aise,* ill at ease. ‖ **aisé** [-é] *adj.* easy; comfortable; free; well-to-do; well-off.

aisselle [èsèl] *f.* armpit.

aîtres [ètr] *m. pl.* ins and outs.

ajonc [àjoⁿ] *m.* furze, gorse.

ajouré [àjûré] *adj.* perforated; open-work; pierced; fretwork.

ajournement [àjûrnemaⁿ] *m.* adjournment; postponement; subpoena; deferment (mil.). ‖ **ajourner** [-é] *v.* to adjourn; to postpone; to stay; to delay; to defer (mil.); to fail, to refer.

ajouter [àjûté] *v.* to add; to join; *ajouter foi à,* to give credit to.

ajuster [àjüsté] *v.* to adjust; to set; to adapt; to fit; to aim at; to arrange; to settle. ‖ **ajusté** [-té] *adj.* tight-fitting. ‖ **ajusteur** [-œr] *m.* fitter.

alambic [àlaⁿbìk] *m.* still.

alanguissement [àlaⁿgìsmaⁿ] *m.* languor; weakness; droopiness.

alarme [àlàrm] *f.* alarm. ‖ **alarmer** [-é] *v.* to frighten; to alarm; *s'alarmer,* to take fright; to be alarmed.

albâtre [àlbâtr] *m.* alabaster.

alcool [àlkòl] *m.* alcohol; spirits; hard liquor; *alcool à brûler,* denatured alcohol. ‖ **alcoolisme** [-ìsm] *m.* alcoholism.

aléa [àléá] *m.* risk; hazard. ‖ **aléatoire** [-twàr] *adj.* risky, chancy, contingent; problematical.

alène [àlèn] *f.* awl.

alentour [àlaⁿtûr] *adv.* around, round about; *m. pl.* neighbo(u)rhood; vicinity; surroundings.

alerte [àlèrt] *f.* alarm, warning, alert; *adj.* alert; vigilant; brisk, quick; spry; crisp.

alevin [àlvĩ] *m.* fry, young fish.

alezan [àlzaⁿ] *m., adj.* chestnut, sorrel [cheval], *alezan roux,* red bay.

algarade [àlgàràd] *f.* quarrel; scolding; dressing-down; prank.

algèbre [àljèbr] *f.* algebra. ‖ **algébrique** [-ìk] *adj.* algebraic.

Algérie [àljéri] *f.* Algeria. ‖ **algérien** [-yĩ] *m., adj.*ª Algerian.

algue [àlg] *f.* seaweed.

alibi [àlìbì] *m.* alibi.

aliénation [àlyénàsyoⁿ] *f.* alienation; transfer, derangement (med.). ‖ **aliéné** [-é] *m.* lunatic, madman, maniac; *adj.* insane. ‖ **aliéner** [-é] *v.* to alienate; to unhinge; to estrange; to transfer [propriété]; *s'aliéner,* to lose.

alignement [àlìɲmaⁿ] *m.* alignment; line; dressing (mil.). ‖ **aligner** [-é] *v.* to draw up (mil.); to line up; to align; *s'aligner,* to dress (mil.); to fall into line; *s'aligner avec,* to take on.

aliment [àlìmaⁿ] *m.* aliment; food; sustenance. ‖ **alimentation** [-tàsyoⁿ] *f.* rationing; subsistence; food; nourishment; feeding; feed (mech.). ‖ **alimenter** [-té] *v.* to feed; to supply (mech.), *s'alimenter,* to eat; to lay in.

alinéa [àlìnéá] *m.* paragraph, indentation.

aliter [àlìté] *v.* to confine to bed; to keep in bed; *s'aliter,* to take to one's bed.

alizé [àlìzé] *m.* trade wind.

allaiter [àlèté] *v.* to suckle, to feed.

allant [àlaⁿ] *m.* go; liveliness; dash; *adj.* active, busy, buoyant.

allécher [àlléshé] *v.* to allure; to attract; to tempt.

allée [àlé] *f.* alley; walk; path; drive; *allées et venues,* comings and goings.

allège [àlèj] *adj.* © unloaded.

alléger [àlléjé] *v.* to lighten; to alleviate; to relieve; to unburden; *s'alléger,* to grow lighter.

allégorie [àllégòrî] *f.* allegory.

allègre [àllègr] *adj.* lively, cheerful. ‖ *allégresse* [àllégrès] *f.* liveliness; cheerfulness; joy.

alléguer [àllégé] *v.* to adduce; to allege; to assign; to cite, to plead.

Allemagne [àlmàñ] *f.* Germany. ‖ *allemand* [àlmaⁿ] *m.*, *adj.* German.

aller [àlé] *v.* to go; to proceed; to move; *m.* departure; outward journey; one-way ticket; *aller à pied,* to walk; *aller à cheval,* to ride; *aller en voiture,* to ride, to drive; *aller en bateau,* to sail; *comment allez-vous?,* how are you?; *aller chercher,* to go for; *allons!,* come on!; *cela vous va,* it fits you, it suits you; *il y va de sa vie,* his life is at stake; *aller à la dérive,* to drift; *s'en aller,* to go away, to depart; to die; *au pis aller,* at the worst; *aller et retour,* Am. round-trip ticket, Br. return ticket.

allergie [àlèrjî] *f.* allergy.

alliage [àlyàj] *m.* alloy. ‖ *alliance* [-yàⁿs] *f.* alliance; union; marriage; wedding ring. ‖ *allié* [-yé] *m.* ally; kin. ‖ *allier* [-yé] *v.* to ally; to unite; to alloy; to combine; to blend [couleurs]; *s'allier,* to ally; to alloy; to harmonize; to marry into [à une famille].

alligator [àlìgàtòr] *m.* alligator.

allô! [àlô] *interj.* hullo!; hallo!

allocation [àllòkàsyoⁿ] *f.* allocation; allowance; assignment; allotment; dole [chômage]; *pl.:* family allowance [allocations familiales].

allocution [àllòküsyoⁿ] *f.* address, speech, allocution.

allongement [àloⁿjmaⁿ] *m.* lengthening; extension; elongation. ‖ *allonger* [-é] *v.* to lengthen, to extend; to stretch; to elongate; to lift [tir]; *s'allonger,* to grow longer; to stretch out; to lie down at full length; to fall [visage].

allouer [àlûé] *v.* to allow; to grant; to allocate; to award; to allot.

allumage [àlümàj] *m.* kindling, lighting, ignition (mech.); *couper l'allumage,* to switch off the ignition. ‖ *allumer* [-é] *v.* to light; to kindle; to inflame; to set fire to; to stir up [passions]; *s'allumer,* to catch fire. ‖ *allumette* [-èt] *f.* match. ‖ *allumeur* [-œr] *m.* igniter (mech.); lighter. ‖ *allumeuse* [-èz] *f.* vamp, tease.

allure [àlür] *f.* gait; manner; aspect; style; behavio(u)r; walk, pace; rate of march (mil.); turn; *à toute allure,* at top speed; *régler l'allure,* to set the pace; *d'allures libres,* fast; *d'allure louche,* suspicious-looking.

allusion [àllüzyoⁿ] *f.* allusion, hint; *faire allusion à,* to refer to.

aloès [àlòès] *m.* aloe.

aloi [àlwà] *m.* legal tender; quality; *de bon aloi,* genuine.

alors [àlòr] *adv.* then; so; in such a case; *alors que,* whereas; *et alors?,* so what?; *alors même que,* even though.

alose [àlôz] *f.* shad.

alouette [àlwèt] *f.* lark.

alourdir [àlûrdîr] *v.* to make heavy; to weigh down; to dull [esprit]; *s'alourdir,* to become heavy.

aloyau [àlwàyô] *m.* sirloin.

alpage [àlpàj] *m.* mountain pasture.

alphabet [àlfàbè] *m.* alphabet; reading-primer. ‖ *alphabétique* [-étîk] *adj.* alphabetical.

alpinisme [àlpinîsm] *m.* mountaineering. ‖ *alpiniste* [-îst] *m., f.* alpinist; moutain-climber.

altérable [àltéràbl] *adj.* alterable. ‖ *altérant* [-aⁿ] *adj.* thirst-producing. ‖ *altération* [-àsyoⁿ] *f.* adulteration; deterioration; debasement; faltering [voix]; heavy thirst [soif]; inflecting [musique].

altercation [àltèrkàsyoⁿ] *f.* altercation, dispute.

altérer [àltéré] *v.* to alter; to change; to adulterate; to spoil; to fade; to make thirsty; *s'altérer,* to undergo a change; to alter; to degenerate; to deteriorate; to twist.

alternance [àltèrnaⁿs] *f.* alternation; rotation (agr.). ‖ *alternatif* [-àtîf] *adj.* alternate, alternative. ‖ *alternative* [-àtîv] *f.* alternative, option. ‖ *alterner* [-é] *v.* to alternate; to rotate.

altier [àltyé] *adj.* haughty, proud. ‖ *altitude* [-îtüd] *f.* altitude, height. ‖ *alto* [àltô] *m.* alto, viola.

aluminium [àlümìnyòm] *m.* alumin(i)um.

alunir [àlünîr] *v.* to land on the moon. ‖ *alunissage,* landing on the moon.

alvéole [àlvéòl] *m.* cell [miel]; pit cavity; socket [dent]; alveolus (med.).

amabilité [àmàbìlîté] *f.* amiability; affability; kindness.

amadou [àmàdû] *m.* amadou; Am. punk; tinder. ‖ *amadouer* [-wé] *v.* to wheedle; to soften up; to coax; to get round.

amaigrir [àmègrîr] *v.* to make thin; to emaciate; to grow thin; to slim. ‖

amaigrissement [-ìsmaⁿ] *m.* growing thin; thinning down; emaciation; slimming; wasting away.

amalgame [àmàlgàm] *m.* amalgam; medley. ‖ *amalgamer* [-é] *v.* to amalgamate; to blend.

amande [àmaⁿd] *f.* almond. ‖ *amandier* [-yé] *m.* almond-tree.

amant [àmaⁿ] *m.* lover; paramour.

amariner (s') [sàmàrìné] *v.* to find one's sea-legs.

amarre [àmàr] *f.* mooring rope; hawser; cable. ‖ *amarrer* [-é] *v.* to moor, to cable, to berth; to secure; to lash [cordage].

amas [àmà] *m.* heap, pile; hoard; mass; accumulation. ‖ *amasser* [-sé] *v.* to heap up; to amass; to hoard; *s'amasser,* to pile up, to crowd together; to gather.

amateur [àmàtœr] *m.* lover, amateur, dilettante; fan; bidder.

ambages [aⁿbàj] *f. pl.* circumlocution; *sans ambages,* forthrightly, outspokenly.

ambassade [aⁿbàsàd] *f.* embassy; errand, mission. ‖ *ambassadeur* [-œr] *m.* ambassador.

ambiance [aⁿbyaⁿs] *f.* environment; surroundings; atmosphere; spirit.

ambigu [aⁿbìgü] *adj.** ambiguous; cryptic, doubtful, shady. ‖ *ambiguïté* [-güìté] *f.* ambiguity.

ambitieux [aⁿbìsyë] *adj.** ambitious. ‖ *ambition* [-yoⁿ] *f.* ambition.

ambre [aⁿbr] *m.* amber.

ambulance [aⁿbülaⁿs] *f.* ambulance; surgical hospital (mil.); dressing-station. ‖ *ambulancier* [-yé] *m.* orderly (med.). ‖ *ambulant* [aⁿbülaⁿ] *adj.* travel(l)ing; itinerant; *marchand ambulant,* hawker, peddler.

âme [âm] *f.* soul; spirit; sentiment; heart; feeling; bore [canon]; core [câble]; soundpost [violon]; *âme damnée,* creature, tool, stooge; *grandeur d'âme,* magnanimity.

améliorer [àmélyòré] *v.* to improve; to ameliorate; to better; *s'améliorer,* to ameliorate, to grow better; to mend.

aménagement [àménàjmaⁿ] *m.* arrangement; equipment; fitting up; preparation; fixtures [maison]; set-up. ‖ *aménager* [àménàjé] *v.* to prepare; to fit up; to plan; to harness.

amende [àmaⁿd] *f.* fine; penalty; forfeit; *amende honorable,* apology. ‖ *amender* [-dé] *v.* to amend, to improve; *s'amender,* to mend one's ways; to improve; to reform.

amener [àmné] *v.* to bring; to lead; to conduct; to introduce [style]; to

induce; to occasion; to haul down (naut.); to strike [pavillon]; to lower [voile]; *s'amener,* to arrive, to turn up, to roll up.

aménité [àménìté] *f.* charm, graciousness; *pl.* compliments (ironique).

amenuiser [àmᵉnüìzé] *v.* to pare; to whittle; to reduce; *s'amenuiser,* to dwindle, to decrease.

amer [àmèr] *adj.** bitter; *m.* bitters.

américain [àmérìkàⁿ] *m., adj.** American. ‖ *américaniser* [-àⁿìzé] *v.* to Americanize. ‖ *amérindien* [-rìⁿdyìⁿ] *adj.** Amerindian. ‖ *Amérique* [àmérìk] *f.* America.

amerrir [àmérîr] *v.* to alight on the water (aviat.).

amertume [àmèrtüm] *f.* bitterness.

ameublement [àmëblᵉmaⁿ] *m.* furniture; furnishings.

ameuter [àmëté] *v.* to train [chiens]; to stir up, to rouse [foule]; *s'ameuter,* to rise; to mob.

ami [àmì] *m.* friend; *petite amie,* mistress, girl-friend. ‖ *amiable* [àmyàbl] *adj.* amicable, friendly; *à l'amiable,* amicably, by mutual agreement.

amiante [àmyaⁿt] *f.* asbestos.

amical [àmìkàl] *adj.* friendly; amicable; *amicale* *f.* friendly society.

amidon [àmìdoⁿ] *m.* starch. ‖ *amidonner* [-òné] *v.* to starch.

amincir [àmìⁿsîr] *v.* to thin, to reduce; *s'amincir,* to slenderize, to slim, to grow thinner.

amiral [àmìràl] *m.** admiral; *adj.** flagship *contre-amiral* *m.* rear admiral. ‖ *amirauté* [àmìrôté] *f.* admiralship; admiralty, *Br.* Admiralty House.

amitié [àmìtyé] *f.* friendship; affection; kindness; *mes amitiés à,* my kindest regards to.

ammoniac [àmònyàk] *adj.* ammoniac. ‖ *ammoniaque* *f.* ammonia.

amnésie [àmnézî] *f.* amnesia.

amnistie [àmnìstî] *f.* amnesty. ‖ *amnistier* [-tyé] *v.* to amnesty.

amoindrir [àmwìⁿdrîr] *v.* to lessen; to reduce, to belittle; to mitigate; *s'amoindrir,* to diminish.

amollir [àmòlîr] *v.* to soften; to unman; to enervate; to weaken.

amonceler (s') [sàmoⁿslé] *v.* to heap up; to drift; to bank up.

amont [àmoⁿ] *m.* upstream water; head waters; *en amont,* upriver.

amorçage [àmòrsàj] *m.* priming [canon]; capping [obus]; starting (electr.); baiting [poisson]. ‖ *amorce* [àmòrs] *f.* primer; priming; percussion cap; fuze (electr.); detonator;

beginning (fig.). ‖ **amorcer** [-é] *v.* to prime [canon]; to start; to embark upon; to bait [poisson].

amorphe [àmòrf] *adj.* amorphous, shapeless; flabby; slack.

amortir [àmòrtír] *v.* to deaden [son, douleur]; to muffle; to subdue; to absorb [choc]; to pay off [argent]; to amortize. ‖ **amortissement** [-ìsmaⁿ] *m.* abatement; deadening; absorption [choc]; redemption [finance]; soundproofing [son]; *fonds d'amortissement,* sinking funds. ‖ **amortisseur** [-ìsœr] *m.* snubber; shock-absorber; shocksnubber; fender; dashpot; damper (electr.).

amour [àmúr] *m.* love; affection; passion; *mal d'amour,* lovesickness; *f. pl.* **premières amours,** calf-love; (*faire l'amour* does not mean « make love », and is not in polite use); *amour-propre,* self-pride; self-respect. ‖ **s'amouracher** [sàmúràshé] *v.* to fall in love (*de,* with), to fall for. ‖ **amourette** [àmúrèt] *f.* passing fancy, crush. ‖ **amoureux** [-é] *adj.** loving, enamoured; *m.* lover, sweetheart.

amovible [àmòvíbl] *adj.* revocable [poste]; removable; detachable.

amphibie [aⁿfìbí] *adj.* amphibious; *m.* amphibian.

amphithéâtre [aⁿfìtéátr] *m.* amphitheater; *Br.* amphitheatre.

ample [aⁿpl] *adj.* broad; ample; wide; spacious. ‖ **ampleur** [-ær] *f.* width; fullness; intensity; volume. ‖ **ampliation** [-làsyoⁿ] *f.* amplification; certified copy (jur.). ‖ **amplificateur** [-lfìkàtœr] *m.* amplifier [radio]; enlarger (phot.); *adj.** magnifying, amplifying. ‖ **amplifier** [-ifyé] *v.* to amplify, to magnify; to enlarge. ‖ **amplitude** [-ltüd] *f.* amplitude; vastness; extent; scope.

ampoule [aⁿpúl] *f.* ampulla; phial; bulb (electr.); blister (med.). ‖ **ampoulé** [-lé] *adj.* bombastic.

amputation [aⁿpütàsyoⁿ] *f.* amputation; reduction, curtailment; cuttingdown, cut. ‖ **amputer** [-é] *v.* to amputate; to curtail.

amure [àmür] *f.* tack of sail. ‖ **amurer** [-ré] *v.* to board the tack.

amusant [àmüzaⁿ] *adj.* amusing, diverting. ‖ **amusement** [-maⁿ] *m.* amusement; entertainment; diversion; recreation. ‖ **amuser** [-é] *v.* to amuse; to divert; to fool [créanciers]; *s'amuser,* to amuse oneself, to have a good time; to enjoy oneself. ‖ **amusette** [-zèt] *f.* plaything; child's play.

amygdale [àmìdàl] *f.* tonsil.

an [aⁿ] *m.* year; *avoir six ans,* to be six years old; *le jour de l'an,* New

Year's day; *bon an mal an,* taking one year with another; *l'an dernier,* last year.

anachorète [ànàkòrèt] *m.* anchorite, anchoret, hermit.

anachronique [ànàkrònìk] *adj.* anachronistic. ‖ **anachronisme** [-ìsm] *m.* anachronism.

analgésie [ànàljézí] *f.* analgesia. ‖ **analgésique** [-ìk] *adj.,* *m.* analgesic.

analogie [ànàlòjí] *f.* analogy. ‖ **analogique** [-ìk] *adj.* analogical. ‖ **analogue** [ànàlòg] *adj.* analogous, similar; counterpart.

analyse [ànàlìz] *f.* analysis. ‖ **analyser** [-lzé] *v.* to analyse. ‖ **analytique** [ànàlìtìk] *adj.* analytical.

ananas [ànàná] *m.* pineapple.

anarchie [ànàrshí] *f.* anarchy. ‖ **anarchiste** [-ìst] *m.,* *f.* anarchist.

anathème [ànàtèm] *m.* anathema; curse.

anatomie [ànàtòmí] *f.* anatomy. ‖ **anatomique** [-ìk] *adj.* anatomical.

ancestral [aⁿsèstràl] *adj.** ancestral. ‖ **ancêtre** [aⁿsètr] *m.* ancestor; forefather, forebear; gaffer.

anchois [aⁿshwá] *m.* anchovy.

ancien [aⁿsyⁿ] *adj.** ancient; old; elder; former; senior; early; past; bygone; *ancien élève,* alumnus; *Br.* old boy; **anciennement** [-syènmaⁿ] *adv.* formerly. ‖ **ancienneté** [aⁿsyènté] *f.* seniority; oldness; antiquity.

ancrage [aⁿkràj] *m.* anchoring, anchorage. ‖ **ancre** [aⁿkr] *f.* anchor; brace [construction]; *jeter l'ancre,* to cast anchor; *lever l'ancre,* to weigh anchor. ‖ **ancrer** [-é] *v.* to anchor; to brace; to tie; to secure; *s'ancrer,* to establish oneself, to dig in; to become rooted.

andain [aⁿdⁿ] *m.* swath.

andouille [aⁿdúy] *f.* chitterlings; (pop.) fool, boob, ninny, sap.

andouiller [aⁿdúyé] *m.* antler, tine [of antler].

âne [àn] *m.* ass, donkey; *bonnet d'âne,* dunce's cap; *coup de pied de l'âne,* last straw; *dos d'âne,* ridge.

anéantir [ànéaⁿtír] *v.* to annihilate; to exhaust; to overwhelm; to blast; to destroy. ‖ **anéantissement** [-ìsmaⁿ] *m.* annihilation; destruction; ruin; prostration.

anecdote [ànèkdòt] *f.* anecdote. ‖ **anecdotique** [-tìk] *adj.* anecdotic, anecdotal.

anémie [ànémí] *f.* an(a)emia. ‖ **anémier** [-yé] *v.* to make an(a)emic; to debilitate. ‖ **anémique** [-ìk] *adj.* an(a)emic.

anémone [ànémòn] *f.* anemone, windflower; sea-anemone.

ânerie [ânrî] *f.* stupidity. ‖ *ânesse* [-ès] *f.* she-ass.

anesthésie [ànèstézî] *f.* an(a)esthesia. ‖ *anesthésier* [-yé] *v.* to an(a)esthetize. ‖ *anesthésiste* [-ìst] *m.*, *f.* anaesthetist.

anévrisme [ànévrìsm] *m.* aneurism.

anfractuosité [ɑⁿfràktüòzìté] *f.* anfractuosity; sinuosity; winding [route]; rugged outlines [terrain].

ange [ɑⁿj] *m.* angel; *être aux anges*, to walk on air. ‖ *angélique* [-élìk] *adj.* angelic; *f.* angelica.

angine [ɑⁿjìn] *f.* tonsillitis; quinsy; angina (med.).

anglais [ɑⁿglè] *m.* English; Englishman; English language; *adj.* English. ‖ *anglaise* [-glèz] *f.* Englishwoman; Italian hand [écriture]; *pl.* ringlets.

Angleterre [ɑⁿglᵉtèr] *f.* England. ‖ *anglican* [ɑⁿglìkaⁿ] *m.*, *adj.* Anglican. ‖ *angliciser* [-ìslzé] *v.* to anglicize. ‖ *anglo-normand* [ɑⁿglônòrmɑⁿ] *adj.* Anglo-Norman; *les îles Anglo-Normandes*, the Channel Isles. ‖ *anglophile* [-fîl] *m.*, *adj.* Anglophil(e); pro-English. ‖ *anglo-saxon* [-sàksoⁿ] *m.*, *adj.** Anglo-Saxon; Anglo-American.

angoisse [ɑⁿgwàs] *f.* anguish; agony; spasm; distress; anxiety; *poire d'angoisse*, choke-pear. ‖ *angoisser* [-é] *v.* to anguish, to distress.

anguille [ɑⁿgìy] *f.* eel; *anguille de mer (congre)*, conger.

angulaire [ɑⁿgülèr] *adj.* angular; *pierre angulaire*, cornerstone. ‖ *anguleux* [-ë] *adj.** angular.

anicroche [ànìkròsh] *f.* hitch, snag.

animal [ànìmàl] *m.** animal, beast; *adj.** animal, brutish.

animateur [ànìmàtœr] *m.* animator; moving spirit; *adj.** animating, lifegiving. ‖ *animation* [-àsyoⁿ] *f.* animation, liveliness; excitement; quickening. ‖ *animer* [ànìmé] *v.* to animate; to quicken; to enliven; to stir up.

animosité [ànìmòzìté] *f.* animosity, hostility; spite.

anis [ànî] *m.* aniseed.

ankylose [ɑⁿkìlòz] *f.* anchylosis; cramp; stiffness. ‖ *ankyloser* [-é], *s'ankyloser* *v.* to stiffen.

annales [ànnàl] *f. pl.* records, annals.

anneau [ànnô] *m.** ring; link; ringlet; hoop; *anneau brisé*, split ring.

année [àné] *f.* year.

annelé [ànlé] *adj.* ringed; annulate, annulose.

annexe [ànnèks] *f.* annex; appendix; enclosure; supplement; *adj.* annexed, enclosed; *lettre annexe*, covering letter. ‖ *annexer* [-é] *v.* to annex. ‖ *annexion* [-yoⁿ] *f.* annexation.

annihilation [ànnììlàsyoⁿ] *f.* annihilation. ‖ *annihiler* [ànnììlé] *v.* to annihilate; to annul.

anniversaire [ànìvèrsèr] *m.* anniversary, birthday.

annonce [ànoⁿs] *f.* announcement; publication; advertisement; notification; banns. ‖ *annoncer* [-é] *v.* to announce; to declare; to proclaim; to usher in; to presage; to foretell; to advertize; *s'annoncer bien*, to be promising. ‖ *annonceur* [-œr] *m.* advertizer; announcer [radio]. ‖ *annonciateur* [-syàtœr] *adj.** foreboding; *m.* announcer. ‖ *Annonciation* [-syàsyoⁿ] *f.* Annunciation, Lady Day. ‖ *annoncier* [-yé] *m.* advertizing agent.

annotation [ànnòtàsyoⁿ] *f.* annotation; note. ‖ *annoter* [-é] *v.* to annotate.

annuaire [ànnüèr] *m.* yearbook; directory; annual; almanac; *annuaire du téléphone*, telephone directory. ‖ *annuel* [ànnüèl] *adj.** annual; yearly. ‖ *annuité* [ànnüìté] *f.* annuity.

annulaire [ànnülèr] *adj.* annular; ring-shaped; *m.* fourth finger; ring-finger.

annulation [ànnülàsyoⁿ] *f.* cancellation; annulment. ‖ *annuler* [-é] *v.* to annul; to repeal; to nullify; to cancel; to rescind; to reverse; *s'annuler*, to counterbalance, to cancel each other.

anoblir [ànòblîr] *v.* to ennoble; *Br.* to raise to the peerage. ‖ *anoblissement* [-ìsmaⁿ] *m.* ennoblement.

anodin [anòdⁿ] *adj.* anodyne; mild; harmless.

anomalie [ànòmàlî] *f.* anomaly.

ânon [ânoⁿ] *m.* ass's foal; (fam.) fool. ‖ *ânonner* [ànòné] *v.* to drone, to hem and haw.

anonymat [ànònìmà] *m.* anonymity. ‖ *anonyme* [-îm] *adj.* anonymous, nameless; Inc. Ltd. (comm.).

anorak [ànòràk] *m.* anorak, windjacket.

anormal [ànòrmàl] *adj.** abnormal.

anse [ɑⁿs] *f.* handle; ear [pot]; loop [corde]; creek; cove (geogr.).

antagonisme [ɑⁿtàgònìsm] *m.* antagonism. ‖ *antagoniste* [-ìst] *m.*, *adj.* antagonist.

antan [ɑⁿtaⁿ] *m.* yesteryear.

antécédent [ɑⁿtésédaⁿ] *m.* antecedent; *adj.* previous.

antenne [ɑⁿtèn] *f.* aerial; antenna; feeler; lateen yard (naut.); branch line (railw.).

antérieur, -e [ɑⁿtéryœr] *adj.* previous; former; anterior; prior. ‖ **antériorité** [-lòrìté] *f.* priority.

anthracite [ɑⁿtràsìt] *m.* anthracite; stone coal.

anthrax [ɑⁿtràks] *m.* anthrax.

anthropophage [ɑⁿtròpòfàj] *m.* cannibal. ‖ **anthropophagie** [-ì] *f.* cannibalism.

antiaérien [ɑⁿtìàéryìⁿ] *adj.** antiaircraft.

antialcoolisme [-àlkòlìsm] *m.* teetotalism, prohibitionism.

antiaveuglant [-àvèg[lɑⁿ] *adj.* antidazzle, antiglare.

antibrouillard [-brûyàr] *m. inv.* foglight; demister.

antichambre [ɑⁿtìshɑⁿbr] *f.* anteroom; waiting room; *faire antichambre chez,* to dance attendance on.

antichar [ɑⁿtìshàr] *m.* antitank weapon; *adj.* antitank.

anticipation [ɑⁿtìsìpàsyoⁿ] *f.* anticipation; encroachment; *par anticipation,* in advance. ‖ **anticiper** [-é] *v.* to anticipate; to forestall; to encroach.

anticonceptionnel [ɑⁿtìkoⁿsèpsyonèl] *m., adj.** contraceptive.

antidérapant [ɑⁿtìdéràpɑⁿ] *adj.* nonskidding, non-slipping; *m.* non-skid tire.

antidote [ɑⁿtìdòt] *m.* antidote.

antienne [ɑⁿtyèn] *f.* anthem; antiphon; story (fam.).

antigel [ɑⁿtìjèl] *m.* antifreeze.

antigivre [ɑⁿtìjìvr] *m.* de-icer; *adj.* de-icing.

Antilles [ɑⁿtìy] *f. pl.* West Indies; *mer des Antilles,* Caribbean Sea.

antilope [ɑⁿtìlòp] *f.* antelope.

antiparasite [ɑⁿtìpàràzìt] *m.* suppressor [télévision].

antipathie [ɑⁿtìpàtì] *f.* antipathy, aversion. ‖ **antipathique** [-ìk] *adj.* unlikable; uncongenial.

antipodes [ɑⁿtìpòd] *m. pl.* antipodes.

antiquaire [ɑⁿtìkèr] *m.* antiquary; antique-dealer. ‖ **antique** [ɑⁿtìk] *adj.* antique, ancient. ‖ **antiquité** [-ìté] *f.* antiquity; *magasin d'antiquités,* old curiosity shop.

antisémite [ɑⁿtìsémìt] *adj.* anti-Semitic; *m.* anti-Semite. ‖ **antisémitisme** [-tìsm] *m.* anti-Semitism.

antiseptique [ɑⁿtìsèptìk] *m., adj.* antiseptic.

antre [ɑⁿtr] *m.* den; lair.

anxiété [ɑⁿksyété] *f.* anxiety; concern. ‖ **anxieux** [-yè] *adj.** anxious; uneasy.

aorte [àòrt] *f.* aorta.

août [û] *m.* August.

apache [àpàsh] *m.* apache; tough, hooligan, hoodlum.

apaisement [àpèzmɑⁿ] *m.* appeasement; quieting; calming. ‖ **apaiser** [-é] *v.* to appease; to pacify; to calm; to soothe; to allay; to lull; to quell; to satisfy [faim]; to quench [soif]; to assuage [douleur]; *s'apaiser,* to subside; to quieten down; to cool down [colère]; to calm down (personne).

apanage [àpànàj] *m.* appanage.

aparté [àpàrté] *m.* aside; private conversation.

apathie [àpàtì] *f.* apathy. ‖ **apathique** [-ìk] *adj.* apathic.

apatride [àpàtrìd] *m., f.* stateless person.

apercevoir [àpèrsᵉvwàr] *v.** to perceive; to catch sight of; to glimpse; *s'apercevoir,* to realize, to be aware of, to notice. ‖ **aperçu** [àpèrsü] *m.* glimpse; insight; summary; outline; approximation; rough estimate; view.

apéritif [àpérìtìf] *m.* appetizer.

à-peu-près [àpëprè] *m.* approximation.

apeuré [àpëré] *adj.* scared, frightened; timid.

aphone [àfòn] *adj.* voiceless.

aphte [àft] *m.* aphta; gum-boil.

apiculteur [àpìkültœr] *m.* beekeeper. ‖ **apiculture** [-ür] *f.* apiculture; beekeeping.

apitoiement [àpìtwàmɑⁿ] *m.* compassion. ‖ **apitoyer** [-yé] *v.* to arouse pity in; to move; *s'apitoyer,* to feel pity; to condole.

aplanir [àplànìr] *v.* to level; to smooth; to plane; to iron out, to be removed [difficultés].

aplatir [àplàtìr] *v.* to flatten; to clench [rivet]; to plaster down [cheveux]; to knock out [personne]; *s'aplatir,* to flatten out; to collapse; to grovel.

aplomb [àploⁿ] *m.* equilibrium; perpendicularity; uprightness; balance; self-possession; coolness; cheek; stand [cheval]; *d'aplomb,* vertical, plumb, steady; *ça vous remettra d'aplomb,* that will set you up.

apocalypse [àpòkàlìps] *f.* apocalypse; book of Revelation.

apogée [àpòjé] *m.* apogee; zenith; peak; apex.

apologétique [àpòlòJétĭk] *f.* apologetics. ‖ **apologie** [-ĭ] *f.* apologia, vindication, defense.

apoplectique [àpòplèktĭk] *adj.* apoplectic. ‖ **apoplexie** [àpòplèksĭ] *f.* apoplexy; cerebral hemorrhage; *attaque d'apoplexie*, stroke.

apostasie [àpòstàzĭ] *f.* apostasy; *Br.* ratting (fam.). ‖ **apostasier** [-àzyé] *v.* to apostatize; to abandon. ‖ **apostat** [-à] *m.* apostate.

apostille [àpòstĭy] *f.* note, sidenote. ‖ **apostiller** [-iyé] *v.* to annotate; to endorse [requête].

apostolat [àpòstòlà] *m.* apostolate. ‖ **apostolique** [-ĭk] *adj.* apostolic; papal.

apostrophe [àpòstròf] *f.* apostrophe; reprimand. ‖ **apostropher** [-é] *v.* to apostrophize; to scold.

apothéose [àpòtéòz] *f.* apotheosis; glorification; finale.

apothicaire [àpòtĭkèr] *m.* apothecary.

apôtre [àpôtr] *m.* apostle; *bon apôtre*, hypocrite.

apparaître [àpàrètr] *v.** to appear; to come into sight; to become visible.

apparat [àpàrà] *m.* show, pomp, display, state.

appareil [àpàrèy] *m.* apparatus; plant; machine; mechanism; instrument; device; plane (aviat.); camera (phot.); set (radio); telephone; appliance (surg.); show, pomp, display. ‖ **appareillage** [-àj] *m.* fitting up; installation; preparation; outfit; equipment; accessories; getting under way (naut.); matching [couleurs]; pairing, mating. ‖ **appareiller** [-é] *v.* to install; to fit up; to spread [filet]; to trim [voile]; to get under way (naut.); *s'appareiller*, to pair.

apparence [àpàràⁿs] *f.* appearance; semblance; likelihood; trace; *sauver les apparences*, to save face, to keep up appearances. ‖ **apparent** [-àⁿ] *adj.* visible; noticeable; apparent; conspicuous; *peu apparent*, inconspicuous.

apparentement [àpàràⁿtmàⁿ] *m.* electoral alliance; pooling (or) linking arrangements. ‖ **apparenter** [àpàràⁿté] *v.* to connect; to ally [mariage].

appariteur [àpàrĭtœr] *m.* usher; attendant; beadle; laboratory assistant.

apparition [àpàrĭsyoⁿ] *f.* apparition; appearance; vision.

appartement [àpàrt^emàⁿ] *m.* flat; apartment; rooms; quarters.

appartenir [àpàrt^enĭr] *v.** to belong; to suit; to concern; to fit; to appertain to; *s'appartenir*, to be one's own master.

appas [àpà] *m. pl.* charms; bust. ‖ **appât** *m.* bait; allurement. ‖ **appâter** [-é] *v.* to lure with bait; to entice.

appauvrir [àpôvrĭr] *v.* to impoverish; to weaken; to thin [vin]; *s'appauvrir*, to become impoverished.

appeau [àpô] *m.** decoy; bird-call.

appel [àpèl] *m.* appeal, call; roll call; callover; summons; muster (mil.); *appel téléphonique*, telephone call; *faire l'appel*, to call the roll; *faire appel à*, to appeal to; to call on; *interjeter appel*, to lodge an appeal; *juger en appel*, to hear on appeal (jur.). ‖ **appeler** [àplé] *v.* to call; to name; to summon; to call in; to call for; to hail; to require; to send for; to draft (mil.); *en appeler à*, to appeal to; *s'appeler*, to be called; to be named; to be termed; *je m'appelle Jean*, my name is John. ‖ **appellation** [àpèllàsyoⁿ] *f.* name; term; trade-mark.

appendice [àpīⁿdĭs] *m.* appendix (med.); supplement; annex; appendage. ‖ **appendicite** [-ĭt] *f.* appendicitis.

appentis [àpàⁿtĭ] *m.* lean-to, penthouse; shed; out-house.

appesantir [àp^ezaⁿtĭr] *v.* to make heavy; to weigh down; *s'appesantir*, to grow heavy; to dwell on.

appétissant [àpétĭsàⁿ] *adj.* appetizing. ‖ **appétit** [-ĭ] *m.* appetite.

applaudir [àplòdĭr] *v.* to applaud; to clap; to approve; to praise; to acclaim; to compliment; to commend. ‖ **applaudissements** [-ĭsmàⁿ] *m. pl.* applause; clapping; cheers; acclamation.

applicable [àplĭkàbl] *adj.* applicable, appropriate. ‖ **application** [-àsyoⁿ] *f.* application; assiduity; diligence; industry; sedulousness; laying-on; *mettre en application*, to apply; to administer. ‖ **applique** [àplĭk] *f.* ornament; wall bracket; bracket candlestick, sconce; mounting, setting. ‖ **appliquer** [-é] *v.* to apply; to put on, to lay on; to put to use; to carry out; to enforce; *s'appliquer*, to apply; to apply oneself; to devote oneself (à, to); to work hard (à, at).

appoint [àpwīⁿ] *m.* addition; contribution; odd money; balance. ‖ **appointements** [-tmàⁿ] *m. pl.* salary; emoluments. ‖ **appointer** [-té] *v.* to put on salary; to pay a salary to; to sharpen [crayon].

appontement [àpoⁿtmàⁿ] *m.* wooden pier; flying bridge; landing stage. ‖ **apponter** [-é] *v.* to deck-land (aviat.).

apport [àpòr] *m.* contribution; share [capital]; deposit; bringing up (mil.). ‖ **apporter** [-té] *v.* to bring; to fetch; to supply; to provide; to produce.

apposer [àpôzé] *v.* to affix; to place; to add; to stick [affiche]; to insert;

to put [signature]. ‖ **apposition** [-ìsyoⁿ] *f.* affixing; apposition.

appréciable [àprésyàbl] *adj.* appreciable; noticeable. ‖ **appréciation** [-yàsyoⁿ] *f.* appreciation; estimation; estimate; valuation. ‖ **apprécier** [-yé] *v.* to appraise; to estimate; to appreciate; to value; to esteem.

appréhender [àpréaⁿdé] *v.* to apprehend; to dread, to fear; to arrest. ‖ **appréhension** [-syoⁿ] *f.* apprehension; fear; dread; arrest.

apprendre [àpraⁿdr] *v.** to learn; to inform; to find out; to teach; *ça t'apprendra,* serve you right.

apprenti [àpraⁿtì] *m.* apprentice; beginner. ‖ **apprentissage** [-sàj] *m.* apprenticeship.

apprêt [àprè] *m.* preparation; dressing [nourriture]; finish (techn.); sizing [encollage]; affectation, « frills ». ‖ **apprêtage** [-tàj] *m.* dressing; sizing (techn.). ‖ **apprêter** [-té] *v.* to prepare; to dress; to finish; to prime; to cook; *s'apprêter,* to get ready; to dress; to be imminent, to be brewing.

apprivoiser [àprìvwàzé] *v.* to tame; to domesticate; *s'apprivoiser,* to grow tame; to become more sociable; to get used (*avec,* to).

approbateur [àpròbàtœr] *adj.** approving; *m.* approver. ‖ **approbatif** [-àtìf] *adj.** approving. ‖ **approbation** [-àsyoⁿ] *f.* approval; approbation; consent.

approchable [àpròshàbl] *adj.* approachable, accessible. ‖ **approchant** [-aⁿ] *adj.* approximating. ‖ **approche** [àpròsh] *f.* approach; advance; oncoming. ‖ **approcher** [-é] *v.* to approach; to draw near; to bring up; *s'approcher de,* to draw near to.

approfondi [àpròfoⁿdì] *adj.* elaborate; careful; extensive; thorough. ‖ **approfondir** [-îr] *v.* to deepen; to master; to fathom; to excavate; to go deeply into.

appropriation [àpròprìàsyoⁿ] *f.* appropriation; embezzlement; allocation; adaptation. ‖ **s'approprier** [sàpròprìyé] *v.* to appropriate.

approuver [àprûvé] *v.* to approve; to agree to; to consent to; to authorize; to pass.

approvisionnement [àpròvìzyoⁿmaⁿ] *m.* supplying; supplies (mil.); victualing, catering; stock; store; provisioning. ‖ **approvisionner** [-é] *v.* to supply; to feed (mil.); to store; to victual; *s'approvisionner,* to get in supplies.

approximatif [àpròksìmàtìf] *adj.** approximate; approximative.

appui [àpüì] *m.* support; backing; prop; stay; bearing (mech.); docu-

ments *à l'appui,* supporting documents; *être sans appui,* to be unprotected; to be friendless; *appui de fenêtre,* window-sill; *point d'appui,* fulcrum, purchase; *appui-bras,* arm-rest. ‖ **appuyer** [-yé] *v.* to support; to strengthen; to second; to lean; to stress; *s'appuyer sur,* to lean against; to rest on; to depend on; to rely on.

âpre [âpr] *adj.* rough, harsh; bitter, tart; peevish, severe; ruthless; keen; crabbed; grasping; rasping.

après [àprè] *prep.* after; *adv.* afterwards; later; *d'après,* according to; *après que,* after; *après tout,* after all; *après-demain,* the day after tomorrow; *après-diner,* evening; *après-midi,* afternoon; *après-guerre,* afterwar period.

âpreté [àpreté] *f.* roughness; bitterness; sharpness; asperity; acrimony; sourness; tartness.

à-propos [àpròpô] *m.* relevance, opportuneness.

apte [àpt] *adj.* fit, apt; suitable; qualified; appropriate. ‖ **aptitude** [-ltüd] *f.* aptitude; capacity; turn (*à,* for); qualification; fitness; efficiency; qualities.

apurement [àpürmaⁿ] *m.* audit. ‖ **apurer** [àpüré] *v.* to audit.

aquaplane [àkwàplàn] *m.* surf-board, aquaplane.

aquarelle [àkwàrèl] *f.* water colo(u)r. ‖ **aquarelliste** [-ìst] *m.,* *f.* water-colo(u)rist.

aquarium [àkwàryòm] *m.* aquarium. ‖ **aquatique** [-àtìk] *adj.* aquatic; watery, marshy.

aqueduc [akdük] *m.* aqueduct; culvert; conduit.

aquilon [àkìloⁿ] *m.* North wind.

arabe [àràb] *m. f., adj.* Arab; Arabic; Arabian.

arabesque [àràbèsk] *f.* arabesque.

arable [àràbl] *adj.* arable; tillable.

arachide [àràshìd] *f.* groundnut, peanut; *beurre d'arachide,* © peanut butter.

araignée [arèñé] *f.* spider; grapnel.

arbalète [àrbàlèt] *f.* crossbow.

arbitrage [àrbìtràj] *m.* arbitration; arbitrage (comm.). ‖ **arbitraire** [-èr] *adj.* arbitrary; despotic; discretionary; lawless; *m.* good pleasure, discretion. ‖ **arbitre** [àrbìtr] *m.* arbitrator; adjudicator; referee; umpire; disposer; *libre arbitre,* free-will. ‖ **arbitrer** [-é] *v.* to arbitrate; to umpire, to referee.

arborer [àrbòré] *v.* to raise; to erect; to set up; to hoist; to fly [pavillon]; to step [mât]; to flaunt, to sport.

arboriculteur [àrbòrĭkültœr] *m.* arboriculturist, nurseryman. ‖ *arbre* [àrbr] *m.* tree; arbor, shaft, spindle, axle (mech.). ‖ *arbrisseau* [-ĭsô] *m.* shrub; sapling. ‖ *arbuste* [àrbüst] *m.* shrub.

arc [àrk] *m.* bow; arch; arc [cercle]; *tir à l'arc*, archery; *arc-en-ciel m.* rainbow.

arcade [àrkàd] *f.* arcade; passageway; arch.

arc-boutant [àrkbûtan] *m.* flying-buttress; prop, stay. ‖ *arc-bouter v.* to buttress; *s'arc-bouter*, to lean, to set one's back [*contre*, against]; to brace up.

arceau [àrsô] *m.** arch; hoop.

archaïque [àrkàĭk] *adj.* archaic.

arche [àrsh] *f.* ark; arch [pont].

archéologie [àrkéòlòjĭ] *f.* arch(a)eology. ‖ *archéologue* [-òg] *m.* arch(a)eologist.

archet [àrshè] *m.* bow.

archevêché [àrshevèshé] *m.* archbishopric; archbishop's palace. ‖ *archevêque* [-èk] *m.* archbishop.

archicomble [àrshĭcônbl] *adj.* packed.

archipel [àrshĭpèl] *m.* archipelago.

architecte [àrshĭtèkt] *m.* architect. ‖ *architecture* [-ür] *f.* architecture. ‖

archives [àrshĭv] *f.* archives, records.

arçon [àrson] *m.* saddlebow.

ardemment [àrdàman] *adv.* ardently, eagerly. ‖ *ardent* [àrdan] *adj.* burning; hot; scorching; eager, fervent; ardent, passionate; earnest; raging. ‖ *ardeur* [-œr] *f.* ardo(u)r; heat; earnestness; eagerness; spirit, mettle.

ardoise [àrdwàz] *f.* slate; debt; score. ‖ *ardoisière* [-yèr] *f.* slate quarry.

ardu [àrdü] *adj.* steep; abrupt; arduous; difficult, knotty; uphill.

arène [àrèn] *f.* arena; *pl.* amphitheater; *Br.* amphitheatre; ring.

arête [àrèt] *f.* fishbone; bridge; crest, ridge; chamfer [moulure]; angle.

argent [àrjan] *m.* silver; money; *argent comptant*, cash; *argent disponible*, available money; *argent liquide*, ready money; *argent monnayé*, silver currency. ‖ *argenterie* [-trî] *f.* silver, silver-plate, silverware, flatware. ‖ *argentin* [-tin] *adj.* tinkling; silvery; argentine.

argile [àrjĭl] *f.* clay; *argile réfractaire*, fireclay.

argot [àrgô] *m.* slang. ‖ *argotique* [-òtĭk] *adj.* slangy.

arguer [àrgüé] *v.* to deduce; to argue; to plead; to allege. ‖ *argument* [-üman] *m.* argument, reasoning; evidence; summary, outline. ‖ *argumenter* [-ümanté] *v.* to argue. ‖ *argutie* [-üsî] *f.* quibble, cavil.

aride [àrĭd] *adj.* arid, dry; sterile; barren. ‖ *aridité* [-ĭté] *f.* aridity.

aristocratie [àrĭstòkràsî] *f.* aristocracy.

arithmétique [àrĭtmétĭk] *f.* arithmetic; arithmetic book.

arlequin [àrlekin] *m.* harlequin; *en arlequin*, in motley.

armagnac [àrmànyàk] *m.* Armagnac brandy.

armateur [àrmàtœr] *m.* ship outfitter; ship owner. ‖ *armature* [-ür] *f.* frame; brace; armature (electr.); key signature (mus.); backbone, core (fig.). ‖ *arme* [àrm] *f.* weapon, arm; branch of the service; *à armes égales*, on equal terms; *arme de choc*, striking weapon; *être sous les armes*, to be under arms; *faire des armes*, to fence; *faire ses premières armes*, to make one's first campaign; *passer par les armes*, to shoot; *prise d'armes*, military review, parade. ‖ *armée* [àrmé] *f.* army (mil.); crowd, host, army (fig.); *armée de l'air*, air force; *armée de mer*, navy, fleet, sea forces; *armée de terre*, land forces; *zone des armées*, theater of operations. ‖ *armement* [àrmeman] *m.* armament, arming; equipment; commissioning (naut.); manning (techn.); loading, cocking [armes]. ‖ *armer* [àrmé] *v.* to arm; to equip; to fortify; to reinforce; to sheathe; to man, to commission (naut.); to load [canon]; to cock [arme à feu]; to mount [machine]; to wind (electr.); to set [appareil]; to dub [chevalier]. ‖ *armistice* [-ĭstĭs] *m.* armistice.

armoire [àrmwàr] *f.* wardrobe; locker; cupboard.

armoiries [àrmwàrĭ] *f. pl.* arms, armorial bearings; coat of arms. ‖ *armorier* [àrmòryé] *v.* to emblazon.

armure [àrmür] *f.* armo(u)r; weave (techn.). ‖ *armurier* [-yé] *m.* armo(u)rer; gunsmith.

aromate [àròmàt] *m.* aromatic substance. ‖ *aromatiser* [-ĭzé] *v.* to give flavo(u)r, aroma (à, to).

arôme [àrôm] *m.* aroma, flavo(u)r.

arpent [àrpan] *m.* acre. ‖ *arpentage* [-tàj] *m.* land surveying; land measuring; survey. ‖ *arpenteur* [-tœr] *m.* land surveyor.

arpète [àrpèt] *f.* milliner's apprentice.

arquer [àrké] *v.* to bend; to arch; to curve; to camber.

arrachage [àràshàj] *m.* pulling up, uprooting. ‖ *arracher* [àràshé] *v.* to

tear out, to tear away; to pull out; to uproot, to extract; to draw [dents]; to wrench [clou], to strip; to extort; *d'arrache-pied*, unremittingly, at a stretch.

arraisonnement [àrèzònmaⁿ] *m.* boarding, hailing, visiting of a ship. ‖ *arraisonner* [àrèzòné] *v.* to hail, to board, to visit (naut.).

arrangement [àraⁿjmaⁿ] *m.* arrangement, adjustment, ordering; agreement, terms, understanding; adaptation. ‖ *arranger* [-é] *v.* to arrange, to adjust, to set in order, to get up, to organize, to settle [querelle]; to fit, to be convenient, *s'arranger*, to manage, to contrive, to come to terms, to settle matters (*avec* with); to get oneself up.

arrérages [àréràj] *m. pl.* arrears.

arrestation [àrèstàsyoⁿ] *f.* arrest; apprehension ‖ *arrêt* [àrè] *m.* stop, stoppage, stopping, halt; interruption; sentence, award, judgment, attachment (jur.); detention, seizure; *aux arrêts*, under arrest. *arrêt de mort*, death sentence; *chien d'arrêt*, pointer; *maison d'arrêt*, prison *prononcer un arrêt*, to pass sentence ‖ *arrêté* [-té] *m.* decision; order, ordinance, decree; bylaw; *adj.* decided, determined; settled. ‖ *arrêter* [-té] *v.* to stop, to check; to arrest; to fix, to fasten; to draw up, to determine, to decide; to settle [comptes]; to engage, to hire [employé, chambre]; to cast off [maille]; *s'arrêter*, to stop; to halt; to pause; to cease.

arrhes [àr] *f. pl.* earnest money; deposit.

arrière [àryèr] *m.* rear [armée]; stern (naut.); back part; *à l'arrière*, aft; *en arrière*, behind; backward(s); in arrears, *arrière-garde*, rear-guard; *arrière-goût*, aftertaste; *arrière-grand-mère*, great-grandmother, *arrière-grand-père*, great-grandfather, *arrière-pensée*, ulterior motive, *arrière-petit-fils*, great-grandson, *arrière-petite-fille*, great-grand-daughter, *arrière-plan*, background; *arrière-saison*, *Am* late fall, *Br* late autumn; *arrière-train*, back, rear part [véhicule]; trailer hind quarters [animal]. ‖ *arriéré* [àryéré] *adj.* overdue; backward; antiquated.

arrimer [àrìmé] *v.* to stow (naut.); to trim; to pack (aviat.).

arrivage [àrìvàj] *m.* arrival; new consignment [marchandises]. ‖ *arrivée* [-é] *f.* arrival [personne]; coming; inlet, intake (techn.); winning post; finish. ‖ *arriver* [-é] *v.* to arrive, to come; to happen; *en arriver à*, to come to; *arriver à*, to succeed in, to manage to, to reach. ‖ *arriviste* [-ìst] *m., f.* pusher, thruster, climber.

arrogance [àrògans] *f.* arrogance; haughtiness ‖ *arrogant* [-gaⁿ] *adj.* arrogant, overbearing ‖ *s'arroger* [sàròjé] *v.* to arrogate to oneself, to assume [privilège].

arrondir [àroⁿdîr] *v.* to make round; to round off, to rub down [angles]; to round [période], *s'arrondir*, to become round, to fill out. ‖ *arrondissement* [-ìsmaⁿ] *m.* rounding off; district, ward [ville].

arrosage [àrôzàj] *m.* watering, wetting, moistening, sprinkling; irrigation; basting, dilution [vin]. ‖ *arroser* [-é] *v.* to water, to wet; to moisten, to sprinkle, to baste, to bribe; *ça s'arrose*, that calls for celebration. ‖ *arrosoir* [-wàr] *m.* watering can; sprinkler.

arsenal [àrsⁿàl] *m.* arsenal; armory; dockyard; navy yard (naut.).

arsenic [àrsⁿìk] *m.* arsenic.

art [àr] *m.* art; skill; artfulness; knack; artificiality.

artère [àrtèr] *f.* artery (med.); thoroughfare [rue]. ‖ *artériel* [àrtéryèl] *adj.* arterial.

arthrite [àrtrìt] *f.* arthritis.

artichaut [àrtìshô] *m.* artichoke; spiked barrier (mil.).

article [àrtìkl] *m.* article; item; thing; commodity, clause; entry; matter, subject, stipulation, provision; *articles de Paris* fancy goods, *faire l'article*, to show off, to vaunt; *à l'article de la mort*, at the point of death.

articulation [àrtìkülàsyoⁿ] *f.* articulation joint, utterance; connection, coupling deployment (mil.). ‖ *articuler* [-é] *v.* to articulate; to link; to joint; to pronounce, to utter; to subdivide (mil.).

artifice [àrtìfìs] *m.* artifice; guile; contrivance, stratagem; expedient; *feu d'artifice*, fireworks. ‖ *artificiel* [-yèl] *adj.* artificial ‖ *artificier* [-yé] *m.* pyrotechnist. ‖ *artificieux* [-yé] *adj.* artful, cunning

artillerie [àrtìyrî] *f.* artillery; ordnance, mounted guns; *artillerie de campagne*, field artillery. ‖ *artilleur* [-ïyœr] *m.* artilleryman; artillerist; gunner.

artisan [àrtìzaⁿ] *m.* artisan, craftsman; agent (fig.). ‖ *artisanat* [-zànà] *m.* handicraft; craftsmen *m. pl.*

artiste [àrtìst] *m.* artist, performer. ‖ *artistique* [-ìk] *adj.* artistic.

as [às] *m.* ace.

ascendance [àsaⁿdaⁿs] *f.* ancestry. ‖ *ascendant* [-aⁿ] *adj.* ascending; upward; mounting, rising; *m.* ascendant; ascendency; influence; *pl.* ancestry; *prendre de l'ascendant sur*, to gain advantage over. ‖ **ascenseur** [àsaⁿsœr] *m. Am.* elevator; *Br.* lift. ‖ **ascension** [-yoⁿ] *f.* ascent; Ascension; climb.

ascèse [àsèz] *f.* asceticism. ‖ **ascète** [-sèt] *m., f.* ascetic.

asepsie [àsèpsî] *f.* asepsis. ‖ **aseptiser** [-tîzé] *v.* to asepticize.

asile [àzîl] *m.* asylum; retreat; home, shelter, refuge; haven.

aspect [àspè] *m.* aspect; sight; appearance; look; point of view.

asperge [àspèrj] *f.* asparagus. ‖ **asperger** [-é] *v.* to sprinkle; to spray.

aspérité [àspérîté] *f.* asperity, roughness, harshness.

aspersion [àspèrsyoⁿ] *f.* sprinkling, spraying.

asphyxie [àsfìksî] *f.* asphyxia. ‖ **asphyxier** [-yé] *v.* to asphyxiate, to suffocate.

aspic [àspîk] *m.* asp, serpent, coral snake; aspic.

aspirant [àspîraⁿ] *m.* candidate; midshipman (naut.); officer candidate (mil.). ‖ **aspirateur** [-àtœr] *m.* suction van; vacuum cleaner; aspirator (mech.). ‖ **aspiration** [-àsyoⁿ] *f.* aspiration; inspiration (med.); inhaling; suction; longing; intake. ‖ **aspirer** [-é] *v.* to aspire; to inspire, to inhale; to breathe in, to suck in; to desire; to long (à, for).

assagir [àsàjîr] *v.* to make wiser; to sober, to steady.

assaillant [àsàyaⁿ] *m.* assailant; besieger; aggressor. ‖ **assaillir** [àsàyîr] *v.** to attack; to besiege; to assault; to assail.

assainir [àsènîr] *v.* to make healthier; to decontaminate; to purify; to cleanse. ‖ **assainissement** [-îsmaⁿ] *m.* cleansing, purifying; sanitation; disinfecting; decontamination; hygiene; reform, reorganization.

assaisonnement [àsèzònmaⁿ] *m.* seasoning; flavo(u)ring; dressing. ‖ **assaisonner** [-é] *v.* to season, to dress; to give zest to.

assassin [àsàsîⁿ] *m.* murderer; assassin. ‖ **assassinat** [-inà] *m.* murder; assassination. ‖ **assassiner** [-iné] *v.* to murder; to assassinate; to pester.

assaut [àsô] *m.* assault, attack; onslaught; match; bout; *donner l'assaut,* to storm, to charge; *enlever d'assaut,* to take by storm; *monter à l'assaut,* to storm.

assèchement [àsèshmaⁿ] *m.* drying, draining. ‖ **assécher** [àsèshé] *v.* to dry, to drain.

assemblage [àsaⁿblàj] *m.* assemblage; gathering, collection; assembly; combination; connection, coupling (electr.);

joint (techn.). ‖ **assemblée** [-é] *f.* assembly; meeting; congregation; gathering; company. ‖ **assembler** [-é] *v.* to gather; to bring together; to muster; to assemble, to join; to fit together; to joint, to connect (electr.); to collect; *s'assembler,* to assemble, to meet; to be joined.

assener [àsⁿé] *v.* to strike; to land [coup]; to hit.

assentiment [àsaⁿtìmaⁿ] *m.* agreement, consent.

asseoir [àswàr] *v.** to seat, to set; to settle, to fix; to place; to lay; to establish [impôt]; *s'asseoir,* to sit down; to settle.

assermenté [àsèrmaⁿté] *adj.* sworn-in; on oath; juror. ‖ **assermenter** [-é] *v.* to swear in.

assertion [àsèrsyoⁿ] *f.* assertion.

asservir [àsèrvîr] *v.* to enslave; to subject. ‖ **asservissement** [-ìsmaⁿ] *m.* slavery, subjection; bondage.

assesseur [àsèsœr] *m.* assessor; assistant.

assez [àsè] *adv.* enough; rather; fairly; sufficiently; *j'en ai assez!,* I'm fed up with it!; *assez!,* that will do!

assidu [àsîdü] *adj.* assiduous, diligent; regular. ‖ **assiduité** [-üìté] *f.* assiduity, diligence.

assiégeant [àsyéjaⁿ] *m.* besieger. ‖ **assiéger** [-é] *v.* to besiege; to surround; to beset; to mob; to dun.

assiette [àsyèt] *f.* plate (vaisselle]; seat [cheval]; trim (naut.); stable position; basis. ‖ **assiettée** [-é] *f.* plateful, plate.

assignation [àsîñàsyoⁿ] *f.* assignment; summons; subpoena. ‖ **assigner** [-é] *v.* to assign, to allot; to fix, to appoint; to allocate, to earmark; to summon, to cite; to subpoena (jur.); to sue (en, for).

assimilable [àsîmìlàbl] *adj.* assimilable; comparable. ‖ **assimilation** [-àsyoⁿ] *f.* assimilation. ‖ **assimiler** [-é] *v.* to assimilate; to compare; to give an equivalent status to; to digest.

assis [àsì] *p. p. of s'asseoir; adj.* seated, sitting; established. ‖ **assise** [-îz] *f.* foundation; seating; layer, stratum, bed, course (techn.); seat [cavalier]; *pl.* Assizes, criminal court (jur.).

assistance [àsìstaⁿs] *f.* audience, spectators, bystanders; congregation; presence, attendance; assistance; *assistance publique,* public relief administration; *assistance sociale,* social welfare work; *assistance maritime,* salvage; *assistance judiciaire,* free legal aid. ‖ **assistant** [-aⁿ] *m.* assistant; helper; onlooker, bystander, spectator.

‖ **assister** [-é] v. to assist; to aid, to help; **assister à**, to attend, to be present at.

association [àsòsyàsyoⁿ] f. association; partnership; combination; coupling (electr.); gang. ‖ **associer** [-yé] v. to associate, to unite; to join up; to connect (electr.); **s'associer**, to share; to join; to participate; to go into partnership with; to sympathize with. ‖ **associé** [-yé] m. partner; associate [société savante].

assoiffé [àswàfé] adj. thirsty, thirsting; parched; eager.

assolement [àsòlmaⁿ] m. (crop)-rotation. ‖ **assoler** [-é] v. to rotate.

assombrir [àsoⁿbrîr] v. to darken; to sadden, to make gloomy; to cloud; **s'assombrir**, to darken; to become cloudy; to cloud over.

assommant [àsòmaⁿ] adj. deadly dull; boring; tiresome, plaguy; stunning. ‖ **assommer** [àsòmé] v. to fell; to knock on the head, to stun; to bore, to plague, to pester. ‖ **assommoir** [-wàr] m. bludgeon, blackjack; loaded cane; breakback trap; low dive, Am. deadfall, dram shop.

assomption [àsoⁿpsyoⁿ] f. assumption.

assortiment [àsòrtìmaⁿ] m. matching; assortment, range; variety; suitability; set. ‖ **assortir** [-îr] v. to match; to pair; to assort; to stock [comm.]; **s'assortir**, to match.

assoupir [àsûpîr] v. to make sleepy, drowsy; to soothe [douleur]; **s'assoupir**, to become drowsy; to doze off; to wear off [douleur]. ‖ **assoupissement** [-ìsmaⁿ] m. drowsiness; doze, nap; sloth.

assouplir [àsûplîr] v. to make supple, to break in; **s'assouplir**, to become supple (or) more tractable. ‖ **assouplissement** [-ìsmaⁿ] m. breaking in; relaxation [formalités].

assourdir [àsûrdîr] v. to deafen; to muffle [son]; to tone down.

assouvir [àsûvîr] v. to satiate; to satisfy; to glut; to gratify; **s'assouvir**, to gorge, to be sated (de, with).

assujettir [àsüjétîr] v. to subjugate, to subdue; to compel; to fix, to fasten; to tie down; to secure; **s'assujettir**, to subject oneself. ‖ **assujettissement** [-ìsmaⁿ] m. subjugation; fastening; securing; dependence.

assumer [àsümé] v. to assume, to take upon oneself.

assurance [àsüraⁿs] f. assurance; self-confidence; certainty; pledge, security, safety; guarantee; insurance; **assurance contre les accidents du travail**, workmen's compensation insurance;

assurances sociales, social security; **assurance contre l'incendie**, fire insurance. ‖ **assurer** [-é] v. to assure; to secure; to fasten; to insure; to affirm; to ensure [résultat]; **s'assurer**, to ascertain, to make sure; to secure, to get hold (de, of); to get insured; to seize (mil.); to apprehend.

astérisque [àstérìsk] m. asterisk.

asthénie [àsténí] f. debility.

asthme [àsm] m. asthma.

asticot [àstìkô] m. maggot, gentle. ‖ **asticoter** [-té] v. to harass, to tease; to nag.

astiquer [àstìké] v. to polish; to scour; to smarten.

astral [àstràl] adj.* astral, starry. ‖ **astre** [àstr] m. heavenly body; star.

astreindre [àstrⁿdr] v.* to subject; to compel, to force; to bind. ‖ **astringent** [-ìⁿjaⁿ] adj. astringent; binding; styptic.

astrologie [àstròlòjí] f. astrology. ‖ **astrologue** [-ôg] m. astrologer.

astronef [àstrònèf] m. space-ship.

astronome [àstrònòm] m. astronomer. ‖ **astronomie** [-í] f. astronomy.

astuce [àstüs] f. guile, craftiness; wile, trick. ‖ **astucieux** [-yé] adj.* crafty, astute, artful.

atavique [àtàvìk] adj. atavistic.

atelier [àt•lyé] m. workshop; studio; repair shop [réparations].

atermoiement [àtèrmwàmaⁿ] m. delay; renewal (jur.); pl. procrastination, shilly-shally. ‖ **atermoyer** [-àyé] v. to put off; to defer; to procrastinate; to dally.

athée [àté] m., f. atheist, nullifidian; adj. atheistic. ‖ **athéisme** [-ìsm] m. atheism.

athlète [àtlèt] m., f. athlete. ‖ **athlétique** [-étìk] adj. athletic. ‖ **athlétisme** [-étìsm] m. athletics.

Atlantique [àtlaⁿtìk] m. Atlantic Ocean.

atlas [àtlàs] m. atlas.

atmosphère [àtmòsfèr] f. atmosphere. ‖ **atmosphérique** [-érìk] adj. atmospheric.

atoll [àtòl] m. atoll, coral island.

atome [àtòm] m. atom; speck [poussière]; jot. ‖ **atomique** [-ìk] adj. atomic. ‖ **atomiser** [-zé] v. to atomize, to pulverize.

atone [àtòn] adj. atonic; unstressed; dull, vacant. ‖ **atonie** [-í] f. atony, sluggishness.

atours [àtûr] m. pl. finery.

atout [àtû] m. trump; courage; setback.

atrabilaire [àtràbilèr] adj. atrabilious, melancholy; cantankerous.

âtre [âtr] m hearth.

atroce [àtròs] adj. atrocious, dreadful, grim, cruel; heinous. ‖ **atrocité** [-lté] f. atrocity, atrociousness.

atrophie [àtròfí] f. atrophy; emaciation; withering. ‖ **atrophier** [-yé] v. to atrophy.

attabler (s') [sàtàblé] v. to sit down to table.

attachant [àtàshaⁿ] adj. winning, endearing, attractive, arresting. ‖ **attache** [àtàsh] f bond, tie, link; cord; strap, attachment, paper clip, joint, brace (mech.); port d'attache, home port. ‖ **attacher** [-é] v. to attach; to fasten, to tie, to attract; to attribute; s'attacher, to attach oneself; to cling; to devote oneself; s'attacher aux pas de, to dog the steps of.

attaque [àtàk] f. attack; assault; onset; attaque d'apoplexie, apoplectic stroke, attaque de nerfs, fit of hysterics. ‖ **attaquer** [-é] v. to attack; to assail; to assault; to contest; to lead [cartes]; to operate (techn.); to corrode; to tackle; s'attaquer à, to attack, to fall upon; to grapple with.

attardé [àtàrdé] adj. belated, behindhand; old-fashioned; backward; m. laggard ‖ **attarder** [-é] v. to delay; to make late; s'attarder, to delay, to linger, to dawdle.

atteindre [àtiⁿdr] v.* to reach, to attain; to hit [cible]; to strike; to overtake; to affect, to injure. ‖ **atteinte** [-iⁿt] f. reach; stroke, blow; shock, touch; harm, injury.

attelage [àtlàj] m. harnessing; team, yoke; coupling (techn.). ‖ **atteler** [-é] v. to harness; to couple; to yoke; s'atteler à, to set to; to buckle to; to get down to. ‖ **attelle** [àtèl] f. splint; pl. hames.

attenant [àt⁰na⁰] adj. adjoining, adjacent; neighbo(u)ring.

attendant (en) [⁰⁰nàta⁰da⁰] adv. meanwhile, prep. pending; en attendant que, until. ‖ **attendre** [àta⁰dr] v. to wait for, to await; to expect; to look forward to; to long for; to stop; faire attendre, to keep waiting; s'attendre à, to expect.

attendrir [àta⁰drír] v. to make tender; to soften [viande]; to move, to touch; se laisser attendrir, to become tender; to be affected, to be moved; s'attendrir, to become tender; to soften, to be moved (fig.). ‖ **attendrissement** [-lsma⁰] m. making tender; hanging [viande]; emotion; pity.

attendu [àta⁰dü] prep. considering; on account of; m. ground, reason

adduced; attendu que, considering that; whereas.

attentat [àta⁰tà] m. criminal attempt; outrage attentat à la pudeur, indecent assault. offense against public morals.

attente [àta⁰t] f. wait, waiting; expectation, salle d'attente, waiting room.

attenter [àta⁰té] v. to make a criminal attempt (à, on); attenter à ses jours. to attempt suicide.

attentif [àta⁰tíf] adj.* attentive, careful, heedful, mindful. ‖ **attention** [-syo⁰] f attention; care; heed; faire attention à, to pay attention to; to mind, to heed, attention!, look out! mind! ‖ **attentionné** [-syòné] adj. considerate.

attentisme [àta⁰tìsm] m. sitting-on-the-fence policy.

atténuation [àténüàsyo⁰] f. extenuation, attenuation, mitigation; reduction. ‖ **atténuer** [-üé] v. to extenuate; to attenuate, to reduce; s'atténuer, to soften; to die down; to lessen.

atterrer [àtèré] v. to astound, to dismay; to stun.

atterrir [àtèrír] v. to make land; to ground (naut.); to land (aviat.). ‖ **atterrissage** [-lsàj] m. landfall; alighting; grounding, landing; train d'atterrissage. under-carriage.

attestation [àtèstàsyo⁰] f. attestation; testimonial; certificate; character, affidavit. ‖ **attester** [-é] v. to certify, to testify; to vouch.

attiédir [àtyédír] v. to cool; to warm; to damp, s'attiédir, to cool down.

attifer [àtífé] v. to dress up, to get up; s'attifer, to rig oneself up.

attirable [àtìràbl] adj. attractable. ‖ **attirail** [-ày] m outfit; gear, tackle; pomp. ‖ **attirance** [-a⁰s] f. attraction. ‖ **attirant** [-a⁰] adj. attractive. ‖ **attirer** [-é] v. to draw; to attract; to entice; to lure, to allure; to decoy; to win; s'attirer, to bring upon oneself.

attiser [àtìzé] v. to stir up; to poke; to arouse.

attitré [àtìtré] adj. appointed, regular, customary; recognized.

attitude [àtìtüd] f. attitude; posture, pose.

attraction [àtràksyo⁰] f. attraction; attractiveness; pl. variety entertainment; floor show.

attrait [àtrè] m. attraction; charm; liking, lure.

attrape [àtràp] f. trap, snare; trick, hoax, attrape-mouches, flypaper; attrape-nigaud, boobytrap. ‖ **attraper** [-é] v. to entrap; to trick; to catch; to scold (fam.).

attrayant [àtrèyàⁿ] *adj.* attractive.

attribuer [àtrìbüé] *v.* to attribute; to ascribe; to assign; to allot; to grant. ‖ **attribut** [-ü] *m.* attribute. ‖ **attribution** [-üsyoⁿ] *f.* conferment; allocation; *pl.* competence, powers, duties.

attrister [àtrìsté] *v.* to grieve; to sadden; to darken; *s'attrister,* to become sad; to mope; to lour.

attroupement [àtrûpmaⁿ] *m.* mob; unlawful assembly; disorderly gathering; riot. ‖ **attrouper** [-é] *v.* to gather; to assemble; *s'attrouper,* to assemble, to crowd, to flock together.

au [ô], *see* à.

aubaine [ôbèn] *f.* godsend; windfall.

aube [ôb] *f.* dawn, daybreak.

aube [ôb] *f.* paddle, float.

aubépine [ôbépìn] *f.* hawthorn; whitethorn; may.

auberge [ôbèrj] *f.* inn, tavern; *auberge de jeunesse,* youth hostel.

aubergine [ôbèrjìn] *f.* eggplant.

aubergiste [ôbèrjìst] *m.,* *f.* innkeeper, landlord, host.

aucun [ôkuⁿ] *adj., pron.* not any, none, any; *d'aucuns,* some people. ‖ *aucunement* [-ünmaⁿ] *adv.* by no means, not at all, in no way.

audace [ôdàs] *f.* daring, boldness, audacity; cheek; *payer d'audace,* to face the music. ‖ **audacieux** [-yë] *adj.** bold, audacious; daring.

au-dehors [ôd∘ôr] *adv.* outside; abroad. ‖ *au-delà* [ôdlà] *adv.* more; longer; beyond; *m.* beyond. ‖ *au-delà de loc. prép.* beyond, over, past. ‖ *au-dessous* [ôdsü] *adv.* below. ‖ *au-dessus* [ôdsü] *adv.* over; above. ‖ *au-devant* [ôdvaⁿ] *adv.* forward, ahead; *aller au-devant de,* to go to meet.

audience [ôdyaⁿs] *f.* sitting, session; hearing; *audience publique,* open court. ‖ **auditeur** [-ìtœr] *m.* listener, hearer; auditor (comptes); prosecutor (jur.). ‖ **auditif** [-ìtìf] *adj.** auditory. ‖ **audition** [-lsyoⁿ] *f.* hearing; recital; auditing (comm.); audition. ‖ **auditoire** [-ìtwàr] *m.* auditorium; audience; attendance; congregation; court-room. ‖ **audio-visuel** [ôdyòvìzüèl] *adj.** audio-visual.

auge [ôj] *f.* trough; manger.

augmentation [ôgmaⁿtàsyoⁿ] *f.* increase, enlargement; raise; rise [prix]. ‖ **augmenter** [-é] *v.* to increase, to enlarge; to raise, to rise.

augure [ôgür] *m.* augur; augury, omen; *de bon augure,* auspicious; *de mauvais augure,* ominous.

aujourd'hui [ôjûrdüì] *adv.* today; nowadays; *d'aujourd'hui en huit, en quinze,* today week, fortnight.

aulne [ôn] *m.* alder [arbre].

aulx [ô] *pl. of* ail.

aumône [ômôn] *f.* alms, charity; *faire l'aumône,* to give alms. ‖ **aumônerie** [-rì] *f.* chaplaincy; chaplainship. ‖ **aumônier** [-yé] *m.* chaplain.

auparavant [ôpàràvaⁿ] *adv.* before; beforehand; previously.

auprès [ôprè] *adv.* near; close to; close by; *auprès de,* beside, near; *auprès de la Cour,* attached to the Court.

auquel [ôkèl], *see lequel.*

auréole [ôréòl] *f.* aureole, halo; halation (phot.).

auriculaire [ôrìkülèr] *adj.* auricular; *m.* little finger.

aurifère [ôrìfèr] *adj.* auriferous, goldbearing. ‖ **aurifier** [-yé] *v.* to fill, to stop with gold.

aurore [ôrôr] *f.* dawn, daybreak; *aurore boréale,* northern lights.

auscultation [ôskültàsyoⁿ] *f.* auscultation. ‖ **ausculter** [-é] *v.* to auscultate, to sound.

auspices [ôspìs] *m. pl.* auspice, omen.

aussi [ôsì] *adv.* also; as; so; therefore; *aussi bien,* besides, for that matter; *moi aussi,* so am I, so do I. ‖ **aussitôt** [ôsìtô] *adv.* immediately; at once; directly; forthwith; *aussitôt que,* as soon as.

austère [ôstèr] *adj.* austere, severe, sober; stern. ‖ **austérité** [-érìté] *f.* austerity, sternness.

autant [ôtaⁿ] *adv.* as much, as many; so much; so many; *d'autant plus que,* all the more as; especially as; *en faire autant,* tò do the same; *autant le faire vous-même,* you might as well do it yourself; *autant que,* as far as.

autel [ôtèl] *m.* altar.

auteur [ôtœr] *m.* author, originator; writer, composer; perpetrator; *droits d'auteur,* royalties.

authenticité [ôtaⁿtìsìté] *f.* authenticity, genuineness. ‖ **authentifier** [-ìfyé] *v.* to authenticate. ‖ **authentique** [-ìk] *adj.* authentic; certified [document].

auto [ôtô] *f.* car, motor. ‖ **auto-école** [-ékôl] *f.* driving school.

autobus [ôtòbüs] *m.* motorbus, bus.

autocar [ôtòkàr] *m.* motor coach.

autochenille [ôtòshnìy] *f.* halftrack vehicle; caterpillar-tractor.

autoclave [ôtòklàv] *m.* sterilizer; *adj.* self-regulating.

autocuiseur [òtòkülżær] *m.* pressure cooker, self-cooker.

autodidacte [òtòdîdàkt] *m., f.* self-taught person.

autodrome [òtòdròm] *m.* motor-racing track.

autographe [òtògràf] *adj.* autographic; *m.* autograph.

automate [òtòmàt] *m.* automaton. ‖ *automatique* [-ĭk] *adj.* automatic, self-acting.

automitrailleuse [òtòmìtràyéz] *f.* combat car.

automne [òtòn] *m.* autumn, *Am.* fall.

automobile [òtòmòbìl] *f.* automobile; car; *adj.* self-propelled; *canot automobile*, motor boat. ‖ *automobiliste* [-ĭst] *m., f.* motorist, automobile driver.

automotrice [òtòmòtrìs] *f.* railcar.

autonome [òtònòm] *adj.* autonomous. ‖ *autonomie* [-ĭ] *f.* autonomy, self-government; independance; range.

autopsie [òtòpsî] *f.* autopsy; post-mortem.

autorail [òtòrày] *m.* railcar.

autorisation [òtòrîzàsyòn] *f.* authorization; permission; leave; license; warrant. ‖ *autoriser* [-ĭzé] *v.* to authorize; to empower; to permit; *s'autoriser*, to take the liberty; to ground oneself (*de*, on). ‖ *autoritaire* [-ĭtèr] *adj.* authoritarian; high-handed. ‖ *autorité* [-ĭté] *f.* authority; legal power; *avoir de l'autorité sur*, to have power over; *faire autorité en*, to be an authority on.

autoroute [òtòrût] *f.* motor highway, turnpike, express way.

autostop [òtòstòp] *m.* hitch-hiking; *Am.* thumbing rides; *faire de l'autostop*, to hitch-hike, *Am.* to thumb a ride; to bum a ride (fam.).

autour [òtûr] *adv.* about, around.

autre [òtr] *adj., pron.* other; another; different; further; else; *quelqu'un d'autre*, someone else; *l'un ou l'autre*, either; *ni l'un ni l'autre*, neither; *l'un et l'autre*, both; *l'un l'autre*, each other, one another; *tout autre*, anyone else; *une tout autre femme*, quite a different woman; *autre chose*, something else; *à d'autres!*, tell that to the marines! ‖ *autrefois* [-fwà] *adv.* formerly, of old, in the past. ‖ *autrement* [-màn] *adv.* otherwise.

Autriche [òtrîsh] *f.* Austria. ‖ *autrichien* [-yĭn] *m., adj.** Austrian.

autruche [òtrüsh] *f.* ostrich.

autrui [òtrüĭ] *m.* others, other people.

auvent [òvàn] *m.* penthouse; weatherboard; porch roof; hood.

aux [ò], *see à.*

auxiliaire [òksîlyèr] *adj.* auxiliary; subsidiary; *m.* auxiliary, assistant; *bureau auxiliaire*, sub-office.

auxquels [òkèl], *see lequel.*

avachir [àvàshîr] *v.* to soften; *s'avachir*, to lose shape; to become sloppy.

aval [àvàl] *m.* downstream.

aval [àvàl] *m.* endorsement (comm.).

avalanche [àvàlansh] *f.* avalanche.

avaler [àvàlé] *v.* to swallow, to gulp down; to gobble; to lower; to pocket [affront]; to inhale [fumée].

avaliser [àvàlĭzé] *v.* to indorse.

à-valoir [àvàlwàr] *m.* instalment.

avance [àvàns] *f.* advance; progress; loan (comm.); lead, travel (mech.); *avoir de l'avance sur*, to be ahead of; *d'avance*, beforehand; *être en avance*, to be fast; *prendre de l'avance*, to take the lead. ‖ *avancé* [-é] *adj.* advanced; forward; progressive; over-ripe [fruit]; high [viande]. ‖ *avancement* [-màn] *m.* promotion; projection; advancement; progress; pitch (techn.); *recevoir de l'avancement*, to be promoted. ‖ *avancer* [-é] *v.* to move forward; to advance; to promote, to push; to hasten; to proceed, to progress; to be fast [montre]; to pay in advance; *s'avancer*, to move forward, to advance; to jut out; to go too far.

avanie [àvànî] *f.* affront, snub.

avant [àvàn] *prep.* before; in front of; *adv.* beforehand; previously; forward; *m.* bow (naut.); forward [football]; front, fore part; *en avant*, forward; in front; *plus avant*, further; *avant que*, before; *avant-bras*, forearm; *avant-coureur*, forerunner; precursor; harbinger; scout; *avant-dernier*, penultimate; next to last; last but one; *avant-garde*, advance guard, vanguard; *avant-goût*, foretaste; *avant-hier*, the day before yesterday; *avant-midi*, © forenoon, morning; *avant-port*, outer harbo(u)r; *avant-poste*, outpost; *avant-première*, dress rehearsal; private view; *avant-projet*, rough draft; preliminary plan; *avant-propos*, introduction; foreword; *avant-scène*, proscenium; *avant-train*, limber (mil.); forecarriage [véhicule]; forequarters [animal]; *avant-veille*, two days before.

avantage [àvantàĵ] *m.* advantage, profit; benefit; gain; *donner l'avantage*, to give odds; *tirer avantage de*, to turn to advantage. ‖ *avantager* [-ĵé] *v.* to benefit; to give an advantage to; to become. ‖ *avantageux* [-ë] *adj.** advantageous, profitable; becoming; conceited, self-satisfied (fig.).

avare [àvàr] *m., f.* miser, niggard; *adj.* miserly, avaricious, stingy. ‖ *avarice* [-ĭs] *f.* avarice; stinginess.

avarie [àvàrî] *f.* damage, injury; *pl.* deterioration; *subir une avarie,* to be damaged. ‖ **avarier** [-yé] *v.* to spoil, to damage.

avatar [àvàtàr] *m.* avatar; transformation; *pl.* vicissitudes, ups and downs.

avec [àvèk] *prep., adv.* with.

avenant [àvnaⁿ] *adj.* prepossessing, comely; *m.* codicil, rider, clause (jur.); *à l'avenant,* in keeping, appropriate, to match.

avènement [àvènmaⁿ] *m.* coming; arrival; advent, accession.

Avent [àvaⁿ] *m.* Advent.

aventure [àvaⁿtür] *f.* adventure; chance, luck, venture; *dire la bonne aventure,* to tell fortunes; *à l'aventure,* at random. ‖ **aventurer** [-é] *v.* to risk; *s'aventurer,* to venture, to take risks. ‖ **aventureux** [-ë] *adj.** venturesome, risky, reckless. ‖ **aventurier** [-yé] *m.* adventurer.

avenu [àvnü] *adj.; nul et non avenu,* null and void.

avenue [àvnü] *f.* avenue, drive.

avérer [àvéré] *v.* to establish, to authenticate; *s'avérer,* to prove, to turn out.

averse [àvèrs] *f.* shower, downpour.

aversion [àvèrsyoⁿ] *f.* aversion, dislike; reluctance.

avertir [àvèrtîr] *v.* to warn, to notify. ‖ **avertissement** [-ìsmaⁿ] *m.* warning; foreword; notification. ‖ **avertisseur** [-ìsœr] *m.* warning signal; hooter; alarm [feu]; call bell; horn [auto]; callboy (theat.).

aveu [àvë] *m.** admission; avowal; confession; consent; acknowledgment; *sans aveu,* disreputable.

aveuglant [àvœglaⁿ] *adj.* blinding; glaring; overpowering, categorical, indubitable. ‖ **aveugle** [àvœgl] *m.* blind man; *f.* blind woman; *adj.* blind, sightless. ‖ **aveuglement** [-ᵉmaⁿ] *m.* blinding; blindness [moral]. ‖ **aveugler** [-é] *v.* to blind; to dazzle; to hoodwink; to stop [fuite]. ‖ **aveuglette (à l')** [-ᵉt] *adv.* blindly, gropingly.

aviateur [àvyàtœr] *m.* airman; aviator, flyer. ‖ **aviation** [àvyàsyoⁿ] *f.* aviation; air force; flying; airplanes.

aviculture [àvìkültür] *f.* bird fancying; poultry farming.

avide [àvìd] *adj.* greedy, eager (for); keen (on). ‖ **avidité** [-ìté] *f.* avidity; greediness; eagerness.

avilir [àvìlîr] *v.* to debase, to degrade, to lower. ‖ **avilissement** [-ìsmaⁿ] *m.* debasement, degradation, depreciation.

aviné [àvìné] *adj.* tipsy, drunk.

avion [àvyoⁿ] *m.* airplane, plane; *Br.* aeroplane; *avion de tourisme,* private airplane; *avion radio-commandé,* wireless-controlled airplane; *avion à réaction,* jet; *par avion,* by airmail.

aviron [àvìroⁿ] *m.* oar, scull, © paddle; rowing. ‖ **avironner** [-òné] *v.* © to paddle, to row.

avis [àvì] *m.* opinion; guess; advice; notice; notification; intimation; warning; *à mon avis,* in my opinion; *changer d'avis,* to change one's mind; *jusqu'à nouvel avis,* until further notice; *sauf avis contraire,* unless I hear to the contrary. ‖ **avisé** [-zé] *adj.* shrewd, sagacious. ‖ **aviser** [-zé] *v.* to catch sight of; to inform, to notify; to advise; *s'aviser de,* to think about; to dare, to find a way.

aviso [àvìzô] *m.* dispatch boat.

aviver [àvìvé] *v.* to brighten; to touch up [couleurs]; to revive [feu]; to burnish [métal]; to sharpen [outils]; to irritate [plaie].

avocat [àvòkà] *m.* barrister; counsel; lawyer; advocate, pleader, counsel(l)or; *avocat général, Br.* Public Prosecutor, *Am.* Attorney general.

avocat [àvòkà] *m.* avocado [fruit].

avoine [àvwàn] *f.* oats.

avoir [àvwàr] *m.* property; possession; credit; fortune; *v.** to have; to possess; to hold; *avoir chaud,* to be warm; *il y a trois jours,* three days ago; *qu'est-ce qu'il y a?,* what is the matter?; *en avoir contre,* to have a grudge against.

avoisinant [àvwàzìnaⁿ] *adj.* neighbouring; nearly. ‖ **avoisiner** [é] *v.* to adjoin; to border on; to be near to.

avortement [àvòrtᵉmaⁿ] *m.* miscarriage; failure; abortion. ‖ **avorter** [-é] *v.* to miscarry, to abort; *se faire avorter,* to cause oneself to miscarry.

avouable [àvwàbl] *adj.* avowable. ‖ **avoué** [àvwé] *m.* solicitor. ‖ **avouer** [àvwé] *v.* to admit, to acknowledge; to own to; to ratify; to endorse.

avril [àvrìl] *m.* April; *poisson d'avril,* April fool joke.

axe [àks] *m.* axis; axle; spindle; pin; line; *axe de manivelle,* crankshaft. ‖ **axer** [-é] *v.* to center.

axiome [àksyòm] *m.* axiom.

ayant [èyaⁿ] *pr. p.* of *avoir.* ‖ **ayant droit** [-drwà] *m.* rightful claimant.

azotate [àzòtàt] *m.* nitrate. ‖ **azote** [àzòt] *m.* nitrogen.

azur [àzür] *m.* azure, blue; *la Côte d'Azur,* the Riviera.

azyme [àzìm] *adj.* unleavened.

B

baba [bàbà] *m.* sponge-cake steeped in rum.

baba [bàbà] *adj.* (pop.) flabbergasted, amazed; *en rester baba*, to be dumb-founded.

babeurre [bàbœr] *m.* buttermilk.

babil [bàbîl] *m.* prattle [enfants]; twittering [oiseaux]. ‖ *babillard* [-lyàr] *m.* chatterer, © notice-board; *adj.* talkative, garrulous.

babine [bàbîn] *f.* pendulous lip; chop.

babiole [bàbyòl] *f.* toy, plaything; curio; gewgaw.

bâbord [bàbòr] *m.* port (naut.).

babouche [bàbûsh] *f.* Turkish slipper.

bac [bàk] *m.* ferry-boat; tank; tub; sink; vat (techn.); *passer en bac*, to cross on the ferry.

bac [bàk] *abbrev. for baccalauréat.*

baccalauréat [bàkàlòréà] *m.* second-ary school leaving-certificate, *Am.* bachelor's degree.

bacchanale [bàkànàl] *f.* orgy.

bâche [bàsh] *f.* canvas cover.

bachelier [bàsh·lyé] *m.* bachelor [Académie].

bachique [bàshîk] *adj.* Bacchic.

bachot [bàshô] *m.* dinghy; wherry.

bachot [bàshô] *m.* (pop.), see *bacca-lauréat.*

bacille [bàsîl] *m.* bacillus.

bâcler [bàklé] *v.* to bar, to bolt [porte]; to close; to hustle; to patch up; to hurry over [travail].

bactérie [bàktérî] *f.* [usually *pl.*] bacteria. ‖ *bactériologie* [-lòlòjî] *f.* bacteriology.

badaud [bàdô] *m.* stroller; gaper, *Am.* rubber-neck. ‖ *badauder* [-dé] *v.* to stroll about; to gape.

baderne [bàdèrn] *f.* fender (naut.); *vieille baderne*, old fog(e)y.

badigeon [bàdìjoⁿ] *m.* whitewash; distemper [murs]. ‖ *badigeonner* [-òné] *v.* to paint; to daub; to whitewash.

badin [bàdiⁿ] *m.* joker, banterer; *adj.* playful. ‖ *badinage* [-inàj] *m.* banter. ‖ *badiner* [-iné] *v.* to toy, to trifle; to dally; to tease.

bafouer [bàfwé] *v.* to ridicule, to scoff at, to gibe at.

bafouillage [bàfûyàj] *m.* nonsense. ‖ *bafouiller* [-ûyé] *v.* to stammer; to splutter [moteur]; to talk nonsense.

bâfrer [bàfré] *v.* (pop.) to guzzle, to gorge; to stuff oneself with.

bagage [bàgàj] *m.* baggage; luggage; *plier bagage*, to pack up and leave; *dépôt des bagages*, luggage office; *bagages non accompagnés*, luggage in advance.

bagarre [bàgàr] *f.* scuffle, brawl; free fight; quarrel. ‖ *se bagarrer* [s·bàgàré] *v.* to scuffle.

bagatelle [bàgàtèl] *f.* trifle; love-making; *interj.* nonsense!

bagne [bàñ] *m.* convict prison; hulk.

bagnole [bàñòl] *f.* cart; (fam.) car.

bagou(t) [bàgû] *m.* (fam.) glibness; *avoir du bagout*, to have the gift of the gab.

bague [bàg] *f.* ring; band.

baguenauder [bàgnôdé] *v.* (pop.) to loaf; to waste time.

baguette [bàgèt] *f.* stick; wand; rod; bread [pain]; beading (techn.).

bahut [bàü] *m.* chest; cupboard.

bai [bè] *adj.* bay [cheval].

baie [bè] *f.* bay (geogr.).

baie [bè] *f.* berry (bot.).

baignade [bèñàd] *f.* bathe, dip. ‖ *baigner* [-é] *v.* to bathe; to bath; to steep; to wash [côte]; *se baigner*, to take a bath; to have a bathe. ‖ *baigneur* [-œr] *m.* bather. ‖ *baignoire* [-wàr] *f.* bath, bathtub; lower box, baignoire (theat.).

bail [bày] (*pl.* **baux** [bô]) *m.* lease; *prendre une maison à bail*, to lease a house.

bâillement [bàymaⁿ] *m.* yawn; gap-ing. ‖ *bâiller* [bàyé] *v.* to yawn; to gape; to be ajar [porte].

bailleur [bàyœr] *m.* giver; lessor; *bailleur de fonds*, silent partner, fi-nancial backer.

bâillon [bàyoⁿ] *m.* gag. ‖ *bâillonner* [bàyòné] *v.* to gag.

bain [biⁿ] *m.* bath; bathing; *salle de bains*, bathroom; *bains publics*, public baths; *bain-douche*, shower bath; *bain-marie*, water-bath, *Br.* jacketed saucepan, *Am.* double-boiler.

baïonnette [bàyònèt] *f.* bayonet.

baisemain [bèzmiⁿ] *m.* hand-kissing.

baiser [bèzé] *m.* kiss.

baisse [bès] *f.* lowering; going down [eaux]; ebb [marée]; fall [prix]; *en baisse*, falling. ‖ *baisser* [bèsé] *v.* to lower; to let down [vitre]; to turn down [lampe]; to hang [tête]; to dip, to dim [phares]; to sink; to decline; to drop; to abate; *se baisser*, to stoop; to bend down.

bajoue [bàjû] *f.* chap, chop, jowl.

Bakélite [bàkélìt] *f.* (trade-mark) Bakelite.

bal [bàl] *m.* ball; dance.

balade [bàlàd] *f.* (fam.) stroll; ramble; excursion. ‖ *balader* [-é] *v.* (fam.) to take for a walk; *envoyer balader*, to chuck away; to send packing; *se balader*, to go for a stroll. ‖ *baladeur* [-œr] *m.* saunterer; selector rod [auto]. ‖ *baladeuse* [-ëz] *f.* handcart; trouble lamp, inspection lamp.

balafre [bàlàfr] *f.* gash; scar. ‖ *balafrer* [-é] *v.* to gash, to slash.

balai [bàlè] *m.* broom; brush; mop; carpet-sweeper.

balance [bàlã⁵s] *f.* balance; scales, weighing-machine; hesitation; *faire pencher la balance*, to turn the scale; *faire la balance*, to strike a balance. ‖ *balancement* [-mᵃⁿ] *m.* rocking; swinging; harmony; indecision. ‖ *balancer* [-é] *v.* to balance, to poise; to waver; to sway, to swing; to hesitate; *se balancer*, to swing; to rock; to ride [bateau]. ‖ *balancier* [-yé] *m.* pendulum [horloge]; balance-wheel [montre]; balancing-pole; screw-press (mech.). ‖ *balançoire* [-wàr] *f.* see-saw, swing.

balayage [bàlèyàj] *m.* sweeping; brushing; scanning. ‖ *balayer* [-èyé] *v.* to sweep; to sweep up [poussière]; to scan [télévision]; to scour [mer]. ‖ *balayeur* [-èyœr] *m.* sweeper, scavenger; *balayures*, sweepings.

balbutiement [bàlbüsîmᵃⁿ] *m.* stammering. ‖ *balbutier* [-yé] *v.* to stammer; to mumble.

balcon [bàlkoⁿ] *m.* balcony; dress-circle (theat.); pulpit (naut.).

baldaquin [bàldàkìⁿ] *m.* canopy; tester.

baleine [bàlèn] *f.* whale; whale-bone; corset-bone. ‖ *baleiner* [-é] *v.* to stiffen. ‖ *baleinier* [-yé] *adj.*＊ whaling [industrie]; *m.* whaler [navire]; whale-fisher [pêcheur]; *baleinière*, whale-boat.

balise [bàlìz] *f.* beacon; ground-light (aviat.); *balise flottante*, buoy. ‖ *baliser* [-é] *v.* to beacon (naut.); to buoy, to mark; to provide landing-lights (aviat.).

balistique [bàlìstìk] *f.* ballistics; gunnery; *adj.* ballistic.

balivernes [bàlìvèrn] *f. pl.* nonsense.

ballade [bàlàd] *f.* ballad.

ballant [bàlãⁿ] *m.* swing; *adj.* dangling; swinging; slack [corde].

ballast [bàlàst] *m.* ballast.

balle [bàl] *f.* husk, chaff [avoine].

balle [bàl] *f.* pack; bale [coton].

balle [bàl] *f.* ball; bullet (mil.); shot; (pop.) franc; map [figure].

ballerine [bàlrîn] *f.* ballet-dancer. ‖ *ballet* [bàlè] *m.* ballet.

ballon [bàloⁿ] *m.* balloon; ball; football; ball-signal (naut.); flask (chem.); rounded hill-top; *envoyer un ballon d'essai*, to put out a feeler. ‖ *ballonnement* [-ònmᵃⁿ] *m.* swelling; bloat; flatulence. ‖ *ballonner* [-òné] *v.* to swell out; to balloon; to distend; to bulge.

ballot [bàlô] *m.* pack, bundle; ninny, sucker. ‖ *ballottage* [-òtàj] *m.* tossing; shaking; second ballot [élections]. ‖ *ballottement* [-òtmᵃⁿ] *m.* tossing. ‖ *ballotter* [-òté] *v.* to toss about; to shake, to jolt; to rattle [porte]; (fig.) to put off.

balluchon [bàlüshoⁿ] *m.* bundle.

balnéaire [bàlnéér] *adj.* watering; *station balnéaire*, spa, bathing resort.

balourd [bàlûr] *adj.* dense, doltish; *m.* lout, clod-hopper. ‖ *balourdise* [-dîz] *f.* blunder, stupid mistake.

baluchon, *see* balluchon.

balustrade [bàlüstràd] *f.* balustrade; handrail. ‖ *balustre* [-lüstr] *m.* baluster, banister.

bambin [bãⁿbìⁿ] *m.* urchin, youngster; (fam.) kid, brat.

bambocheur [bãⁿbòshœr] *m.* (pop.) reveller; carouser.

bambou [bãⁿbû] *m.* bamboo.

ban [bãⁿ] *m.* proclamation; applause; *le ban et l'arrière-ban*, every man Jack; *mettre au ban*, to outlaw, to banish; *pl.* banns [mariage].

banal [bànàl] *adj.*＊ commonplace; banal; trite; hackneyed. ‖ *banalité* [-ité] *f.* commonplace, banality, triteness.

banane [bànàn] *f.* banana.

banc [bãⁿ] *m.* bench, seat, pew [église]; bench (mech.); bank; shoal [sable]; school [poissons]; *banc de neige*, Ⓒ snow-bank; *banc des témoins*, witness-box.

bancaire [bãⁿkèr] *adj.* bank, banking.

bancal [bãⁿkàl] (*pl.* **bancals**) *adj.* bandy-legged; unsteady.

bandage [bãⁿdàj] *m.* bandaging; bandage; *Br.* tyre, *Am.* tire (techn.); winding up [ressort]; *bandage herniaire*, truss.

bande [bãⁿd] *f.* band, strip; stripe; belt [terre]; cine-film; sound-track, tape; list (naut.); wrapper; *donner de la bande*, to list, to heel over.

bande [baⁿd] *f.* band, party, gang; troop; pack [loups]; flock; *bande noire*, set of terrorists.

bandeau [baⁿdô] *m.** headband; diadem; bandage.

bander [baⁿdé] *v.* to bind up, to bandage; to draw, to bend; to tighten; to strain; to be tight; *bander les yeux*, to blindfold; *se bander*, to be bent.

banderole [baⁿdrôl] *f.* streamer; sling (mil.); pennant.

bandit [baⁿdì] *m.* bandit, gangster; (fam.) rogue, ruffian, *Am.* hijacker.

bandoulière [baⁿdûlyèr] *f.* shoulder-strap; *en bandoulière*, slung over the shoulder.

banlieue [baⁿlyë] *f.* suburb, outskirts; *de banlieue*, suburban.

banne [bàn] *f.* coal cart; basket, hamper; tilt, tarpaulin.

banni [bànì] *m.* outcast; outlaw; exile; *adj.* banished.

bannière [bànyèr] *f.* flag; banner; ensign; shirt-tail.

bannir [bànìr] *v.* to outlaw, to exile.

banque [baⁿk] *f.* bank; banking; *billet de banque*, banknote; *banque par actions*, joint-stock bank; *faire sauter la banque*, to break the bank [jeu]; *banque du sang*, blood bank.

banqueroute [baⁿkrût] *f.* bankruptcy; failure; *faire banqueroute*, to go bankrupt. || *banqueroutier* [-yé] *m.* fraudulent bankrupt; bankrupt trader.

banquet [baⁿkè] *m.* feast, banquet. || *banqueter* [-té] *v.* to feast, to banquet.

banquette [baⁿkèt] *f.* bench, seat; bank [terre]; bunker [golf].

banquier [baⁿkyé] *m.* banker.

banquise [baⁿkîz] *f.* ice-floe, ice-pack, ice-field.

baptême [bàtèm] *m.* baptism, christening; *nom de baptême*, Christian name. || *baptiser* [bàtìzé] *v.* to baptize, to christen; to name; to nickname; to water down.

baquet [bàkè] *m.* tub, bucket.

bar [bàr] *m.* bass [poisson].

bar [bàr] *m.* bar [hôtel, café].

baragouin [bàràgwìⁿ] *m.* (pop.) gibberish. || *baragouiner* [-ìné] *v.* to gibber; *baragouiner le français*, to murder French.

baraque [bàràk] *f.* hut, shed, shanty; booth; hovel. || *baraquement* [-maⁿ] *m.* hutting; hutments.

baratin [bàràtìⁿ] *m.* spiel, line, ballyhoo. || *baratiner* [-tìné] *v.* to speechify, to gas.

baratte [bàràt] *f.* churn. || *baratter* [-é] *v.* to churn [lait].

barbare [bàrbàr] *m.* barbarian; *adj.* barbaric; uncivilized; barbarous, cruel. || *barbarie* [-ì] *f.* barbarity. || *barbarisme* [-ìsm] *m.* barbarism (gramm.).

barbe [bàrb] *f.* beard; whiskers; burr (techn.); *se faire la barbe*, to shave; *rire dans sa barbe*, to laugh up one's sleeve; (pop.) *la barbe!*, shut up! || *barbeau* [-ô] *m.* barbel [poisson]; cornflower (bot.). || *barbelé* [-é] *adj.* barbed. || *barber* [-é] *v.* to bore stiff. || *barbet* [-è] *m.* water-spaniel. || *barbiche* [-ìsh] *f.* short beard; goatee. || *barbillon* [-ìyoⁿ] *m.* barb. || *barbon* [bàrboⁿ] *m.* greybeard, old fogey.

barbiturique [bàrbìtürìk] *m.* barbiturate; *adj.* barbituric.

barboter [bàrbôté] *v.* to dabble; to splash; to bubble [gaz]. || *barboteur* [-èr] *m.* paddler; bubbler (techn.). || *barboteuse* [-ëz] *f.* rompers; washing-machine. || *barbot(t)e* [-ôt] *f.* © catfish; © illegal gambling-house.

barbouillage [bàrbûyàj] *m.* daubing; scrawl; scribble. || *barbouiller* [-ûyé] *v.* to daub; to sully; (fam.) to mess up.

barbu [bàrbü] *adj.* bearded.

barde [bàrd] *m.* bard, poet.

barde [bàrd] *f.* pack-saddle; slice of bacon. || *barder* [-é] *v.* to bard [volaille]; to cover with.

barder [bàrdé] *v.* to carry away; (fam.) to toil; (pop.) *ça barde!*, it's tough going!

barème [bàrèm] *m.* ready-reckoner; scale [salaires]; graph.

baril [bàrì] *m.* barrel, keg, cask. || *barillet* [-yè] *m.* small barrel, keg; cylinder [revolver].

bariolage [bàryôlàj] *m.* motley; gaudy colo(u)r scheme. || *barioler* [-é] *v.* to checker; to paint gaudily; to variegate.

barman [bàrmàn] *m.* barman, *Am.* bartender.

barnum [bàrnòm] *m.* showman; shindy.

baromètre [bàrômètr] *m.* barometer; *baromètre enregistreur*, barograph. || *barométrique* [-étrìk] *adj.* barometric.

baron [bàroⁿ] *m.* baron. || *baronne* [-òn] *f.* baroness.

baroque [bàrôk] *m.* baroque; *adj.* baroque; curious, odd, strange.

barque [bàrk] *f.* boat; barque; *bien conduire sa barque*, to manage one's affairs well. || *barquette* [-èt] *f.* skiff; small boat; shaped tart.

barrage [bàràj] *m.* barring, closing [rues]; barrier; obstruction; dam, weir (mech.); barrage (mil.); *barrage de*

route, road block. ‖ **barre** [bàr] *f.* bar; rod; helm (naut.); ingot [or]; bar [jur.]; stroke; bar-line (mus.); stripe; bore [rivière]; *barre de connexion,* tierod [auto]; *barre d'appui,* handrail; *paraître à la barre,* to appear before the Court; *barre de plage,* surf. ‖ **barreau** [-ô] *m.** bar, rail; rung [échelle]; bar (jur.); *être reçu au barreau,* Br. to be called to the bar; *Am.* to pass the bar. ‖ **barrer** [-é] *v.* to bar; to stop; to cross out; *Br.* to cross [chèque]; to steer (naut.); © to lock (a door); *rue barrée,* no thoroughfare; *se barrer,* to buzz off (pop.). ‖ **barrette** [-èt] *f.* small bar; connecting strip (electr.).

barrette [bàrèt] *f.* biretta; cardinal's cap; hair-slide; spray.

barreur [bàrœr] *m.* helmsman; cox.

barricade [bàrìkàd] *f.* barricade. ‖ **barricader** [-é] *v.* to barricade.

barrière [bàrìyèr] *f.* barrier; obstacle; turnpike; gate [passage à niveau]; starting-post [courses].

barrique [bàrìk] *f.* hogshead, butt, barrel, cask; barrel roll.

baryton [bàrìtoⁿ] *m., adj.* baritone.

bas [bâ] *m.* lower part; bottom; foot; small; stocking; *adj.** low; small; mean; *adv.* low; *en bas,* below; *aller en bas,* to go downstairs; *à bas...!,* down with...!; *faire main basse sur,* to lay hands on; *au bas mot,* at the lowest estimate; *bas-fonds,* underworld; shallows (naut.); *bas-côté,* aisle; *bas-relief,* low-relief.

basalte [bàzàlt] *m.* basalt.

basane [bàzàn] *f.* sheepskin; basil. ‖ **basané** [-é] *adj.* tanned, sunburnt, swarthy.

bascule [bàskül] *f.* weighing-machine; seesaw; *wagon à bascule,* tip-waggon; *Am.* dump-cart. ‖ **basculer** [-é] *v.* to rock; to tip up; *faire basculer,* to dip [fanal, phare]. ‖ **basculeur** [-œr] *m.* tilter; *basculeur de phares,* dipper [autos].

base [bâz] *f.* base; base-line; bottom; basis, ground, foundation; *jeter les bases,* to lay the foundations; *sans base,* unfounded; *base navale,* naval base; *de base,* basic.

basoche [bàzòsh] *f.* the bar, the legal profession.

basque [bàsk] *m., adj.* Basque; *f.* skirt, tail.

basse [bâs] *see bas; f.* bass (mus.); cello; shoal, reef (naut.); *basse-cour,* farmyard. ‖ **bassesse** [-ès] *f.* baseness; base action; vulgarity; *faire des bassesses,* to stoop to some humiliating expedient.

basset [bàsè] *m.* basset hound.

bassin [bàsⁿ] *m.* basin; lake [artificiel]; tank (techn.); dock; pelvis (anat.); bed-pan. ‖ **bassine** [bàsⁿ] *f.* pan; preserving pan; basin. ‖ **bassiner** [-é] *v.* to warm [lit]; to bathe; (pop.) to annoy. ‖ **bassinet** [-è] *m.* small basin. ‖ **bassinoire** [-wàr] *f.* warming-pan; bore (fam.).

bastion [bàstyoⁿ] *m.* bastion.

bastringue [bàstrⁿg] *m.* honky-tonk joint; row, racket.

bât [bâ] *m.* pack-saddle; *cheval de bât,* pack-horse.

bataille [bàtày] *f.* battle; *bataille rangée,* pitched battle; *livrer bataille à,* to join battle with. ‖ **batailler** [-àyé] *v.* to fight; to struggle. ‖ **batailleur** [-àyœr] *adj.* fighting; quarrelsome. ‖ **bataillon** [-àyoⁿ] *m.* battalion.

bâtard [bâtàr] *m., adj.* bastard; crossbred; mongrel [animaux]; kind of French bread; degenerate [race]. ‖ **bâtardise** [-dîz] *f.* bastardy.

bateau [bàtô] *m.** boat, ship; *bateau à vapeur,* steamer; *bateau de pêche,* fishing-boat; *bateau de sauvetage,* lifeboat; *monter un bateau à quelqu'un,* to pull someone's leg; *bateau-citerne,* tanker; *bateau-feu,* lightship; *bateau-hôpital,* hospital-ship; *bateau-mouche,* small passenger steamer.

bateleur [bàtᵉlœr] *m.* mountebank.

batelier [bàtᵉlyé] *m.* boatman.

bâter [bâté] *v.* to saddle; *un âne bâté,* a silly ass.

bâti [bâtì] *m.* framing; body [moteur]; tacking. ‖ **bâtiment** [-màⁿ] *m.* edifice, building; vessel (naut.). *bâtiment marchand,* merchant ship. ‖ **bâtir** [bâtîr] *v.* to build, to construct; to tack [couture]; to baste; *terrain à bâtir,* building-site; *un homme bien bâti,* a well-built man. ‖ **bâtisse** [-ìs] *f.* masonry; building.

batifoler [bàtìfòlé] *v.* to frolic, to romp.

batiste [bàtìst] *f.* batiste, cambric.

bâton [bâtoⁿ] *m.* stick, staff; baton (mil.); truncheon [police]; wand; © bat [baseball]; *à bâtons rompus,* by fits and starts; *bâton ferré,* alpenstock; *bâton d'or,* wall-flower. ‖ **bâtonner** [-òné] *v.* to beat; to cudgel.

battage [bàtàj] *m.* beating [tapis]; churning; threshing; field of fire (mil.); boosting. ‖ **battant** [-àⁿ] *m.* door; clapper [cloche]; *adj.* banging; beating; pelting [pluie]; flying [pavillon]; *porte battante,* swing-door; folding-door. ‖ **batte** [bàt] *f.* beater. ‖ **battement** [-màⁿ] *m.* beating; clapping; palpitation; pulsation (techn.). ‖ **batterie** [-rî] *f.* gun-site; roll [tambour]; battery (mil.; electr.); set [cuisine]. ‖

batteur [-œr] *m.* beater; *batteur de pavé,* loafer; *batteur de pieux,* pile-driver. || **batteuse** [-ëz] *f.* threshing-machine. || **battoir** [-wàr] *m.* bat; beetle [linge]. || **battre** [bàtr] *v.* to beat; to thrash; to thresh; to mint [monnaie]; to defeat; to scour [campagne]; to shuffle [cartes]; to throb; to clap; *se battre,* to fight. || **battu** [bàtü] *adj.* beaten; wrought [fer]. || **battue** *f.* beat [chasse]. || **batture** [-ür] *f.* © strand.

baudet [bôdè] *m.* donkey.

bauge [bôj] *f.* lair; filthy hovel.

bavard [bàvàr] *m.* gossiper; *adj.* talkative, garrulous. || **bavardage** [-dàj] *m.* gossip; chatter. || **bavarder** [-dé] *v.* to gossip; to chatter, to chat; to blab; to tattle. || **bavasser** [-àsé] *v.* © to gossip; to blab.

bave [bàv] *f.* dribble; drivel; slobber; slime. || **baver** [-é] *v.* to dribble; to drivel; to slobber; to ooze. || **bavette** [-èt] *f.* bib; *tailler une bavette,* to gossip. || **baveux** [-ë] *adj.** dribbling; drooling; runny [omelette]. || **bavoir** [-vwàr] *m.* bib. || **bavure** [-ür] *f.* smear; beard [moulage]; burr; seam.

bayer [bàyé] *v.* to gape.

bazar [bàzàr] *m.* bazaar; © charity sale; bargain stores, five-and-ten; *tout le bazar,* the whole caboodle. || **bazarder** [-dé] *v.* (fam.) to sell off.

béant [béàⁿ] *adj.* gaping; yawning.

béat [béà] *adj.* smug, complacent; quiet. || **béatifier** [-tìfyé] *v.* to beatify (eccles.). || **béatitude** [-tìtüd] *f.* beatitude, bliss; complacency.

beau, belle [bô, bèl] (**bel,** *m.* before a vowel or a mute *h*) *m.** beau; beautiful; fine [temps]; *f.* beauty; deciding game; *adj.** beautiful, fair, handsome; smart, fashionable, elegant; fine, noble; good [temps]; splendid; excellent; comfortable; *une belle occasion,* a fine opportunity; *se faire beau,* to smarten oneself up; *au beau milieu,* in the very middle; *de plus belle,* more than ever; *tout beau!,* careful!; *avoir beau,* in vain [e. g. *j'ai beau chercher,* it's no use my looking]; *beau-fils,* stepson; *beau-frère,* brother-in-law; *beau-père,* step-father; father-in-law; *beaux-arts,* fine arts.

beaucoup [bôkû] *adv.* much; *m.* a great deal, many; much; *beaucoup de gens,* many people; *de beaucoup, à beaucoup près,* by far.

beaupré [bôpré] *m.* bowsprit.

beauté [bôté] *f.* beauty; loveliness.

bébé [bébé] *m.* baby; doll.

bec [bèk] *m.* beak, bill [oiseaux]; snout [poissons]; nose [outil]; spout; nib; *le bec dans l'eau,* in the lurch; *bec de gaz,* gas-burner; (pop.) *fermer ton bec!,* shut up!; **bec-de-cane,** lever-handle; **bec-de-lièvre,** hare-lip.

bécarre [békàr] *adj., m.* natural (mus.).

bécasse [békàs] *f.* woodcock; goose. || **bécassine** [-ìn] *f.* snipe; little goose (fam.).

bêchage [bèshàj] *m.* digging. || **bêche** [bèsh] *f.* spade; **bêche-de-mer,** sea-slug. || **bêcher** [-é] *v.* to dig, or delve.

becqueter [bèkté] *v.* to peck; to pick [up]; (fam.) to kiss.

bedaine [b°dèn] *f.* (fam.) stomach, paunch; pot; pot-belly.

bédane [bédàn] *m.* cold chisel.

bedeau [b°dô] *m.** beadle; verger (eccles.).

bedonner [b°dòné] *v.* (fam.) to grow stout, paunchy, pot-bellied.

bée [bé] *adj. f.*; *bouche bée,* agape, open-mouthed; gaping.

bégaiement [bégèmaⁿ] *m.* stammering. || **bégayer** [-èyé] *v.* to stammer, to stutter.

bègue [bèg] *m., f.* stammerer; *adj.* stammering.

béguin [bégiⁿ] *m.* mobcap; sweet-heart; infatuation.

beigne [bèñ] *f.* biff, cuff (pop.); © *m.* doughnut. || **beignet** [-yè] *m.* fritter, doughnut.

béjaune [béjôn] *m.* freshman; green-horn; tyro.

bêlement [bèlmaⁿ] *m.* bleating. || **bêler** [-é] *v.* to bleat, to blat.

belette [b°lèt] *f.* weasel.

beige [bèj] *m., f., adj.* Belgian. || *Belgique* [-ìk] *f.* Belgium.

bélier [bélyé] *m.* ram; battering ram (mil.); hydraulic ram.

bellâtre [bèlâtr] *m.* beau, fop; *adj.* dandified.

belle, see **beau.**

belligérant [bèllìjéraⁿ] *m., adj.* belligerent. || **belliqueux** [bèllìkë] *adj.** bellicose, warlike; quarrelsome.

bémol [bémòl] *m.* flat (mus.).

bénédictin [bénédìktiⁿ] *m., adj.* Benedictine. || **bénédiction** [-ìksyoⁿ] *f.* blessing; godsend, windfall.

bénéfice [bénéfìs] *m.* benefit; gain, profit; living, benefice (eccles.); premium. || **bénéficiaire** [-yèr] *m.* recipient; payee. || **bénéficier** [-yé] *v.* to profit; to benefit.

benêt [b°nè] *m.* simpleton, sap; *adj. m.* stupid, simple.

bénévole [bénévòl] *adj.* kind; benevolent; unpaid [services]; *infirmière bénévole*, voluntary nurse.

bénin, bénigne [bénⁱⁿ, bénìñ] *adj.* benign, kind; mild. ‖ *bénignité* [bénìñté] *f.* kindness; mildness.

bénir [bénír] *v.** to bless, to consecrate; *Dieu vous bénisse!*, God bless you! ‖ *bénitier* [-ìtyé] *m.* holy water vessel; stoup.

benjamin [bⁱnjàmⁱⁿ] *m.* junior, youngest child; darling.

benjoin [bⁱnjwⁱⁿ] *m.* benzoin, gum benjamin (bot.).

benne [bèn] *f.* hamper; basket; tub; *Am.* dump truck.

benzine [bⁱnzîn] *f.* benzine.

béquille [békỳy] *f.* crutch; stand [bicyclette]; prop, leg (naut.); tail-skid (aviat.).

bercail [bèrkày] *m.* sheepfold; fold (eccles.).

berceau [bèrsô] *m.** cradle; bed (techn.); vault (arch.); arbo(u)r. ‖ *bercer* [-é] *v.* to rock; to lull; to soothe [chagrin]; to delude; *se bercer*, to rock; *se bercer d'un espoir*, to cherish a hope. ‖ *berceuse* [-ēz] *f.* swing-cot; © rocking-chair; lullaby.

béret [bérè] *m.* tam-o'-shanter; beret.

berge [bèrj] *f.* bank [rivière, chemin, fossé]; parapet (mil.).

berger [bèrjé] *m.* shepherd. ‖ *bergère* [-èr] *f.* shepherdess; easy chair. ‖ *bergerie* [-ᵉrî] *f.* sheep-pen. ‖ *bergeronnette* [-ᵉrònèt] *f.* wagtail (oiseau).

berlue [bèrlü] *f.* faulty vision; *avoir la berlue*, to get all things all wrong.

berne [bèrn] *f.;* *mettre le pavillon en berne*, to fly the flag at half-mast. ‖ *berner* [-é] *v.* to fool, to make fun of, to deceive.

bernique! [bèrnìk] *interj.* nothing doing! ; no luck !

besicles [bᵉzìkl] *f. pl.* (fam.) specs, giglamps, cheaters.

besogne [bᵉzòñ] *f.* work, task, job. ‖ *besogner* [-é] *v.* to labour, to drudge. ‖ *besogneux* [-ē] *adj.** needy, hard-up.

besoin [bᵉzwⁱⁿ] *m.* need, want; poverty; *au besoin*, in case of need; *avoir besoin de*, to want; *est-il besoin?*, is it necessary ?

bestial [bèstyàl] *adj.** bestial, brutish. ‖ *bestiaux* [-yô] *m. pl.* livestock. ‖ *bestiole* [-yòl] *f.* tiny beast.

bêta [bètá] *m.* simpleton, block-head.

bétail [bétày] *m.* cattle; livestock.

bête [bèt] *f.* beast, animal; fool; *bête de somme*, pack animal, beast of burden; *bête à bon Dieu*, lady-bird;

bête puante, © skunk (*fr.* moufette); *bête noire*, pet aversion; *bonne bête*, good sort; *faire la bête*, to play the fool; *chercher la petite bête*, to be over-critical; *adj.* silly, stupid. ‖ *bêtifier* [-ìfyé] *v.* to play the fool. ‖ *bêtise* [-îz] *f.* a mere trifle; blunder; folly; nonsense; mistake; silliness.

béton [bétⁿ] *m.* concrete; *béton armé*, reinforced concrete; ferro-concrete.

bette [bèt] *f.* white beet. ‖ *betterave* [-ràv] *f.* beetroot, beet; mangel-wurzer; sugar-beet.

beuglement [bēglᵉmⁿ] *m.* bellowing; lowing [bétail]. ‖ *beugler* [-é] *v.* to bellow, to low.

beurre [bœr] *m.* butter; *un œil au beurre noir*, a black eye. ‖ *beurrer* [-é] *v.* to butter. ‖ *beurrier* [-yé] *m.* butter-man; butter-dish; *adj.* butter-producing.

beuverie [bēvrî] *f.* drinking bout.

bévue [bévü] *f.* blunder, slip, boner.

biais [byè] *m.* skew (techn.); slant; bias; expedient; tuck [couture]; *en biais*, askew; *regarder de biais*, to throw a side-glance; *chercher un biais pour*, to find an easy way of; *adj.* skew; sloping; oblique. ‖ *biaiser* [-zé] *v.* to slant, to cut aslant; to use evasions.

bibelot [bìblô] *m.* knick-knack, trinket, curio.

biberon [bìbrⁿ] *m.* feeding-bottle; tippler. ‖ *biberonner* [-òné] *v.* to tipple, to booze, to liquor up.

bibi [bìbì] *m.* number one (myself); tile (fam.).

bibite [bìbìt] *f.* © insect.

Bible [bìbl] *f.* Bible.

bibliographie [bìblìògràfî] *f.* bibliography. ‖ *bibliographique* [-gràfìk] *adj.* bibliographical. ‖ *bibliomane* [-màn] *m.* book collector. ‖ *bibliophile* [-fìl] *m.* book-lover. ‖ *bibliothécaire* [-tékèr] *m.* librarian. ‖ *bibliothèque* [-tèk] *f.* library; reading-room; bookcase; bookshelf.

biblique [bìblìk] *adj.* Biblical.

bicarbonate [bìkàrbònàt] *m.* bicarbonate.

biceps [bìsèps] *m., adj.* biceps.

biche [bìsh] *f.* hind, doe, roe.

bichon [bìshⁿ] *m.* lap-dog. ‖ *bichonner* [-òné] *v.* to curl; to make smart; to caress.

bicoque [bìkòk] *f.* hovel; shack; *Am.* shanty; dump (fam.).

bicorne [bìkòrn] *m.* cocked hat.

bicyclette [bìsìklèt] *f.* bicycle, cycle; *aller à bicyclette*, to cycle; *bicyclette de course*, racing cycle.

bidet [bìdè] *m.* nag; bidet (hyg.); trestle.

bidon [bìdoⁿ] *m.* tin, can, drum [essence]; water-bottle (mil.). ‖ *bidon-ville* [-vìl] *m.* shanty-town.

bielle [byèl] *f.* tie-rod; crank-arm; *bielle motrice,* connecting-rod (mech.); *bielle de soupape,* valve push-rod.

bien [byiⁿ] *m.* good; welfare; possession, estate, property, wealth, goods; *adv.* well; right, proper; really; many; comfortable; *un homme de bien,* a good man; *biens immeubles,* real property; *faire du bien,* to do good; *être bien avec,* to be on good terms with; *vouloir bien,* to be willing; *être bien,* to be comfortable, to be good-looking; *bien des gens,* many people. *aussi bien que,* as well as; *bien que,* although; *tant bien que mal,* so-so, after a fashion; *bien-aimé,* beloved; *bien-être,* comfort; well-being; welfare; *bien-fondé,* cogency, merit; *bien-fonds,* real estate; landed property.

bienfaisance [byiⁿfⁿzaⁿs] *f.* beneficence; charity; *bureau de bienfaisance,* relief committee. ‖ *bienfaisant* [-aⁿ] *adj.* charitable; beneficial. ‖ *bienfait* [byiⁿfè] *m.* good turn, kindness; benefit. ‖ *bienfaiteur, trice* [-tœr, -trìs] *m., f.* benefactor, *f.* benefactress.

bienheureux [byiⁿnèrë] *adj.* * *m.* blissful; blessed; *m. pl.* the blessed, the blest.

bienséance [byiⁿséaⁿs] *f.* propriety, decorum. ‖ *bienséant* [-éaⁿ] *adj.* decent, becoming, seemly.

bientôt [byiⁿtô] *adv.* soon; before long; *à bientôt !,* see you shortly !, *Am.* so long !

bienveillance [byiⁿvèyaⁿs] *f.* benevolence; *par bienveillance,* out of kindness. ‖ *bienveillant* [-èyaⁿ] *adj.* benevolent.

bienvenu [byiⁿvnü] *m., adj.* welcome; *soyez le bienvenu !,* welcome ! ‖ *bienvenue* [-ü] *f.* welcome; *souhaiter la bienvenue à,* to welcome.

bière [byèr] *f.* beer; *bière blonde,* pale ale.

bière [byèr] *f.* coffin.

biffer [bìfé] *v.* to cross out, to strike out, to cancel [mot].

biffin [bìfiⁿ] *m. Am.* junkman; (fam.) foot-slogger.

bifteck [bìftèk] *m.* beefsteak.

bifurcation [bìfürkàsyoⁿ] *f.* bifurcation; fork [route]; junction (railw.). ‖ *bifurquer* [bìfürké] *v.* to fork; to bifurcate; to branch off [route]; to shunt (electr.).

bigame [bìgàm] *m.* bigamist; *adj.* bigamous. ‖ *bigamie* [-î] *f.* bigamy.

bigarré [bìgàré] *adj.* motley, variegated. ‖ *bigarrer* [-é] *v.* to mottle, to checker. ‖ *bigarrure* [-ür] *f.* mixture, variegation, motley.

bigle [bìgl] *adj.* squint-eyed.

bigot [bìgô] *m.* bigot; *adj.* bigoted, over-devout. ‖ *bigoterie* [-òtrî] *f.* bigotry.

bigoudi [bìgûdî] *m.* curling pin, hair-curler.

bijou [bìjû] *m.* * jewel, gem. ‖ *bijouterie* [-trî] *f. Br.* jewellery, *Am.* jewelry; jeweler's shop. ‖ *bijoutier* [-tyé] *m.* jeweler.

bilan [bìlaⁿ] *m.* balance-sheet; statement; schedule (comm.); *déposer son bilan,* to file a petition in bankruptcy.

bilatéral [bìlàtéràl] *adj.* * bilateral; two-sided.

bile [bìl] *f.* bile, gall; anger; *se faire de la bile,* to worry, to get worked up. ‖ *biliaire* [-yèr] *adj.* biliary; *canal biliaire,* bile-duct. ‖ *bilieux* [-yë] *adj.* * bilious; choleric, cross, testy; morose; cantankerous.

bilingue [bìliⁿg] *adj.* bilingual. ‖ *bilinguisme* [-üïsm] *m.* bilingualism.

billard [bìyàr] *m.* billiards; billiard-table; billiard-room.

bille [bîy] *f.* small ball [billard]; marble [jeu]; block, log [bois]; (pop.) nut; dial.

billet [bìyè] *m.* note, letter; circular; notice, bill (comm.); ticket; bank-note; *billet doux,* love-letter; *billet de faire-part,* wedding, funeral announcement; *billet simple,* single ticket; *billet d'aller et retour,* return ticket; *billet à vue,* bill payable at sight; *billet de logement,* billeting order (mil.); *billet à ordre,* promissory note.

billevesées [bìlᵛzé] *f. pl.* nonsense, crazy ideas; rubbish.

bimensuel [bìmaⁿsüèl] *adj.* * twice-monthly. ‖ *bimestriel* [-mèstriyèl] *adj.* * bimonthly.

bimoteur [bìmòtœr] *adj.* twin-engined; *m.* bimotored plane.

binette [bìnèt] *f.* hoe (agr.).

binette [bìnèt] *f.* (pop.) face, mug.

binocle [bìnòkl] *m.* eye-glasses; pince-nez.

biographe [bìògràf] *m.* biographer. ‖ *biographie* [-î] *f.* biography. ‖ *biographique* [-ik] *adj.* biographical.

biologie [bìòlòjî] *f.* biology. ‖ *biologique* [-ìk] *adj.* biological. ‖ *biologiste* [-ìst] *m., f.* biologist.

biplace [bìplàs] *adj., m. f.* two-seater.

bique [bìk] *f.* she-goat, nanny-goat; old nag. ‖ *biquet* [-è] *m.* kid.

bis [bì] *adj.* brown; *pain bis*, brown bread.

bis [bìs] *adv.* twice, again, repeat; ditto; encore!; *n° 32 bis*, n° 32 A [maisons].

bisannuel [bìzànnüèl] *adj.** bi-annual.

bisbille [bìzbîy] *f.* (fam.) bickering, quarrel; *en bisbille*, at loggerheads.

biscornu [bìskòrnü] *adj.* two-horned; odd; misshapen, distorted; inconsequent [argument].

biscotte [bìskòt] *f.* rusk. ‖ *biscuit* [bìsküì] *m.* biscuit, *Am.* cracker; *biscuit de mer*, ship's biscuit, hard tack; *biscuit à la cuiller*, *Br.* sponge-finger, *Am.* lady-finger.

bise [bîz] *f.* north wind.

biseau [bìzô] *m.** chamfer, bevel; bevelling. ‖ *biseauter* [-té] *v.* to bevel; to cheat [cartes].

bismuth [bìsmüt] *m.* bismuth.

bison [bìzoⁿ] *m.* bison, buffalo.

bissecteur, -trice [bìsèktœr, -trìs] *adj.* bisecting; *f.* bisector, bisectrix. ‖ *bissection* [bìsèksyoⁿ] *f.* bisection.

bisser [bìsé] *v.* to encore (theat.).

bissextile [bìssèkstìl] *adj.; année bissextile*, leap-year.

bistouri [bìstûrî] *m.* lancet, knife.

bistre [bìstr] *m.* bistre; *adj.* blackish-brown. ‖ *bistré* [-é] *adj.* brown, swarthy.

bistro [bìstrô] *m.* pub; publican; *le bistro du coin*, the local.

bitume [bìtüm] *m.* bitumen, asphalt; tar; *bitumé*, tarred.

bivouac [bìvwàk] *m.* bivouac. ‖ *bivouaquer* [-é] *v.* to bivouac.

bizarre [bìzàr] *m.* queer thing; strange part; *adj.* bizarre, odd, curious, strange. ‖ *bizarrerie* [-rî] *f.* oddness, peculiarity; whim.

bizut [bìzü] *m.* (fam.) fresher, freshman.

bla-bla-bla [blàblàblà] *m.* claptrap, blah, bunkum, *Am.* baloney.

blackbouler [blàkbûlé] *v.* to blackball, to turn down.

blafard [blàfàr] *adj.* pale, wan; livid.

blague [blàg] *f.* tobacco-pouch; humbug, nonsense; fib; banter; gag; *sans blague?*, you don't say? ‖ *blaguer* [blàgé] *v.* to chaff; to joke. ‖ *blagueur* [blàgœr] *m.* humbug; wag; *adj.** bantering; scoffing.

blaireau [blèrô] *m.** badger (zool.); shaving-brush; brush [peintre].

blâmable [blâmàbl] *adj.* blamable. ‖ *blâme* [blâm] *m.* blame; *vote de blâme*, vote of censure. ‖ *blâmer* [-é]

v. to blame; to censure; to reprimand; to find fault with.

blanc, blanche [blaⁿ, blaⁿsh] *m.* white; white part; white man; blank; bull's-eye [cible]; blank cartridge; breast [volaille]; *f.* billiard ball; minim (mus.); *adj.* white, pale; clean, spotless; blank; *chèque en blanc*, blank check; *chauffer à blanc*, to make white-hot; *blanc de chaux*, whitewash; *saigner à blanc*, to bleed white; *magasin de blanc*, *Br.* linen drapery, *Am.* household linen store; *nuit blanche*, sleepless night; *arme blanche*, cold steel; *blanc-bec*, greenhorn; *blanc-seing*, blank signature; full power. ‖ *blanchâtre* [blaⁿshâtr] *adj.* whitish. ‖ *blanche, see blanc.* *blancheur* [-œr] *f.* whiteness, pallor; purity. ‖ *blanchiment* [-ìmaⁿ] *m.* bleaching. ‖ *blanchir* [-îr] *v.* to whiten, to blanch; to bleach; to clean, to launder; to fade; to turn grey. ‖ *blanchissage* [-ìsàj] *m.* washing. ‖ *blanchisserie* [-ìsrî] *f.* laundry. ‖ *blanchisseur* [-ìsœr] *m.* laundry-man; bleacher (text.). ‖ *blanchisseuse* [-ìsëz] *f.* washerwoman; laundress.

blaser [blàzé] *v.* to blunt; to surfeit; *il est blasé*, he is jaded, blasé.

blason [blàzoⁿ] *m.* blazon, coat-of-arms; heraldry.

blasphème [blàsfèm] *m.* blasphemy; © oath, swear word. ‖ *blasphémer* [-émé] *v.* to blaspheme; to curse; © to swear.

blatte [blàt] *f.* cockroach, black-beetle.

blé [blé] *m.* corn; wheat; *blé de Turquie*, © *blé d'Inde*, maize, *Am.* Indian corn; *blé noir*, buck wheat.

blême [blèm] *adj.* pale, wan; ghastly. ‖ *blêmir* [îr] *v.* to grow pale, to blanch.

bléser [blézé] *v.* to lisp.

blessant [blèsaⁿ] *adj.* wounding, offensive [remarque]. ‖ *blessé* [é] *m.* casualty. ‖ *blesser* [-é] *v.* to wound; to hurt; to offend; to jar upon; *se blesser*, to hurt oneself; to take offense. ‖ *blessure* [-ür] *f.* wound, injury.

blet [blè] *adj.** over-ripe.

blette [blèt] *f.* white beet.

bleu [blë] *m.* blue; blue mark; bruise; recruit (mil.); blueprint; *adj.* blue; underdone [viande]; *bleu ciel*, sky blue; *bleu marine*, navy blue; *passer au bleu*, to blue; *colère bleue*, violent anger, towering rage; *conte bleu*, fairy tale; *en rester bleu*, to be flabbergasted; *pl.* overalls, dungarees. ‖ *bleuâtre* [-âtr] *adj.* bluish. ‖ *bleuet* *m.* cornflower; © blueberry, bilberry, whortleberry [*fr.* myrtille]. ‖ *bleuir* [îr] *v.* to make blue; to turn blue. ‖ *bleuter* [-té] *v.* to tinge with blue.

blindage [blin̄dàj] *m.* armo(u)r-plating. ‖ **blinder** [-é] *v.* to armo(u)r, to protect; to timber; to sheet; to screen (electr.); *voitures blindées*, armo(u)red vehicles.

bloc [blòk] *m.* block; memorandum pad; mass; lump; (pop.) clink; *en bloc*, wholesale; *visser à bloc*, to screw right in; *bloc de correspondance*, writing tablet. ‖ **blocage** [-àj] *m.* blocking; locking; jamming on. ‖ **blockhaus** [-ôs] *m.* blockhouse; conning-tower [sous-marin]. ‖ **blocus** [üs] *m.* blockade; *faire le blocus de*, to blockade; *forcer le blocus*, to run the blockade.

blond [blon] *m.*, *adj.* blond; *adj.* fair; flaxen; pale [bière]. ¦ **blonde** [blon̄d] *f.* © sweetheart. ‖ **blondeur** [-dœr] *f.* blondness. ‖ **blondin** [-din̄] *m.*, *adj.* fair-haired. ‖ **blondir** [-dîr] *v.* to grow yellow.

bloquer [blòké] *v.* to block up; to blockade; to besiege; to stop [chèque]; to jam on [freins]; to lock (mech.); *se bloquer*, to get jammed.

blottir (se) [s⁹blòtîr] *v.* to squat; to crouch; to nestle; to huddle up.

blouse [blûz] *f.* blouse; smock; overall. ‖ **blouson** [zon] *m.* wind-cheater, wind-breaker.

bluet [blüè] *m.* cornflower.

bluff [blœf] *m.* bluff. ‖ **bluffer** [-é] *v.* to bluff; to pull a fast one. ‖ **bluffeur** [-œr] *m.* bluffer.

blutage [blütàj] *m.* bolting; sifting. ‖ **bluter** [-é] *v.* to bolt, to sift. ‖ **blutoir** [-wàr] *m.* sieve.

boa [bòà] *m.* boa.

bobard [bòbàr] *m.* tall story.

bobèche [bòbèsh] *f.* candle-ring; socket.

bobine [bòbîn] *f.* bobbin, spool, reel; roll; drum (techn.); coil (electr.); inductor; (fam.) mug, map. ‖ **bobiner** [-iné] *v.* to wind, to spool.

bobo [bòbô] *m.* (fam.) pain, sore.

bocal [bòkàl] *m.** glass jar; bowl; globe; *mettre en bocal*, to bottle.

bock [bòk] *m.* glass of beer; enema.

bœuf [bœf, *pl.* bë] *m.* ox; beef; *bœuf en conserve*, corned beef.

boire [bwàr] *m.* drink; drinking; *v.** to drink; to absorb; to imbibe; to swallow [insultes]; to drink in; *boire comme un trou*, to drink like a fish; *chanson à boire*, drinking song.

bois [bwà] *m.* wood; forest; timber; fire-wood; antler(s) [cerf]; wood-wind (mus.); *bois ronds*, spars; *cabane de bois ronds*, © log-cabin; *bois contre-plaqué*, plywood; *sous-bois*, under-growth. ‖ **boisage** [-zàj] *m.* timbering;

afforestation. ‖ **boisé** [-zé] *adj.* wooded; timbered. ‖ **boisement** [-zman] *m.* tree-planting. ‖ **boiser** [-zé] *v.* to panel; to timber; to plant with trees. ‖ **boiserie** [-zrî] *f.* joinery; woodwork; wainscoting, panelling.

boisseau [bwàsô] *m.** bushel.

boisson [bwàson] *f.* drink; *pris de boisson*, intoxicated; in liquor.

boîte [bwàt] *f.* box, case; Br. tin; Am. can; (pop.) prison; *boîte aux lettres*, Br. letter-box; Am. mail-box; *boîte de vitesses*, gear-box; *boîte de nuit*, night-club; *en boîte*, Br. tinned, Am. canned; *mettre en boîte*, to pull someone's leg.

boiter [bwàté] *v.* to halt, to hobble, to limp, to be lame. ‖ **boiteux** [-ë] *adj.** lame; rickety.

boîtier [bwàtyé] *m.* box, case; box-maker.

boitiller [bwàtiyé] *v.* to hobble.

bol [bòl] *m.* bowl, basin.

bolcheviste [bòlsh⁹vìst] *m.*, *f.* Bolchevist. ‖ **bolchevisme** [-ìsm] *m.* Bolchevism.

bolduc [bòldük] *m.* tape, colored ribbon.

boléro [bòlérò] *m.* bolero.

bolide [bòlìd] *m.* meteorite; racing-car; Am. hot-shot; thunderbolt.

bombance [bon̄bans] *f.* feasting, riot, revel, junket.

bombardement [bon̄bàrdman] *m.* bombing; shelling; bombardment. ‖ **bombarder** [-é] *v.* to shell; to bombard. ‖ **bombardier** [-yé] *m.* bombardier; bomber (aviat.).

bombe [bon̄b] *f.* bomb; depth-charge; *à l'épreuve des bombes*, bomb-proof; *en bombe*, like a rocket; *faire la bombe*, to go on a spree. ‖ **bomber** [-é] *v.* to bulge; to bend; to swell; to camber [route]; *se bomber*, to bulge.

bon, bonne [bon, bòn] *m.* order, voucher; bond, draft; *adj.* good; simple; kind; clever; fit, proper, right; witty large; fine; well paid [emploi]; lucky [étoile]; *adv.* well; nice; fast; [*comp meilleur*, better, *sup. le meilleur*, the best]; *bon de poste*, postal order; *bon du trésor*, treasury bond; *bonne année!*, a happy New Year!; *bonne compagnie*, elegant society; *il fait bon*, the weather is fine; *à quoi bon?*, what's the use?; *pour de bon*, in earnest, for good and all.

bonasse [bònàs] *adj.* easy-going, good-hearted.

bonbon [bon̄bon] *m.* Br. sweet, Am. candy. ‖ **bonbonnerie** [-ònrî] *f.* confectionery. ‖ **bonbonnière** [-ònyèr] *f.*

sweetmeat-box; candy-box; snug little house.

bond [boⁿ] m. jump, bound, leap; spring; *je vous ai fait faux bond,* I left you in the lurch.

bonde [boⁿd] f. plug; bung [tonneau]; bung-hole; sluice-gate. ‖ *bonder* [-é] v. to fill up; *salle bondée,* packed house.

bondieuserie [boⁿdyēzᵉrǐ] f. pietism; pl. church ornaments.

bondir [boⁿdîr] v. to bound, to jump; to leap; to spring; to bounce; to caper.

bonheur [bònœr] m. happiness; bliss; good luck; success; *par bonheur,* luckily; *au petit bonheur,* haphazardly.

bonhomie [bònòmǐ] f. simplicity, good nature, heartiness. ‖ *bonhomme* [bònòm] m. man, fellow, chap; simple-minded man; bolt (mech.); *un faux bonhomme,* a humbug, a hypocrite.

boni [bònǐ] m. bonus, profit, allowance; surplus.

bonification [bònǐfǐkàsyoⁿ] f. improvement; allowance; rebate (comm.). ‖ *bonifier* [-yé] v. to better; to allow; *se bonifier,* to improve.

boniment [bònǐmoⁿ] m. patter, claptrap; compliments.

bonjour [boⁿjûr] m. good day; good morning; good afternoon.

bonne [bòn] adj., see *bon;* f. maid, servant; *bonne à tout faire,* general servant; *bonne d'enfant,* children's nurse; *bonne-maman,* grandma.

bonnement [bònmoⁿ] adv.; *tout bonnement,* clearly, plainly.

bonnet [bònè] m. cap; *gros bonnet,* bigwig, Am. big shot; *opiner du bonnet,* to nod assent; *avoir la tête près du bonnet,* to be quick-tempered. ‖ *bonneterie* [bòntrǐ] f. haberdashery, hosiery. ‖ *bonnetier* [bòntyé] m. haberdasher, hosier. ‖ *bonnette* [bònèt] f. bonnet; supplementary lens (phot.). ‖ *bonnichon* [-nǐshoⁿ] m. child's cap.

bonsoir [boⁿswàr] m. good evening; good night.

bonté [boⁿté] f. goodness, kindness; *ayez la bonté de,* be so good as to.

b o q u e t e a u [bòktô] m.* copse, spinney.

borax [bòràks] m. borax.

bord [bòr] m. edge, border; side, shore [mer]; bank; brim [chapeau]; verge [ruine]; tack (naut.); *à bord du bateau,* on board ship; *médecin du bord,* ship's doctor. ‖ *bordage* [dàj] m. hemming, bordering; bulwarks (naut.).

bordeaux [bòrdô] m. Bordeaux wine; claret.

bordée [bòrdé] f. board; tack; broadside; volley; watch (naut.); *bordée de neige,* ⓒ heavy snowfall; spree.

bordel [bòrdèl] m. (pop.) brothel.

border [bòrdèl] v. to hem, to border.

bordereau [bòrdᵉrô] m.* memorandum; statement; docket, schedule; register; note; *bordereau de versement,* pay-in slip.

bordure [bòrdür] f. border; bordering; edge; rim; Br. kerb, Am. curb [trottoir].

borgne [bòrñi] adj. one-eyed; disreputable, shady; *rue borgne,* blind alley.

borique [bòrǐk] adj. boracic. ‖ *boriqué* [-é] adj. containing boracic.

bornage [bòrnàj] m. settling the boundary staking; demarcation. ‖ *borne* [bòrn] f. boundary, limit; milestone, landmark; terminal (electr.); bollard (naut.), *dépasser les bornes,* to overstep the bounds; *pour aller au delà d'un the bornes,* to go beyond a joke. ‖ *borné* [-é] adj. narrow, limited, cramped, restricted. ‖ *borner* [-é] v. to set limits; to limit; to confine.

bosquet [bòskè] m. grove; shrubbery.

bosse [bòs] f. hump; lump; bump; dent; knob; relief [art] *avoir la bosse de,* to have a gift for. ‖ *bosseler* [-lé] v. to emboss; to batter. ‖ *bossoir* [-wàr] m. davit (naut.). ‖ *bossu* [-ü] adj. hunchbacked. ‖ *bossuer* [üé] v. to batter.

bot [bô] adj. *pied bot,* club-foot.

botanique [bòtànǐk] adj. botanical; f. botany.

botte [bòt] f. bunch [fleurs], truss [foin], sheaf [blé].

botte [bòt] f. thrust [escrime].

botte [bòt] f. boot; *bottes d'égoutier,* waders.

botteler [bòtlé] v. to bind, to truss.

botter [bòté] v. to put on shoes, boots, to kick; to suit. ‖ *bottier* [-yé] m. shoemaker, bootmaker. ‖ *bottillon* [bòtǐyoⁿ] m. bottee.

Bottin [bòtǐⁿ] m. (trade-mark) French directory, social register.

bottine [bòtǐn] f. ankle-boot.

bouc [bûk] m. he-goat; goatee [barbe]; *bouc émissaire,* scape-goat, fall guy.

boucan [bûkoⁿ] m. (pop.) row, racket, shindy, noise.

bouchage [bûshàj] m. stopping; corking; plugging.

bouche [bûsh] f. mouth; opening; muzzle [canon]; nozzle; orifice; *bouche de chaleur,* hot-air grating; *bouche de métro,* subway entrance; *bouche à feu,* piece of artillery; *bouche d'incendie,* fire-hydrant, Am. fire-plug;

faire la petite bouche, to be finicky. ‖ **bouché** [-é] *adj.* stoppered; corked; bottled; clogged; stupid, dense. ‖ **bouchée** [-é] *f.* mouthful. ‖ **boucher** [-é] *v.* to stop (up), to cork; to shut up; *se boucher*, to become obstructed.

boucher [bûshé] *m.* butcher. ‖ **boucherie** [-rî] *f.* butcher's shop; slaughter, massacre.

bouche-trou [bûsh-trû] *m.* stop-gap; substitute.

bouchon [bûshoⁿ] *m.* cork, stopper, plug, bung; sign; inn, public-house; float [pêche]; wisp [paille]. ‖ **bouchonner** [òné] *v.* to rub down.

boucle [bûkl] *f.* buckle; ear-ring; curl; lock [cheveux]; loop, ring. ‖ **bouclé** [-é] *adj.* curly, curled. ‖ **boucler** [-é] *v.* to curl; to buckle; to loop; to strap; to lock up. ‖ **bouclette** [-èt] *f.* ringlet.

bouder [bûdé] *v.* to sulk; to fight shy of; to be cool towards. ‖ **bouderie** [rî] *f.* sulkiness. ‖ **boudeur** [-œr] *adj.* sullen, sulky.

boudin [bûdⁿ] *m.* Br. black pudding, Am. blood-sausage; spring; flange [roue]; beading.

boudoir [bûdwàr] *m.* boudoir.

boue [bû] *f.* mud, mire; sediment; dirt; slush, sludge.

bouée [bûé] *f.* buoy; *bouée de sauvetage*, life-buoy.

boueur [bûœr] *m.* scavenger; Br. dustman, Am. garbage-collector; street cleaner. ‖ **boueux** [bûё] *adj.* muddy; dirty; sloppy, squashy.

bouffant [bûfaⁿ] *adj.* puffed, full, ample. ‖ **bouffée** [-é] *f.* puff, whiff, gust [vent]; flush (med.); fit, outburst. ‖ **bouffi** [-î] *adj.* puffy; bloated; swollen. ‖ **bouffissure** [-isür] *f.* swelling; puffiness; bombast.

bouffon [bûfoⁿ] *m.* fool, jester; buffoon, prankster; *adj.* farcical, ludicrous, jocular.

bougeoir [bûjwàr] *m.* candle-stick.

bougeotte [bûjòt] *f.* *avoir la bougeotte*, to have the fidgets.

bouger [bûjé] *v.* to stir; to move; to budge; to make a move, to act.

bougie [bûjî] *f.* taper; candle; candle-power; *bougie d'allumage*, Br. sparking-plug, Am. spark plug.

bougon [bûgoⁿ] *m.* grumbler, croaker, grouser; *adj.* grumbling. ‖ **bougonner** [-òné] *v.* to grumble.

bougre [bûgr] *m.* fellow, chap, guy.

bouillabaisse [bûyàbès] *f.* Provençal fish-soup.

bouillant [bûyaⁿ] *adj.* boiling; hot; hot-tempered. ‖ **bouilleur** [bûyœr] *m.* boiler; distiller. ‖ **bouilli** [bûyî] *m.*

boiled beef. ‖ **bouillie** [bûyî] *f.* pap, pulp; gruel; mess. ‖ **bouillir** [bûyîr] *v.** to boil; *faire bouillir*, to boil. ‖ **bouilloire** [bûywàr] *f.* Br. kettle, Am. teakettle. ‖ **bouillon** [bûyoⁿ] *m.* broth, soup; bubble; restaurant; unsold copies [journaux]; *bouillon d'onze heures*, poison. ‖ **bouillonnement** [bûyònmaⁿ] *m.* bubbling, effervescence, seething; boiling. ‖ **bouillonner** [-é] *v.* to boil; to seethe; to bubble; to foam; to froth; to puff [couture]. ‖ **bouillotte** [bûyòt] *f.* footwarmer; hot-water bottle.

boulange [bûlaⁿj] *f.* baker's trade. ‖ **boulanger** [-jé] *m.* baker. ‖ **boulangerie** [-rî] *f.* baking; bakery; baker's shop.

boule [bûl] *f.* ball; bowl; (pop.) nut, noddle; *boule de neige*, snowball; *boule de gomme*, gum-drop; *jouer aux boules*, to play bowls; *perdre la boule*, to go nuts; *se mettre en boule*, to get spiky.

bouleau [bûlô] *m.** birch [arbre].

bouledogue [bûldòg] *m.* bulldog.

bouler [bûlé] *v.* to roll along; to pad; to fluff; *envoyer bouler*, to send packing. ‖ **boulet** [-è] *m.* shot; ball; (fig.) drag, millstone. ‖ **boulette** [-èt] *f.* meatball; blunder.

boulevard [bûlvàr] *m.* boulevard; bulwark.

bouleversement [bûlvèrs•maⁿ] *m.* overthrow, confusion; bewilderment. ‖ **bouleverser** [-é] *v.* to upset; to disrupt; to throw into confusion.

bouline [bûlîn] *f.* bowline.

boulon [bûloⁿ] *m.* bolt; pin. ‖ **boulonner** [-òné] *v.* to bolt (down).

boulot, -otte [bûlò, -òt] *adj.* fat, plump, tubby (person); *m.* (fam.) work, grind. ‖ **boulotter** [-òté] *v.* (fam.) to grub up; to tuck in.

bouquet [bûkè] *m.* bunch; cluster [arbres]; aroma [vin]; crowning-piece [feu d'artifice]; *c'est le bouquet!*, that's the last straw! ‖ **bouquetière** [-tyèr] *f.* flower-girl.

bouquin [bûkⁿ] *m.* (fam.) old book. ‖ **bouquiner** [-kiné] *v.* to pore over books; to browse among bookstalls. ‖ **bouquiniste** [-inìst] *m.* second-hand book dealer.

bourbeux [bûrbё] *adj.** miry, muddy. ‖ **bourbier** [-yé] *m.* slough; mire; mess, fix.

bourde [bûrd] *f.* fib, humbug; mistake; blunder; boner; thumper.

bourdon [bûrdoⁿ] *m.* omission (typogr.).

bourdon [bûrdoⁿ] *m.* humblebee; drone bass; great bell. ‖ **bourdonnement** [-ònmaⁿ] *m.* humming; buzz; head noises, singing [d'oreilles].

bourdonner [-òné] *v.* to hum; to buzz; to murmur.

bourg [bûr] *m.* borough; market-town. ‖ **bourgade** [-gàd] *f.* large village. ‖ **bourgeois** [bûrjwà] *m.* citizen, townsman, middle-class person; (fam.) Philistine, capitalist; *adj.* middle-class; *common cuisine bourgeoise,* plain cooking *pension bourgeoise,* boarding-house; *en bourgeois,* in plain clothes. ‖ **bourgeoisie** [-zî] *f.* middle-class; *droit de bourgeoisie,* freedom of a city.

bourgeon [bûrjoⁿ] *m.* bud; pimple. ‖ **bourgeonnement** [-ònmaⁿ] *m.* budding, sprouting. ‖ **bourgeonner** [-òné] *v.* to bud, to shoot; *un visage bourgeonné,* a pimply face.

bourgeron [bûrjⁱ•roⁿ] *m.* overall; fatigue dress; jumper.

Bourgogne [bûrgòñ] *f.* Burgundy. ‖ **bourguignon** [-gìñoⁿ] *adj.** Burgundian.

bourlinguer [bûrlⁱⁿgé] *v.* to wallow, to strain, to make heavy going; to navigate, to knock about.

bourrade [bûràd] *f.* blow, knock, thump.

bourrage [bûràj] *m.* stuffing; padding; swotting; (fam.) *bourrage de crâne,* tripe, eyewash; brainwashing.

bourrasque [bûràsk] *f.* squall.

bourratif [bûràtìf] *adj.** stodgy, filling.

bourre [bûr] *f.* fluff, flock [laine]; padding; floss; cotton-waste; wad.

bourreau [bûrô] *m.** hangman; executioner; tormentor.

bourrelet [bûrlè] *m.* pad; draught-excluder; bulge; fender (naut.); flange [roue]; roll [de graisse].

bourrelier [bûrlyé] *m.* saddler. ‖ **bourrellerie** [-èlrî] *f.* harness-maker's shop; harness trade.

bourrer [bûré] *v.* to stuff; to pad; to cram; to ram in; to beat, to trounce.

bourrique [bûrìk] *f.* she-ass; block-head, dolt.

bourru [bûrü] *adj.* shaggy; rough; rude; surly; peevish.

bourse [bûrs] *f.* purse; bag; stock-exchange; funds; scholarship. ‖ **boursier** [-yé] *m.* scholar, bursar, scholarship-holder; speculator; purse-maker (comm.).

boursoufler [-é] *v.* to bloat; to puff up; to swell; to blister; to inflate. ‖ **boursouflure** [-ûr] *f.* swelling; blister [peinture]; turgidity, bombast.

bousculade [bûskülàd] *f.* jostling; scrimmage; rush. ‖ **bousculer** [-é] *v.* to jostle, to hustle; to upset, to knock over; to bully; to rush; *se bousculer,*

to scramble, to push about; to hurry; to scuffle.

bouse [bûz] *f.* cow-dung.

boussole [bûsòl] *f.* compass; *perdre la boussole,* to be all at sea; to be off one's rocker.

boustifaille [bûstìfày] *f.* (pop.) food, grub.

bout [bû] *m.* end, extremity; tip; bit; *au bout du compte,* after all; *à bout,* tired out, worn out; exasperated, out of patience; *joindre les deux bouts,* to make both ends meet; *à bout portant,* point-blank; *tenir le bon bout,* to get the whip-hand.

boutade [bûtàd] *f.* whim; sally; *par boutades,* by fits and starts.

boute-en-train [bûtaⁿtrⁱⁿ] *m.* teaser; (fam.) life and soul of the party, merry fellow.

bouteille [bûtèy] *f.* bottle; *bouteille Thermos,* Thermos flask (nom déposé); *mettre en bouteille,* to bottle; *bouteille à gaz,* gas cylinder; *prendre de la bouteille,* to age.

boutique [bûtìk] *f.* shop; store; booth; stall; boutique; *parler boutique,* to talk shop. ‖ **boutiquier** [-yé] *m.* shopkeeper.

bouton [bûtoⁿ] *m.* bud [fleur]; pimple; button; stud [chemise]; door-knob; handle; *bouton-d'or,* buttercup. ‖ **boutonner** [-òné] *v.* to bud; to button. ‖ **boutonnière** [-ònyèr] *f.* button-hole; rosette.

bouture [bûtür] *f.* cutting, slip (hort.). ‖ **bouturer** [-é] *v.* to strike, to plant cuttings; to shoot suckers (hort.).

bouvier [bûvyé] *m.* cowherd; drover. ‖ **bouvillon** [-iyoⁿ] *m.* bullock, young bullock, steer.

bouvreuil [bûvrœy] *m.* bullfinch.

bovin [bòvⁱⁿ] *adj., m.* bovine.

box [bòks] *m.* cubicle; box stall; dock; stand.

boxe [bòks] *f.* boxing; sparring. ‖ **boxer** [-é] *v.* to box, to spar. ‖ **boxeur** [-œr] *m.* boxer.

boyau [bwàyô] *m.** bowel, gut; hose-pipe; communication trench (mil.); *corde à boyau,* catgut.

boycottage [bòìkòtàj] *m.* boycotting. ‖ **boycotter** [-é] *v.* to boycott.

bracelet [bràslè] *m.* bracelet, armlet; watch-strap; bangle; *bracelet-montre,* wrist-watch.

braconnage [bràkònàj] *m.* poaching. ‖ **braconner** [-é] *v.* to poach. ‖ **braconnier** [-yé] *m.* poacher.

brader [bràdé] *v.* to sell off. ‖ **braderie** [-rì] *f.* clearance-sale, *Am.* rummage sale.

braguette [bràgèt] *f.* fly, flies [pantalon].

braillard [bràyàr] *m.* bawler, noisy brat; *adj* noisy, obstreperous, shouting; brawling. ‖ **brailler** [bràyé] *v.* to bawl, to squall.

braire [brèr] *v.** to bray; to blubber [enfants], to boohoo.

braise [brèz] *f.* glowing wood embers, live coals; (pop.) oof. ‖ **braiser** [-é] *v.* to braise.

bramer [bràmé] *v.* to bell [animal].

brancard [brankàr] *m.* stretcher; shaft [voiture] ‖ **brancardier** [-dyé] *m.* stretcher-bearer

branchage [branshàj] *m.* branches, boughs [arbres]; branchery. ‖ **branche** [bransh] *f.* branch, bough; arm [lunettes], blade [hélice]; leg [compas]; side [famille], line [commerciale]; *vieille branche*, old chap. ‖ **branchement** [-man] *m.* tapping; connection, junction. ‖ **brancher** [-é] *v.* to roost; to perch; to connect; to plug in (electr.); to branch (electr.). ‖ **branchette** [-èt] *f.* twig.

branchies [branshî] *f. pl.* gills.

brandir [brandîr] *v.* to brandish, to flourish; to wave.

branlant [branlan] *adj.* tottering, shaky; loose [dent]. ‖ **branle** [branl] *m.* shaking, tossing; swinging; start; impulse; *mettre en branle*, to set in motion; *branle-bas*, clearing the decks (naut.); disturbance. ‖ **branler** [-é] *v.* to shake; to be loose, to be unsteady; to rock; to wag; to be in danger.

braquage [bràkàj] *m.* pointing, aiming; steering [auto]. ‖ **braquer** [-é] *v.* to point, to level, to aim; to deflect (aviat.); to lock [roues]; *braquer les yeux sur*, to stare at.

bras [brà] *m.* arm; handle; hand; *avoir le bras long*, to be very influential; *manquer de bras*, to be shorthanded; *à tour de bras*, with might and main; *bras dessus, bras dessous*, arm in arm.

braséro [bràzéró] *m.* charcoal-pan, brazier ‖ **brasier** [-yé] *m.* brazier; furnace blaze

brasillement [bràzîlyman] *m.* glittering [métal], spluttering. ‖ **brasiller** [-lyé] *v.* to sparkle; to splutter; to grill; to sizzle.

brasse [bràs] *f.* fathom (naut.); breast - stroke [nage]; pitch-stirrer (techn.). ‖ **brassée** [-é] *f.* armful. ‖ **brasser** [-é] *v.* to brace (naut.).

brasser [bràsé] *v.* to brew; to mix; to handle; to hatch [complot]; to stir up. ‖ **brasserie** [-rî] *f.* brewing; brewery; restaurant. ‖ **brasseur** [-œr] *m.* brewer; *brasseur d'affaires*, big business man.

brassière [bràsyèr] *f.* shoulder-strap; child's bodice; *brassière de sauvetage*, life-jacket.

bravache [bràvàsh] *m.* bully; swaggerer. ‖ **bravade** [-àd] *f.* bravado; bragging. ‖ **brave** [bràv] *adj.* brave; honest; good, nice, smart; *un homme brave*, a brave man; *un brave homme*, a worthy man, a decent fellow ‖ **braver** [-é] to brave, to defy, to dare. ‖ **bravo** [-ó] *m* bravo, cheer, *interj.* bravo!, well done! ‖ **bravoure** [-ûr] *f.* courage bravery.

brebis [brœbî] *f.* ewe; sheep; *brebis galeuse* black sheep.

brèche [brèsh] *f.* breach; notch [lame], gap; hole; *une brèche à l'honneur*, a breach of hono(u)r.

bréchet [bréshè] *m.* breast-bone.

bredouillage [brœdûyàj] *m.* stammering, muttering ‖ **bredouille** [brœdûy] *adj.* *revenir bredouille*, to return empty-handed. ‖ **bredouiller** [-é] *v.* to stammer, to stutter; to mumble.

bref [brèf] *m.* brief; *adj.** brief, short; concise, short, *adv.* briefly, in short; *parler bref*, to speak curtly.

breloque [brœlòk] *f.* trinket, charm, breloque [bijou]; dismiss (naut.); *battre la breloque* to go pit-a-pat [cœur], to go badly [pendule], to have a screw loose [personne].

Bretagne [brœtàñ] *f.* Brittany; *la Grande-Bretagne*, Great Britain.

bretelle [brœtèl] *f.* strap, sling (mil.); shoulder-strap; *pl.* braces, *Am.* suspenders

breton [brœton] *m.*, *adj.** Breton.

breuvage [brœvàj] *m.* drink; beverage; draught.

brevet [brœvè] *m.* patent; warrant; certificate. *Am.* degree [diplôme]; licence, commission (mil.), badge (de scout); *brevet de pilote*, pilot's licence; *brevet de capitaine*, master's certificate. ‖ **breveté** [-té] *m.* patentee; *adj.* patent, certificated. *Am.* holding a degree. ‖ **breveter** [-té] *v.* to patent [invention]; to license.

bribes [brîb] *f. pl.* scraps, bits.

bric-à-brac [brìkàbràk] *m.* curios; bits and pieces, odds and ends.

bricolage [brìkòlàj] *m.* tinkering, pottering, *Am.* puttering about. ‖ **bricole** [brìkòl] *f.* breast-harness; strap; brace; ricochet; backstroke; odd job; trifle. ‖ **bricoler** [-é] *v.* to tinker; to do odd jobs; *Am.* to putter; *qu'est-ce que tu bricoles?*, what are you up to? ‖ **bricoleur** [-œr] *m.* handyman; *Am.* putterer.

bride [brìd] *f.* bridle, reins; ribbon [chapeau]; loop; tie (mech.); flange;

à bride abattue, at full speed; *lâcher la bride à*, to give rein to; *tourner bride*, to turn back. ‖ **brider** [-é] *v.* to bridle; to check; to curb; to truss [volaille]; to flange (techn.); *yeux bridés*, narrow eyes.

bridge [brĭdj] *m.* bridge [jeu]. ‖ **bridger** [-é] *v.* to play bridge.

brièveté [brĭèvté] *f.* brevity, shortness, concision.

brigade [brĭgàd] *f.* brigade (mil.); gang [travailleurs]; squad [police]; body [hommes]; shift(-work). ‖ **brigadier** [-yé] *m.* corporal (mil.); sergeant [police]; foreman.

brigand [brĭgaⁿ] *m.* brigand; robber; rogue. ‖ **brigandage** [-dàj] *m.* plunder; robbery.

briguer [brĭgé] *v.* to court; to solicit; to intrigue for; to canvass for.

brillant [brĭyaⁿ] *m.* brightness, brilliance; shine, sheen, polish; glitter; brilliant [diamant]; *adj.* bright, shining, sparkling; wonderful; talented; dashing; dazzling. ‖ **briller** [brĭyé] *v.* to shine; to sparkle; to blaze; to glitter; to glare; to be conspicuous.

brimade [brĭmàd] *f. Br.* ragging, *Am.* hazing. ‖ **brimer** [-é] *v. Br.* to rag, *Am.* to haze; to bully.

brimborion [brĭⁿbòrĭoⁿ] *m.* bauble, knick-knack.

brin [brĭⁿ] *m.* shoot, blade [herbe]; thread, strand; bit; sprig [bruyère]; *un beau brin de fille*, a fine figure of a girl.

brindille [brĭⁿdĭy] *f.* twig.

brio [brĭyô] *m.* brio, dash, spirit.

brioche [brĭyòsh] *f.* brioche; bun; (fam.) pot-belly.

brique [brĭk] *f.* brick; cake [savon]; brick-red. ‖ **briquet** [-è] *m.* tinder-box; cigarette lighter; *battre le briquet*, to strike a light. ‖ **briqueterie** [-trî] *f.* brickyard. ‖ **briquettes** [-èt] *f. pl.* patent fuel, briquettes.

bris [brĭ] *m.* breaking open; breaking loose; wreckage (naut.). ‖ **brisant** [-zaⁿ] *m.* breaker; reef, shoal; *adj.* breaking; bursting.

brise [brĭz] *f.* breeze.

brisé [brĭzé] *adj.* broken; tired out; folding [porte]. ‖ **brisées** [-é] *f. pl.* tracks; footsteps. ‖ **brisement** [-maⁿ] *m.* breaking. ‖ **briser** [-é] *v.* to break; to shatter; *brisons là*, let's leave it at that; *se briser*, to break *brise-bise*, draught-protector; *brise-circuit*, circuit-breaker; *brise-glace*, ice-breaker; *brise-lames*, breakwater, groyne.

bristol [brĭstòl] *m.* visiting-card.

britannique [brĭtànĭk] *adj.* British; *m. f.* Briton, Britisher.

broc [brô] *m.* jug; pitcher.

brocantage [bròkaⁿtàj] *m.* second-hand dealing. ‖ **brocanteur** [-tœr] *m.* second-hand dealer.

brochage [bròshàj] *m.* stitching; brocading. ‖ **broche** [bròsh] *f.* spit [à rôtir]; skewer; spindle; pin (mech.); peg [tente]; knitting-needle; brooch, breast-pin; *pl.* tusks [sanglier]. ‖ **brocher** [-é] *v.* to stitch; to brocade; to emboss; to scamp; *un livre broché*, a paper-bound book.

brochet [bròshè] *m.* pike [poisson].

brochette [bròshèt] *f.* skewer; pin (techn.); spitful; row.

brocheur [bròshœr] *m.* book-stitcher. ‖ **brochure** [-ür] *f.* brochure; booklet; pamphlet.

brodequin [bròdkĭⁿ] *m.* sock, buskin [théâtr.]; half-boot; ammunition-boot.

broder [bròdé] *v.* to embroider; to romance. ‖ **broderie** [-rî] *f.* embroidery; embellishment (fig.). ‖ **brodeur, -euse** [-œr, -ëz] *m., f.* embroiderer, embroideress.

broiement, see *broyement*.

bromure [bròmür] *m.* bromide.

broncher [bròⁿshé] *v.* to stumble; to trip; to move; to falter; *sans broncher*, without flinching.

bronches [bròⁿsh] *f. pl.* bronchia. ‖ **bronchite** [-ĭt] *f.* bronchitis. ‖ **broncho-pneumonie** [bròⁿkôpnëmònĭ] *f.* broncho-pneumonia.

bronze [bròⁿz] *m.* bronze; *cœur de bronze*, heart of iron. ‖ **bronzer** [-é] *v.* to bronze; to tan; to harden [cœur].

brosse [bròs] *f.* brush; ☯ drinking spree; *prendre une brosse*, ☯ to get drunk; *brosse à cheveux*, hairbrush; *brosse à dents*, tooth-brush; *cheveux en brosse*, crew-cut; *pl.* brushwood. ‖ **brosser** [-é] *v.* to brush; to scrub; to paint; (pop.) to thrash.

brou [brû] *m.* husk, shuck; *brou de noix*, walnut stain.

brouette [brûèt] *f.* wheelbarrow. ‖ **brouettée** [-é] *f.* barrow-load. ‖ **brouetter** [-é] *v.* to wheel in a barrow.

brouhaha [brûàà] *m.* noise, uproar; commotion; hubbub.

brouillage [brûyàj] *m.* jamming [radio]; interference [radio].

brouillamini [brûyàmĭnĭ] *m.* (fam.) disorder, confusion.

brouillard [brûyàr] *m.* fog; mist; waste-book. ‖ **brouillasser** [brûyàsé] *v.* to drizzle.

brouille [brûy] *f.* disagreement, difference; *être en brouille avec*, to be on bad terms with. ‖ **brouiller** [-é] *v.* to mix up; to confuse; to shuffle [cartes]; to jam [radio]; to interfere [radio]; to scramble [œufs]; *brouiller les cartes,* to spread confusion; *se brouiller,* to get dim; to become confused; to fall out [amis]. ‖ *brouillon* [-oⁿ] *m.* rough copy; *Br.* wastebook, *Am.* scratch-pad; *adj.** untidy; blundering.

broussailles [brûsây] *f. pl.* bush, brushwood; briars; *en broussaille,* unkempt, shaggy. ‖ *broussailleux* [-ë] *adj.** bushy. ‖ *brousse* [brûs] *f.* bush.

brouter [brûté] *v.* to browse, to graze; to jump [outil]; to chatter [moteur]. ‖ *broutilles* [-tîy] *f. pl.* twigs; brushwood; mere trifles.

broyement [brwàmaⁿ] *m.* pounding, crushing. ‖ *broyer* [-àyé] *v.* to pound, to pulverize; to crush; to grind. ‖ *broyeur* [-àyœr] *m.* pounder, breaker; grinder; crusher.

bru [brü] *f.* daughter-in-law.

bruine [brüîn] *f.* drizzle, Scotch mist. ‖ *bruiner* [-îné] *v.* to drizzle.

bruire [brüîr] *v.* to rustle; to murmur; to whisper. ‖ *bruissement* [brüîsmaⁿ] *m.* murmuring; rustling; soughing; humming; whispering.

bruit [brüî] *m.* noise; clatter; din; clang [métal]; report; rumo(u)r; turmoil; stir; sensation; *bruit sourd,* thud; *le bruit court que,* it is rumo(u)red that. ‖ *bruitage* [brüîtàj] *m.* sound effects.

brûlage [brülàj] *m.* burning; singeing [cheveux]. ‖ *brûlant* [-aⁿ] *adj.* burning, on fire; scorching; ardent. ‖ *brûler* [-é] *v.* to burn; to singe; to scorch; to scald [avec des liquides]; to be hot; to yearn; to hurry; *se brûler la cervelle,* to blow one's brains out; *brûler le pavé,* to tear along the street; *brûler une étape,* to pass through without stopping; *à brûle-pourpoint,* point-blank. ‖ *brûlerie* [-rî] *f.* brandy-distillery. ‖ *brûleur* [-œr] *m.* gas-burner; brandy distiller; incendiary. ‖ *brûloir* [-wàr] *m.* coffee roaster. ‖ *brûlot* [-lô] *m.* flare (aviat.); firebrand (fig.); © gnat. ‖ *brûlure* [-ür] *f.* burn; scald; blight (agr.).

brume [brüm] *f.* mist; fog. ‖ *brumeux* [-ë] *adj.** foggy; hazy; misty.

brun [bruⁿ] *m.* brown; *adj.* brown; dark; dusk; *une brune,* a brunette. ‖ *brunante* [brünaⁿt] *f.* © nightfall, dusk. ‖ *brunâtre* [brünâtr] *adj.* brownish. ‖ *brunir* [-îr] *v.* to tan, to become brown; to burnish. ‖ *brunissage* [-îsàj] *m.* burnishing. ‖ *brunisseur* [-îsœr] *m.* burnisher. ‖ *brunissoir* [-îswàr] *m.* burnisher [outil].

brusque [brüsk] *adj.* blunt, brusque, abrupt, rough; sudden; sharp. ‖ *brusquer* [-é] *v.* to be blunt with; to hustle

[gens]; to hurry [choses]. ‖ *brusquerie* [-erî] *f.* brusqueness, abruptness.

brut [brüt] *adj.* raw, unworked; in the rough; gross (comm.); crude [huile]; unrefined [sucre]; rough [diamant]; *revenu brut,* gross returns. ‖ *brutal* [-àl] *adj.** brutal; unfeeling; savage; rough; crude; fierce; plain [vérité]. ‖ *brutaliser* [-àlîzé] *v.* to bully; to ill-treat. ‖ *brutalité* [-àlîté] *f.* brutality; cruelty; roughness. ‖ *brute* [brüt] *f.* brute; ruffian.

Bruxelles [brüsèl] *f.* Brussels.

bruyant [brüyaⁿ] *adj.* noisy, loud; boisterous; clamorous; riotous; rollicking [rire]; resounding (fig.).

bruyère [brüyèr] *f.* heath; heather; briar; *coq de bruyère,* grouse.

bu [bü] *p. p. of boire.*

buanderie [büaⁿdrî] *f.* wash-house, laundry-room.

buccal [bükàl] *adj.** of the mouth.

bûche [büsh] *f.* log; block; billet [bois]; (fam.) blockhead; *bûche de Noël,* yule-log; *ramasser une bûche,* to have a spill. ‖ *bûcher* [-é] *m.* woodshed; wood-stack; stake (hist.); pyre; *v.* to rough-hew; © to cut down, to fell trees; (fam.) to grind, *Br.* to swot. ‖ *bûcheron* [-roⁿ] *m.* wood-cutter, lumberjack. ‖ *bûcheur* [-œr] *m.* (fam.) hard worker, plodder, *Br.* swotter, *Am.* grind, digger; grub.

bucolique [bükòlîk] *adj., f.* bucolic, pastoral.

budget [büdjè] *m.* budget; estimates; *boucler le budget,* to make both ends meet. ‖ *budgétaire* [-étèr] *adj.* budgetary; financial.

buée [büé] *f.* steam, vapo(u)r.

buffet [büfè] *m.* sideboard; cupboard; dresser; buffet; refreshment room; *Am.* sandwich-counter; organcase.

buffle [büfl] *m.* buffalo; buff [cuir]; strop [pour rasoir].

buis [büî] *m.* boxwood; palm [bénit].

buisson [büîsoⁿ] *m.* bush; hedge; thicket. ‖ *buissonneux* [-ònë] *adj.** bushy. ‖ *buissonnier* [-ònyé] *adj.* living in the bush; *faire l'école buissonnière,* to play truant, *Am.* to play hookey.

bulbe [bülb] *m.* bulb [plante].

bulle [bül] *f.* bubble; blister; seal; Papal bull; *papier bulle,* Manila paper.

bulletin [bültⁿ] *m.* bulletin; report; form; receipt; list; ticket; check; *bulletin de vote,* ballot-paper, voting-paper; *bulletin météorologique,*

weather report; *bulletin de bagages,*
Br. luggage-ticket, *Am.* baggage-check.

buraliste [büràlìst] *m.* clerk [poste];
receiver [régie]; tobacconist.

bure [bür] *f.* frieze, homespun [tissu];
frock [robe]; sackcloth (fig.).

bureau [bürô] *m.** bureau, writing-
desk; office; shop; staff; board [di-
recteurs]; *bureau de tabac,* tobacco
shop; *bureau de poste,* post-office; *le*
Deuxième Bureau, the Intelligence
Department (mil.); *chef de bureau,*
head of a department. ‖ *bureaucrate*
[-kràt] *m.* bureaucrat. ‖ *bureaucratie*
[-kràsî] *f.* bureaucracy; (fam.) red
tape. ‖ *bureaucratique* [-kràtík] *adj.*
bureaucratic.

burette [bürèt] *f.* cruet; oil-can;
oiler.

burin [bürìⁿ] *m.* burin; graver;
etching needle. ‖ *buriner* [-ìné] *v.* to
engrave; to mark; to swot (fam.).

burlesque [bürlèsk] *adj.* burlesque;
comical, ludicrous.

burnous [bürnû] *m.* burnous, *Am.*
burnoose.

buse [büz] *f.* buzzard; (fam.) dunce,
dolt, nitwit.

buse [büz] *f.* nozzle (techn.); mill-
race; air-shaft [mine]; choke.

busqué [büské] *adj.* hooked.

buste [büst] *m.* bust; *en buste,* half-
length.

but [bü(t)] *m.* mark; aim; target;
home; goal; objective; purpose; *de*
but en blanc, bluntly; *droit au but,* to
the point.

butane [bütàn] *m.* butane.

butée [büté] *f.* abutment; thrust;
arrester (techn.). ‖ *buter* [-é] *v.* to
abut; to butt; to knock against; to
trip; to prop.; (pop.) to bump off;
c'est un esprit buté, he's an obstinate
creature; *se buter,* to be determined;
to bump into.

butin [bütìⁿ] *m.* booty, plunder,
spoils. ‖ *butiner* [-ìné] *v.* to loot, to
pillage; to gather honey [abeilles].

butoir [bütwàr] *m.* buffer [trains].

butte [büt] *f.* mound; hillock; bank;
butts (mil.); *être en butte à,* to be
exposed to. ‖ *butter* [-é] *v.* to bank up,
to earth up. ‖ *buttoir* [-wàr] *m. Br.*
ridging-plough, *Am.* ridging-plow.

buvable [büvàbl] *adj.* drinkable;
(pop.) acceptable. ‖ *buvard* [-àr] *m.*
blotting-paper. ‖ *buvette* [-èt] *f.*
refreshment bar; pump-room [villes
d'eau]. ‖ *buveur* [-œr] *m.* drinker;
toper; *buveur d'eau,* teetotaler. ‖ *bu-*
voter [-òté] *v.* to sip.

byzantin [bìzaⁿtìⁿ] *m., adj.* Byzan-
tine.

C

c', see *ce.*

ça [sà] see *cela.*

çà [sà] *adv.* here; hither; *çà et là,*
here and there.

cabale [kàbàl] *f.* cabala; cabal, faction; intrigue; © canvassing. ‖ *caba-*
ler [-é] *v.* © to canvass. ‖ *cabaleur*
[-œr] *m.* © canvasser. ‖ *cabalistique*
[-ìstîk] *adj.* cabalistic.

caban [kàbaⁿ] *m.* greatcoat.

cabane [kàbàn] *f.* hut, shed; cabin;
hutch [lapins]; *cabane à sucre,* ©
saphouse. ‖ *cabanon* [-oⁿ] *m.* small
cabin; bungalow; padded cell.

cabaret [kàbàrè] *m.* tavern, pot-
house; restaurant. ‖ *cabaretier* [-tyé]
m. inn-keeper; publican.

cabas [kàbà] *m.* basket; market-bag.

cabèche [kàbèsh] *f.* noddle (fam.).

cabestan [kàbestaⁿ] *m.* capstan.

cabillaud [kàbìyô] *m.* fresh cod.

cabillot [kàbìyô] *m.* toggle pin.

cabine [kàbìn] *f.* cabin; berth (naut.);
car [ascenseur]; cab [grue, locomo-

tive]; *Br.* telephone kiosk, call-box,
Am. telephone booth. ‖ *cabinet* [-è]
m. closet; office; ministry, government; consulting-room; collection;
cabinet; case; toilet; *cabinet noir,*
dark-room; *cabinet de toilette,* dressing-room; lavatory; *cabinet de travail,*
study.

câble [kâbl] *m.* cable; *câble de re-*
morque, tow-line, hawser. ‖ *câbler* [-é]
v. to cable [télégramme]; to wire up
(electr.). ‖ *câblogramme* [-ògràm] *m.*
cable, cablegram.

caboche [kàbòsh] *f.* nail; hobnail;
(pop.) head, pate, noddle. ‖ *cabochon*
[-oⁿ] *m.* cabochon [pierre]; brass nail
[clou]; noddle (fam.).

cabosse [kàbòs] *f.* bump. ‖ *cabosser*
[-é] *v.* to bump; to batter; to bash in.

cabot [kàbò] *m.* ham actor; corporal
[soldat]; tyke [chien].

cabotage [kàbòtàj] *m.* coasting-trade.
‖ *caboter* [-é] *v.* to coast. ‖ *caboteur*
[-œr] *m.* coaster, coasting-vessel.

cabotin [kàbòtìⁿ] *m.* ham-actor;
strolling player. ‖ *cabotinage* [-ìnàj]

m. barn-storming [d'acteur]; histrion-ism; self-advertisement.

caboulot [kàbûlô] *m.* low pub, dive.

cabrer (se) [s⁰kàbré] *v.* to rear, to shy, to buck; to revolt, to kick, to jib; to nose up (aviat.).

cabri [kàbrî] *m.* kid.

cabriole [kàbriòl] *f.* caper, leap. ‖ **cabrioler** [-é] *v.* to caper about, to cut capers. ‖ **cabriolet** [-è] *m.* cabriolet, cab.

caca [kàkà] *m.* (pop.) cack.

cacahuète [kàkàwèt] *f.* peanut.

cacao [kàkàò] *m.* (bot.) cacao; (culin.) cocoa. ‖ **cacaoté** [-té] *adj.* cocoa-flavoured.

cacatoès [kàkàtòès] *m.* cockatoo, parakeet.

cachalot [kàshàlô] *m.* cachalot, sperm whale.

cache [kàsh] *f.* hiding-place; screen, mask (phot.); **cache-cache**, hide-and-seek; **cache-col**, scarf; **cache-nez**, muffler; **cache-poussière**, dust-coat; **cache-sexe**, slip, Bikini. ‖ **cacher** [kà-shé] *v.* to hide, to conceal; to make a secret of; **se cacher**, to hide; to avoid.

cachet [kàshè] *m.* seal; stamp; ticket; mark; trade-mark; cachet (med.); fee; *avoir du cachet*, to have distinction; to look authentic; *lettre de cachet*, warrant of arrest. ‖ **cachetage** [kàsh-tàj] *m.* sealing. ‖ **cacheter** [kàshté] *v.* to seal (up). ‖ **cachette** [-èt] *f.* hiding-place; *en cachette*, secretly, by stealth. ‖ **cachot** [-ô] *m.* dungeon; jail. ‖ **cachotterie** [-òtrî] *f.* mysterious ways; *faire des cachotteries*, to have secrets. ‖ **cachottier** [-òtyé] *m.* secretive fellow; *adj.*⁺ mysterious, reticent.

cachou [kàshû] *m.* cachou.

cacophonie [kàkòfònî] *f.* cacophony. ‖ **cacophonique** [-ìk] *adj.* cacophonous, discordant.

cactus [kàktüs] *m.* cactus.

cadastre [kàdàstr] *m.* land registry; Ordnance Survey.

cadavérique [kàdàvérìk] *adj.* cadaverous; *rigidité cadavérique*, rigor mortis. ‖ **cadavre** [kàdàvr] *m.* dead body, cadaver, corpse; carcass.

cadeau [kàdô] *m.*⁺ gift, present.

cadenas [kàdnà] *m.* padlock; clasp. ‖ **cadenasser** [-sé] *v.* to padlock; to fasten [bracelet].

cadence [kàdⁿs] *f.* cadence, rhythm, fall (lit.); cadenza (mus.); *en cadence*, rhythmically. ‖ **cadencer** [-é] *v.* to set the rhythm.

cadet [kàdè] *m.* younger son; cadet mil.); caddie [golf]; young man; *adj.*⁺ younger, junior, youngest; *mon cadet*

de deux ans, my junior by two years; *le cadet de mes soucis*, the least of my worries.

cadran [kàdraⁿ] *m.* face, dial; *cadran solaire*, sun-dial. ‖ **cadrat** [-à] *m.* quadrat. ‖ **cadratin** [-àtⁿ] *m.* em-quad. ‖ **cadre** [kàdr] *m.* frame; framework; outline, limits; setting [scène]; sphere; cadre, staff (mil.); cot (naut.); *les cadres*, staff; high-grade, employees; *cadre de réception*, frame aerial. ‖ **cadrer** [-é] *v.* to tally, to agree; to fit in; to center.

caduc, -uque [kàdük] *adj.* decrepit, decaying; frail, feeble [voix]; deciduous (bot.); null, lapsed (jur.); *mal caduc*, epilepsy.

caducée [kàdüsé] *m.* caduceus, Mercury's wand.

cafard [kàfàr] *m.* cockroach; sneak; humbug; *adj.* sneaking; sanctimonious; *avoir le cafard*, to be in the dumps, to have the blues.

cafarder [kàfàrdé] *v.* to carry tales.

cafardeux [kàfàrdè] *adj.*⁺ browned off.

café [kàfé] *m.* coffee; café; *café nature*, black coffee; *café en poudre*, soluble coffee; pub. ‖ **caféine** [-éîn] *f.* caffeine. ‖ **cafétéria** [-téryà] *f.* © cafeteria. ‖ **cafetier** [-tyé] *m.* café-owner; publican. ‖ **cafetière** [-tyèr] *f.* coffee-pot.

cage [kàj] *f.* cage; hen-coop; frame (constr.); shaft; well; cover, casing; (pop.) prison, clink; *cage à billes*, ball-race (mech.). ‖ **cageot** [-jô] *m.* hamper.

cagneux [kàñè] *adj.*⁺ knock-kneed.

cagnotte [kàñòt] *f.* pool, kitty.

cagot [kàgô] *m.* bigot; *adj.* sanctimonious.

cagoule [kàgûl] *f.* cowl, hood.

cahier [kàyé] *m.* note-book; exercise-book; official reports.

cahot [kàò] *m.* jolt. ‖ **cahotement** [-tmaⁿ] *m.* jolting. ‖ **cahoter** [-té] *v.* to jolt; to jog, to jerk. ‖ **cahoteux** [-tè] *adj.*⁺ rough, bumpy [route].

cahute [kàüt] *f.* hut; hovel; cabin.

caille [kày] *f.* quail [oiseau].

caillebotis [kàybòtì] *m.* grating; duckboards (mil.).

caillebotte [kàybòt] *f.* curds. ‖ **caillebotter** [-é] *v.* to curdle; to clot.

cailler [kàyé] *v.* to curdle; to clot [sang]; *lait caillé*, clotted milk, curds; *caille-lait*, rennet.

caillot [kàyò] *m.* clot.

caillou [kàyû] *m.*⁺ pebble, small stone; cobble. ‖ **caillouteux** [-tè] *adj.*⁺ pebbly, stony, flinty. ‖ **cailloutis** [-tì] *m.* rubble, heap of broken stones; rough surface.

caisse [kès] *f.* case, box; till; cash-box; cash; pay-desk; fund; drum; body [véhicule]; *caisse d'épargne*, savings-bank; *grosse caisse*, big drum; *argent en caisse*, cash in hand; *faire la caisse*, to balance the cash; *caisse à eau*, water-tank. ‖ *caissette* [-èt] *f.* small box. ‖ *caissier* [-yé] *m.* cashier; teller; treasurer. ‖ *caisson* [-oⁿ] *m.* caisson; locker (naut.); boot [auto]; *se faire sauter le caisson*, to blow one's brains out.

cajoler [kàjòlé] *v.* to cajole, to coax, to wheedle.

cal [kàl] *m.* callosity.

calage [kàlàj] *m.* propping; wedging.

calamité [kàlàmité] *f.* calamity, disaster. ‖ *calamiteux* [-ë] *adj.** calamitous.

calcaire [kàlkèr] *m.* limestone; *adj.* calcareous, chalky.

calciner [kàlsìné] *v.* to calcine, to burn, to char.

calcium [kàlsyòm] *m.* calcium.

calcul [kàlkül] *m.* reckoning; calculation; computation; estimation, estimate; calculus; *faux calcul*, miscalculation. ‖ *calculateur, -trice* [-àtœr, -trìs] *m., f.* calculator, reckoner; scheming, calculating. ‖ *calculer* [-é] *v.* to calculate; to compute; to reckon; to deliberate; to forecast. ‖ *calculeux* [-ë] *adj.** calculous.

cale [kàl] *f.* hold [bateau]; *cale de construction*, stocks; *cale sèche*, dry dock; *eau de cale*, bilge water.

cale [kàl] *f.* wedge, chock; prop; packing.

calé [kàlé] *adj.* well versed, well up; *p. p. of caler.*

calebasse [kàlbàs] *f.* calabash; gourd.

calèche [kàlèsh] *f.* calash, calèche.

caleçon [kàlsoⁿ] *m.* drawers, *Br.* pants, *Am.* shorts.

calembour [kàlⁿbûr] *m.* pun. ‖ *calembredaine* [-ʳdèn] *f.* nonsense, foolishness; quibble.

calendes [kàlⁿd] *f. pl.* calends. ‖ *calendrier* [kàlⁿdryé] *m.* calendar; almanac.

calepin [kàlpⁿ] *m.* note-book.

caler [kàlé] *v.* to draw water, to have draught (naut.).

caler [kàlé] *v.* to wedge, to chock; to prop (up); to jam; to stall [moteur]; to key [poulie]; to lower; to adjust; (pop.) to flinch.

calfat [kàlfà] *m.* ca(u)lker. ‖ *calfatage* [-tàj] *m.* ca(u)lking. ‖ *calfater* [-té] *v.* to ca(u)lk.

calfeutrer [kàlfëtré] *v.* to stop up the chinks of; *se calfeutrer*, to shut oneself up.

calibrage [kàlìbràj] *m.* calibrating; gauging; trimming (phot.). ‖ *calibre* [kàlìbr] *m.* bore, calibre [canon]; size; gauge (techn.); former; template; *compas de calibre*, callipers. ‖ *calibrer* [-é] *v.* to calibrate; to gauge; to trim.

calice [kàlìs] *m.* chalice (eccles.).

calice [kàlìs] *m.* calyx (bot.).

calicot [kàlìkò] *m.* calico, *Am.* unbleached muslin; counter-jumper.

calife [kàlìf] *m.* caliph.

Californie [kàlìfòrnî] *f.* California.

califourchon (à) [àkàlìfûrshoⁿ] *adv.* astride.

câlin [kâlⁿ] *m.* wheedler; *adj.* wheedling, cajoling; coaxing. ‖ *câliner* [-ìné] *v.* to wheedle; to fondle, to caress. ‖ *câlinerie* [-ìnrî] *f.* cajolery; coaxing; caressing.

calleux [kàlë] *adj.** horny, callous; hard. ‖ *callosité* [-òzìté] *f.* callosity; *avec callosité*, callously.

calligraphie [kàlìgràfî] *f.* calligraphy, penmanship. ‖ *calligraphier* [-fyé] *v.* to calligraph.

calmant [kàlmaⁿ] *m.* sedative, anodyne (med.); *adj.* calming, soothing. ‖ *calme* [kàlm] *m.* calm, calmness, stillness; composure; *adj.* calm, still, quiet. ‖ *calmer* [-é] *v.* to calm, to quieten; to soothe; to pacify; *se calmer*, to abate, to calm down.

calomniateur, -trice [kàlòmnyàtœr, -trìs] *m., f.* slanderer; *adj.* slanderous; libel(l)ous. ‖ *calomnie* [-î] *f.* calumny, slander, libel. ‖ *calomnier* [-yé] *v.* to slander; to libel. ‖ *calomnieux* [-yë] *adj.** slanderous; libel(l)ous.

calorie [kàlòrî] *f.* *Br.* calory, *Am.* calorie. ‖ *calorifère* [-ìfèr] *m.* heating-apparatus, stove. ‖ *calorifique* [-ìfìk] *adj.* calorific. ‖ *calorifuge* [-ìfüj] *adj.* heat-insulating. ‖ *calorifuger* [-ìfüjé] *v.* to insulate.

calot [kàlò] *m.* cap; forage-cap (mil.). ‖ *calotin* [-tⁿ] *m.* (pop.) churchy person. ‖ *calotte* [-t] *f.* skull-cap; slap in the face, cuff; the cloth, priesthood. ‖ *calotter* [-té] *v.* (fam.) to box someone's ears.

calque [kàlk] *m.* fair copy; tracing. ‖ *calquer* [-é] *v.* to copy; to trace; to transfer [tricot]; *papier à calquer*, tracing-paper.

calumet [kàlümè] *m.* calumet; pipe.

calvaire [kàlvèr] *m.* calvary, wayside cross; cross.

calviniste [kàlvìnìst] *m., f.* calvinist; *adj.* calvinistic.

calvitie [kàlvìsî] *f.* baldness.

camail [kàmày] *m.* cape (eccles.); cloak.

camarade [kàmàràd] *m.*, *f.* comrade, fellow, mate. ‖ *camaraderie* [-rî] *f.* comradeship, friendship; clique.

camard [kàmàr] *adj.* snubnosed. ‖ *Camarde* [-d] *f.* (pop.) the Death.

cambouis [kanbûî] *m.* cart-grease; dirty oil.

cambré [kanbré] *adj.* bent, cambered, arched, bowed [jambes]. ‖ *cambrer* [-é] *v.* to bend, to camber, to arch [pieds]; *se cambrer,* to brace oneself up; to warp.

cambriolage [kanbrìòlàj] *m.* house-breaking, burglary. ‖ *cambrioler* [-é] *v.* to burgle; to break into [maison]. ‖ *cambrioleur* [-œr] *m.* housebreaker, burglar; yegg.

cambrure [kanbrür] *f.* camber; bend; arch; curve; instep.

cambuse [kanbüz] *f.* store-room (naut.). ‖ *cambusier* [-yé] *m.* store-keeper; steward's mate.

came [kàm] *f.* cam; lifter (mech.); *arbre à cames,* camshaft.

caméléon [kàméléon] *m.* chameleon; turncoat, trimmer.

camélia [kàmélyà] *m.* camellia (bot.).

camelot [kàmlô] *m.* street hawker. ‖ *camelote* [-òt] *f.* cheap articles, junk, trash, rubbish.

camera [kàmèrà] *f.* cine-camera.

camériste [kàmérìst] *f.* maid of honour; chamber-maid.

camion [kàmyon] *m.* wag(g)on; *Br.* lorry, *Am.* truck. ‖ *camionnage* [-yònàj] *m.* cartage; trucking; hauling. ‖ *camionnette* [-yònèt] *f. Br.* small lorry, *Am.* light truck; delivery-van. ‖ *camionneur* [-yònœr] *m. Br.* lorry-driver, *Am.* truck driver.

camisole [kàmìzòl] *f.* camisole; *camisole de force,* strait-jacket.

camomille [kàmòmîy] *f.* camomile.

camouflage [kàmûflàj] *m.* camou-flage; black-out. ‖ *camoufler* [-é] *v.* to camouflage (mil.); to disguise; to conceal; to black-out.

camouflet [kàmûflè] *m.* camouflet; snub.

camp [kan] *m.* camp; side; faction, party; *camp volant,* temporary shelter.

campagnard [kanpànàr] *m.* rustic, countryman; *adj.* rustic; country.

campagne [kanpàñ] *f.* open country; countryside; campaign (mil.); field (mil.); cruise (naut.); *à la campagne,* in the country; *en pleine campagne,*

out in the open; *battre la campagne,* to rave.

camper [kanpé] *v.* to camp; to fix; *se camper,* to pitch one's camp; to plant oneself. ‖ *campeur* [-për] *m.* camper.

camphre [kanfr] *m.* camphor. ‖ *camphré* [-é] *adj.* camphorated.

camping [kanpìng] *m.* camping; *faire du camping,* to go camping, to camp out.

campos [kanpò] *m.* (fam.) day off; holiday.

camus [kàmü] *adj.* snub-nosed; pug-nosed [chien].

Canada [kànàdà] *m.* Canada; *au Canada,* in Canada; *canadien* [yin] *m.*, *adj.* Canadian. ‖ *canadienne* [-yèn] *f.* sheepskin jacket.

canaille [kànày] *f.* (pop.) rabble; riffraff; scum; blackguard, scoundrel, spiv, heel; *adj.* low, coarse. ‖ *canaillerie* [-rî] *f.* dirty trick, roguery.

canal [kànàl] *m.* canal; channel; conduit; pipe (mech.); passage (bot.); duct; flue; feeder; ditch. ‖ *canalisation* [-ìzàsyon] *f.* canalisation [rivière]; draining; mains (mech.); pipe-line. ‖ *canaliser* [-ìzé] *v.* to canalize; to lay pipes; to make navigable [rivière].

canapé [kànàpé] *m.* couch, sofa.

canard [kànàr] *m.* duck; drake; hoax; false news; sensationalist news-paper, *Br.* rag (pop.); wrong note (mus.); lump of sugar dipped in brandy or coffee. ‖ *canardeau* [-dô] *m.* duck-ling. ‖ *canarder* [-dé] *v.* to fire at, to pepper [navire]; to pitch [navire].

canari [kànàrî] *m.* canary.

canasson [kànàson] *m.* (fam.) jade, hack, nag.

cancan [kankan] *m.* cancan; gossip.

cancer [kansèr] *m.* cancer; *le Cancer,* the Crab, Cancer (astr.). ‖ *cancéreux* [-érë] *m.* cancer sufferer; *adj.* can-cerous. ‖ *cancérigène* [érìjèn] *adj.* carcinogenic.

cancre [kankr] *m.* crab; cray-fish; dunce, duffer.

cancrelat [kankrelà] *m.* cockroach.

candélabre [kandélàbr] *m.* branched candlestick, candelabrum.

candeur [kandœr] *f.* ingenuousness, artlessness, guilelessness; cando(u)r.

candi [kandî] *adj.* candied.

candidat [kandìdà] *m.* candidate. ‖ *candidature* [-tür] *f.* candidature; *poser sa candidature à,* to put up for.

candide [kandìd] *adj.* ingenuous, art-less, guileless. ‖ *candidement* [-man] *adv.* ingenuously.

cane [kàn] *f.* duck.

caner [kàné] *v.* (pop.) to funk it, to chicken out.

caneton [kàntoⁿ] *m.* duckling.

canette [kànèt] *f.* duckling; can [bière]; spool [machine à coudre].

canevas [kànvà] *m.* canvas; outline, plan, groundwork.

cangue [kàⁿg] *f.* cangue.

caniche [kànìsh] *m.* poodle.

caniculaire [kànìkülèr] *adj.* sultry [temps]; *les jours caniculaires*, the dog-days. ‖ **canicule** [-ül] *f.* dog-days.

canif [kànìf] *m.* penknife, pocket-knife.

canin [kànìⁿ] *adj.* canine, dog [exposition]. ‖ **canine** [-ìn] *f.* canine [dent].

caniveau [kànìvò] *m.** gutter.

canne [kàn] *f.* cane, stick; rod; walking-stick; *sucre de canne*, cane-sugar; *canne à sucre*, sugar-cane; *canne à pêche*, fishing-rod.

canneler [kànlé] *v.* to groove, to flute (arch.); to corrugate.

cannelle [kànèl] *f.* cinnamon.

cannelure [kànlür] *f.* channel; groove, fluting (arch.); corrugation.

cannette, *see* **canette.**

cannibale [kànìbàl] *m.*, *f.* cannibal. ‖ **cannibalisme** [-ìsm] *m.* cannibalism.

canoë [kànòé] *m.* canoe. .

canon [kànoⁿ] *m.* cannon; gun; barrel; glass of wine; *poudre à canon*, gun-powder; *à canon rayé*, rifled; *coup de canon*, gunshot.

canon [kànoⁿ] *m.* canon (eccles.; mus.); *droit canon*, canon law. ‖ **canonique** [-ònìk] *adj.* canonical. ‖ **canonisation** [-ònìzàsyoⁿ] *f.* canonization. ‖ **canoniser** [-ònìzé] *v.* to canonize.

canonnade [kànònàd] *f.* gun-fire, cannonade. ‖ **canonnerie** [-rî] *f.* gun-foundry. ‖ **canonnier** [-yé] *m.* gunner, artilleryman. ‖ **canonnière** [-yèr] *f.* gunboat [navire]; pop-gun [jouet].

canot [kànò] *m.* boat; dinghy; pinnace; © canoe; *canot de sauvetage*, life-boat; *canot glisseur*, speed-boat. ‖ **canotage** [-òtàj] *m.* rowing, boating, canoeing. ‖ **canoter** [-òté] *v.* to go in for boating. ‖ **canotier** [-òtyé] *m.* boatman; oarsman; straw-hat, boater.

cantatrice [kaⁿtàtrìs] *f.* singer.

cantine [kaⁿtìn] *f.* canteen (mil.); equipment-case; school-canteen; dining-hall; ‖ **cantinier** [-ìnyé] *m.* canteen-manager.

cantique [kaⁿtìk] *m.* canticle; sacred song, hymn.

canton [kaⁿtoⁿ] *m.* canton, district; section. ‖ **cantonade** [kaⁿtònàd] *f.* wings (theat.); *à la cantonade*, off-stage. ‖ **cantonal** [-òⁿàl] *adj.** district. ‖ **cantonnement** [-òⁿmaⁿ] *m.* billeting, quartering; quarters (mil.). ‖ **cantonner** [-òⁿé] *v.* to billet, to quarter [soldats]; to confine; to divide into districts. ‖ **cantonnier** [-òⁿyé] *m.* roadman, roadmender.

canular [kànülàr] *m.* hoax, leg-pull.

canule [kànül] *f.* nozzle. ‖ **canuler** [-é] *v.* (pop.) to bore.

caoutchouc [kàûtshû] *m.* india-rubber; raincoat, solid tire; *pl.* galoshes, rubbers; *anneau en caoutchouc*, elastic band; *caoutchouc durci*, vulcanite. ‖ **caoutchouter** [-té] *v.* to rubberize, to treat with rubber.

cap [kàp] *m.* cape; head (naut.); course; *de pied en cap*, from head to foot; *mettre le cap sur*, to steer for, to head for; *doubler un cap*, to round a cape.

capable [kàpàbl] *adj.* capable, able, of good abilities.

capacité [kàpàsìté] *f.* capacity; ability, qualification (jur.).

caparaçonner [kàpàràsòné] *v.* to caparison.

cape [kàp] *f.* cape; hood; cloak, gown; *rire sous cape*, to laugh up one's sleeve; *être à la cape* (naut.), to be hove to.

capharnaüm [kàfàrnàòm] *m.* lumber-room.

capillaire [kàpìllèr] *adj.* capillary. ‖ **capillarité** [-àrìté] *f.* capillarity (phys.).

capilotade [kàpìlòtàd] *f.* hash; *mettre en capilotade*, to knock to smithereens; to beat to a pulp.

capitaine [kàpìtèn] *m.* captain; skipper; master-mariner; lieutenant-commander; commander; chief, leader; *capitaine de port*, harbo(u)r-master.

capital [kàpìtàl] *m.** capital, assets; *adj.** capital; essential, principal; outstanding [importance]; *peine capitale*, death-penalty. ‖ **capitale** [-àl] *f.* capital [ville, lettre]. ‖ **capitaliser** [-àlìzé] *v.* to capitalize; to save. ‖ **capitalisme** [-àlìsm] *m.* capitalism. ‖ **capitaliste** [-àlìst] *m.*, *f.* capitalist; *adj.* capitalistic.

capitation [kàpìtàsyoⁿ] *f.* poll-tax.

capiteux [kàpìtö] *adj.** heady [vin], strong; sexy [femme].

capiton [kàpìtoⁿ] *m.* silk-flock, stuffing. ‖ **capitonner** [-òné] *v.* to pad, to upholster.

capitulation [kàpìtülàsyoⁿ] *f.* capitulation, surrender. ‖ **capituler** [-é] *v.* to capitulate, to surrender; to yield.

capoc [kàpòk] *m.* kapok.

capon [kàpoⁿ] *m.* coward, sneak; *adj.* afraid, cowardly. ‖ *caponner* [-òné] *v.* to funk; to sneak.

caporal [kàpòràl] *m.** corporal; shag [tabac]. ‖ *caporaliser* [-izé] *v.* to Prussianize. ‖ *caporalisme* [-îsm] *m.* narrow militarism.

capot [kàpô] *m.* hooded greatcoat; cloak; bonnet, hood [auto]; cowling (aviat.); cover.

capot [kàpô] *m.* *faire capot*, to capsize, to turn turtle; *être capot*, to have lost all the tricks [cartes].

capote [kàpòt] *f.* greatcoat; bonnet; hood.

capoter [kàpòté] *v.* to capsize, to overturn; to turn turtle (naut.); to heel right over; to nose over (aviat.).

câpre [kâpr] *f.* caper (bot.).

caprice [kàprìs] *m.* caprice, whim, fancy. ‖ *capricieux* [-yë] *adj.** capricious, whimsical; moody, temperamental.

Capricorne [kàprìkòrn] *m.* Capricorn.

capsulage [kàpsülàj] *m.* capsuling, capping. ‖ *capsule* [kàpsül] *f.* capsule; percussion-cap; cap [bouteille]; seal. ‖ *capsuler* [-é] *v.* to seal, to cap [bouteille].

captage [kàptàj] *m.* water-catchment; picking up [courant]. ‖ *captation* [-àsyoⁿ] *f.* captation; inveiglement (jur.). ‖ *capter* [-é] *v.* to collect; to pick up [radio]; to win insidiously; to canalize; to recover (ind.).

captieux [kàpsyë] *adj.** insidious, cunning; specious, fallacious.

captif [kàptîf] *m.* captive; prisoner; *adj.** captive. ‖ *captiver* [-ìvé] *v.* to enslave; to win; to captivate, to enthrall; to bewitch. ‖ *captivité* [-ìvìté] *f.* captivity, bondage.

capture [kàptür] *f.* capture; seizure; prize. ‖ *capturer* [-é] *v.* to capture; to seize; to arrest.

capuchon [kàpüshoⁿ] *m.* hood; cowl (eccles.); cap [stylo].

capucin [kàpüsiⁿ] *m.* Capuchin friar. ‖ *capucine* [-în] *f.* Capuchin nun; nasturtium (bot.); band [fusil].

caque [kàk] *f.* keg; herring-barrel.

caquet [kàkè] *m.* cackle [poules]; gossip, chatter; gift of the gab; *rabattre le caquet*, to take someone down a peg. ‖ *caquetage* [kàktàj] *m.* gossiping. ‖ *caqueter* [kàkté] *v.* to cackle; to chatter, to gossip, to jaw; to prattle.

car [kàr] *conj.* for; because; as.

car [kàr] *m.* motor-coach; bus.

carabine [kàràbîn] *f.* carbine, rifle. ‖ *carabiné* [-îné] *adj.* sharp; stiff [histoire]; raging [fièvre]; violent, heavy [rhume]. ‖ *carabinier* [kàràbìnyé] *m.* carabineer; constable.

caracoler [kàràkòlé] *v.* to caracole, to prance.

caractère [kàràktèr] *m.* character; nature; temperament; characteristic; feature; expression; handwriting; letter; ideograph; type (typogr.); notation marks (mus.); *un caractère*, a case; *bon caractère*, good temper; *mauvais caractère*, bad disposition; *avoir caractère pour*, to have authority for. ‖ *caractériel* [-téryèl] *adj.** temperamental. ‖ *caractériser* [-érizé] *v.* to caracterize; *se caractériser*, to be distinguished (*par*, by). ‖ *caractéristique* [-érìstîk] *f.* characteristic, salient feature; *adj.* typical, distinctive, specific.

carafe [kàràf] *f.* glass decanter; bottle. ‖ *carafon* [-oⁿ] *m.* small decanter.

carambolage [kàraⁿbòlàj] *m.* cannon [billard]; collision. ‖ *caramboler* [-é] *v.* to cannon, to carom; to collide with, to run into.

caramel [kàràmèl] *m.* caramel; burnt sugar, butter-scotch; taffy. ‖ *caraméliser* [-mélìzé] *v.* to caramelize; to colour with caramel.

carapace [kàràpàs] *f.* carapace, shell.

carat [kàrà] *m.* carat.

caravane [kàràvàn] *f.* caravan; trailer; conducted tour; party of tourists. ‖ *caravansérail* [kàràvaⁿséràÿ] *m.* caravanserai, caravansary.

carbonate [kàrbònàt] *m.* carbonate. ‖ *carbonaté* [-é] *adj.* carbonized. ‖ *carbone* [kàrbòn] *m.* carbon; *papier carbone*, carbon paper. ‖ *carbonique* [-ìk] *adj.* carbonic. ‖ *carboniser* [-izé] *v.* to carbonize, to char; to burn to death.

carburant [kàrbüraⁿ] *m.* motor-fuel.

carburateur [kàrbüràtœr] *m.* carburet(t)or. ‖ *carburation* [-àsyoⁿ] *f.* carburet(t)ing; vaporization.

carbure [kàrbür] *m.* carbide. ‖ *carburer* [-é] *v.* to vaporize; (fam.) to go strong.

carcajou [kàrkàjû] *m.* wolverine, glutton.

carcan [kàrkaⁿ] *m.* iron collar, carcan; (pop.) jade; gawk.

carcasse [kàrkàs] *f.* carcass; framework, skeleton, shell [construction]; casing [pneu].

cardage [kàrdàj] *m.* carding. ‖ *carde* [kàrd] *f.* bur, teasel; carding-brush

67 CAR — CAR

(text.). ‖ **carder** [-é] v. to card, to comb. ‖ **cardeuse** [-ëz] f. carding-machine.

cardiaque [kàrdyàk] adj. cardiac; crise cardiaque, heart attack.

cardigan [kàrdìgaⁿ] m. cardigan.

cardinal [kàrdìnàl] m.*, adj.* cardinal.

cardiogramme [kàrdìògràm] m. cardiogram. ‖ **cardiologie** [-lòjî] f. cardiology. ‖ **cardiologue** [-lòg] m., f. cardiologist.

carême [kàrèm] m. Lent; figure de carême, gloomy face; comme mars en carême, unfailingly; carême-prenant, Shrovetide.

carence [kàraⁿs] f. insolvency (jur.); deficiency (med.).

carène [kàrèn] f. hull; pompe de carène, bilge-pump. ‖ **caréner** [-éné] v. to careen (naut.); to streamline (aviat.).

caressant [kàrèsaⁿ] adj. caressing, tender. ‖ **caresse** [kàrès] f. caress, endearment. ‖ **caresser** [-é] v. to caress, to fondle, to stroke [animal]; to cherish [espoir].

cargaison [kàrgèzoⁿ] f. cargo, freight; shipload.

cargo [kàrgô] m. cargo-boat, tramp-steamer.

caribou [kàrìbû] m. cariboo.

caricatural [kàrìkàtùràl] adj.* caricatural. ‖ **caricature** [kàrìkàtür] f. caricature. ‖ **caricaturer** [-é] v. to caricature. ‖ **caricaturiste** [-ìst] m. caricaturist.

carie [kàrî] f. caries, decay; blight (bot.). ‖ **carier** [kàryé] v. to rot; dent cariée, decayed tooth.

carillon [kàrìyoⁿ] m. carillon, chime, peal. ‖ **carillonner** [-òné] v. to chime; to jingle; to sound; to announce. ‖ **carillonneur** [-ònœr] m. bell-ringer.

carlin [kàrlⁿ] m. pug-dog.

carlingue [kàrlⁿg] f. keelson (naut.); cabin, cockpit (aviat.).

carme [kàrm] m.*, adj. Carmelite [moine]. ‖ **carmélite** [-élìt] f. Carmelite [religieuse].

carmin [kàrmⁿ] m. carmine, crimson, deep red. ‖ **carminer** [-ìné] v. to dye, to colo(u)r with carmine.

carnage [kàrnàj] m. carnage, slaughter, butchery; raw meat.

carnassier [kàrnàsyé] m. carnivore; adj.* carnivorous. ‖ **carnassière** [-yèr] f. game-bag.

carnation [kàrnàsyoⁿ] f. flesh colo(u)r; complexion.

carnaval [kàrnàvàl] (pl. carnavals) m. carnival. ‖ **carnavalesque** [-èsk] adj. carnavalesque.

carne [kàrn] f. nag, jade; tough meat (pop.); brute.

carnet [kàrnè] m. note-book; carnet de chèques, Br. cheque-book, Am. checkbook; carnet de banque, pass-book; carnet de timbres, book of stamps; carnet-répertoire, address-book.

carnier [kàrnyé] m. game-bag.

carnivore [kàrnìvòr] adj. carnivorous; flesh-eating.

carotte [kàròt] f. carrot; plug [tabac]; trick, hoax, take-in; tirer une carotte à quelqu'un, to swindle someone. ‖ **carotter** [-é] v. (fam.) to wangle; to humbug.

caroube [kàrûb] f. carob. ‖ **caroubier** [-byé] m. locust-tree, carob-tree.

carpe [kàrp] m. wrist.

carpe [kàrp] f. carp [poisson].

carpette [kàrpèt] f. rug.

carquois [kàrkwà] m. quiver.

carré [kàré] m. square; landing [maison]; messroom (naut.); adj. square; well-set; downright, straight-forward; tête carrée, obstinate fellow.

carreau [kàrô] m.* diamonds [cartes]; window-pane; floor, square brick; tile; pit-head [mine]; à carreaux, checked [étoffe]; (fam.) se tenir à carreau, to be cautious; rester sur le carreau, to lie dead.

carrefour [kàrfûr] m. crossroads; open square; intersection.

carrelage [kàrlàj] m. tiling. ‖ **carreler** [-é] v. to pave with tiles; to draw squares; to checker.

carrelet [kàrlè] m. sewing awl; packing-needle; sail-needle; square dipping-net.

carrément [kàrémaⁿ] adv. squarely; firmly; bluntly.

carrer [kàré] v. to square; se carrer, to swagger; to recline.

carrier [kàryé] m. quarryman. ‖ **carrière** [-yèr] f. quarry (techn.); career, vocation, course; donner libre carrière à, to give free rein to.

carriole [kàryòl] f. light cart; old crock, Am. jalopy.

carrossable [kàròsàbl] adj. carriageable. ‖ **carrosse** [kàròs] m. state-coach; rouler carrosse, to be well off, to live in style. ‖ **carrosserie** [-rî] f. body [auto]; coach-building. ‖ **carrossier** [-yé] m. coach-builder, body-builder.

carrousel [kàrûzèl] m. tournament; merry-go-round; carrousel.

carrure [kàrür] *f.* breadth of shoulders.

cartable [kàrtàbl] *m.* satchel; drawing portfolio.

carte [kàrt] *f.* card; list; menu; ticket; map; chart (naut.); *carte postale*, postcard; *carte blanche*, full powers; *cartes sur table*, above-board; *carte routière*, road-map; *partie de cartes*, game of cards; *carte-lettre*, letter-card.

cartel [kàrtèl] *m.* cartel, trust (comm.); coalition.

cartel [kàrtèl] *m.* challenge; truce; clock, dial-case.

carter [kàrtèr] *m.* gear-case; sump.

cartilage [kàrtilàj] *m.* cartilage; gristle. ‖ *cartilagineux* [-inè] *adj.** gristly.

cartographe [kàrtògràf] *m., f.* map-maker, chart-maker. ‖ *cartographie* [-î] *f.* cartography, mapping.

cartomancie [kàrtòmansî] *f.* cartomancy. ‖ *cartomancienne* [-syèn] *f.* fortune-teller.

carton [kàrton] *m.* pasteboard; cardboard; cardboard box; portfolio; cartoon; carton; target; cancel (typogr.); mount (phot.); *carton-pâte*, papier mâché. ‖ *cartonnage* [-ònàj] *m.* boarding. ‖ *cartonner* [-òné] *v.* to bind in boards, to put in stiff covers. ‖ *cartonnerie* [-ònrî] *f* cardboard nanufactory (or) trade. ‖ *cartonneur* [-ònœr] *m.* binder. ‖ *cartonnier* [-ònyé] *m.* cardboard-seller; cardboard file; filing cabinet; set of filing cases.

cartouche [kàrtúsh] *m.* cartouche.

cartouche [kàrtúsh] *f.* cartridge, round; refill [stylo]. ‖ *cartouchière* [-yèr] *f.* cartridge-pouch.

cas [kà] *m.* case; instance; circumstance; *en aucun cas*, under no circumstances; *faire cas de*, to think highly of; *faire peu de cas de*, to make light of; *au cas où*, in case; *en tout cas*, at all events, in any case.

casanier [kàzànyé] *adj.** stay-at-home; *m.* homebody.

casaque [kàzàk] *f.* coat, jacket; jumper; blouse; *tourner casaque*, to turn coat. ‖ *casaquin* [-kin] *m.* jumper.

cascade [kàskàd] *f.* cascade; waterfall; peals [de rires]. ‖ *cascader* [-é] *v.* to cascade; to go the pace. ‖ *cascadeur* [-dœr] *m.* stunt man.

case [kàz] *f.* hut, small house; compartment; pigeon-hole; square [échecs]; box [poste].

caséine [kàzéìn] *f.* casein.

casemate [kàzmàt] *f.* casemate; underground stronghold.

caser [kàzé] *v.* to put away; to file; to settle; to accommodate; to marry off; *se caser*, to settle down; to find a home, an employment.

caserne [kàzèrn] *f.* barracks. ‖ *caserner* [-é] *v.* to billet, to quarter; to send into barracks.

casier [kàzyé] *m.* rack; pigeon-hole; filing-cabinet; wine-bin, bottle-rack; music cabinet, canterbury; *casier judiciaire*, police record.

casino [kàzìnò] *m.* casino.

casoar [kàzòàr] *m.* cassowary; plume.

casque [kàsk] *m.* helmet; head-phones (telegr.); *casque blindé*, crash-helmet. ‖ *casquer* [-é] *v.* (fam.) to fork out [argent]. ‖ *casquette* [-èt] *f.* cap.

cassable [kàsàbl] *adj.* breakable. ‖ *cassant* [-an] *adj.* brittle; crisp; gruff, short.

cassation [kàsàsyon] *f.* cassation, repeal; *Cour de cassation*, Supreme Court of Appeal.

casse [kàs] *f.* breaking; breakage; damage; *casse-cou*, dangerous place; dare-devil; *casse-croûte*, snack, © snack-bar; *casse-noisette*, nut-cracker; *casse-tête*, club, truncheon; uproar; puzzle.

casse [kàs] *f.* case (typogr.). ‖ *casseau* [kàsò] *m.** half-case; fount-case (typogr.).

cassement [kàsman] *m.* worry; breaking. ‖ *casser* [-é] *v.* to break, to smash; to crack; to demote, to reduce to the ranks.

casserole [kàsròl] *f.* saucepan, stewpan; (fam.) old crock, *Am.* jalopy. ‖ *casserolée* [-é] *f.* panful.

cassette [kàsèt] *f.* casket; case; money-box.

casseur [kàsœr] *m.* breaker, smasher; *adj.** clumsy, destructive; *casseur d'assiettes*, blusterer.

cassis [kàsìs] *m.* black-currant; black-currant brandy.

cassis [kàsì] *m.* water-bar, furrow-drain across the road.

cassonade [kàsònàd] *f.* brown sugar.

cassoulet [kàsúlè] *m.* cassoulet, casserole-dish.

cassure [kàsür] *f.* break, fracture; breakage; crease [tissu].

castagnettes [kàstàñèt] *f. pl.* casta-nets.

caste [kàst] *f.* caste; *esprit de caste*, class consciousness.

castel [kàstèl] *m.* castle, manor.

castillan [kàstìyan] *m., adj.** Castilian.

castor [kàstòr] *m.* beaver.

castration [kàstràsyoⁿ] *f.* castration; gelding. || *castrer* [-é] *v.* to geld, to castrate; to emasculate.

casuel [kàzüèl] *m.* fee; *adj.** accidental, fortuitous, casual.

casuiste [kàzüïst] *m.* casuist. || *casuistique* [-ïk] *f.* casuistry.

cataclysme [kàtàklïsm] *m.* cataclysm, disaster; upheaval.

catacombes [kàtàkoⁿb] *f. pl.* catacombs.

catalepsie [kàtàlèpsï] *f.* catalepsy. || *cataleptique* [-tïk] *m.*, *f.*, *adj.* cataleptic.

catalogue [kàtàlòg] *m.; Br.* catalogue; *Am.* catalog; list. || *cataloguer* [-ògé] *v.* to catalog(ue).

catalyse [kàtàlïz] *f.* catalysis.

Cataphote [kàtàfòt] *m.* (trade-mark) reflector; cat's eye.

cataplasme [kàtàplàsm] *m.* poultice.

catapulte [kàtàpült] *f.* catapult. || *catapulter* [-té] *v.* to catapult; to hurl (fam.).

cataracte [kàtàràkt] *f.* waterfall; cataract (med.).

catarrhe [kàtàr] *m.* catarrh.

catastrophe [kàtàstròf] *f.* catastrophe, disaster, calamity. || *catastrophé* [-fé] *adj.* (fam.) wrecked, come to grief. || *catastrophique* [-fïk] *adj.* catastrophic.

catch [kàtsh] *m.* all-in wrestling.

catéchiser [kàtéshïzé] *v.* to catechize; (fam.) to lecture. || *catéchisme* [-ïsm] *m.* catechism. || *catéchiste* [-ïst] *m.*, *f.* catechist. || *catéchumène* [kàtékümèn] *m.*, *f.* catechumen.

catégorie [kàtégòrï] *f.* category, class. || *catégorique* [-ïk] *adj.* categorical; emphatic; clear; flat.

cathédrale [kàtédràl] *f.* cathedral.

cathode [kàtòd] *f.* cathode.

catholicisme [kàtòlïsïsm] *m.* Catholicism. || *catholicité* [-ïté] *f.* Catholicity, orthodoxy; the Catholic world. || *catholique* [kàtòlïk] *m.*, *f.*, *adj.* Catholic.

cauchemar [kôshmàr] *m.* nightmare; bugbear.

causal [kòzàl] *adj.* causal (gramm.).

cause [kôz] *f.* cause, motive; case, trial; reason; *à cause de*, on account of; *et pour cause*, for a good reason; *un ayant cause*, an assign; *avocat sans cause*, briefless barrister. || *causer* [kôzé] *v.* to cause.

causer [kôzé] *v.* to talk, to chat; to blab; || *causerie* [-rï] *f.* chat; informal talk. || *causette* [-èt] *f.* chit-chat. ||

causeur [-œr] *m.* talker; *adj.* chatty. || *causeuse* [-èz] *f.* settee, sofa.

causticité [kôstïsïté] *f.* causticity. || *caustique* [kôstïk] *m.*, *adj.* caustic.

cauteleux [kôt•lë] *adj.*° cunning, sly, crafty; wary, fawning.

cautère [kôtèr] *m.* cautery. || *cautérisation* [-érïzàsyoⁿ] *f.* cauterization. || *cautériser* [-érïzé] *v.* to cauterize.

caution [kôsyoⁿ] *f.* security, guarantee, bail; caution-money; deposit; *sujet à caution*, unreliable; *se porter caution pour*, to go bail for; to stand surety for. || *cautionnement* [-yònmaⁿ] *m.* surety (comm.). || *cautionner* [-yòné] *v.* to stand surety for.

cavalcade [kàvàlkàd] *f.* cavalcade; procession; pageant.

cavalerie [kàvàlrï] *f.* cavalry. || *cavalier* [-yé] *m.* rider, horseman; partner [danse]; knight [échecs]; escort; *adj.*° riding; haughty; off-hand; jaunty; flippant.

cave [kàv] *f.* vault; wine-cellar; cellar; liqueur cabinet; *adj.* hollow. || *caveau* [kàvô] *m.*° cellar, vault. || *caverne* [kàvèrn] *f.* cavern, cave; den. || *caverneux* [-ë] *adj.*° cavernous, hollow.

caviar [kàvyàr] *m.* caviar(e).

cavité [kàvïté] *f.* hollow, cavity.

ce [s•] (ce becomes *c'* before *être*) *demonstr. pron.* he; she; it; this; that; they; these; those; which; what; *c'est un livre*, it is a book; *c'est une femme*, she is a woman; *ce sont des hommes*, they are men; *c'est ce que je craignais*, it is what I feared; *c'est à vous de*, it is for you to; *il n'est pas chez lui*, *ce qui est dommage*, he is out, which is a pity; *c'est qu'il est parti*, the fact is he has gone; *pour ce qui est de*, as for; *ce disant...*, so saying..., *ç'a été vrai*, it was true; *qu'est-ce que c'est?*, what is it?; *est-ce que vous savez?*, do you know?; *c'est-à-dire*, that is to say; i.e. (*id est*, that is).

ce, cette [s•, sèt] (pl. *ces* [sè]) [ce becomes *cet* before a word beginning with a vowel or a mute *h*] *demonstr. adj.* this, that, pl. these, those; *ce chien-ci*, this dog; *cet homme*, this man; *cette femme-là*, that woman.

ceci [s•sï] *demonstr. pron.* this.

cécité [sésïté] *f.* blindness.

cédant [sédaⁿ] *m.* assignor, grantor. || *céder* [-é] *v.* to give up; to transfer; to hand over; to yield; to submit; to resign; to give way.

cédille [sédïy] *f.* cedilla (gramm.).

cédrat [sédrà] *m.* citron; citron-tree.

cèdre [sèdr] *m.* cedar, © American thuya.

cédule [sédül] f. notification; schedule [taxes]; script; note.

ceindre [sɛ̃dr] v.* to gird; to bind; to surround; to wreathe.

ceinture [sɛ̃tür] f. belt, girdle; waist; circle; enclosure *ceinture fléchée* © arrow sash; *se serrer la ceinture,* to tighten one's belt. ‖ **ceinturer** [-é] v. to girdle; to encircle; to surround.

cela [sēlà] (*fam. ça* [sà]) *demonstr. pron.* that; *c'est cela,* that is it; that's right; *comment cela?,* what?, how so?; *comme ci, comme ça,* so so, middling; *comme ça,* thus, like that; *ça y est l,* that's that !

célébration [sélébràsyoⁿ] f. celebration. ‖ **célèbre** [sélèbr] *adj.* celebrated, famous. ‖ **célébrer** [sélébré] v. to celebrate; to extol. ‖ **célébrité** [sélébrité] f. celebrity.

celer [sēlé] v. to hide, to conceal.

céleri [sélrì] m. celery.

célérité [sélérìté] f. speed, swiftness, rapidity; alacrity.

céleste [sélèst] *adj.* heavenly, celestial; divine.

célibat [sélìbà] m. celibacy. ‖ **célibataire** [-tèr] m. bachelor; f. spinster; *adj.* unmarried; single.

celle, celles, see *celui.*

cellier [sélyé] m. cellar; store-room.

cellulaire [sélülèr] *adj.* cellular; *voiture cellulaire,* police-van, Black Maria; *Am.* paddy wagon. ‖ **cellule** [sélül] f. cell. ‖ **cellulite** [-ìt] f. cellulitis.

Celluloïd [sélülòïd] m. (trade-mark) Celluloid.

celtique [sèltìk] m., *adj.* Celtic.

celui, celle [sēlüi, sèl] (*pl. ceux, celles* [sē, sèl]) *demonstr. pron.* he; him; she; the one that; *pl.* they, those; them; *celui qui parle,* he who speaks; *à celui qui parle,* to him who speaks; *celui de mon père,* my father's; *celui-ci,* the latter; this one; *celui-là,* the former; that one.

cémenter [sémaⁿté] v. to case-harden.

cénacle [sénàkl] m. Upper Room; coterie, group.

cendre [saⁿdr] f. cinders, ash. ‖ **cendré** [-é] *adj.* ash-colo(u)red, ashy. ‖ **cendrée** [-é] f. dust-shot; cinder-track. ‖ **cendrier** [-ìyé] m. ash-tray; ash-pan. ‖ **Cendrillon** [-ìyoⁿ] f. Cinderella; sit-by-the-fire (fam.).

Cène [sèn] f. Last Supper; communion.

cénobite [sénòbìt] m. coenobite.

cénotaphe [sénòtàf] m. cenotaph.

censé [saⁿsé] *adj.* supposed; reputed. ‖ **censeur** [-œr] m. censor; critic; vice-principal [lycée]. ‖ **censure** [-ür] f. censure, blame; censorship. ‖ **censurer** [-üré] v. to censor; to blame; to criticize; to censure.

cent [sènt, © sèn] m. cent [© m. et f.].

cent [saⁿ] m., *adj.* one hundred, a hundred; *deux cent douze,* two hundred and twelve; *deux cents ans,* two hundred years; *cinq pour cent,* five per cent. ‖ **centaine** [-tèn] f. about a hundred; a hundred; *plusieurs centaines d'hommes,* several hundred men.

centaure [saⁿtôr] m. centaur.

centenaire [saⁿtnèr] m. centenary; centenarian; *adj.* a hundred years old.

centiare [saⁿtyàr] m. one square meter.

centième [saⁿtyèm] m., *adj.* hundredth.

centigrade [saⁿtìgràd] *adj.* centigrade. ‖ **centigramme** [-ìgràm] m. centigram. ‖ **centilitre** [-ìlìtr] m. centilitre. ‖ **centime** [-ìm] m. centime. ‖ **centimètre** [-ìmètr] m. Br. centimetre, Am. centimeter.

central [saⁿtràl] m.* telephone exchange; *adj.* central; *centrale,* generating station; jail. ‖ **centralisation** [-ìzàsyoⁿ] f. centralization. **centraliser** [-ìzé] v. to centralize. ‖ **centre** [saⁿtr] m. Br. centre, Am. center; middle. ‖ **centrer** [-é] v. to center; to adjust. ‖ **centrifuge** [saⁿtrìfüj] *adj.* centrifugal. ‖ **centripète** [-pèt] *adj.* centripetal.

centuple [saⁿtüpl] m., *adj.* hundredfold. ‖ **centupler** [-plé] v. to centuple, to centuplicate.

cep [sèp] m. vine-stock. ‖ **cépage** [sépàj] m. vine-plant.

cèpe [sèp] m. flap mushroom.

cependant [sēpaⁿdaⁿ] *adv.* meanwhile; *conj.* yet, however, nevertheless.

céphalalgie [séfàlàljì] f. headache. ‖ **céphalée** [-é] f. headache. ‖ **céphalique** [-ìk] *adj.* cephalic.

céramique [séràmìk] f. ceramics; *adj.* ceramic. ‖ **céramiste** [-ìst] m., f. ceramist.

cerceau [sèrsô] m.* hoop.

cercle [sèrkl] m. circle, ring; hoop [tonneau]; company; group; club. ‖ **cercler** [-é] v. to encircle; to hoop; to ring; to tire.

cercueil [sèrkœy] m. coffin; shell.

céréale [séréàl] f., *adj.* f. cereal; *pl.,* © breakfast food.

cérébral [sérébràl] *adj.* cerebral; *fatigue cérébrale,* brain-fag.

cérébro-spinal [sérébrôspìnàl] *adj.* cerebro-spinal.

cérémonial [sérémònyàl] *m.*, *adj.* ceremonial, etiquette ‖ **cérémonie** [-î] *f.* ceremony. pomp. fuss. *visite de cérémonie,* formal visit. ‖ **cérémonieux** [-yé] *adj.* ceremonious, formal.

cerf [sèr] *m.* stag, hart; *cerf-volant,* paper kite; stag-beetle.

cerfeuil [sèrfœy] *m.* chervil.

cerise [s*ə*rîz] *f.* cherry; *adj.* cherry-red. ‖ **cerisier** [-yé] *m.* cherry-tree; cherry-wood.

cerne [sèrn] *m.* ring, circle. ‖ **cerné** [-é] *adj.* encircled; *avoir les yeux cernés,* to have rings under the eyes. ‖ **cerner** [-é] *v.* to surround; to encompass; to hem in. ‖ **cernure** [-ür] *f.* ring; blue ring.

certain [sèrtì*n*] *adj.* certain, sure; fixed; positive; *chose certaine,* a certainty; *certaines choses,* some things.

certes [sèrt] *adv.* to be sure, indeed.

certificat [sèrtìfìkà] *m.* certificate, attestation, testimonial; character testimonial. ‖ **certification** [-syo*n*] *f.* certification; witnessing (jur.). ‖ **certifier** [sèrtìfyé] *v.* to certify, to vouch, to attest; to witness [signature].

certitude [sèrtìtüd] *f.* certainty.

cérumen [sérümèn] *m.* cerumen, ear-wax.

cerveau [sèrvô] *m.** brain; mind; *rhume de cerveau,* cold in the head; *cerveau brûlé,* hot-head; *cerveau creux,* dreamer.

cervelas [sèrvəlà] *m.* saveloy, cervelat.

cervelet [sèrvəlè] *m.* cerebellum.

cervelle [sèrvèl] *f.* brains (anat.); mind; *sans cervelle,* brainless, *se creuser la cervelle,* to rack one's brains.

cessant [sèsa*n*] *adj.* ceasing, suspending; *toute affaire cessante,* strait away. ‖ **cessation** [sèsàsyo*n*] *f.* cessation, suspension, stoppage. ‖ **cesse** [sès] *f.* cease, ceasing. ‖ **cesser** [-é] *v.* to stop, to cease, to leave off; *cessez-le-feu,* cease-fire.

cessible [sèsìbl] *adj.* transferable (jur.). ‖ **cession** [-yo*n*] *f.* transfer, assignment (jur.). ‖ **cessionnaire** [-yònèr] *m.* transferee, assignee (jur.).

cet, cette, *see* ce.

cétacé [sétàsé] *m.*, *adj.* cetacean.

ceux, *see* celui.

chacal [shàkàl] (*pl.* chacals) *m.* jackal.

chacun [shàku*n*] *pron.* each; each one; everybody; *chacun son goût,* every man to his taste.

chafouin [shàfwì*n*] *m.*, *adj.* sly-looking, weasel-faced (person).

chagrin [shàgrì*n*] *m.* grief, sorrow, trouble. vexation *adj.* sorry, sad; gloomy. sullen; fretful. ‖ **chagriner** [-iné] *v.* to afflict, to grieve; to annoy; se chagriner, to be distressed.

chahut [shàü] *m.* (pop.) uproar; rag. ‖ **chahuter** [-té] *v.* (pop.) to kick up a row; to barrack; to boo.

chai [shè] *m.* wine-store.

chaîne [shèn] *f.* chain, link; fetters; necklace. sequence; train [idées] bondage. warp (text.); boom [port]; series; range [montagnes]; *travail à la chaîne,* assembly-line work. ‖ **chaînette** [-èt] *f.* small chain. ‖ **chaînon** [-o*n*] *m* link.

chair [shèr] *f.* flesh; meat; pulp [fruit]; *chair de poule,* gooseflesh; *chair à canon,* bullet bait.

chaire [shèr] *f.* chair; pulpit; rostrum; tribune; professorship.

chaise [shèz] *f.* chair, seat; *chaise électrique,* the chair; *chaise longue,* reclining-chair, chaise-longue. ‖ **chaisière** [-yèr] *f.* pew-opener; chair-attendant.

chaland [shàla*n*] *m.* barge, lighter.

chaland [shàla*n*] *m.* customer, purchaser.

châle [shâl] *m.* shawl.

chalet [shàlè] *m.* chalet; cottage.

chaleur [shàlœr] *f.* heat, warmth; glow; ardo(u)r. ‖ **chaleureux** [-ë] *adj.* warm; ardent; cordial; hearty.

chaloupe [shâlûp] *f.* ship's boat; launch; sloop; © boat, rowboat.

chalumeau [shàlümô] *m.** (drinking-) straw; reed, pipe; blow-pipe.

chalut [shàlü] *m.* trawl; drag-net. ‖ **chalutier** [-tyé] *m.* trawler.

chamarrer [shàmàré] *v.* to bedeck; to trim.

chambranle [sho*n*bra*n*l] *m.* frame.

chambre [sho*n*br] *f.* room; chamber; cabin (naut.); *chambre à coucher,* bedroom; *chambre à air,* inner tube [pneu]; *les deux Chambres,* Parliament; *chambre noire,* dark-room; *femme de chambre,* housemaid; *garder la chambre,* to keep to one's room. ‖ **chambrée** [-é] *f.* roomful; barrack room. ‖ **chambrer** [-é] *v.* to lock up; to bring to room temperature.

chameau [shàmô] *m.** camel; (pop.) dirty dog.

chamois [shàmwà] *m.* chamois; chamois leather.

champ [sha*n*] *m.* field, open country; scope; range; ground, space; *champ de courses,* race-course; *champ visuel,* field of vision.

Champagne [sha⁰pàñ] *f.* Champagne [région]; *m.* champagne; *fine champagne,* liqueur brandy.

champêtre [sha⁰pètr] *adj.* rural, rustic pastoral; country.

champignon [sha⁰piñoⁿ] *m.* mushroom, peg, ⟨fam.⟩ accelerator pedal [auto]. ‖ **champignonnière** [-ònyèr] *f.* mushroom-bed.

champion [sha⁰pyoⁿ] *m.* champion. ‖ **championnat** [-yònà] *m.* championship.

chance [shaⁿs] *f.* chance; luck; fortune; blessing; risk; odds.

chancelant [shaⁿslaⁿ] *adj.* tottering, staggering. ‖ **chanceler** [shaⁿslé] *v.* to reel, to stagger, to totter; to falter. ‖ **chancellement** [shaⁿsèlmaⁿ] *m.* unsteadiness.

chancelier [shaⁿselyé] *m.* chancellor. ‖ **chancelière** [-lyèr] *f.* foot-muff. ‖ **chancellerie** [shaⁿsèlrî] *f.* chancellery.

chanceux [shaⁿsë] *adj.** lucky; hazardous, risky; uncertain.

chancre [shaⁿkr] *m.* ulcer; canker; *chancreux,* ulcerous; cankered.

chandail [shaⁿdày] *m.* sweater.

Chandeleur (la) [shaⁿdëlœr] *f.* Candlemas.

chandelier [shaⁿdelyé] *m.* candlestick; chandler. ‖ **chandelle** [shaⁿdèl] *f.* candle; icicle; snot (pop.); *en voir trente-six chandelles,* to see stars.

chanfrein [shaⁿfrîⁿ] *m.* forehead; chamfer.

change [shaⁿj] *m.* change; exchange (comm.), *agent de change.* stockbroker; *lettre de change.* bill of exchange *bureau de change* foreign exchange office; *cours du change,* rate of exchange. *donner le change* to mislead, to side-track. ‖ **changeant** [-aⁿ] *adj.* variable fickle unsettled [temps]. ‖ **changement** [-maⁿ] *m* change, alteration; *changement de vitesse,* gearchange. Am. gearshift. ‖ **changer** [-é] *v.* to change to exchange to alter; to shift [vitesses]; *changer d'avis,* to change one's mind. *se changer,* to change; to change one's clothing; *se changer en,* to change into. ‖ **changeur** [-œr] *m.* money-changer.

chanoine [shànwàn] *m.* canon. ‖ **chanoinesse** [-ès] *f.* canoness.

chanson [shaⁿsoⁿ] *f.* song; nonsense. ‖ **chansonner** [-òné] *v.* to lampoon. ‖ **chansonnier** [-ònyé] *m.* song-writer; song-book.

chant [shaⁿ] *m.* side, edge; *de chant,* edgewise.

chant [shaⁿ] *m.* singing; song; canto [poème].

chantage [shaⁿtàj] *m.* blackmail. ‖ **chantant** [-taⁿ] *adj.* harmonious, musical; ⟨ing-song. ‖ **chanter** [shaⁿté] *v.* to sing; to crow [coq]; to celebrate; *si ça vous chante,* if it suits you; *faire chanter,* to blackmail; **chanteur,** singer: crooner.

chantier [shaⁿtyé] *m.* timber-yard; coal-yard; dockyard; shipyard; building yard, ⟨ lumber camp; stocks; *sur le chantier,* in hand.

chantonner [shaⁿtòné] *v.* to hum. ‖ **chantre** [shaⁿtr] *m.* chanter; cantor; chorister; songster.

chanvre [shaⁿvr] *m.* hemp.

chaos [kàô] *m.* chaos, confusion. ‖ **chaotique** [-tîk] *adj.* chaotic.

chaparder [shàpàrdé] *v.* (pop.) to swipe. to scrounge, to filch, to pinch, Am. to lift.

chape [shàp] *f.* cope (eccles.); covering; cap; tread [pneu]; strap [moteur]. ‖ **chapeau** [shàpô] *m.** hat; cap [stylo]; cover; *chapeau bas,* hat in hand; *chapeau haut de forme,* top-hat.

chapelain [shàplⁿ] *m.* chaplain.

chapelet [shàplè] *m.* rosary, beads; string [oignons]; series.

chapelier [shàpelyé] *m.* hatter, Am. milliner.

chapelle [shàpèl] *f.* chapel; coterie.

chapelure [shàplür] *f.* bread-crumb topping.

chaperon [shàproⁿ] *m.* hood; coping [mur]. chaperon. ‖ **chaperonner** [-òné] *v.* to chaperon.

chapiteau [shàpîtô] *m.** cornice; head; top; capital.

chapitre [shàpîtr] *m.* chapter; chapter-house (eccles.); subject; item. ‖ **chapitrer** [-tré] *v.* to admonish.

chapon [shàpoⁿ] *m.* capon.

chaque [shàk] *adj.* each, every.

char [shàr] *m.* chariot; truck, wag(g)on; *char d'assaut,* tank (mil.).

charabia [shàràbyà] *m.* (fam.) gibberish, gobbledegook.

charbon [shàrboⁿ] *m.* coal; blight (agr.), anthrax (vet.); carbuncle (med.), *charbon de bois,* charcoal; *sur des charbons ardents,* on tenter-hooks. ‖ **charbonnage** [-ònàj] *n.* coal-mining; colliery. ‖ **charbonner** [-òné] *v.* to char; to sketch in charcoal. ‖ **charbonnier** [-ònyé] *m.* coal-man; coalhole; collier (naut.); coal-dealer.

charcuterie [shàrkütrî] *f.* porkbutcher's shop (or trade, or meat); Am. delicatessen. ‖ **charcutier** [-yé] *m.* pork-butcher.

chardon [shàrdoⁿ] *m.* thistle.

chardonneret [shàrdònrè] *m.* gold-finch.

charge [shàrj] *f.* burden, load; cost; charge; post; place; responsibility; caricature; *c'est à ma charge*, it's my responsibility; *femme de charge*, housekeeper. || **chargé** [-é] *adj.* laden, loaded; entrusted; burdened; full; overcast [ciel]. *m. chargé d'affaires*, envoy. || **chargement** [-•ma^n] *m.* load; cargo; consignment . loading . charging [accumulateur]; registration [lettre]. || **charger** [-é] *v.* to load; to burden; to charge; to entrust; to indict; to register; *se charger*, to undertake, to take it upon oneself; *je m'en charge*, I'll see to it. || **chargeur** [-jœr] *m.* stoker; cassette; loader; loading clip; charger.

chariot [shàryò] *m.* wagon, trolley; carriage (mech.); cradle (naut.).

charitable [shàrìtàbl] *adj.* charitable. || **charité** [-é] *f.* charity; alms; kindness.

charivari [shàrìvàrì] *m.* charivari; din.

charlatan [shàrlàta^n] *m.* charlatan, quack; *charlatanisme*, charlatanism.

charmant [shàrma^n] *adj.* charming, delightful. || **charme** [shàrm] *m.* spell, charm. || **charmer** [-é] *v.* to charm; to please, to delight. || **charmeur** [-œr] *m., adj.** charmer.

charmille [shàrmîy] *f.* arbour.

charnel [shàrnèl] *adj.** carnal; sensual. || **charnier** [-nyé] *m.* charnel-house.

charnière [shàrnyèr] *f.* hinge.

charnu [shàrnü] *adj.* fleshy; brawny; pulpy [fruits].

charogne [shàròñ] *f.* carrion.

charpente [shàrpa^nt] *f.* timber-work; framework; frame. || **charpenter** [-é] *v.* to frame, to construct. || **charpentier** [-yé] *m.* carpenter; ship-wright.

charpie [shàrpî] *f.* lint.

charretée [shàrté] *f.* cart-load. || **charretier** [-yé] *m.* carter. || **charrette** [shàrèt] *f.* cart. || **charrier** [-yé] *v.* to cart, to carry; to wash down; to drift ice. || **charroi** [shàrwà] *m.* cartage; transport (mil.).

charron [shàro^n] *m.* wheelwright.

charrue [shàrü] *f. Br.* plough, *Am.* plow.

charte [shàrt] *f.* charter; deed.

chartreux [shàrtrë] *m., adj.** Carthusian.

chas [shâ] *m.* eye [aiguille].

chasse [shàs] *f.* hunt; hunting, shooting; play (mech.); pursuit, chase;

chasse d'eau, flush; *chasse-mouches* fly-swatter; *chasse-neige*, snowplow. || **chasser** [-é] *v.* to hunt; to spin [roue]; to pursue, to chase; to drive away; to dismiss; *chasser sur ses ancres*, to drag anchor. || **chasseur** [-œr] *m.* hunter, sportsman, page-boy, messenger boy, *Am.* bell-hop; fighter (aviat.); mountain infantry (mil.).

châsse [shâs] *f.* reliquary (eccles.).

chassieux [shàsyë] *adj.* gummy; bleary-eyed.

châssis [shâsì] *m.* frame; sash [fenêtre] . chassis [auto]; under-carriage (aviat.); glass-frame (agric.).

chaste [shàst] *adj.* pure, chaste. || **chasteté** [-•té] *f.* chastity.

chat, chatte [shà, shàt] *m., f.,* cat; tag [jeu]; *avoir un chat dans la gorge*, to have a frog in one's throat; *pas un chat*, not a soul.

châtaigne [shàtèñ] *f.* chestnut. || **châtaignier** [-yé] *m.* chestnut-tree (*or* -wood).

châtain [shâta^n] *adj.* brown, chestnut-brown, light-brown.

château [shâtò] *m.** castle; palace; country seat, manor; *châteaux en Espagne*, castles in the air; *château d'eau*, water-tower; *château de cartes*, house of cards. || **châtelain** [shàtla^n] *m.* squire, lord of the manor; landowner.

châtier [shâtyé] *v.* to punish, to chastise; to improve [style]; *châtiment*, chastisement, punishment.

chatoiement [shàtwàma^n] *m.* sparkle; glistening; sheen.

chaton [shàto^n] *m.* kitten; catkin.

chaton [shàto^n] *m.* bezel, setting; stone [pierres].

chatouille [shàtûy] *f.* tickle. || **chatouillement** [shàtûyma^n] *m.* tickle, tickling, titillation. || **chatouiller** [shàtûyé] *v.* to tickle; to gratify; to titillate; (fam.) to thrash, *chatouilleux*, ticklish; touchy, sensitive; sore [point]; punctilious [honneur].

chatoyer [shàtwàyé] *v.* to shimmer; to gleam, to glisten, to sparkle.

châtrer [shâtré] *v.* to castrate; to geld [animaux]; to prune.

chatteries [shàtrî] *f. pl.* delicacies.

chatterton [shàtérto^n] *m.* insulating tape, Chatterton's compound.

chaud [shô] *m.* heat, warmth; *adj.* hot, warm; ardent, animated; violent; bitter; eager; *adv.* hot; *avoir chaud*, to be hot; *il fait chaud*, it is hot, warm. || **chaudière** [-dyèr] *f.* boiler, furnace; kitchen boiler. || **chaudron** [-dro^n] *m.* cauldron; *chaudronnerie*, copper wares; boiler-making; **chaudronnier**, brazier, coppersmith

chauffage [shôfàj] *m* heating, warming; **chauffage central**, central heating.

chauffard [shôfàr] *m.* speedster, hit-and-run driver

chauffe [shôf] *f.* heating, overheating; stoking, firing, **chauffe-eau**, water-heater. | **chauffer** [-é] *v* to warm, to heat; to overheat; to become hot; to burn; to stoke up, to sweat **chauffer au rouge**, to make red-hot. | **chauffeur** [-œr] *m.* stoker, fireman, chauffeur [auto]; driver.

chauler [shôlé] *v.* to lime; to lime-wash.

chaume [shôm] *m.* thatch; stubble; **chaumière**, thatched cottage.

chaussée [-é] *f.* road; roadway; causeway; bank.

chausser [-é] *v.* to put on [chaussures]; to supply foot-wear; to fit, to suit; **il chausse du 43**, he takes size 43 (in shoes); **chausse-pied**, shoe-horn.

chausses [shôs] *f. pl.* breeches, hose.

chaussette [-èt] *f.* sock. | **chausson** [-ô] *m.* slipper; apple turn-over [cuisine]. | **chaussure** [-ür] *f.* footwear, foot-gear; boot, shoe.

chauve [shôv] *m.* bald head; *adj.* bald; bare [mont]; **chauve-souris**, *f.* bat (zool.).

chauvin [shôvin] *m.*, *adj.* chauvinist, jingoist; **chauvinisme**, chauvinism, *Am.* spread-eagleism.

chaux [shô] *f.* lime; **chaux éteinte**, slaked lime; **chaux vive**, quicklime; **pierre à chaux**, lime-stone; **four à chaux**, lime-kiln.

chavirer [shàviré] *v.* to capsize [bateau], to overturn; to upset.

chef [shèf] *m.* head; principal; chef [cuisine]; chief, chieftain, superior, master; leader; foreman, ganger, major [bataillon] conductor [orchestre], **chef de rayon**, floor-walker **chef de service**, departmental manager, **chef d'état-major**, chief of staff, **de mon propre chef**, on my own authority; **chef-d'œuvre**, masterpiece, **chef-lieu**, chief town, *Br.* county town; *Am.* county seat. | **cheftaine** [-tèn] *f.* scout-mistress.

cheik [shèk] *m.* sheik.

chelem [shlèm] *m.* slam.

chélidoine [kélidwàn] *f.* celandine.

chemin [shemin] *m.* way; road; path; course; **chemin faisant**, on the way; **chemin battu**, beaten track; **faire son chemin**, to thrive, to get on well; **chemin de fer**, railway, railroad; **il n'y va pas par quatre chemins**, he does not mince matters. | **chemineau** [sheminô] *m.* tramp, *Am.* hobo.

cheminée [sheminé] *f.* chimney; flue; funnel (naut.); smoke-stack; fire-place, mantelpiece.

cheminer [sheminé] *v.* to tramp, to plod on.

cheminot [sheminô] *m.* railwayman.

chemise [shemîz] *f.* shirt [hommes], chemise [femmes], wrapper, folder, cover, jacket (techn.); case, **chemise de nuit**, night-dress; **chemiser**, to line; to jacket (techn.), **chemisier**, shirt-maker; blouse; shirtwaist.

chenal [shenàl] *m.* channel; fairway; **petits poissons des chenaux**, © smelt, small cod.

chenapan [shnàpan] *m.* scamp, rascal.

chêne [shèn] *m.* oak; **chêne vert**, holm, ilex; **de chêne**, oaken.

chenet [shenè] *m.* fire-dog, andiron.

chenil [shenì] *m.* dog-kennel.

chenille [shenîy] *f.* caterpillar; track; chenille (text.).

chenu [shenü] *adj.* old; hoary; snowy.

cheptel [shèptèl] *m.* cattle, livestock.

chèque [shèk] *m. Br.* cheque; *Am.* check; voucher; coupon.

cher [shèr] *adj.* dear, beloved, costly, expensive; *adv.* dear, dearly; **moins cher**, cheaper; **la vie chère**, the high cost of living; **rendre cher**, to endear; **se vendre cher**, to fetch a high price.

chercher [shèrshé] *v.* to look for, to seek; to search; to try; **aller chercher**, to fetch, to get; **envoyer chercher**, to send for, **chercher à tâtons**, to grope for. | **chercheur** [-œr] *m.* seeker, inquirer, investigator, searcher; *adj.* inquiring, searching.

chère [shèr] *f.* living, fare, cheer; **faire bonne chère**, to live well, to fare well; *adj.*, see **cher**.

chéri [shèrì] *m.*, *adj.* dearest, darling. | **chérir** [-îr] *v.* to cherish, to love dearly.

cherté [shèrté] *f.* dearness, expensiveness, costliness; high price.

chérubin [shérübin] *m.* cherub.

chétif [shétìf] *adj.* puny, weak; mean; paltry; wretched, pitiful.

cheval [shevàl] *m.* horse; horse-power [auto]; **cheval de course**, race-horse; **cheval de bât**, pack-horse; **cheval de bataille**, charger; pet subject; **aller à cheval**, to go on horseback, to ride; **être à cheval sur**, to sit astride; to be a stickler for; **monter sur ses grands chevaux**, to ride one's high horse; **chevaux de bois**, merry-go-round.

chevaleresque [sh⁰vàlrèsk] *adj.* chivalrous. ‖ **chevalerie** [-î] *f.* chivalry.

chevalet [sh⁰vàlè] *m.* support, stand; trestle; sawing-horse; bridge [violon]; easel [art]; prop, buttress.

chevalier [sh⁰vàlyé] *m.* knight; *chevalier servant*, suitor; *chevalier d'industrie*, swindler.

chevalière [sh⁰vàlyèr] *f.* signet-ring.

chevalin [sh⁰vàlⁱⁿ] *adj.* equine; *boucherie chevaline*, horse butcher's shop.

chevaucher [sh⁰vôshé] *v.* to ride; to sit astride; to overlap.

chevelure [sh⁰vlür] *f.* hair; head of hair; scalp; coma, tail.

chevet [sh⁰vè] *m.* head, bedhead [lit]; *livre de chevet*, bedside book.

cheveu [sh⁰vë] *m.** (a) hair; *pl.* hair, hairs; *se faire couper les cheveux*, to have one's hair cut; *couper un cheveu en quatre*, to split hairs; *tiré par les cheveux*, far-fetched.

cheville [sh⁰víy] *f.* peg, pin; ankle; padding [discours]; stopgap [vers]; *cheville ouvrière*, king-bolt; mainspring; *se fouler la cheville*, to sprain one's ankle; *ne pas arriver à la cheville de*, to be far inferior to. ‖ **cheviller** [-lyé] *v.* to peg, to bolt, to pin together; to pad out (fig.).

chèvre [shèvr] *f.* goat, she-goat; sawhorse (mech.); gin (mech.). ‖ **chevreau** [sh⁰vrô] *m.** kid(-skin). ‖ **chèvrefeuille** [shèvr⁰fëy] *m.* honeysuckle. ‖ **chevrette** [sh⁰vrèt] *f.* kid; shrimp; tripod. ‖ **chevreuil** [-œy] *m.* roe, roedeer; venison. ‖ **chevrier** [-lyé] *m.* goatherd. ‖ **chevron** [-ⁿ] *m.* rafter; stripe (mil.). ‖ **chevronné** [sh⁰vrôné] *adj.* experienced.

chevrotement [ch⁰vròtma] *m.* quivering; quavering. ‖ **chevroter** [-é] *v.* to kid; to bleat; to quiver; to quaver; to tremble.

chevrotine [ch⁰vròtìn] *f.* buckshot.

chez [shé] *prep.* at; with; to; in; among; at ...'s house; at home; to ...'s house; care of [lettres]; *je suis chez mon frère*, I am at my brother's; *je viens de chez ma tante*, I am coming from my aunt's; *je suis chez moi*, I am at home; *je suis chez vous*, I am at your house; *faites comme chez vous*, make yourself at home; *chez les Français*, among the French; in the French character; *chez Racine*, in (the works of) Racine.

chic [shìk] *m.* chic, high style; *adj.* chic, stylish, smart; *chic type*, decent fellow, good sort.

chicane [shìkàn] *f.* cavil, pettyfogging, quibble; *chercher chicane à*, to pick a quarrel with. ‖ **chicaner** [-é] *v.*

to quarrel, to cavil, to quibble. ‖ *chicanerie* [-rî] *f.* quibbling, chicanery. ‖ *chicaneur* [-œr] *m.* pettifogger, quarrel-picker; *adj.** argumentative, pettifogging. ‖ *chicanier* [-yé] *adj.* quibbling; *m.* pettifogger, quibbler.

chiche [shìsh] *adj.* miserly, stingy, mean, niggardly; *pois chiches*, chick peas; *interj. Chiche!*, I dare you!

chichi [shìshî] *m.* fuss, frills.

chicorée [shìkòré] *f.* endive; chicory.

chicot [shìkò] *m.* stump, stub.

chien [shyⁱⁿ] *m.* dog; cock [arme à feu]; *chien courant*, beagle; *chien d'arrêt*, pointer; *chien de berger*, collie, sheep dog; *chien de chasse*, hound *chien esquimau*, husky, *chienloup*, wolfhound, police dog; *chienne*, bitch, she-dog; *chiendent* [-daⁿ] *m.* twitch, snag, rub (fam.).

chiffon [shìfoⁿ] *m.* rag. ‖ **chiffonner** [-òné] to crumple, to ruffle; to provoke, to irritate. ‖ **chiffonnier** [-ònyé] *m.* rag-picker, junkman; chiffonnier, *Am.* dresser.

chiffre [shìfr] *m.* figure, digit; code; cipher, mark, amount, total; monogram. **chiffrer** [-é] *v.* to calculate, to add up; to encode, to cipher; to reckon; to figure out.

chignole [shìñòl] *f.* hand-drill (techn.); flivver [voiture].

chignon [shìñoⁿ] *m.* chignon; bun (fam.).

chimère [shìmèr] *f.* chimera, idle fancy. *chimérique*, visionary.

chimie [shìmî] *f.* chemistry; *chimique*, chemical; artificial; **chimiste**, chemist.

chimpanzé [shìⁿpaⁿzé] *m.* chimpanzee.

chiner [shìné] *v.* to mottle [tissu]; to josh, to chaff.

Chinois [shìnwà] *adj., m.* Chinese.

chiot [shyô] *m.* puppy.

chiourme [shyûrm] *f.* chain-gang.

chiper [shìpé] *v.* (pop.) to filch, to pilfer, to swipe.

chipie [shìpî] *f.* (pop.) mean, sour woman.

chipoter [shìpòté] *v.* to pick at food, to be finicky in eating; to haggle.

chique [shìk] *f.* quid [tabac]; chigoe.

chiqué [shìké] *m.* make-believe; fuss; eye-wash.

chiquenaude [shìknôd] *f.* light blow, tap, fillip; snap of the fingers.

chiquer [shìké] *v.* to chew tobacco.

chiromancie [kìròmaⁿsî] *f.* chiromancy, palmistry. ‖ **chiromancien** [-yⁱⁿ] *m.* palmist.

chiropracteur [kìròpràktœr] *m.* chiropractor. || *chiropraticien* [-pràtìsyìⁿ] *m.* © chiropractor. || *chiropratique* [-tîk] *f.* © chiropractic. || *chiropraxie* [-pràksî] *f.* chiropratic.

chirurgical [shìrürjìkàl] *adj.* surgical. || *chirurgie* [shìrürjî] *f.* surgery. || *chirurgien* [-yìⁿ] *m.* surgeon.

chlore [klòr] *m.* chlorine. || *chloroforme* [-òfòrm] *m.* chloroform. || *chloroformer* [-òfòrmé] *v.* to chloroform. || *chlorure* [-ür] *m.* chloride.

choc [shòk] *m.* shock; clinck; bump; clash; collision; crash; impact.

chocolat [shòkòlà] *m.* chocolate; *Am.* chocolate candy; *tablette de chocolat,* bar of chocolate; *chocolater,* to cover with chocolate; *chocolaterie,* chocolate factory.

chœur [kœr] *m.* choir; chorus.

choir [shwàr] *v.** to fall.

choisir [shwàzìr] *v.* to choose.

choix [shwà] *m.* choice, option, election, range, collection, selection; *au choix,* by choice; *de choix,* first class, first rate.

chômage [shòmàj] *m.* unemployment; *en chômage,* unemployed, out of work; *indemnité de chômage,* dole. || *chômer* [-é] *v.* to stop working, to be idle; *jour chômé,* day off. || *chômeur* [-œr] *m.* unemployed worker.

chope [shòp] *f.* beer mug. || *chopine* [-ìn] *f.* (fam.) bottle; © pint. || *chopiner* [-é] *v.* (fam.) to crack a bottle.

choquer [shòké] *v.* to shock, to offend; to clink [verres]; to strike against; *se choquer,* to take offense.

choral [kòràl] *adj.* choral. || *choriste* [-ìst] *m.* choir singer. || *chorus* [-üs] *m.* chorus; *faire chorus,* to chime in.

chose [shòz] *f.* thing; matter, affair; *petite chose,* trifle, titbit; *où en sont les choses?,* how do matters stand?; *Monsieur Chose,* Mr. What's-his-name; *tout chose,* all abashed, uncomfortable; out-of-sorts.

chou [shú] *m.** cabbage; cream puff; dear, darling; *choux de Bruxelles,* Brussels sprouts; *chou frisé,* kale; *faire chou blanc,* to draw a blank; *chou à la crème,* cream puff; *chou-fleur,* cauliflower. || *chouchou* [shúshú] *m.* (fam.) pet; blue-eyed boy. || *chouchouter* [-té] *v.* (fam.) to pet.

choucroute [shúkrút] *f.* sauerkraut.

chouette [shwèt] *f.* owl; *adj.* (fam.) splendid, *Am.* swell.

choyer [shwàyé] *v.* to fondle, to pet, to cherish.

chrême [krèm] *m.* chrism.

chrétien [krétyìⁿ] *m.,* *adj.** Christian. || *chrétienté* [-té] *f.* Christendom. || *Christ* [krìst] *m.* Christ; crucifix. || *christianiser* [krìstyànìzé] *v.* to Christianize. || *christianisme* [krìstyànìsm] *m.* Christianity.

chrome [kròm] *m.* chromium.

chronique [krònîk] *f.* chronicle, review, news; *adj.* chronic. || *chroniqueur* [-œr] *m.* chronicler. || *chronologie* [krònòlòjî] *f.* chronology; *chronologique,* chronological. || *chronomètre* [krònòmètr] *m.* chronometer, stop-watch; *chronométrer,* to time; *chronométreur,* time-keeper.

chrysanthème [krìzaⁿtèm] *m.* chrysanthemum.

chuchotement [shüshòtmaⁿ] *m.* whispering. || *chuchoter* [-é] *v.* to whisper.

chute [shüt] *f.* fall, drop; downfall; overthrow; ruin; collapse.

ci [sì] *demonstr. pron.* this; *adv.* here; *cet homme-ci,* this man; *par-ci par-là,* here and there; now and then; *ci-après,* *ci-dessous,* below; *ci-contre,* opposite; *ci-dessus,* above; *ci-devant,* previously; formerly; *ci-gît,* here lies; *ci-joint,* enclosed.

cible [sìbl] *f.* target; butt.

ciboire [sìbwar] *m.* pyx, ciborium.

ciboule [sìbúl] *f.* Welsh onion, scallion. || *ciboulette* [-lèt] *f.* chives.

ciboulot [sìbúlò] *m.* (fam.) pate.

cicatrice [sìkàtrìs] *f.* scar. || *cicatriser* [-ìzé] *v.* to heal up; to scar; *se cicatriser,* to cicatrize, to skin over, to scar over.

cidre [sìdr] *m.* cider.

ciel [syèl] (*pl.* *cieux* [syë], sometimes *ciels*) *m.* Heaven, Paradise; sky, firmament; top, roof (mech.); *pl.* heavens; climes, climates; *à ciel ouvert,* unroofed; out of doors.

cierge [syèrj] *m.* candle; taper.

cigale [sìgàl] *f.* cicada.

cigare [sìgàr] *m.* cigar. || *cigarette* [-èt] *f.* cigarette.

cigogne [sìgòñ] *f.* stork.

ciguë [sìgü] *f.* hemlock.

cil [sìl] *m.* eye-lash. || *ciller* [sìyé] *v.* to blink, to wink.

cimaise [sìmèz] *f.* dado, cyma.

cime [sìm] *f.* top, summit, peak.

ciment [sìmaⁿ] *m.* cement; *béton de ciment,* concrete. || *cimenter* [-té] *v.* to cement; to consolidate; to strengthen.

cimetière [sìmtyèr] *m.* cemetery, graveyard, churchyard.

cinéaste [sìnéàst] *m.* film-producer.

cinéma [sìnémà] *m.* cinema; *Am.* motion-picture theater, movie-house, movies (fam.); *Br.* pictures (fam.); *cinémathèque,* film-store, film-library; *cinématographier,* to cinematograph, to film.

cinglant [sìnglaⁿ] *adj.* lashing; bitter, biting; scathing.

cinglé [sìnglé] *adj.* (pop.) *il est cinglé,* he's not all there, *Br.* he's off his head. ‖ *cingler* [-é] *v.* to whip, to lash.

cingler [sìnglé] *v.* to sail, to scud along, to steer (naut.).

cinq [sìⁿk] *m., adj.* five; *cinq hommes,* five men; *le cinq avril,* April the fifth. ‖ *cinquantaine* [-aⁿtèn] *f.* about fifty, fifty or so. ‖ *cinquante* [-aⁿt] *adj.* fifty. ‖ *cinquantième* [-aⁿtyèm] *m., adj.* fiftieth. ‖ *cinquième* [-yèm] *m., adj.* fifth.

cintre [sìⁿtr] *m.* curve, arch, bend; coat-hanger. ‖ *cintrer* [-é] *v.* to arch, to curve.

cirage [sìràj] *m.* waxing, polishing; boot-polish, shoe-polish, blacking.

circoncire [sìrkoⁿsìr] *v.* to circumcise; *circoncision,* circumcision.

circonférence [sìrkoⁿféraⁿs] *f.* circumference; girth; perimeter.

circonflexe [sìrkoⁿflèks] *adj.* circumflex.

circonlocution [sìrkoⁿlòküsyoⁿ] *f.* circumlocution.

circonscription [sìrkoⁿskrìpsyoⁿ] *f.* circumscribing; division, district; constituency, electoral district.

circonscrire [sìrkoⁿskrîr] *v.* to circumscribe; to encircle; to limit.

circonspect [sìrkoⁿspèkt] *adj.* wary, guarded, circumspect, cautious. ‖ *circonspection* [-èksyoⁿ] *f.* circumspection, caution, wariness.

circonstance [sìrkoⁿstaⁿs] *f.* circumstance, event; *circonstances atténuantes,* extenuating circumstances; *de circonstance,* special, fit for the occasion. ‖ *circonstanciel* [-syèl]* circumstantial; adverbial.

circonvenir [sìrkoⁿvnîr] *v.* to impose upon; to get round.

circonvolution [sìrkoⁿvòlüsyoⁿ] *f.* circumvolution; windings; convolution.

circuit [sìrküï] *m.* circuit, circumference; roundabout way; tour; *coup de circuit,* ⓒ home run; *ouvrir le circuit,* to switch on.

circulaire [sìrkülèr] *f., adj.* circular.

circulation [sìrkülàsyoⁿ] *f.* circulation; traffic; currency; *circulatoire,* circulatory. ‖ *circuler* [sìrkülé] *v.* to circulate; to flow; to move about; to move on.

cire [sîr] *f.* wax; *cire à cacheter,* sealing-wax. ‖ *cirer* [-é] *v.* to wax, to polish; *cireur,* polisher; bootblack; *cireuse,* waxer, floor-polisher.

ciron [sìroⁿ] *m.* mite.

cirque [sìrk] *m.* circus; cirque.

cisailles [sìzây] *f. pl.* shears, nippers. ‖ *cisailler* [-é] *v.* to shear, to nip, to clip.

ciseau [sìzô] *m.** chisel; *pl.* scissors, shears. ‖ *ciseler* [-lé] *v.* to chisel; to carve; to cut; to chase [argent]. ‖ *ciselure* [-lür] *f.* chissel(l)ing; delicate carving.

citadelle [sìtàdèl] *f.* citadel. ‖ *citadin* [sìtàdiⁿ] *m.* townsman.

citation [sìtàsyoⁿ] *f.* citation; quotation; summons, subpoena (jur.).

cité [sìté] *f.* city, large town; group of dwellings; housing development; workers' flats; students' hostels; *droit de cité,* rights of a citizen.

citer [sìté] *v.* to quote; to summons (jur.); to cite; to mention; to subpoena (jur.).

citerne [sìtèrn] *f.* cistern, tank.

cithare [sìtàr] *f.* cithara; cither, zither.

citoyen [sìtwàyiⁿ] *m.* citizen.

citron [sìtroⁿ] *m.* lemon; lemon-colo(u)r; *citronnade,* lemonade, lemon-squash; *citronnier,* lemon-tree; lemon-wood.

citrouille [sìtrûy] *f.* pumpkin.

civet [sìvè] *m.* stew.

civière [sìvyèr] *f.* hand-barrow; stretcher; litter.

civil [sìvìl] *m.* civilian; layman; private life; *adj.* civic, civil; polite; *en civil,* in plain clothes, in mufti; *droit civil,* common law. ‖ *civilisation* [-ìzàsyoⁿ] *f.* civilization. ‖ *civiliser* [-ìzé] *v.* to civilize; *se civiliser,* to become civilized. ‖ *civilité* [-ìté] *f.* civility, courtesy, *pl.* compliments. ‖ *civique* [sìvìk] *adj.* civic; civil.

claie [klè] *f.* hurdle; screen; tray.

clair [klèr] *m.* light, clearness; *adj.* clear, bright, light; obvious; thin [soupe]; *adv.* clearly; *tirer au clair,* to clarify, to bring to light; *vert clair,* light green; *voir clair,* to see clearly; to see through; *claire-voie,* clerestory (arch.); lattice-work. ‖ *clairet* [-è] *m.* light-red wine; *adj.* light, pale; thin. ‖ *clairière* [-yèr] *f.* glade, clearing.

clairon [klèroⁿ] *m.* bugle; bugler.

clairsemé [klèrsᵉmé] *adj.* scattered; sparse, thinly-sown; thin. ‖ *clairvoyance* [-vwàyaⁿs] *f.* clairvoyance;

shrewdness, perspicacity; **clairvoyant**; clairvoyant; shrewd, clearsighted.

clameur [klàmœr] *f.* clamo(u)r; outcry; shout.

clan [klaⁿ] *m.* clan; clique.

clandestin [klaⁿdèstìⁿ] *adj.* clandestine, secret; underhand; covert; stealthy; illicit; underground. ‖ **clandestinité** [-tìnìté] *f.* clandestineness; underground movement.

clapet [klapè] *m.* valve; sluice, clapper; rectifier (electr.).

clapier [klapyé] *m.* burrow; hutch.

clapotement [klàpòtmaⁿ] *m.* lapping, plashing [eau].

claque [klàk] *f.* slap, smack; hired applauders (theat.), claque; *pl.* © rubbers.

claquer [klàké] *v.* to smack; to clap [mains]; to snap [doigts]; to crack [fouet]; to bang [porte]; (pop.) to kick the bucket; *il claque des dents,* his teeth are chattering. ‖ **claquettes** [-èt] *f. pl.* tap-dancing.

clarine [klàrìn] *f.* cattle-bell. ‖ **clarinette** [-èt] *f.* clarinet; clarinetist.

clarté [klàrté] *f.* light, clearness; brightness, gleam; limpidity.

classe [klâs] *f.* class, rank; kind; *Br.* form, *Am.* grade [lycée]; class-room. ‖ **classement** [-maⁿ] *m.* classification; filing. ‖ **classer** [-é] *v.* to classify; to catalog(ue); to grade; to file. ‖ **classeur** [-œr] *m.* file, filing-cabinet.

classicisme [klàsìsìsm] *m.* classicism.

classification [klàsìfìkàsyoⁿ] *f.* classification. ‖ **classifier** [-ìfyé] *v.* to classify; to sort out.

classique [klàsìk] *adj.* classical; classic; standard; *m.* classic; standard work; classicist.

claudication [klôdìkàsyoⁿ] *f.* lameness; halting.

clause [klôz] *f.* clause; section (jur.).

clavecin [klàvsìⁿ] *m.* harpsichord, clavichord.

clavette [klàvèt] *f.* pin, key, cotter.

clavicule [klàvìkül] *f.* clavicle, collarbone.

clavier [klàvyé] *m.* keyboard; manual [orgue].

clé *or* **clef** [klé] *f.* key; spanner, wrench (mech.); clef (mus.); *clé anglaise,* monkey wrench, adjustable spanner; *sous clé,* under lock and key; *clef de voûte,* keystone; *fausse clé,* skeleton key.

clémence [klémaⁿs] *f.* clemency, mercy; mildness [temps]. ‖ **clément** [klémaⁿ] *adj.* clement; merciful; mild; lenient.

clémentine [klémaⁿtìn] *f.* tangerine.

clerc [klèr] *m.* clergyman; clerk (jur.); *pas de clerc,* blunder.

clergé [klèrjé] *m.* clergy; the cloth.

clérical [klérìkàl] *adj.** clerical.

cliché [klìshé] *m.* plate, block (typogr.); negative (phot.); cliché, stock phrase; *prendre un cliché,* to make an exposure.

client [klìaⁿ] *m.* client, customer, fare (comm.); patient (med.); guest [hôtel]. ‖ **clientèle** [-tèl] *f.* custom; customers, clients (comm.); practice [avocat]; connection.

cligner [klìñé] *v.* to wink; to blink.

clignotant [klìñòtaⁿ] *adj.* twinkling; flickering; blinking; *m.* winker, blinker; turn indicator. ‖ **clignoter** [klìñòté] *v.* to blink; to flicker; to twinkle [étoile].

climat [klìmà] *m.* climate; region; mood; *climatique,* climatic; *climatiser,* to air-condition.

clin [klìⁿ] *m.* clin d'œil, wink; *en un clin d'œil,* in the twinkling of an eye.

clinique [klìnìk] *f.* clinic; nursinghome; *adj.* clinical.

clinquant [klìⁿkaⁿ] *m.* tinsel; foil; showiness; *adj.* showy, gaudy.

clique [klìk] *f.* drum and bugle band; set, clique; gang.

cliquet [klìkè] *m.* catch; ratchet (mech.); pawl.

cliquetis [klìktì] *m.* clang [métal]; rattling; clatter; chinking [verres]; clash [armes]; jingling; *Br.* pinking [moteur].

cloaque [klòàk] *m.* cesspool; sink.

clochard [klòshàr] *m.* tramp, *Am.* hobo.

cloche [klòsh] *f.* bell; dish-cover; bell-jar; (pop.) idiot, dope. ‖ **clocher** [-é] *v.* to limp, to hobble; *il y a quelque chose qui cloche,* there's something not quite right.

clocher [klòshé] *m.* belfry; steeple; *course au clocher,* steeple-chase.

cloison [klwàzoⁿ] *f.* partition; dividing wall; bulkhead (naut.); *cloison étanche,* water-tight bulkhead. ‖ **cloisonner** [-é] *v.* to partition off.

cloître [klwâtr] *m.* cloister; monastery; convent; *vie de cloître,* cloistered life. ‖ **cloîtrer** [-é] *v.* to cloister; to confine.

clopiner [klòpìné] *v.* to hobble, to limp.

cloque [klòk] *f.* blister; swelling; blight [arbres].

clore [klòr] *v.** to close, to enclose; to end. ‖ **clos** [klô] *m.* enclosure, close; vineyard. ‖ **clos** *adj.* closed; shut in; finished. ‖ **clôture** [klôtür] *f.* enclosure, fence; closing, closure. ‖ **clôturer** [-é] *v.* to enclose; to close down; to conclude.

clou [klû] *m.* nail; spike; boil (med.); high spot, climax; pawn-shop, *Am.* hock shop; (pop.) jail, clink; *mettre au clou,* to pawn. ‖ **clouer** [-é] *v.* to nail; to pin down; to rivet; to non-plus; *être cloué au lit,* to be bed-ridden. ‖ **clouter** [klûté] *v.* to nail; to stud.

club [klœb] *m.* club.

coagulation [kòàgülàsyon] *f.* coagulation, congealing. ‖ **coaguler** [-é] *v.* to coagulate, to congeal, to clot, to curdle [lait].

coaliser (se) [sᵉkòàlìzé] *v.* to form a coalition, to unite. ‖ **coalition** [kòàlìsyon] *f.* coalition, union, league.

coasser [kòàsé] *v.* to croak [grenouille].

coassocié [kòàsòsyé] *m.* copartner.

cobaye [kòbày] *m.* guinea-pig.

cobra [kòbrà] *m.* cobra.

cocaïne [kòkàïn] *f.* cocaine.

cocarde [kòkàrd] *f.* cockade; roundel.

cocasse [kòkàs] *adj.* droll, funny, odd.

coccinelle [kòksìnèl] *f.* ladybird.

coche [kòsh] *m.* coach.

coche [kòsh] *f.* nick, notch. ‖ **cocher** [-é] *v.* to nick, to notch.

cocher [kòshé] *m.* driver, cabman; *porte cochère,* carriage-entrance, main gate.

cochon [kòshon] *m.* pig, hog; pork; (pop.) filthy swine; *cochon d'Inde,* guinea-pig; *adj.** (pop.) beastly. ‖ **cochonner** [kòshòné] *v.* to pig; to bungle [un travail]. ‖ **cochonnerie** [-nrî] *f.* filth; trash; smut; lousy trick.

coco [kòkò] *m.* noix de coco, coco-nut. ‖ **cocotier** [kòkòtyé] *m.* coconut palm.

cocotte [kòkòt] *f.* chickabiddy; loose woman, *Am.* floozy; stew-pan (culin.); paper hen; *Cocotte Minute,* pressure cooker (trade-mark).

code [kòd] *m.* code; law; statute-book. ‖ **codifier** [kòdìfyé] *v.* to codify [lois]; to code [message].

coefficient [kòèfìsyan] *m.* coefficient; factor.

cœur [kœr] *m.* heart; courage; feelings; core [centre]; *pl.* hearts [cartes]; *à cœur joie,* to one's heart's content; *le cœur brisé,* broken-hearted; *de bon cœur,* gladly, heartily; *en avoir le*

cœur net, to get it off one's chest; to get to the bottom of the matter; *par cœur,* by heart; *si le cœur vous en dit,* if you feel inclined; *un homme de cœur,* a brave man.

coffre [kòfr] *m.* chest, box; coffer; mooring buoy (naut.); *coffre-fort,* strong-box; safe. ‖ **coffrer** [-é] *v.* to lock up; (fam.) to put in jail. ‖ **coffret** [-è] *m.* casket; locker; tool-box; *coffret de sûreté,* © safety deposit box.

cognac [kòñàk] *m.* cognac, brandy.

cognée [kòñé] *f.* axe, hatchet. ‖ **cogner** [-é] *v.* to knock; to hammer; to drive in [clou]; to hit, to bump against; to thump; to pound.

cohérence [kòérans] *f.* coherence. ‖ **cohérent** [-an] *adj.* coherent.

cohésion [kòézyon] *f.* cohesion, co-hesiveness.

cohorte [kòòrt] *f.* cohort.

cohue [kòü] *f.* crush; throng; press.

coi, coite [kwà, kwàt] *adj.* quiet, silent.

coiffe [kwàf] *f.* cap; head-dress; lining. ‖ **coiffé** [-é] *adj.* covered, wearing a hat; arranged [cheveux]; *né coiffé,* born with a silver spoon in one's mouth. ‖ **coiffer** [-é] *v.* to cover [tête]; to suit [chapeau]; to do [cheveux]; *se coiffer,* to do one's hair; to wear [chapeau], to be infatuated [de, with]. ‖ **coiffeur, -euse** [-œr, -ëz] *m., f.* hairdresser. ‖ **coiffure** [-ür] *f.* head-gear; hair-style; hairdressing.

coin [kwin] *m.* corner; nook; patch [terre]; stamp, die; wedge, chock; *au coin du feu,* by the fire-side. ‖ **coincer** [-sé] *v.* to wedge; *se coincer,* to stick, to jam.

coïncidence [kòinsìdans] *f.* coincidence; **coïncident,** coincident. ‖ **coïncider** [-é] *v.* to coincide.

coing [kwin] *m.* quince.

coke [kòk] *m.* coke.

col [kòl] *m.* neck [bouteille]; collar; pass (geogr.); *faux col,* detachable collar; *col-bleu,* bluejacket.

colère [kòlèr] *f.* anger, wrath, passion; *adj.* choleric, passionate; *en colère,* angry. ‖ **coléreux** [-éré] *adj.** irascible, hot-tempered. ‖ **colérique** [-érìk] *adj.* choleric; bilious.

colifichet [kòlìfìshè] *m.* gew-gaw; *pl.* fancy-goods.

colimaçon [kòlìmàson] *m.* snail; *escalier en colimaçon,* spiral staircase.

colique [kòlìk] *f.* colic, stomach-ache.

colis [kòlì] *m.* parcel, package; bundle; *par colis postal,* by parcel post; *pl.* luggage.

collaborateur, -trice [kòllàbòràtœr, -trìs] *m.*, *f.* collaborator; colleague, co-worker; contributor. ‖ *collaboration* [-àsyoⁿ] *f.* collaboration. ‖ *collaborer* [-é] *v.* to collaborate; to contribute [publication].

collage [kòlàj] *m.* pasting; gluing. ‖ *collant* [-aⁿ] *adj.* adhesive, sticky; tight, close-fitting.

collation [kòlàsyoⁿ] *f.* collation; checking; snack, light meal. ‖ *collationner* [-yòné] *v.* to collate, to compare; to check; to have a snack.

colle [kòl] *f.* glue, gum; paste; poser, difficult question.

collecte [kòlèkt] *f.* collect (eccles.); collection. ‖ *collecteur* [-œr] *m.* collector; tax-collector; *m.*, *adj.* commutator (electr.); *égout collecteur,* main sewer. ‖ *collectif* [-ìf] *adj.*° collective, joint. ‖ *collection* [kòlèksyoⁿ] *f.* collection; *collectionner,* to collect; *collectionneur,* collector. ‖ *collectivité* [kòlèktìvìté] *f.* collectivity; community.

collège [kòlèj] *m.* college; *Br.* secondary grammar school, high school; *collège électoral;* electoral body, *Am.* electoral college. ‖ *collégien, -enne* [-yìⁿ, -yèn] *m.*, *f.* schoolboy, schoolgirl.

collègue [kòllèg] *m.*, *f.* colleague.

coller [kòlé] *v.* to stick; to paste; to glue; to clarify [vins]; to fit closely; (pop.) to fail, to plough [candidat]; *Am.* to flunk; *se coller,* to cling together.

collet [kòlè] *m.* collar; cape; neck [outil]; flange [tuyau]; snare, trap; *collet monté,* prissy, straight-laced; *prendre au collet,* to collar; to snare.

collier [kòlyé] *m.* necklace; collar; ring; *coup de collier,* big effort.

colline [kòlìn] *f.* hill.

collision [kòllìzyoⁿ] *f.* collision; shock; conflict; clash.

colloque [kòllòk] *m.* parley; conversation; symposium.

collutoire [kòllütwàr] *m.* gargle.

colmater [kòlmàté] *v.* to warp (geol.); to clog; to seal up [brèche], to fill in [trou].

colombe [kòloⁿb] *f.* dove; *colombier,* dovecote; pigeon-hole (typogr.).

colon [kòloⁿ] *m.* colonial; colonist, settler; planter.

côlon [kôloⁿ] *m.* colon (anat.).

colonel [kòlònèl] *m.* colonel.

colonial [kòlònyàl] *m.*, *adj.*° colonial. ‖ *colonialisme* [-lsm] *m.* imperialism. ‖ *colonie* [-ì] *f.* colony, settlement; *colonie de vacances,* holiday camp. ‖ *colonisateur, -trice* [-ìzàtœr, -trìs] *m.*,

f. colonizer; *adj.* colonizing. ‖ *colonisation* [-ìzàsyoⁿ] *f.* colonization, settling. ‖ *coloniser* [-ìzé] *v.* to colonize, to settle.

colonne [kòlòn] *f.* pillar, column; *colonne vertébrale,* spinal column, backbone.

colophane [kòlòfàn] *f.* rosin.

coloquinte [kòlòkìⁿt] *f.* colocynth; noddle (fam.).

colorant [kòlòràⁿ] *m.* dye; *adj.* colo(u)ring. ‖ *coloration* [-àsyoⁿ] *f.* colo(u)ring. ‖ *coloré* [-é] *adj.* highly colo(u)red; florid, ruddy [teint]. ‖ *colorer* [-é] *v.* to colo(u)r, to dye. ‖ *colorier* [-yé] *v.* to colour. ‖ *coloris* [-ì] *m.* colo(u)ring, colo(u)r.

colossal [kòlòsàl] *adj.*° colossal, gigantic. ‖ *colosse* [kòlòs] *m.* colossus.

colporter [kòlpòrté] *v.* to hawk, to peddle; to spread [nouvelles]; *colporteur,* hawker, *Br.* pedlar; *Am.* peddler; newsmonger [nouvelles].

coltiner [kòltìné] *v.* to porter; to lug.

coma [kòmà] *m.* coma.

combat [koⁿbà] *m.* combat, battle; fight; struggle; contest; engagement; *mettre hors de combat,* to disable. ‖ *combatif* [-tìf] *adj.*° pugnacious. ‖ *combativité* [-tìvìté] *f.* pugnaciousness. ‖ *combattant* [-taⁿ] *m.* fighter; *ancien combattant,* ex-serviceman, *Am.* veteran. ‖ *combattre* [-tr] *v.*° to fight, to contend; to oppose; to struggle.

combien [koⁿbyìⁿ] *adv.* (followed by *v.* or *adj.*) how many; how much; *combien de,* how much; how many; how far [distance]; *combien de fois,* how often.

combinaison [koⁿbìnèzoⁿ] *f.* combination, arrangement; plan; flying suit; overalls; combinations; slip [femme]. ‖ *combine* [koⁿbìn] *f.* (pop.) plan, scheme, racket. ‖ *combiné* [-é] *m.* combined set; radiogram. ‖ *combiner* [-iné] *v.* to combine; to devise; *se combiner,* to combine.

comble [koⁿbl] *m.* heaped measure; height, summit; roof, roofing; *adj.* brimful, full up; *ça, c'est le comble,* that's the last straw; *de fond en comble,* from top to bottom; *salle comble,* packed house. ‖ *combler* [-é] *v.* to fill up; to heap up; to make good [déficit]; to gratify [désir]; to fill [lacune].

combustible [koⁿbüstìbl] *m.* fuel; *adj.* combustible. ‖ *combustion* [-yoⁿ] *f.* combustion, burning.

comédie [kòmédì] *f.* comedy; acting; play; pretence; farce. ‖ *comédien, -enne* [-yìⁿ, -yèn] *m.*, *f.* comedian; actor, player; hypocrite.

comestible [kòmèstìbl] *m.* provisions; *pl.* foodstuffs; victuals; *adj.* eatable, edible.

comète [kòmèt] *f.* comet.

comique [kòmìk] *m.* comedian, humorist; comic art; funny side; humo(u)r; *adj.* comic, comical, funny.

comité [kòmìté] *m.* committee, board; *en petit comité*, a select party, making a small group.

commandant [kòmɑⁿdɑⁿ] *m.* major (mil.); commanding officer; commodore (naut.); squadron-leader (aviat.); *adj.* commanding. ‖ **commande** [kòmɑⁿd] *f.* order; control (techn.); drive (techn.); lever; *sur commande*, to order; *levier de commande*, control lever, stick (aviat.); *bulletin de commande*, order-form. ‖ **commandement** [-mɑⁿ] *m.* command, order, commandment; authority. ‖ **commander** [-é] *v.* to order, to command; to govern; to overlook, to dominate; to control. ‖ **commanditaire** [-itèr] *m. Br.* sleeping partner, *Am.* silent partner; backer, angel (theat.). ‖ **commandite** [-ìt] *f.* limited liability (comm.); *en commandite*, limited joint-stock. ‖ **commanditer** [-té] *v.* to finance, to stake; to angel.

comme [kòm] *adv.* as, like; how; in the way of; *conj.* as; *faites comme moi*, do as I do; *comme il entrait*, as he was entering, on entering; *comme il est bon*, how kind he is; *comme mort*, almost dead.

commémoratif [kòmmèmòràtìf] *adj.* commemorative. ‖ **commémoration** [-àsyoⁿ] *f.* commemoration. ‖ **commémorer** [-é] *v.* to commemorate.

commençant [kòmɑⁿsɑⁿ] *m.* beginner. ‖ **commencement** [-mɑⁿ] *m.* beginning, start, outset. ‖ **commencer** [-sé] *v.* to commence, to begin, to start; to open.

commensal [kòmɑⁿsàl] *m.* commensal; table-companion; guest.

comment [kòmɑⁿ] *adv.* how; *interj.* what! why!

commentaire [kòmɑⁿtèr] *m.* commentary; comment; note; remark. ‖ **commentateur** [-àtœr] *m.* commentator. ‖ **commenter** [-é] *v.* to comment upon; to criticize.

commérage [kòméràj] *m.* gossip.

commerçant [kòmèrsɑⁿ] *m.* tradesman, merchant, trader; *adj.* mercantile; commercial; shopping. ‖ **commerce** [kòmèrs] *m.* trade, commerce; intercourse; *commerce de détail*, retail trade. ‖ **commercer** [-é] *v.* to trade, to deal. ‖ **commercial** [-yàl] *adj.* commercial, trading, business; **commercialiser**, to commercialize.

commère [kòmèr] *f.* fellow-sponsor at baptism; gossip; crony.

commettre [kòmètr] *v.* to commit; to entrust; to perpetrate.

commis [kòmì] *p. p., adj., see commettre; m.* clerk; agent; shop-assistant; *commis voyageur, Br.* commercial travel(l)er, *Am.* drummer, travel(l)ing salesman.

commisération [kòmìzéràsyoⁿ] *f.* commiseration, pity.

commissaire [kòmìsèr] *m.* commissioner; superintendent [police]; purser [bateau]; *commissaire-priseur*, valuer; auctioneer. ‖ **commissariat** [àryà] *m.* commissioner's office; police station.

commission [kòmìsyoⁿ] *f.* commission; committee; message, errand. ‖ **commissionnaire** [-yònèr] *m.* commission-agent (comm.); messenger; errand-boy. ‖ **commissionner** [-yòné] *v.* to commission.

commissure [kòmìsür] *f.* commissure; corner of the lips.

commode [kòmòd] *f.* chest of drawers; *adj.* convenient; handy; good-natured. ‖ **commodité** [-ìté] *f.* convenience, comfort.

commotion [kòmòsyoⁿ] *f.* disturbance, commotion; shock (electr.); concussion (med.). ‖ **commotionner** [-né] *v.* to shock.

commuer [kòmüé] *v.* to commute.

commun [kòmuⁿ] *m.* joint property; generality; common people; *pl.* outbuildings; *adj.* common, usual; vulgar; *faire cause commune avec*, to side with. ‖ **communal** [kòmünàl] *adj.* common [terre], communal. ‖ **communauté** [-òté] *f.* community, society; Commonwealth.

commune [kòmün] *f.* parish; *Chambre des Communes, Br.* House of Commons.

communiant [kòmünyɑⁿ] *m.* communicant.

communicatif [kòmünìkàtìf] *adj.* communicative. ‖ **communication** [-àsyoⁿ] *f.* communication; message.

communier [kòmünyé] *v.* to take Holy Communion, to communicate. ‖ **communion** [-nyoⁿ] *f.* communion.

communiqué [kòmünìké] *m.* official news, bulletin. ‖ **communiquer** [-é] *v.* to communicate, to impart, to transmit; to circulate; *se communiquer*, to spread.

communisme [kòmünìsm] *m.* communism. ‖ **communiste** [-ìst] *m., f.* communist.

commutateur [kòmütàtœr] *m.* commutator (electr.); switch.

compact [koⁿpàkt] *adj.* compact, close.

compagne [koⁿpàñ] *f.* companion; wife; mate, partner. ‖ **compagnie** [-ñ] *f.* company, society; party; fellowship; *tenir compagnie,* to keep company. ‖ **compagnon** [-oⁿ] *m.* companion, fellow, comrade; mate, partner.

comparable [koⁿpàràbl] *adj.* comparable. ‖ **comparaison** [-èzoⁿ] *f.* comparison.

comparaître [koⁿpàrètr] *v.* to appear in court (jur.).

comparatif [koⁿpàràtìf] *m.,* *adj.*° comparative. ‖ **comparer** [koⁿpàré] *v.* to compare; to liken.

comparse [koⁿpàrs] *m.,* *f.* supernumerary; confederate.

compartiment [koⁿpàrtìmaⁿ] *m.* compartment; division; partition. ‖ **compartimenter** [-té] *v.* to compart.

comparution [koⁿpàrüsyoⁿ] *f.* appearance (jur.).

compas [koⁿpà] *m.* compasses; compass (naut.). ‖ **compassé** [-sé] *adj.* formal, stiff; regular.

compassion [koⁿpàsyoⁿ] *f.* compassion, pity.

compatibilité [koⁿpàtìbìlìté] *f.* compatibility. ‖ **compatible** [koⁿpàtìbl] *adj.* compatible; suitable.

compatir [koⁿpàtìr] *v.* to sympathize, to bear with; *compatissant,* compassionate, tender; sympathetic.

compatriote [koⁿpàtrìòt] *m.* compatriot, fellow-countryman.

compensateur, -trice [koⁿpaⁿsàtœr, -trìs] *m.* compensator; *adj.*° compensating (techn.). ‖ **compensation** [-àsyoⁿ] *f.* compensation; balancing (techn.). ‖ **compenser** [koⁿpaⁿsé] *v.* to compensate; to make up for; to adjust [compas].

compère [koⁿpèr] *m.* fellow-sponsor at baptism; compère; accomplice; comrade, old fellow (fam.), pal; *compère-loriot,* sty (med.).

compétence [koⁿpétaⁿs] *f.* competence, authority, powers (jur.); skill, ability; *compétent,* competent; cognizant (jur.).

compétiteur, -trice [koⁿpétìtœr, -trìs] *m., f.* competitor, rival. ‖ **compétition** [-ìsyoⁿ] *f.* competition, rivalry.

compilateur, -trice [koⁿpìlàtœr, -trìs] *m., f.* compiler. ‖ **compilation** [-syoⁿ] *f.* compiling; compilation. ‖ **compiler** [-lé] *v.* to compile.

complaire [koⁿplèr] *v.* to please; *se complaire à,* to take pleasure in. ‖ **complaisance** [koⁿplèzaⁿs] *f.* obligingness; complacency; self-satisfac-

tion; *complaisant,* obliging; complacent, self-satisfied.

complément [koⁿplémaⁿ] *m.* complement; object (gramm.). ‖ **complémentaire** [-tèr] *adj.* complementary.

complet [koⁿplè] *m.* suit. ‖ **complet, -plète** [-plè, -plèt] *adj.* complete; entire; whole; full; *au complet,* full up. ‖ **compléter** [-été] *v.* to complete, to fill up.

complexe [koⁿplèks] *m.* complex (psych.); *adj.* complex, complicated. ‖ **complexion** [-yoⁿ] *f.* constitution; temperament. ‖ **complexité** [-ìté] *f.* complexity.

complication [koⁿplìkàsyoⁿ] *f.* complication; complexity.

complice [koⁿplìs] *m., f.* accomplice; party, accessory; *adj.* abetting; knowing. ‖ **complicité** [ìté] *f.* complicity; aiding and abetting (jur.).

compliment [koⁿplìmaⁿ] *m.* compliment; congratulation; flattery; *pl.* greetings; kindest regards. ‖ **complimenter** [-té] *v.* to compliment; to congratulate.

compliqué [koⁿplìké] *adj.* complicated, elaborate, intricate. ‖ **compliquer** [-é] *v.* to complicate.

complot [koⁿplò] *m.* plot, conspiracy; scheme. ‖ **comploter** [-òté] *v.* to plot, to conspire; to be up to.

comportement [koⁿpòrtmaⁿ] *m.* behavior. ‖ **comporter** [-té] *v.* to admit of; to comprise; to require; to involve; *se comporter,* to behave.

composant [koⁿpòzaⁿ] *m., adj.* component. ‖ **composé** [-é] *m.* compound; *adj.* compound; composed; impassive [visage]; composite. ‖ **composer** [-é] *v.* to compose; to compound; to set (typogr.); to arrange. ‖ **compositeur, -trice** [-ìtœr, -trìs] *m., f.* composer; compositor (typogr.). ‖ **composition** [koⁿpòzìsyoⁿ] *f.* composing, composition; type-setting, agreement; mixture (med.); theme, examination paper.

compote [koⁿpòt] *f.* stewed fruit.

compréhensible [koⁿpréaⁿsìbl] *adj.* comprehensible, understandable. ‖ **compréhensif** [-ìf] *adj.*° comprehensive; understanding. ‖ **compréhension** [-yoⁿ] *f.* understanding, grasp.

comprendre [koⁿpraⁿdr] *v.*° to understand, to grasp, to comprehend; to include, to cover; *se comprendre,* to be understood; to understand each other.

compresse [koⁿprès] *f.* compress (med.). ‖ **compresseur** [-ær] *m.* compressor; supercharger [moteur]; *rouleau compresseur,* road-roller. ‖ **compression** [-yoⁿ] *f.* compression; repression; restriction.

comprimé [koⁿprìmé] *adj.* compressed; *m.* tablet (med.). ‖ *comprimer* [-é] *v.* to compress; to check, to restrain.

compris [koⁿprì] *p. p., adj., see comprendre; non compris,* exclusive of; *y compris,* including.

compromettant [koⁿpròmètaⁿ] *adj.* dangerous, bad. ‖ *compromettre* [-ètr] *v.* to compromise; to endanger; to jeopardize; to impair.

compromis [koⁿpròmì] *m.* compromise. ‖ *compromission* [-syoⁿ] *f.* compromising with one's conscience.

comptabiliser [koⁿtàbìlìzé] *v.* to enter into the books. ‖ *comptabilité* [koⁿtàbìlìté] *f.* book-keeping, accountancy; accountancy department. ‖ *comptable* [-àbl] *m.* book-keeper, accountant; *adj.* responsible. ‖ *comptant* [-aⁿ] *m.* cash, ready money; *adj.* ready [argent]; *au comptant,* for cash. ‖ *compte* [koⁿt] *m.* account; count; reckoning; number; *à compte,* on account; *en fin de compte,* after all; *faire entrer en ligne de compte,* to take into account; *mettre sur le compte de,* to impute to; *se rendre compte de,* to realize; *compte courant,* current account; *tenir compte de,* to take into consideration; *compte rendu,* account, report; *régler un compte,* to settle an account. ‖ *compter* [-é] *v.* to reckon, to count; to rely. ‖ *compteur* [-œr] *m.* computer; counter; meter. ‖ *comptoir* [-twàr] *m.* counter; bar; department; agency; branch; bank.

compulser [koⁿpülsé] *v.* to go through.

comté [koⁿté] *m.* county.

comte [koⁿt] *m.* count, Br. earl. ‖ *comtesse* [-ès] *f.* countess.

concasser [koⁿkàsé] *v.* to break up, to pound, to crush.

concave [koⁿkàv] *adj.* concave.

concéder [koⁿsédé] *v.* to allow, to grant, to concede.

concentration [koⁿsaⁿtràsyoⁿ] *f.* concentration. ‖ *concentrer* [-é] *v.* to concentrate; to intensify; to focus; *lait concentré,* condensed milk; *concentré de viande,* meat extract.

conception [koⁿsèpsyoⁿ] *f.* conception; idea; point of view.

concernant [koⁿsèrnaⁿ] *prep.* concerning, regarding. ‖ *concerner* [-é] *v.* to concern, to affect.

concert [koⁿsèr] *m.* concert. ‖ *concerter* [-té] *v.* to concert; to plan.

concession [koⁿsèsyoⁿ] *f.* concession, grant; plot. ‖ *concessionnaire* [-yònèr] *m., f.* grantee; licence-holder; patentee; concessionnaire.

concevable [koⁿsèvàbl] *adj.* conceivable. ‖ *concevoir* [koⁿsèvwàr] *v.** to conceive; to imagine; to devise.

concierge [koⁿsyèrj] *m., f.* hallporter; door-keeper; janitor; caretaker.

conciliabule [koⁿsìlyàbül] *m.* confabulation; secret meeting.

conciliant [koⁿsìlyaⁿ] *adj.* conciliatory. ‖ *conciliation* [-yàsyoⁿ] *f.* conciliation. ‖ *concilier* [-yé] *v.* to conciliate, to reconcile; to win over.

concis [koⁿsì] *adj.* concise, brief; *concision,* conciseness, brevity.

concitoyen [koⁿsìtwàyiⁿ] *m.* fellowcitizen.

conclave [koⁿklàv] *m.* conclave.

concluant [koⁿklüaⁿ] *adj.* conclusive. ‖ *conclure* [-ür] *v.** to conclude, to finish; to infer. ‖ *conclusion* [-üzyoⁿ] *f.* conclusion; termination; finding, opinion (jur.).

concombre [koⁿkoⁿbr] *m.* cucumber.

concordance [koⁿkòrdaⁿs] *f.* concordance, agreement; sequence (gramm.). ‖ *concorde* [koⁿkòrd] *f.* agreement, harmony. ‖ *concorder* [koⁿkòrdé] *v.* to agree, to concur.

concourir [koⁿkürìr] *v.** to converge; to vie, to compete [pour, for]; to co-operate [à, in]. ‖ *concours* [koⁿkûr] *m.* concourse, gathering; co-operation; help; competitive examination; competition; match.

concret, -crète [koⁿkrè, -krèt] *adj.* concrete; actual; solid. ‖ *concrétiser* [-tìzé] *v.* to concretize.

conçu [koⁿsü] *p. p. of concevoir.*

concubinage [koⁿkübìnàj] *m.* concubinage. ‖ *concubine* [koⁿkübìn] *f.* concubine.

concurrence [koⁿküraⁿs] *f.* rivalry; competition; *faire concurrence à,* to compete with. ‖ *concurrent* [-aⁿ] *m.* competitor, rival; candidate; *adj.* competitive, rival.

concussion [koⁿküsyoⁿ] *f.* misappropriation of funds, embezzlement; extortion.

condamnable [koⁿdànàbl] *adj.* blameworthy. ‖ *condamnation* [-àsyoⁿ] *f.* conviction, sentence (jur.); blame, censure, reproof. ‖ *condamné* [-é] *m.* convict; condemned person. ‖ *condamner* [-é] *v.* to condemn; to sentence (jur.); to censure; to reprove.

condensateur [koⁿdaⁿsàtœr] *m.* condenser (electr.); *adj.* condensing. ‖ *condensation* [-àsyoⁿ] *f.* condensation. ‖ *condensé* [-é] *m.* digest. ‖ *condenser* [-é] *v.* to condense; *condenseur,* condenser (mech.).

condescendance [ko^{n}dèsa^{n}da^{n}s] *f.* condescension. ‖ *condescendre* [ko^{n}dèsa^{n}dr] *v.* to comply; to condescend; to deign.

condiment [ko^{n}dìma^n] *m.* condiment; spice.

condisciple [ko^{n}dìsìpl] *m.* schoolfellow, school-mate; fellow-student.

condition [ko^{n}dìsyo^n] *f.* condition, state, circumstances; rank; *pl.* terms; *à condition*, on condition. ‖ *conditionnel* [-yònèll] *m.*, *adj.* conditional. ‖ *conditionnement* [-yònma^n] *m.* conditioning; wrapping. ‖ *conditionner* [-né] *v.* to condition; to wrap up.

condoléances [ko^{n}dòléa^{n}s] *f.* *pl.* condolence; *sincères condoléances*, deepest sympathy.

conducteur, -trice [ko^{n}düktœr, -trìs] *m.*, *f.* conductor; leader; driver [voiture]; *adj.* conducting.

conduire [ko^{n}düìr] *v.** to lead, to conduct, to guide; to direct; to steer [naut.]; to drive [auto]; to convey, to look after, to manage, to run [affaires]; *se conduire*, to behave; to find one's way. ‖ *conduit* [ko^{n}düì] *m.* conduit, pipe, passage, duct; *conduit principal*, main. ‖ *conduite* [ko^{n}düìt] *f.* conducting, guidance; driving, management, command; channel, pipe; behavio(u)r; *changer de conduite*, to mend one's ways.

cône [kôn] *m.* cone.

confection [ko^{n}fèksyo^n] *f.* making; manufacture; ready-made clothes. ‖ *confectionner* [-yòné] *v.* to make up, to manufacture; *confectionneur*, outfitter, clothier.

confédération [ko^{n}fédéràsyo^n] *f.* confederation. ‖ *confédérer* [-é] *v.* to confederate, to unite.

conférence [ko^{n}féra^{n}s] *f.* conference; lecture; consultation (med.). ‖ *conférencier* [-yé] *m.* lecturer.

conférer [ko^{n}féré] *v.* to compare [documents]; to award; to confer.

confesser [ko^{n}fèsé] *v.* to confess; to avow; to own up to; *se confesser*, to confess one's sins; *confesseur*, confessor; *confession*, confession, avowal.

confiance [ko^{n}fya^{n}s] *f.* confidence, trust; *confiance en soi*, self-confidence. ‖ *confiant* [-ya^n] *adj.* trusting, confident; trustful; sanguine.

confidence [ko^{n}fìda^{n}s] *f.* confidence, secret. ‖ *confident* [-a^n] *m.* confidant; sociable. ‖ *confidente* [-a^{n}t] *f.* confidante. ‖ *confidentiel* [-yèll] *adj.** confidential, private, secret.

confier [ko^{n}fyé] *v.* to entrust; to disclose [nouvelles]; *se confier*, to confide; to rely [à, on].

configuration [ko^{n}fìgüràsyo^n] *f.* configuration, outline.

confiner [ko^{n}fìné] *v.* to border upon; to confine. ‖ *confins* [ko^{n}fì^n] *m.* *pl.* confines, limits, borders.

confire [ko^{n}fìr] *v.** to preserve, to pickle.

confirmation [ko^{n}fìrmasyo^n] *f.* confirmation. ‖ *confirmer* [-é] *v.* to confirm; to corroborate, to bear out; to ratify.

confiscation [ko^{n}fìskàsyo^n] *f.* confiscation, seizure, forfeiture.

confiserie [ko^{n}fìzrî] *f.* confectionery, confectioner's shop, *Am.* candy shop. ‖ *confiseur* [-œr] *m.* confectioner.

confisquer [ko^{n}fìské] *v.* to confiscate.

confit [ko^{n}fì] *p. p.*, *adj.*, see *confire*; *fruits confits*, preserved fruit. ‖ *confiture* [-tür] *f.* jam, preserve.

conflagration [ko^{n}flàgràsyo^n] *f.* conflagration.

conflit [ko^{n}flì] *m.* conflict, strife, clash.

confluent [ko^{n}flüa^n] *m.* confluence, meeting [eaux].

confondre [ko^{n}fo^{n}dr] *v.* to confound, to confuse; to intermingle; *se confondre*, to blend; to be lost; to be confused.

conformation [ko^{n}fòrmàsyo^n] *f.* conformation. ‖ *conforme* [ko^{n}fòrm] *adj.* consistent; identical; *conformément*, in accordance [à with]. ‖ *conformer* [-é] *v.* to shape, to form; *se conformer*, to conform. ‖ *conformisme* [-ìsm] *m.* conventionalism; conformity; orthodoxy. ‖ *conformiste* [-ìst] *m.*, *f.* formalist, conventionalist; conformist. ‖ *conformité* [-ìté] *f.* conformity.

confort [ko^{n}fòr] *m.* comfort. ‖ *confortable* [-tàbl] *adj.* comfortable.

confraternel [ko^{n}fràtèrnèl] *adj.** brotherly, fraternal. ‖ *confraternité* [ko^{n}fràtèrnìté] *f.* brotherhood.

confrère [ko^{n}frèr] *m.* colleague. ‖ *confrérie* [-frérî] *f.* confraternity; guild.

confrontation [ko^{n}fro^{n}tasyo^n] *f.* collation; confrontation. ‖ *confronter* [ko^{n}fro^{n}té] *v.* to confront; to compare [textes].

confus [ko^{n}fü] *adj.* confused, mixed; obscure; dim; indistinct; muffled; embarrassed; at a loss. ‖ *confusion* [-zyo^n] *f.* confusion, disorder; embarrassment.

congé [ko^{n}jé] *m.* leave, holiday; discharge (mil.); dismissal; permit; clearance [bateau]; *un jour de congé*, a day off; *prendre congé*, to take leave; *donner congé*, to dismiss; *demander*

son congé, to give notice. ‖ **congédier** [-dyé] v. to dismiss, to discharge, to lay off.

congélation [koⁿjélàsyoⁿ] f. coagulation; freezing. ‖ **congeler** [koⁿjlé] v. to congeal, to solidify; to freeze.

congénère [koⁿjénèr] s. congener; like, fellow.

congénital [koⁿjénitàl] adj.* congenital, inborn.

congère [koⁿjèr] f. snowdrift.

congestion [koⁿjèstyoⁿ] f. congestion (med.); congestion pulmonaire, pneumonia; congestionné, flushed [visage]; se congestionner, to become congested; to flush up; to turn purple in the face.

congratuler [koⁿgràtülé] v. to congratulate.

congrégation [koⁿgrégàsyoⁿ] f. congregation (eccles.); brotherhood.

congrès [koⁿgrè] m. congress. ‖ **congressiste** [-sìst] s. member of a congress.

congru [koⁿgrü] adj. adequate; suitable; portion congrue, bare living, congrûment, duly, correctly.

conique [konìk] adj. conical; tapering.

conjecture [koⁿjèktür] f. conjecture, guess, surmise; conjecturer, to conjecture, to surmise.

conjoint [koⁿjwiⁿ] adj. joint; wedded, married (jur.); m. pl. husband and wife.

conjonction [koⁿjoⁿksyoⁿ] f. conjunction.

conjoncture [koⁿjoⁿktür] f. conjuncture, juncture.

conjugaison [koⁿjügèzoⁿ] f. conjugation.

conjugal [koⁿjügàl] adj.* conjugal.

conjuguer [koⁿjügé] v. to conjugate; to couple, to combine.

conjuration [koⁿjüràsyoⁿ] f. conspiracy, plot; entreaties. ‖ **conjurer** [-é] v. to conspire, to plot; to exorcise; to entreat.

connaissable [konèsàbl] adj. recognizable. ‖ **connaissance** [-aⁿs] f. knowledge; learning; acquaintance; consciousness; prendre connaissance de, to take note of; perdre connaissance, to faint; en connaissance de cause, knowingly; sans connaissance, unconscious. ‖ **connaisseur** [-œr] m. connoisseur, expert; adj.* expert. ‖ **connaître** [konètr] v.* to know, to be aware of; to understand; to experience; faire connaître, to bring to one's knowledge, to communicate; to make known; se connaître, to be acquaint-

ed; ne plus se connaître, to be beside oneself; se connaître en, to be an expert in.

connexion [konèksyoⁿ] f. connection, lead (electr.).

connivence [konìvaⁿs] f. connivance, complicity.

connu [konü] adj. known, discovered; p. p. of connaître.

conquérant [koⁿkéraⁿ] m. victor, conqueror; adj. conquering. ‖ **conquérir** [-érir] v.* to conquer, to subdue; to win over. ‖ **conquête** [-èt] f. conquest; acquisition.

conquis p. p. of conquérir.

consacrer [koⁿsàkré] v. to consecrate; to dedicate; to devote; expression consacrée, stock phrase.

consanguin [koⁿsaⁿgiⁿ] adj. consanguinean, consanguineous.

conscience [koⁿsyaⁿs] f. conscience; consciousness; conscientiousness; avoir conscience de, to be aware of; cas de conscience, matter of conscience, scruple; consciencieux, conscientious. ‖ **conscient** [koⁿsyaⁿ] adj. conscious, aware.

conscrit [koⁿskrì] m. recruit, conscript (mil.), Am. draftee.

consécration [koⁿsékràsyoⁿ] f. consecration.

consécutif [koⁿsékütìf] adj.* consecutive; following upon.

conseil [koⁿsèy] m. advice; resolution; council; meeting of directors; counsel (jur.); adviser; conseil d'administration, board of directors; conseil municipal, town council; un bon conseil, a good piece of advice; prendre conseil de, to take counsel of; conseil de guerre, council of war; court-martial. ‖ **conseiller** [-é] v. to advise, to recommend. ‖ **conseiller** [-é] m. council(l)or; adviser.

consentement [koⁿsaⁿtmaⁿ] m. consent, assent. ‖ **consentir** [-ìr] v. to consent, to agree; to authorize, to grant.

conséquence [koⁿsékaⁿs] f. consequence, issue, result, sequel; importance; en conséquence, accordingly; as a result; sans conséquence, of no importance. ‖ **conséquent** [-aⁿ] adj. consistent; following; par conséquent, therefore.

conservateur, -trice [koⁿsèrvàtœr, -trìs] m., f. conservative; keeper; guardian; curator; adj. conservative; preservative. ‖ **conservation** [-àsyoⁿ] f. preservation, conservation. ‖ **conservatoire** [-àtwàr] m. school, academy; adj. conservative [mesures]. ‖ **conserve** [koⁿsèrv] f. preserve; tinned food, Am.

canned food; *conserves au vinaigre*, pickles; *de conserve*, together, in convoy. ‖ **conserver** [-é] *v.* to preserve, to keep, to maintain; *se conserver*, to keep [nourriture].

considérable [koⁿsìdéràbl] *adj.* considerable; extensive; important; notable. ‖ **considération** [-àsyoⁿ] *f.* consideration; motive; esteem. ‖ **considérer** [-é] *v.* to consider; to contemplate; to gaze on; to regard; to ponder.

consignation [koⁿsìñàsyoⁿ] *f.* consignment; deposit. ‖ **consigne** [koⁿsìñ] *f.* order, instructions; detention [lycée]; *Br.* cloakroom [gare], *Am.* baggage-room, check-room. ‖ **consigner** [-ìñé] *v.* to deposit; to consign; to check [bagages]; to register; to detain; to confine to barracks (mil.).

consistance [koⁿsìstaⁿs] *f.* consistency, firmness. ‖ **consistant** [-aⁿ] *adj.* consistent, firm, compact, stiff. ‖ **consister** [-é] *v.* to consist, to be made [en, of].

consistoire [koⁿsìstwàr] *m.* consistory.

consœur [koⁿsœr] *f.* sister-member, colleague.

consolateur, -trice [koⁿsòlàtœr, -trìs] *m., f.* consoler, comforter; *adj.* consoling. ‖ **consolation** [-àsyoⁿ] *f.* consolation, solace. ‖ **consoler** [-é] *v.* to console, to comfort.

consolidation [koⁿsòlìdàsyoⁿ] *f.* consolidation; healing [fracture]; funding. ‖ **consolider** [-é] *v.* to consolidate; to fund [dettes]; to heal up (med.).

consommateur, -trice [koⁿsòmàtœr, -trìs] *m., f.* consumer; customer [restaurant]. ‖ **consommation** [-àsyoⁿ] *f.* consumption; consummation; drink. ‖ **consommé** [-é] *m.* broth, soup; *adj.* consummate. ‖ **consommer** [-é] *v.* to consume; to use up; to waste; to complete.

consomption [koⁿsoⁿpsyoⁿ] *f.* wasting, decline.

consonne [koⁿsòn] *f.* consonant.

consort [koⁿsòr] *m.* consort; *pl.* associates, confederates.

conspirateur, -trice [koⁿspìràtœr, -trìs] *m., f.* conspirator. ‖ **conspiration** [-àsyoⁿ] *f.* conspiracy, plot. ‖ **conspirer** [-é] *v.* to conspire, to plot; to tend.

conspuer [koⁿspüé] *v.* to run down; to boo; to conspue.

constamment [koⁿstàmaⁿ] *adv.* steadily; continually, constantly. ‖ **constance** [-aⁿs] *f.* steadiness, constancy. ‖ **constant** [-aⁿ] *adj.* steadfast; invariable, constant. ‖ **constante** [aⁿt] *f.* constant (math.).

constatation [koⁿstàtàsyoⁿ] *f.* authentic fact; statement; verification; confirmation. ‖ **constater** [-é] *v.* to report; to state; to establish; to confirm; to ascertain, to verify.

constellation [koⁿstèllàsyoⁿ] *f.* constellation. ‖ **consteller** [-é] *v.* to constellate; to stud [bijoux].

consternation [koⁿstèrnàsyoⁿ] *f.* consternation, dismay. ‖ **consterner** [-é] *v.* to dismay, to astound.

constipation [koⁿstìpàsyoⁿ] *f.* constipation. ‖ **constiper** [-é] *v.* to constipate.

constituant [koⁿstìtüaⁿ] *adj.* component, constituent. ‖ **constituer** [-üé] *v.* to constitute, to settle; to establish. ‖ **constitutif** [-tìf] *adj.** constitutive, basic.

constitution [koⁿstìtüsyoⁿ] *f.* constitution; establishing; formation; settlement; health; **constitutionnel,** constitutional.

constriction [koⁿstrìksyoⁿ] *f.* constriction.

constructeur [koⁿstrüktœr] *m.* builder, constructor. ‖ **constructif** [-tìf] *adj.** constructive. ‖ **construction** [-syoⁿ] *f.* construction, building; structure; *en construction,* building; on the stocks [bateau]. ‖ **construire** [koⁿstrüîr] *v.** to build, to construct.

consubstantiation [koⁿsübstaⁿsyàsyoⁿ] *f.* consubstantiation.

consul [koⁿsül] *m.* consul. ‖ **consulat** [-à] *m.* consulate; consulship.

consultant [koⁿsültaⁿ] *adj.* consultant, consulting; *avocat consultant,* lawyer, counsel. ‖ **consultatif** [-àtìf] *adj.** consultative, advisory. ‖ **consultation** [-àsyoⁿ] *f.* consultation; conference. ‖ **consulter** [-é] *v.* to consult, to refer to; *se consulter,* to consider, to deliberate.

consumer [koⁿsümé] *v.* to consume, to use up.

contact [koⁿtàkt] *m.* contact; relation; connection (electr.).

contagieux [koⁿtàjyë] *adj.** contagious, infectious, catching. ‖ **contagion** [-yoⁿ] *f.* contagion, infection.

contamination [koⁿtàmìnàsyoⁿ] *f.* contamination; pollution. ‖ **contaminer** [koⁿtàmìné] *v.* to contaminate, to infect (med.); to pollute.

conte [koⁿt] *m.* tale, story.

contemplatif [koⁿtaⁿplàtìf] *adj.** contemplative. ‖ **contemplation** [koⁿtaⁿplàsyoⁿ] *f.* contemplation. ‖ **contempler** [koⁿtaⁿplé] *v.* to contemplate; to gaze upon; to reflect upon, to ponder.

contemporain [koⁿtɑⁿpòriⁿ] *m., adj.* contemporary.

contenance [koⁿtnɑⁿs] *f.* capacity; bearing. countenance; *perdre contenance*, to be put out of countenance; to lose face ‖ **contenir** [-êr] *v.* to include. to contain, to hold, to restrain, to control; *se contenir*, to contain oneself; to refrain; to forbear.

content [koⁿtɑⁿ] *adj.* contented glad, pleased. happy satisfied ‖ **contentement** [-tmaⁿ] *m.* contentment, satisfaction. ‖ **contenter** [-té] *v.* to content, to satisfy, to gratify.

contentieux [koⁿtɑⁿsyë] *m.* litigable questions, *adj.* contentious; *bureau du contentieux*, disputed claims department.

contenu [koⁿtnü] *adj.* reserved; stified; restrained; *m.* contents.

conter [koⁿté] *v.* to tell, to relate.

contestable [koⁿtèstàbl] *adj.* questionable, debatable. ‖ **contestation** [-àsyoⁿ] *f.* dispute. ‖ **contester** [-é] *v.* to dispute, to question; to contend.

conteur [koⁿtœr] *m.* narrator; storyteller.

contexte [koⁿtèkst] *m.* context.

contigu, uë [koⁿtïgü] *adj.* adjoining, adjacent.

continent [koⁿtïnɑⁿ] *adj.* continent, modest.

continent [koⁿtïnɑⁿ] *m.* continent; mainland. ‖ **continental** [-tàl] *adj.* continental.

contingence [koⁿtïⁿjɑⁿs] *f.* contingency. ‖ **contingent** [-aⁿ] *m* quota; contingent; *adj.* contingent. ‖ **contingenter** [-aⁿté] *v.* to fix quotas for.

continu [koⁿtïnü] *adj.* continuous, continual, unbroken; uninterrupted, direct (electr.). ‖ **continuateur, -trice** [-àtœr, -trïs] *m., f.* continuator **continuation** [-àsyoⁿ] *f.* continuation continuance, carrying on. ‖ **continuel** [-èl] *adj.* continual, unceasing. ‖ **continuer** [-é] *v.* to continue; to carry on, to keep on; to prolong; *se continuer*, to last, to be continued.

contondant [koⁿtoⁿdaⁿ] *adj.* bruising, contusive.

contorsion [koⁿtòrsyoⁿ] *f.* contortion. ‖ **contorsionner** [-syòné] *v.* to contort.

contour [koⁿtûr] *m.* contour; outline; circuit [ville]. ‖ **contourner** [-né] *v.* to outline; to go round; to distort; to evade.

contracter [koⁿtràkté] *v.* to contract; to catch [rhume]; to acquire [habitude]; to incur; *se contracter*, to contract, to shrink; to shrivel. ‖ **contraction** [-àksyoⁿ] *f.* contraction, narrowing; shrinking.

contradicteur [koⁿtràdîktœr] *m.* opposer, opponent ‖ **contradiction** [-ïksyoⁿ] *f* contradiction inconsistency. ‖ **contradictoire** [-ïktwàr] *adj* contradictory inconsistent, conflicting; *examen contradictoire*, cross-examination.

contraindre [koⁿtrïndr] *v.** to compel, to force. to coerce; to restrain; *se contraindre*, to restrain oneself. ‖ **contrainte** [koⁿtrïnt] *f.* constraint, compulsion, embarrassment; *par contrainte* under duress.

contraire [koⁿtrèr] *m., adj.* contrary, opposite, adverse; *au contraire*, on the contrary.

contrariant [koⁿtràryaⁿ] *adj.* trying, vexatious. tiresome; provoking; contradictious ‖ **contrarier** [koⁿtràryé] *v.* to thwart, to oppose; to annoy, to vex. ‖ **contrariété** [-té] *f.* difficulty; clash; annoyance, vexation.

contraste [koⁿtràst] *m.* contrast; **contraster**, to contrast.

contrat [koⁿtrà] *m.* contract, deed, agreement; settlement [mariage]; *dresser un contrat*, to draw up a deed; *passer un contrat*, to execute a deed.

contravention [koⁿtràvɑⁿsyoⁿ] *f.* infringement, minor offense; *dresser une contravention à*, to summons.

contre [koⁿtr] *prep.* against; *adv.* near; *tout contre*, close by; *cinq contre un*, five to one; **contre-attaque**, counter-attack; *en contrebas*, lower down; *à contrecœur*, reluctantly; **contre-enquête**, counter-inquiry; **contre-expertise**, countervaluation; **contre-indication**, contra-indication (med.), **contre-jour**, back-lighting, false light; **contre-projet**, counterplan; counter-bill [parlement]; **contre-torpilleur**, destroyer; **contre-voie**, wrong side of the train; *à contre-voie*, up the down track.

contrebalancer [koⁿtrebàlaⁿsé] *v.* to counterbalance, to compensate.

contrebande [koⁿtrebaⁿd] *f.* contraband goods, smuggling; *faire la contrebande*, to smuggle. ‖ **contrebandier** [-yé] *m.* smuggler.

contrebasse [koⁿtrebàs] *f.* doublebass, contrabass; double-bass player.

contrecarrer [koⁿtrekàré] *v.* to thwart [projets].

contrecoup [koⁿtrekû] *m.* rebound; jar; after-effect.

contredire [koⁿtredîr] *v.** to contradict, to gainsay; to be inconsistent; *contredit*, contradiction; *sans contredit*, unquestionably.

contrée [koⁿtré] *f.* country, region.

contrefaçon [koⁿtr*fàsoⁿ] *f.* counterfeit, forgery; counterfeiting. ‖ *contrefaire* [koⁿtr*fèr] *v.* to forge, to counterfeit; to ape, to imitate; to feign. ‖ **contrefait** [-è] *adj.* forged, counterfeit; feigned; deformed.

contrefort [koⁿtr*fòr] *m.* buttress; spur (geogr.).

contremaître [koⁿtr*mètr] *m.* overseer, foreman; first mate (naut.).

contrepartie [koⁿtr*pàrtî] *f.* counterpart; compensation.

contrepoids [koⁿtr*pwà] *m.* counterweight, counterbalance.

contrepoison [koⁿtr*pwàzoⁿ] *m.* antidote, counter-poison.

contrer [koⁿtré] *v.* to cross, to thwart.

contresens [koⁿtr*saⁿs] *m.* misinterpretation; nonsense; opposite direction.

contresigner [koⁿtr*sìñé] *v.* to countersign.

contretemps [koⁿtr*taⁿ] *m.* mishap; inconvenience; disappointment; syncopation (mus.); *à contretemps,* inopportunely; out of time; syncopated (mus.).

contrevent [koⁿtr*vaⁿ] *m.* outside shutter.

contrevérité [koⁿtr*vérìté] *f.* untruth.

contribuable [koⁿtrìbüàbl] *adj.* taxpayer; *adj.* taxable. ‖ **contribuer** [-üé] *v.* to contribute. ‖ **contribution** [-üsyoⁿ] *f.* contribution; tax; duty, excise.

contrister [koⁿtrìsté] *v.* to afflict.

contrit [koⁿtrî] *adj.* contrite. ‖ **contrition** [koⁿtrìsyoⁿ] *f.* contrition, repentance.

contrôlable [koⁿtrôlàbl] *adj.* able to be checked. ‖ *contrôle* [koⁿtrôl] *m.* roll (mil.); controller's office; boxoffice (theat.); hall-mark; checking; inspection; supervision; control. ‖ *contrôler* [-é] *v.* to check, to verify; to examine; to stamp; to control. ‖ *contrôleur* [-œr] *m.* inspector; supervisor; controller; driver [métro]; ticket collector.

contrordre [koⁿtròrdr] *m.* countermand.

controverse [koⁿtròvèrs] *f.* controversy.

convaincre [koⁿvíⁿkr] *v.** to convince; to convict. ‖ *convaincu* [koⁿvíⁿkü] *adj.* earnest, convinced; convicted.

convalescence [koⁿvàlèsaⁿs] *f.* convalescence. ‖ *convalescent* [-aⁿ] *m.*, *adj.* convalescent.

convenable [koⁿvnàbl] *adj.* proper, fit; appropriate; expedient; becoming;

suitable; decent. ‖ **convenance** [koⁿvnaⁿs] *f.* fitness, propriety; decency; expediency; convenience. ‖ *convenir* [-nîr] *v.* to suit; to be convenient; to agree, to admit; to arrange; to be agreeable (à, to); *il convient que,* it is fitting that; *c'est convenu,* that's settled.

convention [koⁿvaⁿsyoⁿ] *f.* convention; agreement; *pl.* clauses; *conventionnel,* conventional.

converger [koⁿvèrjé] *v.* to converge.

conversation [koⁿvèrsàsyoⁿ] *f.* conversation, talk. ‖ *converser* [-é] *v.* to converse, to talk together.

conversion [koⁿvèrsyoⁿ] *f.* conversion; change.

converti [koⁿvèrtî] *adj.* converted; *m.* convert. ‖ *convertir* [koⁿvèrtîr] *v.* to convert; to change; to transform; *se convertir,* to be converted. ‖ *convertissable* [-ìsàbl] *adj.* convertible.

convexe [koⁿvèks] *adj.* convex.

conviction [koⁿvìksyoⁿ] *f.* conviction.

convier [koⁿvyé] *v.* to invite; to incite.

convive [koⁿvîv] *m.*, *f.* guest.

convocation [koⁿvòkàsyoⁿ] *f.* convocation; summons; calling-up (mil.).

convoi [koⁿvwà] *m.* convoy; train; funeral procession; supply column; escort.

convoiter [koⁿvwàté] *v.* to covet, to desire. ‖ *convoitise* [-îz] *f.* lust, covetousness; longing.

convoler [koⁿvòlé] *v.* to marry, to remarry.

convoquer [koⁿvòké] *v.* to summon; to call up (mil.); to be called for interview.

convoyer [koⁿvwàyé] *v.* to convoy; to escort.

convulsif [koⁿvülsìf] *adj.** convulsive. ‖ *convulsion* [koⁿvülsyoⁿ] *f.* convulsion; spasm. ‖ *convulsionner* [-syòné] *v.* to convulse.

coopération [kòòpéràsyoⁿ] *f.* co-operation. ‖ *coopérative* [-àtìv] *f.* co-operative. ‖ *coopérer* [-é] *v.* to co-operate, to work together.

coordination [kòòrdìnàsyoⁿ] *f.* co-ordination. ‖ *coordonner* [-òné] *v.* to co-ordinate, to arrange.

copain [kòpíⁿ] *m.* (pop.) pal, chum, *Am.* buddy.

copeau [kòpô] *m.** shaving, chip [bois]; cutting; *pl.* turnings [métal].

copie [kòpî] *f.* copy, imitation; transcript. ‖ *copier* [kòpyé] *v.* to copy, to transcribe; to reproduce; to imitate.

copieux [kòpyë] *adj.** copious, abundant, plentiful.

copiste [kòpìst] *m.* copier, copyist.

copropriétaire [kòpròpryétèr] *m.*, *f.* joint tenant.

coq [kòk] *m.* cock, rooster; *au chant du coq*, at cock-crow; *comme un coq en pâte*, in clover sitting pretty; *poids coq*, bantam-weight; *coq-à-l'âne*, cock-and-bull story.

coque [kòk] *f.* shell [œuf]; body (mech.), bottom, hull [bateau]; kink [corde]; *œuf à la coque*, boiled egg.

coqueluche [kòklüsh] *f.* whooping-cough; favo(u)rite.

coquet [kòkè] *adj.** coquettish; smart, spruce, stylish; dainty.

coquetier [kòktyé] *m.* egg-merchant; egg-cup.

coquette [kòkèt] *f.* coquette, flirt.

coquetterie [kòkètrî] *f.* coquetry; coyness, smartness, daintiness.

coquillage [kòkìyàʃ] *m.* shell; shell-fish. ‖ **coquille** [kòkìy] *f.* shell [escargot, huître]; misprint (typogr.).

coquin [kòkìⁿ] *m.* scamp, rascal; hussy (f.); *adj.* roguish, rascally. ‖ **coquinerie** [-rî] *f.* knavish trick; knavishness.

cor [kòr] *m.* horn; corn [pied].

corail [kòrày] *m.** coral.

corbeau [kòrbô] *m.** crow, raven; corbel (arch.); grappling-iron (naut.).

corbeille [kòrbèy] *f.* basket; flower-bed; dress-circle (theat.); wedding-presents.

corbillard [kòrbìyàr] *m.* hearse.

cordage [kòrdàʃ] *m.* rope, cordage; stringing [raquette], gear (naut.); rigging. ‖ **corde** [kòrd] *f.* rope, cord, line; string [violon], chord (geom.), hanging; *à cordes*, stringed (instrument); *usé jusqu'à la corde*, threadbare; *cordeau*, string; chalk-line *cordée*, roped climbing party, *cordelette*, string; *cordelière*, girdle, fillet (arch.).

cordial [kòrdyàl] *m.** cordial; *adj.** cordial, hearty, warm. ‖ **cordialité** [-ité] *f.* cordiality, heartiness.

cordon [kòrdoⁿ] *m.* strand, twist [câble]; cord; girdle; *cordon sanitaire*, sanitary cordon, *Am.* quarantine line; *cordon-bleu*, first-rate cook.

cordonnerie [kòrdònrî] *f.* shoemaking; shoemaker's shop.

cordonnet [kòrdònè] *m.* braid, cord.

cordonnier [kòrdònyé] *m.* shoemaker, cobbler.

coricide [kòrìsìd] *m.* corn-plaster.

cormoran [kòrmòràⁿ] *m.* cormorant.

cornac [kòrnàk] *m.* mahout.

cornaline [kòrnàlîn] *f.* cornelian.

corne [kòrn] *f.* horn; hoof; shoe-horn; dog's-ear [livre]. ‖ **cornée** [-é] *f.* cornea.

corneille [kòrnèy] *f.* rook, crow; *bayer aux corneilles*, to stand gaping, *Am.* to rubberneck.

cornemuse [kòrnᵉmüz] *f.* bagpipe.

corner [kòrné] *v.* to hoot; to trumpet; to ring [oreilles]. ‖ **cornet** [-è] *m.* cornet; trumpet; hooter [auto]. ‖ **cornette** [-èt] *f.* mob-cap.

cornichon [kòrnìshoⁿ] *m.* gherkin; (pop.) duffer, mug, clot.

cornouiller [kòrnûyé] *m.* cornel-tree; dogwood.

cornu [kòrnü] *adj.* horned. ‖ **cornue** *f.* retort (chem.).

corollaire [kòròllèr] *m.* corollary; deduction; inference.

corolle [kòròl] *f.* corolla.

corporation [kòrpòràsyoⁿ] *f.* corporation; *corporatif*, corporative; *corporatisme*, corporatism.

corporel [kòrpòrèl] *adj.** corporeal; corporal, bodily.

corps [kòr] *m.* body; matter; corps (mil.), group; *à corps perdu*, desperately; *perdu corps et biens*, lost with all hands; *corps à corps*, hand to hand; *corps de bâtiment*, main building; *corps de garde*, guard-room; *corps diplomatique*, diplomatic body; *prendre corps*, to materialize.

corpulence [kòrpülaⁿs] *f.* corpulence, stoutness. ‖ **corpulent** [-aⁿ] *adj.* corpulent, stout.

corpuscule [kòrpüskül] *m.* corpuscle; particle.

correct [kòrèkt] *adj.* correct; accurate. ‖ **correcteur, -trice** [-œr, -trìs] *m.*, *f.* corrector; proof-reader. ‖ **correctif** [-ìf] *adj.**, *m.* corrective. ‖ **correction** [kòrèksyoⁿ] *f.* correction; punishment; correctness; *maison de correction*, reformatory. ‖ **correctionnel** [-yònèl] *adj.** correctional; *tribunal correctionnel*, court of summary jurisdiction, police court.

corrélation [kòrrélàsyoⁿ] *f.* correlation, connection.

correspondance [kòrèspoⁿdaⁿs] *f.* correspondence; connection [transport], *Am.* transfer-point; dealings. ‖ **correspondant** [-aⁿ] *m.* correspondent; *adj.* corresponding. ‖ **correspondre** [kòrèspoⁿdr] *v.* to correspond; to communicate; to agree.

corridor [kòrìdòr] *m.* corridor.

corrigé [kòrìjé] *m.* key, crib. ‖ **corriger** [-é] *v.* to correct; to read [épreuves]; to reform; to adjust; to punish; *se corriger d'une habitude*, to break oneself of a habit.

corroborer [kòrròbòré] v. to corro-borate, to confirm; to support.

corroder [kòrròdé] v. to corrode.

corrompre [kòroⁿpr] v. to corrupt; to taint; to pollute; to deprave; to bribe; **se corrompre**, to spoil, to putrefy; to become corrupt.

corrosif [kòrròzìf] adj.* corrosive.

corrupteur, -trice [kòrüptœr, -trìs] m., f. corrupter; briber; adj. corrupt-ing. ‖ **corruption** [kòrüpsyoⁿ] f. cor-ruption; bribing; graft.

corsage [kòrsàj] m. bust; bodice [robe]; blouse.

corsaire [kòrsèr] m. corsair; calf-length jeans [pantalon], Am. clam-diggers, pedal-pushers.

corsé [kòrsé] adj. strong; full-bodied [vin]; spicy [histoire].

corselet [kòrsᵉlè] m. corselet, bodice.

corser [kòrsé] v. to strengthen, to stiffen; **se corser**, to take a turn for the worse.

corset [kòrsè] m. corset. ‖ **corsetier** [-ᵉtyé] m. corset-maker.

cortège [kòrtèj] m. retinue; proces-sion; cortège funèbre, funeral.

cortisone [kòrtizòn] f. cortisone.

corvée [kòrvé] f. fatigues (mil.); fatigue party; drudgery, irksome task.

corvette [kòrvèt] f. corvette, sloop.

cosaque [kòzàk] m. cossack.

cosmétique [kòsmétìk] m., adj. cos-metic.

cosmique [kòsmìk] adj. cosmic.

cosmographie [kòsmògràfì] f. cos-mography.

cosmonaute [kòsmonôt] m. cosmo-naut.

cosmopolite [kòsmòpòlìt] m., adj. cosmopolitan.

cosmos [kòsmòs] m. cosmos.

cosse [kòs] f. pod, husk; shell.

cossu [kòsü] adj. well-off, rich.

costaud [kòstô] adj. hefty, Am. husky; m. tough, guy, muscleman.

costume [kòstüm] m. costume, dress; suit; **costumer** (se) to dress; **se costumer en**, to dress up as; bal costumé, fancy-dress ball.

cote [kòt] f. quota, share; quotation (comm.); classification [bateaux]; alti-tude; favo(u)r.

côte [kôt] f. rib; slope; hill; coast, shore; côte à côte, side by side; cô-telé, ribbed, corduroy (text.).

côté [kôté] m. side; district; aspect; direction; à côté de, beside; de côté, askew; sideways; d'un côté, on the one hand; du côté de, in the direction of.

coteau [kòtô] m.* hill, hillock, knoll.

côtelette [kôtlèt] f. cutlet [veau], chop [porc]; pl. (pop.) sideboards.

coter [kòté] v. to quote; to assess; to classify; to rate; to number.

cotillon [kòtìyoⁿ] m. petticoat; cotil-lon.

cotisation [kòtìzàsyoⁿ] f. subscrip-tion; assessment [taxes]; dues; quota. ‖ **cotiser (se)** [sᵉkòtìzé] v. to sub-scribe.

coton [kòtoⁿ] m. cotton; coton hydro-phile, cotton-wool (med.); **cotonnade**, cotton fabric; cotton goods; **coton-neux**, cottony; fleecy; downy.

côtoyer [kôtwàyé] v. to skirt; to hug [côte]; to coast; to border on.

cou [kû] m. neck; cou-de-pied, instep.

couard [kwàr] m. coward; adj. cowardly. ‖ **couardise** [-dìz] f. coward-ice.

couchant [kûshaⁿ] m. west; sunset; wane; adj. setting [soleil]; lying. ‖ **couche** [kûsh] f. bed, couch; class [sociale]; stratum, layer, film [glace]; coat [peinture]; confinement; fausse couche, miscarriage. ‖ **coucher** [-é] m. night's lodging; sunset; v. to put to bed; to lay down; to spread [pein-ture]; to sleep; **se coucher**, to lie down; to go to bed; to set [soleil]. ‖ **couchette** [-èt] f. cot; bunk (naut.); berth [train].

coucou [kûkû] m. cuckoo; cuckoo-clock; cowslip (bot.).

coude [kûd] m. elbow; angle, bend; jouer des coudes, to elbow one's way. ‖ **coudée** [-é] f. cubit. ‖ **coudoyer** [-wàyé] v. to elbow, to jostle.

coudre [kûdr] v.* to sew, to stitch; machine à coudre, sewing-machine.

couenne [kwàn] f. bacon-rind; crack-ling.

coulage [kûlàj] m. casting [métal]; leakage; scuttling [bateau]. ‖ **coulant** [-aⁿ] adj. running, flowing; fluent, easy. ‖ **coulée** [-é] f. flow; tapping [métal]; running-hand [écriture]. ‖ **couler** [-é] v. to flow, to run; to leak; to trickle; to cast [métal]; to pour; to founder; to sink; **se couler**, to creep; to slide.

couleur [kûlœr] f. colo(u)r; paint; dye; complexion; suit [cartes]; pre-tence; marchand de couleurs, chandler.

couleuvre [kûlœvr] f. snake.

coulisse [kûlìs] f. groove, slot; slide; backstage; wing (theat.); à coulisse, sliding; dans les coulisses, behind the scenes. ‖ **coulisser** [-é] v. to provide with slides; to run up; to slide. ‖ **cou-lissier** [-yé] m. outside broker.

couloir [kûlwàr] m. corridor, passage; strainer.

coup [kû] *m.* blow, knock; stroke (mech.); hit; thrust; stab [couteau]; shot; beat; sound; blast; wound; turn, move; deed; *après coup,* as an afterthought; *tout d'un coup,* all at once; *boire un coup,* to have a drink; *sous le coup de,* under the influence of; *coup de coude,* nudge; *coup de pied,* kick; *coup de soleil,* sunstroke; *coup de feu,* shot; *coup de main,* surprise attack, raid; helping hand; know-how; *coup d'œil,* glance, sight; *coup de tête,* rash impulse; *manquer son coup,* to miss, to fail; *donner un coup de main,* to give a hand; *coup de téléphone,* telephone call.

coupable [kûpábl] *m.,* *f.* culprit; *adj.* guilty.

coupant [kûpaⁿ] *m.* edge; *adj.* cutting, sharp.

coupe [kûp] *f.* cut; cutting; section; felling [arbres]; *coupe de cheveux,* haircut; *coupe transversale,* cross-section; *sous la coupe de quelqu'un,* under someone's thumb; *coupe-circuit,* cut-out; *coupe-file,* police pass; *coupe-gorge,* cut-throat; *coupe-papier,* paper-knife, letter opener; *coupelle* [-èl] *f.* cupel; *couper* [-é] *v.* to cut; to cut off; to intercept; to interrupt; to water down; to ring off [téléphone]; *se couper,* to contradict oneself; to intersect; *couperet* [-rè] *m.* chopper; knife, blade.

couperosé [kûprôzé] *adj.* blotchy.

couplage [kûplàj] *m.* coupling; connection; *couple* [kûpl] *m.* couple, pair; brace [faisans]; *f.* couple, two; yoke [bœufs]; *coupler,* to couple.

couplet [kûplè] *m.* couplet; verse [chanson].

coupon [kûpoⁿ] *m.* coupon; ticket; remnant; *coupon-réponse international,* international reply coupon.

coupure [kûpür] *f.* cut; paper money; clipping.

cour [kûr] *f.* court; courtyard; courtship; *faire la cour à,* to court, to woo, to make love to.

courage [kûràj] *m.* courage, gallantry, pluck; *courageux* [-è] *adj.** brave, courageous, gallant, plucky.

couramment [kûràmaⁿ] *adv.* fluently, readily.

courant [kûraⁿ] *m.* current, stream; draught; course; *adj.* running, current; *fin courant,* at the end of the present month; *courant d'air,* Br. draught, Am. draft; *au courant de,* conversant with.

courbatu [kûrbàtü] *adj.* stiff in the joints; *courbature* [-r] *f.* aching, stiffness; *courbaturer,* to tire out; to stiffen.

courbe [kûrb] *f.* curve; graph; contour; *adj.* curved; *courber* [-é] *v.* to bend, to curve; *se courber,* to bend, to stoop; *courbette* [kûrbèt] *f.* curvet; *faire des courbettes,* to bow and scrape; to kowtow; *courbure* [-bür] *f.* curvature; curve; camber.

coureur [kûrœr] *m.* runner, racer; philanderer, Am. wolf; rover, gadabout; *coureur de(s) bois,* © coureur de(s) bois, bush-ranger; *coureuse* [-èz] *f.* slut, trollop (fam.).

courge [kûrj] *f.* gourd; pumpkin.

courir [kûrîr] *v.** to run; to be current; to pursue, to run after; to hunt; *courir le monde,* to travel widely, to roam the world over.

couronne [kûrôn] *f.* crown, coronet; wreath; rim [roue]; foolscap; *couronnement* [-maⁿ] *m.* crowning, coronation; *couronner* [-é] *v.* to crown; to wreath; to reward.

courrier [kûryé] *m.* courier; messenger; mail; letters; *par retour du courrier,* by return mail; *courriériste* [-rìst] *m.* columnist; par writer.

courroie [kûrwà] *f.* strap; belt (mech.).

courroucer [kûrûsé] *v.* to anger, to incense; to enrage; *courroux* [kûrû] *m.* (lit.) wrath, ire, anger.

cours [kûr] *m.* course; stream; lapse [temps]; avenue; path; currency; price; lessons; series of lectures; *donner libre cours à,* to give free rein to; *au cours de,* during; *long cours,* foreign travel.

course [kûrs] *f.* run; course; race; trip; cruise (naut.); ride; errand; stroke (mech.); *course de taureaux,* bull-fight; *faire des courses,* to go on errands; to go shopping; *coursier,* courser, steed; errand-boy.

court [kûr] *adj.* short, brief; *adv.* short; *à court de,* short of; *court-circuit,* short-circuit; *court-circuiter,* to short-circuit; *court-métrage,* short; *court-vêtu,* short-skirted.

courtage [kûrtàj] *m.* brokerage, commission.

courtier [kûrtyé] *m.* broker.

courtisan [kûrtìzaⁿ] *m.* courtier; *courtisane* [-àn] *f.* courtesan; *courtisanerie* [-ànrî] *f.* toadyism; *courtiser* [-é] *v.* to court; to toady to; to suck up to (pop.); to make love to.

courtois [kûrtwà] *adj.* courteous, well-bred; *courtoisie,* courtesy.

couru [kûrü] *p. p. of courir.*

cousette [kûzèt] *f.* dressmaker's assistant.

cousin [kûzⁿ] *m.* cousin; *cousin germain,* first cousin.

cousin [kûzin] m. gnat, midge.

coussin [kûsin] m. cushion; **coussinet**, pad, small cushion; bearing; chair [rail].

cousu [kûzü] adj. sewn; cousu d'or, rolling in money; p. p. of **coudre**.

coût [kû] m. cost; pl. expenses. || **coûtant** [-tan] adj. costing; au prix coûtant, at cost price.

couteau [kûtô] m.* knife; coup de couteau; stab; à couteaux tirés, at daggers drawn; **coutelas**, butcher's knife, cutlass; **coutelier**, cutler; **coutellerie**, cutlery; cutler's shop.

coûter [kûté] v. to cost; coûter cher, to be expensive; coûte que coûte, at all costs; **coûteux**, expensive.

coutume [kûtüm] f. custom, habit; avoir coutume de, to be accustomed to; **coutumier**, customary.

couture [kûtür] f. sewing, needlework; seam; battre à plate couture, to beat hollow; maison de couture, dressmaker's shop; **couturier**, ladies' tailor; **couturière**, dressmaker.

couvée [kûvé] f. clutch [œufs]; brood.

couvent [kûvan] m. convent, nunnery; monastery; convent-school.

couver [kûvé] v. to sit on [œufs]; to brood; to hatch [complot]; to brew [orage]; to smoulder; couver des yeux, to gaze at; to gloat over.

couvercle [kûvèrkl] m. lid, cover, cap (mech.).

couvert [kûvèr] m. table things; house-charge [restaurant]; cover; shelter; adj. covered; hidden; obscure; mettre le couvert, to lay the table; restez couvert, keep your hat on.

couverture [kûvèrtür] f. coverlet, rug, blanket; cover; protection; roofing; margin (fin.).

couveuse [kûvèz] f. sitting hen; incubator; brooder, hatcher. || **couvi** [-i] adj. addled.

couvreur [kûvrœr] m. slater, thatcher, tiler; cover-point.

couvrir [kûvrîr] v.* to cover; to defray [frais]; to wrap up; to protect; to screen; to roof; se couvrir, to put on one's hat; to clothe oneself; to become overcast [ciel]; **couvre-chef**, hat, head-dress; **couvre-feu**, curfew; **couvre-lit**, bedspread; **couvre-pied**, quilt.

crabe [kràb] m. crab.

crachat [kràshà] m. spit, spittle. || **cracher** [-é] v. to spit; to cough up [argent]; c'est son père tout craché, he's the living image of his father. || **crachin** [-in] m. mizzle, drizzle. || **crachoir** [-wàr] m. spitoon; tenir le crachoir, to monopolize the conversation. || **crachoter** [-òté] v. to sputter.

craie [krè] f. chalk.

craindre [krindr] v.* to fear; to be anxious for. || **crainte** [krint] f. fear, dread; sans crainte, fearless; de crainte, for fear. || **craintif** [krintif] adj.* timid; fearful.

cramoisi [kràmwàzí] m., adj. crimson; scarlet.

crampe [kranp] f. cramp (med.).

crampon [kranpon] m. cramp, brace; stud [bottes]; staple; (pop.) bore. || **cramponner** [-òné] v. to clamp; (pop.) to pester; se cramponner, to cling to.

cran [kran] m. notch; cog [roue]; catch; avoir du cran, to be plucky, to have guts (fam.).

crâne [krân] m. skull; adj. plucky; jaunty. || **crâner** [-é] v. to swagger, to swank; to brazen it out. || **crânerie** [-rî] f. pluck, daring.

crapaud [kràpô] m. toad; baby-grand [piano]; low arm-chair.

crapet [kràpè] m. © crapet soleil, sunfish; crapet calicot, calico bass; crapet gris, rock bass.

crapule [kràpül] f. debauchee; blackguard; crapuleux, debauched; lewd, filthy, foul.

craqueler [kràklé] v. to crackle. || **craquelure** [-lür] f. crack, flaw. || **craquement** [-man] m. cracking, creaking. || **craquer** [-é] v. to crack, to creak; to strike [allumette]; to split.

crasse [kràs] f. filth, dirt; dirty trick; stinginess; adj. crass [ignorance]. || **crasseux** [-ë] adj.* dirty, filthy; stingy.

cratère [kràtèr] m. crater.

cravache [kràvàsh] f. riding-whip. || **cravacher** [-é] v. to horsewhip, to flog; to spur on, to goad on.

cravate [kràvàt] f. tie, necktie. || **cravater** [-é] v. to collar.

crayeux [krèyë] adj.* chalky.

crayon [krèyon] m. pencil; crayon pastel, crayon; **crayonnage**, pencil sketch; **crayonner**, to sketch.

créance [kréans] f. credence, belief; credit; debt; créance hypothécaire, mortgage; lettres de créance, credentials; **créancier**, creditor.

créateur, -trice [kréàtœr, -tris] m., f. creator, inventor; adj. creative, inventive. || **création** [kréàsyon] f. creation; invention; setting up. || **créature** [kréàtür] f. creature.

crécelle [krésèl] f. rattle; voix de crécelle, grating voice.

crèche [krèsh] f. cradle; crib; day-nursery; manger.

crédibilité [krédîbilîté] f. credibility.

crédit [krédì] *m.* credit; trust (comm.); repute; loan; *faire crédit à,* to give credit; *crédit foncier,* loan society; *à crédit.* on credit. ‖ **créditer** [-té] *v.* to credit [*de,* with]. ‖ **créditeur** [-tœr] *m.* creditor.

credo [krédô] *m.* creed.

crédule [krédül] *adj.* credulous. ‖ **crédulité** [-ìté] *f.* credulity.

créer [kréé] *v* to create; to bring out.

crémaillère [krémayèr] *f.* pot-hook; rack (mech.); *pendre la crémaillère,* to give a house-warming.

crématoire [krémàtwàr] *adj.* crematory; *four crématoire,* crematorium.

crème [krèm] *f.* cream; *crème glacée,* ice cream; **crémerie,** dairy; buttery [restaurant]; **crémière,** dairymaid; cream-jug.

crémone [krémòn] *f.* casement bolt.

créneau [krénô] *m.** battlement. ‖ **créneler** [krénlé] *v.* to embattle; to tooth [roue]; to notch; to mill [monnaie].

créole [kréòl] *m., f., adj.* creole.

créosote [kréòzòt] *f.* creosote.

crêpe [krèp] *f.* pancake.

crêpe [krèp] *m.* crape. ‖ **crêpelé** [krèplé] *adj.* crimped. ‖ **crêper** [krèpé] *v.* to crimp; *se crêper le chignon,* to tear each other's hair.

crépi [krépì] *adj., m.* rough-cast. ‖ **crépir** [krépìr] *v.* to rough-cast.

crépiter [krépìté] *v.* to crackle; to patter [pluie].

crépu [krépü] *adj.* crisp, fuzzy [cheveux]; crinkled.

crépuscule [krépüskül] *m.* twilight, dusk.

cresson [krèson] *m.* cress, water-cress; **cressonnière,** water-cress bed.

crête [krèt] *f.* crest; ridge; summit; comb [coq].

crétin [krétin] *m.* cretin, idiot; blockhead.

cretons [kreton] *m. pl.* © greaves, potted mince of pork [*Fr.* = rillettes].

creuser [krèzé] *v.* to hollow out; to excavate; to dig; to sink [puits]; *Br.* to plough, *Am.* to plow [sillon]; *se creuser,* to grow hollow; to rise [mer]; to grow gaunt [joues]; *se creuser la tête,* to rack one's brains.

creuset [krèzè] *m.* crucible.

creux [krè] *m.* hollow, cavity; trough [vague]; pit [estomac]; *adj.** hollow, empty; sunken; slack [période].

crevaison [krɘvèzon] *f.* puncture; bursting; **crevant** [-an] *adj.* killing; fagging.

crevasse [krɘvàs] *f.* crevice, split; chink; chap [mains].

crever [krɘvé] *v.* to split, to burst; to poke out [yeux]; to puncture [pneu]; (pop.) to die; *crever de faim,* to starve.

crevette [krɘvèt] *f.* shrimp; prawn.

cri [krì] *m.* cry; shout; shriek; *le dernier cri,* the latest fashion. ‖ **criailler** [-âyé] *v.* to bawl; to grouse. ‖ **criant** [-yan] *adj.* glaring, shocking. ‖ **criard** [-yàr] *adj.* crying; shrill [voix]; pressing [dettes]; loud, gaudy [couleurs].

crible [krìbl] *m.* sieve; screen (techn.). ‖ **cribler** [-é] *v.* to sift; to riddle; *criblé de dettes,* head over ears in debt.

cric [krìk] *m.* jack; lever.

cricket [krìkèt] *m.* cricket.

criée [krié] *f.* auction. ‖ **crier** [-é] *v.* to cry, to shout, to scream; **crieur,** bawler; hawker; *crieur public,* town-crier.

crime [krìm] *m.* crime; felony (jur.); *crime d'incendie,* arson.

criminel [krìmìnèl] *m.* criminal; *adj.* criminal; unlawful.

crin [krin] *m.* horsehair; coarse hair.

crinière [krìnyèr] *f.* mane.

crique [krìk] *f.* creek, cove.

criquet [krìkè] *m.* locust; cricket (ent.); small pony; (pop.) little shrimp.

crise [krìz] *f.* crisis; fit; attack (med.); *crise nerveuse,* nervous breakdown, *crise du papier,* paper shortage.

crispation [krìspàsyon] *f.* contraction; twitching. ‖ **crisper** [krìspé] *v.* to contract; to shrivel; *cela me crispe,* that gets on my nerves; *se crisper,* to wince; to move convulsively.

crisser [krìsé] *v.* to grate; to squeak [freins]; to rasp.

cristal [krìstàl] *m.* crystal; cut glass. ‖ **cristallin** [-in] *m.* lens [œil]; *adj.* crystalline, crystal-clear. ‖ **cristalliser** [-ìzé] *v.* to crystallize.

critère [krìtèr], **critérium** [krìtéryòm] *m.* criterium; test.

critiquable [krìtìkàbl] *adj.* criticizable. ‖ **critique** [krìtìk] *m.* critic; *f.* criticism, review; *adj.* critical; decisive; crucial. ‖ **critiquer** [-é] *v.* to criticize; to find fault with; to nag; to censure.

croassement [kròàsman] *m.* caw [corbeau]; croak. ‖ **croasser** [kròàsé] *v.* to caw; to croak.

croc [krô] *m.* hook; tooth, fang [loup]; tusk [sanglier]; *croc-en-jambe,* trip up. ‖ **croche** [kròsh] *f.* quaver (mus.); *double croche,* semi-quaver; *triple croche,* demi-semi-quaver; *adj.* © bent, twisted, curved,

crooked [prop. et fig.]. ‖ **crocher** [-é] v. to hook. ‖ **crochet** [-ɛ̀] m. hook; crochet-hook; skeleton key; square bracket (typogr.); *dentelle au crochet*, crochet-work; *faire un crochet*, to swerve. ‖ **crocheter** [-té] v. to crochet; to pick [serrure]. ‖ **crochu** [-ü] adj. hooked; crooked.

crocodile [kròkòdil] m. crocodile.

croire [krwàr] v.* to believe; to think; *croire à*, to believe in; *s'en croire*, to be conceited.

croisade [krwàzàd] f. crusade.

croisé [krwàzé] m. crusader, twill (text.); adj. crossed; folded [bras]; twilled (text.); *mots croisés*, cross-word puzzle. ‖ **croisée** [-é] f. crossing; transept [église]; casement-window. ‖ **croisement** [-maⁿ] m. crossing; intersection; cross-breed. ‖ **croiser** [-é] v. to cross; to meet; to cruise (naut.). ‖ **croiseur** [-œr] m. cruiser. ‖ **croisière** [-yèr] f. cruise. ‖ **croisillon** [-lyoⁿ] m. cross-bar; lattice.

croissance [krwàsaⁿs] f. growth; increase. ‖ **croissant** [-aⁿ] m. crescent roll; crescent; bill-hook; adj. growing; increasing.

croître [krwàtr] v.* to grow; to increase; to lengthen.

croix [krwà] f. cross; *en croix*, crosswise; *Croix-Rouge*, Red Cross.

croquer [kròké] v. to crunch; to sketch; *croquer le marmot*, to cool one's heels; *croque-mort*, undertaker's assistant.

croquet [kròkɛ̀] m. croquet.

croquis [kròkì] m. sketch, rough draft; outline.

crosne [krôn] m. Chinese artichoke.

crosse [kròs] f. crook, crozier; butt [fusil]; stick, club [golf]; lacrosse [sport].

crotte [kròt] f. dirt; mud; dung [animal]; interj. bother! ‖ **crotter** [-é] v. to dirty. ‖ **crottin** [-ìⁿ] m. horse-dung, droppings.

crouler [krûlé] v. to collapse; to totter; to crumble; *faire crouler*, to bring down.

croup [krûp] m. croup (med.).

croupe [krûp] f. croup, rump [animal]; brow [colline]; *monter en croupe*, to ride behind.

croupetons (à) [àkrûpetoⁿ] adv. squatting.

croupi [krûpì] adj. stagnant, foul.

croupier [krûpyé] m. croupier.

croupière [krûpyèr] f. crupper; *tailler des croupières à*, to make rough work for.

croupion [krûpyoⁿ] m. rump; parson's nose, *Am.* pope's nose.

croupir [krûpîr] v. to stagnate; to wallow [personnes].

croustillant [krûstìyaⁿ] adj. crisp, spicy [histoire].

croûte [krût] f. crust, rind [fromage]; scab; (pop.) daub [tableau]; old fossil; *casser la croûte*, to have a snack; *croûter*, to grub (pop.); *croûton*, bit of crust; (pop.) duffer.

croyable [krwàyàbl] adj. believable. ‖ **croyance** [krwàyaⁿs] f. belief; creed; faith. ‖ **croyant** [krwàyaⁿ] m. believer; adj. believing; *les croyants*, the faithful.

cru [krü] p. p. of **croire**.

cru [krü] adj. raw, crude, uncooked; rude, coarse; *monter à cru*, to ride bareback; *lumière crue*, hard light, glaring light.

cru [krü] m. wine region; vineyard; *grands crus*, high-class wines; *vin du cru*, local wine; *de votre cru*, of your own making.

crû [krü] p. p. of **croître**.

cruauté [krüôté] f. cruelty.

cruche [krüsh] f. pitcher, jar, jug; blockhead; *cruchon*, small jug; mug of beer; stoneware hot-water bottle; pig; dolt; duffer (fam.).

crucial [krüsyàl] adj.* crucial.

crucifier [krüsìfyé] v. to crucify. ‖ **crucifix** [krüsìfì] m. crucifix. ‖ **crucifixion** [-ksyoⁿ] f. crucifixion.

crudité [krüdìté] f. crudity, coarseness; rawness; raw vegetables.

crue [krü] f. rise, swelling; *en crue*, in flood.

cruel [krüɛ̀l] adj.* cruel, harsh, pitiless; painful.

crustacé [krüstàsé] m. crustacean, shellfish.

crypte [krìpt] f. crypt.

cryptogame [krìptògàm] m. cryptogam.

cryptogramme [krìptògràm] m. cryptogram.

cubage [kübàj] m. cubage; cubic content. ‖ **cube** [küb] m. cube; adj. cubic; *cuber*, to cube; *cubique*, cubic; *cubisme*, cubism.

cueillette [kœyèt] f. picking; harvest-time. ‖ **cueillir** [kœyîr] v.* to pick, to pluck, to gather; (fam.) to nab.

cuiller or **cuillère** [külyèr] f. spoon; *cuiller à soupe*, table-spoon; *cuiller à entremets*, dessert-spoon. ‖ **cuillerée** [külyré] f. spoonful; *cuillerée à café*, tea-spoonful.

cuir [küir] m. leather; skin, hide; (fam.) bloomer [prononciation]; *cuir à rasoir*, razor-strop; *cuir chevelu*, scalp.

cuirasse [küìràs] *f.* armo(u)r ; *plaque de cuirasse,* armo(u)r-plate. ‖ **cuirassé** [-é] *m.* battleship ; *adj.* armo(u)red. ‖ **cuirasser** [-é] *v.* to armo(u)r ; to protect ; to harden. ‖ **cuirassier** [-yé] *m.* cuirassier.

cuire [küîr] *v.** to cook ; to bake [four] ; to boil [eau] ; to burn [soleil] ; to smart ; *faire cuire,* to cook ; *il lui en cuira,* he'll be sorry for it ; **cuisant,** smarting ; bitter.

cuisine [küìzîn] *f.* kitchen ; cookery ; cooking ; galley (naut.) ; *faire la cuisine,* to do the cooking. ‖ **cuisiner** [-ìné] *v.* to cook ; to pump, to grill (pop.). ‖ **cuisinier** [-ìnyé] *m.* cook, chef. ‖ **cuisinière** [-ìnyèr] *f.* cook ; kitchen range, cooker, kitchen stove.

cuisse [küîs] *f.* thigh ; leg [poulet]. ‖ **cuisseau** [-ô] *m.** leg.

cuisson [küìsonⁿ] *f.* cooking, baking ; smarting pain.

cuissot [küìsô] *m.* haunch.

cuistre [küìstr] *m.* pedant.

cuit [küì] *adj.* cooked, baked, done ; *trop cuit,* overdone ; *cuit à point,* done to a turn. ‖ **cuite** [küìt] *f.* baking ; *prendre une cuite,* to get drunk, to have one too many.

cuivre [küîvr] *m.* copper ; *cuivre jaune,* brass ; *les cuivres,* the brass (mus.) ; **cuivré,** copper-colo(u)red ; bronzed. ‖ **cuivrer** [küìvré] *v.* to copper ; to bronze.

cul [kü] *m.* (pop.) backside ; bottom ; *cul-de-jatte,* legless cripple ; *cul-de-lampe,* pendant ; tail-piece (typogr.) ; *cul-de-sac,* blind alley ; dead end.

culasse [külàs] *f.* breech [arme à feu] ; combustion head.

culbute [külbüt] *f.* somersault ; tumble ; cropper (fig.). ‖ **culbuter** [-é] *v.* to throw over ; to topple over ; to upset ; to take a tumble. ‖ **culbuteur** [-œr] *m.* tipping device ; valve rocker ; tumbler.

culinaire [külìnèr] *adj.* culinary.

culminant [külmìnanⁿ] *adj.* culminating, highest. ‖ **culminer** [-é] *v.* to culminate.

culot [külô] *m.* base, bottom ; residue ; lastborn ; (pop.) nerve, *Br.* cheek ; *avoir du culot, Br.* to be cheeky, *Am.* to have a lot of nerve.

culotte [külòt] *f.* breeches ; trousers, *Am.* pants ; rump [bœuf] ; *culottes courtes,* shorts. ‖ **culotter** [-é] *v.* to season [pipe] ; *se culotter,* to put one's trousers on ; to season, to color [pipe].

culpabilité [külpàbìlìté] *f.* guilt.

culte [kült] *m.* worship ; form of worship ; cult ; sect.

cultivable [kültìvàbl] *adj.* arable. ‖ **cultivateur, -trice** [-àtœr, -trìs] *m., f.* farmer, cultivator. ‖ **cultivé** [-é] *adj.* cultivated ; cultured [personne]. ‖ **cultiver** [-é] *v.* to cultivate, to till ; to raise [blé].

culture [kültür] *f.* culture ; cultivation ; tillage. ‖ **culturel** [-èl] *adj.** cultural.

cumul [kümül] *m.* lumping ; cumulation , pluralism ; accumulation. ‖ **cumuler** [kümülé] *v.* to hold a plurality (of offices) ; to cumulate ; to pluralize.

cupide [küpîd] *adj.* greedy, grasping, covetous. ‖ **cupidité** [-ìté] *f.* greed, cupidity ; graspingness.

curable [küràbl] *adj.* curable. ‖ **curatif** [küràtìf] *adj.** curative.

cure [kür] *f.* rectory ; living (eccles.).

cure [kür] *f.* care ; cure ; treatment ; *cure-dents,* tooth-pick.

curé [küré] *m.* parson, parish priest, rector, vicar.

curée [küré] *f.* quarry ; rush, scramble.

curer [küré] *v.* to clean out ; to pick [dents], to dredge [rivière] ; *curetage,* cleansing ; *curette,* scraper (med.).

curieux [küryë] *adj.** interested ; inquisitive , odd, curious ; *m.* sightseer. ‖ **curiosité** [-yòzìté] *f.* curiosity ; *pl.* sights.

curseur [kürsœr] *m.* slide, runner.

cutané [kütàné] *adj.* cutaneous, of the skin.

cuticule [kütìkül] *f.* cuticle.

cuti-réaction [kütìréàksyonⁿ] *f.* skin-test.

cuve [küv] *f.* vat ; tank ; cistern ; *cuvée,* vatful. ‖ **cuver** [küvé] *v.* to ferment, to work. ‖ **cuvette** [-èt] *f.* basin ; wash-bowl ; dish ; pan [cabinet]. ‖ **cuvier** [-yé] *m.* wash-tub.

cyanure [syànür] *m.* cyanide.

cycle [sìkl] *m.* cycle ; **cyclique,** cyclic. ‖ **cyclisme** [-ìsm] *m.* cycling. ‖ **cycliste** [-ìst] *m., f.* cyclist. ‖ **cyclomoteur** [sìklòmòtœr] *m.* auto-cycle.

cyclone [sìklòn] *m.* cyclone.

cygne [sìñ] *m.* swan ; *jeune cygne,* cygnet.

cylindrage [sìlìⁿdràj] *m.* road-rolling ; mangling. ‖ **cylindre** [sìlìⁿdr] *m.* cylinder ; roller ; **cylindrique,** cylindrical.

cymaise v. **cimaise.**

cynique [sìnîk] *m.* cynic ; *adj.* cynical ; impudent ; unblushing, barefaced [mensonge] ; **cynisme,** cynicism ; shamelessness.

cyprès [sìprè] *m.* cypress.

cystite [sìstìt] *f.* cystitis.

D

d', see de.

dactylographe [dàktĭlògràf] *m.*, *f.* typist; *m.* © typewriter. ‖ *dactylographie* [-ĭ] *f.* typing, typewriting. ‖ *dactylographier* [-yé] *v.* to type.

dada [dàdà] *m.* gee-gee; hobby; fad.

dague [dàg] *f.* dagger; dirk.

daigner [dèñé] *v.* to deign, to condescend.

daim [dĭⁿ] *m.* deer; buckskin, suède [peau]. ‖ *daine* [dèn] *f.* doe.

dais [dè] *m.* canopy; dais.

dallage [dàlàj] *m.* paving; tiled floor. ‖ *dalle* [dàl] *f.* paving-stone, flagstone; floor tile. ‖ *daller* [-é] *v.* to pave.

daltonisme [dàltònĭsm] *m.* colo(u)r-blindness.

dam [dàⁿ] *m.* damnation; displeasure.

damassé [dàmàsé] *adj.* damask.

dame [dàm] *f.* (married) lady; queen [cartes, échecs]; king [dames], rowlock [rame]; *jouer aux dames*, Br. to play draughts, Am. to play checkers.

dame-jeanne [dàmjàn] *f.* demijohn.

damer [dàmé] *v.* to crown [dames]; to ram [terre]; *damer le pion à*, to outwit. ‖ *damier* [-yé] *m.* check [étoffe]; *Br.* draught-board, *Am.* checker-board.

damnation [dànàsyòⁿ] *f.* damnation. ‖ *damner* [dàné] *v.* to damn.

dandiner (se) [sᵉdàⁿdìné] *v.* to waddle; to strut.

danger [dàⁿjé] *m.* danger, peril; risk; jeopardy; *dangereux*, dangerous.

dans [dàⁿ] *prep.* in; within; during; into; from; *boire dans une tasse*, to drink out of a cup; *dans les 200 francs*, about 200 francs; *dans le temps*, formerly.

danse [dàⁿs] *f.* dance, dancing; *danse de Saint-Guy*, St. Vitus's dance. ‖ *danser* [-é] *v.* to dance; *il m'a fait danser*, he led me a dance; *danseur*, dancer; ballet-dancer; partner [danse].

dard [dàr] *m.* dart; sting; burning ray [soleil]; *darder*, to hurl; to spear.

dartre [dàrtr] *f.* herpes, scurf.

date [dàt] *f.* date; *en date de*, under date of. ‖ *dater* [-é] *v.* to date; *à dater de ce jour*, from to-day. ‖ *dateur* [-ær] *m.* date-marker.

datte [dàt] *f.* date; *dattier*, date-palm.

dauphin [dòfĭⁿ] *m.* dolphin; dauphin (hist.).

daurade [dôràd] *f.* gilt-head.

davantage [dàvaⁿtàj] *adv.* more [quantité]; longer [espace, temps].

davier [dàvyé] *m.* dental forceps; davit (naut.).

de [dᵉ] *prep.* (de becomes d' before a vowel and a mute *h*, *du* replaces *de le*, *des* replaces *de les* [of the, from the]) of; from; by; on; with; any; some; than; from; at; *de Paris à Rome*, from Paris to Rome; *il tira un couteau de sa poche*, he pulled a knife out of his pocket; *estimé de ses amis*, esteemed by his friends; *de nom*, by name; *il tombe de fatigue*, he is ready to drop with fatigue; *je bois du thé*, I drink tea; *il a du pain*, he has some bread; *d'un côté*, on one side; *plus de cinq*, more than five; *il se moque de moi*, he laughs at me; *de vingt à trente personnes*, between twenty and thirty people.

dé [dé] *m.* dice; domino; tee [golf].

dé [dé] *m.* thimble.

déambuler [déaⁿbŭlé] *v.* to stroll about, to saunter.

débâcle [débàkl] *f.* breaking up; disaster; downfall; collapse; rout.

déballage [débàlàj] *m.* unpacking. ‖ *déballer* [-é] *v.* to unpack.

débandade [débaⁿdàd] *f.* confusion; rout, stampede, flight. ‖ *débander* [-é] *v.* to disband (mil.); *se débander*, to disband; to disperse.

débander [débaⁿdé] *v.* to relax; to loosen; to unbandage.

débarbouiller [débàrbŭyé] *v.* to wash [visage]; *se débarbouiller*, to wash one's face; to clean up (fam.); *débarbouillette*, *f.* © facecloth.

débarcadère [débàrkàdèr] *m.* wharf, landing stage (naut.); arrival platform.

débardeur [débàrdær] *m.* stevedore.

débarquement [débàrkᵉmaⁿ] *m.* disembarkment, landing; unloading; detraining (mil.); arrival. ‖ *débarquer* [-é] *v.* to disembark, to land; to unload; to detrain (mil.).

débarras [débàrà] *m.* riddance; lumber-room; storeroom. ‖ *débarrasser* [-sé] *v.* to rid; to clear; *se débarrasser de*, to get rid of; to extricate oneself from.

débat [débà] *m.* dispute; discussion; debate; contest; *pl.* court hearing; proceedings.

débattre [débàtr] *v.** to discuss; *se débattre*, to struggle.

débauche [débôsh] *f.* debauch; fling (fam.). || *débauché* [-é] *m.* debauchee; rake; *adj.* debauched, dissolute. || *débaucher* [-é] *v.* to debauch; to lead astray; to discharge, to lay off; *se débaucher,* to go astray, to become dissolute.

débet [débè] *m.* debit balance, balance due.

débile [débîl] *adj.* feeble, weak, frail, puny. || *débilité* [-îté] *f.* weakness, debility; deficiency. || *débiliter* [-îté] *v.* to weaken; to debilitate (med.).

débiner [débîné] *v.* (fam.) to run down, to crab; *se débiner* (fam.) to run each other down; to hop it, *Am.* to scram.

débit [débì] *m.* sale; retail shop; output; delivery; *débit de boissons,* public-house, *Am.* tavern, café; *débit de tabac,* tobacconist's shop.

débit [débì] *m.* debit; *portez à mon débit,* debit me with.

débitant [débìtaⁿ] *m.* dealer, retailer; *débitant de boissons,* publican, *Am.* bartender; *débitant de tabac,* tobacconist. || *débiter* [-é] *v.* to retail, to sell (com.); to debit (fin.); to cut up [bois]; to give out, to discharge; to recite; to utter. || *débiteur* [-œr] *m.* debtor; *compte débiteur,* debit account.

déblaiement [déblèmaⁿ] *m.* clearing; digging out, excavating. || *déblayer* [-èyé] *v.* to remove, to clear away.

déblatérer [déblàtéré] *v.* to utter; to bluster out; to rail (*contre,* against).

débloquer [déblòké] *v.* to free, to release; to relieve; to unlock; to take off; to go astray (fam.).

déboire [débwàr] *m.* disappointment; let-down; nasty taste.

déboiser [débwàzé] *v.* to deforest; to clear of trees.

déboîter [débwàté] *v.* to dislocate, to put out of joint; to disconnect.

débonnaire [débònèr] *adj.* debonair; good natured, easy-going.

débordant [débòrdaⁿ] *adj.* protruding; outflanking (mil.); overflowing; exuberant; bursting (*de,* with). || *débordé* [débòrdé] *adj.* overflowing [rivière]; overwhelmed [travail]. || *débordement* [-⁰maⁿ] *m.* overflowing, flood; dissipation; invasion; outflanking (mil.). || *déborder* [-é] *v.* to overflow; to run over; to jut out; to sheer off (naut.); to outflank (mil.); to trim (techn.).

débouché [débûshé] *m.* outlet; way out; opening; market (comm.); expedient. || *déboucher* [-é] *v.* to open; to uncork; to clear; to lead (*dans,* into); to emerge; to debouch (mil.).

déboulonner [débûlòné] *v.* to un-rivet, to unbolt; to debunk (pop.).

débourrer [débûré] *v.* to remove the stuffing from; to extract the wad from [fusil]; to clean out [pipe].

débours [débûr] *m.* outlay, expenses. || *débourser* [-sé] *v.* to lay out, to disburse, to spend.

debout [d⁰bû] *adv.* upright; standing (up); on its hind legs [animal]; out of bed; *interj.* up you get!, *se tenir debout,* to stand.

débouter [débûté] *v.* to nonsuit; to dismiss (jur.); to reject.

déboutonner [débûtòné] *v.* to un-button.

débraillé [débràyé] *adj.* untidy; scarcely decent; loose.

débrancher [débraⁿshé] *v.* to disconnect [électr.].

débrayage [débrèyàj] *m.* disengaging, declutching; uncoupling; clutch pedal. || *débrayer* [-èyé] *v.* to disengage, to declutch, to let out the clutch.

débrider [débrìdé] *v.* to unbridle [cheval]; to stop.

débris [débrì] *m.* debris, remains, wreckage; *pl.* waste products; rubbish; rubble.

débrouillard [débrûyàr] *m.* (fam.) resourceful person, *Am.* go-getter; *adj.* (fam.) resourceful, all there. || *débrouiller* [-ûyé] *v.* to disentangle; to clear up; to sort out; *se débrouiller,* to manage; to see it through.

début [débü] *m.* beginning, start, outset; first move [jeux]; *faire ses débuts,* to make one's first appearance; *débutant(e),* beginner; novice; debutante. || *débuter* [-té] *v.* to begin; to have first move [jeux]; to make one's first appearance.

deçà [d⁰sà] *adv.* on this side; *en deçà de,* on this side of.

décacheter [dékàshté] *v.* to unseal, to open.

décade [dékàd] *f.* decade; period of ten days.

décadence [dékàdaⁿs] *f.* decadence, decline, decay. || *décadent* [-aⁿ] *adj.* decadent, declining.

décaféiné [dékàféìné] *adj.* decaffeinated, caffeine-free.

décalcifier [dékàlsìfyé] *v.* to decalcify; *se décalcifier,* to become decalcified.

décaler [dékàlé] *v.* to unwedge; to shift, to alter; to readjust.

décalitre [dékàlìtr] *m.* decalitre.

décalquer [dékàlké] *v.* to transfer; to trace off; *papier à décalquer,* tracing-paper.

décamper [dékaⁿpé] *v.* to decamp; to move off; to clear out; to make off, to bolt.

décapant [dékàpaⁿ] *m.* pickle; paint (or) varnish (or) polish remover; scouring solution. || *décaper* [dékàpé] *v.* to scour; to scrape; to cleanse.

décapiter [dékàpìté] *v.* to decapitate, to behead.

décapsuler [dékàpsülé] *v.* to remove the crown cork of.

décatir [dékàtìr] *v.* to sponge; to take the gloss off (text.); *se décatir,* to become worn.

décédé [désédé] *m., adj.* deceased, departed, defunct. || *décéder* [-é] *v.* to die, to decease (jur.).

déceler [déslé] *v.* to disclose; to betray; to reveal.

décembre [désaⁿbr] *m.* December.

décemment [désàmaⁿ] *adv.* decently. || *décence* [désaⁿs] *f.* decency, decorum; *décent,* decent, becoming, proper; *peu décent,* unseemly.

décentraliser [désaⁿtràlìzé] *v.* to decentralize.

déception [désèpsyoⁿ] *f.* deception; disappointment.

décerner [désèrné] *v.* to award; to confer; to bestow; to issue [mandat d'arrêt].

décès [désè] *m.* decease (jur.).

décevant [désvaⁿ] *adj.* deceptive; misleading; disappointing. || *décevoir* [-wàr] *v.** to deceive; to disappoint.

déchaînement [déshènmaⁿ] *m.* unbridling, letting loose; outburst; fury. || *déchaîner* [-é] *v.* to let loose; *se déchaîner,* to rage; to break loose; to break [orage].

déchanter [déshaⁿté] *v.* to alter one's tone; to sing small, to come down a peg (pop.).

décharge [déshàrj] *f.* unloading; discharge release, acquittal (jur.); outlet; relief; volley (mil.); lumber-room. || *décharger* [-é] *v.* to unload, to unlade; to discharge; to relieve; to vent; to acquit; to dismiss; *se décharger,* to discharge; to go off, to fire [fusil]; to give vent to; *déchargeur,* docker; stevedore; coal-heaver; lightning conductor.

décharné [déshàrné] *adj.* lean, emaciated, skinny, fleshless; gaunt.

déchaussé [déshôsé] *adj.* barefooted; bare; gumless [dents]; *se déchausser,* to take off one's shoes.

dèche [dèsh] *f.* (pop.). straits.

déchéance [déshéaⁿs] *f.* downfall; decay [morale]; forfeiture; deprivation of civil rights; expiration.

déchet [déshè] *m.* loss; decrease; waste, scrap; refuse; offal [viande].

déchiffrer [déshìfré] *v.* to decipher; to decode [messages]; to read at sight (theat.), to sight-read (mus.).

déchiqueter [déshìkté] *v.* to hack, to slash, to tear up, to tear to shreds, to mangle.

déchirant [déshìraⁿ] *adj.* heart-rending. || *déchirement* [-maⁿ] *m.* tearing, rending; laceration; pang. || *déchirer* [-é] *v.* to rend, to tear (up); to defame. || *déchirure* [-ür] *f.* tear, rent; laceration.

déchoir [déshwàr] *v.** to fall off, to decay, to decline; *déchu* [-ü] *adj.* fallen; expired [police]; disqualified.

décidé [désìdé] *adj.* decided, determined; resolute. || *décider* [-é] *v.* to decide, to settle; to rule (jur.); to persuade; *se décider,* to make up one's mind, to resolve.

décigramme [désìgràm] *m.* decigram.

décilitre [désìlìtr] *m.* decilitre.

décimal [désìmàl] *adj.** decimal.

décimer [désìmé] *v.* to decimate; to deplete.

décimètre [désìmètr] *m.* decimeter.

décisif [désìzìf] *adj.** decisive; conclusive. || *décision* [-yoⁿ] *f.* decision; ruling (jur.); resolution.

déclamation [déklàmàsyoⁿ] *f.* declamation; ranting. || *déclamatoire* [-àtwàr] *adj.* declamatory; ranting. || *déclamer* [-é] *v.* to declaim; to rant.

déclaration [déklàràsyoⁿ] *f.* declaration, announcement, proclamation. || *déclarer* [-é] *v.* to declare; to proclaim, to make known; to certify; to notify; *se déclarer,* to declare oneself; to break out [feu].

déclassé [déklàsé] *m.* social outcast; *adj.* obsolete; come down in the world. || *déclasser* [-é] *v.* to bring down in the world; to declare obsolete.

déclencher [déklaⁿshé] *v.* to unlatch; to disengage (mech.); to set in motion; to launch [attaque].

déclic [déklìk] *m.* catch; pawl; trigger; *pl.* nippers.

déclin [déklìⁿ] *m.* decline, decay, wane [lune]; ebb [marée]. || *déclinaison* [-nèzoⁿ] *f.* declination, variation [boussole]; declension (gramm.). || *décliner* [-ìné] *v.* to decline; to refuse; to state [nom]; to wane; to deviate [boussole].

déclouer [déklûé] *v.* to unnail.

décocher [dékòshé] *v.* to shoot, to let fly; to discharge.

décoiffer [dékwàfé] *v.* to remove someone's hat; to take someone's hair down; to disarrange.

décollage [dékòlàǯ] *m.* unsticking; ungluing; taking-off (aviat.). ‖ **décoller** [-é] *v.* to unstick; to disengage; to loosen; to take off (aviat.); **se décoller,** to come off.

décolleté [dékòlté] *adj.* wearing a low dress; low-necked [robe].

décoloration [dékòlòràsyoⁿ] *f.* discolo(u)ration, bleaching, fading. ‖ **décolorer** [-é] *v.* to discolo(u)r; to fade; to bleach; **se décolorer,** to fade; to lose one's colo(u)r.

décombres [dékoⁿbr] *m. pl.* rubbish; debris, rubble.

décommander [dékòmoⁿdé] *v.* to cancel; to countermand.

décomposer [dékoⁿpòzé] *v.* to decompose; to decay; to distort [traits]; **se décomposer,** to decompose, to rot; to become distorted. ‖ **décomposition** [-ìsyoⁿ] *f.* decomposition; rotting, decay; distortion [traits].

décompte [dékoⁿt] *m.* deduction; balance due. ‖ **décompter** [-é] *v.* to deduct; to be disappointed.

déconcerter [dékoⁿsèrté] *v.* to disconcert; to upset; to put out.

déconfit [dékoⁿfì] *adj.* discomfited; crest-fallen. ‖ **déconfiture** [-tür] *f.* ruin; insolvency.

déconnecter [dékònèkté] *v.* to disconnect; to switch off.

déconseiller [dékoⁿsèyé] *v.* to advise against, to dissuade.

déconsidérer [dékoⁿsìdéré] *v.* to discredit; **se déconsidérer,** to belittle oneself.

décontenancer [dékoⁿtnaⁿsé] *v.* to put out of countenance, to abash, to mortify; **se décontenancer,** to lose countenance.

décontracter [dékoⁿtràkté] *v.* to relax.

déconvenue [dékoⁿvnü] *f.* disappointment; trying mishap; discomfiture; failure.

décor [dékòr] *m.* decoration; set (theat.); *pl.* scenery. ‖ **décorateur** [-àtœr] *m.* decorator; stage-designer. ‖ **décoratif** [-àtìf] *adj.* decorative, ornamental. ‖ **décoration** [-àsyoⁿ] *f.* decoration; insignia; medal. ‖ **décorer** [-é] *v.* to decorate; to ornament.

décortiquer [dékòrtìké] *v.* to husk [riz]; to shell [noix].

décorum [dékòròm] *m.* decorum, propriety.

découcher [dékûshé] *v.* to sleep out; to stay out all night.

découler [dékûlé] *v.* to trickle; to flow; to be derived, to follow (de, from).

découper [dékûpé] *v.* to carve; to cut out; to cut up; to stamp out [métal]; **se découper,** to stand out (sur, against).

découplé [dékûplé] *adj.* strapping, well built. ‖ **découpler** [-é] *v.* to uncouple; to unleash.

découragement [dékûràǯmaⁿ] *m.* discouragement, despondency. ‖ **décourager** [-é] *v.* to discourage, to dishearten; **se décourager,** to lose heart.

décousu [dékûzü] *adj.* unstitched; unconnected, disjointed; loose; desultory [tir].

découvert [dékûvèr] *m.* overdraft; uncovered balance; open ground (mil.); *adj.* uncovered; open; exposed, bare; overdrawn [compte]; *à découvert,* in the open. ‖ **découverte** [-èrt] *f.* discovery; detection; *aller à la découverte,* to explore, to reconnoitre (mil.). ‖ **découvrir** [-rîr] *v.* to uncover; to expose, to lay bare; to find out, to detect; to discover.

décrasser [dékràsé] *v.* to clean, to scour; to scrape; to decarbonize [moteur].

décrépit [dékrépì] *adj.* decrepit, worn out; broken-down; delapidated. ‖ **décrépitude** [-tüd] *f.* decrepitude.

décret [dékrè] *m.* decree, order; *décret-loi, Br.* order in council, *Am.* executive order. ‖ **décréter** [dékrété] *v.* to decree, to enact; to issue a writ against (jur.).

décrier [dékrìé] *v.* to decry, to disparage; to discredit; to run down.

décrire [dékrîr] *v.°* to describe; to depict.

décrocher [dékròshé] *v.* to unhook; to unsling; to take down; to take off; to disconnect; to disengage (mil.); *décrochez-moi-ça,* reach-me-down, ready-made suit; old clothes shop.

décroître [dékrwâtr] *v.°* to decrease, to diminish; to shorten; to subside; to wane [lune].

décrotter [dékròté] *v.* to clean, to brush up; to scrape; *décrotteur,* shoe-black; *décrottoir,* door-scraper.

décrue [dékrü] *f.* fall, subsidence; decrease.

déçu [désü] *p. p. of* decevoir.

déculotter [dékülòté] *v.* to unbreech; **se déculotter,** to take off one's breeches.

décupler [dékûplé] *v.* to decuple; **se décupler,** to increase tenfold.

dédaigner [dédèñé] *v.* to scorn; to disregard, to slight; to disdain. ‖ **dédaigneux** [-ё] *adj.°* scornful, disdainful, contemptuous. ‖ **dédain** [dédìⁿ] *m.* scorn, disdain, contempt.

dédale [dédàl] *m.* maze, labyrinth; intricacy (fig.).

dedans [dᵉdaⁿ] *m.* inside, interior; *adv.* in, inside, within; *au-dedans de*, within; *en dedans*, inside; *mettre quelqu'un dedans*, to take someone in.

dédicace [dédìkàs] *f.* dedication. ‖ **dédicacer** [-é] *v.* to dedicate.

dédier [dédyé] *v.* to dedicate; to inscribe [livre]; to devote.

dédire [dédìr] *v.* to disown; to retract; to refute; *se dédire*, to retract, to take back. ‖ **dédit** [dédì] *m.* renunciation; retractation; withdrawal; breaking [promesse]; forfeit; penalty.

dédommagement [dédòmàĵmaⁿ] *m.* indemnity; compensation, damages. ‖ **dédommager** [-é] *v.* to indemnify, to compensate.

dédouaner [dédwàné] *v.* to clear through the Customs.

dédoublement [dédûblᵉmaⁿ] *m.* dividing into two; duplication; *dédoublement de la personnalité*, dual personality. ‖ **dédoubler** [dédûblé] *v.* to divide into two; to unline [habit]; to undouble [étoffe]; to form single file (mil.).

déduction [déduksyoⁿ] *f.* deduction; inference. ‖ **déduire** [dédüīr] *v.** to deduce, to infer; to deduct.

défaillance [défàyaⁿs] *f.* fainting, swoon; shortcoming; lapse; failure. ‖ **défaillir** [-àỹîr] *v.** to faint; to fail; to become feeble; to default (jur.).

défaire [défèr] *v.** to undo; to defeat; to pull down; to unpack; *se défaire*, to come undone, to come apart; to get rid; to take one's coat off. ‖ **défait** [défè] *adj.* undone; defeated; drawn [visage]; wan; wasted [traits]. ‖ **défaite** [défèt] *f.* defeat; evasion, shift, poor excuse; disposal (comm.).

défalquer [défàlké] *v.* to deduct; to write off [dette].

défaut [défô] *m.* defect; blemish; default; lack; absence; shortcoming; flaw (techn.); *sans défaut*, faultless; *à défaut de*, for want of; in place of; *mettre en défaut*, to baffle; *vous nous avez fait défaut*, we have missed you; *prendre en défaut*, to catch napping.

défavorable [défàvòràbl] *adj.* unfavo(u)rable; disadvantageous. ‖ **défavoriser** [défàvòrìzé] *v.* to disadvantage.

défectif [défèktîf] *adj.** defective, faulty. ‖ **défection** [-èksyoⁿ] *f.* defection; *faire défection*, to desert. ‖ **défectueux** [-èktüë] *adj.** faulty, defective. ‖ **défectuosité** [-èktüòzìté] *f.* defect, flaw.

défendable [défaⁿdàbl] *adj.* defensible; tenable. ‖ **défendeur, -eresse** [-èr, -ᵉrès] *m.*, *f.* defendant. ‖ **défendre** [défaⁿdr] *v.* to defend, to protect; to uphold; to forbid, to prohibit; *à son corps défendant*, reluctantly; in self-defense; *il ne put se défendre de rire*, he couldn't help laughing.

défense [défaⁿs] *f.* Br. defence, Am. defense; protection; justification; prohibition; plea (jur.); counsel; tusk [éléphant]; fender (naut.); *défense de fumer*, no smoking; *faire défense*, to forbid; *légitime défense*, self-defense; *défense passive*, air-raid precautions. ‖ **défenseur** [-œr] *m.* defender; supporter; counsel for defense. ‖ **défensif** [-ìf] *adj.** defensive.

déférence [déféraⁿs] *f.* deference, regard, respect, esteem. ‖ **déférer** [-é] *v.* to award; to submit (jur.); to impeach; to comply (*à*, with); to refer (jur.).

déferler [défèrlé] *v.* to unfurl; to break [vagues].

défi [défì] *m.* challenge; *lancer un défi à*, to challenge. ‖ **défiance** [-yaⁿs] *f.* mistrust, suspicion; diffidence. ‖ **défiant** [-yaⁿ] *adj.* distrustful, wary, cautious.

déficience [défìsyaⁿs] *f.* deficiency. ‖ **déficient** [-yaⁿ] *adj.*, *m.* deficient.

déficit [défìsìt] *m.* deficit, shortage; deficiency.

défier [défyé] *v.* to challenge; to dare; to brave; to defy; *se défier*, to beware; to distrust.

défigurer [défìgüré] *v.* to disfigure; to distort [vérité]; to deface; to mar.

défilé [défìlé] *m.* defile, pass; gorge; march past, parade. ‖ **défiler** [-é] *v.* to file off; to march past.

défini [défìnì] *adj.* definite; defined; fixed; *passé défini*, past historic, preterite (gramm.). ‖ **définir** [-îr] *v.* to define; *se définir*, to become clear. ‖ **définissable** [-ìsàbl] *adj.* definable. ‖ **définitif** [-ìtìf] *adj.** definitive; final; standard [œuvre]; *à titre définitif*, permanently. ‖ **définition** [-ìsyoⁿ] *f.* definition.

déflagration [déflàgràsyoⁿ] *f.* deflagration.

déflation [déflàsyoⁿ] *f.* deflation; devaluation.

déflorer [déflòré] *v.* to deflower; to stale, to spoil.

défoncer [défoⁿsé] *v.* to stave in; to break up [terre, routes]; *se défoncer*, to break up; to give way.

déformation [défòrmàsyoⁿ] *f.* deformation; distorsion. ‖ **déformer** [-é] *v.* to deform, to put out of shape; to distort [faits]; to buckle; *se déformer*, to get out of shape; to warp [bois].

défraîchi [défrèshì]* *adj.* Br. shop-soiled, Am. shop-worn.

défrayer [défrèyé] *v.* to defray; to entertain.

défricher [défrìshé] *v.* to clear, to reclaim [terrain]; to break up.

défroque [défròk] *f.* cast-off clothing. ‖ **défroqué** [-é] *adj.* unfrocked.

défunt [défuⁿ] *adj.* defunct, late, deceased.

dégagé [dégàjé] *adj.* unconstrained; free and easy; off-hand [manière]. ‖ **dégagement** [-maⁿ] *m.* release; escape; relief; disengagement; redemption [prêt sur gages]. ‖ **dégager** [-é] *v.* to redeem [prêt sur gages]; to disengage; to rescue; to release; to make out [signification]; to emit; *se dégager*, to get out of, to escape, to be emitted; to be revealed [vérité].

dégarnir [dégàrnîr] *v.* to strip; to dismantle; to unrig [voilier]; to unfurnish; *se dégarnir*, to part with; to be stripped.

dégât [dégâ] *m.* damage; devastation, havoc.

dégel [déjèl] *m.* thaw. ‖ **dégeler** [déjlé] *v.* to thaw.

dégénérer [déjénéré] *v.* to degenerate, to decline; *dégénérescence*, degeneration (med.).

dégingandé [déjingàndé] *adj.* ungainly, gawky, loosely built.

déglinguer [dégli[n]gé] *v.* (fam.) to dislocate.

déglutition [déglütìsyoⁿ] *f.* swallowing, deglutition.

dégoiser [dégwàzé] *v.* (fam.) to rattle off (or) on.

dégonfler [dégoⁿflé] *v.* to deflate; to debunk; *Br.* to climb down (fam.); *se dégonfler*, to subside, to collapse; to funk it (fam.).

dégorger [dégòrjé] *v.* to disgorge; to unstop; to flow out; to overflow.

dégoter [dégòté] *v.* (pop.) to pick up, to ferret out.

dégourdir [dégûrdîr] *v.* to take the chill off [eau]; to revive; to stretch [jambes]; to smarten up; *se dégourdir*, to feel warmer; to stretch; to become more alert; *dégourdi*, lively, sharp, smart.

dégoût [dégû] *m.* disgust, aversion; dislike. ‖ **dégoûtant** [-aⁿ] *adj.* disgusting, loathsome, nauseating, revolting. ‖ **dégoûté** [-té] *adj.* disgusted; fastidious, squeamish. ‖ **dégoûter** [-té] *v.* to disgust, to repel, to nauseate, to sicken; *se dégoûter*, to take a dislike (*de*, to).

dégoutter [dégûté] *v.* to drip, to trickle.

dégradation [dégràdàsyoⁿ] *f.* degradation, reduction to the ranks (mil.);

gradation, shading off [couleurs]; damage. ‖ **dégrader** [-é] *v.* to degrade; to demote, to reduce to the ranks (mil.); to damage, to deface; to shade off; to tone down [couleurs]; *se dégrader*, to debase oneself.

dégrafer [dégràfé] *v.* to unhook; to unfasten.

dégraissage [dégrèsàj] *m.* cleaning; skimming. ‖ **dégraisser** [-é] *v.* to clean; to scour; to skim; to impoverish [terre].

degré [dəgré] *m.* degree; stage; step; *à ce degré de*, to this pitch of.

dégrever [dégrəvé] *v.* to reduce, to relieve [impôts]; to free.

dégriser [dégrìzé] *v.* to sober down, to cool down.

dégrossir [dégrôsîr] *v.* to rough out; to lick into shape (fam.).

déguenillé [dégənìyé] *adj.* tattered, ragged, in rags.

déguerpir [dégèrpîr] *v.* (pop.) to clear out; *Am.* to beat it.

déguisement [dégìzmaⁿ] *m.* disguise; *sans déguisement*, openly. ‖ **déguiser** [dégìzé] *v.* to disguise; to conceal.

déguster [dégüsté] *v.* to taste; to sample; to sip; to relish.

dehors [dəòr] *m.* outside; exterior; appearances; *adv.* outside; abroad; in the offing, spread [voiles]; *en dehors du sujet*, beside the point; *mettre dehors*, to turn out; to oust; to sack, to lay off.

déjà [déjà] *adv.* already, before.

déjection [déjèksyoⁿ] *f.* evacuation; dejection (med.).

déjeter [déjté] *v.* to warp [bois]; to buckle [métal]; *se déjeter*, to warp, to buckle.

déjeuner [déjœné] *m.* breakfast; lunch; *v.* to breakfast; to lunch; *petit déjeuner*, breakfast.

déjouer [déjûé] *v.* to baffle; to foil, to outwit, to thwart, to upset.

delà [dəlà] *adv.*, *prep.*, beyond; *au-delà de*, beyond, above; *par-delà les mers*, beyond the seas; *l'au-delà*, the next world.

délabré [délàbré] *adj.* ruined; dilapidated; ramshackle, tumbledown; shattered [santé].

délacer [délàsé] *v.* to unlace; to undo [souliers]; *se délacer*, to come undone.

délai [délè] *m.* delay; respite; reprieve (jur.); *à court délai*, at short notice; *dernier délai*, deadline.

délaisser [délèsé] *v.* to forsake, to desert, to abandon; to relinquish (jur.).

délassant [délàsaⁿ] *adj.* relaxing; recreating. ‖ **délassement** [délàsmaⁿ] *m.* relaxation. ‖ **délasser** [-é] *v.* to relax, to rest; *se délasser,* to relax; to take a rest.

délation [délàsyoⁿ] *f.* informing, denunciation, squealing (pop.).

délavé [délàvé] *adj.* washed out; wishy-washy.

délayer [délèyé] *v.* to dilute; to spin out [discours].

délectable [délèktàbl] *adj.* delectable, delicious, delightful. ‖ *délectation* [-àsyoⁿ] *f.* delight, enjoyment. ‖ *délecter* [-é] *v.* to delight; *se délecter,* to take delight (à, in), to relish; to revel.

délégation [délégàsyoⁿ] *f.* delegation; assignment; allotment. ‖ *délégué* [-égé] *m.,* *adj.* delegate; deputy. ‖ *déléguer* [-égé] *v.* to delegate; to assign.

délester [délèsté] *v.* to unballast [bateau]; to unload; to relieve (fig.).

délibération [délìbéràsyoⁿ] *f.* deliberation; discussion; decision. ‖ *délibéré* [-é] *adj.* deliberate; resolute; *m.* consultation (jur.). ‖ *délibérer* [-é] *v.* to deliberate; to resolve.

délicat [délìkà] *adj.* delicate; dainty; nice, tricky [question]; fastidious [mangeur]; fragile; embarrassing; sensitive; awkward [situation]; *procédés peu délicats,* unscrupulous behavio(u)r; *faire le délicat,* to be finicky. ‖ *délicatesse* [-tès] *f.* delicacy; fragility; fastidiousness; *pl.* niceties.

délice [délìs] *m.* (*f.* in *pl.*) delight, pleasure; *faire ses délices de,* to be the delight of. ‖ *délicieux* [-yë] *adj.** delicious, delightful, charming; lovely.

délictueux [délìktüé] *adj.** unlawful, punishable; *acte délictueux,* *Br.* offense, *Am.* offense, misdemeano(u)r.

délié [délìé] *adj.* slim, thin; glib [langue]; nimble [esprit]. ‖ *délier* [délìé] *v.* to untie, to undo; to release; *sans bourse délier,* without spending a penny.

délimitation [délìmìtàsyoⁿ] *f.* delimitation; demarcation. ‖ *délimiter* [-é] *v.* to fix the boundaries of; to define [pouvoirs].

délinquant [délìⁿkaⁿ] *m.* delinquent, offender.

délirant [délìraⁿ] *adj.* frantic, frenzied; rapturous; delirious. ‖ *délire* [délîr] *f.* delirium; frenzy, ecstasy; *avoir le délire,* to be delirious, to rave, to wander. ‖ *délirer* [-ìré] *v.* to be delirious; to rave.

délit [délì] *m.* misdemeano(u)r; offence; *en flagrant délit,* in the very act, red-handed.

délivrance [délìvraⁿs] *f.* delivery; rescue; childbirth; issue [billets]. ‖ *délivrer* [-é] *v.* to deliver; to rescue; to issue [billets].

déloger [délòjé] *v.* to dislodge; to remove; to go away; to drive away, to turn out; to oust.

déloyal [délwàyàl] *adj.** disloyal; false; dishonest; treacherous; unfair; foul [jeu]. ‖ *déloyauté* [délwàyôté] *f.* disloyalty, treachery.

déluge [délüj] *m.* deluge, flood.

déluré [délüré] *adj.* smart, wide-awake, knowing, sharp, no fool.

démagogue [démàgòg] *m.* demagogue.

démailler [démàyé] *v.* to unpick; *se démailler,* to run, *Br.* to ladder [bas].

demain [d^emìⁿ] *m., adv.* to-morrow; *demain matin,* to-morrow morning; *demain en huit,* to-morrow week; *à demain,* good-bye till to-morrow; *après-demain,* the day after to-morrow.

démancher [démaⁿshé] *v.* to unhaft [outil]; to put out of joint; to shift [violon].

demande [d^emaⁿd] *f.* request; question; inquiry; demand (comm.); claim; *sur demande,* on application. ‖ *demander* [-é] *v.* to ask; to ask for; to beg, to request; to wish, to want; to apply for; to order; *demander à quelqu'un,* to ask someone; *demander quelqu'un,* to ask for someone; *on est venu vous demander,* someone called for you; *se demander,* to wonder. ‖ *demandeur, -eresse* [-œr, -ᵉrès] *m., f.* plaintiff (jur.).

démangeaison [démaⁿjèzoⁿ] *f.* itching. ‖ *démanger* [-é] *v.* to itch.

démanteler [démaⁿtlé] *v.* to dismantle.

démaquillage [démàkìyàj] *m.* cleansing. ‖ *se démaquiller* [s^edémàkìyé] *v.* to take off one's make-up.

démarcation [démàrkàsyoⁿ] *f.* demarcation, boundary.

démarche [démàrsh] *f.* step; walk; gait; conduct; *faire des démarches pour,* to take steps to. ‖ *démarcheur* [-œr] *m.* canvasser, *Am.* solicitor.

démarquer [démàrké] *v.* to mark down [prix]; to remove the marks from.

démarrer [démàré] *v.* to cast off [bateau]; to start [voiture]; to slip moorings. ‖ *démarreur* [-œr] *m.* self-starter; crank.

démasquer [démàské] *v.* to unmask, to expose; to divulge.

démêlé [démélé] *m.* dispute; contest. ‖ *démêler* [-é] *v.* to unravel; to make out; to extricate; to contend.

démembrer [démaⁿbré] *v.* to dismember.

déménagement [déménàjmaⁿ] *m.* removal moving *voiture de déménagement* furniture van. ‖ **déménager** [-é] *v.* to remove to move out . (fam.) to be out of one's mind. ‖ **déménageur** [-œr] *m* furniture remover.

démence [démaⁿs] *f.* insanity, lunacy, folly, madness.

dément [démaⁿ] *m.*, *adj.* insane.

démenti [démaⁿtì] *m.* denial, contradiction. ‖ **démentir** [-îr] *v.* to give the lie to. to contradict ; to refute ; to belie ; *se démentir*, to contradict oneself ; to fail

démériter [démérité] *v.* to be blameworthy to forfeit the esteem (*de*, of).

démesure [dém°zür] *f.* excessiveness ; disproportion. ‖ **démesuré** [dém°züré] *adj.* inordinate, huge, beyond measure ; out of all proportion , excessive.

démettre [démètr] *v.°* to dislocate, to put out of joint ; to dismiss ; *se démettre*, to resign ; to give up.

demeure [d°mœr] *f.* dwelling, residence ; delay ; *à demeure*, fixed ; *mettre en demeure de*, to order to. ‖ **demeuré** [-é] *adj.*, *m.* mentally deficient ‖ **demeurer** [-é] *v.* to live, to reside ; to dwell ; to stay, to remain ; *au demeurant*, after all, on the whole.

demi [d°mì] *m.*, *adj.* half ; *à demi*, by halves ; *une demi-heure*, half an hour ; *une heure et demie*, one hour and a half ; *il est une heure et demie*, it is half past one ; *demi-cercle*, semicircle ; *demi-teinte*, half-tint, halftone, mezzotint ; *demi-ton*, semitone ; *demi-tour*, half-turn; about turn (mil.).

démission [démìsyoⁿ] *f.* resignation. ‖ **démissionner** [-yòné] *v.* to resign.

démobilisation [démòbìlìzàsyoⁿ] *f.* demobilization. ‖ **démobiliser** [-é] *v.* to demobilize.

démocrate [démòkràt] *m.*, *f.* democrat. ‖ **démocratie** [-àsì] *f.* democracy.

démodé [démòdé] *adj.* old-fashioned, out of date, antiquated.

demoiselle [d°mwàzèl] *f.* young lady ; spinster , rowlock (naut.) ; dragon-fly (ent.) ; *demoiselle d'honneur*, bridesmaid.

démolir [démòlîr] *v.* to demolish, to pull down ; to overthrow ; to ruin, to wreck. ‖ **démolition** [-ìsyoⁿ] *f.* demolition, pulling down ; *pl.* rubbish.

démon [démoⁿ] *m.* demon, devil ; fiend ; imp.

démonétiser [démònétìzé] *v.* to demonetize ; to withdraw.

démonstrateur [démoⁿstràtœr] *m.* demonstrator. ‖ **démonstratif** [-àtìf] *adj.°* demonstrative. ‖ **démonstration** [-àsyoⁿ] *f.* demonstration ; show of force (mil.) ; proof (math.).

démontable [démoⁿtàbl] *adj.* detachable , collapsible. ‖ **démonter** [-é] *v.* to unseat to dismantle , to take to pieces to upset (fig.), *se démonter*, to get out of order, to run down [montre] ; to be disconcerted ; *démonte-pneu*, Br tyre-lever, *Am.* tire-iron.

démontrer [démoⁿtré] *v.* to demonstrate to show

démoraliser [démòràlìzé] *v.* to demoralize to dishearten

démordre [démòrdr] *v.* to let go ; to give in to desist

démunir (se) [s°démünîr] *v.* to part with , to deprive oneself of.

dénaturé [dénàtüré] *adj.* unnatural ; cruel , perverted, depraved ; *alcool dénaturé* , methylated spirit. ‖ **dénaturer** [-é] *v.* to distort ; to misrepresent ; to pervert

dénégation [dénégàsyoⁿ] *f.* denial.

déni [dénì] *m* denial ; refusal.

déniaiser [dényèzé] *v.* to wise up.

dénicher [dénìshé] *v.* to take from the nest , to find, to unearth.

denier [d°nyé] *m.* small coin, penny ; cent ; money ; *les deniers publics*, public funds.

dénigrer [dénìgré] *v.* to disparage, to run down.

dénivellation [dénìvèllàsyoⁿ] *f.* unevenness , gradients ; subsidence.

dénombrer [dénoⁿbré] *v.* to take a census of , to count, to enumerate.

dénomination [dénòmìnàsyoⁿ] *f.* name , denomination. ‖ **dénommer** [dénòmé] *v* to name, to denominate

dénoncer [dénoⁿsé] *v.* to denounce ; to betray ; to expose. ‖ **dénonciateur**, *-trice* [dénoⁿsyàtœr, -trìs] *m.*, *f.* informer, *Am* stool-pigeon (pop.). ‖ **dénonciation** [-yàsyoⁿ] *f* denunciation ; notice of termination [traité].

dénoter [dénòté] *v.* to denote, to show, to mark.

dénouement [dénûmaⁿ] *m.* untying ; result , solution. dénouement (theat.) ‖ **dénouer** [dénûé] *v.* to untie, to unravel ; *se dénouer*, to come undone ; to be solved , to end.

dénoyauter [dénwàyòté] *v.* to stone, *Am.* to pit.

denrée [daⁿré] *f.* commodity ; produce , *denrées alimentaires*, foodstuffs.

dense [daⁿs] *adj.* dense ; thick. ‖ **densité** [-ìté] *f.* denseness, density ; compactness ; fullness, substance.

dent [daⁿ] *f.* tooth ; prong [fourchette], cog [roue] ; *mal aux dents*, toothache ; *sans dents*, toothless ; *serrer les dents*, to set one's teeth ; *avoir une dent contre*, to have a grudge against; *sur les dents,* fagged, worn out. ‖ *dentaire* [-tèr], *dental* [-tàl] *adj.* dental. ‖ *denté* [-é] *adj.* toothed; *roue dentée.* cogwheel.

denteler [dãⁿtlé] *v.* to indent; to notch; to cog [roue]; to serrate.

dentelle [dãⁿtèl] *f.* lace; lace-work. ‖ *dentelure* [dãⁿtlür] *f.* perforation [timbre]; indentation; dogtooth (techn.).

dentier [dãⁿtyé] *m.* denture, set of false teeth, plate. ‖ *dentifrice* [-lfrìs] *m.* dentifrice, tooth-paste , *adj.* dental. *dentiste* [-lst] *m.,f.* dentist. ‖ *dentition* [-ìsyoⁿ] *f.* teething; set of teeth. ‖ *denture* [-ür] *f.* set of teeth; teeth (mech.).

dénuder [dénüdé] *v.* to lay bare; to strip.

dénuement [dénümãⁿ] *m.* destitution, poverty. ‖ *dénuer* [-üé] *v.* to strip; to deprive.

dépannage [dépànàj] *m.* repairs [auto]; breakdown service. ‖ *dépanner* [-é] *v.* to repair; to help (fig.).

dépareillé [dépàrèyé] *adj.* odd; incomplete; unmatched.

départ [dépàr] *m.* departure, start, sailing [bateau]; setting out; *sur le départ,* on the point of leaving; *départ lancé,* flying start; *point de départ,* starting point.

département [dépàrt⋅mãⁿ] *m.* department; *Br.* Ministry; section; province; *départemental,* departmental.

départir [dépàrtîr] *v.*⋆ to distribute, to allot, to dispense; *se départir de,* to give up; to break from.

dépasser [dépâsé] *v.* to pass, to go beyond, to exceed; to overtake; to project beyond; *dépasser à la course,* to outrun.

dépayser [dépèìzé] *v.* to take out of one's element; to remove from home; *être dépaysé,* to be uprooted, to be at a loss; *se dépayser,* to leave home; to go abroad.

dépecer [dép⋅sé] *v.* to cut up; to dismember.

dépêche [dépèsh] *f.* dispatch; message; telegram, wire (fam.). ‖ *dépêcher* [-é] *v.* to hasten; to expedite; to dispatch; *se dépêcher,* to hurry up, to make haste.

dépeindre [dépⁱndr] *v.*⋆ to depict; to describe.

dépeinturer [dépⁱntüré] *v.* © to remove paint [from wall, etc.].

dépenaillé [dépnàyé] *adj.* (fam.) in rags, in tatters.

dépendance [dépãⁿdãⁿs] *f.* dependency [pays]; dependence; subordination; *pl.* offices; outbuildings; annexes. ‖ *dépendre* [dépãⁿdr] *v.* to depend (*de,* on).

dépendre [dépãⁿdr] *v.* to take down, to unhang.

dépens [dépãⁿ] *m. pl.* cost, expense, charges, costs (jur.). ‖ *dépense* [dépãⁿs] *f.* expenditure, outlay; consumption [gaz]; pantry; *dépenses de bouche.* living expenses; *dépense de temps,* waste of time. ‖ *dépenser* [-é] *v.* to spend; to expend; *se dépenser,* to be spent; to spare no effort; to waste one's energy. ‖ *dépensier* [-yé] *adj.*⋆ extravagant, spendthrift.

déperdition [dépèrdìsyoⁿ] *f.* waste; loss; leakage.

dépérir [dépérîr] *v.* to decline, to pine away, to dwindle.

dépeupler [dépœplé] *v.* to depopulate; to thin [forêt].

dépilatoire [dépìlàtwàr] *adj.,* *m.* depilatory.

dépister [dépìsté] *v.* to hunt out, to track down, to ferret out; to throw off the scent; to outwit.

dépit [dépì] *m.* spite, resentment, grudge; *en dépit de,* in spite of; *par dépit,* out of spite. ‖ *dépiter* [-té] *v.* to vex, to spite; *se dépiter,* to be annoyed; to be hurt.

déplacé [déplàsé] *adj.* unbecoming, improper. ‖ *déplacement* [-mãⁿ] *m.* displacement; removal; travel(l)ing; movement [bateau]; *frais de déplacement,* travel(l)ing expenses. ‖ *déplacer* [-é] *v.* to displace; to dislodge, to move; to have a displacement of [bateau]; to replace; *se déplacer,* to move; to travel.

déplaire [déplèr] *v.*⋆ to offend, to displease; *il me déplaît,* I don't like him; *ne vous en déplaise,* with all due deference to you; *se déplaire,* to dislike. ‖ *déplaisant* [déplèzãⁿ] *adj.* disagreable, unpleasant. ‖ *déplaisir* [-îr] *m.* displeasure, vexation; grief.

dépliant [déplìyãⁿ] *m.* folder. ‖ *déplier* [-lyé] *v.* to unfold. ‖ *déploiement* [déplwàmãⁿ] *m.* deployment (mil.); show, display; unfolding.

déplorable [déplòràbl] *adj.* deplorable, lamentable; wretched. ‖ *déplorer* [-é] *v.* to deplore; to lament, to mourn.

déployer [déplwàyé] *v.* to unfold; to unfurl [voile]; to spread out; to display; to deploy (mil.).

déplu [déplü] *p. p. of* déplaire.

déplumer [déplümé] *v.* to pluck; *se déplumer,* to moult; (pop.) to grow bald.

dépoli [dépòlì] *adj.* ground; frosted.

déportation [dépòrtàsyoⁿ] *f.* deportation. ‖ *déporté* [dépòrté] *adj.* deported, displaced; transported; *m.* deportee. ‖ *déportements* [-⋅mãⁿ] *m. pl.* misconduct, misbehavio(u)r.

déporter [-é] v. to deport; se dépor-ter, to desist.

déposant [dépòzaⁿ] m. depositor; deponent, witness (jur.). ‖ déposer [-é] v. to deposit [argent]; to put down; to leave; to depose; to give evidence; to introduce [projet de loi]. ‖ déposi-taire [-itèr] m., f. trustee; agent. ‖ déposition [-isyoⁿ] f. deposition; state-ment (jur.).

déposséder [dépòsédé] v. to disposs-sess; to deprive. ‖ dépossession [dé-posésyoⁿ] f. dispossession; eviction.

dépôt [dépô] m. deposit; handing in [télégramme]; store, depot; ware-house; police station; bond [douane]; sediment; dump; en dépôt, on sale; in stock.

dépoter [dépòté] v. to unpot; to decant.

dépotoir [dépòtwàr] m. dump.

dépouille [dépúy] f. skin [animal]; slough [serpent]; pl. spoils, booty; dépouille mortelle, mortal remains. ‖ dépouillement [-maⁿ] m. despoiling; scrutiny; count [scrutin]. ‖ dépouiller [-é] v. to skin; to strip; to plunder; to rob; to cast off; to inspect; to count [scrutin]; to go through [cour-rier]; to study [documents].

dépourvu [dépúrvü] adj. destitute, devoid; au dépourvu, unawares.

dépoussiérer [dépûsyéré] v. to dust.

dépravation [dépràvàsyoⁿ] f. de-pravity, corruption. ‖ dépraver [-é] v. to deprave, to pervert, to corrupt.

dépréciation [déprésyàsyoⁿ] f. de-preciation; wear and tear. ‖ déprécier [-yé] v. to depreciate; to belittle; to disparage; to devalue.

déprédation [déprédasyoⁿ] f. depre-dation.

dépression [déprèsyoⁿ] f. depression; hollow; fall in pressure. ‖ déprimer [déprimé] v. to depress; se déprimer, to get depressed; to get dejected.

depuis [d^epü̈] adv., prep. since; from; for; after; depuis combien?, since when?; je suis ici depuis trois semaines, I have been here for three weeks.

dépuratif [dépüràtïf] adj.*, m. depu-rative; blood-cleansing.

députation [dépütàsyoⁿ] f. deputa-tion; se présenter à la députation, to put up for Parliament. ‖ député [-é] m. deputy; member of Parliament, Br. M. P., Am. Congressman. ‖ dépu-ter v. to depute; to delegate.

déraciner [déràsïné] v. to uproot, to eradicate.

déraillement [déràymaⁿ] m. derail-ment, railway accident. ‖ dérailler [-é] v. to go off the rails; faire dérailler, to derail. ‖ dérailleur [-œr] m., gear-shift, three-speed gear [bicyclette].

déraison [dérèzoⁿ] f. unreasonable-ness, want of sense. ‖ déraisonnable [-ònàbl] adj. unreasonable; unwise; senseless, absurd, foolish. ‖ déraison-ner [-òné] v. to talk nonsense, to rave.

dérangement [déraⁿ|maⁿ] m. dis-turbance, disorder; trouble; fault (mech.). ‖ déranger [-é] v. to derange; to bother, to disturb; to upset [pro-jets]; se déranger, to get out of order [machine]; to trouble; to live a wild life.

dérapage [déràpàj] m. skidding; dragging (naut.). ‖ déraper [-é] v. to skid [auto]; to drag its anchor [ba-teau]; to weigh anchor.

dératisation [déràtïzasyoⁿ] f. derat-isation. ‖ dératiser [-é] v. to exter-minate rats.

dérèglement [dérègl^emaⁿ] m. disor-der; irregularity [pouls]; dissoluteness. ‖ dérégler [déréglé] v. to upset; to unsettle; se dérégler, to get out of order [montre]; to lead an abandoned life, to run wild (fig.).

dérider (se) [s^edérïdé] v. to brighten up, to become serene.

dérision [dérïzyoⁿ] f. derision, mock-ery; tourner quelqu'un en dérision, to make a laughing-stock of someone. ‖ dérisoire [-wàr] adj. ridiculous, absurd, ludicrous.

dérivatif [dérïvàtïf] adj.* derivative. ‖ dérivation [-àsyoⁿ] f. derivation; diversion; shunting, shunt (electr.); drift (mil.); loop [ch. de fer].

dérive [dérîv] f. leeway (naut.); à la dérive, adrift.

dériver [dérïvé] v. to drift (naut.).

dériver [dérïvé] v. to derive (de, from); to spring (de, from); to divert; to shunt (electr.).

dermatologie [dèrmàtòlòjî] f. derma-tology.

dernier [dèrnyé] m., adj.* last, latest; final; closing [prix]; utmost [impor-tance]; mettre la dernière main à, to give the finishing touch to. ‖ derniè-rement [-yèrmaⁿ] adv. recently, lately.

dérobade [déròbàd] f. escape; evad-ing, evasion. ‖ dérober [déròbé] v. to steal; to hide; se dérober, to steal away; to hide; to swerve [cheval]; to elude, to evade, to shirk; à la dérobée, stealthily, on the sly.

dérogation [dérògàsyoⁿ] f. deroga-tion. ‖ déroger [déròjé] v. to derogate (à, from); to lower oneself, to stoop.

déroulement [dérûlmaⁿ] m. passing; unfolding. ‖ dérouler [dérûlé] v. to unroll; to unreel; to unfold; se dérou-ler, to unfold; to take place; to develop.

déroute [dérût] *f.* rout; *mettre en déroute,* to rout; *en pleine déroute,* in full flight. ‖ **dérouter** [-é] *v.* to put off the track; to bewilder, to baffle; to lead astray.

derrière [dèryèr] *adv.* behind; astern (naut.). *prep.* behind. after. astern of (naut.). *m* back, rear; bottom. backside (fam.), stern (naut.). *par-derrière.* from the rear, from behind; *pattes de derrière,* hind legs.

des [dé, dè], *see* de.

dès [dè] *prep.* from, since; upon; as early as; *dès lors,* from then on; *dès aujourd'hui,* from today; *dès que,* as soon as

désabuser [dézàbûzé] *v.* to undeceive; to disillusion; *se désabuser,* to have one's eyes opened.

désaccord [dézàkòr] *m.* discord; dissension, disagreement; *en désaccord,* at variance. ‖ **désaccorder** [-é] *v.* to set at variance; to untune (mus.); *se désaccorder,* to get out of tune.

désaffecter [dézàfèkté] *v.* to deconsecrate (eccles.); to release (jur.).

désaffection [dézàfèksyon] *f.* disaffection, *se désaffectionner,* to lose one's affection (*de,* for).

désagréable [dézàgréàbl] *adj.* disagreeable. unpleasant, nasty.

désagréger [dézàgréjé] *v.* to disintegrate, *se désagréger,* to break up; to disaggregate

désagrément [dézàgrémàn] *m.* unpleasantness, source of annoyance; inconvenience. discomfort.

désaltérer [dézàltéré] *v.* to refresh, to quench (someone's) thirst.

désamorcer [dézàmòrsé] *v.* to uncap.

désappointement [dézàpwintmàn] *m.* disappointment. ‖ **désappointer** [-é] *v.* to disappoint

désapprobateur, -trice [dézàpròbàtœr, -trìs] *adj.* disapproving. ‖ **désapprobation** [-àsyon] *f.* disapprobation, disapproval. ‖ **désapprouver** [dézàprûvé] *v.* to disapprove of, to object to; to disagree with.

désarçonner [dézàrsòné] *v.* to unseat; to dumbfound, to flabbergast (pop.).

désarmement [dézàrmemàn] *m.* disarmament, laying up (naut.). ‖ **désarmer** [-é] *v.* to disarm; to lay up, to decommission [navire]; to unload [canon]; to uncock [fusil].

désarroi [dézàrwà] *m.* confusion, disorder, disarray.

désastre [dézàstr] *m.* disaster; *désastreux,* desastrous.

désavantage [dézàvàntàj] *m.* disadvantage; drawback. ‖ **désavantager**

[-é] *v.* to put at a disadvantage, to handicap. ‖ **désavantageux** [-ë] *adj.* disadvantageous. unfavourable; prejudicial detrimental.

désaveu [dézàvë] *m.* disavowal, denial. repudiation disowning. ‖ **désavouer** [dézàvûé] *v.* to disown, to deny; to repudiate to disclaim.

descendance [dèsàndàns] *f.* descent; descendant. ‖ **descendant** [-àn] *m.* descendant offspring. *adj.* descending, going down downward. ‖ **descendre** [désàndr] *v.* to descend; to come down, to go down; to take down; to let down. *descendre de cheval,* to dismount *descendre de l'autobus,* to get off the bus. *descendre à l'hôtel,* to stop at the hotel. *tout le monde descend,* all change. ‖ **descente** [-ànt] *f.* descent, slope. declivity; raid; rupture; dismounting [cheval]; downstroke [piston]; *descente de bain,* bathmat; *descente de justice,* search (jur.).

descriptif [dèskrìptìf] *adj.* descriptive. ‖ **description** [-ìpsyon] *f.* description.

désemparer [dézànpàré] *v.* to disable; to leave; *sans désemparer,* without stopping, *être désemparé,* to be in distress (or) at a loss (or) helpless.

désenchantement [dézànshàntmàn] *m.* disenchantment; disillusion. ‖ **désenchanter** [-é] *v.* to disenchant; to disillusion

désensibiliser [dézànsìbìlìzé] *v.* to desensitize

déséquilibre [dézékìlìbr] *m.* lack of balance ‖ **déséquilibrer** [-é] *v.* to unbalance. to throw out of balance.

désert [dézèr] *m.* desert, wilderness; *adj.* deserted, desert; lonely; wild.

déserter [dézèrté] *v.* to desert; to forsake to abandon. ‖ **déserteur** [-tœr] *m* deserter. ‖ **désertion** [-syon] *f.* desertion.

désertique [dézèrtìk] *adj.* desert, barren

désespérant [dézèspéràn] *adj.* hopeless. heart-breaking. ‖ **désespéré** [-éré] *adj* desperate, hopeless; disheartened. *en désespéré,* like mad. ‖ **désespérer** [-éré] *v.* to despair, to be disheartened. to drive to despair. ‖ **désespoir** [-wàr] *m.* despair, desperation; *en désespoir de cause,* as a last resource, as a desperate shift.

déshabillé [dézàbìyé] *m.* wrap; *en déshabillé* in dishabille; in undress. ‖ **déshabiller** [-é] *v.* to undress, to strip, to disrobe

déshabituer [dézàbìtüé] *v.* to disaccustom, *se déshabituer,* to rid oneself of the habit (*de,* of).

désherber [dézèrbé] *v.* to weed.

déshériter [dézérìté] *v.* to disinherit.

déshonneur [dézònœr] *m.* dishono-o(u)r, disgrace. ‖ **déshonorant** [-òraⁿ] *adj.* dishono(u)ring, disgraceful. ‖ **déshonorer** [-òré] *v.* to dishono(u)r, to disgrace; to defile.

déshydrater [dézìdràté] *v.* to dehydrate.

désignation [dézìñàsyoⁿ] *f.* designation; appointment, nomination. ‖ **désigner** [-é] *v.* to designate; to appoint; to indicate; **désigner du doigt**, to point out.

désillusion [dézìllüzyoⁿ] *f.* disillusion. ‖ **désillusionner** [-yòné] *v.* to disillusion.

désinence [dézìnaⁿs] *f.* ending.

désinfectant [dézìⁿfèktaⁿ] *m., adj.* disinfectant. ‖ **désinfecter** [-é] *v.* to disinfect; to fumigate; to decontaminate. ‖ **désinfection** [dézìⁿfèksyoⁿ] *f.* disinfection.

désintégration [dézìⁿtégràsyoⁿ] *f.* disintegration; splitting, fission. ‖ **désintégrer** [-é] *v.* to disintegrate; to split; **se désintégrer**, to disintegrate.

désintéressé [dézìⁿtérèsé] *adj.* unselfish, disinterested. ‖ **désintéressement** [-maⁿ] *m.* unselfishness; impartiality. ‖ **désintéresser** [-é] *v.* to indemnify; to buy out; **se désintéresser**, to give up; to take no further interest.

désintoxication [dézìⁿtòksìkàsyoⁿ] *f.* detoxication. ‖ **désintoxiquer** [-é] *v.* to detoxicate.

désinvolte [dézìⁿvòlt] *adj.* free, easy; off-hand, airy; detached. ‖ **désinvolture** [-ür] *f.* off-handedness; ease, freedom; cheek, nerve (fam.).

désir [dézìr] *m.* desire, wish. ‖ **désirable** [-ìràbl] *adj.* desirable; **peu désirable**, undesirable. ‖ **désirer** [-ìré] *v.* to desire, to wish; to want, **cela laisse à désirer**, it's not altogether satisfactory. ‖ **désireux** [-ìrë] *adj.** desirous, eager.

désistement [dézìst^emaⁿ] *m.* standing down, withdrawal.

désister (se) [s^edézìsté] *v.* to withdraw; to desist (*de*, from); to waive; to renounce.

désobéir [dézòbéìr] *v.* to disobey; **désobéir à quelqu'un**, to disobey someone. ‖ **désobéissance** [-ìsaⁿs] *f.* disobedience. ‖ **désobéissant** [-ìsaⁿ] *adj.* disobedient.

désobligeant [dézòblìjaⁿ] *adj.* disobliging; uncivil; unpleasant. ‖ **désobliger** [-é] *v.* to disoblige; to displease.

désœuvré [dézœvré] *adj.* idle, at a loose end; unoccupied, unemployed.

désolant [dézòlaⁿ] *adj.* distressing, sad; most annoying. ‖ **désolation** [-àsyoⁿ] *f.* desolation; devastation; distress. ‖ **désoler** [-é] *v.* to grieve; to annoy; to lay waste.

désolidariser (se) [s^edésòlìdàrìzé] *v.* to dissociate oneself (*de*, from).

désopilant [dézòpìlaⁿ] *adj.* (fam.) side-splitting.

désordonné [dézòrdòné] *adj.* disorderly; untidy; unruly. ‖ **désordre** [dézòrdr] *m.* disorder, confusion; chaos; untidiness; *pl.* riots, disturbances.

désorganisation [dézòrgànìzàsyoⁿ] *f.* disorganization. ‖ **désorganiser** [-é] *v.* to disorganize; to upset; to confuse.

désorienter [dézòryaⁿté] *v.* to mislead; to bewilder; **tout désorienté**, all at sea.

désormais [dézòrmè] *adv.* henceforth, hereafter, from now on; for the future.

désossé [dézòsé] *adj.* boneless; boned.

despote [dèspòt] *m.* despot; **despotique**, despotic; **despotisme**, despotism.

desquels, desquelles, *see* **lequel.**

dessaisir [dèsèzìr] *v.* to dispossess; **se dessaisir de**, to part with, to give up, to relinquish.

dessaler [dèsàlé] *v.* to unsalt; to soak (viande); to sharpen (someone's) wits; **se dessaler**, to learn a thing or two.

dessécher [désèshé] *v.* to dry up, to wither; to steel, to harden.

dessein [dèsìⁿ] *m.* design, scheme, project, plan; intention; **à dessein**, on purpose; **sans dessein**, unintentionally, © stupid, foolish; **avoir le dessein de**, to intend to.

desserrer [dèsèré] *v.* to loosen; to unclamp; to unscrew (écrou); to release (frein).

dessert [dèsèr] *m.* dessert.

desservir [dèsèrvìr] *v.** to clear (table); to clear away; to do an ill turn to; to disserve.

desservir [dèsèrvìr] *v.* to serve (transport); to ply between; to officiate at (eccles.).

dessin [dèsìⁿ] *m.* drawing; sketch; plan; pattern; **dessin à main levée**, free-hand drawing; **dessin animé**, animated cartoon. ‖ **dessinateur, -trice** [dèsìnàtœr, -trìs] *m., f.* drawer; pattern-designer; draughtsman. ‖ **dessiner** [-ìné] *v.* to draw, to sketch; to design; to lay out (jardin); to show; **se dessiner**, to stand out; to loom up; to appear; to take form.

dessouler [désûlé] *v.* to sober up.

dessous [d^esû] *m.* lower part, under side; *adv.* under, underneath, beneath, below; *prep.* under; **vêtements de dessous**, underclothes; **les dessous**, the seamy side.

dessus [dᵉsü] *m.* top, upper side; lid; treble (mus.); advantage; *adv.* on; over, above; *prep.* on, upon; above, over; *prendre le dessus*, to get the upper hand.

destin [dèstⁱⁿ] *m.* fate, destiny. ‖ *destinataire* [dèstⁱnàtèr] *m.*, *f.* addressee; payee. ‖ *destination* [-àsyoⁿ] *f.* destination; *à destination de*, addressed to [colis], bound for [bateau]. ‖ *destinée* [-é] *f.* fate, destiny. ‖ *destiner* [-é] *v.* to destine; to intend; *se destiner*, to intend to enter [profession].

destituer [dèstìtüé] *v.* to dismiss, to discharge. ‖ *destitution* [-üsyoⁿ] *f.* dismissal; removal.

destrier [dèstryé] *m.* steed.

destructeur, -trice [dèstrüktœr, -trìs] *m.*, *f.* destructor, destroyer; *adj.* destructive. ‖ *destructif* [-tìf] *adj.** destructive. ‖ *destruction* [dèstrüksyoⁿ] *f.* destruction, destroying; demolition.

désuet [désüè] *adj.** obsolete.

désunion [dézünyoⁿ] *f.* separation; disunion.

désunir [dézünìr] *v.* to separate, to divide, to disunite; *se désunir*, to come apart; to fall out.

détachement [détàshmaⁿ] *m.* detaching; detachment (mil.); indifference, unconcern. ‖ *détacher* [-é] *v.* to detach; to unfasten, to undo; to separate; to detail (mil.); *se détacher*, to come loose; to separate, to part; to stand out.

détacher [détàshé] *v.* to clean.

détail [détày] *m.* detail; particular; trifle; retail (comm.); detailed account; *marchand au détail*, retail dealer. ‖ *détaillant* [-aⁿ] *m.* retailer. ‖ *détailler* [-é] *v.* to detail; to relate in detail; to retail; to divide up.

détaler [détàlé] *v.* to scamper away.

détecter [détèkté] *v.* to detect. ‖ *détection* [-syoⁿ] *f.* detection. ‖ *détective* [détèktìf] *m.* detective.

déteindre [détⁱⁿdr] *v.** to take the colo(u)r out of; to lose colo(u)r, to fade.

dételer [détlé] *v.* to unyoke, to unharness; to ease off; to say good-bye to romance (fam.).

détendre [détaⁿdr] *v.* to slacken, to loosen; *se détendre*, to relax, to ease.

détenir [détnìr] *v.** to detain; to hold; to keep back.

détente [détaⁿt] *f.* relaxation; slackening; easing; expansion; trigger [fusil]; power stroke [moteur]; *dur à la détente*, close-fisted (fig.).

détention [détaⁿsyoⁿ] *f.* detention; imprisonment; detainment; holding. ‖ *détenu* [détnü] *m.* prisoner; *adj.* detained, imprisoned.

détergent [détèrjaⁿ] *adj.*, *m.* detergent.

détérioration [détéryòràsyoⁿ] *f.* damage; deterioration, wear and tear. ‖ *détériorer* [-é] *v.* to damage; to impair; to make worse.

déterminant [détèrmìnaⁿ] *m.* determinant; *adj.* determinating. ‖ *détermination* [-àsyoⁿ] *f.* resolution; determination. ‖ *déterminer* [-é] *v.* to determine, to settle; to ascertain; to induce; to cause; *se déterminer*, to make up one's mind, to resolve. ‖ *déterminisme* [-ìsm] *m.* determinism.

déterrer [détéré] *v.* to disinter; to unearth.

détersif [détèrsìf] *adj.**, *m.* detergent.

détestable [détèstàbl] *adj.* detestable, hateful. ‖ *détester* [-é] *v.* to detest, to hate.

détonateur [détònàtœr] *m.* detonator; fog-signal [chemin de fer]. ‖ *détonation* [-àsyoⁿ] *f.* detonation, report [arme à feu]. ‖ *détoner* [-é] *v.* to detonate, to explode.

détour [détùr] *m.* detour, roundabout way; bend; winding; ruse; *sans détour*, straightforward. ‖ *détourné* [-né] *adj.* out of the way; circuitous, roundabout; indirect. ‖ *détournement* [-nᵉmaⁿ] *m.* diversion; embezzlement [fonds]; abduction. ‖ *détourner* [-né] *v.* to divert [rivière]; to avert; to parry [coup]; to turn away; to misappropriate; to embezzle; *se détourner*, to give up; to turn away.

détracteur, -trice [détràktœr, -trìs] *m.*, *f.* detractor; slanderer; maligner; defamer.

détraqué [détràké] *adj.* out of order; deficient; crazy, cracked; unsettled. ‖ *détraquer* [détràké] *v.* to put out of order; to upset; to derange; *se détraquer*, to break down.

détremper [détraⁿpé] *v.* to moisten, to soak.

détresse [détrès] *f.* distress; danger; grief; *signal de détresse*, distress signal, S.O.S.

détriment [détrìmaⁿ] *m.* detriment; cost, loss; prejudice.

détritus [détrìtüs] *m.* detritus; refuse; rubbish.

détroit [détrwà] *m.* strait, channel.

détromper [détroⁿpé] *v.* to undeceive; *détrompez-vous!*, don't you believe it!

détrôner [détrôné] *v.* to dethrone; to debunk.

détrousser [détrûsé] *v.* to rob.

détruire [détrüìr] *v.** to destroy, to demolish, to pull down; to ruin; to overthrow.

dette [dèt] *f.* debt; obligation; *dettes actives*, assets; *dettes passives*, liabilities; *faire des dettes*, to run into debt.

deuil [dœy] *m.* mourning; bereavement.

deux [dë] *m.* two; second; *adj.* two; *tous les deux*, both; *Henri II*, Henry the Second; *le deux mai*, the second of May; *tous les deux jours*, every other day; *deux fois*, twice. || **deuxième** [-zyèm] *m., f., adj.* second.

dévaler [dévâlé] *v.* to run down.

dévaliser [dévâlìzé] *v.* to rob, to rifle.

dévalorisation [dévâlòrìzàsyoⁿ] *f.* devaluation, fall in value, depreciation. || **dévaloriser** [-é] *v.* to devalorize.

dévaluation [dévâlüàsyoⁿ] *f.* devaluation. || **dévaluer** [-é] *v.* to devaluate.

devancer [d^evaⁿsé] *v.* to precede; to outstrip; to forestall. || **devancier** [-yé] *m.* predecessor.

devant [d^evaⁿ] *m.* front, forepart; *adv.* in front, before, ahead; *prep.* in front of, before, ahead of; *pattes de devant*, forelegs; *prendre les devants*, to go on ahead; *devant la loi*, in the eyes of the law. || **devanture** [-tür] *f.* front; shop-front.

dévaster [dévàsté] *v.* to devastate, to ravage, to lay waste, to wreck.

déveine [dévèn] *f.* ill-luck, bad luck.

développement [dévlòpmaⁿ] *m.* development; spreading out; gear ratio [auto]. || **développer** [-é] *v.* to develop; to expand; to spread out, to unfold; to expound upon [texte]; *se développer*, to develop; to expand; to improve; to spread out.

devenir [d^ev^enìr] *v.* * to become; to grow; to turn; *qu'est-il devenu?*, what has become of him?

déverser [dévèrsé] *v.* to incline; to lean; to slant; to warp [bois]; to pour off; to tip; *se déverser*, to flow out.

déviation [dévyàsyoⁿ] *f.* deviation, variation, swerving. || **déviationnisme** [-ìsm] *m.* deviationism. || **déviationniste** [-ìst] *m., f.* deviationist.

dévider [dévìdé] *v.* to unwind, to reel off. || **dévidoir** [-wàr] *m.* winder; cable-drum (electr.).

dévier [dévyé] *v.* to deviate, to swerve; to diverge; to deflect; *se dévier*, to warp [bois]; to grow crooked; to curve (med.).

devin, devineresse [d^eviⁿ, -ìnrès] *m., f.* soothsayer; fortune-teller. || **deviner** [-ìné] *v.* to guess; to find out. || **devinette** [-ìnèt] *f.* riddle; puzzle.

devis [d^evì] *m.* estimate.

dévisager [dévìzàjé] *v.* to stare at.

devise [d^evîz] *f.* motto; currency. || **deviser** [-ìzé] *v.* to chat, to have a chat, to talk.

dévisser [dévìsé] *v.* to unscrew.

dévitaliser [dévìtàlìzé] *v.* to devitalize.

dévoiler [dévwàlé] *v.* to unveil, to reveal, to disclose; to unmask; to discover.

devoir [d^evwàr] *m.* duty; exercise; home-work [écolier]; *pl.* respects; *v.* * to owe; to have to; must; should, ought; *vous devriez le faire*, you ought to do it; *vous auriez dû le faire*, you should have done it; *je vous dois dix francs*, I owe you ten francs; *il doit partir demain*, he is to leave tomorrow.

dévolu [dévòlü] *m.* claim; choice; *adj.* devolved; fallen.

dévorer [dévòré] *v.* to devour; to consume; to squander [fortune]; to swallow [insulte]; *dévorer des yeux*, to gloat over; to gaze upon.

dévot [dévô] *m.* devotee, devout person; *adj.* devout, pious; sanctimonious. || **dévotion** [-òsyoⁿ] *f.* devotion; devoutness, piety.

dévouement [dévûmaⁿ] *m.* self-sacrifice; devotion; devotedness. || **dévouer** [-ûé] *v.* to devote; to dedicate.

dévoyé, -ée [dévwàyé] *m., f.* pervert; *adj.* depraved, perverted.

dévoyer [dévwàyé] *v.* to lead astray; *se dévoyer*, to stray.

dextérité [dèkstérìté] *f.* dexterity, ability, skill, cleverness.

diabète [dyàbèt] *m.* diabetes; *diabétique*, diabetic.

diable [dyàbl] *m.* devil; jack-in-the-box [jouet]; trolley; porter's barrow, *Am.* porter's dolly; *un pauvre diable*, a poor wretch; *tirer le diable par la queue*, to be hard up. || **diablerie** [-erî] *f.* devilry, fun. || **diablotin** [-òtiⁿ] *m.* imp; little devil; cracker. || **diabolique** [-òlìk] *adj.* diabolical, fiendish; devilish.

diaconesse [dyàkònès] *f.* deaconess.

diacre [dyàkr] *m.* deacon.

diadème [dyàdèm] *m.* diadem.

diagnostic [dyàgnòstìk] *m.* diagnosis. || **diagnostiquer** [-é] *v.* to diagnose.

diagonale [dyàgònàl] *f.* diagonal.

diagramme [dyàgràm] *m.* diagram.

dialecte [dyàlèkt] *m.* dialect. || **dialectique** [dyàlèktìk] *f.* dialectics; *adj.* dialectic.

dialogue [dyàlòg] *m.* dialogue. || **dialoguer** [-ògé] *v.* to converse, to talk; to put in the form of a dialogue.

diamant [dyàmaⁿ] *m.* diamond.

diamètre [dyàmɛtr] *m.* diameter.

diapason [dyàpàzoⁿ] *m.* tuning-fork; diapason; pitch.

diaphane [dyàfàn] *adj.* diaphanous, transparent.

diaphragme [dyàfràgm] *m.* diaphragm; sound-box; midriff.

diapositive [dyàpòzìtìv] *f.* transparency.

diapré [dyàpré] *adj.* mottled, variegated.

diarrhée [dyàré] *f.* diarrhea.

diatribe [dyàtrìb] *f.* diatribe; harangue.

dichotomie [dìkòtòmî] *f.* dichotomy; fee-splitting.

dictateur [dìktàtœr] *m.* dictator. ‖ **dictature** [-ür] *f.* dictatorship.

dictée [dìkté] *f.* dictation. ‖ **dicter** [-é] *v.* to dictate.

diction [dìksyoⁿ] *f.* diction; delivery; style.

dictionnaire [dìksyònèr] *m.* dictionary; lexicon; *dictionnaire géographique,* gazetteer.

dicton [dìktoⁿ] *m.* saying, proverb; saw.

didactique [dìdàktìk] *adj.* didactic.

dièse [dyɛz] *m.* sharp (mus.).

diète [dyɛt] *f.* diet; regimen; *à la diète,* on a low diet. ‖ **diététicien** [dyététìsyèⁿ] *m.* dietetician, *Am.* dietician. ‖ **diététique** [-tìk] *f.* dietetics.

dieu [dyë] (*pl. dieux*) *m.* god; God; *à Dieu ne plaise,* God forbid; *mon Dieu!,* dear me! good gracious!

diffamation [dìfàmàsyoⁿ] *f.* defamation. ‖ **diffamatoire** [-twàr] *adj.* defamatory, libellous. ‖ **diffamer** [dìfàmé] *v.* to defame, to libel, to slander.

différence [dìférãⁿs] *f.* difference, disparity, discrepancy. ‖ **différencier** [-ⁿsyé] *v.* to differentiate, to distinguish. ‖ **différend** [-ⁿⁿ] *m.* difference, dispute, quarrel. ‖ **différent** [-ⁿⁿ] *adj.* different, unlike. ‖ **différentiel** [-ⁿsyèl] *m., adj.*ª differential. ‖ **différer** [-é] *v.* to differ; to defer, to put off, to postpone.

difficile [dìfìsìl] *adj.* difficult, hard; awkward, hard to please; fastidious, finicky; squeamish. ‖ **difficulté** [dìfìkülté] *f.* difficulty; disagreement; obstacle; trouble; *faire des difficultés,* to raise objections.

difforme [dìfòrm] *adj.* misshapen, deformed. ‖ **difformité** [-lté] *f.* deformity, malformation.

diffus [dìfü] *adj.* diffused; diffuse [style]. ‖ **diffuser** [-zé] *v.* to diffuse; to publish; to broadcast. ‖ **diffusion** [-zyoⁿ] *f.* diffusion; propagation; broadcasting; wordiness, verbosity.

digérer [dìjéré] *v.* to digest; to assimilate; to swallow [insulte]. ‖ **digeste** [-ɛst] *m.* digest; selection. ‖ **digestible** [-ɛstìbl] *adj.* digestible. ‖ **digestif** [-ɛstìf] *m., adj.*ª digestive. ‖ **digestion** [-ɛstyoⁿ] *f.* digestion.

digital [dìjìtàl] *adj.*ª digital; *empreintes digitales,* fingerprints.

digne [dìñ] *adj.* dignified; worthy, deserving; *digne d'éloges,* praiseworthy. ‖ **dignitaire** [-ltèr] *m.* dignitary. ‖ **dignité** [-lté] *f.* dignity.

digression [dìgrèsyoⁿ] *f.* digression.

digue [dìg] *f.* dike; dam; sea-wall; jetty; breakwater; embankment; barrier; obstacle (fig.).

dilapidation [dìlàpìdàsyoⁿ] *f.* squandering, peculation, wasting. ‖ **dilapider** [dìlàpìdé] *v.* to squander; to waste; to misappropriate.

dilatation [dìlàtàsyoⁿ] *f.* dilatation. ‖ **dilater** [dìlàté] *v.* to dilate, to expand; to distend (med.).

dilemme [dìlɛm] *m.* dilemma, quandary.

diligence [dìlìjãⁿs] *f.* diligence, industry; haste, speed; stage-coach. ‖ **diligent** [-ⁿ] *adj.* diligent, industrious, hard-working.

diluer [dìlüé] *v.* to dilute, to water down.

diluvien [dìlüvyèⁿ] *adj.*ª diluvial.

dimanche [dìmãⁿsh] *m.* Sunday; *dimanche des Rameaux,* Palm Sunday.

dimension [dìmãⁿsyoⁿ] *f.* size, dimension.

diminuer [dìmìnüé] *v.* to diminish; to lessen; to reduce; to lower; to shorten [voile]; to abate; to decrease; to fall off. ‖ **diminutif** [-ütìf] *m., adj.*ª diminutive. ‖ **diminution** [-üsyoⁿ] *f.* diminution; reduction; decrease; abatement; impairment; shortening [robe]; lessening.

dinde [dìⁿd] *f.* turkey(-hen); goose (fig.), foolish woman. ‖ **dindon** [dìⁿdoⁿ] *m.* turkey-cock; dupe.

dîner [dìné] *v.* to dine, to have dinner; *m.* dinner; dinner-party. ‖ **dinette** [dìnɛt] *f.* dolls' dinner-party; snack meal. ‖ **dîneur** [-œr] *m.* diner.

diocèse [dyòsɛz] *m.* diocese.

diphtérie [dìftérî] *f.* diphtheria.

diplomate [dìplòmàt] *m.* diplomat. ‖ **diplomatie** [-àsî] *f.* diplomacy; tact; ‖ **diplomatique** [-àtìk] *adj.* diplomatic.

diplôme [dìplôm] *m.* diploma, certificate. ‖ **diplômé** [dìplômé] *adj., m.* certificated, graduated.

dire [dîr] *m.* speech, words; allegation; statement, account; *v.*ª to say; to tell; to recite [poème]; to bid; to order; *d'après ses dires*, from what he says; *on dit*, it is said, people say; *qu'en dites-vous?*, what do you think of it?; *vous l'avez dit*, exactly, Am. you said it; *on m'a dit de le faire*, I was told to do it; *cela ne me dit rien*, that conveys nothing to me; that does not appeal to me.

direct [dìrèkt] *adj.* direct; straight; through; express [train]. ‖ *directeur, -trice* [-tœr, -trìs] *m.* director, *f.* directress; manager, *f.* manageress; head; principal, governor; leader; editor; *adj.* directing, controlling, head. ‖ **direction** [-syoⁿ] *f.* direction; management, manager's office; steering gear (mech.); *mauvaise direction*, mismanagement, wrong way. ‖ *directive* [-tìv] *f.* directive, instruction.

dirigeable [dìrìjàbl] *m.* airship; *adj.* dirigible. ‖ *dirigeant* [-aⁿ] *m.* ruler, leader; *adj.* ruling, leading. ‖ *diriger* [-é] *v.* to direct, to manage; to steer (naut.); to conduct (mus.); to lead; to aim [fusil]; to plan; *se diriger*, to make one's way; to behave.

discernement [dìsèrnᵉmaⁿ] *m.* discernment; discrimination. ‖ *discerner* [-é] *v.* to discern, to perceive; to discriminate.

disciple [dìsìpl] *m.* disciple, follower.

discipline [dìsìplìn] *f.* discipline, order. ‖ *discipliner* [-ìné] *v.* to discipline.

discontinuer [dìskoⁿtìnüé] *v.* to discontinue.

discordant [dìskòrdaⁿ] *adj.* dissonant, discordant; conflicting; clashing, jarring. ‖ *discorde* [dìskòrd] *f.* discord, dissension.

discothèque [dìskòtèk] *f.* record library.

discourir [dìskûrîr] *v.* to discourse. ‖ *discours* [dìskûr] *m.* speech; discourse; talk; language; treatise.

discourtois [dìskûrtwà] *adj.* discourteous, unmannerly, rude.

discrédit [dìskrédì] *m.* discredit, disrepute. ‖ *discréditer* [-té] *v.* to bring into discredit to disparage.

discret [dìskrè] *adj.* discreet; cautious; quiet, modest, discrete (math.). ‖ *discrétion* [-ésyoⁿ] *f.* discretion; prudence, reserve; mercy; *à discrétion*, unlimited; as much as you want.

disculper [dìskülpé] *v.* to exonerate, to exculpate, to clear, to vindicate.

discussion [dìsküsyoⁿ] *f.* discussion; debate argument.

discuter [dìskúté] *v.* to discuss, to debate, to question; to argue.

disert [dìzèr] *adj.* eloquent; fluent.

disette [dìzèt] *f.* scarcity, dearth, want, lack, shortage.

diseur [dìzœr] *m.* speaker; reciter; *diseur de bonne aventure*, fortuneteller.

disgrâce [dìsgrâs] *f.* disgrace, disfavo(u)r; misfortune; adversity. ‖ *disgracier* [-àsyé] *v.* to disgrace, to dismiss from favo(u)r. ‖ *disgracieux* [-yё] *adj.* ungracious; awkward; uncouth; ugly; unpleasant.

disjoindre [dìzjwìⁿdr] *v.* to separate, to disunite; *se disjoindre*, to come apart.

disjoncteur [dìsjoⁿktœr] *m.* switch; circuit-breaker.

dislocation [dìslòkàsyoⁿ] *f.* dislocation; dispersal; dismemberment. ‖ *disloqué* [-é] *m.* contortionist. ‖ *disloquer* [dìslòké] *v.* to dislocate; to put out of action; to disband; to disperse; to break up.

disparaître [dìspàrètr] *v.* to disappear; to vanish; *faire disparaître*, to remove, to do away with; *soldat disparu*, missing soldier.

disparate [dìspàràt] *f.* disparity; *adj.* ill-assorted, ill-matched.

disparition [dìspàrìsyoⁿ] *f.* disappearance; disappearing.

disparu [dìspàrù] *p. p. of* disparaître.

dispendieux [dìspaⁿdyё] *adj.* expensive.

dispensaire [dìspaⁿsèr] *m.* dispensary, surgery; welfare center.

dispense [dìspaⁿs] *f.* exemption; certificate of exemption. ‖ *dispenser* [-é] *v.* to dispense; to excuse, to exempt; to distribute.

disperser [dìspèrsé] *v.* to disperse; to split up; to scatter. ‖ *dispersion* [-yoⁿ] *f.* dispersion; scattering; rout (mil.) breaking up; leakage (electr.)

disponibilité [dìspoⁿìbìlìté] *f.* availability disposal; *pl.* available funds; *en disponibilité*, unattached (mil.). ‖ *disponible* [-ìbl] *adj.* available; spare; vacant.

dispos [dìspô] *adj.* alert; fit; cheerful; all right.

disposer [dìspôzé] *v.* to dispose; to arrange, to prepare; to provide (jur.); *l'argent dont je dispose*, the money at my disposal, the money I have available. ‖ *dispositif* [-ìtìf] *m.* apparatus, device, contrivance, gadget. ‖ *disposition* [-ìsyoⁿ] *f.* disposition, arrangement; disposal, clause (jur.); tendency; state [esprit], humo(u)r; *à votre entière disposition*, fully at your disposal.

disproportion [dìspròpòrsyoⁿ] *f.* disproportion. ‖ *disproportionné* [-syòné] *adj.* disproportionate.

dispute [dìspút] *f.* dispute, quarrel; *chercher dispute à*, to pick a quarrel with. ‖ *disputer* [-é] *v.* to dispute, to wrangle ; to contest ; to contend for ; to play [match] ; *se disputer*, to quarrel ; to argue.

disquaire [dìskèr] *s.* record-dealer.

disqualification [dìskàlìfìkàsyoⁿ] *f.* disqualification. ‖ *disqualifier* [-yé] *v.* to disqualify.

disque [dìsk] *m.* disc ; signal [chemin de fer] ; plate [embrayage] ; record ; *disque longue durée*, long-playing record.

dissection [dìssèksyoⁿ] *f.* dissection.

dissemblable [dìssaⁿblàbl] *adj.* dissimilar, unlike. ‖ *dissemblance* [-aⁿs] *f.* unlikeness ; dissimilarity.

disséminer [dìsémìné] *v.* to disseminate ; *se disséminer*, to spread.

dissension [dìsaⁿsyoⁿ] *f.* discord, dissension. ‖ *dissentiment* [-aⁿtìmaⁿ] *m.* disagreement, dissent.

disséquer [dìsséké] *v.* to dissect.

dissertation [dìsèrtàsyoⁿ] *f.* dissertation ; treatise ; essay, composition. ‖ *disserter* [-é] *v.* to discourse, to hold forth.

dissidence [dìssìdaⁿs] *f.* dissent ; dissidence. ‖ *dissident* [-aⁿ] *adj.* dissident ; *m.* dissident ; dissenter.

dissimulateur, -trice [dìsìmülàtœr, -trìs] *m., f.* dissembler. ‖ *dissimulation* [-àsyoⁿ] *f.* deceit ; dissimulation ; concealment. ‖ *dissimulé* [-é] *adj.* secretive, deceptive. ‖ *dissimuler* [-é] *v.* to dissemble, to conceal ; to hide ; to cover up ; to affect indifference to ; *se dissimuler*, to hide.

dissipateur, -trice [dìsìpàtœr, -trìs] *m., f.* spendthrift ; *adj.* wasteful, extravagant. ‖ *dissipation* [-àsyoⁿ] *f.* dissipation ; waste ; inattention ; foolish conduct [lycée]. ‖ *dissiper* [-é] *v.* to dissipate ; to waste ; to disperse, to dispel ; to divert ; *se dissiper*, to pass away ; to amuse oneself ; to become dissipated.

dissocier [dìssòsyé] *v.* to dissociate.

dissolu [dìssòlü] *adj.* dissolute. ‖ *dissolution* [-syoⁿ] *f.* dissoluteness ; dissolution ; solution [liquide].

dissolvant [dìssòlvaⁿ] *m., adj.* solvent.

dissonance [dìssònaⁿs] *f.* dissonance ; discord (mus.). ‖ *dissonant* [-aⁿ] *adj.* discordant ; jarring.

dissoudre [dìssûdr] *v.*° to dissolve ; to disintegrate ; to dispel.

dissuader [dìssüàdé] *v.* to dissuade (*de*, from). ‖ *dissuasion* [-zìoⁿ] *f.* dissuasion.

distance [dìstaⁿs] *f.* distance ; interval ; *commande à distance*, remote control. ‖ *distancer* [-é] *v.* to outrun,

to outstrip. ‖ *distant* [dìstaⁿ] *adj.* distant ; aloof.

distendre [dìstaⁿdr] *v.* to distend ; to pull [muscle].

distillation [dìstìllàsyoⁿ] *f.* distillation. ‖ *distiller* [-é] *v.* to distil ; to exude. ‖ *distillerie* [-rî] *f.* distillery.

distinct [dìstìⁿ] *adj.* distinct ; different ; separate ; audible (voix). ‖ *distinctif* [-ktìf] *adj.*° distinctive, characteristic. ‖ *distinction* [-ksyoⁿ] *f.* distinction ; difference ; good breeding ; discrimination ; polished manners ; *sans distinction*, indiscriminately.

distingué [dìstìⁿgé] *adj.* distinguished ; refined ; eminent. ‖ *distinguer* [-gé] *v.* to distinguish ; to discern ; to make out, to perceive ; to single out ; to hono(u)r ; *se distinguer*, to gain distinction ; to be conspicuous.

distorsion [dìstòrsyoⁿ] *f.* distortion.

distraction [dìstràksyoⁿ] *f.* absence of mind ; amusement ; recreation ; inattention.

distraire [dìstrèr] *v.* to separate ; to divert ; to amuse, to entertain ; to distract. ‖ *distrait* [dìstrè] *adj.* inattentive ; absent-minded.

distribuer [dìstrìbüé] *v.* to distribute ; to deal out ; to issue. ‖ *distributeur, -trice* [-ütœr, -trìs] *m., f.* distributor ; *Br.* petrol pump, *Am.* gasoline pump ; ticket-clerk. ‖ *distribution* [-üsyoⁿ] *f.* distribution ; delivery [courrier] ; issue ; cast (theat.) ; arrangement ; valve-gear (mech.).

dit [dì] *m.* saying, maxim ; *adj., p. p.,* see *dire.*

diurne [dìürn] *adj.* diurnal, day.

divagation [dìvàgàsyoⁿ] *f.* divagation, wandering, incoherence ; desultoriness. ‖ *divaguer* [dìvàgé] *v.* to divagate ; to wander ; to ramble.

divan [dìvaⁿ] *m.* divan.

divergence [dìvèrjaⁿs] *f.* divergence ; difference. ‖ *divergent* [-aⁿ] *adj.* divergent ; diverging. ‖ *diverger* [-é] *v.* to branch off, to diverge.

divers [dìvèr] *adj.* diverse, miscellaneous ; varying ; several ; various ; sundry. ‖ *diversifier* [-sìfyé] *v.* to diversify, to vary. ‖ *diversion* [-syoⁿ] *f.* diversion ; change. ‖ *diversité* [-sìté] *f.* diversity ; variety.

divertir [dìvèrtîr] *v.* to divert, to amuse ; to entertain ; to distract. ‖ *divertissement* [-ìsmaⁿ] *m.* entertainment ; amusement ; pastime ; game ; divertissement (theatr.).

dividende [dìvìdaⁿd] *m.* dividend.

divin [dìvìⁿ] *adj.* holy ; divine ; sublime ; heavenly.

divination [dìvìnàsyoⁿ] *f.* divination, fortune-telling ; sooth-saying.

diviniser [dìvìnìzé] *v.* to divinize; to exalt. ‖ **divinité** [dìvìnìté] *f.* divinity, deity; Godhead.

diviser [dìvìzé] *v.* to divide; to share; to separate. ‖ **diviseur** [-œr] *m.* divider; divisor (math.); factor (math.). ‖ **divisible** [-ìbl] *adj.* divisible. ‖ **division** [-yoⁿ] *f.* division; branch; portion; dissension; double bar (mus.).

divorce [dìvòrs] *m.* divorce; *demander le divorce*, to sue for divorce. ‖ **divorcer** [-é] *v.* to divorce.

divulgation [dìvülgàsyoⁿ] *f.* divulgement, disclosure. ‖ **divulguer** [-gé] *v.* to divulge; to reveal.

dix [dìs] ([dîz] before a vowel or a mute *h,* [dì] before a consonant) *m.,* *adj.* ten; tenth [date]; the tenth [roi]; *dix-sept,* seventeen; *dix-huit,* eighteen; *dix-neuf,* nineteen; *dix-septième,* seventeenth; *dix-huitième,* eighteenth; *dix-neuvième,* nineteenth. ‖ **dixième** [dìzyèm] *m., f., adj.* tenth.

dizaine [dìzèn] *f.* half a score; about ten.

docile [dòsìl] *adj.* docile; meek; obedient; submissive. ‖ **docilité** [-ìté] *f.* docility; obedience; meekness.

dock [dòk] *m.* dock (naut.); warehouse.

docte [dòkt] *adj.* learned.

docteur [dòktœr] *m.* doctor; physician. ‖ **doctoral** [-òràl] *adj.*° doctor's; pedantic; pompous. ‖ **doctorat** [-òrà] *m.* doctorate, Doctor's degree. ‖ **doctoresse** [-òrès] *f.* lady-doctor.

doctrine [dòktrìn] *f.* doctrine; tenet.

document [dòkümaⁿ] *m.* document; proof. ‖ **documentaire** [-tèr] *adj.* documentary. ‖ **documentaliste** [-lìst] *s.* research assistant. ‖ **documentariste** [-rìst] *s.* documentary director. **documentation** [-syoⁿ] *f.* documentation, documents. ‖ **documenter** [-té] *v.* to document; *bien documenté sur,* having a detailed knowledge of.

dodeliner [dòdlìné] *v.* to dandle [enfant]; to wag, to nod [tête].

dodu [dòdü] *adj.* plump, chubby.

dogmatique [dògmàtìk] *adj.* dogmatic; *dogmatisme,* dogmatism.

dogue [dòg] *m.* mastiff.

doigt [dwà] *m.* finger; toe; digit; *à deux doigts de,* within an ace of; *montrer du doigt,* to point at. ‖ **doigté** [-té] *m.* fingering (mus.); adroitness; tact.

doléance [dòléaⁿs] *f.* complaint; grievance.

dolent [dòlaⁿ] *adj.* painful; doleful; mournful.

dollar [dòlàr] *m.* dollar.

domaine [dòmèn] *m.* domain; realm; estate; property; land; sphere (fig.); *domaine public,* public property.

dôme [dôm] *m.* dome; cupola; vault [ciel].

domesticité [dòmèstìsìté] *f.* domesticity; household; domesticated state. ‖ **domestique** [dòmèstìk] *m., f.* servant; *adj.* domestic; menial. ‖ **domestiquer** [-é] *v.* to domesticate, to tame.

domicile [dòmìsìl] *m.* domicile; residence; abode; dwelling; address; *franco à domicile, Br.* carriage paid, *Am.* free delivery. ‖ **domicilié** [-yé] *adj.* domiciled.

dominante [dòmìnaⁿt] *f.* leading characteristic; dominant (mus.). ‖ **dominateur, -trice** [dòmìnàtœr, -trìs] *adj.* domineering; ruling. ‖ **domination** [-àsyoⁿ] *f.* domination, rule. ‖ **dominer** [-é] *v.* to dominate; to rule; to prevail; to overlook.

dominical [dòmìnìkàl] *adj.*° dominical; *oraison dominicale,* Lord's prayer.

dommage [dòmàj] *m.* damage, harm, injury, loss; *quel dommage!,* what a pity!; *dommages-intérêts,* damages. ‖ **dommageable** [-àbl] *adj.* prejudicial.

dompter [doⁿté] *v.* to tame; to break in [cheval]; to subdue; to master. ‖ **dompteur** [-œr] *m.* tamer; trainer; subduer (fig.).

don [doⁿ] *m.* gift, present; donation; talent; knack. ‖ **donataire** [dònàtèr] *m.* beneficiary. ‖ **donateur, -trice** [-àtœr, trìs] *m., f.* donor, giver. ‖ **donation** [-àsyoⁿ] *f.* donation; contribution, gift.

donc [doⁿk] *conj.* then; therefore; now; so; hence; whence; well, so, now; *allons donc,* come on; nonsense; you don't mean it.

donjon [doⁿjoⁿ] *m.* keep; turret; donjon.

donne [dòn] *f.* deal [cartes]. ‖ **donnée** [-é] *f.* datum (*pl.* data); fundamental idea; theme. ‖ **donner** [-é] *v.* to give; to bestow; to present; to attribute; to supply; to yield [récoltes]; to deal [cartes]; to strike; to look; to overlook [ouvrir sur]; *donner dans le piège,* to fall into the trap. ‖ **donneur** [-œr] *m.* giver; dealer [cartes]; donor [sang]; informer [dénonciateur].

dont [doⁿ] *pron.* whose, of whom; of which; by whom; by which; from whom; from which; among which; among which; about whom; about which; *voici dix crayons, dont deux rouges,* here are ten pencils, including two red ones.

doper [dòpé] *v.* to dope; to buck up.

dorade [dòràd] *f.* gilt-head (v. DAURADE); sea-bream.

doré [dòré] *adj.* gilt, gilded; golden; *m.* © wall-eyed pike, yellow pike.

dorénavant [dòrénàvaⁿ] *adv.* henceforth.

dorer [dòré] *v.* to gild; to brown [viande]; to egg [gâteau].

dorloter [dòrlòté] *v.* to coddle; to pamper.

dormant [dòrmaⁿ] *m.* sash; *adj.* sleeping, dormant; stagnant [eau]. ‖ *dormeur* [-œr] *m.* sleeper; sluggard. ‖ *dormir* [-îr] *v.* to sleep; to lie still; to be latent; to stagnate; *une histoire à dormir debout*, a tall story; a boring tale; *dormir comme une souche*, to sleep like a log. ‖ *dormitif* [-ìtìf] *m.* sleeping-draught; soporific. ‖ *dortoir* [dòrtwàr] *m.* dormitory; sleeping-quarters.

dorure [dòrür] *f.* gilt; browning.

doryphore [dòrìfòr] *m.* potato bug, Colorado beetle.

dos [dô] *m.* back; ridge (geogr.); *faire le gros dos*, to set up one's back [chat] *en dos d'âne*, ridged; saddle-back; hump [pont].

dosage [dòzàj] *m.* dosing; measuring out. ‖ *dose* [dôz] *f.* dose; amount. ‖ *doser* [-é] *v.* to dose; to measure out.

dossier [dòsyé] *m.* back [chaise]; record; file; brief [avocat]; documents, papers.

dot [dòt] *f.* dowry; *coureur de dots*, fortune-hunter. ‖ *dotation* [-àsyoⁿ] *f.* endowment, foundation. ‖ *doter* [-é] *v.* to endow; to give a dowry to.

douane [dwàn] *f.* customs; custom-house, duty. ‖ *douanier* [-yé] *m.* customs officer. *adj.* customs.

doublage [dûblaj] *m.* lining [pardessus]; plating. ‖ *double* [dûbl] *m.* double; duplicate. *adj.* double, two-fold; deceitful; dual [commande]; double feature (cinem.); *double-croche*, semi-quaver, *4m.* sixteenth note. ‖ *doublé* [-é] *m.* gold-plated metal. ‖ *doubler* [-é] *v.* to double; to fold in two; to line [pardessus]; to plate [métal]; to pass; to overtake [auto]; to understudy (theat.); to dub [film]. ‖ *doublure* [-ür] *f.* lining; understudy.

douce [dûs], see **doux**; *douce-amère*, *f.* woody nightshade, bitter-sweet. ‖ *douceureux* [-rë] *adj.* sweetish, sickly, cloying; smooth-tongued. ‖ *douceur* [-œr] *f.* sweetness; softness; gentleness; mildness; *pl.* sweets, sweet things.

douche [dûsh] *f.* douche; shower-bath. ‖ *doucher* [-é] *v.* to give (somebody) a shower-bath; to douche; to douse; to cool off (fig.); *se doucher*, to shower.

douer [dwé] *v.* to endow; *doué* [-é] *adj.* gifted.

douille [dûy] *f.* socket; casing; cartridge case; boss [roue].

douillet [dûyè] *adj.* soft; sensitive; delicate; effeminate; cosy, snug.

douleur [dûlœr] *f.* pain; suffering; ache; sorrow, grief; pang. ‖ *douloureux* [dûlûrë] *adj.* painful; aching; sorrowful, sad.

doute [dût] *m.* doubt; misgiving; suspicion; *sans doute*, doubtless; no doubt. ‖ *douter* [-é] *v.* to doubt; to question; to mistrust; *se douter*, to suspect; *je m'en doutais*, I thought as much. ‖ *douteux* [-ë] *adj.* doubtful, dubious; questionable; uncertain.

douve [dûv] *f.* moat; stave [tonneau].

doux, douce [dû, dûs] *adj.* soft; sweet; mild; gentle; smooth; fresh [eau]; *filer doux*, to submit; to sing small; *tout doux*, gently; *en douce*, on the quiet.

douzaine [dûzèn] *f.* dozen; *une demi-douzaine*, half a dozen. ‖ *douze* [dûz] *m.*, *adj.* twelve; *le douze juin*, the twelfth of June. ‖ *douzième* [-yèm] *m.*, *f.*, *adj.* twelfth.

doyen [dwàyìⁿ] *m.* dean; doyen; senior; *adj.* senior; eldest.

dragée [dràjé] *f.* sugar-plum; sugared almond; pill (med.).

dragon [dràgoⁿ] *n.* dragon; dragoon (mil.). ‖ *dragonne* [-òn] *f.* tassel.

drague [dràg] *f.* dredger; drag-net; drag. ‖ *draguer* [dràgé] *v.* to dredge; to drag. ‖ *dragueur* [-œr] *m.* dredger; *dragueur de mines*, minesweeper.

drain [drìⁿ] *m.* drain; drain-pipe. ‖ *drainer* [drèné] *v.* to drain.

dramatique [dràmàtìk] *adj.* dramatic. ‖ *dramatiser* [-ìzé] *v.* to dramatize. ‖ *dramaturge* [-ürj] *m.* dramatist, playwright. ‖ *drame* [dràm] *m.* drama; play; tragedy (fig.).

drap [drà] *m.* cloth; sheet [lit]; pall. ‖ *drapeau* [-pô] *m.* flag; standard; colo(u)rs (mil.); *sous les drapeaux*, in the services. ‖ *draper* [-pé] *v.* to drape; to hang with cloth. ‖ *draperie* [-prî] *f.* drapery; cloth-trade. ‖ *drapier* [-pyé] *m.* draper, clothier.

drave [dràv] *f.* © drive, log-running [Fr. = flottage]. ‖ *draver* [-é] *v.* © to float; to drive. ‖ *draveur* [-œr] *m.* © driver, wood-floater, raftsman, logger.

dressage [drèsàj] *m.* training; fitting up; breaking [cheval]. ‖ *dresser* [-é] *v.* to erect; to raise; to lay; to set out; to draw up [liste]; to pitch [tente]; to train; to drill; to prick up [oreilles]; *se dresser*, to rise. ‖ *dresseur* [-œr] *m.* trainer, adjuster. ‖ *dressoir* [-wàr] *m.* dresser, sideboard.

drogue [dròg] *f.* drug; chemical; rubbish. ‖ *droguer* [dròjé] *v.* to drug; to physic. ‖ *droguerie* [rì] *f.* drysalter's shop, drugstore. ‖ *droguiste* [-ìst] *m.* Br. drysalter.

droit, -e [drwà, àt] *m.* law; right; fee; *f.* the right hand; the right [pol.];

adj. straight; right [angle]; upright; vertical; virtuous; *adv.* straight; honestly; *faire son droit*, to study law; *droits de douane*, customs duty; *avoir droit à*, to have a right to; *donner droit à*, to entitle to; *tenir la droite*, to keep to the right; *tout droit*, straight on. ‖ **droiture** [-tür] *f.* uprightness; straightforwardness; integrity.

drôle [drôl] *m.* rascal, scamp; *adj.* droll, funny; odd, queer. ‖ **drôlerie** [-rî] *f.* drollery; jest, *Am.* gag.

dromadaire [dròmàdèr] *m.* dromedary.

dru [drü] *adj.* vigorous, sturdy; dense; thick; close-set; *adv.* thick; fast; vigorously; hard.

druide [drüîd] *m.* druid.

du [dü], *see* de.

dû, due [dü] *p. p. of devoir;* *m.* what is due; *adj.* due; owing.

dualité [düàlìté] *f.* duality.

dubitatif [dübìtàtìf] *adj.** dubitative.

duc [dük] *m.* duke; horned owl. ‖ **duché** [-é] *m.* dukedom; duchy. ‖ **duchesse** [-shès] *f.* duchess; duchess pear (bot.); duchess satin.

duègne [düèñ] *f.* duenna.

duel [düèl] *m.* duel; *se battre en duel*, to fight a duel.

dûment [düman] *adv.* duly; in due form; properly.

dune [dün] *f.* dune, sand-hill; *pl.* downs.

duo [düô] *m.* duet.

dupe [düp] *f.* dupe. ‖ **duper** [-é] *v.* to dupe, to fool, to take in. ‖ **duperie** [-rî] *f.* dupery, trickery. ‖ **dupeur** [-œr] *m.* trickster, cheat, *Am.* sharper.

duplicata [düplìkàtà] *m.* duplicate, copy. ‖ **duplicateur** [-œr] *m.* duplicator.

duplicité [düplìsìté] *f.* duplicity, double-dealing.

duquel [dükèl], *see* **lequel**.

dur [dür] *adj.* hard; tough; difficult; hard-boiled; harsh; hardened; unfeeling; *adv.* hard; *dur d'oreille*, hard of hearing.

durable [düràbl] *adj.* durable; lasting; solid. ‖ **durant** [-aⁿ] *prep.* during; *sa vie durant*, his whole life long.

durcir [dürsîr] *v.* to harden. ‖ **durcissement** [-ìsmaⁿ] *m.* hardening, toughening, stiffening.

durée [düré] *f.* duration; wear; time. ‖ **durer** [-é] *v.* to endure, to last; to hold out; to wear well [étoffe]; to continue; *le temps me dure*, I find life dull.

dureté [dürté] *f.* hardness; harshness; difficulty; unkindness; hardheartedness.

durillon [dürìyoⁿ] *m.* corn [pied]; callosity.

duvet [düvè] *m.* down; fluff. ‖ **duveté** [düvté], **duveteux** [düvtë] *adj.** downy, fluffy.

dynamique [dìnàmìk] *f.* dynamics; *adj.* dynamic. ‖ **dynamisme** [-ìsm] *m.* dynamism.

dynamite [dìnàmît] *f.* dynamite. ‖ **dynamiter** [-é] *v.* to dynamite; to blow up.

dynamo [dìnàmô] *f.* dynamo.

dynastie [dìnàstî] *f.* dynasty.

dysenterie [dìsaⁿtrî] *f.* dysentery.

dyspepsie [dìspèpsî] *f.* dyspepsia. ‖ **dyspeptique** [tìk] *adj.* dyspeptic.

E

eau [ô] *f.* water; rain; juice [fruit]; wet; perspiration; *eau douce*, fresh water; *ville d'eaux*, watering-place; *faire eau*, to spring a leak (naut.); *être en eau*, to be dripping with perspiration; *eau de Javel*, chlorinated water; *eau-de-vie*, brandy; spirits; *eau-forte*, etching; nitric acid.

ébahir [ébàîr] *v.* to astound, to dumbfound, to stupefy; to flabbergast. ‖ **ébahissement** [-ìsmaⁿ] *m.* amazement, astonishment.

ébats [ébà] *m. pl.* frolics, sports, gambols. ‖ **ébattre (s')** [sébàtr] *v.* to frolic, to gambol, to frisk about.

ébauche [ébôsh] *f.* sketch; outline; rough draft. ‖ **ébaucher** [-é] *v.* to rough out, to sketch; to rough-hew. ‖ **ébauchoir** [-wàr] *m.* roughing-chisel.

ébène [ébèn] *f.* ebony. ‖ **ébéniste** [-ìst] *m.* cabinet-maker. ‖ **ébénisterie** [-ìstᵉrî] *f.* cabinet work; cabinetmaking.

éberlué [ébèrlüé] *adj.* flabbergasted.

éblouir [éblüîr] *v.* to dazzle; to fascinate. ‖ **éblouissement** [-ìsmaⁿ] *m.* dazzle; glare; dizziness.

ébonite [ébònìt] *f.* ebonite, vulcanite.

éborgner [ébòrñé] *v.* to blind in one eye, to put (someone's) eye out; to disbud (hort.).

éboueur [ébüœr] *m.* scavenger.

ébouillanter [ébüyaⁿté] *v.* to scald.

éboulement [ébülmaⁿ] *m.* caving in; giving way; fall of earth; landslide. ‖ **ébouler** [-é] *v.* to cave in; to crumble; to slip [terre], to fall. ‖

éboulis [-ì] *m.* debris; fallen earth; scree.

ébouriffer [ébûrîfé] *v.* to ruffle; to dishevel; to startle, to amaze.

ébranlement [ébraⁿlmaⁿ] *m.* shaking; shock; commotion; disturbance. || **ébranler** [-é] *v.* to shake; to loosen [dent]; to set in motion; to disturb; *s'ébranler,* to shake; to totter; to start, to move off.

ébrécher [ébréshé] *v.* to notch; to chip; to jag; to blunt [couteau]; to make inroads upon [fortune]. || **ébréchure** [-ür] *f.* chip; notch.

ébriété [ébrìété] *f.* intoxication, drunkenness, inebriety.

ébrouer (s') [sébrûé] *v.* to snort.

ébruiter [ébrüìté] *v.* to spread, to make known; *s'ébruiter,* to spread, to become known.

ébullition [ébülìsyoⁿ] *f.* ebullition, boiling; commotion, turmoil (fig.).

écaille [ékày] *f.* scale; shell [huître, tortue]; flake; chip. || **écailler** [-é] *v.* to scale; to shell; to open [huître]; *s'écailler,* to peel off; to flake off.

écale [ékàl] *f.* pod [pois]; husk. || **écaler** [-é] *v.* to shell, to husk, to shuck.

écarlate [ékàrlàt] *f., adj.* scarlet.

écarquiller [ékàrkìyé] *v.* to open wide [yeux]; to goggle.

écart [ékàr] *m.* discard; discarding [cartes].

écart [ékàr] *m.* deviation; variation; difference; divergence; error; digression; swerve; *à l'écart,* apart; *faire un écart,* to swerve, to shy; *se tenir à l'écart,* to stand aside; to stand aloof. || **écarté** [-té] *adj.* far apart; lonely; secluded, remote, isolated, out-of-the-way. || **écarteler** [-tºlé] *v.* to quarter. || **écartement** [-tºmaⁿ] *m.* separation; setting aside; gap, space; gauge [rails]. || **écarter** [-té] *v.* to separate; to avert; to ward off, to turn aside; to dispel; to turn down [réclamation]; *s'écarter,* to deviate; to stray; to diverge; to make way for.

ecclésiastique [èklézyàstìk] *m.* clergyman, ecclesiastic; *adj.* clerical, ecclesiastical.

écervelé [ésèrvºlé] *m.* madcap, harum-scarum; *adj.* scatter-brained, wild, thoughtless, flighty.

échafaud [éshâfô] *m.* scaffolding; stand; platform; gallows. || **échafaudage** [-dàj] *m.* scaffolding. || **échafauder** [-é] *v.* to erect scaffolding; to build up.

échalas [éshàlà] *m.* prop; hop-pole; (fam.) lanky person.

échalote [éshàlòt] *f.* shallot.

échancrer [éshaⁿkré] *v.* to indent; to notch; to slope [couture]. || **échancrure** [-ür] *f.* indentation, hollowing out; cut; opening [robe].

échange [éshaⁿj] *m.* exchange; barter. || **échanger** [-é] *v.* to exchange; to barter, to trade; to swap (fam.); to reciprocate.

échanson [éshaⁿsoⁿ] *m.* butler.

échantillon [éshaⁿtìyoⁿ] *m.* sample; pattern; specimen; extract. || **échantillonner** [-ìyóné] *v.* to sample; to check.

échappatoire [éshàpàtwàr] *f.* evasion; way out; loop-hole. || **échappé** [-é] *m., adj.* fugitive, runaway. || **échappée** [-é] *f.* escape ·.purt [sport]; short ·pell; vista, glimpse. || **échappement** [-maⁿ] *m.* escape; outlet; exhaust. *tuyau d'échappement,* exhaust-pipe. || **échapper** [-é] *v.* to escape, to avoid; *laisser échapper,* to overlook; to set free; *son nom m'échappe,* his name has slipped my mind; *l'échapper belle,* to have a narrow escape; *s'échapper,* to escape (*de,* from); to slip out; to vanish.

écharde [éshàrd] *f.* splinter; sliver; prickle.

écharpe [éshàrp] *f.* scarf; sash; sling (med.), *en écharpe,* in a sling; across; diagonally.

écharper [éshàrpé] *v.* to slash; to hack (up), to cut to pieces.

échasse [éshàs] *f.* stilt; scaffold-pole. || **échassier** [-syé] *m.* wader; spindle-shanks.

échauder [éshôdé] *v.* to scald.

échauffer [éshôfé] *v.* to heat; to overheat; to warm; to inflame, to incense; *s'échauffer,* to grow warm; to get overheated; to become aroused.

échauffourée [éshôfûré] *f.* rash undertaking; scuffle; term; clash; skirmish, affray.

échéance [éshéaⁿs] *f.* falling due; maturity; term; expiration [bail]; *venir à échéance,* to fall due; *à courte échéance,* short-dated. || **échéant** [-aⁿ] *adj.* falling due; *le cas échéant,* if such be the case; should the occasion arise; if necessary.

échec [éshèk] *m.* check; defeat; failure; reverse, blow; *pl.* chess; *échec et mat,* checkmate; *tenir en échec,* to hold at bay.

échelle [éshèl] *f.* ladder; scale; port (naut.), run [bas]; *échelle double,* pair of steps; *faire la courte échelle,* to give a helping hand; *sur une grande échelle,* on a big scale; *échelle mobile,* sliding scale. || **échelon** [-ºloⁿ] *m.* rung [échelle]; step; degree, echelon (mil.). || **échelonner** [éshlòné] *v.* to grade; to space out; to stagger [congés]; to draw up in echelon (mil.).

écheniller [ésh•nlyé] v. to clear of caterpillars.

écheveau [éshvô] m.* skein, hank.

échevelé [ésh•vlé] adj. dishevelled; tangled; tousled, rumpled; wild.

échine [éshǐn] f. backbone, spine; chine. || **s'échiner** [séshǐné] v. to tire oneself out.

écho [ékô] m. echo; faire écho, to echo.

échoir [éshwàr] v.* to fall due; to expire [bail]; to befall.

échoppe [éshòp] f. stall, booth.

échotier [ékòtyé] m. newsmonger; gossip-writer; columnist.

échouer [éshûé] v. to run aground; to beach; to strand; to fail; to fall through [projet]; faire échouer, to wreck; s'échouer, to run aground.

échu [éshü] p. p. of échoir.

éclabousser [éklàbûsé] v. to splash, to bespatter. || **éclaboussure** [-ür] f. splash.

éclair [éklèr] m. flash of lightning; flash; éclair [pâtisserie]; pl. lightning. || **éclairage** [-àj] m. light; lighting; illumination; scouting (mil.). || **éclaircie** [-sǐ] f. clearing [forêt]; gap, break [nuages]; bright interval [temps]. || **éclaircir** [-sǐr] v. to clear (up); to brighten; to solve; to explain; to elucidate; to thin; s'éclaircir, to clear up; to get thin; to be enlightened. || **éclaircissement** [-sǐsmaⁿ] m. clearing up; explanation; enlightenment; elucidation.

éclairer [éklèré] v. to light; to enlighten; to reconnoitre (mil.). || **éclaireur** [-œr] m. scout.

éclat [éklà] m. burst; explosion; peal [tonnerre]; flash; brightness; luster; brilliance; renown; splendo(u)r; outburst; piece; splinter; rire aux éclats, to laugh heartily; faire un éclat, to create a stir; faux éclat, tawdriness. || **éclatant** [-taⁿ] adj. brilliant; loud; sparkling, glittering; magnificent; obvious. || **éclatement** [-tmaⁿ] m. bursting; explosion. || **éclater** [-té] v. to burst; to explode; to blow up; to break out [feu, rires]; to shatter; to clap [tonnerre]; to flash; faire éclater, to blow up; to burst; to break; laisser éclater, to give vent to [émotions].

éclipse [éklǐps] f. eclipse. || **éclipser** [-é] v. to eclipse; to outshine; to overshadow; s'éclipser, to become eclipsed; to vanish, to disappear.

éclisse [éklǐs] f. splinter; splint (med.); fish-plate [rail].

éclopé [éklòpé] m. cripple; adj. crippled, lame.

éclore [éklòr] v.* to hatch [œufs]; to open; to burst, to blossom; faire

éclore, to hatch; to realize [projet]. || **éclosion** [-ôzyoⁿ] f. hatching; opening; blossoming; breaking forth; dawning; dawn, birth (fig.).

écluse [éklüz] f. lock; sluice; floodgate. || **éclusier** [-zyé] m. lock-keeper.

écœurement [ékœrmaⁿ] m. disgust, nausea. || **écœurer** [-é] v. to sicken, to disgust, to nauseate; to dishearten.

école [ékòl] f. school; school-house; doctrine; instruction; faire école, to set a fashion; école maternelle, nursery school. || **écolier** [-yé] m. schoolboy, pupil, learner; novice, beginner. || **écolière** [-yèr] f. schoolgirl.

éconduire [ékoⁿdüïr] v. to show out; être éconduit, to be met with a polite refusal.

économat [ékònòmà] m. treasurership; steward's office, treasurer's office. || **économe** [ékònòm] m., f. treasurer, steward, bursar [collège]; housekeeper; adj. economical, frugal, thrifty; sparing. || **économie** [-ǐ] f. economy; thrift; saving; pl. savings; faire des économies, to save up. || **économique** [-ǐk] adj. economic [science]; economical, cheap, inexpensive. || **économiser** [-ǐzé] v. to economize; to save, to put by. || **économiste** [-ǐst] m. economist.

écope [ékòp] f. scoop; ladle. || **écoper** [-é] v. to bail out; to be hit; to suffer.

écorce [ékòrs] f. bark [arbre]; peel, rind; outside. || **écorcer** [-sé] v. to bark; to peel.

écorcher [ékòrshé] v. to skin, to flay; to scratch; to graze; to fleece [clients]; to grate on [oreille]; to murder [langue]. || **écorchure** [-ür] f. abrasion; graze; scratch.

écorner [ékòrné] v. to break the horns of; to dog-ear [livre]; to curtail, to reduce.

écornifler [ékòrnǐflé] v. to cadge, to scrounge.

écossais [ékòsè] m. Scot; Scots [dialecte]; adj. Scottish. || **Écosse** [-ékòs] f. Scotland.

écosser [ékòsé] v. to shell, to husk.

écot [ékô] m. share, quota; reckoning; shot.

écoulement [ékûlmaⁿ] m. flow; discharge; outlet; sale, disposal. || **écouler** [-é] v. to flow out; to pass [temps]; to sell, to dispose of; s'écouler, to flow away; to elapse [temps]; to sell.

écourter [ékûrté] v. to shorten; to curtail; to crop.

écoute [ékût] f. listening-post (mil.); listening in, reception [radio]; aux écoutes, eavesdropping. || **écouter** [-é] v. to listen (to); to listen in; to heed, to pay attention; **s'écouter,** to coddle oneself; to indulge oneself. || *écouteur* [-œr] *m.* receiver [téléphone]; headphone; listener; eavesdropper. || *écoutille* [-ĭy] *f.* hatchway.

écran [ékra^n] *m.* screen; filter (phot.).

écrasement [ékrâzma^n] *m.* crushing; defeat; disaster; crash. || *écraser* [-é] *v.* to crush; to run over; to squash; to ruin; to overwhelm; **s'écraser,** to crash (aviat.).

écrémer [ékrémé] *v.* to take the cream off, to skim. || *écrémeuse* [-ëz] *f.* separator.

écrevisse [ékr^{e}vìs] *f.* crayfish.

écrier (s') [sékrìé] *v.* to cry out; to exclaim.

écrin [ékri^n] *m.* casket, case.

écrire [ékrîr] *v.** to write; to write down; to compose; *machine à écrire,* typewriter; *comment ce mot s'écrit-il?* how do you spell that word? || *écrit* [ékrì] *m.* writing pamphlet; written examination. *adj.* written; *par écrit,* in writing. || *écriteau* [-tô] *m.** bill, poster, placard, notice, board. || *écriture* [-tür] *f.* writing; documents, records; entry [comptabilité]. *l'Ecriture sainte,* Holy Writ, *tenir les écritures,* to keep the accounts. || *écrivailleur* [-vàyœr] *m.* scribbler. || *écrivain* [-vi^n] *m.* writer, author; *authoress* [femme].

écrou [ékrû] *m.* nut (mech.).

écrouer [ékrûé] *v.* to imprison, to send to prison.

écroulement [ékrûlma^n] *m.* collapse; crumbling; falling in; downfall; ruin. || *écrouler (s')* [sékrûlé] *v.* to collapse; to fall in; to give way; to crumble; to break up; to come to nothing.

écru [ékrü] *adj.* unbleached; raw [soie], ecru [couleur].

écu [ékü] *m.* shield; crown [monnaie].

écueil [ékœy] *m.* rock; reef; sandbank; danger; temptation.

écuelle [éküèl] *f.* porringer; bowlful.

éculer [ékülé] *v.* to tread down at the heel [chaussures]; *éculé,* down-at-heel.

écume [éküm] *f.* foam [animal, vagues]; froth; lather; scum; *écume de mer,* meerschaum. || *écumer* [-é] *v.* to foam, to froth; to skim; to scour [mer]. || *écumoire* [-wàr] *f.* skimmer.

écureuil [ékürœy] *m.* squirrel.

écurie [ékürî] *f.* stable; stud; boxing school.

écusson [éküso^n] *m.* escutcheon; scutcheon; badge; tab.

écuyer [éküyé] *m.* squire; horseman; riding-master; equestrian. ||

écuyère [-yèr] *f.* horsewoman; equestrienne.

édenté [éda^{n}té] *adj.* broken-toothed; toothless.

édicter [édìkté] *v.* to enact, to decree.

édification [édìfìkàsyo^n] *f.* edification building, erection. || *édifice* [-ìs] *m.* edifice, structure, building. || *édifier* [-yé] *v.* to enlighten; to edify; to build, to erect.

édit [édì] *m.* edict, decree.

éditer [édìté] *v.* to edit; to publish. || *éditeur,* -trice [-œr, -trìs] *m.* editor, *f.* editress; publisher. || *édition* [-syo^n] *f.* edition; issue; publication. || *éditorial* [édìtòryàl] *m.** leading article; *adj.** editorial. || *éditorialiste* [-ìst] *s.* leader writer, *Am.* editorial writer.

édredon [édr^{e}do^n] *m.* eiderdown; eiderdown quilt.

éducateur, -trice [édükàtœr, -trìs] *m., f.* educator; breeder. || *éducatif* [-àtìf] *adj.** educative, educational. || *éducation* [-àsyo^n] *f.* education; training; upbringing; breeding; *sans éducation,* ill-bred. || *éduquer* [édükè] *v.* to bring up; to educate; to train [animaux].

effacé [èfàsé] *adj.* retired; unobtrusive. || *effacer* [èfàsé] *v.* to efface; to delete; to blot out; to erase; to outshine; to retract (aviat.); **s'effacer,** to become obliterated; to wear away; to give way, to stand aside.

effarer [èfàré] *v.* to scare, to bewilder, to fluster, to flurry.

effaroucher [èfàrûshé] *v.* to startle; to scare away; to alarm.

effectif [èfèktìf] *m.* total strength; numbers, complement (naut.); *adj.** effective; positive; actual. || *effectivement* [-ìvma^n] *adv.* effectively; just so; in actual fact. || *effectuer* [-üé] *v.* to effect; to carry out, to execute, to achieve, to accomplish; **s'effectuer,** to be carried out; to be realized; to be performed.

efféminé [éfémìné] *adj.* effeminate.

effervescence [èfèrvèsa^{n}s] *f.* effervescence, excitement. || *effervescent* [-a^n] *adj.* effervescent; over-excited.

effet [èfè] *m.* effect, result; purpose; action; impression; bill (comm.); *pl.* property, belongings; kit, outfit (mil.); *sans effet,* ineffective, ineffectual; *en effet,* indeed; *faire l'effet de,* to look like.

effeuiller [èfèyé] *v.* to pluck off the petals; to thin out the leaves of.

efficace [èfìkàs] *f.* efficacity (theol.); *adj.* efficacious; effectual, effective. || *efficacité* [-ìté] *f.* efficacy, effectiveness; efficiency.

efficient [èfìsya^n] *adj.* efficient.

effigie [èfìjî] *f.* effigy.

effiler [èfìlé] *v.* to unravel, to fray; to taper. ‖ **effilocher** [-òshé] *v.* to ravel out; to fray.

efflanqué [èflⁿké] *adj.* lanky.

effleurer [èflœré] *v.* to graze; to brush; to skim; to touch lightly on; to cross, to come into the mind of.

effluve [èflüv] *m.* effluvium.

effondrer [èfoⁿdré] *v.* to break up [terre]; to stave in; to overwhelm; *s'effondrer*, to cave in; to collapse; to slump [prix].

efforcer (s') [sèfòrsé] *v.* to strive, to do one's best; to endeavour; to strain oneself. ‖ **effort** [èfòr] *m.* effort, exertion; strain.

effraction [èfraksyoⁿ] *f.* house-breaking; *vol avec effraction*, burglary.

effrayant [èfrèyaⁿ] *adj.* dreadful, awful, appalling. ‖ **effrayer** [-èyé] *v* to frighten, to terrify, to scare; *s'effrayer*, to be frightened, to take fright.

effréné [èfréné] *adj.* unbridled, unrestrained.

effriter [èfrìté] *v.* to exhaust; *s'effriter*, to crumble; to weather [roche].

effroi [èfrwà] *m.* fear, terror, fright.

effronté [èfroⁿté] *adj.* shameless; impudent; brazen; saucy [enfant]. ‖ **effronterie** [-rî] *f.* effrontery, impudence, impertinence.

effroyable [èfrwàyàbl] *adj.* frightful; horrible; awful; shocking.

effusion [èfüzyoⁿ] *f.* effusion; outpouring; pouring out, gushing; effusiveness.

égal [égàl] *m.°* equal; *adj.°* equal, alike; regular; even; level, smooth; steady [allure]; *sans égal*, matchless; *ça m'est égal*, it's all the same to me, I don't mind. ‖ **également** [-maⁿ] *adv.* equally; likewise; as well, too. ‖ **égaler** [-é] *v.* to equal; to match; to compare, to put on a par (with). ‖ **égaliser** [-ìzé] *v.* to equalize, to level; to make even. ‖ **égalité** [-ìté] *f* equality; uniformity; regularity; evenness; *à égalité*, equal, deuce [tennis].

égard [égàr] *m.* regard, consideration, respect; *à l'égard de*, with regard to; *par égard pour*, out of respect for; *eu égard à*, considering; *à cet égard*, in this respect.

égarement [égàrmaⁿ] *m.* straying; mislaying; aberration [esprit]; wildness; frenzy; disordered life. ‖ **égarer** [-é] *v.* to lead astray; to mislead; to mislay; *s'égarer*, to lose one's way; to wander [esprit].

égayer [égèyé] *v.* to cheer up; to enliven; to brighten up.

égide [éjìd] *f.* protection.

églantier [églaⁿtyé] *m.* eglantine, sweet briar; wild rose. ‖ **églantine** [-în] *f* wild rose, dog-rose.

église [églîz] *f.* church; *l'Eglise anglicane*, the Church of England.

égoïsme [égòìsm] *m.* egoism, selfishness. ‖ **égoïste** [égòìst] *m.*, *f.* egoist; *adj.* selfish.

égorger [égòrjé] *v.* to slaughter; to kill; to slit (someone's) throat.

égosiller (s') [ségòzìyé] *v.* to sing loudly [oiseau]; to shout like mad [personne].

égout [égû] *m.* drain; sewer; drainage; spout. ‖ **égoutter** [-té] *v.* to drip; to drain (off). ‖ **égouttoir** [-twàr] *m.* plate-rack; drainer.

égratigner [égràtìñé] *v.* to scratch. ‖ **égratignure** [-ür] *f.* scratch.

égrener [égrⁿé] *v.* to pick off [raisins]; to shell; to gin [coton]; *s'égrener*, to fall; to scatter.

éhonté [éoⁿté] *adj.* brazen, shameless, umblushing.

éjectable [éjèktàbl] *adj.* ejector [siège] ‖ **éjection** [-syoⁿ] *f.* ejection.

élaborer [élàbòré] *v.* to elaborate, to work out

élaguer [élàgé] *v.* to prune.

élan [élaⁿ] *m.* elk, eland (zool.).

élan [élaⁿ] *m.* spring, dash, bound; impetus, impulse; outburst. ‖ **élancé** [-sé] *adj.* slim; slender. ‖ **élancement** [-smaⁿ] *m* spring; transport; twinge [douleur] ‖ **élancer** [-sé] *v.* to dart, to shoot; *s'élancer*, to shoot up; to spring, to dart forth.

élargir [élàrjîr] *v.* to enlarge; to widen, to broaden [idées]; to release; *s'élargir*, to get wider; to extend; to stretch [chaussures].

élastique [élàstìk] *m.* elastic; rubber; elastic band; *adj.* elastic; springy.

électeur, -trice [élèktœr, -trîs] *m.*, *f.* voter, elector. ‖ **élection** [élèksyoⁿ] *f.* election; polling, preference, choice; *élection partielle*, by-election. ‖ **électoral** [élèktòràl] *adj.°* electoral.

électricien [élèktrìsyⁿ] *m.* electrician. ‖ **électricité** [élèktrìsìté] *f.* electricity. ‖ **électrique** [-ìk] *adj.* electric, electrical. ‖ **électriser** [-ìzé] *v.* to electrify. ‖ **électro-aimant** [-dèmaⁿ] *m.* electromagnet. ‖ **électrocuter** [-òküté] *v.* to electrocute. ‖ **électronique** [-ònìk] *adj.* electronic, electron; *f.* electronics.

élégamment [élégàmaⁿ] *adv.* elegantly. ‖ **élégance** [-aⁿs] *f.* elegance, stylishness; beauty. ‖ **élégant** [-aⁿ] *adj.* elegant, stylish; tasteful; *m.* person of fashion.

élément [élémaⁿ] *m.* element; cell (electr.); ingredient; *pl.* rudiments, basic principles. ‖ **élémentaire** [-tèr] *adj.* elementary; rudimentary; fundamental, basic.

éléphant [éléfaⁿ] *m.* elephant.

élevage [élvàj] *m.* breeding, rearing; ranch. **élévation** (élévàsyoⁿ] *f.* elevation, raising, lifting; rise; increase; loftiness. ‖ **élève** [élèv] *m.*, *f.* pupil, schoolboy (*f.* schoolgirl), student; disciple; *f.* breeding, seedling. ‖ **élevé** [élvé] *adj.* high, lofty; *mal élevé*, illbred. **élever** [-é] *v.* to raise, to lift; to erect; to set up, to bring up [enfant]; to breed; *s'élever*, to rise (up); to get up; to protest; to amount; to increase. ‖ **éleveur** [-œr] *m.* breeder [animaux].

éligible [élìjìbl] *adj.* eligible; fit.

éliminer [élìmìné] *v.* to eliminate, to get rid of; to cancel out.

élire [élìr] *v.** to elect; to choose; to return [candidat].

élite [élìt] *f.* elite, best, pick, choice; *d'élite*, crack [régiment]; picked [troupes].

élixir [élìksìr] *m.* elixir.

elle, elles [èl] *pron.* she, her; it; *pl.* they, them. *elle-même*, herself; itself.

élocution [élòküsyoⁿ] *f.* elocution, delivery.

éloge [élòj] *m.* praise; eulogy; panegyric. ‖ **élogieux** [-yé] *adj.** laudatory; eulogistic.

éloigné [élwàñé] *adj.* far, remote, distant; absent. ‖ **éloignement** [-maⁿ] *m.* distance, absence, remoteness; removal; dislike, antipathy. ‖ **éloigner** [-é] *v.* to remove; to put away; to avert [soupçons]; to postpone; to alienate; *s'éloigner*, to retire; to go away; to differ; to digress.

éloquence [élòkaⁿs] *f.* eloquence. ‖ **éloquent** [-aⁿ] *adj.* eloquent.

élu [élü] *p. p. of* élire.

élucider [élüsìdé] *v.* to elucidate, to clear up.

éluder [élüdé] *v.* to elude, to dodge, to evade; to shirk.

Elysée [élìzé] *m.* Elysium; Paris residence of the President of the French Republic; *adj.* Elysian.

émacié [émàsyé] *adj.* emaciated.

émail [émày] *m.** enamel; glaze. ‖ **émailler** [-yé] *v.* to enamel; to dot.

émanation [émànàsyoⁿ] *f.* emanation.

émanciper [émàⁿsìpé] *v.* to emancipate; to liberate.

émaner [émàné] *v.* to emanate, to issue; to originate.

émarger [émàrjé] *v.* to sign, to write in the margin; to initial; to draw a salary.

emballage [aⁿbàlàj] *m.* packing; spurt [sport]. ‖ **emballer** [-é] *v.* to pack up; to wrap up; to spurt [sport]; to excite, to fill with enthusiasm; *s'emballer*, to bolt, to run off [cheval]; to race [moteur]; to get excited.

embarcadère [aⁿbàrkàdèr] *m.* landing-stage, wharf, quay; departure platform [gare]. ‖ **embarcation** [-àsyoⁿ] *f.* craft, ship's boat.

embardée [aⁿbàrdé] *f.* lurch, yaw (naut.), swerve [auto].

embarquement [aⁿbàrk°maⁿ] *m.* embarcation, shipment. ‖ **embarquer** [-é] *v.* to embark; to ship; to take on board; (pop.) to arrest; *s'embarquer*, to go aboard; to embark upon; to sail out.

embarras [aⁿbàrà] *m.* obstruction; impediment; difficulty, trouble; embarrassment; trafic jam; *faire des embarras*, to be fussy. ‖ **embarrasser** [-sé] *v.* to embarrass; to hinder; to encumber; to trouble, to puzzle, to perplex; *s'embarrasser*, to be burdened (*de*, with); to get entangled; to be at a loss.

embauche [aⁿbósh] *f.* engaging; job. ‖ **embaucher** [aⁿbóshé] *v.* to hire, to engage; to take on.

embaumé [aⁿbômé] *adj.* balmy. ‖ **embaumer** [-é] *v.* to embalm; to perfume; to smell sweetly of.

embellir [aⁿbèlìr] *v.* to embellish; to doll up; to improve in looks. ‖ **embellissement** [aⁿbèlìsmaⁿ] *m.* embellishment; adornment.

embêtant [aⁿbètaⁿ] *adj.* (fam.) tiresome, annoying. ‖ **embêtement** [-maⁿ] *m.* (fam.) bother; nuisance; worry. ‖ **embêter** [-é] *v.* (fam.) to annoy; to bore; to get on one's nerves.

emblée (d') [daⁿblé] *loc. adv.* there and then; at once; right away; at the outset.

emblème [aⁿblèm] *m.* emblem; symbol; badge.

emboîter [aⁿbwàté] *v.* to encase; to fit in; to set [os]; to can; to box; to clamp, to interlock, to joint; *emboîter le pas à*, to dog s.o.'s footsteps; *s'emboîter*, to fit (*dans*, into).

embolie [aⁿbòlì] *f.* embolism.

embonpoint [aⁿboⁿpwiⁿ] *m.* stoutness, plumpness.

emboucher [aⁿbûshé] *v.* to put to one's mouth, to blow; to bit [cheval]; *mal embouché*, foul-mouthed, coarse. ‖ **embouchure** [-ür] *f.* mouth [rivière]; mouthpiece (mus.); opening.

embourber [aⁿbûrbé] v. to bog; **s'embourber**, to get bogged; to stick in the mud.

embouteillage [aⁿbûtèyàj] m. congestion; bottle-neck; traffic jam; bottling. ‖ **embouteiller** [-èyé] v. to bottle; to bottle up, to block up; to jam [route]; to bottleneck [comm.].

emboutir [aⁿbûtîr] v. to stamp; to beat out; to emboss; **s'emboutir**, to crash; to collide.

embranchement [aⁿbraⁿshmaⁿ] m. branching off; branch-road; road junction; branch-line. ‖ **embrancher** [-é] v. to connect; to join up.

embraser [aⁿbràzé] v. to set on fire; to fire; **s'embraser**, to catch fire, to take fire.

embrassade [aⁿbràsàd] f. kissing. ‖ **embrasse** [aⁿbràs] f. loop; curtainband; arm-rest. ‖ **embrassement** [-maⁿ] m. embrace; hug. ‖ **embrasser** [-é] v. to embrace; to hug; to kiss; to espouse [cause]; to adopt; to include, to take in.

embrasure [aⁿbràzûr] f. embrasure.

embrayage [aⁿbrèyàj] m. coupling, connecting; clutch; putting into gear; **arbre d'embrayage**, clutch-shaft. ‖ **embrayer** [-èyé] v. to couple, to connect; to throw into gear; to let in the clutch [auto].

embrigader [aⁿbrìgàdé] v. to brigade; to enrol.

embrouiller [aⁿbrûyé] v. to tangle up, to embroil; to mix up; to muddle; to confuse.

embrumer [aⁿbrümé] v. to haze; to muddle.

embrun [aⁿbruⁿ] m. spray; fog.

embûche [aⁿbûsh] f. ambush; trap.

embuer [aⁿbüé] v. to mist.

embuscade [aⁿbüskàd] f. ambush. ‖ **embusquer** [-é] v. to post under cover; **s'embusquer**, to lie in wait; to lie hidden; (fam.) to shirk; **un embusqué**, a shirker.

émeraude [émród] f., adj. emerald.

émerger [émèrjé] v. to emerge; to appear, to come into view.

émeri [émrì] m. emery; **papier à l'émeri**, emery-paper.

émérite [émérìt] adj. emeritus; eminent.

émerveillement [émèrvèymaⁿ] m. amazement, wonder, astonishment. ‖ **émerveiller** [-èyé] v. to amaze, to fill with wonder, to astonish; **s'émerveiller**, to wonder, to marvel, to be amazed.

émetteur, -trice [émètœr, -trìs] m. issuer; transmitter; adj. issuing;

broadcasting; transmitting. ‖ **émettre** [émètr] v. to emit [son]; to issue [finances]; to send out; to express [opinion]; to broadcast, to transmit [radio].

émeute [émët] f. riot. ‖ **émeutier** [-yé] m. rioter.

émietter [émyèté] v. to crumble; to waste; **s'émietter**, to crumble away.

émigrant [émìgraⁿ] m. emigrant; adj. emigrating; migratory [oiseau]. ‖ **émigration** [-àsyoⁿ] f. emigration; migration. ‖ **émigré** [-é] m. emigrant; émigré; refugee. ‖ **émigrer** [-é] v. to emigrate.

émincé [émiⁿsé] m. hash; mincemeat; **émincer**, to mince.

éminemment [émìnàmaⁿ] adv. eminently; to a high degree. ‖ **éminence** [-aⁿs] f. eminence; prominence. ‖ **éminent** [-aⁿ] adj. eminent; distinguished; elevated, high.

émissaire [émìssèr] m. emissary; messenger. ‖ **émission** [-yoⁿ] f. emission; issue; broadcasting; transmission; radiation [chaleur].

emmagasiner [aⁿmàgàzìné] v. to store, to warehouse; to store up.

emmailloter [aⁿmàyòté] v. to swaddle; to swathe.

emmancher [aⁿmaⁿshé] v. to haft, to fix a handle to; to fit together; to start, to set about. ‖ **emmanchure** [-ür] f. sleeve-hole, arm-hole.

emmêler [aⁿmèlé] v. to tangle; to mix up; to muddle; to mat.

emménager [aⁿménàjé] v. to move in, Br. to move house; to install.

emmener [aⁿmⁿné] v. to take away; to lead away; to take.

emmitoufler [aⁿmìtûflé] v. to muffle up.

émoi [émwà] m. emotion; commotion; excitement; agitation; anxiety. ‖ **émotif** [émòtìf] adj.* emotional; emotive. ‖ **émotion** [émòsyoⁿ] f. emotion; excitement; agitation; anxiety; feeling. ‖ **émotionnant** [-ònaⁿ] adj. moving; thrilling. ‖ **émotionner** [-òné] v. to move; to thrill. ‖ **émotivité** [-tìvìté] f. emotivity, emotiveness.

émousser [émûsé] v. to blunt; to take the edge off; to dull [sens]; **s'émousser**, to become blunt (or) blunted; to lose its edge [appétit].

émouvant [émûvaⁿ] adj. moving, affecting, touching; thrilling. ‖ **émouvoir** [-wàr] v.* to move; to touch, to affect; to rouse, to stir.

empaqueter [aⁿpàkté] v. to pack up; to wrap up, to do up.

emparer (s') [saⁿpàré] v. to take possession of, to lay hands on, to secure; to seize.

empâter [aⁿpâté] v. to make sticky; to paste to fatten, to cram.

empêchement [aⁿpèshmaⁿ] m. obstacle, hindrance impediment ‖ **empêcher** [-é] ╲ to prevent (de. from); to hinder, to impede, to obstruct, to put a stop to; s'empêcher, to refrain (de, from).

empereur [aⁿprœr] m. emperor.

empeser [aⁿpezé] v. to starch, to stiffen.

empester [aⁿpèsté] v. to infect; to poison. to make (something) stink; to reek of

emphase [aⁿfâz] f. bombast; pomposity; grandiloquence; over-emphasis. ‖ **emphatique** [-àtìk] adj. bombastic; pompous

emphysème [aⁿfizèm] m. emphysema.

empiècement [aⁿpyèsmaⁿ] m. yoke.

empierrer [aⁿpyèré] v. to pave; to metal, to macadamize [route]; to ballast [voie].

empiéter [aⁿpyété] v. to encroach (sur, upon). to infringe; to usurp.

empiler [aⁿpìlé] v. to pile up, to stack; (pop.) to cheat; to rob.

empire [aⁿpìr] m. empire; control; sway; rule authority, mastery.

empirer [aⁿpìré] v to grow worse; to worsen, to make worse; to aggravate; to deteriorate.

empirique [aⁿpìrìk] adj. empirical. ‖ **empirisme** [-ìsm] m. empiricism; empiriste, empiric. empiricist.

emplacement [aⁿplàsmaⁿ] m. site, place, location emplacement (mil.).

emplâtre [aⁿplâtr] m plaster; (pop.) Br. muff. Am milk toast.

emplette [aⁿplèt] f. purchase; aller faire des emplettes. to go shopping.

emplir [aⁿplìr] v. to fill, to fill up.

emploi [aⁿplwà] m. employment. use; post, job function mode d'emploi, directions for use.   **employé** [-yé] m. clerk, assistant [magasin] employee; adj. employed. ‖ **employer** [-yé] v. to employ, to use, to lay out [argent]; to exert; s'employer, to busy oneself, to occupy oneself. ‖ **employeur** [-yœr] m. employer.

empocher [aⁿposhé] v. to pocket.

empoigner [aⁿpwàñé] v. to grip; to grasp; to lay hold of; to arrest, to catch; to thrill; s'empoigner, to grapple.

empois [aⁿpwà] m. starch; dressing (text.).

empoisonnement [aⁿpwàzònmaⁿ] m. poisoning. ‖ **empoisonner** [-é] v. to poison; to corrupt; to infect; to reek of. ‖ **empoisonneur** [-œr] m. poisoner.

emporté [aⁿpòrté] adj. hot-headed; hasty, quick-tempered. ‖ **emportement** [-ᵉmaⁿ] m fit of passion. outburst transport ‖ **emporter** [-é] v to carry away, to take away to remove; to capture l'emporter sur. to prevail over, to get the better of, s'emporter, to flare up, to lose one's temper; to bolt [cheval]

empourprer [aⁿpûrpré] v. to purple; to flush s'empourprer, to glow red; to purple to blush

empreindre [aⁿprɛ̃dr] v. to impress; emprein de. stamped with. ‖ **empreinte** [-ɪⁿt] f. imprint; impress; stamp mark.

empressé [aⁿprèsé] adj. eager; earnest fervent. fussy ‖ **empressement** [-maⁿ] m eagerness, readiness, promptness hurry. ‖ **empresser** (s') [-é] v to hasten; to be eager; to hurry.

emprise [aⁿprîz] f. hold; mastery.

emprisonnement [aⁿprizònmaⁿ] m. imprisonment custody. ‖ **emprisonner** [-é] v to imprison, to confine.

emprunt [aⁿpruⁿ] m. loan, borrowing; d'emprunt. assumed. ‖ **emprunter** [-té] v to borrow, to assume [nom]. to take [route]. ‖ **emprunteur, -teuse** [-tœr, -tèz] m., f. borrower; adj. borrowing.

ému [émü] p. p. of émouvoir.

émulation [émülàsyoⁿ] f. emulation; rivalry ‖ **émule** [émül] m., f. emulator; rival, competitor.

en [aⁿ] prep. in; into; to; in the; in a; at; of; by; like; whilst; while; with; within; from; aller en Amérique, to go to America; il entra en courant, he came running in; en un an, within a year. tout en regrettant, while regretting; en bois, wooden; en bas, below. downstairs, en été, in summer; en avant, forward; agir en homme to act like a man; en-tête, heading headline.

en [aⁿ] pron. of him, of her; of it; of them, for it; for them; from there. some; any; il en parle, he is speaking of it; il en est désolé. he is sorry about it; j'en ai, I have some; combien en voulez-vous?, how many do you want?. prenez-en. take some; il en est aimé. he is loved by her; je ne l'en admire pas moins, I admire him none the less for it.

enamouré [aⁿamüré] adj. amorous; enamoured.

encadrement [aⁿkàdrᵉmaⁿ] m. framing; frame, framework; setting. ‖ **encadrer** [-é] v. to frame; to surround; to officer (mil.).

encaisse [aⁿkès] f. cash in hand, cash balance. ‖ **encaissé** [-é] adj.

encased; boxed-in; sunk [route]. ‖ **encaisser** [-é] v. to pack in cases; to box; to collect [argent]; (pop.) to take punishment. ‖ **encaisseur** [-œr] m. cash-collector; cashier.

encan [aⁿkaⁿ] m. public auction.

encarter [aⁿkàrté] v. to inset; to insert; to card; to card-index; to register.

encastrer [aⁿkàstré] v. to fit in; to embed.

encaustique [aⁿkôstìk] f. encaustic; wax polish, furniture polish. ‖ **encaustiquer** [-ké] v. to polish; to wax.

enceinte [aⁿsⁿt] f. enclosure; walls; precincts; adj. f. pregnant, with child.

encens [aⁿsaⁿ] m. incense. ‖ **encenser** [-sé] v. to incense; to flatter. ‖ **encensoir** [-swàr] m. censer; flattery.

encercler [aⁿsèrklé] v. to encircle, to surround, to hem in; to shut in.

enchaînement [aⁿshènmaⁿ] m. chain; chaining; series; sequence. ‖ **enchaîner** [-é] v. to chain up; to fetter; to connect; to link; to curb, to paralyse (fig.); s'enchaîner, to be linked (or) connected.

enchanté [aⁿshaⁿté] adj. enchanted; delighted; pleased to meet you [présentation]. ‖ **enchanter** [-é] v. to enchant; to bewitch; to enrapture; to delight. ‖ **enchanteur, -eresse** [-œr, -rès] m., f. charmer; enchanter; adj. charming; enchanting; entrancing.

enchâsser [aⁿshâsé] v. to enshrine; to insert, to mount; to set [diamant].

enchère [aⁿshèr] f. bidding, bid; vente aux enchères, auction sale. ‖ **enchérir** [-érîr] v. to bid; to outbid; to raise the price of; to grow dearer; enchérir sur, to outdo, to go one better than.

enchevêtrement [aⁿshevètremaⁿ] m. tangle; confusion. ‖ **enchevêtrer** [-é] v. to entangle; to confuse; to halter [cheval]; to join.

enchifrené [aⁿshìfrené] adj. stuffed up; sniffling.

enclin [aⁿklⁿ] adj. inclined; disposed; prone; apt.

enclos [aⁿklô] m. enclosure; paddock; wall. ‖ **enclore** [-klòr] v. to enclose, to close in.

enclume [aⁿklüm] f. anvil.

encoche [aⁿkòsh] f. notch; slot; pl. thumb-index [livres].

encoignure [aⁿkòñür] f. corner; corner-cupboard.

encolure [aⁿkòlür] f. neck; size in collars; neck-opening [robe].

encombrement [aⁿkoⁿbremaⁿ] m. obstruction; litter; congestion; traffic jam; glut (comm.); overcrowding. ‖

encombrer [-é] v. to obstruct; to block up; to congest; to crowd; to encumber; to litter; s'encombrer, to cumber (or) burden oneself (de, with).

encore [aⁿkòr] adv. again; yet; besides; too; pas encore, not yet; encore un peu, a little more; a little longer; quoi encore?, what else?; encore que, although.

encouragement [aⁿkûràjmaⁿ] m. encouragement; inducement. ‖ **encourager** [-é] v. to encourage; to cheer.

encourir [aⁿkûrîr] v.* to incur.

encrasser [aⁿkràsé] v. to dirty, to soil; to grease; to smear; to stop up, to clog; to soot up [bougie]; to oil up; s'encrasser, to become dirty; to soot up; to clog; to fur; to get choked.

encre [aⁿkr] f. ink; encre de Chine, Indian ink, indelible ink; encre sympathique, invisible ink. ‖ **encrer** [-é] v. to ink. ‖ **encrier** [-ìyé] m. inkstand, inkwell.

encroûter [aⁿkrûté] v. to cover with a crust; to crust; to cake; to roughcast; s'encroûter, to crust; to fossilize, to get rusty.

encyclopédie [aⁿsìklòpédî] f. encyclopedia.

endetter [aⁿdèté] v. to involve in debt; s'endetter, to run into debt.

endeuiller [aⁿdœyé] v. to plunge into mourning; to sadden.

endiablé [aⁿdyàblé] adj. wild; reckless; possessed; furious; mischievous; frantic.

endiguer [aⁿdìgé] v. to dam up; to dyke; to localize; to check.

endive [aⁿdîv] f. endive.

endoctriner [aⁿdòktrìné] v. to indoctrinate; to brainwash.

endolori [aⁿdòlòrì] adj. sore, aching.

endommager [aⁿdòmàjé] v. to damage; to injure.

endormant [aⁿdòrmaⁿ] adj. soporific; boring; humdrum; tedious, wearisome. ‖ **endormi** [-ì] adj. asleep; drowsy, sleepy; dormant; numb [membre]. ‖ **endormir** [-îr] v.* to put to sleep; to lull; to bore; to benumb; to humbug; to deaden [douleur]; s'endormir, to go to sleep, to fall asleep; to slack off (fig.).

endos, endossement [aⁿdô, -òsmaⁿ] m. endorsement. ‖ **endosser** [-òsé] v. to put on [habits]; to take on; to endorse; to back.

endroit [aⁿdrwà] m. place, spot, site; passage; right side [étoffe]; à l'endroit, right side out.

enduire [aⁿdüîr] v.* to coat; to plaster. ‖ **enduit** [-üî] m. coat, coating, plastering; glazing; dressing.

endurance [aⁿdüraⁿs] *f.* endurance; patience; resistance. ‖ **endurant** [-aⁿ] *adj.* enduring; patient; long-suffering.

endurcir [aⁿdürsîr] *v.* to harden; to inure; **s'endurcir**, to harden; to toughen; to become callous.

endurer [aⁿdüré] *v.* to bear, to endure, to put up with, to tolerate.

énergétique [énèrjétìk] *adj.* energizing; *f.* energetics. ‖ **énergie** [énèrjî] *f.* energy; vigo(u)r. ‖ **énergique** [-jìk] *adj.* energetic; vigo(u)rous; strenuous; strong; drastic; emphatic. ‖ **énergumène** [-gümèn] *m., f.* person possessed; wild fanatic; madman; ranter.

énervement [énèrv°maⁿ] *m.* enervation; nervous irritation. ‖ **énerver** [-é] *v.* to enervate; to irritate, to annoy; to get on (someone's) nerves; **s'énerver**, to become excited (or) irritable (or) nervy (or) nervous.

enfance [aⁿfaⁿs] *f.* childhood; infancy; dotage, second childhood. ‖ **enfant** [aⁿfaⁿ] *m., f.* child (*pl.* children); boy; girl, youngster; son; daughter; *enfant terrible*, little terror; *enfant de chœur*, chorister; *enfant trouvé*, foundling. ‖ **enfantement** [-tmaⁿ] *m.* childbirth; production; beginning. ‖ **enfanter** [-té] *v.* to bear, to give birth to, to beget. ‖ **enfantillage** [-tìyàj] *m.* childishness, trifle. ‖ **enfantin** [-tîⁿ] *adj.* childish; infantile.

enfariner [aⁿfàriné] *v.* to flour; to sprinkle with flour.

enfer [aⁿfèr] *m.* hell; *pl.* the underworld, Hades.

enfermer [aⁿfèrmé] *v.* to shut in; to close up; to enclose; to lock in.

enfiévrer [aⁿfyévré] *v.* to make (someone) feverish; to excite, to stir up, to fever.

enfiler [aⁿfilé] *v.* to thread [aiguille]; to string [perles]; to run through; to slip on [habits]; to turn down [rue]; to rake (mil.).

enfin [aⁿfiⁿ] *adv.* at last; finally; in short; that's to say; *interj.* at last! well!

enflammer [aⁿflàmé] *v.* to inflame; to set on fire; to enflame; **s'enflammer**, to catch fire; to become inflamed; to flare up (fig.).

enflé [aⁿflé] *adj.* swollen; bloated; turgid. ‖ **enfler** [-é] *v.* to swell; to puff out; to bloat; to elate; **s'enfler**, to swell; to rise [rivière]; to grow turgid. ‖ **enflure** [-ür] *f.* swelling; turgidity.

enfoncer [aⁿfoⁿsé] *v.* to break in; to break open; to drive in; to stave in; to sink; to cram [chapeau]; to get the better of; to do for (pop.); **s'enfoncer**, to sink; to subside, to go down; to plunge; to embed itself [balle].

enfouir [aⁿfûîr] *v.* to bury; to enclose; to conceal.

enfourcher [aⁿfûrshé] *v.* to sit astride; to mount.

enfreindre [aⁿfrîⁿdr] *v.** to infringe, to break, to transgress [loi].

enfuir (s') [saⁿfûîr] *v.°* to flee, to run away; to elope; to escape; to leak.

enfumer [aⁿfümé] *v.* to blacken (or) to fill with smoke; to smoke out.

engageant [aⁿgàjaⁿ] *adj.* engaging, winning; attractive; pleasing; inviting. ‖ **engagement** [-maⁿ] *m.* engagement; bond; promise; pawning; enlistment (mil.); appointment; action (mil.); entry [sport]; *pl.* liabilities. ‖ **engager** [-é] *v.* to engage; to pledge; to urge; to institute [poursuites]; to involve; to put in gear; to invest; to pawn; to sign on (naut.); to foul; to jam; to begin; to join [bataille]; **s'engager**, to promise; to undertake; to pledge oneself; to engage oneself; to enlist; to get stuck; to foul [ancre]; to enter; to begin.

engeance [aⁿjaⁿs] *f.* brood.

engelure [aⁿjlür] *f.* chilblain.

engendrer [aⁿjaⁿdré] *v.* to engender; to beget; to breed; to produce.

engin [aⁿjîⁿ] *m.* machine, engine; tool; device; trap.

englober [aⁿglòbé] *v.* to unite, to put together; to comprise; to include.

engloutir [aⁿglûtîr] *v.* to swallow up; to engulf; to swallow, to bolt.

engluer [aⁿglüé] *v.* to lime; to catch.

engoncé [aⁿgoⁿsé] *adj.* bundled up.

engorger [aⁿgòrjé] *v.* to block, to choke up, to obstruct, to congest.

engouement [aⁿgûmaⁿ] *m.* obstruction (med.); infatuation.

engourdir [aⁿgûrdîr] *v.* to numb, to benumb; to dull; **s'engourdir**, to grow numb; to become sluggish. ‖ **engourdissement** [-ìsmaⁿ] *m.* numbness; dullness, sluggishness.

engrais [aⁿgrè] *m.* manure; fattening; grass; pasture; *engrais chimique*, fertilizer. ‖ **engraisser** [-sé] *v.* to fatten; to manure; to fertilize [sol]; to thrive; to grow stout.

engrenage [aⁿgrenàj] *m.* gear; gearing; cogwheels; network (fig.); sequence.

engueulade [aⁿg°làd] *f.* (pop.) bawling out. ‖ **engueuler** [-lé] *v.* (pop.) to blow out, to tell off; **s'engueuler** (pop.), to have a row (*avec*, with).

enguirlander [aⁿgìrlaⁿdé] *v.* to garland; (fam.) to smack down.

énigmatique [énìgmàtìk] *adj.* enigmatic; puzzling. ‖ **énigme** [énìgm] *f.* enigma, riddle.

enivrer [aⁿnìvré] v. to intoxicate, to make (someone) drunk; to carry away (fig.); *s'enivrer*, to get drunk; to be intoxicated.

enjambée [aⁿjaⁿbé] f. stride. ‖ *enjamber* [-é] v. to straddle; to stride over; to stride along; to encroach.

enjeu [aⁿjë] m.* stake.

enjoindre [aⁿjwìⁿdr] v. to enjoin, to direct, to order; to call upon.

enjôler [aⁿjôlé] v. to wheedle, to coax; to humbug. ‖ *enjôleur, -euse* [œr, -ëz] m., f. wheedler, cajoler; adj. wheedling, coaxing.

enjoliver [aⁿjòlìvé] v. to beautify; to embellish; to adorn. ‖ *enjoliveur* [-œr] m. wheel-disc, hub-cap.

enjoué [aⁿjwé] adj. playful; sprightly, jaunty; lively, bright.

enlacer [aⁿlàsé] v. to entwine, to interlace; to embrace, to clasp; to hem in.

enlaidir [aⁿlèdîr] v. to disfigure; to make ugly (qqn); to grow ugly.

enlèvement [aⁿlèvmaⁿ] m. removal, carrying off; kidnapping; abduction; storming (mil.). ‖ *enlever* [aⁿlvé] v. to remove; to carry off; to lift up; to take off; to kidnap; to abduct; to storm (mil.); to win [prix]; to urge.

enliser [aⁿlìzé] v. to suck in; *s'enliser*, to sink (dans, in).

enluminer [aⁿlümìné] v. to illuminate; to colo(u)r; to redden, to flush; *enluminé*, flushed, rubicund; *enluminure*, illumination; ruddiness.

ennemi [ènmì] m. enemy, foe; adversary; adj. hostile; opposing, prejudicial.

ennoblir [aⁿnòblîr] v. to ennoble.

ennui [aⁿnüï] m. worry; weariness; tediousness; trouble; nuisance, annoyance; bore. ‖ *ennuyer* [-yé] v. to worry; to annoy, to vex; to bother, to bore; *s'ennuyer*, to be bored; to feel dull; to be fed up (fam.). ‖ *ennuyeux* [-yë] adj.* tedious; annoying; worrying.

énoncé [énoⁿsé] m. statement; wording. ‖ *énoncer* [-é] v. to enunciate; to express; to state.

enorgueillir [aⁿnòrgœyîr] v. to make proud; *s'enorgueillir*, to be proud; to pride oneself (de, on).

énorme [énôrm] adj. enormous, huge, tremendous; monstrous; outrageous; shocking. ‖ *énormité* [-lté] f. enormity; hugeness; shocking thing; outrageousness.

enquérir (s') [saⁿkérîr] v. to inquire, to ask (de, after, about). ‖ *enquête* [aⁿkèt] f. inquiry, investigation. ‖ *enquêter* [aⁿkèté] v. to hold an inquiry, to investigate.

enraciner [aⁿràsìné] v. to root; to dig in; to implant; *s'enraciner*, to take root; to become rooted.

enragé [aⁿràjé] m. madman; adj. mad; enraged; keen, out-and-out; enthusiastic. ‖ *enrager* [-é] v. to enrage; to madden; to be mad (fam.); *faire enrager*, to tease; to drive wild.

enrayer [aⁿrèyé] v. to brake; to check; to lock [roue]; to jam; to stop; to spoke.

enregistrement [aⁿrjìstr°maⁿ] m. registration; entry; recording; registry. ‖ *enregistrer* [-é] v. to register; to record; to score. ‖ *enregistreur* [-œr] m. registrar; recorder; recording apparatus; adj.* recording; self-registering [baromètre].

enrhumer (s') [saⁿrümé] v. to catch a cold; *être enrhumé*, to have a cold.

enrichi [aⁿrìshì] m., adj. upstart, newly rich. ‖ *enrichir* [-îr] v. to enrich; to adorn; *s'enrichir*, to grow rich; to thrive. ‖ *enrichissement* [-ìsmaⁿ] m. enrichment.

enrober [aⁿròbé] v. to coad (de, with).

enrôlement [aⁿrôlmaⁿ] m. enrolment; enlistment (mil.). ‖ *enrôler* [-é] v. to enrol; to recruit; to enlist (mil.); *s'enrôler*, to enlist.

enroué [aⁿrué] adj. hoarse. ‖ *enrouement* [-rûmaⁿ] m. hoarseness. ‖ *s'enrouer* [saⁿrûé] v. to grow hoarse.

enrouler [aⁿrûlé] v. to coil up, to roll up, to wind; *s'enrouler*, to wrap (or) to fold oneself.

ensanglanté [aⁿsaⁿglaⁿté] adj. gory, bloody, blood-stained. ‖ *ensanglanter* v. to bloody; to steep in blood.

enseigne [aⁿsèñ] f. sign, sign-board; standard [drapeau]; m. ensign; sub-lieutenant.

enseignement [aⁿsèñmaⁿ] m. teaching; education; instruction. ‖ *enseigner* [-é] v. to teach; to instruct; to inform; *enseigner l'anglais à quelqu'un*, to teach someone English.

ensemble [aⁿsaⁿbl] m. ensemble; whole; mass; adv. together; at the same time; *dans l'ensemble*, on the whole; *vue d'ensemble*, general view.

ensemencer [aⁿsmaⁿsé] v. to sow.

enserrer [aⁿsèré] v. to enclose, to encompass; to shut in; to hem in; to lock up.

ensevelir [aⁿsevlîr] v. to bury; to shroud; *ensevelissement*, shrouding.

ensoleillé [aⁿsòlèyé] adj. sunny; sunlit. ‖ *ensoleiller* v. to sun; to light up, to brighten.

ensommeillé [aⁿsòmèyé] adj. sleepy, drowsy.

ensorceler [aⁿsòrselé] *v.* to bewitch; to captivate; *ensorceleuse,* witch.

ensuite [aⁿsüït] *adv.* after, afterwards, then; next.

ensuivre (s') [saⁿsüïvr] *v.** to follow, to result, to ensue.

entacher [aⁿtàshé] *v.* to taint; to sully.

entaille [aⁿtày] *f.* notch; groove; cut; gash. ‖ **entailler** [-é] *v.* to notch; to groove; to gash.

entamer [aⁿtàmé] *v.* to make the first cut in; to cut; to open [cartes]; to begin; to broach; to penetrate (mil.).

entasser [aⁿtàsé] *v.* to pile up; to heap up; to accumulate; to crowd together; to hoard [argent].

entendement [aⁿtaⁿdmaⁿ] *m.* understanding. ‖ **entendre** [-aⁿdr] *v.* to hear; to understand; to expect; to intend; to mean; *entendre dire que,* to hear that; *entendre parler de,* to hear of; *laisser entendre,* to hint; *s'entendre,* to agree; to be understood; to be heard; *il s'y entend,* he's an expert at it. ‖ **entendu** [-aⁿdü] *adj.* heard; understood; *Am.* O. K.; capable; *faire l'entendu,* to put on a knowing air; *c'est entendu,* that's settled; *bien entendu,* of course; clearly understood.

entente [aⁿtaⁿt] *f.* skill; understanding; agreement; sense; meaning.

entériner [aⁿtériné] *v.* to confirm, to ratify.

entérite [aⁿtérìt] *f.* enteritis.

enterrement [aⁿtèrmaⁿ] *m.* interment, burial; funeral. ‖ **enterrer** [-é] *v.* to inter, to bury; to shelve [question]; to outlive; *s'enterrer,* to bury oneself; to dig in (mil.); to live in seclusion; to vegetate.

en-tête [aⁿtèt] *f.* heading; headline; printed address; bill-head.

entêté [aⁿtété] *adj.* headstrong, pigheaded; stubborn; infatuated, taken. ‖ **entêtement** [-maⁿ] *m.* obstinacy, stubbornness. ‖ **entêter** [-é] *v.* to give a headache to; to infatuate; to go to one's head; *s'entêter,* to be obstinate; to persist (à, in); to be bent (à, on).

enthousiasme [aⁿtûzyàsm] *m* enthusiasm. ‖ **enthousiasmer** [-é] *v* to fill with enthusiasm; to thrill; to carry (someone) away; *s'enthousiasmer,* to enthuse; to become enthusiastic; to be thrilled. ‖ **enthousiaste** [-yàst] *m., f.* enthusiast; *adj.* enthusiastic.

entiché [aⁿtìshé] *adj.* infatuated (de, with).

entier [aⁿtyé] *m.* entirety; *adj.** whole; entire; complete; total; full; headstrong; outspoken; bluff; *nombre*

entier, integer; *en entier,* in full; *entièreté,* entirety.

entonner [aⁿtòné] *v.* to intone; to strike up; to celebrate [louange].

entonnoir [aⁿtònwàr] *m.* funnel; hollow; crater (mil.).

entorse [aⁿtòrs] *f.* sprain; twist; *se donner une entorse,* to sprain one's ankle.

entortiller [aⁿtòrtïyé] *v.* to twist, to wind; to entangle; to wrap up; to get round; *s'entortiller,* to twine; to get entangled.

entourage [aⁿtûràj] *m.* setting; frame; surroundings; circle; environment; attendants. ‖ **entourer** [-é] *v.* to surround; to encircle; to hem in; to gather round.

entournure [aⁿtûrnür] *f.* arm-hole.

entracte [aⁿtràkt] *m.* entracte, interlude; interval.

entrailles [aⁿtrày] *f. pl.* guts; bowels; womb; pity, mercy.

entrain [aⁿtriⁿ] *m.* liveliness; spirit, go, zest, life. ‖ **entrainement** [-ènmaⁿ] *m.* attraction; drive (mech.); allurement; carrying away; training. ‖ **entrainer** [-èné] *v.* to carry away; to draw along; to involve; to win over; to bring about; to train. ‖ **entraineur** [-ènœr] *m.* trainer; coach; pace-maker. ‖ **entraineuse** [-èz] *f.* dance-hostess, *Am.* B-girl, shill.

entrave [aⁿtràv] *f.* fetter, shackle; impediment; obstacle. ‖ **entraver** [-é] *v.* to fetter, to shackle; to impede, to hinder; to clog.

entre [aⁿtr] *prep.* between; among; amid; into; together; *entre nous,* between ourselves; *il tomba entre leurs mains,* he fell into their hands; *plusieurs d'entre nous,* several of us; [N. B. *s'entre-* or *s'entr'* prefixed to a verb usually means *each other, one another*; *s'entre-tuer,* to kill one another]; *entre-deux,* space between; insertion [couture]; partition; *entretemps,* interval; meanwhile; in the meantime.

entrebâiller [aⁿtrebâyé] *v.* to half-open; *entrebâillé* [-é] *adj.* ajar.

entrecôte [aⁿtrekòt] *f.* ribsteak.

entrecouper [aⁿtrekûpé] *v.* to intersect; to interrupt; to break; *entrecoupé,* broken; jerky.

entrecroiser [aⁿtrekrwàzé] *v.* to interlace; to cross; to intersect.

entrée [aⁿtré] *f.* entry; entrance; admission; access; price of entry; import duty; entrée, first course; beginning; inlet.

entrefaites [aⁿtrefèt] *f. pl.; sur ces entrefaites,* meanwhile, meantime.

entrefilet [aⁿtrefilè] *m.* short newspaper paragraph.

entregent [aⁿtrejaⁿ] *m.* resourcefulness; gumption (fam.).

entrelacer [aⁿtrelàsé] *v.* to interlace; to intertwine.

entremêler [aⁿtremèlé] *v.* to intermingle; to intersperse; to mix.

entremets [aⁿtremè] *m.* sweet dish, *Am.* dessert.

entremetteur [aⁿtremètœr] *m.* go-between; middleman (comm.); pimp. ‖ **entremetteuse** [-tëz] *f.* procuress. ‖ *s'entremettre* [saⁿtremètr] *v.* to intervene; to steep in. ‖ **entremise** [aⁿtremîz] *f.* mediation, intervention, *par l'entremise de*, through.

entrepont [aⁿtrepoⁿ] *m.* between-decks.

entreposer [aⁿtrepôzé] *v.* to store, to warehouse; to bond [douane]. ‖ **entrepôt** [-ô] *m.* store, warehouse; bonded warehouse.

entreprenant [aⁿtreprenaⁿ] *adj.* enterprising. ‖ **entreprendre** [-aⁿdr] *v.*° to undertake; to take in hand; to contract for; to attempt. ‖ **entrepreneur** [-•nœr] *m.* contractor. ‖ **entreprise** [-îz] *f.* enterprise; undertaking; concern; contract; attempt.

entrer [aⁿtré] *v.* to enter, to go in, to come in; to take part, to be concerned; to be included; *entrer en courant*, to run in; *défense d'entrer*, no admittance; *faire entrer*, to show in; *entrer en jeu*, to come into play.

entresol [aⁿtresòl] *m.* mezzanine; entresol.

entretenir [aⁿtrenîr] *v.* to maintain; to keep up; to support, to provide for; to keep in repair; to talk to; *s'entretenir*, to support oneself; to converse; to keep fit. ‖ **entretien** [-yiⁿ] *m.* maintenance; upkeep; keeping up; topic; conversation.

entrevoir [aⁿtrevwàr] *v.*° to catch a glimpse of; to be just able to make out; to foresee; *entrevue*, interview.

entrouvert [aⁿtrûvèr] *adj.* half-open; partly open; ajar [porte]; gaping [abîme].

énumération [énüméràsyoⁿ] *f.* enumeration. ‖ **énumérer** [énüméré] *v.* to enumerate; to number.

envahir [aⁿvàîr] *v.* to invade; to encroach upon; to overrun; to steal over [sensation]. ‖ **envahisseur** [-îsœr] *m.* invader; *adj.* invading.

enveloppe [aⁿvlòp] *f.* envelope; wrapping; wrapper, cover; casing, jacket (mech.); outer cover [auto]; exterior. ‖ **envelopper** [-é] *v.* to envelop; to wrap up; to cover; to involve; to hem in, to surround.

envenimer [aⁿvnìmé] *v.* to inflame (med.); to envenom (fig.).

envergure [aⁿvèrgür] *f.* span; spread; breadth; expanse; extent; scope.

envers [aⁿvèr] *m.* reverse, back; wrong side; seamy side (fig.); *prep.* to; towards; *à l'envers*, inside out; wrong way up.

enviable [aⁿvyàbl] *adj.* enviable. ‖ **envie** [aⁿvî] *f.* envy; longing, desire, fancy, wish; birthmark; hangnail; *avoir envie*, to want; to feel like, to fancy; *cela me fait envie*, that makes me envious. ‖ **envier** [-yé] *v.* to envy; to be envious of; to covet; to long for. ‖ **envieux** [-yë] *adj.*° envious.

environ [aⁿvìroⁿ] *adv.* about, nearly; approximately; *m. pl.* vicinity, neighbo(u)rhood, surroundings. ‖ **environner** [-òné] *v.* to surround.

envisager [aⁿvìzàjé] *v.* to envisage; to consider; to look in the face.

envoi [aⁿvwà] *m.* sending, dispatch; consignment; goods; parcel; package; shipment; remittance [argent].

envol [aⁿvòl] *m.* flight; (aviat.) taking off, take-off; (fig.) soaring. ‖ **envolée** [-é] *f.* flight. ‖ *s'envoler* [saⁿvòlé] *v.* to fly away; to take off (aviat.).

envoûter [aⁿvûté] *v.* to bewitch.

envoyé [aⁿvwàyé] *m.* envoy; messenger. ‖ **envoyer** [-é] *v.*° to send, to dispatch; to forward; to delegate; *envoyer chercher*, to send for. ‖ **envoyeur** [-œr] *m.* sender.

épagneul [épàñœl] *m.* spaniel.

épais [épè] *adj.*° thick; dense; stout; dull [esprit]. ‖ **épaisseur** [-sœr] *f.* thickness; depth; density; dullness. ‖ **épaissir** [-sîr] *v.* to thicken; to become dense; to grow stout.

épanchement [épaⁿshmaⁿ] *m.* effusion; pouring out; effusiveness. ‖ **épancher** [-é] *v.* to pour out; to shed; to open; to vent; *s'épancher*, to overflow; to unbosom oneself.

épanoui [épànwì] *adj.* in full bloom [fleur]; beaming; cheerful. ‖ **épanouir** [-îr] *v.* to open; to expand; to cheer, to brighten; to spread; *s'épanouir*, to open out; to blossom, to bloom; to light up. ‖ **épanouissement** [-ìsmaⁿ] *m.* opening; blooming; full bloom; brightening up; lighting up.

épargnant [épàrñaⁿ] *m.* investor. ‖ **épargne** [épàrñ] *f.* economy; thrift; saving. ‖ **épargner** [-é] *v.* to save, to economize; to spare.

éparpiller [épàrpìyé] *v.* to scatter, to disperse; *s'éparpiller*, to scatter; to be frittered away.

épars [épàr] *adj.* scattered; sparse; dispersed.

épatant [épàtàⁿ] *adj.* (fam.) wonderful, fine, terrific, first-rate, capital, *Am.* swell, great. ‖ **épaté** [-é] *adj.* amazed; flat [nez]. ‖ **épater** [-é] *v.* to flatten, to flabbergast.

épaule [épôl] *f.* shoulder; *coup d'épaule*, lift; shove; help. ‖ **épauler** [-é] *v.* to splay [cheval]; to bring to the shoulder; to back, to support. ‖ **épaulette** [-èt] *f.* epaulette (mil.); shoulder-strap.

épave [épàv] *f.* wreck; wreckage; waif, stray; *épaves flottantes*, flotsam, derelict.

épée [épé] *f.* sword; rapier.

épeler [éplé] *v.* to spell.

éperdu [épèrdü] *adj.* distracted, bewildered; desperate.

éperon [éproⁿ] *m.* spur; ridge; buttress [pont]; cutwater; ram [vaisseau de guerre]. ‖ **éperonner** [-òné] *v.* to spur; to spur on; to ram.

épervier [épèrvyé] *m.* sparrowhawk; sweep-net.

éphémère [éfémèr] *adj.* ephemeral; fleeting, transient; *m.* may-fly.

épi [épi] *m.* ear [blé]; cob; cluster [diamants]; spike (bot.); groyne; salient (typogr.).

épice [épìs] *f.* spice; *pain d'épice*, gingerbread. ‖ **épicé** [-é] *adj* spiced, seasoned; spicy (fig.) ‖ **épicer** [-é] *v.* to spice, to make spicy. ‖ **épicerie** [-rî] *f.* groceries; grocer's shop. ‖ **épicier** [-yé] *m.* grocer.

épidémie [épidémí] *f.* epidemic. ‖ **épidémique** [-ìk] *adj.* epidemic.

épiderme [épìdèrm] *m.* epidermis; cuticle; *il a l'épiderme sensible*, he is thin-skinned.

épier [épyé] *v.* to spy upon; to watch out for; to watch.

épieu [épyë] *m.* pike.

épigraphe [épìgràf] *f.* epigraph; chapter-heading.

épilation [épìlàsyoⁿ] *f.* depilation; removal of hair; plucking [sourcils]. ‖ **épiler** [épìlé] *v.* to depilate; to remove hairs; to pluck [sourcils].

épilepsie [épìlèpsî] *f.* epilepsy. ‖ **épileptique** [-tìk] *adj., m., f.* epileptic.

épinard [épìnàr] *m.* spinach.

épine [épîn] *f.* thorn, prickle; *épine dorsale*, backbone. ‖ **épineux** [-lnë] *adj.* thorny; prickly; ticklish, knotty [question].

épinette [épìnèt] *f.* hen-coop; thornhook; spinet (mus.); © spruce [*Fr.* = épicéa].

épingle [épìⁿgl] *f.* pin; peg; *pl.* pinmoney; *épingle de nourrice*, safety-pin; *coup d'épingle*, pin-prick; *tirer son épingle du jeu*, to get out of a scrape; *tiré à quatre épingles*, spruce, spick and span. ‖ **épingler** [-é] *v.* to pin; to pin up.

épique [épìk] *adj.* epic; eventful.

épiscopal [épìskòpàl] *adj.* episcopal. ‖ **épiscopat** [-pà] *m.* bishopric, episcopacy.

épisode [épìzòd] *m.* episode; incident; **épisodique**, episodic; adventitious; transitory.

épistolaire [épìstòlèr] *adj.* epistolary. ‖ **épître** [épìtr] *f.* epistle.

éploré [éplòré] *adj.* in tears; tearful; distressed; mournful.

éplucher [éplüshé] *v.* to pick; to peel; to clean; to sift; to examine closely; to pick holes in (fig.). ‖ **épluchette** [-èt] *f.* © corn-husking bee. ‖ **épluchures** [-ür] *f. pl.* peelings; refuse, waste.

épointé [épwiⁿté] *adj.* blunt; broken.

éponge [époⁿj] *f.* sponge. ‖ **éponger** [-é] *v.* to sponge up; to sponge down; to mop; to dab.

épopée [épòpé] *f.* epic.

époque [épòk] *f.* epoch, age; time; period.

épouse [épûz] *f.* wife, spouse. ‖ **épouser** [-é] *v.* to marry, to wed; to take up [cause]; to fit.

épousseter [épûsté] *v.* to dust; to brush down.

épouvantable [épûvaⁿtàbl] *adj.* dreadful, frightful, appalling. ‖ **épouvantail** [-ày] *m.* scarecrow; bogy. ‖ **épouvante** [épûvaⁿt] *f.* dread, terror; fright. ‖ **épouvanter** [-é] *v.* to terrify; to appal; to scare, to frighten.

époux [épû] *m.* husband; *pl.* husband and wife.

éprendre (s') [sépraⁿdr] *v.* to fall in love [de, with].

épreuve [éprèv] *f.* proof; trial, test; print (phot.); ordeal; examination; *à l'épreuve du feu*, fire-proof; *mettre à l'épreuve*, to put to the test.

épris [éprì] *adj.* smitten, fond; in love; infatuated [de, with].

éprouver [éprûvé] *v.* to try; to test; to put to the test; to feel, to experience. ‖ **éprouvette** [-èt] *f.* test-tube.

épuisé [épüìzé] *adj.* exhausted; spent; out of print [livre]. ‖ **épuisement** [-maⁿ] *m.* exhaustion, draining; using up; emptying. ‖ **épuiser** [-é] *v.* to exhaust; to consume, to use up; to drain; to wear out, to tire out; *s'épuiser*, to be exhausted; to be sold out; to give out; to run out. ‖ **épuisette** [-èt] *f.* landing-net; scoop.

épuration [épüràsyon] *f.* purifying; refining; filtering; purge. ‖ **épure** [épür] *f.* diagram; plan; working-drawing. ‖ **épurer** [-é] *v.* to cleanse; to purify; to refine; to filter; to clear; to purge.

équarrir [ékàrîr] *v.* to square; to cut up, to quarter.

équateur [ékwàtœr] *m.* equator; Ecuador.

équation [ékwàsyon] *f.* equation.

équerre [ékèr] *f.* square; angle-iron; set square [dessin]; *d'équerre*, square.

équilibre [ékìlîbr] *m.* equilibrium, poise, stability (aviat.), balance. ‖ **équilibrer** [-é] *v.* to poise, to balance. ‖ **équilibriste** [-ìst] *m.*, *f.* tight-rope walker; equilibrist.

équinoxe [ékìnòks] *m.* equinox.

équipage [ékìpàj] *m.* suite, retinue; crew (naut.); equipment; carriage; plight; hunt; turn-out; set; *train des équipages*, Army Service Corps. ‖ **équipe** [ékìp] *f.* train of barges; squad; team, gang; working party (mil.); *chef d'équipe*, foreman. ‖ **équipée** [-é] *f.* prank; crazy enterprise. ‖ **équipement** [-man] *m.* equipment; kit; outfit. ‖ **équiper** [-é] *v.* to equip; to fit out; to man. ‖ **équipier** [-yé] *m.* member of a team.

équitable [ékìtàbl] *adj.* equitable, fair, just.

équitation [ékìtàsyon] *f.* equitation, horse-riding; horsemanship.

équité [ékìté] *f.* fairness, equity.

équivalent [ékìvàlan] *adj.* equivalent. ‖ **équivaloir** [-wàr] *v.* to be equivalent, to be tantamount.

équivoque [ékìvòk] *f.* ambiguity; misunderstanding; *adj.* equivocal, ambiguous; dubious; uncertain.

érable [éràbl] *m.* maple-tree; *érable à sucre*, sugar maple; *eau d'érable*, maple sap; *sirop d'érable*, maple syrup; *sucre d'érable*, maple sugar. ‖ **érablière** [-ìèr] *f.* maple grove.

érafler [éràflé] *v.* to graze, to scratch. ‖ **éraflure** [-ür] *f.* graze, abrasion; scratch.

éraillé [éràyé] *adj.* frayed; bloodshot [yeux]; rough; scratched; harsh [voix].

ère [èr] *f.* era.

érection [érèksyon] *f.* erection; setting up.

éreintement [érintman] *m.* (fam.) exhaustion; slating, harsh criticism. ‖ **éreinter** [-é] *v.* to break the back of; (fam.) to ruin; to tire out, to fag; to slate, to pull to pieces, to run down.

ergot [èrgò] *m.* spur [coq]; dewclaw; catch (mech.); ergot. ‖ **ergoter** [-té] *v.* to quibble, to cavil.

ériger [érìjé] *v.* to erect; to set up; to institute; to raise.

ermite [èrmìt] *m.* hermit.

érosion [éròzyon] *f.* erosion.

érotique [éròtìk] *adj.* erotic. ‖ **érotisme** [-ìsm] *m.* eroticism.

errer [èré] *v.* to err; to be wrong; to stray, to wander; to stroll. ‖ **erreur** [èrœr] *f.* error, mistake, slip; fallacy. ‖ **erroné** [èròné] *adj.* erroneous, mistaken, wrong.

érudit [érüdì] *m.* scholar; *adj.* erudite, learned, scholarly. ‖ **érudition** [-syon] *f.* erudition, learning, scholarship.

éruption [érüpsyon] *f.* eruption; rash (med.).

esbroufe [èsbrüf] *f.* (fam.) swagger.

escabeau [èskàbò] *m.*[e] stool; stepladder.

escadre [èskàdr] *f.* squadron. ‖ **escadrille** [-ìy] *f.* flotilla; squadron (aviat.). ‖ **escadron** [-on] *m.* squadron (mil.); *chef d'escadron*, major.

escalade [èskàlàd] *f.* climbing; scaling; housebreaking (jur.). ‖ **escalader** [-é] *v.* to climb, to scale. ‖ **escale** [èskàl] *f.* port of call; call; *faire escale à*, to call at, to put in at. ‖ **escalier** [-yé] *m.* stairs; staircase; *escalier roulant*, escalator.

escalope [èskàlòp] *f.* cutlet.

escamoter [èskàmòté] *v.* to make (something) vanish; to conjure away; to retract (aviat.); to avoid; to pilfer, to pinch. ‖ **escamoteur** [-œr] *m.* conjurer; sharper (fam.).

escapade [èskàpàd] *f.* escapade; prank.

escargot [èskàrgò] *m.* snail.

escarmouche [èskàrmûsh] *f.* skirmish, brush.

escarpé [èskàrpé] *adj.* steep, precipitous; sheer.

escarpin [èskàrpin] *m.* pump; dancing-shoe.

escarre [èskàr] *f.* scab, bed-sore.

escient [èssyan] *m.* knowledge; *à bon escient*, wittingly.

esclaffer (s') [èsklàfé] *v.* to guffaw, to burst out laughing.

esclandre [èsklandr] *m.* scandal; scene.

esclavage [èsklàvàj] *m.* slavery, bondage. ‖ **esclave** [èsklàv] *m.*, *f.* slave.

escompte [èskont] *m.* discount, rebate. ‖ **escompter** [-é] *v.* to discount; to reckon on, to anticipate.

escorte [èskòrt] *f.* escort; convoy (naut.). ‖ **escorter** [-é] *v.* to escort; to convoy (naut.).

escouade [èskwàd] *f.* squad; gang.

escrime [èskrìm] *f.* fencing. ‖ *s'escrimer* [sèskrìmé] *v.* to fence; to fight; to struggle; to strive. ‖ *escrimeur* [èskrìmœr] *m.* fencer, swordsman.

escroc [èskrô] *m.* crook; fraud; swindler. ‖ *escroquer* [-òké] *v.* to swindle; to cheat out of. ‖ *escroquerie* [-òkrî] *f.* swindling; fraud.

espace [èspàs] *m.* space; interval; gap; room; lapse of time; *f.* space (typogr.). ‖ *espacer* [-àsé] *v.* to space; to space out; to separate; to leave room between.

espadon [èspàdòn] *m.* sword-fish.

espadrille [èspàdrîy] *f.* fibre sandal; beach sandal.

Espagne [èspàñ] *f.* Spain. ‖ *espagnol* [-òl] *m.* Spanish [langue]; Spaniard; *adj.* Spanish.

espagnolette [èspàñòlèt] *f.* window-fastening.

espèce [èspès] *f.* species; sort, kind; nature; instance; *pl.* cash (fin.).

espérance [èspéràns] *f.* hope; expectation. ‖ *espérer* [-é] *v.* to hope, to trust; to hope for; to expect.

espiègle [èspyègl] *m.*, *f.* rogue, mischief; *adj.* roguish, mischievous. ‖ *espièglerie* [-rî] *f.* mischievousness; trick.

espion [èspyon] *m.* spy. ‖ *espionnage* [-yònàj] *m.* espionage, spying. ‖ *espionner* [-yòné] *v.* to spy; to spy on.

esplanade [èsplànàd] *f.* esplanade, promenade.

espoir [èspwàr] *m.* hope; expectation.

esprit [èsprì] *m.* spirit; mind; sense; wit; intelligence; talent; soul; meaning; *plein d'esprit*, very witty; full of fun; *faire de l'esprit*, to play the wit; *un bel esprit*, a wit; *esprit fort*, free thinker; *reprendre ses esprits*, to come to oneself; *présence d'esprit*, presence of mind; *esprit de corps*, fellow-spirit; team spirit; *état d'esprit*, disposition; *esprit de suite*, consistency; *esprit-de-vin*, spirit of wine; *Saint-Esprit*, Holy Ghost.

esquif [èskìf] *m.* small boat, skiff.

esquimau [èskìmò] *m.** Eskimo; choc-ice.

esquinter [èskìnté] *v.* (fam.) to tire out; to slash; to ruin, *Am.* to mess up.

esquisse [èskìs] *f.* sketch; outline; rough plan. ‖ *esquisser* [-é] *v.* to sketch; to outline.

esquiver [èskìvé] *v.* to avoid; to dodge; *s'esquiver*, to steal away, to slip away, to slink off.

essai [èsè] *m.* trial, essay; test; try; attempt; *à l'essai*, on trial; *coup d'essai*, first attempt; *faire l'essai de*, to test.

essaim [èsin] *m.* swarm. ‖ *essaimer* [-é] *v.* to swarm; to emigrate.

essayage [èsèyàj] *m.* testing; trying on; fitting. ‖ *essayer* [-èyé] *v.* to try; to attempt; to taste; to try on [habits]; to assay [métal]; *s'essayer*, to try one's hand (*à*, at). ‖ *essayeur* [-èyœr] *m.* assayer; fitter.

essence [èsans] *f.* essence; species [arbre]; *Br.* petrol, *Am.* gasoline; extract; attar [roses]; *poste d'essence*, filling-station, *Am.* service station.

essentiel [èsansyèl] *m.* gist; main point; *adj.** essential.

essieu [èsyë] *m.** axle; axle-tree.

essor [èsòr] *m.* flight, soaring; scope; *prendre son essor*, to take wing; to leap into action.

essorer [èsòré] *v.* to dry; to wring.

essoufflement [èsûflǝman] *m.* panting; puffing; breathlessness. ‖ *essouffler* [-é] *v.* to wind, to puff (fam.); *s'essouffler*, to get out of breath, to be winded.

essuyer [èsüìyé] *v.* to wipe; to mop up; to dry; to endure, to suffer; to meet with [refus]; *essuie-glace*, windscreen wiper, *Am.* windshield wiper; *essuie-main*, towel.

est [èst] *m.* east; *adj.* east, easterly.

estafette [èstàfèt] *f.* courier; messenger; dispatch-rider (mil.).

estafilade [èstàfilàd] *f.* slash.

estampe [èstanp] *f.* print, engraving; stamp, punch. ‖ *estamper* [-é] *v.* to stamp; to emboss; (pop.) to rook, to fleece. ‖ *estampille* [-îy] *f.* stamp; trade-mark.

esthéticien [èstétìsyin] *m.* aesthetician. ‖ *esthéticienne* [-syèn] *f.* beauty specialist, *Am.* beautician. ‖ *esthétique* [èstétìk] *f.* aesthetics; *adj.* aesthetic; plastic [chirurgie].

estimable [èstìmàbl] *adj.* estimable; worthy; quite good. ‖ *estimation* [-àsyon] *f.* estimation; valuation; estimate. ‖ *estime* [èstìm] *f.* esteem; estimation; guesswork; reckoning. ‖ *estimer* [-ìmé] *v.* to esteem; to deem; to estimate; to value; to think, to consider; to calculate; to reckon.

estival [èstìvàl] *adj.** summer. ‖ *estivant* [-an] *m.* summer visitor.

estomac [èstòmà] *m.* stomach; *mal d'estomac*, stomach-ache. ‖ *estomaquer* [-ké] *v.* to stagger; to take (someone's) breath away.

estompe [èstonp] *f.* stump. ‖ *estomper* [-é] *v.* to stump; to shade off; to soften; to blur.

estrade [èstràd] *f.* platform; stand.

estragon [èstràgoⁿ] *m.* tarragon.

estropié [èstròpyé] *m.* cripple; *adj.* crippled; disabled; lame. ‖ **estropier** [-yé] *v.* to cripple; to maim, to disable; to murder, to distort, to mispronounce.

estuaire [èstüèr] *m.* estuary.

esturgeon [èstürjoⁿ] *m.* sturgeon.

et [-é] *conj.* and; *et... et*, both... and.

étable [étàbl] *f.* cattle-shed; pigsty.

établi [étàblì] *m.* bench; work-bench; *adj.* established, settled. ‖ **établir** [-îr] *v.* to establish; to set up; to settle; to ascertain; to construct; to prove; to lay down; to draw up [projet]; to found; to make out [compte]; *s'établir*, to become established; to establish oneself; to settle. ‖ **établissement** [-îsmaⁿ] *m.* establishment; institution; settlement; concern (comm.), business, firm.

étage [étàj] *m.* story, floor; degree, rank; stage (mech.); stratum, (geol.); *deuxième étage*, *Br.* second floor, *Am.* third floor. ‖ **étager** [-é] *v.* to range in tiers; to stagger [heures]. ‖ **étagère** [-èr] *f.* shelf; shelves; whatnot.

étai [étè] *m.* prop, stay, strut, shore.

étain [étiⁿ] *m.* tin; pewter; *feuille d'étain*, tinfoil.

étalage [étàlàj] *m.* show, display; display of goods; shop-window; frontage; showing off; *faire étalage*, to show off. ‖ **étalagiste** [-ìst] *m.*, *f.* window-dresser; stall-holder. ‖ **étale** [étàl] *m.* slack; *adj.* slack [marée]; steady [brise]. ‖ **étaler** [-é] *v.* to display; to expose for sale; to spread out [cartes]; to stagger [vacances]; to show off; *s'étaler*, to stretch oneself out; to sprawl; to show off; to fall.

étalon [étàloⁿ] *m.* stallion.

étalon [étàloⁿ] *m.* standard; *étalon-or*, gold standard.

étamer [étàmé] *v.* to tin; to tinplate; to silver; to galvanize. ‖ **étameur** [-œr] *m.* tinsmith; tinker; silverer.

étamine [étàmìn] *f.* stamen; buttermuslin.

étanche [étaⁿsh] *adj.* watertight; airtight. ‖ **étancher** [-é] *v.* to stanch, to stem [sang]; to stop; to quench, to slake; to make watertight; to make airtight.

étang [étaⁿ] *m.* pond, pool.

étape [étàp] *f.* stage; halting place.

état [étà] *m.* state; occupation; profession; trade; government; establishment; estate, plight, predicament; estimate; statement of account; list; roster; inventory; condition; *en état de*, fit for; in a position to; *à l'état de neuf*, as good as new; *hors d'état*, useless; *dans tous ses états*, highly upset; *homme d'État*, statesman; *remettre en état*, to put in order; *état civil*, civil status; legal status; *état-major*, general staff; headquarters; *état tampon*, buffer state; *États-Unis*, United States. ‖ **étatisme** [-tìsm] *m.* state control.

étau [étô] *m.*° vice, *Am.* vise.

étayer [étèyé] *v.* to prop, to shore up; to support.

été [été] *m.* summer; *été de la Saint-Martin* [© *été des sauvages, été des Indiens*], Indian summer.

été *p. p. of* être.

éteignoir [étéñwàr] *m.* extinguisher; snuffer; wet blanket (fam.). ‖ **éteindre** [étiⁿdr] *v.*° to extinguish, to put out; to switch off; to quench; to slake; to exterminate, to destroy; to pay off [dette]; to cancel; to dim; to soften; *s'éteindre*, to become extinct; to die out; to subside; to grow dim; to fade.

étendard [étaⁿdàr] *m.* standard, banner, flag, colo(u)rs.

étendre [étaⁿdr] *v.* to extend; to expand; to stretch; to spread out; to dilute; to throw to the ground; *s'étendre*, to lie down; to stretch oneself out; to extend; to enlarge, to dwell (*sur*, upon); to run [couleurs]. ‖ **étendu** [étaⁿdü] *adj.* extensive; widespread; outstretched. ‖ **étendue** [-ü] *f.* extent; expanse; range; stretch; scope.

éternel [étèrnèl] *adj.*° eternal; everlasting; endless, perpetual. ‖ **éterniser** [-ìzé] *v.* to immortalize; to perpetuate; *s'éterniser*, to last for ever; to drag on. ‖ **éternité** [-ìté] *f.* eternity; ages (fam.).

éternuement [étèrnümaⁿ] *m.* sneeze; sneezing. ‖ **éternuer** [-é] *v.* to sneeze.

éther [étèr] *m.* ether. ‖ **éthéré** [-é] *adj.* ethereal; skyey.

éthique [étìk] *f.* ethics.

ethnique [ètnìk] *adj.* ethnic.

étiage [étyàj] *m.* low water; low water mark; level (fig.).

étinceler [étiⁿslé] *v.* to sparkle, to flash, to glitter, to gleam; to twinkle. ‖ **étincelle** [-èl] *f.* spark, flash.

étioler (s') [sétyòlé] *v.* to become sick, emaciated; to blanch.

étiqueter [étìkté] *v.* to label. ‖ **étiquette** [-èt] *f.* label; tag; ticket; etiquette; ceremony.

étirer [étìré] *v.* to pull out, to draw out; to stretch.

étoffe [étòf] *f.* stuff, material, cloth, fabric; condition; worth. ‖ **étoffer** [-é] *v.* to make substantial; to stuff; to stiffen.

étoile [étwàl] *f.* star; decoration; asterisk (typogr.); *à la belle étoile*, in the open; *étoile de mer*, starfish. ‖ **étoilé** [-é] *adj.* starry; starshaped; *la Bannière étoilée*, the Star-Spangled Banner, the Stars and Stripes.

étonnant [étònàⁿ] *adj.* astonishing, surprising, amazing. ‖ **étonnement** [-màⁿ] *m.* surprise, astonishment, amazement, wonder. ‖ **étonner** [-é] *v.* to astonish, to amaze; to shake; *s'étonner*, to be astonished; to wonder; to be surprised.

étouffant [étûfàⁿ] *adj.* suffocating; sultry [temps]; stifling. ‖ **étouffée** [-é] *f.* stew; *à l'étouffée*, braised. ‖ **étouffement** [-màⁿ] *m.* suffocation; stifling; choking. ‖ **étouffer** [-é] *v.* to suffocate, to stifle; to choke; to smother; to damp [bruit]; to stamp out; to hush up [affaire].

étoupe [étûp] *f.* tow; oakum; packing (mech.).

étourderie [étûrdᵉrî] *f.* thoughtlessness; blunder; careless mistake. ‖ **étourdi** [-i] *m.* scatter-brain; *adj.* thoughtless; giddy, scatter-brained. ‖ **étourdir** [-îr] *v.* to stun, to daze; to make dizzy; to deaden, to benumb [engourdir]; to calm, to allay; *s'étourdir*, to forget one's troubles; to be lost (*de*, in). ‖ **étourdissant** [-îsàⁿ] *adj.* stunning, deafening; astounding. ‖ **étourdissement** [-îsmàⁿ] *m.* dizziness, giddiness; dazing; blow (fig.).

étrange [étràⁿj] *adj.* strange; curious, odd, queer, peculiar. ‖ **étranger** [-é] *m.* foreigner; stranger [inconnu]; *adj.*° foreign; strange, unknown; irrelevant; *à l'étranger*, abroad; *affaires étrangères*, foreign affairs. ‖ **étrangeté** [-té] *f.* strangeness, oddness.

étranglement [étràⁿglᵉmàⁿ] *m.* strangulation; narrow passage; constriction; choking. ‖ **étrangler** [-é] *v.* to strangle, to choke, to throttle, to stifle; to constrict.

étrave [étràv] *f.* stem (naut.).

être [ètr] *m.* being; creature; existence; *v.*° to be; to exist; to have [verbe auxiliaire]; to go; to belong; to be able; to be dressed; *il est venu*, he has come; *elle s'était flattée*, she had flattered herself; *c'est à vous*, it is yours; *c'est à vous de jouer*, it is your turn; *il est à souhaiter*, it is to be hoped; *j'ai été voir*, I went to see; *il était une fois*, once upon a time, there was once; *où en êtes-vous de vos études?*, how far have you got in your studies?; *il n'en est rien*, nothing of the sort; *vous avez fini, n'est-ce pas?*, you've finished, haven't you?; *il* •

fait beau, n'est-ce pas?, it is fine, isn't it?; *nous sommes le cinq*, it is the fifth to-day; *n'était mon travail*, if it were not for my work; *j'en suis pour mon argent*, I've lost my money; *c'en est assez*, enough; *toujours est-il que*, the fact remains that; *y être*, see y.

étreindre [étrɛ̃dr] *v.*° to clasp; to grasp; to embrace, to hug; to bind. ‖ **étreinte** [-ɪⁿt] *f.* grasp; grip; embrace, hug.

étrenne [étrèn] *f.* New Year's gift; gift; first use of; *Jour des Etrennes*, Boxing Day. ‖ **étrenner** [-é] *v.* to hand-sel, to christen (fam.); to wear [vêtement] for the first time; to be the first customer of.

étrier [étrié] *m.* stirrup; holder (mech.).

étriller [étrîyé] *v.* to curry, to comb; (fam.) to tan, to thrash.

étriqué [étrîké] *adj.* skimpy.

étroit [étrwà] *adj.* narrow; tight; confined; close; scanty; limited; strict [sens]; *à l'étroit*, cramped for room. ‖ **étroitesse** [-tès] *f.* narrowness; tightness; closeness; narrow-mindedness [esprit].

étude [étüd] *f.* study; research; office; article; essay; school-room; practice [avocat]; *à l'étude*, under consideration; under rehearsal (theat.). ‖ **étudiant** [-yàⁿ] *m.* student; undergraduate; *étudiant en droit*, law student. ‖ **étudier** [-yé] *v.* to study; to read [droit]; to investigate; to prepare; to watch, to observe; *s'étudier*, to try hard; to be very careful; to introspect; to be affected.

étui [étüi] *m.* case; cover; sheath; holster [revolver].

étuve [étüv] *f.* sweating-room; drying-stove; airing-cupboard, hot press; oven (fam.). ‖ **étuver** [-é] *v.* to stew; to steam [légumes]; to dry; to stove; to sterilize.

eucharistie [ëkàrìstî] *f.* eucharist. ‖ **eucharistique** [-tîk] *adj.* eucharistic(al).

eunuque [ënük] *m.* eunuch.

euphorie [ëfòrî] *f.* bliss, euphory.

Europe [ëròp] *f.* Europe. ‖ **européen** [-éⁿ] *adj.*°, *s.* European.

eux [ë] *pron.* they, them; *eux-mêmes*, themselves.

évacuer [évàküé] *v.* to evacuate; to drain; to vacate; to abandon [bateau].

évadé [évàdé] *m.* fugitive. ‖ **évader (s')** [sévàdé] *v.* to escape, to run away; to break loose.

évaluation [évàlüàsyoⁿ] *f.* valuation, estimate; assessment. ‖ **évaluer** [-üé] *v.* to value; to estimate; to assess.

évangélique [évaⁿjélìk] *adj.* Evan-gelic(al). ‖ **évangéliser** [-jélìzé] *v.* to evangelize. ‖ **évangile** [-jìl] *m.* gospel.

évanouir (s') [sévànwîr] *v.* to faint, to swoon; to vanish; to faint away. ‖ **évanouissement** [évànwìsmaⁿ] *m.* fainting, swoon; vanishing; disappear-ance; fading [radio].

évaporation [évàpòràsyoⁿ] *f.* evapo-ration; heedlessness. ‖ **évaporer (s')** [sévàpòré] *v.* to evaporate; to grow flighty.

évasé [évàzé] *adj.* bell-mouthed; splayed; cupped; flared [jupe].

évasif [évàzìf] *adj.*° evasive. ‖ **éva-sion** [-yoⁿ] *f.* evasion; escape, flight; escapism (lit.).

évêché [évèshé] *m.* bishopric, dio-cese, see; bishop's palace.

éveil [évèy] *m.* awakening; alertness; alarm; warning; *en éveil*, on the watch. ‖ **éveillé** [-é] *adj.* awake; wide-awake; keen; alert; lively. ‖ **éveiller** [-é] *v.* to awaken; to rouse; *s'éveiller*, to wake up, to awake.

événement [évènmaⁿ] *m.* event; happening; occurrence; incident; re-sult; emergency.

éventail [évaⁿtày] *m.* fan; range [des salaires].

éventaire [évaⁿtèr] *m.* stall, stand; flower-basket. ‖ **éventé** [-é] *adj.* flat; musty; stale; divulged. ‖ **éventer** [-é] *v.* to fan; to expose to the air; to find out; to let out [secret]; to scent; to get wind of; *s'éventer*, to go flat [vin]; to get stale; to fan oneself; to leak out [secret].

éventrer [évaⁿtré] *v.* to rip open; to gut [poisson]; to disembowel.

éventualité [évaⁿtüàlìté] *f.* eventu-ality, possibility, contingency, occur-rence. ‖ **éventuel** [-üèl] *adj.*° even-tual; contingent, possible; emergency.

évêque [évèk] *m.* bishop.

évertuer (s') [sévèrtüé] *v.* to strive, to do one's utmost.

éviction [évìksyoⁿ] *f.* eviction.

évidemment [évìdàmaⁿ] *adv.* evi-dently, obviously; of course. ‖ **évi-dence** [-aⁿs] *f.* evidence, obviousness; conspicuousness. ‖ **évident** [-aⁿ] *adj.* evident, plain; conspicuous, obvious.

évider [évìdé] *v.* to hollow out; to groove; to cut away.

évier [évìé] *m.* sink.

évincer [évìⁿsé] *v.* to evict, to turn out; to oust; to supplant.

évitable [évìtàbl] *adj.* avoidable. ‖ **éviter** [-é] *v.* to avoid; to shun; to dodge; to swing (naut.).

évocation [évòkàsyoⁿ] *f.* evocation; recalling; raising [esprits]; conjuring up.

évoluer [évòlüé] *v.* to develop, to evolve; to revolve; to go through evolutions. ‖ **évolution** [-üsyoⁿ] *f.* evolution; development. ‖ **évolution-nisme** [-ìsm] *m.* evolutionism.

évoquer [évòké] *v.* to evoke, to bring to mind, to conjure up; to raise [esprit].

exacerber [égzàsèrbé] *v.* to exacer-bate.

exact [ègzàkt] *adj.* exact, correct, accurate; precise; punctual; strict; true.

exaction [ègzàksyoⁿ] *f.* exaction; ex-tortion.

exactitude [ègzàktìtüd] *f.* exactitude, exactness, accuracy, precision; correct-ness; punctuality.

exagération [ègzàjéràsyoⁿ] *f.* exag-geration, overstatement. ‖ **exagérer** [-é] *v.* to exaggerate; to over-estimate; to overrate; to magnify; to go too far (fig.).

exaltation [ègzàltàsyoⁿ] *f.* exalta-tion; glorifying; excitement. ‖ **exalté** [-é] *m.* fanatic; *adj.* heated; excited; hot-headed; exalted. ‖ **exalter** [-é] *v.* to exalt; to extol; to rouse, to excite.

examen [ègzàmⁿ] *m.* examination; investigation; test; survey. ‖ **exami-nateur, -trice** [-ìnàtœr, -trìs] *m., f.* examiner. ‖ **examiner** [-ìné] *v.* to examine; to overhaul; to survey; to look into; to investigate; to scruti-nize.

exaspération [ègzàspéràsyoⁿ] *f.* exas-peration, irritation. ‖ **exaspérer** [-é] *v.* to exasperate, to irritate, to provoke; to aggravate.

exaucer [ègzòsé] *v.* to grant [prière], to fulfil(l) [désir].

excavation [èkskàvàsyoⁿ] *f.* excava-tion; excavating.

excédant [èksédaⁿ] *adj.* excessive. ‖ **excédent** [-aⁿ] *m.* surplus, excess. ‖ **excéder** [-é] *v.* to exceed; to weary, to tire out; to aggravate.

excellence [èksèlaⁿs] *f.* excellence; Excellency [titre]. ‖ **excellent** [-aⁿ] *adj.* excellent; delicious; capital, first-rate (fam.). ‖ **exceller** [-é] *v.* to excel; to surpass.

excentricité [èksaⁿtrìsìté] *f.* eccen-tricity; remoteness. ‖ **excentrique** [èksaⁿtrìk] *m.* eccentric (mech.); *adj.* outlying [quartiers]; odd, peculiar, queer.

excepté [èksèpté] *prep.* except; excepting, save, all but. ‖ **excepter** [-é] *v.* to except, to bar. ‖ **exception** [èksèpsyoⁿ] *f.* exception. ‖ **exception-nel** [-yònèl] *adj.*° exceptional; out of the ordinary; unusual.

excès [èksè] *m.* excess; abuse; *pl.* outrages. ‖ **excessif** [-sìf] *adj.** excessive; unreasonable; undue; extreme; exorbitant.

excitable [èksìtàbl] *adj.* excitable. ‖ **excitant** [-aⁿ] *m.* stimulant (med.); *adj.* exciting, stimulating. ‖ **excitation** [-àsyoⁿ] *f.* excitation; incitement. ‖ **exciter** [-é] *v.* to excite; to stir up; to incite; to stimulate, to rouse; **s'exciter,** to get worked up, to get excited.

exclamation [èksklàmàsyoⁿ] *f.* exclamation. ‖ **exclamer (s')** [sèksklàmé] *v.* to cry out; to exclaim.

exclure [èksklür] *v.** to exclude, to debar; to leave out; to shut out. ‖ **exclusif** [-üzìf] *adj.** exclusive; special (comm.); sole [droit]. ‖ **exclusion** [-üzyoⁿ] *f.* exclusion, debarring; *à l'exclusion de,* excluding. ‖ **exclusivité** [-üzìvìté] *f.* exclusiveness; exclusive right; stage-rights.

excommunier [èkskòmünyé] *v.* to excommunicate.

excrément [èkskrémaⁿ] *m.* excrement.

excroissance [èkskrwàsaⁿs] *f.* excrescence.

excursion [èkskürsyoⁿ] *f.* excursion; tour; ramble; outing; trip; hike.

excusable [èksküzàbl] *adj.* excusable. ‖ **excuse** [èsküz] *f.* excuse; *pl.* apologies. ‖ **excuser** [-é] *v.* to excuse, to pardon; to apologize for; **s'excuser,** to apologize, to excuse oneself; to decline.

exécrable [ègzékràbl] *adj.* execrable; disgraceful; horrible; abominable. ‖ **exécrer** [-é] *v.* to execrate, to loathe, to detest.

exécutant [ègzékütaⁿ] *m.* performer, executant. ‖ **exécuter** [-é] *v.* to execute; to perform; to carry out [projet]; to fulfil(l); to put to death; to distrain on [débiteur]; **s'exécuter,** to be performed; to comply; to yield; to pay up (comm.); to sell off. ‖ **exécuteur, -trice** [-ær, -trìs] *m., f.* performer; executor; executioner; *f.* executrix (jur.). ‖ **exécutif** [-ìf] *m., adj.** executive. ‖ **exécution** [ègzéküsyoⁿ] *f.* execution; performance; fulfil(l)ment; production; enforcement (jur.); *mettre à exécution,* to carry out.

exemplaire [ègzaⁿplèr] *m.* copy [livre]; sample, specimen; model; pattern; *adj.* exemplary. ‖ **exemple** [ègzaⁿpl] *m.* example; copy; instance; precedent; warning, lesson; *par exemple,* for instance; *interj.* well I never!

exempt [ègzaⁿ] *adj.* exempt; free; immune. ‖ **exempter** [-té] *v.* to

exempt, to free, to dispense. ‖ **exemption** [-psyoⁿ] *f.* exemption; freedom; immunity.

exercer [ègzèrsé] *v.* to exercise; to practise; to train; to carry on; to try [patience]; to drill; to exert; **s'exercer,** to practice; to train oneself. ‖ **exercice** [-ìs] *m.* exercise; training; practice; drill (mil.); duties; inspection [douane]; financial year; balance-sheet.

exergue [ègzèrg] *m.* exergue.

exhalaison [ègzàlèzoⁿ] *f.* exhalation; smell; fumes; bouquet. ‖ **exhaler** [ègzàlé] *v.* to exhale; to breathe; to breathe out; to emit, to send forth.

exhausser [ègzôsé] *v.* to raise, to heighten.

exhiber [ègzìbé] *v.* to exhibit; to display; to show off. ‖ **exhibition** [ègzìbìsyoⁿ] *f.* exhibition; production, showing; showing off.

exhorter [ègzòrté] *v.* to exhort, to urge, to encourage.

exhumer [ègzümé] *v.* to exhume, to disinter; to unearth, to bring to light, to dig out (fam.).

exigeant [ègzìĵaⁿ] *adj.* exacting, particular, hard to please. ‖ **exigence** [-aⁿs] *f.* excessive demands; unreasonableness; exigency; requirements. ‖ **exiger** [-é] *v.* to demand; to require; to exact, to insist on. ‖ **exigible** [-ìbl] *adj.* due; demandable.

exigu, -uë [ègzìgü] *adj.* scanty; tiny; small. ‖ **exiguïté** [-ìté] *f.* exiguity; exiguousness.

exil [ègzìl] *m.* exile, banishment. ‖ **exilé** [-é] *m.* exile; *adj.* exiled, banished. ‖ **exiler** [-é] *v.* to exile, to banish; **s'exiler,** to go into exile; to expatriate oneself.

existant [ègzìstaⁿ] *adj.* existing, living; extant. ‖ **existence** [-s] *f.* existence; being; life; *pl.* stock (comm.); *moyens d'existence,* means of livelihood. ‖ **existentialisme** [-syàlìsm] *m.* existentialism. ‖ **exister** [ègzìsté] *v.* to exist, to be; to live; to be extant.

exode [ègzòd] *m.* exodus.

exonérer [ègzònéré] *v.* to exonerate; to exempt; to free; to discharge.

exorbitant [ègzòrbìtaⁿ] *adj.* exorbitant, excessive. ‖ **exorbité** [-é] *adj.* starting out of one's head.

exotique [ègzòtìk] *adj.* exotic. ‖ **exotisme** [-tìsm] *m.* exoticism.

expansif [èkspaⁿsìf] *adj.** expansive; effusive; exuberant; **expansion,** expansion; expansiveness; enlargement.

expatrier [èkspàtrìé] *v.* to expatriate, to exile; **s'expatrier,** to expatriate oneself.

expectative [èkspèktàtîv] *f.* expectancy; prospect.

expédient [èkspédyaⁿ] *m.* expedient; dodge (fam.); makeshift; emergency device; *adj.* expedient. ‖ **expédier** [-yé] *v.* to dispatch; to send off; to forward; to expedite; to ship; to hurry through; to clear [navire]; to draw up [acte]. ‖ **expéditeur, -trice** [-ìtœr, -trîs] *m., f.* sender; shipper; agent; *adj.* forwarding. ‖ **expéditif** [-ìtîf] *adj.*° prompt; expeditious. ‖ **expédition** [-ìsyoⁿ] *f.* expedition; sending, dispatch; shipment; consignment; copy [acte]. ‖ **expéditionnaire** [-ìsyònèr] *m.* sender; forwarding agent; shipper; consigner; copying clerk; *adj.* expeditionary.

expérience [èkspéryaⁿs] *f.* experience, experiment, test; *sans expérience,* inexperienced. ‖ **expérimental** [-ìmaⁿtàl] *adj.*° experimental. ‖ **expérimenter** [-ìmaⁿté] *v.* to experiment; to test.

expert [èkspèr] *m.* expert; specialist; connoisseur; valuer (comm.); *adj.* expert, skilled. ‖ **expertise** [-tîz] *f.* valuation; survey; assessment; expert opinion; expert's report. ‖ **expertiser** [-tìzé] *v.* to value, to appraise; to survey.

expiration [èkspìràsyoⁿ] *f.* expiration; breathing out; termination. ‖ **expirer** [-é] *v.* to expire; to die; to breathe out; to terminate.

explicable [èksplìkàbl] *adj.* explainable, explicable. ‖ **explicatif** [-àtîf] *adj.*° explanatory. ‖ **explication** [-àsyoⁿ] *f.* explanation. ‖ **explicite** [èksplìsìt] *adj.* explicit, express, clear, plain. ‖ **expliquer** [-ìké] *v.* to explain; to expound; to account for; *s'expliquer,* to be explained; to explain oneself.

exploit [èksplwà] *m.* exploit, feat, deed; achievement; writ, summons (jur.); *signifier un exploit à,* to serve a writ on. ‖ **exploitation** [-tàsyoⁿ] *f.* exploitation; working [mine]; cultivation; felling [arbres]; mine. ‖ **exploiter** [-té] *v.* to exploit; to work [mine]; to cultivate; to turn to account; to take advantage of; to oppress. ‖ **exploiteur** [-tœr] *m.* exploiter.

explorateur, -trice [èksplòràtœr, -trîs] *m., f.* explorer; *adj.* exploratory. ‖ **exploration** [-àsyoⁿ] *f.* exploration; scanning [télévision]. ‖ **explorer** [-é] *v.* to explore; to search; to scan [télévision].

exploser [èksplôzé] *v.* to explode; to blow up. ‖ **explosif** [-ìf] *m., adj.*° explosive. ‖ **explosion** [-yoⁿ] *f.* explosion; blowing up; bursting.

exportateur, -trice [èkspòrtàtœr, -trîs] *m., f.* exporter; *adj.* exporting.

‖ **exportation** [-àsyoⁿ] *f.* exportation; export. ‖ **exporter** [-é] *v.* to export.

exposant [èkspôzaⁿ] *m.* exhibitor; exponent (math.); petitioner (jur.). ‖ **exposé** [-é] *m.* report; outline; account; statement. ‖ **exposer** [-é] *v.* to expose; to lay bare; to exhibit; to state; to set forth; to endanger. ‖ **exposition** [-ìsyoⁿ] *f.* exhibition; exposure, statement; account; aspect [maison]; lying in state [corps].

exprès [èksprè] *m.* express; *adv.* on purpose, intentionally. ‖ **exprès, -esse** [-è, -ès] *adj.* express, positive, definite; explicit. ‖ **express** [-s] *m., adj.* express [train]. ‖ **expressif** [-sìf] *adj.*° expressive. ‖ **expression** [-syoⁿ] *f.* expression; utterance; squeezing; phrase; *la plus simple expression,* the simplest terms.

exprimable [èksprìmàbl] *adj.* expressible. ‖ **exprimer** [-é] *v.* to express; to voice; to manifest; to squeeze out [jus].

exproprier [èkspròprìyé] *v.* to expropriate.

expulser [èkspülsé] *v.* to expel; to turn out; to evict; to oust; to eject; to banish. ‖ **expulsion** [-yoⁿ] *f.* expulsion; ejection; ousting; eviction.

expurger [èkspürjé] *v.* to expurgate, to bowdlerize.

exquis [èkskì] *adj.* exquisite; delicious, delightful; choice.

exsangue [èksaⁿg] *adj.* bloodless; exsanguine.

extase [èkstàz] *f.* ecstasy, rapture; trance (med.). ‖ **extasier** [-àzyé] *v.* to transport; to enrapture; *s'extasier,* to go into ecstasies. ‖ **extatique** [-àtìk] *adj.* ecstatic.

extensible [èkstaⁿsìbl] *adj.* extending; expanding. ‖ **extension** [-yoⁿ] *f.* extent; extension; spreading; stretching.

exténuer [èksténüé] *v.* to extenuate; to tire out; to wear out; to exhaust.

extérieur [èkstéryœr] *m.* outside; appearance; foreign countries; exterior [cinéma]; *adj.* exterior, outer, outside, external; foreign; unreserved. ‖ **extérioriser** [-ryòrìzé] *v.* to exteriorize; to manifest; *s'extérioriser,* to unbosom oneself; to be expressed.

extermination [èkstèrmìnàsyoⁿ] *f.* extermination, wiping out. ‖ **exterminer** [-é] *v.* to exterminate; to annihilate; to wipe out.

externe [èkstèrn] *m.* day-pupil; non-resident medical student; *adj.* exterior, outer, external.

extincteur [èkstìⁿktœr] *m.* fire-extinguisher. ‖ **extinction** [-syoⁿ] *f.* extinction; loss [voix].

extirper [èkstîrpé] *v.* to extirpate; to cut out; to eradicate; to uproot.

extorquer [èkstòrké] *v.* to extort. ‖ **extorsion** [-syoⁿ] *f.* extortion.

extra [èkstrà] *m.*, *adv.* extra; *adj.* extra-special; **extra-fin**, superfine.

extraction [èkstràksyoⁿ] *f.* extraction; working [mines]; origin, birth, parentage.

extrader [èkstràdé] *v.* to extradite.

extraire [èkstrèr] *v.* to extract; to pull [dent]; to quarry [pierres]; to extricate. ‖ **extrait** [èkstrè] *m.* extract; excerpt; certificate; statement [compte].

extraordinaire [èkstràòrdìnèr] *adj.* extraordinary; uncommon; special; unusual; wonderful.

extravagance [èkstràvàgaⁿs] *f.* extravagance; absurdity; folly. ‖

extravagant [-aⁿ] *adj.* extravagant; exorbitant; absurd, foolish, wild.

extrême [èkstrèm] *m.* utmost limit; *adj.* extreme; utmost; severe; intense; **extrême-onction**, extreme unction; **Extrême-Orient**, Far East. ‖ **extrémiste** [-émìst] *s.* extremist. ‖ **extrémité** [-émìté] *f.* extremity; very end; tip; extreme; border; urgency; *à l'extrémité*, to extremes.

exubérance [ègzübéraⁿs] *f.* exuberance. ‖ **exubérant** [ègzübéraⁿ] *adj.* exuberant; very rich; superabundant; lush; luxuriant.

exultation [ègzültàsyoⁿ] *f.* exultation, rejoicing. ‖ **exulter** [-é] *v.* to exult, to rejoice.

exutoire [ègzütwàr] *m.* exutory; outlet.

F

fable [fàbl] *f.* fable; story, tale; fiction; myth; untruth.

fabricant [fàbrìkaⁿ] *m.* maker, manufacturer. ‖ **fabrication** [-àsyoⁿ] *f.* making, manufacture; production; forging; fabrication. ‖ **fabrique** [fàbrìk] *f.* factory, works, manufacture; mill [papier]; make. ‖ **fabriquer** [-é] *v.* to make, to make up; to manufacture; to forge; to do, to be up to (fam.).

fabuleux [fàbülë] *adj.** fabulous; incredible; prodigious. ‖ **fabuliste** [-ìst] *m.* fabulist.

façade [fàsàd] *f.* façade, front, frontage; appearances (fig.).

face [fàs] *f.* face; countenance; aspect; front; surface; side [disque]; *faire face à*, to confront; to face; *en face de*, facing, in front of.

facétie [fàsésí] *f.* joke; prank.

facette [fàsèt] *f.* facet.

fâché [fâshé] *adj.* sorry; angry; annoyed, cross, vexed; offended; displeased. ‖ **fâcher** [-é] *v.* to incense, to anger; to grieve; to offend; *se fâcher*, to get angry, to lose one's temper; to quarrel. ‖ **fâcheux** [-ë] *m.* bore; *adj.** tiresome, annoying; vexing; awkward; unfortunate; grievous.

facial [fàsyàl] *adj.** facial.

facile [fàsìl] *adj.* easy; simple; facile; ready; pliable; accommodating; fluent [parole]. ‖ **facilité** [-ìté] *f.* ease; easiness; readiness; fluency [parole]; facility; gift; aptitude; pliancy; *pl.* easy terms [paiement]. ‖ **faciliter** [-ìté] *v.* to facilitate, to make easier, to simplify.

façon [fàsoⁿ] *f.* make; fashioning; work; workmanship; manner, way, mode; sort; *pl.* ceremony; affectation; fuss; *de façon à*, so as to; *de toute façon*, in any case; *en aucune façon*, by no means; *de façon que*, so that; *faire des façons*, to stand on ceremony. ‖ **façonner** [-òné] *v.* to shape; to form, to fashion; to make [robe]; to train; to accustom; to mould.

facteur [fàktœr] *m.* postman; transport agent; carman; porter [gare]; maker; factor (math.). ‖ **factice** [-tìs] *adj.* artificial, imitation, factitious. ‖ **factieux** [-syë] *adj.** factious; *m.* factionist. ‖ **faction** [-syoⁿ] *f.* faction; watch, guard, sentry-duty. ‖ **factionnaire** [-syònèr] *m.* sentry.

facture [fàktür] *f.* make; invoice (comm.); bill; account; *suivant facture*, as per invoice. ‖ **facturer** [-türé] *v.* to invoice. ‖ **facturier** [-ryé] *m.* sales-book; invoice-clerk.

facultatif [fàkültàtìf] *adj.** optional, facultative; *arrêt facultatif*, request stop. ‖ **faculté** [-é] *f.* faculty; option; power; privilege; branch of studies; *pl.* means, resources.

fadaise [fàdèz] *f.* nonsense, twaddle, *Am.* baloney (pop.).

fade [fàd] *adj.* tasteless, insipid; flat. ‖ **fadeur** [-œr] *f.* insipidity; sickliness [odeur]; pointlessness; tameness.

fagot [fàgò] *m.* faggot, bundle of sticks. ‖ **fagoté** [-é] *adj.* dowdy, frumpish (fam.).

faible [fèbl] *m.* weakness, foible; weakling; *adj.* weak, feeble; faint [voix]; light, slight; gentle [pente]; poor; slender [ressources]. ‖ **faiblesse** [-ès] *f.* weakness, feebleness; frailty;

weak point; fainting fit; smallness; poorness; slenderness; deficiency. ‖ **faiblir** [-îr] v. to weaken, to grow weak; to flag, to yield.

faïence [fàyaⁿs] f. earthenware; crockery.

faille [fày] f. fault (geol.). ‖ **failli** [-ì] m. bankrupt. ‖ **faillir** [-îr] v.* to fail; to err; to come near; to just miss; to go bankrupt (comm.); il a failli mourir, he nearly died. ‖ **faillite** [-ìt] f. failure, bankruptcy; faire faillite, to go bankrupt.

faim [fìⁿ] f. hunger; avoir faim, to be hungry; mourir de faim, to be starving.

fainéant [fènéaⁿ] m. idler, sluggard, slacker (fam.); adj. idle, lazy, sluggish; slothful.

faire [fèr] m. doing; technique; style; workmanship; v.* to make [fabriquer]; to cause; to get; to bring forth; to do; to perform; to suit; to fit; to deal [cartes]; to manage; to be [temps]; to play [musique]; to paint [tableau]; to produce; to go [distance]; to say; to pay [frais]; to persuade; to wage [guerre]; cela fait mon affaire, that suits me fine; faites attention, be careful; je lui ferai écrire une lettre, I shall have him write a letter; faites-moi le plaisir de, do me the favo(u)r of; faire savoir, to inform; faire voile, to set sail; se faire, to be done; to happen; to get used to; to become; cela ne se fait pas, that is not done; il peut se faire que, it may happen that; comment se fait-il que, how is it that; se faire comprendre, to make oneself understood; ne vous en faites pas, don't worry; faire-part, announcement, card, notification [mariage, décès]. ‖ **faisable** [f^ezàbl] adj. feasible, practicable.

faisan, -ane [f^ezaⁿ, -àn] m., f. pheasant, m.; hen-pheasant, f. ‖ **faisander** [-dé] v. to hang [viande].

faisceau [fèsô] m.* bundle; cluster; pile, stack [armes]; pencil [lumière]; pl. fasces.

faiseur [f^ezœr] m. maker, doer; quack, humbug.

fait [fè] m. fact; deed; act; feat, achievement; case; matter; point; adj. made; done; settled; used; ripe; grown; au fait, de fait, indeed; être au fait de, to be informed of; fait d'armes, feat of arms; fait divers, item of news; prendre sur le fait, to catch in the act; en venir au fait, to come to the point; c'en est fait de, it's all up with; c'est bien fait pour vous, it serves you right; fait-tout, stew-pan.

faîte [fèt] m. ridge [toit]; summit, top; peak, height (fig.).

faix [fè] m. burden, load.

falaise [fàlèz] f. cliff; bluff.

fallacieux [fàlàsyë] adj.* fallacious.

falloir [fàlwàr] v.* to be necessary; il lui faut un crayon, he needs a pencil; il faut qu'elle vienne, she must come; il fallait appeler, you should have called; comme il faut, proper; correct; respectable; gentlemanly; lady-like; il s'en faut de beaucoup, far from it; peu s'en fallut qu'il ne mourût, he very nearly died.

falot [fàlô] m. lantern.

falot [fàlô] adj. queer, quaint, droll, odd, amusing; wan, dull [lumière].

falsification [fàlsìfìkàsyoⁿ] f. falsification; adulteration; forgery, debasement; tampering with. ‖ **falsifier** [fàlsìfyé] v. to falsify; to counterfeit; to adulterate [nourriture]; to sophisticate; to forge; to debase; to tamper with.

famélique [fàmélìk] m. starveling; adj. starving, famished.

fameux [fàmë] adj.* famous, renowned, celebrated; Br. capital, Am. marvelous, swell (fam.).

familial [fàmìlyàl] adj.* family, domestic. ‖ **familiale** [-yàl] f seven-seater saloon, Am. seven-passenger sedan. ‖ **familiariser** [fàmìlyàrìzé] v. to familiarize. ‖ **familiarité** [-ìté] f familiarity, intimacy; pl. liberties. ‖ **familier** [fàmìlyé] adj.* family, domestic; familiar; well-known; intimate; colloquial. ‖ **famille** [fàmîy] f. family; household.

famine [fàmîn] f. famine, starvation.

fanal [fànàl] m.* lantern; beacon; signal-light; navigation light.

fanatique [fànàtìk] m., f. fanatic; adj. fanatical. ‖ **fanatisme** [-ìsm] m. fanaticism.

fane [fàn] f. top; haulm.

faner [fàné] v. to cause to fade; to make hay; to toss; se faner, to fade; to droop. ‖ **faneur** [-œr] m. haymaker.

fanfare [faⁿfàr] f. brass band; fanfare; flourish (mus.). ‖ **fanfaron** [-oⁿ] m. boaster, braggart, swaggerer; adj.* boastful, bragging. ‖ **fanfaronnade** [-ònàd] f. brag, boasting, bluster. ‖ **fanfaronner** [-òné] v. to brag, to bluster, to boast.

fanfreluche [faⁿfrêlüch] f. fal-lal.

fange [faⁿj] f. mud, mire; filth, dirt; ooze. ‖ **fangeux** [-ë] adj.* muddy; dirty, filthy.

fanion [fànyoⁿ] m. flag pennon (mil.). ‖ **fanon** [fànoⁿ] m. pendant (eccles.); dewlap [bœuf]; fetlock [cheval]; whalebone.

fantaisie [faⁿtèzî] f. fancy, whim, caprice; imagination; fantasia (mus.); articles de fantaisie, fancy goods. ‖

fantaisiste [-ìst] *adj.* whimsical; fanciful; *m.* fanciful person.

fantasque [faⁿtàsk] *adj.* fantastic; changeable, flighty.

fantassin [faⁿtàsìⁿ] *m.* infantryman, foot-soldier.

fantastique [faⁿtàstìk] *adj.* fantastic, fanciful; incredible; outrageous.

fantôme [faⁿtôm] *m.* phantom, ghost, spectre; shadow.

faon [faⁿ] *m.* fawn.

farce [fàrs] *f.* stuffing, force-meat [cuisine]; farce, low comedy; trick, practical joke. ‖ *farceur* [-œr] *m.* wag, humorist; practical joker. ‖ *farcir* [-îr] *v.* to stuff.

fard [fàr] *m.* paint; make-up; rouge; artifice; disguise (fig.).

fardeau [fàrdô] *m.* ᵉ burden, load.

farder [fàrdé] *v.* to paint; to make up; to disguise; *se farder,* to make up, to paint.

farfelu [fàrf•lü] *adj.* hare-brained; *m.* whipper-snapper.

farine [fàrìn] *f.* meal, flour; oatmeal [avoine]; *farine lactée,* malted milk. ‖ *farineux* [-ë] *adj.* ᵉ mealy, floury, farinaceous.

farouche [fàrûsh] *adj.* wild, fierce, savage; cruel; shy, timid [peureux]; sullen.

fascicule [fàsìkül] *m.* fascic(u)le; small bundle; part, section [publication].

fascination [fàsìnàsyoⁿ] *f.* fascination, charm. ‖ *fasciner* [-é] *v.* to fascinate; to entrance, to charm.

faste [fàst] *m.* pomp, display, ostentation; *adj.* lucky; auspicious.

fastidieux [fàstìdyë] *adj.* ᵉ tedious, dull; irksome; tiresome.

fastueux [fàstüë] *adj.* ᵉ ostentatious, showy; splendid, sumptuous.

fat [fàt] *m.* fop; conceited idiot; *adj.* foppish; conceited, vain.

fatal [fàtàl] *adj.* fatal, inevitable; *c'est fatal,* it's bound to happen. ‖ *fatalisme* [-ìsm] *m.* fatalism. ‖ *fatalité* [-ìté] *f.* fatality; fate; calamity; misfortune.

fatigant [fàtìgaⁿ] *adj.* tiring, wearisome, fatiguing; tiresome. ‖ *fatigue* [fàtìg] *f.* fatigue, tiredness, weariness; hard work. ‖ *fatigué* [fàtìgé] *adj.* tired, weary, jaded [cheval]; threadbare [vêtement]; well-thumbed [livre]. ‖ *fatiguer* [-é] *v.* to fatigue, to tire, to weary; to overwork, to strain; *se fatiguer,* to get tired; to tire oneself out; to grow sick [*de,* of].

fatuité [fàtüìté] *f.* conceit, self-satisfaction; foppishness.

faubourg [fôbûr] *m.* suburb; outskirts. ‖ *faubourien* [-ryìⁿ] *adj.* ᵉ suburban; *Am.* downtown; common, vulgar.

faucher [fôshé] *v.* to mow, to reap; to mow down (fig.); to sweep by fire (mil.); to pinch (pop.). ‖ *faucheur* [-œr] *m.* mower reaper. ‖ *faucheuse* [-ëz] *f.* mowing-machine, reaper. ‖ *faucheux* [-ë] *m.* field spider, daddylonglegs.

faucille [fôsîy] *f.* sickle, reaping-hook.

faucon [fôkoⁿ] *m.* falcon, hawk.

faufiler [fôfìlé] *v.* to tack; to slip in; to insert; *se faufiler,* to creep in; to slip in; to insinuate oneself.

faune [fôn] *f.* fauna; set (fig.).

faussaire [fôsèr] *m.*; *f.* forger. ‖ *fausser* [-é] *v.* to falsify, to pervert; to bend, to warp; to force [serrure]; to break [parole]; to throw out of tune (mus.); *fausser compagnie à,* to give the slip to. ‖ *fausseté* [-té] *f.* falseness; falsehood; treachery.

faute [fôt] *f.* fault; error; mistake; want, lack; *faute de,* for want of; *sans faute,* without fail.

fauteuil [fôtœy] *m.* armchair; chair [président]; wheel chair [roulant]; seat; stall (theat.).

fautif [fôtìf] *adj.* ᵉ wrong, faulty, incorrect; guilty.

fauve [fôv] *m.* wild beast; *adj.* tawny; musky [odeur]. ‖ *fauvette* [-èt] *f.* warbler.

faux [fô] *f.* scythe.

faux, fausse [fô, fôs] *m.* falsehood; forgery; *adj.* false, untrue, wrong, erroneous; inaccurate; imitation, sham; forged; fraudulent; out of tune (mus.); *adv.* falsely; out of tune (mus.); *faux pas,* slip; *faire fausse route,* to be on the wrong track; *faux col,* shirt-collar, detachable collar; *faux-fuyant,* evasion, subterfuge; *faux frais,* incidentals; *faux-monnayeur,* counterfeiter; *faux-semblant,* false pretence.

faveur [fàvœr] *f.* favo(u)r; kindness; boon; privilege; fashion, vogue; ribbon [ruban]; *conditions de faveur,* preferential terms; *billet de faveur,* complimentary ticket. ‖ *favorable* [fàvòràbl] *adj.* favo(u)rable, propitious; advantageous. ‖ *favori, -ite* [-ì, -ìt] *adj., f., adj.* favo(u)rite; *m. pl.* side-whiskers. ‖ *favoriser* [-ìzé] *v.* to favo(u)r; to encourage; to patronize; to facilitate; to assist. ‖ *favoritisme* [-ìtìsm] *m.* favo(u)ritism.

fébrile [fébrìl] *adj.* febrile; feverish.

fécond [fékoⁿ] *adj.* fruitful, fertile; productive; prolific. ‖ *féconder* [-dé] *v.* to fecundate, to fertilize; to impregnate. || **fécondité** [-ìté] *f.* fertility; fecundity; fruitfulness.

fécule [fékül] *f.* starch; fecula. || **féculent** [-a^n] *m.* starchy food; *adj.* starchy, faeculent.

fédéral [fédéràl] *adj.** federal; *m.* © the Federal Government. || **fédération** [-àsyo^n] *f.* federation. || **fédéré** [-é] *adj.* federate.

fée [té] *f.* fairy; *conte de fées*, fairytale. || **féerie** [-rî] *f.* fairy scene; enchantment; pantomime; fairy-play; magic spectacle. || **féerique** [-rìk] *adj.* fairy; magic; enchanting.

feignant [fènya^n] *adj.*, *m.* (pop.) *see* **fainéant.**

feindre [fi^ndr] *v.** to feign, to sham, to pretend; to limp [cheval]. || **feinte** [f^nt] *f.* sham, pretence; bluff; make-believe; feint [boxe].

fêler [fèlé] *v.* to crack.

félicitation [félìsìtàsyo^n] *f.* congratulation. || **féliciter** [-é] *v.* to congratulate, to compliment.

félin [féli^n] *adj.*, *m.* cat-like; feline.

fêlure [fèlür] *f.* crack; fracture.

femelle [f^mèl] *f.* female.

féminin [fémìni^n] *adj.* feminine; female; womanly; womanish.

femme [fàm] *f.* woman [*pl.* women]; wife.

fenaison [f^nèzo^n] *f.* haymaking.

fendre [fa^ndr] *v.* to split, to cleave; to rend [air]; to slit; to break through [foule]; to crack; *se fendre*, to split, to crack; to cough up (fam.).

fenêtre [f^nètr] *f.* window; sash.

fente [fa^nt] *f.* crack, fissure, split; slit; gap; chink; cranny; crevice; opening; slot.

féodal [féòdàl] *adj.** feudal.

fer [fèr] *m.* iron; sword; shoe [cheval]; curling-tongs; flat-iron; *pl.* fetters, chains; captivity; forceps (med.); *fil de fer*, wire; *fer forgé*, wrought iron; *fer-blanc*, tin. || **ferblanterie** [fèrbla^ntrî] *f.* tin ware, tin goods; tin-shop (ind.). || **ferblantier** [-yé] *m.* tinsmith.

férié [féryé] *adj. jour férié*, public holiday, Bank Holiday.

ferlouche [fèrlûsh] *f.* © ferlouche (pie-filling).

fermage [fèrmàj] *m.* rent; tenant farming.

ferme [fèrm] *f.* farm; farming; farming lease [bail]; truss (techn.); *adj.* firm, rigid, steady, fast, fixed; stiff; resolute; definite; *adv.* firmly, fast.

fermé [fèrmé] *adj.* shut, closed; exclusive; impenetrable; impervious.

ferment [fèrma^n] *m.* ferment. || **fermentation** [-tàsyo^n] *f.* fermentation; excitement; unrest. || **fermenter** [-té] *v.* to ferment.

fermer [fèrmé] *v.* to close, to shut; to close down; to fasten; to switch off [lumière]; to turn out [gaz]; to clench [poing]; to lock [à clé]; to bolt [au verrou].

fermeté [fèrm^té] *f.* firmness; steadiness; steadfastness; constancy.

fermeture [fèrm^tür] *f.* shutting, closing; fastening; *fermeture à glissière*, zipper, zip fastener.

fermier [fèrmyé] *m.* farmer; farm tenant. || **fermière** [-yèr] *f.* farmer's wife.

fermoir [fèrmwàr] *m.* clasp, catch, fastener.

féroce [féròs] *adj.* ferocious, fierce, savage, wild. || **férocité** [-ìté] *f.* fierceness, ferocity.

ferraille [fèràỳ] *f.* scrap-iron, old iron; junk. || **ferré** [-é] *adj.* fitted with iron; shod; well up in (fam.); hobnailed [soulier]. || **ferrer** [-é] *v.* to fit with iron; to shoe [cheval]; to strike [poisson]; to metal [route]. || **ferrure** [-ür] *f.* iron fitting; iron-work.

fertile [fèrtîl] *adj.* fertile; rich. || **fertiliser** [-ìzé] *v.* to fertilize. || **fertilisation** [-ìzàsyo^n] *f.* fertilization. || **fertilité** [-ìté] *f.* fertility; abundance; fruitfulness.

féru [férü] *adj.* smitten; struck.

férule [férül] *f.* cane; sway.

fervent [fèrva^n] *m.* enthusiast; fan (fam.); *adj.* fervent, earnest. || **ferveur** [-œr] *f.* fervo(u)r, earnestness.

fesse [fès] *f.* buttock; *pl.* bottom, backside; *fesse-mathieu*, skinflint. || **fessée** [-é] *f.* spanking. || **fesser** [-é] *v.* to spank.

festin [fèsti^n] *m.* feast, banquet.

feston [fèsto^n] *m.* festoon. || **festonner** [-òné] *v.* to festoon; to scallop [ourlet].

festoyer [fèstwàyé] *v.* to feast; to regale.

fête [fèt] *f.* feast; festival; holiday; birthday; patron saint's day; *faire fête à*, to fête; *fête-Dieu*, Corpus Christi. || **fêter** [-é] *v.* to keep [fête]; to fête; to entertain; to celebrate.

fétiche [fétìsh] *m.* fetish; mascot. || **fétichisme** [-ìsm] *m.* fetishism.

fétide [fétìd] *adj.* fetid, stinking, rank; **fétidité**, fetidness.

fétu [fétü] *m.* straw.

feu [fë] *m.** fire; conflagration; flame; heat; firing [armes]; fire-place [foyer]; light; ardour spirit; *arme à feu*, fire-arm; *faire feu sur*, to fire at; *feu de* joie, bonfire ; *feu d'artifice,* fireworks ; *mettre le feu à,* to set fire to ; *à petit feu,* over a slow fire ; *donnez-moi du feu,* give me a light ; *faire long feu,* to hang fire, to misfire.

feu [-ë] *adj.* late ; deceased.

feuillage [fœyàʒ] *m.* foliage, leaves. ‖ **feuille** [fœy] *f.* leaf ; sheet [papier]. ‖ **feuillet** [-ɛ] *m.* leaf ; form ; sheet. ‖ **feuilleté** [-té] *m.* puff paste. ‖ **feuilleter** [-té] *v.* to turn over the leaves of ; to thumb through ; to skim through [livre] ; to make flaky [pâte]. ‖ **feuilleton** [-tɔⁿ] *m.* serial story. ‖ **feuillu** [-ü] *adj.* leafy.

feutre [fœtr] *m.* felt ; felt hat. ‖ **feutré** [-é] *adj.* felty ; stealthy, soft [pas].

fève [fɛv] *f.* bean ; broad bean.

février [févrìyé] *m.* February.

fiançailles [fyaⁿsày] *f. pl.* engagement, betrothal. ‖ *fiancé,* -ée [-sé] *m.* fiancé ; *f.* fiancée. ‖ **se fiancer** [sᵉfyaⁿsé] *v.* to become engaged.

fibre [fïbr] *f. Br.* fibre, *Am.* fiber ; grain [bois] ; feeling. ‖ **fibreux** [-ë] *adj.*° fibrous, stringy.

fibrome [fïbrôm] *m.* fibrous tumo(u)r.

ficeler [fislé] *v.* to tie up, to do up. ‖ **ficelle** [fisèl] *f.* string, pack-thread, twine ; (pop.) trick, dodge.

fiche [fish] *f.* peg ; pin ; counter [cartes] ; slip [papier] ; form ; index-card ; label ; chit ; plug (electr.). ‖ **ficher** [-é] *v.* to stick in ; to drive in ; (pop.) to do ; to put ; to give ; to throw ; *se ficher,* to laugh (*de,* at) ; *je m'en fiche,* I don't care a hang. ‖ **fichier** [-yé] *m.* card-index ; card-index cabinet. ‖ **fichu** [-ü] *m.* neckerchief ; *adj.* (pop.) lost, done for ; *mal fichu,* wretched, out of sorts.

fictif [fïktïf] *adj.*° fictitious. ‖ **fiction** [fïksyoⁿ] *f.* fiction ; fabrication ; figment ; invention.

fidèle [fïdèl] *adj.* faithful ; loyal ; accurate ; exact [copie] ; *m. pl. les fidèles,* the faithful ; the congregation (eccles.). ‖ **fidélité** [-ïté] *f.* faithfulness, fidelity ; loyalty ; accuracy.

fieffé [fíéfé] *adj.* arrant, consummate.

fiel [fyèl] *m.* bile, gall [animaux] ; spleen ; malice, venom.

fier (se) [sᵉfyé] *v.* to rely (*à, on*) ; to trust [*à, to*].

fier [fyèr] *adj.*° proud ; haughty ; (fam.) fine, precious. ‖ **fierté** [-té] *f.* pride ; dignity ; haughtiness.

fièvre [fyèvr] *f.* fever ; ague ; heat, excitement (fig.) ; *fièvre aphteuse,* foot-and-mouth disease. ‖ **fiévreux** [-ë] *adj.*° feverish ; fever-ridden ; excited.

fifrelin [fifrœlⁿ] *m.* farthing, *Am.* red cent.

figaro [fïgàrð] *m.* barber.

figer [fïʒé] *v.* to coagulate, to congeal ; *se figer,* to congeal, to clot ; to set [visage] ; to freeze [sourire] ; to stiffen [personne].

fignoler [fïñòlé] *v.* to finick over.

figue [fïg] *f.* fig. ‖ **figuier** [fïgyé] *m.* fig-tree.

figurant [fïgüraⁿ] *m.* supernumerary, super (theat.). ‖ **figuration** [-àsyoⁿ] *f.* figuration, representation ; extras (theat.). ‖ **figure** [fïgür] *f.* figure ; face ; type ; appearance ; court-card [cartes]. ‖ **figuré** [-é] *adj.* figurative ; *au figuré,* figuratively. ‖ **figurer** [-é] *v.* to represent ; to act ; to figure ; to appear ; *se figurer,* to imagine, to fancy.

fil [fïl] *m.* thread ; wire ; edge [lame] ; string ; linen ; grain [bois] ; clue ; course ; *fil à plomb,* plumb-line. ‖ **filament** [-àmaⁿ] *m.* filament. ‖ **filant** [-aⁿ] *adj.* flowing ; ropy [vin] ; shooting [étoile]. ‖ **filasse** [-às] *f.* tow ; oakum. ‖ **filateur** [-àtœr] *m.* spinning-mill owner ; spinner ; informer. ‖ **filature** [-àtür] *f.* spinning-mill, cotton-mill ; spinning ; tracking, shadowing. ‖ **file** [fïl] *f.* file ; rank ; queue. ‖ **filer** [-é] *v.* to spin ; to draw out ; to pay out [câble] ; to spin out (fig.) ; to shadow ; to flow ; to smoke [lampe] ; to run off ; to sneak away ; *filer à l'anglaise,* to take French leave. ‖ **filet** [-ɛ] *m.* thread ; fillet [bœuf] ; trickle ; dash [citron] ; thread [vis] ; snare ; net [pêche] ; luggage rack ; *coup de filet,* catch, haul.

filial [fïlyàl] *adj.*° filial. ‖ **filiale** [fïlyàl] *f.* subsidiary company ; sub-branch.

filière [fïlyèr] *f.* draw-plate ; usual channels (fig.).

filin [fïlⁿ] *m.* rope.

fille [fïy] *f.* girl ; maid ; daughter ; sister [religieuse] ; (fam.) whore ; *jeune fille,* girl. ‖ **fillette** [-èt] *f.* little girl.

filleul [fïyœl] *m.* godson. ‖ **filleule** [fïyœl] *f.* god-daughter.

film [fïlm] *m.* film, motion picture, *Am.* movie. ‖ **filmer** [-é] *v.* to film.

filon [fïloⁿ] *m.* vein, lode ; (fam.) cushy job ; bonanza.

filou [fïlû] *m.* crook ; sharper ; swindler ; crook.

fils [fïs] *m.* son ; boy ; lad (fam.).

filtre [fïltr] *m.* filter ; strainer ; percolator [cafetière] ; drip-coffee [café]. ‖ **filtrer** [-é] *v.* to filter ; to strain ; to percolate ; to leak out.

fin [fⁿ] *f.* end ; termination, conclusion ; close ; *fin de semaine* © weekend ; object, aim, purpose ; extremity ; *à la fin,* in the long run ; at last ; *mettre fin à,* to put an end to.

fin [fin] *adj.* fine; refined; pure; choice; slender; sly, artful; subtle; delicate; small; keen, quick [oreille]; *adv.* fine, finely; absolutely.

final [finăl] *adj.** final, last; ultimate.

finance [finaⁿs] *f.* finance; ready money; *pl.* resources; *le ministère des Finances,* Br. the Exchequer, Am. the Treasury. || *financer* [-é] *v.* to finance, to supply with money. || *financier* [-yé] *m.* financier; *adj.** financial; stock [marché].

finasser [finăsé] *v.* to finesse. || *finasserie* [-rì] *f.* trickery, foxiness; *pl.* wiles.

fine [fin] *f.* liqueur brandy.

finesse [finès] *f.* finesse; fineness; nicety; thinness; delicacy; shrewdness; acuteness.

fini [finì] *m.* finish; finishing touch; *adj.* ended, finished; settled; over; accomplished; finite. || *finir* [- îr] *v.* to finish, to end; to cease, to leave off; to be over; to die. || *finissant* [-ìsaⁿ] *m.* © senior, graduating student.

fioriture [fyòrìtür] *f.* flourish.

firmament [firmămaⁿ] *m.* firmament, heavens.

firme [firm] *f.* firm.

fisc [fisk] *m.* treasury; taxes, Br. Inland Revenue; Am. Internal Revenue. || *fiscal* [-ăl] *adj.** fiscal.

fissure [fìsür] *f.* fissure, crack, split, cleft, crevice.

fixe [fìks] *m.* fixed salary; *adj.* fixed; steady; fast; firm; regular; settled. || *fixer* [-é] *v.* to fix; to fasten; to settle; to stare at; to decide; to determine; to hold; to attract [attention]; *se fixer,* to settle down; to get fixed.

flacon [flàkoⁿ] *m.* small bottle; flask; vial, phial.

flagellation [flàjèllàsyoⁿ] *f.* flagellation, scourging. || *flageller* [flàjèllé] *v.* to scourge.

flageoler [flàjòlé] *v.* to shake, to tremble.

flageolet [flàjòlè] *m.* flageolet.

flagorner [flàgòrné] *v.* to flatter; to fawn upon.

flagrant [flàgraⁿ] *adj.* flagrant, obvious; glaring, rank.

flair [flèr] *m.* scent; sense of smell; flair. || *flairer* [-é] *v.* to smell; to scent; to detect.

flamant [flàmaⁿ] *m.* flamingo.

flambant [flaⁿbaⁿ] *adj.* blazing; *flambant neuf,* brand-new. || *flambeau* [-ô] *m.** torch; candlestick. || *flambée* [-bé] *f.* blaze; rocketing [prix]. || *flamber* [-é] *v.* to flame; to blaze; to singe; to sterilize. || *flamboiement* [-wàmaⁿ] *m.* blaze. || *flamboyant* [-wàyaⁿ] *adj.*

flamboyant (arch.); blazing; flaming. || *flamboyer* [-wàyé] *v.* to blaze, to flame; to flash; to gleam.

flamme [flàm] *f.* flame; passion, love; pennant (mil.); *en flammes,* ablaze. || *flammèche* [flàmèsh] *f.* flake (or) burning particle of fire.

flan [flaⁿ] *m.* custard tart; flong (typogr.); *à la flan,* botched; all flummery.

flanc [flaⁿ] *m.* side, flank; *sur le flanc,* laid up; done up.

flancher [flaⁿshé] *v.* to flinch; to give in; to break down [auto].

flanelle [flànèl] *f.* flannel.

flâner [flâné] *v.* to stroll; to lounge about; to saunter; to loaf. || *flânerie* [-rì] *f.* lounging; idling. || *flâneur* [-œr] *m.* stroller; loafer, lounger.

flanquer [flaⁿké] *v.* to flank.

flanquer [flaⁿké] *v.* to throw, to chuck (fam.); to land, to deal [coups].

flaque [flàk] *f.* puddle, pool.

flasque [flàsk] *adj.* flabby, limp.

flatter [flàté] *v.* to flatter; to caress, to stroke; to please; to pretend, to claim; to boast of. || *flatterie* [-rì] *f.* flattery. || *flatteur* [-œr] *m.* flatterer; sycophant; *adj.** flattering; gratifying; pleasing.

fléau [fléô] *m.** flail; beam [balance]; scourge; pest, plague (fig.).

flèche [flèsh] *f.* arrow; spire [église]; pole; jib [grue]; sag; *monter en flèche,* to shoot up. || *fléchette* [fléshèt] *f.* dart.

fléchir [fléshîr] *v.* to bend; to give way; to weaken; to move to pity.

flegmatique [flègmàtìk] *adj.* phlegmatic; stolid; calm, cool. || *flegme* [flègm] *m.* phlegm; coolness.

flétrir [flétrîr] *v.* to fade; to wither; to wilt; to blight. || *flétrissure* [-ìsür] *f.* withering, fading.

flétrir [flétrîr] *v.* to brand; to stain (fig.). || *flétrissure* [-ìsür] *f.* brand; blot.

fleur [flœr] *f.* flower; blossom; prime; bloom; *à fleur de,* level with. || *fleuret* [-è] *m.* foil [escrime]; drill [mine]. || *fleurette* [-èt] *f.* floweret; *conter fleurette,* to flirt. || *fleurir* [-îr] *v.** to flower, to bloom; to thrive; to decorate with flowers. || *fleuriste* [-ìst] *m.,* *f.* florist.

fleuve [flœv] *m.* river.

flexibilité [flèksìbìlìté] *f.* flexibility; suppleness. || *flexible* [-ìbl] *adj.* pliant; flexible; *m.* flex (electr.). || *flexion* [-yoⁿ] *f.* bending, sagging, flexion.

flic [flìk] *m.* (fam.) cop, Br. bobby; slop, flattie; Am. flat-foot.

flirt [flœrt] *m.* flirt; flirting. ‖ **flirter** [-é] *v.* to flirt.

flocon [flòkon] *m.* flake [neige]; flock [laine]. ‖ **floconneux** [-ònë] *adj.* flaky; fluffy.

floraison [flòrèzon] *f.* blossoming; blossom-time.

florissant [flòrìsan] *adj.* flourishing, thriving.

flot [flô] *m.* wave; tide; crowd; flood (fig.); *à flot*, afloat; *à flots*, in torrents; *se mettre à flot*, to get up to date.

flottage [flòtàj] *m.* floating, drive. ‖ **flottaison** [-èzon] *f.* floating; water-line (naut.). ‖ **flotte** [flòt] *f.* fleet; navy; (fam.) rain, water. ‖ **flottement** [-man] *m.* swaying; wavering, hesitation. ‖ **flotter** [-é] *v.* to float; to waver, to hesitate, to drive. ‖ **flotteur** [-œr] *m.* raftsman; float (techn.); buoy [bouée]. ‖ **flottille** [-ìy] *f.* flotilla.

flou [flû] *m.* softness; haziness; *adj.* soft; blurred; hazy; fuzzy, foggy [photo]; fluffy [cheveux].

fluctuer [flüktüé] *v.* to fluctuate.

fluide [flüíd] *m.*, *adj.* fluid.

flûte [flüt] *f.* flute; tall champagne glass; long thin roll of bread; *interj.* bother !, *Br.* blow it !

flux [flü] *m.* flux; flow; *le flux et le reflux*, the ebb and flow. ‖ **fluxion** [-ksyon] *f.* inflammation; congestion.

foi [fwà] *f.* faith, belief; trust, confidence; evidence [preuve]; *de bonne foi*, in good faith; *digne de foi*, reliable, trustworthy; *qui fait foi*, authentic, conclusive.

foie [fwà] *m.* liver.

foin [fwiⁿ] *m.* hay.

foire [fwàr] *f.* fair; spree.

foirer [fwàré] *v.* to hang fire [fusée]; to strip [vis]; to flop (fam.).

fois [fwà] *f.* time, occasion ; *une fois*, once; *deux fois*, twice; *combien de fois*, how often; *à la fois*, at the same time; *encore une fois*, once more; *une fois que*, when, once; *une seule fois*, only once.

foison [fwàzon] *f.* plenty, abundance. ‖ **foisonner** [-òné] *v.* to be plentiful, to abound; to swarm; to swell; to buckle.

fol, see **fou**. ‖ **folâtre** [fòlâtr] *adj.* playful, frisky. ‖ **folâtrer** [-é] *v.* to frolic, to frisk; to gambol. ‖ **folie** [fòlî] *f.* madness; folly; mania; *aimer à la folie*, to love to distraction; *faire des folies*, to act extravagantly, to be overgenerous. ‖ **folle**, see **fou**.

fomenter [fòmanté] *v.* to foment; to stir up.

foncé [fonsé] *adj.* dark, deep. ‖ **foncer** [-é] *v.* to drive in, to bore [puits]; to deepen; to darken; to rush, to charge; *se foncer*, to darken, to deepen.

foncier [fonsyé] *adj.** landed; real; fundamental; thorough; *propriétaire foncier*, landowner.

fonction [fonksyon] *f.* function; office; duty; working; *faire fonction de*, to act as. ‖ **fonctionnaire** [-yònèr] *m.*, *f.* official; civil servant. ‖ **fonctionnement** [-nᵉman] *m.* working; functioning. ‖ **fonctionner** [-yòné] *v.* to function; to work; to act.

fond [fon] *m.* bottom; bed [mer]; foundation; gist; essence; basis; background [tableau]; back; *à fond*, thoroughly; *au fond*, in reality; after all.

fondamental [fondàmantàl] *adj.** fundamental; radical; essential; basic.

fondateur, -trice [fondàtœr, -trìs] *m.*, *f.* founder. ‖ **fondation** [-àsyon] *f.* founding; foundation; basis; endowment [legs]. ‖ **fondé** [-é] *adj.* founded; authorized; *m. fondé de pouvoir*, proxy (jur.); manager (comm.). ‖ **fondement** [-man] *m.* base; foundation; *sans fondement*, groundless. ‖ **fonder** [-é] *v.* to found; to ground, to base, to justify.

fonderie [fondrî] *f.* casting; smelting; foundry; smelting works. ‖ **fondeur** [fondœr] *m.* founder; smelter. ‖ **fondre** [fondr] *v.* to melt; to thaw; to smelt [fer]; to cast [statue]; to dissolve; to soften (fig.); to blend [couleurs]; to swoop, to pounce; *fondre en larmes*, to burst into tears.

fondrière [fondrièr] *f.* bog, quagmire; hollow; pot-hole.

fonds [fon] *m.* land, estate; stock-in-trade; fund; business; *pl.* cash; capital; *fonds de commerce*, business concern; *bon fonds*, good nature.

fontaine [fontèn] *f.* fountain; spring; source.

fonte [font] *f.* melting; smelting; casting; thawing [neige]; cast iron; fount (typogr.).

forage [fòràj] *m.* boring, drilling; bore-hole.

forain [fòriⁿ] *adj.* alien, foreign; travel(l)ing, itinerant; *marchand forain*, hawker; *fête foraine*, fair.

forban [fòrban] *m.* pirate; bandit.

forçat [fòrsà] *m.* convict.

force [fòrs] *f.* force; strength; might; vigo(u)r; power; authority; violence; *pl.* forces, troops; *à force de*, by dint of; *force majeure*, absolute necessity, overpowering circumstances. ‖ **forcément** [-éman] *adv.* necessarily; inevitably.

forcené [fòrsᵉné] *m.* madman; *adj.* frantic, mad, frenzied.

forceps [fòrsèps] *m.* forceps.

forcer [fòrsé] *v.* to force; to compel, to oblige; to take by storm (mil.); to run [blocus]; to break open; to break through [traverser]; to strain; to increase [augmenter]; to pick [serrure] to exaggerate; to win (admiration).

forer [fòré] *v.* to drill, to bore.

forestier [fòrèstyé] *m.* forester; *adj.* forest.

foret [fòrè] *m.* drill; bit; gimlet.

forêt [fòrè] *f.* forest.

forfait [fòrfè] *m.* crime. ‖ *forfaiture* [-tür] *f.* forfeiture; prevarication.

forfait [fòrfè] *m.* contract; *travail à forfait,* job work; work by contract.

forfait [fòrfè] *m.* forfeit; *déclarer forfait,* to give it up.

forfanterie [fòrfaⁿtrî] *f.* bragging, boasting.

forge [fòrj] *f.* forge, smithy; iron-works. ‖ *forger* [-é] *v.* to forge; to hammer; to invent; to coin [mot]; to make up; *se forger,* to fancy. ‖ *forgeron* [-ᵉroⁿ] *m.* blacksmith.

formaliser (se) [sᵉfòrmàlîzé] *v.* to take offense. ‖ *formalisme* [fòrmàlìsm] *m.* formalism; conventionalism. ‖ *formalité* [fòrmàlìté] *f.* form, formality; ceremoniousness.

format [fòrmà] *m.* size; format [livre]. ‖ *formation* [-syoⁿ] *f.* formation; making; development. ‖ *forme* [fòrm] *f.* form; shape; former (techn.); pattern; mould; last [chaussures]; procedure; *pl.* shoe-trees; etiquette; *en forme,* fit, in fine fettle. ‖ *formel* [-èl] *adj.* formal; categorical; express; strict. ‖ *former* [-é] *v.* to form; to fashion, to shape; to mould; to constitute; *se former,* to take shape; to form; to be formed; to be trained.

formidable [fòrmìdàbl] *adj.* formidable, dreadful; (fam.) terrific, tremendous, *Am.* swell.

formulaire [fòrmülèr] *m.* formulary. ‖ *formule* [fòrmül] *f.* formula; form; prescription; phrase. ‖ *formuler* [-é] *v.* to draw up; to formulate; to lay down; to express; to lodge [plainte].

fort [fòr] *m.* strong man; strong point; center; fortress; *adj.* strong; robust; clever; good; skilful; thick; large; ample; stout; heavy [mer]; high [vent]; big, steep [pente]; severe; difficult; *se faire fort de,* to undertake to; *adv.* very; loud; strongly; *au plus fort du combat,* in the thick of the fight. ‖ *forteresse* [-tᵉrès] *f.* fortress, stronghold. ‖ *fortifiant* [-tìfyaⁿ] *m.* tonic; *adj.* fortifying, invigorating, bracing. ‖ *fortification* [-tìfìkàsyoⁿ] *f.* fortification. ‖ *fortifier* [-tìfyé] *v.* to fortify; to invigorate; to strengthen. ‖ *fortin* [-tⁿ] *m.* fortlet.

fortuit [fòrtüî] *adj.* fortuitous, chance, accidental; casual.

fortune [fòrtün] *f.* fortune; chance; luck; wealth; *mauvaise fortune,* misfortune. ‖ *fortuné* [-é] *adj.* fortunate; happy; rich, well-off.

fosse [fôs] *f.* pit; hole; trench; grave; den [lions]. ‖ *fossé* [fôsé] *m.* ditch; trench; moat [douve]. ‖ *fossette* [-èt] *f.* dimple. ‖ *fossile* [-ìl] *m.*, *adj.* fossil. ‖ *fossoyeur* [-wàyœr] *m.* grave-digger.

fou, folle [fû, fòl] *adj.* [fol, *m.*, before a vowel or a mute *h*] mad, insane; crazy; wild; frantic; silly, stupid; enormous, tremendous; passionately fond; *m., f.* madman, *m.*; madwoman, *f.*; lunatic; maniac; jester; gannet [oiseau]; bishop [échecs]; *devenir fou,* to go mad; *rendre fou,* to drive mad; *maison de fous,* lunatic asylum, madhouse; *un monde fou,* a fearful crowd.

foudre [fûdr] *f.* thunder; lightning; thunderbolt; *coup de foudre,* bolt from the blue; love at first sight. ‖ *foudroyant* [-wàyaⁿ] *adj.* terrifying; terrific; crushing; overwhelming. ‖ *foudroyer* [-wàyé] *v.* to strike down; to blast; to dumbfound; to confound; to strike dead.

fouet [fwè] *m.* whip, lash; birch; whipcord; egg-whisk [cuisine]. ‖ *fouetter* [-té] *v.* to whip, to lash; to flog, to birch; to stimulate, to rouse; to beat [œufs].

fougère [fûjèr] *f.* fern; bracken.

fougue [fûg] *f.* fire, mettle, dash, spirit. ‖ *fougueux* [fûgë] *adj.* fiery; impetuous; spirited [cheval].

fouille [fûy] *f.* excavation; search. ‖ *fouiller* [-é] *v.* to excavate; to dig; to search [personne]; to pry; to rummage. ‖ *fouillis* [-î] *m.* jumble, mess.

fouine [fûîn] *f.* stone-marten. ‖ *fouiner* [-é] *v.* to nose about.

foulard [fûlàr] *m.* foulard [étoffe]; silk handkerchief; silk neckerchief; kerchief; scarf.

foule [fûl] *f.* crowd; multitude; throng; mob; fulling [drap]; crushing; *venir en foule,* to flock. ‖ *fouler* [-é] *v.* to tread; to trample down; to tread upon; to press; to crush; to full [drap]; to wrench, to twist [cheville]. ‖ *foulon* [-oⁿ] *m.* fuller. ‖ *foulure* [-ür] *f.* wrench, sprain.

four [fûr] *m.* oven; bakehouse; kiln [chaux]; furnace; (pop.) failure.

fourbe [fûrb] *m., f.* cheat, rascal; *adj.* rascally, deceitful. ‖ *fourberie* [-ᵉrî] *f.* cheating; deceit; trickery; swindle.

fourbi [fûrbî] *m.* (fam.) whole caboodle.

fourbir [fûrbîr] v. to furbish, to polish up.

fourbu [fûrbü] adj. broken-down; exhausted, tired out.

fourche [fûrsh] f. fork; pitchfork; en fourche, forked. || **foucher** [-é] v. to fork, to branch off; to slip [langue]. || **fourchette** [-èt] f. fork, table fork; wishbone. || **fourchu** [-ü] adj. forked; cloven [pied]; branching.

fourgon [fûrgoⁿ] m. wagon; van; Br. luggage van, Am. freight car, baggage car. || **fourgonnette** [-ònèt] f. delivery van (or) truck.

fourmi [fûrmî] f. ant; avoir des fourmis, to have pins and needles. || **fourmilière** [-lyèr] f. ant-hill; ants' nest. || **fourmiller** [-yé] v. to swarm; to tingle.

fournaise [fûrnèz] f. furnace. || **fourneau** [-ô] m.° furnace; stove; cooker; kitchen-range; bowl [pipe]; chamber [mine]; haut fourneau, blast furnace.

fourni [fûrnî] adj. supplied; abundant; thick; bushy.

fournil [fûrnîl] m. bakehouse.

fourniment [fûrnìmaⁿ] m. kit, equipment. || **fournir** [-îr] v. to furnish, to supply, to provide with; to stock; to draw (comm.). || **fournisseur** [-isœr] m. supplier, caterer; tradesman; ship-chandler. || **fourniture** [-ìtür] f supplying; pl. supplies; equipment.

fourrage [fûrâj] m. forage, fodder; foraging (mil.). || **fourrager** [-é] v. to forage; to rummage, to search; to ravage.

fourré [fûré] m. thicket; adj. thick; wooded; furry; lined with fur; filled.

fourreau [fûrô] m.° sheath; scabbard; sleeve; case, cover.

fourrer [fûré] v. to line with fur; to stuff; to poke. || **fourreur** [-œr] m. furrier. || **fourrure** [-ür] f. fur; skin; lining.

fourvoyer [fûrvwàyé] v. to lead astray; se fourvoyer, to go astray.

foutaise [fûtèz] f. (pop.) twaddle, bunkum.

foyer [fwàyé] m. hearth; fire-place; fire-box [machine]; furnace; home; focus (geom.); seat (med.); foyer (theat.); home, hostel.

fracas [fràkâ] m. crash; din, shindy. || **fracasser** [-àsé] v. to shatter; to smash to pieces.

fraction [fràksyoⁿ] f. fraction; portion; group [politique]. || **fractionnement** [-syònmaⁿ] m. fractionation; splitting up. || **fractionner** [-syòné] v. to divide into fractions; to split up. || **fracture** [-tür] f. fracture (med.); breaking open. || **fracturer** [-türé] v. to fracture (med.); to force, to break open; to break (gramm.).

fragile [fràjìl] adj. fragile; brittle; frail. || **fragilité** [-ìté] f. fragility; brittleness; frailty.

fragment [fràgmaⁿ] m. fragment; bit; extract. || **fragmentaire** [-tèr] adj. fragmentary. || **fragmenter** [-té] v. to break up.

fraîche, see frais. || **fraîcheur** [frèshœr] f. freshness; coolness; bloom [fleur]. || **fraîchir** [-îr] v. to freshen, to grow colder; to cool down.

frais, fraîche [frè, frèsh] adj. fresh; cool; recent; new-laid [œufs]; new [pain]; wet [peinture]; m. cool; coolness; fresh breeze; au frais, in a cool place; adv. freshly; newly.

frais [frè] m. pl. cost, expenses, charge; outlay; fees; costs (jur.); à peu de frais, at little cost; se mettre en frais, to go to expense; faire les frais de, to bear the cost of; aux frais de, at the charge of.

fraise [frèz] f. ruff [col]; wattle; countersink (techn.); drill [dentiste].

fraise [frèz] f. strawberry. || **fraisier** [-yé] m. strawberry-plant.

framboise [fraⁿbwàz] f. raspberry. || **framboisier** [-yé] m. raspberry-bush.

franc [fraⁿ] m. franc.

franc, -che [fraⁿ, -sh] adj. frank; free; candid, open; downright, straightforward; natural [fruits]; fair [jeu]; franc de port, carriage paid; postpaid [lettre]; parlez franc, speak your mind; franc-maçon, freemason.

français [fraⁿsè] m. French [langue]; Frenchman; adj. French; les Français, the French. || **française** [-sèz] f. Frenchwoman. || **France** [fraⁿs] f. France.

franchement [fraⁿshmaⁿ] adv. frankly, candidly; really. || **franchir** [-îr] v. to jump over; to pass over; to clear; to cross; to weather [cap]; to overcome. || **franchise** [-îz] f. frankness, openness; exemption; freedom, immunity; en franchise, duty-free; franchise de port, post-free.

franco [fraⁿkô] adv. free of charge.

frange [fraⁿj] f. fringe.

frappant [fràpaⁿ] adj. conspicuous; striking. || **frappe** [fràp] f. minting; striking; impression, stamp. || **frapper** [-é] v. to strike, to hit; © to bat; to knock [porte]; to mint [monnaie]; to punch; to type; to ice [boisson]; frapper du pied, to stamp; se frapper, to get alarmed (fam.). || **frappeur** [-œr] m. © batter.

frasque [fràsk] f. prank.

fraternel [fràtèrnèl] adj.° brotherly, fraternal. || **fraterniser** [-ìzé] v. to fraternize. || **fraternité** [-ìté] f. brotherhood, fraternity.

fraude [fròd] *f.* fraud, deception; *faire entrer en fraude*, to smuggle in. || **frauder** [-é] *v.* to defraud, to cheat; to smuggle. || **fraudeur** [-œr] *m.* defrauder, cheat; smuggler. || **frauduleux** [-ülë] *adj.°* fraudulent; bogus, *Am.* phony.

frayer [frèyé] *v.* to clear, to open up [chemin]; to rub; to spawn [poissons]; to associate, to mix; to wear thin; *se frayer un passage à travers*, to break through.

frayeur [frèyœr] *f.* fright; terror; dread; fear.

fredaine [frədèn] *f.* prank.

fredonner [frədoné] *v.* to hum; to trill.

frégate [frégàt] *f.* frigate; frigate-bird.

frein [frlⁿ] *m.* brake [voiture]; bit [cheval]; curb, restraint; *mettre un frein à*, to curb. || **freiner** [-é] *v.* to brake, to put on the brakes; to restrain.

frelater [frəlàté] *v.* to adulterate.

frêle [frèl] *adj.* frail; weak.

frelon [frəloⁿ] *m.* hornet.

frémir [frémîr] *v.* to quiver; to shake, to tremble; to shudder; to rustle [feuillage]; to sigh [vent]. || **frémissement** [-lsmoⁿ] *m.* quivering, tremor, shuddering; rustling; sighing [vent].

frêne [frèn] *m.* ash, ash-tree.

frénésie [frénézî] *f.* frenzy. || **frénétique** [-étïk] *adj.* frantic, frenzied.

fréquemment [frékàmoⁿ] *adv* frequently. || **fréquence** [-oⁿs] *f* frequency. || **fréquent** [-oⁿ] *adj.* frequent; rapid. || **fréquentation** [-oⁿtàsyoⁿ] *f* frequenting, frequentation. || **fréquenter** [-oⁿté] *v.* to frequent; to visit, to associate with.

frère [frèr] *m.* brother; monk, friar.

fresque [frèsk] *f.* fresco.

fret [frè] *m.* freight; load, cargo; chartering. || **fréter** [frété] *v.* to charter; to freight. || **fréteur** [-tœr] *m.* charterer.

frétiller [frétlyé] *v.* to wriggle; to frisk about; to wag.

fretin [frətlⁿ] *m.* fry.

friable [frlyàbl] *adj.* friable, crumbly.

friand [frlⁿ] *adj.* dainty; *friand de*, fond of, partial to. || **friandise** [-dîz] *f.* tit-bit, delicacy; liking for good food.

friche [frîsh] *f.* fallow land; *être en friche*, to lie fallow.

friction [frlksyoⁿ] *f.* friction (mech.); rubbing; massage. || **frictionner** [-yòné] *v.* to rub; to massage; to shampoo [tête].

frigorifier [frlgòrlfyé] *v.* to refrigerate; *viande frigorifiée*, frozen meat. || **frigorifique** [-îk] *adj.* refrigerating, chilling.

frileux [frïlë] *adj.°* chilly.

frimas [frlmâ] *m.* rime; hoar-frost.

fringant [frlⁿgoⁿ] *adj.* brisk, dapper, smart; frisky [cheval].

friper [frlpé] *v.* to crush, to crumple. || **fripier** [-yé] *m.* old clothes dealer ragman; *Am.* junkman.

fripon [frlpoⁿ] *m.* rascal, scamp; *adj.°* roguish. || **friponnerie** [-dnrî] *f.* roguery; roguish trick.

frire [frîr] *v.°* to fry.

frise [frîz] *f.* frieze.

frisé [frlzé] *adj.* curly, crisp. || **friser** [-é] *v.* to curl, to wave; to verge upon; to go near to.

frisson [frlsoⁿ] *m.* shudder; shiver; thrill. || **frissonner** [-òné] *v.* to shudder; to shiver; to quiver.

frites [frlt] *f. pl.* fried potatoes, chips, French fries. || **friture** [-ür] *f.* frying; frying fat; fried fish; crackling; sizzling.

frivole [frlvòl] *adj.* frivolous; trifling. || **frivolité** [-lté] *f.* frivolity; trifle; tatting.

froid [frwà] *m.* cold; coldness; *adj.* cold; chilly; frigid; *en froid*, on chilly terms; *avoir froid*, to be cold; *il fait froid*, it is cold. || **froideur** [-dœr] *f* coldness; chilliness; indifference.

froisser [frwàsé] *v.* to crumple; to bruise; to ruffle; to offend, to hurt; *se froisser*, to get ruffled; to take offense.

frôler [frôlé] *v.* to graze; to brush past; to rustle.

fromage [fròmàj] *m.* cheese; (fam.) *Br.* cushy job, *Am.* snap. || **fromagerie** [-rî] *f* cheesemonger's, *Am.* cheese store; cheese-dairy.

froment [fròmoⁿ] *m.* wheat.

fronce [froⁿs] *f.* gather; crease. || **froncement** [-moⁿ] *m* puckering; frown [sourcils]. || **froncer** [-é] *v.* to pucker, to wrinkle; to gather; *froncer les sourcils*, to frown; to scowl.

frondaison [froⁿdèzoⁿ] *f.* foliage; foliation.

front [froⁿ] *m.* front; forehead, brow face, impudence; *de front,* *abreu faire front à*, to face || **frontalier** [-tàlyé] *adj.°* frontier *m* borderer, frontiersman. || **frontière** [-tyèr] *f.* border; frontier; boundary

frottement [fròtmoⁿ] *m* rubbing; chafing, friction. || **frotter** [-é] *v.* to rub; to scrub; to polish; to strike [allumette].

frousse [frûs] *f.* fear; *Br.* funk.

fructifier [früktĭfyé] *v.* to bear fruit. || **fructueux** [-üë] *adj.* fruitful, profitable; lucrative.

frugal [frügàl] *adj.* frugal.

fruit [früĭ] *m.* fruit; advantage, profit; result. || **fruitier** [-tyé] *m.* greengrocer; *adj.* fruit-bearing; *arbre fruitier*, fruit-tree.

fruste [früst] *adj.* defaced; rough, unpolished.

frustrer [früstré] *v.* to frustrate; to baulk; to defraud.

fugace [fügàs] *adj.* transient, fleeting. || **fugitif** [fügĭtĭf] *m.* runaway, fugitive; *adj.* fugitive; fleeting; passing, transient. || **fugue** [füg] *f.* escapade; fugue (mus.).

fuir [füĭr] *v.* to fly, to flee, to run away; to leak [tonneau]; to recede; to shun, to avoid. || **fuite** [füĭt] *f.* flight; escape; leak, leakage [liquide].

fulgurant [fülgüràn] *adj.* flashing.

fulminer [fülmĭné] *v.* to fulminate; to thunder forth.

fumée [fümé] *f.* smoke; fumes; steam. || **fumer** [-é] *v.* to smoke; to steam; to fume; *fume-cigarette*, cigarette-holder.

fumer [fümé] *v.* to dung, to manure [terre].

fumet [fümè] *m.* flavo(u)r; scent. || **fumeur** [-œr] *m.* smoker. || **fumeux** [-ë] *adj.* smoky; hazy, nebulous.

fumier [fümyé] *m.* dung; manure [engrais]; dung-hill.

fumiste [fümĭst] *m.* stove-setter; (pop.) joker, crackpot, wag. || **fumisterie** [-rī] *f.* hoax, bunkum, hooey.

fumoir [-wàr] *m.* smoke house, smoking-room.

funèbre [fünèbr] *adj.* funeral; dismal, gloomy, funereal. || **funérailles** [-érày] *f. pl.* funeral.

funeste [fünèst] *adj.* fatal, deadly.

funiculaire [fünĭkülèr] *m.* cable-railway; *adj.* funicular.

furet [fürè] *m.* ferret. || **fureter** [-té] *v.* to ferret; to pry, to nose about; to rummage.

fureur [fürœr] *f.* fury, rage; passion; *faire fureur*, to be all the rage. || **furie** [-ī] *f.* fury, rage. || **furieux** [-yë] *adj.* mad, furious, raging.

furoncle [fürònkl] *m.* boil; furuncle (med.).

furtif [fürtĭf] *adj.* furtive, stealthy.

fusain [füzĭn] *m.* charcoal; charcoal sketch.

fuseau [füzô] *m.* spindle; tapering (or) peg-top trousers. || **fusée** [-é] *f.* fuse; flare; rocket. || **fuselage** [-làj] *m.* fuselage. || **fuselé** [-lé] *adj.* spindle-shaped; tapering, slender [doigts].

fuser [füzé] *v.* to spread; to fuse, to melt; to burn slowly. || **fusible** [-ĭbl] *m.* fuse; fuse-wire; *adj.* fusible.

fusil [füzĭ] *m.* rifle; gun; steel; whetstone; *à portée de fusil*, within shot; *coup de fusil*, shot; (pop.) fleecing. || **fusillade** [-yàd] *f.* shooting. || **fusiller** [-yé] *v.* to shoot.

fusion [füzyòn] *f.* fusion; melting; merger (comm.). || **fusionner** [-yòné] *v.* to amalgamate, to merge; to blend.

fût [fû] *m.* stock [fusil]; handle; shaft [colonne]; barrel, cask, tun.

futaie [fütè] *f.* forest.

futé [füté] *adj.* sharp, cunning.

futile [fütĭl] *adj.* futile, idle, trifling; useless. || **futilité** [-ĭté] *f.* trifle, futility.

futur [fütür] *m.* future (gramm.); intended husband; *adj.* future. || **future** *f.* intended wife.

fuyant [füĭyàn] *adj.* flying, fleeing; fleeting, transient; receding [front]; shifty, evasive, foxy [regard]. || **fuyard** [füĭyàr] *m.* runaway, fugitive; coward.

G

gabardine [gàbàrdĭn] *f.* gabardine; twill raincoat.

gabarit [gàbàrĭ] *m.* mould [moule]; model [navires]; template; gauge.

gâche [gâsh] *f.* staple; wall-hook.

gâcher [gâshé] *v.* to mix; to waste; to bungle; to spoil.

gâchette [gâshèt] *f.* trigger [fusil]; catch; pawl (mech.).

gâchis [gâshĭ] *m.* wet mortar; mess, hash (fig.).

gaffe [gàf] *f.* boat-hook; gaff; (fam.) blunder, bloomer. || **gaffer** [-é] *v.* to

hook; (fam.) to blunder. || **gaffeur** [-œr] *m.* (fam.) blunderer.

gage [gàj] *m.* pledge; pawn; stake [enjeu]; token [preuve]; forfeit; *pl.* wages; hire; *mettre en gage*, to pawn; *prêteur sur gages*, pawnbroker.

gageure [gàjür] *f.* wager; stake; risky shot.

gagner [gàñé] *v.* to gain; to win; to earn [salaire]; to reach; to overtake; to win over; to spread; *se gagner*, to be contagious; *gagne-pain*, breadwinner; livelihood.

gai [gè] *adj.* gay; merry; jolly, cheerful; lively, bright. ‖ *gaieté* [gèté] *f.* mirth, merriment; cheerfulness.

gaillard [gàyàr] *m.* fellow, chap; good fellow; *adj.* merry, jolly, cheery; strong; bold; free, broad [libre].

gain [giⁿ] *m.* gain, profit, earning.

gaine [gèn] *f.* case, casing; sheath; girdle [corset].

galamment [gàlàmàⁿ] *adv.* gallantly; courteously. ‖ *galant* [-àⁿ] *m.* lover; ladies' man; *adj.* elegant; gallant; gay; courteous. ‖ *galanterie* [-àⁿtrî] *f.* politeness; gallantry; love-affair.

galantine [gàlàⁿtîn] *f.* galantine.

galbe [gàlb] *m.* lines; curves; outline; contours, shapeliness

gale [gàl] *f.* mange; scabies (med.).

galère [gàlèr] *f.* galley.

galerie [gàlrî] *f.* gallery; © perron; balcony (theat.); spectators; arcade.

galet [gàlè] *m.* pebble; roller (mech.); *pl.* shingle.

galette [gàlèt] *f.* tart; *Br.* girdle-cake; ship's biscuit; (pop.) brass, oof, dough.

galimatias [gàlìmàtyà] *m.* gibberish.

gallon [gàloⁿ] *m.* *gallon impérial,* imperial gallon; *gallon américain,* US gallon.

galoche [gàlòsh] *f.* clog; galosh, *Am.* rubber.

galon [gàloⁿ] *m.* braid; lace; stripe (mil.); © measuring tape. ‖ *galonner* [-òné] *v.* to braid; to trim with lace.

galop [gàlò] *m.* gallop; *au grand galop,* at full gallop. ‖ *galoper* [-òpé] *v.* to gallop. ‖ *galopin* [-òpiⁿ] *m.* urchin; scamp.

galurin [gàlüriⁿ] *m.* topper, tile, lid (fam.).

galvaniser [gàlvànìzé] *v.* to galvanize; to zinc.

gambade [gàⁿbàd] *f.* gambol; caper. ‖ *gambader* [-é] *v.* to frisk about, to gambol.

gamelle [gàmèl] *f.* bowl; porringer; mess-tin (mil.).

gamin [gàmiⁿ] *m.* urchin, street-arab; little imp; *adj.* roguish. ‖ *gamine* [-în] *f.* girl; street-girl.

gamme [gàm] *f.* scale, gamut (mus.); range; tone, tune (fig.).

ganglion [gàⁿglìoⁿ] *m.* ganglion.

gangrène [gàⁿgrèn] *f.* gangrene, mortification; corruption. ‖ *gangrener* [gàⁿgrøné] *v.* to gangrene, to mortify; to corrupt.

ganse [gàⁿs] *f.* braid, piping; loop.

gant [gàⁿ] *m.* glove. ‖ *ganter* [-té] *v.* to glove; *se ganter,* to put on gloves.

garage [gàràj] *m.* garage [auto]; parking [autos]; docking (naut.); shunting; *voie de garage,* siding. ‖ *garagiste* [-ìst] *m.* garage owner, garage man.

garant [gàràⁿ] *m.* surety; bail; security, guarantee. ‖ *garantie* [-tî] *f.* safeguard; guarantee; warranting; pledge; security. ‖ *garantir* [-tîr] *v.* to warrant; to guarantee; to vouch for; to insure; to protect.

garçon [gàrsoⁿ] *m.* boy; © son; lad; young man; bachelor; waiter [café]; *garçon d'honneur,* best man. ‖ *garçonnier* [-sònyé] *adj.*° boyish. ‖ *garçonnière* [-sònyèr] *f.* bachelor's quarters.

garde [gàrd] *m.* guard; watchman; keeper; warder; guardsman (mil.); *f.* guard; care; watch; protection; keeping; custody; nurse; guards (mil.); end-paper [livre]; fly-leaf [page]; *de garde,* on guard; *sur ses gardes,* on one's guard; *prendre garde,* to beware; *garde à vous !,* attention !; *garde-barrière,* gate-keeper; *garde-boue, Br.* mudguard, *Am.* fender; *garde champêtre,* rural policeman; *garde-chasse,* gamekeeper; *garde-côte,* coastguard; coastguard vessel; *garde-fou,* parapet; railing; *garde-malade, m.* male nurse; *f.* nurse; *garde-manger,* larder, pantry; *garde-robe,* wardrobe; closet, privy. ‖ *garder* [-é] *v.* to keep; to preserve; to retain; to guard; to protect, to defend; to keep watch on; *se garder,* to protect oneself; to keep [fruits]; to beware; to abstain. ‖ *gardien* [-yiⁿ] *m.* guardian; keeper; attendant; warder; *gardien de la paix,* policeman.

gare [gàr] *f.* station; *interj.* beware !, look out !; *chef de gare,* station-master; *gare maritime,* harbo(u)r-station; *gare aérienne,* air-port.

garenne [gàrèn] *f.* warren; preserve; *lapin de garenne,* wild rabbit.

garer [gàré] *v.* to shunt [train]; to park; to garage [auto]; to dock [bateau]; *se garer,* to shunt; to move out of the way.

gargariser [gàrgàrìzé] *v.* to gargle. ‖ *gargarisme* [-ìsm] *m.* gargle; gargling.

gargote [gàrgòt] *f.* cook-shop, *Am.* hash-house.

gargouille [gàrgúy] *f.* gargoyle (arch.); water-spout. ‖ *gargouiller* [-é] *v.* to gurgle; to rumble.

garnement [gàrnmàⁿ] *m.* scamp.

garni [gàrnì] *m.* furnished room; *adj.* furnished; trimmed. ‖ *garnir* [-îr] *v.* to adorn; to furnish; to trim; to line [doubler]; to fill; to stock [magasin]; to garrison. ‖ *garnison* [-zoⁿ] *f.* garrison. ‖ *garniture* [-tür] *f.* fittings; trimmings; set; packing, lining.

garrot [gàrô] *m.* garrot; withers. ‖
garrotter [gàròté] *v.* to bind down;
to strangle.

gaspillage [gàspìyàj] *m.* waste; squandering. ‖ **gaspiller** [-ìyé] *v.* to waste;
to squander; to spoil.

gastrite [gàstrìt] *f.* gastritis. ‖ **gastronome** [-ònòm] *m.*, *f.* gastronome. ‖
gastronomie [-ònòmî] *f.* gastronomy.

gâteau [gâtô] *m.** cake; tart; *gâteau
de miel*, honeycomb.

gâter [gâté] *v.* to spoil; to pamper
[enfant]; to damage; to taint [viande];
se gâter, to deteriorate. ‖ **gâterie** [-rî]
f. treat; spoiling. ‖ **gâteux** [-ë] *m.* old
dotard; *adj.** doddering. ‖ **gâtisme**
[-ìsm] *m.* dotage.

gauche [gôsh] *f.* left hand; left-hand
side; left-wing party; *adj.* left; crooked; awkward, clumsy; *à gauche*, on
the left; *tourner à gauche*, to turn
left; *tenir sa gauche*, to keep to the
left. ‖ **gaucher** [-é] *adj.** left-handed. ‖
gaucherie [-rî] *f.* awkwardness; clumsiness. ‖ **gauchir** [-îr] *v.* to warp; to
buckle. ‖ **gauchissement** [-ìsmaⁿ] *m.*
warping; buckling.

gaufre [gôfr] *f.* waffle; wafer; honeycomb. ‖ **gaufrer** [-é] *v.* to emboss; to
goffer, to crimp. ‖ **gaufrette** [-èt]
f. wafer biscuit. ‖ **gaufrier** [-ìyé] *m.*
waffle-iron.

gaule [gôl] *f.* pole; fishing-rod.

gaver [gàvé] *v.* to cram; to stuff; *se
gaver*, to gorge.

gaz [gàz] *m.* gas.

gaze [gàz] *f.* gauze.

gazelle [gàzèl] *f.* gazelle.

gazette [gàzèt] *f.* gazette; newspaper; gossip (fam.).

gazeux [gàzë] *adj.** gaseous; aerated.

gazon [gàzoⁿ] *m.* grass; turf; lawn
[pelouse].

gazouillement [gàzûymaⁿ] *m.* warbling, twittering [oiseaux]; babbling. ‖
gazouiller [-ûyé] *v.* to warble, to
twitter [oiseaux]; to prattle [enfant];
to babble. ‖ **gazouillis**, see *gazouillement*.

geai [jè] *m.* jay.

géant [jéaⁿ] *m.* giant, *f.* giantess;
adj. gigantic.

geindre [jìⁿdr] *v.* to moan; to whimper; to whine.

gel [jèl] *m.* frost, freezing.

gélatine [jélàtîn] *f.* gelatin. ‖ **gélatineux** [-në] *adj.* gelatinous.

gelée [jºlé] *f.* frost; jelly. ‖ **geler** [-é]
v. to freeze.

gémir [jémîr] *v.* to moan; to groan;
to lament, to bewail. ‖ **gémissement**
[-ìsmaⁿ] *m.* groan; moan; groaning.

gemme [jèm] *f.* gem; *adj. sel gemme*,
rock-salt.

gênant [jènaⁿ] *adj.* annoying; bothersome; embarrassing.

gencive [jaⁿsîv] *f.* gum (anat.).

gendarme [jaⁿdàrm] *m.* gendarme;
constable; (pop.) virago; red herring.
‖ **gendarmerie** [-ºrî] *f.* constabulary;
Gendarmerie royale, Ⓒ Royal Canadian Mounted Police.

gendre [jaⁿdr] *m.* son-in-law.

gêne [jèn] *f.* rack [torture]; uneasiness; discomfort; difficulty, trouble;
want; financial need, straits; *sans gêne*,
free and easy; familiar. ‖ **gêné** [-é]
adj. uneasy; embarrassed; awkward;
short of money, hard up. ‖ **gêner** [-é]
v. to cramp, to constrict; to pinch
[soulier]; to embarrass; to inconvenience; to hamper; to hinder; to
trouble; *se gêner*, to constrain oneself; to go to trouble, to put oneself
out.

généalogie [jénéàlòjî] *f.* genealogy;
lineage; pedigree.

général [jénéràl] *m.* adj.** general;
en général, generally. ‖ **générale** [-àl]
f. general's wife; alarm call; dress-rehearsal. ‖ **généralisation** [-ìzàsyoⁿ]
f. generalisation. ‖ **généraliser** [-ìzé]
v. to generalize. ‖ **généralissime**
[-ìsm] *m.* commander-in-chief. ‖ **généralité** [-ìté] *f.* generality.

générateur, -trice [jénéràtœr, -trìs]
m., *f.* generator; *m.* dynamo; *adj.*
generating; productive. ‖ **génération**
[-àsyoⁿ] *f.* generation.

généreux [jénéré] *adj.** generous, liberal; abundant.

générique [jénérîk] *adj.* generic; *m.*
production credits and cast.

générosité [jénéròzìté] *f.* generosity,
liberality.

genêt [jºnè] *m.* broom; *genêt épineux*, gorse, furze.

gêneur [jènœr] *m.* intruder; nuisance;
spoil-sport.

génial [jényàl] *adj.** full of genius,
inspired. ‖ **génie** [-î] *m.* genius; character; spirit; engineers; *soldat du
génie*, engineer, sapper.

genièvre [jºnyèvr] *m.* juniper-tree;
juniper-berry; gin.

génisse [jénìs] *f.* heifer.

genou [jºnû] *m.** knee; ball-and-socket (mech.); *se mettre à genoux*, to
kneel down.

genre [jaⁿr] *m.* genus, kind, family;
way; gender (gramm.); style; fashion; manners; *le genre humain*, mankind.

gens [jaⁿ] *m. pl.* [preceded by an *adj.*,
this word is *f.*]; people, folk; peoples.

gentiane [jaⁿsyàn] *f.* gentian.

gentil [jɑⁿtî] adj.* nice; kind; pleasing. ‖ **gentilhomme** [-yòm] m. nobleman; gentleman. ‖ **gentillesse** [-yès] f. graciousness; politeness.

géographe [jéŏgrâf] s. geographer. **géographie** [jéŏgrâfî] f. geography. **géographique** [-îk] adj. geographical.

geôle [jôl] f. gaol; jail; prison. **geôlier** [-yé] m. gaoler, jailer.

géologie [jéŏlŏjî] f. geology.

géométrie [jéŏmétrî] f. geometry. **géométrique** [-îk] adj. geometrical.

gérance [jérɑⁿs] f. management; board of directors.

géranium [jérànyòm] m. geranium.

gérant [jérɑⁿ] m. director, manager.

gerbe [jèrb] f. sheaf; spout [eau]; shower [étincelles]; spray [fleurs].

gercer [jèrsé] v. to crack; to chap. ‖ **gerçure** [-ûr] f. crack, fissure; chap.

gérer [jéré] v. to manage; to administer; *mal gérer*, to mismanage.

germain [jèrmⁿ] adj. *cousin germain*, first cousin; *issu de germain*, second cousin.

germe [jèrm] m. germ; shoot; seed; origin. ‖ **germer** [-é] v. to germinate; to shoot, to sprout.

gésir [jézîr] v.* to lie.

gestation [jèstàsyoⁿ] f. gestation.

geste [jèst] m. gesture; motion; sign. ‖ **gesticuler** [-îkülé] v. to gesticulate.

gestion [jèstyoⁿ] f. administration, management.

gibecière [jìbsyèr] f. game-bag.

gibet [jìbè] m. gibbet, gallows.

gibier [jìbyé] m. game.

giboulée [jìbûlé] f. sudden shower; April shower.

gicler [jìklé] v. to squirt, to spurt. ‖ **gicleur** [-œr] m. jet; nozzle.

gifle [jîfl] f. slap; box on the ear. ‖ **gifler** [-é] v. to slap (someone's) face; to box (someone's) ears.

gigantesque [jìgɑⁿtèsk] adj. gigantic, giant. ‖ **gigantisme** [-tîsm] m. giantism, gigantism.

gigot [jìgô] m. leg of mutton; *pl.* hind legs [cheval]. ‖ **gigoter** [-té] v. to kick; to jig; to fidget.

gilet [jìlè] m. waistcoat; vest; cardigan [tricot].

gingembre [jⁱⁿjɑⁿbr] m. ginger.

girafe [jìrâf] f. giraffe.

girofle [jìrôfl] m. clove; *clou de girofle*, clove. ‖ **giroflée** [-é] f. stock; wall-flower; smack.

girouette [jìrûèt] f. weathercock, vane.

gisement [jîzmɑⁿ] m. bed, layer; vein [minerai]; bearing (naut.).

gitan, -ane [jîtɑⁿ, -àn] m., f. gipsy.

gîte [jît] m. shelter, refuge; lodging; lair [animal]; seam, vein, bed [mine]; f. list, heeling (naut.).

givre [jîvr] m. rime, hoar-frost; *givré* [-é] adj. frosted, rimy, rimed.

glabre [glâbr] adj. hairless, smooth; clean-shaven, beardless [visage].

glace [glàs] f. ice; ice-cream; icing [cuisine]; glass, mirror; chill (fig.); ‖ *glacé* [-é] adj. freezing, icy cold; frigid; iced; frozen; glazed; glossy [étoffe]; candied. ‖ **glacer** [-é] v. to chill; to freeze; to ice; to glaze. ‖ **glacial** [-yàl] adj.* glacial, icy; frosty; biting [vent]. ‖ **glacier** [-yé] m. glacier; ice-cream seller. ‖ **glacière** [-yèr] f. ice-house; refrigerator. ‖ **glaçon** [-oⁿ] m. floe; cake of ice; icicle.

glaïeul [glàyœl] m. gladiolus.

glaire [glèr] f. glair.

glaise [glèz] f. clay; potter's clay; loam.

glaive [glèv] m. glaive, sword.

gland [glɑⁿ] m. acorn; tassel [rideau]. ‖ **glande** [glɑⁿd] f. gland.

glaner [glàné] v. to glean.

glapir [glàpîr] v. to yelp; to yap; to squeak.

glas [glâ] m. knell; tolling.

glauque [glôk] adj. glaucous, sea-green.

glissade [glìsàd] f. slip; sliding; slide; glide. ‖ **glissant** [-ɑⁿ] adj. sliding; slippery. ‖ **glissement** [-mɑⁿ] m. slipping; sliding; slip. ‖ **glisser** [-é] v. to slip; to slide; to skid [roue]; to glide (aviat.); *se glisser*, to slip, to creep. ‖ **glissière** [-yèr] f. slide. ‖ **glissoire** [-wàr] f. slide. ⊙ toboggan slide.

global [glòbàl] adj.* total, inclusive; gross. ‖ **globe** [glòb] m. globe, sphere; orb; eyeball [œil]. ‖ **globule** [-ül] m. globule.

gloire [glwàr] f. glory; fame; pride; halo; *se faire gloire de*, to glory in. ‖ **glorieux** [glŏryё] m. braggart; adj.* glorious; vainglorious, conceited. ‖ **glorification** [-ìfikàsyoⁿ] f. glorification. ‖ **glorifier** [-ìfyé] v. to glorify; *se glorifier*, to boast; to glory (*de*, in). ‖ **gloriole** [-yòl] f. vainglory; swank (fam.).

glose [glôz] f. comment, criticism; commentary. ‖ **gloser** [-zé] v. to gloss; to carp at.

glossaire [glòsèr] m. glossary.

glotte [glòt] f. glottis.

glousser [glûsé] v. to cluck [poule]; to gobble [dinde]; to chuckle.

glouton [glûtoⁿ] *m.* glutton; *adj.** greedy, gluttonous. ‖ *gloutonnerie* [-ònrî] *f.* gluttony.

glu [glü] *f.* glue; bird-lime. ‖ *gluant* [-aⁿ] *adj.* sticky, gluey, gummy.

glucose [glükôz] *m.* glucose.

glycérine [glìsérîn] *f.* glycerine.

gobelet [gòblè] *m.* cup; goblet; mug. ‖ *gober* [gòbé] *v.* to swallow, to gulp down; to take in (fig.); to have a great admiration for. ‖ *gobeur* [-œr] *m.* (pop.) guzzler; gull; sucker; simpleton; *adj.* credulous.

goder [gòdé] *v.* to pucker, to crease; to bag [pantalon].

godet [gòdè] *m.* mug; cup; bowl; bucket; flare [couture]; *à godets,* flared.

goéland [gòèlaⁿ] *m.* sea-gull. ‖ *goélette* [-èt] *f.* schooner. ‖ *goémon* [gòémoⁿ] *m.* seaweed; wrack.

goguenard, -arde [gògnàr, ard] *adj.* jeering; scoffing.

goinfre [gwiⁿfr] *m.* (pop.) glutton, guzzler. ‖ *goinfrerie* [-erî] *f.* gluttony.

goître [gwàtr] *m.* goiter; wen (fam.).

golf [gòlf] *m.* golf; *terrain de golf,* golf links.

golfe [gòlf] *m.* gulf; bay.

gomme [gòm] *f.* gum; india-rubber. ‖ *gommer* [gòmé] *v.* to gum; to erase.

gond [goⁿ] *m.* hinge; *sortir de ses gonds,* to fly into a rage.

gondole [goⁿdòl] *f.* gondola. ‖ *gondoler* [goⁿdòlé] *v.* to warp; to blister; to cockle.

gonflement [goⁿfleˡmaⁿ] *m.* inflating, inflation; swelling; distension [estomac]; blowing up; bulging. ‖ *gonfler* [-é] *v.* to inflate [pneus]; to blow up; to swell; to distend [estomac]; to puff up. ‖ *gonfleur* [-œr] *m.* air-pump.

gong [goⁿg] *m.* gong.

goret [gòrè] *m.* young pig, piglet; dirty pig (fig.).

gorge [gòrj] *f.* throat, neck; breast, bosom; gorge; gullet; pass; defile; groove (techn.); *à pleine gorge,* at the top of one's voice; *mal à la gorge,* sore throat. ‖ *gorgée* [-é] *f.* draught; gulp; *petite gorgée,* sip. ‖ *gorger* [-é] *v.* to gorge; to cram; *se gorger,* to stuff oneself.

gorille [gòrîy] *m.* gorilla.

gosier [gòzyé] *m.* throat; gullet.

gosse [gòs] *m.,* *f.* kid, youngster; brat; tot.

gothique [gòtìk] *m.,* *adj.* Gothic.

gouailleur [gûàyœr] *adj.* waggish; jeering.

goudron [gûdroⁿ] *m.* tar; pitch; coaltar [de houille]. ‖ *goudronner* [-òné] *v.* to tar; *toile goudronnée,* tarpaulin.

gouffre [gûfr] *m.* gulf, abyss; chasm.

goujat [gûjà] *m.* hodman; farmhand; cad, blackguard. ‖ *goujaterie* [-rî] *f.* caddishness.

goujon [gûjoⁿ] *m.* gudgeon [poisson].

goulot [gûlô] *m.* neck [bouteille].

goulu [gûlü] *adj.* greedy, gluttonous.

goupille [gûpîy] *f.* pin; bolt; gudgeon.

gourd [gûr] *adj.* benumbed; stiff; numb. ‖ *gourde* [gûrd] *f.* gourd (bot.); flask; water-bottle; (fam.) fathead, *Am.* dumbbell.

gourdin [gûrdiⁿ] *m.* cudgel, club.

gourmand [gûrmaⁿ] *m.* glutton; gourmand, gormandizer; *adj.* greedy; gluttonous. ‖ *gourmander* [-dé] *v.* to guzzle; to chide; to rebuke. ‖ *gourmandise* [-dîz] *f.* greediness, gluttony; *pl.* sweetmeats.

gourme [gûrm] *f.* impetigo; rash; strangles [cheval]; *jeter sa gourme,* to sow one's wild oats. ‖ *gourmé* [-é] *adj.* stiff, formal.

gourmet [gûrmè] *m.* gourmet, epicure.

gourmette [gûrmèt] *f.* curb; bracelet; chain.

gousse [gûs] *f.* pod, shell; clove [ail]. ‖ *gousset* [-è] *m.* arm-pit; gusset; fob pocket.

goût [gû] *m.* taste; flavo(u)r; smell; liking, fancy, preference; manner, style. ‖ *goûter* [-té] *m.* snack, lunch; *v.* to taste; to enjoy, to relish, to appreciate; to eat a little, to have a snack.

goutte [gût] *f.* drop; drip; spot, little bit; gout (med.). ‖ *gouttière* [-yèr] *f.* gutter; spout; cradle (med.); *pl.* eaves.

gouvernail [gûvèrnày] *m.* rudder; helm. ‖ *gouvernante* [-aⁿt] *f.* governess; housekeeper. ‖ *gouvernement* [-emaⁿ] *m.* government; management; care. ‖ *gouverner* [-é] *v.* to govern, to rule, to control; to manage; to take care of; to steer (naut.). ‖ *gouverneur* [-œr] *m.* governor; tutor.

grabat [gràbà] *m.* pallet; humble bed.

grabuge [gràbüj] *m.* (fam.) row, rumpus.

grâce [grâs] *f.* grace; gracefulness, charm; favo(u)r; mercy; pardon (jur.); *pl.* thanks; *coup de grâce,* finishing stroke; *grâce à,* thanks to, owing to; *action de grâces,* thanksgiving. ‖ *gracier* [-yé] *v.* to pardon, to reprieve. ‖ *gracieux* [-yè] *adj.** graceful, pleasing; gracious; courteous; *à titre gracieux,* free of charge.

gracile [gràsìl] *adj.* slender, slim. ‖ **gracilité** [-îté] *f.* gracility, slimness.

grade [gràd] *m.* rank, grade; degree (univ.). ‖ **gradé** [-é] *m.* non-commissioned officer. ‖ **gradin** [-iⁿ] *m* step; bench; *en gradins*, in tiers. ‖ **graduation** [-üàsyoⁿ] *f.* scale; graduation. ‖ **graduel** [-üèl] *adj.*° gradual. ‖ **graduer** [-üé] *v.* to grade; to graduate.

grain [grìⁿ] *m.* grain; seed; bean [café]; bead; speck, particle; texture; squall [vent]; *grain de beauté*, mole; beauty spot; *à gros grains*, coarse-grained. ‖ **graine** [grèn] *f.* seed; berry; *mauvaise graine*, bad lot. ‖ **grainetier** [-tyé] *m.* seed-merchant.

graissage [grèsàj] *m.* greasing; lubrication; oiling. ‖ **graisse** [grès] *f.* grease; fat. ‖ **graisser** [-é] *v.* to grease; to lubricate; to oil; (pop.) to bribe. ‖ **graisseux** [-ö] *adj.*° greasy; fatty; oily; ropy [vin].

grammaire [gràmmèr] *f.* grammar. ‖ **grammairien** [-ryiⁿ] *m.* grammarian. ‖ **grammatical** [-màtikàl] *adj.*° grammatical.

gramme [gràm] *m.* gram.

gramophone [gràmòfòn] *m.* record-player, gramophone, *Am.* phonograph.

grand [graⁿ] *m.* great man; adult, grown-up; *adj.* great; big; large; tall; high; wide; extensive; grown-up; noble, majestic; fashionable; high-class [vin]; *un homme grand*, a tall man; *un grand homme*, a great man; **grand-mère**, grandmother; **grand-messe**, high mass; **grand-oncle**, great-uncle; **grand-père**, grandfather; **grands-parents**, grandparents; **grand-tante**, great-aunt. ‖ **grandeur** [-dœr] *f* size; height; greatness; nobleness; grandeur; scale; importance; extent; magnitude; *grandeur naturelle*, life-size. ‖ **grandiose** [-dyôz] *adj.* grand, impressive, splendid. ‖ **grandir** [-dîr] *v.* to grow tall; to grow up; to increase; to enlarge.

grange [graⁿj] *f.* grange; barn.

granit [grànìt] *m.* granite.

granule [grànül] *m.* granule. ‖ **granulé** [-é] *adj.* granulated, granular. ‖ **granuleux** [-ö] *adj.*° granulous.

graphique [gràfìk] *m.* graph, diagram; *adj.* graphic.

grappe [gràp] *f.* bunch; cluster. ‖ **grappin** [gràpiⁿ] *m.* grapnel; grappling-iron; hook; grab.

gras, grasse [grâ, grâs] *m.* fat; *adj.* fat; fatty; greasy; oily; plump, stout, obese; thick, heavy, broad, smutty [indécent]; *jour gras*, meat day. ‖ **grassouillet** [-sûyè] *adj.* plump, chubby, podgy.

gratification [gràtifikàsyoⁿ] *f.* bonus; gratuity, tip. ‖ **gratifier** [-yé] *v.* to

reward; to favo(u)r; to bestow on, to confer.

gratin [gràtiⁿ] *m.* gratin; smart set (fig.).

gratitude [gràtìtüd] *f.* gratitude, gratefulness, thankfulness.

gratter [gràté] *v.* to scrape; to scratch; to cross out [mot]; to out-distance, to pass; to graft; *gratte-ciel*, skyscraper. ‖ **grattoir** [-wàr] *m.* scraper; eraser.

gratuit [gràtüì] *adj.* free; gratuitous; wanton. ‖ **gratuité** [-té] *f.* gratuitousness.

grave [gràv] *adj.* grave; solemn; sober [visage]; important; serious; low, deep (mus.).

graver [gràvé] *v.* to engrave; to etch [eau-forte]; to imprint (fig.). ‖ **graveur** [-œr] *m.* engraver; etcher.

gravier [gràvyé] *m.* gravel; grit.

gravir [gràvîr] *v.* to climb; to ascend; to clamber up.

gravité [gràvìté] *f.* gravity; seriousness; deepness (mus.).

gravure [gràvür] *f.* engraving; etching [eau-forte]; print; line-engraving [au trait]; copper-plate engraving [taille-douce]; woodcut [bois].

gré [gré] *m.* will, wish, pleasure; liking; taste; agreement; consent; *bon gré mal gré*, willy nilly; *contre son gré*, unwillingly; *savoir gré*, to be grateful (de, for).

gredin [grⁿdiⁿ] *m.* scoundrel, rogue.

gréement [grémaⁿ] *m.* rigging; gear. ‖ **gréer** [gréé] *v.* to rig; to rig up.

greffe [grèf] *m.* registry; clerk's office.

greffe [grèf] *f.* graft; grafting. ‖ **greffer** [-é] *v.* to graft.

greffier [grèfyé] *m.* registrar; clerk of the court.

greffon [grèfoⁿ] *m.* graft, scion.

grêle [grèl] *adj.* slender; thin; shrill [voix]; small [intestin].

grêle [grèl] *f.* hail; shower (fig.). ‖ **grêler** [-é] *v.* to hail; to damage by hail; to pock-mark. ‖ **grêlon** [-oⁿ] *m.* hail-stone.

grelot [grⁿló] *m.* small bell; sheep-bell. ‖ **grelotter** [-òté] *v.* to shiver; to shake; to tinkle [cloche].

grenade [grⁿnàd] *f.* pomegranate; grenade. ‖ **grenadier** [-yé] *m.* pomegranate-tree; grenadier (mil.).

grenaille [grⁿnày] *f.* small grain; lead shot [de plomb]; granulated metal.

grenier [grⁿnyé] *m.* granary; hayloft [foin]; corn-loft [grain]; garret, attic; lumber-room.

grenouille [grᵉnûy] *f.* frog.

grenu [grᵉnü] *adj.* grained; granular; grainy.

grès [grè] *m.* sandstone; stoneware.

grésil [grézìl] *m.* sleet; hail. ‖ *grésiller* [-ìyé] *v.* to sleet; to patter [bruit].

grève [grèv] *f.* shore; bank; beach; strike; *en grève*, on strike; *grève perlée*, Br. go-slow strike. *Am.* slow-down strike; *grève sur le tas*, sit-down strike.

grever [grᵉvé] *v.* to burden; to mortgage; to encumber; to saddle.

gréviste [grévìst] *m.*, *f.* striker.

gribouillage [grìbûyàj] *m.* scribble, scrawl; daub [peinture]. ‖ *gribouiller* [-ûyé] *v.* to scribble, to scrawl; to daub.

grief [grièf] *m.* grievance; complaint; cause for complaint.

grièvement [grièvmaⁿ] *adv.* grievously, gravely, sorely; deeply.

griffe [grìf] *f.* claw; talon; catch (techn.); signature; signature stamp; *coup de griffe*, scratch. ‖ *griffer* [-é] *v.* to scratch; to claw; to stamp. ‖ *griffonnage* [-ònàj] *m.* scrawl, scribble. ‖ *griffonner* [-òné] *v.* to scrawl, to scribble.

grignoter [grìñòté] *v.* to nibble; to pick at; to munch.

gril [grì] *m.* gridiron, grill. ‖ *grillade* [grìyàd] *f.* piece of roast; grilled meat, grill; grilling; roasting; broiling; toasting; wire-netting grating. ‖ *grillage* [-àj] *m.* lattice; grating; grid. ‖ *grille* [grìy] *f.* grate; grating; iron gate; railing; grid [radio]. ‖ *griller* [-ìyé] *v.* to grill; to roast; to broil; to toast [pain]; to calcine; to scorch; to burn; to rail in.

grillon [grìyoⁿ] *m.* cricket.

grimace [grìmàs] *f.* grimace, grin, wry face; humbug; sham; *faire des grimaces*, to make faces. ‖ *grimacer* [-é] *v.* to grimace; to grin; (fam.) to simper; to pucker.

grimer [grìmé] *v.* to make up.

grimper [grìⁿpé] *v.* to climb; to creep up; to clamber up.

grincement [grìⁿsmaⁿ] *m.* creaking [porte]; grating; gnashing [dents]. ‖ *grincer* [-é] *v.* to creak [porte]; to grate; to gnash [dents]. ‖ *grincheux* [grìⁿshë] *m.* (pop.) grouser; *adj.** grumpy, testy; surly; touchy; sulky; crabbed.

grippe [grìp] *f.* grippe; influenza, flu (fam.); *prendre en grippe*, to take a dislike to. ‖ *grippé* [-é] *adj.* down with the flu. ‖ *gripper* [-é] *v.* to seize up; to jam; (fam.) to snatch.

gris [grì] *adj.* grey; dull [temps]; (fam.) tipsy. ‖ *grisâtre* [-zâtr] *adj.*

greyish. ‖ *griser* [-zé] *v.* to intoxicate. ‖ *griserie* [-zrì] *f.* intoxication; exhilaration. ‖ *grisonner* [-zòné] *v.* to turn grey, to go grey.

grive [grîv] *f.* thrush.

grivois [grìvwà] *adj.* broad, licentious, spicy [histoire].

grog [gròg] *m.* grog.

grognement [gròñmaⁿ] *m.* grunt; growl; snarl; grumbling. ‖ *grogner* [-é] *v.* to grunt; to growl; to snarl; to grouse, to grumble. ‖ *grognon* [-oⁿ] *m.* grumbler; *adj.* grumbling, peevish.

groin [grwìⁿ] *m.* snout.

grommeler [gròmlé] *v.* to mutter; to growl; to grumble.

grondement [groⁿdmaⁿ] *m.* rumble; rumbling; roaring; boom [mer]. ‖ *gronder* [-é] *v.* to roar; to growl; to rumble [tonnerre]; to scold; to chide. ‖ *gronderie* [-rî] *f.* scolding.

gros, grosse [grô, grôs] *adj.* big; large; stout; thick; fat; coarse [grossier]; foul [temps]; heavy [mer]; pregnant; swollen; teeming; *en gros*, on the whole; roughly; wholesale [marchand]; *gros mots*, abuse.

gros [grô] *m.* bulk, main part; wholesale trade (comm.); *en gros*, approximately (fig.).

groseille [gròzèy] *f.* currant; gooseberry [à maquereau].

grosse [grôs] *adj.*, *see* gros; *f.* gross, twelve dozen; large-hand [écriture]; engrossed copy. ‖ *grossesse* [-ès] *f.* pregnancy. ‖ *grosseur* [-œr] *f.* size; bulk; swelling. ‖ *grossier* [-yé] *adj.** coarse; gross; rude [impoli]; vulgar; rough; boorish. ‖ *grossièreté* [-yèrté] *f.* coarseness; roughness; rudeness; grossness; coarse language; *pl.* abuse. ‖ *grossir* [-îr] *v.* to increase; to enlarge; to magnify; to swell [enfler]; to grow bigger. ‖ *grossiste* [-ìst] *m.* wholesaler.

grotesque [gròtèsk] *adj.* grotesque; absurd, fantastic, odd.

grotte [gròt] *f.* grotto; cave.

grouillement [grûymaⁿ] *m.* crawling; swarming; rumbling. ‖ *grouiller* [grûyé] *v.* to swarm, to crawl, to teem, to be alive (*de*, with), to hustle (fam.).

groupe [grûp] *m.* group; cluster [étoiles]; clump [arbres]; division; unit (mil.). ‖ *groupement* [-maⁿ] *m.* group; grouping; trust, pool. ‖ *grouper* [-é] *v.* to group; to concentrate [efforts]; *se grouper*, to gather.

grue [grü] *f.* crane; (pop.) prostitute, whore, streetwalker.

grumeau [grümò] *m.** clot; lump.

gruyère [grüyèr] *m.* gruyere cheese.

gué [gé] *m.* ford; *passer une rivière à gué*, to ford a river.

guenille [gₑnîy] *f.* rag, *pl.* tatters.

guenon [gₑnoⁿ] *f.* she-monkey; fright.

guêpe [gẽp] *f.* wasp. ‖ **guêpier** [gépyé] *m.* wasps' nest; bee-eater [oiseau]; tricky situation.

guère [gèr] *adv.* hardly; little; scarcely; *il ne tardera guère à arriver,* it won't be long before he comes; *je n'en ai guère,* I've hardly any.

guéret [géré] *m.* fallow ground; ploughed land.

guéridon [géridoⁿ] *m.* pedestal table.

guérilla [gériyà] *f.* guerilla warfare; band of guerillas. ‖ **guérillero** [-èrò] *m.* guerilla.

guérir [gérîr] *v.* to cure; to heal; to recover; to get back to health. ‖ **guérison** [-ìzoⁿ] *f.* cure; healing; recovering, recovery. ‖ **guérissable** [-ìsàbl] *adj.* curable; medicable. ‖ **guérisseur** [-ìsœr] *adj.* healing; *m.* healer.

guérite [gérît] *f.* sentry-box (mil.); signal-box [chemin de fer]; look-out; shelter.

guerre [gèr] *f.* war, warfare; feud, quarrel; *faire la guerre à,* to wage war against; *le ministère de la Guerre, Br.* the War Office; *Am.* Department of Defense, the Pentagon; *d'avant-guerre,* pre-war. ‖ **guerrier** [-yé] *m.* warrior; *adj.** warlike. ‖ **guerroyer** [-wàyé] *v.* to wage war.

guet [gè] *m.* watch; look-out; patrol; *faire le guet,* to be on the look-out; **guet-apens,** ambush; snare, trap; foul play; treacherous scheme.

guêtres [gètr] *f. pl.* gaiters; spats; leggings.

guetter [gété] *v.* to watch [occasion]; to watch for, to lie in wait for. ‖ **guetteur** [-œr] *m.* watchman; look-out man; signalman.

gueule [gœl] *f.* mouth [animaux]; opening; muzzle [canon]; (pop.) mug, jaw. ‖ **gueuler** [-é] *v.* to bawl. ‖ **gueuleton** [-toⁿ] *m.* (pop.) slap-up meal.

gueuse [gëz] *f.* pig-iron [fonte]; sow [moule].

gueux, gueuse [gë, gëz] *m., f.* tramp; vagabond; beggar; scoundrel; *adj.* poor, poverty-stricken.

gui [gì] *m.* mistletoe.

guichet [gìshè] *m.* wicket-gate; entrance; turnstile; barrier; booking-office window; pay-desk; cash-desk; counter.

guide [gìd] *m.* guide; guide-book; *f.* rein. ‖ **guider** [gìdé] *v.* to guide; to lead; to drive [cheval]; to steer [bateau]. ‖ **guidon** [-oⁿ] *m.* foresight [fusil]; handle-bar [bicyclette]; pennant (naut.).

guigne [gìñ] *f.* black cherry; (pop.) bad luck; ill luck; *Am.* jinx.

guigner [gìñé] *v.* to peer; to peep at; to ogle, to covet.

guignol [gìñòl] *m.* Punch and Judy show; puppet show; puppet.

guignolée [gìñòlé] *f.* © house-to-house collection for the poor.

guillemets [gìymè] *m. pl.* inverted commas, quotation marks.

guilleret [gìyrè] *adj.** sprightly, lively, gay; smart; over-free.

guillotine [gìyòtîn] *f.* guillotine; *fenêtre à guillotine,* sash-window. ‖ **guillotiner** [-ìné] *v.* to guillotine.

guimauve [gìmòv] *f.* marshmallow.

guimbarde [gìⁿbàrd] *f.* wagon; jew's-harp (mus.); (pop.) bone-shaker, rattletrap, *Am.* jalopy.

guindé [gìⁿdé] *adj.* stiff; stilted.

guirlande [gìrlaⁿd] *f.* garland, wreath; festoon.

guise [gîz] *f.* way, manner; fancy; *à votre guise,* as you like, as you will; *en guise de,* by way of.

guitare [gìtàr] *f.* guitar. ‖ **guitariste** [-rìst] *s.* guitarist.

gymnase [jìmnâz] *m.* gymnasium. ‖ **gymnastique** [jìmnàstìk] *f.* gymnastics; *adj.* gymnastic.

H

The French h is never aspirated as in English; no liaison should be made when the phonetic transcription is preceded by ', while in other cases initial h is mute.

habile [àbìl] *adj.* skilful, clever; artful, cunning, sharp; expert; qualified (jur.). ‖ **habileté** [-té] *f.* skill, ability; cleverness; cunning, artfulness [ruse].

habiliter [àbìlìté] *v.* to capacitate; to empower, to entitle.

habillement [àbìymaⁿ] *m.* clothing; clothes; dress; apparel; suit [com-plet]. ‖ **habiller** [-ìyé] *v.* to dress; to clothe; to prepare; to trim; to fit; *habillé,* clad; *s'habiller,* to dress, to get dressed; to dress up.

habit [àbì] *m.* dress; habit (eccles.); coat; dress-coat [de soirée]; *pl.* clothes.

habitant [àbìtaⁿ] *m.* inhabitant; dweller; inmate; resident; © farmer

[Fr. = paysan]. ‖ **habitat** [-à] *m.* habitat. ‖ **habitation** [-àsyoⁿ] *f.* habitation; home; dwelling, abode, residence. ‖ **habiter** [-é] *v.* to live in, to inhabit, to dwell at; to live, to reside; to occupy [maison].

habitude [àbìtüd] *f.* habit; custom, practice; use; *avoir l'habitude de*, to be used to; *d'habitude*, usually. ‖ **habitué** [-üé] *m.* frequenter, regular attendant. ‖ **habituel** [-üèl] *adj.* usual, customary, regular, habitual. ‖ **habituer** [-üé] *v.* to habituate, to accustom; to inure [endurcir]; *s'habituer*, to grow accustomed, to get used.

hache [àsh] *f.* axe; hatchet. ‖ **hacher** [-é] *v.* to chop; to hew; to hack up; to hash [viande]; to mince. ‖ **hachereau** [-rô] *m.* hatchet. ‖ **hachis** [-ì] *m.* hash, mince; minced meat. ‖ **hachoir** [-wàr] *m.* chopper; chopping-board. ‖ **hachuré** [-üré] *adj.* streaked.

hagard [àgàr] *adj.* haggard; drawn; wild-looking; staring.

haie [è] *f.* hedge, hedgerow; line, row; hurdle; *faire la haie*, to line the streets.

haillon [àyoⁿ] *m.* rag; *pl.* tatters.

haine [èn] *f.* hate, hatred; detestation. ‖ **haineux** [-ë] *adj.* hateful; full of hatred.

haïr [àìr] *v.* to hate, to detest, to loathe. ‖ **haïssable** [àìsàbl] *adj.* hateful, odious, detestable.

halage [àlàj] *m.* hauling; towing.

hâle [âl] *m.* tanning, browning; sunburn; tan; tanned complexion. ‖ **hâlé** [-é] *adj.* tanned, sunburnt; weather-beaten.

haleine [àlèn] *f.* breath; wind.

haler [àlé] *v.* to haul; to haul in; to tow; to heave.

hâler [àlé] *v.* to tan, to brown; to burn; to sunburn.

haleter [àlté] *v.* to puff, to pant, to blow; to gasp.

halle [àl] *f.* covered market, market hall.

hallucinant [àlüsìnaⁿ] *adj.* hallucinating, haunting.

halte [àlt] *f.* halt, stop; stopping-place; wayside station; *interj.* hold on! halt!

hamac [àmàk] *m.* hammock.

hameau [àmô] *m.* hamlet.

hameçon [àmsoⁿ] *m.* hook; fish-hook; bait (fig.).

hampe [aⁿp] *f.* shaft [lance]; staff, pole; stem.

hanche [aⁿsh] *f.* hip; haunch [cheval]; *les poings sur les hanches*, arms akimbo.

handicap [aⁿdìkàp] *m.* handicap. ‖ **handicaper** [-é] *v.* to handicap.

hangar [aⁿgàr] *m.* hangar (aviat.); shed; penthouse.

hanneton [àntoⁿ] *m.* may-bug, cockchafer; scatterbrain (fig.).

hanter [aⁿté] *v.* to haunt; to frequent; to keep company with. ‖ **hantise** [-ìz] *f.* obsession.

happer [àpé] *v.* to snap up, to snatch, to catch; to waylay.

harangue [àraⁿg] *f.* harangue; address, speech. ‖ **haranguer** [àraⁿgé] *v.* to harangue; to address.

harasser [àràsé] *v.* to exhaust, to wear out.

harceler [àrsºlé] *f.* to harass; to harry; to worry; to pester, to nag.

hardi [àrdì] *adj.* audacious, bold; daring; rash; impudent, saucy. ‖ **hardiesse** [-yès] *f.* boldness; temerity; effrontery, impudence; audacity, cheek; pluck, daring; rashness. ‖ **hardiment** [-ìmaⁿ] *adv.* boldly, audaciously.

hareng [àraⁿ] *m.* herring; *hareng fumé*, kipper. ‖ **harengère** [-jèr] *f.* fish-wife.

hargneux [àrñë] *adj.* surly; peevish; bad-tempered; nagging [femme]; harsh, cross [ton].

haricot [àrìkò] *m.* haricot, bean, kidney-bean; *haricots verts*, Br. French beans, Am. string beans.

harmonie [àrmònì] *f.* harmony; concord; accord, agreement. ‖ **harmonieux** [-yë] *adj.* harmonious; tuneful, melodious. ‖ **harmonique** [-ìk] *m.*, *adj.* harmonic. ‖ **harmoniser** [-ìzé] *v.* to harmonize; to match.

harnacher [àrnàshé] *v.* to harness; to rig out [personnes]. ‖ **harnais** [-è] *m.* harness; gearing (mech.); saddlery; trappings.

harpe [àrp] *f.* harp.

harpie [àrpì] *f.* harpy; shrew.

harpiste [àrpìst] *s.* harp-player.

harpon [àrpoⁿ] *m.* harpoon; wall-staple. ‖ **harponner** [-òné] *v.* to harpoon; to waylay.

hasard [àzàr] *m.* chance, luck; risk; danger; hazard; *au hasard*, at random; *par hasard*, by chance. ‖ **hasardé** [-dé] *adj.* hazardous, risky, rash, bold, foolhardy. ‖ **hasarder** [-dé] *v.* to hazard, to venture; to risk. ‖ **hasardeux** [-dë] *adj.* perilous, risky, venturous; bold, daring.

hâte [ât] *f.* haste, hurry; eagerness; *à la hâte*, hastily, in a hurry; *avoir hâte*, to be eager; to be in a hurry; to long (*de*, to). ‖ **hâter** [-é] *v.* to hasten; to speed up; to expedite; to force [fruits]; **se *hâter***, to hurry up, to make haste. ‖ ***hâtif*** [-ìf] *adj.** hasty; premature; early; ill-considered.

hausse ['ôs] *f.* rise, *Am.* raise; backsight [fusil]; range (mil.); *à la hausse*, on the rise. ‖ ***haussement*** [-maⁿ] *m.* raising; *haussement d'épaules*, shrug. ‖ ***hausser*** [-é] *v.* to lift; to raise; to increase; to shrug [épaules]; to rise, to go up. ‖ ***haussière*** [-yèr] *f.* hawser. ‖ ***haut*** ['ô] *adj.* height; top; summit; *adj.* high; tall; lofty; elevated; important, eminent, great; loud [voix]; erect [tête]; haughty; *adv.* high; high up; haughtily; aloud; *en haut*, upstairs; up above; at the top; *vingt pieds de haut, haut de vingt pieds*, twenty feet high; ***haut-fond***, shoal, shallows; ***haut-le-cœur***, retching; nausea, ***haut-le-corps***, start, jump; ***haut-parleur***, loudspeaker. ‖ ***hautain*** [-ôtìⁿ] *adj.* haughty; lofty. ‖ ***hauteur*** [-ôtœr] *f.* height; altitude; eminence, hill; pitch (mus.); arrogance, haughtiness; position (naut.); *être à la hauteur de*, to be equal to; to be a match for; to be up to.

hâve ['âv] *adj.* wan; emaciated; gaunt, drawn, haggard.

havre ['àvr] *m.* harbour, haven.

hebdomadaire [èbdòmàdèr] *adj.* weekly; *m.* weekly publication, weekly (fam.).

héberger [ébèrjé] *v.* to lodge; to harbo(u)r.

hébéter [ébété] *v.* to stupefy; to daze; to stun. ‖ ***hébétude*** [-tüd] *f.* daze; hebetude.

hécatombe [ékàtoⁿb] *f.* hecatomb.

hélas! [élàs] *interj.* alas!

héler ['élé] *v.* to hail; to call.

hélice [élìs] *f.* screw; propellor; *en hélice*, spiral.

hélicoptère [élìkòptèr] *m.* helicopter.

hémisphère [émìsfèr] *m.* hemisphere.

hémorragie [émòràjì] *f.* hemorrhage, bleeding.

hennir ['ènìr] *v.* to neigh; to whinny.

herbe [èrb] *f.* grass; herb, plant; weed [maùvaise]; *herbe à puces*, © poison-ivy; seaweed [marine]; *fines herbes*, herbs for seasoning; *en herbe*, unripe; budding (fig.). ‖ ***herbeux*** [-é] *adj.** grassy. ‖ ***herboriste*** [-òrìst] *m.*, *f.* herbalist.

héréditaire [érédìtèr] *adj.* hereditary. ‖ ***hérédité*** [-é] *f.* heredity; heirship.

hérisser ['érìsé] *v.* to bristle up; to ruffle [plumes]; to cover with spikes; **se *hérisser***, to bristle; to stand on end; to get ruffled [personne]. ‖ ***hérisson*** [-oⁿ] *m.* hedgehog; sea-urchin [de mer]; row of spikes; sprocket-wheel; flue-brush.

héritage [érìtàj] *m.* heritage, inheritance; heirloom. ‖ ***hériter*** [-é] *v.* to inherit, to come into. ‖ ***héritier, -ière*** [-yé, yèr] *m.* heir; *f.* heiress.

hermétique [èrmétìk] *adj.* hermetic; airtight; abstruse.

hermine [èrmîn] *f.* ermine, stoat. ‖ ***herminette*** [-ìnèt] *f.* adze.

hernie [èrnî] *f.* hernia, rupture.

héroïne [éròìn] *f.* heroine [personnage]; heroin [stupéfiant]. ‖ ***héroïque*** [éròìk] *adj.* heroic, heroical. ‖ ***héroïsme*** [éròìsm] *m.* heroism.

héron ['éroⁿ] *m.* heron, hern.

héros ['éró] *m.* hero.

herse ['èrs] *f.* harrow; portcullis. ‖ ***herser*** [-é] *v.* to harrow, to drag [champ].

hésitation [ézìtàsyoⁿ] *f.* hesitation; hesitancy, wavering; faltering [pas]; misgiving. ‖ ***hésiter*** [-é] *v.* to hesitate, to waver; to falter.

hétéroclite [étéròklìt] *adj.* unusual, strange; eccentric; incongruous.

hêtre ['ètr] *m.* beech, beech-tree.

heure [œr] *f.* hour; o'clock; time; moment; period; *quelle heure est-il?*, what time is it?; *six heures dix*, ten (minutes) past six, six ten; *six heures moins dix*, ten (minutes) to six; *six heures et demie*, half past six; *c'est l'heure*, time is up; *heure légale*, standard time; *heure d'été*, summer time, daylight-saving time; *dernière heure*, last-minute news; *être à l'heure*, to be on time, to be punctual; *heures supplémentaires*, overtime; *de bonne heure*, early; *tout à l'heure*, just now, a few minutes ago; presently, in a few minutes; *à tout à l'heure*, so long!, see you presently, see you later.

heureusement [œrèzmaⁿ] *adv.* happily; fortunately; successfully.

heureux [œrë] *adj.** happy; glad, pleased, delighted; lucky, fortunate, favo(u)red, blessed; successful, prosperous; auspicious, favo(u)rable; pleasing, apt, felicitous [phrase].

heurt ['œr] *m.* shock; blow. ‖ ***heurter*** ['œrté] *v.* to knock, to hit, to strike; to jostle, to bump; to run into, to crash with, to collide with; to shock, to offend, to wound [sensibilité]; to clash, to jar [couleurs]; to ram, to barge into (naut.); to stub [pied]; **se *heurter***, to collide; to clash (fig.).

hibou ['ìbû] *m.** owl; *jeune hibou*, owlet.

hideux ['ìdë] *adj.** hideous; horrible, frightful, appalling, shocking.

hier [yèr] *adv.* yesterday; *hier soir*, last night, last evening.

hiérarchie [yéràrshĭ] *f.* hierarchy. ‖ **hiérarchique** [-chĭk] *adj.* hierarchical.

hilarant [ĭlàraⁿ] *adj.* mirth-provoking, exhilarating; *gaz hilarant*, laughing-gas.

hippique [ĭpĭk] *adj.* hippic, equine; *concours hippique*, horse-show; *Br.* race-meeting, *Am.* race-meet. ‖ **hippodrome** [-ɒdròm] *m.* hippodrome, circus; race-track, race-course.

hippopotame [ĭpòpòtàm] *m.* hippopotamus.

hirondelle [ĭrɒdèl] *f.* swallow; small river steamer.

hirsute [ĭrsüt] *adj.* hirsute, hairy, shaggy; unkempt; rough, boorish.

hisser [ʼĭssé] *v.* to hoist, to heave, to lift, to raise, to pull up, *Am.* to heft.

histoire [ĭstwàr] *f.* history; story, tale, narration, narrative; yarn (fam.); invention, fib; thing, affair, matter; *faire des histoires*, to make a fuss, to make a to-do. ‖ **historien** [ĭstòryaⁿ] *m.* historian, chronicler, recorder; narrator. ‖ **historique** [-ĭk] *adj.* historic; historical; *m.* historical account, recital, chronicle.

histrion [ĭstrìyoⁿ] *m.* histrion; mountebank.

hiver [ĭvèr] *m.* winter. ‖ **hiverner** [-né] *v.* to winter, to spend the winter; to hibernate.

hocher [ʼòshé] *v.* to shake, to toss, to nod, to wag. ‖ **hochet** [-è] *m.* rattle [de bébé]; toy, bauble.

hollandais [ʼòlɒdè] *adj.* Dutch; *m.* Dutchman. ‖ **Hollande** [ʼòlɒd] *f.* Holland; Netherlands.

homard [ʼòmàr] *m.* lobster.

homélie [òmélĭ] *f.* homily.

homéopathie [òméòpàtĭ] *f.* homœopathy. ‖ **homéopathique** [-tĭk] *adj.* homœopathic.

homicide [òmĭsĭd] *adj.* murderous, homicidal; *m.* murder [volontaire]; manslaughter [involontaire].

hommage [òmàj] *m.* homage, respect, veneration, tribute, esteem; service; acknowledgment, token, gift, testimony; *pl.* respects, compliments; *rendre hommage*, to do homage, to pay tribute.

homme [òm] *m.* man; *pl.* men; mankind; *homme d'affaires*, businessman; *homme de peine*, laborer.

homologuer [òmòlògé] *v.* to homologate; to ratify; to recognize.

honnête [ònèt] *adj.* honest, hono(u)rable, upright, decent; respectable; genteel, courteous, well-bred; seemly, becoming, decorous [conduite]; advantageous, reasonable, moderate [prix]; virtuous [femme]; *honnêtes gens*, decent people; *procédés honnêtes*, square dealings. ‖ **honnêteté** [-té] *f.* honesty, integrity, uprightness; civility, politeness; decency, respectability, seemliness; reasonableness, fairness.

honneur [ònœr] *m.* hono(u)r, rectitude, probity, integrity; repute, credit; respect; chastity; virtue; distinction; court-card [cartes]; *pl.* regalia, hono(u)rs, preferments.

honorable [ònòràbl] *adj.* hono(u)rable; respectable, reputable, creditable. ‖ **honoraire** [-èr] *adj.* honorary; *m. pl.* fee, fees, honorarium; stipend; retainer [avocat]. ‖ **honorer** [-é] *v.* to hono(u)r, to respect; to do hono(u)r to; to be an hono(u)r to; to meet [obligation]; *s'honorer*, to pride oneself (*de*, on). ‖ **honorifique** [-ĭfĭk] *adj.* honorary, titular [titre].

honte [ʼoⁿt] *f.* shame, disgrace, discredit; reproach; confusion, bashfulness; *avoir honte*, to be ashamed; *sans honte*, shameless; *faire honte à*, to make ashamed, to put to shame. ‖ **honteux** [-ë] *adj.** ashamed; shameful, disgraceful, scandalous; bashful, shy.

hôpital [ôpĭtàl] *m.** hospital, infirmary; alms-house, poor-house, asylum [hospice].

hoquet [ʼòkè] *m.* hiccough, hiccup; hic; gasp. ‖ **hoqueter** [-té] *v.* to hiccup; to hiccough.

horaire [òrèr] *m.* time-table, schedule; *adj.* horary, hourly; per hour.

horizon [òrĭzoⁿ] *m.* horizon, skyline; sea-line; outlook; scope (fig.). ‖ **horizontal** [-tàl] *adj.** horizontal.

horloge [òrlòj] *f.* clock; time-piece, time-keeper, chronometer. ‖ **horloger** [-é] *m.* watch-maker, clock-maker. ‖ **horlogerie** [-rĭ] *f.* watch-making, clock-making; watch and clock-trade; clockmaker's shop; *mouvement d'horlogerie*, clockwork.

hormis [ʼòrmĭ] *prep.* except, but, save, excepting.

horreur [òrœr] *f.* horror, dread; abhorrence, loathing, repulsion, repugnance, disgust; atrocity, heinousness; *avoir en horreur*, to abhor, to detest, to abominate; *faire horreur à*, to horrify, to disgust. ‖ **horrible** [-ĭbl] *adj.* horrible, awful, dreadful, fearful, frightful, horrid; appalling, ghastly, gruesome. ‖ **horrifiant** [-ĭfyaⁿ] *adj.* horrifying. ‖ **horrifier** [-ĭfyé] *v.* to horrify, to appal.

hors [ʼòr] *prep.* out of, outside of; without; but, except, save; beyond, past; *hors de combat*, disabled, out of action; *hors de saison*, unseasonable; *hors de doute*, unquestionable; *hors-d'œuvre*, hors-d'œuvre, appetizer; digression, irrelevancy; outwork, outbuilding (arch.); **hors-la-loi,** outlaw; **hors-texte,** bookplate.

hortensia [òrtaⁿsyà] *m.* hydrangea.

hospice [òspîs] *m.* hospice; asylum, refuge; alms-house; home, institution. ‖ *hospitalier* [-itàlyé] *adj.** hospitable; welcoming. ‖ *hospitaliser* [-itàlìsé] *v. Br.* to send to hospital, *Am.* to hospitalize; to admit to a home. ‖ *hospitalité* [-itàlìté] *f.* hospitality; hospitableness; harbo(u)rage.

hostile [òstîl] *adj.* hostile, unfriendly, opposed, adverse, contrary, inimical. ‖ *hostilité* [-ìté] *f.* hostility, enmity, opposition.

hôte, hôtesse [ôt, ôtès] *m., f.* host, *m.*; hostess, *f.*; innkeeper; landlord, *m.*; landlady, *f.*; guest, visitor; lodger; occupier, inmate; *table d'hôte,* table d'hôte, regular *or* ordinary meal. ‖ *hôtel* [ôtèl] *m.* hotel, hostelry, inn; mansion, town-house, private residence; public building; *hôtel meublé,* lodging-house. ‖ *hôtelier* [-ⁱlyé] *m.* hotel-keeper, innkeeper; landlord; host; hosteller [monastère]. ‖ *hôtellerie* [-èlrî] *f.* hostelry, inn, hotel; hotel trade; guest-house.

hotte [òt] *f.* basket; pannier, dosser; hod [maçon]; hood, canopy [cheminée].

houblon [ûblòⁿ] *m.* hop.

houe ['û] *f.* hoe.

houille ['ûy] *f.* coal; *houille blanche,* water-power; *houille brune,* lignite. ‖ *houiller* [-é] *adj.** coal; coal-bearing. ‖ *houillère* [-èr] *f.* coal-mine, coal-pit; colliery.

houle ['ûl] *f.* swell, surge, billows. ‖ *houleux* [-lë] *adj.** swelling; stormy; tumultuous.

houppe ['ûp] *f.* tuft, bunch; pompon; tassel, bob; crest, topknot [cheveux]; powder-puff [poudre]. ‖ *houppette* [-èt] *f.* powder-puff.

hourra ['ûrà] *m., interj.* hurrah.

housse ['ûs] *f.* covering; dust-sheet; *Am.* slip-cover; garment-bag; sparetire cover [auto]; propeller-cover (aviat.); saddle-cloth.

houx ['û] *m.* holly, holly-tree.

hoyau ['wàyô] *m.** mattock, grubbing-hoe; pickaxe.

huard [üàr] *m.* © loon.

hublot [üblô] *m.* scuttle, port-hole.

huche ['üsh] *f.* bin.

hue! ['ü] *interj.* gee!

huer ['üé] *v.* to boo, to hoot, to jeer; to shout, to whoop; to halloo [chasse].

huile [üil] *f.* oil; *huile de table,* salad oil; *huile de coude,* elbow-grease. ‖

huiler [-é] *v.* to oil; to lubricate; to grease; to exude oil. ‖ *huileux* [-ë] *adj.** oily, greasy. ‖ *huilier* [-yé] *m.* oil-can; cruet-stand; oil-maker; oil-merchant.

huissier [üìsyé] *m.* process-server; usher, monitor; beadle.

huit [üt] *m., adj.* eight; eighth [date, titre]; *huit jours,* a week; *d'aujourd'hui en huit,* to-day week, a week from to-day. ‖ *huitaine* [-èn] *f.* about eight; week. ‖ *huitième* [-yèm] *m., f., adj.* eighth.

huître [üîtr] *f.* oyster.

humain [ümⁱⁿ] *adj.* human; humane [bon]; *m.* human being; *pl.* humanity, mankind, men. ‖ *humaniser* [ümànìzé] *v.* to humanize, to civilize; to soften, to mollify. ‖ *humanitaire* [-ìtèr] *adj., s.* humanitarian. ‖ *humanité* [-ìté] *f.* humanity; human nature; mankind; humaneness, kindness; *pl.* humanities, classical studies.

humble [üⁿbl] *adj.* humble, lowly, modest; mean.

humecter [ümèkté] *v.* to dampen, to moisten, to wet.

humer [ümé] *v.* to inhale; to suck up; to sip.

humeur [ümœr] *f.* humo(u)r; disposition, temperament, mood, spirits; fancy; caprice; ill-humo(u)r; temper, anger; *avec humeur,* peevishly; crossly.

humide [ümîd] *adj.* damp, moist, humid, wet, dank; muggy [temps]. ‖ *humidifier* [-ìfyé] *v.* to humidify. ‖ *humidité* [ümìdìté] *f.* humidity, moisture, dampness, wetness, dankness; mugginess [temps].

humilier [ümìlyé] *v.* to humiliate, to mortify, to humble; to abase. ‖ *humilité* [-ìté] *f.* humility, humbleness.

humoriste [ümòrìst] *adj.* humorous, humoristic; *m., f.* humorist. ‖ *humour* [-ûr] *m.* humo(u)r; comic sense.

hune ['ün] *f.* top (naut.); *hune de vigie,* crow's-nest.

huppe ['üp] *f.* tuft, crest; hoopoe [oiseau]. ‖ *huppé* [-é] *adj.* tufted; smart, swell (fam.).

hurlement [ürlᵉmaⁿ] *m.* howl, howling, yelling, roaring, roar; bellow, bellowing. ‖ *hurler* [-é] *v.* to howl, to yell, to roar; to bellow; to bawl.

hurluberlu [ürlübèrlü] *adj.* scatter-brained; *m.* harum-scarum.

hutte ['üt] *f.* hut, cabin, shanty, shed.

hyacinthe [yàsⁱⁿt] *m.* hyacinth.

hydraulique [ìdrôlîk] *adj.* hydraulic; *f.* hydraulics; *force hydraulique,* water-power.

hydravion [idràvyoⁿ] *m.* hydroplane, sea-plane.

hydrogène [idròjèn] *m.* hydrogen.

hygiène [ìjyèn] *f.* hygiene; sanitation. || **hygiénique** [-yénìk] *adj.* hygienic, healthful; sanitary.

hymne [ìmn] *m.* hymn; song; anthem [national].

hypnose [ipnôz] *f.* hypnosis. || **hypnotiser** [ìpnòtìzé] *v.* to hypnotize.

hypocrisie [ipòkrìzî] *f.* hypocrisy; cant. || **hypocrite** [-ìt] *adj.* hypocritical; *m.*, *f.* hypocrite.

hypothécaire [ipòtékèr] *adj.* on mortgage. || **hypothèque** [ìpòtèk] *f.* mortgage. || **hypothéquer** [-éké] *v.* to hypothecate, to mortgage.

hypothèse [ìpòtèz] *f.* hypothesis; assumption, supposition, theory.

hystérie [ìstérî] *f.* hysteria. || **hystérique** [-ìk] *adj.* hysteric, hysterical.

I

ici [ìsì] *adv.* here; now, at this point; *ici-bas,* on earth.

idéal [ìdéàl] *adj.** ideal; imaginary, visionary; *m.** ideal. || **idéalisme** [-ìsm] *m.* idealism. || **idéaliste** [-ìst] *adj.* idealistic; *m.*, *f.* idealist.

idée [ìdé] *f.* idea; notion, conception; mind; intention, purpose; whim, fancy; hint, suggestion.

identification [ìdaⁿtìfìkàsyoⁿ] *f.* identification, identifying. || **identifier** [-ìfyé] *v.* to identify. || **identique** [-ìk] *adj.* identical; equal, equivalent. || **identité** [-ìté] *f.* identity; *carte d'identité,* identification card, identity card.

idiot [ìdyô] *adj.* idiotic, absurd, senseless, stupid; *m.* idiot; fool, silly ass, *Am.* nut (pop.). || **idiotie** [-sî] *f.* idiocy; stupidity; piece of nonsense.

idiotisme [ìdyòtìsm] *m.* idiomatic expression; idiom.

idole [ìdòl] *f.* idol; god.

idylle [ìdìl] *f.* idyl(l); romance.

igloo [ìglû] *m.* igloo.

ignifuge [ìgnìfüj] *adj.* non-inflammable, fireproof.

ignoble [ìñyòbl] *adj.* ignoble; lowborn; vile, base; beastly, filthy; disgraceful, contemptible. || **ignominie** [ìñyòmìnì] *f.* ignominy, disgrace.

ignorance [ìñòraⁿs] *f.* ignorance. || **ignorant** [-oⁿ] *adj.* ignorant; uninformed; illiterate; unlearned; unaware; *m.* ignoramus, dunce. || **ignorer** [-é] *v.* to be unaware of, to be ignorant of, not to know, to ignore [passer sous silence].

il, ils [ìl] *pron.* he; it; she [bateau]; *pl.* they.

île [ìl] *f.* island, isle.

illégal [ìllégàl] *adj.** illegal, unlawful, illicit. || **illégitime** [illéjìtìm] *adj.* illegitimate [enfant]; unlawful [mariage]; unwarranted [réclamation]; spurious [titre]. || **illégitimité** [-ìté] *f.* illegitimacy.

illettré [ìllètré] *adj.* uneducated; illiterate.

illicite [ìllìsìt] *adj.* illicit; foul [coup]; unallowed.

illimité [ìllìmìté] *adj.* boundless, unlimited, unbounded; indefinite.

illisible [ìllìzìbl] *adj.* illegible; unreadable.

illogique [ìllòjìk] *adj.* illogical. || **illogisme** [-ìsm] *m.* illogicality.

illumination [ìllümìnàsyoⁿ] *f.* illumination; lighting; flood-lighting [projecteur]; *pl.* lights; inspiration (fig.); enlightenment. || **illuminer** [-né] *v.* to illuminate; to light up; to enlighten; to brighten.

illusion [ìllüzyoⁿ] *f.* illusion, delusion, fallacy; self-deception; chimera. || **illusionner** [-yòné] *v.* to delude, to deceive. || **illusoire** [-wàr] *adj.* illusory, illusive; deceptive.

illustration [ìllüstràsyoⁿ] *f.* illustration; picture; illustrating; illustriousness, renown; explanation, elucidation, expounding; *pl.* notes. || **illustrer** [-é] *v.* to render illustrious; to illustrate [livre]; to elucidate, to annotate; *s'illustrer,* to become famous.

îlot [ìlô] *m.* islet; block [maisons].

image [ìmàj] *f.* image; picture; likeness, resemblance; effigy; idea, impression; simile; metaphor; *pl.* imagery. || **imaginable** [-ìnàbl] *adj.* imaginable. || **imaginaire** [-ìnèr] *adj.* imaginary, fancied, fictitious. || **imaginatif** [-ìnàtìf] *adj.** imaginative. || **imagination** [-ìnàsyoⁿ] *f.* imagination; conception; fancy, invention, conceit. || **imaginer** [-ìné] *v.* to imagine; to conceive; to fancy, to suppose; *s'imaginer,* to imagine oneself; to conjecture; to delude oneself.

imbécile [iⁿbésìl] *adj.* imbecile, idiotic; half-witted; silly, foolish; *m.* imbecile; fool, simpleton, ninny, fathead, *Am.* nut (pop.). || **imbécillité** [-ìté] *f.* imbecility, feeble-mindedness, silliness; nonsense.

imberbe [iⁿbèrb] *adj.* beardless, smooth-chinned.

imbiber [iⁿbíbé] v. to soak, to steep; to imbue, to impregnate; to imbibe; *imbibé d'eau*, wet.

imbu [iⁿbü] adj. imbued.

imbuvable [iⁿbüvàbl] adj. undrinkable; insufferable (fam.).

imitable [ìmìtàbl] adj. imitable. ‖ *imitateur* [-tœr] m. imitator. ‖ *imitatif* [-tìf] adj.* imitative. ‖ *imitation* [ìmìtàsyoⁿ] f. imitation; imitating, copying; forgery; mimicking. ‖ *imiter* [-é] v. to imitate, to copy; to forge; to mimic, to ape.

immaculé [ìmmàkülé] adj. immaculate, stainless, undefiled.

immangeable [iⁿmaⁿjàbl] adj. inedible, uneatable.

immanquable [iⁿmaⁿkàbl] adj. impossible to miss; inevitable.

immatriculer [ìmmàtrìkülé] v. to matriculate; to register.

immédiat [ìmmédyà] adj. immediate; near, close; direct; urgent.

immense [ìmmaⁿs] adj. immense, huge, vast. ‖ *immensité* [-ìté] f. immensity; vastness; boundlessness; hugeness.

immerger [ìmmèrjé] v. to immerse, to plunge, to dip. ‖ *immersion* [-syoⁿ] f. immersion, plunging, dipping; submergence, submersion (naut.).

immeuble [ìmmœbl] m. real estate, realty, landed property; building, edifice; premises.

immigrant [ìmmìgraⁿ] m. immigrant. ‖ *immigration* [-àsyoⁿ] f. immigration. ‖ *immigrer* [-é] v. to immigrate.

imminent [ìmmìnaⁿ] adj. imminent, impending.

immiscer [ìmmìsé] v. to mix up; to involve; *s'immiscer*, to interfere, to intrude. ‖ *immixtion* [-ksyoⁿ] f. interference, meddling.

immobile [ìmmòbìl] adj. motionless, immobile, unmoving; unshaken, steady. ‖ *immobiliser* [-ìzé] v. to immobilize (mil.); to fix; to lock up [argent]; to convert, to realize (comm.); *s'immobiliser*, to stop. ‖ *immobilité* [-ìté] f. immobility, motionlessness.

immodéré [ìmmòdéré] adj. immoderate, inordinate, intemperate.

immonde [ìmmoⁿd] adj. unclean, foul, filthy.

immoral [ìmmòràl] adj.* immoral. ‖ *immoralité* [-ìté] f. immorality, licentiousness.

immortalité [ìmmòrtàlìté] f. immortality. ‖ *immortel* [-èl] adj.* immortal, everlasting, undying; imperishable; m. immortal.

immunité [ìmmünìté] f. immunity; privilege; exemption [impôts].

impair [iⁿpèr] adj. odd, uneven; m. blunder, bloomer (fam.).

impardonnable [iⁿpàrdònàbl] adj. unforgivable; unpardonable.

imparfait [iⁿpàrfè] adj.* imperfect, defective; unfinished; m. imperfect.

impartial [iⁿpàrsyàl] adj.* impartial, unbiassed, unprejudiced. ‖ *impartialité* [-ìté] f. impartiality, fair-mindedness.

impartir [iⁿpàrtìr] v. to grant; to invest; to allow, to bestow.

impassibilité [iⁿpàsìbìlìté] f. impassibility, impassiveness. ‖ *impassible* [iⁿpàsìbl] adj. impassive, impassible, unfeeling; unmoved; unimpressionable; unperturbed.

impatience [iⁿpàsyaⁿs] f. impatience, intolerance; eagerness, longing; fidgeting. ‖ *impatient* [-yaⁿ] adj. impatient, intolerant; eager; all agog; restless. ‖ *impatienter* [-yaⁿté] v. to provoke, to get (someone) out of patience, to irritate; *s'impatienter*, to lose patience, to become impatient.

impayable [iⁿpèyàbl] adj. inestimable, invaluable, priceless; (fam.) screaming, killing, *Br.* capital, ripping.

impeccable [iⁿpèkàbl] adj. impeccable, faultless; flawless.

impénétrable [iⁿpénétràbl] adj. impenetrable; impervious [imperméable]; inscrutable [visage]; unfathomable [mystère]; close [secret].

impératif [iⁿpéràtìf] adj.* imperative; imperious; m. imperative (gramm.).

impératrice [iⁿpéràtrìs] f. empress.

imperceptible [iⁿpèrsèptìbl] adj. imperceptible, undiscernible.

imperfection [iⁿpèrfèksyoⁿ] f. imperfection; incompleteness; defect, fault; flaw, blemish.

impérial [iⁿpéryàl] adj.* imperial. ‖ *impériale* [-yàl] f. roof, top, upperdeck [autobus]; imperial, tuft [barbe].

impérieux [iⁿpéryë] adj.* imperious; domineering; peremptory; urgent.

impérissable [iⁿpérìsàbl] adj. imperishable; unperishing.

imperméable [iⁿpèrméàbl] adj. impermeable, waterproof, watertight; impervious; m. waterproof, raincoat.

impersonnel [iⁿpèrsònèl] adj.* impersonal.

impertinence [iⁿpèrtìnaⁿs] f. impertinence; pertness, nerve, cheek; irrelevance (jur.). ‖ *impertinent* [-aⁿ] adj. impertinent, saucy, pert, nervy, cheeky; flippant; irrelevant (jur.).

imperturbable [iⁿpèrtürbàbl] adj. imperturbable, unmoved, phlegmatic.

impétueux [iⁿpétüë] *adj.** impetuous, hasty, precipitate, headlong; passionate. ‖ *impétuosité* [-üòzìté] *f.* impetuosity.

impie [iⁿpî] *adj.* impious, ungodly; irreligious; blasphemous; *m.* unbeliever. ‖ *impiété* [-pyété] *f.* impiety; impious deed.

impitoyable [iⁿpìtwàyàbl] *adj.* pitiless; unmerciful; ruthless; unrelenting.

implacable [iⁿplàkàbl] *adj.* implacable, unpardoning.

implication [iⁿplìkàsyoⁿ] *f.* implication.

implicite [iⁿplìsìt] *adj.* implicit, implied; tacit. ‖ *impliquer* [-ìké] *v.* to imply; to implicate.

implorer [iⁿplòré] *v.* to implore, to beseech, to entreat.

impoli [iⁿpòlì] *adj.* impolite, rude. ‖ *impolitesse* [-tès] *f.* rude act; impoliteness; discourtesy.

importance [iⁿpòrtaⁿs] *f.* importance; largeness, considerableness; consequence; social position, authority, credit; self-conceit. ‖ *important* [-aⁿ] *adj.* important, considerable; weighty; self-important, bumptious (fam.); *m.* essential point, main thing.

importateur, -trice [iⁿpòrtàtœr, -trìs] *m.*, *f.* importer [marchandises]; *adj.* importing. ‖ *importation* [-àsyoⁿ] *f.* importation; import. ‖ *importer* [-é] *v.* to import.

importer [iⁿpòrté] *v.* to matter; to import, to be of consequence; *n'importe comment*, no matter how, anyhow, anyway; *n'importe quoi*, no matter what, anything; *qu'importe?*, what's the difference?

importun [iⁿpòrtuⁿ] *adj.* importunate, obtrusive, bothersome, troublesome, unseasonable *m.* pestering person, bore. ‖ *importuner* [-üné] *v.* to importune, to bother, to pester, to bore, to trouble, to inconvenience; to badger (fam.); to dun [débiteur]. ‖ *importunité* [-ünìté] *f.* importunity.

imposable [iⁿpòzàbl] *adj.* taxable. ‖ *imposant* [-aⁿ] *adj.* imposing impressive; commanding, stately. ‖ *imposer* [-é] *v.* to impose, to prescribe, to assign, to inflict [tâche]; to enforce, to lay down [règlement], to tax, to charge; to thrust, to force (à upon); to lay on [mains], *s'imposer*, to assert oneself, to command attention, to obtrude oneself; to be called for ‖ *imposition* [-ìsyoⁿ] *f.* imposition; laying on [mains]; prescribing [tâche]; tax, duty.

impossibilité [iⁿpòsìbìlìté] *f.* impossibility. ‖ *Impossible* [-ìbl] *adj.* impossible; impracticable.

imposteur [iⁿpòstœr] *m.* impostor, deceiver, fake, *Am.* phony (pop.).

impôt [iⁿpô] *m.* tax, duty; taxation.

impotent [iⁿpòtaⁿ] *adj.* impotent; crippled; *m.*, *f.* cripple, invalid.

impraticable [iⁿpràtìkàbl] *adj.* impracticable, unfeasible; unworkable; impassable.

imprécis [iⁿprésì] *adj.* unprecise. ‖ *imprécision* [-zyoⁿ] *f.* vagueness; haziness; looseness.

imprégner [iⁿpréñé] *v.* to impregnate.

impression [iⁿprèsyoⁿ] *f.* pressing, impressing; impression, impress; mark, stamp; printing; print; issue, edition; feeling; sensation. ‖ *impressionnant* [-yònaⁿ] *adj.* impressive; moving, stirring. ‖ *impressionner* [-yòné] *v.* to impress, to affect, to move; to make an impression on.

imprévisible [iⁿprévìzìbl] *adj.* unforeseeable, unpredictable.

imprévoyant [iⁿprévwàyaⁿ] *adj.* improvident. ‖ *imprévu* [-ü] *adj.* unforeseen, unexpected, unlooked-for; sudden.

imprimé [iⁿprìmé] *adj.* printed; *m.* printed form, paper, book; *pl.* printed matter. ‖ *imprimer* [-é] *v.* to print; to communicate [mouvement]; to impress, to stamp; to prime [toile]. ‖ *imprimerie* [-rî] *f.* printing; printing-office; printing works. ‖ *imprimeur* [-œr] *m.* printer

improbabilité [iⁿpròbàbìlìté] *f.* unlikelihood; improbable event. ‖ *improbable* [iⁿpròbàbl] *adj.* improbable, unlikely.

improductif [iⁿpròdüktìf] *adj.** unproductive; idle [argent].

impropre [iⁿpròpr] *adj.* unfit, unsuitable; improper. ‖ *impropriété* [-lété] *f.* impropriety, incorrectness.

improviser [iⁿpròvìzé] *v.* to improvise; to do (something) extempore; to ad-lib (fam.).

imprudence [iⁿprüdaⁿs] *f.* imprudence, rashness; unwariness, heedlessness ‖ *imprudent* [-aⁿ] *adj.* imprudent; heedless, unwary, fool-hardy; incautious.

impudence [iⁿpüdaⁿs] *f.* impudence; immodesty, shamelessness; cheek. ‖ *impudent* [-aⁿ] *adj.* impudent; immodest, shameless, cheeky, saucy, *Am.* nervy. ‖ *impudeur* [-œr] *f.* shamelessness; lewdness

impuissant [iⁿpüìsaⁿ] *adj.* powerless, helpless, incapable, impotent; ineffective, vain; unavailing.

impulsif [iⁿpülsìf] *adj.** impulsive; impetuous. ‖ *impulsion* [-yoⁿ] *f.* impulse, urge; impetus; stimulus, prompting.

impuni [iⁿpünĭ] *adj.* unpunished. ‖ **impunité** [-té] *f.* impunity.

impur [iⁿpür] *adj.* impure, unclean; tainted; unchaste, lewd. ‖ **impureté** [-té] *f.* impurity, uncleanliness, unchastity, lewdness.

imputer [iⁿpüté] *v.* to impute, to ascribe, to attribute; to charge, to debit, to deduct [compte].

inabordable [inàbòrdàbl] *adj.* unapproachable; prohibitive [prix].

inaccessible [inàksèsìbl] *adj.* inaccessible, unattainable.

inaccoutumé [inàkûtümé] *adj.* unaccustomed; unusual; inhabitual; unwonted.

inachevé [inàshvé] *adj.* unfinished.

inaction [inàksyoⁿ] *f.* inaction; dullness [affaires].

inadapté [inàdàpté] *adj.* misfit.

inadvertance [inàdvèrtaⁿs] *f.* inadvertence, unwariness; oversight.

inamovible [inàmòvìbl] *adj.* permanent, irremovable.

inappréciable [inàprésyàbl] *adj.* inappreciable; invaluable.

inattendu [inàtaⁿdü] *adj.* unexpected; unlooked-for.

inattention [inàtaⁿsyoⁿ] *f.* heedlessness; absent-mindedness; inattention.

inaugurer [inôgüré] *v.* to inaugurate, to open; to institute; to unveil [monument]; to usher in [époque].

incapable [iⁿkàpàbl] *adj.* incapable, unfit; unable; incompetent; unqualified. ‖ **incapacité** [-àsité] *f.* incapacity; inability; incompetency; disability [jur.].

incartade [iⁿkàrtàd] *f.* freak; prank, folly; indiscretion; outburst.

incassable [iⁿkàsàbl] *adj.* unbreakable.

incendie [iⁿsaⁿdĭ] *m.* fire, conflagration; arson. ‖ **incendier** [-yé] *v.* to set fire to.

incertain [iⁿsèrtⁿ] *adj.* uncertain, doubtful, questionable; unreliable; unsettled [temps]. ‖ **incertitude** [-ìtüd] *f.* uncertainty, incertitude; perplexity; suspense; instability; dubiousness; unsettled state [temps].

incessant [iⁿsèsaⁿ] *adj.* unceasing, ceaseless; uninterrupted.

incidence [iⁿsidaⁿs] *f.* incidence.

incident [iⁿsìdaⁿ] *m.* incident, occurrence, happening; difficulty; hitch; mishap; *adj.* incidental; incident.

incision [iⁿsìzyoⁿ] *f.* notch; incision; cutting; lancing (med.); tapping [arbre].

inciter [iⁿsìté] *v.* to incite, to urge on, to egg on; to induce.

inclinaison [iⁿklìnèzoⁿ] *f.* inclination, slope, slant, declivity; list [bateau]; nod [tête]. ‖ **inclination** [-àsyoⁿ] *f.* inclination, bent, cant, propensity; bowing [corps]; nod [tête]; attachment. ‖ **incliner** [-é] *v.* to incline, to cant, to bend; to slope, to tilt, to lean; to list [bateau]; to dip [aiguille]; *s'incliner,* to bow; to bank (aviat.); to heel (naut.); to slant; to slope; to yield, to give in (fig.).

inclure [iⁿklür] *v.** to enclose, to include; to insert (jur.). ‖ **inclusif** [-üzìf] *adj.** inclusive.

incohérence [iⁿkòéraⁿs] *f.* incoherence. ‖ **incohérent** [-raⁿ] *adj.* incoherent.

incolore [iⁿkòlôr] *adj.* colourless.

incomber [iⁿkoⁿbé] *v.* to be incumbent; to devolve (à, upon).

incommode [iⁿkòmòd] *adj.* inconvenient; uncomfortable; unhandy [outil]; troublesome. ‖ **incommoder** [-é] *v.* to inconvenience, to hinder; to disturb, to trouble; to disagree with [nourriture].

incomparable [iⁿkoⁿpàràbl] *adj.* incomparable, unrivalled, peerless.

incompatible [iⁿkoⁿpàtìbl] *adj.* incompatible.

incompétent [iⁿkoⁿpétaⁿ] *adj.* incompetent; unqualified (jur.).

incomplet [iⁿkoⁿplè] *adj.** incomplete, unfinished.

incompréhensible [iⁿkoⁿpréaⁿsìbl] *adj.* incomprehensible, unintelligible. ‖ **incompréhension** [-syoⁿ] *f.* incomprehension.

inconduite [iⁿkoⁿdüìt] *f.* misbehavio(u)r, misconduct (jur.).

inconnu [iⁿkònü] *adj.* unknown, unheard-of; *m.* stranger.

inconscience [iⁿkoⁿsyaⁿs] *f.* unconsciousness. ‖ **inconscient** [-yaⁿ] *m.,* *adj.* unconscious.

inconséquent [iⁿkoⁿsékaⁿ] *adj.* inconsistent, inconsequent.

inconsidéré [iⁿkoⁿsìdéré] *adj.* inconsiderate, thoughtless; unconsidered.

inconsistance [iⁿkoⁿsìstaⁿs] *f.* inconsistency, flabbiness.

inconstant [iⁿkoⁿstaⁿ] *adj.* inconstant, fickle; changeable.

incontestable [iⁿkoⁿtèstàbl] *adj.* incontestable, unquestionable, indisputable; incontrovertible.

inconvenance [iⁿkoⁿvnaⁿs] *f.* unsuitableness, impropriety; indecency. ‖ **inconvenant** [-aⁿ] *adj.* improper, indecorous, unbecoming; indecent.

inconvénient [iⁿkoⁿvényaⁿ] *m.* disadvantage, drawback; inconvenience.

incorporer [iⁿkòrpòré] *v.* to incorporate, to embody; to mix.

incorrect [iⁿkòrèkt] *adj.* incorrect; inaccurate; unbusinesslike. ‖ *incorrigible* [-ìjìbl] *adj.* incorrigible; unamendable.

incrédule [iⁿkrédül] *adj.* incredulous; unbelieving; *m.* unbeliever. ‖ *incroyable* [iⁿkrwàyàbl] *adj.* unbelievable. ‖ *incroyant* [-yaⁿ] *adj.* unbelieving; *m.* unbeliever.

inculpation [iⁿkülpàsyoⁿ] *f.* charge, indictment. ‖ *inculpé* [-é] *m.* accused, defendant. ‖ *inculper* [-é] *v.* to charge, to indict.

inculquer [iⁿkülké] *v.* to inculcate.

inculte [iⁿkült] *adj.* uncultivated, waste; rough.

incursion [iⁿkürsyoⁿ] *f.* inroad, foray, raid, incursion.

indécis [iⁿdésì] *adj.* undecided; vague; blurred; irresolute, wavering. ‖ *indécision* [-zyoⁿ] *f.* irresolution; uncertainty.

indéfini [iⁿdéfinì] *adj.* indefinite; undefined; *passé indéfini*, present perfect (gramm.). ‖ *indéfinissable* [-sàbl] *adj.* undefinable; hard to describe; nondescript.

indéfrisable [iⁿdéfrizàbl] *f.* permanent wave.

indélicat [iⁿdélìkà] *adj.* indelicate, coarse; tactless; dishonest, unscrupulous.

indémaillable [iⁿdémàyàbl] *adj.* ladder-proof, *Am.* non-run, runproof.

indemne [iⁿdèmn] *adj.* undamaged, uninjured, unscathed. ‖ *indemniser* [-ìzé] *v.* to indemnify, to make good. ‖ *indemnité* [-ìté] *f.* indemnity, allowance, grant; *indemnité de chômage*, unemployment benefit.

indéniable [iⁿdényàbl] *adj.* undeniable.

indépendance [iⁿdépaⁿdaⁿs] *f.* independence.

indéréglable [iⁿdéréglabl] *adj.* foolproof; never-failing.

indescriptible [iⁿdèskrìptìbl] *adj.* indescribable.

index [iⁿdèks] *m.* forefinger; index [livre]; pointer; black-list; Index. ‖ *indexer* [-é] *v.* to index; to peg.

indicateur, -trice [iⁿdìkàtœr, -trìs] *adj.* indicatory, indicating; *m.* indicator, gauge, guide; directory; timetable; pointer; informer, police spy. ‖ *indicatif* [-àtìf] *adj.** indicative; indicatory; *m.* call sign [radio]. ‖ *indication* [-àsyoⁿ] *f.* indication; sign, token; mark; declaration (jur.); stage-direc-

tions (theat.). ‖ *indice* [iⁿdìs] *m.* indication, sign; clue; landmark (naut.); index; trace (comm.).

indicible [iⁿdìsìbl] *adj.* unspeakable, inexpressible; unutterable.

indifférence [iⁿdiféraⁿs] *f.* indifference, apathy. ‖ *indifférent* [-aⁿ] *adj.* indifferent; unaffected (à, by); unconcerned; emotionless; unimportant; trifling; inert.

indigence [iⁿdìjaⁿs] *f.* indigence; lack, want.

indigène [iⁿdìjèn] *adj.* indigenous; *m., f.* native.

indigent [iⁿdìjaⁿ] *adj.* indigent, needy; *m.* pauper; *pl.* the poor, the needy, the destitute.

indigeste [iⁿdìjèst] *adj.* indigestible; stodgy. ‖ *indigestion* [-tyoⁿ] *f.* indigestion; surfeit.

indignation [iⁿdìñàsyoⁿ] *f.* indignation. ‖ *indigne* [iⁿdìñ] *adj.* unworthy; undeserving; scandalous, worthless; disqualified, debarred (jur.). ‖ *indigné* [-é] *adj.* indignant. ‖ *indigner* [-é] *v.* to shock; to anger; *s'indigner*, to be indignant. ‖ *indignité* [-ìté] *f.* unworthiness; indignity; vileness; disqualification (jur.).

indiquer [iⁿdìké] *v.* to indicate; to point out; to denote; to appoint; to prescribe; to outline, to sketch; to betoken; to recommend; to denounce.

indirect [iⁿdìrèkt] *adj.* indirect; devious; oblique; circumstantial.

indiscipliné [iⁿdìsìplìné] *adj.* undisciplined, unruly.

indiscret [iⁿdìskrè] *adj.** indiscreet; inquisitive; prying, nosy (fam.); telltale, blabbing (fam.). ‖ *indiscrétion* [-ésyoⁿ] *f.* indiscretion, indiscreetness.

indiscutable [iⁿdìskütàbl] *adj.* indisputable, unquestionable. ‖ *indiscuté* [-té] *adj.* unquestioned; beyond question.

indispensable [iⁿdìspaⁿsàbl] *adj.* indispensable; requisite; vital; staple [nourriture].

indisponible [iⁿdìspònìbl] *adj.* unavailable; entailed (jur.).

indisposer [iⁿdìspòzé] *v.* to indispose, to upset, to disagree with [nourriture]; to antagonize; to disaffect. ‖ *indisposition* [-ìsyoⁿ] *f.* indisposition, upset; illness; disinclination.

indistinct [iⁿdìstiⁿ] *adj.* indistinct; hazy, vague; blurred; dim [lumière].

individu [iⁿdìvìdü] *m.* individual; person; fellow, chap, guy, character, customer (fam.); self. ‖ *individuel* [-üèl] *adj.** individual, personal; private; respective.

indivisible [iⁿdìvìzìbl] *adj.* indivisible.

indolent [ⁱⁿdòlaⁿ] *adj.* indolent, slothful, sluggish.

indolore [ⁱⁿdòlòr] *adj.* painless.

indomptable [ⁱⁿdoⁿtàbl] *adj.* indomitable; untamable; unruly, wayward; unconquerable. ‖ *indompté* [-té] *adj.* untamed; uncontrolled, ungoverned.

indubitable [ⁱⁿdübìtàbl] *adj.* unquestionable, undeniable.

induction [ⁱⁿdüksyoⁿ] *f.* induction. ‖ *induire* [-üⁱr] *v.* to induce; to infer; to imply.

indulgence [ⁱⁿdüljaⁿs] *f.* indulgence, leniency; forbearance. ‖ *indulgent* [-aⁿ] *adj.* indulgent, lenient, condoning, long-suffering.

indûment [ⁱⁿdümaⁿ] *adv.* unduly; improperly.

industrie [ⁱⁿdüstrî] *f.* industry; activity; trade, manufacture; skill, dexterity. ‖ *industriel* [-lèl] *adj.* industrial; manufacturing; *m.* industrialist; manufacturer; mill-owner. ‖ *industrieux* [-ìë] *adj.* industrious, busy; skilful, ingenious.

inébranlable [ⁱnébraⁿlàbl] *adj.* unshakeable, steady, steadfast; unyielding; unflinching.

inédit [ⁱnédì] *adj.* unpublished; unedited; *m.* unpublished material; original matter.

ineffaçable [ⁱnéfàsàbl] *adj.* ineffaceable; ineradicable; indelible.

inefficace [ⁱnéfìkàs] *adj.* ineffective, inefficacious, unavailing. ‖ *inefficacité* [-ìté] *f.* inefficacy; inefficiency.

inégal [ⁱnégàl] *adj.* unequal; uneven; irregular [pouls]; shifting, changeable [vent]; unequable [temperament]; disproportioned (fig.). ‖ *inégalité* [-ìté] *f.* inequality; disparity; unevenness; ruggedness.

inélégant [ⁱnélégaⁿ] *adj.* inelegant.

inéligible [ⁱnélìjìbl] *adj.* ineligible.

inéluctable [ⁱnélüktàbl] *adj.* ineluctable.

inepte [ⁱnèpt] *adj.* inept, stupid, idiotic, fatuous. ‖ *ineptie* [ⁱnèpsî] *f.* ineptness, ineptitude, absurdity.

inépuisable [ⁱnépüìzàbl] *adj.* inexhaustible; never-failing.

inerte [ⁱnèrt] *adj.* inert; inactive; passive. ‖ *inertie* [ⁱnèrsî] *f.* inertia; listlessness.

inespéré [ⁱnèspéré] *adj.* unhoped-for, unexpected.

inestimable [ⁱnèstìmàbl] *adj.* inestimable, invaluable.

inévitable [ⁱnévìtàbl] *adj.* inevitable, unavoidable.

inexact [ⁱnègzàkt] *adj.* inexact, inaccurate; unpunctual. ‖ *inexactitude*

[-ìtüd] *f.* inaccuracy, inexactitude; unpunctuality; unreliability.

inexpérience [ⁱnèkspéryaⁿs] *f.* inexperience. ‖ *inexpérimenté* [-ìmaⁿté] *adj.* inexperienced, unpractised; untried, untested. ‖ *inexpert* [ⁱnèkspèr] *adj.* inexpert.

inexplicable [ⁱnèksplìkàbl] *adj.* inexplicable, unexplainable, unaccountable. ‖ *inexpliqué* [-ké] *adj.* unexplained, unaccounted for.

inexprimable [ⁱnèksprìmàbl] *adj.* inexpressible; unspeakable.

infaillible [ⁱⁿfàyìbl] *adj.* infallible.

infaisable [ⁱⁿfᵉzàbl] *adj.* unfeasible.

infâme [ⁱⁿfâm] *adj.* infamous; vile, squalid. ‖ *infamie* [-àmî] *f.* infamy; ignominy; infamous deed (or) expression.

infanterie [ⁱⁿfaⁿtrî] *f.* infantry.

infatigable [ⁱⁿfàtìgàbl] *adj.* indefatigable, tireless.

infect [ⁱⁿfèkt] *adj.* stinking; noisome; filthy. ‖ *infecter* [-é] *v.* to infect, to contaminate; to pollute; to stink.

inférieur [ⁱⁿféryœr] *adj.* inferior; lower, nether; subordinate; *m.* inferior, underling, subaltern, subordinate. ‖ *infériorité* [-yòrìté] *f.* inferiority.

infernal [ⁱⁿfèrnàl] *adj.* infernal; hellish; diabolical, devilish.

infester [ⁱⁿfèsté] *v.* to infest.

infidèle [ⁱⁿfìdèl] *adj.* unfaithful; faithless, misleading; infidel, heathen; unbelieving; *m.* infidel, unbeliever. ‖ *infidélité* [-élìté] *f.* infidelity; faithlessness, unfaithfulness; inaccuracy; unbelief; unfaithful act.

infini [ⁱⁿfìnî] *adj.* infinite; endless; *m.* infinity, infinite. ‖ *infinité* [-té] *f.* infinity; great number.

infirme [ⁱⁿfìrm] *adj.* infirm; disabled, crippled; *m., f.* invalid, cripple. ‖ *infirmerie* [-rî] *f.* infirmary; sickward, sick-room; sick-bay (naut.). ‖ *infirmier* [-yé] *m.* attendant; male nurse; ambulance man; orderly (mil.). ‖ *infirmière* [-yèr] *f.* nurse; attendant. ‖ *infirmité* [-ìté] *f.* infirmity, disability; frailty (fig.).

inflammation [ⁱⁿflàmàsyoⁿ] *f.* inflammation.

inflation [ⁱⁿflàsyoⁿ] *f.* inflation.

inflexible [ⁱⁿflèksìbl] *adj.* inflexible, unbending; unyielding.

inflexion [ⁱⁿflèksyoⁿ] *f.* inflexion; modulation [voix].

infliger [ⁱⁿflìjé] *v.* to inflict.

influence [ⁱⁿflüaⁿs] *f.* influence; ascendancy. ‖ *influent* [-üaⁿ] *adj.* influential; powerful.

influenza [iⁿflüaⁿzà] f. influenza, flu (fam.).

influer [iⁿflüé] v. to influence; to affect; to exert influence.

informateur, -trice [iⁿfòrmàtær, -trìs] s. informant, informer. ‖ **information** [iⁿfòrmàsyoⁿ] f. information; inquiry; investigation; pl. news items, Am. new coverage [presse]; Br. news, Am. newcast [radio].

informe [iⁿfòrm] adj. unformed; shapeless; unshapely; informal; irregular (jur.).

informer [iⁿfòrmé] v. to inform; to notify; to investigate, to inquire (jur.); s'informer, to inquire; to ask about.

infortune [iⁿfòrtün] f. misfortune. ‖ **infortuné** [-é] adj. unfortunate, unlucky, luckless, hapless.

infroissable [iⁿfrwàsàbl] adj. uncreasable, wrinkle-proof.

infructueux [iⁿfrüktüë] adj.* unfruitful, unfructuous; unsuccessful; unavailing; fruitless.

infuser [iⁿfüzé] v. to infuse; to instil; to steep [thé]; infusion, infusion, steeping.

ingénieur [iⁿjényær] m. engineer; ingénieur du son, Br. monitor man, Am. sound man. ‖ **ingénieux** [-yë] adj.* ingenious. ‖ **ingéniosité** [-yò-zìté] f. ingenuity.

ingénu [iⁿjénü] adj. ingenuous, artless, unsophisticated. ‖ **ingénue** [-ü] f. artless girl; ingénue (theat.). ‖ **ingénuité** [-ìté] f. ingenuousness.

ingrat [iⁿgrà] adj. ungrateful, thankless; unproductive; unpleasing; repellent [travail]; plain [visage]. ‖ **ingratitude** [-tìtüd] f. ingratitude, thanklessness.

ingrédient [iⁿgrédyaⁿ] m. ingredient; constituent.

inguérissable [iⁿgérisabl] adj. incurable; inconsolable.

ingurgiter [iⁿgürjìté] v. to ingurgitate; to swallow; to wolf.

inhabile [inàbìl] adj. unskilful, inexpert; incompetent (jur.).

inhabitable [inàbìtàbl] adj. uninhabitable; untenantable.

inhabitué [inàbìtüé] adj. unaccustomed, unhabituated. ‖ **inhabituel** [-èl] adj.* unusual.

inhérent [inéraⁿ] adj. inherent, intrinsic.

inhumain [inümiⁿ] adj. inhuman.

inhumer [inümé] v. to bury, to inter, to inhume.

inimitié [inìmìtyé] f. enmity, hostility; unfriendliness.

iniquité [inìkìté] f. iniquity.

initial [inìsyàl] adj.* initial; starting [prix]. ‖ **initiale** [-yàl] f. initial [lettre]. ‖ **initiative** [inìsyàtìv] f. initiative. ‖ **initier** [-yé] v. to initiate.

injecter [iⁿjèkté] v. to inject; injecté de sang, bloodshot, congested. ‖ **injection** [-èksyoⁿ] f. injection; enema, douche (med.).

injonction [iⁿjoⁿksyoⁿ] f. injunction, order.

injure [iⁿjür] f. insult, offense; injury; pl. abuse. ‖ **injurier** [-yé] v. to insult, to abuse; to call (someone) names; to revile. ‖ **injurieux** [-yë] adj.* insulting, abusive, injurious, offensive.

injuste [iⁿjüst] adj. unjust, unfair. ‖ **injustice** [-tìs] f. injustice; unfair action. ‖ **injustifiable** [-tìfyàbl] adj. unjustifiable. ‖ **injustifié** [-tìfyé] adj. unjustified.

inlassable [iⁿlàsàbl] adj. untiring; tireless, indefatigable.

inné [inné] adj. innate, inborn.

innocence [inòsaⁿs] f. innocence; guiltlessness; harmlessness; artlessness, guilelessness. ‖ **innocenter** [-aⁿté] v. to absolve; to justify.

innombrable [innoⁿbràbl] adj. innumerable, numberless.

innovation [innòvàsyoⁿ] f. innovation; novelty.

inoffensif [inòfaⁿsìf] adj.* inoffensive; innocuous.

inondation [inoⁿdàsyoⁿ] f. inundation. ‖ **inonder** [-é] v. to flood; to overwhelm; to overflow; to glut [marché].

inopiné [inòpìné] adj. unexpected, unlooked for.

inopportun [inòpòrtuⁿ] adj. inopportune; untimely.

inoubliable [inübliàbl] adj. unforgettable.

inouï [inwì] adj. unheard-of.

inoxydable [inòksìdàbl] adj. rustproof; stainless [métal].

inquiet [iⁿkyè] adj.* anxious, uneasy, apprehensive; disturbed; upset; agitated. ‖ **inquiéter** [-yété] v. to disturb, to trouble, to alarm; to make anxious or uneasy; s'inquiéter, to be anxious, to worry; to be concerned (de, about). ‖ **inquiétude** [-yétüd] f. anxiety, concern, apprehension, uneasiness.

inquisition [iⁿkìzìsyoⁿ] f. inquisition; inquiry.

insaisissable [iⁿsèzìsàbl] adj. unseizable, imperceptible; not attachable (jur.); elusive, slippery.

insalubre [iⁿsàlübr] unhealthy; insanitary.

insatiable [iⁿsàsyàbl] adj. insatiable.

inscription [iⁿskrìpsyoⁿ] *f.* inscription; registration, entry, matriculation; enrolment; conscription (naut.). ‖ *inscrire* [-îr] *v.* to inscribe, to write down; to enter, to enroll; *s'inscrire*, to register.

insecte [iⁿsèkt] *m.* insect; bug (fam.). ‖ *insecticide* [-ìsìd] *m., adj.* insecticide.

insensé [iⁿsaⁿsé] *adj.* mad, insane; senseless, extravagant; *m.* madman.

insensibilisation [iⁿsaⁿsìbìlìzàsyoⁿ] *f.* anaesthetization. ‖ *insensibiliser* [-zé] *v.* to anaesthetize. ‖ *insensibilité* [-té] *f.* insensibility; insensitiveness. ‖ *insensible* [iⁿsaⁿsìbl] *adj.* insensible; insensitive; unfeeling; indifferent; unconscious; imperceptible; unaffected (à, by).

inséparable [iⁿsépàràbl] *adj.* inseparable.

insérer [iⁿséré] *v.* to insert; to wedge in, to sandwich in.

insigne [iⁿsìñ] *adj.* signal; notorious, arrant; *m.* badge, emblem; *pl.* insignia.

insignifiant [iⁿsìñìfyaⁿ] *adj.* insignificant; trifling, nominal [somme]; vacuous [visage].

insinuer [iⁿsìnüé] *v.* to insinuate, to hint, to suggest, to imply; to insert (med.); *s'insinuer*, to insinuate oneself; to worm one's way.

insipide [iⁿsìpìd] *adj.* insipid, tasteless; flat; uninteresting.

insistance [iⁿsìstaⁿs] *f.* insistence. ‖ *insister* [-é] *v.* to insist; to persist; to stress; *n'insistez pas*, don't keep on.

insolation [iⁿsòlàsyoⁿ] *f.* sunstroke.

insolence [iⁿsòlaⁿs] *f.* insolence, pertness, incivility; insolent remark. ‖ *insolent* [-aⁿ] *adj.* insolent, pert; saucy, cheeky; *Am.* nervy; *m.* insolent person.

insolvable [iⁿsòlvàbl] *adj.* insolvent.

insomnie [iⁿsòmnî] *f.* sleeplessness, insomnia.

insonorisation [iⁿsònòrìzàsyoⁿ] *f,* sound-proofing.

insouciance [iⁿsûsyaⁿs] *f.* unconcern, jauntiness; carelessness; heedlessness. ‖ *insouciant* [-yaⁿ] *adj.* carefree, jaunty; careless, thoughtless.

insoumis [iⁿsûmî] *adj.* unsubdued; refractory, unruly; insubordinate; *m.* absentee, *Am.* draft-dodger.

insoutenable [iⁿsûtnàbl] *adj.* untenable; indefensible; unbearable.

inspecter [iⁿspèkté] *v.* to inspect; to survey. ‖ *inspecteur, -trice* [-œr, -trìs] *m., f.* inspector; *m.;* inspectress, *f.;* surveyor; overseer; *Br.* shop-walker, *Am.* floor-walker. ‖ *inspection* [-syoⁿ] *f.* inspection; inspectorship.

inspiration [iⁿspìràsyoⁿ] *f.* inspiration; prompting.

instable [iⁿstàbl] *adj.* unstable; unsteady, rickety.

installer [iⁿstàlé] *v.* to install; to fit up; to settle; to induct [officier]; to stow (naut.); *s'installer*, to take up one's abode; to set up.

instamment [iⁿstàmaⁿ] *adv.* insistently, urgently.

instance [iⁿstaⁿs] *f.* instancy, entreaty; immediacy; suit (jur.). ‖ *instant* [-aⁿ] *m.* instant; jiffy (fam.). ‖ *instantané* [-aⁿtàné] *adj.* instantaneous; *m.* snapshot [photo]. ‖ *instantanéité* [-néìté] *f.* instantaneousness. ‖ *instantanément* [-némaⁿ] *adv.* immediately, at once.

instigation [iⁿstìgàsyoⁿ] *f.* instigation; inducement.

instinct [iⁿstîⁿ] *m.* instinct. ‖ *instinctif* [-ktìf] *adj.* instinctive.

instituer [iⁿstìtüé] *v.* to institute; to found; to appoint; to initiate (jur.). ‖ *instituteur, -trice* [-ütœr, -trìs] *m., f.* schoolteacher, *m., f.;* schoolmistress, *f.;* tutor, *m.;* governess, *f.*

instruction [iⁿstrüksyoⁿ] *f.* instruction, tuition, schooling, education; knowledge; training (mil.); direction; investigation (jur.). ‖ *instruire* [iⁿstrüîr] *v.* to instruct, to teach; to inform; to train, to drill (milit.); to investigate, to examine (jur.); *s'instruire*, to learn, to educate oneself, to improve one's mind.

instrument [iⁿstrümaⁿ] *m.* instrument; implement, tool; agent; document; *instrumentiste*, instrumentalist.

insu [iⁿsü] *m.* unawareness; *à l'insu de*, without the knowledge of; *à mon insu*, unknown to me.

insuffisant [iⁿsüfìzaⁿ] *adj.* insufficient, deficient, inefficient.

insulaire [iⁿsülèr] *adj.* insular; *s.* islander.

insulte [iⁿsült] *f.* insult; taunt, jibe; abuse. ‖ *insulter* [-é] *v.* to insult; to revile, to abuse; to jeer at, to jibe at.

insupportable [iⁿsüpòrtàbl] *adj.* unbearable, unendurable; insufferable; provoking.

insurgé [iⁿsürjé] *m., adj.* insurgent. ‖ *insurger (s')* [siⁿsürjé] *v.* to revolt, to rebel, to rise.

insurmontable [iⁿsürmoⁿtàbl] *adj.* insuperable; unconquerable; unsurmountable.

insurrection [iⁿsürèksyoⁿ] *f.* insurrection, rising; uprising. ‖ *insurrectionnel* [-ònèl] *adj.* insurrectional, insurrectionary.

intact [iⁿtàkt] *adj.* intact; untouched, undamaged, unscathed; unblemished [réputation].

intarissable [iⁿtàrìsàbl] *adj.* inexhaustible; perennial [source]; long-winded (fam.).

intégral [iⁿtégràl] *adj.** integral, whole; unexpurgated [texte].

intègre [iⁿtègr] *adj.* upright, honest; incorruptible. ‖ **intégrité** [-égrìté] *f.* integrity; entirety.

intellectuel [iⁿtèllèktüèl] *m.*, *adj.** intellectual.

intelligence [iⁿtèllìjaⁿs] *f.* understanding, intelligence, intellect; agreement, terms; *d'intelligence avec*, in collusion with, *Am.* in cahoots with. ‖ **intelligent** [-aⁿ] *adj.* intelligent; clever, shrewd, brainy (fam.). ‖ **intelligibilité** [-ìbìlìté] *f.* intelligibility. ‖ **intelligible** [-ìbl] *adj.* intelligible; understandable; audible.

intempérance [iⁿtaⁿpéraⁿs] *f.* intemperance; insobriety.

intempéries [iⁿtaⁿpérì] *f. pl.* bad weather.

intempestif [iⁿtaⁿpèstìf] *adj.** untimely, ill-timed, unseasonable.

intendance [iⁿtaⁿdaⁿs] *f.* intendance, stewardship; managership; commissariat (milit.); office [lycée]. ‖ **intendant** [-aⁿ] *m.* intendant; steward; paymaster (naut.); commissariat officer (milit.).

intense [iⁿtaⁿs] *adj.* intense; loud [bruit]; heavy [canonnade]; intensive [propagande]; deep [couleur]; high [fièvre]; strong [courant]; bitter [froid]; strenuous [vie]. ‖ **intensifier** [-ìfyé] *v.* to intensify. ‖ **intensité** [-ìté] *f.* intensity, intenseness; force [vent]; brilliancy [lumière]; depth [couleur]; bitterness [froid].

intenter [iⁿtaⁿté] *v.* to bring, to initiate (jur.). ‖ **intention** [iⁿtaⁿsyoⁿ] *f.* intention, intent, purpose; meaning, drift; wish; *avoir l'intention de*, to intend, to mean. ‖ **intentionné** [-yòné] *adj.* disposed. ‖ **intentionnel** [-yònèl] *adj.** intentional, deliberate.

intercéder [iⁿtèrsédé] *v.* to intercede, to mediate.

intercepter [iⁿtèrsèpté] *v.* to intercept; to shut out; to tap.

intercession [iⁿtèrsèsyoⁿ] *f.* intercession, mediation.

interdiction [iⁿtèrdìksyoⁿ] *f.* interdiction; prohibition, forbidding; suspension; banishment. ‖ **interdire** [-ìr] *v.** to interdict, to veto, to prohibit, to forbid; to bewilder, to dumbfound. ‖ **interdit** [-ì] *adj.* forbidden, prohibited; out of bounds, *Am.* off limits (mil.); non-plussed, abashed, dumbfounded; *m.* interdict (jur.; eccles.); *sens interdit*, no thoroughfare.

intéressant [iⁿtérèsaⁿ] *adj.* interesting; advantageous, attractive [prix]. ‖ **intéressé** [-é] *adj.* interested; concerned; self-seeking; stingy; *m.* interested party. ‖ **intéresser** [-é] *v.* to interest; to concern; to attract, to be interesting to; *s'intéresser*, to become interested, to take an interest (*à*, in). ‖ **intérêt** [-è] *m.* interest; share, stake; benefit; concern; self-interest; *par intérêt*, out of selfishness; *sans intérêt*, uninteresting.

intérieur [iⁿtéryœr] *m.* interior, inside; home; inner nature; *adj.* interior, inner; inward; domestic; inland (naut.).

interlocuteur [iⁿtèrlòkütœr] *m.* interlocutor. ‖ **interlocutrice** [-trìs] *f.* interlocutress.

intermède [iⁿtèrmèd] *m.* interlude.

intermédiaire [iⁿtèrmédyèr] *adj.* intermediate; *m.* intermediary, go-between, neutral; middleman (comm.); medium.

interminable [iⁿtèrmìnàbl] *adj.* interminable, endless, never-ending.

intermittent [iⁿtèrmìtaⁿt] *adj.* intermittent; irregular; alternating.

internat [iⁿtèrnà] *m.* living-in; boarding-in [école]; boarding-school; internship (med.); boarders.

international [iⁿtèrnàsyòⁿàl] *adj.** international.

interne [iⁿtèrn] *adj.* internal, inner; resident; *m.* boarder; resident; intern (med.). ‖ **interner** [-é] *v.* to intern; to confine; *interné*, internee.

interpeller [iⁿtèrpèlé] *v.* to interpellate; to question; to summon to answer (jur.).

interposer [iⁿtèrpòzé] *v.* to interpose.

interprétation [iⁿtèrprétasyoⁿ] *f.* interpretation, interpreting; rendering; reading. ‖ **interprète** [-èt] *m.*, *f.* interpreter; translator; expositor. ‖ **interpréter** [-été] *v.* to interpret; to translate; to render; to expound.

interrogateur, -trice [iⁿtèrògàtœr, -trìs] *adj.* interrogative; questioning; *m.*, *f.* questioner, interrogator; examiner. ‖ **interrogatif** [-tìf] *adj.** interrogative. ‖ **interrogation** [-syoⁿ] *f.* interrogation, questioning. ‖ **interrogatoire** [-wàr] *m.* interrogation, examination (jur.); questioning (mil.). ‖ **interroger** [iⁿtèròjé] *v.* to interrogate, to question, to examine.

interrompre [iⁿtèroⁿpr] *v.* to interrupt; to stop, to suspend; to break [voyage]; to cut in, to break in [conversation]. ‖ **interrupteur, -trice** [-üptœr, -trìs] *adj.* interrupting; *m.* interrupter; switch, contact-breaker, circuit-breaker (electr.); cut-out (electr.). ‖ **interruption** [-üpsyoⁿ] *f.*

interruption; stopping; severance [communication]; breaking in [conversation]; breaking off (electr.); stoppage [travail].

intersection [iⁿtèrsèksyoⁿ] *f.* intersection; crossing.

interurbain [iⁿtèrürbⁱⁿ] *adj.* interurban; *m.* interurban; *Am.* long distance, *Br.* trunk line [téléph.].

intervalle [iⁿtèrvàl] *m.* interval; distance; period [temps]; *par intervalles,* off and on; *dans l'intervalle,* in the meantime.

intervenir [iⁿtèrvⁿîr] *v.* to intervene; to interfere; to occur.

intervertir [iⁿtèrvèrtîr] *v.* to invert, to reverse, to transpose.

intestin [iⁿtèstⁿ] *m.* intestine; bowel; gut; *adj.* internal; domestic; civil; intestine.

intime [iⁿtⁱm] *adj.* intimate, close, inward; private; secret; *m.* familiar, close friend, intimate.

intimer [iⁿtⁱmé] *v.* to intimate; to notify; to summons (jur.).

intimider [iⁿtⁱmⁱdé] *v.* to intimidate, to cow; to browbeat, to bully.

intimité [iⁿtⁱmⁱté] *f.* intimacy, closeness; familiarity; *dans l'intimité,* in private.

intituler [iⁿtⁱtülé] *v.* to entitle; *s'intituler,* to style oneself.

intolérable [iⁿtòléràbl] *adj.* intolerable, unbearable. ‖ **intolérance** [-àⁿs] *f.* intolerance; illiberality.

intonation [iⁿtònàsyoⁿ] *f.* intonation; pitch, ring [voix].

intoxication [iⁿtòksîkàsyoⁿ] *f.* poisoning. ‖ **intoxiquer** [-é] *v.* to poison.

intransigeant [iⁿtraⁿzìjaⁿ] *adj.* intransigent, uncompromising, unbending; peremptory.

intrépide [iⁿtrépîd] *adj.* intrepid, fearless.

intrigue [iⁿtrîg] *f.* intrigue; plot; love-affair; lobbyism; underhand manœuvres. ‖ **intriguer** [-îgé] *v.* to puzzle; to intrigue; to scheme, to plot; to elaborate.

introduction [iⁿtròdüksyoⁿ] *f.* introduction, introducing; presentation; admission (mech.); foreword. ‖ **introduire** [-üîr] *v.* to introduce; to usher; to lead in; to show in; to admit (mech.); *s'introduire,* to get in.

introuvable [iⁿtrûvàbl] *adj.* undiscoverable; unobtainable.

intrus [iⁿtrü] *adj.* intruding; *m.* intruder.

intuition [iⁿtüïsyoⁿ] *f.* intuition.

inusable [inüzàbl] *adj.* indestructible; everlasting; long-wearing.

inusité [inüzîté] *adj.* unusual; obsolete; little used.

inutile [inütîl] *adj.* useless, unavailing, fruitless, unprofitable; needless. ‖ **inutilisable** [-ìzàbl] *adj.* unusable. ‖ **inutilisé** [-ìzé] *adj.* unused; untapped [ressources]. ‖ **inutilité** [-ìté] *f.* uselessness, inutility; unprofitableness; fruitlessness.

invalide [iⁿvàlîd] *adj.* invalid, infirm; disabled; rickety [meuble]; null and void (jur.); *m.* invalid; disabled soldier; pensioner. ‖ **invalider** [-é] *v.* to invalidate; to nullify; to quash [élection]. ‖ **invalidité** [-ìté] *f.* invalidism; disability; nullity (jur.).

invariable [iⁿvàryàbl] *adj.* invariable, unvarying, unchanging.

invasion [iⁿvàzyoⁿ] *f.* invasion.

invective [iⁿvèktîv] *f.* invective; abuse. ‖ **invectiver** [iⁿvèktîvé] *v.* to rail; to abuse.

invendable [iⁿvaⁿdàbl] *adj.* unsaleable. ‖ **invendu** [-ü] *adj.* unsold; *m.* left over.

inventaire [iⁿvaⁿtèr] *m.* inventory, stock-taking; list, schedule; *faire l'inventaire,* to take stock.

inventer [iⁿvaⁿté] *v.* to invent; to discover; to contrive; to make up [histoire]; to coin [phrase]. ‖ **inventeur, -trice** [-ær, -trîs] *m.*, *f.* inventor, discoverer; contriver; finder (jur.); *adj.* inventive. ‖ **inventif** [-ìf] *adj.* inventive. ‖ **invention** [iⁿvaⁿsyoⁿ] *f.* invention, contriving, devising; inventiveness, discovery; coining; fib.

inventorier [iⁿvaⁿtòryé] *v.* to enter on an inventory; to take stock of.

inverse [iⁿvèrs] *adj.* inverted, inverse, contrary; reverse. ‖ **inverser** [-sé] *v.* to invert; to reverse.

investigateur, -trice [iⁿvèstîgàtær, -trîs] *m.*, *f.* investigator, inquirer; *adj.* investigating, searching [regard].

investir [iⁿvèstîr] *v.* to invest; to entrust; to blockade (mil.).

invétéré [iⁿvétéré] *adj.* inveterate.

invisible [iⁿvîzîbl] *adj.* invisible.

invitation [iⁿvîtàsyoⁿ] *f.* invitation; request. ‖ **invité** [-é] *adj.* invited, bidden; *m.* guest. ‖ **inviter** [-é] *v.* to invite; to request; to incite.

involontaire [iⁿvòloⁿtèr] *adj.* involuntary; unintentional.

invoquer [iⁿvòké] *v.* to invoke; to call forth [upon]; to refer to (jur.).

invraisemblable [iⁿvrèsaⁿblàbl] *adj.* unlikely, implausible, tall.

iode [yòd] *m.* iodine.

ion [yoⁿ] *m.* ion.

irai [ìré] *future of aller.*

iris [ìrìs] *m.* iris; flag (bot.).

irlandais [ìrlɑⁿdè] *adj.* Irish; *m.* Irishman. || *Irlande* [-ɑⁿd] *f.* Ireland, Eire.

ironie [ìrònì] *f.* irony. || *ironique* [-ìk] *adj.* ironical.

irréalisable [ìrréàlìzàbl] *adj.* unrealizable; impossible.

irrecevable [ìrrᵉsᵉvàbl] *adj.* inadmissible; inacceptable.

irrécupérable [ìrréküpéràbl] *adj.* irretrievable.

irrécusable [ìrréküzàbl] *adj.* unimpeachable; unchallengeable (jur.).

irréel [ìrréèl] *adj.** unreal.

irréfléchi [ìrréfléshì] *adj.* unconsiddered, thoughtless; inconsiderate. || *irréflexion* [-flèksyoⁿ] *f.* thoughtlessness.

irrégularité [ìrrégülàrìté] *f.* irregularity. || *irrégulier* [-lyé] *adj.** irregular; anomalous; erratic [pouls]; broken [sommeil].

irrémédiable [ìrrémédyàbl] *adj.* irremediable; incurable.

irréparable [ìrrépàràbl] *adj.* irreparable; irretrievable.

irréprochable [ìrrépròshàbl] *adj.* irreproachable; blameless; unimpeachable [témoin].

irrésolu [ìrrézòlü] *adj.* irresolute; unsolved [problème].

irrespectueux [ìrrèspèktüë] *adj.** disrespectful, uncivil.

irrespirable [ìrrèspìràbl]. *adj.* unbreathable, irrespirable.

irresponsabilité [ìrrèspoⁿsàbìlìté] *f.* irresponsibility. || *irresponsable* [-àbl] *adj.* irresponsible.

irrigation [ìrrìgàsyoⁿ] *f.* irrigation; flooding.

irritable [ìrrìtàbl] *adj.* irritable; sensitive [peau]; peevish. || *irritation* [-àsyoⁿ] *f.* irritation; inflammation (med.). || *irriter* [-é] *v.* to irritate; to provoke; to vex; to inflame (med.).

irruption [ìrrüpsyoⁿ] *f.* irruption; raid; inrush.

islandais [ìslɑⁿdè] *adj.* Icelandic; *s.* Icelander. || *Islande* [-lɑⁿd] *f.* Iceland.

isolant [ìzòlɑⁿ] *isolateur*, *-trice* [-àtœr, -trìs] *adj.* insulating; *m.* insulator. || *isolement* [-mɑⁿ] *m.* isolation, loneliness; insulation (electr.). || *isoler* [-é] *v.* to isolate; to segregate; to insulate (electr.). || *isoloir* [-wàr] *m.* insulator; polling-booth.

Israël [ìsraèl] *m.* Israel. || *israélien* [-élyⁱⁿ] *adj.*, *s.* Israeli. || *israélite* [-élìt] *adj.*, *s.* Israelite.

issu [ìsü] *adj.* born; sprung (*de*, from). || *issue* [-ü] *f.* issue, end; upshot, result; outlet, egress; *pl.* offal.

isthme [ìsm] *m.* isthmus.

italique [ìtàlìk] *m.*, *adj.* italic.

itinéraire [ìtìnérèr] *m.* itinerary, route; guide-book.

ivoire [ìvwàr] *f.* ivory.

ivre [ìvr] *adj.* drunk, intoxicated, inebriated; tipsy (fam.). || *ivresse* [ìvrès] *f.* intoxication; drunkenness, inebriation; rapture, ecstasy (fig.). || *ivrogne, -esse* [-òñ, -ès] *m.*, *f.* drunkard, tippler, toper; boozer, sot (pop.). || *ivrognerie* [-òñrî] *f.* wine-bibbing.

J

jabot [jàbò] *m.* crop [oiseau]; frill, jabot [chemise].

jacasser [jàkàsé] *v.* to chatter; *Am.* to yak.

jachère [jàshèr] *f.* fallow.

jacinthe [jàsiⁿt] *f.* hyacinth; bluebell.

jade [jàd] *m.* jade.

jadis [jàdìs] *adv.* formerly, of old.

jaguar [jàgwàr] *m.* jaguar.

jaillir [jàyîr] *v.* to gush, to spurt out; to shoot forth; to fly [étincelles]; to flash [lumière]. || *jaillissement* [-yìsmɑⁿ] *m.* gushing, spouting; jet; springing forth; flash.

jais [jè] *m.* jet.

jalon [jàloⁿ] *m.* surveying-staff; range-pole; landmark; aiming-post, alignment picket (milit.). || *jalonner* [-òné] *v.* to stake out, to mark out.

jalouser [jàlûzé] *v.* to envy. || *jalousie* [jàlûzî] *f.* jealousy; venetian-blind, sun-blind. || *jaloux* [-û] *adj.**, *s.* jealous; envious; unsafe.

jamais [jàmè] *adv.* ever; never; *ne...jamais*, never, not ever; *à jamais*, forever.

jambage [jɑⁿbàj] *m.* jamb [porte]; post [fenêtre]; cheek [cheminée]; down-stroke, pot-hook [écriture].

jambe [jɑⁿb] *f.* leg; shank; stone pier [maçonnerie]; stay-rod [auto]. || *jambière* [-yèr] *f.* legging; leg-guard; greave (arch.). || *jambon* [-oⁿ] *m.* ham. || *jambonneau* [-òñò] *m.** ham knuckle, small ham.

jante [jɑⁿt] *f.* felloe, felly [roue]; rim (auto).

janvier [jaⁿvyé] *m.* January.

japper [jàpé] *v.* to yelp, to yap.

jaquette [jàkèt] *f.* morning coat, tail-coat [homme]; jacket [dame].

jardin [jàrdiⁿ] *m.* garden; park; *pl.* grounds. ‖ *jardinage* [-inàj] *m.* gardening; garden-produce. ‖ *jardinier* [-inyé] *m.* gardener. ‖ *jardinière* [-inyèr] *f.* gardener; flower stand; spring cart; mixed vegetables.

jargon [jàrgoⁿ] *m.* jargon, lingo; gibberish.

jarre [jàr] *f.* earthenware jar.

jarret [jàrè] *m.* hock, ham, hamstring, hough; shin [bœuf]. ‖ *jarretelle* [-tèl] *f.* stocking suspender, garter. ‖ *jarretière* [-tyèr] *f.* garter; sling [fusil].

jars [jàr] *m.* gander.

jaser [jàzé] *v.* to chatter, to gossip, to prattle, to babble; to blab (fam.); to chat. ‖ *jaseur* [-œr] *adj.* talkative.

jasmin [jàsmiⁿ] *m.* jasmine.

jaspe [jàsp] *m.* jasper.

jatte [jàt] *f.* flat bowl.

jauge [jôj] *f.* gauge; gauging-rod; tonnage, burden (naut.); *Br.* petrol-gauge, *Am.* gasoline-gauge [auto]; trench [horticulture]. ‖ *jauger* [-é] *v.* to gauge, to measure; to size up.

jaunâtre [jônàtr] *adj.* yellowish, sallow.

jaune [jôn] *adj.* yellow; *m.* yellow; yolk [œuf]; strikebreaker, scab, *Br.* blackleg [grève]; *rire jaune,* to give a sickly smile. ‖ *jaunir* [-îr] *v.* to yellow; to turn yellow. ‖ *jaunisse* [-ìs] *f.* jaundice.

javelle [jàvèl] *f.* swath.

javelliser [jàvèlìzé] *v.* to chlorinate.

je [jᵉ] *pron.* I.

jeannette [jànèt] *f.* sleeve-board [repassage].

jet [jè] *m.* throw, cast; jet, gush, spurt [liquide]; flash [lumière]; casting [métal]; jetsam (naut.; jur.); shoot, sprout (bot.); *armes de jet,* projectile weapons; *jet d'eau,* fountain, spray; *du premier jet,* at the first try. ‖ *jetée* [jᵉté] *f.* jetty, pier; mole, breakwater. ‖ *jeter* [-é] *v.* to throw, to fling, to cast, to toss; to hurl; to throw away, to cast down; to let go; to drop [ancre]; to utter [cri]; to lay [fondements]; to jettison (naut.); to discharge (med.); *se jeter,* to throw oneself, to jump, to plunge; to pounce (*sur,* on); to rush; to flow, to empty [rivière]. ‖ *jeton* [-oⁿ] *m.* token, tally, mark; counter; *jeton de téléphone,* telephone token, *Am.* slug (fam.).

jeu [jë] *m.** play; sport; game, pastime; fun, frolic; acting [acteur]; execution, playing [musicien]; gambling, gaming; set [échecs]; pack, *Am.* deck [cartes]; stop [orgue]; action, activity (fig.); working (mech.); *jeu de mots,* pun; *franc jeu,* fair play.

jeudi [jëdì] *m.* Thursday; *jeudi saint,* Maundy Thursday.

jeun (à) [àjuⁿ] *adv. phr.* fasting; on an empty stomach.

jeune [jœn] *adj.* young; youthful; juvenile; younger, junior; recent; new; early, unripe, green; immature; *m., f.* young person; *jeune fille,* girl, young lady; *jeune homme,* youngster, youth, stripling; lad; *jeunes gens,* young people; young men; youth.

jeûne [jën] *m.* fast, fasting, abstinence. ‖ *jeûner* [-é] *v.* to fast, to abstain.

jeunesse [jœnès] *f.* youth, young days; boyhood, girlhood; young people; youthfulness, freshness, prime; newness [vin]. ‖ *jeunet* [jœnè] *adj.** youngish, rather young.

joaillerie [jòàyᵉrì] *f.* jewellery, *Am.* jewelry. ‖ *joaillier* [-yé] *m.* jeweller, *Am.* jeweler.

joie [jwà] *f.* joy, delight, gladness, elation; gaiety, mirth, merriment, glee; exhilaration.

joindre [jwiⁿdr] *v.** to join; to link; to unite, to combine; to bring together; to adjoin; to enclose [enveloppe]; to clasp [mains]; *se joindre,* to join, to unite; to adjoin. ‖ *joint* [jwiⁿ] *adj., p. p., see joindre; m.* joint, join, junction, coupling; seam (metall.); packing (mech.); *pièces jointes,* enclosures. ‖ *jointure* [-tür] *f.* joint; articulation; knuckle [doigt].

joli [jòlì] *adj.* pretty; good-looking; nice; attractive; piquant, nice, fine [ironique]. ‖ *joliesse* [-lyès] *f.* prettiness.

jonc [joⁿ] *m.* rush; cane, rattan; guard ring [bijou]; © wedding ring.

joncher [joⁿshé] *v.* to strew, to litter.

jonction [joⁿksyoⁿ] *f.* junction, joining; meeting; connector (electr.).

jongler [joⁿglé] *v.* to juggle. ‖ *jongleur* [-œr] *m.* juggler; trickster.

jonque [joⁿk] *f.* junk [bateau].

jonquille [joⁿkìy] *f.* jonquil.

joue [jû] *f.* cheek; *coucher en joue,* to aim at.

jouer [jwé] *v.* to play; to toy, to trifle; to speculate, to gamble; to stake; to act, to perform, to show (theat.); to feign; to warp, to shrink, to swell [boiserie]; to function (mech.); to fit loosely (mech.); *jouer au tennis,* to play tennis; *jouer du piano,* to play the piano; *jouer des coudes,* to elbow one's way; *se jouer,* to play, to sport, to frolic; to be played; *se jouer de,* to make game of, to make light of. ‖

jouet [jwè] *m.* plaything, toy. ‖
joueur [jwœr] *m.* player; performer;
actor; gambler, gamester; speculator
[Bourse].

joufflu [jûflü] *adj.* chubby, chubby-
cheeked.

joug [jûg] *m.* yoke; bondage; slavery (fig.).

jouir [jûr] *v.* to enjoy; to revel (*de*,
in); to possess [faculté]. ‖ *jouissance*
[-isans] *f.* enjoyment, delight; use,
possession, tenure; fruition. ‖ *jouis-
seur* [-isœr] *m.* pleasure seeker.

joujou [jûjû] *m.*° plaything, toy.

jour [jûr] *m.* day; daylight, light,
lighting; dawn, day-break; day-time;
aperture, opening, gap, chink; open-
work [couture]; *demi-jour*, half-light,
twilight; *grand jour*, broad daylight;
jour de fête, holiday; *de nos jours*,
in our time, nowadays; *donner le jour
à*, to bring to light; to give birth to;
au jour le jour, from hand to mouth.

journal [jûrnàl] *m.*° journal, diary,
record; newspaper; gazette; day-book
(comm.); log-book (naut.); *les journaux*, the press; *style de journal*, jour-
nalese. ‖ *journalier* [-yé] *adj.*° daily,
everyday; variable; *m.* day-labo(u)rer,
journey-man. ‖ *journalisme* [-ism] *m.*
journalism. ‖ *journaliste* [-ist] *m.* journalist, reporter, pressman, newspaper-
man; columnist; journalizer (comm.).
‖ *journalistique* [-istik] *adj.* journal-
istic.

journée [jûrné] *f.* day; daytime;
day's work; day's journey; *toute la
journée*, all day long; *femme de journée*, charwoman; *à la journée*, by the
day. ‖ *journellement* [-èlman] *adv.*
daily, every day.

joute [jût] *f.* Ⓒ game, match.

joyau [jwàyô] *m.*° jewel, gem.

joyeux [jwàyè] *adj.*° joyous, joyful,
merry, elated, blithe.

jubilé [jübîlé] *m.* jubilee; fiftieth
anniversary; golden wedding. ‖ *jubiler*
v. to exult; to gloat.

jucher [jüshé] *v.* to roost; to perch.

judiciaire [jüdîsyèr] *adj.* judicial, forensic. ‖ *judicieux* [-yè] *adj.*° judicious, sensible, well-advised.

judo [jüdô] *m.* judo.

juge [jüj] *m.* judge; magistrate, justice; arbiter; *pl.* bench; *juge d'instruction*, examining magistrate; *juge de
paix*, justice of the peace. ‖ *jugement*
[-man] *m.* judgment; verdict, decision;
decree; opinion; trial; sentence; discrimination, sense. ‖ *juger* [-é] *v.* to
judge; to try [accusé]; to adjudicate;
to decide; to pass sentence on; to
consider, to think; to believe, to deem.

jugulaire [jügülèr] *f.* chin-strap. ‖
juguler [-é] *v.* to jugulate; to choke.

juif, juive [jüîf, -ïv] *adj.* Jewish;
m. Jew, *f.* Jewess.

juillet [jüîyè] *m.* July.

juin [jüïⁿ] *m.* June.

julienne [jülyèn] *f.* vegetable soup.

jumeau, -melle [jümô, -mèl] *m.*°, *f.*,
adj.° twin; double. ‖ *jumeler* [-mⁿlé]
v. to couple; to reinforce. ‖ *jumelles*
[-èl] *f. pl.* binoculars; field-glasses;
opera-glasses.

jument [jümaⁿ] *f.* mare.

jungle [jûⁿgl] *f.* jungle.

jupe [jüp] *f.* skirt. ‖ *jupon* [-oⁿ] *m.*
petticoat, underskirt, *Am.* half-slip.

juré [jüré] *adj.* sworn; *m.* juror, juryman. ‖ *jurement* [-maⁿ] *m.* swearing,
oath. ‖ *jurer* [-é] *v.* to swear; to vow,
to take oath; to blaspheme; to clash,
to jar [couleurs].

juridiction [jürîdïksyoⁿ] *f.* jurisdiction; domain, venue (jur.); department
(fig.). ‖ *juridique* [-dïk] *adj.* juridical,
legal. ‖ *jurisprudence* [jürîsprüdaⁿs] *f.*
jurisprudence. ‖ *juriste* [-rïst] *s.* jurist.

juron [jüroⁿ] *m.* oath, blasphemy,
curse, swear-word.

jury [jürî] *m.* jury; selection committee, examining board [concours].

jus [jü] *m.* juice; gravy [viande];
(pop.) coffee; (pop.) electric current.

jusant [jüzaⁿ] *m.* ebb-tide, ebb.

jusque [jüsk] *prep.* until, till; as far
as, up to; even to, down to; *jusqu'ici*,
so far, up to now; *jusqu'où*, how far;
jusqu'à quand, how long.

juste [jüst] *adj.* just, equitable;
righteous; fair, lawful; proper, fit, apt;
exact [mot]; accurate, correct; sound;
tight; *adv.* just, exactly; precisely;
true (mus.); barely, scarcely; *m.*
virtuous person, upright man. ‖ *justesse* [-ès] *f.* exactness, correctness,
accuracy; appropriateness; *de justesse*, just in time.

justice [jüstïs] *f.* justice, righteousness, equity; jurisdiction; courts of
justice, judges; legal proceedings; *Palais de Justice*, law-courts; *traduire en
justice*, to prosecute. ‖ *justicier* [-syé]
m. justiciary.

justificateur [jüstïfïkàtœr] *adj.* justificatory. ‖ *justificatif* [-tïf] *adj.* justificative; *pièce justificative*, voucher,
supporting document. ‖ *justification*
[-àsyoⁿ] *f.* justification, vindication;
line adjustment (typogr.). ‖ *justifier*
[jüstïfyé] *v.* to justify, to vindicate; to
give proof of; to adjust (typogr.).

jute [jüt] *m.* jute.

juteux [jütè] *adj.*° juicy.

juvénile [jüvénïl] *adj.* youthful;
juvenile.

juxtaposer [jükstàpòzé] *v.* to juxta-
pose.

K

kakatoès [kàkàtoès] *m.* cockatoo.

kaki [kàkì] *adj., m.* khaki.

kangourou [kaⁿgûrû] *m.* kangaroo.

képi [képì] *m.* kepi.

kermesse [kèrmès] *f.* charity fête; village fair.

kilogramme [kìlògràm] *m.* kilogram. ‖ *kilomètre* [-òmètr] *m.* kilometer. ‖ *kilométrage* [-òmètràj] *m.* mileage.

kimono [kìmònò] *m.* kimono.

kiosque [kyòsk] *m.* kiosk, stand; news-stand; flower-stall; conning-tower [sous-marin]; band-stand (mus.).

Klaxon [klàksoⁿ] *m.* (trade-mark) horn, klaxon, hooter. ‖ *klaxonner* [-né] *v.* to hoot, to honk.

kleptomane [klèptòmàn] *s.* klepto-maniac.

krach [kràk] *m.* financial crash, smash, collapse.

kyrielle [kìryèl] *f.* long rigmarole; string [de, of].

kyste [kìst] *m.* cyst.

L

l' art., pron., see le.

la [là] *art., pron.,* see le.

là [là] *adv.* there; *cet homme-là,* that man; *là-dessus,* thereupon; *là-haut,* up there; *là-bas,* down there, over yonder.

labeur [làbœr] *m.* labo(u)r, toil.

laboratoire [làbòràtwàr] *m.* labora-tory.

laborieux [làbòryë] *adj.** laborious, hard-working; toilsome; painstaking.

labour [làbûr] *m.* ploughing, tillage. ‖ *labourable* [-àbl] *adj.* arable, tillable. ‖ *labourer* [-é] *v.* Br. to plough, Am. to plow; to till; to furrow. ‖ *laboureur* [-œr] *m.* farm-hand; Br. ploughman, Am. plowman.

labyrinthe [làbìrìⁿt] *m.* labyrinth, maze.

lac [làk] *m.* lake.

lacer [làsé] *v.* to lace.

lacérer [làséré] *v.* to tear; to lace-rate; to slash (à); to maul.

lacet [làsè] *m.* lace, shoestring, boot-lace; noose, snare [chasse]; turning, winding, hairpin bend [route].

lâche [lâsh] *adj.* loose, slack; lax, slipshod; cowardly; dastardly; *m.* coward, dastard. ‖ *lâcher* [-é] *v.* to release; to slacken, to loosen; to drop; to set free, to let go. ‖ *lâcheté* [-té] *f.* cowardice.

lacis [làsì] *m.* network (mil.).

lacrymogène [làkrìmòjèn] *adj.* tear-producing, tear-exciting; *gaz lacrymo-gène,* tear-gas.

lacs [lâ] *m.* noose, snare; toils.

lacté [làkté] *adj.* milky.

lacune [làkün] *f.* gap, blank; hiatus.

lacustre [làküstr] *adj.* lacustral, lake.

lad [làd] *m.* stable-boy.

ladre [làdr] *adj.* leprous; stingy; *m.* leper; miser; skinflint. ‖ *ladrerie* [làdrᵉrì] *f.* leprosy; meanness, stingi-ness; measles [porc].

lagune [làgün] *f.* lagoon.

laïc, laïque [làìk] *adj.* laic; lay, secular; *m.* layman; *pl.* the laity. ‖ *laïciser* [làìsìzé] *v.* to secularize. ‖ *laï-cité* [-té] *f.* secularity, undenomina-tionalism.

laid [lè] *adj.* ugly; unsightly; plain, Am. homely. ‖ *laideron* [-droⁿ] *m.* ugly person; fright (fam.). ‖ *laideur* *f.* ugliness; plainness, Am. homeliness.

laie [lè] *f.* wild sow.

lainage [lènàj] *m.* wool(l)en goods. ‖ *laine* [lèn] *f.* wool; worsted. ‖ *laineux* [-ë] *adj.** woolly, fleecy.

laisse [lès] *f.* leash. ‖ *laisser* [-é] *v.* to leave; to let, to allow, to permit; to quit, to abandon; *laisser-aller, m.* unconstraint; carelessness; *laissez-passer m.* permit, pass.

lait [lè] *m.* milk; *lait de chaux,* whitewash. ‖ *laitage* [-tàj] *m.* dairy products. ‖ *laitance* [-aⁿs] *f.* milt; soft roe. ‖ *laiterie* [-trì] *f.* dairy; dairy-farming. ‖ *laitière* [-tyèr] *f.* dairy-maid; milkmaid; *adj.* milch [vache].

laiton [lètoⁿ] *m.* brass.

laitue [lètü] *f.* lettuce.

laïus [làüs] *m.* (fam.) speech.

lambeau [laⁿbò] *m.** strip, scrap, shred, bit; rag.

lambiner [laⁿbìné] *v.* (fam.) to dawdle, to loiter.

lambris [laⁿbrì] *m.* wainscoting; wall-lining; panelling.

lame [làm] *f.* lamina, thin plate [mé-tal]; blade; foil; wave.

lamé [làmé] *adj.* spangled; *m.* lamé.

lamentation [làmaⁿtàsyoⁿ] *f.* lament-ation, wailing; complaint. ‖ *lamenter* [làmãⁿté] v. to lament; *se lamenter*, to lament, to bewail, to deplore, to bemoan.

laminer [làmìné] v. to laminate, to roll. || *laminoir* [-wàr] m. rolling-mill, flatting-mill.

lampadaire [lɑⁿpàdèr] m. standard lamp; candelabrum. || *lampe* [lɑⁿp] f. lamp; radio tube; *lampe à alcool*, spirit-lamp; *lampe de poche*, Br. torch, Am. flashlight. || *lampion* [-yoⁿ] m. illumination-lamp; Chinese lantern. || *lampiste* [-ìst] m. lamp-maker; lamp-lighter; Am. fall guy (pop.).

lance [lɑⁿs] f. spear; lance; nozzle; *lance-flammes*, flame-thrower; *lance-torpille*, torpedo-tube. || *lancement* [-mɑⁿ] m. throwing, flinging; launching [bateau]; swinging [hélice]. || *lancer* [-é] v. to throw, to fling, to cast; to launch (naut.); to fire [torpille]; © to pitch [base-ball], to shoot [hockey]; *se lancer*, to rush, to dash, to dart; *se lancer dans*, to embark on; © to shoot [hockey]. || *lancette* [-èt] f. lancet. || *lanceur* [-œr] m. © pitcher [base-ball]. || *lanciner* [-ìné] v. to twinge, to lancinate.

landau [lɑⁿdò] m.* landau.

lande [lɑⁿd] f. moor, wasteland, heath.

langage [lɑⁿgàj] m. language, speech; *langage chiffré*, coded text.

lange [lɑⁿj] m. swaddling-cloth.

langoureux [lɑⁿgûré] adj.* languid, languishing.

langouste [lɑⁿgûst] f. lobster; crayfish. || *langoustine* [-tìn] f. Norway lobster, Dublin prawn, scamp, Am. prawn.

langue [lɑⁿg] f. tongue; language; strip of land; gore [terre]; *mauvaise langue*, backbiter, mischief-maker, scandalmonger; *langues vivantes*, modern languages; *donner sa langue au chat*, to give up.

langueur [lɑⁿgœr] f. languor, languidness; dullness (comm.). || *languir* [lɑⁿgîr] v. to languish, to pine; to mope; to decline; to drag, to be dull (comm.); *languissant*, languid, listless.

lanière [lànyèr] f. thong, lash.

lanterne [lɑⁿtèrn] f. lantern; street-lamp. || *lanterner* [-é] v. (fam.) to dilly-dally, to lag.

lapider [làpìdé] v. to stone.

lapin [làpìⁿ] m. rabbit; *peau de lapin*, cony; *poser un lapin à qqn*, to let s.o. down, Am. to stand s.o. up.

lapsus [làpsüs] m. slip.

laquais [làkè] m. lackey; flunkey.

laque [làk] f. lac; m. lacquer. || *laquer* [-é] v. to lacquer.

larcin [làrsìⁿ] m. larceny, pilfering.

lard [làr] m. bacon; back-fat; *lard salé*, © salt pork; *fèves au lard*, © pork and beans. || *larder* [-dé] v. to lard, to interlard; to inflict [coups]. || *lardon* [-doⁿ] m. lardoon; gibe; kid (pop.).

largable [làrgàbl] adj. releasable. || *largage* [-gàj] m. letting go; unfurling.

large [làrj] adj. broad, wide; generous; big, ample; lax; m. room, space; breadth, width; offing; open-sea. || *largesse* [-ès] f. liberality; bounty, largesse. || *largeur* [-œr] f. breadth, width.

larguer [làrgé] v. to loosen, to slacken; to unfurl.

larme [làrm] f. tear; drop. || *larmoyer* [-wàyé] v. to water [yeux]; to weep, to snivel.

larron [làroⁿ] m. robber.

larve [làrv] f. larva; grub.

larynx [làrìⁿks] m. larynx.

las, lasse [lâ, lâs] adj. tired, weary.

lascar [làskàr] m. (fam.) tough guy.

lascif [làsìf] adj.* lewd.

lasser [làsé] v. to weary, to tire. || *lassitude* [-ìtüd] f. lassitude, fatigue; tiredness; weariness.

latent [làtɑⁿ] adj. latent; hidden.

latéral [làtéràl] adj.* lateral; *rue latérale*, side-street, cross-street.

latin [làtìⁿ] m. Latin; adj. Latin; lateen (naut.).

latitude [làtìtüd] f. latitude; freedom; scope, range.

latte [làt] f. lath.

lauréat [lòréà] m., adj. laureate. || *laurier* [lòryé] m. laurel, bay tree; hono(u)r.

lavable [làvàbl] adj. washable. || *lavabo* [-àbò] m. wash-stand; lavatory. || *lavage* [-àj] m. washing; scrubbing; dilution; (pop.) popping, Am. hocking.

lavande [làvɑⁿd] f. lavender.

lavasse [làvàs] f. slops.

lave [làv] f. lava.

lavement [làvmɑⁿ] m. washing; enema. || *laver* [-é] v. to wash; to bathe; to cleanse. || *lavette* [-èt] f. dish-mop; dish-cloth. || *laveuse* [-ëz] f. washerwoman, scrubwoman; washing-machine. || *lavoir* [-wàr] m. wash-house, washing-place; scullery.

laxatif [làksàtìf] m., adj.* laxative.

layette [lèyèt] f. baby-linen, layette.

le [l^e] def. art. m. (*l'* before a vowel or a mute h) (f. *la*, pl. *les*) the; pron. m. 'him; it (f. her; it), pl. them).

lé [lé] m. width, breadth [tissu].

leader [lîdœr] m. leader.

lèchefrite [lèshfrìt] *f.* dripping-pan. ‖ **lécher** [léshé] *v.* to lick; to elaborate, to over-polish.

leçon [lesoⁿ] *f.* reading; lecture; lesson; advice.

lecteur, -trice [lèktœr, -trìs] *m.*, *f.* reader; foreign assistant (univ.). ‖ **lecture** [-ür] *f.* reading; perusal.

légal [légàl] *adj.* legal; statutory; lawful, licit; forensic [médecine]. ‖ **légaliser** [-ìzé] *v.* to legalize; to certify, to authenticate. ‖ **légalité** [-ìté] *f.* legality, lawfulness, law.

légataire [légàtèr] *m.*, *f.* legatee; *légataire universel,* residuary legatee, general legatee.

légation [légàsyoⁿ] *f.* legation.

légendaire [léjⁿdèr] *adj.* legendary. ‖ **légende** [-ⁿd] *f.* legend; caption; inscription; motto; key.

léger [léjé] *adj.* light; slight; thoughtless, frivolous; gentle; fickle; wanton. ‖ **légèreté** [-èrté] *f.* lightness, nimbleness, agility; slightness; weakness; levity; flightiness; fickleness; frivolity.

légiférer [léjìféré] *v.* to legislate.

légion [léjyoⁿ] *f.* legion.

législateur, -trice [léjìslàtœr, -trìs] *m.*, *f.* legislator, lawgiver; *adj.* legislative. ‖ **législation** [-àsyoⁿ] *f.* legislation, law-giving. ‖ **législature** [-àtür] *f.* legislature; session. ‖ **légiste** [léjìst] *m.* legist; *médecin légiste,* medical expert.

légitime [léjìtìm] *adj.* legitimate, lawful; rightful. ‖ **légitimer** [-ìmé] *v.* to legitimate; to justify; to recognize [titre]. ‖ **légitimité** [-ìmìté] *f.* lawfulness; justness, legitimacy.

legs [lèg *or* lè] *m.* legacy, bequest. ‖ **léguer** [légé] *v.* to bequeath, to leave, to will.

légume [légüm] *m.* vegetable; *grosse légume,* bigwig, *Br.* big bug, *Am.* big shot, wheel (pop.). ‖ **légumier** [-yé] *m.* vegetable dish.

lendemain [lⁿdmⁿ] *m.* next day, morrow, the day after.

lent [lⁿ] *adj.* slow, sluggish. ‖ **lenteur** [-tœr] *f.* slowness; sluggishness; backwardness; dilatoriness.

lentille [lⁿtìy] *f.* lentil; lens; freckle.

léopard [léopàr] *m.* leopard.

lèpre [lèpr] *f.* leprosy. ‖ **lépreux** [-prë] *adj.* leprous; *m.* leper. ‖ **léproserie** [-pròzrì] *f.* lazar-house, leprosary.

lequel [lekèl] (*f.* laquelle, pl. m. lesquels, pl. f. lesquelles) *pron. m.* who [sujet]; whom [complément]; which, that [choses]; *interrog. pron.* which, which one? *duquel,* of whom; whose; from which; of which (one)? *desquels,*

of whom; whose; from which; of which (ones)? *auquel,* to which; to whom; to which(one)? *auxquels,* to which; to whom; to which (ones)?

les [lè] *pl. of* le.

léser [lézé] *v.* to wrong; to injure; to endanger; *lèse-majesté,* high treason.

lésiner [lézìné] *v.* to be stingy, to stint; *Am.* to dicker; to haggle.

lessive [lèsìv] *f.* wash, washing; lye-wash; washing-powder. ‖ **lessiveuse** [-ìvèz] *f.* washing-machine.

lest [lèst] *m.* ballast; sinkers.

leste [lèst] *adj.* brisk, nimble; quick; agile; unscrupulous, sharp; spicy.

lester [lèsté] *v.* to ballast; to weight.

lettre [lètr] *f.* letter; *pl.* literature, letters; *lettre recommandée,* registered letter; *en toutes lettres,* in full; *à la lettre,* literally, word for word. ‖ **lettré** [-é] *adj.* lettered; *m.* scholar; well-read man.

leur [lœr] *pron.* them, to them; *poss. adj.* their; *le leur, la leur, les leurs,* theirs.

leurre [lœr] *m.* lure; decoy; bait; allurement, catch (fig.). ‖ **leurrer** [-é] *v.* to lure; to decoy; to bait; to entice; *se leurrer,* to delude oneself.

levain [levⁿ] *m.* yeast.

levant [levⁿ] *m.* east; Levant.

levée [levé] *f.* raising, lifting; closing, adjourning [séance]; uprising; levying (mil.); embankment, causeway; collection [poste]; gathering (récolte); breaking-up, striking [camp]; swell [mer]; weighing [ancre]; trick [cartes]. ‖ **lever** [-é] *v.* to lift, to raise; to adjourn [séance]; to weigh [ancre]; to collect [poste]; to draw [plan]; to shrug [épaules]; to remit [condamnation]; *m.* raising, rise; levee (mil.); sunrise [soleil]; *se lever,* to rise, to arise; to get up, to stand up; to clear up [ciel]. ‖ **levier** [-yé] *m.* lever.

lèvre [lèvr] *f.* lip.

levrette [levrèt] *f.* greyhound bitch. ‖ **lévrier** [lévrìyé] *m.* greyhound.

levure [levür] *f.* yeast; baking-powder; barm [bière].

lexique [lèksìk] *m.* lexicon.

lézard [lézàr] *m.* lizard; idler, lounger (fam.). ‖ **lézarde** [-d] *f.* split, crevice, chink. ‖ **lézarder** [-dé] *v.* to crack, to split; to bask in the sun; to idle, to loaf, to lounge.

liaison [lyèzoⁿ] *f.* joining; connection; linking; acquaintance, intimacy; communications, liaison (mil.); slur (mus.); love-affair, liaison; *faire la liaison,* to link two words together (gramm.).

liasse [lyàs] *f.* bundle, packet; wad.

libelle [lìbèl] *m.* lampoon; libel (jur.). || *libeller* [-lé] *v.* to draw up, to word [documents]; to fill out [chèque].

libellule [lìbèllül] *f.* dragonfly, *Am.* darning-needle.

libéral [lìbéràl] *adj.* liberal, generous; broad, wide. || *libéralité* [-ìté] *f.* liberality. || *libérateur, -trice* [-àtœr, -trìs] *m., f.* liberator, deliverer rescuer; *adj.* liberating. || *libération* [-àsyoⁿ] *f.* liberation, freeing, releasing; exemption (mil.); discharge [prisonnier]. || *libérer* [-é] *v.* to liberate, to release; to set free; to discharge.

liberté [lìbèrté] *f.* liberty, freedom.

libertin [lìbèrtìⁿ] *adj.* licentious, wayward; *m.* libertine. || *libertinage* [-tìnàj] *m.* profligacy.

libraire [lìbrèr] *m., f.* bookseller, bookdealer. || *librairie* [-ì] *f.* bookshop; book-trade.

libre [lìbr] *adj.* free; open, unoccupied, vacant; *libre-échange*, freetrade; *libre-service*, self-service; self-service store.

lice [lìs] *f.* lists; bitch.

licence [lìsaⁿs] *f.* licence, leave, permission; licentiate's degree; licentiousness. || *licencié* [-yé] *m.* licentiate; licence-holder; *licencié ès lettres*, master of arts. || *licencier* [-yé] *v.* to dismiss, to discharge; to disband (mil.). || *licencieux* [-yé] *adj.* licencious, loose.

licite [lìsìt] *adj.* licit.

licol, licou [lìkòl, lìkû] *m.* halter.

lie [lì] *f.* lees, dregs; scum.

liège [lyèj] *m.* cork; float [pêche].

lien [lyìⁿ] *m.* tie, bond, link; connection. || *lier* [lyé] *v.* to bind, to fasten; to link, to connect; *lier connaissance*, to strike up an acquaintance.

lierre [lyèr] *m.* ivy.

liesse [lyès] *f.* gaiety.

lieu [lyë] *m.* place; locality, spot; grounds, reason, cause; *au lieu de*, instead of; *avoir lieu*, to take place, places; *en premier lieu*, firstly; *lieudit*, place, locality.

lieue [lyë] *f.* league.

lieutenant [lyëtnaⁿ] *m.* lieutenant.

lièvre [lyèvr] *m.* hare.

lignage [lìñàj] *m.* lineage. || *ligne* [lìñ] *f.* line; cord; row, range; *ligne aérienne*, airline; *à la ligne*, indent. || *lignée* [-é] *f.* issue; offspring, progeny; stock.

ligoter [lìgòté] *v.* to bind, to tie up; *Am.* to hog-tie.

ligue [lìg] *f.* league. || *liguer* [lìgé], *se liguer* *v.* to league.

lilas [lìlà] *m.* lilac.

limace [lìmàs] *f.* slug. || *limaçon* [-oⁿ] *m.* snail.

limaille [lìmày] *f.* filings.

limande [lìmaⁿd] *f.* dab; slap (pop.).

limbes [lìⁿb] *m. pl.* limbo.

lime [lìm] *f.* file. || *limer* [-é] *v.* to file; to polish.

limitation [lìmìtàsyoⁿ] *f.* limitation, restriction; marking off. || *limite* [lìmìt] *f.* limit; boundary; maximum [vitesse]. || *limiter* [-ìté] *v.* to limit; to restrict. || *limitrophe* [-ìtròf] *adj.* bordering, adjacent, abutting.

limoger [lìmòjé] *v.* to supersede (milit.); to bowler-hat, to sack, *Am.* to shelve.

limon [lìmoⁿ] *m.* mud, clay, loam; lime (bot.).

limonade [lìmònàd] *f.* lemonade.

limpide [lìⁿpìd] *adj.* limpid; pellucid. || *limpidité* [-ìté] *f.* limpidity, limpidiness, clarity.

lin [lìⁿ] *m.* flax; linen.

linceul [lìⁿsœl] *m.* shroud.

linéaire [lìnéèr] *adj.* linear.

linge [lìⁿj] *m.* linen; calico. || *lingerie* [-rî] *f.* linen-drapery; linen-room; linen-trade; underwear; undergarment.

lingot [lìⁿgò] *m.* ingot.

linguiste [lìⁿgüìst] *m.* linguist. || *linguistique* [-ìk] *adj.* linguistic; *f.* linguistics.

linoléum [lìnòléòm] *m.* linoleum.

linon [lìnoⁿ] *m.* lawn.

linotte [lìnòt] *f.* linnet; *tête de linotte*, feather-brained.

linteau [lìⁿtò] *m.* lintel.

lion [lyoⁿ] *m.* lion. || *lionceau* [-sò] *m.* lion cub. || *lionne* [lyòn] *f.* lioness.

lippe [lìp] *f.* thick lower lip; blubber lip; *faire la lippe*, to pout.

liquéfier [lìkéfyé] *v.* to liquefy.

liqueur [lìkœr] *f.* liquor; liqueur; solution (chem.).

liquidation [lìkìdàsyoⁿ] *f.* liquidation; settlement; clearance sale; winding up (comm.). || *liquide* [lìkìd] *m., adj.* liquid, fluid; *argent liquide*, ready money. || *liquider* [-é] *v.* to liquidate; to settle; to wind up (comm.).

liquoreux [lìkòré] *adj.* sweet, luscious, juicy.

lire [lìr] *v.* to read; to peruse.

lis [lìs] *m.* lily; *fleur de lis*, fleur de lis.

liséré [lìzéré] *adj.* edged, bordered, piped; *m.* border, edging.

liseron [lìzronˣ] *m.* bindweed.

liseuse [lìzëz] *f.* bed jacket; book-wrapper; reading lamp. ‖ **lisible** [lìzìbl] *adj.* legible, readable.

lisière [lìzyèr] *f.* selvedge, list; edge, border, skirt [forêt]; leading-strings (fig.).

lisse [lìs] *adj.* smooth, sleek, slick. ‖ **lisser** [-é] *v.* to sleek; to preen; to smooth, to polish, to gloss; to glaze.

liste [lìst] *f.* list, roll; roster (mil.); panel [jurés].

lit [lì] *m.* bed; bedstead; layer, stratum; bottom [rivière]. ‖ **literie** [lìtrì] *f.* bedding, bedclothes. ‖ **litière** [lì-tyèr] *f.* litter.

litige [lìtìj] *m.* litigation; lawsuit.

litre [lìtr] *m.* Br. litre, Am. liter.

littéraire [lìtérèr] *adj.* literary. ‖ **littéral** [lìtéràl] *adj.** literal. ‖ **littérature** [-àtür] *f.* literature.

littoral [lìtoràl] *adj.** littoral; *m.** coast-line, littoral.

liturgie [lìtürjì] *f.* liturgy.

livide [lìvìd] *adj.* livid, ghastly.

livraison [lìvrèzonˣ] *f.* delivery; part, instalment [livre]; copy, issue [revue].

livre [lìvr] *m.* book; register; journal; *livre de bord,* ship's register; *grand livre,* ledger.

livre [lìvr] *f.* pound [poids; monnaie].

livrée [lìvré] *f.* livery. ‖ **livrer** [-é] *v.* to deliver; to surrender; to wage [bataille]; *se livrer,* to devote oneself, to give oneself over (à, to); to indulge (à, in).

livret [lìvrè] *m.* booklet; libretto; *livret militaire,* service record; *livret de l'étudiant,* student's handbook; scholastic record book.

livreur [lìvrœr] *m.* delivery-man.

local [lòkàl] *adj.** local; *m.** premises. ‖ **localiser** [-àlìzé] *v.* to localize; to locate. ‖ **localité** [-àlìté] *f.* locality. ‖ **locataire** [-àtèr] *m.* tenant; lodger; hirer, renter, lessee (jur.). ‖ **location** [-àsyonˣ] *f.* hiring; letting, renting; tenancy; booking, reservation; *bureau de location,* booking-office, box-office; *prix de location,* rent; *location-vente,* hire-purchase system.

locomotive [lòkòmòtìv] *f.* locomotive, engine. ‖ **locomotrice** [-trìs] *f.* electric engine.

locution [lòküsyonˣ] *f.* idiom, phrase.

loge [lòj] *f.* hut, cabin; lodge [concierge]; kennel [chien]; box (theat.); dressing-room [artiste]. ‖ **logement** [-manˣ] *m.* lodging, housing; dwelling, accommodation, Br. diggings, digs; quarters, billet (mil.); container (comm.); *indemnité de logement,* housing allotment. ‖ **loger** [-é] *v.* to

lodge; to put up; to quarter, to billet (mil.); to house, to live. ‖ **logeuse** [-ëz] *f.* landlady.

logique [lòjìk] *adj.* logical; *f.* logic.

logis [lòjì] *m.* house, home, dwelling.

loi [lwà] *f.* law; rule; *hors la loi,* outlaw; *projet de loi,* bill.

loin [lwinˣ] *adv.* far, distant; *de loin,* at a distance; *de loin en loin,* at long intervals. ‖ **lointain** [-tinˣ] *adj.* remote, far off; *m.* distance.

loir [lwàr] *m.* dormouse, loir.

loisible [lwàzìbl] *adj.* permissible; optional.

loisir [lwàzìr] *m.* leisure, spare time, time off.

long, longue [lonˣ, lonˣg] *adj.* long; slow; *m.* length; *le long de,* along; *à la longue,* in the long run; *dix mètres de long,* ten meters long. ‖ **longe** [lonˣj] *f.* tether; thong [fouet]; lunge, lunging rein.

longe [lonˣj] *f.* loin [veau].

longer [lonˣjé] *v.* to pass along, to go along; to extend along. ‖ **longévité** [-vìté] *f.* longevity. ‖ **longitude** [-ìtüd] *f.* longitude. ‖ **longtemps** [lonˣtanˣ] *adj.* long; a long time. ‖ **longueur** [lonˣgœr] *f.* length; slowness. ‖ **longue-vue** [-vü] *f.* telescope, field-glass, spy-glass.

looping [lüpìnˣ] *m.* loop.

lopin [lòpinˣ] *m.* patch, plot, allotment.

loquace [lòkwàs or -kàs] *adj.* loquacious, talkative; garrulous. ‖ **loquacité** [-ìté] *f.* loquacity, talkativeness.

loque [lòk] *f.* rag; *en loques,* falling to pieces, in tatters.

loquet [lòkè] *m.* latch, clasp.

loqueteux [lòktë] *adj.** ragged.

lorgner [lòrñé] *v.* to ogle, to leer at. ‖ **lorgnette** [-èt] *f.* opera-glasses. ‖ **lorgnon** [-onˣ] *m.* pince-nez, eye-glasses.

lors [lòr] *adv.* then; *lors de,* at the time of; *lors même que,* even when. ‖ **lorsque** [lòrske] *conj.* when.

losange [lòzanˣj] *m.* lozenge, diamond.

lot [lò] *m.* portion, share, lot; prize; *gros lot,* Am. jackpot. ‖ **loterie** [lòtrì] *f.* lottery. ‖ **loti** [-tì] *adj.* provided for; *mal loti,* badly off.

lotion [lòsyonˣ] *f.* lotion.

lotir [lòtìr] *v.* to allot; to parcel out. ‖ **lotissement** [-ìsmanˣ] *m.* allotment; development [terrain].

louable [lûàbl] *adj.* laudable, praise-worthy. ‖ **louange** [lûãˣj] *f.* praise.

louche [lûsh] *f.* soup-ladle; basting-spoon; reamer (mech.).

louche [lûsh] *adj.* cross-eyed; squinting; ambiguous; suspicious; fishy,

Am. phony (pop.). ‖ **loucher** [-é] *v.* to squint; (fam.) to cast longing eyes (*vers*, at).

louer [lûé] *v.* to rent, to hire; to book, to reserve.

louer [lûé] *v.* to praise, to laud, to commend; *se louer*, to be pleased, to be well satisfied (*de*, with).

loufoque [lûfôk] *adj.* (fam.) daft, nutty.

loup [lû] *m.* wolf; mask; crow-bar; error; *loup de mer*, sea-dog, old salt; *à pas de loup*, stealthily; *loup-cervier*, lynx; *loup-garou*, werewolf.

loupe [lûp] *f.* wen (med.), excrescence; burr [arbre]; lens, magnifying glass [optique].

louper [lûpé] *v.* to miss; to botch, to bungle.

lourd [lûr] *adj.* heavy, **Am.** hefty; clumsy; dull-witted; sultry close [temps]. ‖ **lourdeur** [-dœr] *f* heaviness; ponderousness, clumsiness, dullness; mugginess, sultriness [temps].

loustic [lûstîk] *m.* (fam.) wag.

loutre [lûtr] *f.* otter; *peau de loutre*, sealskin.

louve [lûv] *f.* she-wolf. ‖ **louveteau** [-tô] *m.* wolf-cub.

louvoyer [lûvwàyé] *v.* to tack (naut.); to manœuvre; to be evasive.

loyal [lwàyàl] *adj.* fair, straightforward; on the level (fam.); loyal, faithful. ‖ **loyauté** [lwàyôté] *f.* honesty; fairness, loyalty.

loyer [lwàyé] *m.* rent, rental.

lu [lü] *p. p.* of lire.

lubie [lübî] *f.* whim, crotchet, fad.

lubrifiant [lübrîfyàⁿ] *m.* lubricant; *adj.* lubricating.

lucarne [lükàrn] *f.* dormer, attic-window gable-window; skylight.

lucide [lüsîd] *adj.* lucid, clear-headed. ‖ **lucidité** [-té] *f* lucidity.

luciole [lüsyôl] *f* firefly.

lucratif [lükràtîf] *adj.* lucrative.

luette [lüèt] *f* uvula.

lueur [lüœr] *f.* gleam, glimmer, glow, flash, glare; ray.

luge [lüj] *f.* luge, toboggan.

lugubre [lügübr] *adj.* dismal, gloomy; lugubrious.

lui [lüi] *pron.* him, to him; her, to her; *c'est lui*, it is he; *à lui*, his.

luire [lüîr] *v.* to shine, to gleam.

lumière [lümyèr] *f.* light; lamp; enlightenment. ‖ **luminaire** [-inèr] *m.* luminary ‖ **lumineux** [-inè] *adj.* luminous. ‖ **luminosité** [-inôzîté] *f.* luminosity, sheen.

lunaire [lünèr] *adj.* lunar. ‖ **lunatique** [lünàtîk] *adj.* moonstruck; whimsical.

lunch [lunsh] *m.* luncheon, lunch; buffet-lunch.

lundi [lundî] *m.* Monday.

lune [lün] *f.* moon; *lune de miel*, honeymoon; *clair de lune*, moonlight. ‖ **lunette** [-èt] *f.* spyglass; *pl.* spectacles, eye-glasses.

luron [lüroⁿ] *m.* jolly chap.

lustre [lüstr] *m.* luster, gloss; chandelier. ‖ **lustrer** [-é] *v.* to glaze, to gloss, to polish up.

luth [lüt] *m.* lute.

lutin [lütⁿ] *m.* imp, elf, goblin.

lutrin [lütrⁿ] *m.* lectern.

lutte [lüt] *f.* wrestling; fight, struggle, tussle, strife. ‖ **lutter** [-é] *v.* to wrestle; to struggle, to contend, to fight. ‖ **lutteur** [-œr] *m* wrestler; fighter.

luxation [lüksàsyoⁿ] *f* luxation.

luxe [lüks] *m* luxury, profusion.

luxueux [lüksüè] *adj.* luxurious.

luxure [lüksür] *f.* lewdness. ‖ **luxurieux** [-yè] *adj.* lewd.

luzerne [lüzèrn] *f.* lucern; **Am.** alfalfa.

lycée [lîsé] *m.* lycée, secondary school [France]

lymphatique [lⁿfàtîk] *adj.* lymphatic; *lymphe*, lymph.

lyncher [lⁿshé] *v.* to lynch.

lynx [lⁿks] *m.* lynx.

lyre [lîr] *f.* lyre. ‖ **lyrique** [-îk] *adj.* lyrical, lyric. ‖ **lyrisme** [-îsm] *m.* lyricism.

M

ma [mà] *poss. adj. f.* my; *see* mon.

maboul [màbûl] *adj.* (fam.) crazy.

macabre [màkàbr] *adj.* gruesome.

macaron [màkàroⁿ] *m* macaroon. ‖ **macaroni** [-ònî] *m* macaroni.

macédoine [màsédwàn] *f.* diced vegetables; cut-up fruit, fruit salad; hotch-potch (fig.).

macérer [màséré] *v.* to macerate.

mâche [mâsh] *f.* corn-salad. ‖ **mâchefer** [-fèr] *m.* clinker; dross. ‖ **mâcher** [-é] *v.* to chew, to munch, to masticate.

machin [màshⁿ] *m.* thing, gadget, **Am.** gimmick; what's-his-name, so-and-so. ‖ **machinal** [-nàl] *adj.* mechanical, unconscious, involuntary. ‖ **machination** [-nàsyoⁿ] *f.* plot, scheming. ‖ **machine** [-în] *f.* machine;

engine; dynamo (electr.); *pl.* machinery. ‖ *machiner* [-ìné] *v.* to plot, to scheme; to supply (mech.). ‖ *machiniste* [-ìnìst] *m.* engineer; bus driver; stage-hand, scene-shifter (theat.).

mâchoire [mâshwàr] *f.* jaw, jaw-bone; clamp. ‖ *mâchonner* [-shòné] *v.* to chew; to mutter.

maçon [màsòⁿ] *m.* mason, bricklayer. ‖ *maçonnerie* [-ònrî] *f.* masonry; stonework.

maculer [màkùlé] *v.* to stain.

madame [màdàm] *f.* (*pl.* **mesdames**) Mrs.; madam.

madeleine [màdlèn] *f.* sponge-cake.

mademoiselle [màdmwàzèl] *f.* (*pl.* **mesdemoiselles**) Miss; young lady.

madré [màdré] *adj.* sly, *Am.* cagey.

magasin [màgàzìⁿ] *m.* shop *Am.* store; warehouse. ‖ *magasinage* [-zìnàj] *m.* storing; © shopping. *magasiner* [-é] *v.* © to go shopping. ‖ *magasinier* [-nyé] *m.* warehouse man, storeman.

magicien [màjìsyìⁿ] *m.* magician, wizard. ‖ *magie* [-jî] *f.* magic. ‖ *magique* [màjìk] *adj.* magic(al).

magistrat [màjìstrà] *m.* magistrate, judge. ‖ *magistrature* [-tür] *f.* magistrature, magistracy

magnanime [màñànìm] *adj.* magnanimous; *magnanimité*, magnanimity.

magnétique [màñétìk] *adj.* magnetic. ‖ *magnétophone* [màñétòfòn] *m.* tape recorder.

magnifique [màñìfìk] *adj.* magnificent, splendid, glorious, generous.

mai [mè] *m.* May; May-pole.

maigre [mègr] *adj.* thin, lean, skinny; scrawny, gaunt, meagre; scanty lean meat. ‖ *maigreur* [-œr] *f.* thinness; scantiness, emaciation. ‖ *maigrir* [-îr] *v.* to grow thin.

maille [mây] *f.* stitch; link; mesh, mail. ‖ *maillon* [-òⁿ] *m.* mail.

maillot [màyô] *m.* swaddling clothes; bathing-suit; tights; jersey, singlet.

main [mìⁿ] *f.* hand; handwriting; quire [papier]; *main-d'œuvre*, manual labo(u)r; manpower.

maint [mìⁿ] *adj.* many a; *maintes fois*, many times.

maintenant [mìⁿtnàⁿ] *adv.* now. ‖ *maintenir* [-îr] *v.** to maintain; to keep; to support; to uphold; *se maintenir*, to remain; to continue. ‖ *maintien* [mìⁿtyìⁿ] *m.* maintenance, upholding, keeping; bearing.

maire [mèr] *m.* mayor. ‖ *mairie* [-î] *f.* town hall.

mais [mè] *conj.* but.

maïs [màìs] *m.* maize, Indian corn; *Am.* corn.

maison [mèzòⁿ] *f.* house; firm; home; household family; *maison de rapport*, apartment house. ‖ *maisonnette* [-ònèt] *f.* cottage, bungalow.

maître [mètr] *m.* master; ruler; owner teacher [école]; petty officer (naut.); *adj.* chief, main; *maître d'hôtel*, steward, head-waiter; *maître chanteur*, blackmailer. ‖ *maîtresse* [-ès] *f.* mistress, teacher [école]; *adj.* chief. ‖ *maîtrise* [-ìz] *f.* mastery. ‖ *maîtriser* [-ìzé] *v.* to master, to overcome; to control; to deal with; *se maîtriser*, to control oneself.

majesté [màjèsté] *f.* majesty. ‖ *majestueux* [-üë] *adj.** majestic; stately.

majeur [màjœr] *adj.* major, greater, of age *m.* major; middle finger. ‖ *major* [-òr] *m.* regimental adjutant (mil.), *état-major*, staff. ‖ *majorité* [-òrìté] *f.* majority; coming of age; legal age

majuscule [màjüskül] *adj.* capital; *f.* capital letter.

mal [màl] *m.** evil; hurt, harm; pain; wrong disease; *adv.* badly, ill; uncomfortable; *mal au cœur*, nausea; *mal à la tête*, headache; *pas mal*, presentable good-looking; not bad; *pas mal de* s large number, a good many.

malade [màlàd] *adj.* ill, sick; diseased; *m f.* patient. ‖ *maladie* [-î] *f.* illness sickness, malady, disease, ailment. *maladif* [-îf] *adj.** sickly, unhealthy, ailing.

maladresse [màlàdrès] *f.* clumsiness; blunder *maladroit* [-wà] *adj.* clumsy, awkward blundering; *m.* duffer.

malaise [màlèz] *m.* discomfort, uneasiness ‖ *malaisé* [-é] *adj.* difficult.

malappris [màlàprì] *adj.* ill-bred; *m.* boor, *Am.* slob.

malaxer [màlàksé] *v.* to mix; to knead to work.

malchance [màlshàⁿs] *f.* bad luck; mishap *malchanceux* [-ë] *adj.** unlucky, luckless.

mâle [mâl] *m.*, *adj.* male.

malédiction [màlédìksyòⁿ] *f.* curse.

maléfique [màléfìk] *adj.* maleficent, baleful.

malencontreux [màlàⁿkòⁿtrë] *adj.** untoward, unhappy; ill met.

malentendu [màlàⁿtàⁿdü] *m.* misunderstanding, misapprehension.

malfaisant [màlfzàⁿ] *adj.* harmful; mischievous, ‖ *malfaiteur* [-tœr] *m.* evil-doer, scoundrel.

malfamé [màlfàmé] *adj.* ill-famed.

malgré [màlgré] *prep.* despite.

malheur [màlœr] *m.* misfortune; unhappiness. ‖ *malheureux* [-ë] *adj.** unhappy; unfortunate; wretched, trivial; *s.* unfortunate person; *pl.* the destitute.

malhonnête [màlònèt] *adj.* dishonest; impolite, indecent. ‖ *malhonnêteté* [-tè] *f.* dishonesty, improbity; dishonest act, sharp practice.

malice [màlìs] *f.* malice, trick. ‖ *malicieux* [-syë] *adj.** mischievous, impish, arch.

malin, -igne [màlî, -îñ] *adj.* malignant; wicked; cunning, sharp, sly; *m.* devil Evil One.

malle [màl] *f.* trunk; mail-bag. ‖ *mallette* [-èt] *f.* suitcase.

malsain [màlsî] *adj.* unhealthy.

maltraiter [màltrèté] *v.* to maltreat, to ill-use; to manhandle.

malveillance [màlvèyañs] *f.* malevolence, ill-will; evil intent; foul play; criminal machination.

malversation [màlvèrsàsyoñ] *f.* embezzlement.

maman [màmañ] *f.* mama; mother; mummy (fam.).

mamelle [màmèl] *f.* breast; udder. ‖ *mamelon* [màmloñ] *m.* nipple; dug; hillock; boss, swell (mech.).

manche [mañsh] *m.* handle; haft; stick [balai]; joy-stick (aviat.).

manche [mañsh] *f.* sleeve; hose [eau]; shaft [air]; rubber, game [cartes]; set [tennis]; *la Manche,* the English Channel. ‖ *manchette* [-èt] *f.* cuff, wristband; headline [journal]; *pl.* handcuffs (pop.). ‖ *manchon* [-oñ] *m.* muff; casing, socket (techn.); flange (mech.). ‖ *manchot* [-ô] *adj.* one-armed; *m.* one-armed person.

mandarin [mañdàrî] *m.* mandarin. ‖ *mandarine* [-în] *f.* tangerine, mandarine.

mandat [mañdà] *m.* mandate; commission; warrant (jur.); money-order, draft (fin.); *mandat-poste,* postal money-order. ‖ *mandataire* [-tèr] *m.* mandatory; agent; trustee; attorney.

manège [mànèj] *m.* horsemanship, riding; wile, stratagem; treadmill; merry-go-round [foire].

manette [mànèt] *f.* hand-lever.

mangeoire [mañjwàr] *f.* manger; feeding-trough. ‖ *manger* [-é] *v.* to eat; to squander [argent]; to corrode [métal]; to fret [corde].

maniable [mànyàbl] *adj.* manageable; tractable.

maniaque [mànyàk] *m., f., adj.* maniac. ‖ *manie* [-î] *f.* mania; craze.

manier [mànyé] *v.* to handle; to feel; to ply.

manière [mànyèr] *f.* manner, way; affectation; deportment; *de manière que,* so that; *de manière à,* so as to. ‖ *maniéré* [-yéré] *adj.* affected.

manifestant [mànìfèstañ] *m.* demonstrator. ‖ *manifestation* [-àsyoñ] *f.* manifestation; demonstration (pol.). ‖ *manifeste* [-fèst] *adj.* manifest, evident, obvious; *m.* manifesto. ‖ *manifester* [-é] *v.* to manifest, to reveal; to show; to demonstrate.

manipuler [mànìpülé] *v.* to manipulate; to handle; to wield; to key [télégraphe].

manitou [mànìtû] *m.* Manitou.

manivelle [mànìvèl] *f.* crank; winch.

mannequin [mànkî] *m.* manikin; dummy; fashion model.

manœuvre [mànœvr] *f.* working, managing; handling [bateau]; drill (mil.); rigging (naut.); control (aviat.); intrigue; *m.* unskilled workman. ‖ *manœuvrer* [-é] *v.* to work; to ply; to shunt; to scheme; *Br.* to manœuvre, *Am.* to maneuver.

manomètre [mànòmètr] *m.* manometer, pressure-gauge.

manque [mañk] *m.* lack, want, need; deficiency, shortage; breach [parole]. ‖ *manqué* [-é] *adj.* missed; unsuccessful, abortive. ‖ *manquer* [-é] *v.* to lack, to want; to fail; to miss; *manquer de tomber,* to nearly fall.

mansarde [mañsàrd] *f.* attic, garret; dormer-window; *mansardé,* mansard-roofed.

manteau [mañtô] *m.** coat, cloak, mantle; mantelpiece [cheminée].

manucure [mànükür] *f.* manicure.

manuel [mànüèl] *m.* hand-book; *adj.** manual.

manufacture [mànüfàktür] *f.* factory; mill; works; plant. ‖ *manufacturer* [-é] *v.* to manufacture.

manuscrit [mànüskrì] *m.* manuscript; *adj.* hand-written.

manutention [mànütañsyoñ] *f.* handling; manipulation; commissary, *Am.* post-exchange; bakery; store-house (mil.).

maquereau [màkrô] *m.** mackerel [poisson]; pimp [personne].

maquette [màkèt] *f.* model, figure; mock-up; dummy [livre].

maquillage [màkìyàj] *m.* make-up; grease-paint (theat.); working-up (phot.). ‖ *maquiller* [-yé] *v.* to make up; to fake; *se maquiller,* to make up, to paint.

maquis [màkì] *m.* scrub; underground resistance forces, maquis [guerre]; (fig.) maze.

marais [màrè] *m.* marsh, swamp.

marasme [màràsm] *m.* despondency; stagnation; dumps.

marâtre [màràtr] *f.* step-mother; unkind mother.

marauder [màrôdé] *v.* to maraud; to filch; to crawl, to cruise [taxi].

marbre [màrbr] *m.* marble; slab; *sur le marbre*, at press, *Am.* on the press. ‖ *marbrer* [-é] *v.* to marble; to mottle.

marc [màr] *m.* marc [raisin]; grounds [café]; dregs.

marchand [màrshaⁿ] *m.* merchant, dealer, tradesman, shopkeeper; *adj.* marketable; commercial [ville]. ‖ *marchander* [-dé] *v.* to haggle, to bargain. ‖ *marchandise* [-dîz] *f.* merchandise, goods, wares.

marche [màrsh] *f.* step, stair [escalier]; tread; walk; march (mil.); running [machine]; *marche arrière*, backing; reverse.

marché [màrshé] *m.* deal, bargain, contract; market; transaction; *marché aux puces*, flea market, thieves' market; *bon marché*, cheap; *faire marché avec*, to contract.

marchepied [màrsh•pyé] *m.* step; footstool; foot-board, folding-steps [voiture]; running-board [auto] stepladder [escabeau]. ‖ *marcher* [màrshé] *v.* to tread; to walk, to march; to work, to run [machine]; *faire marcher* (fam.), to spoof, *Am.* to kid.

mardi [màrdì] *m.* Tuesday; *mardi gras*, Shrove Tuesday.

mare [màr] *f.* pool, pond. ‖ *marécage* [-ékà] *m.* fen, marshland; bog, swamp; quagmire. ‖ *marécageux* [-ékàjë] *adj.* marshy, boggy.

maréchal [màréshàl] *m.** marshal; farrier [ferrant].

marée [màré] *f.* tide, flow; sea fish; *marée basse*, low-tide; *marée haute*, high-tide.

marelle [màrèl] *f.* hopscotch [jeu].

marge [màrj] *f.* border, edge; fringe; margin [page]; scope, lee-way. ‖ *margelle* [-èl] *f.* curb.

marguerite [màrg•rìt] *f.* (bot.) daisy, marguerite; *Marguerite*, Margret, Maggie, Peggy.

mari [màrì] *m.* husband. ‖ *mariage* [-yàj] *m.* marriage; wedlock, matrimony; wedding; nuptials. ‖ *marié* [-yé] *adj.* married; *m.* bridegroom. ‖ *mariée* [-yé] *f.* bride. ‖ *marier* [-yé] *v.* to marry; to unite; to blend [couleurs]; *se marier*, to get married, to marry, to wed.

marin [màrìⁿ] *m.* sailor; mariner, seaman; *adj.* marine; nautical; sea-going. ‖ *marinades* [-ìnàd] *f. pl.* © pickles. ‖ *marine* [-ìn] *f.* navy; sea-front; sea-

scape [tableau]. ‖ *mariner* [-ìné] *v.* to pickle; to marinade. ‖ *marinier* [-ìnyé] *m.* bargee, waterman.

maringouin [màrìⁿgwìⁿ] *m.* © gnat, mosquito.

marionnette [màryònèt] *f.* puppet.

maritime [màrìtîm] *adj.* maritime.

marmelade [màrm•làd] *f.* marmalade; compote.

marmite [màrmìt] *f.* kettle, pot; heavy shell (mil.). ‖ *marmiton* [-oⁿ] *m.* scullion; kitchen-hand, cook's helper.

marmonner [màrmòné] *v.* to mutter; to mumble.

marmot [màrmô] *m.* brat. ‖ *marmotte* [-òt] *f.* marmot, *Am.* woodchuck. ‖ *marmotter* [-òté] *v.* to mutter, to mumble.

Maroc [màròk] *m.* Morocco. ‖ *marocain* [-ìⁿ] *m.*, *adj.* Moroccan.

maronner [màròné] *v.* (fam.) to grumble, to growl.

maroquin [màròkìⁿ] *m.* Morocco leather ‖ *maroquinerie* [-ìnrì] *f.* leather goods (or) trade.

marotte [màròt] *f.* fad.

marquant [màrkaⁿ] *adj.* conspicuous; striking; prominent. ‖ *marque* [màrk] *f.* mark; trade-mark, brand; distinction; *vin de marque*, choice wine. ‖ *marquer* [-é] *v.* to mark, to stamp, to brand; to indicate, to denote, to testify. ‖ *marqueterie* [-etrî] *f.* inlaid-work.

marquis [màrkì] *m.* marquis, marquess. ‖ *marquise* [-îz] *f.* marchioness; marquee; glass-roof; glass-porch; awning.

marraine [màrèn] *f.* godmother; sponsor.

marron [màroⁿ] *m.* chestnut; blow [coup]; *adj.* maroon, chestnut-colo(u)red. ‖ *marronnier* [-ònyé] *m.* chestnut-tree.

mars [màrs] *m.* March [mois]; Mars [planète].

marsouin [màrswìⁿ] *m.* porpoise; sea-hog.

marteau [màrtô] *m.** hammer; knocker [porte]; striker [horloge]; hammer-head [poisson]; *marteau-pilon*, power-hammer; forging-press. ‖ *marteler* [-•lé] *v.* to hammer; to batter out.

martial [màrsyàl] *adj.** martial.

martinet [màrtìnè] *m.* tilt-hammer (metall.); cat-o'-nine-tails [fouet]; clothes-beater; martlet [oiseau].

martingale [màrtìⁿgàl] *f.* martingale; half-belt.

martin-pêcheur [màrtìⁿpèchœr] *m.* kingfisher.

martre [màrtr] *f.* marten.

martyr [màrtîr] *m.* martyr. ‖ *martyre* [-îr] *m.* martyrdom. ‖ *martyriser* [-îrîzé] *v.* to torment; to martyr.

mascarade [màskàràd] *f.* masquerade.

masculin [màskülin] *adj.* masculine; male; mannish.

masque [màsk] *m.* mask. ‖ *masquer* [-é] *v.* to mask; to conceal.

massacre [màsàkr] *m.* massacre, slaughter.

massage [màsàj] *m.* massage.

masse [màs] *f.* mass; bulk; heap; crowd [gens]; mace [arme]; sledgehammer.

masser [màsé] *v.* to mass; to massage. ‖ *massif* [-îf] *m.* clump; cluster; *adj.** massive, bulky; solid [or]; heavy.

massue [màsü] *f.* club.

mastic [màstìk] *m.* putty. ‖ *mastiquer* [-é] *v.* to masticate, to chew; to putty.

masure [màzür] *f.* shanty, hovel, shack.

mat [màt] *m.* mate [échecs].

mat [màt] *adj.* mat, dull, flat.

mât [mâ] *m.* mast; pole.

matamore [màtàmòr] *m.* swashbuckler, braggart.

matelas [màtlà] *m.* mattress; pad. ‖ *matelasser* [-sé] *v.* to pad; to stuff.

matelot [màtlô] *m.* sailor, seaman.

mater [màté] *v.* to checkmate [échecs]; to subdue.

matérialiser [màtéryàlìzé] *v.* to materialize. ‖ *matérialisme* [-lìsm] *m.* materialism. ‖ *matériel* [-yèl] *m.* working-stock; apparatus; *adj.** material; corporeal, real; *matériel sanitaire*, medical supplies.

maternel [màtèrnèl] *adj.** maternal.

mathématicien [màtémàtìsyin] *m.* mathematician. ‖ *mathématique* [-ìk] *adj.* mathematical. ‖ *mathématiques* [-ìk] *f. pl.* mathematics.

matière [màtyèr] *f.* material; matter, substance; subject.

matin [màtin] *m.* morning.

mâtin [mâtin] *m.* mastiff.

matinal [màtìnàl] *adj.** early rising; morning, matutinal. ‖ *matinée* [-é] *f.* morning, forenoon; afternoon performance (theat.).

matois [màtwà] *adj.* sly, foxy.

matou [màtû] *m.* tom-cat.

matraque [màtràk] *f.* bludgeon.

matrice [màtrìs] *f.* uterus; matrix; die; original; master record.

matricule [màtrìkül] *f.* roll, register; registration; *m.* serial-number.

maturation [màtüràsyon] *f.* maturation. ‖ *maturité* [màtürìté] *f.* maturity; ripeness; full growth.

maudire [môdîr] *v.** to curse, to imprecate. ‖ *maudit* [-ì] *adj.* cursed, accursed; execrable, damnable.

maugréer [môgréé] *v.* to curse.

maure [môr] *m.* Moor; *adj.* Moorish.

maussade [môsàd] *adj.* surly, sullen, sulky; glum; grumpy, crusty; dull, cloudy [temps].

mauvais [môvè] *adj.* evil, ill; wicked, bad; unpleasant, nasty; wrong; harmful; sharp [langue]; *il fait mauvais*, it's bad weather.

mauve [môv] *adj.* mauve, purple; *f.* mallow.

maux [mô] *pl.* of *mal*.

maxillaire [màksìlèr] *m.* jaw-bone.

maxime [màksìm] *f.* maxim.

mazout [màzût] *m.* oil fuel; crude oil; *Am.* mazut.

me [me] *pron.* me, to me; myself.

méandre [méandr] *m.* meander, winding.

mécanicien [mékànìsyin] *m.* mechanic, artificer; mechanician; machinist; engine-driver, *Am.* engineer (railw.). ‖ *mécanique* [-ìk] *adj.* mechanical; *f.* mechanics; mechanism, machinery. ‖ *mécanisme* [-ìsm] *m.* mechanism; works, machinery.

méchanceté [méshansté] *f.* wickedness, naughtiness, mischievousness; unkindness, ill-nature. ‖ *méchant* [méshan] *adj.* wicked, evil; naughty; miserable; sorry.

mèche [mèsh] *f.* wick [chandelle]; tinder [briquet]; fuse [mine]; cracker, *Am.* snapper [fouet]; lock, wisp [cheveux]; bit, drill (mech.); *de mèche avec*, in collusion with.

mécompte [mékont] *m.* miscalculation, miscount; disappointment.

méconnaître [mékònètr] *v.** to fail to recognize; to misappreciate; to belittle; to disown.

mécontent [mékontan] *adj.* discontented, dissatisfied; *m.* malcontent. ‖ *mécontentement* [-tman] *m.* discontent, dissatisfaction; displeasure.

mécréant [mékréan] *m.* unbeliever.

médaille [médàl] *f.* medal.

médecin [médsin] *m.* doctor, physician. ‖ *médecine* [-ìn] *f.* medicine; physic; dose, drug.

médiane [médyàn] *f.* median.

médiateur [médyàtœr] *m.* mediator. ‖ *médiation* [-syon] *f.* mediation. ‖ *médiatrice* [-trìs] *f.* mediatrix.

médical [médĭkằl] *adj.** medical. ‖
médicament [-àmằⁿ] *m.* medicine;
medicament; **médication,** medication;
médicinal, medicinal.

médiéval [médyévằl] *adj.** medi-
(a)eval.

médiocre [médyòkr] *adj.* mediocre,
middling, indifferent; *m.* mediocrity;
ordinary. ‖ **médiocrité** [-ĭté] *f.* mediocrity; poorness; slenderness.

médire [médĭr] *v.** to slander, to
vilify. ‖ **médisance** [ĭzằⁿs] *f.* slander,
scandal-mongering.

méditation [médĭtàsyoⁿ] *f.* meditation. ‖ **méditer** [médĭté] *v.* to medi-
tate; to think over (ou) of; to plan,
to contemplate.

médius [médyüs] *m.* middle finger.

méduse [médüz] *f.* jelly-fish.

méfait [méfè] *m.* misdeed.

méfiance [méfyằⁿs] *f.* distrust. ‖ *méfier (se)* [s°méfyé] *v.* to mistrust; to
be on one's guard.

mégarde [mégàrd] *f.* inadvertence;
par mégarde, inadvertently.

mégère [méjèr] *f.* shrew, termagant,
scold.

mégot [mégô] *m.* butt [cigarette];
stump [cigare].

meilleur [mèyœr] *adj.* better; *meilleur marché,* cheaper; *le meilleur,* the
best.

mélancolie [mélằⁿkòlĭ] *f.* melancholy, mournfulness, gloom. ‖ *mélancolique* [-lĭk] *adj.* melancholy, glum,
downcast, mopish.

mélange [mélằⁿj] *m.* mixture, blend.
‖ *mélanger* [-é] *v.* to mix, to blend,
to mingle; *se mélanger,* to mix, to get
mixed, to mingle.

mélasse [mélàs] *f.* molasses, treacle.

mêlée [mèlé] *f.* conflict, fray, melee,
scramble, scuffle. ‖ *mêler* [-é] *v.* to
mix, to mingle, to blend; to jumble,
to tangle; to shuffle [cartes]; *se mêler,*
to mingle; to interfere, to meddle (de,
with); to take a hand (de, in).

mélèze [mélèz] *m.* larch.

mélodie [mélòdĭ] *f.* melody. ‖ *mélodieux* [-dyë] *adj.** melodious.

melon [m°loⁿ] *m.* melon; bowler
[chapeau].

membrane [mằⁿbràn] *f.* membrane;
web [palmipède].

membre [mằⁿbr] *m.* member; limb
[corps].

même [mèm] *adj.* same; self; very;
adv. even; *de même,* likewise; *être à
même de,* to be able to.

mémoire [mémwàr] *f.* memory;
recollection, remembrance; *de mémoire,* by heart; *m.* memorandum;

memorial; report (jur.); memoir, dissertation. ‖ *mémorable* [-mòràbl] *adj.*
memorable, noteworthy; eventful.

menace [m°nàs] *f.* threat, menace. ‖
menacer [-é] *v.* to threaten; to menace
(de, with).

ménage [ménằj] *m.* housekeeping,
housework; household goods; couple;
femme de ménage, charwoman. ‖ *ménager* [-é] *v.* to save, to spare; to
adjust; *adj.* domestic; thrifty, sparing.
‖ *ménagère* [-èr] *f.* housewife.

mendiant [mằⁿdyằⁿ] *m.* beggar;
mixed nuts. ‖ *mendicité* [-lsĭté] *f.*
begging; beggardom; beggary. ‖ *mendier* [-yé] *v.* to beg.

menée [m°né] *f.* track [chasse];
scheming, intrigue. ‖ *mener* [-é] *v.*
to lead; to conduct, to guide; to drive;
to steer; to manage [entreprise].

ménestrel [ménèstrèl] *m.* minstrel,
gleeman.

méningite [ménĭⁿjĭt] *f.* meningitis.

menotte [m°nòt] *f.* small hand; *pl.*
handcuffs, manacles.

mensonge [mằⁿsoⁿj] *m.* lie, untruth,
fib, falsehood.

mensualité [mằⁿsüàlĭté] *f.* monthly
payment. ‖ *mensuel* [-èl] *adj.**
monthly.

mensurable [mằⁿsüràbl] *adj.* measurable; *mensuration,* mensuration.

mental [mằⁿtàl] *adj.** mental. ‖ *mentalité* [-ĭté] *f.* mentality; turn of mind.

menteur, -teuse [mằⁿtœr, -tēz] *adj.*
lying, fibbing, mendacious; *m.* liar.

menthe [mằⁿt] *f.* mint.

mention [mằⁿsyoⁿ] *f.* mention. ‖
mentionner [-òné] *v.* to mention; to
specify.

mentir [mằⁿtĭr] *v.** to lie, to fib.

menton [mằⁿtoⁿ] *m.* chin.

menu [m°nü] *adj.* small, tiny; slender,
slim; petty, trifling; *m.* menu, bill of
fare; detail.

menuet [m°nüè] *m.* minuet.

menuiserie [m°nüĭzrĭ] *f.* joinery,
woodwork, carpentry. ‖ *menuisier*
[-yé] *m.* joiner, carpenter.

méprendre (se) [s°méprằⁿdr] *v.** to
mistake, to misjudge; to be mistaken.

mépris [méprĭ] *m.* contempt, scorn.
‖ *méprisable* [-zàbl] *adj.* contemptible,
despicable. ‖ *méprisant* [-zằⁿ] *adj.*
contemptuous, scornful.

méprise [méprĭz] *f.* mistake.

mépriser [méprĭzé] *v.* to despise, to
scorn; to slight.

mer [mèr] *f.* sea.

mercantile [mèrkằⁿtĭl] *adj.* mercantile; money-grubbing. ‖ *mercanti-
lisme* [-ĭsm] *m.* mercenary spirit.

mercenaire [mèrsᵉnèr] *m.*, *adj.* mercenary.

mercerie [mèrserî] *f.* haberdashery; *Am.* notions shop, notions.

merci [mèrsî] *f.* mercy, discretion; *m.* thanks, thank you.

mercier [mèrsyé] *m.* haberdasher.

mercredi [mèrkrᵉdî] *m.* Wednesday; *mercredi des Cendres*, Ash Wednesday.

mercure [mèrkür] *m.* mercury, quick-silver.

mercuriale [mèrküryàl] *f.* remonstrance; market price-list.

merde [mèrd] *f.* excrement; dung, shit [not in decent use]; *interj.* oh hell!

mère [mèr] *f.* mother; dam [animaux]; source, reason (fig.); *adj.* mother, parent; *maison mère*, head office.

méridien [mérìdyiⁿ] *m.*, *adj.* meridian. ‖ *méridional* [-yònàl] *m.** southerner; *adj.** southern.

merise [merîz] *f.* wild cherry, gean. ‖ *merisier* [mᵉrìzyé] *m.* wild cherry tree.

mérite [mérìt] *m.* merit, worth. ‖ *mériter* [-é] *v.* to merit, to deserve. ‖ *méritoire* [-wàr] *adj.* deserving, praiseworthy, commendable.

merlan [mèrlaⁿ] *m.* whiting [poisson].

merle [mèrl] *m.* blackbird.

merveille [mèrvèy] *f.* marvel, wonder; *à merveille*, wonderfully. ‖ *merveilleux* [-ë] *adj.** marvelous, wonderful; *m.* supernatural element, marvellous.

mes [mè] *poss. adj. pl.* my; *see mon.*

mésalliance [mézàlyaⁿs] *f.* misalliance. ‖ *mésallier* [-lyé] *v.* to misally; *se mésallier*, to marry beneath one's station.

mésange [mézaⁿj] *f.* titmouse, tomtit.

mésaventure [mézàvaⁿtür] *f.* misadventure, mishap, mischance.

mésentente [mézaⁿtaⁿt] *f.* misunderstanding, disagreement.

mésestimer [mézèstìmé] *v.* to underestimate, to underrate, to undervalue.

mésintelligence [méziⁿtèllìjaⁿs] *f.* disagreement; misunderstanding.

mesquin [mèskiⁿ] *adj.* mean, shabby; paltry, petty [caractère]; stingy [personne]. ‖ *mesquinerie* [-ìnrî] *f.* meanness; stinginess; mean action.

mess [mès] *m.* officers' mess.

message [mèsàj] *m.* message. ‖ *messager* [-é] *m.* messenger; carrier. ‖ *messagerie* [-rî] *f.* carrying trade; parcel delivery [service]; shipping line

[maritime]; stage-coach office [bureau].

messe [mès] *f.* mass (eccles.).

messieurs [mèsyë] *m. pl.* gentlemen, sirs; Messrs.; *see monsieur.*

mesurable [mᵉzüràbl] *adj.* measurable. ‖ *mesure* [-ür] *f.* measure; extent; gauge, standard; moderation, decorum (fig.); bar (mus.); *à mesure que*, in proportion as, as; *en mesure de*, in a position to; *sur mesure*, made to order [vêtement]. ‖ *mesurer* [-üré] *v.* to measure; to calculate; *se mesurer avec*, to cope with.

mésuser [mézüzé] *v.* to misuse.

métairie [métèrî] *f.* small farm.

métal [métàl] *m.** metal; bullion [barres]. ‖ *métallique* [-lìk] *adj.* metallic. ‖ *métallurgie* [-lürjî] *f.* metallurgy; smelting. ‖ *métallurgique* [-jìk] *adj.* metallurgic. ‖ *métallurgiste* [-jìst] *m.* metallurgist.

métamorphose [métàmòrfôz] *f.* metamorphosis. ‖ *métamorphoser* [-zé] *v.* to metamorphose.

métaphore [métàfòr] *f.* metaphor.

métayer [métèyé] *m.* tenant-farmer, *Am.* share-cropper.

météorologie [météòròlòjî] *f.* meteorology; *la Météo*, the weather bureau.

méthode [métòd] *f.* method, system; way. ‖ *méthodique* [-ìk] *adj.* methodical, systematic.

méticuleux [métìkülë] *adj.** meticulous, punctilious; overscrupulous.

métier [métyé] *m.* trade, profession, craft; loom [à tisser]; handicraft [manuel].

métis, -sse [métìs] *adj.* cross-bred, half-caste [personne]; hybrid [plante]; *m.* half-breed; mongrel; cross-bred; mestizo, metif, metis.

métrage [métràj] *m.* measurement; metric length; footage, length [film]. ‖ *mètre* [mètr] *m.* meter; yardstick (fam.); tape-measure [ruban]; metre [vers]. ‖ *métrique* [-ìk] *adj.* metric.

métro [métrô] *m.* underground railway, *Br.* tube, *Am.* subway.

métropole [métròpòl] *f.* metropolis; capital. ‖ *métropolitain* [-ìtiⁿ] *adj.* metropolitan; *m. see métro.*

mets [mè] *m.* food, viand, dish.

mettable [mètàbl] *adj.* wearable. ‖ *metteur* [-tœr] *m.* setter, layer; *metteur en scène*, director; producer (theat.). ‖ *mettre* [mètr] *v.** to put, to lay, to place, to set; to put on [vêtement]; to devote [soins]; *mettre bas*, to bring forth, to drop [animaux]; *mettre en colère*, to anger, *Am.* to madden; *mettre en état*, to enable; *mettre au point*, to adjust; to focus [lentille];

to perfect [invention]; to tune [moteur]; to clarify [affaire]; se *mettre*, to place oneself; to stand; to go, to get; *se mettre à*, to begin, to start; *s'y mettre*, to set about it.

meuble [mœbl] *m.* furniture; *pl.* furnishings; *adj.* movable, loose. ‖ **meubler** [-é] *v.* to furnish; to stock; to store (fig.).

meuglement [mëgləmaⁿ] *m.* lowing, mooing. ‖ **meugler** [-é] *v.* to low; to moo [vache].

meule [mœl] *f.* millstone; grindstone; stack, cock, rick [foin]; round [fromage].

meunier [mënyé] *m.* miller.

meurtre [mœrtr] *m.* murder. ‖ **meurtrier** [-lyé] *m.* murderer; *adj.*° murderous, deadly. ‖ **meurtrière** [-lyèr] *f.* murderess; loop-hole [château fort]. ‖ **meurtrir** [-îr] *v.* to bruise. ‖ **meurtrissure** [-lsür] *f.* bruise.

meute [mët] *f.* pack [chiens].

mévente [mévaⁿt] *f.* slump, stagnation (comm.).

mi [mĭ] *adv.* half, mid, semi-; *Mi-Carême*, mid-Lent; *à mi-chemin*, half-way; *à mi-hauteur*, half-way up.

miaulement [myôlmaⁿ] *m.* mewing, caterwauling. ‖ **miauler** [myôlé] *v.* to mew, to miaow.

mica [mǐkà] *m.* mica.

miche [mĭsh] *f.* round loaf [pain].

micheline [mĭshlĭn] *f.* electric railcar.

micro [mĭkrò] *m.* (fam.) mike.

microbe [mĭkròb] *m.* microbe, germ.

microfilm [mĭkròfĭlm] *m.* microfilm.

microphone [mĭkròfòn] *m.* microphone, mike (fam.).

microscope [mĭkròskòp] *m.* microscope; *microscopique*, microscopic.

microsillon [mĭkròsĭyoⁿ] *m.* long-playing record; minigroove.

midi [mĭdĭ] *m.* midday, noon, twelve o'clock; south (geogr.).

mie [mĭ] *f.* crumb, soft part [pain].

miel [myèl] *m.* honey. ‖ **mielleux** [-ë] *adj.*° honeyed, sugary [paroles]; bland [sourire].

mien, mienne [myĭⁿ, myèn] *poss. pron. m., f.* mine.

miette [myèt] *f.* crumb [pain]; bit.

mieux [myë] *m., adv.* better; *le mieux*, the best; *à qui mieux mieux*, in keen competition; *aimer mieux*, to prefer.

mièvre [myèvr] *adj.* finical, affected.

mignard [mĭñàr] *adj.* dainty; mincing, simpering. ‖ **mignon** [-oⁿ] *adj.*° dainty, tiny, darling, *Am.* cute; *m.* darling, pet.

migraine [mĭgrèn] *f.* migraine, sick headache.

mijoter [mĭjòté] *v.* to stew, to simmer; (fam.) to plot, to concoct.

mil [mĭl], see mille.

milan [mĭlaⁿ] *m.* kite [oiseau].

milieu [mĭlyë] *m.*° middle, midst; medium; sphere [social]; surroundings; middle course; underworld, gangsterdom; *le juste milieu*, the golden mean.

militaire [mĭlĭtèr] *adj.* military; *m.* soldier, military man. ‖ **militariser** [-àrĭzé] *v.* to militarize. ‖ **militarisme** [-àrĭsm] *m.* militarism.

millage [mĭlàj] *m.* © mileage.

mille [mĭl] *m., adj.* thousand, a thousand, one thousand; *Mille et Une Nuits*, Arabian Nights; *mille-pattes*, centipede.

mille [mĭl] *m.* mile. ‖ **milliaire** [mĭlyèr] *adj.* milliary; *borne milliaire*, milestone.

milliard [mĭlyàr] *m.* milliard, billion. ‖ **milliardaire** [-lyàrdèr] *m., adj.* millionaire. ‖ **millième** [-yèm] *m., adj.* thousandth. ‖ **millier** [-lyé] *m.* thousand, about a thousand. ‖ **million** [-yoⁿ] *m.* million. ‖ **millionième** [-yònyèm] *adj.* millionth. ‖ **millionnaire** [-yònèr] *m., f., adj.* millionaire.

mime [mĭm] *m.* mime; mimic. ‖ **mimer** [mĭmé] *v.* to mime; to mimic, to ape. ‖ **mimétisme** [-tĭsm] *m.* mimicry. ‖ **mimique** [mĭmĭk] *f.* mimicry; dumb show, *Am.* pantomime.

mimosa [mĭmòzà] *m.* mimosa.

minable [mĭnàbl] *adj.* shabby.

minauder [mĭnòdé] *v.* to simper, to smirk.

mince [mĭⁿs] *adj.* thin; slender, slight, slim; scanty [revenu]; flimsy [prétexte]. ‖ **minceur** [-œr] *f.* thinness; slenderness, slimness; scantiness.

mine [mĭn] *f.* appearance, look, mien, aspect; *avoir bonne mine*, to look well; *pl.* airs, simperings.

mine [mĭn] *f.* mine; ore [fer]; lead [crayon]; fund (fig.). ‖ **miner** [mĭné] *v.* to mine; to undermine; to consume. ‖ **minéral** [-rè] *m.* ore. ‖ **minéral** [-éràl] *adj.*° mineral; inorganic [chimie].

minet [mĭnè] *m.* pussy, tabby, puss.

mineur [mĭnœr] *adj.* minor; under age; *m.* minor.

mineur [mĭnœr] *m.* miner, collier; sapper (mil.).

miniature [mĭnyàtür] *f.* miniature.

minime [mĭnĭm] *adj.* tiny. ‖ **minimum** [-ĭmòm] *m., adj.* minimum.

ministère [mìnìstèr] *m.* agency; ministry; office; cabinet; department; *Ministère public.* public prosecutor (jur.); *ministère des Affaires étrangères,* Br. Foreign Office. *4m* Department of State. **ministériel** [-éryèl] *adj.** ministerial. ‖ **ministre** [mìnìstr] *m.* minister; secretary; clergyman; *ministre des Finances,* Br. Chancellor of the Exchequer, Am. Secretary of the Treasury.

minorité [mìnòrìté] *f.* minority; nonage (jur.).

minotier [mìnòtyé] *m.* flour-miller.

minuit [mìnùï] *m.* midnight.

minuscule [mìnüskül] *adj.* tiny, wee; *f.* small letter, lower-case letter.

minute [mìnüt] *f.* minute; draft. ‖ **minuter** [-té] *v.* to time. ‖ **minuterie** [-rî] *f.* time-switch. ‖ **minutie** [mìnüsî] *f.* minuteness, detail, trifle, minutiae. ‖ **minutieux** [-yë] *adj.** minute, detailed, thorough, painstaking.

mioche [myòsh] *m.*, *f.* urchin, kiddie, tot; brat.

mirabelle [mìràbèl] *f.* mirabelle plum.

miracle [mìràkl] *m.* miracle. ‖ **miraculeux** [-àkülé] *adj.** miraculous.

mirage [mìràj] *m.* mirage.

mire [mîr] *f.* sighting, aiming [fusil]; surveyor's rod. ‖ **mirer** [mìré] *v.* to aim at [viser]; to hold against the light.

miroir [mìrwàr] *m.* mirror, looking-glass. ‖ **miroiter** [mìrwàté] *v.* to flash; to glisten; to shimmer [eau]; to sparkle [joyau].

mis [mì] *adj.* dressed; *see* mettre.

misaine [mìzèn] *f.* foresail.

mise [mîz] *f.* placing, putting; bid [enchères]; stake [jeu], dress, attire; *mise à exécution,* carrying-out; *mise au point,* rectification; tuning-up (techn.); *mise en scène,* staging [theat.]; *être de mise,* to be suitable (ou) appropriate. ‖ **miser** [mìzé] *v.* to bid; to stake; to count (*sur,* on) [fig.].

misérable [mìzéràbl] *m.*, *f.* wretch, miserable person; outcast; *adj.* miserable; destitute; worthless. ‖ **misère** [mìzèr] *f.* misery, trifle. ‖ **miséricorde** [mìzérìkòrd] *f.* mercy. ‖ **miséricordieux** [-yë] *adj.** merciful, compassionate.

mission [mìsyoⁿ] *f.* mission. ‖ **missionnaire** [-yònèr] *m.* missionary.

mitaine [mìtèn] *f.* mitten.

mite [mìt] *f.* moth; tick. ‖ **mité** [-é] *adj.* moth-eaten, mity. ‖ **miteux** [-tœ] *adj.** shabby.

mitiger [mìtìjé] *v.* to mitigate.

mitoyen [mìtwàyìⁿ] *adj.** mean, middle; intermediate; party [mur].

mitraille [mìtrây] *f.* grape-shot. ‖ **mitrailler** [-àyé] *v.* to machine-gun, to strafe. ‖ **mitraillette** [-àyèt] *f.* sub-machine-gun. ‖ **mitrailleuse** [-àyëz] *f.* machine-gun.

mitre [mìtr] *f.* miter.

mixeur [mìksœr] *m.* mixer, Am. muddler, swizzlestick [cocktail].

mixte [mìkst] *adj.* mixed; joint. ‖ **mixture** [-ür] *f.* mixture.

mobile [mòbìl] *adj.* mobile, movable. unstable, changeable; detachable (mech.); *m.* moving body; driving power; mover, motive ‖ **mobilier** [-yé] *m.* furniture; *adj.* movable, transferable (jur.). ‖ **mobilisation** [-ìzàsyoⁿ] *f* mobilization liquidation (fin.). ‖ **mobiliser** [-ìzé] *v.* to mobilize; to liquidate ‖ **mobilité** [-ìté] *f.* mobility, movableness; changeableness; instability. fickleness.

moche [mòsh] *adj.* (pop.) rotten, lousy [conduite]; shoddy [travail]; ugly; dowdy [personne].

modalité [mòdàlìté] *f.* modality, method, scheme.

mode [mòd] *f.* fashion, mode; manner; vogue; *à la mode,* fashionable; *m.* method, mode; mood (gramm.); *mode d'emploi.* directions for use.

modèle [mòdèl] *m.* model, pattern; *adj.* exemplary. ‖ **modeler** [mòdlé] *v.* to model; to mould; to shape, to pattern.

modérateur, -trice [mòdéràtœr, -trìs] *adj.* moderating, restraining. ‖ **modération** [-àsyoⁿ] *f* moderation. ‖ **modérer** [-é] *v.* to moderate, to restrain; to regulate (mech.).

moderne [mòdèrn] *m.*, *adj.* modern. ‖ **moderniser** [-ìzé] *v.* to modernize, to bring up to date.

modeste [mòdèst] *adj.* modest; unassuming [person]; quiet, simple. ‖ **modestie** [-î] *f.* modesty.

modification [mòdìfìkàsyoⁿ] *f.* modification. ‖ **modifier** [-yé] *v.* to modify, to change, to alter.

modique [mòdîk] *adj.* moderate, reasonable [prix]; slender [ressources].

modiste [mòdîst] *f.* milliner, modiste.

moduler [mòdülé] *v.* to modulate.

moelle [mwàl] *f.* marrow; medulla (anat.); pith, core, marrow (fig.); *moelle épinière,* spinal cord. ‖ **moelleux** [-lœ] *adj.** soft; downy; juicy.

moellon [mwàloⁿ] *m.* quarry-stone.

mœurs [mœr, mœrs] *f. pl.* morals; manners, customs, ways; habits [animaux].

moi [mwà] *pron.* me, to me [complément]; I [sujet]; *m.* self, ego; *c'est à moi,* it is mine; *c'est moi,* it is I; *moi-même,* myself.

moignon [mwàñoⁿ] *m.* stump.

moindre [mwiⁿdr] *adj.* less, lesser, smaller; lower [prix]; *le moindre*, the least; the slightest.

moine [mwàn] *m.* monk, friar; bed-warmer; long light (naut.). ‖ *moineau* [-ô] *m.* sparrow.

moins [mwiⁿ] *adv.* less; fewer; *prep.* minus, less; *m.* dash (typogr.); *à moins que*, unless; *le moins*, the least; *au moins, du moins*, at least.

mois [mwâ] *m.* month; month's pay; *par mois*, monthly.

moisir [mwàzîr] *v.* to mildew, to mould. ‖ *moisissure* [-zìsür] *f.* mould, mildew.

moisson [mwàsoⁿ] *f.* harvest; harvest time. ‖ *moissonner* [-òné] *v.* to harvest, to reap; to gather. ‖ *moissonneur* [-sònœr] *m.* harvester, reaper. ‖ *moissonneuse* [-ònëz] *f.* harvester, reaper; *moissonneuse-batteuse*, combine harvester.

moite [mwàt] *adj.* moist, damp, clammy. ‖ *moiteur* [-œr] *f.* moistness; perspiration.

moitié [mwàtyé] *f.* half, moiety; (pop.) wife, better half.

mol [mòl] *adj.*, see mou.

molaire [mòlèr] *f.* molar [dent].

môle [môl] *m.* mole, pier; break-water.

molécule [mòlékül] *f.* molecule.

molester [mòlèsté] *v.* to molest.

molle [mòl] *adj.*, see mou.

mollesse [mòlès] *f.* softness; flabbiness; slackness; indolence. ‖ *mollet* [-è] *adj.* softish; coddled [œufs]; *m.* calf [jambe]. ‖ *molletière* [mòltyèr] *f.* legging; puttees [bande]. ‖ *molleton* [-oⁿ] *m.* swanskin; flannel; duffel; bunting; quilting. ‖ *mollir* [mòlîr] *v.* to soften; to slacken; to subside [vent].

mollusque [mòlüsk] *m.* mollusc; (fig.) molly-coddle.

moment [mòmaⁿ] *m.* moment; *pour le moment*, for the time being; *par moments*, at times. ‖ *momentané* [-tàné] *adj.* momentary; temporary. ‖ *momentanément* [-tànémaⁿ] *adv.* momentarily; temporarily.

momie [mòmî] *f.* mummy; old fogey; sleepy-head; fossil (fam.).

mon [moⁿ] *poss. adj. m.* (*f.* ma, *pl.* mes) my.

monacal [mònàkàl] *adj.* ‖ monastic.

monarchie [mònàrshî] *f.* monarchy. ‖ *monarque* [-àrk] *m.* monarch.

monastère [mònàstèr] *m.* monastery; convent [nonnes]; *monastique*, monastic.

monceau [moⁿsô] *m.* ‖ heap, pile.

mondain [moⁿdⁿ] *adj.* mundane, worldly, earthly; *m.* worldly-minded person, man-about-town. ‖ *mondanité* [-ànìté] *f.* worldliness; society news [journal]; *pl.* fashionable gatherings. ‖ *monde* [moⁿd] *m.* world; people; family; society; crowd; *tout le monde*, everybody; *recevoir du monde*, to entertain. ‖ *mondial* [-yàl] *adj.* ‖ world-wide; world [guerre].

monétaire [mònétèr] *adj.* monetary.

moniteur, -trice [mònìtœr, -trìs] *m.*, *f.* monitor, monitress; coach [sports].

monnaie [mònè] *f.* money, coin; currency; change; *monnaie légale*, legal tender; mint [hôtel]. ‖ *monnayer* [-yé] *v.* to coin, to mint; to cash in on (fig.). ‖ *monnayeur* [-yœr] *m.* coiner, minter; *faux-monnayeur*, counterfeiter.

monologue [mònòlòg] *m.* monologue; soliloquy; *monologuer*, to soliloquize.

monopole [mònòpòl] *m.* monopoly. ‖ *monopoliser* [-lzé] *v.* to monopolize.

Monoprix [mònòprì] *m.* one-price shop.

monosyllabe [mònòsìllàb] *m.* monosyllable; *adj.* monosyllabic.

monotone [mònòtòn] *adj.* monotonous; dull, stale, humdrum. ‖ *monotonie* [-î] *f.* monotony; sameness.

monseigneur [moⁿsèñœr] *m.* my lord; your grace [duc]; your royal highness [prince]; *pince-monseigneur*, crowbar, jemmy [cambrioleur]. ‖ *monsieur* [m•syë] (*pl.* messieurs [mésyë]) *m.* Mr.; sir; man, gentleman.

monstre [moⁿstr] *m.* monster; freak; *adj.* huge, colossal, enormous, prodigious. ‖ *monstrueux* [-üë] *adj.* ‖ monstrous; unnatural; huge, colossal; dreadful. ‖ *monstruosité* [-üòzìté] *f.* monstrosity.

mont [moⁿ] *m.* mount, mountain; hill; *par monts et par vaux*, up hill and down dale; *mont-de-piété*, pawn-shop. ‖ *montage* [-tàj] *m.* carrying up, hoisting; setting, mounting [joyau]; assembling [appareil]; equipping [magasin]; wiring (electr.); editing [film].

montagnard [moⁿtàñàr] *m.* mountaineer, highlander. ‖ *montagne* [-àñ] *f.* mountain. ‖ *montagneux* [-àñë] *adj.* ‖ mountainous, hilly.

montant [moⁿtaⁿ] *adj.* rising, ascending, uphill; high-necked [robe]; *m.* upright; leg; pillar; pole [tente]; riser [escalier]; stile [porte]; stanchion (naut.). ‖ *monte* [moⁿt] *f.* mounting; covering; *monte-charge*, hoist, freight elevator. ‖ *montée* [-é] *f.* rising; rise; ascent, gradient, up grade. ‖ *monter* [-é] *v.* to climb, to ascend, to mount, to go up; to ride [cheval]; to stock [magasin]; to get on, *Am.* to board [train]; to set [joyau]; to carry up, to bring up; to rise [prix]; to connect up (electr.); *se monter,* to amount; to equip oneself; to get excited.

montre [mo^ntr] *f.* show, display; shop-window, watch; clock [auto]; *montre-bracelet,* wrist-watch. ‖ **montrer** [-é] *v.* to show; to display, to exhibit; to indicate; to denote; *se montrer,* to show oneself; to appear.

monture [mo^ntür] *f.* mount [cheval]; mounting, assembling [machine]; setting [joyau]; frame [lunettes]; equipment; cargo.

monument [mònümä^n] *m.* monument, memorial; historic building; *pl.* sights. ‖ **monumental** [-tàl] *adj.** monumental; (fam.) colossal.

moquer [mòké] *v.* to mock, to ridicule, to scoff at; to deride; *se moquer de,* to make fun of, to laugh at; *s'en moquer,* not to care. ‖ **moquerie** [mòkrî] *f.* scoffing, ridicule, derision.

moquette [mòkèt] *f.* moquette, carpeting.

moqueur [mòkœr] *adj.** mocking, scoffing; *m.* mocker, scoffer.

moral [mòràl] *adj.** moral; ethical; mental, intellectual; *m.* morale. ‖ **morale** [-àl] *f.* morals; ethics, moral [fable]. ‖ **moraliser** [-àlizé] *v.* to moralize. ‖ **moralité** [-àlité] *f.* morality; morality play.

morbide [mòrbîd] *adj.* morbid, sickly, unhealthy.

morceau [mòrsô] *m.** piece, morsel; bit, scrap, fragment; lump [sucre]; piece of music. ‖ **morceler** [mòrsºlé] *v.* to cut up, to parcel out; to divide.

mordant [mòrdä^n] *adj.* corrosive; biting, caustic; mordacious; *m.* corrosiveness; mordancy, causticity. ‖ **mordiller** [-îyé] *v.* to nibble; to bite playfully.

mordoré [mòrdòré] *adj.* reddish brown, bronze-coloured.

mordre [mòrdr] *v.* to bite; to gnaw; to corrode; to catch [roue]; to criticize; to sting.

morfondre [mòrfo^ndr] *v.* to freeze; *se morfondre,* to mope; to be bored; to kick one's heels.

morgue [mòrg] *f.* haughtiness, arrogance; mortuary, morgue.

moribond [mòribo^n] *adj.* moribund, dying; *m.* dying person.

morigéner [mòrìjéné] *v.* to chide, to scold, to rate.

morille [mòrîy] *f.* morel.

morne [mòrn] *adj.* dejected, gloomy, cheerless; dismal, dreary, bleak [paysage]; glum, dejected [personne].

morose [mòrôz] *adj.* morose; gloomy.

mors [mòr] *m.* bit [harnais]; jaw [étau].

morse [mòrs] *m.* walrus.

morsure [mòrsür] *f.* bite; sting.

mort [mòr] *adj.* dead; lifeless; stagnant [eau]; out [feu]; *m.* dead person, deceased; corpse; dummy [cartes]; death; *jour des morts,* All Souls' Day; *mort-né,* still-born; *morte-saison,* slack season, off-season. ‖ **mortalité** [-tàlité] *f.* mortality, death-rate. ‖ **mortel** [-tèl] *adj.** mortal; fatal [accident]; deadly [péché]; deadly dull [soirée]; *m.* mortal.

mortier [mòrtyé] *m.* mortar.

mortifier [mòrtifyé] *v.* to mortify; to humiliate; to hang [gibier].

mortuaire [mòrtüèr] *adj.* mortuary; *drap mortuaire,* pall; *salon mortuaire,* ⊚ funeral home.

morue [mòrü] *f.* cod.

morve [mòrv] *f.* glanders (vet.); mucus, snot. ‖ **morveux** [-væ] *adj.** snotty; *m.* whipper-snapper.

mosaïque [mòzàïk] *f.* mosaic.

mosquée [mòské] *f.* mosque.

mot [mô] *m.* word; note, letter; *mot d'ordre,* countersign; key-note; *bon mot,* joke, witticism.

moteur, -trice [mòtœr, -tris] *adj.* motive, propulsive; *motory* (anat.); *m.* mover; motor; *f.* motor-carriage.

motif [mòtîf] *adj.* motive; *m.* motive, incentive; grounds (jur.).

motion [mòsyo^n] *f.* motion; proposal.

motiver [mòtivé] *v.* to motivate.

motocyclette [mòtòsìklèt] *f.* motorcycle; *motocycliste,* motor-cyclist. ‖ **motoriser** [-rìzé] *v.* to motorize.

motrice, see **moteur.**

motte [mòt] *f.* mound; clod, lump; turf [gazon].

mou, molle [mû, mòl] (*mol, m.,* before a vowel or a mute *h*) *adj.* soft; weak; flabby, flaccid [chair]; lax; spineless (fig.).

mou [mû] *m.* lights, lungs.

mouchard [mûshàr] *m.* sneak, informer, police-spy, *Am.* stool-pigeon. ‖ **moucharder** [-dé] *v.* to spy; to blab.

mouche [mûsh] *f.* fly; beauty-patch; button [fleuret]; bull's eye [cible]; *prendre la mouche,* to take offence.

moucher [mûshé] *v.* to wipe (someone's) nose; to snuff [chandelle]; to trim [cordage]; *moucher qqn,* to put s. o. in his place; *se moucher,* to blow one's nose.

moucheron [mûshro^n] *m.* gnat, midge.

moucheté [mûshté] *adj.* spotty, speckled, flecked.

mouchoir [mûshwàr] *m.* handkerchief.

moudre [mûdr] *v.** to grind, to mill; to thrash.

moue [mû] *f.* pout; *faire la moue*, to pout.

mouette [mûèt] *f.* gull, seamew.

mouffette [mûfèt] *f.* skunk.

moufle [mûfl] *f.* mitt; muffle; pulley-block (mech.).

mouflon [mûflon] *m.* moufflon.

mouillage [mûyàj] *m.* moistening, dampening; watering [vin]; anchoring (naut.); laying [mine]; *être au mouillage*, to ride at anchor. ‖ *mouiller* [mûyé] *v.* to wet, to moisten, to dampen; to cast, to drop [ancre]; to lay [mine]; to moor (naut.); to palatalize [consonne]; *se mouiller*, to water [yeux]; to get wet [personne].

mouise [mwîz] *f.* (pop.) poverty.

moulage [mûlàj] *m.* casting, moulding; founding (metall.); plaster cast. ‖ *moule* [mûl] *m.* mould; matrix.

moule [mûl] *f.* mussel [coquillage]; simpleton [naïf]; molly-coddle [mou].

moulé [mûlé] *adj.* moulded; cast; block [lettres]. ‖ *mouler* [-é] *v.* to cast; to mould; to found [fer]; to fit tightly [robe].

moulin [mûlin] *m.* mill; *moulin à vent*, windmill; *moulin à café*, coffee-mill. ‖ *moulinet* [-inè] *m.* winch; reel [canne à pêche]; turnstile; paddle-wheel; twirl [escrime].

moulure [mûlür] *f.* mo(u)lding.

mourant [mûran] *adj.* dying, expiring; fading, faint; *m.* dying person. ‖ *mourir* [-îr] *v.** to die, to expire; to perish; to go out [feu]; to be out [jeu].

mousquet [mûskè] *m.* musket. ‖ *mousquetaire* [-tèr] *m.* musketeer. ‖ *mousqueton* [-ton] *m.* cavalry magazine rifle; snap-hook.

mousse [mûs] *m.* ship's boy, cabinboy, deck-boy.

mousse [mûs] *f.* moss; froth, foam; head [bière]; suds, lather [savon]; whipped cream.

mousseline [mûslîn] *f.* muslin.

mousser [mûsé] *v.* to froth, to foam; to lather [savon]; to effervesce, to fizz [eau gazeuse]; *se faire mousser*, to advertize oneself. ‖ *mousseux* [-é] *adj.** mossy; frothy, foaming; lathery, *Am.* sudsy; sparkling [vin].

mousson [mûson] *f.* monsoon.

moussu [mûsü] *adj.* mossy; moss-grown.

moustache [mûstàsh] *f.* mustache; whiskers [chat].

moustiquaire [mûstìkèr] *f.* mosquito-net. ‖ *moustique* [-ìk] *m.* mosquito; gnat; sand-fly.

moût [mû] *m.* must [vin]; wort [bière].

moutard [mûtàr] *m.* (pop.) kid.

moutarde [mûtàrd] *f.* mustard.

mouton [mûton] *m.* sheep; mutton [viande]; ram, monkey (mech.); decoy, prison spy (pop.); *pl.* white-caps, white horses [mer]. ‖ *moutonneux* [-ônè] *adj.** fleecy [ciel]; frothy, foamy [mer]. ‖ *moutonnier* [-nyé] *adj.** sheeplike.

mouture [mûtür] *f.* grinding, milling; grist.

mouvant [mûvan] *adj.* actuating [force]; moving, mobile; shifting; *sables mouvants*, quicksand. ‖ *mouvement* [-man] *m.* movement; motion; change; traffic [circulation]; works, action (mech.); impulse. ‖ *mouvementé* [-manté] *adj.* animated, lively; eventful [vie]; undulating [terrain]. ‖ *mouvoir* [-wàr] *v.** to drive, to propel; to actuate; *se mouvoir*, to move, to stir.

moyen [mwàyin] *adj.** middle; average, mean; medium; *m.* means; way, manner; medium; *pl.* resources; *Moyen Age*, Middle Ages; *au moyen de*, by means of; *moyenâgeux*, medieval. ‖ *moyennant* [mwàyènan] *prep.* by means of. ‖ *moyenne* [mwàyèn] *f.* average; mean; pass-mark [école].

moyeu [mwàyè] *m.** hub, nave, boss [roue].

mû [mü], see *mouvoir*.

mucosité [mükòzìté] *f.* mucus, mucosity.

mue [mü] *f.* moulting [oiseaux]; shedding [animaux]; sloughing [reptiles]; breaking [voix]; mew [faucon]; coop [volaille]. ‖ *muer* [-é] *v.* to change; to moult; to shed; to slough; to break [voix]; *se muer*, to change (en, into).

muet [müè] *adj.** dumb, mute; speechless; silent; *m.* mute, dumb person.

mufle [müfl] *m.* snout, muzzle [animal]; cad, rotter, skunk [personne]. ‖ *muflerie* [-rî] *f.* caddishness; rotten trick.

mugir [müjîr] *v.* to bellow [taureau]; to low [vache]; to roar, to boom [mer]; to moan, to howl [vent]. ‖ *mugissement* [-ìsman] *m.* bellowing; lowing; roaring, booming, moaning; howling.

muguet [mügè] *m.* lily of the valley; thrush (med.).

mulâtre, -tresse [mülâtr, -très] *m.* mulatto; *f.* mulatress.

mule [mül] *f.* she-mule [bête].

mule [mül] *f.* mule, slipper.

mulet [mülè] *m.* mule. ‖ *muletier* [mültyé] *m.* muleteer.

mulot [mülò] *m.* field-mouse.

multicolore [mültìkòlòr] *adj.* multi-coloured, *Am.* parti-colored.

multiforme [mültìfòrm] *adj.* multi-form.

multiple [mültìpl] *adj.* multiple, manifold; multifarious; *m.* multiple. ‖ *multiplication* [-ìkàsyo] *f.* multiplication; geár-ratio, step-up (mech.). ‖ *multiplier* [-ìyé] *v.* to multiply; to step up (mech.).

multitude [mültìtüd] *f.* multitude; crowd, throng; heap, lots.

municipal [münìsìpàl] *adj.** municipal. ‖ *municipalité* [-ìté] *f.* municipality, township, corporation.

munificence [münìfìsa^ns] *f.* munificence; *avec munificence,* munificently.

munir [münîr] *v.* to furnish, to supply, to fit, to equip, to provide (*de,* with); to arm, to fortify (mil.). ‖ *munition* [-ìsyo^n] *f.* munitioning; provisioning; stores, supplies; ammunition (mil.).

muqueuse [mükœz] *f.* mucous membrane. ‖ *muqueux* [mükë] *adj.** mucous.

mur [mür] *m.* wall; *mur mitoyen,* party-wall; *franchir le mur du son,* to break through the sound-barrier.

mûr [mür] *adj.* ripe; mellow; mature.

muraille [müràỳ] *f.* high defensive wall; side (naut.). ‖ *mural* [-àl] *adj.** mural; wall.

mûre [mür] *f.* mulberry; brambleberry, blackberry.

mûrement [mürma^n] *adv.* maturely.

murer [müré] *v.* to wall in, to block up.

mûrir [mürîr] *v.* to ripen, to mature.

murmure [mürmür] *m.* murmur; hum [voix]; whisper [chuchotement]; muttering, grumbling. ‖ *murmurer* [-é] *v.* to murmur; to whisper; to grumble, to complain.

musaraigne [müzàrèñ] *f.* shrew-mouse.

musarder [müzàrdé] *v.* to dawdle; to idle; to dilly-dally; to fribble away one's time.

musc [müsk] *m.* musk; musk-deer.

muscade [müskàd] *f.* nutmeg.

muscle [müskl] *m.* muscle, brawn, sinew. ‖ *musclé* [-é] *adj.* brawny, athletic. ‖ *musculaire* [-ülèr] *adj.* muscular. ‖ *musculeux* [-ülë] *adj.** muscular, brawny; beefy [personne].

museau [müzô] *m.** muzzle, snout; nose.

musée [müzé] *m.* museum.

museler [müzlé] *v.* to muzzle; to gag, to silence. ‖ *muselière* [-^elyèr] *f.* muzzle.

muser [müzé] *v.* to idle, to dawdle.

musette [müzèt] *f.* bagpipe (mus.); bag, satchel, pouch; nose-bag [cheval].

muséum [müzéòm] *m.* museum.

musical [müzìkàl] *adj.** musical. ‖ *musicalité* [-ìté] *f.* musicality; music-alness. ‖ *musicien* [-ìsyi^n] *m.* musician; bandsman. ‖ *musique* [müzìk] *f.* music; band. ‖ *musiquette* [-kèt] *f.* cheap music.

musquer [müské] *v.* to musk; *poire musquée,* musk-pear; *rat musqué,* muskrat.

musulman [müzülma^n] *m.* Mohammedan, Moslem.

mutation [mütàsyo^n] *f.* change, mutation, alteration; transfer. ‖ *muter* [-é] *v.* to transfer.

mutilation [mütìlàsyo^n] *f.* mutilation, maiming; defacement; garbling [texte]. ‖ *mutiler* [-é] *v.* to mutilate, to maim; to deface; to garble.

mutin [mütì^n] *adj.* unruly; mutinous; insubordinate [soldat]; *m.* mutineer, rioter. ‖ *mutiner* [-ìné] *v.* to incite to rebellion; *se mutiner,* to revolt; to mutiny. ‖ *mutinerie* [-ìnrî] *f.* rebellion; mutiny; roguishness.

mutisme [mütìsm] *m.* dumbness, muteness; silence.

mutualiste [mütüàlìst] *s.* mutualist. ‖ *mutualité* [-ìté] *f.* mutuality; reciprocity; mutual insurance. ‖ *mutuel* [mütüèl] *adj.** mutual, reciprocal; *secours mutuels,* mutual benefit [société]; *mutuellement,* mutually, reciprocally.

myope [myòp] *adj.* myopic, *Br.* short-sighted, *Am.* nearsighted. ‖ *myopie* [-î] *f.* myopia.

myosotis [myòzòtìs] *m.* forget-me-not, myosotis.

myriade [mìryàd] *f.* myriad.

myrrhe [mîr] *f.* myrrh.

myrte [mîrt] *m.* myrtle. ‖ *myrtille* [mîrtỳ] *f.* whortleberry, blueberry.

mystère [mìstèr] *m.* mystery; secrecy; mystery play. ‖ *mystérieux* [-éryë] *adj.** mysterious; enigmatic; uncanny. ‖ *mysticisme* [-ìsìsm] *m.* mysticism. ‖ *mystification* [-ìfìkàsyo^n] *f.* mystification; hoax. ‖ *mystifier* [-ìfyé] *v.* to mystify; to hoax, to fool, to spoof. ‖ *mystique* [-ìk] *m., f.* mystic [personne]; *f.* mystical theology; *adj.* mystic, mystical.

mythe [mìt] *m.* myth; legend, fable. ‖ *mythique* [-ìk] *adj.* mythical. ‖ *mythologie* [-òlòjî] *f.* mythology.

N

nabot [nàbò] *m.* dwarf, midget.

nacelle [nàsèl] *f.* skiff, wherry, dinghy (naut.); pontoon-boat (mil.); gondola [dirigeable]; nacelle, cockpit (aviat.).

nacre [nàkr] *f.* mother of pearl. ‖ *nacré* [-é] *adj.* nacreous, pearly.

nage [nàj] *f.* swimming; rowing; pulling (naut.); stroke [natation]; rowlock; *en nage*, bathed in perspiration. ‖ *nageoire* [-wàr] *f.* fin. ‖ *nager* [-é] *v.* to row, to pull; to scull; to swim; to wallow in [opulence]; to be all at sea (fam.).

naguère [nàgèr] *adv.* lately; erstwhile.

naïf, -ïve [naïf, -ïv] *adj.* naïve, artless, ingenuous, unaffected; credulous, guileless, unsophisticated; (fam.) green.

nain [nin] *m.* dwarf, midget, pygmy; (fam.) runt; *adj.* dwarfish, stunted.

naissance [nèsaⁿs] *f.* birth; extraction; beginning; rise [rivière]. ‖ *naître* [nètr] *v.** to be born; to originate; to begin; to dawn.

naïveté [nàïvté] *f.* artlessness, simplicity, ingenuousness, naïveté, guilelessness; (fam.) greenness.

nantir [naⁿtìr] *v.* to provide. ‖ *nantissement* [naⁿtìsmaⁿ] *m.* security; lien, hypothecation.

napalm [nàpàlm] *m.* napalm.

naphtaline [nàftàlìn] *f.* moth-balls.

nappe [nàp] *f.* tablecloth, cloth, cover; sheet [eau]; layer [brouillard]. ‖ *napperon* [-roⁿ] *m.* napkin; doily; place-mat; tea-cloth.

narcisse [nàrsìs] *m.* narcissus.

narcotique [nàrkòtìk] *m.*, *adj.* narcotic.

narguer [nàrgé] *v.* to flout; to jeer at; to set at defiance.

narine [nàrìn] *f.* nostril.

narquois [nàrkwà] *adj.* bantering.

narrateur, -trice [nàràtœr, -trìs] *m.*, *f.* narrator, relater, teller. ‖ *narration* [-syoⁿ] *f.* narration, narrative. ‖ *narrer* [-é] *v.* to narrate, to relate, to tell.

nasal [nàzàl] *adj.** nasal. ‖ *nasale* [-àl] *f.* nasal. ‖ *naseau* [-ô] *m.** nostril. ‖ *nasillard* [-ìyàr] *adj.* nasal; snuffling; twanging. ‖ *nasiller* [-ìyé] *v.* to twang.

nasse [nàs] *f.* wicker-trap.

natal [nàtàl] *(pl. natals) adj.* native, natal. ‖ *natalité* [-ìté] *f.* birth-rate.

natation [nàtàsyoⁿ] *f.* swimming.

natif [nàtìf] *adj.** native; natural, inborn.

nation [nàsyoⁿ] *f.* nation. ‖ *national* [-syònàl] *adj.** national. ‖ *nationaliser* [-nàlìzé] *v.* to nationalize. ‖ *nationalité* [-yònàlìté] *f.* nationality; citizenship.

nativité [nàtìvìté] *f.* nativity.

natte [nàt] *f.* mat, matting [paille]; plait, braid; (fam.) pigtail [cheveux]. ‖ *natter* [-é] *v.* to plait, to braid; to mat.

naturalisation [nàtüràlìzàsyoⁿ] *f.* naturalization; stuffing [taxidermie]. ‖ *naturaliser* [-é] *v.* to naturalize; to stuff.

nature [nàtür] *f.* nature; kind, constitution, character; temperament, disposition; *adj.* plain; *nature morte*, still-life. ‖ *naturel* [-èl] *adj.** natural; unaffected; native; innate; illegitimate [enfant]; *m.* naturalness; character. ‖ *naturellement* [-èlmaⁿ] *adv.* naturally; of course.

naufrage [nôfràj] *m.* shipwreck. ‖ *naufragé* [-é] *adj.* shipwrecked; *m.* shipwrecked person, castaway.

nauséabond [nôzéàboⁿ] *adj.* nauseous; evil-smelling. ‖ *nausée* [-é] *f.* nausea; seasickness; loathing, disgust. ‖ *nauséeux* [-éœ] *adj.** nauseous, nauseating; loathsome.

nautique [nôtìk] *adj.* nautical; aquatic [sports].

naval [nàvàl] *(pl. navals) adj.* naval, nautical.

navet [nàvè] *m.* turnip; daub, dud; unsuccessful play, Am. turkey (pop.).

navette [nàvèt] *f.* shuttle; incensebox; *faire la navette*, to ply between, to go to and fro.

navigable [nàvìgàbl] *adj.* navigable [rivière]; seaworthy [bateau]; airworthy (aviat.). ‖ *navigation* [-àsyoⁿ] *f.* navigation. ‖ *naviguer* [nàvìgé] *v.* to navigate, to sail.

navire [nàvìr] *m.* ship, vessel; *navire marchand*, merchantman.

navrant [nàvraⁿ] *adj.* heart-rending; harrowing; agonizing. ‖ *navré* [-é] *adj.* heart-broken; grieved; sorry.

nazi [nàzì] *m.*, *adj.* Nazi.

ne [nə] *adv.* no; not.

né [né] *adj.* born; *il est né*, he was born.

néanmoins [néaⁿmwiⁿ] *adv.* nevertheless, however; yet, still.

néant [néaⁿ] *m.* nothingness, naught, nullity.

nébuleux [nébülœ] *adj.** nebulous, cloudy, misty; turbid [liquide]; gloomy [visage]; obscure [théorie].

nécessaire [nésèsèr] adj. necessary, needed; m. necessities of life; indispensable; outfit, kit. ‖ **nécessite** [-ité] f. necessity, need, want. ‖ **nécessiter** [-ité] v. to necessitate, to require, to entail. ‖ **nécessiteux** [-itë] adj.* necessitous, needy, destitute.

nécrologe [nékròlòj] m. obituary list. ‖ **nécrologie** [-jí] f. necrology, obituary. ‖ **nécrologique** [-jìk] adj. obituary.

néerlandais [néèrlɑⁿdè] adj., m. Dutch.

nef [nèf] f. nave [église]; ship, vessel [poétique].

néfaste [néfàst] adj. ill-omened, baneful; ill-fated; pernicious.

nèfle [nèfl] f. medlar.

négatif [négàtîf] m., adj.* negative. ‖ **négation** [-àsyoⁿ] f. negation, denial; negative (gramm.).

négligé [néglìjé] adj. neglected, careless, slovenly, sloppy, slipshod; m. undress; dishabille; informal dress. ‖ **négligeable** [-àbl] adj. negligible; trifling. ‖ **négligence** [-ɑⁿs] f. negligence, neglect. ‖ **négligent** [-ɑⁿ] adj. negligent, neglectful; slack, remiss. ‖ **négliger** [-é] v. to neglect; to slight; to disregard, to overlook, to omit.

négoce [négòs] m. trade, business; trafficking. ‖ **négociant** [-yɑⁿ] m. merchant; trader; wholesaler. ‖ **négociateur, -trice** [-yàtœr, -trìs] m., f. negotiator, transactor. ‖ **négociation** [-yàsyoⁿ] f. negotiation; transaction (comm.). ‖ **négocier** [-yé] v. to trade, to traffic; to negotiate [traité]; to deal (avec, with).

nègre [nègr] m. negro; ghost writer, Am. stooge [écrivain]. ‖ **négresse** [négrès] f. negress. ‖ **négrier** [négrìyé] m. slave-trader; slave-ship. ‖ **négrillon** [-yoⁿ] m. nigger-boy.

neige [nèj] f. snow. ‖ **neiger** [-é] v. to snow. ‖ **neigeux** [-é] adj.* snowy; snow-covered.

nénuphar [nénüfàr] m. water-lily.

néon [néoⁿ] m. neon.

nerf [nèr] m. nerve; sinew; vein [feuille]; cord [reliure]; rib, fillet (arch.). ‖ **nerveux** [-vë] adj.* nervous; sinewy, wiry; vigorous, terse [style]; excitable, fidgety; responsive [voiture]. ‖ **nervosité** [-vòzìté] f. nervousness, irritability, fidgets, edginess. ‖ **nervure** [-vür] f. nervure, rib; vein; fillet, moulding (arch.); piping [couture].

net, nette [nèt] adj. clean, spotless; net [prix]; clear; plain; distinct (phot.); adv. flatly. ‖ **netteté** [-té] f. cleanness, cleanliness; distinctness [image]; clarity, sharpness (phot.); vividness; flatness [refus]. ‖ **nettoiement, nettoyage** [-wàmɑⁿ, -wàyàj]

m. cleaning, clearing; scouring; mopping-up (mil.); nettoyage à sec, dry-cleaning. ‖ **nettoyer** [-wàyé] v. to clean, to clear; to scour; to plunder; to mop up (mil.).

neuf [nœf] m., adj. nine; ninth [titre, date].

neuf, neuve [nœf, nœv] adj. new; brand-new; remettre à neuf, to renovate.

neurasthénie [nœràsténí] f. neurasthenia.

neutraliser [nœtràlìzé] v. to neutralize. ‖ **neutralité** [-té] f. neutrality. ‖ **neutre** [nœtr] adj. neuter; neutral.

neuvaine [nœvèn] f. novena. ‖ **neuvième** [nœvyèm] m., adj. ninth.

neveu [nⁱvë] m.* nephew.

névralgie [névràljí] f. neuralgia. ‖ **névralgique** [-jìk] adj. neuralgic; point névralgique, nerve-centre. ‖ **névrose** [névròz] f. neurosis. ‖ **névrosé** [-zé] adj. neurotic.

nez [nè] m. nose; snout [animaux]; nose [bateau, avion]; nez à nez, face to face; piquer du nez, to nose-dive.

ni [nì] conj. nor, or; neither... nor; ni moi non plus, nor I either.

niais [nìè] adj. simple, foolish, silly; Am. dumb; m. fool, simpleton, booby, Am. dumbbell. ‖ **niaiserie** [-zrî] f. silliness; twaddle.

niche [nìsh] f. kennel [chien]; niche, nook (archit.).

niche [nìsh] f. trick, prank.

nichée [nìshé] f. nestful; brood. ‖ **nicher** [-é] v. to nest; (fam.) to hang out; se nicher, to nest; to nestle.

nickel [nìkèl] m. nickel.

nid [nì] m. nest; nid d'abeilles, waffle weave [tissu].

nièce [nyès] f. niece.

nielle [nyèl] f. smut, blight [blé].

nier [nyé] v. to deny; to repudiate [dette].

nigaud [nìgô] adj. simple, silly; m. booby, simpleton.

nitouche [nìtûsh] f. demure girl; faire la sainte nitouche, to look as if butter would not melt in one's mouth.

nitrate [nìtràt] m. nitrate.

niveau [nìvô] m.* level; standard; au niveau de, even with. ‖ **niveler** [-lé] v. to level, to even up; to true up (mech.). ‖ **nivellement** [-èlmɑⁿ] m. levelling; surveying; contouring [terre].

noble [nòbl] adj. noble; stately; high-minded; m. noble(man). ‖ **noblesse** [-ès] f. nobility; nobleness.

noce [nòs] f. wedding; spree, Am. binge; pl. marriage, nuptials. ‖ **noceur** [-œr] m. reveller, roisterer; fast liver.

nocif [nòsìf] *adj.* noxious.

noctambule [nòktaⁿbül] *s.* noctambulist; night-prowler.

nocturne [nòktürn] *adj.* nocturnal; *m.* nocturne.

Noël [nòèl] *m.* Christmas, Noel; yuletide; Christmas carol.

nœud [në] *m.* knot; bow [carré]; hitch, bend (naut.); gnarl [bois], node, joint [tige]; knuckle [doigt]; *nœud coulant,* slip-knot, noose; *nœud papillon,* bow-tie.

noir [nwàr] *adj.* black; dark; gloomy [idées]; wicked; (fam.) drunk; *m.* black, Negro; bruise (med.). ‖ *noirâtre* [-âtr] *adj.* blackish, darkish. ‖ *noirceur* [-sœr] *f.* blackness; darkness; gloominess; smudge; atrocity [crime]. ‖ *noircir* [-sìr] *v.* to blacken; to darken; to sully; to besmirch; to scribble on [papier].

noise [nwàz] *f.* quarrel; *chercher noise à quelqu'un,* to try to pick a quarrel with someone.

noisetier [nwàztyé] *m.* hazel-tree. ‖ *noisette* [-èt] *f.* hazel-nut. ‖ *noix* [nwà] *f.* walnut; nut; cushion [veau].

nom [nòⁿ] *m.* name; noun (gramm.); *nom de plume,* pen-name; *nom de famille,* family name, last name; *petit nom,* first name; given name; *nom et prénoms,* full name.

nomade [nòmàd] *adj.* nomadic; *m., f.* nomad.

nombre [nòⁿbr] *m.* number; *bon nombre de,* a good many; *nombre entier,* integer. ‖ *nombreux* [-ë] *adj.* numerous; multifarious; manifold.

nombril [nòⁿbrì] *m.* navel.

nomenclature [nòmaⁿklàtür] *f.* nomenclature, list.

nominal [nòmìnàl] *adj.* nominal; *appel nominal,* roll-call. ‖ *nominatif* [-àtìf] *m.* nominative; subject (gramm.); *adj.* registered [titres].

nommer [nòmé] *v.* to name; to mention; to appoint; *se nommer,* to be named; to give one's name.

non [nòⁿ] *adv.* no; not.

nonce [nòⁿs] *m.* nuncio.

nonchalance [nòⁿshàlaⁿs] *f.* languidness; nonchalance. ‖ *nonchalant* [-aⁿ] *adj.* nonchalant; languid; supine.

non-lieu [nòⁿlyë] *m.* no true bill; *obtenir un non-lieu,* to be discharged.

nonne [nòn] *f.* nun.

nonobstant [nònòbstaⁿ] *prep.* notwithstanding.

non-sens [nòⁿsaⁿs] *m.* meaningless act; nonsense.

nord [nòr] *m.* north; *perdre le nord,* to lose one's bearings.

normal [nòrmàl] *adj.* normal; usual; natural; standard. ‖ *normaliser* [-ìzé] *v.* to normalize, to standardize.

normand [nòrmaⁿ] *adj., m., f.* Norman. ‖ *Normandie* [-dì] *f.* Normandy.

norme [nòrm] *f.* norm.

nos [nô] *poss. adj. pl.* our; *see* **notre.**

nostalgie [nòstàljì] *f.* nostalgia, home-sickness. ‖ *nostalgique* [-ìk] *adj.* nostalgic; home-sick.

notable [nòtàbl] *adj.* notable, noteworthy; distinguished; *m.* person of distinction.

notaire [nòtèr] *m.* notary.

notamment [nòtàmaⁿ] *adv.* especially, particularly.

note [nòt] *f.* note, memo(randum), minute; annotation; notice; mark, *Am.* grade [école]; bill, account [hôtel]; repute; note (mus.). ‖ *noter* [-é] *v.* to note; to notice; to mark; to jot down. ‖ *notice* [-ìs] *f.* notice, account; review. ‖ *notification* [nòtìfìkàsyoⁿ] *f.* notification, advice. ‖ *notifier* [-é] *v.* to notify; to intimate; to signify.

notion [nòsyoⁿ] *f.* notion, idea; smattering.

notoire [nòtwàr] *adj.* well-known; manifest; notorious [brigand]. ‖ *notoriété* [-òrìété] *f.* notoriety, notoriousness; repute, reputation.

notre [nòtr] *poss. adj.* (*pl.* **nos**) our.

nôtre [nôtr] *poss. pron.* ours; our own.

nouer [nûé] *v.* to tie, to knot; to establish [relations]; *se nouer,* to kink, to twist; to cling; to knit; to be anchylosed. ‖ *noueux* [-ë] *adj.* knotty; gnarled [mains]; arthritic [rhumatisme].

nouilles [nûy] *f.* noodle; (fam.) nincompoop.

nourrice [nûrìs] *f.* nurse, wet-nurse; service-tank (tech.); feed-pipe (aviat.). ‖ *nourricier* [-yé] *m.* foster-father; *adj.* nutritious, nutritive. ‖ *nourrir* [nûrìr] *v.* to feed, to nourish; to nurse, to suckle [enfant]; to foster [haine]; to harbo(u)r [pensée]; to cherish [espoir]; to maintain, to sustain [feu] (mil.). ‖ *nourrissant* [-ìsaⁿ] *adj.* nourishing, nutritive, nutritious; rich [aliment]. ‖ *nourrisson* [-ìsoⁿ] *m.* nursling, suckling; foster-child. ‖ *nourriture* [-ìtür] *f.* feeding; food, nourishment.

nous [nû] *pron.* we [sujet]; us, to us [complément]; ourselves; each other; *chez nous,* at our house.

nouveau, -elle [nûvô, -èl] *adj.* (**nouvel,** *m.,* before a vowel or a mute *h*) new; new-style, recent, fresh; novel; another, additional, further; *nouvel an,* new year; *de nouveau,* again; *à nouveau,* anew, afresh; *nouveau-né,* new-born child. ‖ **nouveauté** [-té] *f.* newness, novelty; change, innovation; fancy article, latest model. ‖ **nouvelle** [nûvèl] *f.* news, tidings; short story.

novateur, -trice [nòvàtær, -trìs] *m., f.* innovator; *adj.* innovating.

novembre [nòvᵃbr] *m.* November.

novice [nòvìs] *m.* novice; probationer; tyro; apprentice; *adj.* inexperienced, green; new (en, into).

noyade [nwàyàd] *f.* drowning.

noyau [nwàyô] *m.* stone, kernel, Am. pit [fruit]; nucleus [atome]; group, knot; cell (fig.).

noyer [nwàyé] *v.* to drown; to flood, to inundate; **se noyer**, to be drowned [accident]; to drown oneself [suicide]; to flounder (fig.).

noyer [nwàyé] *m.* walnut-tree.

nu [nü] *adj.* naked, nude; bare; plain, unadorned; *m.* nude; nudity; **nu-pieds**, bare-footed; **nu-tête**, bareheaded.

nuage [nüàj] *m.* cloud; *nuage artificiel*, smoke screen. ‖ **nuageux** [-ê] *adj.* cloudy; overcast; nebulous.

nuance [nüᵃs] *f.* shade hue nuance, gradation. ‖ **nuancé** [nüᵃsé] *adj.* delicately shaded; delicately expressive. ‖ **nuancer** [-sé] *v.* to shade; to blend.

nucléaire [nükléèr] *adj.* nuclear.

nudité [nüdìté] *f.* nudity, nakedness.

nue [nü] *f.* high cloud; *pl.* skies. ‖ **nuée** [-é] *f.* cloud; swarm, host.

nuire [nüîr] *v.* to harm, to hurt; to be injurious. ‖ **nuisible** [nüìzìbl] *adj.* hurtful, harmful, noxious, detrimental, prejudicial.

nuit [nüì] *f.* night.

nul, nulle [nül] *adj.* no, not one; nul, void; *pron.* no one, nobody, not one. ‖ **nullement** [-mᵃ] *adv.* not at all; in no way, by no means. ‖ **nullité** [-lté] *f.* nullity, invalidity; nothingness; nonexistence; nonentity [personne].

numéraire [nümérèr] *adj.* legal [monnaie]; numerary [valeur]; *m.* metallic currency, specie; cash. ‖ **numéral** [-àl] *adj.* numeral. ‖ **numérique** [-îk] *adj.* numerical. ‖ **numéro** [-ô] *m.* number; issue [périodique]; turn [music-hall]. ‖ **numéroter** [-òté] *v.* to number; to page [livre].

nuptial [nüpsyàl] *adj.* wedding; marriage; bridal.

nuque [nük] *f.* nape, scruff of the neck.

nutritif [nütrìtìf] *adj.* nutritive. ‖ **nutrition** [-ìsyoⁿ] *f.* nutrition.

O

obéir [òbéîr] *v.* to obey; to comply; to respond (aviat.). ‖ **obéissance** [-ìsaⁿs] *f.* obedience; compliance, submission; pliancy. ‖ **obéissant** [-ìsaⁿ] *adj.* obedient, compliant, dutiful; submissive; responsive.

obélisque [òbélìsk] *m.* obelisk.

obèse [òbèz] *adj.* obese, fat. ‖ **obésité** [òbézìté] *f.* obesity, corpulence, stoutness, portliness.

objecter [òbjèkté] *v.* to raise an objection, to object. ‖ **objectif** [-tìf] *adj.* objective; *m.* objective aim end lens (phot.), target aim. ‖ **objection** [-syoⁿ] *f.* objection. ‖ **objet** [òbjè] *m.* object, thing; article; complement (gramm.); subject.

obligation [òblìgàsyoⁿ] *f.* obligation, duty; bond [Bourse]; debenture (comm.); favo(u)r, liability (mil.). ‖ **obligatoire** [-àtwàr] *adj.* obligatory; compulsory.

obligeance [òblìjaⁿs] *f.* obligingness. ‖ **obligeant** [-aⁿ] *adj.* obliging; kind, civil. ‖ **obliger** [-é] *v.* to oblige, to constrain, to bind.

oblique [òblìk] *adj.* oblique; slanting; devious, crooked [moyens]. ‖ **obliquer** [-é] *v.* to oblique; to slant; to incline; to swerve.

oblitérer [òblìtéré] *v.* to obliterate; to cancel, to deface [timbre-poste].

obole [òbòl] *f.* obol; farthing, mite.

obscène [òbsèn] *adj.* obscene; lewd; smutty. ‖ **obscénité** [-énìté] *f.* obscenity; lewdness.

obscur [òbskür] *adj.* dark; gloomy; somber; obscure; abstruse [sujet]; indistinct, dim; lowly, humble [naissance]; unknown [écrivain]. ‖ **obscurcir** [-sîr] *v.* to obscure, to darken; to dim; to fog; **s'obscurcir**, to grow dark, to darken, to cloud over [ciel]. ‖ **obscurcissement** [-sìsmaⁿ] *m.* darkening, dimness. ‖ **obscurité** [-ìté] *f.* obscurity; darkness; obscureness; vagueness gloom.

obsédant [òbsédaⁿ] *adj.* haunting; obsessive. ‖ **obséder** [-é] *v.* to obsess; to beset; to importune.

obsèques [òbsèk] *f. pl.* obsequies; funeral.

obséquieux [òbsékyë] *adj.* obsequious; servile. ‖ **obséquiosité** [-kyòzìté] *f.* obsequiousness; oily pleading.

observance [òbsèrvaⁿs] *f.* observance, keeping. ‖ **observateur, -trice** [-àtær, -trìs] *m., f.* observer; spotter (mil.); *adj.* observant. ‖ **observation**

[-àsyoⁿ] f. observation. ‖ **observatoire** [-àtwàr] m. observatory. ‖ **observer** [-é] v. to observe, to notice; to remark; to keep [règlements]; s'*observer*, to be careful, to be cautious; to be on one's guard.

obsession [òbsèsyoⁿ] f. obsession.

obstacle [òbstàkl] m. obstacle, hindrance, impediment; jump, fence [course].

obstination [òbstìnàsyoⁿ] f. obstinacy, stubbornness. ‖ **obstiner** [-é] v. to make (someone) obstinate; s'*obstiner*, to persist; to grow obstinate.

obstruction [òbstrüksyoⁿ] f. obstruction; blocking; *Am.* filibustering [politique]; choking, clogging (techn.). ‖ **obstruer** [òbstrüé] v. to obstruct; to block; to choke; to throttle; to jam.

obtempérer [òbtaⁿpéré] v. to comply, to accede.

obtenir [òbtᵉnîr] v.* to obtain, to get, to procure.

obturateur [òbtüràtœr] m. stopper; obturator; shutter; stop-valve. ‖ **obturation** [-syoⁿ] f. obturation; filling [dent]. ‖ **obturer** [òbtüré] v. to stop, to seal, to obturate; to fill [dent].

obtus [òbtü] adj. blunt; obtuse, dull [personne].

obus [òbü] m. shell. ‖ **obusier** [-zyé] m. howitzer.

obvier [òbvyé] v. to obviate.

occasion [òkàzyoⁿ] f. opportunity, chance, occasion; bargain; motive; d'*occasion*, second-hand. ‖ **occasionner** [-yòné] v. to occasion, to cause, to provoke, to give rise to.

occident [òksìdaⁿ] m. Occident, West. ‖ **occidental** [-tàl] adj.* Occidental, Western.

occulte [òkült] adj. occult; secret. ‖ **occultisme** [-tìsm] m. occultism.

occupant [òküpaⁿ] adj. occupying; engrossing; m. occupant. ‖ **occupation** [-àsyoⁿ] f. occupation; occupancy; business, employment, work. ‖ **occupé** [-é] adj. occupied; engaged; busy [personne, téléphone]. ‖ **occuper** [-é] v. to occupy; to inhabit, to reside in; to hold (mil.); to employ; to fill [temps]; s'*occuper*, to keep busy; to be interested (de, in); to look after.

occurrence [òküraⁿs] f. occurrence; emergency, juncture, occasion; en l'*occurrence*, under the circumstances.

océan [òséaⁿ] m. ocean, sea.

ocre [òkr] f. ochre.

octobre [òktòbr] m. October.

octroi [òktrwà] m. concession, granting; dues, toll; toll-house. ‖ **octroyer** [-é] v. to grant, to concede, to allow; to bestow (on).

oculaire [òkülèr] adj. ocular; m. eyepiece, ocular; *témoin oculaire*, eyewitness. ‖ **oculiste** [-ìst] m. oculist.

ode [òd] f. ode.

odeur [òdœr] f. odo(u)r, scent, smell.

odieux [òdyë] adj.* odious; hateful [personne]; heinous [crime]; m. odiousness, hatefulness.

odorant [òdòraⁿ] adj. odorous, fragrant, odoriferous. ‖ **odorat** [-à] m. olfactory sense; smell. ‖ **odoriférant** [-rìféraⁿ] adj. fragrant.

œdème [édèm] m. oedema, *Am.* edema.

œil [œy] m. (pl. **yeux** [yë]) eye; opening; hole; *coup d'œil*, glance; *faire de l'œil*, to ogle; **œil-de-bœuf**, bull's-eye [fenêtre]; **œil-de-perdrix**, soft corn [callosité]. ‖ **œillade** [-àd] f. glance, ogle, leer. ‖ **œillère** [-èr] f. blinker, *Am.* blinder [cheval]; eyecup (med.). ‖ **œillet** [-è] m. eyelet; pink; carnation (bot.).

œuf [œf, pl. ë] m. egg; ovum (biol.); spawn, roe [poisson]; *œufs sur le plat*, fried eggs; *œufs à la coque*, softboiled eggs; *œuf dur*, hard-boiled egg; *œufs brouillés*, scrambled eggs.

œuvre [œvr] f. work; production; society, institution [bienfaisance]; m. wall, foundation; complete works; opus. ‖ **œuvrer** [-é] v. to work.

offense [òfaⁿs] f. offense; transgression; contempt (jur.). ‖ **offenser** [-é] v. to offend; to injure, to shock; s'*offenser*, to take offense (de, at). ‖ **offenseur** [-œr] m. offender. ‖ **offensif** [-ìf] adj. offensive [armes]. ‖ **offensive** [-ìv] f. offensive (mil.).

office [òfìs] m. office, functions, duty; employment; f. butler's pantry; servants' hall. ‖ **officiel** [-yèl] adj.* official; formal [visite]. ‖ **officier** [-yé] m. officer; v. to officiate. ‖ **officieux** [-yë] adj.* officious; unofficial; m. busybody.

offrande [òfraⁿd] f. offering; offertory (eccles.). ‖ **offre** [òfr] f. offer; bid [enchères]; tender [contrat]; proposal. ‖ **offrir** [-ìr] v.* to offer; to proffer, to give, to present; to bid [enchères]; to tender [contrat]; s'*offrir*, to offer oneself; to volunteer [personne]; to turn up [chance].

offusquer [òfüské] v. to obscure; to obfuscate, to befog, to cloud; to dazzle [yeux]; to offend, to shock (someone); s'*offusquer*, to become clouded; to take offense, to be huffy.

ogive [òjìv] f. rib; gothic arch; ogive.

ogre, ogresse [ògr, ògrès] m. ogre, f. ogress.

oie [wâ] f. goose.

oignon [òñoⁿ] m. onion; bulb [tulipe]; bunion [callosité]; (pop.) watch, turnip.

oindre [wìⁿdr] *v.* to oil; to anoint.

oiseau [wàzô] *m.* bird; (fam.) *Am.* guy; *jeune oiseau*, fledgling; *oiseau-mouche*, humming-bird.

oiseux [wàzë] *adj.* idle; useless. || *oisif* [-ìf] *adj.* lazy; unemployed; uninvested [capital]. || *oisiveté* [-ìvté] *f.* idleness, sloth.

oison [wàzoⁿ] *m.* gosling.

oléagineux [òlèàjìnë] *adj.* oleaginous; *m.* oil-seed.

olive [òlìv] *f.* olive. || *olivier* [-yé] *m.* olive-tree.

ombilical [oⁿbìlìkàl] *adj.* umbilical.

ombrage [oⁿbràj] *m.* shade [arbre]; umbrage, offense. || *ombrager* [-é] *v.* to shade; to screen. || *ombrageux* [-ë] *adj.* shy, skittish [cheval]; touchy, suspicious [personne]. || *ombre* [oⁿbr] *f.* shadow; shade; gloom; ghost [revenant]. || *ombrelle* [-èl] *f.* parasol, sunshade. || *ombrer* [-é] *v.* to shade; to darken. || *ombreux* [-ë] *adj.* shady.

omelette [òmlèt] *f.* omelet.

omettre [òmètr] *v.* to omit, to leave out, to skip, to overlook; to fail, to neglect. || *omission* [-ìsyoⁿ] *f.* omission; oversight.

omnibus [òmnìbüs] *m.* omnibus, bus.

omnipotent [òmnìpòtaⁿ] *adj.* omnipotent. || *omniscient* [-sjaⁿ] *adj.* all-knowing.

omoplate [òmòplàt] *f.* shoulder-blade, scapula, omoplate.

on [oⁿ] *indef. pron.* one, people, they, we, you, men, somebody; *on dit*, it is said; *on-dit*, rumo(u)r.

once [oⁿs] *f.* ounce; bit.

oncle [oⁿkl] *m.* uncle.

onction [oⁿksyoⁿ] *f.* oiling; unction; anointing; unctuousness. || *onctueux* [-tüë] *adj.* unctuous, oily; suave, bland; mellow.

onde [oⁿd] *f.* wave; undulation; billow; corrugation [tôle]; *grandes ondes*, long waves [radio]; *onde sonore*, sound-wave. || *ondée* [-é] *f.* shower. || *ondoyant* [-wàyaⁿ] *adj.* undulating, waving; billowy; swaying; changeable, fluctuating. || *ondoyer* [-wàyé] *v.* to undulate, to wave, to ripple; to waver. || *ondulant* [-ülaⁿ] *adj.* undulating; waving; flowing. || *ondulation* [oⁿdülàsyoⁿ] *f.* waving, flowing; undulation; wave. || *ondulé* [-ülé] *adj.* undulating, rolling; wavy [cheveux]; corrugated [tôle]; curly-grained [bois]. || *onduler* [-ülé] *v.* to undulate, to ripple; to wave [cheveux]; to corrugate [tôle]. || *onduleux* [-ülë] *adj.* undulous, wavy, sinuous.

onéreux [ònéré] *adj.* onerous; burdensome; heavy; costly.

ongle [oⁿgl] *m.* nail [doigt]; claw [animal]; talon [faucon]; *coup d'ongle*, scratch.

onguent [oⁿgaⁿ] *m.* ointment, unguent, salve, liniment.

onze [oⁿz] *m.*, *adj.* eleven; eleventh [titre, date]. || *onzième* [-yèm] *m.*, *adj.* eleventh.

opale [òpàl] *f.* opal.

opaque [òpàk] *adj.* opaque.

opéra [òpérà] *m.* opera.

opérateur, -trice [òpéràtær, -trìs] *m.*, *f.* operator. || *opération* [-àsyoⁿ] *f.* operation; transaction. || *opératoire* [-àtwàr] *adj.* operative. || *opérer* [-é] *v.* to operate; to effect, to bring about; to perform.

opérette [òpérèt] *f.* operetta.

opiner [òpìné] *v.* to opine; to nod in approval. || *opiniâtre* [-yâtr] *adj.* stubborn, opinionated, obstinate; unyielding. || *opiniâtreté* [-yâtr⁹té] *f.* obstinacy, stubbornness. || *opinion* [-yoⁿ] *f.* opinion.

opium [òpyòm] *m.* opium.

opportun [òpòrtuⁿ] *adj.* opportune, timely, convenient. || *opportunité* [-ünîté] *f.* opportuneness, seasonableness, timeliness; expediency.

opposant [òpòzaⁿ] *adj.* opposing, adverse; *m.* opponent, adversary. || *opposé* [-é] *adj.* opposite; opposed; facing. || *opposer* [-é] *v.* to oppose; to compare, to contrast; *s'opposer à*, to be opposed to. || *opposition* [-ìsyoⁿ] *f.* opposition; contrast.

oppresser [òprèsé] *v.* to oppress; to lie heavy on; to squeeze, to crush, to cramp. || *oppresseur* [-sœr] *adj.* oppressive; *m.* oppressor. || *oppressif* [-ìf] *adj.* oppressive. || *oppression* [-yoⁿ] *f.* oppression.

opprimer [òprìmé] *v.* to oppress, to crush, to underfoot.

opprobre [òpròbr] *m.* opprobrium, shame, disgrace.

opter [òpté] *v.* to choose.

opticien [òptìsyaⁿ] *m.* optician.

optimisme [òptìmìsm] *m.* optimism. || *optimiste* [-ìst] *m.*, *f.* optimist; *adj.* optimistic.

option [òpsyoⁿ] *f.* option, choice.

optique [òptìk] *f.* optics; perspective; *adj.* optical.

opulence [òpülaⁿs] *f.* opulence. || *opulent* [-aⁿ] *adj.* opulent, wealthy, rich; buxom [poitrine].

opuscule [òpüskül] *m.* pamphlet, tract, booklet.

or [òr] *m.*, *adj.* gold.

or [òr] *conj.* now; but.

oracle [òràkl] *m.* oracle.

orage [òrà] *m.* storm; disturbance, turmoil (fig.). || **orageux** [-ë] *adj.* stormy; threatening [temps]; lowering [ciel].

oraison [òrèzoⁿ] *f.* orison; oration.

oral [òràl] *adj.*, *m.* oral.

orange [òraⁿ] *f.* orange. || **orangé** [òraⁿjé] *adj.* orange-coloured, orangy; *m.* orange. || **orangeade** [-jàd] *f.* orangeade. || **oranger** [-é] *m.* orange-tree.

orateur [òràtœr] *m.* orator. || **oratoire** [-wàr] *adj.* oratorical; *m.* oratory; chapel.

orbe [òrb] *m.* orb; globe; sphere. || **orbite** [-ìt] *f.* orbit; socket (anat.).

orchestre [òrkèstr] *m.* orchestra; *chef d'orchestre*, conductor; bandmaster. || **orchestrer** [-é] *v.* to score, to orchestrate.

orchidée [òrkìdé] *f.* orchid.

ordinaire [òrdìnèr] *adj.* ordinary, usual, customary, common; *m.* custom; daily fare; mess (mil.); *d'ordinaire*, usually, ordinarily; *peu ordinaire*, unusual.

ordinal [òrdìnàl] *adj.* ordinal.

ordinateur [òrdìnàtœr] *m.* computer.

ordonnance [òrdònaⁿs] *f.* order, arrangement; disposition; ordinance; prescription (med.); judgment (jur.); orderly (mil.). || **ordonnancement** [-maⁿ] *m.* order to pay. || **ordonnateur, -trice** [òrdònàtœr, -trìs] *m.*, *f.* arranger; master of ceremonies; *adj.* directing, managing. || **ordonné** [-é] *adj.* orderly, regulated; tidy; ordained (eccles.). || **ordonner** [-é] *v.* to order, to command, to direct; to arrange; to tidy; to prescribe (med.).

ordre [òrdr] *m.* order, command; arrangement, sequence; orderliness, tidiness; discipline; class, category; array [bataille]; *pl.* holy orders; *numéro d'ordre*, serial number; *de premier ordre*, first-class.

ordure [òrdür] *f.* dirt, filth, muck; garbage, refuse, rubbish; dung; lewdness. || **ordurier** [-yé] *adj.* filthy, lewd; scurrilous.

orée [òré] *f.* verge, skirt, edge, border.

oreille [òrèy] *f.* ear; hearing; handle [anse]; *prêter l'oreille*, to listen attentively. || **oreiller** [-é] *m.* pillow. || **oreillette** [-èt] *f.* auricle. || **oreillons** [-oⁿ] *m. pl.* mumps (med.).

orfèvre [òrfèvr] *m.* goldsmith. || **orfèvrerie** [-rî] *f.* goldsmith's trade; gold plate.

organe [òrgàn] *m.* organ (anat.); voice; agent, means, medium, instrument; part (mech.). || **organique** [-ìk] *adj.* organic. || **organisateur, -trice**

organizer; *adj.* organizing. || **organisation** [-ìzàsyoⁿ] *f.* organization; structure; organizing. || **organiser** [-ìzé] *v.* to organize; to form; to arrange; *s'organiser*, to get into working order; to settle down. || **organisme** [-ìsm] *m.* organism; system (med.); organization, body.

organiste [òrgànìst] *m.* organist.

orge [òrj] *f.* barley.

orgelet [òrj•lè] *m.* stye (med.).

orgie [òrjî] *f.* orgy; profusion, riot [couleurs].

orgue [òrg] *m.* (*f.* in *pl.*) organ (mus.).

orgueil [òrgœy] *m.* pride, conceit. || **orgueilleux** [-ë] *adj.* proud, conceited, bumptious.

orient [òryaⁿ] *m.* Orient, East; water [perle]. || **orientable** [-tàbl] *adj.* swivelling; revolving. || **oriental** [-tàl] *adj.* Oriental, Eastern. || **orientation** [-tàsyoⁿ] *f.* orientation; direction; bearings. || **orienter** [-té] *v.* to orient; to take bearings; to direct; *s'orienter*, to find one's bearings, to get one's position. || **orienteur** [-tœr] *m.* orientator; *orienteur professionnel*, vocational guide.

orifice [òrìfìs] *m.* orifice, hole, opening, aperture.

originaire [òrìjìnèr] *adj.* originating, native; *m.*, *f.* native; original member. || **original** [-àl] *adj.*, *m.* original [texte]; inventive; *s.* eccentric (personne). || **origine** [òrìjìn] *f.* origin; beginning; source. || **originel** [-ìnèl] *adj.* primordial, original, primitive.

orignal [òrìñàl] *m.* ©︎ moose.

oripeau [òrìpô] *m.* tinsel; *pl.* rags.

orme [òrm] *m.* elm-tree.

ornement [òrn•maⁿ] *m.* ornament, adornment, embellishment, trimming. || **ornemental** [-tàl] *adj.* ornamental, decorative. || **ornementation** [-tàsyoⁿ] *f.* ornamentation. || **ornementer** [-té] *v.* to ornament. || **orner** [òrné] *v.* to ornament, to adorn, to decorate, to trim; to enrich (fig.).

ornière [òrnyèr] *f.* rut; groove.

orphelin [òrf•lıⁿ] *m.* orphan; *adj.* orphaned. || **orphelinat** [-ìnà] *m.* orphanage. || **orpheline** [-ı̀n] *f.* orphan-girl.

orteil [òrtèy] *m.* toe.

orthodoxe [òrtòdòks] *adj.* orthodox. || **orthodoxie** [-ksî] *f.* orthodoxy.

orthographe [òrtògràf] *f.* spelling, orthography; *faute d'orthographe*, misspelling. || **orthographier** [-yé] *v.* to spell.

ortie [òrtî] *f.* nettle.

orvet [òrvè] m. blind-worm.

os [òs, pl. ô] m. bone.

oscillation [òsìllàsyoⁿ] f. oscillation; swing; vibration (mech.); fluctuation [marché]. ‖ **osciller** [-é] v. to oscillate; to sway; to swing; to rock; to waver [personne]; to fluctuate [marché].

osé [òzé] adj. bold, daring.

oseille [òzèy] f. sorrel.

oser [òzé] v. to dare, to venture.

osier [òzyé] m. osier, willow (bot.); wicker.

ossature [òsàtür] f. frame, skeleton [corps]; ossature [bâtiment]; carcass (aviat.). ‖ **ossements** [-maⁿ] m. pl. bones, remains [morts]. ‖ **osseux** [-é] adj.* bony; osseous [tissu]. ‖ **ossifier** [-ìfyé] v. to ossify. ‖ **ossuaire** [-òsüèr] m. ossuary.

ostensible [òstaⁿsìbl] adj. ostensible, patent. ‖ **ostensoir** [-wàr] m. monstrance (eccles.). ‖ **ostentateur, -trice** [òstaⁿtàtœr, -trìs] adj. ostentatious, showy. ‖ **ostentation** [-àsyoⁿ] f. ostentation, show, display.

otage [òtàj] m. hostage; guarantee, surety; security.

otarie [òtàrî] f. otary, sea-lion.

ôter [òté] v. to remove, to take off; to doff; to subtract, to deduct; s'ôter, to get out of the way.

ou [û] conj. or; either...or; else.

où [û] adv. where; when [temps]; at which, in which.

ouananiche [wànànîsh] f. © landlocked salmon, wananish.

ouaouaron [wàwàroⁿ] m. © bullfrog.

ouate [ûàt] f. wadding; cotton-wool. ‖ **ouater** [-é] v. to wad; to pad; to quilt; to soften; to blur.

oubli [ûblì] m. forgetting, neglect; forgetfulness; oblivion; omission, oversight. ‖ **oubliable** [-àbl] adj. forgettable. ‖ **oublier** [ûblyé] v. to forget; to neglect; to overlook; s'oublier, to forget oneself, to be careless. ‖ **oubliettes** [-lyèt] f. pl. secret dungeon. ‖ **oublieux** [-lyé] adj.* forgetful; oblivious; unmindful.

ouest [wèst] m. west; adj. west, western.

oui [wì] adv. yes.

ouï-dire [wìdîr] m. hearsay. ‖ **ouïe** [wî] f. hearing; ear (mech.); pl. gills.

ouistiti [wìstìtì] m. wistiti.

ouragan [ûràgaⁿ] m. hurricane, storm, gale, tempest.

ourdir [ûrdîr] v. to warp [tissu]; to hatch, to weave [complot, intrigue].

ourler [ûrlé] v. to hem; ourler à jour, to hemstitch. ‖ **ourlet** [-è] m. hem; rim [oreille].

ours [ûrs] m. bear. ‖ **ourse** f. she-bear; la Grande Ourse, Ursa Major, Great Bear. ‖ **oursin** [-iⁿ] m. sea-urchin. ‖ **ourson** [-oⁿ] m. bear-cub.

outarde [ûtàrd] f. bustard; © Canada goose.

outil [ûtì] m. tool, implement. ‖ **outillage** [-yàj] m. tool set, tool kit; gear, equipment, machinery [usine]. ‖ **outiller** [-yé] v. to equip with tools.

outrage [ûtràj] m. outrage. ‖ **outrager** [-é] v. to outrage, to insult; to desecrate. ‖ **outrageux** [-é] adj.* insulting, scurrilous.

outre [ûtr] f. goatskin, leather-bottle.

outre [ûtr] prep. beyond; in addition to; adv. further; en outre, besides, moreover; passer outre, to go on; to ignore, to overrule (jur.). ‖ **outré** [-é] adj. excessive, undue; infuriated, indignant.

outrecuidance [ûtreküìdaⁿs] f. self-conceit; cocksureness; cheek; **outrecuidant**, overweening, presumptuous; cocksure (fam.); **outre-mer**, overseas; **outrepasser**, to exceed; to exaggerate.

outrer [ûtré] v. to exaggerate; to overdo; to infuriate.

ouvert [ûvèr] adj. open, opened. ‖ **ouverture** [-tür] f. opening; aperture; overture (mus.); mouth [baie]; broadmindedness; heures d'ouverture, business hours.

ouvrable [ûvràbl] adj. workable; jour ouvrable, working-day. ‖ **ouvrage** [-àj] m. work; product. ‖ **ouvragé** [-àjé] adj. wrought; figured. ‖ **ouvré** [-é] adj. worked [bois]; wrought [fer].

ouvre-boîtes [ûvrebwàt] m. tin-opener, Am. can-opener. ‖ **ouvre-huîtres** [-üìtr] m. oyster-knife.

ouvreur [ûvrœr] m. opener; usher (theat.). ‖ **ouvreuse** [-èz] f. usherette (theat.).

ouvrier [ûvrìyé] m. worker; workman; craftsman; labo(u)rer; adj.* working, operative; classe ouvrière, working class. ‖ **ouvrière** [-yèr] f. workwoman; worker bee [abeille].

ouvrir [ûvrîr] v.* to open; to unfasten, to unlock [porte]; to turn on [lumière]; to cut through [canal]; to begin, to start [débat]; s'ouvrir, to open; to unburden oneself.

ovaire [òvèr] m. ovary.

ovale [òvàl] adj. oval; egg-shaped.

ovation [òvàsyoⁿ] f. ovation. ‖ **ovationner** [-syònè] v. to acclaim.

oxygène [òksìjèn] m. oxygen. ‖ **oxygéné** [-éné] adj. oxygenated; peroxide [eau].

P

pacage [pàkàʒ] *m.* pasture-land; pasturage.

pacificateur, -trice [pàsìfìkàtœr, -trìs] *m., f.* pacifier; *adj.* pacifying. ‖ **pacification** [-fìkàsyoⁿ] *f.* pacification. ‖ **pacifier** [pàsìfyé] *v.* to pacify, to appease. ‖ **pacifique** [-ìk] *adj.* pacific, peaceful. ‖ **pacifisme** [-fìsm] *m.* pacifism.

pacotille [pàkòtìy] *f.* shoddy goods, trash.

pacte [pàkt] *m.* pact, agreement. ‖ **pactiser** [-ìzé] *v.* to come to terms, to make a pact.

pagaie [pàgè] *f.* paddle.

pagaïe, pagaille [pàgày] *f.* disorder, clutter, mess, muddle.

paganisme [pàgànìsm] *m.* paganism.

page [pàʒ] *f.* page; *à la page*, up to date.

page [pàʒ] *m.* page-boy, *Am.* bellhop.

paie [pè] *f.* wages [ouvrier]; *jour de paie*, pay-day. ‖ **paiement** [-màⁿ] *m.* payment; disbursement.

païen [pàyⁿ] *m., adj.** pagan, heathen.

paillasse [pàyàs] *f.* straw mattress, pallet; draining-board, *Am.* drain-board, deserter; *m.* clown. ‖ **paillasson** [-oⁿ] *m.* mat, matting; door-mat. ‖ **paille** [pày] *f.* straw; chaff [balle] flaw [joyau]; *paille de fer*, iron shavings, steel wool; *tirer à la courte paille*, to draw straws.

pailleter [pàyté] *v.* to spangle. ‖ **paillette** [-èt] *f.* spangle; flake; flaw [joyau].

pain [pⁿ] *m.* bread; loaf; cake, bar [savon]; lump [sucre]; *pain grillé*, toast; *petit pain*, roll; *pain bis*, brown bread; *pain complet*, whole-wheat bread; *pain d'épice*, gingerbread; *pain de mie*, sandwich loaf.

pair [pèr] *m.* peer; equal; par; *adj.* equal; even [numéro]; *au pair*, for board and lodging. ‖ **paire** [pèr] *f.* pair; couple; brace [perdrix]; yoke [bœufs].

paisible [pèzìbl] *adj.* peaceful.

paître [pètr] *v.** to graze, to crop, to feed, to put to grass; to browse, to graze on.

paix [pè] *f.* peace; quiet; reconciliation.

pal [pàl] *m.* pale.

palais [pàlè] *m.* palace; law-courts; palate (med.).

palan [pàlaⁿ] *m.* pulley-block, tackle.

pâle [pâl] *adj.* pale, pallid; wan; ashen.

palefrenier [pàlfrⁿyé] *m.* stableman, groom, ostler.

paletot [pàltô] *m.* overcoat, greatcoat.

palette [pàlèt] *f.* blade [aviron]; paddle [roue]; palette [artiste]; bat, *Am.* paddle [jeu].

pâleur [pâlœr] *f.* paleness, pallor, pallidness, wanness.

palier [pàlyé] *m.* landing; stage; plummer-block (mech.); level (aviat.); gradation.

pâlir [pâlîr] *v.* to grow pale, to blanch; to fade; to be on the wane (fig.).

palissade [pàlìsàd] *f.* paling, fence, palisade; stockade.

palissandre [pàlìsaⁿdr] *m.* rosewood.

pallier [pàlyé] *v.* to palliate, to mitigate, to alleviate.

palme [pàlm] *f.* palm-branch. ‖ **palmé** [-é] *adj.* palmate (bot.); web-footed. ‖ **palmier** [-yé] *m.* palm-tree. ‖ **palmipède** [-ìpèd] *m., adj.* palmiped; web-footed.

palpable [pàlpàbl] *adj.* palpable; tangible; obvious. ‖ **palper** [-é] *v.* to feel, to touch; to palpate (med.).

palpitation [pàlpìtàsyoⁿ] *f.* palpitation; throb; fluttering [pouls]. ‖ **palpiter** [-é] *v.* to palpitate; to throb, to beat [cœur]; to flicker.

pamphlet [paⁿflè] *m.* lampoon, satire.

pamplemousse [paⁿplemûs] *m.* grapefruit.

pan [paⁿ] *m.* nap; section; face [prisme]; piece; side, section, panel [mur]; patch, stretch [ciel].

panacée [pànàsé] *f.* cure-all.

panache [pànàsh] *m.* plume, tuft; trail [fumée]; stripe [couleurs]; swagger, flourish. ‖ **panaché** [-é] *adj.* plumed; feathered; variegated; mixed, assorted; *m.* shandy.

panais [pànè] *m.* parsnip.

panaris [pànàrì] *m.* whitlow, felon.

pancarte [paⁿkàrt] *f.* placard, bill; label; show card.

pancréas [paⁿkréàs] *m.* pancreas. ‖ **pancréatique** [-tìk] *adj.* pancreatic.

panier [pànyé] *m.* basket; hamper; pannier, hoop-skirt; (fam.) *panier à salade*, prison van, Black Maria, *Am.* paddy-wagon.

panique [pànìk] *f., adj.* panic.

panne [pàn] *f.* hog's fat.

panne [pàn] *f.* breakdown, mishap; *en panne*, out of order, *Am.* on the blink (fam.); hove to (naut.); *panne de moteur*, engine trouble.

panneau [pànô] *m.** snare, net [chasse]; panel [bois]; bulletin-board [affiches]; hatch (naut.).

panorama [pànòràmà] *m.* panorama; view-point; panoramic view.

panse [paⁿs] *f.* belly (fam.), paunch.

pansement [paⁿsmaⁿ] *m.* dressing. ‖ *panser* [-é] *v.* to dress; to groom [cheval].

pantalon [paⁿtàloⁿ] *m.* long pants, trousers, pair of pants; drawers, knickers.

panteler [paⁿtlé] *v.* to pant.

panthère [paⁿtèr] *f.* panther.

pantin [paⁿtⁱⁿ] *m.* jumping-jack; puppet [personne].

pantoufle [paⁿtûfl] *f.* slipper.

paon [paⁿ] *m.* peacock.

papa [pàpà] *m.* papa, daddy, dad.

papal [pàpàl] *adj.** papal. ‖ *papauté* [-ôté] *f.* papacy. ‖ *pape* [pàp] *m.** pope.

paperasse [pàpràs] *f.* useless paper. ‖ *paperasserie* [-rî] *f.* red tape.

papeterie [pàptrî] *f.* paper-shop; stationery; paper-manufacturing. ‖ *papetier* [-tyé] *m.* stationer; paper-manufacturer. ‖ *papier* [-yé] *m.* paper; document; *papier buvard*, blotting paper; *papier collant*, sticking-tape; *papier écolier*, foolscap; *papier d'emballage*, wrapping paper; *papier à lettres*, writing paper; *papier peint*, wall-paper; *papier pelure*, tissue paper, onion-skin paper; *papier de soie*, silk paper; *papier de verre*, sand-paper.

papillon [pàpⁱyoⁿ] *m.* butterfly; leaflet; fly-bill [affiche]; rider [document]; throttle [auto]; bow-tie [nœud]; giddy-head [personne]. ‖ *papillonner* [-yòné] *v.* to flutter; to flit about; to hover.

papillote [pàpⁱyòt] *f.* curl-paper. ‖ *papilloter* [pàpⁱyòté] *v.* to blink [yeux]; to twinkle, to flicker [lumière]; to dazzle, to glitter; to curl [cheveux].

papoter [pàpòté] *v.* to tittle-tattle.

pâque [pâk] *f.* Passover.

paquebot [pàkbô] *m.* passenger-liner, packet-boat, steamer.

pâquerette [pâkrèt] *f.* daisy.

Pâques [pâk] *f. pl.* Easter.

paquet [pàkè] *m.* package, parcel; bundle; mail.

par [pàr] *prep.* by; per; through; from; *par exemple*, for example, for instance; *par la fenêtre*, out of the window; *par ici*, this way; *par trop*, far too much; *par-dessous*, underneath, below; *par-dessus*, over, above; *par-dessus le marché*, into the bargain.

parachever [pàràshevé] *v.* to perfect, to complete.

parachute [pàràshüt] *m.* parachute. ‖ *parachuter* [-té] *v.* to parachute. ‖ *parachutiste* [-ìst] *m.* parachutist; paratrooper.

parade [pàràd] *f.* parade, show, ostentation; checking [cheval]; parry [escrime]. ‖ *parader* [-é] *v.* to parade; to strut; to show off.

paradis [pàràdì] *m.* paradise; top gallery, cheap seats, *Br.* the gods, *Am.* peanut gallery (theat.).

paradoxe [pàràdòks] *m.* paradox.

parages [pàràj] *m. pl.* localities [océan]; latitudes, regions (naut.); parts, quarters, vicinity.

paragraphe [pàràgràf] *m.* paragraph.

paraître [pàrètr] *v.** to appear; to seem; to look; to be published, to come out [livre]; *vient de paraître*, just out.

parallèle [pàràllèl] *f.*, *adj.* parallel; *m.* parallel, comparison.

paralyser [pàràlìzé] *v.* to paralyse; to incapacitate. ‖ *paralysie* [-î] *f.* paralysis; palsy.

parapet [pàràpè] *m.* parapet; breastwork [château fort].

paraphe [pàràf] *m.* paraph; initials.

parapluie [pàràplüì] *m.* umbrella.

parasite [pàràzìt] *m.* parasite; sponger, hanger-on [personne]; interference, *Am.* (pop.) bugs [radio]; *adj.* parasitic.

parasol [pàràsòl] *m.* parasol, sunshade; visor (auto).

paratonnerre [pàràtònèr] *m.* lightning-rod, lightning-conductor.

paravent [pàràvaⁿ] *m.* folding screen.

parc [pàrk] *m.* park; enclosure; paddock [chevaux]; pen [bestiaux]; fold [moutons]; bed [huîtres].

parcelle [pàrsèl] *f.* fragment, particle; lot, plot; bit, grain.

parce que [pàrskᵉ] *conj.* because.

parchemin [pàrshemⁱⁿ] *m.* parchment; sheepskin.

parcimonie [pàrsìmònî] *f.* parsimony. ‖ *parcimonieux* [-nyœ] *adj.** parsimonious, sparing.

parcourir [pàrkûrîr] *v.** to travel through, to go over, to traverse; to examine, to peruse; to look over [texte]; to cover [distance]. ‖ *parcours* [pàrkûr] *m.* distance covered; course, way, road, route.

pardessus [pàrd°sū] m. overcoat, greatcoat, top-coat.

pardon [pàrdoⁿ] m. pardon; forgiveness; excuse me; pilgrimage [Bretagne]. ‖ **pardonner** [-òné] v. to pardon, to forgive, to excuse.

pare-brise [pàrbrīz] m. wind-screen, Am. windshield. ‖ **pare-chocs** [shòk] m. bumper-bar.

pareil [pàrèy] adj.° like, alike, similar; equal, same, identical; such, like that; m. equal, match.

parement [pàrmaⁿ] m. adorning; ornament; cuff [manche]; facing [col]; dressing [pierre]; Br. kerb, Am. curbstone.

parent [pàraⁿ] m. relative, kinsman, pl. parents, relatives; plus proche parent, next-of-kin. ‖ **parenté** [-té] f. kinship, relationship; consanguinity; kindred, relations; affinity (fig.).

parenthèse [pàrantèz] f. parenthesis; bracket; digression.

parer [pàré] v. to adorn, to deck out; to trim; to array.

parer [pàré] v. to avoid, to ward off; to guard against, to avert, to obviate; to parry [boxe, escrime]; to reduce sail (naut.).

paresse [pàrès] f. laziness, idleness, sloth. ‖ **paresseux** [-ë] adj.° lazy, idle, slothful; m. idler, loafer; sloth.

parfait [pàrfè] adj. perfect, faultless, flawless; m. perfect (gramm.); ice-cream; adv. fine.

parfois [pàrfwà] adv. sometimes, at times, occasionally, now and then.

parfum [pàrfuⁿ] m. perfume; scent, fragrance; flavo(u)r [glace]; bouquet [vin]. ‖ **parfumer** [-ümé] v. to perfume, to scent. ‖ **parfumeur** [-mœr] m. perfumer.

pari [pàrì] m. bet, wager; betting; pari mutuel, mutual stake; totalizator system. ‖ **parier** [pàryé] v. to bet.

Paris [pàrì] m. Paris. ‖ **parisien** [-zyiⁿ] adj.° Parisian.

parjure [pàrjür] m. perjury; perjurer; adj. perjured, forsworn. ‖ **parjurer (se)** [-é] v. to perjure oneself, to forswear oneself.

parlant [pàrlaⁿ] adj. speaking, talking; life-like [portrait]; eloquent [geste]. ‖ **Parlement** [-°maⁿ] m. legislative assembly; Br. Parliament, Am. Congress. ‖ **parlementaire** [-°maⁿtèr] adj. parliamentary; Am. Congressional; m. Br. Member of Parliament, Am. Congressman. ‖ **parlementer** [-°maⁿté] v. to parley. ‖ **parler** [-pàrlé] v. to speak, to talk; to converse; m. speech; accent; dialect. ‖ **parleur** [-œr] m. talker, speaker; announcer. ‖ **parloir** [-wàr] m. parlo(u)r. ‖ **parlote** [-òt] f. empty chatter.

parmi [pàrmì] prep. among, amid.

parodie [pàròdì] f. parody. ‖ **parodier** [-yé] v. to parody, to travesty, to burlesque.

paroi [pàrwà] f. partition-wall; inner side.

paroisse [pàrwàs] f. parish. ‖ **paroissial** [-yàl] adj. parochial. ‖ **paroissien** [-yiⁿ] m. parishioner; prayer book.

parole [pàròl] f. word; utterance; promise; parole (mil.); speech, speaking, delivery; eloquence; avoir la parole, to have the floor.

paroxysme [pàròksìsm] m. paroxysm; culminating point.

parquer [pàrké] v. to pen [bestiaux]; to fold [moutons]; to put in paddock [cheval]; to park [auto]; to enclose. ‖ **parquet** [-è] m. floor, flooring; public prosecutor's department; ring [Bourse]. ‖ **parqueter** [-té] v. to floor.

parrain [pàriⁿ] m. godfather; sponsor. ‖ **parrainer** [-né] v. to sponsor.

parricide [pàrìsìd] s. parricide; adj. parricidal.

parsemer [pàrs°mé] v. to strew, to sprinkle; to stud, to spangle.

part [pàr] f. share, part, portion; participation; place where; à part, apart, separately, aside; except for; autre part, elsewhere; d'une part... d'autre part, on one hand... on the other hand; d'autre part, besides; de part et d'autre, on all sides; de part en part, through and through; de la part de, from, by courtesy of; nulle part, no-where. ‖ **partage** [-tàj] m. division; sharing, allotment, apportionment; partition, share, portion, lot. ‖ **partager** [-tàjé] v. to share; to divide; to apportion; to split; to halve [en deux]; se partager, to come in two, to divide; to differ; to fork.

partenaire [pàrt°nèr] s. partner; sparring partner [boxe].

parterre [pàrtèr] m. flower-bed; pit (theat.).

parti [pàrtì] m. party [politique]; side; choice, course; decision; advantage, profit; match [mariage]; detachment (mil.); parti pris, foregone conclusion; prendre son parti de, to resign oneself to; tirer parti de, to turn to account.

partial [pàrsyàl] adj.° partial; biased, one-sided. ‖ **partialité** [-lté] f. partiality, bias, one-sidedness.

participation [pàrtìsìpàsyoⁿ] f. participation; participation aux bénéfices, profit-sharing. ‖ **participe** [pàrtìsìp] m. participle. ‖ **participer** [-é] v. to participate; to take part (à, in); to share; to partake.

particularité [pàrtìkülàrìté] *f.* particularity; detail; peculiarity.

particule [pàrtìkül] *f.* particle.

particulier [pàrtìkülyé] *adj.** particular, special; peculiar; characteristic; uncommon; private [chambre, leçon]; *m.* individual.

partie [pàrtì] *f.* part; party, game; match, contest; lot; line of business (comm.); *partie civile,* plaintiff; *partie double,* double entry (comm.); *partie nulle,* tied score. ‖ *partiel* [pàrsyèl] *adj.** partial.

partir [pàrtîr] *v.** to depart, to leave, to go, to be off; to set out, to start; to go off [fusil]; to emanate, to spring from; *à partir de,* from, starting with.

partisan [pàrtìzaⁿ] *m.* partisan, follower; upholder, supporter; backer [politique].

partitif [pàrtìtîf] *adj.** partitive.

partition [pàrtìsyoⁿ] *f.* score (mus.).

partout [pàrtû] *adv.* everywhere, all over, on all sides, in every direction; all [tennis].

parure [pàrür] *f.* adornment, ornament; finery.

parution [pàrüsyoⁿ] *f.* publication.

parvenir [pàrv•nîr] *v.** to arrive; to reach; to succeed (*à,* in). ‖ *parvenu* [-ü] *m.* upstart, parvenu.

pas [pâ] *m.* step, pace, stride, gait, walk; footprint; threshold [seuil]; pass, passage; straits (geogr.); thread [vis]; *adv.* no; not; *faux pas,* slip; misstep.

pas [pâ] *adv.* not, no, none.

pascal [pàskàl] *adj.* paschal; Easter.

passable [pàsàbl] *adj.* passable, acceptable. ‖ *passablement* [-•maⁿ] *adv.* rather, fairly, tolerably.

passage [pàsàj] *m.* passage; lane; extract [livre]; transition, arcade [voûté]; *passage clouté,* pedestrian crossing, *Am.* pedestrian lane; *passage à niveau,* railway crossing, *Am.* grade crossing. ‖ *passager* [-é] *adj.** fleeting; transitory; momentary; migratory; *s.* passer-by; passenger. ‖ *passant* [pàsaⁿ] *adj.* busy, frequented, *s.* passer-by, wayfarer; *en passant,* by the way. ‖ *passe* [pâs] *f.* passing, passage; permit, pass; thrust, pasado [escrime]; situation, predicament; navigable channel (naut.); overplus (typogr.); *adv.* all right; let it be so; *mauvaise passe,* bad fix; *mot de passe,* password; *passe-droit,* unjust favo(u)r; *passe-lacet,* bodkin; *passe-partout,* master-key; *passe-passe,* sleight-of-hand; *passe-temps,* pastime; *passe-thé,* tea-strainer. ‖ *passé* [-é] *adj.* past; gone; vanished; faded; *m.*

past; past tense (gramm.). ‖ *passer* [pàsé] *v.* to pass; to go; to cross; to die; to pass away; to vanish; to fade; to spend [temps]; to sift [farine]; to strain [liquide]; to put on [vêtement]; to take, to undergo [examen]; to excuse [erreur]; *se passer,* to happen, to take place; to cease; to elapse [temps]; *se passer de,* to do without, to dispense with; to refrain from.

passeport [pàspòr] *m.* passport.

passereau [pàsró] *m.** sparrow.

passerelle [pàsrèl] *f.* foot-bridge; gangway; bridge (naut.).

passeur [pàsœr] *m.* ferryman.

passible [pàsìbl] *adj.* passible; liable, subject.

passif [pàsîf] *adj.** passive; *m.* passive; liabilities, debt (comm.).

passion [pàsyoⁿ] *f.* passion; craze. ‖ *passionnant* [-yònaⁿ] *adj.* entrancing, thrilling, fascinating. ‖ *passionné* [-yòné] *adj.* passionate, impassioned, ardent, warm, eager; *m.* enthusiast, (fam.) fan. ‖ *passionner* [-yòné] *v.* to impassion; to excite; to fascinate; *se passionner,* to be impassioned.

passoire [pàswàr] *f.* strainer; colander [légumes].

pastel [pàstèl] *m.* pastel; crayon; *adj.* pastel.

pastèque [pàstèk] *f.* water-melon.

pasteur [pàstœr] *m.* minister, pastor; shepherd.

pasteuriser [pàstœrìzé] *v.* to pasteurize.

pastiche [pàstìsh] *m.* pastiche.

pastille [pàstìy] *f.* pastille, lozenge.

pastoral [pàstòràl] *adj.** pastoral. ‖ *pastorale* [-ràl] *f.* pastoral play, pastoral poem.

patate [pàtàt] *f.* sweet potato; (fam.) spud.

pataud [pàtó] *m.* clumsy-footed puppy; lout. ‖ *patauger* [-òjé] *v.* to flounder; to wallow; to paddle, to wade.

pâte [pât] *f.* paste; dough, batter [cuisine]; kind, mould. ‖ *pâté* [-é] *m.* pie, patty, pasty; paste [foie]; block [maisons]; clump [arbres]; blot [encre]. ‖ *pâtée* [-é] *f.* coarse food; dog food; mash [volaille].

patelin [pàtlⁿ] *adj.* fawning; *m.* wheedler.

patelin *m.* (fam.) small town; native village.

patent [pàtaⁿ] *adj.* patent; obvious. ‖ *patente* [-aⁿt] *f.* licence; tax (comm.); bill of health (naut.).

patère [pàtèr] *f.* hat-peg, coat-peg; curtain-hook.

paternel [pàtèrnèl] adj.* paternal, fatherly. || **paternité** [-ìté] f. paternity, fatherhood.

pâteux [pâtë] adj.* pasty, clammy; thick, dull [voix].

pathétique [pàtétìk] adj. pathetic, moving; m. pathos.

pathos [pàtòs] m. bathos; affected pathos, bombast.

patience [pàsyans] f. patience, endurance, forbearance; perseverance; solitaire [cartes]. || **patient** [-yan] adj. patient, enduring, forbearing; m. sufferer; patient. || **patienter** [-yanté] v. to exercise patience; to wait patiently.

patin [pàtin] m. skate; runner [traîneau]; skid (aviat.); shoe (mech.); base, flange (railw.); trolley [transbordeur]; patten (arch.); patin à roulettes, roller-skate. || **patinage** [-nàj] m. skating; skidding. || **patiner** [-ìné] v. to skate; to skid, to slip. || **patineur** [-ìnœr] m. skater. || **patinoire** [-nwàr] f. skating-rink.

pâtir [pâtìr] v. to suffer.

pâtisserie [pâtìsrî] f. pastry; pastry shop; pastry-making; pl. cakes. || **pâtissier** [-yé] m. pastry-cook.

patois [pàtwà] m. dialect, patois; jargon, lingo.

pâtre [pâtr] m. herdsman; shepherd.

patriarche [pàtrìàrsh] m. patriarch.

patrie [pàtrì] f. fatherland, native land; mother country; home.

patrimoine [pàtrìmwàn] m. patrimony, inheritance.

patriote [pàtrìyòt] m., f. patriot. || **patriotique** [-ìk] adj. patriotic. || **patriotisme** [-ìsm] m. patriotism.

patron [pàtron] m. patron; protector; master; proprietor, boss; skipper (naut.); pattern, model. || **patronner** [-òné] v. to patronize; to protect; to pattern; to stencil. || **patronyme** [-ònîm] m. surname.

patrouille [pàtrúy] f. patrol; section (aviat.).

patte [pàt] f. paw [animal]; foot [oiseau]; leg [insecte]; flap [poche, enveloppe]; tab, strap [vêtement]; hasp, fastening; à quatre pattes, on all fours; graisser la patte, to bribe; patte-d'oie, crow's-foot [ride].

pâturage [pâtüràj] m. grazing; pasture; pasture-land. || **pâturer** [-é] v. to graze, to pasture; to feed.

paume [pôm] f. palm [main]; tennis [jeu]. || **paumer** [-é] v. (fam.) to lose.

paupière [pôpyèr] f. eyelid.

paupiette [pôpyèt] f. olive, Am. bird.

pause [pôz] f. pause, stop; rest. || **pauser** [-é] v. to pause; to wait.

pauvre [pôvr] adj. poor; needy, penurious, indigent; scanty; unfortunate, wretched; m., f. pauper; beggar; pauvre d'esprit, dull-witted. || **pauvreté** [-eté] f. poverty, indigence; wretchedness; poorness, banality.

pavé [pàvé] m. paving-stone; paving-block; street; sur le pavé, out of work. || **paver** [-é] v. to pave.

pavillon [pàvìyon] m. pavilion; tent; canopy; detached building; cottage; horn [phonographe]; flag, colo(u)rs (naut.).

pavoiser [pàvwàzé] v. to deck out; to dress (naut.).

pavot [pàvô] m. poppy.

paye, see **paie**. || **payement,** see **paiement**. || **payer** [pèyé] v. to pay; to pay for; to defray [frais]; to remunerate, to requite; to expiate, to atone for; payer d'audace, to brazen it out; payer de sa personne, to risk one's skin; se payer, to be paid; to treat oneself to; se payer la tête de, to make fun of (someone); s'en payer, to have a good time. || **payeur** [pèyœr] m. payer; disburser; pay-master (mil.).

pays [pèï] m. country, land; region; fatherland, home, birthplace; mal du pays, homesickness. || **paysage** [-zàj] m. landscape; scenery. || **paysan** [-zan] m., adj.* peasant, rustic; countryman.

peau [pô] f.* skin; hide, pelt; leather [animal], rind, peel, husk [fruit, légume]; coating, film [lait].

pêche [pèsh] f. peach [fruit].

pêche [pèsh] f. fishing; catch; angling [ligne].

péché [péshé] m. sin; trespass; transgression; péché mignon, besetting sin. || **pécher** [-é] v. to sin; to trespass; to offend.

pêcher [pèshé] m. peach-tree.

pêcher [pèshé] v. to fish; to angle; to drag up. || **pêcherie** [-rî] f. fishery; fishing-ground. || **pêcheur** [-œr] m. fisher, fisherman, angler.

pécheur, -eresse [péshœr, rès] m., f. sinner, offender; trespasser, transgressor; adj. sinning; sinful.

pécore [pékòr] f. (fam.) goose.

pécuniaire [pékünyèr] adj. pecuniary.

pédagogie [pédàgòjî] f. pedagogy. || **pédagogique** [-ìk] adj. pedagogical. || **pédagogue** [pédàgòg] m., f. pedagogue.

pédale [pédàl] f. pedal; treadle; pédale d'embrayage, clutch [auto]. || **pédaler** [-é] v. to pedal, to bicycle. || **pédalier** [-yé] m. crank-gear; pedalboard [orgue]; pedalier. || **pédalo** [pédàlò] m. pedal-craft, pedal-boat.

pédant [pédaⁿ] *adj.* pedantic, priggish; *m.* pedant, prig. ‖ **pédantisme** [-ìsm] *m* pedantry.

pédestre [pédèstr] *adj.* pedestrian.

pédicure [pédìkür] *m.*, *f.* chiropodist.

pègre [pègr] *f.* underworld, *Am.* gangsterdom.

peigne [pèñ] *m.* comb; clam. ‖ **peigner** [-é] *v.* to comb; to card [laine]. ‖ **peignoir** [-wàr] *m.* dressing-gown, neglige; bath-robe; wrapper.

peinard [pénàr] *adj.* (pop.) quiet, sly; *m.* slacker.

peindre [pìⁿdr] *v.*° to paint; to portray; to depict.

peine [pèn] *f* punishment; penalty; pain, affliction, grief, sorrow; trouble, difficulty, labo(u)r, toil; *à peine,* hardly, scarcely; *faire de la peine à,* to hurt, to grieve; *être en peine de,* to be at a loss to; *valoir la peine,* to be worthwhile; *se donner la peine de,* to take the trouble to; *sous peine de,* under penalty of, under pain of. ‖ **peiner** [-é] *v.* to pain, to grieve; to toil, to labo(u)r; *se peiner,* to grieve, to fret.

peintre [pìⁿtr] *m.* painter. ‖ **peinture** [-ür] *f.* paint; painting, picture; *attention à la peinture,* fresh paint, wet paint. ‖ **peinturer** [-é] *v.* © to paint. ‖ **peinturlurer** [-ürlüré] *v.* to daub.

péjoratif [péjòràtìf] *adj.*° pejorative, depreciatory, disparaging.

pelage [pºlàj] *m.* pelt, coat; wool, fur; skinning, peeling.

pêle-mêle [pèlmèl] *m.* disorder, jumble, mess; confusion; *adv.* pellmell, confusedly, helter-skelter, promiscuously.

peler [pºlé] *v.* to peel, to skin, to pare, to strip.

pèlerin [pèlrìⁿ] *m.* pilgrim. ‖ **pèlerinage** [-ìnàj] *m.* pilgrimage. ‖ **pèlerine** [-ìn] *f.* cape, tippet.

pelle [pèl] *f.* shovel, scoop, spade; dustpan; (fam.) cropper.

pellicule [pèlìkül] *f.* film; dandruff, scurf [cuir chevelu].

pelote [pºlòt] *f.* ball; pin-cushion; pelota [jeu]. ‖ **peloton** [-oⁿ] *m.* ball; group; platoon; squad [exécution]. ‖ **pelotonner** [-tòné] *v.* to wind into a ball; *se pelotonner,* to coil oneself up, to snuggle.

pelouse [pºlüz] *f.* lawn, grass plot.

peluche [pºlüsh] *f.* plush. ‖ **pelucheux** [-ö] *adj.*° fluffy, plushy.

pelure [pºlür] *f.* peel, rind, paring; onionskin [papier].

pénal [pénàl] *adj.*° penal. ‖ **pénaliser** [-ìzé] *v.* to penalize. ‖ **pénalité** [-ìté] *f.* penalty.

penaud [pºnô] *adj.* abashed, crestfallen, sheepish.

penchant [paⁿshaⁿ] *m.* slope, declivity; leaning, tilt, inclination; propensity, bent, tendency; *adj.* sloping, inclined, leaning ‖ **pencher** [-é] *v.* to tilt, to slope, to incline, to bend; to lean; *se pencher,* to stoop over, to bend; to slope, to be inclined.

pendable [paⁿdàbl] *adj.* meriting the gallows; abominable, scurvy [tour]. ‖ **pendaison** [-èzoⁿ] *f* hanging. ‖ **pendant** [-aⁿ] *m* pendant; counterpart; *adj.* pendent hanging, depending; *prep.* during, *pendant que,* while. ‖ **pendeloque** [-lòk] *f.* ear-drop, earring. ‖ **pendentif** [-aⁿtìf] *m* pendentive (arch.); pendant ‖ **penderie** [-rî] *f.* closet, wardrobe. ‖ **pendiller** [paⁿdìyé] *v.* to dangle ‖ **pendre** [paⁿdr] *v.* to hang; to suspend; to be hanging. ‖ **pendu** [paⁿdü] *m* person hanged; *adj.* hung, hanging, hanged [personne]. ‖ **pendule** [paⁿdül] *m.* pendulum; *f.* clock, time-piece.

pêne [pèn] *m.* bolt; latch.

pénétrant [pénétraⁿ] *adj.* penetrating; keen, searching, impressive; acute; piercing [froid]. ‖ **pénétration** [-àsyoⁿ] *f.* penetration, acuteness; insight. ‖ **pénétrer** [-é] *v.* to penetrate, to go through; to enter; to affect; to pierce; to see through (someone); to go deep into [pays].

pénible [pénìbl] *adj.* painful, laborious; wearisome; distressing.

péniche [pénìsh] *f.* canal-boat; barge; landing-craft (mil.); cutter (douane).

pénicilline [pénìsìlìn] *f.* penicillin.

péninsule [pénìⁿsül] *f.* peninsula.

pénitence [pénìtaⁿs] *f.* penitence, repentance; penance, punishment; penalty [jeux]. ‖ **pénitent** [-aⁿ] *m.* penitent. ‖ **pénitentiaire** [-aⁿsyèr] *adj.* penitentiary.

pénombre [pénoⁿbr] *f.* penumbra; gloom; dusk; shadowy light.

pensée [paⁿsé] *f.* pansy [fleur].

pensée [paⁿsé] *f* thought; sentiment, opinion; notion, idea; conviction; *arrière-pensée,* ulterior motive. ‖ **penser** [-é] *v.* to think; to reflect; to consider; *pensez-vous !,* just imagine! I don't believe it! ‖ **penseur** [-œr] *m.* thinker. ‖ **pensif** [-ìf] *adj.*° pensive, thoughtful; wistful.

pension [paⁿsyoⁿ] *f.* boarding-house; boarding-school; payment for board; pension, annuity. ‖ **pensionnaire** [-yònèr] *m.*, *f.* boarder; in-pupil; pensioner. ‖ **pensionnat** [-yònà] *m.* boarding-school. ‖ **pensionner** [-yòné] *v.* to pension off.

pensum [pìⁿsòm] *m.* imposition, *Am.* extra work.

pentagone [pᵉⁿtàgòn] *m.* pentagon.

pente [pᵃⁿt] *f.* slope, declivity; incline, gradient; tilt, pitch [toit]; propensity, bent; *aller en pente*, to slope.

Pentecôte [pᵃⁿtkôt] *f.* Whitsuntide.

pénurie [pénürî] *f.* scarcity, dearth, want; shortage; penury.

pépie [pépî] *f.* pip, roup.

pépin [pépîⁿ] *m.* kernel, pip, stone, pit; gamp [parapluie]; hitch, snag [ennui]. ‖ **pépinière** [-ìnyèr] *f.* nursery garden; seedbed; professional preparatory school.

pépite [pépît] *f.* nugget.

perçant [pèrsãⁿ] *adj.* piercing; sharp; shrill; penetrating, keen [œil]. ‖ **percée** [-sé] *f.* clearing; break-through (mil.); run-through [rugby]. ‖ **percement** [-mᵃⁿ] *m.* piercing; boring; perforation; tunneling.

percepteur [pèrsèptœr] *m.* tax-collector. ‖ **perceptible** [-tìbl] *adj.* perceptible; audible; collectable. ‖ **perception** [-syoⁿ] *f.* perception; gathering; collector's office.

percer [pèrsé] *v.* to pierce; to bore, to drill; to perforate; to broach; to penetrate; to open; to become known; to break through (mil.); to cut through [rue]. ‖ **perceuse** [-èz] *f.* borer.

percevoir [pèrsᵉwàr] *v.* to perceive; to collect.

perchaude [pèrshôd] *f.* © American perch.

perche [pèrsh] *f.* perch [poisson].

perche [pèrsh] *f.* perch, pole, rod. ‖ **percher** [-é] *v.* to perch, to roost. ‖ **perchoir** [-wàr] *m.* roost.

perclus [pèrklü] *adj.* impotent; anchylosed; stiff.

percolateur [pèrkòlàtœr] *m.* percolator; coffee-percolator.

percussion [pèrküsyoⁿ] *f.* percussion. ‖ **percuter** [-üté] *v.* to strike.

perdant [pèrdᵃⁿ] *adj.* losing; *m.* loser. ‖ **perdition** [-lsyoⁿ] *f.* loss; wreck; perdition (eccles.); distress (naut.). ‖ **perdre** [pèrdr] *v.* to lose; to waste; to ruin; to forfeit; *perdre de vue*, to lose sight of; *se perdre*, to be lost; to lose one's way; to spoil [aliment]; to fall into disuse.

perdreau [pèrdrô] *m.** young partridge.

perdrix [pèrdrì] *f.* partridge.

perdu [pèrdü] *adj.* lost; ruined; wrecked; spoilt; spent [balle].

père [pèr] *m.* father; sire; *pl.* forefathers.

péremptoire [pérᵃⁿptwàr] *adj.* peremptory.

pérennité [pérènìté] *f.* perennity.

péréquation [pérékwàsyoⁿ] *f.* equalizing.

perfection [pèrfèksyoⁿ] *f.* perfection. ‖ **perfectionnement** [-yònmᵃⁿ] *m.* perfecting, improvement; *école de perfectionnement*, finishing school. ‖ **perfectionner** [-yòné] *v.* to perfect, to improve; *se perfectionner*, to improve one's knowledge; to make oneself more skilful.

perfide [pèrfìd] *adj.* perfidious, false, faithless. ‖ **perfidie** [-î] *f.* perfidy, treachery; false-heartedness. ‖ **perforatrice** [pèrfòràtrìs] *f.* boring-machine, drill. ‖ **perforer** [-é] *v.* to perforate, to bore; *cartes perforées*, punched cards.

péril [pérìl] *m.* peril, danger; jeopardy; risk. ‖ **périlleux** [pérìyë] *adj.** perilous, dangerous; hazardous.

périmé [pérìmé] *adj.* lapsed, expired, overdue, forfeit; out of date.

périmètre [pérìmètr] *m.* perimeter.

période [péryòd] *f.* period; age, era, epoch; phase (med.). ‖ **périodique** [-ìk] *m.* periodical; *adj.* periodic.

péripétie [pérìpésî] *f.* sudden change; catastrophe; vicissitude; mishap.

périphrase [pérìfrâz] *f.* circumlocution; periphrasis.

périr [pérìr] *v.* to perish; to die. ‖ **périssable** [-ìsàbl] *adj.* perishable.

perle [pèrl] *f.* pearl; bead. ‖ **perlé** [-é] *adj.* pearly. ‖ **perler** [-é] *v.* to bead.

permanence [pèrmànãⁿs] *f.* permanence; offices; *en permanence*, without interruption. ‖ **permanent** [-ᵃⁿ] *adj.* permanent, lasting. ‖ **permanente** [-ᵃⁿt] *f.* permanent wave, perm.

perméable [pèrméàbl] *adj.* permeable; pervious.

permettre [pèrmètr] *v.** to permit, to allow, to let; *vous permettez?*, allow me?; *se permettre*, to take the liberty (of). ‖ **permis** [-ì] *m.* permit; permission; pass; licence. ‖ **permission** [-ìsyoⁿ] *f.* permission; leave, furlough (mil.); *permissionnaire*, soldier on furlough.

permuter [pèrmüté] *v.* to permute.

pernicieux [pèrnìsyë] *adj.** pernicious, noxious, baneful, malignant.

péroné [péròné] *m.* fibula.

péronnelle [pérònèl] *f.* pert woman.

pérorer [péròré] *v.* to perorate.

perpétrer [pèrpétré] *v.* to perpetrate; to commit.

perpétuel [pèrpétüèl] *adj.** perpetual; endless, everlasting. ‖ **perpétuer** [-üé] *v.* to perpetuate. ‖ **perpétuité** [pèrpétüìté] *f.* perpetuity; *à perpétuité*, for life, for ever.

perplexe [pèrplèks] *adj.* perplexed; puzzled. ‖ **perplexité** [-ìté] *f.* perplexity, puzzlement.

perquisition [pèrkìzìsyoⁿ] *f.* perquisition, search. ‖ **perquisitionner** [-yòné] *v.* to search.

perron [pèroⁿ] *m.* front steps, perron, *Am.* stoop.

perroquet [pèròkè] *m.* parrot; topgallant sail (naut.).

perruche [pèrüsh] *f.* parakeet.

perruque [pèrük] *f.* wig; periwig.

persécuter [pèrséküté] *v.* to persecute; to importune; to harass, to pester. ‖ **persécution** [-üsyoⁿ] *f.* persecution; importunity.

persévérance [pèrsévéraⁿs] *f.* perseverance. ‖ **persévérer** [-é] *v.* to persevere; to persist.

persienne [pèrsyèn] *f.* shutter; blind, persienne.

persiflage [pèrsìflàj] *m.* persiflage; banter, chaff. ‖ **persifler** [-flé] *v.* to banter.

persil [pèrsì] *m.* parsley.

persistance [pèrsìstaⁿs] *f.* persistence. ‖ **persistant** [-aⁿ] *adj.* persistent; perennial (bot.). ‖ **persister** [-é] *v.* to persist.

personnage [pèrsònàj] *m.* personage, person; character (theat.). ‖ **personnalité** [-àlìté] *f.* personality; person. ‖ **personne** [pèrsòn] *f.* person; body; *indef. pron. m.* no one, nobody, not anyone. ‖ **personnel** [-èl] *adj.*° personal; individual; *m.* personnel, staff of employees. ‖ **personnifier** [-ìfyé] *v.* to personify; to impersonate; to embody.

perspective [pèrspèktìv] *f.* perspective; prospect; *en perspective,* in view, in prospect.

perspicace [pèrspìkàs] *adj.* perspicacious, shrewd. ‖ **perspicacité** [-ìté] *f.* perspicacity, shrewdness, insight; acumen; clearsightedness.

persuader [pèrsüàdé] *v.* to persuade, to induce; to convince. ‖ **persuasif** [-üàzìf] *adj.*° persuasive; convincing. ‖ **persuasion** [-üàzyoⁿ] *f.* persuasion.

perte [pèrt] *f.* loss; waste; leakage; defeat (mil.); casualty (mil.); discharge (med.); *à perte de vue,* as far as the eye can see.

pertinent [pèrtìnaⁿ] *adj.* pertinent, relevant.

perturbateur, -trice [pèrtürbàtœr, -trìs] *m., f.* disturber, upsetter; *adj.* disturbing; upsetting. ‖ **perturbation** [-syoⁿ] *f.* perturbation; disorder; upheaval; *perturbations atmosphériques,* atmospherics. ‖ **perturber** [-bé] *v.* to perturb.

pervenche [pèrvaⁿsh] *f.* periwinkle.

pervers [pèrvèr] *adj.* perverse; depraved [goût]; warped [esprit]; wicked; *m.* evil-doer, pervert [sexuel]. ‖ **perversité** [-sìté] *f.* perversity, perverseness. ‖ **pervertir** [-tîr] *v.* to pervert; to corrupt.

pesage [pºzàj] *m.* weighing; paddock. ‖ **pesant** [-aⁿ] *adj.* heavy, ponderous, *Am.* hefty; dull [esprit]. ‖ **pesanteur** [-aⁿtœr] *f.* weigh; gravity; heaviness, *Am.* heftiness; dullness [esprit]. ‖ **peser** [-é] *v.* to weight; to be heavy; to bear on, to press; to consider, to think over.

pessimisme [pèsìmìsm] *m.* pessimism. ‖ **pessimiste** [-ìst] *m., f.* pessimist; *adj.* pessimistic.

peste [pèst] *f.* plague, pestilence; pest (fam.). ‖ **pester** [-é] *v.* to swear, to rave (*contre,* at). ‖ **pestiféré** [-ìféré] *adj.* plague-stricken. ‖ **pestilence** [-ìlaⁿs] *f.* pestilence.

pet [pè] *m.* fart; *pet-de-nonne,* fritter, doughnut.

pétale [pétàl] *f.* petal.

pétarade [pétàràd] *f.* farting; crackling [feu d'artifice]; backfire [moteur]. ‖ **pétarader** [-é] *v.* to pop; to pop back; to backfire; to crackle. ‖ **pétard** [-àr] *m.* petard; firecracker; row, din; bum; six-shooter, *Am.* heater. ‖ **pétillant** [-lyaⁿ] *adj.* crackling; sparkling [vin, yeux]. ‖ **pétillement** [-lymaⁿ] *m.* crackling; sparkling [vin, yeux]; fizzing [eau]. ‖ **pétiller** [-yé] *v.* to crackle; to sparkle; to fizz.

petit [pºtì] *adj.* small, little; short; petty, slight; *m.* little one, little boy; cub, pup, whelp [animaux]; *petit enfant,* tot; *tout petit,* tiny, wee; *petit à petit,* by degrees, little by little; **petite-fille,** grand daughter; *petit-fils,* grandson; *petit-lait,* whey, buttermilk. ‖ **petitesse** [-tès] *f.* smallness; shortness; meanness; pettiness; narrow-mindedness; mean action.

pétition [pétìsyoⁿ] *f.* petition.

pétrifier [pétrìfyé] *v.* to petrify; to dumbfound.

pétrin [pétrìⁿ] *m.* kneading-trough; mess (fam.). ‖ **pétrir** [-ìr] *v.* to knead; to mould.

pétrole [pétròl] *m.* petroleum; mineral oil; kerosene. ‖ **pétrolier** [-yé] *m.* tanker, oiler [bateau]; *adj.*° relating to oil; *industrie pétrolière,* oil industry.

pétulance [pétülaⁿs] *f.* sprightliness; friskiness.

peu [pè] *m.* little; few; a little bit; *adv.* little; few; not very; *peu de chose,* mere trifle.

peuplade [pœplàd] *f.* tribe; people. ‖ **peuple** [pœpl] *m.* people; *adj.* plebeian. ‖ **peupler** [-é] *v.* to people; *se peupler*, to become peopled, to be populous.

peuplier [pœplìyé] *m.* poplar.

peur [pœr] *f.* fear, dread, fright; *avoir peur*, to be afraid; *faire peur*, to frighten; *de peur que*, lest; *de peur de*, for fear of. ‖ **peureux** [-ë] *adj.** fearful.

peut-être [pœtètr] *adv.* perhaps, maybe; possibly.

phalange [fàlaⁿj] *f.* phalanx; host.

phalène [fàlèn] *f.* moth.

phare [fàr] *m.* lighthouse; beacon; headlight [auto].

pharmacie [fàrmàsì] *f.* pharmacy; *Br.* chemist's, *Am.* drugstore; medicine-chest. ‖ **pharmacien** [-y¹ⁿ] *m.* apothecary; *Br.* chemist; *Am.* druggist; **pharmaceutique**, pharmaceutical.

phase [fâz] *f.* phase; stage, period.

phénomène [fénòmèn] *m.* phenomenon; prodigy; character (fam.).

philosophe [fìlòzòf] *m.* philosopher; *adj.* philosophical. ‖ **philosophie** [-ï] *f.* philosophy.

phonographe [fònògràf] *m.* phonograph, record-player, gramophone.

phoque [fòk] *m.* seal.

phosphate [fòsfàt] *m.* phosphate. ‖ **phosphore** [-òr] *m.* phosphorus.

photographe [fòtògràf] *m.* photographer, cameraman. ‖ **photographie** [-ï] *f.* photography; photograph. ‖ **photographier** [-yé] *v.* to photograph; **photocopie**, photostat, photoprint, photocopy.

phrase [frâz] *f.* phrase; sentence.

physicien [fìzìsy¹ⁿ] *m.* physicist.

physionomie [fìzìònòmï] *f.* countenance, aspect, look; physiognomy.

physique [fìzìk] *f.* physics; natural philosophy; *m.* physique, natural constitution; outward appearance; *adj.* physical, material; bodily.

piaffer [pyàfé] *v.* to paw the ground, to prance; to fume; to fidget; to swagger.

piailler [pyàyé] *v.* to chirp, to cheep; to squall.

pianiste [pyànìst] *m.*, *f.* pianist. ‖ **piano** [-ó] *m.* piano; *piano droit*, upright piano; *piano à queue*, grand piano; *piano demi-queue*, baby-grand piano.

piastre [pyàstr] *f.* © dollar.

pic [pìk] *m.* pick, pickaxe; peak [montagne]; *à pic*, steep, sheer,

vertical; apeak (naut.); *in the nick of time, just in time.*

pic [pìk] *m.* woodpecker [oiseau].

pichenette [pìchnèt] *f.* (fam.) fillip, flick, flip.

pichet [pìshè] *m.* pitcher.

pick-up [pìkœp] *m.* record-player, gramophone, pick-up, reproducer.

picorer [pìkòré] *v.* to peck, to pick up; to pilfer (fig.).

picotement [pìkòtmaⁿ] *m.* tingling, prickling. ‖ **picoter** [pìkòté] *v.* to prick, to peck; to tingle.

picotin [pìkòt¹ⁿ] *m.* peck.

pie [pì] *f.* magpie; *adj.* piebald; *pie-grièche*, shrike.

pièce [pyès] *f.* piece; bit, fragment; document; head [bétail]; barrel, cask; apartment, room; play; coin; medal; *pièce d'eau*, artificial pond; *pièce à conviction*, material or circumstancial evidence; *mettre en pièces*, to tear to pieces.

pied [pyé] *m.* foot; leg [meuble]; base; stalk [plante]; head [céleri]; *avoir pied*, to have a footing; *pieds nus*, barefoot; *au pied de la lettre*, literally; *coup de pied*, kick; *fouler aux pieds*, to tread on; to trample; *lâcher pied*, to turn tail; *mettre sur pied*, to set up; to establish; *doigt de pied*, toe; *cou-de-pied*, instep; *pied-à-terre*, temporary lodging; *pied-bot*, club-footed person; *pied-de-biche*, presser-foot; *pied-de-roi*, © folding rule; claw. ‖ **piédestal** [pyédèstàl] *m.* pedestal.

piège [pyèj] *m.* trap, snare; pitfall. ‖ **piéger** [pyéjé] *v.* to snare, to trap.

pierre [pyèr] *f.* stone; *pierre à aiguiser*, grind stone; *pierre d'achoppement*, stumbling-block; *pierre à fusil*, flint; *pierre de taille*, free-stone. ‖ **pierreries** [-rï] *f. pl.* precious gems. ‖ **pierreux** [-ë] *adj.** stony, gritty; calculous (med.).

piété [pyété] *f.* piety.

piétiner [pyétìné] *v.* to stamp; to paw the ground; to trample.

piéton [pyétòⁿ] *m.* pedestrian.

piètre [pyètr] *adj.* shabby, paltry; poor; lame; wretched.

pieu [pyë] *m.** stake, pile, post.

pieuvre [pyëvr] *f.* octopus, poulpe, devil-fish.

pieux [pyë] *adj.** pious, devout.

pigeon [pìjòⁿ] *m.* pigeon; *pigeon voyageur*, carrier-pigeon. ‖ **pigeonnier** [-ònyé] *m.* pigeon-house, dove-cot.

piger [pìjé] *v.* (fam.) to get it; to twig.

pigment [pìgmaⁿ] *m.* pigment. ‖ **pigmenté** [-té] *adj.* pigmented.

pignon [pìñoⁿ] *m.* gable; chain-wheel; pinion [roue].

pile [pìl] *f.* pile, heap; pier [pont]; cell, battery (electr.).

pile [pìl] *f.* reverse, tail [pièce de monnaie]; *pile ou face*, heads or tails.

piler [pìlé] *v.* to pound, to crush, to pulverise, to grind.

pilier [pìlyé] *m.* pillar, column, post; prop; supporter.

pillage [pìyàj] *m.* pillage, plunder; looting, pilfering, waste. ‖ *pillard* [pìyàr] *m.* plunderer; *adj.* pillaging, predatory, plundering. ‖ *piller* [pìyé] *v.* to pillage, to loot, to pilfer, to plunder; to ransack; to filch, to pirate.

pilon [pìloⁿ] *m.* pestle; beetle, rammer, stamper; *mettre au pilon*, to pulp. ‖ *pilonner* [-òné] *v.* to pound, to ram, to mill, to stamp.

pilotage [pìlòtàj] *m.* piloting. ‖ *pilote* [pìlòt] *m.* pilot; guide; *pilote d'essai*, test pilot. ‖ *piloter* [-é] *v.* to pilot; to guide.

pilotis [pìlòtì] *m.* pile-work, pile-foundation, piling; *sur pilotis*, on piles.

pilule [pìlül] *f.* pill.

pimbêche [pìⁿbèch] *f.* (fam.) old cat.

piment [pìmaⁿ] *m.* pimento; all-spice. ‖ *pimenter* [-té] *v.* to spice; to render piquant.

pimpant [pìⁿpaⁿ] *adj.* natty, spruce, smart, trim, natty.

pin [pìⁿ] *m.* pine-tree, fir-tree.

pince [pìⁿs] *f.* pinch; pincers, nippers, pliers, tweezers; crowbar; claw [langouste]; toe [cheval]; grip [main]; tongs [sucre]; *pince-monseigneur*, burglar's jemmy; *pince-nez*, pince-nez, bowless eye-glasses. ‖ *pincé* [-é] *adj.* pinched; affected; stiff.

pinceau [pìⁿsô] *m.* paint-brush; pencil.

pincée [pìⁿsé] *f.* pinch. ‖ *pincer* [-é] *v.* to pinch; to nip; to bite; to compress; to grip; to pluck [guitare]; to purse [lèvres]; (pop.) to nab, to arrest. ‖ *pincette* [-èt] *f.* nip; tweezers, nippers; tongs. ‖ *pinçon* [-oⁿ] *m.* pinch-mark.

pinède [pìnèd] *f.* pine-wood.

pingouin [pìⁿgwìⁿ] *m.* razorbill; auk.

pingre [pìⁿgr] *adj.* (fam.) stingy; skinflint.

pinson [pìⁿsoⁿ] *m.* finch; chaffinch.

pintade [pìⁿtàd] *f.* guinea-fowl, guinea-hen.

pinte [pìⁿt] *f.* pint, © quart.

pioche [pyòsh] *f.* pickaxe, pick, mattock. ‖ *piocher* [-é] *v.* to pick; to grind (fam.).

piolet [pyòlè] *m.* ice-axe.

pion [pyoⁿ] *m.* pawn [échecs]; man [dames]; study master, *Am.* proctor [école]. ‖ *pionnier* [-ònyé] *m.* pioneer; trail-blazer.

pipe [pìp] *f.* pipe; tube. ‖ *pipeau* [-ô] *m.** shepherd's pipe, reed-pipe; bird-call; bird-snare; pipe (mus.) ‖ *piper* [-é] *v.* to peep; to lure [oiseaux]; to load [dés].

piquant [pìkaⁿ] *adj.* prickling, stinging; pointed, sharp; biting; pungent; piquant; witty; *m.* prickle; sting; thorn [épine]; quill [porc-épic]; spike; piquancy, pith; pungency; zest.

pique [pìk] *f.* pike; *m.* spade [cartes]; pique, tiff [querelle]. ‖ *pique-bois* [pìkbwà] *m.* © woodpecker.

piqué [pìké] *adj.* quilted; pinked [tissu]; sour [vin]; *m.* nose-dive (aviat.). ‖ *piquer* [-é] *v.* to prick, to sting; to bite; to puncture; to stitch; to quilt; to stab; to insert; to nettle, to pique; to poke; to nose-dive (aviat.); *se piquer*, to prick oneself; to pride oneself; to take offence; to sour [vin]; *pique-assiette*, sponger, parasite; *pique-nique*, picnic. ‖ *piquet* [-è] *m.* peg, stake, post; picket (mil.); piquet [cartes]. ‖ *piqueter* [-té] *v.* to stake out; to picket; to dot, to spot. ‖ *piquette* [-èt] *f.* thin wine. ‖ *piqueur* [-œr] *m.* huntsman; outrider; stitcher, sewer. ‖ *piqûre* [-ür] *f.* sting, prick; bite; puncture; injection, vaccination, *Am.* shot (med.); stitching, sewing; quilting.

pirate [pìràt] *m.* pirate. ‖ *piraterie* [-rì] *f.* piracy.

pire [pìr] *adj.* worse; *le pire*, the worst.

pirouette [pìrûèt] *f.* pirouette, whirling. ‖ *pirouetter* [-é] *v.* to pirouette, to twirl.

pis [pì] *m.* udder, dug.

pis [pì] *adv.* worse; *le pis*, the worst; *pis-aller*, last resource; makeshift.

piscine [pìsìn] *f.* swimming-pool.

pissenlit [pìsaⁿlì] *m.* dandelion.

pistache [pìstàch] *f.* pistachio-nut; *adj.* pistachio-green.

piste [pìst] *f.* track; race-course; trail, clue, scent; landing strip, runway (aviat.); ring [cirque]. ‖ *pister* [-té] *v.* to track; to shadow.

pistolet [pìstòlè] *m.* pistol.

piston [pìstoⁿ] *m.* piston; sucker [pompe]; valve [cornet]; (fam.) influence, backing, pull. ‖ *pistonner* [-òné] *v.* to recommend, to back, to push, to help to get on.

piteux [pìtë] *adj.** piteous, woeful; pitiable, sorry. ‖ *pitié* [-yé] *f.* pity, mercy, compassion.

piton [pìtoⁿ] *m.* screw-ring, ringbolt; peak [montagne].

pitoyable [pìtwàyàbl] *adj.* pitiable, pitiful, piteous; compassionate, sympathetic; wretched, despicable.

pitre [pìtr] *m.* clown; buffoon.

pittoresque [pìtòrésk] *adj.* picturesque; colourful; *m.* picturesqueness, vividness.

pivert [pìvèr] *m.* green woodpecker.

pivoine [pìvwàn] *f.* paeony.

pivot [pìvô] *m.* pivot, pin, axis, spindle, stud, swivel; fulcrum [levier]; tap-root [racine]. ‖ **pivoter** [-òté] *v.* to pivot, to revolve, to hinge, to swivel.

placage [plàkàj] *m.* veneering.

placard [plàkar] *m.* cupboard, wall-press, closet; bill, poster, placard, notice; panel [porte]. ‖ **placarder** [-dé] *v.* to post, to stick, to placard.

place [plàs] *f.* place; position; stead; space, room; seat, reservation (theat.); job, employment, post; locality, spot; square [publique]; town, fortress; *sur place*, on the spot; *à la place de*, instead of. ‖ **placement** [-maⁿ] *m.* placing; sale, disposal (comm.); investing [argent]; hiring, engaging; *bureau de placement*, *Br.* labour exchange, *Am.* employment agency. ‖ **placer** [-é] *v.* to place; to put, to set; to seat [spectateurs]; to get employment for; to sell, to dispose of (comm.); to invest [argent].

placide [plàsìd] *adj.* placid, calm, tranquil, quiet.

placier [plàsyé] *m.* canvasser; salesman; agent.

plafond [plàfoⁿ] *m.* ceiling. ‖ **plafonnier** [-ònyé] *m.* ceiling-light.

plage [plàj] *f.* beach, shore.

plagiat [plàjyà] *m.* plagiarism, plagiary. ‖ **plagier** [-jyé] *v.* to plagiarize.

plaider [plèdé] *v.* to plead; to litigate; to allege; to intercede. ‖ **plaideur** [-œr] *m.* litigant, petitioner; suitor. ‖ **plaidoirie** [-wàrî] *f.* pleading; barrister's speech. ‖ **plaidoyer** [-wàyé] *m.* plea; argument.

plaie [plè] *f.* wound; sore; plague, scourge, affliction.

plaignant [plèñaⁿ] *m.* plaintiff, prosecutor; *adj.* complaining.

plain [pliⁿ] *adj.* level; *de plain-pied avec*, flush with, on a par with.

plaindre [pliⁿdr] *v.** to pity; to be sorry for; to sympathize with; to grudge; *se plaindre*, to complain; to grumble; to moan.

plaine [plèn] *f.* plain.

plainte [pliⁿt] *f.* complaint; lamentation; reproach; *déposer une plainte*, to file a complaint. ‖ **plaintif** [-ìf] *adj.** plaintive, complaining, doleful; querulous.

plaire [plèr] *v.* to please; to be pleasing; *s'il vous plaît*, if you please; *plaît-il?*, I beg your pardon ?, what did you say ?; *la pièce m'a plu*, I enjoyed the play; *se plaire*, to delight (*à*, in); to please one another; to be content.

plaisant [plèzaⁿ] *m.* jester, joker; *adj.* pleasant; humorous, amusing, funny. ‖ **plaisanter** [-té] *v.* to jest, to joke; to trifle. ‖ **plaisanterie** [-trî] *f.* jest, joke; witticism; wisecrack (fam.); humo(u)r. ‖ **plaisantin** [-tiⁿ] *m.* jester, practical joker.

plaisir [plèzîr] *m.* pleasure, delight; will, consent; diversion; *avec plaisir*, willingly; *à plaisir*, gratuitously; designedly; *faire plaisir à*, to please.

plan [plaⁿ] *m.* plan, scheme, project; plane surface; map; wing (aviat.); distance, ground [tableau]; *adj.* even, level, flat; *plan du métro*, subway map; *premier plan*, foreground; *arrière-plan*, background.

planche [plàsh] *f.* plank, board; shelf; plate [métal]; bed [légumes]; *pl.* stage (theat.); *planchette*, small plank. ‖ **plancher** [-é] *m.* floor, floor-board [auto].

planer [plàné] *v.* to hover, to soar; to plane, to make smooth; *vol plané*, glide.

planétaire [plànétèr] *adj.* planetary. ‖ **planète** [plànèt] *f.* planet.

planeur [plànœr] *m.* sail-plane, glider.

planification [plànìfìkàsyoⁿ] *f.* planning. ‖ **planifier** [-fyé] *v.* to plan, to blueprint.

plant [plaⁿ] *m.* young plant, slip; sapling; plantation. ‖ **plantation** [-tàsyoⁿ] *f.* planting, plantation. ‖ **plante** [plaⁿt] *f.* plant; sole [pied]; seaweed [mer]. ‖ **planter** [-é] *v.* to plant; to set up; to leave flat, to give the slip to, to jilt. ‖ **planteur** [-œr] *m.* planter. ‖ **plantoir** [-wàr] *m.* dibble, planting-tool. ‖ **planton** [-oⁿ] *m.* orderly (mil.); *de planton*, on duty.

plantureux [plaⁿtürë] *adj.** plentiful, copious, abundant; fertile, prolific.

plaque [plàk] *f.* plate [métal]; plaque; badge, tag; slab [marbre]; *plaque tournante*, turn-table (railw.). ‖ **plaquer** [-é] *v.* to plate [métal]; to veneer [bois]; to strike [accord]; (fam.) to jilt, to leave flat. ‖ **plaquette** [-èt] *f.* small plate; thin slab; small book, pamphlet, booklet, brochure.

plastique [plàstìk] *f.* plastic art; *m.* plastic goods; *adj.* plastic.

plastron [plàstroⁿ] *m.* breast-plate; plastron; shirt-front, dicky. ‖ *plastronner* [-òné] *v.* to pose, to strut.

plat [plà] *adj.* flat; level, even; dull [style]; straight [cheveux]; calm [mer]; *m.* dish; *plate-bande*, flower bed; moulding (arch.); *plate-forme*, platform.

platane [plàtàn] *m.* plane-tree.

plateau [plàtô] *m.** tray; table-land, plateau; scale [balance]; platform, stage (theat.).

platée [plàté] *f.* dishful.

platine [plàtĭn] *f.* plate [serrure]; screw-plate [fusil]; platen [presse].

platine [plàtĭn] *m.* platinum.

platitude [plàtĭtüd] *f.* platitude, banal remark; flatness, dullness; obsequiousness; cringing attitude.

platonique [plàtònĭk] *adj.* platonic; useless.

plâtre [plâtr] *m.* plaster. ‖ *plâtrer* [-é] *v.* to plaster. ‖ *plâtrier* [-tryé] *m.* plasterer.

plausible [plôzĭbl] *adj.* plausible.

plèbe [plèb] *f.* common people; plebs.

plébiscite [plébĭssĭt] *m.* plebiscite.

plein [plĭⁿ] *adj.* full; filled; replete; complete, entire, whole; solid [pneu]; pregnant, full [animaux]; (fam.) drunk; *m.* full; full part; full tide; middle; *plein jour*, broad daylight; *plein hiver*, dead of winter; *pleine mer*, high seas; *faire le plein*, to fill the tank [auto]. ‖ *plénipotentiaire* [plénipòtaⁿsyèr] *m.*, *adj.* plenipotentiary. ‖ *plénitude* [-ĭtüd] *f.* plenitude, fullness, completeness, abundance.

pléthore [plétòr] *f.* superabundance. ‖ *pléthorique* [-rĭk] *adj.* overabundant; overcrowded.

pleur [plœr] *m.* tear. ‖ *pleurer* [-é] *v.* to weep, to cry; to mourn; to run, to water [yeux]. ‖ *pleurnicher* [-nishé] *v.* to whimper, to whine, to snivel. ‖ *pleurnicheur* [-nĭshœr] *adj.** whimpering, snivelling; *m.* whimperer, sniveller, cry-baby.

pleutre [plœtr] *m.* coward.

pleuvoir [plœvwàr] *v.** to rain; *il pleut à verse*, it's pouring.

plèvre [plèvr] *f.* pleura.

pli [plĭ] *m.* fold, pleat; wrinkle, pucker, crease; habit; envelope, cover; letter, note; curl [lèvre]; undulation [terrain]; *sous ce pli*, enclosed, herewith; *mise en plis*, wave, hair-set [cheveux]. ‖ *pliable* [-yàbl] *adj.* pliable, foldable, flexible. ‖ *pliage* [-yàj] *m.* folding, creasing. ‖ *pliant* [-yaⁿ] *adj.* pliant, flexible; docile [caractère]; collapsible [chaise]; *m.* folding-stool; camp-stool.

plier [-yé] *v.* to fold; to bend; to yield. ‖ *plieuse* [-yëz] *f.* folding-machine.

plinthe [plĭⁿt] *f.* plinth; skirting-board.

plissement [plĭsmaⁿ] *m.* wrinkling [front]; pursing [lèvres]; plication (geol.). ‖ *plisser* [plĭsé] *v.* to pleat, to fold; to crease; to crumple, to crinkle; to pucker.

plomb [ploⁿ] *m.* lead; fuse (electr.); shot, bullet; weight, sinker; plummet [sonde]; lead seal [sceau]; *à plomb*, upright; perpendicular; *fil à plomb*, plumb-line; *faire sauter un plomb*, to blow out a fuse. ‖ *plombage* [-bàj] *m.* leading, plumbing; sealing [douane]; filling, *Br.* stopping [dents]. ‖ *plomber* [-bé] *v.* to lead; to plumb; to seal; to fill, *Br.* to stop [dents]. ‖ *plomberie* [-brî] *f.* plumbery; lead industry; lead-works. ‖ *plombier* [-byé] *m.* plumber; leadworker; *adj.* related to lead.

plongée [ploⁿjé] *f.* plunge, dive; submersion; submergence [sous-marin]; dip, slope [terrain]; declivity (arch.). ‖ *plongeon* [-oⁿ] *m.* plunge, dive [natation]; diver [oiseau]. ‖ *plonger* [-é] *v.* to plunge, to dive; to submerge [sous-marin]; to immerse, to dip; to pitch [bateau]; to thrust. ‖ *plongeur* [-œr] *m.* diver; dish-washer, scullery-boy; plunger (mech.).

ployer [plwàyé] *v.* to bend; to bow; to give way, to yield; to ploy (mil.).

pluie [plüî] *f.* rain; shower; *pluie battante*, pelting rain, downpour.

plumage [plümàj] *m.* plumage, feathers. ‖ *plume* [plüm] *f.* feather, plume; quill, pen. ‖ *plumeau* [-ô] *m.** feather-duster. ‖ *plumer* [-é] *v.* to pluck, to plume; (fam.) to fleece. ‖ *plumier* [-yé] *m.* pen-box; pencil-case. ‖ *plumitif* [-ĭtĭf] *m.* (fam.) scribbler, pen-pusher.

plupart [plüpàr] *f.* the most, the majority, the greater part, the bulk; *la plupart des gens*, most people; *pour la plupart*, mostly.

pluraliser [plüràlĭzé] *v.* to pluralize. ‖ *pluralité* [-té] *f.* plurality.

pluriel [plüryèl] *m.*, *adj.* plural.

plus [plü] *adv.* more; *m.* more; most; plus (math.); *plus âgé*, older; *ne... plus*, no longer; *au plus*, at most; *de plus*, furthermore; *non plus*, neither, either; *de plus en plus*, more and more; *plus-que-parfait*, pluperfect (gramm.); *plus-value*, increment value.

plusieurs [plüzyœr] *adj.*, *pron.* several.

plutôt [plütô] *adv.* rather, sooner; on the whole; instead.

pluvieux [plüvyë] *adj.** rainy, wet.

pneu [pnë] *m*. Br. tyre, Am. tire. ‖ **pneumatique** [-màtìk] *adj*. pneumatic; Br. tyre, Am. tire; *m*. express letter [Paris].

pneumonie [pnëmònî] *f*. pneumonia (med.).

pochade [pòshàd] *f*. rapid sketch, rough sketch. ‖ **pochard** [-àr] *m*. drunkard, sot. ‖ **poche** [pòsh] *f*. pocket; pouch; sack, bag. ‖ **poché** [-é] *adj*. poached [œuf]; black [œil]. ‖ **pochette** [-èt] *f*. small pocket; pocket book [allumettes]; fancy handkerchief [mouchoir]. ‖ **pochoir** [-wàr] *m*. stencil plate; *peinture au pochoir*, stencilling.

poêle [pwàl] *m*. stove; cooker.

poêle [pwàl] *m*. pall [pompes funèbres].

poêle [pwàl] *f*. frying-pan. ‖ **poêlon** [-loⁿ] *m*. pan, pipkin.

poème [pòèm] *m*. poem. ‖ **poésie** [pòèzî] *f*. poetry; poem. ‖ **poète** [pòèt] *m*. poet. ‖ **poétesse** [pòètès] *f*. poetess. ‖ **poétique** [-ìk] *adj*. poetic; poetical; *f*. poetics.

poids [pwà] *m*. weight; heaviness; importance; load, burden; *poids lourd*, heavy, Br. lorry, Am. truck.

poignant [pwàñaⁿ] *adj*. agonizing; heart-rending; sharp.

poignard [pwàñàr] *m*. dagger, poniard; dirk. ‖ **poignarder** [-dé] *v*. to stab, to pierce. ‖ **poigne** [pwàñ] *f*. grasp, grip. ‖ **poignée** [-é] *f*. handful; handle [porte]; hilt [épée]; grip [revolver]; haft [outil]; handshake [main]. ‖ **poignet** [-è] *m*. wrist; wristband, cuff.

poil [pwàl] *m*. hair; fur; nap, pile [velours]; bristle [brosse]; down, pubescence [plante]. ‖ **poilu** [-ü] *adj*. hairy, shaggy, nappy [tissu]; *m*. French soldier.

poinçon [pwàⁿsoⁿ] *m*. punch; stamp, die; awl; chisel; piercer, pricker [broderie]; puncheon; *poinçon de contrôle*, hall-mark. ‖ **poinçonner** [-òné] *v*. to punch; to prick; to stamp; to cancel; to hall-mark. ‖ **poinçonneur** [-ònœr] *m*. puncher.

poindre [pwìⁿdr] *v*.° to break, to dawn [aube]; to sprout [plante].

poing [pwìⁿ] *m*. fist; hand.

point [pwìⁿ] *m*. point; speck, dot; stitch, pain [med.]; instant; degree; Br. full stop, Am. period; *adv*. not, no, none; *point d'interrogation*, question mark; *deux-points*, colon; *points de suspension*, suspension dots; *point-virgule*, semi-colon; *arriver à point*, to come in the nick of time; *cuit à point*, cooked medium-well; *sur le point de*, about to; *sur ce point*, on that score, in that respect; *point mort*, Br. neutral, Am. dead center [auto].

pointage [pwìⁿtàj] *m*. levelling, pointing; checking; time-keeping [ouvrier]. ‖ **pointe** [pwìⁿt] *f*. point, nail; fichu; cape, foreland; tip, peak; sting, pungency; witticism; touch; dawn [jour]; *pointe de vitesse*, spurt; *pointe sèche*, dry-point engraving; *pointe des pieds*, tiptoe. ‖ **pointer** [-é] *v*. to point; to pierce; to mark; to check; to aim, to lay [fusil]. ‖ **pointeur** [-èr] *m*. pointer, marker; checker; gunlayer. ‖ **pointillé** [-ìyé] *adj*. dotted [ligne]; stippled; *m*. dotted line. ‖ **pointiller** [-ìyé] *v*. to dot; to stipple; to perforate; to bicker. ‖ **pointilleux** [-ìyë] *adj*.° particular, punctilious; fastidious. ‖ **pointu** [-ü] *adj*. pointed, sharp. ‖ **pointure** [-ür] *f*. size.

poire [pwàr] *f*. pear; powder-flask; bulb (electr.); (fam.) dupe, (pop.) sucker.

poireau [pwàrô] *m*.° leek. ‖ **poireauter** [-té] *v*. (pop.) to dance attendance.

poirier [pwàryé] *m*. pear-tree.

pois [pwà] *m*. pea; polka dot [dessin]; *petits pois*, green peas; *pois cassés*, split peas.

poison [pwàzoⁿ] *m*. poison.

poissarde [pwàsàrd] *f*. fish-wife.

poisse [pwàs] *f*. (pop.) tough luck; jinx.

poisseux [pwàsë] *adj*.° pitchy, gluey, sticky.

poisson [pwàsoⁿ] *m*. fish; *poisson d'avril*, April Fool joke; *poisson rouge*, goldfish. ‖ **poissonnerie** [-ònrî] *f*. fishmarket. ‖ **poissonnière** [-ònyèr] *f*. fish-kettle; fish-wife.

poitrail [pwàtràÿ] *m*. breast.

poitrinaire [pwàtrìnèr] *m*., *f*., *adj*. consumptive. ‖ **poitrine** [pwàtrìn] *f*. breast, chest, bosom; bust.

poivre [pwàvr] *m*. pepper. ‖ **poivrer** [-é] *v*. to pepper; to spice. ‖ **poivrier** [-ìyé] *m*. pepper-shrub; pepper-shaker. ‖ **poivron** [-oⁿ] *m*. pimento, Jamaica pepper. ‖ **poivrot** [-ô] *m*. drunkard, tippler.

poix [pwà] *f*. pitch; *poix sèche*, resin.

polaire [pòlèr] *adj*. polar. ‖ **polarisation** [pòlàrìzàsyoⁿ] *f*. polarization. ‖ **polariser** [-rìzé] *v*. to polarize. ‖ **polarité** [-rìté] *f*. polarity. ‖ **pôle** [pôl] *m*. pole.

polémique [pòlémìk] *f*. controversy, polemics; *adj*. polemical. ‖ **polémiquer** [-mìké] *v*. to polemize. ‖ **polémiste** [-mìst] *s*. polemist.

poli [pòlì] *m*. polish, gloss; *adj*. buffed; polished, glossy; (fig.) polite, civil, courteous.

police [pòlìs] *f*. policy [assurance].

police [pòlìs] *f.* police; policing; *agent de police*, policeman; *Br.* bobby, *Am.* cop (fam.); *salle de police*, guardroom; *faire la police*, to keep order. ‖ *policer* [-é] *v.* to civilize, to establish law and order.

polichinelle [pòlìshìnèl] *m.* Punch; buffoon (fig.).

policier [pòlìsyé] *m.* police constable; policeman; detective; *adj.** police.

polir [pòlìr] *v.* to polish, to buff. ‖ *polissoir* [-ìswàr] *m.* polishing tool; buffer.

polisson [pòlìsoⁿ] *m.* scamp, rascal; mischievous child; *adj.* naughty; licentious, indecent, depraved.

politesse [pòlìtès] *f.* politeness; civility; urbanity; compliment.

politicien [pòlìtìsyèⁿ] *m.* politician. ‖ *politique* [-ìk] *f.* politics; policy; *adj.* political; politic, prudent.

pollen [pòllèn] *m.* pollen.

polluer [pòllüé] *v.* to pollute, to defile; to profane.

poltron [pòltroⁿ] *m.* coward; *adj.** cowardly, craven, pusillanimous. ‖ *poltronnerie* [-ònrî] *f.* cowardice, poltroonery.

polycopier [pòlìkòpyé] *v.* to manifold, to mimeograph.

pommade [pòmàd] *f.* pomade, ointment, salve, unguent.

pomme [pòm] *f.* apple; knob, ball; head [chou, laitue]; cone [pin]; *pomme de terre*, potato.

pommeau [pòmô] *m.** pommel; knob. ‖ *pommelé* [-lé] *adj.* dappled, mottled; cloudy.

pommette [pòmèt] *f.* cheek-bone; knob; ball ornament. ‖ *pommier* [-yé] *m.* apple tree.

pompe [poⁿp] *f.* pomp, ceremony; display, parade; state; *entrepreneur de pompes funèbres*, undertaker, funeral director, *Am.* mortician.

pompe [poⁿp] *f.* pump. ‖ *pomper* [-é] *v.* to pump; to suck in.

pompeux [poⁿpë] *adj.** pompous.

pompier [poⁿpyé] *m.* fireman.

pompiste [poⁿpìst] *s.* pump assistant, filling-station mechanic.

pompon [poⁿpoⁿ] *m.* pompon, tuft, tassel.

pomponner (se) [s*poⁿpòné] *v.* to titivate, to smarten oneself up.

ponce [poⁿs] *f.* pumice. ‖ *poncer* [-é] *v.* to pumice; to pounce.

ponction [poⁿksyoⁿ] *f.* puncture; tapping [poumon]; pricking.

ponctualité [poⁿktüàlìté] *f.* punctuality, promptness.

ponctuation [poⁿktüàsyoⁿ] *f.* punctuation.

ponctuel [poⁿktüèl] *adj.** punctual, prompt, exact.

pondération [poⁿdéràsyoⁿ] *f.* ponderation, balance, equilibrium. ‖ *pondéré* [-é] *adj.* poised; weighed; moderate, sensible; considered.

pondeuse [poⁿdëz] *f.* egg-layer. ‖ *pondre* [poⁿdr] *v.* to lay eggs.

pont [poⁿ] *m.* bridge; deck [bateau]; *pont aérien*, air-lift; *pont-levis*, drawbridge; *faire le pont*, to bridge the gap; *pont arrière*, differential, rearaxle (mech.).

pontife [poⁿtìf] *m.* pontiff.

ponton [poⁿtoⁿ] *m.* bridge of boats; pontoon; convict ship.

popote [pòpòt] *adj.* (fam.) stay-at-home; *f.* mess; cooking.

populace [pòpülàs] *f.* populace; mob, rabble. ‖ *populaire* [-èr] *adj.* popular; vulgar, common. ‖ *popularité* [-àrìté] *f.* popularity. ‖ *population* [-àsyoⁿ] *f.* population. ‖ *populeux* [-ë] *adj.** populous. ‖ *populo* [-o] *m.* (fam.) riff-raff, rabble.

porc [pòr] *m.* pork; pig, hog, swine; dirty person (fig.).

porcelaine [pòrs*lèn] *f.* china, chinaware.

porc-épic [pòrképìk] *m.* porcupine, *Am.* hedge-hog.

porche [pòrsh] *m.* porch, portal.

porcher [pòrshé] *m.* swine-herd. ‖ *porcherie* [-*rî] *f.* pig-sty.

pore [pòr] *m.* pore. ‖ *poreux* [-ë] *adj.** porous; permeable; unglazed.

port [pòr] *m.* port, harbo(u)r; sea-port town; wharf, quay; haven; *arriver à bon port*, to arrive safely, to reach safe harbo(u)r.

port [pòr] *m.* carrying; transport; carriage; carrying charges; postage; bearing, gait; tonnage, burden (naut.).

portage [pòrtàj] *m.* portage. ‖ *portager* [-é] *v.* © to portage.

portail [pòrtày] *m.* portal, gate.

portant [pòrtàⁿ] *adj.* bearing, carrying (mech.); *m.* bearer, upright; stay, strut; tread [roue]; *bien portant*, in good health; *à bout portant*, point-blank. ‖ *portatif* [-àtìf] *adj.** portable.

porte [pòrt] *f.* gate, door; gateway, doorway, entrance; eye [agrafe]; *adj.* portal (anat.); *porte cochère*, carriage entrance; *porte à tambour*, revolving door; *mettre à la porte*, to evict, to expel, to oust; to sack; to fire; *porte-fenêtre*, *Br.* French window, *Am.* French door; *porte-à-porte*, door-to-door transport, house-to-house canvassing.

porté [pòrté] *adj.* inclined, disposed, prone; carried; worn; *porté manquant,* reported missing. ‖ *portée* [-é] *f.* bearing; span; litter, brood [animaux]; projection; reach; scope; compass [voix]; import; comprehension; stave (mus.); *à portée de la main,* within reach, to hand. ‖ *porter* [-é] *v.* to carry; to bear, to support; to wear [vêtements]; to take; to bring; to strike, to deal, to aim [coup]; to inscribe, to enter (comm.); to induce, to incline, to prompt; to produce [animaux]; to pass [jugement]; to shoulder [armes]; *se porter,* to proceed, to go; to be [santé]; to offer oneself [candidat]; to be worn [vêtement]; *porte-avions,* aircraft carrier, *Am.* flat-top; *porte-bagages,* carrier, luggage-rack; *porte-bonheur,* talisman, good-luck piece; *porte-bouteilles,* bottle-stand; coaster; *porte-cartes,* card-case; *porte-cigarette,* cigarette-holder; *porte-couteau,* knife-rest; *porte-crayon,* pencil-case; *porte-drapeau,* colo(u)r-bearer; *porte-étendard,* standard-bearer; *portefaix,* street-porter; dock hand, stevedore; *portefeuille,* portfolio; bill-fold, pocket-book; *portemanteau,* portmanteau; coat-stand; coat-hanger; davit (naut.); *porte-mine,* pencil-case; eversharp pencil; *porte-monnaie,* purse; *porte-musique,* music - stand; music - case; *porte-parapluies,* umbrella stand; *porte-parole,* spokesman, mouthpiece; *porte-plume,* penholder; *porte-savon,* soap-dish; *porte-serviettes,* towel-rod; napkin-ring; *porte-voix,* megaphone, speaking tube. ‖ *porteur* [-œr] *m.* porter; bearer, carrier.

portier [pòrtyé] *m.* door-keeper; janitor. ‖ *portière* [-yèr] *f.* door [voiture]; door-curtain. ‖ *portillon* [-lyon] *m.* wicket-gate; side-gate (railw.).

portion [pòrsyon] *f.* portion, part, share; allowance; helping; *portion congrue,* bare subsistence.

portique [pòrtìk] *m.* portico; crossbeam [sports]; awning [chemin de fer].

porto [pòrtò] *m.* port wine.

portrait [pòrtrè] *m.* portrait, likeness, picture. ‖ *portraitiste* [-tìst] *s.* portrait-painter.

pose [pòz] *f.* putting, laying, posting; stationing (mil.); pose, attitude, posture; posing; affectation; time-exposure (phot.). ‖ *posé* [pòzé] *adj.* staid, grave, sedate; poised. ‖ *poser* [-é] *v.* to put, to set; to lay; to rest, to lie; to pose; to ask [question]; to post, to station (mil.); to put down (math.); to pitch (mus.); *se poser,* to alight, to perch [oiseau]; to land [avion]; to come up [question].

positif [pòzìtìf] *adj.°* positive, certain,

definite; matter-of-fact, practical [esprit]; actual, real; *m.* positive print (phot.); solid reality (fig.).

position [pòzìsyon] *f.* position; situation; condition; standing.

posologie [pòzòlòjì] *f.* dosage.

possédé [pòsédé] *adj.* possessed; *m.* madman. ‖ *posséder* [-é] *v.* to possess, to own; to have; to hold; to be master of [science], to dominate (someone). ‖ *possesseur* [pòsèsœr] *m.* possessor, owner. ‖ *possessif* [-sìf] *adj.°* possessive. ‖ *possession* [-yon] *f.* possession, ownership; property, belonging; perfect knowledge.

possibilité [pòsìbìlìté] *f.* possibility. ‖ *possible* [pòsìbl] *adj.* possible; *faire tout son possible,* to do one's best, to do all one can.

postal [pòstàl] *adj.°* postal.

poste [pòst] *f.* post-office; mail; post [relais]; *poste restante,* general delivery, *Br.* to be called for; *mettre à la poste,* to mail, to post.

poste [pòst] *m.* post, station; guard-house; guards (mil.); employment, position, post, job; entry, item, heading (comm.); signal-box (railw.); berth, quarters (naut.); *poste de T.S.F.,* *Br.* wireless, *Am.* radio set; *poste de secours,* medical aid station, first-aid station; *poste de télévision,* television set; *poste d'essence,* petrol-pump, *Am.* filling station; *poste d'incendie,* fire-house, fire-station.

poster [pòsté] *v.* to post, to mail.

postérieur [pòstéryœr] *adj.* posterior, subsequent, later; behind, back; *m.* behind, backside, rear.

postérité [pòstérìté] *f.* posterity.

posthume [pòstüm] *adj.* posthumous.

postiche [pòstìsh] *adj.* superadded; bogus, mock, dummy, false, sham; *m.* postiche; hair-pad, *Am.* rat.

postier [pòstyé] *m.* post-office employee, postal clerk.

postulant [pòstülan] *m.* applicant; candidate; postulant. ‖ *postulat* [-à] *m.* postulate. ‖ *postuler* [-é] *v.* to apply for, to solicit.

posture [pòstür] *f.* posture.

pot [pò] *m.* pot; jar, jug, can; *pot pourri,* hodge-podge; *pot aux roses,* secret plot; *pot-au-feu,* soup-pot; (fig.) stay-at-home; *pot-de-vin,* tip; bribe, graft, hush-money, rake-off (pop.); *pot-pourri,* medley.

potable [pòtàbl] *adj.* potable, drink-able; acceptable (fam.).

potache [pòtàsh] *m.* schoolboy.

potage [pòtàj] *m.* soup; pottage. ‖ *potager* [-é] *m.* kitchen garden; *adj.* vegetable.

potasse [pòtàs] *f.* potash. || *potassium* [-yòm] *m.* potassium.

pote [pòt] *m.* (pop.) chum, pal, *Am.* buddy.

poteau [pòtô] *m.** post, stake; pole; *poteau indicateur*, signpost.

potelé [pòtlé] *adj.* plump, chubby, pudgy; dimpled.

potence [pòtaⁿs] *f.* gallows, gibbet.

potentiel [pòtaⁿsyèl] *adj.** potential; *m.* potentiality.

poterie [pòtrî] *f.* pottery; earthenware; *poterie de grès*, stoneware.

potiche [pòtìsh] *f.* porcelain vase.

potier [pòtyé] *m.* potter; pewterer.

potin [pòtîⁿ] *m.* (fam.) row, din; scandal, piece of gossip. || *potiner* [pòtìné] *v.* to gossip.

potion [pòsyoⁿ] *f.* potion, draft.

potiron [pòtìroⁿ] *m.* pumpkin.

pou [pû] *m.** louse (*pl.* lice).

poubelle [pûbèl] *f.* metal garbage-can; dust-bin.

pouce [pûs] *m.* thumb; big toe; inch; ⓒ hitch-hiking; *faire du pouce*, ⓒ to hitch-hike.

poudre [pûdr] *f.* powder; dust; gun-powder; *café en poudre*, soluble coffee, powdered coffee; *sucre en poudre*, granulated sugar; *poudre de riz*, rice powder, face powder. || *poudrer* [-é] *v.* to powder. || *poudrerie* [-erî] *f.* gunpowder factory; ⓒ blizzard, drifting snow. || *poudreux* [-é] *adj.** dusty, powdery; (*neige*) *poudreuse*, powdered snow. || *poudrier* [-lyé] *m.* woman's powder box, compact. || *poudrière* [-lyèr] *f.* powder-magazine.

pouffer [pûfé] *v.* to burst out laughing.

pouilleux [pûyé] *adj.** lice-infested, lousy.

poulailler [pûlàyé] *m.* hen-house, chicken-roost; poultry-cart; gallery, cheap seats, *Br.* gods, *Am.* peanut gallery (theat.).

poulain [pûlîⁿ] *m.* colt, foal; pony-skin [fourrure]; trainee; promising youngster.

poularde [pûlàrd] *f.* fat pullet. || *poule* [pûl] *f.* hen; fowl; pool [jeu]; mistress; tart [femme]; *chair de poule*, gooseflesh; *poule mouillée*, milksop, timid soul. || *poulet* [-è] *m.* chicken; love-letter.

pouliche [pûlìsh] *f.* filly.

poulie [pûlî] *f.* pulley.

poulpe [pûlp] *m.* octopus, devil-fish.

pouls [pû] *m.* pulse.

poumon [pûmoⁿ] *m.* lung.

poupe [pûp] *f.* stern, poop (naut.).

poupée [pûpé] *f.* doll; puppet; bandaged finger. || *poupin* [-pîⁿ] *adj.* chubby. || *poupon* [-oⁿ] *m.* baby. || *pouponner* [-pòné] *v.* to mother; to nurse. || *pouponnière* [-ònyèr] *f.* public nursery, creche, *Am.* day nursery.

pour [pûr] *prep.* for; on account of; for the sake of; as for; in order to; *pour ainsi dire*, as it were, so to speak; *pour que*, so that, in order that.

pourboire [pûrbwàr] *m.* tip, gratuity.

pourceau [pûrsô] *m.** pig, hog, swine.

pour-cent [pûrsaⁿ] *m.* percent. || *pourcentage* [-tàj] *m.* percentage.

pourchasser [pûrshàsé] *v.* to pursue; to chase; to hound.

pourfendre [pûrfaⁿdr] *v.* to cleave asunder; to lunge at.

pourlécher [pûrléshé] *v.* to lick all over; *se pourlécher les babines*, to lick one's lips.

pourparlers [pûrpàrlé] *m. pl.* parley, conference, negotiations.

pourpoint [pûrpwîⁿ] *m.* doublet.

pourpre [pûrpr] *m.* purple colo(u)r; crimson; *adj.* purple; crimson.

pourquoi [pûrkwà] *adv.* why.

pourrir [pûrîr] *v.* to rot, to spoil; to corrupt; to decay, to putrefy. || *pourriture* [-lür] *f.* rot, rottenness, putrefaction; corruption.

poursuite [pûrsüît] *f.* pursuit; prosecution; lawsuit, legal action. || *poursuivant* [-üìvaⁿ] *m.* candidate, applicant; plaintiff, prosecutor. || *poursuivre* [pûrsüìvr] *v.** to pursue; to seek; to annoy, to beset; to proceed with; to go through with; to prosecute; to carry on [procès]; to continue.

pourtant [pûrtaⁿ] *adv.* yet, still, however, nevertheless.

pourtour [pûrtûr] *m.* circumference, periphery.

pourvoi [pûrvwà] *m.* appeal (jur.); petition. || *pourvoir* [-wàr] *v.** to attend to; to see to; to furnish, to supply; to provide for, to make provision for; *se pourvoir*, to provide oneself; to petition; *se pourvoir en cassation*, to appeal for a reversal of judgment; || *pourvu* [-ü] *adj.* provided; *pourvu que*, provided (that), so long as.

pousse [pûs] *f.* shoot, sprout. || *poussée* [-é] *f.* push, shove, pressure. || *pousser* [-é] *v.* to push, to shove; to impel, to incite; to urge on; to thrust; to utter [cri]; to heave [soupir]; to grow, to sprout.

poussette [pûsèt] *f.* go-cart; push-chair, *Am.* stroller.

poussier [pûsyé] *m.* coal-dust. || *poussière* [-yèr] *f.* dust; powder; pollen; spray [eau]; remains [des

morts]. ‖ **poussiéreux** [-yérë] *adj.* [*]
dusty; dust-colo(u)red.

poussif [pûsîf] *adj.* [*] broken-winded,
short-winded, pursy, wheezy.

poussin [pûsîⁿ] *m.* chick, chicken.

poutre [pûtr] *f.* beam; girder; truss.
‖ **poutrelle** [-èl] *f.* small beam.

pouvoir [pûvwàr] *m.* power; might;
authority; command, government; *v.*[*]
to be able; to have power; to be
possible; *je peux,* I can; *il se peut,* it
is possible, it may be.

prairie [prèrî] *f.* meadow, prairie.

praline [pràlîn] *f.* praline.

praticable [pràtîkàbl] *adj.* practicable, feasible; passable [chemin]; *m.*
practicable, movable stage prop. ‖
praticant [-îkaⁿ] *adj.* church-going;
m. church-goer. ‖ **praticien** [-îsyîⁿ] *m.*
practitioner. ‖ **pratique** [-îk] *f.* practice; method, usage, habit; customers,
clientele, clients; *adj.* practical, busi-
ness-like; matter-of-fact; convenient;
expedient, advantageous, profitable. ‖
pratiquer [-îké] *v* to practise; to
exercise [profession]; to frequent, to
associate with; to open; to contrive,
to build; to cut [chemin]; to pierce
[trou]; to be a church-goer (eccles.).

pré [pré] *m.* meadow.

préalable [préàlàbl] *adj.* previous;
preliminary; prior; anterior; *m.* preliminary.

préambule [préaⁿbül] *m.* preamble.

préau [préó] *m.*[*] covered playground.

préavis [préàvì] *m.* forewarning;
advance notice.

précaire [prékèr] *adj.* precarious;
risky, insecure; delicate [santé].

précaution [prékôsyoⁿ] *f.* precaution;
caution, circumspection, care, pru-
dence. ‖ **précautionner** [-yòné] *v.* to
caution, to warn; to admonish; *se
précautionner,* to be cautious, to take
precautions. ‖ **précautionneux** [-në]
adj.[*] cautious, wary, prudent.

précédent [présédaⁿ] *adj.* preceding,
previous, prior, precedent; former;
m. precedent. ‖ **précéder** [-é] *v.* to
precede, to antecede; to antedate; to
take precedence (over).

précepte [présèpt] *m.* precept, rule;
principle, maxim; law, injunction. ‖
précepteur, -trice [-œr, -trìs] *m.,* *f.*
tutor, teacher. ‖ **préceptorat** [-tòrà]
m. tutorship.

prêche [prèsh] *m.* sermon. ‖ **prêcher**
[-é] *v.* to preach; to sermonize; to
exhort; to advocate.

précieux [présyë] *adj.*[*] precious,
costly; valuable, affected, finical, over-
nice. ‖ **préciosité** [-yòzìté] *f.* affectation, preciosity.

précipice [présîpîs] *m.* precipice,
cliff; abyss, chasm, void, gulf.

précipitation [présîpîtàsyoⁿ] *f.* pre-
cipitancy, hurry, haste; precipitation
(chem.). ‖ **précipiter** [-é] *v.* to precipitate, to hurl, to dash down; to
hustle, to hurry, to hasten, to accelerate; *se précipiter,* to precipitate oneself, to hurl oneself; to rush forward,
to dash, to spring forth, to dart; to
hurry, to hasten; to swoop down.

précis [présî] *m.* summary, résumé,
précis; *adj.* precise, accurate, exact;
fixed, formal; terse; concise. ‖ **préciser** [-zé] *v.* to state precisely, to
define, to specify, to stipulate. ‖ **précision** [-zyoⁿ] *f.* precision, preciseness;
accuracy, correctness; definiteness,
conciseness.

précité [présîté] *adj.* above-mentioned, afore-said.

précoce [prékòs] *adj.* precocious,
early, premature, forward. ‖ **précocité**
[-îté] *f.* precocity.

préconçu [prékoⁿsü] *adj.* precon-
ceived, foregone [opinion].

préconiser [prékonizé] *v.* to advocate, to recommend, to extol.

précurseur [prékürsœr] *m.* forerunner, precursor; harbinger; *adj.*
premonitory.

prédécesseur [prédésèsœr] *m.* predecessor.

prédestination [prédèstìnàsyoⁿ] *f.*
predestination. ‖ **prédestiner** [prédès-
tìné] *v.* to predestinate; to foredoom.

prédicateur [prédîkàtœr] *m.* preach-
er ‖ **prédication** [-àsyoⁿ] *f.* preaching.

prédiction [prédîksyoⁿ] *f.* prediction,
forecast, prophecy, augury.

prédilection [prédìlèksyoⁿ] *f.* predilection; bias; taste; preference; *de
prédilection,* favo(u)rite.

prédire [prédîr] *v.*[*] to predict, to
foretell.

prédisposer [prédîspòzé] *v.* to predispose.

prédominance [prédòmìnaⁿs] *f.* predominance, ascendancy, prevalence. ‖
prédominer [-é] *v.* to predominate, to
prevail.

prééminent [préémìnaⁿ] *adj.* pre-
eminent; prominent; superior.

préexister [préégzìsté] *v.* to pre-
exist.

préfabriquer [préfàbrìké] *v.* to prefabricate.

préface [préfàs] *f.* preface, foreword,
introduction. ‖ **préfacer** [-sé] *v.* to
preface.

préfecture [préfèktür] *f.* prefecture;
préfecture de police, police headquarters; police department.

préférable [préféràbl] *adj.* preferable. ‖ *préféré* [-é] *adj.* preferred, favo(u)rite. ‖ *préférence* [-aⁿs] *f.* preference. ‖ *préférer* [-é] *v.* to prefer. ‖ *préférentiel* [-aⁿsjèl] *adj.* preferential.

préfet [préfè] *m.* prefect; administrator of a department (France); *préfet de police*, chief commissioner of police; *préfet maritime*, port-admiral.

préjudice [préjüdîs] *m.* injury, hurt, detriment, damage, prejudice. ‖ *préjudiciable* [-yàbl] *adj.* prejudicial, detrimental, injurious, hurtful, damaging. ‖ *préjudiciel* [-yèl] *adj.** interlocutory.

préjugé [préjüjé] *m.* prejudice, bias, prejudgment; presumption, assumption. ‖ *préjuger* [-é] *v.* to prejudge.

prélasser (se) [s•prélàsé] *v.* to lounge, to relax.

prélat [prélà] *m.* prelate.

prélèvement [prélèvmaⁿ] *m.* previous deduction; advance withholding; appropriation; drawing; sample (med.). ‖ *prélever* [prélvé] *v.* to deduct beforehand, to withhold beforehand; to set aside, to levy; to take (med.).

préliminaire [prélîmìnèr] *m.*, *adj.* preliminary.

prélude [prélüd] *m.* prelude. ‖ *préluder* [-é] *v.* to prelude.

prématuré [prémàtüré] *adj.* premature; untimely.

préméditation [préméditàsyoⁿ] *f.* premeditation. ‖ *préméditer* [-é] *v.* to premeditate.

prémices [prémîs] *f. pl.* first-fruits; firstlings; beginnings (fig.).

premier [pr•myé] *adj.** first, foremost, principal, chief; best; primeval, ancient; former [de deux]; prime [nombre]; *m.* chief, head, leader; *Br.* first floor, *Am.* second floor; leading man (theat.); *Premier ministre*, Prime Minister, Premier; *matières premières*, raw materials. ‖ *première* [-yèr] *f.* first performance, opening night (theat.); forewoman. ‖ *premièrement* [-yèrmaⁿ] *adv.* first, firstly.

prémisse [prémîs] *f.* premise.

prémonition [prémònìsyoⁿ] *f.* premonition, foreboding. ‖ *prémunir* [-ünîr] *v.* to forewarn, to caution; se *prémunir*, to guard; to protect oneself; to take precautions.

prenable [pr•nàbl] *adj.* seizable; corruptible. ‖ *prenant* [-aⁿ] *adj.* prehensile; engaging, captivating; *partie prenante*, payee. ‖ *prendre* [praⁿdr] *v.** to take; to get; to seize; to buy [billet]; to grasp; to capture; to eat, to have [repas]; to coagulate, to set, to congeal [liquide]; to catch [froid, feu]; to make [décision]; *prendre le*

large, to stand out to sea (naut.); *à tout prendre*, on the whole; *se prendre*, to catch, to be caught; to cling, to grasp; *s'en prendre à*, to blame, to attack (someone); *s'y prendre*, to go about it. ‖ *preneur* [pr•nœr] *m.* taker; captor; lessee.

prénom [prénoⁿ] *m.* name, first name, given name, Christian name. ‖ *se prénommer* [s•prénómé] *v.* to be called.

préoccupation [préòküpàsyoⁿ] *f.* preoccupation; anxiety, worry. ‖ *préoccuper* [-é] *v.* to preoccupy; to disturb, to worry, to trouble; to prejudice; *se préoccuper*, to busy oneself (de, with); to attend (de, to); to bother; to care.

préparateur, -trice [prépàràtœr, -trìs] *m., f.* preparer, maker, assistant; demonstrator; coach, tutor; (fam.) crammer [école]. ‖ *préparatifs* [-àtîf] *m. pl.* preparation. ‖ *préparation* [-àsyoⁿ] *f.* preparation, preparing. ‖ *préparatoire* [-àtwàr] *adj.* preparatory; preliminary. ‖ *préparer* [-é] *v.* to prepare, to make ready; to arrange; *se préparer*, to prepare oneself; to be in the wind [événement]; to loom [malheur]; to brew [orage].

prépondérant [prépoⁿdéraⁿ] *adj.* preponderant; deciding [voix].

préposé [prépòzé] *m.* official in charge, superintendent, overseer; employee; keeper. ‖ *préposer* [-é] *v.* to appoint, to designate, to put in charge. ‖ *préposition* [prépòzìsyoⁿ] *f.* preposition.

prérogative [prérògàtîv] *f.* prerogative, privilege.

près [prè] *adv.* near; close (de, to); *à peu près*, almost, pretty near.

présage [prézàj] *m.* presage, portent, foreboding; omen. ‖ *présager* [-é] *v.* to presage, to bode, to portend; to predict, to augur.

presbyte [prèzbìt] *adj.* presbyopic, long-sighted, *Am.* far-sighted.

presbytère [prèzbìtèr] *m.* parsonage, vicarage; rectory; manse.

prescience [prèsyaⁿs] *f.* prescience, foreknowledge, foresight.

prescription [prèskrìpsyoⁿ] *f.* prescription; specification, limitation (jur.). ‖ *prescrire* [-îr] *v.** to prescribe; to enjoin; to specify, to stipulate.

présence [prézaⁿs] *f.* presence; attendance; bearing; appearance. ‖ *présent* [-aⁿ] *m.* present; present tense; gift; *adj.* present; attentive to. ‖ *présentable* [prézaⁿtàbl] *adj.* presentable. ‖ *présentateur* [-tàtœr] *m.* presenter. ‖ *présentation* [-àsyoⁿ] *f.* presentation; exhibition; introduction. ‖ *présenter* [-é] *v.* to present, to offer; to show, to exhibit; to introduce; se pré-senter, to appear; to occur; to arise [problème], to introduce oneself [personne]; to sit [à un examen].

préservatif [prézèrvàtìf] *m., adj.*[e] preservative contraceptive (med.). ‖ **préservation** [-àsyoⁿ] *f.* preservation, protection. ‖ **préserver** [-é] *v.* to preserve; to protect.

présidence [prézìdàⁿs] *f.* presidency, chairmanship. ‖ **président** [-àⁿ] *m.* president, chairman; presiding judge; speaker (of the *Br.* House of Commons, *Am.* House of Representatives). ‖ **présidentiel** [-àⁿsyèl] *adj.*[e] presidential. ‖ **présider** [-é] *v.* to preside over.

présomptif [prézoⁿptìf] *adj.*[e] presumptive, presumed; *héritier présomptif*, heir-apparent. ‖ **présomption** [-syoⁿ] *f.* presumption, self-conceit. ‖ **présomptueux** [-tüé] *adj.*[e] presumptuous, presuming; self-conceited.

presque [prèsk] *adv.* almost, nearly, all but; *presqu'île*, peninsula.

pressant [prèsàⁿ] *adj.* pressing, urgent; earnest; importunate. ‖ **presse** [près] *f.* press, printing press; crowd; haste, hurry, pressure; impressment (mil.); *presse-papiers*, paper-weight; *presse-purée*, potato-masher. ‖ **pressé** [-é] *adj.* pressed; crowded; close; serried; *in a hurry*, pressing; eager.

pressentiment [prèsàⁿtìmàⁿ] *m.* presentiment; misgiving, apprehension, *Am.* hunch. ‖ **pressentir** [-îr] *v.* to have a presentiment; to sound (someone) out.

presser [prèsé] *v.* to press, to squeeze; to crowd; to hasten, to hurry; to urge, to entreat; to pull [détente]; *se presser*, to press; to crowd; to hurry. ‖ **pression** [-yoⁿ] *f.* pressure; tension; stress, strain; snap [bouton]; *bière à la pression*, draught beer, *Am.* steam beer. ‖ **pressoir** [-wàr] *m.* press; squeezer; push button. ‖ **pressurer** [-üré] *v.* to press; to squeeze; to grind down; to oppress; to bleed white.

prestance [prèstàⁿs] *f.* commanding appearance, good presence.

prestation [prèstàsyoⁿ] *f.* tax-money; required service; *prestation de serment*, taking of an oath.

preste [prèst] *adj.* nimble, agile, deft; quick, brisk; quick-witted.

prestidigitateur [prèstìdìjìtàtœr] *m.* conjuror, juggler, sleight of hand artist. ‖ **prestidigitation** [-àsyoⁿ] *f.* conjuring, juggling, legerdemain, sleight-of-hand, prestidigitation.

prestige [prèstìj] *m.* prestige. ‖ **prestigieux** [-jyœ] *adj.*[e] dazzling, marvellous.

présumer [prézümé] *v.* to presume, to suppose, to assume.

présure [prézür] *f.* rennet.

prêt [prè] *adj* ready, prepared; *prêt-à-porter*, ready-to-wear, ready-made.

prêt [prè] *m.* loan, lending; *prêt-bail*, lend-lease.

prétendant [prétàⁿdàⁿ] *m.* candidate; pretender [au trône]; suitor [amoureux]. ‖ **prétendre** [prétàⁿdr] *v.* to pretend, to claim, to assert, to affirm, to maintain, to intend, to mean; to aspire ‖ **prétendu** [-ü] *adj.* alleged, pretended, supposed, so-called, would-be.

prétentieux [prétàⁿsyè] *adj.*[e] pretentious, assuming, conceited, vain; affected; showy. ‖ **prétention** [-yoⁿ] *f.* pretention, claim, allegation; pretense; demand, conceit.

prêter [prèté] *v* to lend; to ascribe, to attribute; to impart; to bestow; to stretch [tissu], *prêter serment*, to take oath, to swear; *se prêter*, to lend oneself; to yield, to favo(u)r. ‖ **prêteur** [-œr] *m* lender; bailor; *prêteur sur gages*, pawnbroker.

prétexte [prétèkst] *m.* pretext, pretense, excuse, blind. ‖ **prétexter** [-é] *v.* to pretend, to allege.

prêtre [prètr] *m.* priest; minister.

preuve [prœv] *f.* proof; evidence, testimony; test; *faire preuve de*, to show; to display.

prévaloir [prévàlwàr] *v.*[e] to prevail; *se prévaloir*, to take advantage, to presume upon, to avail oneself; to pride oneself (de, on).

prévaricateur, -trice [prévàrìkàtœr, -trìs] *adj.* dishonest; *m., f.* dishonest official. ‖ **prévarication** [-àsyoⁿ] *f.* abuse of trust, breach, default.

prévenance [prévnàⁿs] *f.* considerateness, obligingness; attention. ‖ **prévenant** [prévnàⁿ] *adj.* obliging, kind; attentive, considerate; prepossessing, engaging. ‖ **prévenir** [-îr] *v.* to precede; to forestall; to warn, to caution; to prejudice; to prevent; to anticipate [besoins].

préventif [prévàⁿtìf] *adj.*[e] preventive. ‖ **prévention** [-àⁿsyoⁿ] *f.* prejudice, bias; accusation; confinement pending trial.

prévenu [prévnü] *adj.* prejudiced, biased; warned; forestalled; accused, indicted; *m.* prisoner, accused person.

prévision [prévìzyoⁿ] *f.* prevision, forecast; anticipation; estimate. ‖ **prévoir** [-wàr] *v.*[e] to foresee, to forecast, to gauge; to anticipate. ‖ **prévoyance** [-wàyàⁿs] *f.* foresight; caution. ‖ **prévoyant** [-wàyàⁿ] *adj.* provident; careful, prudent, cautious. ‖

prévu [-ü] *adj.* foreseen, anticipated, provided, allowed.

prie-Dieu [prìdyë] *m.* kneeling-chair, prayer-stool.

prier [prié] *v.* to pray; to entreat, to beseech, to request, to beg; to invite; *je vous en prie,* I beg of you; you are welcome; don't mention it. ‖ *prière* [prìyèr] *f.* prayer; request, entreaty.

primaire [prìmèr] *adj.* primary, elementary.

primauté [prìmòté] *f.* primacy.

prime [prìm] *f.* premium; prize, bonus; bounty, subsidy; encouragement; *faire prime,* to be highly appreciated.

prime [prìm] *adj.* first; prime (math.); *de prime abord,* at first. ‖ *primer* [-é] *v.* to surpass, to excel; to award prizes to. ‖ *primesautier* [-sòtyé] *adj.* impulsive, spontaneous. ‖ *primeur* [-œr] *f.* early product; newness; freshness.

primevère [prìm°vèr] *f.* primrose.

primitif [prìmìtìf] *adj.* first, early, primitive, aboriginal; pristine; *m.* primitive.

primo [prìmò] *adv.* firstly, in the first place.

primordial [prìmòrdyàl] *adj.* primordial, primeval.

prince [prì°s] *m.* prince. ‖ *princesse* [-ès] *f.* princess. ‖ *princier* [-yé] *adj.* princely.

principal [prì°sìpàl] *adj.* principal, chief, main; staple [nourriture]; *m.* principal; main thing; headmaster. ‖ *principauté* [-pòté] *f.* principality, princedom. ‖ *principe* [prì°sìp] *m.* principle; rudiment, element; source, basis, motive.

printanier [prì°tànyé] *adj.* vernal, spring-like. ‖ *printemps* [prì°ta°] *m.* spring, springtime.

prioritaire [prìòrìtèr] *adj.* priority, priority-holder; *m.* priority-holder. ‖ *priorité* [prìòrìté] *f.* priority; precedence; right of way [route].

pris [prì] *p. p.* of *prendre; adj.* taken, caught, captured, seized; congealed, set [liquide]. ‖ *prise* [prìz] *f.* capture, taking, seizure; prize; hold, handle; quarrel; plug (electr.); dose (med.); pinch [tabac]; coupling [auto]; *pl.* fighting, close quarters; *donner prise,* to give a hold; *lâcher prise,* to let go one's hold; *être aux prises avec,* to grapple with; *prise d'armes,* parade under arms; *prise de bec,* squabble, wrangle; *prise de courant,* wall socket, outlet plug (electr.); *prise d'eau,* hydrant; *prise de vues,* shooting of the film, taking of pictures [cinéma].

priser [prìzé] *v.* to estimate; to value; to esteem.

priser [prìzé] *v.* to inhale snuff; to snuff up.

priseur [prìzœr] *m.* appraiser.

prisme [prìsm] *m.* prism.

prison [prìzo°] *f.* prison, penitentiary; *Br.* gaol, *Am.* jail. ‖ *prisonnier* [-ònyé] *m.* prisoner, captive; *adj.* emprisoned; captive.

privation [prìvàsyo°] *f.* privation, deprivation, loss; want, need. ‖ *privauté* [-òté] *f.* familiarity, liberty. ‖ *priver* [-é] *v.* to deprive; to bereave; *se priver,* to deprive oneself; to do without; to stint oneself; to abstain (*de,* from).

privilège [prìvìlèj] *m.* privilege; license; prerogative. ‖ *privilégier* [-éjyé] *v.* to privilege, to license.

prix [prì] *m.* price, cost; rate, return; prize, reward, stakes; *prix de revient, prix de fabrique,* cost price; *prix de gros,* wholesale price; *prix courant,* market price; *prix homologué,* established price; *prix unique,* one-price.

probabilité [pròbàbìlìté] *f.* probability, likelihood. ‖ *probable* [-àbl] *adj.* probable, likely.

probant [pròba°] *adj.* convincing; cogent; probative (jur.).

probe [pròb] *adj.* honest, upright, straightforward. ‖ *probité* [-ìté] *f.* integrity, probity.

problématique [pròblémàtìk] *adj.* problematic(al); questionable. ‖ *problème* [-èm] *m.* problem, question; difficulty.

procédé [pròsédé] *m.* proceeding; behavio(u)r, conduct; process. ‖ *procéder* [-é] *v.* to come from, to originate in; to institute proceedings (jur.). ‖ *procédure* [-ür] *f.* practice, procedure; proceedings.

procès [pròsè] *m.* (law)suit, action; trial; case; *intenter un procès,* to institute proceedings.

procession [pròsèsyo°] *f.* procession; parade.

processus [pròsèsüs] *m.* process, method; progress, march; evolution.

procès-verbal [pròsèvèrbàl] *m.* official report; proceedings.

prochain [pròshì°] *adj.* next; nearest; proximate; immediate; *m.* neighbo(u)r; fellow being. ‖ *prochainement* [-ènma°] *adv.* shortly, soon. ‖ *proche* [pròsh] *adj.* near; *m. pl.* near relations, relatives, next of kin.

proclamation [pròklàmàsyo°] *f.* proclamation, announcement. ‖ *proclamer* [-é] *v.* to proclaim.

procréateur, -trice [pròkréàtœr, -trìs] *adj.* procreative; *m., f.* procreator, parent. ‖ *procréer* [pròkréé] *v.* to procreate.

procuration [pròkürásyoⁿ] f. pro-curation, power of attorney, proxy. || **procurer** [-é] v. to procure, to get, to obtain. || **procureur** [-œr] m. procu-rator; proxy.

prodigalité [pròdìgàlìté] f. prodigal-ity, extravagance, lavishness.

prodige [pròdìj] m. prodigy, mar-vel. || **prodigieux** [-yè] adj.* prodigious, stupendous.

prodigue [pròdìg] adj. prodigal, lav-ish; wasteful, thriftless; m. prodigal, spendthrift, squanderer; l'Enfant pro-digue, the Prodigal Son. || **prodiguer** [-ìgé] v. to be prodigal of, to lavish; to waste, to squander.

producteur, -trice [pròdüktœr, -trìs] m., f. grower; producer; adj. product-ive, producing. || **productif** [-tìf] adj.* productive, fruitful, bearing, yielding. || **production** [-syoⁿ] f. production; output. || **produire** [pròdùïr] v.* to produce; to yield; to show; se pro-duire, to occur, to happen. || **produit** [-üì] m. produce, production; prep-aration; proceeds, profit; product (math.); produit pharmaceutique, pa-tent medicine, Br. chemist's prepara-tion, Am. drug; produits de beauté, cosmetics; produits chimiques, chem-icals.

proéminence [pròémìnaⁿs] f. protu-berance, projection; prominence, prom-inency (fig.). || **proéminent** [pròémì-naⁿ] adj. prominent; protuberant; projecting; salient.

profanateur, -trice [pròfànàtœr, -trìs] m., f. profaner, desecrator. || **profanation** [-àsyoⁿ] f. profanation, desecration, sacrilege. || **profane** [prò-fàn] adj. profane; secular, temporal; m., f. outsider; layman. || **profaner** [-é] v. to profane, to desecrate; to defile.

proférer [pròféré] v. to utter.

professer [pròfèsé] v. to profess; to teach; to practise. || **professeur** [-œr] m. professor, teacher. || **profession** [-yoⁿ] f. profession; declaration; occu-pation, trade, calling, business. || **pro-fessionnel** [-yònèl] adj.* professional. || **professoral** [-òràl] adj.* professorial, || **professorat** [-òrà] m. professorship; teaching profession; teacher's calling.

profil [pròfìl] m. profile, side-face; outline, silhouette. || **profiler** [-é] v. to shape, to contour; to outline, to streamline.

profit [pròfì] m. profit, gain; benefit; expediency; mettre à profit, to turn to account. || **profitable** [-tàbl] adj. profitable, expedient, advantageous. || **profiter** [-té] v. to profit (de, by); to benefit; to avail oneself, to take ad-vantage (de, of). || **profiteur** [-tœr] m. profiteer.

profond [pròfoⁿ] adj. profound; deep; low; vast; heavy [soupir]; sound [sommeil]; dark [nuit]. || **pro-fondeur** [-dœr] f. depth; profundity; penetration [esprit].

profusion [pròfüzyoⁿ] f. profusion, abundance, plenty.

progéniture [pròjénìtür] f. off-spring, progeny.

prognathe [pròvgnàt] adj. underhung [mâchoire]; prognathous [personne].

programme [pròvgràm] m. program; bill, list; platform [politique]; curric-ulum, syllabus [études].

progrès [pròvgrè] m. progress; im-provement, headway, advancement. || **progresser** [-sé] v. to progress. || **pro-gressif** [-sìf] adj.* progressive. || **pro-gression** [-syoⁿ] f. progression, advance-ment. || **progressiste** [-sìst] adj. pro-gressive; s. progressist.

prohiber [pròìbé] v. to prohibit, to forbid. || **prohibitif** [-ìtìf] adj. prohibi-tive. || **prohibition** [-ìsyoⁿ] f. prohi-bition, forbidding; Am. outlawing of alcoholic beverages.

proie [prwà] f. prey, prize, booty, spoil; quarry [chasse].

projecteur [pròjèktœr] m. search-light, floodlight. || **projectile** [-tìl] m. projectile, missile. || **projection** [-syoⁿ] f. projection; éclairage par projection, floodlighting.

projet [pròjè] m. project, plan, scheme, design; projet de loi, bill. || **projeter** [pròjté] v. to project, to throw out; to plan, to intend.

prolétaire [pròlétér] m., f., adj. pro-letarian. || **prolétariat** [-àryà] m. pro-letariat; proletarianism. || **prolétarien** [-ryìⁿ] adj.* proletarian.

prolifération [pròlìféràsyoⁿ] f. proli-feration. || **proliférer** [-féré] v. to pro-liferate.

prolixe [pròlìks] adj. prolix, diffuse, verbose, long-winded.

prolongation [pròloⁿgàsyoⁿ] f. pro-longation, lengthening, protraction. || **prolonge** [pròloⁿj] f. lashing-rope. || **prolongement** [-maⁿ] m. extension, prolonging, continuation. || **prolonger** [-é] v. to prolong, to protract, to lengthen, to extend.

promenade [pròmnàd] f. walk, walk-ing; stroll; promenade; excursion; drive, ride [en voiture]; row, sail, cruise [en bateau]; faire une prome-nade, to take a walk. || **promener** [-é] v. to take out walking; to turn [regard]; se promener, to walk, to go for a walk (stroll, ride, drive, row, sail). || **promeneur** [-œr] f. walker, stroller; rider. || **promenoir** [-wàr] m. promenade, covered walk; strolling gallery.

promesse [pròmẽs] *f.* promise, pledge, assurance; promissory note. ‖ **prometteur, -euse** [pròmẽtœr, -ēz] *adj.* attractive, promising. ‖ *promettre* [-ètr] *v.°* to promise, to pledge; to be promising; *se promettre,* to resolve; to hope; to promise oneself. ‖ *promis* [-ì] *adj.* promised; intended, pledged, *m.* fiancé, betrothed.

promiscuité [pròmìsküìté] *f.* promiscuity, promiscuousness.

promontoire [pròmõtwàr] *m.* promontory, foreland, headland, cape.

promoteur, -trice [pròmòtœr, -trìs] *m., f.* promoter. ‖ *promotion* [-òsyoⁿ] *f.* promotion, advancement, preferment. ‖ *promouvoir* [-mûvwàr] *v.°* to promote.

prompt [proⁿ] *adj.* prompt, quick, speedy, swift; hasty. ‖ *promptitude* [-tìtüd] *f.* promptitude, promptness, quickness.

promu [pròmü] *adj.* promoted.

promulguer [pròmülgé] *v.* to promulgate; to publish, to issue.

prône [prõn] *m.* prone. ‖ *prôner* [-é] *v.* to preach, to sermonize; to extol, to advocate.

pronom [prònoⁿ] *m.* pronoun.

prononcer [prònoⁿsé] *v.* to pronounce; to declare; to pass, to return, to bring in [jugement]. ‖ *prononciation* [-yàsyoⁿ] *f.* pronunciation.

pronostic [prònòstìk] *m.* prognostic, forecast; pre-indication; prognosis (med.).

propagande [pròpàgaⁿd] *f.* propaganda; advertising, *Am.* ballyhoo.

propagation [pròpàgàsyoⁿ] *f.* propagation. ‖ *propager* [-àjé] *v.* to propagate, to spread.

propension [pròpaⁿsyoⁿ] *f.* propensity; proneness.

prophète [pròfèt] *m.* prophet, seer, prophesier. ‖ *prophétie* [-ésî] *f.* prophecy. ‖ *prophétiser* [-étìzé] *v.* to prophesy, to foretell.

propice [pròpìs] *adj.* propitious.

proportion [pròpòrsyoⁿ] *f.* proportion, ratio; rate; size, dimension. ‖ *proportionner* [-yòné] *v.* to proportion, to adjust.

propos [pròpô] *m.* discourse, talk, words; remark, utterance; purpose; *à propos,* by the way; relevant, pertinent. ‖ *proposer* [-zé] *v.* to propose; to offer; *se proposer,* to plan, to intend. ‖ *proposition* [-zìsyoⁿ] *f.* proposition, proposal; motion, suggestion.

propre [pròpr] *adj.* clean, neat, tidy; proper, correct, fitting, appropriate; own; peculiar; right [sens]; *m.* characteristic, attribute; property; proper

sense. ‖ **propreté** [-°té] *f.* cleanliness, neatness, tidiness; honesty, decency.

propriétaire [pròprìétèr] *m.* owner, proprietor landlord. ‖ *propriété* [-é] *f.* property realty, estate; ownership; quality, characteristic; propriety, correctness

propulser [pròpülsé] *v.* to propel. ‖ *propulseur* [pròpülsœr] *m.* propeller; *adj.* propelling propulsive.

prorogation [pròrògàsyoⁿ] *f.* prorogation, prolongation. ‖ *proroger* [-jé] *v.* to extend, to prorogue.

prosaïque [pròzàïk] *adj.* prosaic; flat, dull, matter-of-fact.

proscrire [pròskrîr] *v.°* to prohibit, to proscribe, to outlaw; to banish. ‖ *proscrit* [-krî] *adj.* proscribed, forbidden; *m.* proscript, outlaw.

prose [pròz] *f.* prose.

prospecteur [pròspèktœr] *m.* prospector, miner. ‖ *prospection* [-syoⁿ] *f.* prospection; prospecting; canvassing (comm.).

prospectus [pròspèktüs] *m.* prospectus, handbill, blurb (fam.).

prospère [pròspèr] *adj.* prosperous, thriving. ‖ *prospérer* [-éré] *v.* to flourish, to prosper, to thrive, to succeed. ‖ *prospérité* [-érìté] *f.* prosperity, welfare, prosperousness.

prosterner (se) [s°pròstèrné] *v.* to prostrate oneself, to bow down.

prostituée [pròstìtüé] *f.* prostitute, harlot, whore, strumpet. ‖ *prostituer* [-üé] *v.* to prostitute.

prostration [pròstràsyoⁿ] *f.* prostration. ‖ *prostré* [-tré] *adj.* prostrate.

protagoniste [pròtàgònìst] *s.* protagonist

protecteur, -trice [pròtèktœr, -trìs] *m.* protector; patron; *f.* protectress; patroness; *adj.* protective; patronizing. ‖ *protection* [-syoⁿ] *f.* protection, shelter; cover; defence; support, patronage. ‖ *protectorat* [-tòrà] *m.* protectorate. ‖ *protégé* [pròtéjé] *m.* favo(u)rite, protégé. ‖ *protéger* [-é] *v.* to protect, to shield, to shelter.

protestant [pròtèstaⁿ] *m., adj.* Protestant. ‖ *protestation* [-àsyoⁿ] *f.* protest, protestation. ‖ *protester* [-é] *v.* to protest; to vow; to object; to affirm.

protocole [pròtòkòl] *m.* protocol; etiquette.

prototype [pròtòtìp] *m.* prototype.

protubérance [pròtübéraⁿs] *f.* protuberance.

proue [prû] *f.* prow, stem, bow (naut.); nose (aviat.).

prouesse [prûès] *f.* prowess.

prouver [prûvé] *v.* to prove.

provenance [pròvnaⁿs] *f.* origin, source, provenance; produce.

provenir [pròvnîr] *v.* * to come, to stem, to issue, to proceed, to spring.

proverbe [pròvèrb] *m.* proverb.

providence [pròvìdaⁿs] *f.* providence. || **providentiel** [-yèl] *adj.* * providential; opportune.

province [pròvⁱns] *f.* province. || **provincial** [-yàl] *adj.* * provincial; countrified, country-like; *m.* * provincial, country-person.

proviseur [pròvìzœr] *m.* headmaster [lycée].

provision [pròvìzyoⁿ] *f.* provision, stock, store, hoard, supply; funds, cover, deposit (comm.); retaining fee.

provisoire [pròvìzwàr] *adj.* provisional, temporary.

provocant [pròvòkaⁿ] *adj.* provoking, provocative; exciting; alluring, enticing. || **provocateur, -trice** [-àtœr, -trìs] *m.*, *f.* provoker; aggressor, instigator; *adj.* provoking, instigating, abetting; *agent provocateur*, hired agitator; instigating agent. || **provocation** [-àsyoⁿ] *f.* provocation. || **provoquer** [-é] *v.* to provoke, to incite, to bring on; to instigate; to challenge [duel].

proxénète [pròksénèt] *m.* procurer; *f.* procuress.

proximité [pròksìmìté] *f.* proximity, nearness, vicinity.

pruche [prüsh] *f.* © hemlock fir.

prude [prüd] *adj.* prudish; *f.* prude. || **prudence** [-aⁿs] *f.* prudence, discretion, caution; carefulness. || **prudent** [-aⁿ] *adj.* prudent, discreet, cautious. || **pruderie** [-rî] *f.* prudery, prudishness.

prune [prün] *f.* plum. || **pruneau** [-ô] *m.* * prune; (pop.) bruise; bullet. || **prunelle** [-èl] *f.* sloe; sloe-gin; apple of the eye, pupil [œil]. || **prunier** [-yé] *m.* plum-tree.

prurit [prürì] *m.* itching.

psalmodier [psàlmòdyé] *v.* to psalmodize.

psaume [psôm] *m.* psalm.

pseudonyme [psèdònîm] *m.* pseudonym; fictitious name; pen-name.

psychanalyse [psìkànàlîz] *f.* psychoanalysis. || **psychanalyser** [-ìzé] *v.* to psychoanalyse. || **psychanalyste** [-lìst] *m.* psychoanalyst. || **psychiatre** [psìkìàtr] *m.*, *f.* psychiatrist. || **psychiatrie** [-trî] *f.* psychiatry. || **psychique** [psìshìk] *adj.* psychic. || **psychisme** [-shìsm] *m.* psychism.

psychologie [psìkòlòjî] *f.* psychology. || **psychologique** [-ìk] *adj.* psychological. || **psychologue** [psìkòlòg] *m.*, *f.* psychologist.

puant [püaⁿ] *adj.* stinking, smelly; fetid, rank, foul; conceited. || **puanteur** [-tœr] *f.* stench, stink, reek.

public [püblìk] *adj.* * public; open; *m.* public; audience [assistance]. || **publication** [-ìkàsyoⁿ] *f.* publication; publishing; published work. || **publiciste** [-ìsìst] *m.*, *f.* publicist. || **publicitaire** [-ìsìtèr] *adj.* advertising. || **publicité** [-ìsìté] *f.* publicity; advertising; public relations. || **publier** [-lyé] *v.* to publish, to bring out, to issue.

puce [püs] *f.* flea; *adj.* puce-coloured.

puceron [püsroⁿ] *m.* plant-louse.

pudeur [püdœr] *f.* modesty, decency; bashfulness, shyness, reserve. || **pudibond** [-ìboⁿ] *adj.* prudish. || **pudique** [-ìk] *adj.* bashful; chaste.

puer [püé] *v.* to stink, to smell bad.

puériculture [püérìkültür] *f.* rearing of children; child care.

puéril [püérìl] *adj.* childish.

pugilat [püjìlà] *m.* pugilism; set-to.

puis [püì] *adv.* then, afterwards, next, following.

puisatier [püìzàtyé] *m.* well-digger. || **puiser** [-é] *v.* to draw up; to derive, to borrow, to extract (fig.).

puisque [püìsk] *conj.* since, as; seeing that.

puissamment [püìsàmaⁿ] *adv.* powerfully, potently. || **puissance** [-aⁿs] *f.* power; force; influence; strength; degree (math.); influential person; horse-power [auto]. || **puissant** [-aⁿ] *adj.* powerful, strong, mighty; wealthy; influential; numerous; stout, corpulent; (comm.) leading.

puits [püì] *m.* well, shaft, pit [mine]; cockpit (aviat.).

pulluler [püllülé] *v.* to swarm; to throng; to teem.

pulmonaire [pülmònèr] *adj.* pulmonary.

pulpe [pülp] *f.* pulp; pad.

pulsation [pülsàsyoⁿ] *f.* pulsation, beat, throb.

pulvérisateur [pülvérìzàtœr] *m.* pulveriser; atomizer, spray, vaporizer. || **pulvériser** [-é] *v.* to pulverize; to spray; to smash.

punaise [pünèz] *f.* bug, bedbug; *Br.* drawing-pin, *Am.* thumbtack.

punch [püⁿsh] *m.* punch [boisson, sport].

punir [pünîr] *v.* to punish, to chastise. || **punition** [-ìsyoⁿ] *f.* punishment, chastisement; forfeit [jeux].

pupille [püpîy] *s.* ward, minor.

pupille [püpîy] *f.* pupil of the eye.

pupitre [püpìtr] *m.* desk; lectern, reading-stand.

pur [pür] *adj.* pure; innocent; downright; sheer, stark; *pur sang*, pureblooded, thoroughbred.

purée [püré] *f.* puree; mash.

pureté [pürté] *f.* purity, innocence, pureness; chastity; clearness.

purgatif [pürgàtìf] *m., adj.* * purgative. || *purgatoire* [-wàr] *m.* purgatory. || *purge* [pürj] *f.* purge; cleansing; paying off (hypothèque). || *purger* [-é] *v.* to purge; to cleanse; to pay off; *purger une peine*, to serve one's sentence; *se purger*, to take medicine.

purifier [pürìfyé] *v.* to purify, to cleanse; to refine.

purin [pürìⁿ] *m.* liquid manure.

puritain [pürìtⁿ] *adj., m.* puritan.

pus [pü] *m.* pus, matter.

pusillanime [püzìlànìm] *adj.* fainthearted.

pustule [püstül] *f.* blotch; blister.

putain [pütⁿ] *f.* whore [not in decent use].

putois [pütwà] *m.* polecat, skunk.

putréfier [pütréfyé] *v.* to putrefy, to rot, to decompose. || *putride* [-ìd] *adj.* putrid; tainted; rotten, decayed, decomposed.

pyjama [pìjàmà] *m. Br.* pyjamas, *Am.* pajamas.

Q

quadrillage [kàdrìyàj] *m.* chequerwork. || *quadrillé* [-ìyé] *adj.* chequered; ruled in squares.

quadrupède [kàdrüpèd] *m.* quadruped.

quadruple [kwàdrüpl] *adj.* quadruple; fourfold.

quai [kè] *m.* quay, wharf; embankment, mole; platform [gare].

qualificatif [kàlìfìkàtìf] *adj.* * qualifying; m. epithet, name; qualificative (gramm.). || *qualification* [-ìkàsyoⁿ] *f.* qualification. || *qualifier* [-yé] *v.* to qualify; to style; to name.

qualité [kàlìté] *f.* quality; property; excellence; nature; qualification.

quand [kaⁿ] *conj.* when; whenever.

quant [kaⁿ] *adv.* as; *quant à*, as for.

quantitatif [kaⁿtìtàtìf] *adj.* * quantitative. || *quantité* [-é] *f.* quantity, amount, supply.

quarantaine [kàraⁿtèn] *f.* about forty, twoscore; quarantine; Lent. || *quarante* [-aⁿt] *m., adj.* forty. || *quarantième* [-tyèm] *adj., m.* fortieth.

quart [kàr] *m.* quarter, fourth part, quart [litre]; watch (naut.); *adj.* fourth; quartan.

quartier [kàrtyé] *m.* quarter, fourth part; piece, part; district, neighbo(u)rhood; quarter's rent, pay; flap [selle]; haunch [chevreuil]; *quartier général*, headquarters; *quartier-maître*, quartermaster.

quatorze [kàtòrz] *m., adj.* fourteen. || *quatorzième* [-yèm] *m., f., adj.* fourteenth.

quatre [kàtr] *m., adj.* four, fourth; *quatre-vingts*, eighty; *quatre-vingt-dix*, ninety. || *quatrième* [kàtryèm] *m., f., adj.* fourth.

quatuor [kwàtüòr] *m.* quartet.

que [kᵉ] (*qu'* before a vowel) *rel. pron.* whom, that; which; what; *interrog. pron.* what?; why?

que (*qu'* before a vowel) *conj.* that; than; as; when; only, but; *ne... que*, only, nothing but, not until.

que [kᵉ] (*qu'* before a vowel) *adv.* how, how much, how many.

quel [kèl] *adj.* * what, which; what a; *quel dommage !* what a pity !

quelconque [kèlkoⁿk] *indef. adj.* whatever; mediocre, commonplace, undistinguished.

quelque [kèlkᵉ] *adj.* some, any; whatever, whatsoever; *pl.* a few; *adv.* however; some, about; *quelque chose*, something; *quelquefois*, sometimes, at times, now and then; *quelque part*, somewhere, anywhere; *quelqu'un*, someone, anyone, somebody, anybody; *pl.* some, any.

quémander [kémaⁿdé] *v.* to beg (for), to solicit.

qu'en-dira-t-on [kaⁿdìràtòⁿ] *m.* public opinion.

quenouille [kᵉnûy] *f.* distaff.

querelle [kᵉrèl] *f.* quarrel. || *se quereller* [sᵉkèrèlé] *v.* to quarrel.

question [kèstyoⁿ] *f.* question; query, interrogation; matter, issue. || *questionnaire* [-yònèr] *m.* questionnaire, form, blank. || *questionner* [-yòné] *v.* to question, to interrogate, to quiz; to examine.

quête [kèt] *f.* quest, search; collection; beating about [chasse]. || *quêter* [-é] *v.* to go in quest of; to beg; to make a collection. || *quêteur* [-œr] *m.* alms-collector; sidesman, collection-taker.

queue [kë] *f.* tail; stalk, stem; end; rear; billiard-cue; handle; train

[robe]; queue, file, string; *en queue*, in the rear; *faire queue*, to stand in line, to queue up.

qui [kì] *rel. pron.* who, which, that; whom; *qui que ce soit*, anyone whatever.

qui [kì] *interrog. pron.* who [sujet]; whom [complément direct]; *à qui est-ce?* whose is it?; *quiconque*, whoever, whosoever; whomever, whichever; anybody.

quiétude [kyétüd] *f.* quietude.

quignon [kìñoⁿ] *m.* chunk; hunk.

quille [kîy] *f.* keel (naut.).

quille [kîy] *f.* skittle, ninepin, pin [bowling]; *jeu de quilles*, © bowling alley; *jouer aux quilles*, © to bowl. ‖ *quilleur* [-œr] *m.* © bowler.

quincaillerie [kìⁿkàyrî] *f.* *Br.* ironmongery, *Am.* hardware.

quinine [kìnîn] *f.* quinine.

quinte [kìⁿt] *f.* fifth (mus.); quinte [escrime]; fit, paroxysm [toux]; freak, whim (fig.).

quinteux [kìⁿtë] *adj.** moody, cantankerous, crotchety, restive.

quintuple [kìⁿtüpl] *m., adj.* quintuple, fivefold.

quinzaine [kìⁿzèn] *f.* about fifteen; fortnight, two weeks. ‖ *quinze* [kìⁿz] *m., adj.* fifteen; fifteenth; *quinze jours*, fortnight. ‖ *quinzième* [-zyèm] *adj., s.* fifteenth.

quiproquo [kìpròkò] *m.* misunderstanding; mistake, misapprehension.

quittance [kìtaⁿs] *f.* receipt, discharge.

quitte [kìt] *adj.* clear, free; rid; discharged, quit [dette]; *quitte à*, liable to; on the chance of; *nous sommes quittes*, we're even. ‖ *quitter* [-é] *v.* to depart (from); to leave; to give up; to resign [poste]; to take off [vêtements]; *ne quittez pas*, hold the line [téléphone]; *se quitter*, to part, to separate.

quoi [kwà] *rel. pron.* what; *quoi que je fasse*, whatever I may do; *quoi qu'il en soit*, be that as it may, however it may be.

quoi? [kwà] *interrog. pron.* what?

quoique [kwàk] *conj.* although.

quolibet [kòlìbè] *m.* quibble, gibe.

quote-part [kòtpàr] *f.* quota, share.

quotidien [kòtìdyìⁿ] *m., adj.* daily; *adj.** everyday; quotidian [fièvre].

quotient [kòsyaⁿ] *m.* quotient.

R

rabâcher [ràbâshé] *v.* to repeat over and over.

rabais [ràbè] *m.* reduction, discount; rebate; abatement; depreciation [monnaie]; fall [des eaux]. ‖ *rabaisser* [-sé] *v.* to lower; to reduce; to depreciate; to disparage; to humble.

rabat [ràbà] *m.* band [col]; *rabat-joie*, spoil-sport, wet blanket. ‖ *rabatteur* [-tœr] *m.* beater; tout (comm.). ‖ *rabattre* [ràbàtr] *v.* to pull down, to put down; to beat down; to reduce, to diminish; to lower, to humble; to beat up [gibier]; to ward off [coup]; *se rabattre*, to turn off, to change; to come down; to fall on (*sur*, back). ‖ *rabattu* [-ü] *adj.* turned-down; felled.

rabiot [ràbyò] *m.* (fam.) extra profit; pickings; extra work, overtime.

râble [ràbl] *m.* back, saddle [lièvre]. ‖ *râblé* [-é] *adj.* thick-backed [lièvre]; strong, husky, sturdy.

rabot [ràbò] *m.* plane. ‖ *raboter* [-òté] *v.* to plane; to polish; to filch, *Am.* to lift (pop.). ‖ *raboteux* [-ë] *adj.** rough, rugged, uneven; knotty; harsh.

rabougri [ràbùgrì] *adj.* stunted, skimpy; scraggy [végétation].

rabrouer [ràbrûé] *v.* to snub.

racaille [ràkày] *f.* rabble, scum, riffraff (fam.).

raccommodage [ràkòmòdàj] *m.* mending; darning; repairing. ‖ *raccommoder* [-é] *v.* to mend, to darn; to repair; to piece, to patch; to set right, to correct; to reconcile; *se raccommoder*, to make it up again.

raccord [ràkòr] *m.* joining, fitting, junction; connection [lampe]; accord; matching. ‖ *raccorder* [-dé] *v.* to join, to connect.

raccourci [ràkûrsì] *adj.* shortened, abridged; oblate, ellipsoid (geom.); squat [taille], bobbed [cheveux]; *m.* short cut [chemin]; abridgment, digest [livre]; foreshortening [tableau]. ‖ *raccourcir* [-îr] *v.* to shorten, to curtail, to abridge; to grow shorter.

raccrocher [ràkròshé] *v.* to hook up again, to hang up again; to recover, to retrieve; to ring off [téléphone]; (fam.) to solicit; *se raccrocher à*, to clutch at, to cling to, to hang on to.

race [ràs] *f.* race; stock, breed; blood; strain, line, ancestry; tribe; *de race*, pedigreed, pure-bred [chien]; thoroughbred [cheval].

rachat [ràshà] *m.* repurchase; redemption; surrender, cashing in. ‖

racheter [ràshté] v. to repurchase, to buy back; to redeem, to ransom; to compensate, to make up for; to atone for.

rachitique [ràshìtĭk] adj. rickety, rachitic.

racine [ràsîn] f. root; origin.

racisme [ràsĭsm] m. racialism, Am. racism. ‖ **raciste** [ràsĭst] adj., s. racialist, Am. racist.

raclée [ràklé] f. thrashing, hiding, drubbing. ‖ **racler** [-é] v. to scrape, to rake; to pilfer, to steal, to pinch, to lift (pop.). ‖ **racloir** [-wàr] m. scraper, road-scraper. ‖ **raclure** [-ür] f. scrapings.

racoler [ràkòlé] v. (fam.) to enlist; to tout for (comm.); to accost.

raconter [ràkoⁿté] v. to relate, to tell, to narrate, to recount.

rade [ràd] f. roads, roadstead.

radeau [ràdô] m.* raft, float.

radiateur [ràdyàtær] m. radiator. ‖ **radiation** [-yàsyoⁿ] f. radiation.

radiation [ràdyàsyoⁿ] f. obliteration, striking out; deletion.

radical [ràdìkàl] adj.* radical; fundamental; m.* radical; root.

radier [ràdyé] v. to strike out, to obliterate, to cancel; to delete.

radieux [ràdyë] adj.* radiant; beaming [sourire].

radin [ràdⁿ] adj. (pop.) stingy.

radio [ràdìô] f. radio, wireless; X-ray (med.); m. radiogram, wireless message; wireless operator, telegraphist; *radio-activité*, radio-activity; *radiodiffuser*, to broadcast; *radiodiffusion*, broadcast, broadcasting; *radiologie*, radiology; X-ray treatment; *radiologue*, radiologist; *radioreportage*, news broadcast, running commentary; *radiothérapie*, radiotherapy, X-ray treatment.

radis [ràdĭ] m. radish.

radium [ràdyòm] m. radium.

radotage [ràdòtàj] m. drivel, nonsense, twaddle; dotage. ‖ **radoter** [-é] v. to talk drivel or twaddle, to ramble; to be in one's dotage.

radoub [ràdû] m. repairing, graving (naut.); dry-dock [bassin]. ‖ **radouber** [-bé] v. to repair, to mend.

radoucir [ràdûsîr] v. to soften, to make milder; to mitigate, to allay; to appease, to pacify, to mollify.

rafale [ràfàl] f. squall, gust [vent]; burst, volley, storm [tir].

raffermir [ràfèrmîr] v. to fortify, to strengthen; to secure, to make firm.

raffinage [ràfìnàj] m. refining [sucre]; distilling [huile]. ‖ **raffinement**

[-nᵉmaⁿ] m. refinement; subtlety. ‖ **raffiner** [-é] v. to refine; to be over-nice. ‖ **raffinerie** [-rî] f. refinery.

raffoler [ràfòlé] v. to dote (de, on); to be passionately fond (de, of); to be mad (de, about).

rafle [ràfl] f. stalk [raisin]; cob [maïs].

rafle [ràfl] f. foray, round-up, police raid; clean sweep [vol]; haul [pêche]. ‖ **rafler** [-é] v. to sweep off, to carry off; to round up.

rafraîchir [ràfrèshîr] v. to cool; to refresh; to revive; to freshen. ‖ **rafraîchissement** [-ìsmaⁿ] m. cooling; pl. refreshments.

ragaillardir [ràgàyàrdîr] v. to buck up, to cheer.

rage [ràj] f. rabies, hydrophobia, frenzy, rage; violent pain; passion; mania. ‖ **rager** [-é] v. to rage; to fume. ‖ **rageur** [-ær] adj.* choleric, violent-tempered; snappish.

ragot [ràgò] m. (fam.) gossip, tittle-tattle.

ragoût [ràgû] m. stew, ragout; relish, seasoning.

raid [rèd] m. raid, foray, incursion; endurance contest [sport].

raide [rèd] adj. stiff, rigid; tight, taut; stark; inflexible; steep; swift, rapid; (fam.) tall, exaggerated; adv. quickly, suddenly. ‖ **raideur** [-ær] f. stiffness, rigidity; firmness, inflexibility; tightness; steepness; swiftness; tenacity; harshness. ‖ **raidillon** [-lyoⁿ] m. steep path, up-hill stretch. ‖ **raidir** [-îr] v. to stiffen; to be inflexible.

raie [rè] f. ray, skate [poisson].

raie [rè] f. parting [cheveux]; streak, stripe; line, stroke; furrow.

rail [rày] m. rail.

railler [ràyé] v. to banter, to scoff at, to gibe, to heckle; to jest; Am. to twit. ‖ **raillerie** [ràyrî] f. raillery, bantering, jesting; jest; jeer, mock, scoff. ‖ **railleur** [ràyær] adj.* bantering, joking; jeering, scoffing; m. banterer, joker; scoffer.

rainette [rènèt] f. tree-frog; rennet.

rainure [rènür] f. groove; slot, notch; rabbet.

raisin [rèzⁿ] m. grape; *raisins secs*, raisins; *raisins de Corinthe, de Smyrne*, currants, sultanas.

raison [rèzoⁿ] f. reason; sense, sanity; reparation; justice, right; proof, ground; cause, motive; firm (comm.); ratio (math.); claim (jur.); *à raison de*, at the rate of; *avoir raison*, to be right; *donner raison à*, to decide in favo(u)r of; *à plus forte raison*, so much the more; *avoir raison de*, to get the better of; *en raison de*, in consideration of; *raison sociale*, firm name, trade name. ‖ **raisonnable** [-ònằbl] *adj.* reasonable, rational; right, just; sensible; fair, equitable; moderate [prix]. ‖ **raisonnement** [-ònmaⁿ] *m.* reasoning, reason, argument. ‖ **raisonner** [-òné] *v.* to reason; to argue; to consider, to weigh.

rajeunir [ràjœnîr] *v.* to rejuvenate, to renovate, to renew; to grow young again. ‖ **rajeunissement** [-ìsmaⁿ] *m.* rejuvenation, renovation, restoration.

rajouter [ràjûté] *v.* to add again, to add more.

rajuster [ràjüsté] *v.* to readjust; to reconcile (fig.).

râle [ràl] *m.* rail [oiseau].

râle [ràl] *m.* death-rattle; rattling in the throat.

ralenti [ràlaⁿtî] *m.* slow motion [cinéma]; idling [automobile]. ‖ **ralentir** [-tîr] *v.* to slacken, to slow; to lessen; to abate.

râler [ràlé] *v.* to have a rattle in one's throat; (pop.) to grumble.

ralliement [ràllìmaⁿ] *m.* rallying, rally. ‖ **rallier** [-yé] *v.* to rally; to rejoin; **se rallier**, to rally, to assemble; to hug the shore (naut.).

rallonge [ràloⁿj] *f.* extension-piece, extra leaf. ‖ **rallonger** [-é] *v.* to lengthen, to elongate, to eke out; to thin [sauce]; to let out *or* down [jupe]; to put an extra leaf on [table].

rallye [ràlî] *m.* rally; treasure-hunt.

ramage [ràmàj] *m.* floral pattern; warbling, chirping, twittering.

ramassage [ràmàsàj] *m.* collection, gathering up. ‖ **ramasser** [-é] *v.* to gather; to pick up. ‖ **ramassis** [-î] *m.* heap, collection; gang.

rame [ràm] *f.* oar.

rame [ràm] *f.* stick, prop (hort.); tenter-frame [textile].

rame [ràm] *f.* ream [papier]; convoy, string [bateaux]; lift, line [trains].

rameau [ràmô] *m.* bough, branch; subdivision; *dimanche des Rameaux*, Palm Sunday.

ramener [ràmné] *v.* to bring back; to take home; to restore; to recall; **se ramener**, to be reduced, to come down (à, to).

ramer [ràmé] *v.* to stick, to prop.

ramer [ràmé] *v.* to row. ‖ **rameur** [-œr] *m.* rower, oarsman.

ramier [ràmyé] *m.* wood-pigeon.

ramification [ràmìfìkàsyoⁿ] *f.* ramification; subdivision; outgrowth. ‖ **ramifier** [-yé] *v.* to ramify.

ramollir [ràmòlîr] *v.* to soften; to

enervate (fig.); **se ramollir**, to grow soft. ‖ **ramollissant** [-ìsaⁿ] *adj.* softening; enervating.

ramonage [ràmònàj] *m.* chimney-sweeping. ‖ **ramoner** [-é] *v.* to sweep [cheminée]. ‖ **ramoneur** [-œr] *m.* chimney-sweep.

rampe [raⁿp] *f.* slope, incline; banister; footlights (theat.); inclined plane (tech.). ‖ **ramper** [-é] *v.* to creep, to crawl; to crouch, to cringe, to grovel; to fawn, to toady.

ramure [ràmür] *f.* boughs; antlers.

rancart [raⁿkàr] *m.* appointment (pop.); *au rancart* (fam.), on the shelf, cast aside.

rance [raⁿs] *adj.* rancid, rank; rusty (fig.); *m.* rancidness. ‖ **rancir** [-îr] *v.* to grow rancid.

rancœur [raⁿkœr] *f.* ranco(u)r.

rançon [raⁿsoⁿ] *f.* ransom.

rancune [raⁿkün] *f.* ranco(u)r, spite, grudge. ‖ **rancunier** [-yé] *adj.* spiteful, rancorous.

randonnée [raⁿdòné] *f.* circuit, ramble, long walk; round.

rang [raⁿ] *m.* line, row, column, range, rank; order, class; tier; rate [bateaux]; © rang (group of farms along the same road, or the road itself). ‖ **rangée** [-jé] *f.* row, range, file, line, tier. ‖ **ranger** [-jé] *v.* to put in order; to tidy up; to put away; to arrange; to range; to draw up [voitures]; to rate; to rank; to coast (naut.); to keep back, to subdue; **se ranger**, to make way; to draw up (mil.); to fall in (mil.); to mend one's ways.

ranimer [rànìmé] *v.* to revive, to reanimate; to stir up; to rouse, to enliven.

rapace [ràpàs] *adj.* rapacious; predatory; predaceous; ravenous.

rapatriement [ràpàtrìmaⁿ] *m.* repatriation. ‖ **rapatrier** [-lyé] *v.* to repatriate.

râpe [ràp] *f.* grater; rasp; stalk [raisin]. ‖ **râpé** [-é] *adj.* grated, shredded, shabby, threadbare. ‖ **râper** [-é] *v.* to grate; to rasp; to make threadbare.

rapetisser [ràptìsé] *v.* to shorten, to make smaller; to shrink.

râpeux [ràpë] *adj.* rough, raspy, harsh.

rapide [ràpìd] *adj.* rapid, fast, swift, fleet; hasty, sudden; steep; *m.* fast train, express train. ‖ **rapidité** [-ìté] *f.* rapidity, speed.

rapiécer [ràpyésé] *v.* to patch up, to piece.

rapine [ràpìn] *f.* rapine; extortion. ‖ **rapiner** [-né] *v.* to plunder; to pillage.

rappel [ràpèl] *m.* recall, recalling; call [à l'ordre]; repeal, revocation; reminder, recollection; drum signal, bugle call (mil.); curtain-call (theat.). ‖ **rappeler** [ràplé] *v.* to call back, to call again; to recall; to restore [santé]; to summon up, to muster [courage]; to retract; to remind of; *se rappeler*, to remember, to recall, to recollect.

rapport [ràpòr] *m.* report, account; proceeds, profit, revenue; productiveness, bearing; conformity, analogy; relation, connection, relevancy; ratio; communication. ‖ **rapporter** [-té] *v.* to bring back, to take back; to bring in, to yield; to refund; to refer; to repeal; to report; to quote; to post (comm.); to trace (topogr.); to pay, to bring profit (comm.); to retrieve, to fetch [chiens]; *se rapporter*, to relate; to tally (à, with); *s'en rapporter à*, to rely on. ‖ **rapporteur** [-tœr] *m.* reporter; stenographer; chairman; rapporteur; informer, tattle-tale, tale-bearer.

rapprochement [ràpròshma⁽ⁿ⁾] *m.* bringing together; reconciliation; comparison. ‖ **rapprocher** [-é] *v.* to bring together; to reconcile; to compare; *se rapprocher*, to come near again, to draw nearer; to become reconciled; to approach, to approximate.

rapt [ràpt] *m.* abduction, kidnapping, *Am.* snatch (fam.); rape.

raquette [ràkèt] *f.* racket; battledore; snow-shoe. ‖ **raquetteur** [-œr] *m.* ⓒ snow-shoer.

rare [ràr] *adj.* rare, uncommon, unusual; few, scarce, scanty, sparse; slow [pouls]. ‖ **raréfier** [-éfyé] *v.* to rarefy; *se raréfier*, to rarefy, to become scarce. ‖ **rarement** [-ma⁽ⁿ⁾] *adv.* infrequently, rarely, seldom. ‖ **rareté** [-té] *f.* rarity; scarcity; unusualness.

ras [râ] *adj.* close-shaven, smooth-shaven, close-cropped, close-napped, shorn; bare, smooth; flat, low; *à ras de*, level with; *rase campagne*, open country; *rase-mottes*, hedge-hopping. ‖ **rasade** [-zàd] *f.* glassful, brimmer; brim-full glass. ‖ **raser** [-zé] *v.* to shave; to raze; to tear down [édifice]; to graze, to skim; to hug, to skirt [côte, terre]; (pop.) to bore. ‖ **raseur** [-zœr] *m.* shaver; (pop.) bore. ‖ **rasoir** [-zwàr] *m.* razor.

rassasier [ràsàzyé] *v.* to sate, to satiate; to cloy, to surfeit; to satisfy, to fill; *se rassasier*, to eat one's fill; to gorge oneself; to feast.

rassembler [ràsa⁽ⁿ⁾blé] *v.* to reassemble; to gather together; to collect; to muster (mil.).

rasséréner [ràséréné] *v.* to calm, to clear up, to soothe; *se rasséréner*, to be soothed; to recover one's serenity.

rassis [ràsì] *adj.* stale [pain]; settled; calm, staid, sedate; trite, hackneyed (fig.).

rassortir [ràsòrtîr] *v.* to sort, to match again; to restock.

rassurer [ràsüré] *v.* to reassure, to tranquil(l)ize; to strengthen.

rat [rà] *m.* rat; niggard; taper [bougie]; ballet-girl (theat.); miser, niggard, stingy (fam.).

ratatiner [ràtàtìné] *v.* to shrink, to shrivel up; to wrinkle; to wizen.

rate [ràt] *f.* spleen.

raté [ràté] *m.* misfiring [fusil, moteur]; failure, flop; wash-out, flash-in-the-pan (fam.); *adj.* miscarried, ineffectual; bungled.

râteau [râtô] *m.*° rake; raker; scrapper; large comb [peigne]. ‖ **râteler** [-lé] *v.* to rake. ‖ **râtelier** [-°lyé] *m.* rack [écurie]; (pop.) denture.

rater [ràté] *v.* to misfire; to miss [train]; to fail in, to bungle, to muff, to fluff (pop.); to fail, to miscarry.

ratier [ràtyé] *m.* rat-catcher. ‖ **ratière** [-yèr] *f.* rat-trap.

ratifier [ràtìfyé] *v.* to ratify; to confirm; to sanction.

ration [ràsyo⁽ⁿ⁾] *f.* ration, allowance, share. ‖ **rationnel** [-yònèl] *adj.*° rational; reasonable. ‖ **rationnement** [-yònma⁽ⁿ⁾] *m.* rationing. ‖ **rationner** [-yòné] *v.* to ration.

ratisser [ràtìsé] *v.* to rake, to scrape; to fleece (fam.).

rattacher [ràtàshé] *v.* to refasten, to attach again, to connect.

rattraper [ràtràpé] *v.* to catch again, to retake; to catch up with, to overtake; to recover; *se rattraper*, to catch hold; to make up for [perte]; to be recovered [occasion].

rature [ràtür] *f.* erasure, crossing out, cancellation. ‖ **raturer** [-é] *v.* to erase, to cross out, to cancel, to strike out.

rauque [rôk] *adj.* hoarse.

ravage [ràvàj] *m.* ravage, havoc. ‖ **ravager** [-é] *v.* to ravage, to ruin, to devastate, to lay waste.

ravalement [ràvàlma⁽ⁿ⁾] *m.* resurfacing, refinishing; rough-casting, plastering; hollowing out; disparagement (fig.). ‖ **ravaler** [-é] *v.* to resurface; to rough-cast.

ravauder [ràvôdé] *v.* to mend, to darn, to patch.

rave [ràv] *f.* rape.

ravi [ràvì] *adj.* entranced; delighted.

ravier [ràvyé] *m.* radish-dish.

ravigoter [ràvìgòté] *v.* to refresh, to perk up.

ravin [ràvĭⁿ] *m.* ravine; hollow road. ‖ *ravine* [-ĭn] *f.* gully. ‖ *raviner* [-ĭné] *v.* to plough up.

ravir [ràvĭr] *v.* to ravish, to abduct, to kidnap; to rob of; to charm, to delight, to enrapture (fig.).

raviser (se) [sᵉràvĭzé] *v.* to change one's mind, to think better.

ravissant [ràvĭsaⁿ] *adj.* ravishing, delightful; predatory; ravenous. ‖ *ravissement* [-maⁿ] *m.* rapture, ravishment; kidnapping; rape. ‖ *ravisseur* [-œr] *m.* ravisher, kidnapper.

ravitaillement [ràvĭtàymaⁿ] *m.* supplying; replenishment; provisioning; revictual(l)ing; refue(l)ling [carburant]. ‖ *ravitailler* [-é] *v.* to supply; to replenish; to provision, to revictual; to refuel [carburant].

raviver [ràvĭvé] *v.* to revive; to reanimate; to enliven, to rouse.

rayer [rèyé] *v.* to stripe, to streak; to cancel, to scratch, to erase, to expunge, to strike out; to suppress (fig.); to rifle, to groove [fusil].

rayon [rèyoⁿ] *m.* ray, beam [lumière, soleil]; spoke [roue]; radius.

rayon [rèyoⁿ] *m.* shelf; rack; department [magasin]; specialty, *Am.* field [profession]; zone, circuit, sphere, honeycomb; *chef de rayon,* *Br.* shopwalker, *Am.* floorwalker.

rayonnant [rèyònaⁿ] *adj.* radiant, beaming; lambent.

rayonne [rèyòn] *f.* rayon [tissu].

rayonnement [rèyònmaⁿ] *m.* radiance, radiation; effulgence. ‖ *rayonner* [-é] *v.* to radiate; to beam, to shine; to spread abroad.

rayure [rèyür] *f.* stripe; streak, scratch; strike-out, erasure, cancellation; groove rifling [fusil].

raz [râ] *m.* strong current; *raz de marée,* tidal wave, tide-race.

réacteur [réàktœr] *m.* reactor; jet engine; jet plane. ‖ *réactif* [-tĭf] *m.* reagent (chem.); *adj.** reactive. ‖ *réaction* [-syoⁿ] *f.* reaction; conservatism; *avion à réaction,* jet plane. ‖ *réagir* [réàjĭr] *v.* to react.

réalisable [réàlĭzàbl] *adj.* realizable; feasible, practicable. ‖ *réalisation* [-àsyoⁿ] *f.* realization; fulfil(l)ment; conversion into money. ‖ *réaliser* [-é] *v.* to realize; to convert into money; *se réaliser,* to come true. ‖ *réalisme* [réàlĭsm] *m.* realism. ‖ *réaliste* [-ĭst] *m., f.* realist; *adj.* realistic. ‖ *réalité* [-ĭté] *f.* reality; *en réalité,* really, actually.

réanimation [réànĭmàsyoⁿ] *f.* resuscitation.

rébarbatif [rébàrbàtĭf] *adj.** surly; forbidding.

rebelle [rᵉbèl] *m.* rebel; *adj.* rebellious; insurgent, insubordinate; unyielding, obstinate; wayward; refractory. ‖ *rebeller (se)* [sᵉrᵉbèllé] *v.* to revolt, to rebel; to resist. ‖ *rébellion* [rébèlyoⁿ] *f.* rebellion, revolt; insurrection; insubordination.

rebondissement [rᵉboⁿdĭsmaⁿ] *m.* rebound, rebounding; repercussion.

rebord [rᵉbòr] *m.* edge, brim, border.

rebours [rᵉbûr] *m.* wrong way; opposite; *à rebours,* the wrong way; contrary to.

rebrousser [rᵉbrûsé] *v.* to turn up, to brush up [cheveux]; to turn back; to retrace [chemin].

rebuffade [rᵉbüfàd] *f.* rebuff, repulse, snub.

rebut [rᵉbü] *m.* repulse, rebuff, rejection, refusal, refuse, rubbish, garbage; outcast; *lettre au rebut,* deadletter. ‖ *rebuter* [-té] *v.* to rebuff, to repel; to reject, to discard; to refuse, to disallow (jur.); to disgust, to shock; to dishearten.

récalcitrant [rékàlsìtraⁿ] *adj.* recalcitrant, refractory.

recaler [rᵉkàlé] *v.* (fam.) to fail, to plough.

récapitulation [rékàpìtülàsyoⁿ] *f.* recapitulation, summing up; repetition. ‖ *récapituler* [-é] *v.* to recapitulate, to sum up, to summarize.

recel [rᵉsèl] *m.* receiving, fencing; harbouring. ‖ *receler* [-sᵉlé] *v.* to receive; to harbour; to contain. ‖ *receleur* [rᵉslœr] *m.* receiver of stolen goods, fence.

recensement [rᵉsaⁿsmaⁿ] *m.* census, inventory; verification, checking. ‖ *recenser* [-sé] *v.* to count; to register; to inventory; to record; to take a census of.

récent [résaⁿ] *adj.* recent, late, new, fresh.

récépissé [résépìsé] *m.* receipt; acknowledgment.

réceptacle [résèptàkl] *m.* receptacle, container; resort, haunt, nest [criminels]. ‖ *récepteur, -trice* [-tœr, -trìs] *adj.* receiving; *m.* receiver; reservoir; collector [machine]. ‖ *réception* [-syoⁿ] *f.* reception; receiving, receipt; welcome; reception desk. ‖ *réceptionner* [-syòné] *v.* to take delivery. ‖ *réceptionniste* [-ĭst] *m., f.* receptionist, desk clerk.

récession [résèsyoⁿ] *f.* recession.

recette [rᵉsèt] *f.* receipts, returns [argent]; receivership [bureau]; recipe [cuisine].

recevable [rəsəvàbl] *adj.* receivable; admissible. ‖ *receveur* [-œr] *m.* receiver; addressee, collector [impôts]; conductor [tram]; ticket-taker (theat.); © catcher [base-ball]. ‖ *recevoir* [-wàr] *v.** to receive; to get; to incur; to accept, to admit; to welcome; to entertain, to be at home; © to catch [base-ball].

rechange [rəshãj] *m.* replacement, change; *pièce de rechange,* spare part; refill.

réchapper [réchàpé] *v.* to escape; to get off; to be saved (*de,* from).

réchaud [réshô] *m.* hot-plate, burner; *réchaud à alcool,* spirit stove. ‖ *réchauffer* [-é] *v.* to warm over, to heat up; to rekindle.

rêche [rèsh] *adj.* rough [toucher]; sour [goût]; crabbed [moral].

recherche [rəshèrsh] *f.* search, quest, pursuit, research, inquiry, investigation; prospecting; affectation. ‖ *recherché* [-é] *adj.* sought after, in great demand; studied, affected; refined. ‖ *rechercher* [-é] *v.* to seek again, to search after; to investigate; to aspire to; to court.

rechute [rəshüt] *f.* relapse (med.); back-sliding (fig.).

récidive [résidîv] *f.* recidivism, second offense; recurrence. ‖ *récidiver* [-ivé] *v.* to relapse into crime, to repeat an offense. ‖ *récidiviste* [-ivìst] *m.* recidivist, old offender.

récif [résif] *m.* reef.

récipient [résipyaⁿ] *m.* container; recipient; reservoir.

réciprocité [résipròsité] *f.* reciprocity, reciprocation; interchange. ‖ *réciproque* [-ɔk] *adj.* reciprocal, mutual; converse (math.); *f.* the same, the like; converse, reciprocal (math.).

récit [résí] *m.* story, narrative, account, yarn (fam.); report. ‖ *récital* [-tàl] *m.* recital. ‖ *récitation* [-tàsyoⁿ] *f.* recitation, reciting. ‖ *réciter* [-té] *v.* to recite, to rehearse; to repeat; to tell, to narrate.

réclamation [réklàmàsyoⁿ] *f.* claim, demand; complaint, protest, objection; *bureau des réclamations,* Br. claims department, Am. adjustment bureau. ‖ *réclame* [réklàm] *f.* advertisement, advertising; sign; blurb, Am. ballyhoo (pop.); *faire de la réclame,* to advertise; *réclame du jour,* the day's special; *article de réclame,* feature article. ‖ *réclamer* [-é] *v.* to claim, to demand; to reclaim, to claim back; to complain, to object, to protest.

reclus [rəklü] *m.* recluse; *adj.* cloistered. ‖ *réclusion* [réklüzyoⁿ] *f.* seclusion, reclusion; solitary confinement.

recoin [rəkwiⁿ] *m.* nook, recess, cranny.

récolte [rékòlt] *f.* crop, harvest, vintage; collecting, gathering; profits (fig.). ‖ *récolter* [-é] *v.* to harvest, to reap; to gather in.

recommandable [rəkòmandàbl] *adj.* commendable; estimable; recommendable, advisable. ‖ *recommandation* [-àsyoⁿ] *f.* recommendation; reference, introduction; detainer (jur.); registration [postes]. ‖ *recommander* [-é] *v.* to recommend; to charge, to request; to lodge a detainer (jur.); to register, to insure [postes].

recommencer [rəkòmaⁿsé] *v.* to recommence, to begin anew, to start over (again).

récompense [rékoⁿpaⁿs] *f.* reward; requital; award, compensation. ‖ *récompenser* [-é] *v.* to reward, to requite; to recompense, to repay.

réconciliation [rékoⁿsîlyàsyoⁿ] *f.* reconciliation, reconcilement. ‖ *réconcilier* [-yé] *v.* to reconcile; *se réconcilier,* to become friends again, to make it up (*avec,* with).

reconduire [rəkoⁿdüîr] *v.** to reconduct, to escort, to lead back; to see home.

réconfort [rékoⁿfòr] *m.* comfort, relief. ‖ *réconforter* [-té] *v.* to comfort, to cheer up.

reconnaissance [rəkònèsaⁿs] *f.* recognition; gratitude, thankfulness; acknowledgment, avowal; recognizance; pawn-ticket; reconnaissance, reconnoitring, exploration. ‖ *reconnaissant* [-aⁿ] *adj.* grateful, thankful. ‖ *reconnaître* [-ètr] *v.** to recognize; to identify; to discover; to acknowledge, to admit (to); to concede; to reconnoitre, to explore.

reconstituant [rəkoⁿstìtüaⁿ] *m.* tonic; reconstituant, restorative, Am. bracer (fam.). ‖ *reconstituer* [-üé] *v.* to reconstitute, to reorganize.

reconstruction [rəkoⁿstrüksyoⁿ] *f.* reconstruction, rebuilding. ‖ *reconstruire* [-üîr] *v.** to reconstruct, to rebuild.

reconversion [rəkoⁿvèrsyoⁿ] *f.* reconversion.

recopier [rəkòpyé] *v.* to recopy.

record [rəkòr] *m.* record [sports]; *recordman,* record-holder.

recoupement [rəkûpmaⁿ] *m.* cross-checking, verification.

recourber [rəkûrbé] *v.* to bend again, to bend down (ou) back.

recourir [rəkûrîr] *v.** to have recourse, to resort (to); to appeal (jur.). ‖ *recours* [rəkûr] *m.* recourse; refuge, resort, resource; petition, appeal (jur.); *avoir recours à,* to resort to.

recouvrement [r⁹kûvr⁹m⁹ⁿ] *m.* recovery; regaining, debts due.

recouvrer [r⁹kûvré] *v.* to recover, to retrieve, to get again; to recuperate, to recoup.

récréatif [rékréàtìf] *adj.º* recreative, recreational; relaxing. ‖ *récréation* [-syoⁿ] *f.* recreation; play-time, recess, break.

récrier (se) [s⁹rékrìyé] *v.* to exclaim, to cry out; to expostulate, to protest; to be amazed.

récriminer [rékrìmìné] *v.* to recriminate; to countercharge.

recroqueviller (se) [s⁹r⁹kròkvìyé] *v.* to shrivel up [personne]; to cockle [parchemin].

recrue [r⁹krü] *f.* recruit, draftee, inductee. ‖ *recrutement* [-tm⁹ⁿ] *m.* recruitment, engaging, drafting, enlistment, mustering.

rectangle [rèktⁿgl] *m.* rectangle. ‖ *rectangulaire* [-ülèr] *adj.* rectangular, right-angled.

rectifier [rèktìfyé] *v.* to rectify, to set right, to correct, to amend, to adjust; to straighten. ‖ *rectitude* [-ltüd] *m.* rectitude, uprightness, correctness, straightness.

reçu [r⁹sü] *adj.* received; admitted, recognized, customary, upon usual; *m.* receipt; *au reçu de*, upon receipt of; *être reçu*, to pass [examen].

recueil [r⁹kœy] *m.* collection, selection, assortment, miscellany, anthology, compendium. ‖ *recueillement* [-m⁹ⁿ] *m.* gathering; collectedness; mental repose. ‖ *recueillir* [-îr] *v.º* to gather, to get together, to assemble, to collect; to receive, to acquire; to take in, to reap; to shelter, to harbo(u)r; to inherit [succession]; *se recueillir*, to collect one's thoughts, to wrap oneself in meditation.

recul [r⁹kül] *m.* recoil; falling-back, retreat, kick [fusil]. ‖ *reculer* [-é] *v.* to draw back; to put back; to defer, to postpone; to extend [limites]; to retreat, to fall back, to recede; to recoil, to flinch; to go backwards; to rein back [cheval]; *à reculons*, backwards.

récupérable [réküpéràbl] *adj.* recoverable. ‖ *récupération* [-ràsyoⁿ] *f.* recuperation; recovery; salvage. ‖ *récupérer* [-ré] *v.* to recover; to recuperate [pertes]; to salvage.

récurer [réküré] *v.* to scour, to cleanse.

récuser [réküzé] *v.* to challenge, to take exception to (jur.); to impugn, to reject [témoignage]; *se récuser*, to disclaim competence (jur.).

rédacteur, -trice [rédàktœr, -trìs] *m., f.* writer, drafter [documents]; clerk; *rédacteur en chef*, chief editor. ‖ *rédaction* [rédàksyoⁿ] *f.* editing; editorial staff; drawing up; wording; newsroom; essay, composition [école].

reddition [rèdìsyoⁿ] *f.* surrender; rendering [comptes].

rédempteur [rédⁿptœr] *m.* redeemer; *adj.º* redeeming.

redevable [r⁹d⁹vàbl] *adj.* indebted, owing; beholden; *m.* debtor. ‖ *redevance* [-va⁹s] *f.* dues; rent; fees.

rédhibitoire [rédìbìtwàr] *adj.* redhibitory, latent [vice].

rédiger [rédìjé] *v.* to draw up; to edit; to draft, to word, to indite.

redingote [r⁹dⁿgòt] *f.* frock-coat.

redire [r⁹dîr] *v.º* to repeat, to tell again; to reiterate; to criticize. ‖ *redite* [-ìt] *f.* repetition, redundancy; tautology.

redoubler [r⁹dûblé] *v.* to redouble; to increase; to re-line [vêtement].

redoutable [r⁹dûtàbl] *adj.* redoubtable, fearsome, awful. ‖ *redouter* [-é] *v.* to dread, to fear.

redresser [r⁹drèsé] *v.* to re-erect; to straighten up; to put right, to redress, to reform; to right (aviat.); to hold up [tête]; to rebuke, to reprimand; *se redresser*, to straighten up again; to stand erect again; to right oneself, to be righted.

réduction [rédüksyoⁿ] *f.* reduction; abatement, laying-off; letting-out [personnel], subjugation; reducing (mil.); mitigation (jur.).

réduire [rédüîr] *v.º* to reduce, to lessen, to abate, to diminish, to curtail; to boil down; to subjugate; to compel. *se réduire*, to be reduced, to diminish, to dwindle away; to amount (à, to). ‖ *réduit* [-üì] *m.* recess, nook, hovel; *adj.* reduced; brought to, obliged to.

réel [réèl] *adj.º* real, actual; genuine; sterling, material; *m.* reality.

réfection [réfèksyoⁿ] *f.* repairing; rebuilding, recovery.

référence [référa⁹s] *f.* reference; allusion, *pl.* references. ‖ *référer* [-é] *v.* to refer; to allude; to impute, to ascribe; *se référer*, to refer, to relate; to leave it (à, to); *s'en référer*, to confide, to trust (à, to).

référendum [référìⁿdòm] *m.* referendum.

réfléchi [réfléshì] *adj.* reflected; deliberate, reflective, thoughtful; circumspect; wary; reflexive (gramm.). ‖ *réfléchir* [-îr] *v.* to reflect; to mirror;

to reverberate; to think over, to cogitate, to ponder. || **réflecteur** [réflèktœr] m. reflector; adj. reflective. || **reflet** [rºflè] m. reflection; gleam. || **refléter** [rºflété] v. to reflect, to mirror [lumière].

réflexe [réflèks] m., adj. reflex. || **réflexion** [-yoⁿ] f. reflection; thought, consideration; reproach, imputation; *toute réflexion faite*, all things considered.

refluer [rºflüé] v. to reflow, to ebb, to surge back.

reflux [rºflü] m. ebb.

refondre [rºfoⁿdr] v. to remelt; to refit; to recast. || **refonte** [rºfoⁿt] f. recasting, refounding; recoining; remodel(l)ing, correction, repair.

réforme [réfòrm] f. reform, reformation; amendment; discharge (mil.); retirement, pension (mil.). || **réformer** [-é] v. to reform, to rectify, to amend, to improve; to pension, to discharge (mil.).

refoulement [rºfûlmaⁿ] m. repression. || **refouler** [rºfûlé] v. to drive back, to repel; to repress; to choke back.

réfractaire [réfràktèr] adj. refractory; stubborn, intractable, contumacious; m. defaulting conscript, Am. draft-dodger (mil.).

refrain [rºfriⁿ] m. refrain, chorus, burden.

refréner [rºfréné] v. to bridle, to curb, to restrain.

réfrigérateur [réfrìjérátœr] m. refrigerator; ice-box. || **réfrigérer** [réfrìjéré] v. to refrigerate.

refroidir [rºfrwàdîr] v. to chill, to cool; to check, to temper, to dispirit (fig.). || **refroidissement** [-lsmaⁿ] m. cooling, refrigeration; coldness; chill, cold (med.).

refuge [rºfüj] m. refuge, shelter, asylum; protection; pretext, (fam.) dodge. || **réfugié** [réfüjyé] m. refugee; displaced person. || **réfugier (se)** [sºréfüjyé] v. to take refuge, to take shelter; to have recourse.

refus [rºfü] m. refusal, denial; rejection. || **refuser** [-zé] v. to refuse, to reject, to deny, to decline; to withhold, to grudge, to demur; to haul ahead (naut.); to fail, to plough, Am. to flunk [candidat].

réfutation [réfütàsyoⁿ] f. refutation. || **réfuter** [réfüté] v. to refute, to confute, to disprove.

regagner [rºgàñé] v. to regain, to recover, to reach [maison].

regain [rºgiⁿ] m. aftergrowth; revival, rejuvenation (fig.).

régal [régàl] m. treat; delight. || **régaler** [-é] v. to treat to, to regale, to feast, to entertain; *se régaler,* to enjoy oneself, to have a good time.

regard [rºgàr] m. look; glance, gaze, stare; frown, scowl; notice, attention; man-hole; *en regard*, opposite, facing. || **regarder** [-dé] v. to look at, to glance at, to gaze at, to stare at; to look into, to consider; to face, to be opposite; to regard, to concern; to pay heed; *ça me regarde*, that is my own business.

régate [régàt] f. regatta.

régénérer [réjénéré] v. to regenerate.

régent [réjaⁿ] m., adj. regent. || **régenter** [-té] v. to direct; to govern; to domineer.

régie [réjî] f. administration; excise office; collection of taxes.

regimber [rºjiⁿbé] v. to kick; to balk; to jib.

régime [réjîm] m. diet; regimen; government; rules, regulations; regime, system; object, objective case (gramm.); cluster, bunch [bananes]; rate of flow [rivière].

régiment [réjìmaⁿ] m. regiment.

région [réjyoⁿ] f. region, area, sector, zone, district, territory, locality; Am. belt. || **régional** [-yònàl] adj.* local, regional. || **régionalisme** [-yònàlìsm] m. regionalism.

régir [réjîr] v. to rule, to govern, to administer. || **régisseur** [-ìsœr] m. bailiff; stage manager (theat.); assistant director [cinéma].

registre [rºjìstr] m. register, record; account-book (comm.); compass [voix].

réglage [réglàj] m. adjustment, adjusting; regulating; tuning. || **règle** [règl] f. rule; ruler; order; regularity; example; principle, law; pl. menses; *en règle*, in order, correct, regular; *règle à calcul*, slide-rule. || **réglé** [réglé] adj. ruled, lined [papier]; regular, steady, methodical; exact, fixed. || **règlement** [règlºmaⁿ] m. settlement, adjustment [comptes]; regulation, statute; ordinance, by-law, rule. || **réglementaire** [réglºmaⁿtèr] adj. regular, statutory, prescribed; reglementary. || **réglementer** [-é] v. to regulate. || **régler** [réglé] v. to rule, to line [papier]; to regulate, to order; to settle [comptes]; to set, to adjust, to time [horloge].

réglisse [réglìs] f. liquorice.

règne [rèñ] m. reign; prevalence, duration; influence; *règne animal*, animal kingdom. || **régner** [réñé] v. to reign; to rule; to hold sway, to prevail; to reach, to extend.

regorger [rºgòrjé] v. to overflow; to abound (de, in); to be glutted.

régresser [régrésé] v. to regress; to throw back.

regret [rᵉgrè] m. regret; repining, yearning; *à regret*, with reluctance, grudgingly. ‖ **regrettable** [-tàbl] adj. deplorable, regrettable. ‖ **regretter** [-té] v. to regret; to repent, to be sorry for; to lament, to grieve; to miss.

régulariser [régülàrìzé] v. to regularize. ‖ **régularité** [-ìté] f. regularity; punctuality; steadiness; equability; evenness. ‖ **régulier** [régülyé] adj.° regular; punctual, exact; systematic; steady; right, correct, in order; valid; normal; equable; orderly.

réhabiliter [réàbìlìté] v. to rehabilitate; to reinstate; to vindicate; to whitewash (fig.).

rehausser [rᵉôsé] v. to raise, to heighten; to enhance; to set off.

rein [rìⁿ] m. kidney; pl. loins; *mal aux reins*, backache, lumbago.

réincarnation [réìⁿkàrnàsyoⁿ] f. reincarnation. ‖ **réincarner** [-né] v. to reincarnate.

reine [rèn] f. queen; *reine-claude*, greengage plum; *reine-marguerite*, China aster. ‖ **reinette** [-nèt] f. rennet, pippin.

réitérer [réìtéré] v. to reiterate.

rejaillir [rᵉjàyîr] v. to rebound; to splash, to gush, to spurt, to spout; to spring, to leap out; to reflect, to recoil (*sur*, on).

rejet [rᵉjè] m. rejection; throwing out; refusal; transfer [finance]; sprout, shoot [plante]. ‖ **rejeter** [rᵉjté] v. to reject, to throw back, to refuse; to discard, to shake off; to deny, to disallow (jur.); to spurn; to send forth [plantes]; to transfer (comm.). ‖ **rejeton** [-oⁿ] m. shoot, sucker; offspring, scion.

rejoindre [rᵉjwìⁿdr] v.° to rejoin; to reunite; to overtake [rattraper]; *se rejoindre*, to meet, to join up.

réjoui [réjwì] adj. jolly, jovial, merry. ‖ **réjouir** [-îr] v. to gladden, to cheer, to make merry; to divert, to delight, to entertain; *se réjouir*, to rejoice, to be glad, to make merry, to enjoy oneself, to be delighted. ‖ **réjouissance** [-ìsaⁿs] f. rejoicing, merry-making.

relâche [rᵉlâsh] m. intermission, interruption, respite; closing (theat.); f. putting-in, calling at port (naut.). ‖ **relâché** [-é] adj. lax, relaxed, loose, slack, remiss. ‖ **relâchement** [-maⁿ] m. slackening, loosening, relaxing; laxity, remissness; intermission; abatement. ‖ **relâcher** [-é] v. to slacken, to loosen, to relax; to sag; to release, to liberate; to unbend [esprit]; to abate; to touch port.

relais [rᵉlè] m. relay; Am. hook-up [radio]; shift; relay-station; filling-station [auto].

relater [rᵉlàté] v. to relate, to recount, to tell. ‖ **relatif** [-àtìf] adj.* relative, relating, relevant, concerning; m. relative (gramm.). ‖ **relation** [-àsyoⁿ] f. relation, account, report, statement, reference; relevance; connection; communication; pl. connections; *être en relation avec*, to be connected with, to have dealings with. ‖ **relativité** [-àtìvìté] f. relativity.

relaxation [rᵉlàksàsyoⁿ] f. relaxation. ‖ **relaxer** [rᵉlàksé] v. to release, to liberate; to relax.

relayer [rᵉlèyé] v. to relay, to relieve; to take the place of; to change horses; *se relayer*, to take it in turns.

reléguer [rᵉlégé] v. to relegate, to banish, to exile; to consign.

relent [rᵉlaⁿ] m. musty taste; stale smell.

relève [rᵉlèv] f. relief, shift; relieving party. ‖ **relevé** [rᵉlᵉvé] adj. raised, erect; elevated, lofty, pungent, spicy, hot; noble, refined [ton]; m. statement. ‖ **relever** [-é] v. to raise again, to lift again; to rebuild [maison]; to pick up, to take up; to heighten, to enhance; to criticize; to remark; to spice, to season; to survey (topogr.); to depend, to be dependent (*de*, on); to stem (*de*, from); to take bearings (naut.); to relieve [garde]; *relever de maladie*, to recover.

relief [rᵉlyèf] m. relief, embossment; enhancement; pl. left-overs [repas]; *bas-relief*, bas-relief, low relief.

relier [rᵉlyé] v. to connect; to link; to join; to bind [livres]; to hoop [tonneau]. ‖ **relieur** [-yœr] m. bookbinder.

religieux [rᵉlìjyë] adj.° religious; scrupulous; m. monk, friar. ‖ **religieuse** [-ëz] f. nun, sister; double cream-puff [pâtisserie]. ‖ **religion** [-jyoⁿ] f. religion.

reliquaire [rᵉlìkèr] m. reliquary.

reliquat [rᵉlìkà] m. balance, remainder; after-effect (med.).

relique [rᵉlìk] f. relic, vestige.

reliure [rᵉlyür] f. binding [livres].

reluire [rᵉlüîr] v.° to shine, to glisten, to glitter, to gleam.

remanier [rᵉmànyé] v. to manipulate, to handle again, to modify, to alter, to revise, to recast.

remarier (se) [sᵉrᵉmàryé] v. to remarry.

remarquable [rᵉmàrkàbl] adj. remarkable, noteworthy, conspicuous, outstanding, signal. ‖ **remarque** [rᵉmàrk] f. remark, observation, notice, note; comment. ‖ **remarquer** [-é] v. to remark, to note, to observe, to notice; to distinguish.

remblayer [ranblèyé] v. to bank up.

rembourrer [ranbûré] v. to pad, to stuff, to upholster; to pack, to cram, to wad. ‖ **rembourreur** [-œr] m. © upholsterer.

remboursable [ranbûrsåbl] adj. repayable, redeemable. ‖ **remboursement** [-man] m. reimbursement, refund, repayment; contre remboursement, cash on delivery, C. O. D. ‖ **rembourser** [-é] v. to reimburse, to refund, to repay.

remède [remèd] m. remedy, medicine, cure. ‖ **remédier** [remédyé] v. to remedy, to cure, to relieve.

remémorer [remémòré] v. to remind; se remémorer, to remember, to recall.

remerciement [remèrsìman] m. thanking; gratitude; pl. thanks. ‖ **remercier** [-yé] v. to thank; to decline politely, to discharge, to dismiss; to sack, to fire, to oust.

remettre [remètr] v.* to put back; to put again, to replace, to restore, to reinstate; to put off, to delay, to postpone, to defer, to deliver, to hand over, to remit; to confide, to trust; to cure; to forgive; to recognize; se remettre, to recover one's health; to compose oneself; to recommence; to call to mind, to recollect; s'en remettre à, to rely on.

réminiscence [réminìsans] f. reminiscence, recollection.

remise [remîz] f. delivery; remittance; discount, reduction, rebate, commission (comm.); delay, deferment, postponement, remission (jur.); coach-house; shelter (naut.). ‖ **remiser** [-ìzé] v. to house; to put away [véhicule]; (fam.) to put in one's place.

rémission [rémìsyon] f. remission; abatement (med.); subsiding.

remmailler [ranmàyé] v. to graft a patch into.

remonter [remonté] v. to remount, to get up again, to climb again; to re-equip, to restock; to rise; to increase [valeur]; to date back, to have origin; to wind [horloge]; to brace up [santé]; to cheer up [quelqu'un]. ‖ **remontoir** [-twàr] m. watch-key; key.

remontrance [remontrans] f. expostulation, remonstrance, reproof. ‖ **remontrer** [-é] v. to show again; to demonstrate; to expostulate.

remords [remòr] m. remorse.

remorque [remòrk] f. towing; towline; trailer. ‖ **remorquer** [-é] v. to tow, to haul, to drag. ‖ **remorqueur** [-œr] m. tug(-boat).

rémouleur [rémûlœr] m. knife-grinder; tool-sharpener.

remous [remû] m. eddy, backwater; whirlpool; swirl; movement [foule]; public unrest.

rempailleur [ranpàyœr] m. chair-mender.

rempart [ranpàr] m. rampart; bulwark (fig.).

remplaçant [ranplàsan] m. substitute. ‖ **remplacement** [-man] m. replacing, replacement; substitution. ‖ **remplacer** [-é] v. to take the place of, to supplant; to substitute for; to replace, to supersede.

remplir [ranplîr] v. to fill; to fill again, to replenish; to cram, to stuff; to hold, to perform, to keep [fonction]; to fulfil(l) [devoir]; to occupy [temps]; to supply, to stock. ‖ **remplissage** [-ìsàj] m. filling up; padding (fig.).

remporter [ranpòrté] v. to carry back, to take back; to carry off, to take away; to get, to obtain; to win [prix, victoire].

remuer [remüé] v. to stir; to move; to rouse; to turn up; to shake [tête]; to wag [queue]; to fidget; remue-ménage, rummaging, bustle, hubbub; se remuer, to move; to bustle about.

rémunérateur, -trice [rémünéràtœr, -trìs] adj. remunerative, rewarding; profitable. ‖ **rémunération** [-àsyon] f. remuneration, payment. ‖ **rémunérer** [-é] v. to remunerate; to pay for [services].

renâcler [renâklé] v. to snort, to sniff [bête]; to shirk [besogne]; to demur, to balk, to hang back (pop.).

renaissance [renèsans] f. Renaissance, Renascence; rebirth.

renard [renàr] m. fox. ‖ **renarde** [-àrd] f. vixen.

renchérir [ranshérîr] v. to increase in price; to improve on.

rencontre [rankontr] f. meeting, encounter; engagement (mil.); discovery; coincidence. ‖ **rencontrer** [-é] v. to meet, to encounter; to experience; to chance upon; se rencontrer, to meet each other; to be met with, to be found, to tally, to agree.

rendement [randman] m. output, yield, production; efficiency.

rendez-vous [randévû] m. appointment, rendez-vous, date, engagement; place of resort, haunt; meeting-place.

rendre [randr] v. to render, to return, to restore, to give back; to repay, to refund; to bring in, to yield, to produce; to make, to cause to be; to vomit; to void; to exhale, to emit; to express, to convey; to translate;

to give [verdict]; to bear [témoignage]; to do [hommage]; to pay [visite, honneur]. to dispense [justice]. to issue [arrêt]. *rendre l'âme* to die. to give up the ghost. *rendre service,* to be of service. *rendre compte,* to render an account. *se rendre,* to go oneself. to surrender, to yield, to capitulate; *se rendre compte de,* to realize, *se rendre compte de,* to realize, to be aware of.

rêne [rèn] *f* rein.

renfermé [rɑⁿfèrmé] *adj.* self-contained shut up, closed in; *m.* mustiness. ‖ **renfermer** [-é] *v* to shut up, to lock up, to confine; to enclose, to contain. to include; to conceal.

renfler [rɑⁿflé] *v.* to swell, to bulge.

renflouer [rɑⁿflué] *v.* to refloat, to raise; to pull off the rocks [affaire].

renfoncement [rɑⁿfɔⁿsmɑⁿ] *m.* denting in knocking in. recess, dint, dent.

renforcer [rɑⁿfɔrsé] *v.* to reinforce, to strengthen to augment, to increase; to intensify (phot.). ‖ **renfort** [-ɔr] *m.* reinforcement, strengthening piece; help, aid.

renfrogner (se) [sᵉrɑⁿfrɔñé] *v.* to frown, to scowl.

rengaine [rɑⁿgèn] *f.* catch-phrase; *la même rengaine.* the same old story.

rengorger (se) [sᵉrɑⁿgɔrjé] *v.* to puff up one's chest. to give oneself airs.

reniement [rᵉnìmɑⁿ] *m.* denying; disavowal, denial; disavowing. ‖ **renier** [rᵉnyé] *v.* to deny; to disown, to disavow; to abjure, to forswear.

reniflement [rᵉnìflᵉmɑⁿ] *m.* sniff; snuffling. **renifler** [rᵉnìflé] *v.* to sniff, to snuffle, to snivel; to spurn (fig.).

renne [rèn] *m.* reindeer.

renom [rᵉnɔⁿ] *m* renown, fame, celebrity ‖ **renommé** [-ômé] *adj.* renowned, noted, famed. ‖ **renommée** [-ômé] *f* renown, fame, reputation, celebrity

renoncement [rᵉnɔⁿsmɑⁿ] *m.* renouncement renunciation; abnegation; repudiation ‖ **renoncer** [-é] *v.* to renounce to relinquish, to swear off, to abjure. to repudiate to recant, to retract. to disavow to waive, to disown, to disclaim. to give up [succession] to abdicate [trône]. ‖ **renonciation** [-yàsyoⁿ] *f.* renunciation.

renoncule [rᵉnɔⁿkül] *f.* ranunculus.

renouer [rᵉnûé] *v.* to take up again; to renew to resume.

renouveau [rᵉnûvô] *m.?* springtime; renewal ‖ **renouveler** [-lé] *v.* to renew, to renovate, to revive; to regenerate; to recommence, to repeat. ‖ **renouvellement** [-èlmɑⁿ] *m.* renewal, renovation; increase, redoubling.

rénover [rénôvé] *v.* to renew, to renovate to revive

renseignement [rɑⁿsèñmɑⁿ] *m.* information knowledge. intelligence, account *bureau de renseignements, Am.* information booth *Br* inquiry office. **renseigner** [-é] *v* to inform, to give information to teach again; to direct *se renseigner,* to inquire, to obtain information

rente [rɑⁿt] *f* yearly income, revenue; stock fund annuity rent, profit; *rente viagère* life endowment, annuity. ‖ **rentier** [-yé] *m* stockholder, investor annuitant

rentrée [rɑⁿtré] *f.* re-entrance, re-entering reopening reappearance; gathering, in [récolte] warehousing [marchandise] collection [impôts] reappearance return [acteur] ‖ **rentrer** [-é] *v.* to re-enter to come in again; to collect [impôts] to gather in [récolte]; to take in to be contained, to be comprehended to stifle. to suppress [rire]; to indent (typogr.).

renversement [rɑⁿvèrsᵉmɑⁿ] *m.* reversing overturning overthrow; upsetting confusion disorder. upheaval. ‖ **renverser** [-é] *v* to throw down, to turn upside down. to upset, to overthrow, to overturn to spill [liquide]; to throw into disorder. to confuse, to amaze to stupefy to transpose; to reverse [vapeur]. to drive back, to rout; to invert (math mus.); to defeat, to turn out [ministère]; to stagger (fam.). *se renverser,* to overturn, to capsize. to upset. to turn over.

renvoi [rɑⁿvwà] *m* returning, sending back sending away. dismissal, discharge sacking firing. referring [question] adjournment [parlement]; remand (jur.) belch reflection [lumière] echo reverberation [bruit]; repeat (mus.) ‖ **renvoyer** [-yé] *v.* to send back to return, to dismiss, to discharge to fire to refer [affaire]; to dismiss [ministre]. to reject, to refuse; to refer [question] to remand (jur.); to adjourn to postpone, to defer; to reflect [lumière], to echo, to reverberate [bruit]

repaire [rᵉpèr] *m.* den; haunt; nest; hide-out

repaître (se) [sᵉrᵉpètr] *v.* to feed (*de,* on)

répandre [répɑⁿdr] *v.* to pour, to shed, to spill to spread, to diffuse, to distribute to scatter, to screw; to propagate *se répandre,* to go out, to go about to spread over; to be profuse to spread; to gain ground.

réparable [réparàbl] *adj.* reparable. mendable. remediable, *Am.* fixable. ‖ **réparateur, -trice** [-àtœr, -trɪs] *adj.* reparative; restorative, refreshing *m.*, *f.* repairer; restorer; *Am.* fixer. ‖ **réparation** [-àsyon] *f.* reparation; repair, mending, *Am.* fixing; amends, atonement, satisfaction [honneur]. ‖ **réparer** [-é] *v.* to repair, to mend, *Am.* to fix; to make amends for; to retrieve [pertes]; to redress [torts]; to recruit, to restore [forces].

repartie [r•pàrtî] *f.* repartee, retort, rejoinder, reply.

répartir [répàrtîr] *v.* to divide, to distribute, to portion out; to assess. ‖ **répartition** [-ìsyon] *f.* distribution, division; allotment; assessment.

repas [r•pâ] *m.* meal, repast.

repassage [r•pàsàj] *m.* repassing, ironing, pressing [vêtements]; grinding, sharpening [coutellerie]. ‖ **repasser** [-é] *v.* to repass; to call again; to iron, to press; to grind, to sharpen, to whet; to hone [pierre]; to strop [cuir]; to review; to revise; to ponder.

repentir [r•pantîr] *m.* repentance, remorse; regret, contrition, compunction; *se repentir*, *v.** to repent, to be sorry, to regret.

répercussion [répèrküsyon] *f.* repercussion, reverberation; consequence, after-effect. ‖ **répercuter** [-üté] *v.* to reverberate, to echo, to resound.

repère [r•pèr] *m.* reference; mark; landmark; *point de repère*, guide mark, landmark; blaze [arbre]. ‖ **repérer** [-éré] *v.* to mark; to locate, to discover; to blaze.

répertoire [répèrtwàr] *m.* index, card-file, catalog(ue); repertory, repository; directory; stock (theat.).

répéter [répété] *v.* to repeat, to retell; to rehearse (theat.); to reproduce (jur.). ‖ **répétiteur, -trice** [-ìtœr, -trìs] *m.*, *f.* tutor, coach, private teacher; assistant teacher; repeater (telegr.). ‖ **répétition** [-ìsyon] *f.* reiteration, repetition; rehearsal; recurrence, reproduction; private lesson; *répétition générale*, dress rehearsal.

repeupler [r•pœplé] *v.* to repeople, repopulate; to restock; to replant.

répit [répì] *m.* respite, delay, pause; breather; reprieve (jur.).

replet [r•plè] *adj.* fat, bulky.

repli [r•plì] *m.* fold, crease; winding, coil (fig.). ‖ **replier** [-yé] *v.* to fold again, to fold back; to double back; to bend back; to coil [corde]; to force back (mil.); *se replier*, to twist oneself, to fold oneself; to wind, to coil; to writhe; to fall back, to retreat (mil.).

réplique [réplìk] *f.* reply, answer, response, retort, rejoinder, *Am.* comeback (fam.); repeat (mus.); cue (theat.); replica [art]; *donner la réplique*, to give the cue, *Am.* to play the stooge (theat.). ‖ **répliquer** [-é] *v.* to reply, to respond, to retort.

répondant [réponda•n] *m.* respondent; defendant (jur.); security, guarantee. ‖ **répondre** [répondr] *v.* to answer, to respond, to reply; to satisfy, to come up to; to correspond; *répondre de*, to warrant, to be answerable for, to vouch for, to be responsible for, to go bail for. ‖ **réponse** [-ons] *f.* answer, reply, response; rejoinder (jur.).

report [r•pòr] *m.* carrying forward, bringing forward (comm.); carry over [montant]; continuation [Bourse]. ‖ **reportage** [-tàj] *m.* reporting, commentary. ‖ **reporter** [-tèr] *m.* reporter. ‖ **reporter** [-té] *v.* to carry forward (comm.); to carry over [Bourse]; to carry back, to take back; *se reporter*, to refer, to go back, to be carried back [par la mémoire].

repos [r•pô] *m.* rest, repose; quiet, peace, tranquility; sleep; pause (mus.); half-cock [fusil]; *valeur de tout repos*, gilt-edged security. ‖ **reposé** [-pòzé] *adj.* rested, reposed, refreshed; quiet, calm; *à tête reposée*, at leisure. ‖ **reposer** [-zé] *v.* to place again, to set back; to rest, to repose; to refresh; to be based, to be established; to be inactive, to be out of use; to lie fallow [terre]; *se reposer*, to rest; to rely; to alight, to light [oiseaux]; *se reposer sur*, to put one's trust in. ‖ **reposoir** [-zwàr] *m.* temporary altar.

repoussant [r•pûsan] *adj.* repulsive, disgusting, repugnant, offensive, repellent, loathsome; forbidding. ‖ **repoussé** [-é] *adj.* embossed. ‖ **repousser** [-é] *v.* to push again; to drive back, to beat back, to repel; to thrust away, to push aside; to reject, to spurn; to repulse; to rebuff; to grow again, to sprout; to recoil, to kick [fusil]; to deny [accusation]; to decline [offre]; to put off, to postpone [rendez-vous]. ‖ **repoussoir** [-wàr] *m.* driving-bolt, starting-bolt; dentist's punch; set-off, contrast [tableau]; foil [personne].

répréhensible [répréansìbl] *adj.* reprehensible; censurable.

reprendre [r•prandr] *v.** to retake, to recapture, to get back, to recover; to resume, to begin again; to revive; to reprove, to criticize; to repair; to reply; to take root again; to freeze again.

représailles [r•prézàyl] *f. pl.* reprisal, retaliation; *user de représailles*, to retaliate.

représentant [r•prézanta•n] *m.* representative, deputy, delegate; agent (comm.), salesman. ‖ **représentatif** [-àtìf] *adj.** representative. ‖ **représentation** [-àsyon] *f.* representation;

exhibition, display; performance, show (theat.); remonstrance; agency, branch (comm.). ‖ **représenter** [-é] v. to represent; to exhibit, to produce; to perform [pièce]; to depict, to portray, to describe; to typify, to symbolize.

répression [réprèsyoⁿ] f. repression.

réprimande [réprìmɑⁿd] f. reprimand, reproach. ‖ **réprimander** [-é] v. to reprimand, to reprove, to rebuke, to reproach, to chide, to upbraid; to blow up (fam.).

réprimer [réprìmé] v. to repress, to restrain, to curb, to stifle.

repris [r⁰prì] adj. retaken, taken up again; reset [os]; repris de justice, old offender, Br. old lag (pop.), Am. repeater. ‖ **reprise** [-ìz] f. resumption; retaking, recapture; revival, renewal; return [maladie]; repair, darn, mending [couture]; chorus, refrain (mus.); underpinning [construction]; game [cartes]; bout; round; resumption of play [sport]; pick-up [autom.]. ‖ **repriser** [-ìzé] v. to darn, to mend.

réprobateur, -trice [réprⁱbàtœr, -trìs] adj. reprobative, reproachful, reproving. ‖ **réprobation** [-àsyoⁿ] f. reprobation, reproval, censure.

reproche [r⁰prⁱsh] m. reproach, rebuke, reproof; taunt; sans reproche, blameless, unexceptionable. ‖ **reprocher** [-é] v. to reproach with; to blame for; to upbraid; to challenge (jur.); reprocher à quelqu'un d'avoir fait quelque chose, to reproach someone with having done something.

reproduction [r⁰prⁱdüksyoⁿ] f. reproduction; replica, copy. ‖ **reproduire** [-üîr] v.* to reproduce; to reprint; se reproduire, to be reproduced; to reproduce; to multiply; to breed; to recur, to happen again, to occur again.

réprouver [réprⁱvé] v. to reprobate; to disapprove of; to damn, to cast off (theol.).

reptation [rèptàsyoⁿ] f. reptation. ‖ **reptile** [rèptⁱl] m. reptile.

repu [r⁰pü] adj. satiated, glutted, sated, full.

républicain [répüblìkⁱⁿ] m., adj. republican. ‖ **république** [-ìk] f. republic.

répudier [répüdyé] v. to repudiate.

répugnance [répüfiaⁿs] f. repugnance, loathing, repulsion; reluctance, unwillingness; avoir de la répugnance à, to be loath to. ‖ **répugnant** [-aⁿ] adj. repulsive, repugnant, repellent, distasteful, loathsome. ‖ **répugner** [-é] v. to be repugnant; to inspire repugnance; to feel repugnance, to feel loath; to be contrary to.

répulsion [répülsyoⁿ] f. repulsion, beating back; disgust, loathing.

réputation [répütàsyoⁿ] f. reputation, character; good repute, fame; avoir la réputation de, to pass for. ‖ **réputer** [-é] v. to esteem, to repute, to account, to deem.

requérir [r⁰kérîr] v* to request; to require, to exact, to demand; to claim, to summon. ‖ **requête** [-èt] f. request, petition, demand, application; address, suit (jur.).

requin [r⁰kⁱⁿ] m. shark.

requis [r⁰kⁱ] adj. required, requisite; proper, necessary. ‖ **réquisition** [rékìzìsyoⁿ] f. requisition; summons, levy, demand; seizure. ‖ **réquisitionner** [-ìsyôné] v. to requisition, to commandeer; to seize. ‖ **réquisitoire** [-ìtwàr] m. indictment, list of charges; requisitory; stream of reproaches (fam.).

rescapé [rèskàpé] adj. rescued; m. survivor.

rescousse [rèskûs] f. rescue; help.

réseau [rézô] m.* net; network; web, complication (fig.); system [radio, rail]; tracery (arch.); réseau de barbelés, barbed wire entanglements; réseau de résistance, resistance group.

réserve [rézèrv] f. reserve; reservation, caution, wariness, prudence; modesty, shyness; stock, store, supply; storehouse; preserve [gibier]. ‖ **réserver** [-é] v. to reserve; to keep, to intend; to lay by; to book [places]; se réserver, to hedge. ‖ **réserviste** [-ìst] m. reservist. ‖ **réservoir** [-wàr] m. reservoir; tank, cistern, well.

résidence [rézìdaⁿs] f. residence, residency; dwelling; house; place of abode; residentship. ‖ **résident** [-aⁿ] m. resident; representative [diplomate]. ‖ **résider** [-é] v. to reside, to dwell; to lie, to consist.

résidu [rézìdü] m. residue; remnant; remainder, balance [math.]; amount owing (comm.). ‖ **résiduel** [-èl] adj.* residual; supplemental.

résignation [rézìfiàsyoⁿ] f. resignation; relinquishment, renunciation. ‖ **résigner** [-é] v. to resign; to relinquish, to renounce, to give up, to abdicate; se résigner, to resign oneself, to be resigned; to submit, to put up (à, with).

résiliation [rézìlyàsyoⁿ] f. cancelling, abrogation, annulment, invalidation; deletion; rescission. ‖ **résilier** [-yé] v. to cancel, to annul; to delete.

résille [rézîy] f. hair-net; lattice work.

résine [rézîn] f. resin. ‖ **résineux** [-ë] adj.* resinous.

résistance [rézìstaⁿs] *f.* resistance; opposition underground forces [guerre] ‖ **résistant** [-aⁿ] *adj* resistant, unyielding lasting, sturdy, tough. ‖ **résister** [-é] *v* to resist, to oppose, to withstand, to endure, to bear; to hold out

résolu [rézòlü] *p. p. of* résoudre; *adj.* resolved, determined, decided; resolute; solved ‖ **résolution** [-syoⁿ] *f.* resolution decision, determination; resolve solution, reduction, conversion annulment (jur.). ‖ **résolutoire** [-twàr] *adj* resolutory.

résonance [rézònaⁿs] *f.* resonance; repercussion ‖ **résonateur** [rézònàtœr] *m.* resonator ‖ **résonnement** [-maⁿ] *m.* resounding re-echoing, vibration. ‖ **résonner** [-é] *v* to resound; to reverberate, to re-echo; to vibrate; to twang; to ring, to rattle.

résorber [rézòrbé] *v.* to reabsorb; to absorb to imbibe.

résoudre [rézûdr] *v.** to resolve; to solve, to settle [question]; to decide upon, to determine upon; to dissolve, to melt, to break down; to annul (jur.); *se* **résoudre,** to make up one's mind (*à.* to).

respect [rèspè] *m.* respect, regard, deference awe; reverence. ‖ **respectable** [rèspèktàbl] *adj.* respectable, estimable hono(u)rable, reputable. ‖ **respecter** [-é] *v* to respect, to revere, to hono(u)r, to venerate.

respectif [rèspèktìf] *adj.** respective.

respectueux [rèspèktüé] *adj.** respectful, deferential, dutiful [enfant].

respiration [rèspìràsyoⁿ] *f.* respiration, breathing. ‖ **respirer** [-é] *v.* to respire to breathe; to inhale.

resplendir [rèsplaⁿdìr] *v.* to shine brightly to be resplendent; to gleam. ‖ **resplendissante** [-ìsaⁿ] *adj.* resplendent, bright glittering.

responsabilité [rèspoⁿsàbìlìté] *f.* responsibility, accountability; liability (comm.) ‖ **responsable** [-àbl] *adj.* responsible. accountable, answerable; liable (comm.).

resquille [rèskíy] *f.* wangling. ‖ **resquilleur** [rèskìyœr] *m.* gatecrasher; wangler wide boy.

ressac [rⁱ•sàk] *m.* surf.

ressaisir [rⁱ•sèzìr] *v.* to seize again, to catch again; to recover possession of.

ressasser [rⁱ•sàsé] *v.* to harp on.

ressemblance [rⁱ•saⁿblaⁿs] *f.* likeness, resemblance, similarity. ‖ **ressemblant** [-aⁿ] *adj.* like, similar to; resembling ‖ **ressembler** [-é] *v.* to resemble, to look like, to be similar to, to take after;

se **ressembler,** to look alike, to resemble each other; to be similar.

ressemelage [rⁱ•sⁱmlà] *m.* resoling. ‖ **ressemeler** [-é] *v* to resole.

ressentiment [rⁱ•saⁿtìmaⁿ] *m.* resentment ‖ **ressentir** [-ìr] *v.** to feel, to experience to resent, *se* **ressentir,** to feel the effects to resent; to be felt.

resserrer [rⁱ•sèré] *v* to draw closer, to bind tighter, to coop up, to pen in; to restrain to confine; to condense, to compress, to contract.

ressort [rⁱ•sòr] *m.* spring; elasticity, rebound, resiliency; incentive; spur; energy.

ressort [rⁱ•sòr] *m.* jurisdiction; department province (fig.).

ressortir [rⁱ•sòrtìr] *v.** to go out again, to re-exit; to stand out (fig.); to arise, to proceed, to result [de, from]; *faire* **ressortir,** to throw into relief, to point up.

ressortir à [rⁱ•sòrtìr] *v.* to be under the jurisdiction of, to be dependent on.

ressource [rⁱ•sûrs] *f.* resource, expedient, shift, resort, contrivance; *pl.* funds means

ressusciter [rⁱ•süsìté] *v.* to resuscitate, to revive, to resurrect.

restant [rèstaⁿ] *adj.* remaining, surviving, left; *m.* remainder, rest, residue

restaurant [rèstòraⁿ] *m.* restaurant, eating-place ‖ **restaurateur** [-àtœr] *m.* restaurant-keeper restorer [arts]. ‖ **restaurer** [-é] *v* to restore, to refresh; to repair; to re-establish; *se* **restaurer,** to refresh oneself, to take refreshment, to refresh the inner man.

reste [rèst] *m* rest, remainder, residue; trace, vestige; *pl.* remnants, leavings, remains, scraps; relics; leftovers [nourriture]; mortal remains, dead body, *du reste, au reste,* besides, furthermore, moreover; *de reste,* spare, remaining, over and above. ‖ **rester** [-é] *v* to remain, to stay; to be left; to dwell, to continue.

restituer [rèstìtüé] *v.* to return, to refund, to repay; to restore [textes]. ‖ **restitution** [-üsyoⁿ] *f.* restoration, restitution, repayment, returning, handing back.

restreindre [rèstrìⁿdr] *v.** to restrain, to confine, to circumscribe; to limit, to restrict, to stint, to curb, to inhibit. ‖ **restriction** [-ìksyoⁿ] *f.* restriction, restraint, reserve; limitation, curb, check; austerity; *restriction mentale,* mental reservation.

résultat [rézültà] *m.* result, outcome, sequel, upshot; returns [élection]. ‖ **résulter** [-é] *v.* to result, to follow, to ensue.

résumé [rézümé] *m.* summary, summing-up ; recapitulation ; précis ; outline ; *en résumé*, on the whole, after all. ‖ *résumer* [-é] *v.* to sum up ; to give a summary of ; to recapitulate ; to outline.

résurrection [rézürèksyoⁿ] *f.* resurrection ; restoral, revival ; resuscitation.

retable [rɘtàbl] *m.* retable, reredos, altar-piece.

rétablir [rétàblîr] *v.* to re-establish, to set up again ; to restore ; to repair ; to recover [santé] ; to reinstate ; to retrieve ; *se rétablir*, to recover, to get back on one's feet ; to be re-established, to be restored ; to be repaired. ‖ *rétablissement* [-lsmaⁿ] *m.* re-establishment, restoration ; repair ; recovery, reinstatement ; return to health ; revival (comm.).

rétamer [rétámé] *v.* to tin over again, to re-plate ; to re-silver. ‖ *rétameur* [-œr] *m.* tinker.

retard [rɘtàr] *m.* delay, lateness ; slowness [horloge] ; retardation (mus.) ; *être en retard*, to be late. ‖ *retardataire* [-dàtèr] *m.*, *f.* laggard, lagger, loiterer ; defaulter ; late-comer. ‖ *retardement* [-dɘmaⁿ] *m.* retardment ; delay ; putting-off ; *à retardement*, delayed-action [bombe]. ‖ *retarder* [-dé] *v.* to delay, to retard, to defer ; to put back, to set back [horloge] ; to be slow ; to lose time [horloge] ; to be behindhand [personne].

retenir [rɘtnîr] *v.** to hold back ; to retain ; to withhold ; to reserve, to book [places] ; to moderate, to restrain, to curb ; to hinder, to prevent, to hold up ; to carry (math.) ; to engage, to hire ; *se retenir*, to control oneself ; to refrain, to forbear ; to catch hold [à, of], to cling [à, to].

retentir [rɘtaⁿtîr] *v.* to resound, to ring ; to have repercussions ; to rattle. ‖ *retentissant* [-lsaⁿ] *adj.* resounding, echoing ; sonorous. ‖ *retentissement* [-lsmaⁿ] *m.* resounding ; repercussion.

retenu [rɘtnü] *adj.* reserved, discreet ; detained, help up ; booked [place]. ‖ *retenue* [-ü] *f.* reserve ; discretion ; self-control ; detention, keeping in ; stoppage [paie] ; deduction ; carry-over (math.).

réticence [rétïsaⁿs] *f.* reticence, reserve, concealment. ‖ *réticent* [-saⁿ] *adj.* reticent ; hesitant.

rétif [rétif] *adj.** restive, unmanageable ; stubborn ; balky [cheval].

retiré [rɘtîré] *adj.* secluded, sequestered ; retired ; withdrawn. ‖ *retirer* [-é] *v.* to draw again ; to pull back, to withdraw ; to take out, to draw out ; to take away ; to remove, to take off [vêtement] ; to derive, to reap, to get [bénéfice] ; to redeem [dégager] ; *se*

retirer, to withdraw, to retire, to retreat ; to subside, to recede ; to shrink, to contract.

retombée [rɘtoⁿbé] *f.* fall ; fall-out ; springing. ‖ *retomber* [-é] *v.* to fall again ; to fall back.

rétorquer [rétòrké] *v.* to retort, to return [argument] ; to cast back, to hurl back [accusation].

retors [rɘtòr] *adj.* twisted ; artful, crafty, wily, sly.

retouche [rɘtûsh] *f.* retouch, retouching. ‖ *retoucher* [-é] *v.* to retouch ; to touch up, to improve.

retour [rɘtûr] *m.* return ; repetition, recurrence ; change, vicissitude ; reverse ; angle, elbow (arch.) ; reversion (jur.) ; *être de retour*, to be back ; *retour du courrier*, return mail ; *sans retour*, forever, irretrievably ; *retour de flamme*, backfire [moteur] ; *sur le retour*, on the decline. ‖ *retournement* [-nɘmaⁿ] *m.* turning over. ‖ *retourner* [-né] *v.* to return, to go back ; to send back ; to turn over ; to turn up [cartes] ; to think about ; *se retourner*, to turn around ; to veer round.

retracer [rɘtràsé] *v.* to retrace ; to relate ; to recall.

rétracter [rétràkté] *v.* to retract, to disavow, to revoke ; *se rétracter*, to recant ; to retract.

retrait [rɘtrè] *m.* withdrawal.

retraite [rɘtrèt] *f.* retreat ; retirement ; pension ; seclusion, privacy ; shrinking, contraction ; *battre en retraite*, to beat a retreat ; *prendre sa retraite*, to retire. ‖ *retraité* [-é] *adj.* pensioned off, superannuated ; *m.* pensioner.

retranchement [rɘtraⁿshmaⁿ] *m.* retrenchment, abridgment ; entrenchment (mil.). ‖ *retrancher* [-é] *v.* to retrench, to curtail, to cut short ; to cut off ; to diminish ; to subtract, to deduct (math.) ; to entrench (mil.) ; *se retrancher*, to retrench ; to entrench oneself, to dig in (mil.) ; to hedge, to take refuge.

rétréci [rétrésï] *adj.* shrunk, contracted ; restricted ; narrow, cramped. ‖ *rétrécir* [-îr] *v.* to narrow ; to shrink, to contract ; to take in, to straiten ; *se rétrécir*, to shrink, to contract ; to grow narrower. ‖ *rétrécissement* [-ïsmaⁿ] *m.* shrinking ; narrowing ; cramping ; stricture (med.).

rétribuer [rétribüé] *v.* to remunerate, to pay. ‖ *rétribution* [-üsyoⁿ] *f.* salary, pay ; recompense.

rétroactif [rétròàktïf] *adj.** retroactive.

rétrocéder [rétròsédé] *v.* to retrocede, to cede back ; to recede, to go back. ‖ *rétrocession* [-èsyoⁿ] *f.* retrocession ; recession.

rétrograde [rétrògràd] *adj.* retrograde, backward; *s.* back number. ‖ **rétrograder** [-dé] *v.* to retrograde; to reduce to a lower rank.

rétrospectif [rétròspèktìf] *adj.*[*] retrospective. ‖ **rétrospective** [-tìv] *f.* retrospect.

retroussé [r°trûsé] *adj.* turned up; tucked up; snub [nez]. ‖ **retrousser** [-é] *v.* to turn up; to tuck up; to curl up; to roll up.

retrouver [r°trûvé] *v.* to find again, to regain, to recover; *se retrouver,* to meet again.

rétroviseur [rétròvìzœr] *m.* reflector; rear-vision mirror, driving-mirror [auto].

rets [rè] *m.* net; snare; *pl.* toils (fig.).

réuni [réünì] *adj.* reunited; assembled; gathered; joined. ‖ **réunion** [-yon] *f.* reunion; meeting, assembly, party, gathering; junction; collection; reconciliation. ‖ **réunir** [-îr] *v.* to reunite; to bring together again; to gather, to assemble, to muster; to join; to collect; to reconcile; *se réunir,* to reunite, to assemble again; to meet, to gather.

réussi [réüsì] *adj.* successful, well-executed. ‖ **réussir** [-îr] *v.* to succeed, to be successful (*à,* in); to prosper, to thrive; to carry out well, to accomplish successfully. ‖ **réussite** [-ìt] *f.* success; solitaire, patience [cartes].

revanche [r°va°sh] *f.* revenge; retaliation, requital; return; return-match; *en revanche,* in return.

rêvasser [rèvàsé] *v.* to day-dream; to be wool-gathering. ‖ **rêve** [rèv] *m.* dream; illusion; idle fancy; *c'est le rêve,* it's ideal.

rêvche [r°vèsh] *adj.* harsh, rough; cross, crabby, peevish.

réveil [révèy] *m.* waking, awaking, awakening; alarm-clock; disillusionment (fig.); reveille (mil.). ‖ **réveiller** [-èyé] *v.* to awaken, to awake, to wake, to arouse; to rouse up, to stir up, to quicken; to revive, to recall; *se réveiller,* to awake, to awaken, to wake up; to be roused. ‖ **réveillon** [-èyo°] *m.* midnight supper. ‖ **réveillonner** [-òné] *v.* to go to a reveillon; to see the New Year in.

révélateur, -trice [révélàtœr, -trìs] *m., f.* developer (phot.), *m.;* revealer, informer; *adj.* revealing; significant. ‖ **révélation** [-àsyo°] *f.* revelation, discovery, disclosure; avowal; information (jur.). ‖ **révéler** [-é] *v.* to reveal, to discover, to disclose; to develop (phot.).

revenant [r°vna°] *m.* ghost, spirit, specter, phantom.

revendeur [r°va°dœr] *m.* retail dealer, peddler.

revendicateur, -trice [r°va°dìkàtœr, -trìs] *m., f.* claimant. ‖ **revendication** [-àsyo°] *f.* claim, demand; claiming, reclaiming. ‖ **revendiquer** [-é] *v.* to claim, to claim back; to insist on; to assume [responsabilité].

revenir [r°vnîr] *v.*[*] to come again, to come back, to return; to recur; to reappear, to haunt [fantôme]; to begin again; to recover, to revive, to come to; to cost; to amount to; to accrue [bénéfices]; to recant, to withdraw, to retract; *revenir à soi,* to recover, to regain consciousness; *faire revenir,* to half-cook [cuisine]; *je n'en reviens pas,* I can't believe it, I can't get over it. ‖ **revenu** [-ü] *m.* income, revenue.

rêver [rêvé] *v.* to dream; to muse; to rave, to be light-headed; to ponder; to long, to yearn (*de,* for).

réverbération [révèrbérásyo°] *f.* reverberation; reflecting. ‖ **réverbère** [-èr] *m.* street lamp; reverberator.

révérence [révéra°s] *f.* reverence; veneration, awe; curtsy, bow.

rêverie [rèvrî] *f.* reverie, dreaming, musing; raving.

revers [r°vèr] *m.* back, reverse, wrong side, other side; counterpart; lapel, revers [vêtement]; turn-up [pantalon]; cuff [manche]; top [botte]; back-hand stroke [tennis]; misfortune, setback (fig.).

réversible [révèrsìbl] *adj.* revertible [bien]; reversible [tissu].

revêtement [r°vètma°] *m.* revetment, lining, facing, casing [maçonnerie]; retaining wall; veneering. ‖ **revêtir** [r°vètîr] *v.*[*] to clothe again; to put on, to don; to dress, to array; to invest with, to endow with; to assume [personnage]; to cloak (fig.).

rêveur [rêvœr] *adj.*[*] dreaming; dreamy, pensive; *m.* dreamer, muser.

revient [r°vyì°] *m.* cost.

revirement [r°vìrma°] *m.* tacking, tack; sudden turn; transfer (comm.).

réviser [révìzé] *v.* to revise, to review, to examine; to review (jur.); to overhaul [autom.]. ‖ **révision** [-yo°] *f.* revisal, revision, review, re-examination; rehearing (jur.); proof-reading; *conseil de révision, Br.* recruiting board, *Am.* draft board.

revivifier [r°vìvìfyé] *v.* to revivify, to revive.

revivre [r°vìvr] *v.* to live again; to revive.

révocable [révòkàbl] *adj.* revocable, rescindable. ‖ **révocation** [-àsyo°] *f.* revocation; annulment, repeal, cancellation, countermanding; dismissal, removal [fonctionnaire].

revoir [r°vwàr] *v.*[*] to see again; to meet again; to revise, to review, to re-examine; *au revoir*, good-bye; *se revoir*, to meet each other again.

révoltant [révòltaⁿ] *adj.* revolting; shocking, offensive. ‖ *révolte* [révòlt] *f.* revolt, rebellion, mutiny. ‖ *révolté* [-é] *m.* rebel, mutineer, insurgent. ‖ *révolter* [-é] *v.* to cause to revolt; to rouse, to excite; to shock, to disgust, to horrify; *se révolter*, to revolt, to rebel, to mutiny.

révolu [révòlü] *adj.* revolved; accomplished, completed; elapsed, ended. ‖ *révolution* [-syoⁿ] *f.* revolution; revolving; rotation. ‖ *révolutionnaire* [-syònèr] *adj.* revolutionary; *m., f.* revolutionist. ‖ *révolutionner* [-syòné] *v.* to revolutionize; to upset.

revolver [révòlvèr] *m.* revolver, pistol; *poche à revolver*, hip-pocket. ‖ *révolvériser* [-rizé] *v.* (pop.) to shoot up.

révoquer [révòké] *v.* to revoke; to rescind, to countermand; to repeal, to annul; to dismiss, to recall [fonctionnaire].

revue [revü] *f.* review; survey, examination, revision; magazine, periodical publication; critical article; topical revue, *Am.* musical comedy (theat.); *passer en revue*, to review.

révulser [révülsé] *v.* to distort; to twist; to turn upwards [yeux]. ‖ *révulsif* [-sìf] *adj.*,* m.* revulsive. ‖ *révulsion* [-syoⁿ] *f.* revulsion.

rez-de-chaussée [rédshòsé] *m.* ground-level; ground-floor, *Am.* first floor.

rhinocéros [rìnòséròs] *m.* rhinoceros.

rhubarbe [rübàrb] *f.* rhubarb.

rhum [ròm] *m.* rum.

rhumatisme [rümàtìsm] *m.* rheumatism.

rhume [rüm] *m.* cold.

riant [rìaⁿ] *adj.* laughing, smiling, cheerful, pleasant, pleasing.

ricanement [rìkàn°maⁿ] *m.* sneering. ‖ *ricaner* [rìkàné] *v.* to sneer; to snigger; to grin; to giggle.

riche [rìsh] *adj.* rich, wealthy, opulent; abundant, copious; precious, costly, valuable; *m.* rich person; *pl.* the rich. ‖ *richesse* [-ès] *f.* riches, wealth, opulence; copiousness; richness, costliness.

ricin [rìsìⁿ] *m.* castor-oil plant; *huile de ricin*, castor-oil.

ricocher [rìkòshé] *v.* to rebound; to ricochet. ‖ *ricochet* [-è] *m.* ducks and drakes [jeu]; ricochet (mil.); series, chain, succession; *par ricochet*, indirectly.

ride [rìd] *f.* wrinkle, line; pucker; ripple; corrugation; lanyard (naut.). ‖ *ridé* [rìdé] *adj.* wrinkled, lined; puckered; rippled; shrivelled [pomme].

rideau [rìdô] *m.** curtain, drapery; screen; *rideau de fer*, iron curtain; *rideau de fumée*, smoke-screen; *lever le rideau*, curtain-raiser (theat.).

rider [rìdé] *v.* to wrinkle; to pucker; to ripple, to ruffle; to shrivel.

ridicule [rìdìkül] *adj.* ridiculous, laughable, ludicrous; absurd; *m.* ridicule, ridiculousness; quirk, whim. ‖ *ridiculiser* [-ìzé] *v.* to ridicule, to deride, to poke fun at.

rien [ryìⁿ] *m.* nothing, nought, not anything; anything; trifle, mere nothing; love [tennis]; *cela ne fait rien*, it doesn't matter; *de rien*, don't mention it.

rieur [ryœr] *adj.** laughing, joking; mocking; *m.* laugher.

rigide [rìjìd] *adj.* rigid, stiff; firm; erect; taut, tense; strict, severe; unbending, unyielding. ‖ *rigidité* [-ìdìté] *f.* rigidity, stiffness; sternness; harshness; strictness, severity.

rigolade [rìgòlàd] *f.* (pop.) laughter; tomfoolery.

rigole [rìgòl] *f.* channel, trench, small ditch; drain; gutter; furrow. ‖ *rigoler* [-é] *v.* to furrow; to channel; (fam.) to laugh, to have fun, to be merry; *rigolo* (pop.), funny, jolly.

rigoureux [rìgürê] *adj.** rigorous, strict; severe, stern, harsh; inclement [temps]. ‖ *rigueur* [rìgœr] *f.* rigo(u)r, strictness; precision; severity, harshness; sternness, sharpness; inclemency; *à la rigueur*, strictly speaking, if necessary; *de rigueur*, required, enforced.

rillettes [rìyèt] *f. pl.* rillettes, potted minced pork.

rime [rìm] *f.* rhyme; verse. ‖ *rimer* [-é] *v.* to rhyme. ‖ *rimeur* [-œr] *m.* rhymer; rhymester.

rinçage [rìⁿsàj] *m.* rinsing; washing, cleansing. ‖ *rincer* [-é] *v.* to rinse; to wash, to cleanse; *rince-doigts*, finger-bowl. ‖ *rinçure* [-ür] *f.* rincings; slops.

ripaille [rìpày] *f.* feasting; *faire ripaille*, to feast.

riposte [rìpòst] *f.* repartee, retort; riposte, return [escrime]. ‖ *riposter* [-é] *v.* to retort; to return fire (mil.); to parry and thrust [escrime].

rire [rìr] *v.** to laugh (*de*, at); to be favo(u)rable, to be propitious; to jest, to joke; to mock, to scoff; *m.* laugh, laughter, laughing; *fou rire*, uncontrollable laughter; *gros rire*, guffaw.

ris [rì] *m.* reef [voiles].

ris [rì] *m.* sweetbread.

risée [rìzé] *f.* laugh; laughter, mockery, derision; laughing-stock; butt; gust, squall (naut.). ‖ *risette* [-èt] *f.* smile. ‖ *risible* [-ìbl] *adj.* laughable; ridiculous.

risque [rìsk] *m.* risk, hazard, peril, danger; *risque-tout*, dare-devil. ‖ *risqué* [rìské] *adj.* risky, hazardous; daring; risque. ‖ *risquer* [-é] *v.* to risk; to hazard, to venture; to chance, to run the risk of; to be exposed to.

rissoler [rìsòlé] *v.* to brown.

ristourne [rìstûrn] *f.* cancelling, annulment [police d'assurance]; rebate; return, refund.

rite [rìt] *m.* rite, ceremony, ritual. ‖ *rituel* [rìtüèl] *adj.*, *m.* ritual.

rivage [rìvàj] *m.* shore, strand, beach; bank.

rival [rìvàl] *adj.* rival, competitive; *m.* rival, competitor. ‖ *rivaliser* [-ìzé] *v.* to rival, to compete, to vie; to emulate. ‖ *rivalité* [-ìté] *f.* rivalry, competition, emulation.

rive [rìv] *f.* bank, shore, strand.

river [rìvé] *v.* to rivet; to clench.

riverain [rìvrìⁿ] *adj.* riparian; bordering; *m.* riverside resident; wayside dweller.

rivet [rìvè] *m.* rivet; pin, bolt. ‖ *riveter* [-té] *v.* to rivet.

rivière [rìvyèr] *f.* river, stream; necklace [collier].

rixe [rìks] *f.* fight, brawl, scuffle.

riz [rì] *m.* rice; *poudre de riz*, ricepowder; face powder. ‖ *riziculture* [-zìkültür] *f.* rice-growing. ‖ *rizière* [-zyèr] *f.* rice-field, rice-paddy.

robe [ròb] *f.* robe; dress, frock, gown; wrapper; coat [animal]; skin, husk, peel [fruit]; *gens de robe*, lawyers.

robinet [ròbìnè] *m. Br.* tap, *Am.* faucet, cock, spigot.

robuste [ròbüst] *adj.* robust, sturdy; firm, strong. ‖ *robustesse* [-tès] *f.* sturdiness, robustness, strength.

roc [ròk] *m.* rock.

rocaille [ròkày] *f.* rock-work; *jardin de rocaille*, ⓒ rock garden. ‖ *rocailleux* [ròkàyê] *adj.* rocky, flinty, stony; rough, harsh.

rocambolesque [ròkaⁿbòlèsk] *adj.* fantastic, incredible.

roche [ròsh] *f.* rock; boulder; stone, stony mass. ‖ *rocher* [-é] *m.* prominent rock, high rock. ‖ *rocheux* [-ê] *adj.* rocky, stony.

rodage [ròdàj] *m.* running-in, *Am.* breaking-in [moteur]. ‖ *roder* [-é] *v.* to run in [moteur].

rôder [rôdé] *v.* to prowl; to roam, to rove, to ramble; to lurk. ‖ *rôdeur* [-œr] *m.* prowler, roamer, rover, stroller; vagrant; lurker; loafer; beach-comber.

rodomontade [ròdòmoⁿtàd] *f.* bluster, braggadocio.

rogner [ròñé] *v.* to pare, to crop, to trim, to clip, to prune, to lop; to curtail, to retrench [dépenses].

rognon [ròñoⁿ] *m.* kidney.

rognure [ròñür] *f.* paring, clipping; *pl.* shavings, scraps, shreds.

rogue [ròg] *adj.* haughty, arrogant; overbearing, gruff.

roi [rwà] *m.* king; *fête des Rois*, Twelfth Night. ‖ *roitelet* [-tlè] *m.* petty king; wren [oiseau].

rôle [rôl] *m.* roll; roster, catalog(ue); part, character, rôle (theat.); *à tour de rôle*, in turn.

romaine [ròmèn] *f.* romaine lettuce; scale; steelyard [balance].

roman [ròmaⁿ] *adj.* Romance; Romanesque, *Br.* Norman [style].

roman [ròmaⁿ] *m.* novel; romance; *roman-feuilleton*, serial novel; *roman policier*, detective novel.

romance [ròmaⁿs] *f.* love-song, melody; sentimental ballad.

romancer [ròmaⁿsé] *v.* to write in novel form. ‖ *romancier* [-yé] *m.* novelist.

romanesque [ròmànèsk] *adj.* romantic; imaginary, fabulous; *m.* the romantic.

romanichel [ròmànìshèl] *m.* gipsy, romany.

romantique [ròmaⁿtìk] *adj.* romantic; *m.* Romanticist; Romantic genre. ‖ *romantisme* [ròmaⁿtìsm] *m.* romanticism.

rompre [roⁿpr] *v.* to break; to break off, to snap; to break asunder; to break up, to disrupt, to dissolve; to break in, to train, to inure; to interrupt; to refract; to rupture (med.); to upset [équilibre]; to call off [marché]; *rompre avec*, to fall out with; *rompre les rangs*, to fall out (mil.); *à tout rompre*, furiously, enthusiastically; *se rompre*, to break, to break off, to snap; to get used (to). ‖ *rompu* [-ü] *adj.* broken; dead tired, worn-out; *à bâtons rompus*, by fits and starts.

romsteck [roⁿstèk] *m.* rump-steak.

ronce [roⁿs] *f.* bramble; thorn.

ronchonner [roⁿshòné] *v.* to grouse; to bellyache.

rond [roⁿ] *adj.* round, circular; rotund, plump; frank, open, plaindealing; even [somme]; (fam.) tipsy, *Am.* high; *m.* round, ring, circle, disk, orb; (pop.) nickel, cent; *rond-de-cuir*, air-cushion; (pop.) clerk, bureaucrat; *rond-point*, circular intersection, *Br.* circus, *Am.* traffic circle; *rond de serviette*, napkin-ring. ‖ *ronde* [roⁿd] *f.* round, patrol; roundelay; round-hand [écriture]; semi-breve (mus.). ‖ *rondelet* [-lè] *adj.* roundish, plumpish, stoutish; nice, tidy [somme]. ‖ *rondelle* [-èl] *f.* small round, disc; ⓒ puck [hockey]; ring; rundle; washer [robinet]. ‖ *rondement* [-°ma°] *adv.* roundly; straightforwardly. ‖ *rondeur* [-œr] *f.* roundness, rotundity; fullness; openness, frankness; straightforwardness.

ronflant [ro°flɑ°] *adj.* snoring; sonorous; high-sounding, high-flown, pretentious, bombastic [langage]. ‖ *ronflement* [-°ma°] *m.* snore; roaring; whirr; humming. ‖ *ronfler* [-é] *v.* to snore; to snort; to roar [feu]; to hum [toupie]; to rumble.

ronger [ro°jé] *v.* to gnaw, to nibble, to pick; to corrode, to consume, to eat away; to fret, to torment; to prey upon [esprit]; to bite [ongles]; to chafe at [frein]. ‖ *rongeur* [-œr] *adj.** gnawing; corroding; *m.* rodent.

ronronner [ro°rõné] *v.* to purr.

rosace [rõzàs] *f.* rose-window.

rosbif [ròsbìf] *m.* roast beef.

rose [ròz] *f.* rose; rose-colo(u)r; *adj.* pink, rosy, rose-colo(u)red. ‖ *rosé* [rõzé] *adj.* rosy, roseate.

roseau [rõzô] *m.** reed.

rosée [rõzé] *f.* dew.

rosier [rõzyé] *m.* rose-bush.

rosse [ròs] *f.* jade; sarcastic person; *adj.* malicious, vicious. ‖ *rosser* [-é] *v.* to thrash, to flog, to drub, to cudgel.

rossignol [ròsìñòl] *m.* nightingale; (pop.) false key, skeleton key, picklock; (pop.) white elephant, unsaleable article.

rot [rò] *m.* belch, eructation.

rotation [rõtàsyo°] *f.* rotation.

rôti [rõtì] *m.* roast, roast meat. ‖ *rôtie* [rõtì] *f.* toast. ‖ *rôtir* [rõtìr] *v.* to roast; to broil, to grill, to toast; to scorch, to parch (fig.). ‖ *rôtisserie* [-ìsrí] *f.* cook-shop, roast-meat shop; grill-room. ‖ *rôtissoire* [-ìswàr] *f.* roaster, Dutch oven.

rotule [rõtül] *f.* patella, knee-cap.

roturier [rõtüryé] *adj.** plebeian; vulgar, common; *m.* plebeian, commoner, roturier.

rouage [rûàj] *m.* wheelwork, wheels; machinery, gearing; movement [horlogerie].

roucoulement [rûkûlma°] *m.* cooing. ‖ *roucouler* [-é] *v.* to coo.

roue [rû] *f.* wheel; paddle-wheel; torture-wheel; *faire la roue,* to strut, to show off; *roue libre,* free-wheeling [auto]; *roue de secours,* spare wheel.

roué [rûé] *adj.* crafty, artful, cunning, sly, sharp; thrashed [coups]; *m.* roué, rake, profligate; trickster.

rouelle [rûèl] *f.* fillet [veau].

rouer [rûé] *v.* to break upon the wheel; to thrash; to coil [câble]. ‖ *rouerie* [rûrí] *f.* craft, cunning; trickery, duplicity; dodge, trick; fast one.

rouet [rûè] *m.* spinning-wheel.

rouge [rûj] *adj.* red; *m.* red colo(u)r; redness; blush; rouge; *rouge-gorge,* robin. ‖ *rougeâtre* [-àtr] *adj.* reddish. ‖ *rougeaud* [-ô] *adj.* red-faced. ‖ *rougeole* [-òl] *f.* measles. ‖ *rougeoyer* [-wàyé] *v.* to redden; to glow. ‖ *rouget* [-è] *m.* red gurnet [poisson]; harvest bug [insecte]. ‖ *rougeur* [-œr] *f.* redness; flush, blush, glow, colo(u)r; *pl.* red blotches [peau]. ‖ *rougir* [-ìr] *v.* to redden, to flush, to flush.

rouille [rûy] *f.* rust, rustiness; blight, blast, mildew. ‖ *rouillé* [-é] *adj.* rusty; blighted; out of practice. ‖ *rouiller* [-é] *v.* to rust; to blight; to impair.

roulade [rûlàd] *f.* trill; roulade, run (mus.). ‖ *roulant* [-ɑ°] *adj.* rolling; easy [chemin]; running [feu]; (pop.) killing; *fauteuil roulant,* wheel-chair. ‖ *rouleau* [-ô] *m.** roll; rolling-pin; coil; scroll; *au bout de son rouleau,* at one's wit's end. ‖ *roulement* [-ma°] *m.* rolling; roll; rumbling; rattle; rotation. ‖ *rouler* [-é] *v.* to roll; to roll up; to wind up; (pop.) to revolve; to fleece, to cheat, to do; to roll along, to drive, to ride; to ramble, to wander, to stroll [errer]. ‖ *roulette* [-èt] *f.* small wheel; roller, castor, truckle, trundle; bathchair; roulette [jeu]; dentist's drill. ‖ *roulis* [-ì] *m.* rolling, roll, swell [lames]; lurch [bateau]. ‖ *roulotte* [-òt] *f.* gipsy-van, caravan.

rouspéter [rûspété] *v.* (fam.) to protest; to complain; to gripe. ‖ *rouspéteur* [-tœr] *m.* (fam.) grouser, *Am.* griper, groaner.

rousse [rûs], *see* roux.

rousseur [rûsœr] *f.* redness; *tache de rousseur,* freckle. ‖ *roussi* [-ì] *m.* burnt smell. ‖ *roussir* [-ìr] *v.* to singe, to scorch; *faire roussir,* to brown [viande].

route [rût] *f.* road, way; route, direction, path, course; *grand-route,* highway; *en route,* on the way; *faire route vers,* to make for; *faire fausse route,* to take a wrong course, to alter the course (naut.); *compagnon de route,* fellow-travel(l)er; *carte routière,* road map.

routine [rûtìn] *f.* routine, habit, practice. ‖ *routinier* [-yé] *adj.** routine(-like); habitual; routine-minded.

rouvrir [rûvrìr] *v.* to open again, to reopen.

roux, rousse [rû, rûs] *adj.* red-haired; reddish(-brown), russet; *m.* reddish colo(u)r; red-head [personne]; brown sauce.

royal [rwàyàl] *adj.** royal; regal, kingly. ‖ *royalisme* [-ìsm] *m.* royalism. ‖ *royaliste* [-ìst] *m., f., adj.* royalist. ‖ *royaume* [rwàyõm] *m.* kingdom; realm. ‖ *royauté* [rwàyõté] *f.* royalty.

ruade [rüàd] *f.* kick [cheval].

ruban [rübaⁿ] *m.* ribbon; tape; service ribbon; stretch, road [route].

rubéole [rübéɔl] *f.* rubella.

rubicond [rübikoⁿ] *adj.* rubicund, florid.

rubis [rübí] *m.* ruby.

rubrique [rübrìk] *f.* red chalk; rubric; heading, head, title.

ruche [rüsh] *f.* hive [abeilles]; frill, ruche, ruching. ‖ *rucher* [-é] *m.* apiary, set of hives; *v.* to frill.

rude [rüd] *adj.* rough, harsh; rugged, uneven; grating; stern, strict; rude, uncouth, churlish [personne]; violent [choc]; hard, difficult, troublesome [besogne]. ‖ *rudement* [-maⁿ] *adv.* roughly, harshly; severely; awfully. ‖ *rudesse* [-ès] *f.* roughness; ruggedness, harshness; rudeness.

rudiment [rüdìmaⁿ] *m.* rudiment. ‖ *rudimentaire* [-tèr] *adj.* rudimentary; elementary.

rudoyer [rüdwàyé] *v.* to treat roughly, to ill-treat; to bully.

rue [rü] *f.* street; thoroughfare.

ruée [rüé] *f.* rush, surge, flinging, hurling; stampede [chevaux].

ruelle [rüèl] *f.* lane, alley; passage.

ruer [rüé] *v.* to fling, to hurl; to kick [chevaux]; to deal [coups]; *se ruer,* to throw oneself, to rush.

rugir [rüjír] *v.* to roar, to bellow. ‖ *rugissement* [-ìsmaⁿ] *m.* roar, roaring, (fig.) howling.

rugosité [rügòzìté] *f.* rugosity, roughness, unevenness. ‖ *rugueux* [rügé] *adj.* rough, uneven, rugose; gnarled [arbre].

ruine [rüín] *f.* ruin; shambles; decay, decline; overthrow, destruction, downfall. ‖ *ruiner* [-né] *v.* to ruin, to wreck, to lay waste; to spoil; to overthrow, to destroy. ‖ *ruineux* [-ë] *adj.* ruinous; disastrous.

ruisseau [rüísð] *m.* brook, stream, rivulet, creek; gutter [rue]; flood [larmes]; river [sang]. ‖ *ruisselant* [-laⁿ] *adj.* streaming, running, flowing, dripping; trickling. ‖ *ruisseler* [-lé] *v.* to stream, to run down, to flow, to drip, to trickle. ‖ *ruisselet* [-lè] *m.* brooklet, rivulet. ‖ *ruissellement* [-èlmaⁿ] *m.* streaming, running, flowing, dripping; trickling; flood, stream [lumière]; shimmer [pierreries].

rumeur [rümœr] *f.* confused noise, muffled din; hum; roar, uproar, clamo(u)r; report, rumo(u)r.

ruminant [rümìnaⁿ] *adj.* ruminant, ruminating; pondering (fig.); *m.* ruminant. ‖ *ruminer* [-é] *v.* to ruminate, to chew the cud; to ponder, to brood on, to turn over in one's mind (fig.).

rumsteck [ròmstèk] *m.* rump-steak.

rupture [rüptür] *f.* breaking, rupture; discontinuance; parting, separation; falling out; annulment; breach; abrogation; hernia (med.); fracture [os]; loss [équilibre]; breaking off [relations].

rural [rüràl] *adj.*° rural.

ruse [rüz] *f.* cunning, craft, guile; artifice, trick, ruse, dodge, wile; stratagem [guerre]. ‖ *rusé* [-é] *adj.* cunning, crafty, sly, artful, wily, guileful; slick (fam.). ‖ *ruser* [-é] *v.* to dodge; to practise deceit; to double [chasse].

russe [rüs] *m.*, *adj.* Russian. ‖ *Russie* [-í] *f.* Russia.

rustaud [rüstð] *adj.* boorish, loutish; *m.* rustic, clodhopper.

rustique [rüstìk] *adj.* rustic, rural, *Br.* homely, *Am.* homey.

rustre [rüstr] *m.* churl, boor, lout.

rutabaga [rütàbàgà] *m.* Swedish turnip, *Am.* rutabaga.

rutilant [rütìlaⁿ] *adj.* shining, brilliant, glowing, radiant, shimmering; bright red.

rythme [rìtm] *m.* rhythm. ‖ *rythmer* [-é] *v.* to give rhythm to. ‖ *rythmique* [-ìk] *adj.* rhythmic.

S

sa [sà] *poss. adj.* his, her, its, one's.

sabbat [sàbà] *m.* sabbath; row. ‖ *sabbatique* [-tìk] *adj.* sabbatical.

sable [sàbl] *m.* sand, gravel; *sable mouvant,* quicksand. ‖ *sablé* [-é] *adj.* sanded; sandy; *m.* small dry cake. ‖ *sabler* [-é] *v.* to sand, to gravel; to swig, to toss off [vin]. ‖ *sablier* [-ìyé] *m.* hour-glass; sand-box; sandman. ‖ *sablière* [-ìyèr] *f.* sand-pit. ‖ *sablonneux* [-ònè] *adj.*° sandy, gritty.

sabord [sàbòr] *m.* port-hole. ‖ *saborder* [-dé] *v.* to scuttle [bateau].

sabot [sàbð] *m.* sabot, wooden shoe [chaussure]; hoof [pied]; shoe, skid, drag [frein]; socket [socle]; top [jouet] ‖ *sabotage* [-òtàj] *m.* sabotage; scamping, botching, bungling [travail]; sabot-making [chaussures]. ‖ *saboter* [-té] *v.* to sabotage; to botch, to scamp. ‖ *saboteur* [-tœr] *m.* botcher, bungler. ‖ *sabotier* [-òtyé] *m.* sabot-maker.

sabre [sàbr] *m.* sabre, sword, broadsword; sword-fish [poisson].

sac [sàk] *m.* sack, bag; purse; kitbag, knapsack, haversack (mil.); valise,

satchel; wallet [besace]; sac (anat.); pouch [animal]; sackcloth; sacking, pillage; *sac à main*, purse, hand-bag; *sac de couchage*, sleeping-bag; *sac de voyage*, travel(l)ing-case; overnight bag; *vider son sac*, to get it off one's chest.

saccade [sàkàd] *f.* jerk, jolt, start, fit; saccade [bride]. ‖ **saccadé** [-é] *adj.* jerky, abrupt, broken, jolting, irregular, uneven.

saccager [sàkàjé] *v.* to sack, to pillage, to plunder, to ravage, to ransack, to despoil; to play havoc with.

sacerdoce [sàsèrdòs] *m.* priesthood. ‖ **sacerdotal** [-dòtàl] *adj.** sacerdotal, priestly.

sachet [sàshè] *m.* satchel; saddle-bag; courrier's bag; leather money bag; tool-bag [bicyclette].

sacoche [sàkòsh] *f.* saddle-bag; courrier's bag; leather money bag; tool-bag [bicyclette].

sacre [sàkr] *m.* consecration; anointing; coronation; ⓒ oath, swear word. ‖ **sacré** [-é] *adj.* sacred; holy, consecrated; (pop.) damned, cursed, accursed, confounded, blasted. ‖ **sacrement** [-emaⁿ] *m.* sacrament; covenant. ‖ **sacrer** [-é] *v.* to consecrate; to anoint; to crown; (pop.) to curse, to swear.

sacrifice [sàkrifìs] *m.* sacrifice; privation; renunciation; oblation. ‖ **sacrifier** [-yé] *v.* to sacrifice; to immolate; to renounce, to give up; to devote.

sacrilège [sàkrilèj] *adj.* sacrilegious; *m.* sacrilege; sacrilegious person.

sacristain [sàkristⁿ] *m.* sexton, sacristan. ‖ **sacristie** [-î] *f.* sacristy, vestry.

sadique [sàdìk] *adj.* sadistic; *s.* sadist.

safran [sàfraⁿ] *m.*, *adj.* saffron.

sagace [sàgàs] *adj.* sagacious; perspicacious. ‖ **sagacité** [-ité] *f.* sagacity, shrewdness; discernment.

sage [sàj] *adj.* wise; sensible, sage, sapient; discreet; good, well-behaved; virtuous; modest; quiet, gentle [animal]; *m.* wise man, sage; **sage-femme**, midwife. ‖ **sagesse** [-ès] *f.* wisdom, goodness, good behavio(u)r; discretion; steadiness, sobriety; gentleness [animal]; modesty, chastity [femme].

saignant [sèñaⁿ] *adj.* bleeding, bloody; underdone, *Am.* rare [viande]. ‖ **saignée** [-é] *f.* bleeding: blood-letting; trench [écoulement]: drain [ressources]. ‖ **saignement** [-maⁿ] *m.* bleeding. ‖ **saigner** [-é] *v.* to bleed; to drain [ressources]; *se saigner aux quatre veines*, to bleed oneself white.

saillant [sàyaⁿ] *adj.* projecting, protruding, salient; outstanding; *m.* salient (arch.). ‖ **saillie** [sàyî] *f.* start, spurt, gush, sally, witticism; projection, protuberance; rabbet; servicing [animaux].

saillir [sàyîr] *v.** to gush, to spurt, to spout; to project, to protrude.

saillir [sàyîr] *v.* to cover, to service (zool.).

sain [sⁿ] *adj.* healthy, sound, hale; healthful, wholesome; sane; clear (naut.); *sain et sauf*, safe and sound, unscathed.

saindoux [sⁿdû] *m.* lard.

saint [sⁿ] *adj.* holy, sacred; saintly; sainted, sanctified; *m.* saint; **Saint-Esprit**, Holy Ghost; *sainte nitouche*, smooth hypocrite; *la Saint-Jean*, Midsummer Day. ‖ **sainteté** [sⁿtté] *f.* holiness, saintliness; sanctity.

saisie [sèzî] *f.* seizure; execution (jur.); requisitioning (mil.). ‖ **saisir** [-îr] *v.* to seize, to grasp; to comprehend, to understand; to strike, to startle, to impress; to instruct (jur.); to vest (jur.); to lash (naut.); *se saisir de*, to seize, to take hold; to take possession. ‖ **saisissable** [-lsàbl] *adj.* seizable, perceptible. ‖ **saisissant** [-lsaⁿ] *adj.* keen, sharp, piercing; impressive, striking, startling, thrilling; chilly [temps]. ‖ **saisissement** [-lsmaⁿ] *m.* seizure; shock; thrill, access; pang; sudden chill.

saison [sèzoⁿ] *f.* season; cure (med.); *de saison*, seasonable; *marchand des quatre-saisons*, street vendor. ‖ **saisonnier** [-ònyé] *adj.** seasonal.

salade [sàlàd] *f.* salad; mess (fig.). ‖ **saladier** [-yé] *m.* salad-bowl.

salaire [sàlèr] *m.* wages, pay; reward, retribution (fig.).

salaison [sàlèzoⁿ] *f.* salting; salt meat.

salamandre [sàlàmaⁿdr] *f.* salamander; *Salamandre*, stove [poêle].

salarié [sàlàryé] *adj.* salaried, paid; *m.* wage-earner.

salaud [sàlô] *m.* (pop.) dirty person; sloven, slut; rotter, skunk, dirty dog (pop.). ‖ **sale** [sàl] *adj.* dirty, nasty, filthy, foul; coarse, indecent; dingy, squalid; dull [couleurs]; scurvy [tour].

salé [sàlé] *adj.* salted, salt; briny; pungent; broad, loose, coarse (fig.); overcharged [prix]; *m.* salt pork. ‖ **saler** [-é] *v.* to salt; to overcharge; (pop.) to fleece.

saleté [sàlté] *f.* dirtiness; filth; foulness; obscenity, smuttiness.

salière [sàlyèr] *f.* salt-cellar, salt-shaker, eye-socket [cheval].

saligaud [sàligô] *s.* (pop.) filthy beast; rotter; swine.

salin [sàlⁿ] *adj.* saline, salt, briny. ‖ **saline** [-în] *f.* salt works; salt marsh.

salir [sàlîr] *v.* to dirty, to soil; to stain, to taint, to sully, to tarnish. ‖ **salissant** [-lsaⁿ] *adj.* dirtying; soiling; dirty; easily soiled.

salive [sàlìv] *f.* spittle, saliva. ‖ *saliver* [-lvé] *v.* to salivate.

salle [sàl] *f.* hall; large room; ward [hôpital]; house (theat.); *salle à manger*, dining-room; *salle des pas perdus*, antechamber [palais de justice]; waiting-room [gare].

salmigondis [sàlmìgoⁿdì] *m.* salmagundi; hotchpotch.

saloir [sàlwàr] *m.* salting-tub; salt-box; salt-sprinkler.

salon [sàloⁿ] *m.* drawing-room, living-room; exhibition, show.

salopette [sàlòpèt] *f.* coverall, overalls, dungarees, *Am.* jeans.

salpêtre [sàlpètr] *m.* saltpetre, nitre.

salsifis [sàlsìfì] *m.* salsify, oyster-plant.

saltimbanque [sàltìⁿbaⁿk] *m.* showman, tumbler; charlatan.

salubre [sàlübr] *adj.* salubrious, health-giving. ‖ *salubrité* [-ìté] *f.* salubrity, wholesomeness, healthfulness.

saluer [sàlüé] *v.* to salute, to bow to; to greet; to hail. ‖ *salut* [-ü] *m.* safety; salvation; welfare, preservation, escape; salute, salutation; bow, greeting; hail, cheers; *léger salut*, nod; *Armée du Salut*, Salvation Army. ‖ *salutaire* [-ütèr] *adj.* salutary; advantageous, beneficial; healthful. ‖ *salutation* [-ütàsyoⁿ] *f.* greeting; salutation, salute; bow; *pl.* compliments [lettre].

salve [sàlv] *f.* salvo, volley; salute (artill.); burst of applause.

samedi [sàmdì] *m.* Saturday.

sanctifier [saⁿktìfyé] *v.* to sanctify, to hallow, to consecrate.

sanction [saⁿksyoⁿ] *f.* sanction, penalty; approbation, approval. ‖ *sanctionner* [-syòné] *v.* to sanction; to ratify.

sanctuaire [saⁿktüèr] *m.* sanctuary.

sandale [saⁿdàl] *f.* sandal.

sang [saⁿ] *m.* blood; race, parentage, ancestry; *sang-froid*, coolness, self-control, composure; *de sang-froid*, in cold blood. ‖ *sanglant* [-glaⁿ] *adj.* bleeding; bloody; sanguinary; blood-shot; cutting, keen, bitter.

sangle [saⁿgl] *f.* strap, band; belt; saddle-girth. ‖ *sangler* [-é] *v.* to strap; to lace tightly.

sanglier [saⁿglié] *m.* wild boar.

sanglot [saⁿglò] *m.* sob. ‖ *sangloter* [-òté] *v.* to sob.

sangsue [saⁿsü] *f.* leech; blood-sucker; extortioner.

sanguin [saⁿgìⁿ] *adj.* full-blooded, sanguine; blood-colo(u)red, blooded;

vaisseau sanguin, blood-vessel. ‖ *sanguinaire* [-ìnèr] *adj.* sanguinary, blood-thirsty; *f.* bloodwort; bloodstone. ‖ *sanguinolent* [-ìnòlaⁿ] *adj.* blood-stained, sanguinolent.

sanitaire [sànìtèr] *adj.* sanitary; hygienic; medical.

sans [saⁿ] *prep.* without; free from; *sans-cœur*, heartless person; *sans-gêne*, off-handedness; off-handed.

sansonnet [saⁿsònè] *m.* starling.

santé [saⁿté] *f.* health; *maison de santé*, private hospital; mental home.

saoul, saouler, *see* soûl, soûler.

saper [sàpé] *v.* to sap, to undermine. ‖ *sapeur* [-œr] *m.* sapper; *sapeur-pompier*, fireman.

saphir [sàfìr] *m.* sapphire.

sapin [sàpìⁿ] *m.* fir-(tree); spruce.

sarcasme [sàrkàsm] *m.* sarcasm.

sarcelle [sàrsèl] *f.* teal.

sarclage [sàrklàj] *m.* weeding. ‖ *sarcler* [sàrklé] *v.* to weed. ‖ *sarcloir* [-klwàr] *m.* hoe.

sardine [sàrdìn] *f.* sardine.

sardonique [sàrdònìk] *adj.* sardonic.

sarment [sàrmaⁿ] *m.* vine-shoot, vine-branch, sarmentum.

sarrasin [sàràzìⁿ] *m.* Saracen; buck-wheat.

sas [sà] *m.* sieve.

satané [sàtàné] *adj.* (fam.) devilish. ‖ *satanique* [-nìk] *adj.* fiendish.

satellite [sàtèllìt] *m.* satellite; henchman; stooge (fam.).

satiété [sàsyété] *f.* satiety.

satin [sàtìⁿ] *m.* satin. ‖ *satiné* [-ìné] *adj.* satiny; smooth; glazed. ‖ *satinette* [-ìnèt] *f.* sateen.

satire [sàtìr] *f.* satire; lampoon. ‖ *satirique* [-ìrìk] *adj.* satirical.

satisfaction [sàtìsfàksyoⁿ] *f.* satisfaction; contentment; atonement. ‖ *satisfaire* [-èr] *v.* to satisfy; to please; to give satisfaction; to make atonement; to appease [faim]. ‖ *satisfaisant* [-ᵉzaⁿ] *adj.* satisfying, satisfactory. ‖ *satisfait* [-è] *adj.* satisfied, contented, pleased.

saturer [sàtüré] *v.* to saturate.

sauce [sôs] *f.* sauce; gravy. ‖ *saucer* [-é] *v.* to dip in sauce; to drench, to soak. ‖ *saucière* [-yèr] *f.* sauce-dish, gravy-boat.

saucisse [sôsìs] *f.* sausage; kite-balloon (mil.). ‖ *saucisson* [-oⁿ] *m.* (large) sausage; fascine (mil.).

sauf [sôf] *adj.*° safe; unhurt, unscathed; *prep.* save, except, barring; reserving, under; *sauf-conduit*, safe-conduct.

saugrenu [sògrᵉnü] *adj.* nonsensical.

saule [sôl] *m.* willow; *saule pleureur,* weeping-willow.

saumâtre [sômâtr] *adj.* briny; nasty.

saumon [sômoⁿ] *m.* salmon [poisson]; pig, block (techn.).

saumure [sômûr] *f.* brine, pickle.

saupoudrer [sôpûdré] *v.* to powder, to sprinkle, to dust; to intersperse.

saur [sôr] *adj.* dried; *hareng saur,* red herring, bloater.

saut [sô] *m.* leap, jump, spring, bound; vault; omission; *saut périlleux,* acrobatic somersault; *saut de haie,* hurdling. ‖ *sauter* [-té] *v.* to jump, to leap, to bound; to blow up, to explode; to omit; to leave out; to tumble (theat.); to veer, to shift (naut.); to fry quickly [cuisine]; *sauter aux yeux,* to be self-evident, to be obvious; *saute-mouton,* leap-frog. ‖ *sauterelle* [-trèl] *f.* grasshopper, locust. ‖ *sauterie* [-trî] *f.* dancing party, hop, *Am.* shindig (fam.). ‖ *sautillement* [-tîymaⁿ] *m.* hopping, skipping. ‖ *sautiller* [-tîyé] *v.* to hop, to skip.

sauvage [sôvàj] *adj.* savage, wild; untamed, uncivilized; rude, barbarous; shy, timid, unsociable; *m., f.* savage; unsociable person. ‖ *sauvagerie* [-rî] *f.* savagery; ferocity; wildness; shyness, unsociability.

sauvegarde [sôvgàrd] *f.* safeguard; guarantee; shield, protection; manrope (naut.). ‖ *sauvegarder* [-é] *v.* to safeguard; to save.

sauver [sôvé] *v.* to save, to rescue; to salvage; to deliver; to preserve [apparences]; to spare; *se sauver,* to escape; to run away, *Am.* to beat it (fam.). ‖ *sauvetage* [-tàj] *m.* rescue, saving, salvage; *ceinture de sauvetage,* life-belt; *bateau de sauvetage,* lifeboat. ‖ *sauveteur* [-tœr] *m.* rescuer, deliverer; life-saver; *adj.* saving, preserving. ‖ *sauveur* [-œr] *m.* saver, deliverer; Saviour.

savamment [sàvàmaⁿ] *adv.* learnedly, cleverly.

savane [sàvàn] *f.* savanna.

savant [sàvaⁿ] *adj.* learned, erudite; clever; expert; *m.* scholar; scientist; *femme savante,* bluestocking.

savate [sàvàt] *f.* old shoe, easy slipper; sole-plate (mech.); foot boxing [jeu]; bungler, clumsy workman.

saveur [sàvœr] *f.* savo(u)r, taste, flavo(u)r; zest, tang.

savoir [savwàr] *v.** to know, to be aware of; to know how, to be able; to understand; to find out, to learn, to be informed of; to be acquainted with [faits]; *m.* knowledge, learning, scholarship, erudition; *autant que je sache,* as far as I know; *savoir gré,* to be grateful; *à savoir,* namely, viz

(= videlicet); *savoir-faire,* knowingness, knowledgeability; *savoir-vivre,* good manners, social grace, etiquette.

savon [sàvoⁿ] *m.* soap; (pop.) rebuke; *savon à barbe,* shaving-soap. ‖ *savonnage* [sàvònàj] *m.* soaping, washing. ‖ *savonner* [-òné] *v.* to soap; to lather; to rebuke. ‖ *savonnette* [-ònèt] *f.* bar of soap. ‖ *savonneux, -euse* [-òně, -ěz] *adj.* soapy.

savourer [sàvûré] *v.* to relish, to savo(u)r; to enjoy. ‖ *savoureux* [-ě] *adj.** savo(u)ry, tangy, tasty.

scabreux [skàbrě] *adj.** scabrous; salacious, risqué; dangerous.

scalpel [skàlpèl] *m.* scalpel. ‖ *scalper* [-é] *v.* to scalp.

scandale [skaⁿdàl] *m.* scandal. ‖ *scandaleux* [-ě] *adj.** scandalous, shocking. ‖ *scandaliser* [-ìzé] *v.* to scandalize, to shock, to horrify.

scander [skaⁿdé] *v.* to scan; to emphasize.

scaphandre [skàfaⁿdr] *m.* diving-suit. ‖ *scaphandrier* [-ìyé] *m.* deep-sea diver.

scarabée [skàràbé] *m.* beetle.

scarlatine [skàrlàtîn] *f.* scarlet fever, scarlatina.

sceau [sô] *m.** seal; mark; confirmation (fig.).

scélérat [sélérà] *m.* scoundrel. ‖ *scélératesse* [-tès] *f.* villainy.

scellé [sèlé] *m.* seal. ‖ *sceller* [-é] *v.* to seal (up); to fasten, to fix [construction]; to confirm (fig.).

scénario [sénàryô] *m.* scenario; script. ‖ *scénariste* [-rìst] *s.* script-writer, scenario-writer.

scène [sèn] *f.* scene; stage; scenery.

scepticisme [sèptìsìsm] *m.* scepticism, *Am.* skepticism. ‖ *sceptique* [-ìk] *adj.* sceptic, *Am.* skeptic.

sceptre [sèptr] *m.* sceptre.

schéma [shémà] *m.* diagram, scheme. ‖ *schématique* [-màtìk] *adj.* schematic. ‖ *schématiser* [-màtìzé] *v.* to schematize.

schisme [chìsm] *m.* schism.

sciatique [syàtìk] *adj.* sciatic; *f.* sciatica.

scie [sî] *f.* saw; saw-fish; (pop.) bore, trouble, nuisance.

sciemment [syàmaⁿ] *adv.* wittingly, knowingly, consciously; purposely. ‖ *science* [syaⁿs] *f.* science, learning; knowledge; skill, expertness. ‖ *scientifique* [syaⁿtìfìk] *adj.* scientific; *s.* scientist.

scier [syé] *v.* to saw (off). ‖ *scierie* [sìrî] *f.* saw-mill; lumber-mill.

scinder [sìⁿdé] *v.* to divide, to sever.

scintillement [sɛ̃tìymaⁿ] *m.* glitter, twinkling, sparkle ; flickering. ǁ *scintiller* [-ìyé] *v.* to glitter, to twinkle, to sparkle ; to flicker.

scission [sìsyoⁿ] *f.* scission ; secession ; *faire scission,* to secede.

sciure [syür] *f.* sawdust.

scolaire [skòlèr] *adj.* academic ; *année scolaire,* school year. ǁ *scolarité* [-làrìté] *f.* school-attendance.

scrupule [skrüpül] *m.* scruple, qualm, misgiving ; scrupulousness. ǁ *scrupuleux* [-ë] *adj.** scrupulous ; punctilious ; conscientious.

scruter [skrüté] *v.* to scrutinize ; to investigate, to explore.

scrutin [skrütiⁿ] *m.* ballot, poll, vote.

sculpter [skülté] *v.* to sculpture, to carve. ǁ *sculpteur* [-œr] *m.* sculptor, carver. ǁ *sculpture* [-ür] *f.* sculpture, carving.

se [sᵉ] *refl. pron. m.* himself, itself, oneself ; *f.* herself, itself ; *pl.* themselves, each other, one another.

séance [séaⁿs] *f.* sitting ; seat ; meeting, session ; seance ; *séance tenante,* immediately, on the spot. ǁ *séant* [séaⁿ] *adj.* fitting ; *m.* bottom.

seau [sô] *m.** pail, bucket ; scuttle ; bucketful (contenu).

sec, sèche [sèk, sèsh] *adj.* dry, arid ; plain ; cold, unfeeling ; *adv.* dryly, sharply ; *m.* dryness ; dry weather ; *être à sec,* to be broke, to be hard up ; *perte sèche,* dead loss ; *coup sec,* sharp stroke, rap ; *fruit sec,* failure, washout, flop ; *en cinq sec,* in a jiffy.

sécateur [sékàtœr] *m.* pruning-scissors, pruning-shears.

sécession [sésèsyoⁿ] *f.* secession.

sécher [séshé] *v.* to dry ; to dry up ; to cure, to season ; (pop.) to shun, to avoid ; to wither ; *sécher une classe,* to cut class ; *sécher à un examen,* to fail an examination, *Am.* to flunk. ǁ *sécheresse* [-ᵉrès] *f.* dryness ; aridity ; drought ; bareness ; curtness. ǁ *séchoir* [-wàr] *m.* dryer ; drying-room.

second [sᵉgoⁿ] *adj.* second ; another, new ; inferior ; *m.* second ; assistant ; mate, second officer ; *Br.* second floor, *Am.* third floor. ǁ *secondaire* [-dèr] *adj.* secondary ; subordinate. ǁ *seconde* [-oⁿd] *f.* second ; second class ; seconde [escrime]. ǁ *seconder* [-dé] *v.* to second ; to assist.

secouer [sᵉkûé] *v.* to shake, to jog, to jar, to jerk, to jolt ; to rouse ; *se secouer,* to shake oneself ; to bestir oneself, to exert oneself.

secourable [sᵉkûràbl] *adj.* helpful, helping ; relievable. ǁ *secourir* [-îr] *v.** to help, to succo(u)r ; to rescue. ǁ *secouriste* [-ìst] *s.* member of a first-aid association. ǁ *secours* [sᵉkûr] *m.*

help, assistance, aid, succo(u)r ; relief ; rescue ; *au secours !,* help ! ; *premiers secours,* first-aid ; *roue de secours,* spare-wheel.

secousse [sᵉkûs] *f.* shake, jar, jerk.

secret [sᵉkrè] *adj.* secret ; reserved, reticent ; stealthy, secretive ; furtive ; *m.* secret ; secrecy, privacy, mystery ; secret drawer ; solitary confinement. ǁ *secrétaire* [-étèr] *m.* secretary ; writing-desk. ǁ *secrétariat* [-étàryà] *m.* secretariat, secretary's office ; secretaryship.

sécréter [sékrété] *v.* to secrete. ǁ *sécrétion* [-syoⁿ] *f.* secretion.

sectaire [sèktèr] *m., adj.* sectarian. ǁ *secte* [sèkt] *f.* sect ; cult, denomination ; party (fig.).

secteur [sèktœr] *m.* sector ; circuit (electr.).

section [sèksyoⁿ] *f.* section ; division ; portion ; platoon (mil.). ǁ *sectionner* [-yòné] *v.* to divide ; to sever ; to cut up ; to section off.

séculaire [sékülèr] *adj.* secular ; centenarian ; age-old, century-old. ǁ *séculier* [-yé] *adj.** secular, worldly ; temporal, lay.

secundo [sékoⁿdò] *adv.* secondly.

sécurité [sékürìté] *f.* security, safety ; confidence ; guarantee.

sédatif [sédàtìf] *adj.** sedative, quieting ; *m.* sedative.

sédentaire [sédaⁿtèr] *adj.* sedentary ; fixed, settled.

sédiment [sédìmaⁿ] *m.* sediment.

séditieux [sédìsyë] *adj.** seditious. ǁ *sédition* [-yoⁿ] *f.* sedition.

séducteur [sédüktœr] *adj.** seductive ; bewitching ; tempting ; alluring ; *m.* seducer. ǁ *séduction* [-syoⁿ] *f.* seduction ; enticement ; allurement. ǁ *séduire* [sédüìr] *v.** to seduce ; to beguile, to bewitch ; to charm, to win over ; to captivate ; to bribe. ǁ *séduisant* [-üìzaⁿ] *adj.* seductive ; alluring, fascinating, beguiling.

ségrégation [ségrégasyoⁿ] *f.* segregation ; apartheid.

seiche [sèsh] *f.* cuttle-fish, sepia.

seigle [sègl] *m.* rye.

seigneur [sèñœr] *m.* lord ; squire ; nobleman ; Lord (eccles.). ǁ *seigneurie* [-î] *f.* lordship.

sein [sɛ̃ⁿ] *m.* breast ; bosom ; womb ; heart, midst, middle (fig.).

séisme [séìsm] *m.* seism, earthquake.

seize [sèz] *m., adj.* sixteen ; sixteenth (date, titre). ǁ *seizième* [-yèm] *m., adj.* sixteenth.

séjour [séjûr] *m.* sojourn, stay ; residence. ǁ *séjourner* [-né] *v.* to stay, to sojourn, to reside.

sel [sèl] *m.* salt; wit; pungency (fig.); *pl.* smelling-salts.

sélection [séléksyoⁿ] *f.* selection; choice. ‖ **sélectionner** [-yòné] *v.* to select; to choose, to pick out.

selle [sèl] *f.* saddle; stool; faeces (med.). ‖ **seller** [-é] *v.* to saddle. ‖ **sellerie** [-rî] *f.* saddlery, saddle-room. ‖ **sellette** [-èt] *f.* culprits' seat; *mettre sur la sellette,* to cross-question.

selon [sⁿloⁿ] *prep.* according to; *selon que,* according as.

semailles [sⁿmày] *f. pl.* sowing; seed.

semaine [sⁿmèn] *f.* week; week's work; week's wages.

semblable [saⁿblàbl] *adj.* similar, like, such; resembling; *m.* like; match, equal; fellow-creature. ‖ **semblant** [-aⁿ] *m.* appearance, look; pretence, show, feigning, bluff; *faire semblant,* to pretend; *faux semblant,* pretence. ‖ **sembler** [-é] *v.* to seem, to appear.

semelle [sⁿmèl] *f.* sole [chaussure]; foot [bas]; shoe [traîneau]; sleeper, bed-plate [techn.].

semence [sⁿmaⁿs] *f.* seed; semen; tack [clous]. ‖ **semer** [-é] *v.* to sow; to seed; to scatter, to sprinkle; to disseminate; to spread about; to distance; to shed (fam.).

semestre [sⁿmèstr] *m.* half-year, six months; semester, *Am.* term [école]. ‖ **semestriel** [-ìyèl] *adj.* half-yearly, semi-annual.

semeur [sⁿmœr] *m.* sower; disseminator.

sémillant [sémìyaⁿ] *adj.* lively, sprightly.

séminaire [séminèr] *m.* seminary. ‖ **séminariste** [-àrìst] *m.* seminarist.

semis [sⁿmî] *m.* sowing; seed-bed, seedling. ‖ **semoir** [-wàr] *m.* seed-bag; sowing-machine, drill.

semonce [sⁿmoⁿs] *f.* admonishment, talking-to.

semoule [sⁿmúl] *f.* semolina.

sénat [sénà] *m.* senate. ‖ **sénateur** [-tœr] *m.* senator.

sénevé [sénvé] *m.* black mustard.

sénile [sénìl] *adj.* senile, elderly. ‖ **sénilité** [-é] *f.* senility.

sens [saⁿs] *m.* sense, senses, feelings; judgment, wits, intelligence; meaning, import; interpretation; opinion, sentiment; way, direction; *bon sens,* common sense; *sens interdit,* no entry; *sens unique,* one-way; *sens dessus dessous,* upside-down.

sensation [saⁿsàsyoⁿ] *f.* sensation, feeling. ‖ **sensationnel** [-yònèl] *adj.* sensational; dramatic.

sensé [saⁿsé] *adj.* sensible, wise, level-headed.

sensibiliser [saⁿsìbìlìzé] *v.* to sensitize. ‖ **sensibilité** [-ìté] *f.* sensibility, feeling. ‖ **sensible** [saⁿsìbl] *adj.* sensitive; susceptible; perceptible; evident, obvious; lively, acute; tender, sore [chair]; *être sensible à,* to feel. ‖ **sensiblement** [-ᵉmaⁿ] *adv.* obviously; feelingly, keenly, deeply; noticeably, appreciably. ‖ **sensiblerie** [-ᵉrî] *f.* sentimentality; sob-stuff (fam.).

sensitif [saⁿsìtîf] *adj.ᵉ* sensitive, sensory. ‖ **sensoriel** [-sòryèl] *adj.ᵉ* sensorial, sensory.

sensualité [saⁿsüàlìté] *f.* sensuality; voluptuousness. ‖ **sensuel** [saⁿsüèl] *adj.ᵉ* sensual; voluptuous.

sentence [saⁿtaⁿs] *f.* sentence; verdict; aphorism. ‖ **sentencieux** [-yé] *adj.ᵉ* sententious, oracular, dogmatic.

senteur [saⁿtœr] *f.* scent, fragrance; *pois de senteur,* sweet pea.

sentier [saⁿtyé] *m.* path, lane.

sentiment [saⁿtìmaⁿ] *m.* sentiment; feeling; affection; perception; sensibility; opinion. ‖ **sentimental** [-tàl] *adj.ᵉ* sentimental. ‖ **sentimentalité** [-tàlìté] *f.* sentimentality.

sentinelle [saⁿtìnèl] *f.* sentry, sentinel.

sentir [saⁿtîr] *v.ᵉ* to feel; to guess; to perceive; to smell; to scent; to taste of; to seem; *se sentir,* to feel (oneself); to be conscious; to be felt.

séparable [sépàràbl] *adj.* separable; distinguishable. ‖ **séparation** [-àsyoⁿ] *f.* separation, severing; partition [mur]. ‖ **séparer** [-é] *v.* to separate, to divide; to sever; to part [cheveux]; *se séparer,* to separate, to part; to divide; to break up [assemblée]; to disperse, to scatter.

sept [sèt] *m., adj.* seven; seventh [titre, date].

septembre [sèptaⁿbr] *m.* September.

septième [sètyèm] *m., adj.* seventh.

septique [sèptìk] *adj.* septic.

septuagénaire [sèptüàjénèr] *m., f., adj.* septuagenarian.

sépulcral [sépülkràl] *adj.ᵉ* sepulchral; cavernous [voix]. ‖ **sépulcre** [sépülkr] *m.* sepulchre. ‖ **sépulture** [-tür] *f.* sepulture; burial-place, resting-place, tomb.

séquelle [sékèl] *f.* series [choses]; crew, gang [personnes].

séquence [sékaⁿs] *f.* sequence; run.

séquestration [sékèstràsyoⁿ] *f.* sequestration, seclusion. ‖ **séquestre** [sékèstr] *m.* sequestrator; embargo [bateau]. ‖ **séquestrer** [-é] *v.* to sequester; to confine. to keep in confinement.

sérail [sérày] *m.* seraglio.

séraphin [séràfi^n] *m.* seraph [*pl.* seraphim]; © miser, stingy fellow.

serein [se̞ri^n] *adj.* serene, placid. ‖ **sérénité** [séréníté] *f.* serenity.

sergent [sèrja^n] *m.* sergeant; cramp [outil]; iron hook (naut.); *sergent de ville*, policeman.

série [séri̋] *f.* series; break [billard]; succession; sequence; *en série*, standardized, mass produced; *sérier*, to seriate.

sérieux [séryë] *adj.** serious, grave; earnest; true, solid, substantial; *m.* seriousness, gravity.

serin [se̞ri^n] *m.* canary; (pop.) sap, booby; *seriner*, to cram.

seringue [se̞ri^ng] *f.* syringe.

serment [sèrma^n] *m.* oath, promise; *pl.* swearing; *prêter serment*, to be sworn in.

sermon [sèrmo^n] *m.* sermon; lecture. ‖ **sermonner** [-òné] *v.* to lecture, to preach, to sermonize.

serpe [sèrp] *f.* bill-hook, hedge-bill.

serpent [sèrpa^n] *m.* serpent, snake; *serpent à sonnettes*, rattlesnake. ‖ **serpenter** [-té] *v.* to wind, to meander, to twine, to twist.

serpillière [sèrpìyèr] *f.* packing-cloth, sacking.

serpolet [sèrpòlè] *m.* wild thyme.

serre [sèr] *f.* squeeze, pressure; talon, claw [oiseau]; greenhouse, conservatory; *serre chaude*, hot-house. ‖ **serré** [-é] *adj.* close, serried, compact; tight; clenched; concise, terse. ‖ **serrement** [-ma^n] *m.* pressing, squeezing; pang [cœur]; handshake [main]. ‖ **serrer** [-é] *v.* to press, to tighten, to squeeze; to serry; to grip; to condense; to oppress [cœur]; to close [rangs]; to clench [dents, poings]; to skirt, to hug [côte]; to take in [voiles]; to apply, to put on [freins]; *serrer la main à*, to shake hands with; *serre-frein*, brakesman; *se serrer*, to contract; to crowd; to grow tighter; to sink [cœur].

serrure [se̞rür] *f.* lock; *trou de serrure*, keyhole. ‖ **serrurier** [-yé] *m.* locksmith.

sertir [sèrtír] *v.* to set, to mount.

sérum [séròm] *m.* serum.

servage [sèrvàj] *m.* servitude.

servant [sèrva^n] *m.* servant; gunner; *adj.* serving, in-waiting. ‖ **servante** [-a^nt] *f.* maidservant; dumb-waiter. ‖ **serveur** [-œr] *m.* waiter; dealer [cartes]; server [tennis]. ‖ **serveuse** [-éz] *f.* waitress. ‖ **serviable** [-yàbl] *adj.* serviceable, willing, obliging.

service [sèrvìs] *m.* service; attendance; duty; office, function; set [argenterie, vaisselle]; course [plats]; tradesmen's entrance; *service compris*, tip included; *chef de service*, head of department.

serviette [sèrvyèt] *f.* serviette, napkin; towel; briefcase, portfolio; *serviette éponge*, Turkish towel.

servile [sèrvìl] *adj.* servile, menial; mean, base; slavish.

servir [sèrvír] *v.** to serve, to wait on; to help to; to be of service, to assist; to supply; to work, to operate; to be useful; to be in the service (mil.); *servir de*, to serve as, to be used as; *se servir*, to serve oneself, to help oneself; to avail oneself, to make use of; *se servir de*, to use, to avail oneself of.

serviteur [sèrvìtœr] *m.* servant. ‖ **servitude** [-üd] *f.* servitude.

ses [sè] *poss. adj. pl.* his; her; its.

session [sèsyo^n] *f.* session, sitting.

seuil [sœy] *m.* sill, threshold.

seul [sœl] *adj.* alone, by oneself; sole, only, single; mere, bare. ‖ **seulement** [-ma^n] *adv.* only; but; solely, merely.

sève [sèv] *f.* sap; juice; pith.

sévère [sévèr] *adj.* severe, stern, austere; strict; correct. ‖ **sévérité** [-érìté] *f.* severity; sternness, strictness; correctness, austerity.

sévices [sévìs] *m. pl.* ill-treatment, cruelty. ‖ **sévir** [-ír] *v.* to chastise; to rage [guerre].

sevrage [se̞vràj] *m.* weaning. ‖ **sevrer** [se̞vré] *v.* to wean.

sexe [sèks] *m.* sex.

sexualité [sèksüàlité] *f.* sexuality. ‖ **sexuel** [sèksüèl] *adj.** sexual.

seyant [sèya^n] *adj.* becoming, suitable.

shampooing [sha^npûì^n] *m.* shampoo.

short [shòrt] *m.* shorts.

si [sì] *conj.* if; whether; what if.

si [sì] *adv.* yes [après question négative]; so, so much, however much; *si fait*, yes, indeed; *si bien que*, so that.

sidéré [sìdéré] *adj.* thunderstruck; (fam.) flabbergasted. ‖ **sidérer** [sìdéré] *v.* to stupefy.

siècle [syèkl] *m.* century; age, period; world.

siège [syèj] *m.* seat; chair; coachman's box; bench (jur.); siege; see (eccles.); *le Saint-Siège*, the Holy See; *siège social*, head office. ‖ **siéger** [syéjé] *v.* to sit [assemblée]; to have its head office (comm.); to be localized (fig.).

sien, sienne [syi^n, syèn] *poss. pron.* his, hers, its, one's; *les siens*, one's own people.

sieste [syèst] f. siesta, nap.

sifflement [sìfle̊mₐⁿ] m. whistle, whistling, wheezing; whizzing [flèche]; hiss, hissing ‖ **siffler** [-é] v. to whistle, to hiss; to pipe [oiseau]; to whizz; to wheeze, to hiss, to boo (theat.). ‖ **sifflet** [-è] m whistle; hissing; catcall, boo. ‖ **siffloter** [-ôté] v. to whistle lightly, to whistle under one's breath.

signal [sìñàl] m.* signal; sign; watchword, Am wig-wag (railw.; mil.). ‖ **signalement** [-mₐⁿ] m. description [personne]. ‖ **signaler** [-é] v. to signal; to point out, to indicate; to give the description of; Am. to wig-wag (railw.; mil.). ‖ **signalisation** [-lzàsyoⁿ] f. signalling, signal-system; road signs.

signature [sìñàtür] f. signature.

signe [sìñ] m. sign; signal; mark; token, emblem, symbol, indication, badge, clue; omen. ‖ **signer** [-é] v. to sign; to subscribe; to put one's name to; se **signer**, to cross oneself.

signet [sìñè] m. bookmark.

significatif [sìñfikàtèf] adj.* significant, significative; meaningful; expressive; momentous. ‖ **signification** [-àsyoⁿ] f. significance, signification, import, meaning; notification. ‖ **signifier** [sìñìfyé] v. to signify, to mean; to notify; to intimate; to imply, to denote.

silence [sìlₐⁿs] m. silence, stillness; quiet; secrecy; pause; reticence; rest (mus.); passer sous silence, to pass over in silence. ‖ **silencieux** [-yë] adj.* silent, quiet, still; taciturn; noiseless (techn.); m. silencer, Am. muffler [auto].

silex [sìlèks] m. silex; flint.

silhouette [sìlwèt] f. silhouette.

sillage [sìyàj] m. wake; speed, headway.

sillon [sìyoⁿ] m. furrow, groove; track, trail, wake. ‖ **sillonner** [sìyòné] v. Br. to plough, Am. to plow, to furrow; to streak; to groove.

simagrées [sìmàgré] f. pl. affected airs; pretence.

similaire [sìmìlèr] adj. similar; analogous ‖ **similitude** [-ìtüd] f. similitude, similarity.

simple [sìⁿpl] adj. simple; natural; plain; only, bare, mere; easy; simple-minded; natural; single [chambre]; m. simpleton, single [sport]; m. pl. simples [plantes]; simple soldat, private; simple matelot, ordinary seaman. ‖ **simplicité** [-ìsìté] f. plainness; simplicity; simple-mindedness. ‖ **simplification** [-fìkàsyoⁿ] f. simplification. ‖ **simplifier** [-ìfyé] v. to simplify. ‖ **simpliste** [-ìst] adj. over-simple.

simulacre [sìmülàkr] m. image; semblance, appearance, feint, sham.

simulateur, -trice [sìmülàtœr, -trìs] m., f. shammer pretender; malingerer (mil.). ‖ **simulation** [-àsyoⁿ] f. simulation, feigning ‖ **simuler** [-é] v. to simulate, tc pretend, to feign, to sham; to malinger (mil.).

simultané [sìmültàné] adj. simultaneous coincident, synchronous.

sinapisme [sìnàpìsm] m. mustard plaster sinapism.

sincère [sìⁿsèr] adj. sincere; frank, candid open-hearted; genuine. ‖ **sincérité** [-érìté] f. sincerity, frankness; honesty genuineness.

singe [sìⁿj] m monkey, ape; imitator, mimic, hoist, windlass, winch, crab (techn.), (pop.) boss; bully beef (mil.). ‖ **singer** [-é] v. to ape, to imitate, to mimic ‖ **singerie** [-rî] f. monkey trick; grimace mimicry, apery.

singulariser [sìⁿgülàrìzé] v. to singularize, se **singulariser**, to make oneself noticed. ‖ **singularité** [-rìté] f. singularity, peculiarity. ‖ **singulier** [-yé] adj.* singular peculiar, odd, bizarre, strange, queer, conspicuous.

sinistre [sìnìstr] adj. sinister, ominous, threatening, menacing, baleful, lurid, grim, forbidding, dismal; m. disaster; fire, loss. ‖ **sinistré** [-é] m. victim, adj. bomb-damaged, bombed-out; rendered homeless.

sinon [sìnoⁿ] conj. else, or else; otherwise; if not; except, unless.

sinueux [sìnüë] adj.* sinuous, winding, wavy, meandering, twining. ‖ **sinuosité** [-ôzìté] f. sinuosity, winding; meandering.

sinus [sìnüs] m. sinus, antrum (med.); sine (math.). ‖ **sinusite** [-zìt] f. sinusitis.

sioniste [syònìst] s., adj. Zionist.

siphon [sìfoⁿ] m. siphon; trap [évier]. ‖ **siphonner** [-né] v. to siphon.

sire [sìr] m. sire; lord.

sirène [sìrèn] f. siren, mermaid; foghorn, hooter.

sirop [sìrò] m. syrup.

sismique [sìsmìk] adj. seismic.

site [sìt] m. site, location.

sitôt [sìtò] adv. so soon, as soon.

situation [sìtüàsyoⁿ] f. situation, site, location, position, place, job; predicament, plight; report; bearing (naut.). ‖ **situer** [sìtüé] v. to situate, to locate.

six [sìs] m., adj. six, sixth [titre, date]. ‖ **sixième** [sìzyèm] m., f., adj. sixth.

ski [skì] m. ski. ‖ **skieur** [skyœr] m. skier.

slip [slìp] m. slips; panties; briefs.

smoking [smòkìñ] m. dinner-jacket; Am. tuxedo.

snob [snòb] *m.* snob. ‖ **snobisme** [-ìsm] *m.* snobbishness, snobbery.

sobre [sòbr] *adj.* sober, moderate, well-balanced; temperate; abstemious, frugal; restrained; sedate. ‖ **sobriété** [-ìyété] *f.* sobriety; abstemiousness, sedateness; restraint; quietness [vêtements].

sobriquet [sòbrìkè] *m.* nickname.

soc [sòk] *m.* ploughshare.

sociable [sòsyàbl] *adj.* sociable, companionable, affable, convivial.

social [sòsyàl] *adj.** social. ‖ **socialisme** [-ìsm] *m.* socialism. ‖ **socialiste** [-ìst] *m.*, *f.*, *adj.* socialist.

sociétaire [sòsyétèr] *m.* member, associate; partner; stockholder. ‖ **société** [-é] *f.* society; company, firm, association; partnership, fellowship; community; gathering.

socle [sòkl] *m.* socle.

Socquette [sòkèt] *f.* (trade-mark) ankle sock, anklet, bobby-sock.

soda [sòdà] *m.* soda; sparkling-water. ‖ **sodium** [-yòm] *m.* sodium.

sœur [sœr] *f.* sister; nun.

sofa [sòfà] *m.* sofa, divan.

soi [swà] *pers. pron.* oneself; himself, herself, itself; self; *cela va de soi,* that goes without saying; *soi-disant,* self-styled, so-called, alleged; *soi-même,* oneself.

soie [swà] *f.* silk; silken hair; bristle [porc]. ‖ **soierie** [-rî] *f.* silk goods; silk-trade; silk-factory.

soif [swàf] *f.* thirst; *avoir soif,* to be thirsty.

soigner [swànjé] *v.* to take care of, to nurse, to attend to, to take pains with; *se soigner,* to take care of oneself; to nurse oneself; to coddle oneself. ‖ **soigneux** [-ë] *adj.** careful, mindful; attentive; painstaking; solicitous. ‖ **soin** [swìn] *m.* care; attention; *pl.* attentions, solicitude, pains, trouble; *aux bons soins de,* in care of, courtesy of; *soins de beauté,* beauty treatment; *soins médicaux,* medical care; *premiers soins,* first aid.

soir [swàr] *m.* evening; night; afternoon; *ce soir,* tonight. ‖ **soirée** [-é] *f.* evening; evening party.

soit [swà] *see être; adv.* be it so, well and good, all right, agreed; suppose, grant it; *conj.* either, or; whether; *tant soit peu,* ever so little.

soixantaine [swàsàntèn] *f.* three score; about sixty. ‖ **soixante** [-ànt] *adj.,* *m.* sixty; *soixante-dix,* seventy; *soixante-quinze,* seventy-five. ‖ **soixantième** [-àntyèm] *m.,* *f.,* *adj.* sixtieth.

sol [sòl] *m.* ground; soil.

solaire [sòlèr] *adj.* solar [plexus]; sun [rayons]; *cadran solaire,* sun-dial.

soldat [sòldà] *m.* soldier; *Soldat inconnu,* Unknown Warrior.

solde [sòld] *f.* pay.

solde [sòld] *m.* balance owing; selling off, clearance sale; marked-down item; surplus stock; clearance lines, *Am.* broken lots.

solder [sòldé] *v.* to settle, to discharge [compte]; to sell off, to clear out [marchandises].

sole [sòl] *f.* sole [sabot d'un animal].

sole [sòl] *f.* sole [poisson].

soleil [sòlèy] *m.* sun; sunshine; star (fig.); *coup de soleil,* sunstroke.

solennel [sòlànèl] *adj.** solemn; formal, pompous; dignified. ‖ **solenniser** [-ìzé] *v.* to solemnize. ‖ **solennité** [-ìté] *f.* solemnity; ceremony; dignity, gravity.

solidaire [sòlìdèr] *adj.* mutually responsible; interdependent. ‖ **solidariser** [-àrìzé] *v.* to render jointly liable; *se solidariser,* to join in liability; to make common cause. ‖ **solidarité** [-àrìté] *f.* joint responsibility; solidarity; fellowship. ‖ **solide** [sòlìd] *adj.* solid; strong; tough, stout; stalwart; firm, stable; substantial; reliable; solvent; fast [couleur]; *m.* solid. ‖ **solidifier** [-ìfyé] *v.* to solidify. ‖ **solidité** [-ìté] *f.* solidity; firmness.

soliste [sòlìst] *s.* soloist; *adj.* solo.

solitaire [sòlìtèr] *adj.* solitary, single; lonely; desolate; *m.* hermit, recluse; solitaire [diamant]; old boar [sanglier]. ‖ **solitude** [-üd] *f.* solitude, loneliness; seclusion; wilderness, desert.

solive [sòlìv] *f.* joist; *Am.* stud, scantling. ‖ **soliveau** [-ìvò] *m.** small joist; (fam.) block-head; King Log.

sollicitation [sòlìsìtàsyon] *f.* solicitation, entreaty; application (jur.) ‖ **solliciter** [-é] *v.* to solicit, to entreat; to incite, to urge; to impel. ‖ **solliciteur** [-œr] *m.* solicitor; petitioner. ‖ **sollicitude** [-üd] *f.* solicitude, care.

solo [sòlò] *adj.* solo.

soluble [sòlübl] *adj.* soluble, dissolvable. ‖ **solution** [-üsyon] *f.* solution; solving; answer (math.).

solvabilité [sòlvàbìlìté] *f.* solvency. ‖ **solvable** [sòlvàbl] *adj.* solvent.

sombre [sonbr] *adj.* dark; sombre, gloomy; murky; dull, dim; overcast, murky, cloudy [ciel]; melancholy, dismal, glum [personne].

sombrer [sonbré] *v.* to founder (naut.); to sink, to collapse.

sommaire [sòmèr] *adj.* summary, brief; cursory, desultory; concise, abridged; *m.* summary.

sommation [sòmàsyon] *f.* summons, appeal; invitation.

somme [sòm] *f.* burden; *bête de somme*, beast of burden.

somme [sòm] *f.* sum, total; amount; summary; *en somme*, in short; *somme toute*, on the whole.

somme [sòm] *m.* nap, sleep. || *sommeil* [-èy] *m.* sleep; sleepiness, slumber, drowsiness; *avoir sommeil*, to be sleepy. || *sommeiller* [-èyé] *v.* to doze, to drowse, to snooze, to slumber; to lie dormant.

sommelier [sòmᵉlyé] *m.* butler; cellarman, wine-waiter.

sommer [sòmé] *v.* to summon, to call upon.

sommet [sòmè] *m.* top, summit, peak, crest; apex, acme; crown [tête]; extremity (zool.).

sommier [sòmyé] *m.* pack-horse, sumpter-mule; bed-mattress, spring-mattress; wind-chest [orgue]; timber support (mech.).

sommité [sòmìté] *f.* summit, top; head, principal; prominent person.

somnambule [sòmnᵃⁿbül] *m.*, *f.* sleep-walker, somnambulist. || *somnambulisme* [-lìsm] *m.* sleep-walking, somnambulism.

somnifère [sòmnìfèr] *m.* opiate; narcotic. || *somnolence* [-òlãⁿs] *f.* sleepiness, drowsiness. || *somnolent* [-òlãⁿ] *adj.* somnolent, sleepy, drowsy, slumberous. || *somnoler* [-lé] *v.* to doze, to drowse.

somptuaire [sonptüèr] *adj.* sumptuary.

somptueux [sonptüë] *adj.** sumptuous; magnificent; lavish, luxurious. || *somptuosité* [-üòzìté] *f.* sumptuousness; magnificence, splendo(u)r; lavishness, luxury.

son [son] *poss. adj. m.* (*f. sa, pl. ses*) his, her, its, one's.

son [son] *m.* sound, noise.

son [son] *m.* bran.

sonate [sònàt] *f.* sonata.

sondage [sondàj] *m.* sounding; boring (min.); fathoming; probing. || *sonde* [sond] *f.* sounding-line, depth-line, lead (naut.); probe (med.); bore (min.). || *sonder* [-é] *v.* to sound, to fathom; to probe; to bore [mine]; to search, to explore; to plumb (naut.).

songe [sonj] *m.* dream; dreaming. || *songer* [-é] *v.* to dream; to muse, to ponder; to think; to imagine. || *songerie* [-rî] *f.* dreaming; musing; reverie; meditating. || *songeur* [-ær] *adj.** dreamy, thoughtful, musing.

sonnaille [sònày] *f.* bell [bétail]. || *sonner* [-é] *v.* to sound; to ring, to toll; to strike [horloge]. || *sonnerie* [-rî] *f.* tolling, ringing, ring; buzzer; buzzing; bells, chimes; striking, striking part [horloge].

sonnet [sònè] *m.* sonnet.

sonnette [sònèt] *f.* bell; small bell; house bell, hand-bell, door-bell; buzzer, push-button. || *sonneur* [-ær] *m.* bell-ringer; trumpeter.

sonore [sònòr] *adj.* sonorous, resonant; deep-toned. || *sonoriser* [-nòrìzé] *v.* to add the sound-track to [film]; to voice (gramm.). || *sonorité* [-ìté] *f.* sonorousness; resonance.

sophisme [sòfìsm] *m.* sophism. || *sophiste* [-ìst] *s.* sophist; *adj.* sophistical.

sophistiquer [sòfìstìké] *v.* to adulterate; *sophistiqué*, sophisticated.

soporifique [sòpòrìfìk] *adj., m.* soporific.

sorbet [sòrbè] *m.* sorbet; sherbet.

sorcellerie [sòrsèlrî] *f.* sorcery, witchcraft. || *sorcier* [-yé] *m.* wizard, sorcerer. || *sorcière* [-yèr] *f.* witch, sorceress; hag (fam.).

sordide [sòrdìd] *adj.* sordid, filthy, dirty, grubby; squalid; vile, base; mean, avaricious.

sorgho [sòrgó] *m.* sorghum.

sort [sòr] *m.* fate, destiny; lot, condition; hazard, chance; spell, charm.

sorte [sòrt] *f.* sort, kind, species, type; manner, way; cast (typogr.); *de sorte que*, so that; *en quelque sorte*, in a way, as it were.

sortie [sòrtî] *f.* going out, coming out; exit, way out, outlet, escape; excursion, outing; sally, sortie (mil.); outburst; outbreak.

sortilège [sòrtìlèj] *m.* sortilege, witchcraft; spell.

sortir [sòrtîr] *v.** to go out, to come out, to exit; to bring out, to take out; to pull out; to leave, to depart; to deviate; to protrude, to project; to result, to ensue; to recover [santé].

sosie [sòzî] *m.* double.

sot, sotte [sò, sòt] *adj.* stupid, silly, foolish; ridiculous, absurd; *m., f.* fool. || *sottise* [sòtîz] *f.* foolishness, silliness, nonsense.

sou [sû] *m.* sou [monnaie]; penny, copper; *cent sous*, five francs.

soubassement [sûbàsmᵃⁿ] *m.* basement; substructure.

soubresaut [sûbrᵉsó] *m.* jerk, start; jolt; plunge [cheval].

souche [sûsh] *f.* stump, stock; stem; source, origin, root; head, founder [famille]; chimney-stack; counter-foil, stub [chèque, ticket]; tally.

souci [sûsì] *m.* anxiety, care, bother, worry; sollicitude, concern; marigold (bot.); *sans souci*. carefree ‖ **soucier** [-yé] *v.* to trouble, to upset, to bother, to worry; *se soucier*, to care, to mind, to be concerned, to be anxious. ‖ **soucieux** [-yë] *adj.*° anxious, solicitous, concerned, worried.

soucoupe [sûkûp] *f.* saucer; salver.

soudain [sûdĕⁿ] *adj.* sudden, abrupt; *adv.* suddenly, abruptly. ‖ **soudaineté** [-ĕnté] *f.* suddenness, unexpectedness, abruptness.

soude [sûd] *f.* soda.

souder [sûdé] *v.* to solder, to weld, to braze, to cement.

soudoyer [sûdwàyé] *v.* to bribe.

soudure [sûdûr] *f.* solder.

souffle [sûfl] *m.* breath, breathing; expiration, puff [vent]; inspiration (fig.). ‖ **soufflé** [-é] *m.* soufflé; *adj.* puffed [pâte]; amazed (fam.). ‖ **souffler** [-é] *v.* to breathe, to blow; to puff, to pant; to whisper; to prompt (theat.); to blow out [bougie]; to huff [pion]; to diddle (fam.). ‖ **soufflerie** [-erî] *f.* bellows [orgue]; blowing-apparatus. ‖ **soufflet** [-è] *m* bellows; slap, box on the ear; affront ‖ **souffleter** [-*té] *v* to slap, to box the ears; to outrage. ‖ **souffleur** [-œr] *m.* blower; prompter. ‖ **souffleuse** [-ëz] *f.* Ⓒ snow-blower.

souffrance [sûfrⁿs] *f.* suffering, pain; distress, *en souffrance*, suspended, in abeyance. ‖ **souffrant** [-ⁿ] *adj* suffering, in pain; ill, sick, unwell, poorly, ailing; injured; forbearing. ‖ **souffreteux** [-*tĕ] *adj.*° sickly, weak, needy; feeble, languid ‖ **souffrir** [-îr] *v.*° to suffer; to bear, to endure, to undergo; to tolerate; to allow; to be suffering, to be in pain, in trouble; *souffre-douleur*, butt, laughing-stock, whipping-boy, scapegoat.

soufre [sûfr] *m.* sulphur; brimstone. ‖ **soufrer** [-é] *v.* to sulphur.

souhait [sûè] *m.* wish, desire. ‖ **souhaitable** [-tàbl] *adj.* desirable. ‖ **souhaiter** [-té] *v.* to desire; to wish (something) to (someone).

souiller [sûyé] *v.* to soil, to stain, to dirty, to sully, to blemish; to defile. ‖ **souillon** [sûyoⁿ] *m* slut, sloven; slattern; *f.* scullery-wench. ‖ **souillure** [sûyûr] *f.* dirt, spot, stain; blot, blemish.

soûl [sû] *adj.* surfeited, glutted; (pop.) drunk, intoxicated, tipsy, *Am.* high (fam.); satiated, cloyed.

soulagement [sûlàjmⁿ] *m.* relief, alleviation, solace. ‖ **soulager** [-é] *v.* to relieve, to alleviate, to assuage, to allay; to succo(u)r.

soûlard [sûlàr], **soûlaud** [sûlô] *m.* (fam.) drunkard, boozer. ‖ **soûler**

[sûlé] *v.* to fill, to glut; to intoxicate, to inebriate; *se soûler*, to get drunk.

soulèvement [sûlèvmⁿ] *m* heaving, upheaval swelling [vagues]; rising [estomac] insurrection. ‖ **soulever** [sûlvé] *v* to raise, to lift, to heave, to excite to stir up, to provoke; to sicken, *se soulever*, to raise oneself, to rise; to heave; to revolt, to rebel

soulier [sûlyé] *m.* shoe; slipper.

souligner [sûlîñé] *v* to underline, to underscore to emphasize.

soumettre [sûmètr] *v* ° to submit, to defer, to subject, to subdue; to subordinate *se soumettre*, to submit, to yield; to comply, to assent ‖ **soumis** [-ì] *adj* submissive tractable, compliant, docile, subdued ‖ **soumission** [-ìsyoⁿ] *f* submission, compliance; submissiveness, subjection; offer, tender [contrat] ‖ **soumissionner** [-ìsyòné] *v* to tender, to present.

soupape [sûpàp] *f.* valve; plug; *soupape de sûreté*, safety-valve.

soupçon [sûpsoⁿ] *m* suspicion, mistrust, distrust misgiving, idea, inkling, *Am.* hunch (pop.), surmise, conjecture; dash, touch, hint, dab, bit (fig.). ‖ **soupçonner** [-òné] *v* to suspect, *Am.* to have a hunch (pop.); to surmise, to conjecture, to question. ‖ **soupçonneux** [-òñĕ] *adj.*° suspicious, doubtful.

soupe [sûp] *f.* soup; food, grub (pop.); *Am.* chow (mil.).

soupente [sûpaⁿt] *f.* loft, garret.

souper [sûpé] *m.* supper; *v.* to have supper, to sup.

soupeser [sûpᵉzé] *v.* to weigh in one's hand, *Am.* to heft.

soupière [sûpyèr] *f.* soup-tureen.

soupir [sûpîr] *m* sigh, gasp; breath; crotchet-rest (mus.) ‖ **soupirail** [sûpìrày] *m.*° air-hole vent. ‖ **soupirant** [-ìraⁿ] *m* suitor, wooer, lover. ‖ **soupirer** [-ìré] *v* to sigh, to gasp; *soupirer après*, to long for.

souple [sûpl] *adj* supple, pliant, flexible compliant ‖ **souplesse** [-ès] *f.* pliancy, suppleness flexibility; compliance versatility

source [sûrs] *f.* spring; source. ‖ **sourcier** [sûrsyé] *m.* water-diviner, dowser

sourcil [sûrsì] *m.* eyebrow, brow. ‖ **sourciller** [-yé] *v.* to frown; to flinch. ‖ **sourcilleux** [-yë] *adj.*° supercilious.

sourd [sûr] *adj.* deaf, dull; insensible, dead, hollow, muffled [bruit]; secret, underhanded; *m.* deaf person; *sourd-muet*, deaf-mute. ‖ **sourdine** [-dîn] *f.* mute; *en sourdine*, on the sly.

souriant [sûryaⁿ] *adj.* smiling.

souricière [sûrìsyèr] *f.* mouse-trap.

sourire [sûrîr] *v.** to smile; to be favo(u)rable; *m.* smile.

souris [sûrì] *f.* mouse; *pl.* mice.

sournois [sûrnwà] *adj.* sly; sneaking, underhanded. ‖ *sournoiserie* [-zrî] *f.* slyness; cunning.

sous [sû] *prep.* under, beneath, below; on, upon; with, by; in; *sous peu*, before long, in a short while; *sous-bois*, undergrowth; *sous-chef*, deputy head; *sous-cutané*, subcutaneous; *sous-entendu*, understood; implied, hinted; implication, hint; *sous-lieutenant*, second-lieutenant; *sous-louer*, to sub-let, to sub-lease; *sous-main*, writing-pad; *sous-marin*, submarine; *sous-officier*, non-commissioned officer; N. C. O.; *sous-préfet*, sub-prefect; *sous-produit*, by-product; *je soussigné*, I, the undersigned; *sous-sol*, subsoil, substratum; basement, cellar; *sous-titre*, subtitle.

souscripteur [sûskrìptœr] *m.* subscriber. ‖ *souscription* [sûskrìpsyoⁿ] *f.* subscription; signature; underwriting. ‖ *souscrire* [-îr] *v.** to subscribe; to underwrite, to endorse.

soussigné [sûsîñé] *adj.* undersigned.

soustraction [sûstràksyoⁿ] *f.* subtraction; taking away, abstraction. ‖ *soustraire* [-èr] *v.** to subtract; to remove, to lift; *se soustraire*, to withdraw; to shirk [devoir].

soutache [sûtàsh] *f.* braid.

soutane [sûtàn] *f.* cassock, soutane.

soute [sût] *f.* bunker [charbon]; magazine [poudre]; store-room.

soutenir [sûtnîr] *v.** to support, to sustain, to hold up; to maintain, to contend, to uphold, to affirm; to bear, to endure, to stand; to defend [thèse]. ‖ *soutenu* [-ü] *adj.* sustained; constant, unceasing, unremitting.

souterrain [sûtèrⁱⁿ] *adj.* underground, subterranean; *m.* underground gallery; subway [métro].

soutien [sûtyⁱⁿ] *m.* support, prop, stay; supporter, upholder, vindicator; *soutien-gorge*, brassière.

soutirer [sûtìré] *v.* to draw off, to rack, to extract [liqueur]; to tap [vin]; to filch [argent].

souvenance [sûvnaⁿs] *f.* remembrance. ‖ *souvenir* [-îr] *m.* remembrance, recollection, memory; reminder, memento, souvenir, keepsake; *v.** *se souvenir de*, to remember, to recall, to recollect.

souvent [sûvaⁿ] *adv.* often, frequently.

souverain [sûvrⁱⁿ] *m.* sovereign; *adj.* sovereign, supreme; highest, extreme; without appeal (jur.). ‖

souveraineté [-èⁿté] *f.* sovereignty; dominion.

soviet [sòvyèt] *m.* soviet. ‖ *soviétique* [sòvyétìk] *adj.* soviet.

soya [sòyà] *m.* soya-bean, Am. soybean.

soyeux [swàyë] *adj.** silky, silken.

spacieux [spàsyë] *adj.** spacious, roomy, wide, expansive.

sparadrap [spàràdrà] *m.* adhesivetape, court-plaster, sticking-plaster.

spasme [spàsm] *m.* spasm. ‖ *spasmodique* [-òdìk] *adj.* spasmodic; spastic.

spatial [spàsìàl] *adj.** interplanetary; space.

spatule [spàtül] *f.* spatula; butterpat; ski-tip.

speaker [spìkœr] *m.* speaker; announcer, broadcaster [radio].

spécial [spésyàl] *adj.** special, specific, particular; professional, specialistic. ‖ *spécialiser* [-ìzé] *v.* to specialize; to specify; to particularize; *se spécialiser*, to specialize; *Am.* to major [étude]. ‖ *spécialiste* [-ìst] *m., f.* specialist. ‖ *spécialité* [-ìté] *f.* specialty; speciality; knack (fam.).

spécieux [spésyë] *adj.** specious.

spécifier [spésìfyé] *v.* to specify; to stipulate. ‖ *spécifique* [-ìk] *adj.* specific.

spécimen [spésìmèn] *m.* specimen, sample.

spectacle [spèktàkl] *m.* spectacle, sight; play, show. ‖ *spectateur, -trice* [-àtœr, -àtrìs] *m., f.* spectator, onlooker; bystander; *m. pl.* audience.

spectre [spèktr] *m.* spectre, ghost; spectrum [solaire].

spéculateur, -trice [spékülàtœr, trìs] *m., f.* theorizer, speculator. ‖ *spéculatif* [-àtìf] *adj.** speculative. ‖ *spéculation* [-àsyoⁿ] *f.* speculation. ‖ *spéculer* [-é] *v.* to speculate; to ponder; to theorize.

spéléologie [spéléòlòjî] *f.* speleology. ‖ *spéléologue* [-lòg] *s.* speleologist; pot-holer (fam.).

sphère [sfèr] *f.* sphere. ‖ *sphérique* [sférìk] *adj.* spherical.

spirale [spìràl] *f.* spiral.

spiritisme [spìrìtìsm] *m.* spiritualism. ‖ *spiritualité* [-tüàlìté] *f.* spirituality. ‖ *spirituel* [-üèl] *adj.** spiritual; religious; mental, intellectual; humorous, witty; sprightly. ‖ *spiritueux* [-üë] *adj.* spirituous; *m. pl.* spirits.

splendeur [splaⁿdœr] *f.* splendo(u)r, radiance, glory; pomp, magnificence. ‖ *splendide* [-ìd] *adj.* splendid, sumptuous, magnificent.

spoliation [spòlyàsyoⁿ] *f.* spoliation. ‖ *spolier* [-yé] *v.* to despoil, to plunder; to defraud.

spongieux [sponjyë] *adj.* spongy.

spontané [spontàné] *adj.* spontaneous. ‖ *spontanéité* [-éité] *f.* spontaneity, spontaneousness.

sporadique [spòràdĭk] *adj.* sporadic.

sport [spòr] *m.* sport. ‖ *sportif* [-tĭf] *adj.* sporting; *m.* sports lover. ‖ *sportivité* [-tĭvĭté] *f.* sportmanship.

square [skwàr] *m.* park, square.

squelette [skëlèt] *m.* skeleton. ‖ *squelettique* [-tĭk] *adj.* skeletal; thin, emaciate.

stabilisateur, -trice [stàbĭlĭzàtœr, -trĭs] *adj.* stabilizing; *m., f.* stabilizer. ‖ *stabilisation* [-àsyoⁿ] *f.* stabilization, balancing. ‖ *stabiliser* [-é] *v.* to stabilize. ‖ *stabilité* [stàbĭlĭté] *f.* stability, steadfastness. ‖ *stable* [stàbl] *adj.* steady, stable; lasting; steadfast.

stade [stàd] *m.* stadium; stage.

stage [stàj] *m.* stage, period.

stalle [stàl] *f.* stall; seat.

stance [staⁿs] *f.* stanza.

station [stàsyoⁿ] *f.* station; stop; resort. ‖ *stationnaire* [-yònèr] *adj.* stationary. ‖ *stationner* [-yòné] *v.* to station; to stop, to stand, to park.

statistique [stàtĭstĭk] *f.* statistics; *adj.* statistical.

statue [stàtü] *f.* statue.

statuer [stàtüé] *v.* to decree, to ordain, to enact; to make laws.

stature [stàtür] *f.* stature.

statut [stàtü] *m.* statute; ordinance.

sténodactylo(graphe) [sténòdàktĭlògràf] *m., f.* shorthand-typist. ‖ *sténo-(graphe)* [sténògràf] *m., f.* stenographer. ‖ *sténo(graphie)* [-ĭ] *f.* stenography, shorthand. ‖ *sténographier* [-yé] *v.* to take down in shorthand.

stérile [stérĭl] *adj.* sterile, barren; fruitless. ‖ *stériliser* [-ĭzé] *v.* to sterilize; to castrate, to geld. ‖ *stérilité* [-ĭté] *f.* sterility.

stigmate [stĭgmàt] *m.* stigma. ‖ *stigmatisé* [-ĭzé] *adj.* stigmatized; *m.* stigmatist.

stimuler [stĭmülé] *v.* to stimulate, to excite, to stir; to whet [appétit].

stipuler [stĭpülé] *v.* to stipulate, to specify; to contract, to covenant.

stock [stòk] *m.* stock, supply, hoard.

stop! [stòp] *interj.* stop!

stoppage [stòpàj] *m.* invisible mending, reweaving. ‖ *stopper* [-é] *v.* to reweave; to stop, to halt.

store [stòr] *m.* blind, shade; awning.

strapontin [stràpoⁿtĭⁿ] *m.* folding-seat, *Am.* jumpseat.

stratagème [stràtàgèm] *m.* stratagem, dodge. ‖ *stratégie* [-éjĭ] *f.* strategy.

stratosphérique [stràtòsférĭk] *adj.* strato(spheric).

strict [strĭkt] *adj.* strict, severe.

strident [strĭdoⁿ] *adj.* strident, shrill, rasping, jarring.

strophe [stròf] *f.* strophe.

structure [strüktür] *f.* structure.

stuc [stük] *m.* stucco.

studieux [stüdyë] *adj.* studious.

stupéfaction [stüpéfàksyoⁿ] *f.* stupefaction, amazement; bewilderment. ‖ *stupéfait* [-è] *adj.* astounded, stunned, stupefied, speechless. ‖ *stupéfiant* [-yaⁿ] *adj.* stupefying, astounding; *m.* narcotic, stupefacient. ‖ *stupéfier* [-yé] *v.* to stupefy, to amaze, to astound, to dumbfound.

stupeur [stüpœr] *f.* stupor, daze. ‖ *stupide* [-ĭd] foolish, senseless, stupid, *Am.* dumb. ‖ *stupidité* [-ĭdĭté] *f.* stupidity, *Am.* dumbness.

style [stĭl] *m.* style; stylus. ‖ *stylo* [-ô] *m.* fountain-pen; *stylo à bille*, ball-point pen.

suaire [süèr] *m.* shroud.

suave [süàv] *adj.* sweet, agreeable; soft; suave, bland, unctuous. ‖ *suavité* [-ĭté] *f.* sweetness; suavity.

subalterne [sübàltèrn] *adj.* subaltern; *m.* underling, subaltern.

subdivision [sübdĭvĭzyoⁿ] *f.* subdivision; lot, tract [terre].

subir [sübĭr] *v.* to undergo, to submit to; to take [examen].

subit [sübĭ] *adj.* sudden, brusque. ‖ *subitement* [-tmaⁿ] *adv.* suddenly, all at once, all of a sudden.

subjectif [sübjèktĭf] *adj.* subjective.

subjonctif [sübjoⁿktĭf] *m.* subjunctive.

subjuguer [sübjügé] *v.* to subjugate, to subdue; to master.

sublime [süblĭm] *adj.* sublime, lofty; *sublimer* [-mé] *v.* to sublimate.

submerger [sübmèrjé] *v.* to submerge, to inundate; to sink. ‖ *submersion* [-syoⁿ] *f.* submersion; submergence.

subordonné [sübòrdòné] *adj.* subordinate, inferior, subaltern; subservient, dependent. ‖ *subordonner* [-é] *v.* to subordinate.

suborner [sübòrné] *v.* to bribe; to tamper with [témoin]. ‖ *suborneur* [-œr] *m.* suborner, briber.

subséquent [sübséka] *adj.* subsequent, ensuing.

subside [sübsìd] *m.* subsidy.

subsistance [sübzìstаⁿs] *f.* subsistence, sustenance, maintenance; *pl.* provisions, supplies. ‖ **subsister** [-é] *v.* to subsist, to stand; to be extant; to exist, to live.

substance [sübstаⁿs] *f.* substance; matter; gist. ‖ **substantiel** [-yèl] *adj.* substantial; solid, stout.

substantif [sübstаⁿtìf] *m.* substantive, noun.

substituer [sübstìtüé] *v.* to substitute. ‖ **substitut** [-ü] *m.* substitute. ‖ **substitution** [-üsyoⁿ] *f.* substitution.

subterfuge [sübtèrfüj] *m.* evasion, shift, dodge.

subtil [sübtìl] *adj.* subtle, shrewd, subtile; cunning. ‖ **subtiliser** [-ìzé] *v.* to subtilize; to filch. ‖ **subtilité** [-ìté] *f.* subtlety, shrewdness; subtility.

subvenir [sübvᵉnìr] *v.** to supply, to provide. ‖ **subvention** [-аⁿsyoⁿ] *f.* subsidy. ‖ **subventionner** [-аⁿsyòné] *v.* to subsidize.

subversif [sübvèrsìf] *adj.** subversive. ‖ **subversion** [-syoⁿ] *f.* subversion.

suc [sük] *m.* juice, sap; pith.

succédané [süksédàné] *m., adj.* substitute.

succéder [süksédé] *v.* to succeed, to follow; to replace; to inherit.

succès [süksè] *m.* success; *succès fou,* wild success, smash hit.

successeur [süksèsœr] *m.* successor; heir. ‖ **successif** [-ìf] *adj.** successive, consecutive. ‖ **succession** [-yoⁿ] *f.* succession; sequence, series; inheritance.

succinct [süksìⁿ] *adj.* succint, concise, terse.

succomber [sükoⁿbé] *v.* to succumb, to die, to perish; to yield.

succulent [sükülаⁿ] *adj.* succulent, juicy, luscious; tasty, toothsome.

succursale [sükürsàl] *f.* branch agency, sub-office, regional office.

sucer [süsé] *v.* to suck, to absorb; to draw, to drain. ‖ **sucette** [-èt] *f.* sucker, lollipop [bonbon]. ‖ **suceur** [-œr] *adj.* sucking; *m.* sucker; nozzle.

sucre [sükr] *m.* sugar; *pain de sucre,* sugar-lump; *sucre en morceaux,* lump-sugar; *sucre semoule,* granulated sugar; *sucre cristallisé,* coarse sugar; *sucre candi,* crystallized sugar; *sucre d'érable,* © maple sugar; *partie de sucre,* © sugaring party. ‖ *sucres, m. pl.* © maple sugar time; *aller aux sucres,* © to go to a sugaring party. ‖ **sucrer** [-é] *v.* to sugar. ‖ **sucrerie** [-ᵉrî] *f.* sugar-works; *Br.* sweet, *Am.* candy; © maple bush, sugar bush. ‖ **sucrier** [-ìyé] *m.* sugar-bowl.

sud [süd] *m.* south; *du sud,* southern; *sud-est,* south-east; *sud-ouest,* south-west.

suer [süé] *v.* to sweat, to perspire; to ooze [mur]. ‖ **sueur** [süœr] *f.* sweat, perspiration.

suffire [süfîr] *v.** to suffice, to be enough; to be adequate; *se suffire,* to be self-sufficient. ‖ **suffisamment** [-ìzàmаⁿ] *adv.* sufficiently, enough; adequately. ‖ **suffisance** [-ìzаⁿs] *f.* sufficiency; adequacy; self-sufficiency, conceit. ‖ **suffisant** [-ìzаⁿ] *adj.* sufficient, plenty, enough; conceited, self-sufficient.

suffocant [süfòkаⁿ] *adj.* suffocating; startling, stunning. ‖ **suffocation** [-fòkàsyoⁿ] *f.* suffocation, stifling. ‖ **suffoquer** [-é] *v.* to suffocate, to stifle; to choke; to take (s.o. 's) breath away.

suffrage [süfràj] *m.* suffrage, vote.

suggérer [sügjéré] *v.* to suggest; to hint; to prompt, to inspire. ‖ **suggestif** [-èstìf] *adj.** suggestive; evocative. ‖ **suggestion** [-èstyoⁿ] *f.* instigation, incitement, hint; proposal. ‖ **suggestionner** [-èstyòné] *v.* to suggest; to prompt; to influence by means of suggestion.

suicide [süìsìd] *m.* suicide. ‖ **suicider (se)** [sᵉsüìsìdé] *v.* to commit suicide, to kill oneself. ‖ **suicidé** [süìsìdé] *m.* self-murderer, suicide.

suie [süî] *f.* soot.

suif [süìf] *m.* tallow.

suinter [süìⁿté] *v.* to ooze, to seep, to sweat, to drip, to trickle, to leak, to exude.

Suisse [süìs] *f.* Switzerland; *m.* Swiss; beadle; © chipmunk.

suite [süìt] *f.* following, pursuit; continuation; suite, retinue; attendants; order, series, sequence; consequence, result; *tout de suite,* at once, right away; *donner suite à,* to follow up, to carry out; *et ainsi de suite,* and so on, and so forth. ‖ **suivant** [-süìvаⁿ] *adj.* next, following; *prep.* in the direction of; according to; *m.* attendant. ‖ **suivante** [-аⁿt] *f.* lady's maid. ‖ **suivre** [süìvr] *v.** to follow, to pursue; to succeed; to attend [cours, concert]; *à suivre,* to be continued.

sujet, -ette [süjè, -èt] *adj.* subject, liable, prone, exposed, apt (*à,* to); *m.* subject; topic, matter; cause, reason, ground; fellow, person; *au sujet de,* concerning, about. ‖ **sujétion** [-ésyoⁿ] *f.* subjection.

sulfate [sülfàt] *m.* sulphate. ‖ **sulfater** [-té] *v.* to sulphate.

sulfureux [sülfürë] *adj.** sulphurous. ‖ **sulfurique** [-ìk] *adj.* sulphuric. ‖ **sulfurisé** [-ìzé] *adj.* butter, imitation parchment [papier].

sultan [sültaⁿ] *m.* sultan.

sumac [sümàk] *m.* sumac; *sumac vénéneux,* poison-ivy.

superbe [süpèrb] *adj.* superb.

supercherie [süpèrsh°rî] *f.* deceit, fraud, swindle; trickery.

superficie [süpèrfîsî] *f.* area, surface. ‖ *superficiel* [-yèl] *adj.** superficial; shallow [esprit].

superflu [süpèrflü] *adj.* superfluous; redundant; useless; *m.* superfluity.

supérieur [süpéryœr] *adj.* superior; upper, higher; *m.* superior; principal. ‖ *supériorité* [-yòrìté] *f.* superiority; predominance; advantage; seniority [âge].

superlatif [süpèrlàtìf] *adj.*,* *m.* superlative.

supersonique [süpèrsònîk] *adj.* supersonic.

superstitieux [süpèrstìsyë] *adj.** superstitious. ‖ *superstition* [-yoⁿ] *f.* superstition.

supplanter [süplaⁿté] *v.* to supplant, to supersede, to oust.

suppléance [süpléaⁿs] *f.* substitution, deputyship, temporary term. ‖ *suppléant* [-éaⁿ] *adj.* substitute, deputy, acting, temporary. ‖ *suppléer* [-éé] *v.* to replace, to substitute for; to supplement; to supply; to compensate; to deputize for.

supplément [süplémaⁿ] *m.* supplement; extra payment, extra fare. ‖ *supplémentaire* [-tèr] *adj.* supplementary, additional, extra; *heures supplémentaires,* overtime.

supplication [süplìkàsyoⁿ] *f.* supplication, entreaty, beseeching.

supplice [süplîs] *m.* torture; torment, agony. ‖ *supplicier* [-syé] *v.* to torture; to execute.

supplier [süplìyé] *v.* to supplicate, to implore, to entreat, to beseech.

support [süpòr] *f.* support, prop. ‖ *supportable* [-tàbl] *adj.* bearable, tolerable. ‖ *supporter* [-té] *v.* to support, to uphold; to prop, to sustain; to endure, to bear, to suffer; to tolerate. ‖ *supporter* [-tèr] *m.* supporter; fan.

supposé [süpòzé] *adj.* supposed, alleged; assumed; fictitious. ‖ *supposer* [-é] *v.* to suppose, to assume; to imply. ‖ *supposition* [-ìsyoⁿ] *f.* supposition, assumption, surmise.

suppositoire [süpòzìtwàr] *m.* suppository.

suppôt [süpò] *m.* henchman, tool.

suppression [süprèsyoⁿ] *f.* suppression; stoppage; removing; abatement [bruit]. ‖ *supprimer* [süprìmé] *v.* to

suppress, to abolish; to quell; to eliminate; to cancel; to do away with [personne].

suppuration [süpüràsyoⁿ] *f.* suppuration. ‖ *suppurer* [-ré] *v.* to suppurate.

supputer [süpüté] *v.* to reckon.

suprématie [süprémàsî] *f.* supremacy. ‖ *suprême* [-èm] *adj.* supreme, highest, crowning.

sur [sür] *prep.* on, upon; onto; above; over; towards, about [heure]; *sur-le-champ,* right away, immediately; *sur l'heure,* without delay, at once.

sur [sür] *adj.* sour, tart.

sûr [sür] *adj.* sure, certain; safe, secure; assured; reliable, trustworthy; infallible [remède].

surabondance [süràboⁿdaⁿs] *f.* superabundance, profusion. ‖ *surabondant* [-aⁿ] *adj.* superabundant, profuse. ‖ *surabonder* [-é] *v.* to superabound, to overflow with.

suraigu [sürègü] *adj.** high-pitched, shrill, acute (med.).

suralimentation [süràlìmaⁿtàsyoⁿ] *f.* overfeeding. ‖ *suralimenter* [-é] *v.* to overfeed.

surcharge [sürshàrJ] *f.* overloading, overworking; overtax, overcharge; surcharge [timbre].

surcroît [sürkrwà] *m.* increase; surplus; *par surcroît,* in addition.

surdité [sürdìté] *f.* deafness.

sûrement [sürmaⁿ] *adv.* safely, surely, securely; certainly, assuredly. ‖ *sûreté* [sürté] *f.* safety, security; guarantee; sureness, reliability; *la Sûreté,* Criminal Investigation Department, *Am.* Federal Bureau of Investigation.

surette [sürèt] *f.* © sorrel (*Fr.* oseille).

surexciter [sürèksìté] *v.* to overexcite.

surface [sürfàs] *f.* surface; area.

surfaire [sürfèr] *v.** to overcharge; to overrate; to overdo.

surgir [sürJîr] *v.* to rise, to surge, to loom up; to spring up, to bob up.

surhomme [süròm] *m.* superman. ‖ *surhumain* [-ümⁿ] *adj.* superhuman.

surintendant [sürìⁿtaⁿdaⁿ] *m.* superintendent, overseer.

surjet [sürJè] *m.* overcasting, whipping [couture].

surlendemain [sürlaⁿdmⁿ] *m.* two days after, the second day after.

surmenage [sürm°nàJ] *m.* overworking, overexertion, overdoing. ‖ *surmener* [-é] *v.* to overwork, to overexert, to overstrain.

surmonter [sürmoⁿté] *v.* to surmount, to top; to master.

surnaturel [sürnàtürèl] *adj.** supernatural, uncanny, weird, eerie.

surnom [sürnoⁿ] *m.* surname, family name; nickname.

surnombre [sürnoⁿbr] *m.* surplus.

surnommer [sürnômé] *v.* to name, to style; to nickname.

surnuméraire [sürnümérèr] *m., adj.* supernumerary.

suroît [sürwà] *m.* south-west; sou'wester.

surpasser [sürpàsé] *v.* to surpass, to outdo, to excel, to exceed.

surplis [sürplì] *m.* surplice.

surplomber [sürploⁿbé] *v.* to overhang, to jut out over.

surplus [sürplü] *m.* surplus, overplus; *au surplus*, besides, moreover.

surprenant [sürprenaⁿ] *adj.* surprising, amazing, astonishing. ‖ **surprendre** [sürpraⁿdr] *v.** to surprise, to astonish; to intercept; to overhear. ‖ **surprise** [-ìz] *f.* surprise.

surproduction [sürprôdüksyoⁿ] *f.* overproduction.

surréalisme [sürréàlìsm] *m.* surrealism.

sursaut [sürsô] *m.* start, jump. ‖ **sursauter** [-té] *v.* to start; *faire sursauter*, to startle.

surseoir [sürswàr] *v.** to postpone, to suspend, to defer, to delay; to stay [jugement]. ‖ **sursis** [-ì] *m.* delay, respite; reprieve.

surtaxe [sürtàks] *f.* surtax; extra postage, postage due [timbres]. ‖ **surtaxer** [-ksé] *v.* to supertax, to overtax.

surtout [sürtû] *adv.* especially, above all, chiefly, principally.

surveillance [sürvèyaⁿs] *f.* supervision, watching, superintendence, surveillance; observation, lookout (mil.). ‖ **surveillant** [-èyaⁿ] *m.* overseer, inspector, supervisor. ‖ **surveiller** [-èyé] *v.* to superintend, to supervise, to oversee, to watch over; to tend, to look after [machine].

survenir [sürvenìr] *v.** to occur, to happen, to supervene; to drop in.

survie [sürvì] *f.* survival.

survivance [sürvìvaⁿs] *f.* survival; outliving. ‖ **survivant** [-ìvaⁿ] *m.* survivor. ‖ **survivre** [-ìvr] *v.** to survive, to outlive.

survol [sürvòl] *m.* flight over (aviat.); panning [cinéma]. ‖ **survoler** [-é] *v.* to fly over.

sus [süs] *prep.* on, upon; against; *en sus*, over and above, in addition, furthermore.

susceptibilité [süsèptìbìlìté] *f.* susceptibility; sensitiveness, touchiness. ‖

susceptible [-ìbl] *adj.* susceptible, sensitive, touchy; capable (*de*, of), liable (*de*, to).

susciter [süsìté] *v.* to raise up; to instigate; to kindle, to arouse, to stir up; to create.

susdit [süsdì] *adj.* above-mentioned, aforesaid.

suspect [süspè] *adj.* suspicious; questionable; *m.* suspect. ‖ **suspecter** [-kté] *v.* to suspect; to question.

suspendre [süspaⁿdr] *v.* to hang up, to suspend; to hold in abeyance; to defer, to stay [jugement]; to stop [paiement]. ‖ **suspens** [-aⁿ] *m.* suspense; *adj.* suspended; *en suspens*, in abeyance; outstanding. ‖ **suspension** [-aⁿsyoⁿ] *f.* suspension; hanging up, swinging; stoppage; springs [auto].

suspicion [süspìsyoⁿ] *f.* suspicion.

sustenter [süstaⁿté] *v.* to sustain, to nourish, to support.

susurrer [süsüré] *v.* to whisper; to buzz; to rustle, to susurrate.

suture [sütür] *f.* seam; suture, stitching (med.). ‖ **suturer** [-ré] *v.* to suture.

suzerain [süzrⁿ] *m., adj.* suzerain.

svelte [svèlt] *adj.* svelte, slender. ‖ **sveltesse** [-ès] *f.* slenderness.

syllabe [sìllàb] *f.* syllable. ‖ **syllabique** [-ìk] *adj.* syllabic.

symbole [sìⁿbòl] *m.* symbol, emblem. ‖ **symbolique** [-ìk] *adj.* symbolic, emblematic; token [paiement]. ‖ **symboliser** [-ìzé] *v.* to symbolize. ‖ **symbolisme** [-ìsm] *m.* symbolism.

symétrie [sìmétrì] *f.* symmetry. ‖ ‖ **symétrique** [-ìk] *adj.* symmetrical.

sympathie [sìⁿpàtì] *f.* sympathy; liking, attraction, congeniality. ‖ **sympathique** [-ìk] *adj.* sympathetic; attractive, pleasing, appealing. ‖ **sympathiser** [-zé] *v.* to sympathize; to harmonize, to correspond.

symphonie [sìⁿfònì] *f.* symphony.

symptôme [sìⁿptôm] *m.* symptom.

synagogue [sìnàgòg] *f.* synagogue.

syncope [sìⁿkòp] *f.* syncope; faint; *tomber en syncope*, to faint.

syndical [sìⁿdìkàl] *adj.** syndical; *chambre syndicale*, trade-union committee. ‖ **syndicalisme** [-àlìsm] *m.* trade-unionism. ‖ **syndicat** [-à] *m.* trade-union, syndicate; *syndicat d'initiative*, tourists' information bureau. ‖ **syndiqué** [-é] *adj.* syndicated; *m.* trade-unionist. ‖ **syndiquer** [-é] *v.* to syndicate; to form into a trade-union.

synthèse [sìⁿtèz] *f.* synthesis.

systématique [sìstémàtìk] *adj.* systematic, methodical. ‖ **système** [sìstèm] *m.* system, method; plan.

T

ta [tà] *poss. adj. f.* thy, your.

tabac [tàbà] *m.* tobacco. ‖ **tabatière** [-tyèr] *f.* snuff-box.

table [tàbl] *f.* table; meal; switchboard (teleph.); plate [métal]; *table des matières*, table of contents.

tableau [tàblô] *m.*° frame, painting; scene, sight; list, catalog(ue), table; panel [jurés]; board, blackboard, bulletin-board, *Br.* notice board; telegraph-board; switchboard (electr.); indicator-board; *tableau de bord*, dashboard [auto]. ‖ **tabler** [tàblé] *v.* to count [*sur*, on]. ‖ **tablette** [-èt] *f.* tablet; note-book; writing-pad; shelf; bar, slab [chocolat]; lozenge, troche (pharm.). ‖ **tablier** [-lyé] *m.* apron; hood [cheminée].

tabou [tàbù] *adj.* taboo, tabooed; forbidden; *m.* taboo.

tabouret [tàbûrè] *m.* stool.

tache [tàsh] *f.* stain, spot, blot, blob, blur, speck; taint, blemish, flaw.

tâche [tàsh] *f.* task, job.

tacher [tàshé] *v.* to stain, to spot; to taint, to blemish, to mar.

tâcher [tàshé] *v.* to try, to attempt.

tacheter [tàshté] *v.* to fleck, to speckle, to mottle.

tacite [tàsìt] *adj.* tacit, implied. ‖ **taciturne** [-ûrn] *adj.* taciturn.

tacot [tàkò] *m.* (fam.) bone-shaker, *Am.* jalopy [autom.]; puffer (railw.).

tact [tàkt] *m.* feeling, touch; tact, diplomacy. ‖ **tacticien** [-lsyin] *m.* tactician. ‖ **tactique** [-ìk] *adj.* tactical; *f.* tactics.

taffetas [tàftà] *m.* taffeta; *taffetas gommé*, adhesive-tape.

taie [tè] *f.* pillow-case.

taillader [tàyàdé] *v.* to slash.

taille [tày] *f.* cutting; pruning, trimming, clipping; cut, shape; edge [couteau]; tally; waist, figure; stature, height, size, measure; *taille-crayon*, pencil-sharpener; *taille-douce*, copperplate engraving. ‖ **tailler** [-é] *v.* to cut; to prune, to trim, to clip; to tally; to carve; to sharpen [crayon]; to cut out, to tailor [couture]. ‖ **tailleur** [-œr] *m.* tailor; cutter; tailored suit. ‖ **taillis** [-ì] *m.* copse.

tain [tin] *m.* silvering; foil.

taire [tèr] *v.*° to keep secret, to hush up, to suppress, to keep dark; *se taire*, to be quiet, to fall silent.

talc [tàlk] *m.* French chalk; talcum.

talent [tàlàn] *m.* talent, capacity.

taloche [tàlòsh] *f.* (fam.) cuff.

talon [tàlon] *m.* heel; sole [gouvernail]; stock, reserve; pile [cartes]; shoulder [épée]; stub, counterfoil (comm.); beading, bead [pneu]. ‖ **talonner** [-òné] *v.* to follow, to tail, to dog; to dun; to spur [cheval]; to urge on; to pester.

talus [tàlü] *m.* slope, bank.

tambour [tanbûr] *m.* drum; drummer; barrel [horloge]; spool [bobine]; roller [treuil]; tambour, tympanum (anat.); *tambour-major*, drum-major. ‖ **tambouriner** [-ìné] *v.* to thrum.

tamis [tàmì] *m.* sieve, sifter. ‖ **tamiser** [-zé] *v.* to sift, to strain, to screen; to filter through; to bolt; to soften.

tampon [tanpon] *m.* stopper; plug; rubber stamp; buffer (railw.); pad [ouate]. ‖ **tamponnement** [-ònman] *m.* plugging; collision, shock; thumping. ‖ **tamponner** [-òné] *v.* to plug; to rub with a pad, to dab; to collide with, to bump into.

tan [tan] *m.* tan; tan-bark.

tancer [tansé] *v.* to rate.

tanche [tansh] *f.* tench.

tandem [tandèm] *m.* tandem.

tandis [tandì] *adv.* meanwhile; *tandis que*, while, whereas.

tangage [tangàj] *m.* pitching, rocking.

tangent [tanjan] *adj.* tangent(ial). ‖ **tangente** [-ant] *f.* tangent.

tangible [tanjìbl] *adj.* tangible.

tanguer [tangé] *v.* to pitch, to rock.

tanière [tànyèr] *f.* den, lair.

tanin [tànin] *m.* tannin.

tannage [tànàj] *m.* tanning, dressing. ‖ **tanner** [-é] *v.* to tan, to dress, to cure [peaux]; (pop.) to bore. ‖ **tannerie** [-rî] *f.* tannery. ‖ **tanneur** [-œr] *m.* tanner.

tant [tan] *adv.* so much, so many; as much, as many; so; so far; so long, as long; while; *tant pis*, so much the worse; too bad (fam.); *tant s'en faut*, far from it.

tante [tant] *f.* aunt; pansy (pop.).

tantinet [tantìnè] *adv.* (fam.) bit; somewhat.

tantôt [tantô] *adv.* presently, by and by, anon; a little while ago, just now; sometimes, now... now.

taon [tan] *m.* gadfly, horsefly.

tapage [tàpàj] *m.* noise, uproar, racket, din, rumpus. ‖ **tapageur** [-œr] *adj.** noisy, rowdy; gaudy, showy [couleur]; blustering [manière].

tape [tàp] *f.* rap, slap, tap, thump, pat. ‖ **taper** [-é] *v.* to hit, to slap; to smack, to tap; to stamp; to plug; to rap, to bang; to borrow from; to dab [peinture]; to type(write) [à la machine]. ‖ **tapette** [-èt] *f.* bat, carpet-beater; pansy (pop.). ‖ **tapeur** [-œr] *m.* (fam.) cadger.

tapioca [tàpyòkà] *m.* tapioca.

tapir (se) [sⁿtàpîr] *v.* to crouch; to squat; to skulk, to cower; to nestle.

tapis [tàpî] *m.* carpet, rug; cover, cloth; *tapis roulant,* endless belt, assembly line; *tapis-brosse,* door-mat. ‖ **tapisser** [-sé] *v.* to hang with tapestry; to carpet; to paper. ‖ **tapisserie** [-srî] *f.* tapestry; hangings; wallpaper; upholstery; *faire tapisserie,* to be a wallflower. ‖ **tapissier** [-yé] *m.* upholsterer.

tapoter [tàpòté] *v.* to rap, to tap; to drum, to thrum; to strum [piano].

taquet [tàkè] *m.* wedge, angle-block; peg; flange; belaying-cleat (naut.).

taquin [tàkⁿ] *m.* tease; *adj.* teasing. ‖ **taquiner** [-iné] *v.* to tease, to tantalize, to plague, *Am.* to kid (pop.). ‖ **taquinerie** [-inrî] *f.* teasing, *Am.* kidding (pop.).

tarabiscoté [tàràbìskòté] *adj.* (fam.) over-elaborate, overloaded.

tarabuster [tàràbùsté] *v.* (fam.) to harass; to bully.

tard [tàr] *adv.* late; *tôt ou tard,* sooner or later. ‖ **tarder** [-dé] *v.* to delay, to be long (à, in); to tarry, to loiter, to dally; *il me tarde de,* I long to. ‖ **tardif** [-dîf] *adj.** late, tardy; backward; belated.

tare [tàr] *f.* tare [poids]; defect, blemish; taint [héréditaire]. ‖ **taré** [-é] *adj.* degenerate; corrupt.

targette [tàrjèt] *f.* slide-bolt.

targuer (se) [sⁿtàrgé] *v.* to boast, to brag, to pride oneself (de, on).

tarif [tàrîf] *m.* tariff, rate; price-list, schedule of charges; **tarifer,** to tariff.

tarir [tàrîr] *v.* to dry up; to drain; to exhaust; to leave off (fig.). ‖ **tarissable** [-ìsàbl] *adj.* exhaustible. ‖ **tarissement** [-ìsmaⁿ] *m.* draining, exhausting, drying up.

tarte [tàrt] *f.* tart; flan; *Am.* pie; slap; *adj.* stupid. ‖ **tartelette** [-lèt] *f.* tartlet; *Am.* tart. ‖ **tartine** [-în] *f.* slice of bread; (pop.) tirade.

tartre [tàrtr] *m.* tartar; fur.

tas [tà] *m.* heap, pile; lot, set, batch; *mettre en tas,* to heap up, to pile up.

tasse [tàs] *f.* cup; *tasse à café,* coffee-cup; *tasse de café,* cup of coffee.

tasseau [tàsô] *m.** bracket, clamp.

tasser [tàsé] *v.* to heap, to pile up; to compress; to squeeze; to grow thick; *se tasser,* to sink, to subside, to settle; to set [mur]; to shrink with age; to crowd together, to squeeze together.

tâter [tâté] *v.* to feel, to touch; to try, to taste; to prod; to grope; to test; to feel [pouls]; *se tâter,* to think it over (fam.). ‖ **tâtonner** [tâtòné] *v.* to grope, to feel one's way, to fumble; *à tâtons,* fumblingly, gropingly; *chercher à tâtons,* to grope for.

tatouage [tàtûàj] *m.* tattoo. ‖ **tatouer** [-ûé] *v.* to tattoo.

taudis [tôdî] *m.* hovel; *pl.* slums.

taule [tôl] *f.* (pop.) clink.

taupe [tôp] *f.* mole, moleskin. ‖ **taupinière** [-ìnyèr] *f.* mole-hill.

taureau [tòrô] *m.** bull. ‖ **tauromachie** [-màshì] *f.* bull-fighting.

taux [tô] *m.* rate; fixed price.

taxe [tàks] *f.* tax, duty, rate, charge, dues; toll; impost; taxation, fixing of prices; established price; *taxe supplémentaire,* surcharge; late fee. ‖ **taxer** [-é] *v.* to tax; to rate; to fix the price of; to assess; to charge, to accuse (de, with, of).

taxi [tàksì] *m.* taxi(cab).

te [tⁿ] *pers. pron.* you, to you; thee, to thee; yourself; thyself.

technicien [tèknìsyⁿ] *m.* technician. ‖ **technicité** [-ìsìté] *f.* technicality. ‖ **technique** [-îk] *adj.* technical; *f.* technique, technics.

teigne [tèñ] *f.* tinea; ringworm; scurf (bot.).

teindre [tⁿdr] *v.** to dye, to tint; to tinge; to tincture. ‖ **teint** [-tⁿ] *m.* colo(u)r, tint; dye; hue, shade; complexion; *adj.* dyed; *bon teint,* fast colo(u)r. ‖ **teinte** [tⁿt] *f.* tint, colo(u)r, shade, hue; smack, touch; *demi-teinte,* mezzotint. ‖ **teinter** [-é] *v.* to tint; to tinge. ‖ **teinture** [-ür] *f.* dye, dyeing; tinting; tincture [d'iode]. ‖ **teinturerie** [-ürrî] *f.* dyeing; dye-works, dry-cleaner's. ‖ **teinturier** [-üryé] *m.* dyer.

tel, telle [tèl] *adj.* such; like, similar; *pron.* such a one; *tel que,* such as, like; *tel quel,* such as it is, just as it is; *de telle sorte que,* in such a way that; *monsieur Untel (un tel),* Mr. So-and-so.

télécommander [télékòmaⁿdé] *v.* to operate by remote control.

télégramme [télégràm] *m.* telegram, wire.

télégraphe [télégràf] *m.* telegraph. ‖ **télégraphie** [-î] *f.* telegraphy; *télégraphie sans fil,* wireless telegraphy, radio. ‖ **télégraphier** [-yé] v. to telegraph. ‖ **télégraphiste** [-ìst] m., f. telegraphist, telegraph operator.

téléguidé [télégìdé] adj. guided. ‖ **téléguider** [-é] v. to radio-control.

téléobjectif [téléòbjèktìf] m. telephoto lens.

téléphone [téléfòn] m. (tele)phone. ‖ **téléphoner** [-é] v. to (tele)phone, to call, to ring. ‖ **téléphonique** [-ìk] adj. telephonic, telephone. ‖ **téléphoniste** [-ìst] m., f. telephonist; telephone operator.

télescope [tèlèskòp] m. telescope. ‖ **télescoper** [-é] v. to telescope, to crumple up.

téléscripteur [téléskrìptœr] m. teleprinter.

téléspectateur [téléspèktàtœr] m. televiewer.

téléviser [télévìzé] v. to televise. ‖ **téléviseur** [-zœr] m. television set, televisor. ‖ **télévision** [-zyoⁿ] f. television.

tellement [tèlmaⁿ] adv. so, in such a manner; so much, so far; to such a degree; *tellement que*, so that.

téméraire [témérèr] adj. bold, daring, foolhardy, headstrong. ‖ **témérité** [-ìté] f. audacity, temerity; recklessness, rashness.

témoignage [témwàñàj] m. testimony, evidence, witness; testimonial, certificate; token, proof. ‖ **témoigner** [-é] v. to testify, to bear witness to; to show, to prove, to evince, to be a sign of. ‖ **témoin** [témwìⁿ] m. witness; spectator; evidence, proof, mark; second [duel]; *prendre à témoin*, to call to witness; *témoin à charge, à décharge*, witness for the prosecution, for the defense.

tempe [taⁿp] f. temple (anat.).

tempérament [taⁿpéràmaⁿ] m. constitution, temperament; character, temper, disposition; middle-course; *avoir du tempérament*, to be highly sexed; *par tempérament*, constitutionally; *vente à tempérament*, sale on the instalment plan.

tempérance [taⁿpéraⁿs] f. temperance, moderation.

température [taⁿpéràtür] f. temperature. ‖ **tempérer** [-é] v. to temper, to moderate, to assuage; to anneal (metall.); *se tempérer*, to become mild [temps].

tempête [taⁿpèt] f. tempest, storm, blizzard. ‖ **tempêter** [-é] v. to fume; to storm.

temple [taⁿpl] m. temple. ‖ **templier** [-plyé] m. Knight Templar.

temporaire [taⁿpòrèr] adj. temporary; provisional.

temporel [taⁿpòrèl] adj.* temporal, worldly, secular.

temporiser [taⁿpòrìzé] v. to temporize, to procrastinate, to stall off.

temps [taⁿ] m. time, duration, period, term; age, epoch; hour, moment; weather, season; phase (mech.); tense (gramm.); measure (mus.); *à temps*, in time; *de temps en temps*, from time to time; *en même temps*, at the same time; *quel temps fait-il?*, what's the weather like?

tenace [tⁿàs] adj. tenacious; adhesive; clinging; stubborn, obstinate, dogged, persistent; tough, cohesive; retentive [mémoire]; stiff, resistant. ‖ **ténacité** [-ìté] f. tenacity; adhesiveness; stubbornness; toughness; retentiveness; steadfastness [caractère].

tenaille [tⁿày] f. pincers, nippers, pliers. ‖ **tenailler** [-é] v. to gnaw [faim]; to rack [remords].

tenancier [tⁿaⁿsyé] m. tenant; lessee; holder, keeper; tenant-farmer.

tendance [taⁿdaⁿs] f. tendency; bent, leaning, trend, propensity. ‖ **tendancieux** [-syë] adj.* suggestive; tendentious, tendential; one-sided.

tendeur [taⁿdœr] m. spreader [piège]; coupling-iron; shoe-tree [chaussures].

tendon [taⁿdoⁿ] m. tendon, sinew.

tendre [taⁿdr] v. to stretch, to strain; to spread, to lay, to set; to pitch [tente]; to hang; to hold out, to offer, to proffer, to tender; to tend, to lead, to conduce.

tendre [taⁿdr] adj. tender, soft; fond, affectionate; early, young, new.

tendresse [taⁿdrès] f. tenderness, fondness; pl. endearments, caresses.

tendu [taⁿdü], p. p. of **tendre**.

ténèbres [ténèbr] f. pl. darkness, night, gloom, obscurity; uncertainty (fig.). ‖ **ténébreux** [-ébré] adj.* dark, gloomy, overcast, obscure; melancholy; lowering [ciel]; shady, sinister.

teneur [tⁿœr] m. tenor, terms; purport; percentage; grade (metall.).

tenir [tⁿîr] v.* to hold, to have, to possess; to seize, to grasp; to occupy, to take up, to keep; to keep in, to manage; to retain; to deem to regard, to look upon; to maintain; to side with; to hold fast, to adhere, to stick, to hold together, to depend, to result; to be held [marché]; to remain, to persist, to withstand; to be desirous, to be anxious (à, to); to sail close to the wind (naut.); *tenir compte de*, to take into consideration; *tenir tête à*, to resist; *tenir de la place*, to take up room; *il m'a tenu lieu de père*, he has been like a father to me; *je n'y tiens pas*, I don't care for it; *il ne tient qu'à vous de*, it only depends on

you to; *tiens!*, well!, say!, you don't
say!; *se tenir*, to hold fast, to stand;
to adhere, to stick; to consider oneself; to refrain; to be held, to take
place; *s'en tenir à*, to abide by, to
be content with; to stop at; *à quoi
s'en tenir*, what to believe.

tennis [tènìs] *m.* tennis; tennis court.

ténor [ténòr] *m.* tenor.

tension [taⁿsyoⁿ] *f.* tension, strain;
intensity; voltage (electr.); blood
pressure.

tentacule [taⁿtàkül] *m.* tentacle,
feeler.

tentateur [taⁿtàtœr] *adj.** tempting;
m. tempter. ‖ **tentation** [taⁿtàsyoⁿ] *f.*
temptation.

tentative [taⁿtàtìv] *f.* attempt, trial.

tente [taⁿt] *f.* tent; *dresser une tente*,
to pitch a tent.

tenter [taⁿté] *v.* to attempt, to try,
to endeavo(u)r, to strive; to tempt, to
entice, to tantalize.

tenture [taⁿtür] *f.* hangings, tapestry; wall-paper; paper-hanging.

tenu [t^enü] *p. p.* of *tenir*; *adj.* kept,
obliged, bound.

ténu [ténü] *adj.* tenuous; thin, fine.

tenue [t^enü] *f.* holding (assemblée);
session; attitude; behavio(u)r, deport-
ment, bearing; dress (mil.); appearance; seat [cavalier]; steadiness (mil.);
keeping [livres]; holding-note (mus.);
anchor-hold (naut.); *grande tenue*, full
dress (mil.); *petite tenue*, undress
(mil.); *tenue de corvée*, fatigues (mil.);
tenue de ville, street dress; *tenue des
livres*, bookkeeping.

térébenthine [térébaⁿtìn] *f.* turpentine.

tergiversation [tèrjìvèrsàsyoⁿ] *f.* tergiversation; shilly-shallying. ‖ **tergiverser** [tèrjìvèrsé] *v.* to tergiversate,
to practise evasion, to be shifty, to
beat around the bush.

terme [tèrm] *m.* term; relationship;
termination, end; bound, limit; due
date; appointed time; three months;
quarter's rent; word, expression; *pl.*
state, terms, condition; *à long terme*,
long-dated.

terminaison [tèrmìnèzoⁿ] *f.* termination, ending, conclusion. ‖ **terminer**
[-é] *v.* to terminate, to end, to conclude, to finish; to bound.

terminus [tèrmìnüs] *m.* terminus;
terminal point; last stop.

terne [tèrn] *adj.* dull, dim; wan;
lustreless; colo(u)rless, drab; tar-
nished; tame, flat. ‖ **ternir** [-îr] *v.* to
tarnish, to dull, to dim, to deaden;
to sully, to besmirch [réputation]. ‖
ternissure [-nìsür] *f.* dullness; tar-
nished appearance.

terrain [tèrìⁿ] *m.* ground; ground-
plot, site, position; soil, earth; field;
terrain (mil.); formation (geol.); *terrain d'aviation*, airfield.

terrasse [tèràs] *f.* terrace; bank,
earthwork; flat roof, balcony. ‖ **ter-
rasser** [-é] *v.* to embank, to bank up;
to down, to throw, to floor; to overwhelm, to confound. ‖ **terrassier** [-yé]
m. Br. navvy, *Am.* ditch-digger.

terre [tèr] *f.* earth, ground; land,
shore; soil, loam, clay; world; estate,
grounds, property; territory; *terre
cuite*, terra-cotta; *terre à terre*, matter-
of-fact, commonplace; *ventre à terre*,
at full speed; *mettre pied à terre*, to
alight; *terre-plein*, platform, terrace;
road-bed. ‖ **terreau** [-ô] *m.* vegetable
mo(u)ld, compost. ‖ **terrer** [-é] *v.* to
earth up; to clay [sucre]; *se terrer*,
to burrow; to dig in, to entrench oneself. ‖ **terrestre** [-èstr] *adj.* terrestrial,
earthly, worldly; ground.

terreur [tèrœr] *f.* terror; fright, fear,
dread; awe.

terreux [tèrë] *adj.** earthy, clayey;
dull.

terrible [tèrìbl] *adj.* terrible, terrific,
dreadful, awful; unmanageable; *enfant
terrible*, little terror.

terrier [tèryé] *m.* burrow, hole; terrier dog.

terrifier [tèrìfyé] *v.* to terrify.

terrine [tèrìn] *f.* terrine.

territoire [tèrìtwàr] *m.* territory; district; extent of jurisdiction. ‖ **territorial** [-tòryàl] *adj.** territorial.

terroir [tèrwàr] *m.* soil.

terroriser [tèròrìzé] *v.* to terrorize;
to coerce. ‖ **terrorisme** [-rìsm] *m.*
terrorism. ‖ **terroriste** [-rìst] *s.* terrorist.

tertiaire [tèrsyèr] *adj.* tertiary.

tertre [tèrtr] *m.* hillock, mound,
knoll, hump.

tes [tè] *poss. adj. pl.* thy; your.

tesson [tèsoⁿ] *m.* potsherd, shard.

test [tèst] *m.* test, trial.

testament [tèstàmaⁿ] *m.* will, testament.

têtard [tètàr] *m.* tadpole, *Am.* pol-
liwog; pollard, chub.

tête [tèt] *f.* head; head-piece, cra-
nium; leader, head of an establishment; head of hair; front; beginning;
summit, crown, top; vanguard; brains,
sense, judgment; presence of mind,
self-possession; *faire la tête à quelqu'un*, to frown at someone, to be
sulky with someone; *faire une tête*, to
look glum; *faire à sa tête*, to have
one's own way; *une femme de tête*, a

capable woman; **tenir tête à**, to stand up to; *tête de ligne*, rail-head; starting-point; *voiture de tête*, front train; *tête de pont*, bridge-head (mil.); *se monter la tête*, to get worked up; *forte tête*, unmanageable person, strong-minded person; *coup de tête*, rash action; *la tête la première*, head-long; **tête-à-tête**, private interview; sofa, settee, *Am.* love-seat.

tétée [tété] *f.* suck, suckling. ‖**téter** [-é] *v.* to nurse, to suck, to suckle. ‖ **tétine** [-în] *f.* udder, dug; teat, nipple.

têtu [tètü] *adj.* stubborn, headstrong, wilful, obstinate; mulish, pig-headed.

teuf-teuf [tœftœf] *m.* (fam.) puff-puff.

texte [tèkst] *m.* text; textbook, manual; subject; passage.

textile [tèkstîl] *m., adj.* textile.

textuel [tèkstüèl] *adj.* textual; verbatim.

texture [tèkstür] *f.* texture; disposition, arrangement.

thaumaturge [tômàtürj] *m.* thaumaturge; miracle-worker.

thé [té] *m.* tea; tea party; *boîte à thé*, tea-caddy; *thé des bois*, © wintergreen.

théâtral [téâtràl] *adj.* theatrical; stagy; spectacular. ‖ **théâtre** [-âtr] *m.* theater, playhouse; stage, scene, the boards; dramatic art; plays; setting, place of action.

théière [téyèr] *f.* teapot.

thème [tèm] *m.* theme, subject, topic; exercise.

théologie [téòlòjî] *f.* theology. ‖ **théologien** [-jyîⁿ] *m.* theologian.

théorème [téòrèm] *m.* theorem.

théorie [téòrî] *f.* theory; doctrine; training-manual (mil.). ‖ **théorique** [-îk] *adj.* theoretic(al).

thérapeutique [téràpètîk] *adj.* therapeutic; *f.* therapeutics.

thermal [tèrmàl] *adj.* thermal; *eaux thermales*, hot springs. ‖ **thermes** [tèrm] *m. pl.* thermal baths. ‖ **thermie** [-î] *f.* therm. ‖ **thermique** [-îk] *adj.* thermic.

thermomètre [tèrmòmètr] *m.* thermometer.

thermostat [tèrmòstà] *m.* thermostat.

thésauriser [tézòrizé] *v.* to hoard up, to pile up.

thèse [tèz] *f.* thesis.

thon [toⁿ] *m.* tunny-fish, *Am.* tuna.

thym [tiⁿ] *m.* thyme.

tibia [tîbyà] *m.* tibia, shin-bone, shin.

tic [tîk] *m.* tic, twitch.

ticket [tîkè] *m.* ticket, check.

tiède [tyèd] *adj.* lukewarm, tepid; mild, soft; warm [wind]; indifferent (fig.). ‖ **tiédeur** [tyédœr] *f.* tepidness, tepidity, lukewarmness; indifference, coolness (fig.). ‖ **tiédir** [-îr] *v.* to cool, to tepefy, to grow lukewarm.

tien, tienne [tyîⁿ, -èn] *poss. pron.* yours, thine.

tiers, tierce [tyèr, tyèrs] *adj.* third; *m., f.* third; third person; third party. ‖ **tiercé** [tyèrsé] *m.* State run bet on three horses in one race.

tige [tîj] *f.* stem, stalk, tige; trunk [arbre]; shaft [[colonne]; shank [ancre]; leg [botte]; stock [famille]; rod (mech.).

tigre, tigresse [tîgr, tîgrès] *m.* tiger, *f.* tigress.

tillac [tîyàk] *m.* deck (naut.).

tilleul [tîyœl] *m.* lime-tree; linden-tree.

timbale [tiⁿbàl] *f.* kettledrum [musique]; metal cup; pie-dish. ‖ **timbalier** [-yé] *m.* kettledrummer.

timbre [tiⁿbr] *m.* stamp; bell; tone, timbre; snare, cord [tambour]; *droit de timbre*, stamp fee; *timbre-poste*, postage-stamp. ‖ **timbré** [-é] *adj.* stamped [papier]; sonorous; (pop.) cracked, crazy, nuts. ‖ **timbrer** [-é] *v.* to stamp.

timide [tîmîd] *adj.* timid, shy; timorous, apprehensive. ‖ **timidité** [-îté] *f.* timidity, shyness, diffidence.

timon [tîmoⁿ] *m.* pole, shaft; beam [charrue]; tiller (naut.). ‖ **timonier** [-ònyé] *m.* helmsman.

timoré [tîmòré] *adj.* timorous.

tintamarre [tiⁿtàmàr] *m.* (fam.) uproar; din, row; ballyhoo (fig.).

tinter [tiⁿté] *v.* to ring, to toll; to tinkle; to jingle, to chink; to clink; to buzz, to tingle [oreilles].

tintouin [tiⁿtwîⁿ] *m.* (fam.) worry, trouble.

tique [tîk] *f.* tick, cattle-tick.

tir [tîr] *m.* shooting; firing; gunnery (artill.); shooting-match; *tir à la cible*, target-firing.

tirade [tîràd] *f.* tirade; passage.

tirage [tîràj] *m.* drawing, pulling, hauling, traction, towing; towing-path; print (phot.); striking off (typogr.); circulation, number printed [périodiques]; draught [cheminée]; difficulty, obstacle; quarrying, extraction [pierre]; blasting [poudre]; *tirage au sort*, drawing lots, balloting; *tirage à part*, off-print. ‖ **tirailler** [-àyé] *v.* to pull about; to twitch; to tease; to shoot wildly, to fire away; to skirmish, to snipe. ‖ **tirailleur** [-àyœr] *m.* sharpshooter. ‖ **tire** [tîr] *f.* pull, pulling, tug; © molasses candy, taffy, maple taffy; *voleur à la tire*, pickpocket; *tire-au-flanc*, shirker, malingerer; *tire-botte*, bootjack; boothook; *tire-bouchon*, corkscrew; ringlet; *tire-bouton*, buttonhook; *tire-d'aile (à)*, at full speed; *tire-ligne*, drawing-pen; scribing-tool; *tirelire*, money-box. ‖ *tirer* [-é] *v.* to draw, to pull, to drag, to haul, to tug; to stretch; to pull out; to pull off; to draw [ligne]; to wire-draw [métal]; to shoot, to fire; to infer, to deduce; to print, to work off (typogr.); to get, to derive; *tirer vanité de*, to take pride in; *tirer à sa fin*, to draw to a close; *se tirer*, to extricate oneself; to get out; to recover [santé]; to beat it (pop.); *se tirer d'affaire*, to get along, to manage, to pull through; to get out of trouble; *s'en tirer*, to get along, to make ends meet; to pull through, to scrape through.

tiret [tirè] *m.* dash; hyphen.

tirette [tirèt] *f.* curtain cord; slide.

tireur, -euse [tirœr, -êz] *m., f.* marksman, rifleman; *tireuse de cartes*, fortune-teller.

tiroir [tirwàr] *m.* drawer [table]; slide, slide-valve (mech.); episode.

tisane [tizàn] *f.* infusion, decoction; herb tea.

tison [tizoⁿ] *m.* fire-brand, ember, live-coal. ‖ **tisonner** [-òné] *v.* to poke, to stir, to fan a fire. ‖ **tisonnier** [-ònyé] *m.* poker, fire-iron.

tissage [tisàj] *m.* weaving; cloth-mill. ‖ **tissé** [-é] *adj.* woven. ‖ **tisser** [-é] *v.* to weave, to loom; to plait; to spin; to contrive (fig.). ‖ **tisserand** [-ràⁿ] *m.* weaver. ‖ **tissu** [-ü] *m.* texture; textile, goods, fabric; tissue, web; *tissu de mensonges*, pack of lies; *tissu-éponge*, towelling, sponge-cloth, *Am.* terry cloth.

titre [titr] *m.* title, style, denomination; headline; title-page; head, heading; right, claim; standard [monnaie]; voucher; title-deed; bond, stock, share (fin.); diploma, certificate; *pl.* securities; *à juste titre*, deservedly, justly; *à titre de*, by right of, in virtue of; *en titre*, titular, acknowledged; *titre de créance*, proof of debt. ‖ **titrer** [-é] *v.* to confer a title upon; to titrate (chem.).

tituber [titübé] *v.* to stagger, to totter, *Am.* to weave (fam.).

titulaire [titülèr] *adj.* titular; regular; *m., f.* holder, titular. ‖ **titulariser** [-àrizé] *v.* to appoint as titular.

toast [tòst] *m.* toast.

toboggan [tòbògaⁿ] *m.* toboggan.

toc [tòk] *m.* (fam.) sham goods.

tocsin [tòksiⁿ] *m.* alarm-bell.

toge [tòj] *f.* toga; gown.

tohu-bohu [tòübòü] *m.* (fam.). hubbub; invar; confusion.

toi [twà] *pron.* thou, you.

toile [twàl] *f.* linen; cloth; canvas; sail-cloth; painting, picture; curtain (theat.); *pl.* toils; *toile écrue*, unbleached linen; *toile d'avion*, airplane fabric; *toile à matelas*, ticking; *toile de coton*, calico; *toile cirée*, oilcloth; *toile vernie*, oilskin; *toile d'araignée*, spider web, cobweb.

toilette [twàlèt] *f.* toilet, washing, dressing; dressing table; dress, costume; lavatory; *faire sa toilette*, to groom oneself, to dress; *grande toilette*, full dress.

toise [twàz] *f.* fathom; measuring apparatus. ‖ **toiser** [twàzé] *v.* to measure; to size up; to look (someone) up and down.

toison [twàzoⁿ] *f.* fleece; mop, shock [cheveux].

toit [twà] *m.* roof; *sous les toits*, in a garret. ‖ **toiture** [-tür] *f.* roofing.

tôle [tôl] *f.* sheet-iron; boiler-plate; *tôle ondulée*, corrugated iron; *tôle de blindage*, armo(u)r plate.

tolérable [tòléràbl] *adj.* tolerable, bearable. ‖ **tolérance** [-aⁿs] *f.* tolerance; forbearance; allowance (comm.); *par tolérance*, on sufferance; *maison de tolérance*, licensed brothel. ‖ **tolérer** [-é] *v.* to tolerate, to allow; to suffer, to endure, to bear, to put up with; to wink at.

tollé [tòllé] *m.* outcry.

tomate [tòmàt] *f.* tomato.

tombal [toⁿbàl] *adj.; pierre tombale*, tombstone. ‖ **tombe** [toⁿb] *f.* tomb, grave; tombstone. ‖ **tombeau** [-ô] *m.** see tombe.

tomber [toⁿbé] *v.* to fall, to drop down, to tumble down; to sink; to decay; to crash (aviat.); to droop, to dwindle, to fail; to sag; to flag; *tomber sur*, to meet, to run across; to light; *tomber bien*, to happen opportunely, to come at the right time; *tomber mal*, to come at an inopportune moment, to be unlucky; *tomber amoureux de*, to fall in love with; *tomber en poussière*, to crumble into dust; *laisser tomber*, to drop, to throw down. ‖ **tombereau** [toⁿbrô] *m.** tipcart; dumpcart; cart-load.

tombola [toⁿbòlà] *f.* tombola, lottery.

tome [tòm] *m.* tome.

ton [toⁿ] *poss. adj. m.* (*f.* **ta**, *pl.* **tes**) your; thy.

ton [toⁿ] *m.* tone; intonation; manner, style; pitch (mus.); tint, colo(u)r, shade. ‖ **tonalité** [tònàlité] *f.* tonality.

tondeuse [toⁿdĕz] *f.* shearing-machine; clippers; lawn-mower [gazon]. ‖ *tondre* [toⁿdr] *v.* to shear; to mow; to clip; to fleece. ‖ *tondu* [-ü] *adj.* shorn; fleeced.

tonique [tònĭk] *m., adj.* tonic; *f.* stressed syllable; keynote (mus.).

tonitruant [tònĭtrüaⁿ] *adj.* thundering, thunderous. ‖ *tonitruer* [-é] *v.* to thunder.

tonnage [tònáj] *m.* tonnage.

tonne [tòn] *f.* tun; ton [poids]. ‖ *tonneau* [-ô] *m.** cask, tun, barrel; horizontal spin, roll (aviat.); tonneau [auto]; *petit tonneau,* keg. ‖ *tonnelier* [-ᵉlyé] *m.* cooper. ‖ *tonnelle* [-èl] *f.* arbo(u)r, bower.

tonner [tòné] *v.* to thunder; to boom. ‖ *tonnerre* [-èr] *m.* thunder; thunderclap; thunderbolt; *coup de tonnerre,* clap, peal of thunder.

tonsure [toⁿsür] *f.* tonsure. ‖ *tonsurer* [-é] *v.* to tonsure. ‖ *tonte* [toⁿt] *f.* shearing; mowing; clip.

topaze [tòpàz] *f.* topaz.

topinambour [tòpìnaⁿbûr] *m.* Jerusalem artichoke.

topographie [tòpògràfî] *f.* topography; surveying.

toponymie [tòpònìmî] *f.* toponymy.

toquade [tòkàd] *f.* (fam.) fancy, craze, infatuation.

toque [tòk] *f.* toque; cap.

toqué [tòké] *adj.* crazy, cracked, *Am.* goofy, nuts (pop.).

torche [tòrsh] *f.* torch, link; twist [paille]. ‖ *torchis* [-î] *m.* loam; cob. ‖ *torchon* [-oⁿ] *m.* towel, dish-towel; dish-cloth; dust-cloth; twist [paille].

tordant [tòrdaⁿ] *adj.* (pop.) screamingly funny, killing; *c'est tordant,* it's a scream, *Am.* it's a howl. ‖ *tordre* [tòrdr] *v.* to twist, to wring, to wring out; to contort, to disfigure; to wrest; to beat (fam.); *se tordre,* to twist, to writhe; *se tordre de rire,* to be convulsed with laughter.

toréador [tòrèàdòr] *m.* toreador, bullfighter.

tornade [tòrnàd] *f.* tornado.

torpeur [tòrpœr] *f.* torpor.

torpille [tòrpîy] *f.* torpedo; numbfish. ‖ *torpiller* [-îyé] *v.* to torpedo; to mine. ‖ *torpilleur* [-îyœr] *m.* torpedo-boat; *contre-torpilleur,* destroyer.

torréfier [tòrréfyé] *v.* to torrefy, to roast, to grill; to scorch.

torrent [tòràⁿ] *m.* torrent; flow. ‖ *torrentiel* [-syèl] *adj.** torrential; pelting, impetuous.

torride [tòrîd] *adj.* torrid, scorching, broiling, parching.

torsade [tòrsàd] *f.* twisted fringe, twisted cord; coil [cheveux].

torse [tòrs] *m.* torso, trunk; chest.

torsion [tòrsyoⁿ] *f.* twist, twisting.

tort [tòr] *m.* wrong; mistake, fault; injury, harm, hurt; prejudice; *avoir tort,* to be wrong; *à tort,* wrongly; *donner tort à,* to decide against; *faire tort à,* to wrong; *à tort et à travers,* at random, haphazardly.

torticolis [tòrtìkòlî] *m.* stiff neck; wryneck.

tortiller [tòrtìyé] *v.* to twist; to wriggle, to shuffle; to waddle; to twirl; to kink; *se tortiller,* to wriggle, to writhe, to twist, to squirm, to fidget.

tortionnaire [tòrsyònèr] *m.* torturer.

tortue [tòrtü] *f.* tortoise; turtle.

tortueux [tòrtüë] *adj.** tortuous, winding; wily, underhanded (fig.).

torture [tòrtür] *f.* torture. ‖ *torturer* [-é] *v.* to torture, to torment; to put to the rack; to tantalize; to strain, to twist (fig.).

tôt [tô] *adv.* soon, quickly, speedily; early; *le plus tôt possible,* as soon as possible, at your earliest convenience; *tôt ou tard,* sooner or later.

total [tòtàl] *adj.** total, whole, entire, complete; utter, universal; *m.** whole, total, sum-total. ‖ *totalisateur* [-ìzàtœr] *adj.* adding; *m.* adding-machine; totalizator, tote. ‖ *totaliser* [-zé] *v.* to totalize, to tot up, to add up. ‖ *totalitaire* [-ìtèr] *adj.* totalitarian. ‖ *totalitarisme* [-ìtàrìsm] *m.* totalitarianism. ‖ *totalité* [-ìté] *f.* totality, entirety, whole; *en totalité,* as a whole.

toubib [tûbìb] *m.* (fam.) doc, medico.

touchant [tûshaⁿ] *adj.* touching, moving, stirring; *prep.* concerning, regarding, touching. ‖ *touche* [tûsh] *f.* touch, touching; assay, trial; stroke, style [peinture]; key [clavier]; fret [guitare]; hit [escrime]; drove [bétail]; (fam.) look, mien; *touche-à-tout,* meddler, busybody. ‖ *toucher* [-é] *v.* to touch; to handle, to finger, to feel; to move, to affect; to try [métal]; to receive [argent]; to cash [chèque]; to hit [escrime]; to drive [bétail]; to play [guitare]; to call, to put in (naut.); *m.* touch, feeling; *toucher à,* to touch on, to allude to; to concern, to regard; to meddle in, with; to draw near, to approach; to be like; *se toucher,* to touch, to adjoin; to be contiguous; to touch each other.

touffe [tûf] *f.* tuft, wisp; clump, cluster, bunch. ‖ *touffu* [-ü] *adj.* bushy, tufted; thick, dense, close; branchy, leafy; full, luxuriant; plethoric, turgid, bombastic [style].

toujours [tûjûr] *adv.* always, ever, forever; *toujours est-il que*, the fact remains that.

toupet [tûpè] *m.* tuft [cheveux]; forelock [cheval]; (fam.) cheek, nerve, brass; *avoir du toupet*, to be cheeky.

toupie [tûpî] *f.* top; (pop.) head.

tour [tûr] *m.* turn, round, twining, winding; rotation, revolution; circuit, compass; twist, strain; tour, trip, excursion; trick, dodge, wile; manner, style; place, order; lathe [techn.]; turning-box; wheel [potier]; *tour à tour*, by turns.

tour [tûr] *f.* tower; rook, castle [échecs].

tourbe [tûrb] *f.* peat, turf; mob. ‖ **tourbière** [-yèr] *f.* peat-bog.

tourbillon [tûrbìyon] *m.* whirlwind; whirlpool, eddy; whirl, bustle; vortex. ‖ **tourbillonner** [-ìyòné] *v.* to whirl, to eddy, to swirl.

tourelle [tûrèl] *f.* turret.

tourillon [tûrìyon] *m.* axle; arbor; swivel, spindle; trunnion; hinge.

tourisme [tûrìsm] *m.* touring, sight-seeing; tourism. ‖ **touriste** [-ìst] *m.*, *f.* tourist, sight-seer. ‖ **touristique** [-ìstìk] *adj.* touristic.

tourment [tûrmon] *m.* torment; anguish, worry; agony, pain, pang. ‖ **tourmente** [-t] *f.* storm; gale; blizzard; turmoil (fig.). ‖ **tourmenter** [-té] *v.* to torment; to distress; to worry; to bother; to molest; to plague, to tantalize; to tease; *se tourmenter*, to be uneasy, to worry, to fret; to toss.

tournage [tûrnàj] *m.* shooting [cinéma]; turning (techn.).

tournant [tûrnon] *m.* turning, turn, bend; turning-space; expedient; whirl-pool, eddy; *au tournant de la rue*, around the corner. ‖ **tourne-broche** [-ebròsh] *m.* turnspit; roasting-jack. ‖ **tourne-disque** [-dìsk] *m.* record-player. ‖ **tournedos** [-edò] *m.* fillet steak. ‖ **tournée** [-é] *f.* round, turn, visit, journey, trip, tour; circuit. ‖ **tourner** [-é] *v.* to turn; to shape, to fashion; to turn round, to revolve, to whirl, to twirl, to spin; to wind; to express; to get round, to circumvent; to outflank (mil.); to evade, to dodge; to change, to convert; to construe, to interpret; to turn out, to result; to tend; to sour [vin]; to curdle [lait]; to shoot [film]; *la tête me tourne*, I feel giddy; *se tourner*, to turn round, to turn about; to turn, to change. ‖ **tournesol** [-esòl] *m.* sunflower. ‖ **tournevis** [-vìs] *m.* screwdriver, turnscrew. ‖ **tourniquet** [-ìkè] *m.* turnstile, turnpike; revolving stand; swivel; tourniquet. ‖ **tournoi**

tournoi [tûrnwà] *m.* tournament. ‖ **tournoyer** [-wàyé] *v.* to turn round and round, to whirl; to spin; to wheel; to eddy, to swirl. ‖ **tournure** [-ûr] *f.* turn, direction, course; turning [tour]; shape, form, figure; cast [esprit, style]; construction [phrase].

tourte [tûrt] *f.* pie; duffer (fam.).

tourtereau [tûrterò] *m.* young turtle-dove; lover. ‖ **tourterelle** [tûrterèl] *f.* turtle-dove.

tourtière [tûrtyèr] *f.* © meat-pie.

Toussaint [tûsin] *f.* All Saints' day; *la veille de la Toussaint*, Hallowe' en.

tousser [tûsé] *v.* to cough; to hem,

tout, toute [tû, tût] (*pl.* **tous, toutes**) [*tous* as a pronoun is pronounced *tûs*] *adj.* all; whole, the whole of; every; each; any; *pron.* all, everything; *m.* whole, lot; main thing; total (math.); *adv.* quite, entirely, thoroughly, very, wholly; however; *tous les deux*, both of them; *tous les trois jours*, every third day; *tout droit*, straight ahead; *toutes les fois que*, whenever, each time that; *toute la journée*, all day long; *du tout*, not at all; *du tout au tout*, utterly, entirely; *tout nouveau*, quite new; *tout neuf*, brand new; *tout nu*, stark naked; *tout fait*, ready-made; *tout haut*, aloud; *tout à fait*, entirely, completely, wholly, quite, altogether; *tout à l'heure*, just now; presently; *à tout à l'heure!*, see you later!; *tout de même*, just the same, all the same; *tout de suite*, at once, immediately, right away; *tout au plus*, at the very most; *tout en parlant*, while speaking; *tout-à-l'égout*, sewage system. ‖ **toutefois** [tûtfwà] *adv.* however, yet, nevertheless.

toutou [tûtû] *m.* (fam.) doggie.

toux [tû] *f.* cough, coughing.

toxine [tòksîn] *f.* toxin. ‖ **toxique** [-ìk] *adj.* toxic; *m.* poison.

trac [tràk] *m.* funk; stage-fright.

tracas [tràkà] *m.* bother, worry, annoyance; turmoil, bustle; hoist-hole, *Am.* hoist-way. ‖ **tracasser** [-sé] *v.* to worry; to fuss, to fidget.

trace [tràs] *f.* trace, track, mark; footprint; spoor, trail, scent; clue; vestige. ‖ **tracé** [-e] *m.* tracing; sketching; marking out, laying out; outline, sketch, diagram, drawing; graph, plotting [courbe]. ‖ **tracer** [-é] *v.* to trace, to draw, to sketch, to outline; to lay out.

trachée [tràshé] *f.* trachea; **trachée-artère**, windpipe.

tract [tràkt] *m.* tract, *Am.* drop.

tractation [tràktàsyon] *f.* bargaining; negociation; dealing; deal.

tracteur [tràktœr] *m.* tractor, traction-engine. ‖ **traction** [-syoⁿ] *f.* traction ; pulling ; *Br.* draught, *Am.* draft ; motor traction.

tradition [tràdìsyoⁿ] *f.* tradition ; custom. ‖ **traditionnel** [-yònèl] *adj.* traditional.

traducteur, -trice [tràdüktœr, -trìs] *m., f.* translator. ‖ **traduction** [-syoⁿ] *f.* translation ; interpreting ; crib, pony [texte]. ‖ **traduire** [tràdüïr] *v.* to translate ; to interpret ; to prosecute (jur.) ; to decode (radio).

trafic [tràfìk] *m.* traffic ; trade ; trading ; dealings. ‖ **trafiquant** [-aⁿ] *m.* trafficker, racketeer. ‖ **trafiquer** [-é] *v.* to trade, to traffic, to deal.

tragédie [tràjédì] *f.* tragedy. ‖ **tragédien** [-dyiⁿ] *m.* tragedian. ‖ **tragédienne** [-dyèn] *f.* tragedienne. ‖ **tragique** [tràjìk] *adj.* tragic, tragical ; *m.* tragicness ; tragic art.

trahir [tràïr] *v.* to betray ; to deceive, to be false to ; to disclose, to give away [secret] ; to go back on, to fail, to play false. ‖ **trahison** [-ìzoⁿ] *f.* betrayal, treachery, perfidy, foul play ; treason (jur.).

train [triⁿ] *m.* train ; suite, attendants ; pace, rate ; way, course ; noise, clatter ; raft, float ; railway-train ; *train de marchandises*, *Br.* goods train, *Am.* freight train ; *train de voyageurs*, passenger train ; *train omnibus*, slow train, local train, *Am.* accommodation train ; *train direct*, through-train, non-stop train ; *train rapide*, fast express ; *train de luxe*, Pullman-car express ; *train d'atterrissage*, undercarriage ; landing-gear (aviat.) ; *être en train de parler*, to be talking, to be busy talking ; *mettre en train*, to start.

traînard [trènàr] *m.* loiterer, straggler, dawdler, laggard, *Am.* slowpoke (fam.). ‖ **traîne** [trèn] *f.* dragging ; drag [corde] ; train [robe] ; drag-net ; rope's end (naut.) ; *à la traîne*, in tow, astern ; *traîne sauvage*, ⓒ Indian toboggan. ‖ **traîneau** [-ô] *m.** sled, sledge, sleigh. ‖ **traînée** [-é] *f.* trail, track ; train [poudre] ; air lag [bombe] ; street-walker. ‖ **traîner** [-é] *v.* to drag, to draw, to pull, to trail, to haul ; to tow ; to drag on, to drag out [existence] ; to drawl [voix] ; to protract, to spin out [discussion] ; to trail, to draggle ; to lag behind, to straggle ; to linger, to loiter, to dawdle ; to lie about, to litter ; to flag, to droop, to languish ; *traîner en longueur*, to drag on ; *se traîner*, to crawl along, to creep ; to lag ; to hang heavy [temps].

traire [trèr] *v.** to milk [vache] ; to draw [lait].

trait [trè] *m.* pulling ; arrow, dart ; stroke ; streak, bar ; trace [harnais] ; leash [laisse] ; draught, *Am.* draft,

gulp [liquide] ; dash [tiret] ; flash, beam [lumière] ; idea, burst [éloquence] ; cut [scie] ; trait [caractère] ; feature [visage] ; characteristic touch ; act, deed (fig.) ; relation, connection [rapport] ; *tout d'un trait*, at one stretch ; *d'un seul trait*, at one gulp ; *trait d'esprit*, witticism, sally ; *trait d'union*, hyphen.

traite [trèt] *f.* stage, stretch [voyage] ; draft, bill (comm.) ; milking [lait] ; *la traite des blanches*, white-slave traffic ; *tout d'une traite*, at a stretch ; straight off ; at a sitting.

traité [trèté] *m.* treaty, compact, agreement ; treatise. ‖ **traitement** [-maⁿ] *m.* treatment ; reception ; salary, pay, stipend ; *mauvais traitements*, ill-usage. ‖ **traiter** [-é] *v.* to treat, to use, to behave towards, to deal by ; to discuss, to handle, to discourse upon ; to entertain, to receive ; to qualify, to call, to style, to dub ; to negotiate, to transact ; to execute, to do. ‖ **traiteur** [-œr] *m.* restaurant keeper.

traître, -esse [trètr, -ès] *m.* traitor ; villain (theat.) ; *f.* traitress ; *m., f.* treacherous person ; *adj.* treacherous, false ; vicious [animal] ; dangerous. ‖ **traîtrise** [-îz] *f.* treachery ; traitorous deed ; treacherousness.

trajectoire [tràjèktwàr] *f.* trajectory.

trajet [tràjè] *m.* distance, way ; passage, journey, voyage ; course.

trame [tràm] *f.* web, weft, woof ; plot, conspiracy. ‖ **tramer** [-é] *v.* to weave ; to plot, to contrive.

tramway [tràmwè] *m.* *Br.* tramway, tram ; *Am.* streetcar, trolley car.

tranchant [traⁿshaⁿ] *adj.* cutting, sharp ; decisive, sweeping ; peremptory ; salient ; glaring [couleurs] ; *m.* (cutting) edge. ‖ **tranche** [traⁿsh] *f.* slice, chop ; round [bœuf] ; rasher [bacon] ; edge [page] ; book, portion [valeurs] ; cross-section [vie] ; period, series (math.) ; *doré sur tranche*, giltedged. ‖ **tranchée** [-é] *f.* trench ; entrenchment ; *pl.* gripes, colic. ‖ **trancher** [-é] *v.* to slice ; to cut off, to sever, to chop off ; to cut short, to break off ; to settle, to solve [difficulté] ; to contrast, to stand out [couleurs].

tranquille [traⁿkìl] *adj.* quiet, calm, still, serene ; easy, undisturbed. ‖ **tranquillisant** [-ìzaⁿ] *adj.* tranquillizing ; *m.* tranquillizer. ‖ **tranquilliser** [-ìzé] *v.* to tranquillize, to reassure ; to soothe, to calm, to make easy. ‖ **tranquillité** [-lté] *f.* tranquillity.

transaction [traⁿzàksyoⁿ] *f.* transaction ; compromise ; *pl.* dealings.

transatlantique [traⁿzàtlaⁿtìk] *adj.* transatlantic ; *m.* liner ; deck-chair, steamer-chair.

transborder [traⁿsbòrdé] v. to transship; to transfer; to ferry. ‖ **transbordeur** [-œr] m. travel(l)ing-platform; transporter-bridge; aerial ferry [pont]; train-ferry [bac].

transcription [traⁿskrìpsyoⁿ] f. transcription; transcript. ‖ **transcrire** [traⁿskrîr] v.* to transcribe.

transe [traⁿs] f. trance; apprehension; mortal anxiety.

transférer [traⁿsféré] v. to transfer; to convey, to remove; to shift, to move, to postpone; to translate [évêque]; to assign (jur.). ‖ **transfert** [-fèr] m. transfer; removal (comm.).

transfigurer [traⁿsfìgùré] v. to transfigure.

transformateur, -trice [traⁿsfòrmàtœr, -trìs] adj. transforming; m. transformer. ‖ **transformation** [-àsyoⁿ] f. transformation; conversion; wig, toupee. ‖ **transformer** [-é] v. to transform, to change, to alter, to convert.

transfusion [traⁿsfüzyoⁿ] f. transfusion.

transgresser [traⁿsgrèsé] v. to transgress, to trespass against, to break, to infringe against, to contravene. ‖ **transgresseur** [-œr] m. transgressor, trespasser.

transhumer [traⁿzümé] v. to transhume.

transiger [traⁿzìjé] v. to compound, to compromise, to come to terms.

transir [traⁿsîr] v. to chill, to benumb [froid]; to paralyze.

transistor [traⁿzìstòr] m. transistor.

transit [traⁿzìt] m. transit. ‖ **transitaire** [traⁿzìtèr] m. forwarding agent, transport agent.

transitif [traⁿzìtìf] adj.* transitive.

transition [traⁿzìsyoⁿ] f. transition; modulation (mus.). ‖ **transitoire** [-ìtwàr] adj. transitory.

translucide [traⁿslüsìd] adj. translucent.

transmettre [traⁿsmètr] v.* to transmit; to convey, to impart; to forward, to send on, to pass on, to relay; to hand down [héritage]; to transfer, to assign (jur.).

transmission [traⁿsmìsyoⁿ] f. transmission; transference, assignment (jur.); handing down.

transparaître [traⁿspàrètr] v.* to show through. ‖ **transparence** [traⁿspàraⁿs] f. transparency. ‖ **transparent** [-aⁿ] adj. transparent; pellucid.

transpercer [traⁿspèrsé] v. to transpierce, to transfix; to stab.

transpiration [traⁿspìràsyoⁿ] f. perspiration; transpiring. ‖ **transpirer** [-é] v. to perspire.

transplanter [traⁿsplaⁿté] v. to transplant.

transport [traⁿspòr] m. transport, removal; haulage, freight; carriage, conveyance; transfer; balance brought forward (comm.); troop-transport; rapture, ecstasy. ‖ **transporter** [-té] v. to transport, to convey, to remove, to carry; to transfer, to make over (jur.); to carry over (comm.); to enrapture, to ravish (fig.).

transposer [traⁿspôzé] v. to transpose; to transmute.

transvaser [traⁿsvàzé] v. to decant.

transversal [traⁿsvèrsàl] adj.* transversal, transverse; rue transversale, cross-street.

trapèze [tràpèz] m. trapeze; trapezium (geom.).

trappe [tràp] f. trap, pitfall [piège]. ‖ **trapper** [-é] v. © to trap, to hunt by trapping. ‖ **trappeur** [-œr] m. trapper.

trapu [tràpü] adj. thick-set, squat.

traquenard [tràknàr] m. trap; pitfall.

traquer [tràké] v. to beat up [gibier]; to track down [criminel].

traumatisme [trômàtìsm] m. traumatism.

travail [tràvày] m. (pl. travaux) work, labo(u)r, toil; industry; trouble; piece of work, task, job; workmanship; employment, occupation; working, operation; study; travail, childbirth; pl. works, constructions; transactions; proceedings; travaux forcés, hard labo(u)r; travail en série, mass production. ‖ **travailler** [-é] v. to work, to labo(u)r, to toil; to be industrious, to be at work; to fashion, to shape; to strive, to endeavo(u)r; to study, to take pains with; to cultivate, to till [terre]; to overwork, to fatigue; to torment, to obsess; to ferment [vin]; to knead [pâte]; to be strained [bateau]; to warp [bois]; to crack [mur]; to prey on [esprit]. ‖ **travailleur** [-œr] adj.* hard-working, diligent, industrious; painstaking; m. worker, workman, labo(u)rer, toiler. ‖ **travailliste** [-ìst] s. Labour member [député]; member of the Labour Party.

travée [tràvé] f. bay; span [pont].

travers [tràvèr] m. breadth; defect; oddity, eccentricity; bad habit; broadside (naut.); en travers, across, athwart, crosswise; au travers de, à travers, through; de travers, askew, awry, amiss, askance. ‖ **traversée** [-sé] f. passage, crossing, voyage. ‖ **traverser** [-sé] v. to cross, to traverse; to go through, to pass through, to travel through; to run through [percer]; to lie across, to span; to intersect; to penetrate, to drench. || *traversier* [-syé] *m.* cross-bar; © ferry-boat. || *traversin* [-sⁱⁿ] *m.* bolster-pillow; transom; cross-tree (naut.).

travestir [tràvèstîr] *v.* to disguise.

trébucher [trébushé] *v.* to stumble, to trip, to stagger, to totter, to slip; to blunder; to weigh down [monnaie].

trèfle [trèfl] *m.* clover, shamrock; trefoil; clubs [cartes].

tréfonds [tréfoⁿ] *m.* depth.

treille [trèy] *f.* vine-trellis.

treillis [trèyì] *m.* trellis, lattice-work; coarse canvas, sackcloth.

treize [trèz] *m., adj.* thirteen; thirteenth [date, titre]. || *treizième* [-yèm] *m., adj.* thirteenth.

tréma [trémà] *m.* dieresis.

tremble [traⁿbl] *m.* aspen. || *tremblement* [-ᵉmaⁿ] *m.* trembling, shaking, shivering, shuddering, quivering, quaking; quavering; tremor; flickering [lumière]; quaver, tremolo (mus.); *tremblement de terre,* earthquake. || *trembler* [-é] *v.* to tremble, to shake, to quake, to shiver. || *trembloter* [-òté] *v.* to tremble slightly, to quiver; to quaver [voix]; to flicker [lumière]; to flutter [ailes].

trémolo [trémòlò] *m.* tremolo; quaver.

trémousser [trémûsé] *v.* to hustle; to flutter, to flap [ailes]; *se trémousser,* to frisk about.

trempe [traⁿp] *f.* temper [acier]; steeping; dipping, soaking; damping, wetting; character, stamp. || *trempé* [-é] *adj.* wet, soaked, drenched, sopping. || *tremper* [-é] *v.* to steep, to soak, to drench, to sop; to wet, to dampen; to temper [acier]; to water, to dilute [vin]; to imbrue; to dip, *Am.* to dunk. || *trempette* [-èt] *f.* sippet [pain]; dip [bain].

tremplin [traⁿplⁱⁿ] *m.* springboard; diving-board; ski-jump.

trentaine [traⁿtèn] *f.* about thirty. || *trente* [traⁿt] *m., adj.* thirty; thirtieth [date, titre]. || *trentième* [-yèm] *m., f., adj.* thirtieth.

trépan [trépaⁿ] *m.* trepan, trephine. || *trépaner* [-àné] *v.* to trepan.

trépas [trépà] *m.* death, decease. || *trépasser* [trépàsé] *v.* to die.

trépidation [trépìdàsyoⁿ] *f.* vibration, trepidation, jarring; quaking; tremor [terre]; flurry.

trépigner [trépîñé] *v.* to stamp, to trample; to prance, to dance.

très [trè] *adv.* very; most; very much; quite; greatly, highly.

trésor [trézòr] *m.* treasure; treasury; riches; hoard; relics and ornaments [église]. || *trésorerie* [-rî] *f.* treasury; *Br.* Exchequer. || *trésorier* [-yé] *m.* treasurer; paymaster (mil.).

tressage [trèsàj] *m.* tressing, plaiting.

tressaillement [trèsàymaⁿ] *m.* start; shudder, quiver; flutter, disturbance; thrill; wince. || *tressaillir* [-àyîr] *v.ᵒ* to start, to give a start, to jump; to shudder, to quiver; to bound, to throb; to thrill; to wince.

tressauter [trèsôté] *v.* to start.

tresse [très] *f.* braid, tress; tape. || *tresser* [-é] *v.* to weave, to braid, to plait; to wreathe.

tréteau [trétò] *m.*ᵉ trestle; stage.

treuil [trœy] *m.* winch, windlass.

trêve [trèv] *f.* truce.

tri [trì] *m.* sorting; choosing.

triangle [trìaⁿgl] *m.* triangle.

tribord [trìbòr] *m.* starboard.

tribu [trìbü] *f.* tribe.

tribulation [trìbülàsyoⁿ] *f.* tribulation; trial, distress.

tribunal [trìbünàl] *m.*ᵉ tribunal; court of justice, law-court; magistrates. || *tribune* [-ün] *f.* tribune; rostrum, platform; gallery.

tribut [trìbü] *m.* tribute; contribution; tax; debt. || *tributaire* [-tèr] *m., adj.* tributary.

tricher [trìshé] *v.* to cheat, to trick. || *tricheur* [-œr] *m.* cheat, trickster, *Am.* four-flusher (fam.).

tricolore [trìkòlòr] *adj.* tricolour, tricoloured.

tricorne [trìkòrn] *m.* tricorn, three-cornered hat.

tricot [trìkò] *m.* knitting; knitted fabric; sweater, pullover, *Br.* jersey. || *tricoter* [-òté] *v.* to knit.

trident [trìdaⁿ] *m.* trident; three-pronged pitchfork.

trier [trìyé] *v.* to sort (out), to screen; to classify, to arrange; to pick, to choose, to select. || *trieuse* [trìyèz] *f.* sorting-machine; gin.

trifouiller [trìfüyé] *v.* (fam.) to fumble about; to meddle with.

trille [trîy] *m.* trill.

trimbaler [trⁱⁿbàlé] *v.* (fam.) to drag.

trimer [trìmé] *v.* to toil, to drudge.

trimestre [trìmèstr] *m.* quarter; three months; trimester; term, *Am.* session [école]; quarter's salary; quarter's rent. || *trimestriel* [-ìyèl] *adj.*ᵉ quarterly, trimestrical.

tringle [trⁱⁿgl] *f.* rod; curtain-rod.

trinquer [trinké] v. to clink glasses, to touch glasses; to hobnob with.

trio [trìò] m. trio.

triomphal [trìyonfàl] adj.* triumphal. ‖ **triomphateur, -trice** [-àtœr, -trìs] adj. triumphing; m., f. triumpher. **triomphe** [trìyonf] m. triumph. ‖ **triompher** [-é] v. to triumph; to overcome, to master; to excel; to exult, to glory; to boast.

tripe [trìp] f. tripe; guts, entrails. ‖ **triperie** [-rî] f. tripery. ‖ **tripier** [-yé] m. tripe-dealer.

triple [trìpl] adj. triple, treble, threefold. ‖ **triplé** [-é] adj. triplicate; m. triplet. ‖ **tripler** [-é] v. to triple, to treble.

tripot [trìpô] m. gambling-den, gaming-house; bawdy-house. ‖ **tripotée** [-té] f. (fam.) thrashing [coups]; lots [tas]. ‖ **tripoter** [-òté] v. to putter, to mess around, to fiddle about; to handle, to toy with; to finger; to manipulate, to paw; to meddle with; to tamper with; to gamble, to speculate in; to deal shadily. ‖ **tripoteur** [-òtœr] m. intriguer; mischief-maker; shady speculator.

trique [trìk] f. cudgel.

triste [trìst] adj. sad, sorrowful, mournful, downcast, dejected, doleful; glum, blue, moping; woeful; woebegone [visage]; cheerless, gloomy; unfortunate, painful; mean, wretched, paltry. ‖ **tristesse** [-ès] f. sadness, sorrow, gloom, melancholy; dullness.

trivial [trìvyàl] adj.* vulgar, low, coarse; trivial, trite, hackneyed. ‖ **trivialité** [-ìté] f. vulgarity.

troc [tròk] m. exchange; barter; swop.

trogne [tròñ] f. bloated face.

trognon [tròñon] m. core; stump; stalk [chou]; (fam.) darling, pet.

trois [trwà] m., adj. three; third [titre, date]. ‖ **troisième** [-zyèm] m., f., adj. third.

trombe [tronb] f. waterspout; whirlwind [vent].

trombone [tronbòn] m. trombone; paper-clip.

trompe [tronp] f. horn, trump; proboscis; probe [insecte]; trunk [éléphant]; blast-pump [forge].

tromper [tronpé] v. to deceive, to delude, to mislead; to cheat; to betray, to be unfaithful to [époux]; to elude [surveillance]; se tromper, to be mistaken, to be wrong, to make a mistake; to deceive one another; se tromper de chemin, to take the wrong road. ‖ **tromperie** [-rî] f. deceit, deception, cheating; delusion.

trompeter [tronpété] v. to trumpet abroad; to sound the trumpet; to divulge; to scream [aigle]. ‖ **trompette** [tronpèt] f. trumpet; m. trumpeter; nez en trompette, turned-up nose.

trompeur [tronpœr] adj.* deceitful, delusive, misleading, deceptive.

tronc [tron] m. trunk; bole, body, stem [arbre]; parent-stock [famille]; alms-box, poor box; frustum (geom.). ‖ **tronçon** [-son] m. stub, stump, butt, fragment, broken piece; frustum [colonne].

trône [trôn] m. throne. ‖ **trôner** [-é] v. to sit enthroned; to lord it.

tronquer [tronké] v. to truncate; to curtail; to mangle; to garble.

trop [trô] adv. too much, too many; too, over, overly, overmuch, unduly; too far, too long, too often; m. excess, superfluity; de trop, superfluous; unwelcome, unwanted; trop-plein, overflow, surplus.

trophée [tròfé] m. trophy.

tropical [tròpìkàl] adj.* tropical. ‖ **tropique** [tròpìk] m. tropic.

troquer [tròké] v. to exchange, to barter, to truck, Br. to swop, Am. to swap.

trot [trô] m. trot; au petit trot, at a jog-trot. ‖ **trotte** [tròt] f. (fam.) stretch, run, distance. ‖ **trotter** [tròté] v. to trot; to run about; to toddle [enfant]; to scamper [souris]. ‖ **trotteur** [-tœr] m. trotter [cheval]. ‖ **trottiner** [-ìné] v. to trot short; to jog along; to trot about; to toddle [enfant]. ‖ **trottinette** [-ìnèt] f. scooter. ‖ **trottoir** [-wàr] m. footway, footpath; pavement, Am. sidewalk; bordure du trottoir, Br. kerb, Am. curb.

trou [trû] m. hole; gap; cave, pothole; orifice, mouth; cavern (anat.); eye [aiguille]; trou d'homme, manhole; trou d'air, air-pocket; boire comme un trou, to drink like a fish, Am. to have a hollow leg.

trouble [trûbl] adj. turbid, roiled; muddy; murky; cloudy, overcast; dim, dull; confused; m. confusion, disorder, disturbance, turmoil, perturbation, uneasiness; turbidity, muddiness; dispute; pl. broils, dissensions, disorders, riots; trouble-fête, kill-joy, spoil-sport, wet-blanket. ‖ **troubler** [-é] v. to disturb, to stir up, to make muddy, to cloud; to muddle; to disorder, to confuse, to agitate; to perplex, to upset, to disconcert; to mar; to ruffle, to annoy.

trouée [trûé] f. gap, breach; breakthrough. ‖ **trouer** [-é] v. to bore, to pierce, to drill, to breach.

trouille [trûy] f. (pop.) funk, Am. scare.

troupe [trûp] *f.* troop, band; crew, gang, set; company, herd, flock, drove, throng; *pl.* troops, forces. ‖ *troupeau* [-ô] *m.** herd, drove; flock; pack.

trousse [trûs] *f.* bundle; truss; package; saddle-roll; case, kit, pouch. ‖ *trousseau* [-ô] *m.** bunch; kit; outfit [vêtements]; bride's trousseau. ‖ *trousser* [-é] *v.* to bundle up; to tuck up; to truss.

trouvaille [trûvày] *f.* discovery; lucky find. ‖ *trouver* [-é] *v.* to find, to discover, to meet with, to hit upon; to find out; to invent; to think, to deem, to judge, to consider; *objets trouvés*, lost-and-found; *enfant trouvé*, foundling; *se trouver*, to be, to be found; to be located, situated; to feel; to happen, to turn out, to prove; to be met with, to exist; *se trouver mal*, to feel ill, to swoon.

truc [trük] *m.* thing, gadget, whatnot, jigger, *Am.* gimmick (pop.); knack, hang, skill; dodge, trick; machinery (theat.); thingamajig.

trucage [trükàj] *m.* faking, counterfeit; camouflage, dummy work; trick picture [cinéma]; gerrymandering [élection].

truelle [trüèl] *f.* trowel.

truffe [trüf] *f.* truffle (bot.); muzzle [chien].

truie [trüï] *f.* sow.

truite [trüït] *f.* trout.

truquer [trüké] *v.* to fake; to cook; to gerrymander; to cheat.

trust [trœst] *m.* trust. ‖ *truster* [-té] *v.* to monopolize; to trust.

tu, toi, te [tü, twà, tᵉ] *pers. pron.* you; thou; thee (obj.); *c'est à toi*, it is yours, it is thine.

tu *p. p. of* **taire**.

tub [tœb] *m.* tub; (sponge-)bath.

tubage [tübàj] *m.* tubing. ‖ *tube* [tüb] *m.* tube, pipe.

tubercule [tübèrkül] *m.* tuber (bot.); tubercle (med.). ‖ *tuberculeux* [tübèrkülë] *adj.** tubercular (bot.); tuberculous (med.); *m.* consumptive. ‖ *tuberculose* [-ôz] *f.* tuberculosis, consumption.

tuer [tüé] *v.* to kill, to slay; to slaughter, to butcher; to bore to death; to while away [temps]; *se tuer*, to kill oneself, to commit suicide; to be killed, to get killed; to wear oneself out. ‖ *tuerie* [türî] *f.* slaughter, massacre.

tuile [tüïl] *f.* tile; bad luck, *Am.* tough luck (pop.).

tulipe [tülïp] *f.* tulip; tulip-shaped lamp-shade.

tulle [tül] *m.* tulle.

tuméfier [tüméfyé] *v.* to tumefy. ‖ *tumeur* [-œr] *f.* tumo(u)r.

tumulte [tümült] *m.* tumult, hubbub, turmoil, uproar; riot. ‖ *tumultueux* [-üë] *adj.** tumultuous, noisy; riotous; boisterous.

tunique [tünïk] *f.* tunic; membrane.

tunnel [tünèl] *m.* tunnel.

tuque [tük] *f.* ⓒ tuque, stocking cap.

turban [türbaⁿ] *m.* turban.

turbine [türbîn] *f.* turbine. ‖ *turbiner* [-îné] *v.* (pop.) to swoot; to slog, to grind.

turbulent [türbülaⁿ] *adj.* turbulent; wild [enfants]; stormy [vie].

turc, turque [türk] *adj.* Turkish; *m.* Turkish language; *m., f.* Turk; *assis à la turque*, sitting cross-legged.

turf [türf] *m.* turf, racecourse. ‖ *turfiste* [-ïst] *m.* race-goer.

turlupiner [türlüpïné] *v.* (fam.) to bother; to worry.

turne [türn] *f.* (pop.) hovel; digs; den; hole.

turpitude [türpïtüd] *f.* turpitude.

turque, *see* **turc.**

turquoise [türkwàz] *f.* turquoise.

tutelle [tütèl] *f.* tutelage, guardianship; protection. ‖ *tuteur, -trice* [tütœr, -trïs] *m., f.* guardian; *m.* prop [plante].

tutoyer [tütwàyé] *v.* to address as « tu » and « toi ».

tuyau [tüïyô] *m.** pipe, tube; hose; shaft, funnel; chimney-flue; stem [pipe]; tip, pointer, hint (fam.); *avoir des tuyaux*, to be in the know (fam.); *tuyau d'échappement*, exhaust pipe [auto]. ‖ *tuyauter* [-té] *v.* to flute, to frill, to plait; to give a tip-off to; *tuyauter quelqu'un sur*, to put someone up to. ‖ *tuyauterie* [-trî] *f.* pipe system, pipage.

tympan [tⁱⁿpaⁿ] *m.* ear-drum.

type [tïp] *m.* type; standard model; symbol; (fam.) fellow, chap, *Br.* bloke, *Am.* guy (pop.).

typhoïde [tïfòïd] *f.* typhoid.

typhon [tïfoⁿ] *m.* typhoon.

typhus [tïfüs] *m.* typhus.

typique [tïpïk] *adj.* typical.

typographie [tïpògràfî] *f.* typography.

tyran [tïraⁿ] *m.* tyrant. ‖ *tyrannie* [-ànî] *f.* tyranny. ‖ *tyrannique* [-ànïk] *adj.* tyrannical, despotic; high-handed. ‖ *tyranniser* [-ànïzé] *v.* to tyrannize over, to oppress; to bully.

U

ulcère [ülsèr] *m.* ulcer; sore. ǁ *ulcérer* [-éré] *v.* to ulcerate; to fester; to wound, to embitter, to gall.

ultérieur [ültéryœr] *adj.* ulterior, later; further.

ultimatum [ültìmàtòm] *m.* ultimatum. ǁ *ultime* [ültîm] *adj.* ultimate.

ultrason [ültràson] *m.* ultra-sound; supersonic wave. ǁ *ultraviolet* [-vyòlè] *adj.* ultra-violet.

ululer [ülülé] *v.* to hoot, to tu-whoo; to ululate.

un, une [un, ün] *indef. art.* one; a, an (before a vowel); *adj., pron.* one; first; *un à un,* one by one; *les uns les autres,* one another; *les uns... les autres,* some... others; *l'un l'autre,* each other; *l'un et l'autre,* both; *l'un ou l'autre,* either.

unanime [ünànìm] *adj.* unanimous. ǁ *unanimité* [-ìmìté] *f.* unanimity; *à l'unanimité,* unanimously.

uni [ünì] *adj.* united; harmonious (family); uniform; smooth, level, even; plain, all-over [couleur, dessin]. ǁ *unification* [-fìkàsyon] *f.* unification; merger (ind.). ǁ *unifier* [-fyé] *v.* to unify; to unite.

uniforme [ünìfòrm] *adj.* uniform; flat [tarif]; *m.* uniform; regimentals. ǁ *uniformiser* [-ìzé] *v.* to standardize, to make uniform. ǁ *uniformité* [-ìté] *f.* uniformity.

unilatéral [ünìlàtéràl] *adj.* unilateral; one-sided.

union [ünyon] *f.* union; junction, coalition, combination; blending [couleurs]; marriage; society, association; unity, concord, agreement; union-joint, coupling.

unique [ünìk] *adj.* only, sole, single; unique, unrivalled; *fils unique,* only son; *sens unique,* one-way; *prix unique,* one-price [magasin], *Am.* five-and-ten, dime store.

unir [ünîr] *v.* to unite, to join, to combine, to connect; to make one; to smooth; *s'unir,* to unite; to join forces (à, with); to marry.

unisson [ünìson] *m.* unison, harmony; keeping (fig.).

unitaire [ünìtèr] *adj.* unitarian; unitary. ǁ *unité* [-é] *f.* unity.

univers [ünìvèr] *m.* universe. ǁ *universaliser* [-sàlìzé] *v.* to universalize. ǁ *universalité* [-sàlìté] *f.* universality. ǁ *universel* [-sèl] *adj.* universal.

universitaire [ünìvèrsìtèr] *adj.* university, academic; *m., f.* professor, Academic person. ǁ *université* [-é] *f.* university; *Am.* college.

uranium [ürànyòm] *m.* uranium.

urbain [ürbin] *adj.* urban; town. ǁ *urbanisation* [ürbànìzàsyon] *f.* town-development. ǁ *urbaniser* [-ìzé] *v.* to urbanize; to polish up (fam.). ǁ *urbanisme* [-ìsm] *m.* town-planning, city-planning. ǁ *urbaniste* [-ìst] *s.* town-planner. ǁ *urbanité* [ürbànìté] *f.* urbanity.

urée [üré] *f.* urea. ǁ *urémie* [-émî] *f.* uraemia.

urgence [ürjans] *f.* urgency; emergency; pressure; *d'urgence,* immediately. ǁ *urgent* [-an] *adj.* urgent, pressing; instant; *cas urgent,* emergency.

urinaire [ürìnèr] *adj.* urinary. ǁ *urine* [ürìn] *f.* urine. ǁ *uriner* [-ìné] *v.* to urinate.

urne [ürn] *f.* urn, vessel; ballot-box.

urticaire [ürtìkèr] *f.* hives; nettle-rash.

usage [üzàj] *m.* use, using, employment; usage, habit, practice, wont; experience; service, every-day use; wear, wearing-out [vêtements]; *usage externe,* external application; *faire de l'usage,* to wear well. ǁ *usagé* [-é] *adj.* worn. ǁ *usager* [-é] *m.* user; commoner; *usagers du métro,* tube-travellers, *Am.* subway-riders.

usé [üzé] *adj.* worn out; shabby, threadbare [vêtement]; frayed [corde]; commonplace. ǁ *user* [-é] *v.* to use up, to consume; to abrade; to wear out, to wear down; *user de,* to use, to make use of, to avail oneself of; to resort to; *s'user,* to wear away, to wear down; to wear oneself out; to be used; to decay, to be spent.

usinage [üzìnàj] *m.* machining, manufacturing. ǁ *usine* [üzìn] *f.* (manu)-factory, works, plant; mills [textiles, papier]. ǁ *usiner* [-é] *v.* to machine, to tool. ǁ *usinier* [-yé] *m.* manufacturer; mill-owner.

usité [üzìté] *adj.* used, usual.

ustensile [üstansìl] *m.* utensil.

usuel [üzüèl] *adj.* usual, common.

usure [üzür] *f.* usury; wearing out; wear and tear; wearing away, erosion (geol.); *guerre d'usure,* war of attrition. ǁ *usurier* [-yé] *m.* usurer; money-lender.

usurpateur, -trice [üzürpàtœr, -trìs] *m.* usurper, *f.* usurpress; *adj.* usurping; arrogating; encroaching. ǁ *usurpation* [-àsyon] *f.* usurpation; arrogation; encroaching, encroachment. ǁ *usurper* [-é] *v.* to usurp; to arrogate; to encroach.

utérin [ütéri[n]] adj. uterine. ‖ **utérus** [-rüs] m. uterus.

utile [ütìl] adj. useful, serviceable, of use, convenient; expedient, beneficial; m. what is useful; *en temps utile*, in due time. ‖ **utilisable** [-ìzàbl] adj. utilizable. ‖ **utilisation** [-ìzàsyo[n]] f. utilization, use; utilizing. ‖ **utiliser** [-ìzé]

v. to utilize, to use; to make use of. ‖ **utilitaire** [-ìtèr] adj. utilitarian; commercial; utility. ‖ **utilitarisme** [-ìtàrìsm] m. utilitarianism. ‖ **utilité** [-ìté] f. utility, usefulness; useful purpose; service, avail; utility-man (theat.).

utopie [ütòpî] f. utopia. ‖ **utopiste** [-ìst] s. utopian.

V

va, *see* aller.

vacance [vàka[n]s] f. vacancy; Br. abeyance, Am. opening [poste]; pl. vacation, holidays; recess [parlement]; *grandes vacances*, summer vacation. ‖ **vacant** [-a[n]] adj. vacant, unoccupied; tenantless.

vacarme [vàkàrm] m. uproar, din.

vaccin [vàksi[n]] m. vaccine. ‖ **vaccination** [-ìnàsyo[n]] f. vaccination; Am. shot. ‖ **vacciner** [-ìné] v. to vaccinate.

vache [vàsh] f. cow; cow-hide. ‖ **vacher** [-é] m. cowherd.

vacillant [vàsìya[n]] adj. unsteady, shaky; wobbly, staggering [pas]; flickering [lumière]; vacillating [esprit]. ‖ **vaciller** [-lyé] v. to be unsteady, to shake; to wobble; to sway; to stagger, to totter, to reel, to lurch [tituber]; to flicker; to twinkle [étoile]; to vacillate; to hesitate; to be shaky; to waver.

vadrouiller [vàdrûyé] v. (fam.) to gad about; to pub-crawl; to wander about.

vagabond [vàgàbo[n]] m. vagabond, wanderer; vagrant; tramp, Am. hobo, bum; adj. roving; flighty, wayward. ‖ **vagabondage** [-dà] m. vagabondage, vagrancy. ‖ **vagabonder** [-dé] v. to roam, to rove; to wander.

vagin [vàji[n]] m. vagina. ‖ **vaginite** [-ìt] f. vaginitis.

vagir [vàjîr] v. to wail. ‖ **vagissement** [vàjìsma[n]] m. wailing; squeaking [lièvre].

vague [vàg] adj. vague, indefinite; hazy; indeterminate, indecisive; rambling; vacant, uncultivated [terrain]; m. vagueness.

vague [vàg] f. wave, billow.

vaguemestre [vàgmèstr] m. baggage-master (mil.); army postman; navy postman.

vaillance [vàya[n]s] f. valo(u)r. ‖ **vaillant** [vàya[n]] adj. valiant.

vain [vi[n]] adj. vain, fruitless, sham; shadowy; idle, frivolous; vainglorious; *en vain*, vainly, in vain.

vaincre [vi[n]kr] v.* to conquer, to vanquish, to beat, to win; to defeat, to overcome, to worst, to outdo; to master, to surmount [difficulté]. ‖ **vaincu** [vi[n]kü] adj. conquered, beaten. ‖ **vainqueur** [-œr] adj. inv. triumphant; victorious; m. vanquisher, conqueror, winner.

vairon [vèro[n]] m. minnow [poisson].

vaisseau [vèsô] m.* vessel; ship; nave [église]; *brûler ses vaisseaux*, to burn one's boats.

vaisselle [vèsèl] f. table service; tableware; flatware plates and dishes, china; earthenware, crockery [faïence]; *faire la vaisselle*, to wash up, Am. to wash the dishes.

val [vàl] m. vale, dale.

valable [vàlàbl] adj. valid, good; worthwhile; cogent [raison]; available, valid [billet].

valet [vàlè] m. valet, (man-)servant, footman; varlet; groom [écurie]; farmhand [ferme]; hireling, knave, jack [cartes]; claw [techn.).

valétudinaire [vàlétüdìnèr] adj. valetudinary; s. valetudinarian.

valeur [vàlœr] f. value, worth; weight; import, meaning; length of note (mus.); valo(u)r, bravery; asset; pl. bills, paper, stocks, shares, securities; *mettre en valeur*, to emphasize; to enhance; to reclaim [terre]. ‖ **valeureux** [-ë] adj.* valiant, valorous.

valide [vàlìd] adj. valid; good; sound, cogent; able-bodied, fit for service (mil.). ‖ **valider** [-é] v. to validate; to ratify; to authenticate. ‖ **validité** [-ìté] f. validity, availability (jur.); cogency.

valise [vàlîz] f. valise, portmanteau; suitcase; grip; *valise diplomatique*, embassy dispatch-bag.

vallée [vàlé] f. valley. ‖ **vallon** [-o[n]] m. dale, dell, vale; Br. glen. ‖ **vallonné** [vàlòné] adj. undulating.

valoir [vàlwàr] v.* to be worth; to cost; to be equal to, to be as good as; to deserve; to procure, to furnish; *à valoir*, on account; *cela vaut la peine*, that is worthwhile; *valoir mieux*, to be better; *faire valoir*, to make the most of, to turn to account.

valse [vàls] f. waltz. ‖ *valser* [-é] v. to waltz.

valve [vàlv] f. valve.

vamp [vaⁿp] f. vamp.

vampire [vaⁿpîr] m. vampire; bloodsucker (fam.). ‖ *vampirisme* [-ìrìsm] m. vampirism; blood-sucking.

van [vaⁿ] m. winnowing-basket.

vandale [vaⁿdàl] m. vandal. ‖ *vandalisme* [-ìsm] m. vandalism.

vanille [vàníy] f. vanilla.

vanité [vànìté] f. vanity, conceit, self-sufficiency; futility, emptiness; *tirer vanité de*, to be vain of. ‖ *vaniteux* [-ë] adj.* vain, conceited, stuck-up.

vanne [vàn] f. water-gate.

vanneau [vànò] m.* lapwing.

vanner [vàné] v. to winnow, to fan, to sift [grain]; to van [minerai].

vannerie [vànrî] f. basket-making.

vantard [vaⁿtàr] m. bragger, braggart, boaster, vaunter, swaggerer, Am. blow-hard (pop.); adj. boasting, boastful. ‖ *vantardise* [-dîz] f. boasting, bragging, swaggering; braggadocio. ‖ *vanter* [-é] v. to vaunt, to extol; to advocate, to cry up, to boost, to puff, to push; *se vanter*, to boast, to brag.

vapeur [vàpœr] f. vapo(u)r; steam; haze, fume; m. steamer, steamship; *machine à vapeur*, steam-engine. ‖ *vaporeux* [vàpòrë] adj.* vaporous, misty, steamy; filmy, hazy; nebulous. ‖ *vaporisateur* [-ìzàtœr] m. vaporizer; atomizer; sprayer; evaporator. ‖ *vaporiser* [-ìzé] v. to vaporize; to spray.

vaquer [vàké] v. to be vacant [situation]; to be on vacation [école]; to be recessed [parlement]; *vaquer à*, to attend to; to go about [affaires].

varech [vàrèk] m. seaweed, wrack.

vareuse [vàrëz] f. pea-jacket, pilot-jacket; jersey; jumper [marin]; Am. blouse (mil.).

variable [vàryàbl] adj. variable, changeable, unsteady; fickle, inconstant; unequal [pouls]; f. variable (math.). ‖ *variante* [-yaⁿt] f. variant [texte]; pickles (comm.). ‖ *variation* [-yàsyoⁿ] f. variation.

varice [vàrìs] f. varix. ‖ *varicelle* [-èl] f. chicken-pox.

varié [vàryé] adj. varied; various, sundry; variegated; miscellaneous. ‖ *varier* [-yé] v. to vary; to variegate; to diversify; to fluctuate (fin.); to disagree, to differ [opinions]. ‖ *variété* [-yété] f. variety; diversity; variedness; choice.

variole [vàryòl] f. smallpox.

variqueux [vàrìkë] adj.* varicose.

varlope [vàrlòp] f. trying-plane.

vasculaire [vàskülèr] adj. vascular.

vase [vâz] m. vase.

vase [vâz] f. silt, slime, mire, ooze.

vaseline [vàzlîn] f. vaseline, Am. petroleum jelly, petrolatum.

vasistas [vàzìstàs] m. fanlight, Am. transom; casement window.

vasque [vàsk] f. bassin; bowl.

vassal [vàsàl] m.* vassal.

vaste [vàst] adj. vast, wide.

vaticiner [vàtìsìné] v. to vaticinate.

vaudeville [vôdvìl] m. vaudeville.

vaurien [vôryⁿ] m. good-for-nothing, ne'er-do-well.

vautour [vôtûr] m. vulture.

vautrer (se) [sᵉvôtré] v. to wallow, to welter; to sprawl; to revel (fig.).

veau [vô] m.* calf [animal]; veal [viande]; calfskin [cuir].

vécu [vékü] adj. [see *vivre*] lived; authentic; realistic; real.

vedette [vᵉdèt] f. vedette; patrol boat, scout [bateau]; star, leading-man, leading lady (theat.).

végétal [véjétàl] adj.* vegetable; m.* plant. ‖ *végétarien* [-tàryⁿ] m. vegetarian. ‖ *végétation* [-àsyoⁿ] f. vegetation; pl. adenoids (med.). ‖ *végéter* [-é] v. to vegetate.

véhémence [véémaⁿs] f. vehemence. ‖ *véhément* [-aⁿ] adj. vehement.

véhicule [véìkül] m. vehicle; medium (pharm.). ‖ *véhiculer* [-é] v. to convey.

veille [vèy] f. watching, vigil; waking; sleeplessness; sitting up, staying up [nuit]; night watch (mil.); look-out (naut.); eve. ‖ *veillée* [-é] f. evening; night attendance [malade]; watching, Am. wake [mort]; sitting up. ‖ *veiller* [-é] v. to sit up, to stay up, to keep awake; to watch, to be on the look-out (mil.; naut.); to watch over, to look after, to tend, to attend to [malade]; to watch, to wake [mort]; *veiller à*, to see to, to look after. ‖ *veilleur* [-œr] m. watcher; *veilleur de nuit*, night-watchman. ‖ *veilleuse* [-ëz] f. night-light; dimmer-bulb [auto]; *mettre en veilleuse*, to dim [auto].

veinard [vènàr] adj. lucky; m. lucky person. ‖ *veine* [vèn] f. vein; seam, lode [mine]; humo(u)r, luck. ‖ *veiner* [-é] v. to vein; to grain. ‖ *veineux* [-ë] adj.* veiny; venous. ‖ *veinule* [-ül] f. veinlet, veinule. ‖ *veinure* [-ür] f. veining.

vélaire [vélèr] adj. velar; back; uvular; f. back consonant, back vowel.

vêler [vèlé] v. to calve.

vélin [véliⁿ] m. vellum.

velléité [vèlléité] *f.* inclination, whim, slight impulse.

vélo [vélò] *m.* (fam.) bike, cycle. ‖ **vélocité** [vélòsìté] *f.* velocity. ‖ *vélodrome* [-òdròm] *m.* velodrome. ‖ *vélomoteur* [-mòtœr] *m.* motor-assisted bicycle; moped (fam.).

velours [vəlûr] *m.* velvet; *velours côtelé*, corduroy; *velours de coton*, velveteen; *velours de laine*, velours. ‖ *velouté* [-ûté] *adj.* velvety; downy [joue, pêche]; mellow [vin].

velu [vəlü] *adj.* hairy, shaggy.

venaison [vənèzon] *f.* venison.

vénal [vénàl] *adj.*° venal.

vendange [vandanʒ] *f.* vintage, grapegathering; vine-harvest; *pl.* grapes. ‖ *vendanger* [-é] *v.* to harvest grapes. ‖ *vendangeur* [-œr] *m.* vintager; wineharvester.

vendeur [vandœr] *m.* seller, vendor; salesman, dealer, salesclerk, *Br.* shopman, *Am.* storeclerk. ‖ *vendeuse* [-èz] *f.* salesgirl, saleswoman. ‖ *vendre* [vandr] *v.* to sell; to barter; to betray, to give away (fig.); *à vendre*, for sale; *se vendre*, to sell, to be sold.

vendredi [vandrədì] *m.* Friday; *vendredi saint*, Good Friday.

vénéneux [vénéné] *adj.*° poisonous.

vénérable [vénéràbl] *adj.* venerable. ‖ *vénération* [-àsyon] *f.* veneration. ‖ *vénérer* [-é] *v.* to venerate.

vénerie [vénrî] *f.* venery; hunting.

vénérien [vénéryin] *adj.*° venereal.

veneur [vənœr] *m.* huntsman.

vengeance [vanʒans] *f.* revenge; vengeance. ‖ *venger* [-é] *v.* to avenge; *se venger*, to revenge oneself; *se venger de*, to get revenge on. ‖ *vengeur, -eresse* [-œr, -rès] *m., f.* avenger, revenger; *adj.* avenging; vindictive.

véniel [vényèl] *adj.*° venial.

venimeux [vənìmé] *adj.*° venomous; poisonous; malignant. ‖ *venin* [-in] *m.* venom; poison; malice.

venir [vənîr] *v.*° to come, to be coming; to arrive; to reach; to occur, to happen; to grow; to issue, to proceed; to be descended; *je viens de voir*, I have just seen; *venir chercher*, to call for, to come and get; *faire venir*, to send for.

vent [van] *m.* wind; scent [vénerie]; windage (artill.); emptiness (fig.); *sous le vent*, to leeward; *avoir vent de*, to get wind of.

vente [vant] *f.* sale; selling; *vente aux enchères*, auction.

ventilateur [vantìlàtœr] *m.* ventilator, fan, blower. ‖ *ventilation* [-àsyon] *f.* ventilation, airing; separate valuation (jur.); apportionment (comm.).

ventouse [vantûz] *f.* cupping(-glass); air-hole; nozzle [aspirateur]; sucker [sangsue]; air-scuttle (naut.); *appliquer des ventouses*, to cup.

ventre [vantr] *m.* abdomen, belly; stomach, paunch, tummy (fam.); womb; bowels, insides; *à plat ventre*, prone. ‖ *ventricule* [-ìkül] *m.* ventricle. ‖ *ventriloque* [-ìlòk] *adj.* ventriloquous; *s.* ventriloquist. ‖ *ventru* [-ü] *adj.* paunchy, big-bellied.

venu [vənü] *adj.* come; *bienvenu*, welcome; *mal venu*, unwelcome, ill-received; *le premier venu*, the first comer, anybody; *nouveau venu*, newcomer. ‖ *venue* [-ü] *f.* coming, arrival, advent; growth; *allées et venues*, goings and comings.

vêpres [vèpr] *f. pl.* vespers; evensong.

ver [vèr] *m.* worm; maggot, mite; grub, larva; moth; *ver luisant*, glowworm; *ver solitaire*, tape-worm; *ver à soie*, silk-worm.

véracité [véràsìté] *f.* truthfulness; veracity; accuracy.

véranda [vérandà] *f.* verandah.

verbal [vèrbàl] *adj.*° verbal; oral. ‖ *verbaliser* [-ìzé] *v.* to minute; to draw up an official report. ‖ *verbe* [vèrb] *m.* verb; *avoir le verbe haut*, to be loudmouthed, dictatorial. ‖ *verbeux* [-é] *adj.*° wordy, verbose, long-winded, prolix. ‖ *verbiage* [-yàʒ] *m.* wordiness, verbosity. ‖ *verbosité* [-òzìté] *f.* verbosity, long-windedness.

verdâtre [vèrdâtr] *adj.* greenish. ‖ *verdeur* [-œr] *f.* greenness; viridity, sap [bois]; vitality; tartness, acidity; acrimony; freedom, licentiousness.

verdict [vèrdìkt] *m.* verdict.

verdir [vèrdîr] *v.* to grow green; to colo(u)r green; to become covered with verdigris [cuivre]. ‖ *verdoyant* [-wàyan] *adj.* verdant; greenish. ‖ *verdure* [-ür] *f.* verdancy, verdure, greenery, foliage; greens; pot-herbs.

véreux [véré] *adj.*° wormy, maggoty, worm-eaten; rotten; suspicious; shaky; bogus, *Am.* phony.

verge [vèrʒ] *f.* rod, wand, switch; staff; penis; sway; ⓒ yard, yardstick.

verger [vèrʒé] *m.* orchard.

vergeté [vèrʒté] *adj.* streaky.

verglacé [vèrglàsé] *adj.* slippery, icy. ‖ *verglas* [-glà] *m.* glazed frost.

vergogne [vèrgòñ] *f.* shame.

vergue [vèrg] *f.* yard (naut.).

véridique [vérìdìk] *adj.* veracious.

vérificateur [vérìfìkàtœr] *m.* verifier, inspector, checker, tester, comptroller; auditor; gauge, calipers. ‖ *vérification* [-ìkàsyon] *f.* verification;

inspection, checking, testing; auditing; surveying; probate (jur.). ‖ **vérifier** [-yé] v. to verify; to inspect, to check, to test; to overhaul (mech.); to audit; to scrutinize [suffrages].

véritable [vérìtàbl] adj. veritable, true, real, actual, genuine, authentic; veracious; staunch, thorough, downright. ‖ **vérité** [-é] f. truth, verity; fact; truthfulness, sincerity; en vérité, truly, really.

verjus [vèrjü] m. verjuice.

vermeil [vèrmèy] adj. ruby; rosy; m. silver-gilt.

vermicelle [vèrmìsèl] m. vermicelli.

vermine [vèrmîn] f. vermin; rabble.

vermisseau [vèrmìsô] m.* small worm, grub.

vermoulu [vèrmûlü] adj. worm-eaten.

vermouth [vèrmût] m. vermouth.

verni [vèrnì] adj. varnished; glazed; patent [cuir]; toile vernie, oilskin. ‖ **vernir** [vèrnîr] v. to varnish; to polish; to japan; to glaze [céramique]. ‖ **vernis** [-ì] m. varnish, polish, gloss; glaze, glazing. ‖ **vernissage** [-ìsàj] m. varnishing; glazing; varnishing-day. ‖ **vernisser** [-ìsé] v. to glaze. ‖ **vernisseur** [-ìsœr] m. varnisher, polisher.

vérole [véròl] f. smallpox.

verrat [vèrà] m. boar.

verre [vèr] m. glass; lens [lentille]; crystal [montre]; verre de vin, glass of wine; verre à vin, wine-glass; verre à pied, stemmed glass; verre à liqueur, liqueur glass, pony (pop.); verre à vitre, sheet-glass; verre de sûreté, safety-glass; verre pilé, ground glass. ‖ **verrerie** [-°rî] f. glassmaking; glassworks; glass-ware. ‖ **verrière** [-yèr] f. glass casing; stained glass window. ‖ **verroterie** [-òtrî] f. glass trinkets; glass beads, bugle beads.

verrou [vèrû] m. bolt, bar; lock. ‖ **verrouiller** [-yé] v. to bolt, to lock.

verrue [vèrü] f. wart.

vers [vèr] m. verse, line.

vers [vèr] prep. toward(s), to; about.

versant [vèrsaⁿ] m. slope, versant.

versatile [vèrsàtìl] adj. changeable, fickle; variable; versatile (bot.). ‖ **versatilité** [-ìté] f. fickleness, inconstancy, changeableness.

versé [vèrsé] adj. (well) versed, conversant, practised, experienced; poured; paid. ‖ **versement** [-°maⁿ] m. payment; deposit; instalment; pouring; spilling, shedding; issue (mil.). ‖ **verser** [-é] v. to pour [liquide]; to discharge; to spill, to shed [sang, larmes]; to pay in, to deposit [argent]; to upset [voiture]; to issue (mil.).

verset [vèrsè] m. verse.

version [vèrsyoⁿ] f. version.

vert [vèr] adj. green; verdant, grassy; sharp, harsh; tart; fresh, raw; unripe, sour; smutty, off-colo(u)r [histoire]; vigorous, robust, hale; sharp [réplique]; m. green, green colo(u)r, grass; food; tartness; putting-green [golf].

vertébral [vèrtébràl] adj.* vertebral; colonne vertébrale, spinal column. ‖ **vertèbre** [vèrtèbr] f. vertebra.

ver :al [vèrtìkàl] adj.* vertical.

vertige [vèrtìj] m. dizziness, vertigo, giddiness; bewilderment; intoxication (fig.); avoir le vertige, to feel dizzy. ‖ **vertigineux** [-lnë] adj.* vertiginous; dizzy, giddy.

vertu [vèrtü] f. virtue; chastity; faculty; efficacy; en vertu de, by virtue of. ‖ **vertueux** [-ë] adj.* virtuous.

verve [vèrv] f. verve, zest, spirits.

verveine [vèrvèn] f. vervain, verbena.

vésicule [vézìkül] f. vesicle; vésicule biliaire, gall-bladder.

vespasienne [vèspàzyèn] f. street urinal.

vespéral [vèspéràl] adj.* vespertine.

vessie [vèsì] f. bladder.

veste [vèst] f. jacket. ‖ **vestiaire** [-yèr] m. cloakroom, Am. checkroom (theatr.); wardrobe-room, Am. coatroom [école]; hat-and-coat rack [meuble]; hat and coat, things [objets].

vestibule [vèstìbül] m. vestibule.

vestige [vèstìj] m. trace; remains.

vestimentaire [vèstìmaⁿtèr] adj. vestimentary.

veston [vèstoⁿ] m. man's jacket; lounge-coat; veston d'intérieur, smoking-jacket; complet veston, lounge suit, Am. business suit.

vêtement [vètmaⁿ] m. garment; vestment (eccles.); vesture; raiment [poésie]; cloak, disguise (fig.); pl. clothes, clothing, dress, apparel, attire; garb; weeds [deuil].

vétéran [vétéraⁿ] m. veteran; old hand; older boy.

vétérinaire [vétérìnèr] adj. veterinary; m. veterinarian.

vêtir [vètîr] v.* to clothe, to dress; to put on, to don; se vêtir, to get dressed, to dress (oneself); to put on. ‖ **vêtu** [-ü] p. p. of vêtir.

vétuste [vétüst] adj. decrepit, decayed; worn-out.

veuf, veuve [vœf, vœv] m. widower; f. widow; adj. widowed; bereft.

veuillez, see vouloir.

veule [vœl] adj. flabby; cowardly; toneless [voix]; flat [existence].

veuvage [vœvàj] *m.* widowhood, widowerhood, widowed state. ‖ *veuve, see* **veuf**.

vexant [vèksaⁿ] *adj.* vexing, provoking. ‖ *vexation* [vèksàsyoⁿ] *f.* vexation; annoyance, irritation; harassment, plaguing; molestation. ‖ *vexatoire* [-sàtwàr] *adj.* vexatious. ‖ *vexer* [-é] *v.* to vex; to annoy, to provoke, to irritate, to molest; to harass, to plague; *se vexer*, to get vexed, to be chagrined.

viable [vyàbl] *adj.* viable; durable; feasible.

viaduc [vyàdük] *m.* viaduct.

viager [vyàjé] *adj.** for life; *m.* life interest; *rente viagère*, life annuity; *en viager*, at life interest.

viande [vyaⁿd] *f.* meat; flesh.

viatique [vyàtìk] *m.* viaticum; provisions (fam.).

vibrant [vìbraⁿ] *adj.* vibrating, vibrant; resonant; ringing, quivering [voix]; rousing, stirring [discours]. ‖ *vibration* [-àsyoⁿ] *f.* vibration; fluttering (aviat.). ‖ *vibratoire* [-àtwàr] *adj.* vibratory; oscillatory. ‖ *vibrer* [-é] *v.* to vibrate; to tingle.

vicaire [vìkèr] *m.* curate.

vice [vìs] *m.* vice; sin, blemish.

vice-président [vìsprézìdaⁿ] *m.* vice-chairman; vice-president.

vicier [vìsyé] *v.* to vitiate, to pollute; to invalidate [contrat]. ‖ *vicieux* [-yé] *adj.** vicious; defective, faulty, tricky, restive [cheval]; *usage vicieux*, wrong use; *m.* vicious person.

vicinal [vìsìnàl] *adj.** parochial; local.

vicissitude [vìsìsìtüd] *f.* vicissitude; *pl.* ups and downs.

vicomte [vìkoⁿt] *m.* viscount. ‖ *vicomtesse* [-tès] *f.* viscountess.

victime [vìktîm] *f.* victim; casualty.

victoire [vìktwàr] *f.* victory. ‖ *victorieux* [-òryé] *adj.** victorious.

victuailles [vìktüày] *f. pl.* victuals.

vidange [vìdaⁿj] *f.* cleaning out; ullage; draining. ‖ *vidanger* [-é] *v.* to clean out; to drain. ‖ *vidangeur* [-œr] *m.* nightman.

vide [vîd] *adj.* empty; void, vacant, unoccupied; devoid, destitute; *m.* void, vacuum; blank, empty space; gap, cavity, chasm, hole; emptiness, vanity; *à vide*, empty; *vide-poches*, tray, tidy; work-basket. ‖ *vider* [-é] *v.* to empty; to void; to drain, to draw off; to clear out; to bore, to hollow out; to vacate; to eviscerate; to draw [volaille]; to clean, to gut [poisson]; to core [pomme]; to stone [fruit]; to

bail [eau]; to adjust, to settle [querelle, comptes]; to decide, to end [querelle]; to exhaust [esprit].

vie [vî] *f.* life; lifetime; existence, days; vitality; livelihood, living; food, subsistence; profession, way of life; spirit, animation, noise; biography, memoir; *en vie*, alive; *gagner sa vie*, to earn one's living.

vieil, *see* **vieux**. ‖ *vieillard* [vyèyàr] *m.* old man, oldster, old fellow, greybeard; *pl.* the aged, old people. ‖ *vieillerie* [vyèyrî] *f.* old stuff; *pl.* old rubbish; outworn ideas. ‖ *vieillesse* [vyèyès] *f.* oldness; old age. ‖ *vieillir* [vyèyîr] *v.* to age, to grow old; to become obsolete *or* antiquated. ‖ *vieillot* [-ô] *adj.* oldish; wizened [visage]; old-fashioned [idée].

vierge [vyèrj] *f.* virgin, maiden, maid; *adj.* virgin(al), pure; untrodden, unwrought; blank [page]; unexposed (phot.); untarnished [réputation].

vieux, vieille [vyë, vyèy] (*vieil, m.,* before a vowel or a mute *h*), *adj.* old, aged, advanced in years, elderly; ancient, venerable; old-fashioned, old-style [mode]; obsolete; veteran; *m.* old man, oldster, old fellow; *f.* old woman, old lady; *vieille fille*, old maid, spinster.

vif, vive [vîf, vîv] *adj.* alive, live, living; fast, quick; lively, brisk, sprightly; ardent, eager, hasty; hot [feu]; bracing [air]; sharp, smart, alert [esprit]; sparkling [œil]; keen [plaisir]; violent [douleur]; bright, intense, vivid [couleurs]; mettlesome [cheval]; biting, piercing [froid]; *m.* quick; living person; *de vive voix*, by word of mouth, orally; *vif-argent*, quick-silver, mercury.

vigie [vìjî] *f.* lookout man; watch-tower; observation-box (railw.); vigia (naut.); danger-buoy.

vigilance [vìjìlaⁿs] *f.* vigilance, watch-fulness, wakefulness; caution. ‖ *vigilant* [-aⁿ] *adj.* vigilant, watchful, wakeful; cautious. ‖ *vigile* [vìjìl] *f.* vigil, eve.

vigne [vìñ] *f.* vine; vineyard; *vigne vierge*, Virginia creeper. ‖ *vigneron* [-ᵉroⁿ] *m.* wine-grower.

vignette [vìñèt] *f.* vignette.

vignoble [vìñòbl] *m.* vineyard.

vigoureux [vìgûrë] *adj.** vigorous, strong, sturdy; forceful, energetic; stout, stalwart, sound. ‖ *vigueur* [vìgœr] *f.* vigo(u)r, strength; force, power, energy; stamina, endurance, sturdiness, stalwartness; effectiveness; *entrer en vigueur*, to come into effect; *mise en vigueur*, enforcing, enforcement (jur.).

vil [vĭl] *adj.* vile, base; lowly, mean; paltry; *à vil prix*, dirt cheap.

vilain [vĭlⁿ] *adj.* ugly, unsightly; vile, villainous; nasty; undesirable; mean, scurvy, dirty [tour]; shabby; sordid, wretched; *m.* villein, bondman, serf; cad, blackguard, rascal; naughty child.

vilebrequin [vĭlbrᵉkiⁿ] *m.* wimble.

vilenie [vĭlnĭ] *f.* foul deed.

vilipender [vĭlĭpãdé] *v.* to vilipend; to run down.

villa [vĭllà] *f.* villa. ‖ **village** [vĭlàj] *m.* village. ‖ **villageois** [-wà] *m.* villager; countryman; country bumpkin; *adj.* rustic, country.

ville [vĭl] *f.* town, city; *hôtel de ville*, town hall, city hall; *costume de ville*, plain clothes; morning dress; *dîner en ville*, to dine out.

villégiature [vĭllégyàtür] *f.* sojourn in the country; out-of-town holiday; *en villégiature*, on holiday.

vin [vĭⁿ] *m.* wine; *vin ordinaire*, table wine; *vin de marque*, vintage wine; *vin mousseux*, sparkling wine; *vin chaud*, mulled wine.

vinaigre [vĭnĕgr] *m.* vinegar. ‖ **vinaigrer** [-é] *v.* to season with vinegar. ‖ **vinaigrette** [-ĕt] *f.* vinegar dressing.

vindicatif [vĭⁿdĭkàtĭf] *adj.* vindictive, revengeful. ‖ **vindicte** [vĭⁿdĭkt] *f.* contumely; prosecution.

vingt [vĭⁿ] *m.*, *adj.* twenty; a score; twentieth [date, titre]. ‖ **vingtaine** [-tèn] *f.* about twenty; a score. ‖ **vingtième** [-tyèm] *m.*, *f.*, *adj.* twentieth.

vinicole [vĭnĭkòl] *adj.* wine-growing; wine. ‖ **vinification** [-fĭkàsyoⁿ] *f.* vinification.

viol [vyòl] *m.* rape; violation. ‖ **violateur**, **-trice** [-àtœr, -trĭs] *m.*, *f.* violator; infringer, transgressor, breaker; ravisher. ‖ **violation** [-àsyoⁿ] *f.* violation, infringement.

viole [vyòl] *f.* viol.

violence [vyòlãs] *f.* violence; duress (jur.). ‖ **violent** [-ãⁿ] *adj.* violent; fierce; high, buffeting [vent]. ‖ **violenter** [-ãté] *v.* to do violence to; to force; to rape, to ravish. ‖ **violer** [-é] *v.* to violate; to transgress [loi]; to break [promesse]; to rape, to ravish, to outrage [femme].

violet [vyòlè] *adj.* violet, purple. ‖ **violette** [-èt] *f.* violet. ‖ **violine** [vyòlĭn] *adj.* purple.

violon [vyòloⁿ] *m.* violin, fiddle (fam.); violin player; (pop.) Br. quod, Am. clink, cooler (pop.). ‖ **violoncelle** [-sèl] *m.* violoncello. ‖ **violoncelliste** *m.*, *f.* violoncellist. ‖ **violoneux** [-é] *m.* fiddler. ‖ **violoniste** *m.*, *f.* violinist.

viorne [vyòrn] *f.* viburnum.

vipère [vĭpèr] *f.* viper. ‖ **vipérin** [-iⁿ] *adj.* viperine; venomous, viperous.

virage [vĭràj] *m.* turning; veering; swinging round, slewing round; tacking, going about (naut.); bank [piste]; toning (phot.); turn, corner, bend [auto]; *virage sans visibilité*, blind corner. ‖ **virement** [vĭrmaⁿ] *m.* turning; veering; clearing, transfer (comm.). ‖ **virer** [-é] *v.* to turn; to veer; to transfer (comm.); to clear [chèque]; to bank (aviat.); to tack about (naut.); to tone (phot.).

virginal [vĭrjĭnàl] *adj.* maidenly; virginal. ‖ **virginité** [vĭrjĭnĭté] *f.* virginity; maidenhood.

virgule [vĭrgül] *f.* comma.

viril [vĭrĭl] *adj.* virile; male; manly. ‖ **virilité** [-ĭté] *f.* virility.

virtuel [vĭrtüèl] *adj.* virtual.

virtuose [vĭrtüòz] *s.* virtuoso. ‖ **virtuosité** [-ĭté] *f.* virtuosity.

virulence [vĭrülãs] *f.* virulence; malignity. ‖ **virulent** [-aⁿ] *adj.* virulent; malignant; noxious. ‖ **virus** [vĭrüs] *m.* virus.

vis [vĭs] *f.* screw.

visa [vĭzà] *m.* visa, visé [passeport].

visage [vĭzàj] *m.* face, countenance, visage; aspect, look, air.

vis-à-vis [vĭzàvĭ] *m.* person opposite; vis-à-vis; *adv.* opposite; face to face; towards, with respect to.

viscère [vĭsèr] *m.* internal organ.

visée [vĭzé] *f.* aiming; sighting (mil.); *pl.* aims, designs, ambitions. ‖ **viser** [-é] *v.* to aim at; to sight, to take a sight on (topogr.); to have in view; to concern; to allude to, to refer to. ‖ **viseur** [-œr] *m.* aimer; view-finder (phot.); sighting-tube, eyepiece.

visibilité [vĭzĭbĭlĭté] *f.* visibility. ‖ **visible** [-ĭbl] *adj.* visible, perceptible; obvious, evident; accessible; at home, ready to receive.

visière [vĭzyèr] *f.* visor, vizor; peak [casquette]; eye-shade.

vision [vĭzyoⁿ] *f.* vision; (eye)sight; seeing; view; fantasy; phantom. ‖ **visionnaire** [-yònèr] *m.*, *f.* visionary; seer; *adj.* visionary. ‖ **visionner** [-yòné] *v.* to pre-view. ‖ **visionneuse** [-yònèz] *f.* viewer.

visite [vĭzĭt] *f.* visit; call; inspection; examination [douane]; search (jur.); attendance [médecin]; *faire des visites*, to pay calls; *carte de visite*, visiting-card, Am. calling-card. ‖ **visiter** [-é] *v.* to visit; to attend; to examine, to inspect; to tour; to search (jur.). ‖ **visiteur** [-œr] *m.* visitor, caller.

vison [vìzoⁿ] *m.* mink.

visqueux [vìskë] *adj.** viscous, gluey.

visser [vìsé] *v.* to screw.

visuel [vìzüèl] *adj.** visual; *champ visuel,* field of vision.

vital [vìtàl] *adj.** vital; *minimum vital,* basic minimum. ‖ *vitaliser* [-ìzé] *v.* to vitalize. ‖ *vitalité* [-ìté] *f.* vitality; vigo(u)r. ‖ *vitamine* [vìtàmîn] *f.* vitamin.

vite [vìt] *adj.* fast, swift, rapid, speedy, quick; *adv.* fast, swiftly, rapidly, speedily, quickly. ‖ *vitesse* [-ès] *f.* speed, swiftness, rapidity, quickness, fleetness, celerity; velocity [son, lumière]; *gagner de vitesse,* to outrun.

viticole [vìtìkòl] *adj.* viticultural; wine [industrie]. ‖ *viticulteur* [-kültœr] *m.* viticulturalist; wine-grower. ‖ *viticulture* [-ültür] *f.* viticulture.

vitrail [vìtràȷ] *m.* (pl. *vitraux* [vìtrô]) stained *or* leaded glass window. ‖ *vitre* [vìtr] *f.* (window-)pane. ‖ *vitré* [-é] *adj.* glazed; vitreous, glassy; *porte vitrée,* glass door. ‖ *vitrer* [-é] *v.* to equip with glass panes, to glaze. ‖ *vitreux* [-ë] *adj.** vitreous. ‖ *vitrier* [-ìyé] *m.* glazier. ‖ *vitrifier* [-ìfyé] *v.* to vitrify. ‖ *vitrine* [-în] *f.* shop-window, store-window; show-case.

vitriol [vìtrìyòl] *m.* vitriol. ‖ *vitrioler* [-é] *v.* to vitriolize.

vitupération [vìtüpéràsyoⁿ] *f.* vituperation, abuse. ‖ *vitupérer* [-péré] *v.* to vituperate.

vivable [vìvàbl] *adj.* livable-with. ‖ *vivace* [vìvàs] *adj.* long-lived; perennial (bot.); everlasting, enduring, deep-rooted. ‖ *vivacité* [-ìté] *f.* promptness, alertness; hastiness, petulance; acuteness, intensity [discussion]; vividness, brilliancy [couleur]; vivaciousness, sprightliness; mettle [cheval]; readiness [esprit].

vivant [vìvaⁿ] *adj.* alive, living; lively, animated; vivid [image]; modern [langues]; lifelike [portrait]; *m.* living person; lifetime. ‖ *vive* [vìv] *see vif and vivre.* ‖ *viveur* [-œr] *m.* free liver, fast man, gay dog. ‖ *vivier* [-yé] *m.* fish-pond, fish-preserve. ‖ *vivifier* [-ìfyé] *v.* to vivify, to quicken; to enliven, to revive, to exhilarate. ‖ *vivisection* [-ìsèksyoⁿ] *f.* vivisection. ‖ *vivoir* [vìvwàr] *m.* ① living-room. ‖ *vivoter* [-òté] *v.* to live from hand to mouth, to scrape along. ‖ *vivre* [vìvr] *v.** to live, to be alive; to subsist; to board; to last; to behave; *m.* living; board, food; *pl.* provisions, supplies, victuals; rations (mil.); *vive la reine !* long live the Queen ! *vive(nt) les vacances !* hurrah for the holidays !

vizir [vìzìr] *m.* vizier.

vocabulaire [vòkàbülèr] *m.* vocabulary; word-list.

vocal [vòkàl] *adj.** vocal. ‖ *vocalise* [-îz] *f.* vocalizing. ‖ *vocaliser* [-ìzé] *v.* to vocalize.

vocation [vòkàsyoⁿ] *f.* vocation; calling, bent, inclination; call.

vociférer [vòsìféré] *v.* to vociferate, to shout, to yell, to scream, to bawl.

vœu [vë] *m.** vow; wish, desire; *meilleurs vœux,* best wishes.

vogue [vòg] *f.* vogue, fashion, style, craze, fad, rage. ‖ *voguer* [vògé] *v.* to sail; to row; to float, to go, to scud along; to forge ahead (fig.).

voici [vwàsì] *adv.* here is, here are; see here, behold; this is, these are; *le voici qui vient,* here he comes; *voici deux ans qu'il est ici,* he has been here for two years.

voie [vwà] *f.* way; highway; path; means, channel, course (fig.); duct, canal (anat.); leak (naut.); process (chem.); *voie ferrée,* railway (track), Am. railroad; *voie de départ,* runway (aviat.); *voies de fait,* assault and battery (jur.); *voie d'eau,* leak.

voilà [vwàlà] *adv.* there is, there are; see there, behold; that is, those are; *voilà tout,* that's all; *le voilà qui vient,* there he comes.

voile [vwàl] *f.* sail; canvas.

voile [vwàl] *m.* veil; voile; pretence, cover; fog (phot.); *voile du palais,* soft palate. ‖ *voilé* [-é] *adj.* veiled; hazy [ciel]; muffled [tambour]; fogged (phot.); buckled, bent (mech.). ‖ *voiler* [-é] *v.* to veil; to conceal; to dim, to obscure, to blur, to cloud; to muffle [bruit]; to shade [lumière]; to buckle, to bend, to warp (mech.). ‖ *voilette* [-èt] *f.* hat-veil.

voilier [vwàlyé] *m.* sailing-boat. ‖ *voilure* [-ür] *f.* sails; wings, flying surface (aviat.).

voir [vwàr] *v.** to see; to behold, to perceive; to sight; to watch; to witness; to observe, to look at, to view; to inspect; to visit; to attend [malades]; to have to do with; to understand; *faire voir,* to show.

voire [vwàr] *adv.* indeed, even; nay; in truth.

voirie [vwàrî] *f.* Roads Department, Am. Highway Division.

voisin [vwàzîⁿ] *m.* neighbo(u)r; *adj.* neighbo(u)ring, adjacent, adjoining, next; *maison voisine,* next door. ‖ *voisinage* [-ìnàȷ] *m.* neighbo(u)rhood, proximity, vicinity, nearness; *bon voisinage,* neighbo(u)rliness. ‖ *voisiner* [-ìné] *v.* to be neighbo(u)rly, to border, to be adjacent; to be next; to be close [avec, to].

voiture [vwàtür] *f.* carriage, conveyance, vehicle; transportation; *Br.* car, *Am.* automobile; machine; van, cart, wagon; coach (railw.); freight, load; *voiture d'enfant,* perambulator, baby-carriage, pram (fam.); *petites voitures,* costers' barrows; *lettre de voiture,* way-bill, bill of lading; *en voiture!* take your seats!, *Am.* all aboard! ‖ **voiturée** [-é] *f.* cartload; car-load. ‖ **voiturer** [-é] *v.* to convey, to carry, to transport, to cart. ‖ **voiturier** [-yé] *m.* carrier, carter.

voix [vwà] *f.* voice; tone; vote, suffrage; part (mus.); opinion; judgment; speech; *mettre aux voix,* to put to the vote; *de vive voix,* by word of mouth.

vol [vòl] *m.* theft, robbery, thieving, stealing; *vol à la tire,* pickpocketing; *vol à l'étalage,* shop-lifting.

vol [vòl] *m.* flying, soaring; flight; flock, covey [oiseaux]; spread [ailes]; *au vol,* on the wing; *vue à vol d'oiseau,* bird's-eye view.

volage [vòlàj] *adj.* fickle, inconstant.

volaille [vòlày] *f.* poultry; fowl; *marchand de volaille,* poulterer.

volant [vòlaⁿ] *adj.* flying; loose, floating; movable, portable; *m.* shuttlecock [jeu]; sail [moulin], flywheel, hand-wheel (techn.); steering-wheel [auto]; flounce, panel [couture]; *feuille volante,* loose-leaf.

volatil [vòlàtìl] *adj.* volatile. ‖ **volatiliser** [vòlàtìlìzé] *v.* to volatilize; *se volatiliser,* to volatilize, to go into thin air; to burn up [fusée].

volatile [vòlàtìl] *m.* winged creature.

volcan [vòlkaⁿ] *m.* volcano.

volée [vòlé] *f.* flight [oiseau]; volley [cloche, tennis]; shower [coups]; thrashing.

voler [vòlé] *v.* to steal; to rob; to usurp [titre]; to swipe (fam.).

voler [vòlé] *v.* to fly; to soar; to travel fast; *voler à voile,* to glide. ‖ **volet** [-è] *m.* shutter; flap (aviat.). ‖ **voleter** [-té] *v.* to flutter; to skip (fig.).

voleur [vòlœr] *m.* thief, robber, burglar; shoplifter; stealer, pilferer; plunderer; extortioner; *adj.** thievish; fleecing; pilfering.

volière [vòlyèr] *f.* aviary; bird-cage.

volontaire [vòloⁿtèr] *adj.* voluntary; spontaneous; intentional, deliberate; self-willed, wilful, wayward, headstrong, obstinate, stubborn; *m.* volunteer. ‖ **volonté** [-é] *f.* will; willingness; *payable à volonté,* payable on demand, promissory [billet]; *dernières volontés,* last will and testament; *mauvaise volonté,* unwillingness. ‖ **volontiers** [-yé] *adv.* willingly, gladly, readily.

volt [vòlt] *m.* volt. ‖ **voltage** [-àj] *m.* voltage.

volte [vòlt] *f.* volt [escrime]; vaulting [gymnastique]; *volte-face,* about-face; right-about turn; *faire volte-face,* to face about; to reverse one's opinions.

voltige [vòltìj] *f.* trick-riding; acrobatic exercises. ‖ **voltiger** [vòltìjé] *v.* to flutter; to fly about, to flit, to hover; to flap [rideau]; to perform on a tight-rope, on a trapeze; to tumble.

volubile [vòlübìl] *adj.* voluble; glib; volubile, twining (bot.). ‖ **volubilité** [-ìlìté] *f.* glibness, garrulousness.

volume [vòlüm] *m.* volume, tome; bulk, mass; capacity; compass [voix]. ‖ **volumineux** [-ìnê] *adj.** voluminous, large, bulky, massive; capacious.

volupté [vòlüpté] *f.* delight. ‖ **voluptueux** [-üê] *adj.** voluptuous.

volute [vòlüt] *f.* volute; spiral, curl.

vomir [vòmîr] *v.* to vomit; to bring up, to throw up, to spew up; to puke (fam.); to belch forth (fig.). ‖ **vomissement** [-ìsmaⁿ] *m.* vomiting; vomit. ‖ **vomitif** [-ìtìf] *m., adj.** emetic, vomitory.

vorace [vòràs] *adj.* voracious, greedy, ravenous, gluttonous. ‖ **voracité** [-ìté] *f.* voracity, greediness, gluttony; *avec voracité,* greedily, ravenously.

vos [vô] *poss. adj. pl.* your.

votant [vòtaⁿ] *adj.* voting, enfranchised; *m.* voter, poller; *pl.* constituents. ‖ **vote** [vòt] *m.* vote; voting, balloting, poll; returns, decision, result. ‖ **voter** [-é] *v.* to vote; to ballot; to pass, to carry [projet de loi]. ‖ **votif** [vòtìf] *adj.** votive.

votre [vòtr] *poss. adj.* your.

vôtre [vôtr] *poss. pron.* yours.

vouer [vûé] *v.* to vow, to dedicate, to consecrate; to swear; to pledge.

vouloir [vûlwàr] *v.** to want, to wish; to intend; to require; to need; to resolve, to determine; to try, to seek, to attempt, to endeavo(u)r; to admit, to grant; *m.* will; *vouloir dire,* to mean, to signify; *en vouloir à,* to bear (someone) a grudge; *je ne veux pas,* I won't, I refuse; *vouloir bien,* to be willing; *j'ai voulu le voir,* I tried to see him; *sans le vouloir,* unintentionally; *que voulez-vous?,* what do you want?; *je voudrais,* I should like; *je veux que vous sachiez,* I want you to know; *veuillez agréer,* please accept; *de son bon vouloir,* of one's own accord; *mauvais vouloir,* ill will. ‖ **voulu** [-ü] *adj.* required, requisite, deliberate, intentional; wished, desired; due, received; *en temps voulu,* in due time.

vous [vû] *pron.* you; to you; yourself.

voûte [vût] *f.* vault, arch; archway; roof (med.). || **voûté** [-é] *adj.* vaulted, arched, curved, bowed, bent; stooping, stoop-shouldered, round-shouldered.

voyage [vwàyàj] *m.* travel, travel(l)ing; journey, excursion, trip, tour, run; visit, sojourn, stay; *faire un voyage*, to take a trip. || **voyager** [-é] *v.* to travel; to migrate [oiseaux]; to be on the road (comm.); to be transported [marchandises]. || **voyageur** [-œr] *m.* travel(l)er; tourist; passenger; fare [taxi]; commercial travel(l)er (comm.); *adj.** travel(l)ing.

voyance [vwàyà⁰s] *f.* clairvoyance. || **voyant** [vwàyà⁰] *adj.* showy, gaudy, garish, loud, vivid, conspicuous; *m.* seer, clairvoyant, prophet; sighting-slit (techn.); direction roller [auto]; signal.

voyelle [vwàyèl] *f.* vowel.

voyer [vwàyé] *m.* road-surveyor.

voyeur [vwàyœr] *m.* voyeur; Peeping Tom (fam.).

voyou [vwàyû] *m.* hooligan, loafer, street-arab; *Am.* hoodlum.

vrac [vràk] *m. en vrac*, in bulk; wholesale.

vrai [vrè] *adj.* true, truthful, correct; proper, right, accurate, veracious; real, genuine, authentic; downright, arrant, regular, very; legitimate [théâtre]; *adv.* truly, really, indeed; *m.* truth; *à vrai dire*, to tell the truth, actually; *être dans le vrai*, to be right. || **vraiment** [-mà⁰] *adv.* truly, really, in truth; indeed; actually; is that so?, indeed? || **vraisemblable** [vrèsà⁰blàbl] *adj.* likely, probable; plausible. ||

vraisemblablement [-ᵉmà⁰] *adv.* probably, to all appearances, very likely. || **vraisemblance** [vrèsà⁰blà⁰s] *f.* probability, likelihood; verisimilitude.

vrille [vrîy] *f.* gimlet, borer, piercer; tendril (bot.); tail spin (aviat.). || **vriller** [-é] *v.* to bore; to spiral up.

vrombir [vro⁰bîr] *v.* to hum, to buzz [mouche, toupie]; to throb, to purr, to whirr [moteur]. || **vrombissement** [-ìsmà⁰] *m.* buzzing, hum, humming; throbbing, purring, whirring.

vu [vü] *p. p. of voir; adj.* seen, observed; considered; *prep.* regarding; considering; *mal vu*, ill thought of. || **vue** [vü] *f.* sight; view; eyesight; aspect; survey; prospect, outlook; appearance; light; intention, purpose, design; insight, penetration; *à première vue*, at first sight; *en vue de*, with a view to; *à vue d'œil*, visibly; *connaître de vue*, to know by sight; *hors de vue*, out of sight; *prise de vues*, shooting [film]; *en vue*, conspicuous, prominent; *perdre qqn de vue*, to lose touch with s.o.; *à vue de nez*, at a rough guess.

vulcaniser [vülkànìzé] *v.* to vulcanize.

vulgaire [vülgèr] *adj.* vulgar, common; ordinary, everyday; unrefined, coarse; *m.* the common people, the vulgar herd; *langue vulgaire*, vernacular. || **vulgarisateur** [vülgàrìzàtœr] *m.* popularizer; *adj.** popularizing. || **vulgarisation** [vülgàrìzàsyo⁰] *f.* vulgarization. || **vulgariser** [-ìzé] *v.* to vulgarize, to popularize; to coarsen. || **vulgarité** [-ìté] *f.* vulgarity; *vulgarité criarde*, blatancy.

vulnérable [vülnéràbl] *adj.* vulnerable.

W

wagon [vàgo⁰] *m.* (railway) carriage; coach, car; wagon, truck; *wagon de marchandises*, *Br.* goods-van, *Am.* freight-car; *wagon frigorifique*, refrigerator car; *wagon-citerne*, tank-car; *wagon-lit*, sleeping-car, sleeper, *Am.* pullman; *wagon-poste*, *Br.* mail-van, *Am.* mail-car; *wagon-réservoir*, tank-car; *wagon-restaurant*, dining-car, diner; *wagon-salon*, saloon-car, *Am.*

observation car, parlo(u)r car. || **wagonnet** [-ònè] *m.* tilt-truck, tip-wagon, *Am.* dump-truck.

warrant [wàrà⁰] *m.* warrant. || **warranter** [-té] *v.* to warrant, to guarantee.

watt [wàt] *m.* watt.

whisky [wìskì] *m.* whisky, whiskey.

X

xénophobe [ksénòfòb] *s.* xenophobe; **xénophobie**, xenophobia.

xérès [ksérès] *m.* sherry; Jerez. **xylophone** [ksìlòfòn] *m.* xylophone.

Y

y [ĭ] *adv.* there; here; thither; within; *pron.* to it; by it; at it; in it; *il y a*, there is, there are; *il y a dix ans*, ten years ago; *pendant que j'y pense*, while I think of it; *ça y est!* it's done!, that's it!; *vous y êtes?*, do you follow it?, are you with me?, do you get it?; *je n'y suis pour rien*, I had nothing to do with it, I had no part in it; *vous y gagnerez*, you will profit from it.

yacht [yòt, yàk] *m.* yacht.

yaourt [yàûrt] *m.* yogurt, yoghourt.

yeuse [yëz] *f.* holm-oak, holly-oak, ilex.

yeux [yë] *m. pl.* eyes; *see œil.*

yoga [yògà] *m.* yoga. ‖ **yogi** [-gĭ] *m.* yogi.

yole [yòl] *f.* yawl.

yougoslave [yûgòslàv] *adj., m., f.* Jugoslav, Yugoslav. ‖ **Yougoslavie** [-vĭ] *f.* Jugoslavia, Yugoslavia.

youyou [yûyû] *m.* dinghy.

ypérite [ĭpérĭt] *f.* mustard-gas; yperite.

Z

zazou [zàzû] *m.* teddy boy, *Am.* zoot suiter; cool cat.

zèbre [zèbr] *m.* zebra. ‖ **zébrer** [-é] *v.* to stripe, to streak. ‖ **zébrure** [-brür] *f.* stripe, streak; *pl.* striped markings.

zélandais [zélandè] *m.* Zealander; *adj.* pertaining to Zealand. ‖ **Zélande** [-lande] *f.* Zealand; *Nouvelle-Zélande*, New Zealand.

zèle [zèl] *m.* zeal. ‖ **zélé** [zélé] *adj.* zealous, ardent.

zénith [zénĭt] *m.* zenith.

zéphir [zéfĭr] *m.* zephyr.

zéro [zérô] *m.* zero, naught, cipher; freezing point; starting point; love [tennis]; nonentity, nobody (fam.).

zeste [zèst] *m.* peel, twist [citron].

zézaiement [zézèman] *m.* lisp, lisping. ‖ **zézayer** [-èyé] *v.* to lisp.

zibeline [zìblĭn] *f.* sable.

zigzag [zìgzàg] *m.* zigzag; *éclair en zigzag*, forked lightning; *disposé en zigzag*, staggered. ‖ **zigzaguer** [-àgé] *v.* to zigzag; to flit about.

zinc [zĭⁿg] *m.* zinc; spelter [plaques]; (pop.) bar, counter; airplane.

zizanie [zìzànĭ] *f.* zizania; discord.

zodiaque [zòdyàk] *m.* zodiac.

zona [zònà] *m.* zona, shingles.

zone [zôn] *f.* zone, area, region, sector; belt [climat]; circuit, girdle.

zoo [zòò] *m.* zoo. ‖ **zoologie** [zòòlòjĭ] *f.* zoology. ‖ **zoologique** [jìk] *adj.* zoological; *jardin zoologique*, zoo (fam.).

zozoter [zòzòté] *v.* to lisp.

zut! [züt] *interj.* hang it!, darn it!; *Br.* dash it!

ANGLAIS-FRANÇAIS

L'ESSENTIEL DE LA GRAMMAIRE ANGLAISE

L'ARTICLE

L'article défini.

L'article défini THE est invariable. Ex. : *le garçon*, THE BOY ; *la fille*, THE GIRL ; *les rois*, THE KINGS. — Il se prononce [zhî] devant une voyelle ou un *h* muet, et quand il est seul ou fortement accentué. Dans tous les autres cas, on le prononce [zhe].

L'article défini ne s'emploie pas quand le sens est général, devant : 1° les noms pluriels ; 2° les noms abstraits ; 3° les noms de couleur ; 4° les noms de matière (pain, vin, bois, etc.) ; 5° les noms de langage ; 6° MAN et WOMAN. Ex. : *les chats*, CATS ; *la colère*, ANGER ; *le rouge*, RED ; *le pain*, BREAD ; *l'anglais*, ENGLISH.

Mais il faut toujours l'employer, comme en français, quand le sens n'est pas général. Ex. : *l'homme que je vois*, THE MAN THAT I SEE.

L'article indéfini.

L'article indéfini a deux formes :

1° Devant les consonnes (y compris *w, h* et *y* initial, et toute voyelle ou tout groupe de voyelles ayant le son *ye* ou *you*), on emploie la forme a. Ex. : *un homme*, A MAN ; *une dame*, A LADY ; *une maison*, A HOUSE ; *un usage*, A USE [e yous] ;

2° Devant une voyelle ou un *h* muet, on emploie an.

L'article indéfini n'a pas de pluriel. (V. L'ADJECTIF, *Quelque*.)

L'article indéfini s'emploie devant tout nom concret non précédé d'un autre article, d'un possessif ou d'un démonstratif. Ex. : *mon père, officier de marine, était veuf*, MY FATHER, A NAVAL OFFICER, WAS A WIDOWER ; *sans foyer*, WITHOUT A HOME.

L'article partitif. — V. L'ADJECTIF, *Adjectifs indéfinis*.

LE NOM

Pluriel.

On le forme en ajoutant s au singulier (cet *s* se prononce).

Exceptions.

Les noms terminés en o, s, x, z, sh ajoutent es. Ex. : BOX, BOXES ; POTATO, POTATOES. Cependant, les noms en IES restent *invariables*.

- Les noms terminés par ch ajoutent es, sauf lorsque le *ch* se prononce *k*. Ex. : CHURCH, CHURCHES ; MONARCH, MONARCHS.
- Les noms terminés en y forment leur pluriel : 1° en ys quand l'*y* est précédé par une *voyelle* ; 2° en ies quand l'*y* est précédé par une *consonne*. Ex. : BOY, BOYS ; FLY, FLIES ; LADY, LADIES.
- Les noms terminés par fe et dix noms terminés par f (CALF, ELF, HALF, LEAF, LOAF, SELF, SHEAF, SHELF, THIEF, WOLF) forment leur pluriel en ves. Ex. : KNIFE, ELF, SELF : pl. KNIVES, ELVES, SELVES.

● MAN, WOMAN, CHILD, OX font MEN, WOMEN, CHILDREN, OXEN. FOOT, TOOTH, GOOSE font FEET, TEETH, GEESE. MOUSE et LOUSE font MICE et LICE. DEER, SALMON, SHEEP, TROUT, SWINE et GROUSE sont invariables.

Genre des noms.

La plupart des noms anglais sont du masculin quand ils désignent un homme ou un être mâle, du féminin quand ils désignent une femme ou un être femelle, du neutre dans tous les autres cas. PARENT désigne le père ou la mère, COUSIN un cousin ou une cousine; les mots en er comme READER sont du masculin (*lecteur*), du féminin (*lectrice*) ou du neutre (*livre de lecture*).

Les principales exceptions sont : CHILD et BABY, généralement neutres, SHIP, ENGINE, généralement féminins.

Formation du féminin.

Comme en français, le féminin se forme de trois façons :

1° par un mot différent. Ex. : FATHER, BROTHER, SON, BOY ont pour féminin MOTHER, SISTER, DAUGHTER, GIRL ;

2° par un mot composé. Ex. : MILKMAN a pour féminin MILKMAID ;

3° par une désinence. Ex. : LION, ACTOR, PRINCE font au féminin LIONESS, ACTRESS, PRINCESS. WIDOW (*veuve*) fait au masculin WIDOWER (*veuf*).

Le cas possessif.

Le cas possessif ne peut s'employer que lorsque le possesseur est une personne ou un nom de mesure. On le forme en plaçant le nom possesseur, suivi d'une apostrophe et d'un s, devant le nom de l'objet possédé (dont l'article est supprimé). Ex. : *le livre de Bob*, BOB'S BOOK ; *une promenade d'une heure*, AN HOUR'S WALK.

Les noms pluriels terminés par s prennent seulement l'apostrophe. Ex. : *les livres des élèves*, THE PUPILS' BOOKS.

L'ADJECTIF

L'adjectif est invariable et se place *avant* le nom qu'il qualifie. Ex. : *un bon garçon*, A GOOD BOY ; *une bonne fille*, A GOOD GIRL ; *des dames aimables*, KIND LADIES.

Comparatif et superlatif.

Le comparatif et le superlatif des adjectifs de plus de deux syllabes se forment avec les adverbes MORE (*plus*) et THE MOST (*le plus*). Ex. : *plus actif*, MORE DILIGENT ; *la plus élégante*, THE MOST ELEGANT.

Les adjectifs d'une syllabe forment leur comparatif en prenant la désinence er et leur superlatif en prenant la désinence est. Ex. : *petit*, SMALL ; *plus petit*, SMALLER ; *le plus petit*, THE SMALLEST. (V. LE VERBE, *Règle du redoublement de la consonne finale*.)

La plupart des adjectifs de deux syllabes, et notamment tous ceux terminés par y, forment leur comparatif et leur superlatif comme ceux d'une syllabe. Ex. : NARROW, NARROWER, NARROWEST. (Ceux en y prennent ier et iest : LAZY, LAZIER, LAZIEST.)

Comparatifs et superlatifs irréguliers.

● GOOD (*bon*), BETTER (*meilleur*), THE BEST (*le meilleur*).

● BAD (*mauvais*), WORSE (*pire*), THE WORST (*le pire*).

● LITTLE (*petit*), LESS, LESSER (*moindre*), THE LEAST (*le moindre*).

● FAR (*éloigné*), FARTHER, THE FARTHEST.

● OLD (*vieux*) fait OLDER et THE OLDEST dans le sens général, mais ELDER et THE ELDEST dans le sens de *aîné*.

● FORE (*antérieur*) donne FORMER (*premier de deux*, opposé à LATTER, *dernier*) et THE FIRST (*le premier de tous*, opposé à LAST, *dernier*).

L'adjectif numéral cardinal.

● ONE, TWO, THREE, FOUR, FIVE, SIX, SEVEN, EIGHT, NINE, TEN, ELEVEN, TWELVE, THIRTEEN, FOURTEEN, FIFTEEN, SIXTEEN, SEVENTEEN, EIGHTEEN, NINETEEN, TWENTY, TWENTY-ONE...; THIRTY; FORTY; FIFTY; SIXTY; SEVENTY; EIGHTY; NINETY; ONE HUNDRED, ONE HUNDRED AND ONE...; TWO HUNDRED...; ONE THOUSAND...; TWO THOUSAND...; ONE MILLION...

● DOZEN, SCORE (*vingtaine*), HUNDRED, THOUSAND et MILLION prennent un *s* au pluriel quand on les emploie comme substantifs.

L'adjectif numéral ordinal.

● FIRST, SECOND, THIRD, FOURTH, FIFTH, SIXTH, SEVENTH, EIGHTH, NINTH, TENTH, ELEVENTH, TWELFTH, THIRTEENTH, FOURTEENTH, FIFTEENTH, SIXTEENTH, SEVENTEENTH, EIGHTEENTH, NINETEENTH, TWENTIETH, TWENTY-FIRST...; THIRTIETH; FORTIETH; FIFTIETH; SIXTIETH; SEVENTIETH; EIGHTIETH; NINETIETH; HUNDREDTH...; THOUSANDTH...; MILLIONTH.

Adjectifs démonstratifs et possessifs. — V. LE PRONOM.

Adjectifs indéfinis.

● **Quelque** se traduit par SOME OU ANY. SOME s'emploie surtout dans les phrases affirmatives. Ex. : *J'ai quelques livres,* I HAVE SOME BOOKS.

Le véritable sens de ANY étant « n'importe quel », on s'en sert surtout dans les phrases interrogatives, négatives et dubitatives. Ex. : *Je lis n'importe quel livre,* I READ ANY BOOK; *il ne lit aucun livre,* HE DOES NOT READ ANY BOOK (« he does not read some books » voudrait dire : *il y a des livres qu'il ne lit pas*).

L'article partitif se traduit souvent, lui aussi, par SOME OU ANY. Ex. : *Voulez-vous du pain?* WILL YOU HAVE SOME BREAD ?

● **Quelqu'un** : SOMEBODY ; **quelques-uns** : SOME.

● **Personne** : NOBODY, NOT... ANYBODY.

● **Quelque chose** : SOMETHING (**rien** : NOTHING, ou NOT... ANYTHING).

● **Beaucoup de** : MUCH (sing.), MANY (pl.).

● **Peu de** : LITTLE (sing.), FEW (pl.).

● **Un peu de** : A LITTLE (sing.), A FEW (pl.).

● **Chaque** : EACH (sing.), EVERY (collectif).

● **L'un ou l'autre** : EITHER.

● **Ni l'un ni l'autre** : NEITHER.

● **Assez de** : ENOUGH (placé devant ou après le nom).

LE PRONOM

Pronoms personnels sujets.

I, YOU, HE (m.), SHE (f.), IT (neutre); WE, YOU, THEY. Le pronom THOU (*tu*) n'est guère employé que dans les prières pour s'adresser à Dieu; même dans l'intimité, les Anglais et les Américains se disent YOU.

Dans certains cas où le pronom personnel est sujet, on emploie cependant la forme du pronom personnel complément (v. ci-dessous).

Pronoms personnels compléments.

ME, YOU, HIM (m.), HER (f.), IT (n.); US, YOU, THEM (THEE, *toi*, ne se dit qu'à Dieu).

Le pronom personnel complément est utilisé dans les comparaisons (*Il est plus grand que moi*, HE IS TALLER THAN ME) et dans les expressions THAT'S ME (*c'est moi*), THAT'S US (*c'est nous*), etc.

Adjectifs possessifs.

MY (*mon, ma, mes*), YOUR, HIS (m.), HER (f.), ITS (n.); OUR, YOUR, THEIR (tutoiement : THY).

A la troisième personne, l'adjectif possessif, comme le pronom, s'accorde avec le possesseur. Ex. : *son chapeau (de Jean)*, HIS HAT; *(de Jeanne)*, HER HAT; *son toit (de la maison*, neutre), ITS ROOF; *ses livres (de Jean)*; HIS BOOKS; *(de Jeanne)*, HER BOOKS.

Pronoms possessifs.

MINE (*le mien, la mienne, les miens, les miennes*), YOURS, HIS, HERS, ITS (OWN); OURS, YOURS, THEIRS (tutoiement : THINE).

On emploie le pronom possessif pour traduire l'expression « à moi, à toi, etc. ». Ex. : *Ce chat est à toi*, THIS CAT IS YOURS.

Pronoms réfléchis.

MYSELF (*moi-même*), YOURSELF, HIMSELF (m.), HERSELF (f.), ITSELF (n.); OURSELVES, YOURSELVES, THEMSELVES. Toutes les fois que le pronom complément exprime la même personne que le sujet, on le traduit par le pronom réfléchi. Ex. : *Il se flatte*, HE FLATTERS HIMSELF; *Parle pour toi*, SPEAK FOR YOURSELF.

Pronoms indéfinis.

● **On** se traduit le plus souvent par le passif. Ex. : *On m'a puni*, I WAS PUNISHED; *On dit que vous êtes riche*, YOU ARE SAID TO BE RICH.

Autres façons de traduire **on** : *On frappe à la porte*, SOMEBODY IS KNOCKING AT THE DOOR; *on pourrait dire*, ONE MIGHT SAY.

Un Français dira à un Anglais : *En France on boit du vin, en Angleterre on boit de la bière, en Chine on boit du thé*, IN FRANCE WE DRINK WINE, IN ENGLAND YOU DRINK BEER, IN CHINA THEY DRINK TEA.

● **En, y** se traduisent de différentes façons selon qu'ils sont pronoms ou adverbes. Ex. : *J'en parlais*, I WAS SPEAKING OF IT; *j'en viens*, I COME FROM THERE; *donnez-m'en*, GIVE ME SOME; *j'en ai assez*, I HAVE ENOUGH (OF IT); *j'y songe*, I THINK OF IT; *vas-y*, GO THERE.

Adjectifs et pronoms démonstratifs.

THIS (pl. THESE) correspond à « ce...-ci » et indique un objet très proche. Ex. : THIS DAY, *ce jour-ci (aujourd'hui)*; THESE BOOKS, *ces livres (-ci)*;

THIS pronom veut dire « ceci ». THAT (pl. THOSE) correspond à « ce...-là », et comme pronom à « cela ». Ex. : THOSE PEOPLE, *ces gens-là;* ON THAT DAY, *ce jour-là.*

● **Celui de, ceux de...** se traduisent par THAT OF, THOSE OF...

● **Celui qui, ce que :** V. *Pronoms relatifs.*

● **Ce** employé avec le verbe *être* se traduit généralement par IT ou THAT. Ex. : *C'est encore l'hiver,* IT IS STILL WINTER; *C'est tout ce que je peux vous dire,* THAT IS ALL I CAN TELL YOU. Dans certains cas, on ne le traduit pas. Ex. : *Essayer c'est réussir,* TO TRY IS TO SUCCEED.

Pronoms relatifs.

● Le pronom relatif THAT est invariable. Ex. : *l'homme (la femme) qui parle,* THE MAN (THE WOMAN) THAT SPEAKS; *le livre (les livres) que je vois,* THE BOOK (THE BOOKS) THAT I SEE.
Le pronom THAT ne peut s'employer que lorsqu'il introduit une subordonnée déterminative, indispensable au sens de la phrase.

● L'autre pronom relatif, WHO, qu'on peut employer dans presque tous les cas, a quatre formes : WHO (sujet m., f., sing. et pl.), WHOM (compl. m., f., sing. et pl.), WHOSE (cas possessif; v. *dont*) et WHICH (neutre sing. et pl.). Ex. : *l'homme (la femme) qui vient* ou *que je vois,* THE MAN (THE WOMAN) WHO COMES or WHOM I SEE; *les livres qui sont là (que je vois),* THE BOOKS WHICH ARE HERE (WHICH I SEE).

● **Ce qui, ce que** se traduisent par WHAT quand « ce » appartient grammaticalement à la proposition principale et « qui » ou « que » à la subordonnée, par WHICH quand tout le groupe « ce que, ce qui » appartient à la subordonnée. Ex. : *Je sais ce que je dis,* I KNOW WHAT I SAY; *Ce qu'il dit est très intéressant,* WHAT HE SAYS IS VERY INTERESTING; *Je sais ma leçon, ce qui vous surprend,* I KNOW MY LESSON, WHICH SURPRISES YOU.

● **Quoi** se traduit comme *ce qui, ce que.*

● **Celui qui, celle qui,** etc., se traduisent pour les personnes par HE (m.) ou SHE (f.), HIM (m. compl.) ou HER (f. compl.), THEY (pl.), THEM (pl. compl.) suivis de WHO (sujet) ou WHOM (compl.); pour les choses, par THE ONE WHICH (pl. THE ONES WHICH). Ex. : *Celui que vous voyez,* HE WHOM YOU SEE; *je vois celle qui parle,* I SEE HER WHO SPEAKS; *prenez celui (le livre,* neutre) *que vous voudrez,* TAKE THE ONE (WHICH) YOU LIKE.

● **Dont** (ainsi que **de qui, duquel, de laquelle, desquels, desquelles**) se traduit par WHOSE toutes les fois qu'il exprime un rapport de possession et que le possesseur est une personne. Dans les autres cas, il faut décomposer *dont* en « de qui » et traduire séparément les deux mots. Ex. : *L'homme dont je lis le livre,* THE MAN WHOSE BOOK I READ; *l'homme dont je parle,* THE MAN OF WHOM I SPEAK.

● **Où** se traduit par WHERE, même quand il est pronom relatif. Ex. : *Le quartier où s'est déclaré l'incendie,* THE DISTRICT WHERE THE FIRE OCCURRED.

L'ADVERBE

L'adverbe anglais se forme en ajoutant **ly** à l'adjectif. Ex. : POOR, *pauvre;* POORLY, *pauvrement.* Les adjectifs terminés par **y** (sauf ceux en *ly*) forment leur adverbe en **ily.** Ex. : HAPPY, *heureux;* HAPPILY, *heureusement.* Les adjectifs terminés en **ly** sont aussi employés comme adverbes.

LE VERBE

Désinences.

● Les verbes anglais n'ont que trois désinences : s pour la troisième personne du singulier de l'indicatif, ed pour le passé simple et le participe passé (toujours invariable), ing pour le participe présent. Ex. : *Je travaille*, I WORK ; *il travaille*, HE WORKS ; *il travailla*, HE WORKED ; *travaillé*, WORKED ; *travaillant*, WORKING.

● **Règle du redoublement de la consonne finale.** Devant une désinence commençant par une voyelle (**ed, ing** des verbes ; **er, est** du comparatif et superlatif ; **er** suffixe correspondant au français « eur, euse » ; **y, ish** suffixes pour adjectifs ; **en** suffixe verbal, etc.), la consonne finale d'un mot d'une syllabe doit être doublée si elle est précédée par une seule voyelle. Ex. : TO STOP, STOPPING, STOPPED, STOPPER ; RED, REDDER, THE REDDEST, TO REDDEN, REDDISH.

La consonne finale d'un mot de deux ou plusieurs syllabes suit la règle précédente si l'accent porte sur la dernière syllabe. Ex. : TO PREFER, PREFERRED ; TO OFFER, OFFERED.

● **Verbes terminés en « y ».** Lorsque *y* est précédé par une **consonne**, ces verbes forment leur troisième personne du singulier de l'indicatif présent en **ies** et leur passé en **ied**. Ex. : TO STUDY *(étudier) : il étudie*, HE STUDIES ; *étudié*, STUDIED.

● **Verbes terminés par une chuintante ou par une sifflante.** Les verbes qui se terminent en **ch, sh,** ou en **s, x, z** forment leur troisième personne du singulier de l'indicatif présent en **es**. Ex. : TO COACH, HE COACHES ; TO PUSH, HE PUSHES ; TO GUESS, HE GUESSES ; TO RELAX, HE RELAXES ; TO WHIZZ, IT WHIZZES.

● **To do, to go.** Ces verbes prennent un e devant l'*s* à la troisième personne du singulier de l'indicatif présent : HE DOES, HE GOES.

● **Verbes terminés par un « e muet ».** Le *e* tombe devant la désinence **ing** du participe. Ex. : TO COME, COMING ; TO LIKE, LIKING. Toutefois, la terminaison **ie** se change en **y** devant **ing**. Ex. : TO DIE, DYING.

Temps.

● **L'imparfait français** se traduit parfois par le passé simple (ou prétérit), mais le plus souvent par la forme **progressive** (v. plus loin) quand il indique la continuation ou par la forme **fréquentative** (v. plus loin) quand il indique l'habitude.

● **Le passé simple** (ou prétérit) se forme en ajoutant **ed** à l'infinitif ; il a la même forme à toutes les personnes : I WORKED, YOU WORKED, etc. Il s'emploie pour traduire le passé simple français dans tous les cas, et le passé composé lorsque celui-ci exprime une action complètement passée dans un temps qui exclut le présent. Ex. : *Ma montre s'arrêta* (ou *s'est arrêtée*) *hier*, MY WATCH STOPPED YESTERDAY.

● **Le passé composé** se forme comme en français avec l'auxiliaire *avoir* et le participe passé, mais il ne s'emploie que pour indiquer une action qui se continue dans le présent ou qui embrasse une période comprenant le présent. Ex. : *J'ai reçu beaucoup de lettres cette année*, I HAVE RECEIVED MANY LETTERS THIS YEAR.

● **Le présent français** suivi de « depuis » ou précédé de « il y a... que » se traduit par un passé composé en anglais. Ex. : *J'habite Londres depuis six mois* (ou *il y a six mois que j'habite Londres*), I HAVE BEEN LIVING IN LONDON FOR SIX MONTHS.

● **Le futur** anglais se forme au moyen de deux auxiliaires (WILL et SHALL) et de l'infinitif. D'ordinaire, on emploie SHALL pour la 1ʳᵉ personne et WILL pour la 2ᵉ et la 3ᵉ. Ex. : *Je viendrai*, I SHALL COME; *tu iras*, YOU WILL GO; *elle vous verra*, SHE WILL SEE YOU.

A la première personne, WILL indiquerait la volonté; aux autres personnes, SHALL indiquerait le commandement, l'obligation, la promesse ou la menace (v. *Verbes défectifs*).

Dans les propositions subordonnées où le français emploie le futur, l'anglais utilise généralement le présent. Ex. : *Nous mangerons dès qu'il sera là*, WE WILL HAVE LUNCH WHEN HE COMES.

Modes et voix.

● **L'impératif** anglais se forme au moyen de l'auxiliaire LET *(laisser)*, du pronom personnel complément et de l'infinitif, sauf à la 2ᵉ personne, où l'on emploie seulement l'infinitif. Ex. : *Qu'il parle*, LET HIM SPEAK; *parlons*, LET US SPEAK; *parle, parlez*, SPEAK.

● **Le conditionnel** se forme au moyen de deux auxiliaires, SHOULD pour la première personne, WOULD pour la 2ᵉ et la 3ᵉ. Ex. : *Il viendrait*, HE WOULD COME; *j'irais*, I SHOULD GO.

● **Le subjonctif** est très rarement employé en anglais. Il ne diffère de l'indicatif qu'au présent et seulement à la 3ᵉ personne du singulier (qui ne prend pas d's). On traduit le subjonctif français tantôt par l'**indicatif** (notamment après « quoique », « avant que » et « jusqu'à ce que »), tantôt par SHOULD et l'**infinitif** (après « de peur que »), ou par MAY (passé MIGHT) et l'**infinitif** (après « afin que »), parfois par l'**infinitif**. Ex. : *Je veux qu'il travaille*, I WANT HIM TO WORK.

● **L'infinitif** anglais est généralement précédé de TO. Principales exceptions : on n'emploie pas TO après les verbes défectifs (sauf I AM, I HAVE et I OUGHT) et après les verbes de perception *(voir, entendre*, etc.).

● **L'infinitif français** se traduit généralement par l'infinitif. On le traduit par le **participe présent** : 1° après toutes les prépositions; 2° après les verbes de commencement, de continuation ou de fin; 3° quand l'infinitif joue le rôle d'un nom. Ex. : *Avant de parler*, BEFORE SPEAKING; *il cessa de chanter*, HE STOPPED SINGING; *nager est très sain*, SWIMMING IS VERY HEALTHY.

● **Le passif** se conjugue comme en français avec le verbe TO BE et le **participe passé**. Alors qu'en français seuls les verbes transitifs directs peuvent se mettre au passif, en anglais cette possibilité existe aussi pour les verbes transitifs indirects, qui sont alors suivis de leur préposition habituelle. Ex. : *On m'attend chez moi*, I AM WAITED FOR AT HOME.

« Avoir » et « être ».

● **Le verbe « avoir »** se traduit en anglais par TO HAVE, qui garde la même forme (HAVE) à toutes les personnes du présent de l'indicatif, sauf à la troisième du singulier (HAS). Le verbe TO HAVE sert d'auxiliaire du passé à tous les verbes, même neutres et réfléchis. Ex. : *Il est venu*, HE HAS COME; *elle s'était flattée*, SHE HAD FLATTERED HERSELF.

● **Le verbe « être ».** — Ind. pr. : I AM, YOU ARE, HE IS, WE ARE, YOU ARE, THEY ARE. — Passé simple : I WAS, YOU WERE, HE WAS, WE WERE, YOU WERE, THEY WERE. — Passé comp. : I HAVE BEEN, HE HAS BEEN... — Pl.-q.-p. : I HAD BEEN... — Fut. : I SHALL BE, YOU WILL BE... — Fut. ant. : I SHALL HAVE BEEN, YOU WILL HAVE BEEN. — Cond. pr. : I SHOULD BE, YOU WOULD BE... — Cond. passé : I SHOULD HAVE BEEN, YOU WOULD HAVE BEEN... — Subj. : I BE, YOU BE, HE BE... — Subj. passé : I WERE, YOU WERE, HE WERE... — Inf. : TO BE. — Part. pr. : BEING. — Part. passé : BEEN.

Verbes défectifs.

Ils sont fréquemment employés comme auxiliaires.

● **Pouvoir** se traduit par le défectif CAN lorsqu'il indique la **capacité personnelle**, par MAY quand il indique la **permission** ou la **possibilité**.

● **Devoir** se traduit par OUGHT TO quand il indique l'**obligation de la conscience**, par MUST quand il indique l'**obligation extérieure** ou la **nécessité**.

● Les verbes défectifs n'ont que deux formes au plus : CAN fait au passé COULD ; MAY donne MIGHT ; WOULD (passé de WILL) et SHOULD (passé de SHALL) forment l'auxiliaire du conditionnel ; OUGHT et MUST n'ont qu'une forme.

Aux temps qui leur manquent, les verbes défectifs sont remplacés : CAN par TO BE ABLE TO, MAY par TO BE PERMITTED, MUST par TO BE OBLIGED TO. On supplée souvent au conditionnel passé en faisant suivre le verbe de l'infinitif passé. Ex. : *Elle aurait pu dire,* SHE MIGHT HAVE SAID (*elle pourrait avoir dit*).

Conjugaison négative.

Un verbe négatif doit toujours contenir un auxiliaire (sauf aux cas 3° et 4°).

1° Pour conjuguer négativement un verbe auxiliaire, on place NOT après ce verbe. Ex. : *Je veux,* I WILL ; *je ne veux pas,* I WILL NOT.

2° Pour conjuguer négativement un verbe non auxiliaire, on fait précéder l'infinitif de DO NOT au présent de l'indicatif (DOES NOT à la 3ᵉ personne du singulier) et de DID NOT au passé simple (tous les autres temps se conjuguent avec des auxiliaires). Ex. : *Il parle,* HE SPEAKS ; *il ne parle pas,* HE DOES NOT SPEAK ; *il s'arrêta,* HE STOPPED ; *il ne s'arrêta pas,* HE DID NOT STOP.

3° A l'infinitif ou au participe, on place NOT devant le verbe. Ex. : *Ne pas dire,* NOT TO TELL ; *ne voyant pas,* NOT SEEING.

4° Quand la phrase contient un mot négatif autre que NOT (c.-à-d. NOBODY, NOTHING, NOWHERE, etc.), le verbe reste affirmatif. Ex. : *Il voit quelqu'un,* HE SEES SOMEBODY ; *il ne voit personne,* HE SEES NOBODY.

5° L'infinitif négatif en français est parfois traduit par l'impératif : *ne pas se pencher au-dehors,* DO NOT LEAN OUT.

Conjugaison interrogative.

Un verbe interrogatif doit toujours contenir un auxiliaire (sauf lorsque le pronom interrogatif est sujet : *Qui va là?,* WHO GOES THERE ?).

1° Pour conjuguer interrogativement un verbe auxiliaire ou un verbe à un temps composé, on place le sujet après l'auxiliaire. Ex. : *Allez-vous bien?,* ARE YOU WELL ?; *Votre père le saura-t-il?,* WILL YOUR FATHER KNOW IT ?; *Avait-il parlé?,* HAD HE SPOKEN?

2° Pour conjuguer interrogativement un verbe non auxiliaire, au présent ou au passé simple, on retiendra la formule *D.S.I.* : *D* représentant DO pour le présent (DOES pour la 3ᵉ personne du singulier) ou DID pour le passé, *S* représentant le sujet, *I* représentant l'infinitif du verbe. Ex. : *Savez-vous?* (*D* : DO, *S* : YOU, *I* : KNOW) DO YOU KNOW ?; *Votre père voit-il cela?* (*D* : does, *S* : your father, *I* : see) DOES YOUR FATHER SEE THIS?

Verbes réfléchis et réciproques.

● Les verbes réfléchis se forment avec le verbe et le pronom réfléchi. Ex. : *Elle se flatte,* SHE FLATTERS HERSELF. — Beaucoup de verbes réfléchis français se traduisent par des verbes neutres en anglais. Ex. : *Il s'arrêta,* HE STOPPED.

● On forme les verbes réciproques avec les pronoms EACH OTHER (ou ONE ANOTHER). Ex. : *Ils se flattent (mutuellement),* THEY FLATTER EACH OTHER.

Forme progressive.

Particulière à l'anglais, cette forme consiste à employer le verbe *être* avec le participe présent (dans le sens de « être en train de »). Ex. : *Fumez-vous?*, ARE YOU SMOKING ? (« Do you smoke » signifie : « fumez-vous d'habitude, êtes-vous fumeur ? ».)

La forme progressive est commode pour traduire l'imparfait (de continuation) [v. *Imparfait*]. On l'emploie aussi dans l'expression « il y a... que ». Ex. : *Il y a six mois que j'apprends l'anglais*, I HAVE BEEN LEARNING ENGLISH FOR SIX MONTHS.

Pour exprimer le futur immédiat, on emploie **to go to** à la forme progressive. Cette expression peut être remplacée par **to be about to**. Ex. : *Il va pleuvoir*, IT IS GOING TO RAIN ; *Je vais partir*, I AM ABOUT TO GO.

Forme fréquentative.

Elle consiste à employer WOULD (ou USED TO) devant l'infinitif pour indiquer l'habitude (v. *Imparfait*). Ex. : *Je fumais un cigare de temps en temps*, I WOULD SMOKE A CIGAR NOW AND THEN (« used to » indiquerait une habitude plus régulière).

VERBES IRRÉGULIERS

NOTA. — Les verbes qui n'ont qu'une forme dans cette liste ont la même forme au présent, au passé simple et au participe passé.

Les verbes qui ont deux formes sont ceux qui ont une forme identique au passé simple et au participe passé.

Les formes entre parenthèses sont d'autres formes également employées aux mêmes temps.

To abide, abode : demeurer.
To arise, arose, arisen : se lever.
To awake, awoke, awoke (awaked) : s'éveiller.
To be, was, been : être.
To bear, bore, borne (born = né) : porter.
To beat, beat, beaten : battre.
To become, became, become : devenir.
To begin, began, begun : commencer.
To behold, beheld : contempler.
To bend, bent : ployer.
To bereave, bereft (bereaved) : priver.
To beseech, besought : supplier.
To bespeak, bespoke, bespoken : commander.
To bid, bade, bid (bidden) : ordonner.
To bind, bound : lier, relier.
To bite, bit, bit (bitten) : mordre.
To bleed, bled : saigner.
To blow, blew, blown : souffler.
To break, broke, broken : briser.
To breed, bred : élever.
To bring, brought : apporter.
To build, built (builded) : bâtir.
To burn, burnt (burned) : brûler.
To burst : éclater.
To buy, bought : acheter.

To cast : jeter.
To catch, caught : attraper.
To chide, chid, chid (chidden) : gronder.
To choose, chose, chosen : choisir.
To cleave, cleft, cleft (cloven) : fendre.
To cling, clung : se cramponner.
To clothe, clad, clad (clothed) : vêtir.
To come, came, come : venir.
To cost : coûter.
To creep, crept, crept : ramper.
To crow, crew (crowed), crowed : chanter (comme le coq).
To cut : couper.
To dare, durst, dared : oser.
To deal, dealt : trafiquer.
To dig, dug : creuser.
To do, did, done : faire.
To draw, drew, drawn : tirer.
To dream, dreamt (dreamed) : rêver.
To drink, drank, drunk : boire.
To drive, drove, driven : conduire.
To dwell, dwelt : demeurer.
To eat, ate, eaten : manger.
To fall, fell, fallen : tomber.
To feed, fed : nourrir.
To feel, felt : sentir, éprouver.
To fight, fought : combattre.

To find, found : trouver.
To flee, fled : fuir.
To fling, flung : lancer.
To fly, flew, flown : voler.
To forbear, forbore, forborne : s'abstenir.
To forbid, forbade, forbidden : défendre.
To forget, forgot, forgotten : oublier.
To forgive, forgave, forgiven : pardonner.
To forsake, forsook, forsaken : abandonner.
To freeze, froze, frozen : geler.
To get, got : obtenir.
To gild, gilt (gilded) : dorer.
To gird, girt (girded) : ceindre.
To give, gave, given : donner.
To go, went, gone : aller.
To grind, ground : moudre.
To grow, grew, grown : croître.
To hang, hung (hanged = pendu par le bourreau) : pendre.
To have, had : avoir.
To hear, heard : entendre.
To heave, hove (heaved) : se soulever.
To hew, hewed, hewn : tailler.
To hide, hid, hid (hidden) : cacher.
To hit : frapper, atteindre.
To hold, held : tenir.
To hurt : blesser.
To keep, kept : garder.
To kneel, knelt (kneeled) : s'agenouiller.
To knit, knit (knitted) : tricoter.
To know, knew, known : savoir.
To lade, laded, laden : charger.
To lay, laid : étendre.
To lead, led : conduire.
To lean, leant (leaned) : se pencher.
To leap, leapt (leaped) : bondir.
To learn, learnt : apprendre.
To leave, left : laisser.
To lend, lent : prêter.
To let, let : laisser.
To lie, lay, lain : être couché.
To light, lit (lighted) : allumer.
To lose, lost : perdre.
To make, made : faire.
To mean, meant : vouloir dire.
To meet, met : rencontrer.
To mistake, mistook, mistaken : se tromper.
To mow, mowed, mown : faucher.
To pay, paid : payer.
To pen, pent : parquer.
To put : mettre.
To read, read [pron. rèd] : lire.
To rend, rent : déchirer.
To rid : débarrasser.
To ride, rode, ridden : chevaucher.
To ring, rang, rung : sonner.
To rise, rose, risen : se lever.
To run, ran, run : courir.
To saw, sawed, sawn : scier.
To say, said : dire.
To see, saw, seen : voir.
To seek, sought : chercher.
To seethe, sod, sodden : bouillir.

To sell, sold : vendre.
To send, sent : envoyer.
To set : placer.
To sew, sewed, sewn (sewed) : coudre.
To shake, shook, shaken : secouer.
To shape, shaped, shaped (shapen) : façonner.
To shave, shaved, shaved (shaven) : raser.
To shear, shore (sheared), shorn : tondre.
To shed : verser.
To shine, shone : briller.
To shoe, shod : chausser.
To shoot, shot : tirer (un projectile).
To show, showed, shown : montrer.
To shred : lacérer.
To shrink, shrank (shrunk), shrunk : se ratatiner.
To shrive, shrove, shriven : confesser.
To shut : fermer.
To sing, sang, sung : chanter.
To sink, sank, sunk : sombrer.
To sit, sat : être assis.
To slay, slew, slain : tuer.
To sleep, slept : dormir.
To slide, slid, slid (slidden) : glisser.
To sling, slung : lancer.
To slink, slunk : se glisser.
To slit : fendre.
To smell, smelt (smelled) : sentir (une odeur).
To smite, smote, smitten : frapper.
To sow, sowed, sown : semer.
To speak, spoke, spoken : parler.
To speed, sped : se hâter.
To spell, spelt (spelled) : épeler.
To spend, spent : dépenser.
To spill, spilt (spilled) : répandre.
To spin, spun (span), spun : filer.
To spit, spit (spat), spit : cracher.
To split : fendre (en éclats).
To spoil, spoilt (spoiled) : gâter.
To spread : étaler.
To spring, sprang, sprung : jaillir.
To stand, stood : se tenir debout.
To steal, stole, stolen : voler.
To stick, stuck : coller.
To sting, stung : piquer.
To stink, stank, stunk : puer.
To strew, strewed, strewn : joncher.
To stride, strode, stridden : enjamber.
To strike, struck : frapper.
To string, strung : enfiler.
To strive, strove, striven : s'efforcer.
To swear, swore, sworn : jurer.
To sweat : suer.
To sweep, swept : balayer.
To swell, swelled, swollen : enfler.
To swim, swam, swum : nager.
To swing, swung : balancer.
To take, took, taken : prendre.
To teach, taught : enseigner.
To tear, tore, torn : déchirer.
To tell, told : dire.
To think, thought : penser.
To thrive, throve, thriven : prospérer.
To throw, threw, thrown : jeter.
To thrust : lancer.

To tread, trod, trodden : fouler aux pieds.
To understand, understood : comprendre.
To undo, undid, undone : défaire.
To upset : renverser.
To wear, wore, worn : porter, user.
To weave, wove, woven : tisser.
To weep, wept : pleurer.
To win, won : gagner.

To wind, wound : enrouler.
To withdraw, withdrew, withdrawn : retirer.
To withstand, withstood : résister à.
To work, wrought (worked) : travailler.
To wring, wrung : tordre.
To write, wrote, written : écrire.
To writhe, writhed, writhen : se tortiller.

MONNAIES, POIDS ET MESURES ANGLAIS, AMÉRICAINS ET CANADIENS

MONNAIES

En Angleterre (calculées avec la livre à 13 francs).

Farthing (1/4 d.) :			Half-crown (2/6) :	
1/4 de penny	0,013 F		2 shillings et 6 pence ..	1,60 F
Half-penny (1/2 d.) :			Crown (5 s.) : 5 shillings..	3,25 F
1/2 penny	0,027 F		Half-sovereign (10 s.) :	
Penny (1 d.) :	0,05 F		10 shillings	6,50 F
Shilling (1 s.) : 12 pence..	0,65 F		Sovereign (£ 1) :	
Florin (2 s.) : 2 shillings..	1,30 F		20 shillings	13,00 F

- A **five-pound** banknote : un billet de banque de cinq livres ; **a one-pound Treasury note** : une coupure d'une livre.
- La guinée (21 shillings) n'est plus en circulation, mais est encore utilisée pour indiquer le prix de certains objets de luxe.
- Dans le système décimal, la livre anglaise doit être divisée en 100 **new pennies**; la nouvelle monnaie comportera des pièces de 1/2, 2, 5, 10 et 50 new pennies, un new penny équivalant à 2,5 old pennies.

Aux États-Unis (calculées avec le dollar à 5,50 francs).
Le **dollar américain** ($) est divisé en 100 **cents** (1 cent = 0,055 F). On utilise aussi les divisions suivantes : **dime** (10 cents = 0,55 F); **quarter dollar** (1/4 de dollar = 1,40 F); **eagle** (10 dollars = 55,00 F).

Au Canada.
Les unités de monnaies sont les mêmes qu'aux Etats-Unis, mais le **dollar canadien** vaut environ 10 p. 100 de moins que le dollar américain.

POIDS

Système *avoirdupoids*.

Grain (gr.)	0,064 g		Hundredweight (cwt) :	
Dram : 27 grains	1,772 g		112 lb.	50,8 kg
Ounce (oz.)	28,35 g		Ton (t.) : 20 cwts ..	1 017 kg
Pound (lb.) : 16 oz. ..	453,592 g		*Am.* 25 pounds	11,34 kg
Stone (st.) : 14 lb.	6,350 kg		*Am.* 100 pounds	45,36 kg
Quarter (Qr.) : 28 lb. .	12,695 kg		*Am.* A short ton ..	907,18 kg

Système *troy* pour les matières précieuses.

			Am. Central, Quintal.	45,36 kg
Grain (gr.)	0,064 g		Ounce troy : 20 dwts.	31,10 g
Pennyweight (dwt) :			Pound troy : 12 oz. ..	373,23 g
24 grains	1,555 g			

MESURES DE LONGUEUR

Inch (in.) : 12 lines	0,0254 m		Chain : 4 poles	20,116 m
Foot (ft.) : 12 inches ...	0,3048 m		Rood *ou* furlong :	
Yard (yd.) : 3 feet	0,9144 m		40 poles	201,16 m
Fathom (fthm.) : 6 ft. ..	1,8288 m		Mile (m.) : 8 furlongs.	1 609,432 m
Pole, rod, perch : 5,5 yds.	5,0292 m		Knot *ou* nautical mile :	
			2 025 yards	1 853 m

MESURES DE SUPERFICIE

Square inch : 6,451 cm²; square foot : 929 cm²; square yard : 0,8361 m²; rood : 10,11 ares; acre : 40,46 ares.

MESURES DE VOLUME

Cubic inch : 16,387 cm³; cubic foot : 28,315 dm³; cubic yard : 764 dm³.

MESURES DE CAPACITÉ

En Angleterre et au Canada.
Pint : 0,567 litre; quart (2 pints) : 1,135 l; gallon (4 quarts) : 4,543 l; bushel (8 gallons) : 36,347 l; quarter (8 bushels) : 290,780 l.

Aux États-Unis.
Dry pint : 0,551 litre; dry quart : 1,11 l; dry gallon : 4,41 l; peck : 8,81 l; bushel : 35,24 l; liquid gill : 0,118 l; liquid pint : 0,473 l; liquid quart : 0,946 l; liquid gallon : 3,785 l; barrel : 119 l; barrel petroleum : 158,97 l.

LES SONS DE LA LANGUE ANGLAISE
EXPLIQUÉS AUX FRANÇAIS

SIGNE	MOT TYPE ANGLAIS	SON FRANÇAIS VOISIN	EXPLICATION
i	sick	sic	Son anglais entre *sic* et *sec*.
ì	bin	(bo)bine	Le son anglais est plus bref.
î	eel	île	Le son anglais est plus long.
è	beck	bec	Son anglais entre *è* et *é*.
e	a(gain)	re(gain)	C'est notre *e* muet.
ĕ	burr	bœufs	Son entre *bœufs* et *beurre*.
œ	puff	paf	Son entre *paf* et *peuf*.
a	bag	bague	Son entre *bague* et *bègue*.
à	can	canne	Le son anglais est plus bref.
â	palm	pâme	
o	boss	bosse	Son entre *bosse* et *basse*.
au	law	lau(re)	Comme le précédent, mais plus long.
ou	pool	poule	Très long, sauf dans *good*, *book*, etc.
éⁱ	pay	pays	*i* final à peine prononcé.
aⁱ	tie	taille	
aᵒᵘ	cow	caou(tchouc)	*ou* final à peine prononcé.
oᵒᵘ	low	lôhou	Le son *ou* final à peine perceptible, sauf en Angleterre.
èᵉʳ	air	air	Remplacer le son *r* par un *e* muet.
iᵉʳ	dear	dire	Remplacer le son *r* final par un *e* muet. Cet *r* se prononce quand il est lié à une voyelle suivante.
t, d	Placer la langue plus en arrière que pour le son français, et serrer un peu les dents.		
l	Bloquer les bords de la langue et en creuser le centre.		
r	Placer la langue comme pour rouler un *r* et ébaucher le roulement.		
w	C'est le son *ou* très bref que l'on prononce dans *bois*.		
y	Toujours comme dans *yeux* et dans *yes*.		
g, g	Toujours dur (get = guette).		
h	Aspiration, comme dans *hem!*		
th, zh	Le th est tantôt un *s* blésé (avec la langue entre les dents), tantôt un *z* blésé. On prononcera thick comme *sic* avec un *s* blésé et on prononcera breathe (brîzh) comme *brise* avec un *z* blésé.		
ng	C'est le son *ou* très bref que l'on prononce dans *bois*. à *gn* français dans *signe*, mais la base de la langue reste bloquée, ce qui accentue le son nasal.		
ʳ final	Rarement prononcé par les Anglais (sauf quand il se lie à la voyelle initiale du mot suivant), il est plus nettement prononcé par les Irlandais, les Écossais et les Américains, qui le roulent avec plus ou moins de force.		
s	Ne se prononce jamais *z*.		

Accent. — Prononcer plus fortement la voyelle ou diphtongue en italique. Les monosyllabes sont toujours accentués.

Remarques importantes. — Les sons français u, an, on, in, un, eux n'existent pas en anglais. *La prononciation indiquée dans le dictionnaire est toujours la prononciation américaine.*

ANGLAIS - FRANÇAIS

A

a [e, éı] *indef. art.* un, une; *what a ...l,* quel!, quelle!; *such a,* tel, telle.

abandon [eband^en] *v.* abandonner, laisser; *s.* abandon, m.; désinvolture, f. ‖ **abandoned** [-d] *adj.* abandonné, laissé; immoral, déréglé, perdu. ‖ **abandonment** [-m^ent] *s.* abandon, délaissement; désistement, m.

abase [ebéıs] *v.* abaisser; humilier.

abashed [ebasht] *adj.* confus.

abate [ebéıt] *v.* abattre, réduire; faiblir, se calmer. ‖ **abatement** [-m^ent] *s.* diminution; décrue, f.; rabais, m.

abbey [abi] *s.* abbaye, f.

abbot [ab^et] *s.* abbé, m.

abbreviate [ebrîvié^ıt] *v.* abréger; réduire (math.). ‖ **abbreviation** [ebriviésh^en] *s.* abréviation; réduction, f.

abdicate [abdiké^ıt] *v.* abdiquer. ‖ **abdication** [-e^ısh^en] *s.* abdication, f.

abdomen [abd^em^en] *s.* abdomen, m. ‖ **abdominal** [-omn'l] *adj.* abdominal.

abduct [abdœkt] *v.* enlever [rapt]. ‖

abed [ebèd] *adj.* au lit.

aberration [aberé^ısh^en] *s.* aberration, f.; égarement, m.; déviation, divergence, anomalie, f.

abet [ebèt] *v.* inciter.

abhor [ebhau^r] *v.* abhorrer, détester. ‖ **abhorrence** [-r^ens] *s.* horreur, aversion, f.

abide [eba^ıd] *v.* attendre; endurer; séjourner, rester; persister; *to abide by,* se conformer, rester fidèle à; *to abide with,* habiter chez.

ability [ebíl^eti] *s.** capacité, habileté, capacité légale, f.; *pl.* ressources, f.

abject [abdjèkt] *adj.* abject. ‖ **abjectness** [abdjèktnis] *s.* abjection, f.

abjure [abdjou^er] *v.* abjurer.

able [é^ıb'l] *adj.* capable; compétent; **able-bodied,** bon pour le service; *to be able to,* pouvoir, être capable de; **ably,** habilement.

abnegation [abni'gé^ısh^en] *s.* reniement, désaveu; renoncement, m.; *self-abnegation,* abnégation, f.

abnormal [abnaurm'l] *adj.* anormal. ‖ **abnormality** [abnaurmaliti] *s.** anomalie; difformité, f.

aboard [ebaurd] *adv.* à bord; *to go aboard,* embarquer.

abode [ebo^oud] *s.* séjour, domicile, m.; *pret., p. p. of* **to abide.**

abolish [ebálish] *v.* abolir, annuler. ‖ **abolition** [ebelish^en] *s.* abolition, abrogation, f.

abominable [ebâmn^eb'l] *adj.* abominable, horrible. ‖ **abominate** [ebâminé^ıt] *v.* détester. ‖ **abomination** [-e^ısh^en] *s.* abomination, f.

abort [ebau^rt] *v.* avorter. ‖ **abortion** [ebau^rsh^en] *s.* avortement; avorton, m.

abound [eba^ound] *v.* abonder (with, en); regorger (with, de).

about [eba^out] *adv.* autour; à peu près, presque; sur le point de; çà et là; plus ou moins; *prep.* autour de; environ; vers; au sujet de; à, pour; *about eleven,* vers onze heures; *put about,* ennuyé; *to be about,* s'agir de; *to be about to,* être sur le point de.

above [ebœv] *prep.* au-dessus de; (en) plus de, outre; *adv.* en haut, au-dessus, en outre, ci-dessus; *above all,* surtout; **above-mentioned,** susdit; *over and above,* en sus de, en outre.

abreast [ebrèst] *adv.* de front.

abridge [ebridj] *v.* abréger.

abroad [ebraud] *adv.* au loin; (au-)dehors; à l'étranger.

abrogate [abr^egé^ıt] *v.* abroger.

abrupt [ebrœpt] *adj.* abrupt; brusque; heurté [style]. ‖ **abruptly** [-li] *adv.* brusquement.

abscess [absès] *s.** abcès, m.

abscond [ebsko'nd] *v.* déguerpir.

absence [abs^ens] *s.* absence, f.; *absence of mind,* distraction; *leave of absence,* permission, congé. ‖ **absent** [abs^ent] *adj.* absent; distrait; **absent-minded,** distrait; [absènt] *v. to absent oneself,* s'absenter. ‖ **absentee** [abs^entî] *s.* absentéiste, manquant, m.

absolute [abs^elout] *adj.* absolu; complet; formel; certain. ‖ **absolutely** [-li] *adv.* absolument.

absolution [abs^elousheⁿn] *s.* absolution; rémission, f.; acquittement, m.

absolve [absálv] *v.* absoudre; acquitter; délier [obligation].

absorb [ebsau^rb] *v.* absorber. ‖ **absorbent** [-^ent] *adj.* absorbant. ‖ **absorber** [-^er] *s.* amortisseur, m.

absorption [ebsaurpsh^en] *s.* absorption, f.; amortissement, m.; concentration, f.

abstain [ebsté^ın] *v.* s'abstenir. ‖ **abstemious** [-tîmy^es] *adj.* abstème. ‖ **abstinence** [abstin^ens] *s.* abstinence, f.

abstract [abstrakt] *s.* abrégé; extrait, m.; [abstrakt] *adj.* abstrait; *v.* abstraire; soustraire; extraire; résumer. ‖ **abstraction** [abstraksh⁰n] *s.* abstraction; distraction, f.; détournement, m.

absurd [°bsë͞rd] *adj.* absurde. ‖ **absurdity** [-°ti] *s.*° absurdité, f.

abundance [°bænd⁰ns] *s.* abondance, f. ‖ **abundant** [°bænd⁰nt] *adj.* abondant, copieux; opulent.

abuse [°byous] *s.* abus, m.; insulte, f.; [°byouz] *v.* abuser de; médire de; insulter; léser, nuire à. ‖ **abusive** [-siv] *adj.* abusif; insultant, injurieux.

abyss [°bís] *s.*° abîme, m.

acacia [°ké¹sh°] *s.* acacia, m.; *Am.* gomme arabique, f.

academic [akedèmik] *adj.* académique; *Am.* classique. ‖ **academy** [°kad°mi] *s.*° académie; école, f.

accede [aksíd] *v.* accéder, parvenir; atteindre; consentir à.

accelerate [aksèl°ré¹t] *v.* accélérer. ‖ **acceleration** [aksèl°ré¹sh°n] *s.* accélération, f. ‖ **accelerator** [aksèl°ré¹t°r] *s.* accélérateur, m.

accent [aksènt] *s.* accent, m.; [aksènt] *v.* accentuer. ‖ **accentuate** [aksèntyoué¹t] *v.* accentuer. ‖ **accentuation** [aksèntyoué¹sh°n] *s.* accentuation, f.

accept [°ksèpt] *v.* accepter; admettre. ‖ **acceptable** [-°b'l] *adj.* acceptable, agréable. ‖ **acceptance** [-°ns] *s.* acceptation; popularité; lettre de change acceptée, f. ‖ **acceptation** [°ksèpté¹-sh°n] *s.* acception, f.

access [aksès] *s.*° accès, m.; admission; crise, f. ‖ **accessible** [aksès°b'l] *adj.* accessible. ‖ **accessory** [aksès°ri] *adj.* accessoire, secondaire; *s.*° complice m.; *pl.* accessoires, m. pl.

accident [aks°d°nt] *s.* accident, hasard, contretemps, m. ‖ **accidental** [aks°dènt'l] *adj.* accidentel, fortuit; accessoire; occasionnel.

acclaim [°klé¹m] *v.* acclamer. ‖ **acclamation** [akl°mé¹sh°n] *s.* acclamation, f.

acclimate [°kla¹mit] *v.* (s') acclimater. ‖ **acclimation** [akl°mé¹sh°n] *s.* acclimatation, f.

acclivity [°klíviti] *s.*° montée, côte, rampe, f.

accommodate [°kâm°dé¹t] *v.* accommoder; adapter; concilier; loger; rendre service; *to accommodate oneself,* s'adapter. ‖ **accommodation** [°kâm°dé¹sh°n] *s.* accommodement; logement; emménagement, m.; adaptation; conciliation; installation, f.; *accommodation-train, Am.* train omnibus. ‖ **accommodation unit,** bloc de logements, m.

accompaniment [°kæmp°nim°nt] *s.* accompagnement; accessoire, m. ‖ **accompanist** [-ist] *s.* accompagnateur, m. ‖ **accompany** [-i] *v.* accompagner, escorter; faire suivre.

accomplice [°kâmplis] *s.* complice, m.

accomplish [°kâmplish] *v.* accomplir; réaliser. ‖ **accomplished** [-t] *adj.* accompli, effectué; parfait, consommé. ‖ **accomplishment** [-m°nt] *s.* accomplissement, m.; *pl.* arts d'agrément, m.

accord [°kau͞rd] *s.* accord; consentement, m.; convenance, f.; *of one's own accord,* spontanément; *v.* s'accorder, s'entendre; concéder; arranger, régler. ‖ **accordance** [-°ns] *s.* accord, m.; concession; conformité, f. ‖ **according as** [-ingaz] *conj.* suivant que, selon que. ‖ **according to** [-ingtou] *prep.* d'accord avec, conformément à, selon. ‖ **accordingly** [-ingli] *adv.* en conséquence, conformément.

accordion [°kau͞rdy°n] *s.* accordéon, m.

accost [°kaust] *v.* accoster.

account [°kaºunt] *s.* compte; rapport; relevé, m.; estime; importance; cause, f.; *on account of,* à cause de; *of no account,* sans importance; *current account,* compte courant; *on account,* en acompte; *v.* estimer; *to account for,* expliquer. ‖ **accountable** [-°b'l] *adj.* responsable; explicable. ‖ **accountant** [-°nt] *s.* comptable, m.; *chartered accountant,* expert-comptable. ‖ **accounting** [-ing] *s.* comptabilité, f.

accoutre [°kout°r] *v.* accoutrer; équiper.

accredit [°krèdit] *v.* accréditer; mettre sur le compte de.

accrue [°krou] *v.* croître; résulter.

accumulate [°kyoumy°lé¹t] *v.* accumuler; s'entasser. ‖ **accumulation** [°kyoumy°lé¹sh°n] *s.* accumulation, f.; montant [sum], m. ‖ **accumulator** [°kyoumy°lé¹t°r] *s.* accu(mulateur), m.

accuracy [aky°r°si] *s.* exactitude, précision, f. ‖ **accurate** [aky°rit] *adj.* précis, exact, correct.

accursed [°kër͞st] *adj.* maudit.

accusation [aky°zé¹sh°n] *s.* accusation, f. ‖ **accusative** [°kyouz°tiv] *adj., s.* accusatif, m. ‖ **accusatory** [-târi] *adj.* accusateur. ‖ **accuse** [°kyouz] *v.* accuser. ‖ **accuser** [-°r] *s.* accusateur, dénonciateur, m.

accustom [°kæst°m] *v.* habituer, accoutumer; *to get accustomed to,* s'accoutumer à. ‖ **accustomed** [-d] *p. p., adj.* accoutumé; habituel, coutumier.

ace [é¹s] *s.* as; homme supérieur, m.

ache [é¹k] *s.* douleur, f.; *v.* souffrir; faire mal; *headache,* mal de tête; *toothache,* mal de dents.

achieve [etshív] *v.* achever; acquérir; obtenir; accomplir, réaliser; remporter [victory]. || *achievable* [-eb'l] *adj.* faisable. || *achievement* [-mᵉnt] *s.* achèvement; succès, exploit, m.; réalisation; prouesse, réussite, f.

aching [é¹king] *s.* adj. douloureux.

acid [asid] *adj., s.* acide. || *acidify* [eˢsídᵉfa¹] *v.* acidifier; || *acidity* [eˢsídᵉti] *s.* acidité, f. || *acidulate* [eˢsídyᵉlé¹t] *v.* aciduler, aigrir.

acknowledge [eknálidj] *v.* reconnaître, admettre, avouer. || *acknowledgment* [-mᵉnt] *s.* reconnaissance; réponse, f.; remerciement; accusé de réception, m.

acorn [é¹kᵉrn] *s.* gland, m. || *acorncup,* cupule, f.

acoustics [ekoustiks] *s.* acoustique, f.

acquaint [ekwé¹nt] *v.* informer, renseigner; *to acquaint oneself with,* se mettre au courant de; *to get acquainted with,* faire la connaissance de. || *acquaintance* [-ᵉns] *s.* connaissance, f.; *pl.* relations, f. pl.

acquest [ekwèst] *s.* acquisition, f.; acquêt, m.

acquiesce [akwiès] *v.* acquiescer, accéder à. || *acquiescence* [-ᵉns] *s.* acquiescement, m. || *acquiescent* [-ᵉnt] *adj.* accommodant; consentant.

acquire [ekwa¹ᵉr] *v.* acquérir, obtenir; apprendre; *acquirement* [-mᵉnt] *s.* acquisition, f.; connaissances, f. pl. || *acquisition* [akwᵉzishᵉn] *s.* acquisition, f.

acquit [ekwít] *v.* acquitter; exonérer; *to acquit oneself of,* s'acquitter de, se libérer de. || *acquittal* [-'l] *s.* acquittement, m.

acre [é¹kᵉr] *s.* acre, f.; arpent, m.

acrimonious [akrᵉmaunyᵉs] *adj.* acrimonieux. || *acrimony* [akrᵉmoᵒuni] *s.* acrimonie, f.

acrobat [akrᵉbat] *s.* acrobate, m. || *acrobatics* [akrᵉbatiks] *s.* acrobatie, f.

across [ekraus] *prep.* en travers de; à travers; sur, par-dessus; *adv.* en croix; d'un côté à l'autre.

act [akt] *s.* acte, m.; action, f.; *Br.* thèse (univ.), loi (jur.), f.; acte [theater], m.; *v.* agir; exécuter; commettre; faire représenter [play]; jouer [part]; feindre; *to act as,* faire fonction de. || *acting* [-ing] *s.* représentation; action, f.; *adj.* suppléant, intérimaire. || *action* [akshᵉn] *s.* action, f.; geste, m.; fonctionnement [gun]; combat, m.; *pl.* conduite, entreprise, f. || *active* [aktiv] *adj.* actif, alerte. || *activity* [aktivᵉti] *s.* activité, f. || *actor* [aktᵉr] *s.* acteur, m.

actress [aktris] *s.* actrice, f. || *actual* [aktshoue¹] *adj.* réel, véritable. || *actuality* [aktyoualiti] *s.* réalité; existence effective, f. || *actually* [-i] *adv.* réellement, effectivement.

acumen [ekyoumin] *s.* perspicacité, finesse, f.

acute [ekyout] *adj.* aigu, pénétrant. || *acuteness* [-nis] *s.* acuité, perspicacité; finesse, f.; profondeur, f.

adamant [adᵉmant] *adj.* infrangible; inflexible; *s.* diamant, m.

adapt [edapt] *v.* adapter. || *adaptability* [edaptᵉbiliti] *s.* adaptabilité, souplesse, faculté d'adaptation, f. || *adaptation* [adapté¹shᵉn] *s.* adaptation, f.

add [ad] *v.* ajouter, additionner.

adder [adᵉr] *s.* vipère, f.

addict [adikt] *s.* toxicomane; fanatique, m. (sport); [edíkt] *v.* s'adonner à.

addition [edishᵉn] *s.* addition; somme, f.; *in addition to,* en plus de. || *additional* [-'l] *adj.* additionnel, supplémentaire.

addle [adl] *adj.* pourri; croupissant; brouillé, confus; *addle-brained,* écervelé, brouillon.

address [edrès] *s.* adresse, f.; discours, m.; *v.* adresser, interpeller; s'adresser à. || *addressee* [edrèsî] *s.* destinataire, m. || *addresser* [edrès'e] *s.* expéditeur.

adduce [edyous] *v.* fournir, alléguer. || *adduction* [edækshᵉn] *s.* adduction; allégation, f.

adept [edᵉpt] *adj.* expert, initié; [adèpt] *s.* expert; adepte, m.

adequate [adᵉkwit] *adj.* adéquat; proportionné; suffisant.

adhere [edhiᵉr] *v.* adhérer; maintenir [decision]; tenir [promise]. || *adherence* [-rᵉns] *s.* adhérence, f. || *adherent* [-rᵉnt] *adj., s.* adhérent. || *adhesion* [edhijᵉn] *s.* adhésion, f. || *adhesive* [edhisiv] *adj.* adhésif, collant, gommé; *adhesive tape,* sparadrap, taffetas gommé, m.

adjacent [edjé¹sᵉnt] *adj.* adjacent.

adjective [adjiktiv] *s.* adjectif, m.

adjoin [edjo¹n] *v.* toucher à, avoisiner, attenir à. || *adjoining* [-ing] *adj.* contigu, voisin, adjacent.

adjourn [edjë¹rn] *v.* ajourner; différer; proroger; s'ajourner [meeting]; lever [session]. || *adjournment* [-mᵉnt] *s.* ajournement, m.

adjudge [edjædj] *v.* juger; adjuger. || *adjudication* [edjoudiké¹shᵉn] *s.* décision du tribunal, prononcé de jugement, m.

adjunct [adjængkt] *adj., s.* adjoint.

adjure [edjouᵉr] *v.* adjurer.

adjust [ᵉdʒæst] v. ajuster, régler; *to adjust oneself*, se conformer, s'adapter. || **adjustment** [-mᵉnt] s. ajustage, réglage, m.; adaptation, f.; accord harmonieux, m.

administer [ᵉdminᵉstᵉr] v. administrer; gérer; *to administer an oath*, faire prêter serment. || **administration** [ᵉdminᵉstréⁱshᵉn] s. administration; gestion; curatelle, f. || **administrative** [ᵉdminᵉstréⁱtiv] adj. administratif. || **administrator** [ᵉdminᵉstréⁱtᵉr] s. administrateur; curateur (jur.), m.

admirable [admᵉrᵉb'l] adj. admirable. || **admirably** [-i] adv. admirablement.

admiral [admᵉrᵉl] s. amiral; vaisseau amiral, m. || **admiralty** [-ti] s. amirauté, f.; ministère de la Marine, m.

admiration [admᵉréⁱshᵉn] s. admiration, f. || **admire** [ᵉdmaⁱᵉr] v. admirer; estimer; *Am.* éprouver du plaisir à. || **admirer** [ᵉdmaⁱᵉrᵉr] s. admirateur; soupirant, m. || **admiring** [-ring] adj. admiratif.

admissibility [ᵉdmisibíliti] s. admissibilité, recevabilité, f. || **admissible** [-b'l] adj. admissible, acceptable, recevable. || **admission** [ᵉdmíshᵉn] s. admission; concession, f.; aveu (jur.); accès; prix d'entrée, m. || **admit** [ᵉdmít] v. admettre, accepter; convenir de; avouer; permettre, rendre possible; donner entrée. || **admittance** [-ᵉns] s. admission; entrée, f.; accès, m.; droit (m.) d'entrée.

admonish [ᵉdmónish] v. avertir; admonester; diriger, guider; informer. || **admonition** [admᵉníshᵉn] s. admonestation, f.; conseil, m.

ado [ᵉdou] s. agitation, activité; affaire, f.; bruit, m.

adolescence [ad'lèsᵉns] s. adolescence, f. || **adolescent** [-t] adj., s. adolescent.

adopt [ᵉdápt] v. adopter; se rallier à. || **adoptee** [ᵉdáptí] s. adopté, m. f. || **adoption** [ᵉdápshᵉn] s. adoption, f. || **adoptive** [ᵉdáptiv] adj. adoptif.

adoration [adᵉréⁱshᵉn] s. adoration, f. || **adore** [ᵉdauᵉr] v. adorer. || **adorer** [-rᵉr] s. adorateur; soupirant, m.

adorn [ᵉdauʳn] v. orner, parer. || **adornment** [-mᵉnt] s. ornement, m.

adrift [ᵉdríft] adv. à la dérive; à l'aventure; *Am. to be adrift*, divaguer.

adroit [ᵉdroⁱt] adj. adroit.

adulate [adyouléⁱt] v. aduler, flagorner.

adult [ᵉdœlt] adj., s. adulte.

adulterate [ᵉdœltᵉréⁱt] v. adultérer, falsifier; frelater; adj. frelaté; adultérin, adultère. || **adulterer** [ᵉdœltᵉrᵉr] s. amant, adultère, m. || **adultery** [ᵉdœltᵉri] s. adultère, m. || **adulteration** [ᵉdœltᵉréⁱshᵉn] s. falsification, f.; produit falsifié, m.

advance [ᵉdvǎns] v. avancer; hausser [price]; accélérer; anticiper; s. avance; augmentation; promotion, f.; progrès; paiement anticipé; avancement, m.; pl. avances, démarches, f.; *advance corps, Am.* avant-garde. || **advanced** [-t] adj. avancé; en saillie; âgé; avancé, d'avant-garde [opinion]; plus élevé [price]. || **advancement** [-mᵉnt] s. avancement; progrès, m.; promotion; donation (jur.), f.

advantage [ᵉdvǎntidʒ] s. avantage, bénéfice, m.; utilité; supériorité, f.; *to derive (to reap) advantage from*, tirer avantage de. || **advantageous** [advᵉntéⁱdʒᵉs] adj. avantageux; profitable; seyant.

advent [advènt] s. venue, arrivée, f.; *Advent*, Avent, m.

adventure [ᵉdvèntshᵉr] s. aventure; spéculation hasardeuse, f. || **adventurer** [ᵉdvèntshᵉrᵉr] s. aventurier; chevalier d'industrie, m. || **adventurous** [ᵉdvèntshᵉrᵉs] adj. aventureux, entreprenant; *Am.* risqué.

adverb [advᵉrb] s. adverbe, m.

adversary [advᵉrsèri] s.* adversaire, m. || **adverse** [advᵉʳs] adj. adverse; hostile; **adversity** [-ᵉti] s.* adversité; infortune, f.

advert [advᵉʳt] v. faire attention; faire allusion à; parler de. || **advertence** [advᵉʳtᵉns] s. attention, f. || **advertise** [advᵉʳtaⁱz] v. avertir, aviser, informer; faire de la réclame; demander par voie d'annonce. || **advertisement** [advᵉʳtaⁱzmᵉnt] s. avertissement, m.; préface; annonce, réclame, f. || **advertiser** [advᵉʳtaⁱzᵉr] s. annonceur; journal d'annonces, m. || **advertising** [advᵉʳtaⁱzing] s. réclame, f.; *advertising agency*, agence de publicité.

advice [ᵉdvaⁱs] s. avis, conseil, m.; *to seek legal advice*, consulter un avocat; *as per advice*, suivant avis (comm.). || **advisable** [ᵉdvaⁱzᵉb'l] adj. judicieux, prudent; opportun, indiqué, à propos. || **advise** [ᵉdvaiz] v. conseiller; informer, aviser; *to advise with*, prendre conseil de, consulter; *to advise against*, déconseiller. || **advised** [-d] adj. avisé; délibéré, en connaissance de cause. || **adviser, advisor** [-ᵉr] s. conseiller, conseilleur, m.

advocacy [advᵉkᵉsi] s.* plaidoyer, m.; défense, f. || **advocate** [advᵉkit] s. avocat, défenseur, m.; [advᵉkéⁱt] v. plaider pour.

aerate [éⁱᵉréⁱt] v. aérer; *aerated water*, eau gazeuse. || **aeration** [éⁱᵉréⁱshᵉn] s. aération, f. || **aerial** [éⁱriᵉl] adj. aérien; s. antenne, f. || **aerialist** [-ìst] s. *Am.* trapéziste, m., f.

aerodrome [éᵉdroᵒᵘm], *see airport.*

aeronautics [èᵉro'nautiks] *s.* aéronautique, f. ‖ **aeroplane** [éᵉplé¹n], *see airplane.* ‖ **aeropulse** [èᵉraupœls] *s.* avion (m.) à réaction.

aesthetic [èsthètic], *see esthetic.*

afar [ᵉfâr] *adv.* loin, au loin.

affability [afᵉbíᵏleti] *s.* affabilité, f. ‖ **affable** [afᵉb'l] *adj.* affable.

affair [ᵉfèᵉr] *s.* affaire, f.; négoce, m.; chose, f.; événement, m.; fonction; *pl.* affaires, f.

affect [ᵉfèkt] *v.* affecter; émouvoir; afficher; feindre; influer sur. ‖ **affectation** [afikté¹shᵉn] *s.* affectation, ostentation, f. ‖ **affected** [ᵉfèktid] *adj.* affecté; ému; artificiel; feint; *well affected to*, bien disposé envers; *affected by*, influencé par; atteint de. ‖ **affecting** [-ing] *adj.* émouvant, touchant. ‖ **affection** [ᵉfèkshᵉn] *s.* affection, inclination; maladie, f. ‖ **affectionate** [ᵉfèkshᵉnit] *adj.* affectueux.

affidavit [afᵉdé¹vit] *s.* affidavit, m.; déclaration sous serment, f.

affiliate [ᵉfílié¹t] *v.* affilier; s'associer; adopter [child]; [ᵉfílit] *s.* compagnie associée, f.

affinity [ᵉfíneti] *s.* affinité, f.

affirm [ᵉfëᵉm] *v.* affirmer; soutenir; déclarer solennellement.

affirmative [ᵉfëᵉmetiv] *adj.* affirmatif; *s.* affirmative, f.

affix [ᵉfíks] *v.* apposer [signature]; fixer; afficher; [afiks] *s.* affixe, m.

afflict [ᵉflíkt] *v.* affliger; tourmenter. ‖ **affliction** [ᵉflíkshᵉn] *s.* affliction, f.; chagrin, m.; *pl.* infirmités, f. pl.

affluence [aflouᵉns] *s.* opulence; affluence, f. ‖ **affluent** [aflouᵉnt] *adj.* opulent, abondant; cossu; *s.* affluent, m. ‖ **afflux** [aflœks] *s.* afflux, m.; affluence, f.

afford [ᵉfoᵒᵘrd] *v.* donner, fournir; avoir les moyens de.

affray [ᵉfrè¹] *s.* échauffourée, rixe, f.

affront [ᵉfrœnt] *s.* affront, m.; *v.* faire face à; affronter; insulter.

afield [ᵉfíld] *adv.* en campagne; *far afield*, très loin.

afire [ᵉfa¹ᵉr] *adj.* en feu; ardent.

afloat [ᵉfloᵒᵘt] *adj.*, *adv.* à flot, sur l'eau; en circulation [rumor].

afoot [ᵉfout] *adv.* à pied; sur pied; en cours; en route.

aforesaid [ᵉfoᵒᵘrsèd] *adj.* susdit; ci-dessus mentionné; en question. ‖ **aforethought** [-thaut] *adj.* prémédité.

afoul [ᵉfaᵒᵘl] *adj.* en collision; *to run afoul of*, emboutir.

afraid [ᵉfré¹d] *adj.* effrayé; hésitant; *to be afraid*, craindre, avoir peur (*of*, de).

afresh [ᵉfrèsh] *adv.* de nouveau.

after [aftᵉr] *prep.* après; d'après; *adv.* après, plus tard; *conj.* après que, quand; *adj.* ultérieur, postérieur; de l'arrière (naut.); *after my own liking*, d'après mon goût; **aftermath**, regain [crop]; répercussions, séquelles; **afterpiece**, baisser de rideau; **aftertaste**, arrière-goût; **afterthought**, réflexion après coup, explication ultérieure.

afternoon [aftᵉnoun] *s.* après-midi, m., f.

afterwards [aftᵉrwᵉrdz] *adv.* après, ensuite.

again [ᵉgèn] *adv.* de nouveau, aussi; *never again*, jamais plus; *now and again*, de temps à autre.

against [ᵉgènst] *prep.* contre; en vue de; *against the grain*, à contre-poil; *against a bad harvest*, en prévision d'une mauvaise récolte; *over against*, en face de.

age [é¹dj] *s.* âge, m.; époque; maturité; génération, f.; *of age*, majeur; *under age*, mineur; *v.* vieillir; *the Middle Ages*, le Moyen Age. ‖ **aged** [-id] *adj.* âgé; vieux; âgé de; vieilli [wine]; *middle-aged*, entre deux âges.

agency [é¹djᵉnsi] *s.* agence; action, activité; intervention, f. ‖ **agent** [é¹djᵉnt] *s.* agent; représentant; mandataire; moyen, m.

agenda [ᵉdjèndᵉ] *s.* ordre du jour; mémorandum; programme; agenda, m.

aggrandize [agrᵉnda¹z] *v.* agrandir, accroître, exagérer.

aggravate [agrᵉvé¹t] *v.* aggraver; exaspérer. ‖ **aggravation** [agrᵉvé¹shᵉn] *s.* aggravation; irritation, f.

aggregate [agrigit] *s.* total; agrégat, m.; [agrigé¹t] *v.* réunir, rassembler; s'agréger. ‖ **aggregation** [agrigé¹shᵉn] *s.* agrégation; affiliation, foule, f.; assemblage, m.

aggression [ᵉgrèshᵉn] *s.* agression, f. ‖ **aggressive** [ᵉgrèsiv] *adj.* agressif. ‖ **aggressor** [ᵉgrèsᵉr] *s.* agresseur, m.

aggrieve [ᵉgrîv] *v.* chagriner; léser.

aghast [ᵉgast] *adj.* épouvanté.

agile [adjᵉl] *adj.* agile. ‖ **agility** [ᵉdjíleti] *s.* agilité, f.

agitate [adjᵉté¹t] *v.* agiter, troubler; faire campagne pour; machiner; débattre [question]. ‖ **agitation** [adjᵉté¹shᵉn] *s.* agitation; discussion; campagne, f. ‖ **agitator** [adjᵉté¹tᵉr] *s.* agitateur, m.

aglow [ᵉgloᵒᵘ] *adj.* embrasé.

agnate [agné¹t] *adj.* consanguin; apparenté; *s.* agnat, m.

ago [ᵉgoᵒᵘ] *adj.*, *adv.* passé, écoulé; *many years ago*, il y a de nombreuses années; *how long ago?*, combien de temps y a-t-il?

agonize [agᵉna¹z] *v.* torturer; être au supplice; souffrir cruellement. ‖ **agony** [agᵉni] *s.** angoisse, f.; paroxysme, m.; agonie, f. (med.).

agree [ᵉgrî] *v.* s'entendre; être d'accord; consentir; convenir à; concorder; s'accorder (gramm.); **agreed**, d'accord. ‖ **agreeable** [-ᵉb'l] *adj.* agréable, conforme; consentant; concordant. ‖ **agreement** [-mᵉnt] *s.* pacte, contrat; accord commercial, m.; convention, f.; *to be in agreement*, être d'accord; *as per agreement*, comme convenu.

agricultural [agrikœltshᵉrᵉl] *adj.* agricole. ‖ **agriculture** [agrikœltshᵉr] *s.* agriculture, f. ‖ **agriculturist** [-rist] *s.* agriculteur, m.

agued [é¹gyoud] *adj.* fébrile, frissonnant.

ahead [ᵉhèd] *adv.* en avant; devant; de face; *adj.* avant; en avant; *to go ahead*, aller de l'avant; passer le premier; *to look ahead*, penser à l'avenir.

aheap [ᵉhîp] *adv.* en bloc, en tas.

aid [é¹d] *s.* aide, assistance, f.; *v.* aider, secourir; *pl.* subsides, m. pl.

ail [é¹l] *v.* faire mal; affecter douloureusement; *what ails you?*, qu'avez-vous? ‖ **ailment** [-mᵉnt] *s.* malaise, mal, m.; indisposition, f.

aim [é¹m] *s.* but, m.; cible; trajectoire, f.; *v.* viser; pointer [weapon]; porter [blow]; diriger [effort]; *aimless*, sans but.

air [èᵉr] *s.* air, m.; brise; mine; allure, f.; *adj.* aérien; d'aviation; *v.* aérer; exposer; publier; exhiber; *airbed*, matelas pneumatique; *airborne*, aéroporté; *air-conditioning*, climatisation; *airfield*, terrain d'aviation; *air force*, aviation militaire; armée de l'air; *air hostess*, hôtesse de l'air; *airline*, ligne aérienne; *air mail*, poste aérienne; *air raid*, attaque aérienne; *airship*, aéronef; *by air mail*, par avion; *air terminal*, aérogare; *to be on the air*, émettre [radio]; *they put on airs*, ils se donnent des airs. ‖ **aircraft** [èrkraft] *s.* avion, appareil, m.; *aircraft carrier*, porte-avions. ‖ **airman** [èrmᵉn] *s.* aviateur, m. ‖ **airplane** [èrplé¹n] *s.* avion, m. ‖ **airport** [èrpoᵒurt] *s.* aéroport, m. ‖ **airscrew** [èrskrou] *s.* hélice, f. ‖ **airship** [-ship] *s.* dirigeable, m. ‖ **airtight** [èrta¹t] *adj.* hermétique, imperméable à l'air, étanche. ‖ **airy** [èri] *adj.* aéré, ventilé; léger, gracieux; vain, en l'air.

aisle [a¹l] *s.* bas-côté, m.; nef latérale, f.; passage central, m.

ajar [ᵉdjâr] *adj.* entrouvert.

akimbo [ᵉkimboᵒᵘ] *adv. arms akimbo*, les poings sur les hanches.

akin [ᵉkin] *adj.* apparenté [*to*, à]; voisin, proche [*to*, de].

alarm [ᵉlârm] *s.* alarme, alerte; inquiétude, f.; *v.* alarmer, s'alarmer; effrayer; *alarm bell*, tocsin; *alarm box*, avertisseur d'incendie; *alarm clock*, réveille-matin.

alcohol [alkᵉhaul] *s.* alcool, m. ‖ **alcoholic** [-ik] *adj.* alcoolique. ‖ **alcoholism** [-izᵉm] *s.* alcoolisme, m.

alcove [alkoᵒᵘv] *s.* alcôve, f.

alderman [auldᵉrmᵉn] (*pl.* **aldermen** [mᵉn]) *s.* échevin; conseiller municipal, m.

ale [é¹l] *s.* bière, ale, f.

alert [ᵉlᵉ̈rt] *adj.* alerte, vif; *s.* alerte, f.; *v.* alerter.

alfalfa [alfafᵉ] *s.* luzerne, f.

algebra [aldjᵉbrᵉ] *s.* algèbre, f.

alibi ['aliba¹] *s.* alibi, m.; excuse, f.

alien [é¹lyᵉn] *adj.*, *s.* étranger. ‖ **alienate** [-è¹t] *v.* aliéner; détacher, éloigner. ‖ **alienation** [é¹lyᵉné¹shᵉn] *s.* aliénation, f.

alienist [é¹lyᵉnist] *s.* aliéniste, m.

alight [ᵉla¹t] *v.* descendre; mettre pied à terre; se poser [bird]; atterrir, amerrir (aviat.).

alight [ᵉla¹t] *adj.* allumé; éclairé.

align [ᵉla¹n] *v.* aligner; se mettre en ligne.

alike [ᵉla¹k] *adj.* semblable, pareil; *to be alike to*, être égal à; ressembler à; *adv.* également, de la même façon.

aliment ['alimᵉnt] *s.* aliment, m.; ‖ **alimentary** [-ᵉri] *adj.* alimentaire. ‖ **alimentation** [alimᵉnté¹shᵉn] *s.* alimentation, f.

alimony [alimauni] *s.** pension alimentaire après divorce (jur.), f.

alive [ᵉla¹v] *adj.* vivant; vif; actif.

all [aul] *adⁱ.* tout, toute, tous; *adv.* entièrement; *all at once*, tout à coup; *all in*, fatigué; *all out*, complet; *all right*, bien, bon!; *not at all*, pas du tout; *most of all*, surtout; *all in all*, à tout prendre; *that's all*, voilà tout; *all over*, fini; *all-included*, tout compris; *all-in-wrestling*, catch, m.; *all-of-a-sudden*, primesautier; *all-purpose*, tous usages.

allay [ᵉlé¹] *v.* apaiser, calmer.

allegation [alᵉgé¹shᵉn] *s.* allégation; conclusions (jur.), f. ‖ **allege** [ᵉlèdj] *v.* alléguer, prétendre.

allegiance [ᵉlidjᵉns] *s.* fidélité; obéissance, allégeance, f.

allergy [alᵉ̈rdji] *s.** allergie, f.

alleviate [elîvié¹t] *v.* alléger; soulager. || **alleviation** [elîvié¹shⁿn] *s.* allégement, soulagement, m.

alley [ali] *s.* passage, m.; ruelle, f.; *blind alley*, impasse; *to be up one's alley*, être dans ses cordes.

alliance [ela¹ens] *s.* alliance, entente, f. || **allied** [ela¹d] *adj.* allié; parent; connexe.

alligator [al egé¹tᵉʳ] *s.* alligator, m.; *alligator pear*, poire avocat.

allocate [aloké¹t] *v.* assigner; allouer; *Am.* localiser.

allocution [alokyoushⁿn] *s.* allocution, f.

allot [elât] *v.* assigner, répartir.

allow [ela ͦu] *v.* accorder; approuver; allouer; permettre; admettre; *to allow for*, tenir compte de, faire la part de. || **allowable** [-eb'l] *adj.* admissible; permis. || **allowance** [-ens] *s.* allocation; pension; indemnité; ration; remise; concession, tolérance, f.; rabais, m.; *monthly allowance*, mensualité; *travel(l)ing allowance*, indemnité de déplacement.

alloy [alo¹] *s.* alliage; mélange, m.; [elo¹] *v.* allier; altérer; s'allier.

allude [elyoud] *v.* faire allusion.

allure [elyouʳ] *v.* attirer; séduire, charmer. || **allurement** [-mⁿt] *s.* séduction, f.; charme, m. || **alluring** [-ing] *adj.* séduisant.

allusion [elouʒ ͤn] *s.* allusion, f.

ally [ela¹] *v.* allier; unir; *to ally oneself with*, s'allier à; [ala¹] *s.** allié, m.

almanac [aulmᵉnak] *s.* almanach, m.

almighty [aulma¹ti] *adj.* omnipotent, tout-puissant.

almond [âmᵉnd] *s.* amande, f.

almost [aulmo ͦust] *adv.* presque; quasi; *I had almost thrown myself...*, j'avais failli me jeter...

alms [âmz] *s.* aumône; charité, f.; *alms box*, tronc des pauvres, *alms-house*, hospice; *almsman*, vieillard assisté.

aloft [elauft] *adv.* en haut.

alone [elo ͦun] *adj.* seul; isolé; unique; *adv.* seulement; *to let alone*, laisser tranquille; ne pas s'occuper de; renoncer à.

along [elaung] *prep.* le long de; sur; *adv.* dans le sens de la longueur; *along with*, avec, joint à; ainsi que; *all along*, tout le temps, toujours; *come along!* venez donc! *to go along*, passer, s'en aller, longer. || **alongside** [-sa¹d] *prep., adv.* le long de; à côté de; *to come alongside*, accoster, aborder.

aloof [elouf] *adj.* à distance; à l'écart; séparé; distant, peu abordable.

aloofness [-nis] *s.* froideur, réserve, indifférence; attitude distante, f.

aloud [ela ͦud] *adv.* à haute voix.

alp [alp] *s.* alpe, f.; pâturage de montagne, m.; *the Alps*, les Alpes.

alphabet [alfᵉbèt] *s.* alphabet, m. || **alphabetical** [alfᵉbétik'l] *adj.* alphabétique.

alpinist [alpinist] *s.* alpiniste, m., f.

already [aulrèdi] *adv.* déjà.

Alsace [alsas] *s.* Alsace, f. || **Alsatian** [alsé¹shⁿn] *adj., s.* alsacien.

also [aulso] *adv.* de même façon; également; aussi; de plus.

altar [aultᵉʳ] *s.* autel, m.; *altar-cloth*, nappe d'autel; *altar-piece*, *altar-screen*, retable.

alter [aultᵉʳ] *v.* modifier; se modifier. || **alteration** [aulteré¹shⁿn] *s.* remaniement, m.; falsification, f.; changement, m.; modification, f.

altercation [aulterké¹shⁿn] *s.* altercation, f.

alternate [aulternit] *v.* alterner; *adj.* alterné, alternatif, réciproque. || **alternately** [-li] *adv.* alternativement; tour à tour. || **alternating** [-ing] *adj.* alternatif (électr.). || **alternation** [aulterné¹shⁿn] *s.* alternance; alternative, f. || **alternative** [aulterⁿetiv] *s.* alternative, f.; *adj.* alternatif.

although [aulzho ͦu] *conj.* quoique, bien que; quand bien même.

altitude [alt etyoud] *s.* altitude, f.

altogether [ault ᵉgèzhᵉʳ] *adv.* entièrement; absolument; tout compris.

altruism [altrouiz'm] *s.* altruisme, m. || **altruist** [-ist] *s.* altruiste, m., f.

alum [al ͤm] *s.* alun, m.; *v.* aluner.

alumine [elyoumin ͤ] *s.* alumine, f. || **aluminate** [e-yé¹t] *v.* aluminer. || **alumin(i)um** [-ᵉm] *s.* aluminium, m.

alumnus [elœmn ͤs] *(pl. alumni* [-a¹]) *s.* diplômé; ancien élève, m.

always [aulwiz] *adv.* toujours.

am [am], *see* **to be.**

amalgamate [emalgᵉmé¹t] *v.* amalgamer, mélanger; fusionner [shares]. || **amalgamation** [emalgᵉmé¹shⁿn] *s.* mélange, m.; fusion, f.

amanuensis [emanyouènsis] *(pl. amanuenses)* *s.* secrétaire, m., f.

amass [emas] *v.* amasser.

amateur [ametshour] *s.* amateur, m.

amatory [ametauri] *adj.* amoureux; d'amour; érotique.

amaze [emé¹z] *v.* étonner; émerveiller; confondre. || **amazement** [-mⁿt] *s.* étonnement, émerveillement, m. || **amazing** [-ing] *adj.* étonnant.

ambassador [àmbassᵉdᵉr] *s.* ambassadeur, m.

amber [àmbᵉr] *s.* ambre, m.; *adj.* ambré; *v.* ambrer.

ambiance ['aⁿbyaⁿs] *s.* ambiance, f.

ambiguity [àmbigyoᵘᵉti] *s.* ambiguïté, équivoque, f. ‖ *ambiguous* [àmbígyoᵘᵉs] *adj.* ambigu.

ambition [àmbíshᵉn] *s.* ambition, aspiration, f. ‖ *ambitious* [àmbíshᵉs] *adj.* ambitieux.

amble [àmb'l] *s.* amble, m.; *v.* ambler; se promener.

ambulance [àmbyᵉlᵉns] *s.* ambulance, f.; *Ambulance Corps*, Service sanitaire.

ambush [àmbōush] *v.* embusquer; s'embusquer; surprendre dans une embuscade; *s.** embuscade, embûche, f.

ameliorate [ᵉmîlyᵉréⁱt] *v.* améliorer; s'améliorer. ‖ *amelioration* [ᵉmîlyᵉréⁱshen] *s.* amélioration, f.

amenable [ᵉmînᵉb'l] *adj.* soumis, docile; justiciable; responsable.

amend [ᵉméⁱnd] *v.* modifier; corriger; s'amender; s'améliorer; *s. pl.* compensation, f.; dédommagement, m.; *to make amends for*, racheter, dédommager. ‖ *amendment* [ᵉméⁱndmᵉnt] *s.* rectification, f.; amendement, m.; amélioration, f.

American [ᵉmèrᵉkᵉn] *dj.*, *s.* américain. ‖ *americanism* [-iz'm] *s.* américanisme, m.

amethyst [àmᵉthist] *s.* améthyste, f.

amiable [éⁱmiᵉb'l] *adj.* aimable; affable; prévenant; amical.

amicable [àmikᵉb'l] *adj.* amical; à l'amiable [arrangement].

amid [ᵉmíd], **amidst** [-st] *prep.* au milieu de; parmi; entre.

amiss [ᵉmís] *adv.* mal, de travers; *adj.* inconvenant; fautif; impropre; *to take amiss*, prendre mal.

amity [àmᵉti] *s.* amitié, bonnes relations (internationales), f.

ammonia [ᵉmoᵘⁿyᵉ] *s.* ammoniaque, f. ‖ *ammoniac* [-nyak] *adj.* ammoniac. ‖ *ammoniacal* [àmoᵘnaⁱᵉkᵉl] *adj.* ammoniacal.

ammunition [àmyᵉníshᵉn] *s.* munitions, f.; moyens (m.) de défense.

amnesia [àmnîjiᵉ] *s.* amnésie, f. ‖ *amnesic* [-sik] *adj.*, *s.* amnésique, m., f.

amnesty [àmnèsti] *s.** amnistie, f.; *v.* amnistier.

among [ᵉmᵆng], **amongst** [-st] *prep.* au milieu de; entre; parmi; chez.

amorous [àmᵉrᵉs] *adj.* concupiscent; érotique; porté à l'amour; *amorously*, amoureusement.

amortize [ᵉmauʳtaⁱz] *v.* amortir [debt]. ‖ *amortization* [amauʳtᵉzéⁱshᵉn] *s.* amortissement, m.

amount [ᵉmaᵒuⁿt] *v.* s'élever à; se chiffrer; équivaloir; *s.* total, m.; somme, f.; montant, m.; *in amount*, au total; *to the amount of*, jusqu'à concurrence de.

amour [ᵉmoᵘᵉr] *s.* liaison, intrigue, affaire (f.) d'amour.

amphitheater [àmfᵉthiᵉtᵉr] *s.* amphithéâtre, m.

ample [àmp'l] *adj.* ample; spacieux; abondant; suffisant. ‖ *amplifier* [àmplᵉfaⁱᵉr] *s.* amplificateur, m. ‖ *amplify* [àmplᵉfaⁱ] *v.* amplifier; s'étendre sur [subject].

ampoule [ampoul] *s.* ampoule (med.), f.

amputate [àmpyᵉtéⁱt] *v.* amputer. ‖ *amputation* [àmpyᵉtéⁱshen] *s.* amputation, f.

amuse [ᵉmyouz] *v.* amuser, divertir; tromper; s'amuser. ‖ *amusement* [-mᵉnt] *s.* amusement, m. ‖ *amusing* [-ing] *adj.* amusant; *amusement park*, parc des attractions.

an [ᵉn, àn] *indef. art.* un, une.

anachronic [anᵉkraunik] *adj.* anachronique. ‖ *anachronism* [ᵉnakreniz'm] *s.* anachronisme, m.

anaesthesia [anisthîzyᵉ] *s.* anesthésie, f. ‖ *anaesthetic* [anisthétik] *adj.* insensibilisateur; *s.* anesthésique, m. ‖ *anaesthetize* [-taⁱz] *v.* anesthésier.

analogical [anᵉlâdjikᵉl] *adj.* analogique. ‖ *analogous* [ᵉnalᵉgᵉs] *adj.* analogue. ‖ *analogy* [ᵉnalᵉdji] *s.** analogie, f.

analysis [ᵉnalᵉsis] (pl. *analyses* [-îz]) *s.* analyse, f. ‖ *analyze* [anᵉlaⁱz] *v.* analyser.

anarchic [ànâʳkik] *adj.* anarchique. ‖ *anarchy* [anᵉrki] *s.* anarchie, f.

anatomy [ᵉnatᵉmi] *s.** anatomie, f.; dissection, f.

ancestor [ànsèstᵉr] *s.* ancêtre, m. ‖ *ancestral* [-trᵉl] *adj.* ancestral. ‖ *ancestry* [-tri] *s.* lignage, m.

anchor [àngkᵉr] *s.* ancre, f.; *v.* ancrer, mouiller; attacher, fixer. ‖ *anchorage* [-ridj] *s.* ancrage; mouillage; (fig.) havre, m.

anchovy [àntshoᵘvi] *s.** anchois, m.

ancient [éⁱnshᵉnt] *adj.* ancien.

and [ᵉnd, ànd] *conj.* et.

andiron [àndaⁱᵉn] *s.* chenet, m.

anecdote [ànikdoᵒuⁿt] *s.* anecdote, f.

anemia [ᵉnîmiᵉ] *s.* anémie, f. ‖ *anemic* [ᵉnîmik] *adj.* anémique.

anemone [anémauni] *s.* anémone, f.

anew [ᵉnyou] *adv.* de nouveau, à nouveau; à neuf.

angel [é¹ndjᵉl] *s.* ange, m. ‖ **angelic** [àndjèlik] *adj.* angélique.

anger [àngᵉʳ] *s.* colère, f.; *v.* irriter, courroucer.

angina [àndja¹nᵉ] *s.* angine, f.

angle [àngg'l] *s.* hameçon, m.; ligne, f.; *v.* pêcher à la ligne; essayer d'attraper. ‖ **angler** [-ᵉʳ] *s.* pêcheur à la ligne, m.

angle [àngg'l] *s.* angle; point de vue; aspect, m.; *v. Am.* former en angle; présenter sous un certain angle.

angry [ànggri] *adj.* irrité, fâché; en colère.

anguish [ànggwish] *s.** angoisse, f.; tourment, m.; *v.* angoisser.

animadversion [ànᵉmadvᵉ̈rjᵉn] *s.* critique, f.; blâme, m.

animal [anᵉm'l] *adj.*, *s.* animal.

animate [anᵉmit] *v.* animer; encourager; stimuler; exciter; *adj.* animé, vivant. ‖ **animation** [anᵉmé¹shᵉn] *s.* animation; verve, f. ‖ **animator** [animé¹tᵉʳ] *s.* animateur, m.; animatrice, f.

animosity [anᵉmâsᵉti] *s.* animosité, f.

anise [anis] *s.* anis, m.

ankle [àngk'l] *s.* cheville [foot], f.; **ankle-sock**, socquette, f.

annals [an'lz] *s. pl.* annales, f. pl.

annex [anèks] *v.* annexer; joindre; attacher; *s.** annexe, f. ‖ **annexation** [anèksé¹shᵉn] *s.* annexion, f.

annihilate [ᵉna¹élé¹t] *v.* annihiler.

anniversary [anᵉvᵉ̈rsᵉri] *adj.*, *s.** anniversaire.

annotate [anoᵒuté¹t] *v.* annoter. ‖ **annotation** [anoᵒuté¹shᵉn] *s.* annotation, note, f.

announce [ᵉnaᵒuns] *v.* annoncer; présager; prononcer. ‖ **announcement** [-mᵉnt] *s.* avertissement, avis, m.; annonce, f. ‖ **announcer** [-ᵉʳ] *s.* annoncier; speaker [radio] m.; **woman announcer**, speakerine.

annoy [ᵉno¹] *v.* contrarier, importuner. ‖ **annoyance** [-ᵉns] *s.* désagrément, m.; vexation, f. ‖ **annoying** [-ing] *adj.* ennuyeux, contrariant; importun, gênant.

annual [anyouᵉl] *adj.* annuel; annuaire; *s.* plante annuelle, f.; **annually**, annuellement. ‖ **annuity** [ᵉnouᵗi] *s.** annuité, rente, f.

annul [ᵉnœl] *v.* annihiler; annuler; abroger [law]; casser [sentence].

annulary [anyoulᵉri] *adj.*, *s.* annulaire.

annunciate [ᵉnœnshié¹t] *v.* annoncer. ‖ **annunciation** [ᵉnœnsié¹shᵉn] *s.* annonce; annonciation, f.

anoint [ᵉno¹nt] *v.* oindre; sacrer; administrer l'extrême-onction.

anon [ᵉnân] *adv.* immédiatement, bientôt, tout à l'heure.

anonymity [anonᵢmiti] *s.* anonymat, m. ‖ **anonymous** [ᵉnânᵉmᵉs] *adj.* anonyme.

another [ᵉnæzhᵉʳ] *adj.*, *pron.* un autre; un de plus; encore un; autrui; **one another**, l'un l'autre, les uns les autres; réciproquement.

answer [ànsᵉʳ] *s.* réponse; réplique; solution [problem], f.; *v.* répondre; réussir; être conforme à; **to answer for**, répondre de; **to answer the purpose**, faire l'affaire; **to answer the door**, aller ouvrir. ‖ **answerable** [-rᵉb'l] *adj.* admettant une réponse; réfutable; solidaire; responsable, garant; soluble.

ant [ànt] *s.* fourmi, f.; **ant-eater**, fourmilier; **ant-hill**, fourmilière.

antagonism [àntagᵉniz'm] *s.* antagonisme, m. ‖ **antagonist** [-nist] *s.* antagoniste, m. ‖ **antagonize** [-na¹z] *v.* s'aliéner; offusquer.

antecedent [àntᵉsîd'nt] *s.* antécédent, m.; *adj.* antérieur; présumé.

antechamber [àntitshé¹mbᵉʳ] *s.* antichambre, f.

antedate [àntidé¹t] *s.* antidate, f.; *v.* antidater; anticiper sur; devancer.

antenna [àntènᵉ] *pl.* **antennæ** [-nî] *s.* antenne, f.

anterior [antiᵉriᵉʳ] *adj.* antérieur.

anteroom [àntiroum] *s.* antichambre; salle d'attente, f.

anthem [ànthᵉm] *s.* antienne, f.; hymne, chant, m.

anthracite [ànthrᵉsa¹t] *s.* anthracite, m.

antibiotic [antiba¹autik] *s.* antibiotique, m.

antibody [-baudi] *s.** anticorps, m.

antic [antik] *s.* singerie; cabriole, f.; *v. Am.* faire des singeries (or) des cabrioles.

antidote [antidoᵒut] *s.* antidote, m.

anticipate [àntis¹pé¹t] *v.* anticiper; empiéter; prévoir; s'attendre à. ‖ **anticipation** [àntis¹pé¹shᵉn] *s.* anticipation; prévision, f.

antipathy [àntip²ᵉthi] *s.* antipathie, f.

antiquary [àntikwèri] *s.** antiquaire, m., f. ‖ **antiquity** [àntíkwᵉti] *s.** antiquité, f.

antiseptic [àntᵉsèptik] *adj.*, *s.* antiseptique.

antler [àntlᵉʳ] s. andouiller, bois, m.

anvil [ànvil] s. enclume, f.

anxiety [àngza¹ᵉti] s. anxiété, inquiétude, f. || **anxious** [àngkshᵉs] adj. inquiet; désireux; inquiétant; pénible; **anxiously**, anxieusement.

any [èni] adj., pron. quelque; du, de, des; de la; en; quiconque; aucun; nul; personne; n'importe quel; adv. si peu que ce soit; any way, n'importe comment; de toute façon; any time, à tout moment.

anybody [ènibàdi] pron. quelqu'un; personne; n'importe qui.

anyhow [ènihaᵒu] adv. en tout cas.

anyone [èniwœn] pron. = anybody.

anything [ènithing] pron. quelque chose; n'importe quoi; rien; adv. un peu; si peu que ce soit.

anyway [èniwé¹] adv. en tout cas.

anywhere [ènihwèᵉʳ] adv. n'importe où; quelque part; nulle part.

apart [ᵉpàrt] adv. à part, à l'écart; séparé; to move apart, se séparer; s'écarter; to tell apart, distinguer; to set apart, mettre de côté; différencier.

apartment [ᵉpàrtmᵉnt] s. appartement, m.; Br. grande pièce; salle, f.; pl. logement, m.; **apartment-house**, maison meublée.

apathetic [ᵃpᵉthétik] adj. apathique; indifférent; **apathy**, apathie.

ape [é¹p] s. singe, m.; guenon, f.; v. imiter, singer.

aperture [ᵃpᵉrtshᵉʳ] s. ouverture, f.

apex [é¹pèks] s.* sommet; bout [finger], m.; apogée [glory], m.

apiece [ᵉpís] adv. la pièce; chacun.

apocalypse [ᵉpokᵉlips] s. apocalypse, f. [eccles.].

apologetic [ᵉpâl`djètik] adj. relatif à des excuses; **apologetically**, en s'excusant. || **apologize** [ᵉpâl`dja¹z] v. s'excuser. || **apology** [ᵉpâl`dji] s.* apologie; excuse, f.; semblant, substitut, m.; amende honorable, f.

apoplexy [ᵃp`plèksi] s. apoplexie, f.

apostasy [ᵉpaustᵉsi] s. apostasie, f. || **apostatize** [-t`ᵉta¹z] v. apostasier.

apostle [ᵉpâs`l] s. apôtre, m. || **apostleship** [-ship] s. apostolat, m. || **apostolic(al)** [ᵃpᵉstâlik(`l)] adj. apostolique.

apostrophe [ᵉpaustrᵉfi] s. apostrophe, f.; **apostrophize**, apostropher.

appal [ᵉpaul] v. terrifier. || **appalling** [-ing] adj. terrifiant.

apparatus [àpᵉré¹tᵉs] s.* appareil; attirail, m.

apparel [ᵉparᵉl] s. habillement, m.; v. vêtir; équiper; orner.

apparent [ᵉparᵉnt] adj. apparent, évident; heir apparent, héritier présomptif. || **apparently** [-li] adv. apparemment, visiblement. || **apparition** [ᵃpᵉrishᵉn] s. apparition, f.; fantôme, spectre, m.

appeal [ᵉpíl] v. interjeter appel [law]; implorer; en appeler à; avoir recours à; attirer; s. appel; attrait; recours, m.; does that appeal to you? est-ce que cela vous dit quelque chose?

appear [ᵉpiᵉʳ] v. apparaître, paraître; comparaître; sembler; se manifester; it appears that, il appert que (jur.). || **appearance** [ᵉpîrᵉns] s. aspect, m.; apparence; publication; représentation; comparution, f.; semblant, m.; first appearance, début [artist].

appease [ᵉpîz] v. apaiser. || **appeasement** [ᵉpîzmᵉnt] s. apaisement, m.; conciliation, f.

appellant [ᵉpèlᵉnt] adj., s. appelant (jur.). || **appellation** [àpᵉlé¹shᵉn] s. appellation, f.; titre, m. || **appellee** [àpᵉlî] s. intimé (jur.), m.

append [ᵉpènd] v. annexer, joindre; apposer. **appendicitis** [ᵉpèndisa¹tis] s. appendicite, f. || **appendix** [ᵉpèndiks] s.* appendice, m.

appertain [àpᵉrté¹n] v. appartenir.

appetite [àpᵉta¹t] s. appétit; désir, m. || **appetizer** [àpᵉta¹zᵉʳ] s. apéritif, m. || **appetizing** [àpᵉta¹zing] adj. appétissant.

applaud [ᵉplaud] v. applaudir; approuver. || **applause** [ᵉplauz] s. applaudissements, m. pl.

apple [àp`l] s. pomme, f.; apple of the eye, prunelle de l'œil; **apple-pie**, chausson aux pommes; in apple-pie order, en ordre parfait; **apple-polish**, v. Am. faire de la lèche à; **apple-polisher**, s. Am. lèche-bottes, m.; **apple-sauce**, compote de pommes; flagornerie; Am. boniments; Am. blague (slang).

appliance [ᵉpla¹ᵉns] s. mise en pratique, f.; engin; appareil, m.

applicable [àplikᵉb`l] adj. applicable. || **applicant** [àplᵉkᵉnt] s. postulant, candidat; demandeur (jur.), m. || **application** [àplᵉké¹shᵉn] s. application; demande d'emploi; démarche, f.

apply [ᵉpla¹] v. appliquer; infliger; diriger vers; s'appliquer; to apply oneself to, s'appliquer à; to apply for, faire une demande, une démarche; solliciter; to apply to, s'adresser à.

appoint [ᵉpo¹nt] v. désigner; assigner; nommer; établir, instituer; décider; résoudre; équiper. || **appointment** [ᵉpo¹ntmᵉnt] s. nomination; situation, f.; rendez-vous, m.; pl. équipement, m.; installation, f.; mobilier, m.

apportion [ᵉpoᵒurshᵉn] *v.* répartir, distribuer; proportionner. || ***apportionment*** [-mᵉnt] *s.* répartition, f.; prorata, m.

appraisal [ᵉpréⁱz'l] *s.* estimation, évaluation, f. || ***appraise*** [ᵉpréⁱz] *v.* évaluer; estimer. || ***appraiser*** [-ᵉr] *s.* commissaire-priseur, m.

appreciable [ᵉprîshiᵉb'l] *adj.* appréciable. || ***appreciate*** [ᵉprîshiéⁱt] *v.* apprécier; augmenter [price]; *Am.* être reconnaissant de. || ***appreciation*** [ᵉprîshiéⁱshᵉn] *s.* appréciation; hausse [price], f.; *Am.* reconnaissance, f.

apprehend [aprihᵉnd] *v.* appréhender; arrêter; comprendre; supposer. || ***apprehension*** [aprihᵉnshᵉn] *s.* arrestation; compréhension; crainte, f. || ***apprehensive*** [-siv] *adj.* inquiet, anxieux; compréhensif, vif, perceptif.

apprentice [ᵉprèntis] *s.* apprenti; élève; stagiaire, m., f.; *v.* mettre en apprentissage. || ***apprenticeship*** [-ship] *s.* apprentissage, m.

approach [ᵉprooᵘtsh] *v.* approcher; aborder; s'approcher de; *s.* approche, f.; abord, m.; proximité, f.; *pl.* avances, f.; accès, abords; travaux d'approche, m. || ***approachable*** [-ᵉb'l] *adj.* approchable, accessible; abordable.

approbation [aprᵉbéⁱshᵉn] *s.* approbation, f.

appropriate [ᵉprooᵘpriéⁱt] *v.* s'approprier; affecter à; attribuer; [ᵉprooᵘpriit] *adj.* approprié, indiqué. || ***appropriation*** [ᵉprooᵘpriéⁱshᵉn] *s.* somme affectée; destination [sum], f.; crédit, m.; (jur.) détournement, m.

approval [ᵉproᵘv'l] *s.* approbation, ratification, f. || ***approve*** [ᵉproᵘv] *v.* approuver; consentir; *to approve oneself*, se montrer. || ***approving*** [-ing] *adj.* approbateur; approbatif.

approximate [ᵉpråksᵉméⁱt] *v.* approcher, rapprocher; [ᵉpråksᵉmit] *adj.* proche; approximatif. || ***approximately*** [-li] *adv.* presque, environ, approximativement. || ***approximation*** [ᵉprauksiméⁱshᵉn] *s.* approximation, f.; rapprochement, m. || ***approximative*** [-mᵉtiv] *adj.* approximatif.

appurtenance [ᵉpë̇t'nᵉns] *s.* propriété; dépendances; suite, f.

apricot [éⁱprikàt] *s.* abricot, m.

April [éⁱprᵉl] *s.* avril, m.; *April fool joke*, poisson d'avril.

apron [éⁱprᵉn] *s.* tablier, m.

apt [apt] *adj.* apte à; sujet à; doué pour; enclin à; habile. || ***aptitude*** [aptᵉtyoud] *s.* aptitude, capacité, f.

aquarium [ᵉkwèriᵉm] *s.* aquarium, m.

aquatic [ᵉkwatik] *adj.* aquatique; *s.* plante, sport aquatique.

aqueduct [akwidœkt] *s.* aqueduc, m.

Arab [arᵉb] *adj., s.* arabe.

Arabia [ᵉréⁱbyᵉ] *s.* Arabie, f. || ***Arabian*** [-n] *adj.* arabe.

arbiter [årbitᵉr] *s.* arbitre, m. || ***arbitrament*** [årbitrᵉmᵉnt] *s.* arbitrage, m.; sentence, f. || ***arbitrary*** [årbᵉtrèri] *adj.* arbitraire. || ***arbitrate*** [årbᵉtréⁱt] *v.* arbitrer. || ***arbitration*** [årbᵉtréⁱshᵉn] *s.* arbitrage, m. || ***arbitrator*** [årbᵉtréⁱtᵉr] *s.* arbitre, juge, m.

arbor [årbᵉr] *s.* verger; bosquet, m.

arc [årk] *s.* arc, m.

arcade [årkéⁱd] *s.* arcade, f.

arch [årtsh] *s.** arche; voûte, f.; arc (geom.), m.; *v.* jeter un pont, une arche; arquer, courber; *adj.* maniéré; *pref.* principal.

archaic [årkéⁱik] *adj.* archaïque. || ***archaism*** [årkiizᵉm] *s.* archaïsme, m.

archbishop [åtshbishᵉp] *s.* archevêque, m. || ***archbishopric*** [-rik] *s.* archevêché; archiépiscopat, m.

archipelago [årkᵉpèlᵉgoᵒu] *s.* archipel, m.

architect [årkᵉtèkt] *s.* architecte, m. || ***architecture*** [årkᵉtèktshᵉr] *s.* architecture, f.

archives [åkaⁱvz] *s. pl.* archives, f. pl.

archway [årtshwéⁱ] *s.* voûte, f.

arctic [årktik] *adj.* arctique.

ardent [ård'nt] *adj.* ardent; passionné; *ardent spirits*, spiritueux. || ***ardo(u)r*** [årdᵉr] *s.* ardeur, ferveur, f.; zèle, m.

arduous [årdjouᵉs] *adj.* ardu.

are [år] *pl. indic. of to be;* sommes, êtes, sont.

area [èriᵉ] *s.* aire, superficie; région (mil.); cour, f.; quartier, m.

arena [ᵉrînᵉ] *s.* arène, f.; sable, gravier (med.), m.

argue [årgyou] *v.* argumenter; débattre; soutenir [opinion]; prouver; *to argue down*, réduire au silence; *to argue into*, persuader. || ***argument*** [årgyᵉmᵉnt] *s.* argument, m.; preuve; argumentation; discussion, f.; débat, m.; sommaire, m.; (jur.) plaidoyer, m.; thèse, f.

arid [arid] *adj.* aride, sec. || ***aridity*** [ᵉridᵉti] *s.* sécheresse, aridité, f.

arise [ᵉraⁱz] *v.** se lever; s'élever; surgir; provenir; se produire; se révolter (*against*, contre). || ***arisen*** [ᵉriz'n] *p. p. of to arise.*

aristocracy [arᵉståkrᵉsi] *s.** aristocratie; élite, f. || ***aristocrat*** [ᵉristᵉkrat] *s.* aristocrate, m., f. || ***aristocratic*** [ᵉristᵉkratik] *adj.* aristocratique.

arithmetic [ᵉrithmᵉtik] *s.* arithmétique, f.

ark [ârk] *s.* arche, f.; *Noah's ark,* arche de Noé.

arm [ârm] *s.* arme, f.; *v.* (s')armer.

arm [ârm] *s.* bras, m.; *arm in arm,* bras dessus, bras dessous; *at arm's length,* à bout de bras; *arm-hole,* emmanchure.

armada [ârmâdᵉ] *s.* flotte, escadre, f.

armament [ârmᵉmᵉnt] *s.* armement, m.

armature [ârmᵉtshᵉʳ] *s.* arme, armature (arch.); armure (electr.), f.

armchair [ârmtshèr] *s.* fauteuil, m.

armful [ârmfᵉl] *s.* brassée, f.

armistice [ârmᵉstis] *s.* armistice, m.

armo(u)r [ârmᵉʳ] *s.* armure; cuirasse, f.; blindage, m.; *v.* cuirasser, blinder. ‖ *armo(u)red* [ârmᵉrd] *p. p.* blindé, cuirassé. ‖ *armourer* [-rᵉʳ] *s.* armurier, m. ‖ *armo(u)ry* [ârmᵉri] *s.* armurerie, f.; arsenal, m.; armes, f. pl.; *Am.* fabrique (f.) d'armes.

armpit [ârmpit] *s.* aisselle, f.

army [ârmi] *s.* armée; multitude, f.; *adj.* militaire; de l'armée; *army area,* zone de l'armée; *to enter the army,* entrer dans l'armée; *Am. army hostess,* cantinière.

aroma [erooᵘmᵉ] *s.* arome, m. ‖ *aromatic* [arematik] *adj.* aromatique. ‖ *aromatise* [arooᵘmeta¹z] *v.* aromatiser.

arose [erooᵘz] *pret. of to arise.*

around [eraoᵘnd] *adv.* autour, alentour; de tous côtés; *prep.* autour de; *Am.* à travers; çà et là; dans.

arouse [eraoᵘz] *v.* (r)éveiller; stimuler, provoquer, susciter.

arraign [erᵉi¹n] *v.* traduire en justice; accuser. ‖ *arraignment* [-mᵉnt] *s.* mise en accusation, f.

arrange [erᵉi¹ndj] *v.* arranger; disposer; régler [business]; convenir de; fixer; s'entendre pour. ‖ *arrangement* [erᵉi¹ndjmᵉnt] *s.* arrangement; préparatif, m.; transaction; organisation; combinaison, mesure, f.

array [erᵉi¹] *v.* ranger; disposer; orner; faire l'appel (mil.); *s.* ordre, m.; formation [battle], f.; troupe, f.; vêtements; gala, m.; constitution de jury, f.

arrear [eriᵉʳ] *s.* retard, m.; *pl.* arrérages, m.

arrest [erèst] *v.* arrêter; fixer; surseoir; retenir [attention]; prévenir [danger]; *s.* arrêt, m.; arrestation, f.; surséance (jur.), f.; arrêts (mil.), m. pl.

arrival [eraⁱv'l] *s.* arrivée, f.; arrivage, m. ‖ *arrive* [eraⁱv] *v.* arriver; aboutir; survenir.

arrogance [arᵉgᵉns] *s.* arrogance, f. ‖ *arrogant* [arᵉgᵉnt] *adj.* arrogant.

arrogate [arᵉgéⁱt] *v.* s'arroger; attribuer. ‖ *arrogation* [arᵉgéⁱshᵉn] *s.* usurpation; prétentions injustifiées, f.

arrow [arooᵘ] *s.* flèche, f.; *arrow-root,* marante.

arsenal [ârs'nᵉl] *s.* arsenal, m.

arsenic [ârs'nik] *s.* arsenic, m.

arson [ârs'n] *s.* crime d'incendie volontaire, m.

art [ârt] *s.* art; artifice, m.; ruse, f.; *fine arts,* beaux-arts.

arterial [âtiᵉriᵉl] *adj.* artériel; national [road]. ‖ *artery* [ârtᵉri] *s.** artère; grande route, f.; fleuve navigable, m.

artful [ârtᵉl] *adj.* ingénieux, adroit; rusé; artificiel.

arthritis [âthraⁱtis] *s.* arthrite, f. ‖ *arthrosis* [-throoᵘsis] *s.* arthrose, f.

artichoke [ârtitshooᵘk] *s.* artichaut; *Jerusalem artichoke,* topinambour.

article [ârtik'l] *s.* article, m.; *pl.* contrat d'apprentissage, m.; rôle d'équipage (naut.), m.; *v.* mettre en apprentissage; stipuler; passer un contrat (naut.); accuser (jur.).

articulate [ârtikyᵉlit] *adj.* articulé; manifeste; intelligible; [ârtikyᵉléⁱt] *v.* articuler; énoncer. ‖ *articulation* [ârtikyᵉléⁱshᵉn] *s.* articulation, f.

artifice [ârtᵉfis] *s.* artifice, m.; ruse, f. ‖ *artificial* [ârtᵉfishᵉl] *adj.* artificiel; feint; affecté.

artillery [ârtilᵉri] *s.* artillerie, f.; *artillery-man,* artilleur.

artisan [ârtᵉz'n] *s.* artisan, m.

artist [ârtist] *s.* artiste, m., f. ‖ *artistic* [ârtistik] *adj.* artistique; *artistically,* artistiquement, avec art.

artless [âʳtlis] *adj.* peu artistique; gauche; candide; sans artifice; naturel. ‖ *artlessness* [-nis] *s.* ingénuité, f.

as [ᵉz] *adv., conj., prep.* comme; si, aussi; ainsi que; tant que; de même que; puisque; en tant que; *as regards, as for,* quant à; *as if,* comme si; *as it were,* pour ainsi dire; *the same as,* le même que.

ascend [ᵉsènd] *v.* monter; s'élever. ‖ *ascendancy* [-ᵉnsi] *s.* ascendant, m. ‖ *ascension* [ᵉsènshᵉn] *s.* ascension, f. ‖ *ascent* [ᵉsènt] *s.* ascension, montée; remontée, f.

ascertain [asᵉrtéⁱn] *v.* vérifier; confirmer; s'informer; constater.

ascetic [ᵉsétik] *adj.* ascétique; *s.* ascète, m. ‖ *asceticism* [-isiz'm] *s.* ascétisme, m.; ascèse, f.

ascribe [ᵉskraⁱb] *v.* attribuer; imputer.

asepsis [ᵉsepsis] *s.* asepsie, f. ‖ *asepticize* [-tisa¹z] *v.* aseptiser.

ash [ash] *s.** frêne, m.

ash [ash] *s.** cendre, f.; *v.* réduire en cendres; *ash-colo(u)red*, cendré; *ashtray*, cendrier; *Ash Wednesday*, mercredi des Cendres.

ashamed [eshé¹md] *adj.* honteux.

ashore [eshoour] *adv.* à terre; sur terre; échoué; à la côte; *to ashore*, débarquer.

aside [esa¹d] *adv.* à part; à l'écart; de côté; *Am.* en dehors de, à côté de; *aside from, Am.* outre, en plus de; *s.* aparté [theater], m.

ask [ask] *v.* demander; solliciter; inviter; poser [question]; *to ask somebody for something*, demander quelque chose à quelqu'un.

askance [eskàns] *adv.* de travers, de côté, du coin de l'œil.

asleep [eslíp] *adj.* endormi; engourdi; *to fall asleep*, s'endormir; *to be asleep*, dormir.

aslope [esloo¹p] *adv., adj.* en pente.

asparagus [esparegós] *s.** asperge, f.; *asparagus fern*, asparagus.

aspect [aspèkt] *s.* aspect; air, m.; physionomie; orientation, exposition, f.; *in its true aspect*, sous son vrai jour, sous son angle véritable.

aspen [aspen] *s.* tremble [tree], m.

asperity [aspériti] *s.** aspérité, f.; rigueur, âpreté, f.

asphalt [asfault] *s.* asphalte, m.

asphyxiate [asfíksié¹t] *v.* asphyxier. ‖ *asphyxia* [-sie] *s.* asphyxie, f.

aspiration [aspéri¹shen] *s.* aspiration, f.; souffle, m. ‖ *aspirator* [aspe-ré¹ter] *s.* aspirateur, m. ‖ *aspire* [espa¹r] *v.* aspirer; exhaler; ambitionner; se porter [ambition].

ass [as] *s.** âne, imbécile (fam.), m.; *she-ass*, ânesse.

assail [esé¹l] *v.* assaillir, attaquer. ‖ *assailant* [esé¹lent] *s.* agresseur, assaillant, m.

assassin [esassin] *s.* assassin, m. ‖ *assassinate* [esas¹né¹t] *v.* assassiner. ‖ *assassination* [esas¹né¹shen] *s.* assassinat, m.

assault [esault] *s.* assaut (mil.), m.; agression (jur.), m.; attaque, f.; *v.* assaillir, attaquer. ‖ *assaulter* [-er] *s.* assaillant, agresseur, m.

assay [esé¹] *s.* essai [metal], m.; analyse; vérification [weight, quantity], f.; *v.* faire l'essai; titrer; essayer, tenter.

assemble [esèmb'l] *v.* assembler; ajuster, monter; se réunir. ‖ *assembly* [esèmbli] *s.* réunion; assemblée, f.; montage, m.

assent [esènt] *v.* acquiescer, adhérer; *s.* assentiment, m.

assert [esërt] *v.* revendiquer; affirmer. ‖ *assertion* [esër¹shen] *s.* revendication; affirmation, f. ‖ *assertive* [-tiv] *adj.* affirmatif; péremptoire, cassant.

assess [esès] *v.* imposer; évaluer; assigner; taxer. ‖ *assessment* [-ment] *s.* taxation; évaluation; imposition, f.; *reduction of assessment*, dégrèvement d'impôt.

asset [asèt] *s.* qualité, f.; avantage, m.; *pl.* avoirs; actif, capital, m.

assiduity [asedyouéti] *s.** assiduité, f. ‖ *assiduous* [esídjou s] *adj.* assidu; empressé.

assign [esa¹n] *v.* attribuer; affecter (mil.); alléguer [reason]; assigner; nommer; transférer [law]. ‖ *assignment* [esa¹nment] *s.* attribution; cession; affectation (mil.), f.; transfert [property]; *Am.* devoir (educ.), m.

assimilate [esím¹lé¹t] *v.* assimiler; comparer; s'assimiler. ‖ *assimilation* [esimilé¹shen] *s.* assimilation, f.

assist [esíst] *v.* assister, aider; faciliter; contribuer à. ‖ *assistance* [esís-tens] *s.* assistance; aide, f. ‖ *assistant* [esístent] *adj., s.* assistant; adjoint, aide; auxiliaire.

assizes [esa¹ziz] *s. pl.* assises, f. pl.; tribunal, m.

associate [esoo¹shiit] *adj.* associé; *s.* associé; compagnon; confrère, collègue; complice, m.; titre académique; [esoo¹shié¹t] *v.* associer; s'associer. ‖ *association* [esoo¹sié¹shen] *s.* association; société; *pl.* relations, f.

assort [esaurt] *v.* classer, trier; assortir; être assorti; fréquenter. ‖ *assortment* [esaurtment] *s.* classement; tri; assortiment, m.

assuage [eswé¹dj] *v.* assouvir, satisfaire [hunger]; étancher [thirst]; soulager [pain]; apaiser [anger].

assume [esoum] *v.* assumer; prendre; s'emparer de; s'arroger; feindre; présumer. ‖ *assumed* [-d] *adj., p. p.* feint; d'emprunt [name].

assumption [esæmpshen] *s.* prétention; hypothèse; action d'assumer; Assomption, f.

assurance [eshourens] *s.* affirmation, conviction; promesse; assurance; garantie, f.

assure [eshour] *v.* assurer; certifier. ‖ *assuredly* [-idli] *adv.* assurément; avec assurance.

asterisk [asterisk] *s.* astérisque, m.

astern [estër¹n] *adv.* à l'arrière; en arrière; *adj.* arrière.

asthma [asme] *s.* asthme, m.

astonish [estânish] *v.* confondre; étonner. ‖ *astonishing* [-ing] *adj.* étonnant; surprenant. ‖ *astonishment* [-ment] *s.* étonnement, m.

astound [estâ°und] v. stupéfier.

astray [estré¹] adv. hors du chemin; perdu; de travers; dérangé; erroné; to go astray, s'égarer; adj. égaré.

astride [estra¹d] adv. à cheval; à califourchon; jambes écartées.

astringent [estrindjent] adj. astringent; austère; s. astringent, m.

astrologer [astraulaudjer] s. astrologue, m. || **astrology** [-ledji] s. astrologie, f.

astronomer [estrânemer] s. astronome, m. || **astronomy** [estrânemi] s. astronomie, f.

astute [estyout] adj. fin, rusé, sagace.

asunder [esænder] adj. séparé; écarté; adv. coupé en deux.

asylum [esa¹lem] s. asile; hospice, hôpital, m.

at [at] prep. à; au; de; dans; chez; sur; par; I live at my brother's, j'habite chez mon frère; at hand, à portée de la main; at sea, en mer; at any rate, en tout cas; at any sacrifice, au prix de n'importe quel sacrifice; at last, enfin; at this, sur ce.

atavism [atevizm] s. atavisme, m.

ate [é¹t] pret. of to eat.

atheist [e¹thiist] s. athée, m.

athlete [athlît] s. athlète, m. || **athletic** [athlètik] adj. athlétique. || **athletics** [athlètiks] s. gymnastique, f.; athlétisme, m.

atmosphere [atmesfier] s. atmosphère, f. || **atmospheric** [atmesfèrik] adj. atmosphérique.

atoll [atâl] s. atoll, m.

atom [atem] s. atome, m.; molécule, f.; atom bomb, bombe atomique; atom free, dénucléarisé. || **atomic** [etâmik] adj. atomique. || **atomist** [-ist] s. atomiste, m. || **atomize** [-a¹z] v. atomiser, pulvériser, vaporiser.

atone [eto°un] v. expier; racheter; compenser; concilier. || **atonement** [-ment] s. réconciliation; compensation; expiation; rédemption, f.

atrocious [etro°ushes] adj. atroce. || **atrocity** [etrâseti] s.* atrocité, f.

atrophy [atrefi] s. atrophie, f.; v. atrophier.

attach [etatsh] v. attacher; imputer; saisir [law]. || **attachment** [-ment] s. attachement, m.; saisie-arrêt, f. (jur.); embargo, m.

attack [etak] v. attaquer; entamer; commencer; s. attaque, offensive, f. || **attacker** [-er] s. assaillant, m.

attain [eté¹n] v. atteindre; acquérir; parvenir à. || **attainder** [-der] s. condamnation [treason]; flétrissure, f. || **attainment** [-ment] s. acquisition;

réalisation; connaissances, f.; savoir, m.; classical attainments, culture classique.

attempt [etèmpt] s. tentative, f.; effort; essai; attentat, m.; v. tenter; tâcher; attenter à.

attend [etènd] v. faire attention [to, à]; suivre [lessons]; assister à [lectures]; vaquer à [work]. || **attendance** [-ens] s. présence; assistance, f.; soins (med.); service [hotel], m. || **attendant** [-ent] adj. résultant, découlant de; au service de; s. assistant, aide; serviteur, garçon, m.; ouvreuse; pl. suite, f.

attention [etènshen] s. attention, f.; égards, m.; garde-à-vous (mil.), m.; to pay attention to, faire attention à. || **attentive** [etèntiv] adj. attentif.

attenuate [eté¹nyoué¹t] v. atténuer; amaigrir. || **attenuation** [eté¹nyoué¹-shen] s. atténuation, f.

attest [etèst] v. attester; s. témoignage, m.; attestation, f. || **attestation** [atèsté¹shen] s. attestation, f.

attic [atik] s. mansarde, f.; grenier, m.

attire [eta¹r] s. vêtement, m.; parure, f.; v. orner, parer; vêtir.

attitude [ateyoud] s. attitude, f.

attorney [etër̄n¹] s. avoué; mandataire, m.; by attorney, par procuration; Attorney-general, procureur général; Am. procureur du gouvernement; public attorney, procureur de la République.

attract [etrakt] v. attirer. || **attraction** [-shen] s. attrait, m.; séduction, f. || **attractive** [-tiv] adj. attrayant, séduisant.

attribute [atrebyout] s. attribut, m.; [etribyout] v. attribuer, imputer. || **attribution** [atribyoushen] s. attribution; prérogative, f.

attune [etyoun] v. accorder; harmoniser (to, avec).

auburn [aubern] adj. brun-rouge.

auction [aukshen] s. enchère, f.; v. vendre aux enchères; Am. auction-room, salle des ventes. || **auctioneer** [aukshenier] s. commissaire-priseur; courtier inscrit, m.

audacious [audé¹shes] adj. audacieux. || **audacity** [audaseti] s. audace, f.

audible [audeb'l] adj. perceptible [ear]. || **audience** [audiens] s. audience [hearing], f.; spectateurs; auditoire [hearers], m.; assistance, f. || **audio-visual** [audio°vizyoue¹l] adj. audiovisuel. || **audit** [audit] v. apurer; vérifier; s. bilan; apurement, m.; vérification, f.; audit-office, cour des comptes. || **audition** [audishen] s. audition; ouïe, f. || **auditor** [auditer]

s. auditeur; vérificateur, m. ‖ *auditorium* [aud⁰t⁰⁰uri⁰m] s. salle de conférences ou de concerts, f.; parloir, m. ‖ *auditory* [-t⁰ri] adj. auditif; s. auditoire; auditorium, m.

auger [aug⁰ʳ] s. tarière; sonde, f.

aught [aut] pron., s. quelque chose; rien; *for aught I know*, pour autant que je sache.

augment [augm⁰nt] s. accroissement, m.; [augm⁰nt] v. augmenter. ‖ *augmentation* [augm⁰nté¹sh⁰n] s. augmentation, f.

augur [aug⁰ʳ] s. augure, m.; v. augurer.

august [aug⁰st] adj. auguste; s. août, m.

auk [auk] s. pingouin, m.

aunt [ànt] s. tante, f.

auscultate [auskⁱlté¹t] v. ausculter.

auspices [auspisiz] s. auspices, m. ‖ *auspicious* [auspish⁰s] adj. propice, favorable; prospère, fortuné.

austere [austⁱⁱʳ] adj. austère. ‖ *austerity* [austⁱʳ⁰ti] s. austérité f.; *austerity plan*, plan de restrictions.

authenticate [authéntiké¹t] v. authentifier; certifier; homologuer; valider. ‖ *authenticity* [auth⁰ntis⁰ti] s. authenticité, f.

author [auth⁰ʳ] s. auteur, m.

authoritative [⁰thaur⁰té¹tiv] adj. autorisé; qui fait autorité; autoritaire. ‖ *authority* [⁰thaur⁰ti] s. autorité, source, f. ‖ *authorize* [⁰thaura¹z] v. autoriser; justifier.

auto, automobile [auto⁰u] [aut⁰m⁰bíl] s. auto, automobile, f.; *autobahn*, autoroute; *autocar*, autocar.

automat [automat] s. Am. restaurant à service automatique, m. ‖ *automatic* [aut⁰matik] adj. automatique; s. revolver, m.; *automatically*, d'office; automatiquement. ‖ *automation* [aut⁰mé¹sh⁰n] s. automatisation, automation, f. ‖ *automatism* [autaum⁰tiz'm] s. automatisme, m. ‖ *automaton* [-⁰n] (pl. *automata*) s. automate, m.

autonomous [autân⁰m⁰s] adj. autonome. ‖ *autonomy* [autân⁰mi] s. autonomie, f.

autopsy [aut⁰psi] s.* autopsie, f.

autostrada [autostrâd⁰] s. autostrade, f.

autumn [aut⁰m] s. automne, m.

auxiliary [augzíly⁰ri] adj., s.* auxiliaire.

avail [avé¹l] s. utilité, f.; profit, m.; v. servir; être utile; se servir de. ‖ *available* [-b'l] adj. disponible, utilisable; valable, valide [ticket]; *available funds*, disponibilités; *I am available*, je suis à votre disposition.

avaricious [ev⁰rish⁰s] adj. avare.

avenge [evèndj] v. venger. ‖ *avenger* [-⁰ʳ] s. vengeur, m.; vengeresse, f.

avenue [av⁰nyou] s. avenue, f.

average [avridj] adj. moyen; ordinaire; s. moyenne; avarie [ship], f.; v. faire, donner une moyenne de.

averse [evë̀ʳs] adj. opposé; adversaire de; non disposé à. ‖ *aversion* [evë̀ʳj⁰n] s. aversion, f. ‖ *avert* [evë̀ʳt] v. détourner; éviter; empêcher; prévenir [accident]; conjurer [danger].

aviation [é¹vièsh⁰n] s. aviation, f. ‖ *aviator* [é¹viét⁰ʳ] s. aviateur, m.

avidity [vid⁰ti] s. avidité, f.

avoid [evo¹d] v. éviter; annuler [law]. ‖ *avoidable* [-b'l] adj. évitable; annulable.

avouch [eva⁰utsh] v. affirmer, déclarer, assurer; reconnaître, avouer.

avow [eva⁰u] v. avouer; reconnaître. ‖ *avowal* [-el] s. aveu, m.

await [ewé¹t] v. attendre; guetter.

awake [ewé¹k] v.* éveiller; inspirer; exciter [interest]; se réveiller, s'éveiller; adj. éveillé; vigilant. ‖ *awaken* [-⁰n] v. éveiller, réveiller; ranimer; susciter. ‖ *awakening* [-⁰ning] s. réveil; désappointement, m.

award [ewaurd] s. décision, f.; dommages-intérêts (jur.), m. pl.; récompense, f.; prix, m.; v. décider; décerner; accorder.

aware [ewèʳ] adj. au courant de; averti de; qui a conscience de.

away [ewé¹] adv. au loin, loin; *away back*, il y a longtemps, il y a loin; *to keep away*, se tenir à l'écart; *right away*, tout de suite; *going-away*, départ; *ten miles away*, à dix milles de distance; adj. absent, éloigné.

awe [au] s. crainte; terreur, f.; v. inspirer de la crainte. ‖ *awful* [auf⁰l] adj. terrible; formidable. ‖ *awfully* [-i] adv. terriblement; extrêmement.

awhile [⁰hwa¹l] adv. quelque temps; un instant; de si tôt.

awkward [aukw⁰rd] adj. gauche, embarrassé; incommode, gênant. ‖ *awkwardness* [-nis] s. gêne, gaucherie; incommodité, f.

awl [aul] s. alène, f.

awry [era¹] adj., adv. de travers.

axe [aks] s. hache, f.

axis [aksis] (pl. *axes* [aksiz]) s. axe, m.

axle [aks'l] s. essieu; tourillon [wheel], m.; *stub axle*, fusée.

aye [a¹] adv. oui; vote affirmatif.

azure [aj⁰ʳ] adj. azur; s. azur, m.

B

baa [bâ] *s.* bêlement, m.; *v.* bêler.

babble [bab'l] *s.* babil; *v.* babiller; *babbling*, babillard.

baby [bé¹bi] *s.* * bébé; enfant; petit, m.; *adj.* puéril; d'enfant; *v. Am.* dorloter, câliner, cajoler; *baby-carriage*, voiture d'enfant; *baby-linen*, layette; *baby-grand*, demi-queue [piano]; *baby-sitter*, gardienne d'enfant, garde-bébé; *baby-sitting*, garde d'enfants.

bach [batsh] *v. Am.* vivre en célibataire. ‖ *bachelor* [-°l°r] *s.* célibataire; bachelier (univ.), m.

back [bak] *s.* arrière; dos; reins; revers [hand]; verso [sheet], m.; *adj.* d'arrière; *adv.* en arrière; *to be back*, être de retour; *to go back*, aller en arrière; renforcer [wall]; soutenir; endosser [document]; renverser [steam]; reculer; *to back up*, faire marche arrière; soutenir; appuyer; *to backslide*, récidiver; *backache*, mal de reins; *backbite*, dénigrer, médire de; *backbone*, colonne vertébrale, épine dorsale, f.; *backfire*, retour de flamme; *background*, arrière-plan, fond; *backhanded*, déloyal, équivoque; *backhead*, *Am.* occiput; *backing*, appui, soutien, protection; *back-shop*, arrière-boutique; *backstairs*, escalier de service; *backstitch*, point arrière; *backwash*, remous, m. ‖ *backward* [-w°rd] *adj.* en retard; arriéré. ‖ *backwardness* [-w°rdnis] *s.* hésitation; lenteur d'intelligence, f.; défaut d'empressement, m. ‖ *backwards* [-w°rdz] *adv.* en arrière; à la renverse; à rebours.

bacon [bé¹k°n] *s.* lard, m.

bacteriology [baktiriâl°dji] *s.* bactériologie, f.

bad [bad] *adj.* mauvais, méchant; hostile, dangereux, insuffisant [price]; *bad-tempered*, acariâtre; *to look bad*, être mauvais signe; *to be on bad terms with*, être en mauvais termes avec. ‖ *badly* [-li] *adv.* méchamment; mal.

bade [bad] *pret. of* **to bid**.

badge [badj] *s.* insigne; brassard, m.; plaque [policeman], f.

badger [badj°r] *s.* blaireau, m.; *v.* harceler, tourmenter.

badness [badnis] *s.* méchanceté; mauvaise qualité, f.; mauvais état, m.

baffle [baf'l] *v.* déjouer [curiosity]; dérouter; *s.* défaite; chicane; cloison, f.; *baffle-board*, revêtement insonorisant. ‖ *baffling* [-ing] *adj.* déconcertant; *baffling winds*, brises folles.

bag [bag] *s.* sac, m.; valise, f.; *Am.* balle [cotton], f.; *v.* ensacher; chiper; tuer [hunt]; *money-bag*, porte-monnaie.

bagatelle [bag°tél] *s.* bagatelle, f.; divertissement musical; billard, m.

baggage [bagidj] *s.* bagages; équipement, m.; *baggage-car*, fourgon; *baggage-check*, bulletin de bagages; *baggage-tag*, étiquette; *baggage-truck*, chariot à bagages.

bagpipe [bagpa¹p] *s.* cornemuse, f.; *bagpiper*, joueur de cornemuse.

bail [bé¹l] *v.* seau, m.; *v.* vider; écoper (naut.); *to bail out of a plane*, sauter en parachute.

bail [bé¹l] *v.* libérer sous caution; se porter garant de; *s.* caution; liberté sous caution, f.; répondant, m.

bait [bé¹t] *v.* amorcer [fish]; harceler [person]; *s.* appât, m.

baize [bé¹z] *s.* feutrine, f.

bake [bé¹k] *v.* faire cuire au four; *s.* fournée, f.; *half-baked*, prématuré, inexpérimenté, mal fait. ‖ *baker* [-°r] *s.* boulanger; *Am.* petit four, m. ‖ *bakery* [-°ri] *s.* * boulangerie, f.; fournil, m. ‖ *baking* [-ing] *s.* cuisson, cuite, f.; *baking-pan*, tourtière; *baking-powder*, levure anglaise.

balance [bal°ns] *s.* balance, f.; stabilité; indécision, f.; équilibre; compte; bilan; solde [account]; reste, m.; *v.* balancer; équilibrer; solder [account]; *balance-beam*, fléau de balance; *balance-weight*, contrepoids.

balcony [balk°ni] *s.* * balcon, m.

bald [bauld] *adj.* chauve; dénudé; dépouillé; plat [style].

bale [bé¹l] *v.* écoper (naut.); *to bale out*, sauter en parachute.

bale [bé¹l] *s.* ballot [wares, cotton], m.; balle; botte [hay], f.; *v.* emballer.

baleful [bé¹lful] *adj.* nuisible, pernicieux, funeste.

baler [bé¹l°r] *s.* emballeur, m.

balk [bauk] *s.* déception; solive, f.; obstacle; contretemps, m.; *v.* faire obstacle à; contrarier; frustrer; se dérober [horse].

ball [baul] *s.* balle, f.; ballon, m.; boule; bille, f.; boulet, m.; balle [firearms]; boulette [flesh]; pelote [wool], f.; *abbrev. of* baseball; *goof balls*, barbituriques, m.; *v.* mettre en boule, en pelote; *to ball up*, échouer; embrouiller.

ball [baul] *s.* bal, m.
ballad [bal⁰d] *s.* ballade, f.; romance [music], f.
ballast [bal⁰st] *s.* lest; ballast, m.; *v.* lester, ballaster.
ballet [bale¹] *s.* ballet, m.; *ballet-girl,* danseuse, ballerine; *ballet-skirt,* tutu.
ballistics [b⁰lístiks] *s.* balistique, f.
balloon [b⁰loun] *s.* ballon; aérostat, m.; *balloon sleeve,* manche ballon.
ballot [bal⁰t] *s. Am.* bulletin de vote, m.; scrutin secret, m.; *v.* voter; élire; *ballot-box,* urne électorale; *ballot-paper,* bulletin de vote; *second ballot,* ballottage.
balm [bâm] *s.* baume, m.; *v.* embaumer. || *balmy* [-i] *adj.* embaumé; lénifiant; calmant; maboul (pop.).
baloney [b⁰loᵘni] *s. Am.* blague, foutaise, f.; boniment, m.
balsam [bauls⁰m] *s.* baume, m.; balsamine, f.
bamboo [bàmboᵘ] *s.* bambou, m. || *bamboozle* [bàmbouz'l] *v.* duper, tromper, « refaire ».
ban [bàn] *s.* ban; bannissement; embargo, m.; *v.* proscrire; maudire; *marriage ban(n)s,* publications de mariage, bans.
banana [b⁰nan⁰] *s.* banane, f.; *banana boat,* bananier [ship]; *banana tree,* bananier.
band [bànd] *s.* lien; bandage; ruban; orchestre; troupeau, m.; bande, bague [bird], f.; *v.* se liguer; grouper; baguer [bird]. || *bandage* [-idj] *s.* bandage; bandeau, m.; *v.* bander. || *band-box* [-bauks] *s.** carton à chapeau, m.; boîte (f.) à rubans.
bandit [bàndit] *s.* bandit, m.
bandy [bàndi] *v.* renvoyer; échanger; lutter; *adj.* arqué; *bandy-legged,* bancal.
bane [bé¹n] *s.* poison; fléau, m. || *baneful* [-foul] *adj.* empoisonné; pernicieux.
bang [bàng] *v.* cogner; claquer [door]; couper à la chien [hair]; *s.* coup; fracas, m.; détonation; frange [hair], f.; *interj.* pan!
banish [bànish] *v.* bannir; chasser. || *banishment* [-m⁰nt] *s.* exil, m.
banister [bànist⁰r] *s.* balustrade; rampe, f.
bank [bàngk] *s.* berge; digue, f.; talus; banc [sand], m.; *v.* couvrir [fire]; endiguer; faire un talus; virer [plane]; s'amonceler [snow].
bank [bàngk] *s.* banque, f.; *v.* mettre en banque; diriger une banque; *to bank on,* compter sur. || *banker* [-⁰r] *s.* banquier, m. || *banking* [-ing] *s.* opérations bancaires; profession de

banquier, f.; *adj.* bancaire. || *bank-note* [-noᵘt] *s.* billet de banque, m. || *bankrupt* [-rœpt] *s.* banqueroutier, m.; *adj.* en faillite; insolvable; *to go bankrupt,* faire faillite. || *bankruptcy* [-rœptsi] *s.** banqueroute, faillite, f.
banner [bàn⁰r] *s.* bannière, f.; étendard, m.; *Am. adj.* principal, exceptionnel; *banner headline,* titre flamboyant; *v. Am.* titrer en manchettes énormes.
banquet [bàngkwit] *s.* banquet, m.; *v.* banqueter.
banter [bànt⁰r] *v.* plaisanter; taquiner; *s.* plaisanterie; taquinerie, f.
banting [bànting] *s.* régime amaigrissant, m.
baptism [baptiz⁰m] *s.* baptême, m. || *baptize* [bapta¹z] *v.* baptiser.
bar [bâr] *s.* barre; barrière; buvette; mesure [music]; bande [flag], f.; obstacle; bar; lingot; barreau [law], m.; *v.* barrer; annuler; exclure; *to bar oneself in,* se barricader chez soi.
barb [bârb] *s.* barbe [arrow], f.; barbillon, m.; *v.* barbeler; barder; *barbed wire,* fil de fer barbelé.
barbarian [bârbèri⁰n] *adj., s.* barbare. || *barbarous* [bârb⁰r⁰s] *adj.* barbare.
barbecue [bârbikyou] *s. Am.* boucan, gril; animal rôti, m.; *v.* préparer le barbecue.
barbed [bârbd] *adj.* barbelé [wire]; acéré [word]. || *barber* [-b⁰r] *s.* barbier; coiffeur pour hommes, m.
barbiturate [barbityouré¹t] *s.* barbiturique, m. || *barbituric* [-rik] *adj.* barbiturique.
bard [bâ⁰rd] *s.* barde [poet.], m.; barde [bacon], f.; *v.* barder.
bare [bèr] *adj.* nu, dénudé; simple; démuni; manifeste; *v.* découvrir; dénuder; révéler; *barefaced,* éhonté; *barefoot(ed),* nu-pieds; *bare-headed,* nu-tête; *bare-legged,* nu-jambes. || *barely* [-li] *adv.* à peine, tout au plus. || *bareness* [-nis] *s.* nudité, f.; dénuement, m.
bargain [bârgin] *s.* marché, négoce, pacte, m.; emplette; occasion, f.; solde, m.; *v.* traiter; conclure; marchander; *into the bargain,* par-dessus le marché; *at bargain price,* à bas prix; *bargain day,* jour de solde; *bargain counter, Am.* rayon des soldes. || *bargaining* [-ing] *s.* marchandage, m.; négociations, f.
barge [bârdj] *s.* chaland, m.; *v. Am.* transporter par péniche. || *bargee* [ba⁰djî] *s.* marinier, m.
bark [bârk] *s.* écorce, f.; *v.* écorcer; décortiquer; écorcher [leg].
bark [bârk] *s.* aboiement, m.; *v.* aboyer.

barley [bârli] s. orge, f.

barm [bârm] s. levure de bière, f. ‖ **barmy** [-i] adj. écumeux; loufoque (fam.).

barn [bârn] s. grange, f.; grenier; hangar, m.; v. engranger; abriter sous hangar; *streetcar barn*, dépôt de tramways; *barnyard*, cour de ferme, basse-cour; *barn-stormer*, acteur ambulant; *Am.* orateur électoral.

barnacle [bâʳnᵉk'l] s. bernacle; barnacle, f.; crampon, m.

barometer [berâmᵉtᵉʳ] s. baromètre, m.

baron [barᵉn] s. baron, m.; *Am.* magnat de la finance ou du commerce, m. ‖ **baroness** [-is] s.* baronne, f.

barracks [barᵉks] s. caserne, f.; baraquements; abri agricole, m.

barrage [barâj] s. barrage, m.

barrel [barᵉl] s. baril, fût; canon [gun]; tambour [machine]; corps [pump], m.; caque [herring]; hampe [feather]; mesure [corn], f.; v. embariller; bomber [road]; *double-barrel(l)-ed*, à deux coups.

barren [barᵉn] adj. aride, stérile. ‖ **barrenness** [-nis] s. stérilité, f.

barrette [berᵉˡt] s. barrette, f.

barricade [barᵉkéˡd] s. barricade, f.; v. barricader.

barrier [bariᵉʳ] s. barrière, f.; obstacle, m.; limite, f.

barrister [baristᵉʳ] s. avocat, m.

barrow [baroᵘ] s. brouette, f.; diable [porter], m.; baladeuse [coster], f.; brancard, m.; civière, f.; v. brouetter.

barrow [baroᵘ] s. tumulus, m.

bartender [bâʳtendᵉʳ] s. barman, m.

barter [bâʳtᵉʳ] v. troquer; s. troc, m.

base [béˡs] adj. bas; vil. ‖ **baseness** [-nis] s. bassesse, f.

base [béˡs] s. base, f.; v. fonder; établir. ‖ **basement** [-mᵉnt] s. soubassement; sous-sol [story], m.

baseball [béˡsbaul] s. base-ball, m.

bash [bash] v. cogner; cabosser; s.* gnon, m.

bashful [bashfᵉl] adj. timide. ‖ **bashfulness** [-nis] s. timidité, f.

basic [béˡsik] adj. fondamental.

basin [béˡs'n] s. bassin, m.

basis [béˡsis] (pl. bases [béˡsiz]) s. base, f.; fondement, m.

bask [bask] v. se chauffer.

basket [baskit] s. panier, m.; corbeille, f.; *basket-maker*, vannier; *basket-work*, vannerie; *the pick of the basket*, le dessus du panier, l'élite; v. mettre dans un panier; clisser [bottle]. ‖ **basket-ball** [-baul] s. basket(-ball) [game], m.

bass [béˡs] s.* basse [music], contrebasse, f.; adj. grave [music]; *bass-horn*, cor de basset.

bass [bas] s.* bar [fish], m.; perche [fish], f.; *black bass*, *Fr. Can.* achigan, m.; *calico bass*, *Fr. Can.* crapet calicot, m.; *rock bass*, *Fr. Can.* crapet gris, m.

basset [basit] s. basset, m.

bastard [bastᵉrd] adj., s. bâtard. ‖ **bastardize** [-a¹z] v. (s')abâtardir.

baste [béˡst] v. arroser (culin.).

baste [béˡst] v. bâtir [to sew].

baste [béˡst] v. bâtonner, battre.

bat [bat] s. bâton, m.; crosse, f.; battoir [cricket], m.; v. frapper.

bat [bat] s. chauve-souris, f.

bat [bat] v. *Am.* cligner.

batch [batsh] s.* fournée, grande quantité, f.; tas, m.; v. réunir.

bath [bath] s. bain, m.; *bath-house*, cabine de bain; *bath-robe*, peignoir de bain; *bathroom*, salle de bains; *bath-tub*, baignoire. ‖ **bathe** [béˡzh] v. se baigner. ‖ **bather** [-ᵉʳ] s. baigneur, m. ‖ **bathing** [-ing] s. baignade, f.

baton [batᵉn] s. bâton, m.; baguette, f.

battalion [betaly°n] s. bataillon, m.

batter [batᵉʳ] s. pâte, f.

batter [batᵉʳ] s. batteur [baseball], m.; *Fr. Can.* frappeur, m.; v. frapper, heurter; démolir; bossuer; délabrer; taper sur (mil.); *battering gun*, pièce de siège.

battery [bateri] s.* batterie, f.

battle [bat'l] s. bataille, f.; combat, m.; v. combattre; se battre; *battledress*, tenue de campagne; *battlefield*, champ de bataille, f. ‖ **battlement** [-mᵉnt] s. créneau, m.; pl. remparts, m. pl. ‖ **battleship** [-ship] s. cuirassé, m.

bawd [baud] s. proxénète, m., f. ‖ **bawdy** [-i] adj. obscène, ordurier.

bawl [baul] s. cri, m.; v. crier; proclamer; *to bawl out*, enguirlander (fam.).

bay [béˡ] s. baie, f.; *bay-tree*, laurier; *bay-window*, fenêtre, baie.

bay [béˡ] s. abois, m.; *to stand at bay*, être aux abois.

bay [béˡ] adj. bai [color].

bayonet [béˡenit] s. baïonnette, f.; v. attaquer à la baïonnette.

bazaar [bezâr] s. bazar, m.; vente, f.

be [bî] v.* être; se porter, se trouver; *I am well*, je vais bien; *I am hungry*, j'ai faim; *it is fine*, il fait beau; *the hall is twenty feet long*, la salle a vingt pieds de long; *to be born*, naître; *how much is that?*, combien coûte cela ?

beach [bîtsh] *s.** plage; rive; grève, f.; *v.* tirer à sec; *beachcomber,* clochard; *beached,* échoué; *beach-head,* tête de pont.

beacon [bîkᵉn] *s.* signal, m.; balise, f.; phare, m.; *v.* baliser; signaliser.

bead [bîd] *s.* grain (rosary), m.; perle [necklace]; mire [gun]; goutte [sweat], f.; *pl.* chapelet, m.; *v.* orner de perles; *to bead with,* émailler de; *Am. to draw a bead on,* coucher en joue.

beadle [bîd'l] *s.* huissier, appariteur, m.; bedeau, m. ‖ *beadledom* [-daum] *s.* bureaucratie, f.

beak [bîk] *s.* bec [bird], m.; proue [ship], f.; *beak-iron,* bigorne.

beam [bîm] *s.* poutre, f.; fléau [balance]; timon; bau [ship]; rayon [light]; éclat; rayonnement, m.; *v.* briller; rayonner; émettre; *radio beam,* signal par radio. ‖ *beaming* [-ing] *adj.* radieux; rayonnant.

bean [bîn] *s.* fève, f.; haricot; grain [coffee], m.; *green beans, French beans,* haricots verts.

bear [bèr] *s.* ours; baissier [market price], m.; *bear-pit,* fosse aux ours; *ant-bear,* tamanoir.

bear [bèr] *v.** porter; supporter; rapporter; peser sur; *to bear upon,* avoir du rapport; *to bear out,* confirmer; *to bear up,* résister; *to bear with,* excuser; avoir de la patience; *to bear five per cent,* rapporter cinq pour cent; *to bring to bear,* mettre en jeu. ‖ *bearer* [-ᵉʳ] *s.* porteur; support, m.; *ensign-bearer,* porte-drapeau; *fruit-bearer,* arbre fruitier; *stretcher-bearer,* brancardier; *tale-bearer,* cancanier. ‖ *bearing* [-ing] *s.* endurance; relation; applicabilité, f.; relèvement (naut.), m.; conduite, f.; *pl.* tenants et aboutissants, m.; situation, position, f.; *adj.* porteur; productif; *to take bearings,* faire le point [ship]; *child-bearing,* gestation.

beard [bîᵉrd] *s.* barbe, f.; *v.* tirer par la barbe; défier, braver, narguer; *white-beard,* barbon. ‖ *bearded* [-id] *adj.* barbu; *bearded lady,* femme à barbe. ‖ *beardless* [-lis] *adj.* imberbe.

beast [bîst] *s.* bête, f.; animal, m.

beat [bît] *v.** battre; frapper; *s.* battement, m.; pulsation; batterie [drum]; ronde, tournée, f.; *to beat back,* refouler; *to beat in,* enfoncer; *Am. to beat it,* filer, décamper; *that beats everything !,* ça c'est le comble !; *adj.* épuisé, fourbu; *to beat up,* battre, fouetter [eggs]; *dead beat,* éreinté. ‖ *beaten* [-'n] *p. p. of to beat;* *adj.* battu; rebattu. ‖ *beater* [-ᵉʳ] *s.*

batteur; rabatteur; *Am.* vainqueur, m.; *egg-beater,* fouet (culin.); *drumbeater,* tambour [man]. ‖ *beating* [-ing] *s.* battement, m.; raclée; défaite, f.; louvoyage (naut.), m.; *adj.*, *pr. p.* palpitant.

beatitude [biatᵉtyoud] *s.* béatitude, f.

beau [boᵒ] *s.* galant, amoureux, prétendant, m. ‖ *beauteous* [byoutiᵉs] *adj.* beau, belle; accompli. ‖ *beautiful* [byoutᵉfᵉl] *adj.* beau, belle; admirable. ‖ *beautify* [byoutᵉfa¹] *v.* embellir. ‖ *beauty* [byouti] *s.** beauté, f.; *beauty-spot,* grain de beauté; *that's the beauty of it,* c'est le plus beau de l'affaire.

beaver [bîvᵉr] *adj.*, *s.* castor, m.; *beavertree,* magnolia, m.

became [bikéᵊm] *pret. of to become.*

because [bikauz] *conj.* parce que; car; *adv. because of,* à cause de.

beck [bèk] *s.* signe, appel, m.; *at s.o.'s beck and call,* aux ordres de qqn. ‖ *beckon* [bèkᵉn] *v.* faire signe.

become [bikᵉm] *v.** devenir; convenir [suit]; aller bien à; *to become red,* rougir; *to become warm,* s'échauffer; *what has become of you?,* qu'êtes-vous devenu ? ‖ *becoming* [-ing] *adj.* convenable; seyant.

bed [bèd] *s.* lit, m.; plate-bande, f.; gisement; banc [oyster], m.; couche, f.; *v.* coucher; reposer; *ill in bed,* alité; *to tuck up the bed,* border le lit; *sick-bed,* lit de douleur; *single bed,* lit à une place; *double bed,* lit à deux places; *bedbug,* punaise; *bedclothes,* linge de lit; *bed-quilt,* couvre-pieds piqué; *bedside,* chevet; *bed-spring,* ressort du sommier; *folding-bedstead,* lit pliant; *bedtime,* heure du coucher. ‖ *bedded* [-id] *adj.* couché. ‖ *bedding* [-ing] *s.* literie, f.

bee [bî] *s.* abeille, f.; *Am.* réunion de travail, f.; *bee-bread,* pollen; *bee-culture,* apiculture; *bee-garden,* rucher; *bee-hive,* ruche; *to have a bee in one's bonnet,* avoir une araignée au plafond.

beech [bîtsh] *s.** hêtre, m.; *beech-nut,* faine.

beef [bîf] *s.* viande de bœuf, f.; *v. Am.* tuer un bovin; gémir; rouspéter; *beefsteak,* bifteck; *corned-beef,* bœuf salé; *roast beef,* rosbif. ‖ *beefy* [-i] *adj.* costaud; rougeaud.

been [bîn, bèn] *p. p. of to be.*

beer [bîᵉr] *s.* bière, f.; *beer-pull, beer-pump,* pompe à bière.

beet [bît] *s.* bette; betterave, f.; *sugar-beet,* betterave sucrière; *beet-radish,* betterave rouge.

beetle [bît'l] *s.* demoiselle [paving], f.; pilon, m.; *v.* pilonner.

beetle [bīt'l] *s.* escargot, scarabée, m.; *black-beetle*, cafard.

beetle [bīt'l] *v.* surplomber; *beetle-browed*, aux sourcils proéminents.

befall [bifaul] *v.* arriver à, échoir à; avoir lieu. || *befallen*, p. p.; *befell*, pret. of to befall.

befit [bifit] *v.* convenir. || *befitting* [-ing] *adj.* convenable.

before [bifoour] *adv.* avant; devant; auparavant; *conj.* avant que; *before long*, avant peu, sans tarder. || *beforehand* [-hand] *adv.* d'avance; au préalable; à l'avance.

befriend [bifrènd] *v.* traiter en ami; favoriser; venir en aide à.

beg [bèg] *v.* prier; solliciter; mendier; *I beg your pardon*, je vous demande pardon; *to beg the question*, faire une pétition de principe.

began [bigœn] *pret. of to begin.*

beget [bigèt] *v.* engendrer; causer.

beggar [bègᵉʳ] *s.* mendiant, m.; *v.* réduire à la mendicité, ruiner. || *begging* [bèging] *s.* mendicité, f.

begin [bigin] *v.* commencer; débuter; se mettre à; *to begin with*, pour commencer, d'abord. || *beginner* [-ᵉʳ] *s.* commençant; débutant, m. || *beginning* [-ing] *s.* commencement, début, m.; origine, f.; fait initial, m.

begot [bigàt] *pret., p. p. of to beget.* || *begotten*, p. p. of to beget.

begrudge [bigrædj] *v.* donner à contrecœur; envier; lésiner sur.

beguile [bigaïl] *v.* tromper, séduire.

begun [bigœn] *p. p. of to begin.*

behalf [bihaf] *s.* sujet, intérêt, m.; cause, f.; *in his behalf*, en sa faveur; *on behalf of*, au nom de.

behave [bihéïv] *v.* se conduire; se comporter; *behave!*, sois sage! || *behavio(u)r* [-yᵉʳ] *s.* comportement, m.; tenue; manières, f.

behead [bihèd] *v.* décapiter.

beheld [bihèld] *pret., p. p. of to behold.*

behemoth [b'hīmauth] *s.* hippopotame, m.

behind [bihaïnd] *adv.* arrière; derrière; en arrière; en réserve, de côté; *prep.* derrière; *behindhand*, en retard; *s.* arrière [baseball], m.

behold [bihoould] *v.* regarder; contempler; *interj.* voyez! voici! || *beholden* [-'n] *adj.*, p. p. obligé, redevable. || *beholder* [-ᵉʳ] *s.* spectateur, m.; spectatrice, f.

behove [bihouv] *v.* incomber, être du devoir de; être utile (*to*, à).

being [bīïng] *s.* être, m.; existence, f.; *pr. p.* étant; *adj.* existant.

belated [bilétid] *adj.* attardé; en retard; tardif.

belay [biléï] *v.* amarrer; *Am.* arrêter, cesser (colloq.).

belch [bèltsh] *v.* roter; vomir; *Am.* rouspéter, râler (fam.); *s.** éructation, f.

beleaguer [bilīgᵉʳ] *v.* assiéger.

belfry [bèlfri] *s.** beffroi; clocher, m.

Belgian [bèldjiᵉn] *adj.*, *s.* belge.

Belgium [bèldjiᵉm] *s.* Belgique, f.

belie [bilaï] *v.* démentir.

belief [bilīf] *s.* croyance; foi; conviction; opinion, f. || *believable* [bilīvᵉb'l] *adj.* croyable. || *believe* [bilīv] *v.* croire, avoir foi en. || *believer* [-ᵉʳ] *s.* croyant; convaincu, m. || *believing* [-ing] *adj.* croyant; crédule.

belittle [bilit'l] *v.* déprécier; dévaloriser; discréditer. || *belittling* [-ing] *s.* discrédit, m.; dépréciation, f.

bell [bèl] *s.* cloche; clochette; sonnette, f.; *bellboy*, groom d'hôtel; *bell-flower*, campanule; *bell-tower*, beffroi, clocher; *call-bell*, timbre; *jingle-bell*, grelot.

bell [bèl] *v.* bramer.

belle [bèl] *s.* belle, beauté, f.

bellied [bèlid] *adj.* pot-bellied, ventru.

belligerent [bilidjᵉrᵉnt] *adj.*, *s.* belligérant.

bellow [bèloou] *v.* mugir, beugler; hurler; *s.* mugissement, hurlement, m.

bellows [bèlouz] *s.* soufflet, m.

belly [bèli] *s.** ventre; estomac, m.; *v.* gonfler; s'enfler.

belong [bilaung] *v.* appartenir; incomber à; être le propre de; *to belong here*, être à sa place ici, être du pays. || *belongings* [-ingz] *s.* effets, m.; affaires; possessions, f.

beloved [bilœvid] *adj.* bien-aimé.

below [beloou] *adv.* au-dessous; en bas; en aval; ci-dessous; *prep.* au-dessous de; sous; *here below*, ici-bas.

belt [bèlt] *s.* ceinture, f.; ceinturon; bandage (med.), m.; courroie (mech.); zone (geogr.), f.; *v.* ceindre; ceinturer; *belt-line*, ligne de ceinture; *belt-work*, travail à la chaîne.

bemoan [bimooun] *v.* se lamenter.

bench [bèntsh] *s.** banc, m.; banquette, f.; tribunal, m.; magistrature, f.; gradin, m.

bend [bènd] *s.* courbure, f.; tournant [road]; nœud [rope]; pli [limb], salut, m.; inclinaison, f.; *v.** courber, plier; bander [bow]; fléchir [will]; diriger [steps]; fixer [eyes]; appliquer [mind]; enverguer [sail]; se courber; se soumettre à.

beneath [binîth] *prep.* sous; au-dessous de; *adv.* au-dessous : *it is beneath you*, c'est indigne de vous.

benediction [bèn°dîkshen] *s.* bénédiction, f.

benefactor [bèn°faktər] *s.* bienfaiteur, m. ‖ **benefactress** [bèn°faktris] *s.* bienfaitrice, f.

benefice [bén°fis] *s.* bénéfice, m. ‖ **beneficent** [bènèf°s'nt] *adj.* bienfaisant. ‖ **beneficial** [bèn°fishel] *adj.* avantageux; salutaire. ‖ **benefit** [bèn°fit] *s.* profit; bienfait; avantage, m.; *v.* profiter à, être avantageux pour; profiter, tirer profit; *benefit society*, société de secours mutuel; *for the benefit of*, au profit de.

benevolence [bènèv°lens] *s.* bienveillance, f. ‖ **benevolent** [benèvelent] *adj.* bienveillant; charitable [institution].

benign [bina¹n] *adj.* bénin; doux; affable. ‖ **benignant** [b°nignent] *adj.* doux, bienfaisant.

bent [bènt] *s.* penchant, m.; inclination; tendance, f.; *pret., p. p. of to bend*; *adj.* courbé; Fr. Can. croche; penché; tendu [mind]; *to be bent on*, être décidé à.

bequeath [bikwîzh] *v.* léguer. ‖ **bequest** [bikwèst] *s.* legs, m.

bereave [birîv] *v.* priver; perdre, être en deuil de.

berry [bèri] *s.* baie [fruit], f.; grain [coffee], m.

berth [bërth] *s.* couchette [sleeping-car]; cabine [ship], f.; mouillage (naut.); emplacement (naut.), m.; *v.* placer à quai; *to give a wide berth to*, se tenir à l'écart de.

beseech [bisîtsh] *v.* supplier.

beset [bisèt] *v.* assaillir; parsemer; *besetting sin*, péché mignon.

beside [bisa¹d] *prep.* à côté de; hors de; *beside oneself*, hors de soi; *beside the mark*, hors de propos; à côté du but. ‖ **besides** [-z] *adv.* d'ailleurs; en outre; en plus; de plus; *prep.* outre.

besiege [bisîdj] *v.* assiéger. ‖ **besieger** [-er] *s.* assaillant, m.

besmear [bismier] *v.* souiller, barbouiller.

besot [bisaut] *v.* abrutir, hébéter.

besought [bisaut] *pret., p. p. of to beseech*.

bespeak [bispîk] *v.* commander [meal]; réserver [room]; faire prévoir; prouver; *bespoke tailor*, tailleur à façon.

besprinkle [bispringk'l] *v.* asperger; saupoudrer; parsemer.

best [bèst] *adj.* meilleur; le meilleur; le mieux; *to have the best of*, avoir le dessus, l'avantage; *as best I could*, de mon mieux; *in one's best*, sur son trente et un; *to make the best of*, tirer le meilleur parti de; *best-seller*, livre à succès.

bestow [bisto°u] *v.* accorder, donner; consacrer à.

bestride [bistra¹d] *v.* monter; chevaucher; enjamber.

bet [bèt] *v.* parier; *s.* pari, m.

betake [bité¹k] *v.* se rendre (à); avoir recours à; se mettre à. ‖ **betaken** [bité¹k'n] *p. p. of to betake.*

betoken [bito°uk'n] *v.* annoncer; présager; dénoter; révéler.

betook [bitouk] *pret. of to betake.*

betray [bitré¹] *v.* trahir; tromper. ‖ **betrayal** [-el] *s.* trahison, f. ‖ **betrayer** [-er] *s.* traître, m.

betrothal [bitrauthel] *s.* fiançailles, f. ‖ **betrothed** [bitrautht] *s.* fiancé, m.; fiancée, f.

better [bèter] *adj.* meilleur; *adv.* mieux; *v.* améliorer; *s.* supériorité, f.; *pl.* supérieurs, m.; *you had better*, vous feriez mieux; *so much the better*, tant mieux; *to know better*, être fixé; *all the better because*, d'autant mieux que; **betterment**, amélioration, f.

betting [béting] *s.* pari, m.

between [betwîn], **betwixt** [betwikst] *prep.* entre; *adv.* parmi; entre; *between-decks*, entrepont; *between-season*, demi-saison; *betweenwhiles*, dans l'intervalle, de temps en temps.

bevel [bév'l] *s.* biseau; biveau, m.; *adj.* de biais, oblique; *v.* biseauter.

beverage [bévridj] *s.* boisson, f.

bewail [biwé¹l] *v.* se lamenter; déplorer.

beware [biwèr] *v.* prendre garde; *interj.* attention !

bewilder [biwilder] *v.* affoler; dérouter, déconcerter. ‖ **bewilderment** [-ment] *s.* affolement, m.

bewitch [biwitsh] *v.* ensorceler; captiver. ‖ **bewitcher** [-er] *s.* ensorceleur, m. ‖ **bewitchment** [-ment] *s.* ensorcellement; enchantement, m.

beyond [biyånd] *adv.* au-delà; là-bas; *prep.* au-delà de, outre; en dehors de; *the house beyond*, la maison d'à côté; *it is beyond me*, ça me dépasse.

bias [ba¹es] *s.* biais, m.; tendance, f.; préjugé, m.; *adj.* de biais, oblique; *adv.* obliquement; *v.* influencer, détourner; biaiser.

bib [bib] *s.* bavette, f.; *v.* siroter.

Bible [ba¹b'l] *s.* Bible, f. ‖ **biblical** [bíblik'l] *adj.* biblique.

bibliography [bibli'augrefi] *s.* bibliographie. || *bibliophile* [-fa¹l] *s.* bibliophile, m., f.

biceps [ba¹seps] *s.* biceps, m.

bicker [bikᵉʳ] *v.* se chamailler; couler vite. || *bickering* [-ring] *s.* dispute, bisbille, prise (f.) de bec.

bicycle [ba¹sik'l] *s.* bicyclette, f.; *v.* aller à bicyclette. || *bicyclist* [-ist] *s.* cycliste, m., f.

bid [bid] *v.** inviter; ordonner; offrir [price]; demander; souhaiter; *s.* offre; enchère; invitation; demande [cards], f.; *to bid the ban(n)s,* publier les bans; *to call for bids,* mettre en adjudication; *the last bid,* la dernière mise. || *bidden* [bidᵉn] *p. p. of* **to bid**, **to bide**. || *bidding* [-ing] *s.* ordre, m.; enchères, f. pl.

bide [ba¹d] *v.* attendre; endurer; résider; *to bide one's time,* attendre le moment favorable.

biennial [ba¹énial] *adj.* biennal.

bier [bîr] *s.* civière, f.; cercueil, m.

bifurcate [ba¹fᵉrké¹t] *v.* bifurquer. || *bifurcation* [ba¹fᵉrké¹shᵉn] *s.* bifurcation, f.

big [big] *adj.* gros; grand; important; *to talk big,* le prendre de haut; faire le fanfaron; *Br.* big-end, *Am.* big-head, tête de bielle [auto]. || *bigness* [-nis] *s.* grosseur, grande taille, f.

bigamist [bigᵉmist] *s.* bigame, m. || *bigamous* [-ᵉs] *adj.* bigame.

bigot [bigᵉt] *s.* bigot; fanatique, m. || *bigotry* [-tri] *s.* bigoterie, f.

bike [ba¹k] *s. Am.* bécane, f.; *v.* aller à bicyclette.

bilberry [bìlbèri] *s.** myrtille, f.; *Fr. Can.* bleuet, m.

bile [ba¹l] *s.* bile; colère, f.; bile-cyst, vésicule biliaire; bile-stone, calcul biliaire.

bilge [bildj] *s.* fond de cale, m.

bilingual [ba¹lingwᵉl] *adj.* bilingue. || *bilingualism* [-iz'm] *s.* bilinguisme, m.

bilious [bìlyᵉs] *adj.* bilieux; colérique; *bilious attack,* embarras gastrique.

bill [bil] *s.* facture; addition [restaurant]; note [hotel]; traite, f.; billet à ordre (comm.), m.; *Am.* billet de banque; projet de loi, m.; affiche [theatre], f.; programme [theatre], m.; état, m.; table, f.; *v.* facturer; faire un compte; établir une liste; annoncer par affiche; *bill of fare,* menu; *bill of exchange,* lettre de change; *to discount a bill,* escompter un effet; *to settle a bill,* régler une note; *billboard,* tableau d'affichage.

billet [bìlit] *s.* billet, m.; lettre, f.; billet de logement, m.; *v.* donner un billet de logement; loger.

billiards [bìlyᵉrdz] *s.* billard, m.

billion [bìlyᵉn] *s.* billion, m.; *Am.* milliard, m.

billow [bìloᵘ] *s.* vagues; houle, f.; *v.* ondoyer. || *billowy* [bìlᵉwi] *adj.* houleux; ondoyant.

bin [bìn] *s.* coffre, m.; caisse; huche, f.; casier, m.; *v.* ranger en caisse.

binary [ba¹nᵉri] *adj.* binaire.

bind [ba¹nd] *v.** attacher; lier; obliger, forcer; relier [book]. || *binding* [-ing] *s.* reliure, f.; lien, m.; *adj.* obligatoire; *cloth-binding,* reliure en toile.

bindweed [ba¹ndwînd] *s.* liseron, m.

biographer [ba¹ágrᵉfᵉr] *s.* biographe, m., f. || *biography* [-grᵉfi] *s.** biographie, f.

biologist [ba¹álᵉdjist] *s.* biologiste, m., f. || *biology* [-lᵉdji] *s.* biologie, f.

biopsy [ba¹ápsi] *s.* biopsie, f.

birch [bᵉrtsh] *s.** bouleau, m.; verges, f. pl.; *v.* fouetter.

bird [bᵉrd] *s.* oiseau, m.; *early bird,* personne matinale; *bird-lime,* glu; *bird's eye view,* vue à vol d'oiseau.

birth [bᵉrth] *s.* naissance, f.; enfantement, m.; origine, f.; commencement, m.; extraction, f.; *birth certificate,* acte de naissance; *birth-control,* limitation des naissances; *birthday,* anniversaire; *birthplace,* pays natal; *birthrate,* natalité; *birthright,* droit d'aînesse.

biscuit [biskit] *s.* biscuit, m.

bishop [bìshᵉp] *s.* évêque; fou [chess], m. || *bishopric* [-ric] *s.* évêché; épiscopat, m.

bit [bit] *s.* morceau; fragment, m.; mèche [tool], f.; mors [horse], m.; *adv.* un peu; *to champ at the bit,* ronger son frein; *a good bit older,* sensiblement plus âgé; *not a bit,* pas un brin; *pret., p. p. of* **to bite**.

bistoury [bistouri] *s.** bistouri, m.

bistre [bistᵉr] *adj., s.* bistre.

bitch [bitsh] *s.** chienne; femelle; garce, f.

bite [ba¹t] *v.** mordre; piquer [insect]; *s.* morsure, piqûre; bouchée, f. || *bitten* [bitᵉn] *p. p. of* **to bite**.

bitter [bitᵉr] *adj.* amer; âpre; aigre; mordant; cruel; *s. pl.* amers [drink], m. || *bitterly* [-li] *adv.* amèrement, violemment; extrêmement. || *bitterness* [-nis] *s.* amertume; irritation; violence; hostilité; acuité, f. || *bittersweet* [-swit] *s.* douce-amère, f.; *adj.* aigre-doux.

bitumen [bítyoumin] *s.* bitume, m.

bivouac [bívouak] *s.* bivouac, m.; *v.* bivouaquer.

bizarre [bizâr] *adj.* bizarre.

black [blak] *adj.* noir; obscur; sombre; poché [eye]; sinistre, mauvais; *s.* nègre. Noir, m.; *v.* noircir, dénigrer; *Black Monday*, lundi de Pâques; *black-out*, camouflage des lumières. ‖ *blackberry* [-bèrì] *s.* mûre, f. ‖ *blackbird* [-bë͞rd] *s.* merle, m. ‖ *blackboard* [boourd] *s.* tableau noir, m. ‖ *blacken* [-ₑn] *v.* noircir, dénigrer. ‖ *blackjack* [-djak] *s.* Am. assommoir; vingt-et-un [cards], m. ‖ *blackleg* [-lèg] *s.* Br. escroc, tricheur; jaune [strikebreaker], m. ‖ *blackmail* [-mé¹l] *s.* chantage, m.; *v.* faire chanter. ‖ *blackmailer* [-mé¹lₑʳ] *s.* maître chanteur, m. ‖ *blackness* [-nis] *s.* noirceur; couleur noire, f. ‖ *black-pudding* [-pouding] *s.* boudin, m. ‖ *blacksmith* [-smith] *s.* forgeron, m. ‖ *blackthorn* [-thaurn] *s.* prunellier, m. ‖ *blacky* [-i] *s.* Noir; moricaud (pop.), m.

bladder [bladₑʳ] *s.* vessie; vésicule, f.

blade [blé¹d] *s.* feuille; lame [knife], f.; brin [grass]; plat [oar], m.; palette [propeller]; aile d'hélice, f.; *shoulder-blade*, omoplate.

blain [blé¹n] *s.* pustule, f.

blamable [blé¹mₑb'l] *adj.* blâmable. ‖ *blame* [blé¹m] *s.* blâme, m.; *v.* blâmer; reprocher. ‖ *blameless* [-lis] *adj.* irréprochable. ‖ *blameworthy* [blé¹-mₑ-wêrdi] *adj.* blâmable, fautif.

blanch [blàntsh] *v.* blanchir.

bland [blànd] *adj.* doux; aimable.

blandish [blandìsh] *v.* cajoler, aduler.

blank [blàngk] *adj.* blanc; dénudé; vide; vain; en blanc; à blanc; complet, total; blanc, non rimé [verse]; *s.* blanc, m.; lacune, f.; vide, trou, m.; *to look blank*, avoir l'air confondu.

blanket [blàngkit] *s.* couverture, f.; *v.* couvrir; *Am.* inclure sous une rubrique générale; étouffer [scandal]; *blanket ballot*, bulletin électoral général; *blanket statement*, propos (or) énoncé général.

blare [blèr] *v.* retentir; résonner; proclamer; *s.* bruit, fracas, m.

blarney [blâni] *s.* boniment, m.; flagornerie, f.; *v.* embobeliner, flagorner.

blasé [blâzé¹] *adj.* blasé.

blaspheme [blasfîm] *v.* blasphémer. ‖ *blasphemy* [blasfimi] *s.** blasphème, m.

blast [blast] *s.* rafale [wind], f.; éclat [trumpet], m.; explosion [dynamite], f.; souffle [bomb], m.; *v.* exploser; détruire; flétrir [reputation]; *blast furnace*, haut fourneau; *blasting-oil*, nitroglycérine.

blatancy [blé¹t'nsi] *s.* vulgarité, f. ‖ *blatant* [-ₑnt] *adj.* criard; voyant; flagrant, criant.

blaze [blé¹z] *s.* flamme, f.; éclat, m.; *v.* flamber, resplendir; marquer [trees]; *in a blaze*, en feu. ‖ *blazer* [-ₑʳ] *s.* blazer; bobard, m.; *Am.* casserole, f.

blazon [blé¹zₑn] *s.* blason, m.; parade, f.; *v.* blasonner; claironner.

bleach [blîtsh] *v.* blanchir; pâlir. ‖ *bleacher* [-ₑʳ] *s.* blanchisseur, m.; *pl.* *Am.* gradins, m.

bleak [blîk] *adj.* froid, venteux; désolé, lugubre; désert; morne.

blear [blier] *adj.* chassieux [eyes]; indistinct, indécis [outline]; imprécis [mind].

bleat [blît] *v.* bêler; *s.* bêlement, m.

bled [blèd] *pret., p. p. of to bleed*. ‖ *bleed* [blîd] *v.* saigner. ‖ *bleeding* [-ing] *s.* saignement, m.; saignée; hémorragie, f.

blemish [blèmish] *v.* ternir; flétrir; souiller; *s.** défaut, m.; faute, tache, imperfection, f.

blench [blèntsh] *v.* reculer; éviter, fuir; broncher.

blench [blèntsh] *v.* blêmir; pâlir; faire pâlir.

blend [blènd] *s.* mélange, m.; *v.* mélanger, mêler; dégrader [colors]; fondre [sounds]; harmoniser; se mélanger. ‖ *blending* [-ing] *s.* mélange, m.

bless [blès] *v.* bénir. ‖ *blessed* [-id] *adj.* béni; saint; bienheureux; [blèst] *pret., p. p. of to bless*. ‖ *blessing* [-ing] *s.* bénédiction; grâce, f.; bienfait, m.

blest, *see blessed*.

blew [blou] *pret. of to blow*.

blight [bla¹t] *s.* nielle [corn]; rouille; influence perverse, f.; *v.* brouir; gâcher; ruiner [hope].

blind [bla¹nd] *adj.* aveugle; *s.* persiennes; œillère [horse], f.; abat-jour; prétexte; store; masque, m.; *v.* aveugler; *blind lantern*, lanterne sourde; *stone-blind*, complètement aveugle. ‖ *blinder* [-ₑʳ] *s.* œillère; *Am.* persienne, f. ‖ *blindfold* [-foould] *v.* aveugler; bander les yeux à; *adj.* qui a les yeux bandés; *s.* ruse, f. ‖ *blindly* [-li] *adv.* à l'aveuglette. ‖ *blindness* [-nis] *s.* cécité, f.; aveuglement, m. ‖ *blindworm* [-wêrm] *s.* orvet, m.

blink [blingk] *v.* clignoter; cligner des yeux; fermer les yeux sur; *s.* coup d'œil; clignotement, aperçu, m.; lueur, f. ‖ *blinker* [-ₑʳ] *s.* œillère, f. (autom.) clignotant, m. ‖ *blinking* [-ing] *adj.* clignotant; vacillant [flame].

bliss [blís] *s.* félicité; béatitude, f. ‖
blissful [-fᵉl] *adj.* bienheureux. ‖
blissfulness [-fᵉlnis] *s.* béatitude, f.;
bonheur total, m.

blister [blísteʳ] *s.* pustule; ampoule;
boursouflure, f.; *v.* boursoufler.

blithe [blaⁱzh] *adj.* gai; heureux. ‖
blitheness [-nis] *s.* joie, gaieté, f.

blizzard [blízᵉrd] *s.* tempête de
neige; *Fr. Can.* poudrerie, f.; *Am.* attaque violente.

bloat [bloᵘt] *v.* enfler; se gonfler;
adj. Am. prétentieux, « gonflé »; mé-
téorisant [cattle]. ‖ **bloater** [-ᵉʳ] *s.*
hareng saur, m.

block [blâk] *s.* bloc; pâté, îlot
[houses], m.; forme [hat], f.; encombrement, m.; *v.* bloquer; encombrer;
block writing, écriture en lettres d'imprimerie.

blockade [blâké¹d] *s.* blocus; *Am.*
blocage, m.; obstruction, f.; *v.* bloquer, obstruer. ‖ **blockhead** [blâkèd]
s. lourdaud; imbécile, m.

blond(e) [blând] *adj., s.* blond(e).

blood [blœd] *s.* sang, m.; *v.* acharner
[hound]; donner le baptême du sang;
blood bank, banque du sang; *blood
count,* numération globulaire; *blood
group,* groupe sanguin; *blood pressure,* tension artérielle; *blood-sugar,*
glycémie; *blood test,* examen du sang;
blood typing Am. recherche du
groupe sanguin; *blood vessel,* vaisseau sanguin. ‖ **blooded** [-id] *adj.* de
race, pur sang. ‖ **bloodshed** [-shèd] *s.*
effusion de sang, f. ‖ **bloodshot** [-shât]
adj. injecté de sang. ‖ **bloodthirsty**
[-thë̈ʳsti] *adj.* sanguinaire. ‖ **blood-
sucker** [-sœkᵉʳ] *s.* sangsue, f. ‖
bloody [-i] *adj.* sanglant; ensanglanté.

bloom [bloum] *s.* fleur; floraison, f.;
incarnat, m.; *v.* fleurir, s'épanouir. ‖
bloomer [-ᵉʳ] *s.* gaffe, bourde, f. ‖
blooming [-ing] *adj.* en fleur, florissant; *s.* floraison, f.

blossom [blâsᵉm] *s.* fleur, f.;
épanouissement, m.; *Am.* variété de
quartz; *v.* fleurir, s'épanouir.

blot [blât] *s.* tache, f.; pâté [ink],
m.; rature; faute, erreur, f.; *v.* tacher; maculer; buvarder.

blotch [blâtsh] *s.** pustule; éclaboussure; tache, f.; *v.* tacher.

blotter [blâteʳ] *s.* buvard, m.; brouillard (comm.); *Am.* livre de po-
lice, m. ‖ **blotting** [-ing] *adj.* qui
sèche; *blotting-pad,* sous-main; *blotting paper,* buvard.

blouse [blaᵘs] *s.* blouse, chemisette,
f.; chemisier, corsage, m.

blow [bloᵘ] *v.** fleurir, s'ouvrir.

blow [bloᵘ] *v.** souffler; sonner
[trumpet]; s'envoler; *Am.* déguerpir;

s. coup; soufflement; coup de vent,
m.; *to blow a fuse,* faire sauter un
plomb; *to blow one's nose,* se moucher; *to blow out,* éteindre; éclater
[tire]. ‖ **blower** [-ᵉʳ] *s.* souffleur, ventilateur, m.; soufflerie, f. ‖ **blown** [-n]
p. p. of **to blow.**

blowout [bloᵘaᵒᵘt] *s.* éclatement,
m.; crevaison [tire]; ventrée, f.

blowpipe [bloᵘpaⁱp] *s.* chalumeau, m.; sarbacane, f.

blowzy [blaᵒuzi] *adj.* rouge; ébourif-
fée, mal soignée [woman].

blubber [blœbeʳ] *v.* pleurnicher; *s.*
pleurnicherie, f.

bludgeon [blœdjᵉn] *s.* matraque, f.;
v. matraquer.

blue [bloᵘ] *adj.* bleu; triste; *s.* bleu,
ciel, azur, m.; *pl.* mélancolie, f.;
v. bleuir; passer au bleu; *out of the
blue,* soudainement; *to feel blue,* avoir
le cafard; *bluecap,* bluet; *blue light,*
feu de Bengale; *blue-stone,* sulfate de
cuivre. ‖ **bluebell** [-bèl] *s.* jacinthe des
prés, f. ‖ **blueberry** [-bèri] *s.** myrtille,
f.; *Fr. Can.* bleuet, m.

bluff [blœf] *s.* falaise, f.; escarpement; bluff, m.; *adj.* escarpé; rude;
brusque; *v.* bluffer. ‖ **bluffer** [-ᵉʳ] *s.*
bluffeur, m. ‖ **bluffly** [-li] *adv.* rudement, brutalement.

bluing [bloᵘing] *s.* bleu de blanchisseuse, m. ‖ **bluish** [bloᵘish] *adj.*
bleuâtre; *bluish green,* glauque.

blunder [blœndeʳ] *s.* bévue, gaffe,
sottise, f.; *v.* gaffer, commettre une
maladresse. ‖ **blunderer** [-rᵉʳ] *s.* gaf-
feur, m.; maladroit, m.

blunt [blœnt] *adj.* émoussé; obtus,
stupide; brusque, rude; *v.* émousser;
amortir [blow].

blur [blëʳ] *s.* tache; bavochure; buée,
f.; *v.* brouiller; tacher; ternir; estomper; ennuager.

blurb [blëʳb] *s. Am.* réclame; prière
d'insérer [book]; publicité, f.

blurt [blëʳt] *v.* parler à l'étourdi;
gaffer; *to blurt out,* lancer; lâcher
[word].

blush [blœsh] *s.** rougeur, f.; incarnat, m.; *v.* rougir.

bluster [blœsteʳ] *s.* tapage, m.; tempête; forfanterie, f.; *v.* faire une
bourrasque; faire le fanfaron. ‖ **blustering** [-ring] *adj.* fanfaron.

boa [boᵒua] *s.* boa, m.

boar [boᵒuʳ] *s.* verrat; sanglier, m.

board [boᵒuʳd] *s.* planche; table; pension, f.; écriteau; carton; comité;
établi; bord [ship], m.; côte (naut.),
f.; *pl.* le théâtre, m.; *v.* planchéier;
nourrir; prendre pension; aborder;
board and room, pension complète;

Board of Trade, ministère du Commerce; *to board out*, mettre en pension. ‖ **boarder** [-ᵉʳ] *s.* pensionnaire, m., f. ‖ **boarding-house** [ˈɪnghaᵘⁿs] *s.* pension de famille, f. ‖ **boarding-school** [-ingskoul] *s.* pensionnat, m.

boast [boᵒust] *s.* vantardise, f.; *v.* se vanter, s'enorgueillir. ‖ **boastful** [-fᵉl] *adj.* vantard, vaniteux. ‖ **boasting** [-ing] *s.* vantardise, f.

boat [boᵒut] *s.* bateau, m.; embarcation, f. ‖ **boater** [-ᵉr] *s.* canotier, m. ‖ **boathouse** [-haᵒus] *s* hangar à bateaux, m. ‖ **boating** [-ing] *s.* canotage; transport par bateau, m. ‖ **boatman** [-mᵉn] *s.* batelier navigateur, marin, m. ‖ **boatswain** [boᵒsn] *s.* maître (m.) d'équipage.

bob [bâb] *s.* pendant [ear] plomb [line]; gland, m.; lentille [clock]; secousse; monnaie [shilling] coiffure à la Ninon, f.; *v.* secouer par saccades; ballotter; écourter [tail]; pendiller; *to bob up and down*, tanguer; *bob-sleigh*, traîneau.

bobolink [bobᵉlingk] *s.* troupiale, m. [bird]; *Fr. Can.* goglu, m.

bode [boᵒud] *pret., p., p. of to bide.*

bodice [bâdis] *s.* corsage, m.

bodiless [bâdilis] *adj.* immatériel; sans corps. ‖ **bodily** [bâdili] *adj.* corporel; matériel, sensible. *adv.* corporellement; par corps, d'un bloc; unanimement. ‖ **body** [bâdi] *s * corps; code, recueil; corsage; fuselage (aviat.), m.; nef [church]. carrosserie [auto]; masse [water], f., *to come in a body*, venir en masse. *as a body*, dans l'ensemble, collectivement; *the constituent body*, le collège électoral; *body guard*, garde du corps.

bog [bâg] *s.* marais, m.; *v.* embourber; *to bog down*, s'enliser. ‖ **boggy** [-i] *adj.* marécageux.

bog(e)y [boᵒugi] *s.* croquemitaine, m.

bogus [boᵒugᵉs] *adj.* factice; *bogus concern*, attrape-nigaud.

Bohemian [boᵒuhímiᵉn] *adj.* bohémien.

boil [boˈil] *s.* furoncle, m.

boil [boˈil] *v.* bouillir; faire bouillir; *s.* ébullition, f.; *to boil over* déborder en bouillant; *to boil away* × évaporer en bouillant; *to boil down*, faire réduire à l'ébullition, condenser. ‖ **boiler** [-ᵉr] *s.* bouilloire; chaudière, f.; calorifère, m.; *double boiler*, bain-marie.

boisterous [boˈistᵉrᵉs] *adj.* bruyant, tumultueux; turbulent.

bold [boᵒuld] *adj.* hardi; courageux; escarpé [cliff]; gras (typogr.); *bold-faced*, effronté. ‖ **boldly** [-li] *adv.* hardiment. ‖ **boldness** [-nis] *s.* audace; hardiesse; insolence, f.

bolero [belèᵉroᵒu] *s.* boléro, m. (mus.).

bolero [baulᵉroᵒu] *s.* boléro, m. [costume].

Bolivia [baulivíᵉ] *s.* Bolivie, f.; *Bollvian*, bolivien.

Bolshevik [boᵒulshvik] *adj.* bolchevique · *Bolshevist* s. bolcheviste, m., f.

bolster [boᵒulstᵉr] *s.* traversin, m.; *v. to bolster up*, étayer [doctrine]; soutenir [person].

bolt [boᵒult] *s.* verrou; boulon; bond; rouleau [paper], m.; cheville [pin]; flèche [arrow]; culasse [rifle]; foudre [thunder]; fuite, f.; *adj.* rapide et droit; *v.* verrouiller; boulonner; avaler; fuir; bluter; tamiser; *Am.* se retirer d'un parti, s'abstenir de voter. ‖ **bolter** [-ᵉr] *s.* blutoir; *Am.* dissident d'un parti, m.

bomb [bâm] *s.* bombe, f.; *v.* bombarder · *bomb - crater*, entonnoir; *bomb-release*, lancement de bombes; *bomb-shell*, obus; bombe (fig.); *bomb-thrower*, lance-bombes · *bomb-ed-out*, sinistré; *bombing plane*, bombardier (aviat.). ‖ **bombard** [bâmbârd] *v.* bombarder. ‖ **bombardier** [bâmbᵉdîr] *s.* bombardier, m. ‖ **bombardment** [bâmbârdmᵉnt] *s.* bombardement, m.

bombastic [bâmbastik] *adj.* ampoulé, amphigourique.

bomber [bâmᵉr] *s.* bombardier, m.

bonanza [bo'nanzᵉ] *s.* filon, m.

bond [bând] *s.* lien, m.; obligation, f.; *v.* garantir par obligations; entreposer à la douane. ‖ **bondage** [-idj] *s.* esclavage, m.; servitude, f. ‖ **bondsman** [-zmᵉn] *s.* garant, m.; serf, esclave. m.

bone [boᵒun] *s.* os, m.; arête [fish]; baleine [of corset], f.; *v.* désosser; baleiner. *Am.* bûcher, travailler dur; *a bone of contention*, une pomme de discorde; *he is a bag of bones*, il n'a que la peau et les os; *to make no bones about*, n'avoir pas de scrupules à; *I feel it in my bones*, j'en ai le pressentiment. ‖ **boner** [-ᵉr] *s.* bourde, gaffe, boulette, énormité, f.

bonfire [bânfaˈr] *s.* bûcher; feu de joie, m.

bonnet [bânit] *s.* capote, f.; capot [auto]; complice, m.; *v.* coiffer.

bonus [boᵒunᵉs] *s.* prime, f.; boni, m.

bony [boᵒuni] *adj.* osseux; plein d'arêtes.

bonze [bânz] *s.* bonze, m.

boo [bou] *v.* huer; *s. pl.* huées, f.

booby [boubi] *s.*, adj.* nigaud; lourdaud; *booby-trap*, attrape-nigaud; mine-piège (milit.).

boohoo [bouhou] v. braire.

book [bouk] s. livre; registre, m.; *book of tickets*, carnet de tickets; *on the books*, inscrit dans la comptabilité; *order-book*, carnet de commandes; *to book one's place*, louer sa place. ‖ **bookcase** [-kéʲs] s. bibliothèque, f. ‖ **booking** [-ing] s. enregistrement, m. ‖ **bookish** [-ish] adj. pédantesque. ‖ **bookkeeper** [-kîpᵉʳ] s. comptable, m., f. ‖ **bookkeeping** [-kîping] s. comptabilité, f.; *double-entry bookkeeping*, comptabilité en partie double. ‖ **booklet** [-lèt] s. livret, opuscule, m. ‖ **bookseller** [-sèlᵉʳ] s. libraire, m. ‖ **bookshelf** [-shèlf] s. (pl. **bookshelves** [-shèlvz]) s. étagère de bibliothèque, f. ‖ **bookshop** [-shâp], **bookstore** [-stoᵘʳ] s. librairie, f. ‖ **bookstall** [-staul], *Am.* **bookstand** [-stand] s. étalage (m.) de librairie; bibliothèque de gare, f.

boom [boum] s. grondement, m.; boom, emballement des cours, m.; vogue, f.; chaîne, f.; v. gronder [wind]; voguer rapidement; prospérer; augmenter; *boom and bust*, prospérité et dépression.

boon [boun] adj. gai, joyeux.

boon [boun] s. bienfait, m.; faveur, f.

boor [bour] s. rustre; lourdaud, m. ‖ **boorish** [bourish] adj. rustre.

boost [boust] s. *Am.* poussée; augmentation, f.; v. pousser, faire l'article; augmenter [price]. ‖ **booster** [-ᵉʳ] s. amplificateur; survolteur; prôneur, m.; *booster-rocket*, fusée porteuse; *booster-shot*, piqûre de rappel. ‖ **boosting** [-ing] s. battage, m.

boot [bout] s. surplus, m.; *to boot*, en plus, par-dessus le marché.

boot [bout] s. chaussure, botte, bottine, f.; brodequin [torture]; coffre [vehicle]; coup de pied, m.; v. botter; donner un coup de pied. ‖ **bootblack** [-blak] s. cireur de bottes, m.

booth [bouzh] s. cabine; baraque, f.; isoloir, m.

bootlegger [boutlègᵉʳ] s. *Am.* contrebandier (m.) de spiritueux.

bootlick [boutlik] v. *Am.* lécher les bottes, flagorner.

booty [bouti] s.* butin, m.

booze [bouz] s. noce, ribote; gnôle (fam.), f.; v. siroter (fam.); *boozer*, pochard.

border [baurdᵉʳ] s. bord, m.; bordure, frontière, f.; v. border; être limitrophe de; *border-line*, ligne de démarcation; *border-line case*, cas limite.

bore [boᵘʳ] pret. of to bear.

bore [boᵘʳ] v. percer; forer; s. trou; calibre [gun]; mascaret [tide]; alésage (mech.), m.; sonde [mine], f.

bore [boᵘʳ] v. ennuyer, importuner; s. ennui; importun; raseur (fam.), m. ‖ **boredom** [-dᵉm] s. ennui, m. ‖ **boring** [-ing] adj. ennuyeux.

born [baurn] p. p. of to bear; adj. né; inné. ‖ **borne** [baurn] p. p. of to bear.

borough [bᵉroᵘ] s. bourg, m.; cité; circonscription électorale, f.

borrow [bauroᵘ] v. emprunter, « taper ». ‖ **borrowed** [-d] adj. d'emprunt, faux, usurpé. ‖ **borrower** [-ᵉʳ] s. emprunteur, m. ‖ **borrowing** [-ing] s. emprunt, m.

bosom [bouzᵉm] s. sein; cœur; plastron [shirt], m.; *bosom friend*, ami intime.

boss [baus] s.* bosse; butée; protubérance, f.; v. bosseler.

boss [baus] s.* patron, m.; *Am.* politicien influent; adj. de premier ordre; en chef; v. diriger, contrôler; *to boss it*, gouverner. ‖ **bossy** [-i] adj. autoritaire, impérieux.

botany [bâtᵉni] s. botanique, f.

botch [bâtsh] v. rafistoler; saboter, bousiller (fam.).

both [boᵘth] adj., pron., conj. tous les deux; ensemble; à la fois; *both of us*, nous deux; *on both sides*, des deux côtés.

bother [bâzhᵉʳ] s. tracas; ennui; souci, m.; v. ennuyer, tourmenter; se tracasser. ‖ **bothersome** [-sᵉm] adj. ennuyant; inquiétant.

bottle [bât'l] s. bouteille, f.; flacon, m.; botte [hay], f.; v. mettre en bouteille; *to bottle up*, embouteiller, bloquer; *bottle brush*, rince-bouteilles; *bottle cap*, capsule; *bottleneck*, goulot; embouteillage.

bottom [bâtᵉm] s. fond; bout; bas [page], m.; carène (naut.), f.; *bottoms up!* à la vôtre!, *to be at the bottom of*, être l'instigateur de; *bottomless*, sans fond, insondable.

bough [baᵘ] s. rameau, m.

bought [baut] pret., p. p. of to buy.

boulder [boᵘldᵉʳ] s. rocher, m.

boulevard [boulvâʳ] s. boulevard, m.

bounce [baᵘns] v. sauter; se jeter sur; rebondir; faire sauter; se vanter, exagérer; *Am.* expulser, congédier; s. saut, rebondissement; bruit, m.; explosion; vantardise, f.; *Am.* expulsion, f.; renvoi, m.

bound [baᵘnd] adj., p. p. lié, attaché; *Am.* résolu à; tenu; *bound up in*, entièrement pris par; *bound to happen*, inévitable.

bound [baᵘnd] s. limite, f.; bond, m.; adj. à destination de; tenu; v.

borner; bondir; *out of bounds*, accès défendu. ‖ **boundary** [ba^{ou}nd^eri] *s.** borne; frontière, f. ‖ **boundless** [ba^{ou}ndlis] *adj.* illimité, sans borne.

bountiful [ba^{ou}ntf^el] *adj.* libéral, généreux. ‖ **bounty** [ba^{ou}nti] *s.** bonté, f.; largesses, f. pl.; gratification, prime, f.

bouquet [boukéⁱ] *s.* bouquet, m.

bout [ba^{ou}t] *s.* coup; match, m.; partie; crise (med.), f.

bow [ba^{ou}] *s.* salut, m.; inclinaison; proue (naut.), f.; *v.* s'incliner; courber; saluer; ployer, fléchir; *bow-side*, tribord.

bow [bo^{ou}] *s.* arc; archet; nœud; arçon [saddle]. m.; monture [spectacles], f.; *bow-legged*, bancal.

bowels [ba^{ou}elz] *s. pl.* intestins, m. pl.; entrailles, tripes, f. pl.

bower [ba^{ou}er] *s.* tonnelle, f.; boudoir, m.; maisonnette, f.

bowl [bo^{ou}l] *s.* bol; vase rond; fourneau [pipe], m.; boule, f.; *v.* jouer aux boules, jouer aux quilles. rouler [carriage]; servir la balle [game]. ‖ **bowler** [-^er] *s.* joueur, *Fr Can.* quilleur; chapeau melon, m. ‖ **bowling** [-ing] *s.* bowling, jeu de quilles, m.; *bowling-alley*, boulodrome, m.; *bowling-pin*, quille, f.

bowman [bo^{ou}m^en] (*pl* bowmen) *s.* archer, m.

box [bâks] *s.** boîte, malle; loge (theat.), f.; compartiment; carton; banc, box, m.; guérite, cabine, f.; *box-office*, bureau de location.

box [bâks] *s.* buis [wood], m.

box [bâks] *s.** gifle, claque, f.; *v.* gifler; boxer. ‖ **boxer** [-^er] *s.* boxeur, m. ‖ **boxing** [-ing] boxe, f.; *Boxing Day*, jour des étrennes.

boy [boⁱ] *s.* garçon, m.

boycott [boⁱkât] *v.* boycotter; *s.* boycottage, m.

boyhood [boⁱhoud] *s.* enfance, f. ‖ **boyish** [boⁱish] *adj.* puéril; d'enfant; garçonnier.

bra [brâ] *s.* soutien-gorge, m.

brace [bréⁱs] *s.* paire; attache; agrafe (mech.); accolade (typogr.); *pl. Br* bretelles, f.; *v.* attacher consolider, étayer; tonifier, bander. tendre accolader; *carpenter's brace*. vilebrequin; *to brace up*, fortifier, tonifier.

bracelet [bréⁱslit] *s.* bracelet, m.

bracken [brak^en] *s.* fougère, f.

bracket [brakit] *s.* applique, f.; tasseau; crochet (typogr.), m.; *v.* mettre entre crochets; réunir.

brag [brag] *s.* fanfaronnade, f.; *v.* se vanter; *braggart*, fanfaron.

braid [bréⁱd] *s.* galon, m.; tresse; soutache, f.; *v.* tresser.

brain [bréⁱn] *s.* cerveau, m.; cervelle, f.; *v.* casser la tête; faire sauter la cervelle à; *brainstorm*, idée de génie, trouvaille. ‖ **brainwash** [-waush] *v.* faire un lavage de cerveau à; endoctriner. ‖ **brainwashing** [-ing] *s.* lavage de cerveau, endoctrinement, m.

brake [bréⁱk] *s.* frein; bordage (mech.), m.; *v.* ralentir, freiner; enrayer *brake(s)man*, serre-frein.

bramble [bràmb'l] *s.* ronce, f.; *bramble-berry*, mûre, f.; *bramble-rose*, églantine.

bran [bràn] *s.* son [wheat], m.

branch [bràntsh] *s.** branche; succursale. agence; bifurcation, f.; embranchement; affluent, m.; *v.* s'embrancher; se ramifier.

brand [brànd] *s.* tison; stigmate, m.; flétrissure; marque de fabrique; sorte, f.; *v.* stigmatiser, marquer au fer rouge. marquer les bestiaux; *brandnew*, flambant neuf.

brandish [bràndish] *v.* brandir; secouer. agiter.

brandy [bràndi] *s.** brandy, m.; eaude-vie, f.

brass [bra] *s.* cuivre laiton, airain, m.; *adj.* de cuivre; *v.* cuivrer; *brassband*, fanfare; *brass tacks*, le fond de l'affaire, l'essentiel.

brassière [brasiè^r] *s.* soutiengorge, m.

brat [brat] *s.* marmot, gosse, m.

brave [bréⁱv] *adj.* brave; beau, chic; *v.* braver, défier. ‖ **bravery** [-eri] *s.* bravoure; élégance; parure, f.

bravo [bravo^{ou}] *interj.*, *s.* bravo.

brawl [braul] *v.* crier, brailler; *s.* vacarme, m.; querelle, rixe, f.

brawn [braun] *s.* muscle, m.; fromage (m.) de tête; *brawny*, musclé.

bray [bréⁱ] *s.* braiment, m.; *v.* braire.

brazen [bréⁱz'n] *adj.* de cuivre, d'airain, impudent, effronté.

brazier [bréⁱje^r] *s.* chaudronnier; braséro, m.

breach [brîtsh] *s.** brèche; rupture; infraction à, violation de, f.; *v.* ouvrir une brèche dans.

bread [brèd] *s.* pain, m.; *v.* paner; *brown bread*, pain bis; *stale bread*, pain rassis; *bread-crumb*, chapelure; *v.* paner; *bread-winner*, gagne-pain.

breadth [brèdth] *s.* largeur; dimension, f.; lé, m.

break [bréⁱk] *s.* brèche, trouée; interruption, lacune, rupture; baisse [price]; aubaine, f.; *v.** casser, briser; violer [law]; ruiner, délabrer [health]; éclater [storm]; annoncer, faire part de [purpose]; *to break down,* abattre; broyer; *to break out,* éclater [war]; *to break up,* se séparer, (se) disperser, cesser; *to give a break,* donner une chance. ‖ *breakable* [-ᵉb'l] *adj.* cassable. ‖ *breakdown* [bréᵢkdaᵒᵘn] *s.* rupture (f.) de négociations; dépression nerveuse (f.); effondrement; fiasco, m.; panne, f. ‖ *breaker* [-ᵉʳ] *s.* briseur; perturbateur; interrupteur; brisants [waves], m. ‖ *breakfast* [-fᵉst] *s., v.* déjeuner, petit déjeuner; *breakfast food,* Fr. Can. céréales, f. pl.

breast [brèst] *s.* poitrine, f.; sein; poitrail; cœur; sentiment; blanc de volaille, m.; *v.* lutter contre; *to make a clean breast,* faire des aveux complets; *breastbone,* sternum, bréchet; *breastwork,* parapet.

breath [brèth] *s.* souffle, m.; haleine, f.; *v.* respirer, souffler; *out of breath,* à bout de souffle; *to gasp for breath,* haleter.

breathe [brîzh] *v.* respirer; exhaler; souffler; *to breathe one's last,* rendre le dernier soupir; *not to breathe a word,* ne pas souffler mot. ‖ *breather* [-ᵉʳ] *s.* moment de répit, m.; bol d'air, m. ‖ *breathing* [-ing] *s.* respiration, f.; souffle, m.; répit, m.; détente, f.; *breathing-hole,* soupirail. ‖ *breathless* [brèthlis] *adj.* essoufflé; suffocant; étouffant; oppressé; sans vie; en haleine, haletant.

bred [brèd] *pret., p. p. of to breed;* *well-bred,* bien élevé.

breeches [brítshiz] *s. pl.* pantalon, m.

breed [brîd] *s.* race; sorte, espèce, f.; *v.* élever, nourrir; éduquer; engendrer. ‖ *breeder* [-ᵉʳ] *s.* étalon; éleveur; éducateur, m. ‖ *breeding* [-ing] *s.* procréation, f.; éducation, f.; élevage, m.

breeze [brîz] *s.* brise, f. ‖ *breezy* [-i] *adj.* aéré; animé; vif; jovial, désinvolte.

brethren [brèzhrin] *s. pl.* frères; confrères, m. pl.

breve [brîv] *s.* brève (mus.), f. ‖ *breviary* [brîvⁱeri] *s.* * bréviaire, m. ‖ *brevity* [brévᵉti] *s.* * brièveté, f.

brew [brou] *v.* brasser [ale]; tramer; comploter; faire infuser [tea]; *s.* bière, f. ‖ *brewer* [-ᵉʳ] *s.* brasseur, m. ‖ *brewery* [-ᵉri] *s.* * brasserie, f.

briar [braᵢᵉʳ] *s.* ronce, f.; églantier, m.

bribe [braᵢb] *s.* paiement illicite, pot-de-vin, m.; *v.* corrompre. ‖ *bribery* [-ᵉri] *s.* * concussion, f.

brick [brîk] *s.* brique, f.; Am. brave type, bon garçon; *v.* briqueter; *bricklayer,* maçon; *brickwork,* briquetage;

brickyard, briqueterie. ‖ *brickbat* [-bat] *s.* briqueton; brocard, m.; insulte, f.

bridal [braᵢd'l] *adj.* nuptial. ‖ *bride* [braᵢd] *s.* mariée, f.; *the bride and groom,* les nouveaux mariés. ‖ *bridegroom* [-groum] *s.* marié, m. ‖ *bridesmaid* [-zméᵢd] *s.* demoiselle d'honneur, f. ‖ *bridesman* [-zmᵉn] (*pl.* bridesmen) *s.* garçon d'honneur, m.

bridge [bridj] *s.* pont, m.; passerelle (naut.), f.; chevalet [violin]; dos [nose]; prothèse dentaire, f.; jeu de cartes, m.; *v.* jeter un pont sur; *drawbridge,* pont-levis; *bridge-head,* tête de pont.

bridle [braᵢd'l] *s.* bride, f.; frein, m.; restriction, f.; *v.* brider; maîtriser, subjuguer; se rengorger; *bridlepath,* piste cavalière.

brief [brîf] *adj.* bref, concis; *s.* dossier (jur.); sommaire, abrégé; bref apostolique, m.; *v.* abréger, résumer; documenter (on, sur). ‖ *briefly* [-li] *adv.* brièvement. ‖ *briefcase* [-kéᵢs] *s.* portefeuille, m.; serviette; chemise, f. ‖ *briefness* [-nis] *s.* brièveté, f. ‖ *briefs* [-s] *s. pl.* cache-sexe, slip, m.

brier, see briar.

brig [brig] *s.* brick (naut.), m.; Am. prison (fam.), f.

brigade [brigéᵢd] *s.* brigade, f.; *v.* embrigader; *brigadier,* général de brigade.

bright [braᵢt] *adj.* brillant; gai; intelligent; vif [color]; Am. blond [tobacco]. ‖ *brighten* [-'n] *v.* faire briller; égayer; embellir; polir; s'éclairer. ‖ *brightness* [-nis] *s.* éclat, m.; clarté; splendeur; vivacité; gaieté, f.

brilliance [brîlyᵉns] *s.* éclat; lustre; brillant, m.; splendeur, f. ‖ *brilliant* [brîlyᵉnt] *adj.* brillant, éclatant; talentueux. ‖ *brilliantine* [brîlyᵉntîn] *s.* brillantine, f.; [brilyᵉntîn] *v.* brillantiner.

brim [brim] *s.* bord, m.; *v.* remplir jusqu'au bord; être tout à fait plein; *to brim over,* déborder. ‖ *brimmer* [-ᵉʳ] *s.* rasade, f.; verre arasé, m.

brimstone [brimstoᵒᵘn] *s.* soufre, m.

brine [braᵢn] *s.* saumure; eau salée, f.; *v.* plonger dans la saumure; *brinepit,* saline; *briny,* saumâtre, salé; amer.

bring [bring] *v.* * amener, conduire; apporter; coûter, revenir [price]; *to bring along,* apporter, amener; *to bring about,* produire, occasionner; *to bring back,* rapporter, ramener; *to bring down,* faire descendre; humilier, abattre; *to bring forth,* produire; *to bring forward,* avancer, reporter [sum] *to bring in*. introduire; *to bring out*, faire sortir; publier; *to bring off*, renflouer; *to bring up*, élever, nourrir; mettre sur le tapis [subject]. *how much does coal bring?*, combien coûte le charbon?

brink [bringk] *s.* bord, m.

brioche [brioous̆] *s.* brioche, f.

briquette [brikèt] *s.* briquette, f.

brisk [brisk] *adj.* vif, actif (comm.); animé, alerte. ‖ **briskly** [-li] *adv.* allégrement, activement.

bristle [bris'l] *s.* soie [pig], f.; *v.* se hérisser. ‖ **bristly** [-i] *adj.* hérissé.

Britain [brit'n] *s.* Grande-Bretagne, f. ‖ **British** [british] *adj. s.* britannique, anglais. | **Brittany** [brit'ni] *s.* Bretagne, Armorique, f.

brittle [brit'l] *adj.* fragile, cassant; friable. ‖ **brittleness** [-nis] *s.* fragilité, f.

broach [broous̆] *s.** broche, f.; *v.* embrocher; mettre en perce [cask]; entamer [subject].

broad [braud] *adj.* large, vaste, hardi; fort [accent]; tolérant [mind]; clair [hint]; *broad-minded*, à l'esprit large. ‖ **broadcast** [-kast] *s.* radiodiffusion, émission, transmission, f.; *v.* radiodiffuser, émettre; semer à la volée. **broaden** [-'n] *v.* élargir.

brocade [broouké'd] *s.* brocart, m.

broil [bro'l] *s.* querelle, échauffourée, f.; tumulte, m.

broil [bro'l] *v.* griller, rôtir; faire rôtir. ‖ **broiler** [-er] *s.* gril, m.; *Am.* journée torride, f.

broke [broouk] *pret. of to break*; *adj.* ruiné, fauché. ‖ **broken** [-'n] *p. p. of to break*; *adj.* brisé, rompu; délabré, en ruine; fractionnaire [number]; vague [hint]; entrecoupé [voice], *broken French*, mauvais français.

broker [broouker] *s.* courtier brocanteur; prêteur sur gages, m. **brokerage** [broouke'ridj] *s.* courtage, m.; **brokerage fee**, commission de courtier.

bromide [broouma'd] *s.* bromure, m.; raseur, m.; platitude, f.

bronchitis [brânka'tis] *s.* bronchite, f.

bronze [brânz] *s.* bronze, m.; *adj.* bronzé; *v.* bronzer.

brooch [brouts̆] *s.** broche [clasp], f.

brood [broud] *s.* couvée, nichée, foule, flopée, f. (colloq.); *v.* couver; méditer; ruminer; menacer, planer sur. ‖ **brooder** [-er] *s.* couveuse, f.

brook [brouk] *s.* ruisseau, m.

brook [brouk] *v.* supporter.

broom [broum] *s.* genêt; balai, m.; *v.* balayer; **broomstick**, manche à balai.

broth [brauth] *s.* bouillon; potage, m.

brother [brœzher] *s.* frère; collègue, m.; *brother - in - law*, beau-frère. ‖ **brotherhood** [-houd] *s.* fraternité; confraternité; confrérie, f. ‖ **brotherly** [-li] *adj.* fraternel.

brought [braut] *pret., p. p. of to bring.*

brow [braou] *s.* sourcil; front; sommet [hill], m. ‖ **browbeat** [-bìt] *v.* rudoyer, malmener.

brown [braoun] *adj.* brun; sombre; bis; marron; châtain; bronzé; *v.* brunir; *browned off*, déprimé.

browning [braouning] *s.* revolver, m.

browse [braouz] *v.* brouter; bouquiner; *v.* pousse verte, f.

bruise [brouz] *s.* contusion, f.; bleu, m.; *v.* contusionner, meurtrir.

brunette [brounèt] *s.* brunette, f.

brunt [brœnt] *s.* choc; assaut, m.

brush [brœsh] *s.** fourré; pinceau, m.; brosse; escarmouche; friche, f.; *v.* brosser, effleurer; *to brush aside*, écarter; *to brush away*, essuyer, balayer; *to brush up a lesson* repasser une leçon. *brush-off*, coup de balai; *brush-up*, coup de brosse. **brushwood** [-woud] *s.* fourré, m.; broussailles, f. pl.

brusque [brœsk] *adj.* brusque.

brutal [brout'l] *adj.* brutal. ‖ **brutality** [broutalⁱti] *s.** brutalité, f.

brute [brout] *s.* brute, f.; *adj.* brut; bestial, grossier; brutal. ‖ **brutify** [-ifa'] *v.* abrutir. ‖ **brutish** [-ish] *adj.* brutal, bête, grossier.

bubble [bœb'l] *s.* bulle, f.; bouillon, bouillonnement, m.; chimère, f.; *v.* bouillonner, faire des bulles. **bubbly** [-i] *adj.* plein de bulles; mousseux, pétillant, champagnisé.

buck [bœk] *s.* mâle (renne, antilope, lièvre, lapin), *Am.* dollar (fam.), m.

buck [bœk] *s.* ruade, f.; *v.* ruer; désarçonner; *to buck up*, (se) ravigoter.

bucket [bœkit] *s.* seau, baquet; auget [wheel]; piston [pump], m.; *to kick the bucket*, casser sa pipe (fam.).

buckle [bœk'l] *s.* boucle, f.; *v.* boucler; atteler à [work]; *to buckle down*, travailler dur.

buckshee [bœkshì] *adj.* aux frais de la princesse.

buckshot [bœkshât] *s.* chevrotine, f.

buckwheat [bœkhwìt] *s.* sarrazin, m.

bud [bœd] *s.* bourgeon; bouton, m.; *v.* bourgeonner. ‖ **buddy** [-i] *s.* Am.* camarade, copain, m.

budge [bœdj] *v.* bouger; faire bouger.

budget [bœdjit] *s.* budget; sac, m.

buff [bœf] *s.* peau de buffle, f.; chamois, m.; *Am.* fanatique, m.

buff [bœf] *s* coup, soufflet, m.; *blindman's buff*, colin-maillard.

buffalo [bœf'lo⁰ᵘ] *s.* buffle, bison, m.

buffer [bœf•r] *s.* tampon; *Am.* parechocs, m.; *buffer-state*, Etat-tampon; *buffer-stop*, butoir.

buffet [bœfit] *s.* coup, soufflet, m.; *v.* souffleter; cahoter; se débattre (*with*, contre).

buffet [bœfé¹] *s.* buffet; [boufé¹] *s.* restaurant, m.; *Am.* **buffet-car**, wagon-restaurant.

bug [bœg] *s.* punaise, f.; microbe, germe, m. ‖ **bugbear** [-bèr] *s.* croquemitaine, épouvantail, m.; bête noire, f.

bugle [byoug'l] *s.* cor de chasse; clairon, m.; *v.* claironner.

build [bîld] *s.* structure; stature; taille, f.; *v.** bâtir, construire; établir; *to build up*, édifier; *to build upon*, compter sur. ‖ *builder* [-ᵉʳ] *s.* entrepreneur, constructeur, m. ‖ *building* [-ing] *s.* construction, f.; bâtiment, m.; *public building*, édifice public; *adj.* de construction; à bâtir; du bâtiment; *building land*, terrain à bâtir; *building plot*, lotissement. ‖ *built* [bîlt] *adj., p. p.* bâti; façonné.

bulb [bœlb] *s.* bulbe, oignon; globe [eye], m.; ampoule (electr.); poire [rubber], f.

bulge [bœldj] *s.* renflement, m.; bosse, f.; *v.* bomber; faire eau (naut.). ‖ *bulgy* [-i] *adj.* tors.

bulk [bœlk] *s.* masse, f.; volume, m.; *Am.* pile de tabac, f.; *in bulk*, en vrac, en gros; *to bulk large*, faire figure importante. ‖ *bulky* [-i] *adj.* volumineux, massif; lourd.

bull [boul] *s.* taureau; haussier [Stock Exchange]; *Am.* agent de police; boniment, m.; *adj.* de hausse; *v.* provoquer la hausse.

bull [boul] *s.* bulle [papal], f.

bulldozer [bouldoᵒᵘzer] *s.* bulldozer, m.

bullet [boulit] *s.* balle [gun], f.

bulletin [boul•t'n] *s.* bulletin, m.; *v. Am.* publier, annoncer; *bulletin board*, panneau d'affichage.

bullfight [boulfa¹t] *s.* course (f.) de taureaux; corrida, f.; *bullfighter*, torero.

bullfinch [boulfintsh] *s.** *Br.* bouvreuil, m.

bullion [bouly•n] *s.* or en barres; lingot, m.; encaisse métallique, f.

bully [bouli] *s.** matamore, m.; *adj.* fanfaron; jovial; épatant; *v.* intimider; malmener; le faire à l'influence.

bulwark [boulwᵉrk] *s.* fortification; défense, f.; rempart, m.; *pl.* bastingage, m. (naut.).

bum [bœm] *s.* vagabond; écornifleur; débauché, m.; *adj. Am.* de mauvaise qualité, inutilisable; *v.* rouler sa bosse; vivre aux crochets de; écornifler.

bumblebee [bœmb'lbî] *s.* bourdon, m.

bump [bœmp] *s* bosse, f.; coup, m.; *v.* se cogner; heurter; cahoter; *to bump off, Am.* démolir. ‖ *bumper* [-ᵉʳ] *s.* pare-chocs, m.; *adj.* excellent, abondant.

bun [bœn] *s.* brioche (f.) aux raisins; pain au lait, m.; chignon, m.; *Am.* cuite, f.

bunch [bœntsh] *s.** botte [vegetables]; grappe [grapes]; bosse [hump], f.; bouquet; trousseau [keys], m.; *v.* se grouper; réunir; se renfler; faire une bosse.

bundle [bœnd'l] *s.* paquet; fagot, m.; botte; liasse, f.; *v.* botteler; entasser; *to bundle up*, emmitoufler, empaqueter; *to bundle in*, (s')entasser.

bunghole [bœnghoᵒᵘl] *s.* bonde, f.

bungle [bœngg'l] *v.* gâcher, bousiller; *s.* gâchis, m.

bunion [bœny•n] *s.* oignon, m.

bunk [bœngk] *s.* couchette; blague, foutaise, f.; bourrage de crâne, m.; *v.* partager une chambre; se mettre au lit; filer, décaniller (colloq.).

bunny [bœni] *s.** lapin, m.

buoy [bo¹] *s.* bouée, f.; *v.* maintenir à flot; *to buoy up*, soutenir. ‖ *buoyant* [-ᵉnt] *adj.* qui peut flotter; léger; gai, vif; plein de ressort.

bur [bër] *s.* grasseyement, m.; *v.* grasseyer.

burden [bërdᵉn] *s.* fardeau, m.; charge, f; tonnage (naut.), m.; *v.* charger.

burden [bërdᵉn] *s.* refrain, m.; thème, m. [speech]. ‖ *burdensome* [-sᵉm] *adj* lourd, pesant

burdock [bërdâk] *s.* bardane, f.

bureau [byouroᵒᵘ] *s.* bureau; cabinet; secrétaire, m.; *travel bureau*, agence de voyage; *weather bureau*, office de météorologie. ‖ *bureaucracy* [byou'råkrᵉsi] *s.* bureaucratie, f.

burglar [bërglᵉr] *s.* cambrioleur, voleur, m. ‖ *burglarize* [-ra¹z] *v.* cambrioler. ‖ *burglary* [-ri] *s.** cambriolage, m.

burial [bèri•l] *s.* enterrement, m.; *burial-ground*, *burial-place*, cimetière, caveau, tombe.

burlap [bĕᵃlap] *s.* serpillière; toile (f.) à sac.

burly [bĕᵃli] *adj.* corpulent; bien charpenté.

burn [bĕᵃn] *s* brûlure, f.; *v* * brûler; incendier. être enflammé *to burn to ashes*, réduire en cendres. **burner** [-ᵉʳ] * brûleur. bec [lamp] échaud, m. **burning** *ngl* incendie, feu, m.; *adj* brûlant ardent.

burnish [bĕʳnısh] brunir; polir; *s.* brunissage, polissage, éclat, m.

burnt [bĕʳnt] *pret. p. p. of* to burn.

burrow [bĕʳoʷ] *s* terrier, m.; *v.* se terrer, creuser, miner.

bursar [bĕʳsᵃʳ] boursier; économe, m.; **bursary**, économat.

burst [bĕʳst] * éclat, mouvement brusque, élan n explosion, f.; *v.* * éclater, saillir. crever, faire éclater. *to burst open* enfoncer. *to burst into tears*, éclater en sanglots. *pret. of* **to burst.**

bury [bĕri] *v* enterrer. *buried in thought* perdu dans ses pensées.

bus [bœs] *s.* * autobus, bus; omnibus; *Am.* car, m.

bush [boush] *s* * fourré, buisson; arbuste n brousse. *m* friche, f. **bush-fighter**, *tiran* tireur n. **bush-ranger**, Fr. n areur des bois, m.; **maple bush**, *e* an ucrerie, f.

bushel [boush'l] boisseau, m.

bushy [boushi] *adj* touffu, épais.

busily [bızıl] *adv* activement, avec diligence. **business** [bıznıs] *s* affaires cupation n n commerce. négoce n affaires n n bout nis business n envoy n n ent jeu un. **business house** man n merce *to make ta* n ine arger de. **businesslike** *a'k* n méthodique *ik* n ique **businessman** [pl **businessmen**) *s.* homme d'affaires, m.

bust [bœst] buste. m.

bust [bœst] * four, fiasco, m.; *Am.* banqueroute, f. n m. dompter [horse]. réduire à la faillite; faire faillite

bustle [bœs'l] *s* confusion, agitation, f.; remue ménage n. *v* se remuer; s'empresse remuler

busy [bızı] *adj* faire occupé. diligent laboreux **busybody** [-bâdi] *s.* officieux, rdeton indiscret, m. commère, f

but [bœt] *conj. prep.. adv* nais; ne... pas ne. que seulement excepté. auf *but bur* en ins m. *it was bur n moment* n affaire d'un instant. *nothing but* rien que; *but yesterday*, pas plus tard qu'hier.

butcher [boutshᵉʳ] *s.* boucher, m.; *v.* massacrer; *butcher's shop*, boucherie **butchery** [boutshʳi] *s.* carnage, n *Am.* boucherie, f.

butler [bœtlᵉʳ] *s.* sommelier; maître d'hôtel m.

butt [bœt] *s.* bout; derrière trognon; culot négot. m.. crosse [gun]; cible; victime, f.; *butt and nutt*, bout à bout; *the butt of ridicule*, un objet de risée.

butt [bœt] *s.* barrique, f.

butt [bœt] *v.* donner des coups de tête. de cornes coup le tête; coup de corne. botte [fencing], f.; *to butt in* se mêler de ce qui ne vous regarde pas interrompre.

butter [bœtᵉʳ] * beurre, m.; *v.* beurrer **butter-dish**, beurrier **butter-fingered**, maladroit **butter-pat**, coquille le beurre. **buttermilk** [-milk] *s.* babeurre, m. **butterscotch** [-skâtsh] * caramel au beurre, m.

buttercup [bœtᵉʳkœp] *s.* bouton d'or, m.

butterfly [bœtᵉʳflaⁱ] *s.* * papillon, m.

buttocks [bœtœks] *s. pl.* derrière, m.; fesses pl.

button [bœt'n] *s* bouton, m.; *v.* boutonne. **button hook**, tire-bouton. ‖ **buttonhole** [-hoʷl] *s.* boutonnière, f.; *v.* cramponner.

buttress [bœtris] *s.* * arc-boutant, pilier soutien, m.; *v.* soutenir.

buxom [bœksᵉm] *adj.* dodu, potelé; gracieux.

buy [baⁱ] *v.* * acheter; *to buy back*, racheter *to buy up*, accaparer. ‖ **buyer** *s* acheteur, n.

buzz [bœz] * bourdonnement, m.; bourdonner huchoter.

buzzard [bœzᵃʳd] *s.* buse, f.; *Am.* urubu n (fig.) vautour, m.

buzzer [bœzᵉʳ] *s.* vibreur, couineur. m.

by [baⁱ] *prep.* par; de; en; à; près de; envers sur; *by far* le beaucoup. une n me in n n *by twelve*, vers midi à late le *lose by*, tout près *by and by* près, tout à l'heure *by the by*, en passant. incidemment *by the way* propos; *by myself* tout seul n n four, leux n n n n mund, à la fois **bygone** *adj.* passé; tém n n n n n m. **bylaw** *aul n* n règlement *mm n by n bth* n[ij] chemin le urne. n **by-product** [-pradœkt] sous produit, m. **bystander** [standᵉʳ] spectateur, assistant, m. **byword** [-wĕʳd] *s.* proverbe; objet de risée, m.

C

cab [kab] *s.* fiacre ; taxi ; *Am.* abri de locomotive, m. ; *cab-driver*, *cabman*, cocher, chauffeur ; *cab-stand*, station de taxis.

cabbage [kabidj] *s.* chou, m.

cabin [kabin] *s.* cabane ; cabine, *f.*

cabinet [kabinit] *s.* cabinet, m.

cable [ké¹b'l] *s.* câble, m. ; *v.* câbler ; *cablegram*, câblogramme.

cackle [kak'l] *s.* caquet, m. ; *v.* caqueter, bavarder.

cactus [kaktes] (*pl.* cacti [kakta¹]) *s.* cactus, m.

cad [kad] *s.* voyou ; goujat, m.

cadaverous [kedaveres] *adj.* cadavérique ; livide.

cadence [ké¹d'ns] *s.* cadence, f.

cadet [kedèt] *s.* cadet, m.

café [kefé¹] *s.* café, restaurant, m. ‖ *cafeteria* [kafetirie] *s. Am.* restaurant de libre-service, m. ; *Fr. Can.* cafétéria, f. ‖ *caffeine* [kafiìn] *s.* caféine, f. ; *caffeine-free*, décaféiné.

cage [ké¹dj] *s.* cage, f.

cake [ké¹k] *s* gâteau ; tourteau ; pain [soap], m. ; tablette [chocolate], f. ; *v.* recouvrir d'une croûte ; coaguler.

calaboose [kalebous] *s. Am.* taule, f. (fam.).

calamitous [kelamites] *adj.* catastrophique ‖ *calamity* [kelamiti] *s.* calamité, f

calcify [kalsifa¹] *v.* (se) calcifier.

calcine [kalsa¹n] *v.* (se) calciner.

calcium [kalsiem] *s* calcium, m.

calculate [kalkye¹lé¹t] *v.* calculer ; *to calculate on* compter sur ‖ *calculation* [kalkye¹lé¹sh'n] *s* calcul, m. ; conjectures *f* ‖ *calculator* [kalkyelé¹ter] *s* calculateur, m , machine à calculer *f.* ‖ *calculus* [kalkye¹les] (*pl.* calculi [-a¹]) *s.* calcul (med.) ; calcul infinitésimal, m

caldron [kauldren] *s.* chaudron, m.

calendar [kalender] *s.* calendrier, m.

calf [kaf] (*pl* calves [kavz]) *s.* veau ; mollet, m ; *calfskin*, veau [leather] ; *calf love*, amour juvénile. *calf-length trousers*, corsaire pantalon corsaire.

caliber [kaleber] *s* calibre, m. ‖ *calibrate* [kalebré¹t] *v* calibrer.

calico [kaleko⁰u] *s.* * calicot, m. ; indienne f.

calk [kauk] *v.* calfater

call [kaul] *s.* appel, m. ; invitation ; visite ; convocation ; vocation, f. ; coup de fil, m. ; *v.* appeler ; visiter ; téléphoner ; convoquer ; toucher (naut.) ; *to call at a* port, faire escale à un port ; *to call for*, demander ; *to call forth*, faire naître, évoquer ; *to call in*, faire entrer . *to be called*, s'appeler ; *to call up on the phone*, appeler par téléphone ; *call-box*, cabine téléphonique ; *call-number*, numéro de téléphone. ‖ *caller* [-er] *s.* visiteur, m. ‖ *calling* [-ing] *s* appel, m. ; convocation ; vocation, f

callosity [kalàsìti] *s.** callosité, f. ; endurcissement, m. ‖ *callous* [kales] *adj.* calleux . dur. ‖ *callus* [kales] (*pl.* calli [-a¹]) *s* cal, durillon, m.

calm [kâm] *adj., s.* calme ; *v.* calmer, tranquilliser. ‖ *calmness* [-nis] *s.* calme, m. ; tranquillité, f

calorie [kaleri] *s.* calorie, f. ‖ *calorific* [kalerifik] *adj* calorifique.

calumniate [kelœmnié¹t] *v.* calomnier ; *calumny*, calomnie.

calyx [kéliks] (*pl.* calyces [kalisîz]) *s.* calice (bot.), m.

came [ké¹m] *pret. of* to come.

camel [kàm'l] *s.* chameau, m.

camera [kamere] *s.* appareil photographique. m.

camomile [kamoma¹l] *s.* camomille, f , *camomile tea*, camomille.

camouflage [kameflâj] *s.* camouflage, m. ; *v* camoufler

camp [kàmp] *s* camp, m. ; *v.* camper ; *camp-bed*, lit de camp ; *camp-stool*, pliant , *political camp*, parti politique

campaign [kàmpé¹n] *s.* campagne, f. ; *v.* faire campagne

camphor [kàmfer] *s.* camphre, m.

camping [kamping] *s* camping ; campement, m ‖ *campus* [kàmpes] *s.** *Am.* terrain de l'université, m.

can [kàn] *s* pot ; bidon, m. ; boîte ; jarre, f. ; *Fr Can* canette [of beer, soft drink], f. ; *v.* mettre en boîte, en conserve ; *can-opener*, ouvre-boîtes, m.

can [kàn] *v* savoir ; pouvoir ; être capable *who can tell?*, qui le sait ?

Canada [kànede] *s.* Canada, m. ; *Canadian*, canadien.

canal [kenal] *s* canal, m. ‖ *canalization* [kenalezé¹sh'n] *s.* canalisation, f. ‖ *canalize* [kenala¹z] *v.* canaliser.

canary [k^{e}nè^{e}ri] *s.** canari, serin, m.

cancel [kàns'l] *v.* annuler; biffer; décommander, résilier; *s* annulation, f.; deleatur, m.; poinçonneuse, f.

cancer [kàns^{e}^{r}] *s* cancer, m.; ***cancerous,*** cancéreux, ***cancer-producing,*** cancérigène ***cancroid,*** cancériforme; cancroïde

candid [kàndid] *adj.* franc, loyal; impartial, sans prévention.

candidacy [kànd^{e}d^{e}si] *s.** candidature, f. || ***candidate*** [kànd^{e}dé^{1}t] *s.* candidat, m

candied [kandid] *adj.* confit, candi.

candle [kand'l] *s* chandelle, bougie, f.; ***Candlemas,*** Chandeleur, ***candlestick,*** chandelier, bougeoir.

candor [kànd^{e}^{r}] *s* bonne foi; sincérité; loyauté; spontanéité; impartialité, f.

candy [kàndi] *s.** bonbon; candi, m.; ***candy-shop,*** confiserie; *v.* confire; *candied-almonds,* pralines.

cane [ké^{1}n] *s* canne, f.; *v.* bâtonner; canner, ***sugar-cane,*** canne à sucre; ***walking-cane,*** canne

canicular [k^{e}nikyoul^{e}^{r}] *adj.* caniculaire.

canine [ké^{1}na^{1}n] *adj.* canin; *s.* canine, f.

canker [kank^{e}^{r}] *v.* (s') ulcérer; *s.* chancre, ulcère, m.

canned [kànd] *adj.* en conserve, en boîte, ***canned goods,*** conserves alimentaires, ***cannery*** [kàn^{e}ri] *s.* fabrique de conserves, f

cannibal [kanib^{e}l] *s., adj.* cannibale; ***cannibalism,*** cannibalisme, m.; ***cannibalize,*** démonter et réutiliser [engine].

cannon [kàn^{e}n] *s* canon; carambolage [billiards], m ***cannonade*** [kan^{e}né^{1}d] *s* canonnade, f., *v* canonner. | ***cannoneer*** [kan^{e}nîr] *s* canonnier, m.

cannot [kanât] ***can not,*** *see* ***can.***

canoe [k^{e}nou] *s* canot, m.; chaloupe; pirogue, f., *v* canoter

canon [kàn^{e}n] *s* canon, règlement; chanoine, m. || ***canoness*** [-is] *s.** chanoinesse, f || ***canonic*** [k^{e}nânik] *adj.* canonique ***canonization*** [kan^{e}na^{1}zé^{1}sh^{e}n] *s* canonisation, f. || ***canonize*** [kàn^{e}na^{1}z] *v* canoniser

canopy [kan^{e}pi] *s** dais; baldaquin; conopée (eccles.), m.; voûte (fig.), f.

cantaloupe [kàntlo^{ou}p] *s.* melon cantaloup, m

cantankerous [kàntàngk^{e}r^{e}s] *adj.* désagréable, revêche.

canteen [kàntîn] *s.* cantine, f.; bidon, m.

canter [kànt^{e}^{r}] *s.* petit galop, m.; *v.* aller au petit galop.

canticle [kàntik'l] *s.* cantique, m.

canton [kànt^{e}n] *s.* canton, m.; région, f.; [kantân] *v* diviser en cantons; [kàntân] cantonner. || ***cantonment*** [kàntânm^{e}nt] *s* cantonnement, m.

canvas [kànv^{e}s] *s.* grosse toile, toile de tente, f.

canvass [kànv^{e}s] *s.** enquête; inspection; sollicitation des votes, campagne électorale. *Fr. Can.* cabale, f.; *v.* examiner, prospecter, visiter, faire le démarcheur, enquêter, faire une campagne électorale. *Fr. Can.* cabaler; dépouiller le scrutin, ***canvasser*** [-^{e}^{r}] *s.* agent électoral, *Fr. Can.* cabaleur; démarcheur, prospecteur, représentant, m.

canyon [kàny^{e}n] *s.* cañon, m.

cap [kap] *s* bonnet, m.; casquette; toque, calotte, barrette; capsule, f.; *v.* coiffer d'un bonnet; surmonter; capsuler

capability [ké^{1}p^{e}bil^{e}ti] *s.** capacité, aptitude, f. ***capable*** [ké^{1}p^{e}b'l] *adj* capable, compétent || ***capacious*** [k^{e}pé^{1}sh^{e}s] *adj* vaste, ample spacieux || ***capacity*** [k^{e}pas^{e}ti] *s.** capacité; contenance, aptitude; compétence légale, qualité, f.

cape [ké^{1}p] *s* cap, promontoire, m.

cape [ké^{1}p] *s.* collet, m.; pèlerine, f.

caper [ké^{1}p^{e}^{r}] *s.* cabriole, f.; *v.* cabrioler

caper [ké^{1}p^{e}^{r}] *s.* câpre; câprier, m.

capillarity [kapilariti] *s* capillarité, f. || ***capillary*** [k^{e}pil^{e}ri] *adj., s.* capillaire.

capital [kap^{e}t'l] *s* capital, chapiteau, m., capitale, majuscule, f; *adj* capital, excellent, principal ***capitalism*** [-iz^{e}m] *s* capitalisme, m ***capitalist*** [-ist] *s* capitaliste, m ***capitalize*** [-a^{1}z] *v* capitaliser, accumuler, écrire en majuscules, écrire avec une majuscule initiale

capitulate [k^{e}pitsh^{e}lé^{1}t] *v.* capituler. ***capitulation*** [k^{e}pitsh^{e}lé^{1}sh^{e}n] *s.* capitulation, f

capote [k^{e}po^{ou}t] *s.* capote, f.

caprice [k^{e}prîs] *s* caprice, m. || ***capricious*** [k^{e}prish^{e}s] *adj.* capricieux.

capsize [kapsa^{1}z] *v.* chavirer, faire chavirer

capstan [kapst^{e}n] *s.* cabestan, m.

capsule [kaps'l] *s.* capsule, f.

captain [kaptin] *s.* capitaine, m.; *v.* commander

caption [kapsh^{e}n] *s. Am.* sous-titre, m.; légende, f.; chapeau, m.; arrestation, f. (jur.).

captious [kapshes] *adj.* pointilleux; critique captieux.

captivate [kapt•vé¹t] *v.* captiver. ‖ *captive* [kaptiv] *adj.*, *s.* captif, prisonnier. *captivity* [kaptiv•ti] *s.* captivité, f. ‖ *capture* [kaptsh•r] *s.* capture, prise, f.; *v.* capturer.

car [kâr] *s.* voiture; auto, f.; wagon; ascenseur, m. ; *4m.* *car-licence*, carte grise; *car-sickness*, mal des transports *dining-car*, wagon-restaurant; *Am.* *freight-car*, wagon de marchandises.

caramel [karem'l] *s.* caramel, m.

carat [karet] *s.* carat, m.

caravan [karevan] *s.* caravane, f.

carbolic [kârbâlik] *adj.* phénique.

carbon [kârbân] *s.* carbone, m.; *carbon-copy*, double; *carbon-paper*, papier carbone.

carbonate [kârbenit] *s.* carbonate, m.

carbuncle [kârhengk'l] *s.* escarboucle. f. anthrax, m.

carburation [kârberé¹shen] *s.* carburation. f. *carburetor* [kârberé¹ter] *s.* carburateur. m.

carcasse [kârkes] *s.* carcasse, f.; cadavre, m.

card [kârd] *s.* carte; lettre de fairepart; fiche (comm.); rose des vents (naut.), f.; diagramme (mech.) m.; *to play cards*, jouer aux cartes.

card [kârd] *s.* carde, f.; *v.* carder.

cardboard [kârdbo°rd] *s.* carton, m.

cardiac [kârdiak] *adj.* du cœur; cardiaque.

cardinal [kârdin•l] *adj.*, *s.* cardinal.

care [kèr] *s.* soin; souci, m.; attention, f., *v.* se soucier ie faire attention à; *to take care of*, avoir soin de, prendre garde à; *with care fragile* [wares] *care of* aux bons soins de.

careen [kerîn] *v.* caréner (naut.); *s.* carénage, m.

career [kerîr] *s.* carrière; profession; course. f. cours, m.

careful [kèrf•l] *adj.* soigneux; soucieux prudent attentif be careful!, prenez garde! *carefully* [li] *adv.* avec soin attentivement avec anxiété. ‖ *carefulness* [nis] attention vigilance. f. soin souci f. *careless* [kèrlis] *adj.* négligent insouciant. *carelessly* [li] *adv.* négligemment, avec insouciance sans soin. *carelessness* [nis] *s.* négligence, f.

caress [keré¹s] *s.* caresse, f.; *v.* caresser.

caretaker [kèrté¹ker] *s.* gardien, m.

careworn [kèrwo°urn] *adj.* dévoré de souci; rongé d'angoisse.

cargo [kârgo°u] *s.* cargaison, f.; fret, m.; *cargo boat*, cargo.

cariboo [kàrebou] *s. Fr. Can.* caribou. m.

caricature [kariketsher] *s.* caricature, f.; *v.* caricaturer. ‖ *caricaturist* [-rist] *s.* caricaturiste, m.

caries [kèrîîz] *s.* carie, f.

carload [kârlo°ud] *s.* chargement d'un wagon, m.; voiturée, f. ‖ *carman* [-m°n] (*pl. carmen*) *s.* voiturier; camionneur; livreur; *Am.* conducteur de tramway, m.

carnal [kârn'l] *adj.* charnel.

carnation [kârné¹shen] *s.* œillet, m.; carnat, m.

carnival [kârnev'l] *s.* carnaval, m.

carnivorous [kârniveres] *adj.* carnivore.

carol [karel] *s.* chant, cantique, m.; *v.* chanter; *Christmas carol*, noël (mus.).

carom [karem] *s.* carambolage, m.; *v.* caramboler, heurter.

carouse [kera°uz] *v.* festoyer; faire la noce.

carousel [karezèl] *s.* carrousel, m.

carpenter [kârpenter] *s.* charpentier, menuisier, m. ‖ *carpentry* [-ri] *s.* menuiserie charpenterie, f.

carpet [kârpit] *s.* tapis, m.; moquette f. couvrir d'un tapis; mettre sur le tapis [subject]; *bedside carpet*, descente de lit; *carpet-sweeper*, balai mécanique.

carriage [karidj] *s.* voiture, f.; véhicule transport wagon port, attitude *sea carriage*, transport par mer *carriage-paid*, franco; *carriage way*, aie carrossable.

carrier [karier] *s.* porteur; transporteur voiturier m. compagnie de transport f. *airplane carrier*, porteavion disease carrier, porteur de germe nail-carrier, facteur; *carrier wave*, onde porteuse.

carrion [karien] *s.* charogne, f.

carrot [karet] *s.* carotte, f.

carry [kari] *v.* porter; emporter; emmener faire voiter [law] reporter [sum] *to carry away* entraîner, enthousiasmer, remporter [victory]; *to carry on* continuer; *to carry out*, mettre à exécution.

cart [kârt] *s.* charrette, f.; fourgon, m.; transporter dans une charrette, charrier.

cartilage [kârtilidj] *s.* cartilage, m.

cartograph [kârtegraf] *s.* cartographe, m., f. ‖ *cartography* [-i] *s.* cartographie, f.

carton [kârt'n] *s.* carton, m.

cartoon [kârtoͧn] *s.* caricature, f.; dessin animé, m. || **cartoonist** [-ist] *s.* caricaturiste; dessinateur de dessins animés. m.

cartridge [kârtridj] *s.* cartouche, f.; **cartridge-belt**, cartouchière.

carve [kârv] *v.* sculpter; graver; ciseler; découper [meat]; *to carve up*, démembrer. || **carver** [-ᵉr] *s.* sculpteur; graveur, découpeur, m.; **fish-carver**, truelle à poisson. || **carving** [-ing] *s.* sculpture, ciselure, f.; découpage, m.; **carving-knife**, couteau à découper.

cascade [kaskᵉid] *s.* cascade, f.

case [kéⁱs] *s* caisse; taie, trousse, f.; étui; boîtier. écrin. m.

case [kéⁱs] *s* cas; événement; état, m.; condition affaire, cause [law], f.; *in case*, au cas où; *in any case*, en tout cas; **case-history**, dossier médical; **case-law**, jurisprudence.

casement [kéⁱsmᵉnt] *s.* croisée; fenêtre, f.

casern [kᵉzᵉrn] *s.* caserne, f.

cash [kash] *s.* espèces, f. pl.; numéraire; argent comptant, m.; *v.* payer; toucher [check] **cash box**, caisse; **cash payment**, paiement comptant; **cash on delivery** (*c. o. d.*), contre remboursement. || **cashier** [-iᵉr] *s.* caissier, m.

casino [kᵉsinoͧ] *s.* casino, m.

cask [kask] *s.* tonneau, fût, m.

casket [kaskit] *s* cassette, f.; écrin, coffret; *Am.* cercueil, m.

casque [kask] *s.* casque, m.

casserole [kasᵉroͧl] *s.* daubière, f.; ragoût, m.

cassock [kasᵉk] *s.* soutane, f.

cast [kast] *s.* jet, lancement; coup [dice]; mouvement [eye]; moulage, m.; disposition [mind]; distribution [theat.]; interprétation [theat.], f.; *v.* jeter; couler [metal], clicher [print]; monter, distribuer [theat.]; *to cast a ballot*, voter; *to cast about*, chercher de tous côtés, *to cast aside*. mettre de côté, *to cast away*, rejeter, repousser; *to cast in*, partager; *to cast out*, expulser; *to cast lots*. tirer au sort; *to have a cast in the eye*, loucher; *to cast down*, décourager; baisser [eyes]; *pret., p. p. of* **to cast**; **cast-iron**, fonte, en fonte (fig.); d'acier (fig.).

castanets [kastᵉnèts] *s. pl.* castagnettes, f pl.

castaway [kastᵉwéⁱ] *s.* naufragé, m.

caste [kast] *s.* caste, f; *to lose caste*, perdre son prestige social.

castigate [kastᵉgéⁱt] *v.* châtier.

castle [kas'l] *s.* château, m.; tour [chess], f.

castoff [kastauf] *adj.* de rebut.

castor [kastᵉr] *s.* castor, m.; **castor oil**, huile de ricin.

castor [kastᵉr] *s.* saupoudroir, m.; salière. poivrière; roulette [armchair], f

casual [kajouᵉl] *adj.* fortuit; accidentel. *Am* sans cérémonie; à bâtons rompus temporaire, intermittent; désinvolte *s* travailleur temporaire, m. || **casualty** [-ti] *s.* accident; blessé, accidenté. m.; victime, f.; pertes (mil.), f.

cat [kat] *s.* chat, m.; chatte, f.; **cat's eye**, feu arrière [bicycle]; cataphote, m. [reflector].

cataclysm [katᵉkliz'm] *s.* cataclysme. m.

catacomb [katᵉkooͧm] *s.* catacombe. f.

catalepsy [katᵉlèpsi] *s.* catalepsie, f.

catalog(ue) [katlooͧg] *s.* catalogue, m.; *v.* cataloguer.

cataract [katᵉrakt] *s.* cataracte, f.

catarrh [kᵉtâr] *s.* catarrhe, m.

catastrophe [kᵉtastrᵉfi] *s.* catastrophe. f.; **catastrophic**, catastrophique

catch [katsh] *s.* prise, f.; loquet, crampon, air à reprises (mus.), m.; *v.* attraper saisir, *Fr. Can.*, recevoir [baseball], surprendre; donner, appliquer; *to catch fire*. prendre feu; *to catch cold*, prendre froid; *to catch on*, comprendre *catch-as-catch-can*, catch [sport] *to catch up with*, rattraper. || **catcher** [-ᵉr] *s. Fr Can* receveur [baseball] *s.* || **catching** [-ing] *adj.* prenant séduisant contagieux; *s.* prise, f **catchpenny** [-pèni] *s.* attrape-nigaud, m. || **catchy** [-i] *adj.* entraînant facile à retenir, insidieux.

catechesis [katᵉkīsis] *s.* catéchèse, f. || **catechism** [katᵉkiz'm] *s.* catéchisme. m || **catechist** [-kist] *s.* catéchiste, m. f || **catechize** [-kaⁱz] *v.* catéchiser **catechumen** [katikyoumᵉn] *s.* catéchumène. m., f.

categorical [katᵉgaurikˈl] *adj.* catégorique || **category** [katᵉgooͧri] *s.* catégorie. f

cater [kéⁱtᵉr] *v.* approvisionner.

caterpillar [katᵉrpilᵉr] *s.* chenille, f.; profiteu m (colloq.); **caterpillar-tractor**, autochenille.

catfish [katfish] *s.* poisson-chat, m.; *Fr. Can* barbote. f.

cathedral [kᵉthidrᵉl] *s.* cathédrale, f.

catholic [kathᵉlik] *adj., s.* catholique. || **catholicism** [kᵉthâlᵉsiz'm] *s.* catholicisme, m. || **catholicity** [kâthᵉlisiti] *s.* catholicité; universalité, f.

catkin [katkin] *s.* chaton, m. (bot.).

cattle [kat'l] *s.* bétail; bestiaux, m.

caught [kaut] *pret., p. p. of* **to catch.**

cauliflower [kaul°fla°u°r] *s.* chou-fleur, m.

caulk [kauk] *v.* calfeutrer; calfater; *Am.* étanchéifier.

cause [kauz] *s.* cause, f.; *v.* causer; *there is cause to,* il y a lieu de.

causeway [kauzwé¹] *s.* chaussée, f.

caustic [kaustik] *adj., s.* caustique.

cauterize [kaut°ra¹z] *v.* cautériser; endurcir. ‖ **cautery** [-i] *s.°* cautère, m.

caution [kaush°n] *s.* avertissement, m.; précaution; caution, f.; *v.* avertir; mettre en garde; *interj.* attention! ‖ **cautious** [kaush°s] *adj.* circonspect, prudent. ‖ **cautiousness** [-nis] *s.* circonspection, prudence, f.

cavalier [kav°li°r] *adj., s.* cavalier. ‖ **cavalry** [kav'lri] *s.°* cavalerie, f.

cave [ké¹v] *s.* caverne, f.; repaire, m.; *v.* creuser; *to cave in,* s'effondrer, s'affaisser.

cavern [kav°rn] *s.* caverne, f. ‖ **cavernous** [-°s] *adj.* caverneux; cave.

cavity [kav°ti] *s.°* cavité; carie, f.

caw [kau] *s.* croassement, m.; *v.* croasser.

cayman [ké¹m°n] *s.* caïman, m.

cease [sîs] *v.* cesser; arrêter; renoncer à; interrompre; *s.* cessation, cesse; relâche, f.; répit; arrêt, m.; **ceaseless,** incessant.

cecity [sìsiti] *s.* cécité, f.; aveuglement, m.

cedar [sid°r] *s.* cèdre, m.

cede [sîd] *v.* céder.

ceiling [sîling] *s.* plafond, m.; **ceiling price,** prix maximum.

celebrate [sèl°bré¹t] *v.* célébrer. ‖ **celebrated** [-id] *adj.* célèbre. ‖ **celebration** [sèl°bré¹sh°n] *s.* célébration, f. ‖ **celebrity** [s°lèbr°ti] *s.* célébrité, f.

celery [sèl°ri] *s.°* céleri, m.

celestial [s°lèstsh°l] *adj.* céleste.

celibacy [sèl°b°si] *s.* célibat, m. ‖ **celibate** [-bit] *s.* célibataire, m., f.

cell [sèl] *s.* cellule, f.; cachot, m.; pile électrique, f.

cellar [sèl°r] *s.* cave, f.; cellier, m.

Celluloid [sèly°lo¹d] *s.* Celluloïd, m.

cement [s°mènt] *s.* ciment, m.; *v.* cimenter; *reinforced cement,* ciment armé.

cemetery [sèm°t°ri] *s.°* cimetière, m.

censor [sèns°r] *s.* censeur; critique, m.; *v.* censurer. ‖ **censorship** [-ship] *s.* censure; fonction de censeur, f. ‖ **censure** [sènsh°r] *s.* censure, f.; *v.* censurer, blâmer, critiquer.

census [sèns°s] *s.* recensement, m.

cent [sènt] *s.* cent, m.; *Am.* pièce de monnaie, f.; *per cent,* pour cent. ‖ **centenarian** [sèntinè°ri°n] *adj., s.* centenaire, m., f. ‖ **centenary** [sèntin°ri] *adj., s.°* centenaire m. ‖ **centennial** [sentèni°l] *adj., s.* centenaire.

center [sènt°r] *s.* centre; cintre (arch.), m.; *v.* centrer; placer au centre; (se) concentrer.

centigrade [sènt°gré¹d] *adj.* centigrade. ‖ **centigram(me)** [-gram] *s.* centigramme, m. ‖ **centilitre** [-lìt°r] *s.* centilitre, m. ‖ **centimetre** [-mìt°r] *s.* centimètre, m.

centipede [sènt°pîd] *s.* mille-pattes, m.; scolopendre, f.

central [sèntr°l] *adj.* central; *s.* central téléphonique, m. ‖ **centralize** [sèntr°la¹z] *v.* centraliser.

century [sèntsh°ri] *s.°* siècle, m.

ceramics [si'ramiks] *s. pl.* céramique, f.

cereal [siri°l] *adj., s.* céréale.

cerebral [sèribr°l] *adj.* cérébral.

ceremonial [sèr°mo°uni°l] *adj., s.* cérémonial. ‖ **ceremonious** [-ni°s] *adj.* cérémonieux, solennel. ‖ **ceremony** [sèr°mo°uni] *s.°* cérémonie, f.

certain [sër't'n] *adj.* certain, sûr. ‖ **certainly** [-li] *adv.* certainement, assurément. ‖ **certainty** [-ti] *s.* certitude, assurance, f.

certificate [sër'tif°kit] *s.* certificat; diplôme; brevet, m.

certify [sër't°fa¹] *v.* certifier; légaliser; garantir.

certitude [sër't°tyoud] *s.* certitude, assurance, f.

cessation [sèsé¹sh°n] *s.* arrêt, m.; interruption; suspension, f.; *cessation of arms,* armistice.

cession [sèsh°n] *s.* cession, f.

cesspool [sèspoul] *s.* cloaque, m.; fosse d'aisances, f.

chafe [tshé¹f] *v.* chauffer; irriter; frotter; raguer (naut.); s'érailler *[rope]*; s'échauffer.

chaff [tshaf] *s.* balle *[corn]*; paille d'avoine; paille hachée, f.; *v.* railler, plaisanter. ‖ **chaffer** [-°r] *s.* taquin, plaisantin, m.

chaffinch [tshafintsh] *s.* pinson, m.

chafing [tshé¹fing] *s.* irritation, f.

chagrin [sh°grin] *s.* contrariété, f.; désappointement, m.; *v.* contrarier, chagriner.

chain [tshé¹n] *s.* chaîne, f.; *v.* enchaîner; captiver; *Am.* **chain store,** succursale commerciale; **chain stitch,** point de chaînette; **chain work,** travail à la chaîne.

chair [tshèr] *s.* siège, m.; chaise; chaire, f.; *armchair, easy-chair,* fauteuil, f.; *rocking-chair,* fauteuil à bascule. ‖ *chairman* [tshèrmᵉn] (*pl. chairmen*) *s.* président [meeting], m.

chaise [shéⁱz] *s.* cabriolet, m.; chaise de poste, f.

chalice [tshɑlis] *s.* calice, m.

chalk [tshauk] *s.* craie; « ardoise », somme due [account], f.; *v.* marquer à la craie; blanchir; *French chalk,* talc; *to chalk up,* inscrire une somme au compte de; *chalky,* crayeux, blanc.

challenge [tshɑlindj] *s.* défi, m.; provocation; interpellation; sommation; récusation (jur.), f.; *interj.* qui vive?; *v.* défier; revendiquer; interpeller; récuser (jur.); arrêter [sentry]; héler (naut.).

chamber [tshéⁱmbᵉr] *s.* chambre; salle; âme [gun], f.; *air chamber,* chambre à air. ‖ *chamberlain* [-ᵉlin] *s.* chambellan; camérier, m. ‖ *chambermaid* [-méⁱd] *s.* femme de chambre, f.

chameleon [kᵉmǐlyᵉn] *s.* caméléon, m.

chamfer [tshɑmfᵉr] *s.* chanfrein, m.

champagne [shɑmpéⁱn] *s.* champagne [wine], m.

champion [tshɑmpiᵉn] *s.* champion, m.; *v.* défendre, protéger. ‖ *championship* [-ship] *s.* championnat, m.

chance [tshɑns] *s.* sort, hasard, m.; occasion; probabilité, f.; billet de loterie, m.; *adj.* accidentel, fortuit; *v.* survenir; avoir lieu; avoir l'occasion de; risquer; *by chance,* par hasard; *to run a chance,* courir le risque.

chancellery [tshɑnsᵉlᵉri] *s.** chancellerie, f. ‖ *chancellor* [tshɑnsᵉlᵉr] *s.* chancelier; recteur [univ.]; *Am.* juge, m.

chandelier [shɑndᵉlǐᵉr] *s.* lustre, m.

change [tshéⁱndj] *s.* changement; linge de rechange, m.; monnaie; la Bourse, f.; *v.* changer; modifier; *small change,* petite monnaie; *to get change,* faire de la monnaie. ‖ *changeable* [-ᵉb'l] *adj.* variable, changeant; inconstant. ‖ *changer* [-ᵉr] *s.* changeur, m.

channel [tshɑn'l] *s.* canal; chenal; porte-hauban (naut.); lit [river], m.; *the English Channel,* la Manche.

chant [shɑnt] *s.* plain-chant, m.; *v.* psalmodier.

chaos [kéⁱɑs] *s.* chaos, m.

chap [tshap] *s.* gerçure; crevasse, f.; *v.* se gercer, se crevasser.

chap [tshap] *s.* camarade, copain; garçon, individu, type, m.

chapel [tshap'l] *s.* chapelle, f.

chaperon [shapᵉroᵘn] *s.* chaperon, m.; duègne, f.; *v.* chaperonner.

chaplain [tshɑplin] *s.* chapelain, m.; *army chaplain,* aumônier militaire.

chapter [tshɑptᵉr] *s.* chapitre [book]; chapitre des chanoines, m.; *Am.* branche d'une société, f.; *v.* chapitrer.

char [tshâr] *v.* carboniser; *s.* noir animal, m.

char [tshâr] *s.* femme (f) de ménage; *v.* faire des ménages.

character [kariktᵉr] *s.* marque, qualité dominante; réputation, f.; caractère; genre; personnage; rôle (theat.); certificat, m. ‖ *characteristic* [kariktᵉrīstik] *adj., s.* caractéristique. ‖ *characterization* [kariktᵉra¹zéⁱshᵉn] *s.* caractérisation; personnification, f. ‖ *characterize* [-ra¹z] *v.* caractériser.

charcoal [tshârkoᵘl] *s.* charbon de bois, m.; *charcoal-drawing,* fusain.

charge [tshârdj] *s.* charge; accusation, f.; prix, frais, m.; *v.* charger; percevoir; faire payer; grever; accuser, accabler; recharger (electr.); *at my own charge,* à mes frais; *charge account,* compte dans un magasin; *charge prepaid,* port payé. ‖ *charger* [-ᵉr] *s.* cheval de bataille; chargeur; plateau, m.

chariot [tshariᵉt] *s.* char, m.; voiture, f.; *v.* voiturer; rouler carrosse.

charitable [tsharᵉtᵉb'l] *adj.* charitable. ‖ *charity* [tsharᵉti] *s.** charité, offrande; bonnes œuvres, f.; *charity bazaar,* vente de charité; *charity school,* orphelinat.

charlatan [shârlᵉt'n] *s.* charlatan, m.

charm [tshârm] *s.* charme; attrait; talisman, m.; *v.* charmer. ‖ *charming* [-ing] *adj.* charmant.

chart [tshârt] *s.* carte marine, f.; diagramme; graphique, m.; *v.* cartographier; hydrographier.

charter [tshârtᵉr] *s.* charte, f.; affrètement, m.; *v.* affréter; louer; accorder une charte.

charwoman [tshârwoumᵉn] (*pl. charwomen*) *s.* femme de ménage (or) de journée.

chary [tshèⁱri] *adj.* économe, chiche; circonspect, avisé; emprunté.

chase [tshéⁱs] *s.* chasse, poursuite, f.; *v.* chasser, courre.

chase [tshéⁱs] *s.* rainure, ciselure, f.

chasm [kazᵉm] *s.* abîme, m.; crevasse; lacune, f.

chassis [shasì] *s.* châssis, m.

chaste [tshéⁱst] *adj.* chaste, pudique.

chastise [tshasta¹z] *v.* châtier. ‖ *chastisement* [tshastizmᵉnt] *s.* châtiment, m.; punition, f.

chastity [tshast⁰ti] s. chasteté, f.

chasuble [tshazoub'l] s. chasuble, f.

chat [tshat] s. causerie, causette, f.; v. causer, bavarder.

chattels [tshat'ls] s. pl. biens meubles, m. pl.; propriété, f.

chatter [tshat⁰r] s. cri de la pie; cri du singe; claquement de dents; bavardage, m.; jacasserie, f.; v. jaser; jacasser; claquer [teeth]. ‖ **chatterbox** [-bâks] s.* moulin (m.) à paroles (fam.).

chauffeur [shoouf⁰r] s. chauffeur, m.

chauvinist [shoouvinist] s. chauvin, m.

cheap [tshîp] adj., adv., s. bon marché; at a cheap rate, à bas prix; to hold cheap, faire peu de cas de; to feel cheap, se sentir honteux. ‖ **cheapen** [-⁰n] v. marchander; déprécier. ‖ **cheaply** [-li] adv. bon marché. ‖ **cheapness** [-nis] s. bas prix, m.; basse qualité, f.

cheat [tshît] s. escroquerie, f.; escroc; tricheur, m.; v. duper; escroquer; tricher [cards].

check [tshèk] s. échec, m.; rebuffade, f.; frein; obstacle, empêchement; poinçon; chèque bancaire, m. contremarque, f.; Am. note de restaurant, f.; jeton de vestiaire, m.. v. faire échec; réprimer, entraver. enregistrer; contrôler; consigner [luggage]; laisser au vestiaire. ‖ **checkbook** [-bouk] s. carnet de chèques; carnet à souches, m. ‖ **checkroom** [-roum] s. bureau d'enregistrement des bagages; vestiaire, m.; consigne, f. ‖ **checker** [-⁰r] s. pion du jeu de dames; dessin à carreaux; pointeur; contrôleur, m.; v. orner de carreaux; diversifier; **checker board**, damier.

cheek [tshîk] s. joue; bajoue; impudence, f.; **cheekbone**, pommette. ‖ **cheeky** [-i] adj. effronté.

cheep [tshîp] v. gazouiller; piauler, s. gazouillis; piaulement, m.

cheer [tshî⁰r] s. joie; bonne humeur; acclamation; chère [fare], f.; v. encourager; égayer; acclamer; **to cheer up**, réconforter. ‖ **cheerful** [f⁰l] adj. gai, allègre; réconfortant. ‖ **cheerfully** [-f⁰li] adv. allègrement, de bon cœur. ‖ **cheerfulness** [-f⁰lnis] s. allégresse, gaieté, bonne humeur, f. ‖ **cheerless** [-lis] adj. abattu, morne.

cheese [tshîz] s. fromage, m.; **cheese cover**, cloche à fromage; **cheese hopper**, asticot; **cottage cheese**, fromage blanc.

chemical [kèmik'l] adj. chimique; s. produit chimique, m.; **chemical warfare**, guerre des gaz. ‖ **chemist**

[kèmist] s. Br. pharmacien, m.; Am. chimiste, m. ‖ **chemistry** [-ri] s. chimie, f.

cheque [tshèk] s. chèque, m.

chequer [tshék⁰r] s. damier, m.; étoffe (f.) à carreaux; v. quadriller; bigarrer, diaprer; **chequered**, à carreaux; varié, mouvementé.

cherish [tshèrish] v. chérir; soigner; nourrir [hope].

cherry [tshèri] s.* cerise, f.; **cherry stone**, noyau de cerise.

chervil [tshërvil] s. cerfeuil, m.

chess [tshès] s. échecs, m. pl.; **chessboard**, échiquier.

chest [tshèst] s. coffre, m.; caisse, boîte; poitrine, f.; poitrail, m.; **chest of drawers**, commode.

chestnut [tshèsn⁰t] s. châtaigne, f.; marron, m.; plaisanterie, f.; adj. châtain; **chestnut horse**, alezan; **chestnut-tree**, châtaignier.

chew [tshou] s. chique, f.; v. chiquer; mâcher; ruminer, ressasser; **chewing-gum**, chewing-gum.

chicane [shiké¹n] s. chicane, f.; v. chicaner. ‖ **chicanery** [-ri] s.* chicanerie, argutie, chicane, f.

chick [tshik] s. poussin, m.; **chickpea**, pois chiche. ‖ **chicken** [-in] s. poulet, m.; **chicken pox**, varicelle; **chicken-hearted**, poule mouillée.

chicory [tshik⁰ri] s. chicorée; endive, f.

chide [tsha¹d] v.* gronder, réprimander; **chiding**, réprimande.

chief [tshîf] s. chef, m.; adj. principal; **chief justice**, président de la Cour suprême. ‖ **chiefly** [-li] adv. surtout, principalement.

chiffon [shifân] s. gaze, f.

chilblain [tshilblé¹n] s. engelure, f.

child [tsha¹ld] (pl. **children** [tshildr⁰n]) s. enfant, m., f.; **godchild**, filleul; **with child**, enceinte. ‖ **childbirth** [-bër̈th] s. accouchement, m. ‖ **childhood** [-houd] s. enfance, f. ‖ **childish** [-ish] adj. puéril, enfantin. ‖ **childless** [-lis] adj. sans enfants. ‖ **childlike** [-la¹k] adj. enfantin, candide, innocent.

chili [tshîli] s. Am. poivre de Cayenne, piment, m.

chill [tshil] s. froid, refroidissement, m.; adj. glacé; v. glacer; se refroidir; congeler, frigorifier. ‖ **chilly** [-i] adj. froid; frileux; frisquet; réfrigérant.

chim(a)era [k⁰mir⁰] s. chimère, f.

chime [tsha¹m] s. carillon, m.; harmonie, f.; v. carillonner; **to chime in**, placer son mot; **to chime with**, être en harmonie avec.

chimney [tshimni] s. cheminée, f.; **lamp chimney,** verre de lampe; **chimney hook,** crémaillère; **chimney piece,** manteau (m.) de cheminée; **chimney pot,** cheminée extérieure; **chimney sweep,** ramoneur.

chin [tshin] s. menton, m.

China [tsha¹ne] s. Chine, f.; **China aster,** reine-marguerite.

china [tsha¹ne] s. porcelaine, f.; adj. de Chine; de porcelaine, porcelainier; **china closet,** vitrine; **chinaware,** porcelaine.

chinch [tshintsh] s.* Am. punaise, f.

chincough [tshinkâf] s. coqueluche, f.

Chinese [tsha¹niz] adj., s. chinois.

chink [tshingk] s. crevasse, fente, f.; v. fendiller, crevasser.

chink [tshingk] s. tintement, m.; v. faire tinter; tinter.

chip [tship] s. copeau; fragment, m.; Am. incision dans un pin, f.; v. couper, hacher; chapeler; s'effriter; inciser; Am. **to chip in,** placer son mot; mettre son grain de sel.

chipmunk [tshipmœngk] s. tamia, Fr. Can. suisse, m.

chiropractic [ka¹repraktik] s. chiropraxie; ostéopathie, Fr. Can. chiropratique, f. ‖ **chiropractor** [-ter] s. ostéopathe; Fr. Can. chiropraticien, m.

chirp [tshĕrp] s. gazouillement, m.; v. gazouiller. ‖ **chirping** [-ing] s. pépiement, m.

chisel [tshiz'l] s. ciseau, m.; v. ciseler; filouter (pop.).

chivalrous [shiv'lres] adj. chevaleresque. ‖ **chivalry** [shiv'lri] s. chevalerie; courtoisie, f.

chlorine [klo°urin] s. chlore, m. ‖ **chloroform** [klo°uraufaurm] s. chloroforme, m.; v. chloroformer.

chocolate [tshouklit] adj. s. chocolat; **chocolate pot,** chocolatière.

choice [tsho¹s] s. choix; assortiment, m.; alternative, f.; adj. choisi, excellent; **by choice,** par goût, volontairement; **for choice,** de préférence.

choir [kwâ¹er] s. chœur, m.; v. chanter en chœur; **choir-school,** manécanterie, maîtrise.

choke [tsho°uk] v. étouffer; obstruer; étrangler; régulariser [motor]; s. suffocation; constriction, f.; obturateur [auto], m.

cholera [kâlere] s. choléra, m.

choose [tshouz] v.* choisir; décider; préférer; opter; **to pick and choose,** faire son choix.

chop [tshâp] v. taillader; hacher; gercer; s. côtelette, f; coup de hache, de couperet, m. ‖ **chopping** [-ing] s.

coupe, f.; hachage, m.; **chopping-block, chopping-knife,** hachoir.

choral [ko°urel] s. chœur, m.; adj. choral.

chord [kaurd] s. corde [music], f.; accord [music], m.

chore [tsho°ur] s. Am. besogne, f.

chorus [ko°ures] s. chœur, m.; v. chanter, répéter en chœur.

chose [tsho°uz] pret. of **to choose.** ‖ **chosen** [-'n] p. p. of **to choose.**

chrism [krizem] s. chrême, m.

Christ [kra¹st] s. Christ, m. ‖ **christen** [kris'n] v. baptiser. ‖ **christening** [-ing] s. baptême, m. ‖ **christian** [krist-sh°n] adj., s. chrétien; **christian name,** prénom, f. ‖ **christianity** [kristshian°ti] s. christianisme, m.

Christmas [krismes] s. Noël, m., f.; **Christmas Eve,** nuit de Noël; **Christmas log,** bûche de Noël.

chronic [krânik] adj. chronique.

chronicle [krânik'l] s. chronique, f.; v. relater, narrer. ‖ **chronicler** [-er] s. chroniqueur, m.

chronological [krânelâdjik'l] adj. chronologique.

chronometer [krenâmeter] s. chronomètre, m.

chrysalid [kris'lid] s. chrysalide, f.

chrysanthemum [krisânth°mem] s. chrysanthème, m.

chubby [tshœbi] adj. joufflu, dodu.

chuck [tshœk] s. gloussement, m.; v. glousser.

chuck [tshœk] s. tapotement, m.; v. tapoter.

chuckle [tshœk'l] s. rire étouffé; gloussement, m.; v. glousser.

chum [tshœm] s. camarade, copain, m.; **chummy,** intime.

chump [tshœmp] s. bûche, f.; lourdaud, m.

chunk [tshœngk] s. gros morceau; quignon [bread], m. ‖ **chunky** [-i] adj. Am. trapu, grassouillet.

church [tshĕrtsh] s.* église, f.; temple, m. ‖ **churchman** [-men] (pl. **churchmen**) s. ecclésiastique, m. ‖ **churchy** [-i] adj. cagot; calotin. ‖ **churchyard** [-yârd] s. cimetière, m.

churl [tshĕrl] s. rustre; grigou; crin, ronchon, m. (fam.); **churlish,** fruste, mal dégrossi; grincheux; regardant.

churn [tshĕrn] s. baratte, f.; v. baratter; fouetter [cream].

chute [shout] s. glissière, f.; rapide, m.; **coal chute,** manche à charbon; **refuse chute,** vide-ordures.

cicada [siké¹de] s. cigale, f.

cider [saɪdər] s. cidre, m.

cigar [sigár] s. cigare, m.; **cigar-store**, débit de tabac. ‖ **cigarette** [sigerèt] s. cigarette, f.; **cigarette holder**, fume-cigarette; **cigarette case**, étui à cigarettes; **cigarette lighter**, briquet.

cinch [sintsh] s.* Am. sangle, f.; « filon », m.; v. sangler.

cinder [sindər] s. braise; escarbille, f.; pl. cendres, f.

cinema [sínəmə] s. cinéma, m. ‖ **cinematograph** [sinimatəgrâf] s. cinéma, m.; v. cinématographier.

cinnamon [sínəmən] s. cannelle, f.

cipher [saɪfər] s. zéro; chiffre; code secret, m.; v. chiffrer; calculer; **cipherer**, officier du chiffre.

circle [sёrk'l] s cercle; milieu social, m.; v. encercler; circuler, tournoyer.

circuit [sёrkit] s. circuit, parcours, tour; pourtour, m.; tournée rotation, révolution, f.; **circuit breaker**, disjoncteur. ‖ **circuitous** [sёrkyouìtəs] adj. indirect, détourné.

circular [sёrkyeləг] adj., s. circulaire. ‖ **circulate** [sёrkyelé¹t] v. circuler; répandre; **circulating library**, bibliothèque circulante. **circulation** [sёrkyeléʹshən] s. circulation, f.

circumference [sёrkœmfərəns] s. circonférence, périphérie, f. ‖ **circumlocution** [sёrkəmloʰkyoushən] s. circonlocution, f.

circumscribe [sёrkəmskraɪb] v. circonscrire.

circumspect [sёrkəmspèkt] adj. circonspect. ‖ **circumspection** [sёrkəmspèkshən] s. circonspection, f.

circumstance [sёrkəmstans] s. constance, f.; événement; détail, m.; pl. situation de fortune, f.; **in no circumstances**, en aucun cas. ‖ **circumstantial** [sёrkəmstænshəl] adj. circonstancié; accessoire; indirect (jur.).

circus [sёrkəs] s.* cirque; rond-point, m.

cistern [sístёrn] s. citerne, cuve, f.; réservoir, m.; chasse d'eau, f.

citadel [sitéd'l] s. citadelle, f.

citation [saɪtéʹshən] s. citation; mention, f. ‖ **cite** [saɪt] v. citer; mentionner; appeler en justice.

citizen [sítz'n] s. citoyen; civil; citadin; ressortissant, m. ‖ **citizenship** [-ship] s. droit de cité, m.; nationalité, f.

citron [sítrən] s. cédrat, m.

city [síti] s.* cité, ville, f.; adj. urbain; municipal; **city council**, municipalité; **city hall**, mairie; **city item**, Am. nouvelle locale.

civic [sivik] adj. civique. ‖ **civics** [-s] s. Am. instruction civique, f.

civil [sív'l] adj. civil; **civil duty**, devoir civique. ‖ **civilian** [sevílyən] s. civil; **civilian clothes**, habit civil. ‖ **civility** [sevíleti] s.* urbanité, courtoisie, f. ‖ **civilization** [siv'lzéʹshən] s. civilisation, f. ‖ **civilize** [sív'la¹z] v. civiliser. ‖ **civism** [sivíz'm] s. civisme, m.

clad [klad] pret., p. p. of **clothe**.

claim [kléʹm] s. demande; revendication; prétention, f.; droit, titre, m.; v. revendiquer; prétendre à; accaparer (attention). ‖ **claimant** [-ent] s. réclamant; prétendant [throne]; postulant, requérant, m.

clairvoyant [klèrvoʹent] adj. clairvoyant; voyant.

clam [klam] s. peigne [shellfish], m.; palourde, f.; **clam-diggers**, Am. corsaire [trousers].

clamber [klambər] v. grimper.

clammy [klami] adj. visqueux, gluant.

clamor [klamər] s. clameur, f.; v. clamer, vociférer. ‖ **clamorous** [klaméʹrəs] adj. bruyant; revendicateur.

clamp [klàmp] s. crampon, m.; armature; agrafe, f.; v. cramponner; assujettir; marcher lourdement.

clan [klàn] s. clan, m.; **clannish**, attaché à sa coterie, partisan.

clandestine [klàndèstin] adj. clandestin.

clang [klàng] s. sonnerie, f.; bruit métallique, m.; v. sonner, tinter; résonner, retentir. ‖ **clango(u)r** [-ᵉr] s. son éclatant, m.; v. retentir. ‖ **clangorous** [-gᵉrᵉs] adj. retentissant.

clap [klap] s. claquement; coup, m.; v. claquer; taper; battre [wings]; applaudir; **clap of thunder**, coup de tonnerre.

claret [klarᵉt] s. bordeaux [wine], m.

clarify [klarefaʹ] v. clarifier, élucider; s'éclaircir.

clarinet [klarenèt] s. clarinette, f.

clarion [klariᵉn] s. clairon, m.

clarity [klareti] s. clarté, lumière, f.

clash [klash] s.* collision, f.; choc, fracas, m.; v. choquer, heurter; entrer en lutte; résonner; se heurter.

clasp [klasp] s. fermoir; clip, m.; agrafe; étreinte, f.; v. agrafer; étreindre; joindre [hands].

class [klas] s.* classe; leçon; catégorie, f.; cours; ordre; rang, m.; v. classer, classifier; **the lower classes**, le prolétariat. ‖ **classic** [-ik] adj., s. classique; **classic scholar**, humaniste. ‖ **classical** [-ik'l] adj. classique. ‖ **classify** [-ifaʹ] v. classifier. ‖ **classmate** [-méʹt] s. condisciple, m. ‖ **classroom** [-roum] s. salle de classe, f.

clatter [klat**e**r] *s.* fracas; bruit de roue, m.; *v.* résonner; cliqueter; caqueter.

clause [klauz] *s.* article, m.; clause, proposition (gramm.), f.; membre de phrase, m.; avenant, m. (jur.).

clavicle [klavik'l] *s.* clavicule, f.

claw [klau] *s.* griffe; serre [eagle]; pince [crab], f.; valet [bench], m.; *v.* griffer; agripper; égratigner; érafler; gratter (fam.).

clay [klé¹] *s.* argile; glaise, f.; limon, m.; *clayish*, argileux.

clean [klîn] *adj.* propre; pur; net; *adv.* absolument, totalement; *v.* nettoyer; purifier; vider [fish]; *clean-cut*, bien coupé, élégant, net; *clean-handed*, probe. ‖ *cleaner* [-er] *s.* nettoyeur; dégraisseur; cireur, m.; *vacuum cleaner*, aspirateur. ‖ *cleaning* [-ing] *s.* nettoyage, dégraissage, m. ‖ *cleanliness* [klênlinis] *s.* propreté, f. ‖ *cleanly* [klênli] *adv.* proprement; *adj.* propre. ‖ *cleanness* [klinnis] *s.* propreté, f. ‖ *cleanse* [klènz] *v.* nettoyer, purifier. ‖ *cleanser* [klènser] *s.* produit d'entretien, m. ‖ *cleansing* [-ing] *adj.* détersif; *s.* nettoyage, m.; dépuration; purification, f.

clear [klier] *adj.* clair; serein; évident; pur; sans mélange; entier; débarrassé de; *adv.* clairement; entièrement; *v.* clarifier; éclaircir; nettoyer; défricher; débarrasser; disculper; ouvrir [way]; dégager; franchir; liquider; toucher net [sum]; *s.* espace dégagé, m.; *clear loss*, perte sèche; *clear majority*, majorité absolue; *clear profit*, bénéfice net; *to clear the ground*, déblayer le terrain; *to clear the table*, desservir; *the sky clears up*, le ciel s'éclaire; *clear-sighted*, clairvoyant. ‖ *clearance* [-rens] *s.* dégagement; déblaiement; dédouanement; congé (naut.), m.; *clearance sale*, liquidation. ‖ *clearing* [-ring] *s.* éclaircissement; déblaiement; dédouanement, m.; justification, f.; terrain défriché, m.; éclaircie [wood]; liquidation [account]; compensation bancaire, f. ‖ *clearness* [-nis] *s.* clarté, f.

cleat [klît] *s.* taquet; tasseau, m.

cleave [klîv] *v.* fendre. ‖ *cleaver* [-er] *s.* couperet; fendoir, m.

cleave [klîv] *v.* coller, adhérer à; s'attacher à.

clef [klèf] *s.* clef (mus.), f.

cleft [klèft] *s.* fente, fissure, f.; *adj.* fendu, fissuré; *p. p. of to cleave.*

clematis [klèmetis] *s.** clématite, f.

clemency [klèmensi] *s.* clémence, f.; douceur [weather], f. ‖ *clement* [klèment] *adj.* clément, indulgent; doux, clément [weather].

clementina [klèmentîne] *s.* clémentine, f.

clench [klèntsh] *s.** crampon, rivet, m.; *v.* river [nail]; serrer [teeth]; serrer [fist]; empoigner.

clergy [klëfdji] *s.* clergé, m. ‖ *clergyman* [-men] *s.* ecclésiastique, m. ‖ *clerical* [klérik'l] *adj.* ecclésiastique, clérical; de bureau; *clerical work*, travail d'écritures.

clerk [klërk] *s.* clerc; commis; employé; secrétaire municipal; *Am.* vendeur, m.; *law-clerk*, greffier.

clever [klèver] *adj.* habile; intelligent; adroit. ‖ *cleverly* [-li] *adv.* habilement; sagement; bien. ‖ *cleverness* [-nis] *s.* dextérité; habileté; intelligence, ingéniosité; promptitude (f.) d'esprit.

clew [klou] *s. Br.* fil conducteur; indice; écheveau, m.; piste; pelote; trace, f.; *v.* peloter; mettre sur la piste; *to clew up*, carguer.

cliché [klishé¹] *s.* cliché; lieu commun, m.; banalité, f.

click [klik] *s.* cliquetis; clic; clappement [tongue]; bruit métallique, m.; *v.* cliqueter; claquer; *to click the heels*, claquer des talons.

client [kla¹ent] *s.* client, m., cliente, f. ‖ *clientele* [kla¹èntèl] *s.* clientèle, f.; habitués, m. pl. (theatr.).

cliff [klif] *s.* falaise, f.; rocher escarpé, m.; varappe, f.

climate [kla¹mit] *s.* climat [weather], m. ‖ *climatize* [-eta¹z] *v.* acclimater.

climax [kla¹maks] *s.* gradation, f.; comble; faîte, sommet, m.; *v.* culminer; amener au point culminant.

climb [kla¹m] *v.* grimper; gravir; escalader; s'élever; s'ascension, escalade, f.; *to climb down*, descendre; en rabattre, baisser pavillon. ‖ *climber* [-er] *s.* grimpeur; alpiniste, m.; plante grimpante, f.; *Am.* arriviste, m. ‖ *climbing* [-ing] *s.* montée, escalade, f.; arrivisme, m.

clinch [klintsh] *v.* river; serrer; tenir bon; assujettir; *s.** crampon; corps-à-corps [boxing], m.

cling [kling] *v.** se cramponner; adhérer; coller à; s'en tenir, rester attaché [to, à].

clinic [klinik] *s.* clinique, f. ‖ *clinical* [-el] *adj.* clinique.

clink [klingk] *v.* cliqueter; *s.* cliquetis; tintement, m. ‖ *clinker* [-er] *s.* mâchefer, m.; type formidable, m.

clip [klip] *s.* broche; attache, agrafe, f.; *v.* serrer, pincer; agrafer; écourter.

clip [klip] *s.* tonte, f.; coup, m.; *v.* tondre; rogner; couper ras; donner des coups de poing (fam.); *to go a good clip*, marcher à vive allure, « allonger le compas ». ‖ *clipper* [-ᵉʳ] *s.* tondeuse, f.; clipper [ship, plane], m. ‖ *clipping* [-ing] *s.* tonte; taille [hair], f.; *Am.* coupure de presse, f.; *clipping bureau*, argus de la presse.

clique [klik] *s.* clique, coterie, f.

cloak [kloᵒᵘk] *s.* manteau, pardessus, m.; capote, f.; prétexte; masque, m.; *v.* couvrir d'un manteau; masquer, dissimuler. ‖ *cloakroom* [-room] *s.* vestiaire (theat.), m.; consigne (railw.), f.; *Am.* antichambre [Capitole, Washington].

clock [klâk] *s.* horloge; pendule; montre, f.; *adj.* régulier, réglé; *v.* minuter [race]; chronométrer; *alarm clock*, réveille-matin; *to set a clock by*, régler une pendule sur; *the clock is fast*, l'horloge avance; *time-recording clock*, pendule enregistreuse; *clockwise*, dans le sens des aiguilles d'une montre; *clockwork*, rouages.

clod [klâd] *s.* motte de terre, f.; caillot; lourdaud, m.; *v.* s'agglomérer [earth].

clodhopper [klâdhâpᵉʳ] *s.* paysan; cul-terreux, m.; godasse, f.

clog [klâg] *s.* entrave, f.; obstacle, empêchement, m.; galoche, f.; *v.* obstruer; se boucher; s'étouffer.

cloister [klo¹stᵉʳ] *s.* cloître, m.; *v.* cloîtrer; *cloistral*, claustral.

close [kloᵒᵘz] *s.* fin, conclusion; clôture, f.; enclos, m.; *v.* fermer; enfermer; se clore; arrêter [account]; conclure; serrer [ranks]; *to close out*, liquider; *closed session*, huis-clos (jur.).

close [kloᵒᵘs] *adj.* clos, fermé; enclos; mesquin, avare; lourd [weather]; renfermé [air]; suffocant; compact; serré [questioning]; étroit, rigoureux; intime; ininterrompu [bombardment]; appliqué, attentif; littéral [translation]; *adv.* hermétiquement, tout près, tout de suite; *close-fitting*, ajusté, collant; *close-mouthed*, peu communicatif; *close shaven*, rasé de près. ‖ *closely* [-li] *adv.* de près; étroitement; rigoureusement, secrètement. ‖ *closeness* [-nis] *s.* proximité, étroitesse; ladrerie; solitude, f.; rapprochement; isolement; manque d'air, m.; fidélité [translation]; rigueur; texture serrée, f.; caractère renfermé, m.

closet [klâzit] *s.* cabinet, m.; armoire, penderie, f.; *adj.* secret, intime; *v.* conférer secrètement; prendre à part.

closure [kloᵒᵘjᵉʳ] *s.* clôture; conclusion, f.; *v.* clôturer, clore.

clot [klât] *s.* grumeau, caillot, m.; (fam.) idiot, m.; *v.* se cailler, se coaguler.

cloth [klauth] *s.* toile; nappe; étoffe; livrée, f.; tapis de table; tissu; uniforme; drap; torchon, m.; *tea cloth*, nappe à thé; *man of the cloth*, ministre du culte; *American cloth*, toile cirée; *cloth-maker*, drapier. ‖ *clothe* [kloᵒᵘzh] *v.* vêtir; habiller. ‖ *clothes* [kloᵒᵘz] *s. pl.* habits, vêtements; linge, m.; *underclothes*, sous-vêtements; *suit of clothes*, complet; *clothes pin*, pince à linge; *clothes-rack* (or) *-tree*, porte-habits, portemanteau. ‖ *clothier* [kloᵒᵘzhyᵉʳ] *s.* drapier; fabricant de vêtements, m. ‖ *clothing* [kloᵒᵘzhing] *s.* costume; vêtement; linge, m.; fabrication du drap, f.

cloud [klaᵒᵘd] *s.* nuage, m.; foule, nuée, f.; *v.* couvrir de nuages; s'assombrir; se voiler; menacer; ternir; s'amonceler. ‖ *cloudburst* [-bë'st] *s.* averse, trombe, f. ‖ *cloudiness* [-inis] *s.* aspect nuageux; aspect trouble; air sombre, m.; obscurité, f. ‖ *cloudless* [-lis] *adj.* serein, clair, sans nuage. ‖ *cloudy* [-i] *adj.* nuageux, couvert; sombre; trouble [liquid]; nébuleux [idea].

clove [kloᵒᵘv] *s.* clou de girofle, m.; *clove of garlic*, gousse d'ail.

clover [kloᵒᵘvᵉʳ] *s.* trèfle, m.; *to be in clover*, être dans l'abondance.

clown [klaᵒᵘn] *s.* rustre; bouffon, clown, m.; *v.* faire le clown.

cloy [klo¹] *v.* rassasier, repaître; gorger; lasser, dégoûter, blaser.

club [klœb] *s.* massue; trique, f.; trèfle [cards]; club, m.; *v.* frapper, assommer; se réunir; s'associer; *club-foot*, pied-bot; *clubhouse*, club, cercle.

cluck [klœk] *s.* gloussement, m.; *v.* glousser.

clue, see **clew**.

clump [klœmp] *s.* groupe, bloc, m.; bouquet, massif [trees], m.; *Am.* bloc [houses], m.; bruit sourd, m.; *v.* grouper en bouquet; marcher d'un pas lourd.

clumsy [klœmzi] *adj.* engourdi; gauche, maladroit; disgracieux.

clung *pret., p. p. of* to cling.

cluster [klœstᵉʳ] *s.* grappe, f.; bouquet; groupe; essaim [bees], m.; *Am.* entourage [gems], m.; *v.* (se) grouper; se mettre en grappe.

clutch [klœtsh] *s.* prise, f.; griffe, serre; couvée [eggs], f.; embrayage [auto], m.; *v.* saisir, empoigner; accrocher; *to step on the clutch*, débrayer; *to throw in the clutch*, embrayer; *clutch-disc*, disque d'embrayage; *clutch-fork*, embrayeur; *foot clutch*, pédale d'embrayage.

clutter [klœtᵉʳ] *v.* désordre, m.; confusion, f.; *v.* mettre en désordre; rendre confus; se démener, s'affairer.

coach [koᵒutsh] *s.* voiture, f.; car; wagon, m.; entraîneur; répétiteur, m.; *v.* préparer, guider, mettre au courant. ‖ *coachman* [-mᵉn] *s.* conducteur; cocher, m.

coagulate [koᵒuagyᵉléⁱt] *v.* coaguler; se cailler; se coaguler.

coal [koᵒul] *s.* charbon, m.; houille, f.; *v.* approvisionner en charbon; *hard coal*, anthracite; *coal-dust*, poussier; *coal oil*, pétrole.

coalesce [koᵒuelès] *v.* s'unir, se combiner, se fondre.

coalition [koᵒuelishᵉn] *s.* coalition, f.

coarse [koᵒurs] *adj.* grossier; brut; vulgaire. ‖ *coarseness* [-nis] *s.* rudesse; grossièreté, vulgarité, f.

coast [koᵒust] *s.* côte; berge; pente [hill], f.; littoral, m.; *v.* côtoyer; caboter (naut.); *Am.* glisser le long de; *coastal*, côtier; *coastline*, littoral.

coat [koᵒut] *s.* habit, m.; veste; tunique; peau [snake]; robe [animal]; couche [paint], f.; *v.* revêtir, enduire; peindre; goudronner; glacer (culin.); *coated*, chargé [tongue]; couché [paper]. ‖ *coat-hanger*, portemanteau; *to turn one's coat*, tourner casaque. ‖ *coating* [-ing] *s.* enduit, revêtement, m.

coax [koᵒuks] *v.* cajoler; caresser; enjôler, amadouer.

cob [kâb] *s.* épi de maïs; bidet [horse], m.; boule [bread], f.; torchis, m.

cobalt [koᵒubault] *s.* cobalt, m.

cobble [kâb'l] *s.* pavé rond, m.; *v.* paver.

cobble [kâb'l] *v.* raccommoder [shoes]. ‖ *cobbler* [-ᵉʳ] *s.* cordonnier; cobbler [drink], m.; *Am.* tourte aux fruits, f.

cobra [koᵒubrᵉ] *s.* cobra, m.

cobweb [kâbwèb] *s.* toile d'araignée, f.

cocaine [koᵒukéⁱn] *s.* cocaïne, f.

cock [kâk] *s.* coq; oiseau mâle; robinet [tap]; chien [gun], m.; meule [hay], f.; *v.* relever [hat]; armer [gun]; *fuel cock*, robinet d'essence; *cock-eyed*, qui louche; *safety cock*, cran d'arrêt; *cock-sure*, absolument sûr; *cock-a-doodle-doo*, cocorico.

cockade [kâkéⁱd] *s.* cocarde, f.

cockatoo [kâkᵉtoᵘ] *s.* cacatoès, m.

cockchafer [kâktshèⁱfᵉʳ] *s.* hanneton, m.

cockle *s.* clovisse; froissure, f.; faux pli, m.; *v.* (se) froisser; (se) chiffonner.

cockroach* [kâkroᵒutsh] *s.* blatte, f.; cafard, m.

cocktail [kâktéⁱl] *s.* cocktail, m.

cocky [kâki] *adj.* impertinent, insolent; fat; suffisant; tranchant.

cocoa [koᵒukoᵘ] *s.* cacao, m.

coconut [koᵒukᵉnᵉt] *s.* noix de coco, f.

cocoon [kᵉkoun] *s.* cocon, m.

cod [kâd] *s.* morue, f.; *cod-liver oil*, huile de foie de morue.

coddle [kâd'l] *v.* mitonner; choyer; câliner; *Am.* faire mijoter.

code [koᵒud] *s.* code, m.; *v.* chiffrer; *code message*, message chiffré.

codger [kâdjᵉʳ] *s.* type; original; gaillard, m.

codicil [kâdᵉs'l] *s.* codicille, m.

codify [kâdᵉfaⁱ] *v.* codifier.

coefficient [koifishᵉnt] *s.* coefficient, m.

cœnobite [sìnobaⁱt] *s.* cénobite, m.

coerce [koᵒuᵉrs] *v.* contraindre; réprimer. ‖ *coercion* [koᵒuᵉʳshᵉn] *s.* coercition, contrainte; coaction (jur.), f. ‖ *coercive* [koᵉʳsiv] *adj.* coercitif.

coffee [kaufi] *s.* café, m.; *coffee-cup*, tasse à café; *coffee-mill*, moulin à café; *coffee-pot*, cafetière; *coffee-tree*, caféier.

coffer [kaufᵉʳ] *s.* coffre, m.; cassette, f.; *v.* mettre au coffre.

coffin [kaufin] *s.* cercueil, m.; *v.* mettre en bière.

cog [koᵒug] *s.* dent [wheel], f.; rouage, m.; *cogwheel*, roue dentée.

cogent [koᵒudjᵉnt] *adj.* convaincant; puissant [argument].

cogitate [kâdjitéⁱt] *v.* méditer; réfléchir à.

cognate [kâgnéⁱt] *adj.* apparenté; *s.* congénère, parent, m.

coherent [koᵒuhirᵉnt] *adj.* cohérent. ‖ *cohesion* [koᵒuhijᵉn] *s.* cohésion, f.

coiffeur [kwâfᵉʳ] *s.* coiffeur, m. ‖ *coiffure* [kwâfyouʳ] *s.* coiffure [hairdo], f.

coil [koⁱl] *s.* rouleau; repli, m.; spirale, f.; glène [rope]; bobine (electr.), f.; *v.* s'enrouler; lover.

coin [koⁱn] *s.* pièce de monnaie, f.; coin, m.; *v.* battre [money]; inventer; fabriquer; *to pay one in his own coin*, rendre à quelqu'un la monnaie de sa pièce. ‖ *coinage* [-idj] *s.* monnayage, m.; frappe; invention, f.

coincide [koᵒuinsaⁱd] *v.* coïncider. ‖ *coincidence* [koᵒuinsᵉdᵉns] *s.* coïncidence, f.

coke [coᵒuk] *s.* coke, m.

colander [kælᵉndᵉʳ] *s.* tamis, m.

cold [koᵒuld] *adj.* froid; *s.* froid; refroidissement; rhume, m.; *coldcream*, crème de beauté; *to give the* *cold shoulder*, battre froid; *head cold*, rhume de cerveau; *chest cold*, rhume de poitrine. ‖ **coldness** [-nis] *s*. froidure; froideur, f.

cole-seed [koºulsîd] *s*. graine de colza, f.

collaborate [kᵉlaberéᵻt] *v*. collaborer. ‖ **collaboration** [kᵉlaberéᵻshᵉn] *s*. collaboration, f. ‖ **collaborator** [kᵉlaberéᵻtᵉr] *s*. collaborateur, m.; collaboratrice, f.

collapse [kᵉlaps] *v*. s'écrouler; s'effondrer; être démoralisé; *s*. effondrement; évanouissement, m.; prostration, f.

collar [kâlᵉr] *s*. collier [dog]; col [shirt]; collet, m.; *v*. colleter; prendre au collet; *stiff collar*, faux col; *collarbone*, clavicule; *collar size*, encolure.

collateral [kᵉlatᵉrᵉl] *adj*. collatéral; secondaire, accessoire; coïncident; *s*. nantissement; collatéral, m.

colleague [kᵉlîg] *s*. collègue, m., f.

collect [kᵉlèkt] *v*. rassembler; collectionner; percevoir [taxes]; recouvrer [debts]; faire la levée [mail]; s'amasser; *s*. collecte, f.; *to collect oneself*, se ressaisir, se recueillir; *collect on delivery*, en port dû. ‖ **collection** [kᵉlèkshᵉn] *s*. collection; accumulation; perception; collecte; levée [letters], f.; ramassage; encaissement, m.; *to take up a collection*, faire la quête. ‖ **collective** [kᵉlèktiv] *adj*. collectif. ‖ **collector** [kᵉlèktᵉr] *s*. collecteur; percepteur; quêteur; collectionneur, m.

college [kâlidj] *s*. collège; corps constitué, m.; faculté [univ.], f.

collide [kᵉlaᵻd] *v*. entrer en collision; s'emboutir.

collier [kâlyᵉr] *s*. mineur, m.; navire charbonnier, m.

collision [kâlijᵉn] *s*. collision f.; heurt, choc; abordage; conflit, m.

colloquial [kᵉloºukwiᵉl] *adj*. familier; de la conversation courante. ‖ **colloquy** [-i] *s*.* colloque, entretien, m.

collusion [kâlyoujᵉn] *s*. collusion, f.

colon [koºulᵉn] *s*. côlon [anat.], m.

colon [koºulᵉn] *s*. deux-points [ponctuation], m. pl.

colonel [kën'l] *s*. colonel, m.

colonial [kᵉloºuniᵉl] *adj*., *s*. colonial. ‖ **colonist** [kâlᵉnist] *s*. colon, m. ‖ **colonization** [kâlᵉnezéᵻshᵉn] *s*. colonisation, f. ‖ **colonize** [kâlᵉnaᵻz] *v*. coloniser. ‖ **colonizer** [-ᵉr] *s*. colonisateur, m.; colonisatrice, f. ‖ **colony** [kâlᵉni] *s*.* colonie, f.

colo(u)r [kœlᵉr] *s*. couleur, teinte, f.; ton, m.; *pl*. drapeau; *v*. colorer; colorier; teinter; rougir; se colorer;

colo(u)rblind, daltonien. ‖ **colo(u)red** [-d] *adj*. coloré; colorié; de couleur. ‖ **colo(u)rful** [-fᵉl] *adj*. haut en couleurs. ‖ **colo(u)ring** [-ing] *s*. coloration, f.; coloris; prétexte, m. ‖ **colo(u)rless** [-lis] *adj*. incolore, terne.

colossal [kᵉlâs'l] *adj*. colossal. ‖ **colossus** [kᵉlâsᵉs] *s*.* colosse, m.

colt [koºult] *s*. revolver, colt; poulain, m.

column [kâlᵉm] *s*. colonne, f. ‖ **columnist** [-ist] *s*. journaliste, m.

coma [koºumᵉ] *s*. coma, m.; *comatose*, comateux.

comb [koºum] *s*. peigne, m.; étrille; carde; crête [cock, wave], f.; rayon [honey], m.; *v*. peigner; étriller; carder; déferler [wave].

combat [kâmbat] *s*. combat, m.; *v*. combattre, se battre. ‖ **combatant** [kâmbᵉtᵉnt] *adj*., *s*. combattant. ‖ **combative** [-iv] *adj*. combatif.

comber [koºumbᵉr] *s*. cardeur; brisant, m.

combination [kâmbᵉnéᵻshᵉn] *s*. combinaison; coalition; association, f.; syndicat, m.; chemise-culotte, f. ‖ **combine** [kᵉmbaᵻn] —*v*. combiner; s'unir, s'associer; se syndiquer; se liguer; *s*. [ˈkâmbaᵻn] corporation, f.; trust, m.; *combine-harvester*, moissonneuse-batteuse.

combustible [kᵉmbœstᵉb'l] *adj*., *s*. combustible. ‖ **combustion** [kᵉmbœstshᵉn] *s*. combustion, f.

come [kœm] *v*.* venir; arriver; provenir; advenir; parvenir. *p. p. of* **to come**; *to come across*, traverser; venir à l'esprit; *to come away*, s'en aller; *to come back*, retourner; *to come forth*, paraître, être publié; *to come in*, entrer; *to come out*, sortir; *to come of age*, atteindre sa majorité; *to come near*, approcher; *to come on*, avancer; *to come to pass*, se faire, se réaliser; *to come up*, pousser, monter, surgir; *to make a come-back*, se rétablir; faire une rentrée.

comedian [kᵉmidiᵉn] *s*. comédien, comique, m. ‖ **comedy** [kâmᵉdi] *s*. comédie, f.

comely [kœmli] *adj*. gracieux, séduisant, avenant. ‖ **comeliness** [-nis] *s*. beauté, grâce, f.; charme, m.

comestible [kᵉméstib'l] *adj*., *s*. comestible, m.

comet [kâmit] *s*. comète, f.

comfit [kœmfit] *s*. dragée, f.; *comfitmaker*, confiseur.

comfort [kœmfᵉrt] *s*. confort, bienêtre; réconfort, m.; aisance; consolation, f.; *v*. réconforter. ‖ **comfortable** [-ᵉb'l] *adj*. confortable; consolant;

aisé [life]. ‖ *comfortably* [-ᵉb'li] adv. confortablement. ‖ *comforter* [-ᵉʳ] s. consolateur, m.; *Br.* cache-nez; *Am.* couvre-pied, m.; couverture piquée, f. ‖ *comfortless* [-lis] adj. triste; incommode; délaissé.

comic [kámik] adj. comique; s. comique; dessin humoristique, m. ‖ *comical* [-'l] adj. plaisant, drôle.

coming [kœming] adj. prochain; s. venue, arrivée, f.

comma [kámᵉ] s. virgule, f.; *Br.* *inverted commas,* guillemets.

command [kᵉmánd] s. ordre; pouvoir, m.; autorité, maîtrise; région militaire, f.; v. commander; dominer; *to have full command of,* être entièrement maître de. ‖ *commander* [-ᵉʳ] s. commandant, chef, m. ‖ *commandment* [-mᵉnt] s. commandement, m.

commemorate [kᵉmèmᵉréit] v. commémorer. ‖ *commemoration* [kᵉmémârᵉ'shᵉn] s. commémoration; commémoraison, f.

commence [kᵉmèns] v. commencer. ‖ *commencement* [-mᵉnt] s. début, commencement, m.; distribution des diplômes, f.

commend [kᵉmènd] v. recommander; louer; confier. ‖ *commendable* [-ᵉb'l] adj. recommandable, louable. ‖ *commendation* [kâmᵉndéishᵉn] s. recommandation; approbation, f.

commensal [kᵉmènsᵉl] s. commensal, m.

comment [kámᵉnt] s. commentaire, m.; annotation; critique, f.; v. commenter; annoter. ‖ *commentary* [-ᵉri] s.* commentaire, m.; *running commentary,* reportage en direct. ‖ *commentator* [-éitᵉr] s. commentateur, m.

commerce [kámᵉrs] s. commerce international, m.; commerce amoureux, m. ‖ *commercial* [kᵉmë̀rshᵉl] adj. commercial. ‖ *commercialize* [kᵉmœ̀rshᵉlaiz] v. commercialiser.

commiseration [kᵉmizᵉréishᵉn] s. compassion; condoléances, f.

commissary [kâmᵉsèri] s.* délégué; commissaire du gouvernement; intendant militaire; vicaire général, m.; *Am.* coopérative, f.

commission [kᵉmíshᵉn] s. commission; autorisation; mission; gratification; remise; réunion, f.; mandat; brevet (mil.), m.; v. charger de; mandater; armer (naut.). ‖ *commissioner* [-ᵉʳ] s. commissaire; mandataire; gérant, m.

commit [kᵉmít] v. commettre; confier; envoyer; *to commit to memory,* apprendre par cœur; *to commit oneself,* se compromettre; *to commit to prison,* faire incarcérer.

committee [kᵉmíti] s. comité, m.

commodious [kᵉmoᵘudiᵉs] adj. spacieux. ‖ *commodity* [kᵉmádᵉti] s.* produit, m.; denrée, marchandise, f.

commodore [kámᵉdoᵘr] s. chef d'escadre, m.

common [kámᵉn] adj. commun; public; général; familier; usuel; vulgaire; s. terrains communaux, m.; réfectoire; repas, m.; pl. Communes, f.; v. manger en commun; *common law,* droit coutumier; *common prayer,* liturgie anglicane; *common road,* sentiers battus; *common sense,* sens commun. ‖ *commonly* [-li] adv. communément. ‖ *commonness* [-nis] s. fréquence; banalité, f. ‖ *commonplace* [-pléis] adj. banal; s. banalité, f. ‖ *commonweal* [-wil] s. bien public, m.; chose publique, f. ‖ *commonwealth* [-wèlth] s. république; collectivité; confédération, f.; gouvernement, m.

commotion [kᵉmoᵘushᵉn] s. commotion; agitation, f.; trouble, m.

commune [kᵉmyoun] v. converser; *to commune with oneself,* se recueillir; [kámyoun] s. commune, f. ‖ *communicate* [kᵉmyounᵉkéit] v. communiquer; communier. ‖ *communication* [kᵉmyounᵉkéishᵉn] s. communication, f.; message, m. ‖ *communicative* [kᵉmyounᵉkéitiv] adj. communicatif. ‖ *communion* [kᵉmyounyᵉn] s. communion, f. ‖ *communism* [kámyounizᵉm] s. communisme, m. ‖ *communist* [kámyounist] adj., s. communiste. ‖ *community* [kᵉmyounᵉti] s.* communauté, société, f.; *community chest,* fonds commun.

commutation [kâmyoutéishᵉn] s. commutation; substitution, f.; remplacement; échange; paiement anticipé et réduit, m.; *commutation ticket,* *Am.* carte d'abonnement au chemin de fer. ‖ *commutator* [kámyoutéitᵉr] s. commutateur, m. ‖ *commute* [kᵉmyout] v. commuer; *Am.* voyager avec un abonnement. ‖ *commuter* [kᵉmyoutᵉr] s. abonné des chemins de fer, m.

compact [kᵉmpakt] adj. compact, dense; v. condenser; tasser.

compact [kámpakt] s. pacte, m.; poudrier, m.

companion [kᵉmpanyᵉn] s. compagnon, m.; compagne, f. ‖ *companionship* [-ship] s. camaraderie; compagnie, f.; équipe, f. ‖ *company* [kœmpᵉni] s.* compagnie; troupe; société, f. *limited company,* société à responsabilité limitée; *joint-stock company,* société par actions.

comparable [kámpᵉrᵉb'l] adj. comparable. ‖ *comparative* [kᵉmparᵉtiv] adj. comparatif; comparé. ‖ *compare* [kᵉmpèr] v. comparer; s. comparaison, f.; *beyond compare*, incomparable. ‖ **comparison** [kᵉmparis'n] s. comparaison, f.; *by comparison with*, en comparaison de.

compartment [kᵉmpârtmᵉnt] s. compartiment, m.; section, f.

compass [kᵉmpᵉs] s.* enceinte; limites; boussole, f.; enclos; circuit; compas, m.; v. entourer; faire un circuit; atteindre [ends]; *compass card*, rose des vents.

compassion [kᵉmpashᵉn] s. compassion, f. ‖ **compassionate** [-it] adj. compatissant; v. compatir à.

compatibility [kᵉmpati'bíliti] s. compatibilité, f. ‖ **compatible** [-patᵉb'l] adj. compatible.

compatriot [kᵉmpéᵗriᵉt] s. compatriote, m., f.

compel [kᵉmpèl] v. contraindre.

compendious [kᵉmpèndiᵉs] adj. abrégé, compendieux. ‖ **compendium** [-em] m. condensé, abrégé, m.

compensate [kàmpᵉnséᵗt] v. compenser; indemniser. ‖ **compensation** [kàmpᵉnséᵗshᵉn] s. compensation; rémunération, f.; dédommagement, m.

compete [kᵉmpîᵗt] v. concourir, rivaliser; faire concurrence à.

competence [kàmpᵉtᵉns] s. compétence, f. ‖ **competent** [kàmpᵉtᵉnt] adj. compétent; admissible; honnête, suffisant.

competition [kàmpᵉtishᵉn] s. concours, m.; compétition; concurrence, f. ‖ **competitive** [kᵉmpètᵉtiv] adj. compétitif; concurrent; *competitive examination*, concours. ‖ **competitor** [kᵉmpètᵉtᵉr] s. rival, concurrent, compétiteur, m.

compilation [kᵉmpiléᵗshᵉn] s. compilation, f. ‖ **compile** [-paᵗl] v. compiler. ‖ **compiler** [-ᵉr] s. compilateur, m.; compilatrice, f.

complacent [kᵉmplès'nt] adj. content de soi; obligeant.

complain [kᵉmpléᵗn] v. gémir; se plaindre, porter plainte, réclamer. ‖ **complaint** [-t] s. plainte; réclamation; maladie, f.; grief, m.; doléances, f. pl.; élégie, f.; *complaint book*, registre des réclamations.

complaisance [kᵉmpléᵗzᵉns] s. complaisance; obligeance; courtoisie, f. ‖ **complaisant** [-ᵉnt] adj. complaisant, obligeant; courtois.

complement [kàmplᵉmᵉnt] s. complément, effectif, personnel, m.; [kàmplᵉmènt] v. compléter. ‖ **complementary** [kàmpliméntᵉri] adj. complémentaire.

complete [kᵉmplîᵗt] adj. complet; achevé; entier; v. achever, compléter.

‖ **completeness** [-nis] s. plénitude, f. ‖ **completion** [kᵉmplîshᵉn] s. achèvement; accomplissement, m.; conclusion; exécution [contract], f.

complex [kàmplèks] s.* complexe; pl. assemblage, m.; [kᵉmplèks] adj. complexe ‖ **complexion** [kᵉmplèkshᵉn] s. complexion, f. tempérament; teint [skin], m ‖ **complexity** [kᵉmplèksᵉti] s.* complexité, f., complication, f.

compliance [kᵉmplaᵗᵉns] s.* acquiescement, m., complaisance; soumission, f., *in compliance with*, conformément à, d'accord avec ‖ **compliant** [kᵉmplaᵗᵉnt] adj souple, complaisant.

complicate [kàmplᵉkéᵗt] v. compliquer; embrouiller ‖ **complication** [kàmplᵉkéᵗshᵉn] s. complication, f.

complicity [kᵉmplísᵗti] s.* complicité, f

compliment [kàmplᵉmᵉnt] s. compliment, cadeau m.; [kàmplᵉmènt] v. complimenter féliciter, faire un cadeau; *complimentary*, flatteur; gratis, gracieux de faveur [ticket].

comply [kᵉmplaᵗ] v. se plier à; se conformer accéder à; consentir. ‖ *complying* [-ing] adj. accommodant, conciliant, complaisant.

component [kᵉmpoᵘnᵉnt] adj., s. composant

compose [kᵉmpoᵘz] v. composer; apaiser. *to compose oneself*, se calmer, se disposer à. ‖ **composer** [-ᵉr] s. compositeur auteur, conciliateur, m. ‖ **composite** [kᵉmpàzit] adj. composite, varié, s mélange, composé, m. ‖ **composition** [kàmpᵉzishᵉn] s. constitution; composition, transaction, f.; accommodement, compromis, arrangement, m ‖ **composure** [kᵉmpoᵘjᵉr] s. calme, sang-froid, m.

compound [kàmpaᵘnd] s. composé, m.; [kàmpaᵘnd] adj. composé; v. composer mêler, combiner; transiger; *to compound interest*, calculer les intérêts composés

comprehend [kàmprihènd] v. comprendre concevoir inclure. ‖ **comprehensible** [kàmprihènsᵉb'l] adj. compréhensible intelligible ‖ **comprehension** [-shᵉn] s. compréhension, f. ‖ **comprehensive** [-siv] adj. compréhensif; total, d'ensemble ‖ **comprehensively** [-sivli] adv en bloc, en général; avec concision. ‖ **comprehensiveness** [-sivnis] s. concision; étendue; compréhension, f

compress [kàmprès] s.* compresse, f.; *Am*. machine à comprimer le coton; [kᵉmprès] v. comprimer; condenser; tasser. ‖ **compression** [kaumprèshᵉn] s. compression, f. ‖ **compressor** [-ᵉr] s. compresseur, m.

comprise [kᵉmpraᵗz] v. comprendre, renfermer, contenir, inclure.

compromise [kâmprəma'z] *s.* compromis, m.; transaction, f.; *v.* transiger; compromettre, risquer.

comptroller [kəntrəʊlər] *s.* contrôleur; économe intendant, m.

compulsion [kəmpʌlshən] *s.* contrainte, f. **compulsory** [kəmpælsəri] *adj.* obligatoire, forcé; requis; coercitif, contraignant.

computation [kâmpyətə'shən] *s.* supputation estimation, f. calcul. m. ‖ **compute** [kəmpyout] *v.* calculer; supputer, compter. ‖ **computer** [-ər] *s.* ordinateur, m.

comrade [kâmrad] *s.* camarade, m.

concave [kânkè'v] *adj.* concave.

conceal [kənsîl] *v.* cacher, dissimuler; recéler **concealment** [-mənt] *s* dissimulation. f secret mystère; recel, m.

concede [kənsîd] *v.* concéder, accorder; admettre, reconnaître.

conceited [kənsîtid] *adj.* vaniteux, présomptueux suffisant.

conceivable [kənsîvəb'l] *adj.* concevable. **conceive** [kənsîv] *v.* concevoir, imaginer éprouver, ressentir; exprimer, penser; se faire une idée.

concentrate [kânsəntrè't] *v.* concentrer; condenser. ‖ **concentration** [kânsəntrè'shən] *s.* concentration, f.

concept [kânsèpt] *s* concept, m.; idée, opinion, f ‖ **conception** [kənsèpshən] *s* conception, projet. m.

concern [kənsərn] *s* affaire préoccupation entreprise commerciale, f.; souci, m concerner; intéresser; préoccuper *it is no concern of mine* cela ne me regarde pas *to be concerned about* se préoccuper de **concerning** [-ing] *prep.* concernant, au sujet de, relatif à

concert [kânsərt] *s.* concert; accord, m.; [kənsərt] *v.* concerter, organiser.

concession [kənsèshən] *s* concession réduction 4m licence f **concessionaire** [-r] *s* concessionnaire, m.

conciliate [kənsîliè't] *v* concilier; gagner, concilier apaiser **conciliation** [kənsîliè'shən] *s* conciliation réconciliation **conciliatory** [kənsîliètri] *adj* conciliateur; conciliatoire, de conciliation.

concise [kənsa'z] *adj.* concis. ‖ **conciseness** [-nis] *s* concision, f.

conclave [kânklè'v] *s* conclave, m.

conclude [kənkloud] *v* conclure; décider, juger; résoudre **conclusion** [-jən] *s* conclusion, décision, f. ‖ **conclusive** [-siv] *adj* concluant.

concoct [kânkâkt] *v.* concocter, préparer [food]; ourdir, tramer. ‖ **concoction** [kânkâkshən] *s.* mélange, m.; élaboration, machination, f.

concord [kânkaurd] *s.* concorde, f.; accord, pacte, m.

concordance [kənkârdəns] *s.* concordance, f. **concordant** [-ənt] *adj.* concordant, harmonieux.

concrete [kânkrît] *adj.* concret.

concrete [kânkrît] *s.* béton; ciment, m.; cimenter.

concrete [kânkrît] *v.* coaguler, solidifier, congeler.

concubinage [kənkyoubinidj] *s.* concubinage, m.

concur [kənkər] *v.* s'unir; être d'accord, s'accorder. ‖ **concurrence** [kənkərəns] *s* concours, m.; coïncidence approbation, f.

condemn [kəndèm] *v.* condamner. ‖ **condemnation** [kândèmnè'shən] *s.* condamnation, f.

condensation [kândènsè'shən] *s.* condensation, f résumé, abrégé, m. ‖ **condense** [kəndèns] (se) condenser; accourcir. ‖ **condenser** [-ər] *s.* condensateur, m.

condescend [kândisènd] *v.* condescendre **condescension** [kândisènshən] *s* condescendance, f.

condiment [kândəmənt] *s.* condiment, m.

condition [kəndishən] *s.* condition; situation, clause, f.; *pl.* état des affaires, m situation de fortune, f.; 4m travail 1e rattraper (éduc.), n stipuler imiter conditionner mettre en son état; *Am.* ajourner sous conditions (éduc.). ‖ **conditional** [-1] *adj* conditionnel.

condole [kəndoul] *v.* déplorer; faire les condoléances, exprimer sa sympathie, compatir **condolence** [-èns] *s.* condoléances, f. pl.

condone [kəndoun] *v.* pardonner; réparer

conduce [kəndyous] *v* conduire, amener, faire aboutir [to. à]. ‖ **conducive** [-iv] *adj.* contributif, efficace; favorable.

conduct [kândækt] *s.* conduite, f.; comportement, n. [kəndækt] *v.* conduire, diriger **conductor** [-ər] *s.* conducteur; guide; chef, directeur, m.; receveur 4m chef te train, m.; *orchestra conductor*, chef d'orchestre *lightning conductor*, paratonnerre.

conduit [kândit] *s.* conduit, m.; canalisation, f.

cone [koun] *s.* cône; 4m. cornet de glace cake], m. *pine cone*, pomme de pin *cone-shaped*, conique.

confection [kənfèkshən] *s* sucrerie, confiserie, f. v confectionner; confire; faire. ‖ **confectioner** [-ər] *s.* confiseur,

m. ‖ *confectionery* [-èri} *s.* confiserie, f.; bonbons. m pl.

confederacy [kәnfέdәrәsi] *s.*ᵃ confédération, f. ‖ *confederate* [kәnfέdә-rit] *s.* confédéré. m.; *v* confédérer.

confer [kәnfèʳ] *v* conférer comparer; tenir une conférence. gratifier de; communiquer ‖ *conference* [kɑ̂nfә-rᵉns] *s* conférence, f.; entretien; congrès, m.

confess [kәnfès] *v.* (se) confesser; admettre avouer ‖ *confession* [kәn-fέshᵉn] *s* confession. f. ‖ *confessional* [-'l] *s.* confessionnal. m. ‖ *confessor* [kәnfès°ʳ] *s* confesseur, m.

confidant [kɑ̂nfᵉdәnt] *s.* confident, m. ‖ *confide* [kәnfaᵢd] *v* confier; charger; se fier ‖ *confidence* [kɑ̂nfᵉ-dᵉns] *s* confiance assurance confiance, f. ‖ *Am confidence game*, escroquerie *confidence man*, escroc. ‖ *confident* [kɑ̂nfᵉdᵉnt] *adj* confiant, assuré, présomptueux ‖ *confidential* [kɑ̂nfᵉdénshᵉl] *adj* confidentiel, secret; de confiance intime

configuration [kᵉnfigyouré¹shᵉn] *s.* configuration, f

confine [kәnfaⁱn] *s.* confins, m. pl.; limites, f pl. [kᵉnfaⁱn] *v.* confiner; emprisonner limiter *to confine one-self to*, se borner a ‖ *confinement* [-mᵉnt] *s* détention réclusion. limitation, restriction. f couches, f pl.

confirm [kᵉnfɝ̀m] *v* confirmer. ‖ *confirmation* [kɑ̂nfᵉrmé¹shᵉn] *s.* confirmation. f

confiscate [kɑ̂nfiské¹t] *v.* confisquer. ‖ *confiscation* [kɑ̂nfiské¹shᵉn] *s.* confiscation. f

conflagration [kɑ̂nflᵉgré¹shᵉn] *s.* incendie. m conflagration, f.

conflict [kɑ̂nflikt] *s* conflit; antagonisme, m [kᵉnflíkt] *s* s'opposer à; entrer en conflit être en contradiction (*with* avec)

conform [kᵉnfaᵘʳm] *v* (se) conformer; se rallie *conformable* [-eb'l] *adj.* conforme soumis *conformation* [kᵉnfaurmᵉ'shᵉn] *s* conformation adaptation f *conformism* miz'm], *s.* conformisme m *conformist* [-ist] *s.* conformiste m *conformity* [kᵉn-faurmᵉti] *s*ᵃ conformité. f

confound [kɑ̂nfaᵒund] *v* confondre; déconcerte *confound it!* le diable l'emporte! *confounded*, sacré, fieffé, satane fichu

confront [kᵉnfrænt] *v.* confronter, affronter; se rencontrer. ‖ *confrontation* [kɑ̂nfrᵉnté¹shᵉn] *s.* confrontation. f.

confuse [kᵉnfyouz] *v* embrouiller; dérouter confondre bouleverser. ‖ *confusing* [-ing] *adj* confus. déconcertant. ‖ *confusion* [kᵉnfyouʒᵉn] *s.*

confusion, f.; désarroi, désordre; tumulte, m.; honte, f.

confutation [kɑ̂nfyouté¹shᵉn] *s.* réfutation. f. ‖ *confute* [kᵉnfyout] *v.* réfuter.

congeal [kᵉndjɝ̀l] *v.* geler; se congeler; coaguler ‖ *congealment* [-mᵉnt], *congelation* [kɑ̂ndjilé¹shᵉn] *s.* congélation. f

congenial [kᵉndjìnyᵉl] *adj.* en harmonie avec *to be congenial with*, sympathise avec. ‖ *congeniality* [kᵉndjìnⁱalᵉtⁱ] *s* affinité. sympathie, f.

congestion [kᵉndjèstshᵉn] *s.* congestion, f encombrement. m

conglomerate [kᵉnglɑ̂mᵉrit] *adj.* conglomére aggloméré *s* conglomérat, m.; agglomération f [kᵉnglɑ̂mᵉré¹t] *v.* conglomére agglomérer

congratulate [kᵉngrɑ̀tshᵉlé¹t] *v.* féliciter. *congratulation* [kᵉngrɑ̀tshᵉ-lé¹shᵉn] *s.* félicitations, f. pl.; compliment m

congregate [kɑ̂nggrigé¹t] *v.* assembler; se réunir *congregation* [kɑ̂ng-grigé¹shᵉn] *s* réunion congrégation; assemblée des fidèles. f

congress [kɑ̂nggrès] *s*ᵃ congrès, m.; assemblée f *Am* Parlement national de Etats Unis m *congressman*, député membre du Congrès.

congruity [kᵉngrouⁱtⁱ] *s.*ᵃ convenance conformité f accord, m.

conical [kɑ̂nik'l] *adj* conique.

conifer [kouⁿnifᵉʳ] *s* conifère, m.

conjecture [kᵉndjèktshᵉʳ] *s.* conjecture, f. conjecturer

conjugal [kɑ̂ndjuːgᵉl] *adj.* conjugal. ‖ *conjugate* [-gé¹t] *v* unir, accouple conjugue (gramm.). ‖ *conjugation* [kɑ̂ndjᵉgé¹shᵉn] *s.* conjugaison. f

conjunction [kᵉndjæŋkshᵉn] *s.* conjonction rencontre f

conjuncture [kᵉndjæŋktshᵉʳ] *s.* conjoncture situation critique, f.

conjure [kɑ̂ndiⁱ-ʳ] *s* conjurer [magic] [kᵉndʒuⁱou] implore] supplier. ‖ *conjurer* [kɑ̂ndiᵉ-ʳ] *s* prestidigitateur. m *conjuring* [-ing] *s* prestidigitation f *conjuring trick*, tour de passe-passe

connect [kᵉnèkt] *v* joindre, unir; associe [mind] relie [road]. correspondre avec [train] *connection* [kᵉnèkshᵉn] *s* jonction union liaison [gramm famille] parente relations d amitie ou d affaire] clientèle. correspondance communication [train boat]. f groupe parti m.; *to miss connections*, manquer la correspondance; *air connection*, liaison aérienne.

conniption [kᵉnip̣shᵉn] *s.* accès de colère, de passion (slang), m.

connivance [kᵉna¹vᵉns] *s.* connivence, complicité, f. ‖ *connive v.* être de connivence, fermer les yeux [*at*, *sur*]; tremper (*at*, dans).

connoisseur [kânᵉsë̃r] *s.* connaisseur, m.

conquer [kângkᵉʳ] *v.* conquérir; subjuguer. ‖ *conqueror* [-ʳᵉʳ] *s.* conquérant; vainqueur, m. ‖ *conquest* [kânkwèst] *s* conquête, f.

conscience [kânshᵉns] *s.* conscience, f.; *conscience stricken*, pris de remords. ‖ *conscientious* [kânshiènshᵉs] *adj.* consciencieux ‖ *conscious* [kânshᵉs] *adj.* conscient, intentionnel; au courant de, *conscious of*, sensible à. ‖ *consciousness* [-nis] *s.* conscience, connaissance, f.

conscript [kᵉnskrip̣t] *v.* enrôler; [kânskript] *s* conscrit, m.

consecrate [kânsikré¹t] *v.* consacrer; dédier ‖ *consecration* [kânsikré¹-shᵉn] *s* consécration, dédicace, f.

consecutive [kᵉnsèkyᵉtiv] *adj.* consécutif, successif

consent [kᵉnsènt] *v.* consentir; approuver, *s* consentement; accord, m.; acceptation, f

consequence [kânsᵉkwèns] *s.* conséquence, importance f ‖ *consequent* [kânsᵉkwènt] *adj* résultant conséquent. ‖ *consequently* [-li] *adv.* en conséquence par conséquent

conservation [kânsᵉrvé¹shᵉn] *s.* conservation, préservation, f ‖ *conservative* [kᵉnsë̃rvᵉtiv] *adj* conservatif, conservateur *s* conservateur m. ‖ *conservator* [-tᵉʳ] *s* conservateur, m.; *Am.* curateur, m. ‖ *conservatory* [kᵉnsë̃rvᵉtoo̅ʳi] *s* conservatoire [music], m., serre [greenhouse]. f. ‖ *conserve* [kᵉnsœ̃rv] *s* confiture (ou) conserve (f.) de fruits; *v.* mettre en conserve, conserver.

conshie [kânshi] *s.* objecteur (m.) de conscience

consider [kᵉnsidᵉʳ] *v.* considérer. ‖ *considerable* [kᵉnsidᵉrᵉb'l] *adj.* considérable important, éminent; beaucoup de (fam.) ‖ *considerate* [kᵉnsidᵉrit] *adj.* modéré, tolérant prévenant ‖ *consideration* [kᵉnsidré¹shᵉn] *s* considération, réflexion, compensation cause (jur.), f.; motif, mobile jugement, m. ‖ *considering* [kᵉnsidᵉrᵓng] *prep* attendu que, étant donné que vu que.

consign [kᵉnsa¹n] *v.* consigner (comm.) livrer, confier, remettre; expédier [wares] ‖ *consignation* [kânsignéʰshᵉn], *consignment* [kᵉnsa¹nmᵉnt] *s.* expédition; consignation, f.

consist [kᵉnsist] *v.* consister [*in*, en]. **consistency** [-ᵉnsi] *s.*' consistance; stabilité, harmonie; cohésion; solidité, f.; esprit de suite, m. ‖ *consistent* [-ᵉnt] *adj* consistant; cohérent; solide; compatible (*with*, avec).

consolation [kânsᵉlé¹shᵉn] *s.* consolation, f. ‖ *consolatory* [kᵉnsâlᵉtᵉri] *adj.* consolateur. ‖ *console* [kᵉnsoᵒᵘl] *v.* consoler.

consolidate [kᵉnsâlᵉdé¹t] *v.* consolider; combiner; s'unir.

consommé [kânsᵉmé¹] *s.* consommé, bouillon. m

consonant [kânsᵉnᵉnt] *adj.* en harmonie; compatible; sympathique; *s.* consonne. f.

consort [kânsaurt] *s.* époux; consort [prince]; navire d'escorte, m.; conserve, f. (naut.), [kᵉnsaurt] *v.* s'associer (*with*, avec) fréquenter.

conspicuous [kᵉnspikyou̅ᵉs] *adj.* notoire, manifeste remarquable.

conspiracy [kᵉnspirᵉsi] *s.*' conspiration, f ‖ *conspirator* [kᵉnspirᵉtᵉr] *s.* conspirateur. m. ‖ *conspire* [kᵉnspa¹r] *v.* conspirer

conspue [kᵉnspyou] *v.* conspuer.

constable [kænstᵉb'l] *s.* constable, agent de police, m. ‖ *constabulary* [kᵉn'stabyou̅l̓ᵉri] *s.*' police, f.; *adj.* de police.

constancy [kânstᵉnsi] *s.* constance, persévérance, stabilité, f. ‖ *constant* [kânstᵉnt] *adj.* constant; *s.* constante, f

constellate [kânstᵉlé¹t] *v.* consteller. ‖ *constellation* [-shᵉn] *s.* constellation, f

consternation [kanstᵉrné¹shᵉn] *s.* atterrement, m ‖ *consternate* ['kânstᵉne¹tᵢ ⸲ atterrer

constipate [kânstipé¹t] *v.* constiper. ‖ *constipation* [kânstipé¹shᵉn] *s.* constipation, f

constituent [kᵉnstitshou̅ᵉnt] *adj.* constituant constitutif électoral; *s.* élément constituant électeur, commettant, m. ‖ *constitute* [kânstᵉtyout] *v.* constituer, établir. élire, nommer. ‖ *constitution* [kânstᵉtyou̅shᵉn] *s.* constitution (med, jur), f ‖ *constitutional* [-shn'l] *adj.* constitutionnel; *Am.* fédéral, *s* promenade hygiénique. f ‖ *constitutive* [kânstityoutiv] *adj.* constitutif fondamental; constituant; essentiel

constrain [kᵉnstré¹n] *v.* contraindre; gêner, réprimer. ‖ *constraint* [kᵉnstré¹nt] *s* contrainte, f.

constrict [kᵉnstrikt] *v.* contracter; comprimer; resserrer. ‖ *constriction* [-shᵉn] *s.* constriction, f.

construct [kᵉnstrækt] v. construire, fabriquer. ‖ **construction** [kᵉnstrækshᵉn] s. construction texture interprétation. f. **constructive** [kᵉnstræktiv] adj. constructif. **construe** [kᵉnstrou] v expliquer; traduire; construire (gramm.).

consul [kâns'l] s. consul, m. ‖ **consulate** [-it] v consulat, m.

consult [kᵉnsœlt] v consulter; conférer; tenir compte de. **consultation** [kâns'lté'shᵉn] s. consultation, f.

consume [kᵉnsoum] consumer; consommer; absorber ‖ **consumer** [-ᵉr] v consommateur, m.

consummate [kᵉnsˑmé'i] v consommer, achever [kᵉnsˑmit] adj. consommé, achevé parfait. **consummation** [kâns né'shᵉn] s consommation accomplissement m.

consumption [kᵉnsˑmpshᵉn] s. consommation tuberculose, f. ‖ **consumptive** [kᵉnsˑmptiv] adj. tuberculeux destructeur nineux.

contact [kântakt] contact, m.; [kᵉntakt] toucher être en contact; entrer en relations avec **contactor**, interrupteur automatique (électr.).

contagion [kᵉnté'jᵉn] contagion, f. ‖ **contagious** [kᵉnté'djᵉs] adj. contagieux.

contain [kᵉnté'n] v. contenir; enclore inclure refréner se contenir. ‖ **container** [-ᵉr] s récipient, réservoir container m.

contaminate [kᵉntamé'i] v contaminer infecter polluer. **contamination** [kᵉntamé'shᵉn] s. contamination, f.

contemn [kᵉntèm] v mépriser.

contemplate [kânt mplé'i] contempler méditer projeter **contemplation** kânt mplé'shᵉn ontemplation. projet n. **contemplative** [kânt mplé'tiv] adj méditatif, pensif, songeur ontemplatif

contemporary [kᵉntempᵉrèri] adj., s.* contemporain, m.

contempt [kᵉntempt] mépris. dédain, n. défaut m. non comparution, infraction, f. **contemptible** [-ᵉb'l] adj. méprisable. **contemptuous** [-shou°s] adj. méprisant, dédaigneux.

contend [kᵉntènd] v rivaliser de; concourir lutter discuter soutenir [opinion] affirmer prétendre.

content [kᵉntènt] adj content, satisfait; consentant, satisfaire s. contentement; Br. assentiment, vote favorable, m.

content [kântènt] s. contenu; volume, m.; capacité; contenance, f.; *table of contents*, table des matières.

contention [kᵉntènshᵉn] s. contestation; controverse; affirmation, assertion. argument, m. **contentious** [kᵉntènshᵉs] adj. contentieux; litigieux querelleur.

contentment [kᵉntèntmᵉnt] s. contentement n satisfaction, f.

contest [kântèst] lutte rencontre; controverse, dispute épreuve compétition. combat débat n [kᵉntèst] v. lutter, combattre disputer rivaliser (with avec). **contestable** [kᵉntèst°b'l] adj. contestable **contestation** [kântèsté'shᵉn] s. contestation, f.; litige. n.

context [kântèkst] s. contexte, m.

contexture [kᵉntèkstshᵉr] s. texture, ontexture. f.

contiguous [kᵉntigyou°s] adj. contigu, voisin.

continence [kânt°nᵉns] s. continence, f.; empire sur soi, m. **continent** [kânt°nᵉnt] adj. continent, chaste; modéré retenu. sobre.

continent [kânt°nᵉnt] s. continent, m. **continental** [kântᵉnènt'l] adj., continental.

contingency [kᵉntindjènsi] s * contingence éventualité, f. **contingent** [kᵉntindjᵉnt] adj contingent éventuel aléatoire, conditionnel événement contingent, contingent militaire. n.

continual [kᵉntinyou°l] adj. continu, ininterrompu **continually** [-i] adv. continuellement sans interruption. ‖ **continuance** [kᵉntinyou°ns] continuation durée continuité prorogation [law], f **continuation** [kᵉntinyué'shᵉn] continuation, prolongation suite f **continue** [kᵉntinyou] continuer durer prolonger, demeurer with hez persister. **continuity** [kântinyuiti] continuité scénario. n. **continuous** [kᵉntinyou°s] adj. continu permanent (cinéma).

contorsion [kᵉntaurshᵉn] s. contorsion. f.

contour [kântour] s. contour; profil le terrain, m.

contraband [kântrᵉband] s. contrebande, f.

contrabass [kântrᵉbé's] s.* contrebasse f

contraceptive [kântrᵉséptiv] adj. contraceptif. v préservatif. m.

contract [kântrakt] v contrat pacte; marché traité n convention entreprise. [kᵉntrakt] contracter contracter [illness] acquérir abréger [words] froncer [eyebrows] [kântrakt] passer un contrat. **contraction** [kᵉntrakshᵉn] s. contraction, f. ‖

contractor [kᵊntrᴀktᵉr] *s.* contractant; entrepreneur; adjudicataire; fournisseur (mil.), m.

contradict [kântrᵊdíkt] *v.* contredire. ‖ **contradiction** [kântrᵊdíksh*e*n] *s.* contradiction, f.; *beyond all contradiction*, sans contredit. ‖ **contradictory** [kântrᵊdíktᵉri] *adj.* contradictoire.

contrariety [kântrᵊra¹eti] *s.* opposition, f.; désaccord, m. ‖ **contrariness** [kântrᵉrinis] *s.* esprit (m.) de contradiction.

contrary [kântrᵉri] *adj.* contraire, opposé; défavorable; hostile; *s.* contraire, m.; *on the contrary*, au contraire

contrary [kᵊntrᵉᵉri] *adj.* contrariant; obstiné, têtu.

contrast [kântrast] *s.* contraste, m.; [kᵊntrast] *v.* contraster.

contravene [kântrᵊvín] *v.* contrarier, aller à l'encontre de; contredire; contrevenir à.

contribute [kᵊntríbyout] *v.* contribuer. ‖ **contribution** [kântrᵊbyoush*e*n] *s.* apport, m.; contribution; souscription; cotisation, f. ‖ **contributor** [kᵊntríbyᵉtᵉr] *s.* souscripteur, collaborateur, m.

contrite [kântra¹t] *adj.* contrit; de contrition. ‖ **contrition** [kᵊntríshᵊn] *s.* contrition, f.

contrivance [kᵊntra¹vᵉns] *s.* procédé, plans, m.; invention, f.; appareil; expédient, m. ‖ **contrive** [kᵊntra¹v] *v.* inventer; agencer; réussir. ‖ **contriver** [-ᵉr] *s.* inventeur; auteur de complot, m.

control [kᵊntro⁰ᵘl] *s.* contrôle, m.; autorité, influence, f.; levier de commande, frein régulateur (mech.), m.; *control lever*, levier de commande; *v.* contrôler; diriger; refréner; régler; *to control oneself*, se maîtriser. ‖ **controller** [-ᵉr] *s.* contrôleur, appareil de contrôle, m.

controversy [kântrᵊvёrsi] *s.* controverse, polémique, f. ‖ **controvert** [-vёrt] *v.* controverser, débattre; contester.

contumacious [kântyoumé¹sh*e*s] *adj.* contumace, rebelle.

contumelious [kantyoumíli*e*s] *adj.* injurieux; méprisant. ‖ **contumely** [kântyoumíli] *s.* injure, f.; outrage, m.; mépris, dédain, m.

conundrum [kᵊnœdrᵊm] *s.* énigme, devinette, « colle », f.

convalesce [kânvᵊlès] *v.* se rétablir [health]. ‖ **convalescence** [kânvᵊlès'ns] *s.* convalescence, f. ‖ **convalescent** [-n't] *s.* convalescent, m.

convene [kᵊnvín] *v.* assembler, convoquer; citer (jur.); se réunir.

convenience [kᵊnvíny*e*ns] *s.* commodité, convenance, f. ‖ **convenient** [kᵊnvíny*e*nt] *adj.* commode; convenable; loisible, possible; acceptable; pratique.

convent [kânvènt] *s.* couvent, m.

convention [kᵊnvènshᵊn] *s.* convention; bienséance; convenances, f. pl.; usages, m. pl.; assemblée, f.; accord, contrat, m.; ‖ **conventional** [-'l] *adj.* conventionnel, classique.

converge [kᵊnvёᵊdj] *v.* converger.

conversant [kânvёᵊs'nt] *adj.* versé (*with.* dans) familier avec. ‖ **conversation** [kânvёᵊsé¹shᵉn] *s.* conversation, f. ‖ **converse** [kᵊnvёᵊs] *v.* converser, causer, fréquenter; *adj.* inverse, réciproque; [kânvёᵊs] *s.* contrepartie; réciproque; conversation, f.; rapports, m. pl.

conversion [kᵊnvёrshᵉn] *s.* conversion, f.; détournement [law], m. ‖ **convert** [kânvёᵊt] *s.* converti, m.; [kᵊnvёᵊt] *v.* convertir; transformer; changer [into, en]. ‖ **converter** [kânvёᵊtᵉr] *s.* convertisseur; adaptateur; transformateur, m. ‖ **convertible** [kᵊnvёᵊtíb'l] *adj.* convertible; convertissable; décapotable [autom.].

convex [kânvèks] *adj.* convexe; bombé [road].

convey [kᵊnvé¹] *v.* transporter; communiquer, exprimer [thanks]; céder [property]; donner [idea]. ‖ **conveyance** [-ᵉns] *s.* transport; transfert; acte de vente, m.; transmission, f.; *public conveyance,* véhicule de transport en commun.

convict [kânvikt] *s.* condamné, forçat, m.; [kᵊnvíkt] *v.* convaincre de culpabilité; condamner. ‖ **conviction** [kᵊnvíkshᵊn] *s.* conviction; preuve de culpabilité; condamnation, f. ‖ **convince** [kᵊnvíns] *v.* convaincre. ‖ **convincing** [-ing] *adj.* convaincant.

convocation [kânvᵊké¹shᵊn] *s.* convocation, assemblée, f. ‖ **convoke** [kᵊnvo⁰ᵘk] *v.* convoquer.

convoy [kânvo¹] *s.* convoi, m.; escorte, f.; escorteur, m. (naut.); [kᵊnvo¹] *v.* convoyer; escorter, protéger.

convulse [kᵊnvœls] *v.* convulser. ‖ **convulsion** [-shᵊn] *s.* convulsion, f.

cony [ko⁰ᵘni] *s.* lapin [animal, fur], m.; *cony-wool*, poil de lapin.

coo [kou] *s.* roucoulement, m.; *v.* roucouler.

cook [kouk] *s.* cuisinier, m.; cuisinière, f.; coq [naut.], m.; *v.* cuisiner; cuire; préparer; *cook book,* livre de cuisine. ‖ **cooker** [-ᵉr] *s.* cuisinière, f.; cuiseur, m.; *pressure cooker,* autocuiseur (Cocotte Minute). ‖ **cookery** [-ᵉri] *s.* cuisine, f.; art culinaire, m. ‖

cookie, cooky [-i] *s.* petit gâteau ; biscuit, m. ‖ **cooking** [-ing] *s.* cuisson ; cuisine, f.; **cooking utensils,** ustensiles de cuisine, m. pl.

cool [koul] *adj.* frais, fraîche ; calme, froid ; indifférent ; impudent ; évalué sans exagération ; *s.* fraîcheur, f.; frais, m.; *v.* rafraîchir ; calmer ; (se) refroidir. ‖ **cooler** [-er] *s.* réfrigérateur ; garde-frais ; cocktail frais, m.; *Am.* taule (slang), f. ‖ **coolness** [-nis] *s.* fraîcheur ; froideur, f.

coon [koun] *s. Am.* raton [animal] ; nègre (slang), m.

coop [koup] *s.* cage [hens] ; mue, f.; poulailler, m.; *v.* enfermer ; *to coop up,* claquemurer. ‖ **cooper** [-er] *s.* tonnelier, m.

cooperate [koouápéreit] *v.* coopérer. ‖ **cooperation** [koouápéreishen] *s.* coopération, f. ‖ **cooperative** [koouápéreitiv] *adj.* coopératif ; *s.* coopérative, f.

coordinate [koouáurd'néit] *v.* coordonner ; [koouáurd'nit] *adj.* coordonné. ‖ **coordination** [koouáurd'néishen] *s.* coordination, f.

coot [kout] *s.* foulque, f.

cop [káp] *s. Am.* flic, m.; *v.* (fam.) pincer, choper ; *to cop it,* écoper.

cope [koup] *v.* se mesurer ; tenir tête (*with,* à).

copious [koupies] *adj.* copieux.

copper [káper] *s.* cuivre ; sou [coin] ; *Am.* policier, m.; *adj.* cuivré ; en cuivre ; *v.* cuivrer ; **coppersmith,** chaudronnier.

coppice [kápis], **copse** [káps] *s.* taillis, m.

copy [kápi] *s.* copie, f.; double ; exemplaire [book] ; numéro [newspaper], m.; *v.* copier, imiter ‖ **copyright** [-rait] *s.* propriété littéraire, f.; droits d'auteur, m.; *v.* prendre le copyright.

coquette [kouukèt] *s.* coquette, f.

coral [kaurel] *adj., s.* corail.

cord [kaurd] *s.* corde, f.; cordon ; cordage, m.; *pl.* pantalon de velours à côtes ; *spinal cord,* moelle épinière.

cordial [kaurdjel] *adj., s.* cordial. ‖ **cordiality** [kârdialiti] *s.* cordialité, f.

cordon [kaurd'n] *s.* cordon, m.

corduroy [kaurderoi] *s.* velours côtelé, m.; *pl.* pantalon de velours ; *adj.* en velours côtelé ; *Am.* en rondins, fasciné [road] ; *v. Am.* bâtir en rondins.

core [koour] *s.* centre, noyau ; trognon [apple], m.; *v.* dénoyauter.

coreligionist [koourilidjenist] *s.* coreligionnaire, m. f.

cork [kaurk] *s.* liège ; bouchon, m.; *v.* boucher ; *to be corked,* être éreinté ; **cork-tree,** chêne-liège ; **corkscrew,** tire-bouchon.

corn [kaurn] *s.* grain ; blé ; *Am.* maïs, *Fr. Can.* blé d'Inde, m.; **cornhusking bee,** *Fr. Can.* épluchette de blé d'Inde, f.; *v.* saler [corned-beef] ; **cornflower ;** bleuet.

corn [kaurn] *s.* cor [foot], m.

cornea [kânie] *s.* cornée, f.

corned [kârnd] *adj.* en conserve.

cornel [kârn'l] *s.* cornouiller, m.

corner [kaurner] *s.* angle, coin, m.; encoignure, f.; *v.* rencogner ; acculer ; coincer ; accaparer.

cornet [kaurnèt] *s.* cornet à pistons, m.; cornette, f.

cornfield [kaurnfîld] *s. Am.* champ de maïs ; *Br.* champ de blé, d'avoine, de seigle, d'orge, m.

cornice [kaurnis] *s.* corniche, f.

corollary [kerâléri] *s.* corollaire, m.

coronation [kaurenéishen] *s.* couronnement, m.

coroner [kaurener] *s.* coroner ; officier de police judiciaire, m.

coronet [kaurenit] *s.* couronne, f.; diadème, m.

corporal [kaurperel] *adj.* corporel, matériel ; *s.* corporal, m.

corporal [kaurperel] *s.* caporal, m.

corporation [kaurperéishen] *s.* municipalité ; corporation, société, f.; *Am.* organisme, m.; rotondité, bedaine, f. (fam.).

corps [koour] *(pl.* [-z]) *s.* corps (mil.), m.; forces (mil.), f. pl.

corpse [kaurps] *s.* cadavre, m.

corpulence [kaurpyelens] *s.* corpulence, f.

corpuscle [kaurpes'l] *s.* corpuscule ; globule [blood], m.

corral [keral] *s. Am.* enclos, m.; *v.* enfermer dans un enclos ; capturer.

correct [kerèkt] *v.* corriger ; redresser ; *adj.* exact, juste ; conforme. ‖ **correction** [kerèkshen] *s.* correction, f. ‖ **correctly** [-li] *adv.* correctement, exactement. ‖ **correctness** [kerèktnis] *s.* exactitude ; correction ; justesse, f. ‖ **corrector** [kerèkter] *s.* correcteur, m.; correctrice, f.; correctif, m.

correlate [kauréléit] *v.* mettre en relation, relier. ‖ **correlation** [kâriléishen] *s.* corrélation, f. ‖ **correlative** [kerèltiv] *adj., s.* corrélatif.

correspond [kerespánd] *v.* correspondre ; être assorti ; écrire. ‖ **correspondence** [-ens] *s.* correspondance ; harmonie ; relations ; lettres, f.; accord, m. ‖ **correspondent** [-ent] *adj., s.*

correspondant ; **special correspondent,** envoyé spécial [newspaper]. ‖ **corresponding** [-ing] *adj.* correspondant.

corridor [kaur°d°r] *s.* couloir, m.

corroborate [k°râb°ré¹t] *v.* corroborer, confirmer.

corrode [k°ro°ud] *v.* corroder. ‖ **corrosive** [k°ro°usiv] *adj.* corrosif.

corrugated [kârougé¹tid] *adj.* gaufré (paper) ; **corrugated iron,** tôle ondulée.

corrupt [k°ræpt] *v.* corrompre ; pervertir, suborner ; *adj.* dépravé, pervers ; corrompu. ‖ **corruption** [k°ræpshⁿ] *s.* corruption ; dépravation ; concussion, f.

corsage [kaursâj] *s.* bouquet (or) garniture de costume ; corsage, m.

corsair [kausè°r] *s.* corsaire, m.

corset [kaursit] *s.* corset, m. ; **corset bone,** baleine de corset.

cortege [kaurté¹j] *s.* cortège, m.

corvette [kaurvèt] *s.* corvette, f.

cosmetic [kâzmètik] *s.* cosmétique, m. ; *pl.* produits (m. pl.) de beauté.

cosmic [kâzmik] *adj.* cosmique.

cosmopolitan [kâzm°pâlⁱt'n] *adj.* cosmopolite.

cosmos [kâzmâz] *s.* cosmos, m.

cost [kaust] *s.* coût, prix ; frais, m. ; dépens (jur.), m. pl. ; *v.* * coûter ; **cost price,** prix coûtant ; *at any cost,* coûte que coûte ; *to bear the cost of,* faire les frais de ; *pret., p. p. of* to **cost.**

costermonger [kast°rmœngg°r] *s.* marchand (m.) des quatre-saisons.

costly [kaustli] *adj.* coûteux.

costume [kâstyoum] *s.* costume, m. ; [kastyoum] *v.* costumer. ‖ **costumer** [-°r] *s.* Am. costumier, m.

cosy [ko°uzi] *adj.* confortable ; à l'aise ; *s.** causeuse, f. ; couvre-théière, f.

cot [kât] *s.* lit d'enfant, lit pliant, lit de camp, m. ; couchette, f.

cottage [kâtidj] *s.* maisonnette, f.

cotton [kât'n] *s.* coton, m. ; cotonnade, f. ; *adj.* en coton ; **cotton batting,** rouleau de coton cardé ; **cotton mill,** filature de coton ; **cotton wool,** ouate ; *absorbent cotton,* coton hydrophile ; **sewing cotton,** fil à coudre.

couch [kao°utsh] *s.** canapé, divan, m. ; couche (techn.), f. ; *v.* coucher ; étendre une couche ; rédiger ; se coucher, se tapir.

cough [kauf] *s.* toux, f. ; *v.* tousser ; **whooping cough,** coqueluche ; *to cough up,* expectorer.

could [koud] *pret. of* to **can.**

council [kao°uns'l] *s.* assemblée en conseil, f. ; concile, m. ; *City Council,* conseil municipal ; **councilman,** conseiller municipal.

counsel [kao°uns'l] *s.* conseil, avis ; projet ; avocat conseil, m. ; délibération, f. ; *v.* conseiller ; *private counsel,* fondé de pouvoir. ‖ **counselor** [-°r] *s.* conseiller ; avocat, m.

count [kao°unt] *s.* compte ; calcul ; chef d'accusation (jur.) ; dépouillement du scrutin, m. ; *v.* compter.

count [kao°unt] *s.* comte, m.

countenance [kao°unt°n°ns] *s.* physionomie, f. ; aspect, air ; encouragement, m. ; *v.* favoriser, appuyer ; encourager.

counter [kao°unt°r] *s.* comptoir ; compteur, m.

counter [kao°unt°r] *adj.* opposé, contraire, adverse ; *adv.* à l'encontre ; *s.* contraire ; contre [fencing], m. ; *v.* riposter ; s'opposer. ‖ **counteract** [kao°unt°r°akt] *v.* contrecarrer, neutraliser. ‖ **counterbalance** [-bal°ns] *v.* contrebalancer. ‖ **counter-clockwise** [-klâkwa¹z] *adv.* au sens inverse des aiguilles d'une montre. ‖ **counterfeit** [kao°unt°rfit] *s.* contrefaçon, f. ; contrefaire, feindre ; *adj.* faux, contrefait. ‖ **countermand** [kao°unt°rmând] *s.* contrordre, m. ; [-mând] *v.* décommander, donner contrordre. ‖ **counterpane** [-pé¹n] *s.* couverture ; couvre-pieds, m. ‖ **counterpart** [-pârt] *s.* contre-partie, copie, f. ; pendant, m. ‖ **counterpoise** [-po¹s] *s.* contrepoids, m. ; *v.* contrebalancer.

countess [kao°untis] *s.** comtesse, f.

countinghouse [kao°untinghao°us] *s.* bureaux ; comptoir-caisse, m.

countless [kao°untlis] *adj.* innombrable.

country [kœntri] *s.** pays, territoire, m. ; région, contrée ; patrie ; campagne, province, f. ; **country seat,** propriété à la campagne. ‖ **countryman** [-m°n] (*pl.* **countrymen**) *s.* paysan ; compatriote, m.

county [kao°unti] *s.** comté, m. ; division d'un territoire, f.

coup [kou] *s.* coup ; coup de main, m.

coupé [koupé¹] *s.* coupé, m.

couple [kœp'l] *s.* couple, m. ; paire, f. ; *v.* coupler, accoupler ; associer. ‖ **coupling** [-ing] *s.* accouplement, m. ; attache [railway] ; union, f.

coupon [koupân] *s.* coupon [stocks, ticket], m.

courage [k°¹ridj] *s.* courage, m. ‖ **courageous** [k°ré¹dj°s] *adj.* courageux, brave.

courier [kouri°r] *s.* courrier, m.

course [ko°urs] *s.* course ; direction, f. ; cours, courant ; service [meal], m. ;

succession, f.; cours des études, m.; *v.* poursuivre; courir; *race course,* champ de courses; *of course,* naturellement.

court [koᵒurt] *s.* cour [house; king; homage; justice; tribunal], f.; court [tennis], m.; *v.* courtiser; solliciter; *court day,* jour d'audience; *court house,* palais de justice. ‖ *courteous* [kĕrtⁱ°s] *adj.* courtois. ‖ *courtesy* [kĕrt°sⁱ] *s.** courtoisie; politesse; attention aimable, f. ‖ *courtier* [koᵒurtⁱⁱᵉʳ] *s.* courtisan, m. ‖ *courtship* [koᵒurtship] *s.* cour, galanterie, assiduités, f. ‖ *courtyard* [koᵒurtyârd] *s.* cour de maison, f.

cousin [kœz'n] *s.* cousin, m.; cousine, f.; *first cousin,* cousin germain.

cove [koᵒuv] *s.* anse, crique, f.

covenant [kœvᵉn°nt] *s.* contrat, accord, engagement, f.; convention, alliance, f.; *v.* s'engager; stipuler par contrat.

cover [kœvᵉʳ] *s.* couvercle, m.; couverture, housse; protection, f.; abri; déguisement; tapis de table, m.; enveloppe [letter], f.; *v.* couvrir; recouvrir; protéger; inclure; dissimuler; embrasser; s'étendre sur; féconder; couvrir [stocks]; *Am.* assurer un reportage; *cover-girl,* modèle (phot.). ‖ *covering* [-ing] *s.* couverture; enveloppe, f.; abri; revêtement, m. ‖ *covert* [kœvᵉrt] *adj.* voilé, secret, indirect.

covet [kœvit] *v.* convoiter. ‖ *covetous* [-°s] *adj.* avide, cupide. ‖ *covetousness* [-nis] *s.* convoitise; cupidité; avidité, f.

cow [kaᵒu] *s.* vache; femelle des ruminants, f.

cow [kaᵒu] *v.* intimider; atterrer.

coward [kaᵒuᵉrd] *adj.*, *s.* couard, poltron. ‖ *cowardice* [-is] *s.* poltronnerie, f. ‖ *cowardly* [-li] *adj.* poltron; *adv.* lâchement.

cowboy [kaᵒuboᵑ] *s.* cow-boy, m.

cower [kaᵒuᵉr] *v.* ramper de peur ou de honte; s'accroupir; plier l'échine (*before,* devant).

cowl [kaᵒul] *s.* capuchon, m.; capuce, m.; capot, m. (autom.).

cowlick [kaᵒulik] *s.* épi [hair], m.

cowslip [kaᵒuslip] *s.* coucou, m. (bot.).

coy [koᵑ] *adj.* réservé, modeste, timide; coquette et mijaurée.

cozen [kœz'n] *v.* tromper, duper.

crab [krab] *s.* crabe, m.; *crab apple,* pomme sauvage. ‖ *crabbed* [-id] *adj.* aigre, acariâtre; obscur, indéchiffrable.

crack [krak] *s.* craquement; coup de feu, m.; fissure, lézarde, crevasse; *Am.* pointe, méchanceté; toquade, f.;

mensonge, m.; *adj.* excellent; *v.* craquer; muer [voice]; se fendre; fissurer; gercer; casser [nuts]; faire claquer [whip]. ‖ *cracker* [-ᵉʳ] *s.* pétard; craquelin [cake], m. ‖ *crackle* [-'l] *v.* crépiter, pétiller; se craqueler; *s.* crépitement, pétillement, m.; craquelure, f. ‖ *crackling* [-ling] *s.* friton, gratton, m.; grésillement, m.

cradle [kré¹d'l] *s.* berceau; cadre, ber (naut.); cerceau, m.; gouttière, f. (med.); *v.* bercer; endormir; coucher dans un berceau.

craft [kraft] *s.* habileté, adresse; ruse, f.; art, métier; appareil, m. (aviat.); unité (naut.), f. ‖ *craftsman* [-smᵉn] *s.* artisan, m. ‖ *crafty* [-i] *adj.* rusé, astucieux.

crag [krag] *s.* rocher escarpé, m.; varappe, f. ‖ *craggy* [-i] *adj.* à pic; rocailleux.

cram [krám] *v.* s'empiffrer; entasser; bourrer; chauffer [study]; bachoter; se bourrer; *s.* cohue, presse, f.; bourrage, m.; blague, f.

cramp [krámp] *s.* crampe, colique, f.; crampon; étau, m.; crispation, f.; *v.* cramponner; restreindre; gêner; donner des crampes à.

cranberry [krànbèri] *s.** airelle, f.

crane [kré¹n] *s.* grue [bird, machine], f.; *v.* tendre le cou.

crank [krànk] *s.* manivelle; lubie, manie, f.; maniaque (fam.), m.; *v.* faire partir à la manivelle; tourner la manivelle. ‖ *cranky* [-i] *adj.* détraqué; excentrique; revêche.

cranny [kráni] *s.** fente, lézarde, f.

crape [kré¹p] *s.* crêpe [mourning], m.; *v.* crêper [hair].

crash [krash] *s.** fracas, m.; collision; catastrophe, f.; atterrissage brutal; écrasement; krach (fin.), m.; grosse toile de fil, f.; *v.* fracasser; faire du fracas; s'écraser; « casser du bois » (aviat.).

crate [kré¹t] *s.* cadre [frame]; cageot, m.

crater [kré¹tᵉr] *s.* cratère; entonnoir, m.

cravat [krᵉvat] *s.* foulard, m.

crave [kré¹v] *v.* implorer; convoiter; être avide de. ‖ *craving* [-ing] *s.* désir (ou) besoin intense, m.; passion, f.; *adj.* intense; dévorant; passionné.

craw [krau] *s.* langouste, f.

crawl [kraul] *s.* marche lente, f.; crawl [swimming], m.; *v.* ramper; s'insinuer; *to crawl with,* grouiller de.

crayfish [kré¹fish] *s.* écrevisse; langouste, f.; *v.* marcher à reculons; se dérober.

crayon [kré¹ᵉn] s. fusain ; pastel, m. ; v. faire du pastel ; esquisser ; ébaucher [plan].

craze [kré¹z] v. rendre fou ; s. folie ; insanité ; toquade, f. ‖ **crazy** [-i] adj. fou, toqué ; to be crazy about, raffoler de.

creak [krík] v. grincer [door] ; craquer [shoes] ; chanter [insects] ; s. grincement, crissement, m.

cream [krím] s. crème [milk, cosmetic, cookery] ; élite, f. ; jaune crème, m. ; v. écrémer ; battre en crème ; **creamy**, crémeux. ‖ **creamery** [-ᵉri] s.* crèmerie, f.

crease [krís] s. pli, faux pli, m. ; v. plisser ; faire des faux plis ; chiffonner, froisser ; **creaseless**, infroissable ; **creasy**, chiffonné, froissé.

create [krié¹t] v. créer. ‖ **creation** [krié¹shᵉn] s. création, f. ‖ **creative** [krié¹tiv] adj. créateur, créatrice. **creator** [krié¹tᵉr] s. créateur, m. ‖ **creature** [krítshᵉr] s. créature, f.

credence [kríd'ns] s. créance, foi, f. ; crédit, m. ‖ **credentials** [kridénshᵉlz] s. pl. lettres de créance, f. ; certificat, m. ; copie conforme, f. ; pl. pièces d'identité, f. ‖ **credible** [krèdᵉb'l] adj. digne de foi ; croyable, admissible.

credit [krèdit] s. estime ; influence, f. ; crédit ; honneur, mérite, m. ; actif (comm.), m. ; v. croire, attribuer à ; créditer ; fournir à crédit. ‖ **creditable** [-ᵉb'l] adj. honorable, estimable ; louable. ‖ **creditor** [-ᵉr] s. créancier ; crédit, m.

credulity [kridyouliti] s. crédulité, f. ‖ **credulous** [krèdyᵉlᵉs] adj. crédule.

creed [kríd] s. credo, m. ; croyance ; profession de foi, f.

creek [krík] s. crique, f. ; ruisseau, m.

creep [kríp] v.* ramper ; se glisser ; s'insinuer ; se hérisser ; s. pl. appréhension, horreur, f. ; chair de poule, f. ‖ **creeper** [-ᵉr] s. plante grimpante, f. ; grimpereau [bird], m. ; **crept** [krèpt] pret., p. p. of to creep.

crescent [krès'nt] adj., s. croissant.

cress [krès] s. cresson, m.

crest [krèst] s. crête, f. ; cimier ; écusson [heraldry], m. ; **crest-fallen**, abattu, penaud.

cretin [krétin] s. crétin, m.

crevice [krèvis] s. crevasse, f.

crew [krou] s. bande, troupe, f. ; équipage (naut.), m. ; équipe, f. ‖ **crewcut** [-két] s. Am. coupe (f.) de cheveux en brosse.

crib [krib] s. crèche, mangeoire, f. ; petit lit ; coffre [grain], m. ; traduction juxtalinéaire, f. ; v. enfermer, encager ; piller, copier, chiper.

cricket [krîkit] s. grillon, m.

cricket [krîkit] s. cricket [game], m.

crime [kra¹m] s. crime, m. ‖ **criminal** [krîmᵉn'l] adj., s. criminel.

crimp [krîmp] v. gaufrer ; onduler [hair] ; crêper ; tuyauter.

crimson [krîmz'n] adj., s. cramoisi ; pourpre, m.

cringe [krîndj] v. s'accroupir ; s'aplatir ; s. courbette, f.

cripple [krîp'l] s. estropié, boiteux, m. ; v. estropier ; paralyser (fig.).

crisis [kra¹sis] (pl. **crises** [kra¹zìz]) s. crise, f. ; point crucial, m.

crisp [krisp] adj. crépu, frisé ; croustillant, friable [cake] ; vif [fire, repartee] ; frais [lettuce] ; frisquet [wind] ; v. crêper, friser.

criterion [kra¹tirien] s. critérium, critère, m.

critic [kritik] s. critique, m. ‖ **critical** [-'l] adj. critique. ‖ **criticism** [kritᵉsizᵉm] s. critique, f. ‖ **criticize** [kritᵉsa¹z] v. critiquer. ‖ **critique** [kritîk] s. critique, f.

croak [krouᵘk] v. croasser ; coasser ; grogner ; Am. claquer, crever ; descendre, démolir ; s. coassement ; croassement, m.

crochet [krouᵘshé¹] s. crochet [knitting], m. ; v. faire du crochet ; **crochet hook**, crochet [needle].

crock [krâk] s. pot, m. ; cruche, f. ‖ **crockery** [-ᵉri] s. poterie, faïence, f.

crocodile [krâkᵉda¹l] s. crocodile, m.

crony [krouᵘni] s.* commère, f. ; compère ; copain, m.

crook [krouk] s. manche recourbé, m. ; houlette, crosse, f. ; escroc (fam.), m. ; v. courber ; se courber ; s'incurver. ‖ **crooked** [-id] adj. tordu, crochu, Fr. Can. croche ; tortueux ; frauduleux ; voûté, courbé. ‖ **crookedness** [-idnis] s. courbure ; voussure ; tortuosité, perversité, f.

croon [kroun] v. chantonner ; fredonner ; s. fredon, m. ; complainte, f. ‖ **crooner** [-ᵉr] s. chanteur de charme, m.

crop [krâp] s. jabot [bird] ; manche de fouet, m. ; récolte, f. ; coupe, f. [of hair] ; v. épointer ; bretauder ; récolter ; produire. ‖ **cropper** [-ᵉr] s. tondeuse, f. ; agriculteur, m. ; chute, f.

crosier [krouᵘjᵉr] s. crosse (eccles.), f.

cross [kraus] s.* croix, f. ; crucifix ; croisement, m. ; adj. transversal ; contraire, opposé ; maussade, désagréable ; métis ; v. croiser ; traverser ; rencontrer ; contrarier ; barrer [check] ; franchir [door] ; métisser ; **crossword puzzle**, mots croisés. ‖ **crossing** [-ing] s. croisement ; passage ; barrement [check]; signe de croix, m.; contra-riété; traversée [sea], f.; *river-cross-ing*, gué; *railroad crossing*, passage à niveau.

crotchety [krâtshiti] *adj.* fantasque, excentrique; quinteux, acariâtre.

crouch [kraᵒutsh] *v.* se tapir, s'accroupir; s'aplatir (fig.).

croup [kroup] *s.* croupe [horse], f.

croup [kroup] *s.* croup, m.

crouton [kroutân] *s.* croûton, m.

crow [kroᵒu] *s.* corneille, f.; *crow's feet*, pattes d'oie, rides.

crow [kroᵒu] *v.** chanter comme le coq; se vanter, triompher.

crowbar [kroᵒubâr] *s.* pince [lever], f.

crowd [kraᵒud] *s.* foule, multitude, troupe, bande, f.; rassemblement, m.; *v.* pousser, serrer; entasser, affluer; se presser; bonder, encombrer.

crown [kraᵒun] *s.* couronne; pièce de monnaie, f.; fond [hat]; sommet, m.; *v.* couronner; achever; honorer; récompenser.

crozier, see crosier.

crucial [kroushel] *adj.* décisif; éprouvant; critique.

crucible [krouseb'l] *s.* creuset, m.

crucifix [krousefiks] *s.** crucifix, m. ‖ *crucifixion* [krousefíkshen] *s.* crucifixion, f. ‖ *crucify* [krousefa¹] *v.* crucifier.

crude [kroud] *adj.* cru; brut; grossier; fruste.

cruel [krouel] *adj.* cruel. ‖ *cruelty* [-ti] *s.** cruauté, f.

cruet [krouit] *s.* burette, f.; *vinegar cruet*, vinaigrier; *oil cruet*, huilier.

cruise [krouz] *s.* croisière, f.; *v.* croiser; marauder [taxi]. ‖ *cruiser* [-ᵉʳ] *s.* croiseur (naut.); car de police, m.

cruller [kraelᵉʳ] *s.* beignet, m.

crumb [kroem] *s.* miette; mie, f.; *v.* émietter; *crumb-scoop*, ramasse-miettes.

crumble [kraemb'l] *v.* pulvériser; (s')émietter.

crumple [kraemp'l] *v.* froisser, chiffonner; se friper; *Am.* flancher.

crunch [kraentsh] *v.* croquer; broyer; *s.** bruit de broiement, m.

crupper [kraepᵉʳ] *s.* croupière, f.

crusade [krousé¹d] *s.* croisade, f.; *v.* entreprendre une croisade; *crusader*, croisé.

crush [kraesh] *s.** écrasement, m.; cohue, f.; béguin, m.; *v.* écraser; opprimer; dominer; *to crush out*, exprimer, extraire [juice]; réprimer [revolt]; *to crush in*, s'écraser pour entrer; *to crush up*, se serrer.

crust [kraest] *s.* croûte, f.; *v.* faire croûte; couvrir d'une croûte; *crusty*, croûteux; revêche.

crustacean [krousté¹shen] *s.* crustacé, m.

crutch [kraetsh] *s.** béquille, f.

crux [kroeks] *s.** difficulté, f.; point crucial, m.

cry [kra¹] *s.** cri; appel, m.; proclamation; crise de larmes, f.; *v.* crier; pleurer; réclamer; proclamer; *to cry out against*, se récrier contre; *to cry down*, décrier; *to cry up*, vanter; *Am.* cry-baby, pleurnicheur.

crystal [kríst'l] *s.* cristal, m. ‖ *crystalline* [-in] *adj.* cristallin. ‖ *crystallize* [-a¹z] *v.* cristalliser.

cub [kaeb] *s.* petit d'animal; lionceau, louveteau, renardeau, ourson, gosse; débutant, m.

cube [kyoub] *s.* cube, m.; *v.* cuber; *cubic*, cubique; *cubism*, cubisme; *cubist*, cubiste.

cuckoo [koukou] *s.* coucou [bird], m.; *cuckoo clock*, coucou.

cucumber [kyoukœmbᵉʳ] *s.* concombre, m.; *Am.* cucumber tree, magnolia.

cud [kaed] *s.* aliment ruminé, m.; chique, f.

cuddle [kaed'l] *s.* enlacement, m.; *v.* embrasser; s'étreindre; câliner; *to cuddle up*, se pelotonner.

cudgel [kaedjᵉl] *s.* trique, f.; gourdin, m.; *v.* bâtonner, rosser.

cue [kyou] *s.* réplique (theat.); queue [billiards], f.; indication, directive, consigne, f.; mot d'ordre, m.

cuff [kaef] *s.* manchette [sleeve], f.; parement; revers [trousers], m.

cuff [kaef] *s.* soufflet, coup de poing, m.; *v.* gifler; cogner.

cuirass [kwiras] *s.** cuirasse, f.

culinary [kyoulᵉnèri] *adj.* culinaire.

cull [kael] *v.* cueillir; choisir.

culminate [kaelmᵉné¹t] *v.* culminer.

culprit [kaelprit] *s.* inculpé; coupable, m.

cult [kaelt] *s.* culte, m.; secte, f.

cultivate [kaeltᵉvé¹t] *v.* cultiver; civiliser; chérir. ‖ *cultivation* [kaeltᵉvé¹-shen] *s.* culture, f. ‖ *cultivator* [kaeltᵉvé¹tᵉr] *s.* cultivateur, m. ‖ *cultural* [kaeltshᵉrel] *adj.* cultural; culturel. ‖ *culture* [kaeltshᵉr] *s.* culture, f.

culver [kaelvᵉr] *s.* ramier, m.

cumbersome [kaembᵉrsᵉm] *adj.* encombrant; pesant.

cumulative [kyoumyᵉlé¹tiv] *adj.* cumulatif; plural; composé.

cunning [kœning] *adj.* rusé, astucieux; ingénieux; *Am.* attrayant, gentil; *s.* ruse, astuce, adresse, f.; talent, m.

cup [kœp] *s.* coupe; tasse, f.; bol; calice, m.; *v.* mettre des ventouses; *eggcup,* coquetier; *tin cup,* quart (mil.); *wet cup,* ventouse scarifiée. ‖ **cupboard** [kœbᵉrd] *s.* buffet; placard, m. ‖ **cupcake** [-ké¹k] *s.* petit four, m.

cur [kœr] *s.* corniaud; cabot [dog]; être méprisable; chien, m. (fam.).

curate [kyourit] *s.* vicaire, m.

curb [kœrb] *s.* gourmette [horse], f.; frein, m.; margelle du puits, f.; bord du trottoir; marché libre (fin.), m.; *v.* refréner, brider.

curd [kœrd] *s.* (se) cailler; *s.* caillé, m. ‖ **curdle** [-'l] *v.* cailler; se figer, se glacer (fig.).

cure [kyour] *s.* soin spirituel, m.; charge d'âme; cure (med.); guérison, f.; remède, m.; *v.* guérir; remédier; saler [meat]; faire sécher [hay, tobacco]; *cure-all,* panacée; *cureless,* incurable.

curfew [kœrfyou] *s.* couvre-feu, m.

curio [kyourioou] *s.* curiosité; rareté, f. ‖ **curiosity** [kyouriậsᵉti] *s.** curiosité, f.; *curiosity shop,* magasin d'antiquités. ‖ **curious** [kyouriᵉs] *adj.* curieux; inhabituel; étrange.

curl [kœrl] *s.* boucle, spirale, f.; *v.* boucler, friser; s'enrouler; s'élever en volutes; *curly,* bouclé, frisé; *curled cabbage,* chou frisé.

currant [kœrᵉnt] *s.* raisin de Corinthe, m.; groseille, f.; *black currant,* cassis [fruit]; *currant bush,* groseillier; *currant wine,* cassis [liquor].

currency [kœrᵉnsi] *s.** circulation [money]; devise; monnaie en circulation, f.; cours, m. (fig.); *papercurrency,* papier-monnaie. ‖ **current** [kœrᵉnt] *adj.* courant [change]; habituel; *s.* courant, m.; *current price,* prix courant; *current-breaker,* interrupteur (electr.).

curse [kœrs] *s.* malédiction; calamité, f.; *v.* maudire; jurer; *cursed,* maudit.

cursory [kœrsᵉri] *adj.* superficiel, en diagonale [reading].

curt [kœrt] *adj.* bref, cassant; concis.

curtail [kœrté¹l] *v.* rogner, raccourcir; réduire. ‖ **curtailment** [-mᵉnt] *s.* diminution, f.

curtain [kœrt'n] *s.* rideau, m.; *v.* poser des rideaux; voiler.

curtsy [kœrtsi] *s.** révérence, f.

curvature [kœrᵛᵉtshᵉr] *s.* courbure, f. ‖ **curve** [kœrv] *s.* courbe, f.; virage, m.; *v.* (se) courber.

cushion [koushᵉn] *s.* coussin; coussinet (mech.); amortisseur, m.; bande [billiard table], f.; *v.* garnir de coussins; amortir; *air cushion,* coussin pneumatique. ‖ **cushy** [-i] *adj.* ouaté, douillet; pépère (fam.).

custard [kœstᵉrd] *s.* flan, m.; crème renversée, f.

custodian [kœstoᵒudiᵉn] *s.* gardien, m.; conservateur, m. [museum]. ‖ **custody** [kœstᵉdi] *s.** garde, protection; détention, f.; *in custody,* en état d'arrestation.

custom [kœstᵉm] *s.* coutume; habitude; *Br.* clientèle, f.; achalandage, m.; *pl.* droits de douane; *adj.* fait sur mesure; *custom garments,* vêtements sur mesure. ‖ **customary** [-ᵉri] *adj.* coutumier, usel. ‖ **customer** [-ᵉr] *s.* marchand; client, m. ‖ **customhouse** [-haᵒus] *s.* administration, bureaux des douanes; *customhouse official,* douanier.

cut [kœt] *s.* coupure, entaille; blessure; tranchée; tranche; coupe [clothes]; réduction [price]; gravure, planche; parcelle de terre cultivée; coupe de bois, f.; *Am.* tunnel, m.; *v.* couper, tailler, *Fr. Can.* bûcher [trees]; séparer; diminuer [price]; traverser; couper, cingler; prendre un raccourci; creuser [canal, road]; tailler sur un patron [cloth]; manquer [class]; *short cut,* raccourci; *to cut out,* couper (electr.); exclure; *pret., p. p.* of *cut.*

cute [kyout] *adj.* adroit; attirant.

cuticle [kyoutik'l] *s.* cuticule; envie, f.; épiderme, m.

cutlery [kœtlᵉri] *s.* coutellerie, f.

cutlet [kœtlit] *s.* côtelette, f.

cutter [kœtᵉr] *s.* coupeur [wood, cloth]; cotre, cutter (naut.); *Am.* navire garde-côte (naut.); coutre de moissonneuse ou de faucheuse; petit traîneau, m.

cuttlefish [kœt'lfish] *s.** seiche, f.

cyclamen [siklᵉmᵉn] *s.* cyclamen, m.

cycle [sa¹k'l] *s.* cycle, m.; bicyclette, f.; *v.* faire de la bicyclette; revenir par cycle. ‖ **cyclist** [-ist] *s.* cycliste, m. f.

cyclone [sa¹kloᵒun] *s.* cyclone, m.; *cyclone cellar, Am.* abri anti-cyclone.

cylinder [silindᵉr] *s.* cylindre; barillet [revolver]; corps de pompe (mech.), m.

cynic [sinik] *s.* cynique; misanthrope, m. ‖ **cynical** [-'l] *adj.* sceptique; désabusé; sarcastique.

cypress [sa¹prᵉs] *s.** cyprès, m.

cyst [sist] *s.* kyste, m. ‖ **cystitis** [sista¹tis] *s.* cystite, f.

D

dab [dab] *v.* tapoter; *s.* tapotement, m.; tape; touche; tache; empreinte, f. ‖ **dabble** [-'l] *v.* barboter; *to dabble in*, s'occuper un peu de.

dad, daddy [dad, dadi] *s.* papa, m.; *daddy-long-legs*, faucheux.

daffodil [daf•dil] *s.* jonquille, f.; coucou, m.

daft [daft] *adj.* idiot; toqué.

dagger [dag•r] *s.* poignard, m.

dahlia [daly•] *s.* dahlia, m.

daily [dé¹li] *adj.* journalier; *adv.* journellement; *s.•* quotidien [newspaper], m.

dainty [dé¹nti] *adj.* gracieux; délicat; exquis; *s.•* friandise, f.

dairy [dèri] *s.•* laiterie, f.

daisy [dé¹zi] *s.•* pâquerette, f.

dale [dé¹l] *s.* vallon, m.

dally [dali] *v.* badiner; batifoler; flâner, se retarder.

dam [dàm] *s.* digue; écluse, f.; barrage, m.; *v.* endiguer.

damage [dàmidj] *s.* dommage; dégât; préjudice, m.; *pl.* dommages-intérêts; *v.* abîmer; nuire à; s'endommager; *to pay for damages*, dédommager.

dame [dé¹m] *s.* dame; douairière, f.

damn [dàm] *v.* damner; jurer. ‖ **damnation** [damné¹sh•n] *s.* damnation, f.; éreintement, m. ‖ **damned** [-d] *adj.* damné; sacré.

damp [dàmp] *adj.* humide; *s.* humidité, f.; *v.* humidifier; étouffer [fire]; décourager, abattre. ‖ **dampness** [-nis] *s.* humidité, f.

dance [dàns] *s.* danse, f.; bal, m.; *v.* gambader, danser. ‖ **dancer** [-•r] *s.* danseur, danseuse. ‖ **dancing** [-ing] *s.* danse, f.; *dancing-partner*, danseur.

dandelion [dànd'la¹•n] *s.* pissenlit, m.

dandruff [dàndr•f] *s.* pellicules, f. pl.

dandy [dàndi] *s.* dandy, m.; chose élégante, f.; *adj.* Am. élégant, excellent, chic.

danger [dé¹ndj•r] *s.* danger, risque, m. ‖ **dangerous** [-r•s] *adj.* dangereux.

dangle [dàng'l] *v.* pendre, pendiller.

dapple [dap'l] *s.* tacheture, f.; *adj.* tacheté, pommelé; *v.* tacheter, pommeler; se tacheter.

dare [dè•r] *s.* défi, m.; audace, f.; *v.•* oser; défier; affronter; *dare-devil*, casse-cou. ‖ **daring** [-ring] *s.* audace, f.; *adj.* audacieux.

dark [dârk] *adj.* obscur; sombre; noir; ténébreux; foncé; secret; *s.* obscurité; ignorance, f.; noir, secret, m.; *dark-complexioned*, basané, bronzé. ‖ **darken** [-•n] *v.* obscurcir; noircir. ‖ **darkness** [-nis] *s.* obscurité, ténèbres; noirceur, f.

darling [dârling] *adj., s.* chéri.

darn [dârn] *s.* reprise, f.; *v.* repriser; *interj.* maudit soit!; *darning needle*, aiguille à repriser.

darnel [dârn'l] *s.* ivraie, f.

dart [dârt] *s.* dard; trait; brusque mouvement, élan, m.; *v.* lancer; s'élancer.

dash [dash] *s.•* choc; élan; coup de main, m.; impétuosité; petite quantité, dose; course, f.; tiret, m.; *v.* heurter, cogner; lancer; éclabousser; ruiner; déprimer; griffonner; se précipiter. ‖ **dasher** [-•r] *s.* baratton, m.; épateur, m. (colloq.); *Am.* garde-boue, m. ‖ **dashing** [-ing] *adj.* fougueux; brillant; dynamique; tapageur.

data [dé¹t•] *s. pl.* données, f. pl.

date [dé¹t] *s.* datte [fruit], f.

date [dé¹t] *s.* date; échéance, f.; terme; *Am.* rendez-vous, m.; *v.* dater; être daté; *up to date*, à la page; *at short date*, à courte échéance; *to date from*, remonter à; *under the date of*, en date de.

daub [daub] *v.* barbouiller; souiller; plâtrer [trees]; *s.* enduit; barbouillage, m.; croûte, f. [painting].

daughter [daut•r] *s.* fille, f.; *daughter-in-law*, bru; *daughterly*, filial.

daunt [daunt] *v.* intimider, effrayer; *dauntless*, intrépide.

davenport [dav•npo°rt] *s.* secrétaire; *Am.* canapé-lit, m.

dawdle [daud'l] *v.* flâner, musarder.

dawn [daun] *s.* aube, f.; commencement, m.; *v.* poindre; apparaître.

day [dé¹] *s.* jour, m.; journée; époque, f.; âge, m.; *a week from today* (*Br. this day week*), d'aujourd'hui en huit; *today*, aujourd'hui; *to the day*, au jour fixé; *by day*, de jour; *daybreak*, aurore, aube; *day laborer*, journalier [man]; *daylight*, lumière du jour; *day nursery*, garderie d'enfants; *day school*, externat; *daytime*, journée; *day work*, travail à la journée.

daze [dé¹z] *v.* hébéter; étourdir; éblouir; *s.* étourdissement, m.; confusion, f.; ahurissement, m. ‖ **dazzle** [daz'l] *v.* éblouir; *s.* éblouissement, f.

deacon [dîk⁰n] *s.* diacre, m. ‖ **deaconess** [-is] *s.°* diaconesse, f. ‖ **deaconship** [-ship] *s.* diaconat, m.

dead [dèd] *adj.* mort; amorti; inactif; insensible; terne [color]; éteint [fire]; disparu [language]; *s.* mort, m.; période la plus calme, f.; *adv.* extrêmement; droit, directement; net [stop]; **dead center,** point mort (mech.); **dead letter,** lettre au rebut; **dead shot,** excellent tireur; **dead tired,** éreinté; **dead wall,** mur aveugle. ‖ **deaden** [-'n] *v.* amortir; émousser; assourdir. ‖ **deadly** [-li] *adj.* mortel; meurtrier; implacable; *adv.* mortellement; terriblement.

deaf [dèf] *adj.* sourd; **deaf-mute,** sourd-muet. ‖ **deafen** [-⁰n] *v.* assourdir; étourdir. ‖ **deafening** [-ning] *adj.* assourdissant. ‖ **deafness** [-nis] *s.* surdité, f.

deal [dîl] *s.* quantité; donne [cards]; opération commerciale; *Am.* transaction; partie liée (pol.), f.; marché, m.; *v.°* distribuer; faire le commerce (*in,* de); négocier (*with,* avec); *a great deal of,* beaucoup de; *to give a square deal,* se montrer juste envers. ‖ **dealer** [-⁰r] *s.* marchand, négociant, m. ‖ **dealings** [-ingz] *s. pl.* affaires, négociations, f. pl.; commerce, m.

deal [dîl] *s.* bois blanc, sapin, m.; planche, f.; madrier, m.

dealt [dèlt] *pret., p. p. of* to deal.

dean [dîn] *s.* doyen, m. ‖ **deanship** [-ship] *s.* décanat; doyenné, m.

dear [di⁰r] *adj.* cher, aimé; précieux; coûteux; *s.* être cher, m. ‖ **dearly** [-li] *adv.* avec tendresse; chèrement, à prix élevé.

dearth [dër̃th] *s.* disette; pénurie, f.

death [dèth] *s.* mort; fin, f.; décès, m.; **death-bell,** glas; **death rate,** mortalité; **deathless,** immortel; **deathlike,** cadavérique; sépulcral, de mort; **deathly,** mortel; mortellement.

debacle [dé¹bâk'l] *s.* débâcle, f.

debar [dibâr] *v.* exclure, éliminer.

debark [dibârk] *v.* débarquer.

debase [dibé¹s] *v.* avilir; dégrader.

debate [dibé¹t] *s.* débat, m.; discussion, f.; *v.* discuter, débattre. ‖ **debater** [-⁰r] *s.* controversiste, argumentateur, m.

debauch [dibautsh] *s.°* débauche, f.; *v.* débaucher, pervertir. ‖ **debauchee** [débâtshî] *s.* débauché, m. f. ‖ **debauchery** [dibautsh⁰ri] *s.* débauche, corruption, f.

debilitate [dibîlté¹t] *v.* débiliter, déprimer. ‖ **debility** [dibî¹eti] *s.°* débilité, faiblesse, f.

debit [dèbit] *s.* débit; débet; doit, m.; *v.* débiter; passer au débit.

debris [débris] (*pl.* **debris**) *s.* décombres, m. pl.

debt [dèt] *s.* dette; créance, f.; *to run into debt,* s'endetter; **gambling debt,** dette de jeu; **national debt,** dette publique. ‖ **debtor** [-⁰r] *s.* débiteur, m.; débitrice, f.

debut [dibyou] *s.* début, m.

decade [dèké¹d] *s.* décade; décennie, f.

decadence [diké¹d'ns] *s.* décadence, f. ‖ **decadent,** décadent.

decaffeinated [dikⱥfiiné¹tid] *adj.* décaféiné.

decalcify [dikalsifa¹] *v.* décalcifier.

decamp [dikâmp] *v.* décamper; lever le camp.

decant [dikⱥnt] *v.* décanter. ‖ **decanter** [-⁰r] *s.* carafe, f.

decapitate [dikⱥp°té¹t] *v.* décapiter.

decay [diké¹] *s.* délabrement; dépérissement, m.; décadence; carie [teeth], f.; *v.* décliner; dépérir; se délabrer; se carier; se pourrir.

decease [disîs] *s.* décès, m.; *v.* décéder. ‖ **deceased** [-t] *adj., s.* défunt, mort.

deceit [disît] *s.* tromperie, f. ‖ **deceitful** [-f⁰l] *adj.* trompeur. ‖ **deceive** [disîv] *v.* tromper, abuser.

decelerate [disèl°ré¹t] *v.* ralentir.

December [disèmb⁰r] *s.* décembre, m.

decency [dî¹nsi] *s.°* bienséance, f. ‖ **decent** [dis°nt] *adj.* bienséant, décent; convenable, suffisant.

deception [disèps°n] *s.* tromperie; illusion, f.; mécompte, m.

decide [disa¹d] *v.* décider.

decimal [dès⁰m'l] *adj.* décimal; *s.* décimale, f.

decimate [dès°mé¹t] *v.* décimer.

decipher [disa¹f⁰r] *v.* déchiffrer.

decision [disij⁰n] *s.* décision, f.; arrêt; jugement, m. ‖ **decisive** [disa¹siv] *adj.* décisif.

deck [dèk] *s.* pont, tillac (naut.), m.; *Am.* toit [train]; jeu de cartes, m.; *v.* couvrir, orner; **flight deck,** pont d'envol; **fore-deck,** gaillard d'avant; **quarter deck,** gaillard d'arrière.

declaim [diklé¹m] *v.* déclamer. ‖ **declamation** [dèklⁱmé¹shⁱn] *s.* déclamation, f. ‖ **declamatory** [diklâm°t⁰ri] *adj.* déclamatoire.

declaration [dèklⁱré¹shⁱn] *s.* déclaration, f. ‖ **declare** [diklèr] *v.* déclarer; proclamer; affirmer; annoncer [cards]; se déclarer.

declension [diklènsh⁰n] *s.* déclinaison (gramm.); baisse, pente, f. ‖ **decline** [dikla¹n] *v.* incliner, pencher;

baisser [price]; refuser; décliner (gramm.); s. déclin, m.; décadence; pente; baisse [price]; consomption (med.), f.

declivity [diklíveti] s.* pente, déclivité, descente, f.

decode [dikooud] v. déchiffrer.

decompose [dikºmpoºuz] v. (se) décomposer; (se) pourrir. || *decomposition* [dikâmpºzishºn] s. décomposition, f.

decorate [dèkºré¹t] v. décorer; enjoliver. || *decoration* [dèkºré¹shºn] s. décoration; médaille, f.; pavoisement; décor, m. || *decorative* [dèkºré¹tiv] adj. décoratif. || *decorum* [dikoºurºm] s. décorum, m.; bienséance; étiquette, f.

decoy [dikoˡ] s. leurre; appât; piège, m.; v. leurrer, attirer.

decrease [dikrîs] v. décroître; diminuer; [dík̖rîs] s. décroissance, diminution; baisse, décrue, f.

decree [dikrî] s. décret, arrêt, m.; v. décréter, décider.

decrepit [dikrèpit] adj. décrépit.

decrial [dikra¹ºl] s. dénigrement, m. || *decry* [dikra¹] v. décrier, dénigrer.

decuple [dèkyoupˡl] s. décuple; v. décupler.

dedicate [dèdºké¹t] v. dédier. || *dedication* [dèdºké¹shºn] s. dédicace; consécration, f.

deduce [didyous] v. déduire. || *deduct* [didºkt] v. décompter, retrancher. || *deduction* [didækshºn] s. déduction; retenue, f.

deed [dîd] s. action, f.; haut fait; acte, document (jur.), m.; v. transférer par un acte; *deed of gift*, donation; *foul deed*, forfait; *private deed*, acte sous seing privé.

deem [dîm] v. juger; estimer.

deep [dîp] adj. profond; sage, pénétrant; intense [feeling]; foncé [color]; grave [tone]; grand [mourning]; *deep in thought*, absorbé; s. océan; ciel; abîme, m.; profondeur, f.; adv. profondément; tout au fond; intensément. || *deepen* [-ºn] v. approfondir; creuser; assombrir; sombrer [voice]; foncer. || *deepness* [-nis] s. profondeur, f.

deer [diºr] s. daim, cerf, cervidé, m.; *deerhound*, chien courant; *deerskin*, peau de daim.

deface [difé¹s] v. défigurer, mutiler.

defalcation [difalké¹shºn] s. détournement de fonds, m.

defamation [dèfºmé¹shºn] s. diffamation, f. || *defame* [difé¹m] v. diffamer.

default [difault] s. défaut (jur.), m.; déficience, f.; v. faire défaut (jur.);

faillir à. || *defaulter* [-ºr] s. concussionnaire; délinquant; contumace; défaillant; insoumis; réfractaire, m.

defeat [difît] s. défaite, frustration, f.; v. battre, défaire; frustrer; déjouer [plan]; mettre en minorité.

defect [difèkt] s. défaut, m.; imperfection; tare, f. || *defection* [difèkshºn] s. défection, f. || *defective* [-iv] adj. défectueux; déficient; défectif (gramm.).

defence [difèns] s. défense, f. || *defend* [difènd] v. protéger; défendre (jur.). || *defendant* [-ºnt] s. défendeur (jur.), m. || *defender* [-ºr] s. défenseur (jur.), m. || *defense* [difèns] s. défense, f. || *defensive* [-iv] adj. défensif; s. défensive, f.

defer [difêr] v. différer, remettre, ajourner; mettre en sursis (milit.).

defer [difêr] v. déférer; s'en rapporter. || *deference* [dèfºrºns] s. déférence, f. || *deferential* [dèfºrènshºl] adj. respectueux, déférent.

defiance [difa¹ºns] s. défi, m.; résistance, f. || *defiant* [difa¹ºnt] adj. provocant, agressif; défiant.

deficiency [difìshºnsi] s.* manque, défaut, m.; carence, déficience, lacune, f.; déficit, m. || *deficient* [difìshºnt] adj. insuffisant, défectueux; s. débile mental, m. || *deficit* [dèfºsit] s. déficit; découvert, m.

defile [difa¹l] s. défilé, m.; gorge, f.

defile [difa¹l] v. souiller, corrompre. || *defilement* [-mºnt] s. souillure, f.

define [difa¹n] v. définir. || *definite* [dèfºnit] adj. déterminé, précis; défini (gramm.). || *definition* [dèfºnishºn] s. définition, f. || *definitive* [difìnºtiv] adj. définitif, décisif; déterminatif (gramm.).

deflagrate [dèflºgré¹t] v. embraser; prendre feu. || *deflagration* [dèflºgré¹shºn] s. déflagration, f.

deflate [diflé¹t] v. dégonfler. || *deflation* [diflé¹shºn] s. déflation, f.

deflect [diflèkt] v. détourner, dévier; braquer [wheels].

deform [difaurm] v. déformer; défigurer. || *deformed* [-d] adj. difforme || *deformity* [-ºti] s.* difformité, f.

defraud [difraud] v. frustrer, frauder, tromper; léser, faire tort à.

defray [difré¹] v. défrayer; payer.

defrost [difrâst] v. dégivrer; décongeler; *defroster*, dégivreur.

deft [dèft] adj. agile, adroit.

defy [difa¹] v. défier, braver.

degenerate [didjènºrit] adj., s. dégénéré; [-é¹t] v. dégénérer.

deglutition [digloutìshºn] s. déglutition, f.

degradation [dègr⁰dé¹sh⁰n] s. dégradation, f.; avilissement, m. ‖ **degrade** [digré¹d] v. dégrader; avilir.

degree [digrî] s. degré; rang; diplôme (educ.); degré (math., gramm.), m.; puissance (math.), f.; *by degrees*, peu à peu.

degustate [digœsté¹t] v. déguster.

dehydrate [diha¹dré¹t] v. déshydrater; *dehydrated eggs*, œufs en poudre.

de-ice [dî'a¹s] v. dégivrer; **de-icer**, dégivreur.

deign [dé¹n] v. daigner.

deity [dî⁰ti] s.° divinité; déité, f.

dejected [didjèktid] adj. abattu, découragé. ‖ **dejection** [didjèksh⁰n] s. abattement, découragement, m.

delay [dilé¹] s. délai; retard, sursis, m.; v. différer, retarder; tarder.

delectable [dilèkt⁰b'l] adj. délectable, délicieux.

delegate [dèl⁰gé¹t] s. délégué, représentant; *Am.* député, m.; v. déléguer. ‖ **delegation** [dél⁰gé¹sh⁰n] s. délégation, f.

delete [dilît] v. effacer, biffer.

deliberate [dilíb⁰rit] adj. délibéré; prémédité; circonspect; [dilib⁰ré¹t] v. délibérer; peser, examiner. ‖ **deliberation** [dilib⁰ré¹sh⁰n] s. délibération; réflexion; discussion, f.

delicacy [dèl⁰k⁰si] s.° friandise; délicatesse; fragilité; sensibilité, f. ‖ **delicate** [dèl⁰k⁰t] adj. délicat; raffiné; fragile. ‖ **delicatessen** [dèl⁰k⁰té¹s'n] s. plats cuisinés, m. pl.

delicious [dilísh⁰s] adj. délicieux.

delight [dila¹t] s. délice, joie, f.; v. ravir, enchanter; prendre plaisir à. ‖ **delightful** [-f⁰l] adj. délicieux, charmant, ravissant.

delimit [dilímit] v. délimiter.

delineate [dilínié¹t] v. tracer, esquisser; délimiter.

delinquent [dilíngkw⁰nt] adj., s. délinquant (jur.).

delirious [dilíri⁰s] adj. délirant (med.); extravagant; *to be delirious*, délirer. ‖ **delirium** [dilíri⁰m] s. délire, m.

deliver [dilív⁰r] v. délivrer, libérer; exprimer, énoncer; remettre; distribuer [letters]; prononcer [speech]; donner [blow]; accoucher de. ‖ **deliverance** [-r⁰ns] s. délivrance; libération, f. ‖ **deliveree** [dilív⁰rî] s. *Am.* destinataire, m. ‖ **deliverer** [dilív⁰r⁰r] s. libérateur; livreur, m. ‖ **delivery** [dilív⁰ri] s.° délivrance; livraison [goods]; distribution [letters]; élocution, f.; accouchement; service [baseball], m.; **delivery man**, livreur; **delivery truck**, voiture de livraison.

dell [dèl] s. vallon, m.

delouse [dila⁰ᵘs] v. épouiller.

delude [dilo̅u̅d] v. tromper, abuser.

deluge [dèlyoudj] s. déluge, m.; v. inonder.

delusion [dilouj⁰n] s. tromperie; erreur, f.; *optical delusion*, illusion d'optique. ‖ **delusive** [dilousiv] adj. trompeur; illusoire.

delve [dèlv] v. bêcher; fouiller (fig.).

demagogic [dèm⁰gẁjik] adj. démagogique. ‖ **demagogism** [dèm⁰gågiz'm] s. démagogie. ‖ **demagogue** [dèm⁰gaug] s. démagogue, m. ‖ **demagoguery** [dèm⁰gågri], **demagogy** [dém⁰gogi] s. démagogie, f.

demand [dimand] s. exigence; réclamation; prétention; commandes (econ.); sommation (jur.), f.; débouché (comm.), m.; v. exiger; revendiquer; solliciter; s'enquérir. ‖ **demanding** [-ing] adj. exigeant; revendicatif.

demean [dimîn] v. abaisser, avilir.

demeanor [dimîn⁰r] s. conduite, f.; maintien, comportement, m.

demented [dimèntid] adj. dément.

demerit [dimèrit] s. faute, f.; mauvais point (educ.); *Am.* blâme, m.

demobilize [dimo⁰ᵘb'la¹z] v. démobiliser. ‖ **demobilization** [dimo⁰ᵘb'l⁰zé¹sh⁰n] s. démobilisation, f.

democracy [d⁰måkr⁰si] s.° démocratie, f. ‖ **democrat** [dèm⁰krat] s. démocrate, m. ‖ **democratic** [dèm⁰kratik] adj. démocratique. ‖ **democratize** [dimåkr⁰ta¹z] v. (se) démocratiser.

demolish [dimálish] v. démolir. ‖ **demolisher** [-⁰r] s. démolisseur, m. ‖ **demolition** [dim⁰lísh⁰n] s. démolition, f.

demoniac [dimo⁰ᵘniak] adj. démoniaque; s. possédé, m.

demonstrate [dèm⁰nstré¹t] v. démontrer. ‖ **demonstration** [dèm⁰nstré¹sh⁰n] s. démonstration, f. ‖ **demonstrative** [dimánstr⁰tiv] adj. démonstratif; expansif; probant.

demoralize [dimaur⁰la¹z] v. démoraliser; dépraver, pervertir.

demur [dimë̈r] v. objecter; hésiter.

demure [dimyour] adj. grave; prude.

demurrage [dimë̈ridj] s. surestarie (naut.), f.

den [dèn] s. antre, repaire; cabinet de travail, m.

denegation [dînige¹sh⁰n] s. dénégation, f.

denial [dina¹⁰l] s. démenti; refus, déni, m.; dénégation, f.

denigrate [dînigre¹t] v. dénigrer; **denigration**, dénigration; **denigrator**, dénigreur.

denomination [dinâmᵉné¹shᵉn] *s.* dénomination; confession religieuse; valeur d'une coupure [money], f.

denote [dinoᵘt] *v.* dénoter.

denounce [dinaᵒᵘns] *v.* dénoncer; stigmatiser; rompre [treaty].

dense [dèns] *adj.* dense, épais, compact; stupide. ‖ **density** [-ᵉti] *s.* densité; sottise, f.

dent [dènt] *s.* entaille, f.; *v.* entailler. ‖ **dental** [-ᵉl] *adj.* dentaire; *s.* dentale (gramm.), f.; **dental office,** cabinet dentaire. ‖ **dentist** [-ist] *s.* dentiste, m. ‖ **dentistry** [-tistri] *s.* art dentaire, m. ‖ **dentition** [dentïsh°n] *s.* dentition, f. ‖ **denture** [dèntshᵉr] *s.* dentier, m.

denunciation [dinœnsié¹shᵉn] *s.* dénonciation; accusation publique; rupture [treaty], f.; **denunciator,** dénonciateur.

deny [dina¹] *v.* nier; démentir; refuser; *to deny oneself to callers,* ne pas recevoir, interdire sa porte.

deodorize [dioᵘdᵉra¹z] *v.* désodoriser; défruiter [olive oil].

depart [dipârt] *v.* partir; se retirer; mourir. ‖ **departed** [-id] *adj.* absent; défunt. ‖ **department** [-mᵉnt] *s.* département; ministère; service (comm.); rayon, comptoir, m.; administration, section; discipline (univ.); division (mil.), f. ‖ **departure** [-shᵉr] *s.* départ, m.; déviation, f.

depend [dipènd] *v.* dépendre (*on,* de); compter (*on,* sur). ‖ **dependable** [-ᵉb'l] *adj.* digne de confiance, sûr. ‖ **dependence** [-ᵉns] *s.* dépendance; confiance, f. ‖ **dependency** [-ᵉnsi] *s.ᵉ* dépendance; colonie, f. ‖ **dependent** [-ᵉnt] *adj.* dépendant; subordonné (gramm.); *s.* protégé, m.

depict [dipïkt] *v.* peindre; décrire.

depilate [dépilé¹t] *v.* épiler. ‖ **depilation** [dépilé¹shᵉn] *s.* épilation, f. ‖ **depilatory** [dépïlᵉᵗᵉri] *s., adj.* dépilatoire, m.

deplete [diplît] *v.* épuiser, vider.

deplorable [diploᵒᵘrᵉb'l] *adj.* déplorable. ‖ **deplore** [diploᵒᵘr] *v.* déplorer; pleurer.

deploy [diplo¹] *v.* (se) déployer.

depopulate [dipaupyoᵘle¹t] *v.* dépeupler; **depopulation,** dépopulation, f.

deport [dipoᵒᵘrt] *v.* déporter; *to deport oneself,* se comporter. ‖ **deportation** [dipoᵒᵘrté¹shᵉn] *s.* déportation, f. ‖ **deportment** [dipoᵒᵘrtmᵉnt] *s.* comportement, m.

depose [dipoᵒᵘz] *v.* déposer, destituer; témoigner. ‖ **deposit** [dipázit] *v.* mettre en dépôt; consigner; déposer; verser; *s.* dépôt; versement; cautionnement [money]; gisement (geol.),

m.; consignation, f. ‖ **deposition** [dè-pᵉzïsh°n] *s.* déposition; destitution, f.; témoignage; dépôt, m. ‖ **depositor** [dipázitᵉr] *s.* déposant, m. ‖ **depot** [dïpoᵒᵘ] *s.* entrepôt, m.; *Am.* gare, f.

depravation [diprᵉvé¹shᵉn] *s.* dépravation, f. ‖ **deprave** [dipré¹v] *v.* dépraver.

depreciate [diprîshié¹t] *v.* (se) déprécier; faire baisser le prix. ‖ **depreciative** [-iv] *adj.* péjoratif.

depredation [dèprᵉdé¹shᵉn] *s.* déprédation, f.

depress [diprès] *v.* déprimer; humilier; déprécier; accabler. ‖ **depressed** [-t] *adj.* déprimé, abattu. ‖ **depression** [diprèsh°n] *s.* dépression; crise (comm.); baisse, f.; affaissement; dénivellement; découragement, m.

deprive [dipra¹v] *v.* priver.

depth [dèpth] *s.* profondeur; gravité [sound]; vivacité [colors], f., abîme; fond, m.

depurative [dipyourᵉtiv] *adj., s.* dépuratif, m.

deputation [dèpyᵉté¹shᵉn] *s.* députation; délégation, f. ‖ **depute** [dipyout] *v* députer, déléguer. ‖ **deputy** [dèpyᵉti] *s.ᵉ* député, délégué; suppléant, adjoint, m.

derail [diré¹l] *v.* dérailler. ‖ **derailment** [-mᵉnt] *s.* déraillement, m.

derange [diré¹ndj] *v.* déranger; troubler; affoler; rendre fou.

derelict [dèrᵉlikt] *s.* épave, f.; *adj.* abandonné.

deride [dira¹d] *v.* railler; ridiculiser; rire de. ‖ **derision** [dirij°n] *s.* dérision, f.

derivation [dèrivé¹shᵉn] *s.* dérivation, f. ‖ **derivative** [dirïvᵗiv] *s., adj.* dérivé, m. ‖ **derive** [dira¹v] *v.* provenir; tirer; recevoir; déduire; dériver (gramm.).

derm [dœ°rm] *s.* derme, m. ‖ **dermatology** [-ᵉtâlᵉdji] *s.* dermatologie, f.

derogate [dérogé¹t] *v.* déroger; porter atteinte (*from,* à). ‖ **derogation** [dérogé¹shᵉn] *s.* dérogation; atteinte, f.; amoindrissement, m.

descend [disènd] *v.* descendre; déchoir; être transmis par héritage. ‖ **descendant** [-ᵉnt] *adj., s.* descendant. ‖ **descent** [disènt] *s.* descente; origine; extraction; pente; transmission par héritage, f.

describe [diskra¹b] *v.* décrire. ‖ **description** [diskrïpsh°n] *s.* signalement, m.; description; sorte, espèce, f.

descry [diskra¹] *v.* apercevoir, discerner; détecter, découvrir.

desert [dizᵉ°rt] *s.* mérite, m.; sanction, f.

desert [dèzᵉrt] *adj., s.* désert.

desert [dizè⁰rt] *v.* déserter; abandonner. ‖ **deserter** [dizè⁰tᵉr] *s.* déserteur, m. ‖ **desertion** [dizèᵉrshᵉn] *s.* désertion, f.; abandon, m.

deserve [dizè⁰rv] *v.* mériter. ‖ **deserving** [-ing] *adj.* méritant; méritoire; digne (*of*, de).

design [diza¹n] *s.* dessein, projet; plan; dessin, m.; *v.* projeter; faire le plan de, destiner (*for*, à); **designing**, intrigant, **designedly**, à dessein.

designate [dèzigné¹t] *v.* désigner; spécifier, nommer. ‖ **designation** [dèzignéⁱshᵉn] *s.* désignation, f.

designer [diza¹nᵉr] *s.* dessinateur; architecte, intrigant, m.

desirability [diza¹rᵉbílᵉti] *s.* utilité, f. ‖ **desirable** [diza¹rᵉb'l] *adj.* désirable. ‖ **desire** [diza¹r] *s.* désir, m.; *v.* désirer, souhaiter. ‖ **desirous** [dizair⁰s] *adj.* désireux.

desist [dizíst] *v.* cesser.

desk [dèsk] *s.* bureau, pupitre, m.; chaire, f.; **desk clerk**, réceptionniste.

desolate [dès⁰lit] *adj.* désolé désert; dévasté [dès⁰lé¹t] - désoler avager; affliger délaisser, abandonner ‖ **desolation** [dès⁰lé¹shᵉn] *s.* désolation, f.

despair [dispè⁰r] *s.* désespoir, m.; *v.* désespérer. ‖ **despairing** [-ing] *adj.* désespéré.

desperate [dèsprit] *adj.* désespéré, forcené. téméraire très grave (med.); **to do something desperate**, faire un malheur ‖ **desperation** [dèsp⁰ré¹shᵉn] *s.* désespoir, m. témérité désespérée, f.

despicable [dèspik⁰b'l] *adj.* méprisable.

despise [dispa¹z] *v.* mépriser; dédaigner.

despite [dispa¹t] *prep.* en dépit de, malgré.

despoil [dispo¹l] *v.* dépouiller. ‖ **despoliation** [dispoºuliéⁱshᵉn] *s.* spoliation, f.

despond [dispánd] *v.* se décourager. ‖ **despondency** (-ⁿsi] *s.* découragement, m. dépression, f **despondent** [-ⁿt] *adj* abattu, découragé. déprimé.

despot [dèsp⁰t] • **despote** .yran, m. ‖ **despotic** [dispátik] *adj.* despotique. ‖ **despotism** [dèsp⁰tiz⁰m] *s.* despotisme, m.

dessert [dizè⁰rt] *s.* dessert, m.

destination [dèst⁰né¹shᵉn] *s.* destination, f. ‖ **destine** [dèstin] *v.* destiner. ‖ **destiny** [dèst⁰ni] *s.°* destinée, f.; destin, m. *pl.* Parques, f. pl.

destitute [dèst⁰tyout] *adj.* dénué, dépourvu, indigent, nécessiteux. ‖ **destitution** [dèst⁰tyoushᵉn] *s.* dénuement, m.; pauvreté, indigence; destitution, f.

destroy [distro¹] *v.* détruire; exterminer; **to destroy oneself**, se suicider. ‖ **destroyer** [-⁰r] *s.* destructeur; meurtrier destroyer (naut.), m. ‖ **destruction** [distrækshᵉn] *s.* destruction; ruine, f. ‖ **destructive** [distræktiv] *adj.* destructif, destructeur.

desultory [dés⁰lt⁰ri] *adj.* décousu; à bâtons rompus; sans méthode.

detach [ditatsh] *v.* détacher; séparer; retrancher. ‖ **detachment** [-mᵉnt] *s.* détachement (mil.), m; séparation; indifférence, f.

detail [dité¹l] *s.* détail; détachement (mil.), m.; [dité¹l] *v.* détailler; attribuer, assigner; détacher (mil.); **to go into details**, entrer dans les détails.

detain [dité¹n] *v.* détenir; retenir. ‖ **detainer** [-⁰r] *s.* détenteur, f.

detect [ditèkt] *v.* déceler, détecter. ‖ **detection** [ditèkshᵉn] *s.* découverte, f.; fait d'être découvert, m. ‖ **detective** [ditèktiv] *s.* détective, m.; *adj.* révélateur, policier.

detention [ditènshᵉn] *s.* détention, f.; emprisonnement; retard involontaire, m.; retenue, f.

deter [ditèr] *v.* dissuader.

detergent [ditè⁰rdjᵉnt] *adj., s.* détergent, détersif.

deteriorate [ditiriⁱré¹t] *v.* (se) détériorer. ‖ **deterioration** [ditiriⁱré¹shᵉn] *s.* détérioration, f.

determination [ditè⁰m⁰né¹shᵉn] *s.* décision résolution; délimitation; détermination, f ‖ **determine** [ditè⁰rmin] *v.* déterminer, délimiter; décider; résoudre produire.

deterrent [ditèr⁰nt] *adj.* décourageant dissuadant, préventif, *s.* préventif m., force de dissuasion, f.

detest [ditèst] *v* détester. ‖ **detestable** [di'tést⁰b'l] *adj.* détestable.

dethrone [dithroºun] *v* détrôner.

detonate [dèt⁰né¹t] *v* détoner; faire exploser ‖ **detonation** [dèton颹shᵉn] *s.* détonation, f. ‖ **detonator** [dèton颹t⁰r] *s.* détonateur, pétard, m.

detour [dítour] *s.* détour, m.; déviation [way], f.; *v.* prendre un détour, aller par un détour.

detoxicate [ditâksiké¹t] *v.* désintoxiquer. ‖ **detoxication** [ditâksiké¹shᵉn] *s.* désintoxication, f.

detract [ditrakt] *v.* enlever; dénigrer. déroger. ‖ **detractor** [-⁰r] *s.* détracteur, m.

detriment [dètr⁰mᵉnt] *s.* détriment, préjudice, m. ‖ **detrimental** [dètrimént⁰l] *adj.* préjudiciable; désavantageux.

devaluation [dîvalyou'é¹shᵉn] *s.* dévaluation, f.

devastate [dèvᵉsté¹t] v. dévaster, ravager; *devastation*, dévastation, f.

develop [divèlᵉp] v. développer; exposer; exploiter; accroître; développer (phot.); se manifester; se développer. ‖ *developer* [-ᵉr] s. révélateur (phot.), m. ‖ *development* [-mᵉnt] s. développement, m.

deviate [dîvié¹t] v. dévier; s'écarter. ‖ *deviation* [dîvié¹shᵉn] s. déviation, f.; écart, m.

device [diva¹s] s. projet; plan, système; stratagème; mécanisme; appareil; engin, dispositif; procédé, m.; invention; devise, f.; *pl.* désir, m.

devil [dèv'l] s démon, diable; homme méchant ou cruel; apprenti imprimeur, m.; v tourmenter; endiabler; assaisonner fortement (culin.). *devilry*, diablerie; *devil-may-care*, étourdi, insouciant. ‖ *devilish* [-ish] *adj.* diabolique; endiablé.

devious [dîviᵉs] *adj.* détourné; sinueux; dévié.

devise [diva¹z] v. imaginer, inventer; ourdir; léguer; s. legs, m.

devoid [divo¹d] *adj.* dénué, privé, dépourvu (*of,* de.)

devolve [divâlv] v. échoir, transmettre par héritage; incomber (*on, upon,* à).

devote [divoᵘt] v. consacrer; vouer; *to devote oneself to,* se livrer à. ‖ *devoted* [divoᵘtid] *adj.* adonné (*to,* à); dévoué ‖ *devotee* [dévo't'] s. dévot, fervent, m. ‖ *devotion* [divoᵘshᵉn] s. dévotion, consécration, f.; dévouement, m.; *pl.* dévotions, f. pl.

devour [diva᎓ᵘr] v. dévorer.

devout [divaᵘt] *adj.* dévot, pieux; fervent, zélé.

dew [dyou] s rosée, f.; v. couvrir de rosée; humecter; *dewberry*, mûre; *dewdrop*, goutte de rosée; *dewlap*, fanon ‖ *dewy* [-i] *adj* couvert de rosée; pareil à la rosée.

dexterity [dèkstèrᵉti] s. dextérité; adresse, f *dexterous* [dèkstrᵉs] *adj.* adroit, droitier.

diabetes [da¹ᵉbîtis] s. diabète, m.

diadem [da¹ᵉdèm] s. diadème, m.

diagnose [da¹ᵉgnoᵘs] v. diagnostiquer.

diagonal [da¹ag'n'l] s. diagonale, f.

diagram [da¹ᵉgram] s diagramme, m.

dial [da¹ᵉl] s cadran, m.; capter connecté (teleph.) *dial telephone*, téléphone automatique *to dial a number,* composer un numéro (teleph.).

dialect [da¹ᵉlèkt] s dialecte, m.

dialogize [da¹al᎓dja¹z] v dialoguer. ‖ *dialog(ue)* [da¹ᵉlaug] s. dialogue, m.; v. dialoguer.

diameter [da¹amᵉtᵉr] s. diamètre, m

diamond [da¹ᵉmᵉnd] s. diamant; losange (geom.); carreau [cards]; terrain de base-ball, m.

diapason [da¹ᵉpé¹z'n] s. diapason, m

diaper [da¹ᵉpᵉr] s. linge (m.) ni d'abeilles, couche [infant]; serviette hygiénique, f.; v. langer; losanger.

diarrhea [da¹ᵉrî᎓] s. diarrhée, f.

diary [da¹ᵉri] s.* journal particulier; agenda, m.

dibble [dîb'l] s. plantoir, m.

dice [da¹s] s. pl. dés, m.; *dice box*, cornet.

dickens [dîkinz] s. diable, m.

dicker [dîkᵉr] v. Am. marchander.

dictate [dîkté¹t] s. ordre, m.; v. dicter; ordonner ‖ *dictation* [dîkté¹shᵉn] s. dictée, domination, f. ‖ *dictator* [dîkté¹tᵉr] s dictateur, m. ‖ *dictatorship* [-ship] s dictature, f.

diction [dîkshᵉn] s diction, f.

dictionary [dîkshᵉnèri], Br. [dîkshᵉnri] s * dictionnaire, m.

did [did] *pret.* of *to do.*

die [da¹] s (*pl dice* [-s]) s. dé à jouer m.; (*pl. dies* [-z]) coin [tool], m.; ma trice (mech.), f.

die [da¹] v. mourir, périr.

dieresis [da¹ᵉrᵉsis] (*pl. diereses*) s tréma, m.

diet [da¹ᵉt] s. alimentation; nourriture, f.; régime, m.; v nourrir; donner, suivre un régime. *low diet*, diète.

dietetician [da¹ᵉtétîshᵉn] s. diététicien, m. diététicienne, f ‖ *dietetics* [da¹ᵉtetiks] s. pl diététique, f.

differ [difᵉr] v différer n'être pas d'accord (*with,* avec) ‖ *difference* [difrᵉns] s différence divergence, dissension, discussion f différend, m. *it makes no difference* cela ne fait rien. ‖ *different* [difrᵉnt] *adj* différent. ‖ *differentiate* [dif᎓rènshié¹t] v différencier se distinguer *differently* [difrᵉntli] *adv* différemment.

difficult [dif᎓kœlt] *adj* difficile, ardu ‖ *difficulty* [dif᎓kœlti] s * difficulté, f.; embarras d'argent m.

diffidence [dif᎓dᵉns] s manque (m.) d'assurance, ‖ *diffident* [dif᎓dᵉnt] *adj.* dépourvu d'assurance, embarrassé, timide.

diffuse [difyouz] v. diffuser, répandre; [difyous] *adj* répandu, diffus, prolixe. ‖ *diffusion* [difyou᎓ᵉn] s diffusion, f.

dig [dig] v * creuser, bêcher; déterrer; s coup, sarcasme, m.

digest [da¹djèst] s compilation, f.; digeste, m.; [dᵉdjèst] v. digérer; assimiler, compiler. ‖ *digestible* [-ᵉb'l] *adj.* digestible. ‖ **digestion** [dᵊdjᵉs-tshᵉn] *s.* digestion, f. ‖ **digestive** [dᵊdjᵉstiv] *adj.*, *s.* digestif.

digger [digᵉ] *s.* terrassier; chercheur d'or, m.; *digger-up* (fam.), dénicheur.

dignified [dignᵉfaˡd] *adj.* digne, solennel, sérieux, grave. ‖ **dignify** [dignᵉfaˡ] *v.* honorer. ‖ **dignitary** [dignᵉtèri] *s.* dignitaire, m. ‖ **dignity** [dignᵉti] *s.* dignité; gravité; importance, f.

digress [dᵉgrès] *v.* s'écarter du sujet. ‖ **digression** [dᵉgrèshᵉn] *s.* digression, f.

dike [daˡk] *s.* fossé, m.; digue, f.

dilapidate [dᵉlapᵉdéˡt] *v.* dilapider; délabrer; tomber en ruines. ‖ **dilapidation** [dilapidéˡshᵉn] *s.* dilapidation, f.; délabrement, m.

dilatation [daˡlᵉtéishᵉn] *s.* dilatation, f. ‖ **dilate** [daˡléˡt] *v.* dilater, distendre; s'étendre (*on*, sur). ‖ **dilatory** [dilᵉtooᵊri] *adj.* lent, dilatoire.

dilemma [dᵉlèmᵉ] *s.* dilemme, m.

diligence [dilᵉdjᵉns] *s.* diligence; application, f. ‖ **diligent** [dilᵉdjᵉnt] *adj.* diligent, actif, appliqué.

dilute [dilout] *v.* diluer; délayer; baptiser [wine]; édulcorer, adoucir (fig.); se délayer; s'édulcorer.

dim [dim] *adj.* sombre; indistinct; terne; *v.* assombrir, obscurcir, voiler; s'effacer.

dime [daˡm] *s.* *Am.* pièce de dix cents, f.; *dime novel*, roman populaire à bon marché; *dime store*, prix unique, monoprix.

dimension [dᵉmènshᵉn] *s.* dimension, mesure, f.

diminish [dᵉminish] *v.* diminuer, réduire. ‖ **diminution** [dimᵉnyoushᵉn] *s.* diminution, f. ‖ **diminutive** [dᵉminyᵉtiv] *adj.*, *s.* diminutif.

dimmer [dimᵉʳ] *s.* régulateur d'éclairage; réducteur code, m. (autom.).

dimness [dimnis] *s.* pénombre, matité; faiblesse, f. [of light]; imprécision, f. [of memory].

dimple [dimpˡl] *s.* fossette, f.; *v.* creuser des fossettes.

din [din] *s.* vacarme, m.; *v.* assourdir; rabâcher; faire du tintamarre.

dine [daˡn] *v.* dîner; faire dîner; *dining-room*, salle à manger. ‖ **diner** [-ᵉʳ] *s.* dîneur; *Am.* voiture-restaurant, m. ‖ **dinette** [dinèt] *s.* *Am.* coin-repas, m.

dinghy [dìngi] *s.* yole, f.; canot, m.

dingle [dìngˡl] *s.* vallon, m.

dingy [dìndji] *adj.* terne, sale, gris.

dinner [dinᵉʳ] *s.* dîner, déjeuner, m.; *dinner jacket*, smoking; *dinner service*, service de table.

dint [dint] *s.* coup, m.; *by dint of*, à force de, grâce à.

diocese [daˡᵉsis] *s.* diocèse, m.

dip [dip] plongeon; bain [sheep], m.; pente, f.; *v.* immerger, plonger; s'incliner; baisser [headlight]; saluer [flag]; *sheep-dip*, produit désinfectant.

diphtheria [difthiriᵉ] *s.* diphtérie, f.

diphthong [difthaung] *s.* diphtongue, f.

diploma [diplooᵘmᵉ] *s.* diplôme, m.

diplomacy [diplooᵘmᵉsi] *s.* diplomatie, f. ‖ **diplomat** [diplᵉmat] *s.* diplomate, m. ‖ **diplomatic** [diplᵉmatik] *adj.* diplomatique.

dipper [dipᵉʳ] *s.* plongeur, m; louche, f.; martin-pêcheur, m.; *dipper-switch*, basculeur de phares.

dire [daˡᵉr] *adj.* horrible; sinistre.

direct [dᵉrèkt] *adj.* direct; franc; immédiat, imminent; *v.* diriger; guider; indiquer; prescrire; adresser [letter]; *adv.* directement; tout droit. ‖ **direction** [dᵉrèkshᵉn] *s.* direction; instruction; adresse, f.; mode d'emploi, m. ‖ **directive** [dᵉrèktiv] *adj.* directif; *s.* directive, f. ‖ **directness** [dᵉrèktnis] *s.* franchise, spontanéité, f. ‖ **director** [dᵉrèktᵉʳ] *s.* directeur; membre d'un conseil d'administration; conducteur [locomotive]; superviseur, m. ‖ **directory** [dᵉrèktᵉri] *s.* conseil d'administration; répertoire d'adresses, m.; *telephone directory*, annuaire téléphonique.

dirigible [dirᵉdjᵉbˡl] *adj.*, *s.* dirigeable.

dirt [dëʳt] *s.* ordure, boue; saleté; impuretés (mech.), f.; *dirt floor*, plancher en terre battue. ‖ **dirty** [-i] *adj.* sale, crasseux; couvert [weather]; *v.* salir.

disable [diséˡbˡl] *v.* estropier; mettre hors d'usage ou de combat; disqualifier; frapper d'incapacité (jur.); désemparer (naut.).

disabuse [disᵉbyouz] *v.* désabuser.

disadvantage [disᵉdvàntidj] *s.* désavantage, m.; *v.* désavantager; *at a disadvantage*, dans des conditions d'infériorité.

disagree [disᵉgrî] *v.* différer; se disputer (*with*, avec); ne pas convenir. ‖ **disagreeable** [-ᵉbˡl] *adj.* désagréable; incommode. ‖ **disagreement** [-mᵉnt] *s.* désaccord, m.; discordance, f.

disappear [disᵉpiᵉr] *v.* disparaître. ‖ **disappearance** [-rᵉns] *s.* disparition, f.

disappoint [disᵉpoˡnt] *v.* désappointer; décevoir. ‖ **disappointing** [-ing] *adj.* décevant. ‖ **disappointment** [-mᵉnt] *s.* désappointement, m.; contrariété, f.

disapproval [dis°prouv'l] *s.* désapprobation, f. ‖ *disapprove* [dis°prouv] *v.* désapprouver.

disarm [disârm] *v.* désarmer. ‖ *disarmament* [-°m°nt] *s.* désarmement, m.

disarrange [dis°ré¹ndj] *v.* déranger.

disarray [dis°ré¹] *s.* désarroi, désordre, m.; confusion, f.; *in disarray*, en négligé.

disaster [dizast°r] *s.* désastre, m. ‖ *disastrous* [dizastr°s] *adj.* désastreux; catastrophique.

disavow [dis°va°u] *v.* désavouer.

disband [disbānd] *v.* licencier; disperser, se débander.

disbelief [disbilîf] *s.* incrédulité, f. ‖ *disbelieve* [-b°lîv] *v.* ne pas croire (*in*, à); nier.

disburse [disbèrs] *v.* débourser. ‖ *disbursement* [-m°nt] *s.* débours, m.; dépense, f., déboursement, m.

discard [diskârd] *s.* écart [cards], m.; [diskârd] *v.* écarter; rejeter; se défausser.

discern [dizë°n] *v.* discerner; distinguer. ‖ *discernment* [-m°nt] *s.* discernement, m.

discharge [distshârdj] *v.* décharger [load, gun] libérer [prisoner]; congédier [servant] acquitter [debt] remplir [duty], lancer [projectile] rempurer [wound] déchargement acquittement élargissement accomplissement; congé [soldier], débit [river], m.; décharge quittance (comm.); libération. suppuration, f.

disciple [disa¹p'l] *s.* disciple, m.

disciplinary [dis°plin°ri] *adj.* disciplinaire. ‖ *discipline* [-plin] *s.* discipline, f.; *v.* discipliner; punir.

disclaim [disklé¹m] *v.* désavouer; rejeter; se défendre de.

disclose [disklo°uz] *v.* découvrir; divulguer. ‖ *disclosure* [disklo°uj°r] *s.* divulgation, révélation, f.

discolo(u)r [diskœl°r] *v.* décolorer.

discomfit [diskœmfit] *v.* déconfire.

discomfort [diskœmfë°t] *v.* peiner; incommoder gêner; *s.* malaise, m.; gêne, incommodité, f.

disconcert [disk°nsë°t] *v.* déconcerter, embarrasser déranger, gêner.

disconnect [disk°nëkt] *v.* dissocier; séparer débrancher, couper [telephone line]. ‖ *disconnected* [-id] *adj.* détaché, décousu; isolé, désuni; incohérent.

disconsolate [diskâns'lit] *adj.* inconsolable. morose, triste.

discontent [disk°ntènt] *s.* mécontentement, m.; *v.* mécontenter.

discontinuance [disk°ntinyou°ns] *s.* interruption; suspension, solution de continuité, f. ‖ *discontinue* [disk°ntinyou] *v.* interrompre suspendre; cesser; discontinuer. ‖ *discontinuity* [diskânt°nvou°ti] *s.°* discontinuité, f.

discord [diskaurd] *s.* discorde; dissonance, f. ‖ *discordant* [-'nt] *adj.* discordant; dissonant.

discount [diska°unt] *s.* rabais; escompte, m.; *v.* rabattre, déduire [sum], décompter; escompter; faire une remise; réduire à ses justes proportions.

discourage [diskë°ridj] *v.* décourager; dissuader (*from*, de). ‖ *discouragement* [-m°nt] *s.* découragement, m.

discourse [disko°urs] *s.* discours; entretien, m., [disko°urs] *v.* discourir; causer s'entretenir.

discourteous [diskë°ti°s] *adj.* discourtois. ‖ *discourtesy* [diskë°t°si] *s.* discourtoisie, f.

discover [diskœv°r] *v.* découvrir; dévoiler révéler ‖ *discoverer* [-r°r] *s.* découvreur, inventeur, m. ‖ *discovery* [diskœvri] *s.°* découverte; invention révélation, f.

discredit [diskrèdit] *s.* discrédit; doute, m.; *v.* discréditer; perdre confiance en; élever des doutes sur.

discreet [diskrît] *adj.* prudent, circonspect. discret.

discrepancy [diskrèp°nsi] *s.°* différence [account]; discordance, contradiction variation, f.

discrete [diskrît] *adj.* distinct.

discretion [diskrèsh°n] *s.* prudence, circonspection, discrétion; libre disposition f. discernement, m.

discriminate [diskrimné¹t] *v.* distinguer discriminer, *discriminating*, plein de discernement, fin.

discursive [diskë°siv] *adj.* discursif; décousu, incohérent.

discus [diskœs] *s.°* disque, m.

discuss [diskœs] *v.* discuter. ‖ *discussion* [diskœsh°n] *s.* discussion, f.; débat, m.

disdain [disdé¹n] *s.* dédain, mépris, m.; *v.* dédaigner; *disdainful*, dédaigneux.

disease [dizîz] *s.* maladie, f. ‖ *diseased* [-d] *adj.* malade; morbide, maladif nalsain.

disembark [disimbârk] *v.* débarquer. *disembarkation* [disèmbârké¹sh°n] *s.* débarquement, m.

disenchant [disintshânt] *v.* désenchanter, désillusionner.

disengage [dising鹿°dj] *v.* dégager; se libérer; débrayer (mech.).

disentangle [disintăngg'l] *v.* démêler, débrouiller; élucider.

disfigure [disfigyᵉr] *v.* défigurer.

disgorge [disgaurdj] *v.* dégorger.

disgrace [disgré¹s] *s.* disgrâce; honte,
f.; déshonneur, m.; *v.* disgracier; déshonorer; discréditer; *disgraceful,* honteux; dégradant.

disgruntled [disgrænt'ld] *adj.* mécontent, maussade.

disguise [disga¹z] *s.* déguisement, m.;
dissimulation, f.; *v.* déguiser.

disgust [disgæst] *s.* dégoût, m.; *v.*
dégoûter; *disgusting,* répugnant.

dish [dish] *s.** plat; mets, m.; *pl.*
vaisselle, f.; *v.* apprêter, accommoder;
arranger, servir; *dish-cloth,* torchon;
dish-drainer, égouttoir; *dish-mop,*
lavette; *dish-warmer,* chauffe-plat.

dishearten [dishárt'n] *v.* décourager,
démoraliser.

dishevel [dishĕv'l] *v.* écheveler.

dishonest [disănist] *adj.* malhon-
nête; frauduleux. || *dishonesty* [-i] *s.**
malhonnêteté; déloyauté, f. || *dishon-
o(u)r* [disănᵉr] *v.* déshonorer; laisser
protester (comm.); *s.* déshonneur, m.;
protêt, m. (comm.). || *dishono(u)rable*
[-rᵉb'l] *adj.* déshonorant.

disillusion [disilouⱼᵉn] *s.* désillusion,
f.; *v.* désillusionner.

disinfect [disinfĕkt] *v.* désinfecter. ||
disinfectant [-ᵉnt] *s.* désinfectant, m.

disinherit [disinhĕrit] *v.* déshériter.

disintegrate [disint·gré¹t] *v.* (se)
désintégrer; (se) désagréger. || *disin-
tegration* [disintigré¹shᵉn] *f.* désintégration; désagrégation, f.

disinter [disintœr] *v.* déterrer.

disinterested [disint·rᵉstid] *adj.* désintéressé.

disjoin [disdjo¹n] *v.* disjoindre.

disk [disk] *s.* disque, m.

dislike [disla¹k] *s.* antipathie, f.; *v.*
ne pas aimer; *to take a dislike to,*
prendre en grippe; *to be disliked by,*
être mal vu de.

dislocate [dislouⁿké¹t] *v.* disloquer.*

dislodge [dislădj] *v.* déloger.

disloyal [dislau¹ᵉl] *adj.* déloyal. ||
disloyalty [-ti] *s.* déloyauté, f.

dismal [dízm'l] *adj.* lugubre, sombre.

dismantle [dismănt'l] *v.* démanteler
[fort]; dépouiller [clothes]; vider
[house]; désarmer [ship].

dismast [dismast] *v.* démâter.

dismay [dismé¹] *s.* consternation;
stupeur, f.; *v.* terrifier; consterner,
décourager; abattre.

dismiss [dismís] *v.* renvoyer; congédier; révoquer; bannir [thought]; *Am.*
acquitter (jur.); rejeter [appeal]; lever
[meeting]. || *dismissal* [-'l] *s.* congé,
m.; révocation; expulsion, f.

dismount [dismaᵒunt] *v.* descendre de
cheval; démonter [gun, jewel]; désarçonner.

disnature [disné¹tshᵉr] *v.* dénaturer.

disobedience [dis·bí·diᵉns] *s.* dés-
obéissance, f. || *disobedient* [dis·bí-
diᵉnt] *adj.* désobéissant. || *disobey*
[dis·béi] *v.* désobéir à; enfreindre.

disoblige [dis·bla¹dj] *v.* désobliger.

disorder [disaurdᵉr] *s.* désordre;
trouble, m.; anarchie, émeute; confusion; maladie, f.; *v.* déranger; déré-
gler; bouleverser. || *disorderly* [-li] *adj.*
en désordre; déréglé; perturbé; débauché; *adv.* d'une manière désor-
donnée ou déréglée.

disorganization [disaurgᵉn·zé¹shᵉn]
s. désorganisation, f. || *disorganize*
[disárg·na¹z] *v.* désorganiser.

disown [disoᵒun] *v.* désavouer; nier;
renier.

disparage [dispáridj] *v.* déprécier;
dénigrer.

disparate [dispᵉrit] *adj.* disparate.

dispassionate [dispash·nit] *adj.*
calme; impartial; objectif.

dispatch [dispatsh] *s.** envoi, m.;
dépêche; hâte; expédition, f.; *cipher
dispatch,* message chiffré; *v.* expédier; dépêcher; exécuter.

dispel [dispĕl] *v.* dissiper, chasser.

dispensary [dispăns·ri] *s.** dispensaire, m.; officine, pharmacie, f.

dispensation [dispᵉnsé¹shᵉn] *s.* dispensation; exemption; administration;
disposition; dispense; loi religieuse, f.
|| *dispense* [dispĕns] *v.* dispenser;
distribuer; administrer; exempter
(*from,* de); se dispenser (*with,* de);
gasoline dispenser, distributeur
d'essence.

disperse [dispᵉrs] *v.* disperser. || *dis-
persion* [dispᵉrsh·n] *s.* dispersion, f.

dispirited [dispíritid] *adj.* déprimé,
découragé.

displace [displé¹s] *v.* déplacer; muter; supplanter.

display [displé¹] *v.* déployer; étaler;
exhiber, faire étalage de; *s.* déploiement; étalage, m.; exhibition, f.; *display window,* vitrine.

displease [displîz] *v.* déplaire; mécon-
tenter. || *displeasure* [displĕj·ᵉr] *s.* mé-
contentement; déplaisir, m.; colère, f.

disport [dispoᵒurt] *v.* s'amuser; *s.*
divertissement, m.

disposal [dispoᵒuz'l] *s.* disposition;
répartition; dispensation; vente, f.;

‖ *dispose* [dispoᵘz] v. disposer; arranger; vendre, céder; incliner à; *to dispose of*, se défaire de; vaincre. ‖ *disposition* [dispᵉzíshᵉn] s. disposition; aptitude; inclination; humeur; décision, f.; agencement, m.

dispossess [dispᵉzès] v. déposséder.

disproportionate [disprᵉpaursh°nit] *adj.* disproportionné.

disprove [disproᵘv] v. réfuter.

disputable [dispyoutᵉb'l] *adj.* discutable. ‖ *disputation* [dispyouté¹sh°n] *s.* débat, m.; contestation, f. ‖ *dispute* [dispyout] s. dispute; discussion, f.; v. disputer; discuter.

disqualification [diskwâlifiké¹sh°n] *s.* disqualification, f. ‖ *disqualify* [diskwâl·fa¹] v. disqualifier; mettre dans l'incapacité de.

disquiet [diskwa¹ᵉt] *adj.* inquiet; *s.* inquiétude, f.; v. inquiéter.

disregard [disrigárd] v. négliger; dédaigner; *s.* dédain, m.

disreputable [disrèpyᵉtᵉb'l] *adj.* mal famé, discrédité.

disrespect [disrispèkt] *s.* irrespect; manque d'égards, m.

dissatisfaction [dissatisfáksh°n] *s.* insatisfaction, f.; mécontentement, m. ‖ *dissatisfy* [dissatisfa¹] v. mécontenter.

dissect [disèkt] v. disséquer.

dissemble [disèmb'l] v. dissimuler; simuler, feindre.

disseminate [disèm°né¹t] v. disséminer.

dissension [disènsh°n] *s.* dissension, f. ‖ *dissent* [disènt] v. être en désaccord ou en dissidence; *s.* dissentiment, m.; dissidence (eccles.); divergence, f.

dissertation [dis·rté¹sh·n] *s.* dissertation, f.; mémoire, m.; discours, m.

dissever [disèv·r] v. séparer.

dissimilar [disím·l·r] *adj.* différent.

dissimulation [disimy·lé¹sh·n] *s.* dissimulation, f. ‖ *dissimulator* [dismyoulé¹t·r] *s.* dissimulateur, m.; -trice, f.

dissipate [dis·pé¹t] v. dissiper; disperser. ‖ *dissipation* [dis·pé¹sh·n] *s.* dissipation; dispersion, f.

dissociate [disoᵘshié¹t] v. dissocier, séparer.

dissolute [dis·lout] *adj.* dissolu. *dissoluteness* [-nis] *s.* débauche, f. ‖ *dissolution* [dis·loush·n] *s.* dissolution; dispersion, f. ‖ *dissolve* [dizǻlv] v. séparer; disperser; détruire; (se) dissoudre.

dissuade [diswé¹d] v. dissuader. ‖ *dissuasion* [diswé¹j·n] *s.* dissuasion, f.

distaff [dístaf] *s.* quenouille, f.

distance [díst·ns] *s.* distance, f.; lointain, m.; v. distancer, devancer. ‖ *distant* [díst·nt] *adj.* éloigné; distant, hautain.

distaste [dísté¹st] *s.* répulsion, f.; dégoût, m. ‖ *distasteful* [-f·l] *adj.* repoussant, répugnant.

distend [distènd] v. distendre.

distil [distíl] v. distiller. ‖ *distillation* [dis·tlé¹sh·n] *s.* distillation, f. ‖ *distillery* [distíl·rí] *s.°* distillerie, f.

distinct [distíngkt] *adj.* distinct. ‖ *distinction* [distíngsh·n] *s.* distinction, f. ‖ *distinctive* [distíngktiv] *adj.* distinctif. ‖ *distinctness* [-nis] *s.* netteté; différenciation, f.

distinguish [distíngwish] v. distinguer; discerner; différencier. ‖ *distinguishing* [-ing] *adj.* distinctif, caractéristique.

distort [distaurt] v. déformer; fausser; distordre; altérer [truth].

distract [distrakt] v. distraire; détourner; rendre fou. ‖ *distraction* [distraksh·n] *s.* distraction; perturbation, f.; affolement, m.

distrain [distré¹n] v. saisir (jur.).

distress [distrès] *s.°* détresse; saisie (jur.), f.; v. affliger; saisir (jur.).

distribute [distríbyout] v. distribuer; répartir; classifier. ‖ *distribution* [distr·byoush·n] *s.* distribution, répartition, f. ‖ *distributor* [distríbyᵘt·r] *s.* distributeur, m.; concessionnaire, m.

district [dístrikt] *s.* district; arrondissement; quartier, m.; région, f.; circonscription, f.; canton; secteur, m.

distrust [distrʌst] *s.* défiance, méfiance, f.; v. se défier de. ‖ *distrustful* [-f·l] *adj.* défiant, soupçonneux.

disturb [distᵉrb] v. déranger; inquiéter; incommoder. ‖ *disturbance* [distᵉrb·ns] *s.* dérangement; tumulte; ennui; désordre, m.; inquiétude, f.; trouble, m.; émeute; perturbation, f. ‖ *disturber* [distᵉrb·r] *s.* perturbateur, m.

disunion [disyouny·n] *s.* désunion, f. ‖ *disunite* [disyouna¹t] v. désunir.

disuse [disyous] *s.* désuétude, f.; [disyouz] v. ne plus employer.

ditch [ditsh] *s.°* fossé, m.; rigole, f.; v. creuser un fossé; drainer ou arroser [meadow]; *Am.* plaquer.

ditto [ditoᵘ] *s.* dito, idem, m.

ditty [dítí] *s.°* chansonnette, f.

diurnal [da¹ᵉrn'l] *adj.* quotidien.

divan [da¹ván] *s.* divan, m.

dive [da¹v] *s.* plongeon, m.; piqué (aviat.); bistrot, m.; v. plonger; piquer (aviat.). ‖ *diver* [-ᵉr] *s.* plongeur; scaphandrier; plongeon [bird], m.; *pearl diver*, pêcheur de perles.

diverge [dₑvё⁴dj] *v.* diverger; différer. ‖ **divergence** [-ₑns] *s.* divergence, f. ‖ **divergent** [-ₑnt] *adj.* divergent.

divers [da¹vₑʳz] *adj.* divers. ‖ **diverse** [dₑvёˢs] *adj.* différent. ‖ **diversify** [da¹vёˢsifa¹] *v.* diversifier. ‖ **diversion** [dₑvёⁱjₑn] *s.* diversion; distraction, f. **diversity** [dₑvёˢsti] *s.* diversité, f. ‖ **divert** [dₑvёʳt] *v.* dévier; divertir.

divest [da¹vèst] *v.* dévêtir; déposséder, dépouiller.

divide [dₑva¹d] *v.* diviser; séparer; partager; désunir. ‖ **dividend** [div⁴dènd] *s.* dividende (math.; comm.), f. ‖ **dividers** [dₑva¹dⁱʳz] *s. pl.* compas, m.

divination [divₑné⁴shₑn] *s.* divination, f. ‖ **divine** [dₑva¹n] *adj.* divin; *s.* théologien, prêtre, m.; *v.* deviner. ‖ **divinity** [dₑvⁱnⁱti] *s.* divinité; théologie, f.

divisible [dₑvⁱzₑb'l] *adj.* divisible. ‖ **division** [dₑvⁱjₑn] *s.* division, f. ‖ **divisor** [dₑva¹zₑʳ] *s.* diviseur, m.

divorce [dₑvoᵘʳs] *s.* divorce, m.; *v.* divorcer d'avec; prononcer le divorce de. ‖ **divorcee** [divauᵘʳsⁱ] *v.* divorcé, m. f. ‖ **divorcement** [divausmₑnt] *s.* divorce, m.

divulgation [da¹vœlgé⁴shₑn] *s.* divulgation, f. ‖ **divulge** [dₑvœldj] *v.* divulguer.

dizziness [diz'nis] *s.* vertige, m. ‖ **dizzy** [dizl] *adj.* étourdi; *to feel dizzy*, avoir le vertige.

do [dou] *v.*° faire; accomplir; réussir; exécuter; préparer; arranger; se porter; prospérer; travailler; suffire; *he tried to do me*, il a essayé de me refaire; *we cannot do without him*, nous ne pouvons nous passer de lui; *do not lie*, ne mentez pas; *how do you do?*, comment allez-vous?; *he sees us, does he not?*, il nous voit, n'est-ce pas?; *you hate me. I do not*, vous me détestez. Pas du tout; *I must do without*, il faut que je m'en passe; *do stay for dinner with us*, restez donc dîner avec nous; *he is done in*, il est fourbu; *that will do*, cela suffit; *well-to-do*, aisé, cossu; *well done*, bravo, à la bonne heure.

docile [doᵘsa¹l] *adj.* docile. ‖ **docility** [doᵘsilⁱti] *s.* docilité, f.

dock [dâk] *s.* dock; bassin; quai, m.; *dry dock*, cale sèche; *v.* faire entrer dans le dock; diminuer (wages); rogner (off, sur); **docker**, docker.

doctor [dâktₑʳ] *s.* docteur; médecin, m.; *v.* soigner; exercer la médecine; *eye-doctor*, oculiste. ‖ **doctorate** [-rit] *s.* doctorat, m.

doctrine [dâktrin] *s.* doctrine, f.

document [dâkyₑmₑnt] *s.* document, m.; [dâkyₑmènt] *v.* documenter; *document-case*, porte-documents. ‖ **documentary** [dâkyouméntₑri] *adj.* documentaire. ‖ **documentation** [dâkyouménté⁴shₑn] *s.* documentation, f.

dodder [daudₑʳ] *v.* dodeliner du chef; chanceler; traîner la patte (fam.).

dodge [dâdj] *s.* ruse, f.; détour; stratagème, m.; *v.* esquiver; louvoyer; ruser; faire marcher; lanterner.

doe [doᵘ] *s.* femelle du daim, du lapin, du lièvre, f.

doff [dâf] *v.* enlever, ôter.

dog [daug] *s.* chien; chenêt; crampon (mech.), m.; suivre à la piste, chasser; *dogberry tree*, cornouiller; *dog days*, canicule; *dog-rose*, églantine; *doggedly*, avec acharnement; *dog-house*, niche; *dog's ear*, corne à un livre; *dog show*, exposition canine; *dog-tired*, éreinté; *doggish*, hargneux, grincheux; *Am.* plastronneur.

dogma [daugmₑ] *s.* dogme, m.; *dogmatic*, dogmatique, catégorique.

doings [douⁱngz] *s. pl.* agissements, m. pl.; conduite, f.; actions, f. pl.

doldrums [dâldrₑmz] *s. pl.* cafard; marasme, m.; calmes équatoriaux, m. pl.

dole [doᵘl] *s.* distribution gratuite; aumône, f.; secours, m.; *v.* distribuer; *unemployment dole*, indemnité de chômage.

doleful [doᵘlfₑl] *adj.* lugubre; endeuillé; plaintif; dolent, triste.

doll [dâl] *s.* poupée, f.

dollar [dâlₑʳ] *s.* dollar, m.; *Fr. Can.* piastre, f.

dolly [dâli] *s.*° chariot, m.; poupée, f.

dolor [doᵘlₑʳ] *s.* douleur, f.

dolphin [dâlfin] *s.* dauphin [mammal], m.; daurade, f. [fish].

dolt [doᵘlt] *s.* lourdaud, sot, m.

domain [doᵘmé¹n] *s.* domaine, m.

dome [doᵘm] *s.* dôme, m.

domestic [dₑmèstik] *adj.* domestique; privé; national; apprivoisé; *s.* domestique, serviteur, m.

domicile [dâmₑs'l] *s.* domicile, m.; *v.* (se) domicilier.

dominant [dâmₑnₑnt] *adj.* dominant. ‖ **dominate** [dâmₑné¹t] *v.* dominer. ‖ **domination** [dâmₑné¹shₑn] *s.* domination, f. ‖ **domineer** [dâmₑnⁱʳ] *v.* tyranniser, opprimer.

dominion [dₑmⁱnyₑn] *s.* dominion, m.; domination; souveraineté, f.

domino [dâmₑnoᵘ] *s.*° domino [costume, mask, game], m.

don [dân] *v.* mettre, vêtir.

donate [do°°né¹t] *v.* donner, accorder. ‖ **donation** [do°°né¹sh°n] *s.* donation, f.; don, m.

done [dœn] *p. p. of* to do; fait, achevé; *to be done with,* en avoir fini avec; *to be done for,* être épuisé, ruiné; *overdone,* trop cuit.

donee [don¹] *s.* donataire, m.

donkey [dânki] *s.* âne, m.

donor [do°°n°r] *s.* donateur; donneur, m.

doodle [doud'l] *v.* griffonner des petits dessins; *s.* griffonnage, m.

doom [doum] *s.* jugement, m.; sentence; destinée, f.; *doomsday,* jour du jugement dernier; *v.* condamner; destiner, vouer [to, à].

door [do°r] *s.* porte; entrée; portière, f.; *doorframe,* chambranle; *doorkeeper,* portier, huissier; *doorknob,* bouton; *doormat,* paillasson; *doorstep,* pas de porte, seuil; *doorway,* entrée; *next door,* à côté.

dope [do°p] *s.* stupéfiant; opium; *Am.* tuyau (slang); benêt, m.; *v.* droguer, doper; *dope fiend,* morphinomane.

dormer [daurm°r] *s.* lucarne, f.

dormitory [daurm°to°uri] *s.** dortoir, m.

dormouse [daurma°us] *s.* loir, m.

dorsal [daurs'l] *adj.* dorsal.

dosage [do°usidj] *s.* dosage, m.; posologie, f. ‖ **dose** [do°us] *s.* dose, f.; *v.* médicamenter.

dot [dât] *s.* point, m.; *v.* mettre des points; pointiller; *to a dot,* parfaitement, minutieusement; *polka dots,* pois sur étoffe.

dotage [do°utidj] *s.* radotage, m. ‖ **dotard** [do°ut°rd] *s.* radoteur, m.

double [dœb'l] *adj.* double; *s.* double; duplicata; pli; contre [bridge], m.; ruse, duplicité, f.; *v.* doubler; plier; replier; redoubler; serrer [fists]; *adv.* doublement; *double-bedroom,* chambre à deux lits; *double-breasted,* croisé; *double-deal,* duplicité; *double-quick,* pas gymnastique (mil.); *to double-cross,* duper.

doubt [da°ut] *s.* doute, m.; *v.* douter; hésiter; soupçonner; *doubtful,* douteux; indécis; *doubtless,* sans aucun doute, indubitablement.

douche [doush] *s.* douche; injection, f.; bock, m.; *v.* (se) doucher; donner (or) prendre une injection.

dough [do°u] *s.* pâte, f.; argent (slang); *doughboy,* fantassin américain; *doughnut,* beignet, *Fr. Can.* beigne, m.; *doughtray,* pétrin.

doughty [da°uti] *adj.* courageux.

douse [da°us] *v.* tremper, doucher; éteindre.

dove [do°uv] *pret. of* to dive.

dove [dœv] *s.* colombe, f.; pigeon, m.; *dove-cot,* pigeonnier; *dovetail,* queue d'aronde.

dowager [da°ued j°r] *s.* douairière, f.

dowdy [da°udi] *adj.* négligé; mal tenu; fagoté.

dower [da°u°r] *s.* douaire, m.; dot, f.; *v.* donner en douaire; doter.

down [da°un] *s.* dune, f.

down [da°un] *s.* duvet, m.; *downy,* duveteux.

down [da°un] *adv.* en bas; bas; au fond; à terre; *adj.* descendant; déprimé; baissé, abaissé; *prep.* du haut en bas de; *s.* descente, f.; *v.* baisser; descendre; renverser; *the sun is down,* le soleil est couché; *down here,* ici-bas; *to pay down,* verser des arrhes; *downcast,* abattu; *downdraft,* trou d'air (aviat.); *down-stream,* au fil du courant. ‖ **downfall** [-faul] *s.* chute, f. ‖ **downpour** [-po°ur] *s.* averse, f. ‖ **downright** [-ra¹t] *adj.* vertical; franc, catégorique. ‖ **downstairs** [-stèrz] *adv.* en bas; *adj.* du rez-de-chaussée. ‖ **downward** [-w°rd] *adj.* en pente; incliné; *adv.* en descendant; vers le bas; en bas.

dowry [da°uri] *s.** dot, f.; douaire, m.

dowser [da°uz°r] *s.* radiesthésiste, m.

doze [do°uz] *s.* somme, m.; sieste, f.; *v.* sommeiller; s'assoupir.

dozen [dœz'n] *s.* douzaine, f.; *a baker's dozen,* treize à la douzaine.

drab [drab] *adj.* grisâtre; monotone.

draft [draft] *s.* tirage; puisage; plan; brouillon; dessin; virement bancaire; courant d'air; détachement (mil.); tirant d'eau (naut.), m.; circonscription (mil.); boisson; traite (comm.), f.; *pl.* dames [game], f.; *v.* esquisser; dessiner; faire un brouillon; détacher (mil.); *draftee,* conscrit; *draftsman,* dessinateur; *to rough-draft,* ébaucher.

drag [drag] *s.* herse; drague, f.; grappin; frein, sabot; obstacle; drag, m.; trace artificielle du renard [hunting], f.; *v.* traîner; draguer; pêcher à la seine; passer lentement [time]; enrayer [wheel]; chasser sur ses ancres (naut.); chasser le renard [hunting]; *dragnet,* drège; *Am.* rafle.

dragon [drag°n] *s.* dragon, m. ‖ **dragonfly** [drag°nfla¹] *s.** libellule, f.

drain [dré¹n] *s.* drain; conduit d'écoulement; égout, m.; *v.* drainer; assécher; épuiser; vider; s'égoutter. ‖ **drainage** [-¹dj] *s.* drainage; soutirage; assèchement; écoulement, m.

drake [dré¹k] *s.* canard, m.

dram [dram] *s.* drachme [weight], f.; goutte [drink], f.

drama [drâm•] *s.* drame, m. ‖ *dramatic* [dr•matik] *adj.* dramatique. ‖ *dramatist* [drâm•tist] *s.* dramaturge, auteur dramatique, m. ‖ *dramatize* [dram•ta¹z] *v.* dramatiser.

drank [dràngk] *pret. of* to drink.

drape [dré¹p] *s.* draperie, f.; rideau, m.; *v.* draper. ‖ *draper* [-•ʳ] *s.* drapier, marchand de nouveautés, m. ‖ *drapery* [-•ri] *s.*° draperie; étoffes, f.; métier de drapier, m.

drastic [drastik] *adj.* rigoureux.

draught [draft], *see* draft.

draw [drau] *v.*° tirer; haler; extraire; dégainer [sword]; inspirer [breath]; tirer, gagner [lot]; toucher [money]; attirer; tirer [chimney]; tirer sur (comm.); dessiner, esquisser; arracher [teeth]; étirer [wire]; puiser [water]; faire match nul; *to draw up;* pousser [sigh]; rédiger [document]; relever, tirer en haut; *to draw together,* se rapprocher, se rassembler; *s.* lot gagné; tirage du lot; montant obtenu ou touché, m.; partie nulle; attraction, f.; *drawback,* obstacle, handicap; *drawback* (comm.); *drawbridge,* pont-levis. ‖ *drawer* [-•ʳ] *s.* tireur; tiroir, m.; [-•ʳz] *pl.* caleçon, m. ‖ *drawing* [-ing] *s.* tirage, dessin, m.; extraction; attraction; quantité de thé à infuser, f.; *drawing-paper,* papier à dessin; *drawing-pin,* punaise; *drawing-room,* salon. ‖ *drawn* [-n] *p. p. of* to draw.

drawl [draul] *v.* ânonner; *s.* élocution lente et traînante, f.

dray [dré¹] *s.* camion, m.; *drayage,* camionnage.

dread [drèd] *s.* crainte, terreur, f.; *adj.* terrible; *v.* redouter, s'épouvanter. ‖ *dreadful* [-f•l] *adj.* terrifiant; épouvantable, redoutable.

dreadnought [drèdnaut] *s.* dreadnought, m.; ratine [cloth], f.

dream [drîm] *s.* rêve, m.; *v.*° rêver. ‖ *dreamer* [-•ʳ] *s.* rêveur, m. ‖ *dreamily* [-ili] *adv.* rêveusement. ‖ *dreamt* [drèmt] *pret., p. p. of* to dream. ‖ *dreamy* [drîmi] *adj.* rêveur; mélancolique; irréel; vague.

dreary [driri] *adj.* morne; lugubre.

dredge [drèdj] *s.* drague, f.; *v.* draguer; *dredge boat,* dragueur.

dredge [drèdj] *v.* saupoudrer. ‖ *dredger* [-•ʳ] *s.* saupoudroir, m.

dregs [drègz] *s. pl.* lie, f.

drench [drèntsh] *s.*° averse; saucée (colloq.), f.; purge, f. [for animals]; *v.* tremper; inonder; faire boire; purger.

dress [drès] *s.*° habillement, m.; robe, toilette, tenue, f.; *v.* habiller, vêtir;

apprêter; orner; parer; coiffer [hair]; tanner [leather]; cultiver [land]; panser [wound]; pavoiser [ship]; aligner [soldiers]; s'habiller; se parer; s'aligner (mil.); *dress-coat,* habit de soirée; *dress-rehearsal,* répétition générale. ‖ *dresser* [-•ʳ] *s.* coiffeuse, f. ‖ *dressing* [-ing] *s.* toilette; sauce; raclée (fam.), f.; assaisonnement; apprêt (techn.); alignement (mil.), m.; *French dressing,* vinaigrette; *dressing-gown,* robe de chambre. ‖ *dressmaker* [-mé¹k•ʳ] *s.* couturier, m.; couturière, f. ‖ *dressmaking* [-mé¹king] *s.* couture, f. ‖ *dressy* [-i] *adj.* chic, élégant.

drew *pret. of* to draw.

dribble [drib'l] *v.* dégoutter; verser goutte à goutte; dribbler [game]; *s.* goutte, f. ‖ *driblet* [driblit] *s.* goutte; bribe, f.; brin, soupçon, m.

dried [dra¹d] *pret., p. p. of* to dry; *adj.* sec; déshydraté; tapé [pear]. ‖ *drier* [dra¹•ʳ] *s.* séchoir, m.; sécheuse, f.; siccatif, m.

drift [drift] *s.* poussée; tendance; alluvion; dérive (naut.); masse [snow], f.; nuage [dust], m.; *v.* pousser; amonceler; aller à la dérive; s'amasser; être chassé par le vent.

drill [dril] *s.* foret; exercice (mil.), m.; *v.* forer, percer; faire l'exercice; *drill ground,* terrain de manœuvres.

drill [dril] *s.* sillon; semoir, m.; *v.* semer par sillon.

drily [dra¹li], *see* dryly.

drink [dringk] *s.* boisson, f.; alcool, m.; *v.*° boire; *to drink up,* vider [glass]; *to drink in,* écouter attentivement, absorber; *to drink off,* boire d'un trait; *drink-money,* pourboire. ‖ *drinkable* [-•b'l] *adj.* buvable, potable. ‖ *drinker* [-•ʳ] *s.* buveur, m. ‖ *drinking* [-ing] *s.* boire, m.; boisson; ivrognerie, f.; *drinking-bout,* beuverie; *drinking-water,* eau potable.

drip [drip] *s.* égouttement, m.; *v.* dégoutter; *drip-coffee,* café-filtre; *dripping-pan,* lèche-frite.

drive [dra¹v] *s.* promenade en voiture; route carrossable; presse (comm.); vente-réclame (comm.); transmission (mech.); *Am.* touche [cattle], f.; drive [sport], m.; flottage, m.; *Fr. Can.* drave, f.; *v.*° pousser; conduire [auto]; faire marcher, actionner; contraindre; enfoncer [nail]; toucher [cattle]; *Fr. Can.* draver; *driver;* aller en voiture; percer [tunnel]; *he has a lot of drive,* il a beaucoup d'allant; *what are you driving at?,* où voulez-vous en venir?; *driving wheel,* roue motrice.

drivel [driv'l] *v.* baver; radoter; *s.* bave; bêtises, f.

driven [driv⁰n] *p. p. of to drive.* ‖ **driver** [dra¹ver] *s.* conducteur; chauffeur; mécanicien; machiniste; driver [sport]; *Fr. Can.* draveur, m.

drizzle [driz'l] *v.* bruiner; *s.* bruine, f.

droll [dro⁰l] *adj.* drôle, amusant.

dromedary [drăm⁰d⁰ri] *s.° dromadaire, m.

drone [dro⁰n] *s.* bourdon; bourdonnement; parasite, m.; *v.* bourdonner; paresser; vivre en parasite.

droop [droup] *v.* se pencher; languir; s'affaiblir; se voûter; pencher [head]; baisser [eyes]; *s.* affaissement, m.

drop [drăp] *s.* goutte; chute; pendeloque, f.; *v.* laisser tomber; goutter; tomber; jeter [anchor]; lâcher [bombs]; sauter [stitch]; laisser échapper [word]; *cough drop,* pastille contre la toux; *drop curtain,* rideau de théâtre; *dropper, dropping tube,* compte-gouttes.

dropsy [drăpsi] *s.* hydropisie, f.

drought [dra⁰t] *s.* sécheresse, f.

drove [dro⁰uv] *s.* troupeau, m.

drove [dro⁰uv] *pret. of to drive.*

drown [dra⁰un] *v.* noyer; étouffer [sound]; submerger; se noyer.

drowse [dra⁰uz] *v.* sommeiller; somnoler. ‖ **drowsiness** [dra⁰uzinis] *s.* somnolence, f. ‖ **drowsy** [dra⁰uzi] *adj.* somnolent, assoupi; soporifique, endormi; apathique, endormi.

drudge [drŏdj] *v.* peiner, trimer; *s.* trimeur, forçat, esclave, m. ‖ **drudgery,** corvée; besogne harassante; turbin (colloq.).

drug [drŏg] *s.* produit pharmaceutique, m.; drogue f.; stupéfiant, m.; *v.* droguer; *drug-addict,* toxicomane. ‖ **druggist** [-ist] *s.* droguiste, pharmacien, m. ‖ **drugstore** [-sto⁰ur] *s.* pharmacie, droguerie, f.; bazar, m.

druid [drou¹d] *s.* druide, m.

drum [drŏm] *s.* tambour; tympan; cylindre; rouleau, m.; *v.* tambouriner; battre du tambour; *bass drum,* grosse caisse; *drumhead,* peau de tambour; *drum major,* tambour-major; *drumstick,* baguette de tambour. ‖ **drummer** [-⁰r] *s.* tambour [man]; *Am.* commis voyageur, m.

drunk [drŏngk] *p. p. of to drink;* *adj.* ivre; *to get drunk,* prendre une cuite (fam.), *Fr. Can.* prendre une brosse. ‖ **drunkard** [-⁰rd] *s.* ivrogne, poivrot, m. ‖ **drunken** [-⁰n] *adj.* ivre. ‖ **drunkenness** [-⁰nis] *s.* ivresse, ivrognerie, f.

dry [dra¹] *adj.* sec, sèche; desséché; aride; altéré; caustique; ardu; *Am.* antialcoolique; ennuyeux, « rasoir »; *v.* sécher; faire sécher; essuyer [dishes]; se tarir; *s.° Am.* prohibitionniste, m.; *dry goods,* nouveautés; *dry cleaning,* nettoyage à sec; *drysalter,* droguiste; ‖ **dryly** [-li] *adv.* sèchement. ‖ **dryness** [-nis] *s.* sécheresse, dessiccation; aridité, f.

dual [dyou⁰l] *adj.* double; *dual control,* double commande; *dual office,* cumul. ‖ **duality** [dyou⁰liti] *s.° dualité, f.

dub [dŏb] *v.* qualifier; doubler [film]; raboter, aplanir.

dubious [dyou¹bi⁰s] *adj.* douteux; contestable; problématique. ‖ **dubitative** [-bi⁰tiv] *adj.* dubitatif.

duchess [dŏtshis] *s.° duchesse, f.

duck [dŏk] *s.* coutil, m.

duck [dŏk] *s.* canard, m.; cane, f.; *duckling,* caneton.

duck [dŏk] *v.* plonger; immerger; éviter en baissant la tête; *s.* plongeon, m.; esquive, f.

duct [dŏkt] *s.* conduit, m.

ductile [dŏkt'l] *adj.* ductile; docile.

dudgeon [dŏdj⁰n] *s.* colère, f.

due [dyou] *adj.* dû; convenable; échu [bill]; qui doit arriver; *s.* dû; droit, m.; taxe, f.; *due North,* droit vers le Nord; *what is it due to?,* à quoi cela tient-il?; *in due time,* en temps voulu; *the train is due at six,* le train doit arriver à six heures; *town dues,* octroi.

duel [dyou⁰l] *s.* duel, m.; *v.* se battre en duel.

duet [dyouèt] *s.* duo, m. ‖ **duettist** [-ist] *s.* duettiste, m. f.

duffer [dŏf⁰r] *s.* colporteur; faussaire; faux; cancre; sot, m.

dug *pret., p. p. of to dig.* ‖ **dugout** [dŏga⁰ut] *s.* abri, m.; cagna; pirogue, f.

duke [dyouk] *s.* duc, m.; *dukedom,* duché.

dull [dŏl] *adj.* stupide, hébété; borné; traînard; morne, terne; ennuyeux; ralenti [comm.]; triste; gris [sky]; sourd [sound]; pâle [color]; émoussé [blade]; *v.* hébéter, engourdir; ternir; émousser; amortir. ‖ **dullness** [-nis] *s.* stupidité; lenteur; torpeur; tristesse, f.; ennui; engourdissement, m.

duly [dyouli] *adv.* dûment.

dumb [dŏm] *adj.* muet, muette; silencieux; *Am.* stupide; *dumb-waiter,* monte-plat. ‖ **dumbness** [-nis] *s.* mutisme, m.; stupidité, f.

dumfound [dŏmfa⁰und] *v.* abasourdir, confondre, désarçonner, ébahir.

dummy [dŏmi] *s.° mannequin; acteur d'un rôle muet; homme de paille; mort [bridge]; objet factice, m.;

maquette; sucette, f.; *adj.* factice, truqué; agissant comme prête-nom.

dump [dœmp] *s.* dépôt; dépotoir, m.; décharge publique des ordures, f.; *v.* décharger, vider; entasser.

dumps [dœmps] *s. pl.* cafard, m.; idées noires, f. pl.

dumpy [dœmpi] *adj.* trapu, replet.

dun [dœn] *v.* harceler (a debtor); *s.* créancier impatient, m.

dunce [dœns] *s.* ignorant, m.; *dunce's cap*, bonnet d'âne.

dune [dyoun] *s.* dune, f.

dung [dœng] *s.* fumier, m.; crotte, f.; *v.* fumer; *dunghill*, tas de fumier.

dungeon [dœndjᵉn] *s.* cachot, m.

dunk [dœnk] *v.* tremper, faire des mouillettes; faire trempette.

Dunkirk [dœnkë^rk] *s.* Dunkerque.

duo [dyou^{ou}] *s.* duo, m.

dupe [dyoup] *s.* dupe, f.; *v.* duper.

duplicate [dyoupl^ekit] *adj.* double; *s.* double, duplicata, m.; [dyoupl^e-kéⁱt] *v.* copier; établir en double; faire un duplicata; reproduire.

duplicity [dyouplis^eti] *s.*^e duplicité, hypocrisie, f.

durable [dyour^eb'l] *adj.* durable.

duration [dyouréⁱsh^en] *s.* durée, f.

duress [dyou^erès] *s.* contrainte; captivité, f. || *during* [dyouring] *prep.* durant, pendant.

dusk [dœsk] *s.* crépuscule, m.; *Fr. Can.* brunante, f. || *dusky* [-i] *adj.* sombre, obscur; hâlé.

dust [dœst] *s.* poussière; cendres [corpse]; ordures, balayures, f.; poussier, m.; *v.* épousseter; saupoudrer; *saw-dust*, sciure; *dust coat*, cache-poussière; *dust-pan*, pelle à ordures. ||

duster [-^{er}] *s.* torchon, essuie-meuble; *Am.* cache-poussière, m.; *feather-duster*, plumeau, m. || *dusty* [-i] *adj.* poussiéreux; poudreux.

Dutch [dœtsh] *adj., s.* Hollandais, Néerlandais; *Dutch oven*, rôtissoire. || *Dutchman* [-m^en] (*pl.* **Dutchmen**) *s.* Hollandais, m.

dutiable [dyouti^eb'l] *adj.* soumis aux droits de douane. || *dutiful* [dyouti-f^el] *adj.* soumis; déférent; respectueux. || *duty* [dyouti] *s.*^e devoir; respect, m.; tâche, obligation; taxe, imposition, f.; *duty-free*, exempt d'impôt.

dwarf [dwourf] *adj., s.* nain, naine; *v.* rapetisser; arrêter la croissance; réduire (*to*, à).

dwell [dwèl] *v.*^e habiter, demeurer; rester; insister (*on*, sur). || *dweller* [-^{er}] *s.* habitant, résident, m. || *dwelling* [-ing] *s.* habitation, f.; domicile, m. || *dwelt* [-t] *pret., p. p. of* **to dwell**.

dwindle [dwind'l] *v.* diminuer; dépérir; se ratatiner.

dye [daⁱ] *s.* teinture; couleur, f.; *v.* teindre; *Br.* dye-house; *Am.* dye-work, teinturerie. || *dyer* [-^{er}] *s.* teinturier, m.

dying [daⁱing] *adj.* moribond, mourant.

dynamic [daⁱnamik] *adj.* dynamique; énergique; *s. pl.* dynamique, f. || *dynamism* [daⁱn^emiz'm] *s.* dynamisme, m.

dynamite [daⁱn^emaⁱt] *s.* dynamite, f.; *v.* dynamiter, miner. || *dynamiter* [-^{er}] *s.* dynamiteur, m.

dynamo [daⁱn^em^e] *s.* dynamo, f.

dynasty [din^esti] *s.*^e dynastie, f.

dysentery [dis'ntèri] *s.* dysenterie, f.

dyspepsia [dispèpsh^e] *s.* dyspepsie, f.

E

each [îtsh] *adj.* chaque; *pron.* chacun, chacune; *each other*, l'un l'autre.

eager [îg^{er}] *adj.* avide; ardent; impatient. || *eagerness* [-nis] *s.* avidité; ardeur; impatience, f.; zèle, m.

eagle [îg'l] *s.* aigle, m.; *eagle-owl*, grand-duc.

ear [i^{er}] *s.* oreille; anse, f.; épi, m.; *ear-drum*, tympan; *ear-ring*, boucle d'oreille; *ear-trumpet*, cornet acoustique; *ear-wax*, cérumen.

earl [ë^rl] *s.* comte, m.

early [ë^rli] *adv.* tôt, de bonne heure; *adj.* matinal; précoce; prompt; de primeur [fruit]; bas [age].

earn [ë^rn] *v.* gagner; acquérir; mériter; *earnings*, salaire.

earnest [ë^rnist] *adj.* sérieux; sincère; ardent; *s.* sérieux, m.; *in earnest*, sérieusement, pour de bon; *earnest money*, arrhes. || *earnestly* [-li] *adv.* avec sérieux; avec ardeur.

earnings [ë^rningz] *s.* gain, salaire, m.; appointements, m. pl.; bénéfices, m. pl.

earphone [i^{er}fo^{ou}n], **earpiece** [i^{er}-pîs] *s.* écouteur, m. || *earshot* [-shôt] *s.* portée d'ouïe, f.

earth [ë^rth] *s.* terre, f.; monde; univers; sol, m. || *earthen* [-^en] *adj.* en terre; de terre; *earthenware*, poterie, faïence. || *earthly* [-li] *adj.* terrestre; mondain; matériel. || *earthquake* [-kwéⁱk] *s.* tremblement de terre, m. || *earthwork* [-wë^rk] *s.* terrassement,

m. ‖ **earthworm** [-wĕᵣm] *s.* ver de terre; lombric, m. ‖ **earthy** [-i] *adj.* terreux; fruste; truculent.

ease [īz] *s.* aise, confort; soulagement, m.; aisance; facilité; détente, f.; *v.* soulager; détendre; faciliter; mollir (naut.); alléger.

easel [īz'l] *s.* chevalet, m.

easily [izᵉli] *adv.* aisément.

east [īst] *s.* est; orient; levant, m.; *adj.* oriental; *adv.* à l'est, vers l'est, de l'est; *Near East*, Proche-Orient; *Far East*, Extrême-Orient.

Easter [īstᵉr] *s.* Pâques, m. pl.

eastern [īstᵉrn] *adj.* oriental, de l'est. ‖ **eastward** [īstwᵉrd] *adv., adj.* vers l'est.

easy [īzi] *adj.* facile; à l'aise; léger; libre; docile; tranquille; *to feel easy*, se sentir à son aise; *easy-going*, placide, accommodant; *by easy stages*, à petites étapes.

eat [īt] *v.** manger; *to eat up the miles*, dévorer les kilomètres. ‖ **eatables** [ītᵉb'lz] *s. pl.* aliments, m.; choses comestibles, f. ‖ **eaten** [īt'n] *p. p. of to eat*. ‖ **eater** [-ᵉr] *s.* mangeur, m. ‖ **eating-house** [ītingha°us] *s.* restaurant, m.

eaves [īvz] *s.* larmier, m.; *eaves-drop*, écouter aux portes; *eaves-dropper*, espion, indiscret.

ebb [ĕb] *s.* reflux; déclin, m.; baisse, f.; *v.* refluer; décliner; péricliter; *ebb tide*, jusant.

ebony [ĕbᵉni] *s.* ébène, m.

ebullient [ibælyᵉnt] *adj.* bouillonnant, effervescent; exubérant.

ebullition [ĕb·lishᵉn] *s.* ébullition, f.

eccentric [iksèntrik] *adj., s.* excentrique, original. ‖ **eccentricity** [ĕksèntrisiti] *s.** excentricité, f.

ecclesiastic [ikliziastik] *adj., s.* ecclésiastique.

echo [ĕko°u] *s.** écho, m.; *v.* répéter; faire écho, répercuter.

éclair [éᵏᵏlĕᵉr] *s.* éclair, m. (culin.).

eclipse [iklíps] *s.* éclipse, f.; *v.* éclipser; *to become eclipsed*, s'éclipser.

economical [ik·nᵃmik'l] *adj.* économique; économe, épargnant. ‖ **economically** [-'li] *adv.* économiquement. ‖ **economics** [ik·nᵃmiks] *s.* économie politique, f. ‖ **economist** [ikanᵉmist] *s.* économiste, m. ‖ **economize** [ikanᵉmaᵏz] *v.* économiser; ménager; épargner. ‖ **economy** [ikanᵉmi] *s.** économie, parcimonie, frugalité; épargne, f.; système économique, m.

ecstasy [ĕkstᵉsi] *s.** extase, f. ‖ **ecstatic** [ĕkstatik] *adj.* extatique.

eczema [ĕkzimᵉ] *s.* eczéma, m.

eddy [ĕdi] *s.** tourbillon, remous, m. *v.* tourbillonner.

edge [èdj] *s.* tranchant; bord; fil [sword], m.; lisière; tranche [book] acuité, f.; *v.* aiguiser; border; se faufiler; *to set the teeth on edge*, agace, les dents; *gilt-edged*, doré sur tranche

edible [ĕdᵉb'l] *adj., s.* comestible.

edict [īdikt] *s.* édit, m.

edification [ĕdifiké¹shᵉn] *s.* édifica tion, f. ‖ **edificatory** [-tᵉri] *adj.* édifiant. ‖ **edifice** [ĕdᵉfis] *s.* édifice, m. ‖ **edify** [ĕdᵉfa¹] *v.* édifier.

edit [èdit] *v.* réviser; éditer. ‖ **edi tion** [idishᵉn] *s.* édition, f. ‖ **edito** [èditᵉr] *s.* rédacteur en chef; directeu de journal ou de collection, m. ‖ **ed torial** [èd·to°uri·l] *adj., s.* éditoria m.; *Am. editorial writer*, éditorialiste

educate [ĕdjᵉké¹t] *v.* éduquer, élever instruire. ‖ **education** [èdjᵉké¹shᵉn] *s* éducation; pédagogie; études, f. ‖ **educational** [-'l] *adj.* instructif; péda gogique. ‖ **educative** [èdjᵉké¹tiv] *adj* éducatif. ‖ **educator** [èdjᵉké¹tᵉr] *s* éducateur, m.; éducatrice, f.

eel [īl] *s.* anguille, f.; *eel-pout*, ba bote.

efface [ifès] *v.* effacer. ‖ **effacemen** [-mᵉnt] *s.* effacement, m.

effect [ᵉfèkt] *s.* effet, résultat; sens accomplissement, m.; réalisation; ir fluence, f.; *pl.* effets, biens, m. pl.; *v* effectuer, accomplir. ‖ **effective** [-iv *adj.* effectif; efficace; impressionnant en vigueur (jur.); bon pour le servic (mil.). ‖ **effectiveness** [-nis] *s.* effica cité, f.; effet, m.; sensation, f. **effectual** [ᵉfèktshou·l] *adj.* efficace.

effeminate [ᵉfèm·nit] *adj.* effémin

effervescent [èfᵉrvès·nt] *adj.* effer vescent; exubérant, surexcité.

effete [èfīt] *adj.* épuisé; stérile.

efficacious [ĕfiká¹shᵉs] *adj.* efficac ‖ **efficacy** [ĕf·k·si] *s.* efficacité, f.

efficiency [ᵉfish·nsi] *s.* efficience, ‖ **efficient** [ᵉfish·nt] *adj.* efficien compétent; capable; utile.

effigy [ĕf·dji] *s.** effigie, f.

effluvium [ĕflouvi·m] *s.* effluve, m

effort [ĕf·rt] *s.* effort, m.

effrontery [ᵉfrænt·ri] *s.* effronteri impudence, f.

effulgence [ĕfœldjᵉns] *s.* éclat, br lant, m.; splendeur, f.

effusion [ĕfyouj·n] *s.* effusion, épanchement, m. ‖ **effusive** [ĕfyousi *adj.* expansif, démonstratif.

egg [ĕg] *s.* œuf, m.; *boiled egg*, œ à la coque; *fried egg*, œuf sur le pla *hard-boiled egg*, œuf dur; *poache egg*, œuf poché; *scrambled egg*

œufs brouillés; **egg-cup,** coquetier;
eggplant, aubergine; **egg-shell,** coquille d'œuf.

egocentric [égo°uséntrik] *adj.* égocen-
triste. || **egocentricity** [ègo°uséntris°ti]
s. égocentrisme, m. || **egoism**
[égo°uìz'm] *s.* égoïsme, m. || **egoist**
[-ist] *s.* égoïste, m. f. || **egotism** [ìge-
tìz°m] *s.* égotisme, m. || **egotist** [-ist]
s. égotiste, m. f.

egregious [ìgrìdjì°s] *adj.* insigne, notoire, signalé.

Egypt [ìdjìpt] *s.* Égypte, f.; *Egyptian,*
Égyptien, Égyptien.

eider [aìd°r] *s.* eider, m.; *eider-down,*
duvet; édredon, m.

eight [é¹t] *adj.* huit. || **eighth** [-th]
adj. huitième. || **eighty** [-ì] *adj.* quatre-
vingts.

either [ìzh°r] *adj.,* *pron.* l'un ou
l'autre; *conj.* ou bien; *adv.* non plus;
either of them, chacun d'eux; *nor he*
either, ni lui non plus; *in either case,*
dans les deux cas.

eject [idjèkt] *v.* éjecter, expulser. ||
ejection [-sh°n] *s.* expulsion, f.

elaborate [ìlab°rìt] *adj.* compliqué,
recherché; soigné, fini; [ìlab°ré¹t] *v.*
élaborer, produire.

elapse [ìlaps] *v.* s'écouler [time].

elastic [ìlastìk] *adj.* élastique; souple;
s. élastique, m. || **elasticity** [ìlastìs°ti]
s. élasticité, f.

elate [ìlé¹t] *v.* exalter, transporter.

elbow [èlbo°u] *s.* coude, m.; *v.* coudoyer; *to elbow one's way,* jouer des
coudes pour se frayer un chemin; *el-*
bow grease, huile de coude.

elder [èld°r] *adj.* aîné; plus âgé;
ancien; *s.* aîné, ancien; dignitaire
[eccles.], m. || **elderly** [-lì] *adj.* d'un
certain âge. || **eldest** [èldist] *adj.* aîné.

elder [èld°r] *s.* sureau, m.

elect [ìlèkt] *adj.,* *s.* élu; d'élite; *v.*
élire. || **election** [ìlèksh°n] *s.* élection,
f. || **elective** [-tìv] *adj.* électif; électo-
ral; facultatif; *s.* matière à option, f.
|| **elector** [ìlèkt°r] *s.* électeur, m. ||
electoral [ìlèkt°r°l] *adj.* électoral.

electric [ìlèktrìk] *adj.* électrique. ||
electrical [-'l] *adj.* électrique; *elec-*
trical engineering, électrotechnique. ||
electrician [ìlèktrìsh°n] *s.* électri-
cien, m. || **electricity** [ìlèktrìs°ti] *s.*
électricité, f. || **electrify** [ìlèktr°fa¹] *v.*
électrifier; électriser. || **electrocute**
[ìlèktr°kyout] *v.* électrocuter. || **elec-**
trode [ìlèktro°ud] *s.* électrode, f. ||
electromagnet [ìlèktro°umagnìt] *s.*
électro-aimant, m. || **electron** [ìlèk-
trân] *s.* électron, m. || **electronics**
[-ìks] *s.* électronique, f.

elegance [èl°g°ns] *s.* élégance, f. ||
elegant [èl°g°nt] *adj.* élégant.

elegy [èlìdjì] *s.* * élégie, f.

element [èl°m°nt] *s.* élément, m. ||
elementary [-°rì] *adj.* élémentaire;
primaire [school].

elephant [èl°f°nt] *s.* éléphant, m.

elevate [èl°vé¹t] *v.* élever, hausser;
exalter, ennoblir; enthousiasmer. ||
elevation [èl°vé¹sh°n] *s.* élévation;
altitude; exaltation, f. || **elevator**
[èl°vé¹t°r] *s.* ascenseur; élévateur, m.

eleven [ìlèv°n] *adj.* onze.

elicit [ìlìsit] *v.* tirer, arracher [word];
susciter [applause].

eligible [èlìdj°b'l] *adj.* éligible.

eliminate [ìlìm°né¹t] *v.* éliminer. ||
elimination [ìlìm°né¹sh°n] *s.* élimina-
tion, f. || **eliminatory** [ìlìm°né¹tori] *adj.*
éliminatoire.

elixir [ìlìks°r] *s.* élixir, m.

elk [èlk] *s.* élan; *Am.* wapiti, m.

ellipse [ìlìps] *s.* ellipse, f.

elm [èlm] *s.* orme, m.

elocution [èl°kyoush°n] *s.* élocution;
diction, f.

elope [ìlo°up] *v.* s'enfuir (*from,* de);
se faire enlever (*with,* par).

eloquence [èl°kwens] *s.* éloquence, f.
|| **eloquent** [èl°kw°nt] *adj.* éloquent.

else [èls] *adj.* autre; *adv.* autrement;
nothing else, rien d'autre; *or else,* ou
bien; *everything else,* tout le reste;
nowhere else, nulle part ailleurs. ||
elsewhere [-hwè°r] *adv.* ailleurs.

elucidate [ìlous°dé¹t] *v.* élucider;
clarifier. || **elucidation** [ìlous°dé¹sh°n]
s. élucidation, explication, f.; éclaircissement, m.

elude [ìloud] *v.* éluder; échapper à.
|| **elusive** [ìlyousìv] *adj.* évasif, fuyant;
déconcertant.

emaciate [ìmé¹shié¹t] *v.* amaigrir.

emanate [èm°né¹t] *v.* émaner. || *ema-*
nation [èm°né¹sh°n] *s.* émanation, f.

emancipate [ìmans°pé¹t] *v.* éman-
ciper. || **emancipation** [ìmans°pé¹sh°n]
s. émancipation, f.

embalm [ìmbâm] *v.* embaumer.

embankment [ìmbàngkm°nt] *s.*
digue, f.; remblai; quai, m.

embargo [ìmbârgo°u] *s.* embargo, m.

embark [ìmbârk] *v.* (s')embarquer.

embarrass [ìmbâr°s] *v.* embarrasser;
déconcerter; causer des difficultés fi-
nancières. || **embarrassment** [-m°nt]
s. embarras; trouble, m.; gêne pécuniaire, f.

embassy [èmb°sì] *s.* * ambassade, f.

embellish [ìmbèlìsh] *v.* embellir.

ember [èmb°r] *s.* cendre, f.; *pl.*
braises, f.; tison, m.

embezzle [imbèz'l] *v.* détourner [money]. || *embezzlement* [-m^ent] *s.* détournement, m.

embitter [imbit^er] *v.* rendre amer; aigrir [feelings].

emblem [èmbl^em] *s.* emblème, m.

embody [imbôdi] *v.* incorporer; incarner; matérialiser.

embolden [imboould'n] *v.* enhardir.

emboss [imbaus] *v.* gaufrer; frapper; bosseler.

embrace [imbréⁱs] *s.* embrassement, m.; étreinte, f.; *v.* embrasser; inclure; adopter [profession]; *embracement,* embrassement, enlacement.

embroider [imbroⁱd^er] *v.* broder. || *embroidery* [-^eri] *s.* broderie, f.

embryo [èmbrio^u] *s.* embryon, m.

emend [imènd] *v.* corriger.

emerald [èm^erld] *s.* émeraude, f.

emerge [imërdj] *v.* émerger. || *emergency* [-ènsi] *s.* circonstance critique, f.; cas urgent, m.; *Am.* to call « *emergency* », appeler police-secours.

emery [èm^eri] *s.* émeri, m.

emigrant [èm^egr^ent] *adj., s.* émigrant. || *emigrate* [èm^egréⁱt] *v.* émigrer. || *emigration* [èm^egréⁱsh^en] *s.* émigration, f.

eminence [èm^en^ens] *s.* éminence, f. || *eminent* [èm^en^ent] *adj.* éminent; élevé; remarquable.

emissary [èm^esèri] *s.* émissaire, m. agent secret, m.

emission [imísh^en] *s.* émission, f.

emit [imit] *v.* émettre [paper money]; dégager [smoke]; publier [decree].

emotion [imo^ush^en] *s.* émotion, f. || *emotional* [imo^ush^en'l] *adj.* émotionnel; émotif; ému. || *emotive* [imo^utiv] *adj.* émotif. || *emotiveness* [-ivnis] *adj.* émotivité, f.

emperor [èmp^er^er] *s.* empereur, m.

emphasis [èmf^esis] (*pl.* **emphases**) *s.* accent oratoire, m.; force, énergie, f. || *emphasize* [èmf^esaⁱz] *v.* accentuer; appuyer sur; insister. || *emphatic* [imfatik] *adj.* accentué, appuyé.

emphysema [emfisîm^e] *s.* emphysème, m.

empire [èmpaⁱr] *s.* empire, m.

empiric [émpírik] *adj.* empirique. || *empiricism* [émpírisiz'm] *s.* empirisme, m.

employ [imploⁱ] *v.* employer; occuper [time]; *s.* emploi, m. || *employee* [imploⁱî] *s.* employé, m. || *employer* [imploⁱe^r] *s.* employeur, m. || *employment* [-m^ent] *s.* emploi, m.; occupation, charge, f.

emporium [èmpo^uri^em] *s.* entrepôt, magasin, marché, m.

empress [èmpris] *s.* impératrice, f.

emptiness [èmptinis] *s.* vide, m. || *empty* [èmpti] *adj.* vide; stérile; vain; *v.* vider; se jeter [river].

emulate [èmyéⁱt] *v.* rivaliser avec. || *emulation* [émyouléⁱsh^en] *s.* émulation, f. || *emulator* [émyoul^et^er] *s.* émule, m. f.

enable [inéⁱb'l] *v.* habiliter; mettre à même de.

enact [inakt] *v.* décréter, promulguer (jur.).

enamel [inam'l] *s.* émail, m.; *v.* émailler.

enamo(u)r [inam^er] *v.* séduire.

encamp [inkämp] *v.* camper. || *encampment* [-m^ent] *s.* campement, m.

enchain [èntshéⁱn] *v.* enchaîner.

enchant [intshänt] *v.* enchanter; fasciner. || *enchanter* [-^er] *s.* enchanteur, m. || *enchantment* [-m^ent] *s.* enchantement, m.; féerie, f.

encircle [insër'k'l] *v.* encercler.

enclose [inklo^uz] *v.* enclore; enfermer; entourer [surround]; inclure. || *enclosure* [inklo^uj^er] *s.* enclos; pl [letter], m.; clôture, f.

encomium [ènko^umi^em] *s.* éloge; panégyrique, m.

encompass [inkämp^es] *v.* encercler; contenir.

encore [ängkaur] *interj.* bis!; *s.* rappel, bis, m.; *v.* bisser.

encounter [inka^unt^er] *s.* rencontre, bataille, f.; *v.* rencontrer; affronter; combattre.

encourage [inkër^eidj] *v.* encourager; inciter; aider. || *encouragement* [-m^ent] *s.* encouragement, stimulant; soutien, m.

encroach [inkro^utsh] *v.* empiéter (*upon*, sur).

encumber [inkämb^er] *v.* encombrer; charger; gêner; accabler [with, de].

encyclic [ènsaⁱklik] *s.* encyclique, f.

encyclopedia [énsaⁱkl^epîdi^e] *s.* encyclopédie, f. || *encyclopedical* [énsaⁱklopîdik'l] *adj.* encyclopédique.

end [ènd] *s.* fin; extrémité; mort, f.; bout; but, m.; *v.* finir; achever; aboutir; se terminer; mourir; *to secure one's end,* arriver à ses fins; *to make an end to,* en finir avec.

endanger [indéⁱndj^er] *v.* mettre en danger; risquer.

endear [indi^er] *v.* rendre cher, faire aimer. || *endearment* [-m^ent] *s.* caresse; affection, f.

endeavo(u)r [indèv^er] *s.* effort, m.; tentative, f.; *v.* essayer; s'efforcer (*to*, de); tenter.

•nding [ènding] *s.* conclusion; fin, nort, f. ‖ **endless** [èndlis] *adj.* perpé-uel; interminable; incessant.

•ndorse, *see* **indorse**.

•ndow [indaᵒᵘ] *v.* doter; doüer. ‖ **ndowment** [-mᵉnt] *s.* dotation, f.; lon, m.

•ndue [indyou] *v.* douer; investir.

•ndurance [indyouᵣᵉns] *s.* endurance; ésistance, patience, f. ‖ **endure** [indyouᵣ] *v.* durer; endurer; patien-er; supporter, tolérer.

•nema [ènᵉmᵉ] *s.* lavement; broc, m.

•nemy [ènᵉmi] *s.ᵉ* ennemi, m.

•nergetic [ènᵉrdjètik] *adj.* énergique. **energy** [ènᵉrdji] *s.ᵉ* énergie, f.

•nervate [ènᵉrvé¹t] *v.* énerver; débi-iter; [enérvit] *adj.* énervé, abattu, ébilité, affaibli.

•nfeeble [infíb'l] *v.* affaiblir.

•nfold, *see* **infold**.

•nforce [infoᵒᵘrs] *v.* forcer [obe-lience]; faire appliquer [law]; faire aloir [right]. ‖ **enforcement** [-mᵉnt] *s.* . contrainte; exécution; applica-lion, f.

•nfranchise [ènfràntsha¹z] *v.* affran-hir; donner droit de cité ou de vote.

•ngage [ingé¹dj] *v.* engager; garan-ir; attirer [attention]; attaquer; se ancer; employer; embrayer (mech.); engager; se livrer à [business]; s'en-rener (mech.). ‖ **engagement** [-mᵉnt] *s.* fiançailles, f. pl.; occupation; romesse, f.; engagement; combat; ontrat; engrenage (mech.); rendez-ous, m.

•ngender [indjèndᵉr] *v.* engendrer.

•ngine [èndjᵉn] *s.* machine; locomo-ive, f.; engin [war]; moteur, m.; **ngine trouble**, panne de moteur. ‖ **ngineer** [èndjᵉnⁱᵉr] *s.* ingénieur; mé-anicien; soldat du génie, m.; *v.* diri-er la construction de; établir des lans. ‖ **engineering** [-ing] *s.* art de ingénieur; génie, m.; logistique ndustrielle, f.; manigances, f. pl. olloq.).

•ngland [ìnggfᵉnd] *s.* Angleterre, f. **English** [ìngglish] *adj.*, *s.* anglais, f. ‖ **nglishman** [-mᵉn] *s.* Anglais, m. ‖ **nglishwoman** [-woumᵉn] *s.* An-laise, f.

•ngraft [èngràft] *v.* greffer.

•ngrave [ingré¹v] *v.* graver. ‖ **engra-er** [-ᵉr] *s.* graveur, m. ‖ **engraving** ing] *s.* gravure, f.

•ngross [ingroᵒᵘs] *v.* grossoyer writing]; absorber [attention]; mono-oliser.

•ngulf [ingœlf] *v.* engloutir.

enhance [inhàns] *v.* augmenter; in-tensifier; rehausser.

enigma [inígmᵉ] *s.* énigme, f. ‖ **enig-matic(al)** [énigmatik('l)] *adj.* énigma-tique.

enjoin [indjo¹n] *v.* enjoindre; inter-dire (*from*, de).

enjoy [indjo¹] *v.* jouir de; apprécier; savourer; *to enjoy oneself*, se diver-tir; *to enjoy the use of*, avoir l'usu-fruit de. ‖ **enjoyable** [-'b'l] *adj.* agréable, attirant. ‖ **enjoyment** [-mᵉnt] *s.* jouissance, f.; plaisir; usufruit, m.

enkindle [ènkínd'l] *v.* enflammer.

enlarge [inlàrdj] *v.* agrandir, étendre, élargir; s'accroître; commen-ter, s'étendre (*upon*, sur). ‖ **enlar-gement** [-mᵉnt] *s.* agrandissement, développement; accroissement, m.; hypertrophie, f. (med.).

enlighten [inla¹t'n] *v.* éclairer; ins-truire; illuminer.

enlist [inlíst] *v.* enrôler; s'engager. ‖ **enlistment** [-mᵉnt] *s.* recrutement; engagement, m.

enliven [inla¹vᵉn] *v.* animer, égayer; stimuler [business].

enmity [ènmᵉti] *s.* inimitié, f.

ennoble [inoᵒᵘb'l] *v.* ennoblir; ano-blir; grandir.

enormity [inauᵣmiti] *s.ᵉ* énormité, f. ‖ **enormous** [inauᵣmᵉs] *adj.* énorme.

enough [ᵉnœf] *adj.* suffisant; *adv.* assez; *s.* quantité suffisante, f.; *enough to pay*, de quoi payer; *good enough*, assez bon; *more than enough*, plus qu'il n'en faut.

enounce [inoᵒᵘns] *v.* proclamer; énoncer; mentionner. ‖ **enouncement** [-mᵉnt] *s.* proclamation, déclaration; mention, f.

enquire, *see* **inquire**.

enrage [inré¹dj] *v.* enrager.

enrapture [inràptshᵉr] *v.* ravir.

enrich [inrítsh] *v.* enrichir.

enroll [inroᵒᵘl] *v.* enrôler; immatri-culer; s'inscrire. ‖ **enrollment** [-mᵉnt] *s.* enrôlement; enregistrement; re-gistre, rôle, m.

enshroud [ènshraᵒᵘd] *v.* ensevelir.

ensign [èns'n] *s.* enseigne de vais-seau, m.; [ènsa¹n] *s.* enseigne, f.; étendard; insigne, m.

enslave [inslé¹v] *v.* asservir.

ensnare [ènsnèᵉr] *v.* prendre au piège.

ensue [ènsou] *v.* s'ensuivre, résulter.

ensure [inshour] *v.* assurer.

entail [intéil] *v.* léguer (jur.); entraî-ner [consequence].

entangle [intàngg'l] *v.* enchevêtrer, embrouiller.

enter [ènt°r] v. entrer; commencer; prendre part à; s'affilier à; enregistrer [act, address]; notifier (jur.); embrasser [profession].

enteritis [ènt°ra¹tis] s. entérite, f.

enterprise [ènt°rpra¹z] s. entreprise; initiative, f. ‖ *enterprising* [-ing] *adj.* entreprenant.

entertain [ènt°rté¹n] v. recevoir [guest]; accueillir [suggestion]; caresser [hope]; nourrir [project]; divertir, amuser. ‖ *entertaining* [-ing] *adj.* amusant. ‖ *entertainment* [-m°nt] *s.* accueil; divertissement, m.

enthrall [inthraul] v. asservir.

enthusiasm [inthyouzlaz°m] s. enthousiasme, m. ‖ *enthusiast* [-zlast] *s.* enthousiaste, m., f. ‖ *enthusiastic* [-ziastik] *adj.* enthousiaste.

entice [inta¹s] v. attirer, séduire. ‖ *enticement* [-m°nt] *s.* attrait, m.

entire [inta¹r] *adj.* entier, complet, total. ‖ *entirely* [-li] *adv.* entièrement, intégralement. ‖ *entirety* [-ti] *s.* totalité, intégralité, f.

entitle [inta¹t'l] v. intituler; habiliter; donner le droit à.

entity [ènt°ti] *s.* entité, f.

entomb [intoum] v. enterrer.

entrails [èntr°lz] s. entrailles, f. pl.

entrance [èntr°ns] s. entrée; introduction, f.; début; accès; droit d'entrée, m.

entrance [intrèns] v. jeter en transe; ravir.

entreat [intrît] v. supplier, implorer. ‖ *entreaty* [-ti] *s.* supplication, instances, f.

entree [ântré¹] s. entrée [dish], f.

entrust [intrèst] v. confier; remettre, déposer; charger.

entry [èntri] *s.* entrée [passage]; inscription; écriture (comm.); prise de possession (jur.), f.; débuts, m. pl.; *entry form,* feuille d'inscription.

entwine [intwa¹n] v. entrelacer.

enumerate [inyoum°ré¹t] v. énumérer. ‖ *enumeration* [inyoum°ré¹sh°n] *s.* énumération, f.

enunciate [inœnsié¹t] v. énoncer; annoncer; prononcer. ‖ *enunciation* [inœnshié¹sh°n] *s.* énonciation; déclaration; prononciation, f.

envelop [invèl°p] v. envelopper. ‖ *envelope* [ènv°loup] *s.* enveloppe, f.

enviable [ènvi°b'l] *adj.* enviable. ‖ *envious* [ènvi°s] *adj.* envieux.

environ [inva¹r°n] v. environner. ‖ *environment* [-m°nt] *s.* environs; milieu environnant, m. ‖ *environs* [-z] *s.* environs, m. pl.

envisage [invizldj] v. envisager.

envoy [ènvo¹] *s.* envoyé, m.

envy [ènvi] *s.** envie, f.; v. envier.

enwrap [inrap] v. envelopper.

epaulet [èp°lèt] *s.* épaulette, f.

ephemeral [°fèm°r°l] *adj.* éphémère

epic [èpik] *adj.* épique; *s.* épopée, f.

epidemic [èp°dèmik] *adj.* épidémique; *s.* épidémie, f.

epidermal [èpidèm°l] *adj.* épidermique. ‖ *epidermis* [-mis] *s.* épiderme, m.

episcopal [ipîsk°p°l] *adj.* épiscopal. ‖ *episcopate* [ipîsk°pit] *s.* épiscopat, m

episode [èpiso°ud] *s.* épisode, m. ‖ *episodic* [èpîsâdik] *adj.* épisodique.

epistle [ipîs'l] *s.* épître, f.

epitaph [èp°taf] *s.* épitaphe, f.

epoch [èp°k] *s.* époque, f.

equal [îkw°l] *adj.* égal; capable de *s.* égal, pair, m.; v. égaler; *I don',* feel *equal to it,* je ne m'en sens pas la force; *equally,* également. ‖ *equality* [îkwâl°ti] *s.* égalité, f. ‖ *equalize* [îkw°la¹z] v. égaliser; niveler.

equation [ikwé¹j°n] s. équation, f.

equator [ikwé¹t°r] s. équateur, m.

equestrian [ikwèstri°n] *adj.* équestre *s.* cavalier, m.

equilibrium [ikw°librî°m] *s.* équilibre, m.

equip [ikwîp] v. équiper; outiller. ‖ *equipment* [-m°nt] *s.* équipement outillage, m.

equitable [èkwit°b'l] *adj.* équitable ‖ *equity* [èkw°ti] *s.* équité, f.

equivalence [ikwîv°l°ns] *s.* équivalence, f. ‖ *equivalent* [ikwîv°l°nt] *adj.* équivalent.

equivocal [ikwîv°k'l] *adj.* équivoque. ‖ *equivocate* [-ké¹t] v. biaiser

era [î°r°] *s.* ère, époque, f.

eradicate [iradiké¹t] v. déraciner.

erase [iré¹s] v. raturer. ‖ *eraser* [-°r *s.* grattoir, m.; gomme, f. ‖ *erasure* [iré¹j°r] *s.* rature, f.

ere [èr] *prep.* avant de; *conj.* avan que.

erect [irèkt] *adj.* droit; v. ériger dresser; monter [machine].

ermine [ë°rmin] *s.* hermine, f.

erode [iro°ud] v. éroder; corroder. *erosion* [iro°uj°n] *s.* érosion, f.

erotic [irâtik] *adj.* érotique. ‖ *eroti cism* [-isiz°m] *s.* érotisme, m.

err [ë°r] v. errer; se tromper; s'égarer

errand [èr°nd] *s.* commission; course f.; message, m.; *errand boy,* commis sionnaire, coursier, m.

rrant [èr•nt] *adj.* errant.

rroneous [•ro°°ni•s] *adj.* erroné. ‖ **rror** [èr°r] *s.* erreur, f.

rudite [èrouda¹t] *adj.* érudit. ‖ **erudition** [èroudish•n] *s.* érudition, f.

ruption [iræpsh•n] *s.* éruption, f.

scalade [èsk•lé¹d] *v.* escalader; *s.* calade, f.

escape [•skế¹p] *v.* s'échapper; éluder; éviter [pain], échapper à; *s.* évason; fuite [gas], f.; moyen de salut, .; *fire escape,* échelle de sauvetage; .; *caped prisoner,* évadé. ‖ **escapism** ské¹piz•m] *s* évasion, f.

scalator [èsk•lé¹t•r] *s.* escalier rou•nt, m.

schew [èstshou] *v.* éviter.

scort [èskaurt] *s.* escorte, f.; convoi, .; [iskaurt] escorter; convoyer.

scutcheon [iskætsh•n] *s.* écusson, f.

special [•spèsh•l] *adj.* spécial; •pecially, spécialement, surtout.

spionage [èspi•nidj] *s.* espion•ge, m.

spouse [ispa°°z] *v.* épouser.

squire [iskwa¹•r] *s.* Monsieur (court•y title), cavalier, m.

ssay [èsé¹] *s.* essai, m.; [•sé¹] *v.* •sayer, tenter.

ssence [ès'ns] *s.* essence, f. ‖ **essen•al** [ts•nsh•l] *adj.* essentiel.

tablish [•stablish] *v.* établir; ins•ier démontrer; fonder [firm]. ‖ **tablishment** [-m•nt] *s.* établisse•ent, effectifs (mil.), m.; maison de •mmerce, f.

tate [•sté¹t] *s.* état; biens, domaine, .; condition sociale; fortune, f.; •mily estate, patrimoine.

teem [•stîm] estimer, *s* estime, ‖ **estimable** [èst•m•b'l] *adj.* esti•able **estimate** [èst•mit] *s* estima•n, *f* devis n., [•st•mé¹t] *v* estim•r; évaluer juger. **estimation** •st•mé¹sh•n] *s* estimation appréci•n évaluation, f., jugement, m.

trange [•stré¹ndj] *v* aliéner [affec•n] détourner dépayser.

tuary [èstshou•ri] *s.°* estuaire, m.

ch [ètsh] *v.* graver à l'eau-forte; •ching, eau-forte.

ernal [itèr•n'l] *adj.* éternel. ‖ **eter•ty** [itèr•nti] *s.°* éternité, f.

her [îth•r] *s.* éther, m. ‖ **ethereal** •hiri•l] *adj.* éthéré.

hical [èthík'l] *adj.* éthique. ‖ **ethics** •thiks] *s.* morale, éthique, f.

hnography [èthn•gr•fi] *s.* ethno•aphie, f. ‖ **ethnology** [-dji] *s.* ethno•gie, f

etiquette [ètikèt] *s.* étiquette, f.; cérémonial, m.; bonnes manières, f. pl.

ethnic [èthnik] *adj.* ethnique.

etymological [étim•lâdjik•l] *adj.* étymologique. ‖ **etymology** [èt•mâl•dji] *s.°* étymologie, f.

eucalyptus [youk•lípt•s] *s.°* eucalyptus, m.

euphemism [youf•miz•m] *s.* euphémisme, m.

European [your•pi•n] *adj., s.* européen.

euthanasia [youth•né¹zi•] *s.* euthanasie, f.

evacuate [ivakyoué¹t] *v.* évacuer. ‖ **evacuation** [ivakyoué¹sh•n] *s.* évacuation, f. ‖ **evacuee** [ivakyouî] *s.* évacué, m.

evade [ivé¹d] *v.* éviter; éluder; s'évader; s'esquiver.

evaluate [ivalyoué¹t] *v.* évaluer. ‖ **evaluation** [ivalyoué¹sh•n] *s.* évaluation, f.

evangelical [ivàndjèlik'l] *adj.* évangélique.

evaporate [ivap•ré¹t] *v.* (s') évaporer. ‖ **evaporation** [ivap•ré¹sh•n] *s.* évaporation, f.

evasion [ivé¹j•n] *s.* échappatoire; évasion, f. ‖ **evasive** [ivé¹siv] *adj.* évasif; fuyant.

eve [îv] *s.* veille; vigile, f.; soir, m.

even [îv•n] *adj.* égal; uni; plat; équivalent pair [number]; juste; *adv.* même exactement; également; *v.* égaliser aplanir; niveler. *to get even with,* rendre la pareille à, *to be even with,* être quitte avec *even-handed,* équitable *even money,* compte rond; *even now,* à l'instant *even so,* pourtant *even though,* quand même.

evening [îvning] *s* soir, m.

event [ivènt] *s.* événement; incident; résultat; event m. ‖ *eventful* [-f•l] *adj.* mouvementé; mémorable ‖ *eventual* [•shou•l] *adj.* final; éventuel; *eventually,* finalement. ‖ *eventuality* [ivèntshoué°ti] *s.* éventualité, f.

ever [èv•r] *adv* toujours; *if ever,* si jamais; *ever so little,* si peu que ce soit *hardly ever* presque jamais; *ever so much* infiniment. *evergreen* [-grîn] *adj* toujours vert [plant]. ‖ *everlasting* lasting] *adj* perpétuel; *s.* éternité. éternelle [plant], f. ‖ *evermore* mo°°r] *adv* pour jamais.

every [èvri] *adj.* chaque tout, toute, tous *very day,* tous les jours; *every other day,* tous les deux jours, *every now and then,* de temps à autre, *every one,* chacun, tous. ‖ *everybody* [-bâdi] *pron.* tout le monde. ‖ *everyday* [-dé¹] *adj.* quotidien; habituel. ‖ *everyone* [-wœn] *pron.* chacun; tous; tout le monde. ‖ **everything** [-thing] *pron.* tout, toute chose. ‖ **everywhere** [-hwèr] *adv.* partout.

evict [ivíkt] *v.* évincer; expulser. ‖ **eviction** [ivíksh•n] *s.* éviction, f.

evidence [év•d•ns] *s.* évidence; indication; preuve, f.; témoignage (jur.), m. ‖ **evident** [év•d•nt] *adj.* évident, manifeste.

evil [ív'l] *adj.* mauvais; *s.* mal; malheur, m.; *adv.* mal; **evil-doer**, malfaiteur.

evince [ivíns] *v.* montrer; déployer.

evocation [èvo°°ké¹sh•n] *s.* évocation, f. ‖ **evoke** [ivo°°k] *v.* évoquer; provoquer [laughter].

evolution [èv°l“sh•n] *s.* évolution, f. ‖ **evolve** [iválv] *v.* développer.

ewe [you] *s.* brebis, f.

ewer [you°°r] *s.* aiguière, f.

exact [igzakt] *adj.* exact; **exactly**, exactement. ‖ **exactitude** [igzakt•tyoud] *s* exactitude, f.

exact [igzakt] *v.* exiger; commettre des exactions. ‖ **exacting** [-ing] *adj.* exigeant [person]; épuisant [work].

exaggerate [igzadj•ré¹t] *v.* exagérer. ‖ **exaggeration** [igzadj•ré¹sh•n] *s.* exagération, f.

exalt [igzault] *v.* exalter. ‖ **exaltation** [ègzaulté¹sh•n] *s* exaltation, f.

examination [igzam•né¹sh•n] *s.* examen, interrogatoire [prisoner], m.; visite [customs]; instruction (jur.), f.; **examination-paper**, composition, épreuve. ‖ **examine** [igzamin] *v.* examiner; interroger (jur. univ.); visiter (customs). ‖ **examinee** [igzam•ní] *s.* candidat, m. ‖ **examiner** [igzamin°r] *s.* examinateur; juge d'instruction, m.

example [igzàmp'l] *s* exemple, m.

exasperate [igzasp•ré¹t] *v.* exaspérer; irriter. ‖ **exasperation** [igzasp•ré¹sh•n] *s* exaspération, f.

excavate [èksk•vé¹t] *v.* creuser. ‖ **excavation** [èksk•vé¹sh•n] *s.* excavation; fouille, f.

exceed [iksíd] *v.* excéder; outrepasser. **exceedingly**, extrêmement.

excel [iksèl] *v.* exceller; surpasser. ‖ **excellence** [èks'l•ns] *s.* excellence, f. ‖ **excellent** [èks'l•nt] *adj.* excellent.

except [iksèpt] *prep.* excepté; sauf; *conj.* à moins que; *v.* excepter; objecter (*against* contre). ‖ **excepting** [-ing] *prep.* excepté hormis. ‖ **exception** [iksèpsh•n] *s* exception, objection; opposition (jur.), f. ‖ **exceptional** [-'l] *adj.* exceptionnel.

excerpt [èksë°rpt] *v.* prendre un extrait de, extraire; [èksë°rpt] *s.* extrait, m.

excess [iksès] *s.°* excès; dérèglement. **excess baggage**, excédent de bagages ‖ **excessive** [iksèsiv] *adj.* excessif **excessively**, excessivement.

exchange [ikstshé¹ndj] *s.* échange change [money]; bureau central [telephone], m.; Bourse [place]; permutation (mil.), f.; *v.* échanger, troquer changer [money]; permuter (mil.). **rate of exchange**, taux du change.

exchequer [ikstshék°r] *s.* échiquier trésor public, m.

excise [eksa¹z] *s.* impôt indirect, m. *v.* imposer; pressurer; faire une incision dans.

excitable [iksa¹t•b'l] *adj.* excitable ‖ **excitant** [èksit•nt] *s.* excitant, m. ‖ **excitation** [èksité¹sh•n] *s.* excitation f. ‖ **excite** [iksa¹t] *v* exciter; irriter stimuler. ‖ **excited** [-id] *adj.* agité impatient; enthousiasmé. ‖ **excitement** [-m•nt] *s.* excitation; émotion; animation, f. ‖ **exciting** [-ing] *adj.* excitant émouvant; passionnant.

exclaim [iksklé¹m] *v.* s'exclamer protester. ‖ **exclamation** [èkskl•mé¹sh•n] *s.* exclamation, f.; **exclamation mark**, point d'exclamation.

exclude [ikskloud] *v.* exclure. ‖ **excluding** [-ing] *prep.* non compris. **exclusion** [iksklouj•n] *s.* exclusion, ‖ **exclusive** [ikskloustiv] *adj.* exclusif privé, fermé, **exclusive of**, sans compter, non compris

excommunicate [èksk•myoun•ké¹ *v.* excommunier. ‖ **excommunicatio** [èksk•myoun•ké¹sh•n] *s.* excommunication, f.

excoriate [iksko°°rié¹t] *v.* écorche

excrement [èkskrim•nt] *s.* excrément, m.

exculpate [èksk•lpé¹t] *v.* disculpe

excursion [iksk.ë°rj•n] *s* excursion sortie, f.; raid, m. (mil.) digression f.; **excursion train**, train de plaisir. **excursionist** [-ist] *s.* excursionniste m. f.

excusable [ikskyouz•b'l] *adj.* excu sable. ‖ **excuse** [ikskyous] *s.* excuse f.; [ikskyouz] *v* excuser; dispenser d'

execrable [èksikr•b'l] *adj.* exécrable détestable. ‖ **execrate** [-é¹t] *v.* exécre ‖ **execration** [èksikré¹sh•n] *s.* exécr tion, f.

execute [èksikyout] *v.* exécuter accomplir; mettre à mort. ‖ **executic** [èksikyoush•n] *s.* accomplissement, m exécution saisie-exécution (jur.), f. **executioner** [-•°r] *s.* bourreau, m. **executive** tègzékyoutiv] *adj.* exécut ‖ **executor** [igzékyut°r] *s.* exécute testamentaire, m.; [èksikyout°r] *s.* ex cutant, m.

exegesis [èksidjísis] (*pl.* exegeses) exégèse, f.

exemplary [igzèmpl•ri] adj. exemplaire. ‖ **exemplify** [igzèmpl•fa¹] v.
illustrer par des exemples.

exempt [igzèmpt] adj. exempt; v.
exempter. ‖ **exemption** [igzèmpsh•n] s.
exemption, f.

exercise [èks•r'sa¹z] s. exercice;
usage; devoir scolaire, m.; occupation, f.; pl. programme de variétés,
m.; v. exercer; pratiquer; faire de
l'exercice; *to be exercised about,* être
préoccupé par.

exert [igzë•rt] v. exercer; *to exert
oneself,* s'efforcer de; se dépenser. ‖
exertion [igzë•rsh•n] s. effort, m.

exhalation [èks•lé¹sh•n] s. exhalaison, f. ‖ **exhale** [èks-hé¹l] v. émettre;
(s')exhaler

exhaust [igzaust] v. achever; débiliter; s. évacuation (mech.), f.; *to be
exhausted* être à bout de forces. ‖
exhaustion [igzaustsh•n] s. épuisement, m. ‖ **exhaustive** [igzaustiv] adj.
complet.

exhibit [igzîbit] v. exhiber; exposer.
‖ **exhibition** [èks•bîsh•n] s. exhibition;
exposition, f

exhilarate [igzîl•ré¹t] v. égayer.

exhort [igzaurt] v. exhorter. ‖ **exhortation** [ègzâté¹sh•n] s. exhortation, f.

exhume [igzyoum] v. exhumer.

exigency [èks•dj•nsi] s.* exigence;
urgence, f ‖ **exigent** [èks•dj•nt] adj.
exigeant; urgent.

exiguity [èksigyouiti] s. exiguïté, f.
‖ **exiguous** [igzigyou•s] adj. exigu.

exile [ègza¹l] s. exilé; exil, m.; v.
exiler.

exist [ègzîst] v. exister. ‖ **existence**
[-•ns] s. existence, f. ‖ **existent** [-•nt]
adj. existant. ‖ **existentialism** [ègzis-
tènsh•liz'm] s existentialisme, m.

exit [ègzit] s. sortie, f.; v. sortir.

exodus [èks•d•s] s. exode, m.

exonerate [igzán•ré¹t] v. disculper;
exempter dispenser de.

exorbitant [igzaurb•t•nt] adj. exorbitant; extravagant prohibitif.

exorcism [èksau•siz'm] s. exorcisme,
m. ‖ **exorcize** [-a¹z] v. exorciser.

exotic [igzátik] adj. exotique. ‖ **exoticism** [-tisiz'm] s. exotisme, m.

expand [ikspànd] v. étendre; développer, amplifier, se dilater, s'agrandir. ‖ **expanse** [ikspàns] s. étendue, f.
‖ **expansion** [ikspànsh•n] s. expansion, dilatation, f ‖ **expansive**
[ikspànsiv] adj. expansif.

expatriate [èkspé¹trié¹t] v. expatrier.

expect [ikspèkt] v. attendre; s'attendre à; exiger; *what to expect,* à
quoi s'en tenir. ‖ **expectancy** [-•nsi]

s.* expectative; attente, f. ‖ **expectation** [èkspèkté¹sh•n] s. attente; espérance; expectative, f.; pl. espérances.

expectorate [ikspèkt•ré¹t] v. expectorer; **expectoration,** expectoration.

expediency [ikspìdi•nsi] s.* convenance; opportunité, f ; opportunisme,
m. ‖ **expedient** [ikspìdi•nt] adj. opportun; avantageux, s expédient, m.

expedition [èkspidish•n] s. diligence;
hâte; expédition, f ‖ **expeditionary**
[-•ri] adj expéditionnaire. ‖ **expeditious** [èkspidish•s] adj. expéditif.

expel [ikspèl] v expulser.

expend [ikspènd] v. dépenser. ‖
expenditure [-itsh•r] s. dépense, f. ‖
expense [ikspèns] s. dépense, f.;
frais; dépens (jur.), m. pl. ‖ **expensive**
[-iv] adj. coûteux, cher. ‖ **expensiveness** [-ivnis] s. cherté, f.

experience [ikspfri•ns] s. expérience,
f ; v. éprouver, expérimenter; subir
[feeling]. ‖ **experienced** [-t] adj.
expérimenté, expert. ‖ **experiment**
[ikspèr•m•nt] s. expérience, f.; v.
expérimenter. ‖ **experimental** [ikspé-
rimènt'l] adj. expérimental, d'essai. ‖
experimentation [ikspèr•mènté¹sh•n]
s. expérimentation, f.

expert [èkspë•rt] s. expert, spécialiste, m. [ikspë•rt] adj expert. ‖ **expertise** [èkspë•rtîz] s expertise; compétence, f. ‖ **expertness** [èkspë•rtnis] s.
maîtrise, f.

expiate [èkspié¹t] v. expier. ‖ **expiation** [èkspié¹sh•n] s. expiation, f. ‖
expiatory [èkspi•ré¹ri] adj. expiatoire.

expiration [èksp•ré¹sh•n] s. expiration, f. ‖ **expire** [ikspa¹r] v. expirer;
prendre fin, exhaler [air].

explain [iksplé¹n] v expliquer. ‖
explainable [-•b'l] adj explicable. ‖
explanation [èkspl•né¹sh•n] s. explication, f. ‖ **explanatory** [iksplàn•-
to•ri] adj explicatif.

explode [ikspló•d] v. exploser; faire
sauter, discréditer.

exploit [èksplo¹t] s. exploit, m.;
[iksplo¹t] v exploiter, utiliser; abuser
de. ‖ **exploitation** [èksplo¹té¹sh•n] s.
exploitation, f.

exploration [èkspl•ré¹sh•n] s. exploration, f. ‖ **explore** [iksplaur] v. explorer. ‖ **explorer** [-•r] s. explorateur, m.

explosion [ikspló•uj•n] s. explosion,
f. ‖ **explosive** [ikspló•usiv] adj., s.
explosif.

exponent [ikspó•un•nt] s. exposant;
représentant, interprète; exécutant, m.

export [èkspó•urt] s. exportation, f.;
article d'exportation, m.; [ikspó•urt]
v. exporter. ‖ **exportation** [èkspau•
té¹sh•n] s. exportation, f. ‖ **exporter**
[èkspau•t•r] s. exportateur, m.

expose [ikspoᵒᵘz] *v.* exposer; exhiber; démasquer. || **exposition** [èkspⁱzishᵉn] *s.* exposition; exhibition, f.; exposé, m.

expostulate [ikspằstshᵉléⁱt] *v.* gourmander, faire la morale (*with*, à).

exposure [ikspoᵒᵘjᵉr] *s.* exposition; divulgation; pose (phot.), f.

expound [ikspaᵒᵘnd] *v.* expliquer.

express [iksprès] *adj.* exprès; formel; précis; rapide; s.ᵉ exprès [messenger]; express [train], m., *Am.* factage, service de transport des colis, m.; *v.* exprimer, extraire, exposer; envoyer par exprès; *adv.* exprès; d'urgence; rapidement. || **expression** [ikspréⁱshᵉn] *s.* expression, f. || **expressive** [iksprèsiv] *adj.* expressif.

expressly [iksprèsli] *adv.* expressément, explicitement; volontairement.

expropriate [èksproᵒᵘprié¹t] *v.* exproprier; déposséder (fig.).

expulsion [ikspœlshᵉn] *s.* expulsion, f.

expunge [ikspoundj] *v.* effacer; supprimer.

expurgate [èkspᵉrgéⁱt] *v.* expurger.

exquisite [èkskwizit] *adj.* exquis, intense; *exquisite despair*, désespoir atroce. || **exquisiteness** [-nis] *s.* raffinement, m., intensité, f.

exsanguinate [èksằngkwinéⁱt] *v.* saigner à blanc; *exsanguine*, exsangue, anémique.

extant [ikstằnt] *adj.* existant.

extemporaneous [èkstémpᵉréⁱnyᵉs] *adj.* improvisé impromptu. || **extemporization** [èkstémpᵉra¹zéⁱshᵉn] *s.* improvisation, f || **extemporize** [èkstémpᵉra¹z] *v.* improviser.

extend [ikstènd] *v.* étendre; prolonger; accroître, accorder [protection]; s'étendre. || **extension** [ikstènshᵉn] *s.* extension, prolongation prorogation, f.; *extension table* table à rallonges. || **extensive** [ikstènsiv] *adj.* étendu; spacieux. || **extent** [ikstènt] *s.* étendue, f.; *to such an extent*, à tel point.

extenuate [ikstènyoué¹t] *v.* atténuer; amoindrir.

exterior [ikstiriᵉr] *adj., s.* extérieur. || **exteriorization** [èkstiᵉri²ela¹zéⁱshᵉn] *s.* extériorisation, f. || **exteriorize** [èksti²eri²era¹z] *v* extérioriser.

exterminate [ikstër̃mᵉnéⁱt] *v.* exterminer. || **extermination** [ikstër̃mᵉnéⁱshᵉn] *s.* extermination, f.

external [ikstër̃n'l] *adj.* externe.

extinct [ikstíngkt] *adj.* éteint; aboli. || **extinguish** [ikstinggwish] *v.* éteindre, détruire. || **extinguishment** [-mᵉnt] *s.* extinction, f.

extirpate [èkstᵉrpé¹t] *v.* extirper.

extol [iksto°ᵘl] *v.* exalter, glorifier.

extort [ikstaurt] *v.* extorquer. || **extortion** [ikstaurshᵉn] *s.* extorsion, f.

extra [èkstrᵉ] *adj.* supplémentaire, extra; *extra tire*, pneu de secours; *do you have an extra copy?*, avez-vous un exemplaire de trop?; *s* supplément [payment]; figurant [cinema]; extra [workman], m.; édition spéciale, f.; *adv.* extra.

extract [èkstrakt] *s.* extrait, m.; [ikstrakt] *v.* extraire. || **extraction** [ikstraksh°n] *s.* extraction; origine, f.; extrait, m.

extradite [èkstrᵉda¹t] *v.* extrader.

extraneous [ikstré¹niᵉs] *adj.* étranger (*to*, à).

extraordinary [ikstraurd'nᵉri] *adj.* extraordinaire; *extraordinarily*, extraordinairement.

extravagance [ikstravᵉgᵉns] *s.* extravagance, prodigalité, f. gaspillage, m. || **extravagant** [ikstravᵉgᵉnt] *adj.* extravagant; prodigue; exorbitant [price], excessif.

extreme [ikstrîm] *adj.* extrême; ultime, exceptionnel [case], rigoureux; avancé [opinion], *s* extrémité, f.; extrême, m., **extremely**, extrêmement. || **extremity** [ikstrèm¹ti] *s.ᵉ* extrémité, f.; extrême; bout, besoin, danger, m.

extricate [èkstriké¹t] *v* dégager.

extrinsic [èkstrínsik] *adj.* extrinsèque.

extrude [èkstroud] *v* rejeter, expulser; faire saillie, dépasser. || **extrusion** [èkstrouj°n] *s.* expulsion, f.

exuberance [igzyoubᵉrᵉns] *s.* exubérance, f. || **exuberant** [igzyoubᵉrᵉnt] *adj.* exubérant.

exult [igzœlt] *v.* exulter. || **exultation** [ègzœltéⁱshᵉn] *s.* exultation, f.

eye [a¹] *s.* œil; œillet [cloth]; chas [needle]; piton, m., vision, discrimination, f., *v.* observer, examiner; toiser; *to keep an eye on*, ne pas perdre de vue, *hook and eye*, crochet et porte, *to make eyes at*, faire les yeux doux à, *pearl-eye*, cataracte [eye]; **eye-opener**, nouvelle sen-ationnelle, **eye-wash**, collyre; tape-à-l'œil. || **eyeball** [-baul] *s.* globe de l'œil, m. || **eye-brow** [-bra°ᵘ] *s.* sourcil, m. || **eyeglass** [-glas] *s.ᵉ* lorgnon; oculaire, m.; jumelles, lunettes, f. pl. **eyelash** [-lash] *s.ᵉ* cil, m. || **eyelet** [-lit] *s* œillet de lacet, m. || **eyelid** [-lid] *s* paupière, f. || **eyesight** [-sa¹t] *s.* vue, f. || **eyesore** [-so°ᵘr] *s.* mal d'yeux; repoussoir [person], m.

eyot [èit] *s.* îlot, m.

eyrie [èri] *s.* aire [nest]; nichée, f.; nid d'aigle (arch.), m.

F

fable [fé¹b'l] s. fable, f.

fabric [fabrik] s. tissu, textile; ouvrage; édifice, m. ‖ **fabricate** [-é¹t] v. fabriquer; construire; inventer. ‖ **fabrication** [fabriké¹sh°n] s. fabrication; construction; invention, f.

fabulist [fabyoulist] s. fabuliste, m. ‖ **fabulous** [faby°l°s] adj. fabuleux.

façade [f°sâd] s. façade, f.

face [fé¹s] s. face, figure; façade; facette [diamond]; physionomie; apparence; tournure; surface, f.; aspect; cadran [dial]; œil (typogr.). m.; pl. grimace; **face-cloth,** gant de toilette, m.; Fr. Can. débarbouillette, f.; **face-lifting,** chirurgie esthétique; v. affronter; faire face; donner sur [house]; to face a coat, mettre des revers à une veste; to face out, payer d'audace; to about-face, faire demi-tour (mil.).

facet [fasit] s. facette, f.

facetious [f°sish°s] adj. facétieux.

facial [fé¹sh°l] adj. facial.

facilitate [f°sílité¹t] v. faciliter. ‖ **facility** [f°síl°ti] s. facilité, f.

facing [fé¹sing] s. revêtement; revers; parement [cloth]. m.

fact [fakt] s. fait, m.; as a matter of fact, en réalité.

faction [faksh°n] s. faction, f.

factor [fakt°r] s. facteur; agent, m.; v. mettre en facteur. ‖ **factorage** [-ridj] s. courtage; droits de commission, m. pl. ‖ **factory** [faktri] s.* fabrique; usine, f.; atelier, m.

facultative [fakœlt°tiv] adj. facultatif; conditionnel; occasionnel.

faculty [fak'lti] s.* faculté, f.

fad [fad] s. marotte; vogue, f.

fade [fé¹d] v. se flétrir; dépérir; s'évanouir; disparaître.

faery [fè°ri] adj. féerique; s. pays (m.) des fées.

fag [fag] v. peiner; s'éreinter; s. trimeur, manœuvre, m.; (fam.) cigarette, cibiche, f.; fag-end, bout, mégot.

faience [fa¹auns] s. faïence, f.

fail [fé¹l] v. échouer; manquer à; faiblir; faire faillite (comm.); he will not fail to, il ne manquera pas de; without fail, sans faute. ‖ **failure** [-y°r] s. manque; manquement; échec; raté, m.; faillite; panne [current], f.

faint [fé¹nt] adj. faible; épuisé; pusillanime; vague; v. défaillir; s'évanouir; faint-hearted, lâche. ‖ **faintness** [-nis] s. faiblesse; timidité, f.; découragement, m.

fair [fèr] s. foire, f.

fair [fèr] adj. beau; belle; favorable; bon [wind]; clair [complexion]; blond [hair]; juste; moyen; adv. bien, convenablement; au net; en plein; carrément, franchement; v. tourner au beau [weather]; Am. just fair, médiocrement; fair play, franc jeu; fair price, prix honnête; to bid fair to, promettre de; a fair copy, une copie au propre. ‖ **faired** [-d] adj. fuselé; caréné (aviat.). ‖ **fairing** [-ing] s. profilage, carénage, m. (aviat.). ‖ **fairly** [-li] adv. honnêtement; loyalement; passablement. ‖ **fairness** [-nis] s. beauté; équité; honnêteté; bonne foi, f. ‖ **fairway** [-wé¹] s. passe, f.; chenal navigable (naut.); Am. parcours normal, m. [golf].

fairy [fèri] adj. féerique; s.* fée; fairyland, pays des fées.

faith [fé¹th] s. foi; fidélité; croyance; confiance, f.; to break faith, manquer à sa parole. ‖ **faithful** [-f°l] adj. fidèle; loyal. ‖ **faithfully,** loyalement; fidèlement. ‖ **faithfulness** [-nis] s. fidélité; loyauté, f. ‖ **faithless** [-lis] adj. infidèle; déloyal. ‖ **faithlessness** [-lisnis] s. déloyauté; infidélité; incroyance, f.

fake [fé¹k] s. trucage; faux, m.; adj. truqué, falsifié; prétendu, feint; v. truquer, maquiller; feindre.

fakir [fâki°r] s. fakir, m.

falange [f°lândj] s. phalange, f.

falcon [faulk°n] s. faucon, m. ‖ **falconry** [-ri] s. fauconnerie, f.

fall [faul] s. chute; tombée [night]; déchéance; baisse [price]; cascade [water]; décrue [waters], f.; renversement [government]; éboulement [earth]; automne [season], m.; v.* tomber; baisser; succomber; to fall back, se replier (mil.); to fall into a spin, descendre en vrille (aviat.); to fall behind, rester en arrière; to fall out with, se brouiller avec; to fall through, s'échouer; fall guy, « lampiste » (fam.). ‖ **fallen** [-°n] p. p. of to fall. ‖ **falling** [-ing] s. chute, f.; falling away, amaigrissement, affaissement; falling back, repli; falling in, écroulement [building], rassemblement (mil.).

fallow [falo°u] adj. en jachère; s. jachère, f.; v. jachérer.

false [fauls] adj. faux, fausse; false answer, faux témoignage (jur.); to play false, tricher, tromper; falsely, faussement. ‖ **falsehood** [-houd] s. fausseté, f.; mensonge, m. ‖ **falseness** [-nis] s. fausseté; perfidie, f. ‖ **falsification** [fâlsifiké¹sh°n] s. falsification,

f. ‖ **falsify** [-efaⁱ] v. falsifier. ‖ **falsity** [-eti] s. fausseté, f.

falter [faulteʳ] v. chanceler; hésiter; balbutier; s. balbutiement; tremblement; vertige, m.

fame [féⁱm] s. renommée, réputation, f.; of ill fame, mal famé. ‖ **famed** [-d] adj. célèbre, réputé.

familiar [femílyeʳ] adj. familier; intime; familiarisé (with, avec); s. familier, m. ‖ **familiarity** [femiliarᵉti] s.* familiarité, f. ‖ **familiarize** [femílyeraⁱz] v. familiariser. ‖ **family** [famli] s.* famille, f.; family name, nom de famille; family tree, arbre généalogique; to be in a family way, être enceinte.

famine [famⁱn] s. famine, f.

famish [famish] v. affamer; mourir de faim.

famous [féⁱmes] adj. fameux; célèbre; renommé.

fan [fàn] s. éventail; ventilateur; van; Am. amateur, admirateur, m.; v. éventer; vanner [grain]; attiser [fire]; to fan out, se déployer (mil.).

fanatic [fenatik] adj., s. fanatique. ‖ **fanaticism** [fenatᵉsizᵉm] s. fanatisme, m.

fanciful [fànsifᵉl] adj. capricieux; fantasque; fantastique. ‖ **fancy** [fànsi] s.* fantaisie; imagination, f.; goût; caprice, m.; v. s'imaginer; avoir du goût pour; to take a fancy to, s'éprendre de; to fancy oneself, s'imaginer; fancy ball, bal costumé; fancy goods, nouveautés, fantaisies.

fang [fàng] s. croc [dog]; crochet [snake], m.; racine [tooth], f.

fantastic [fàntastik] adj. fantastique; extravagant. ‖ **fantasy** [fàntᵉsi] s.* fantaisie; imagination, f.; caprice, m.

far [fàr] adv. loin; au loin; adj. lointain; éloigné; reculé; far and wide, de tous côtés; in so far as, dans la mesure où; as far as, aussi loin que, autant que; how far? jusqu'où; so far, jusqu'ici; far from it, tant s'en faut; by far, de beaucoup; farfetched, recherché; faraway, lointain.

farce [fàrs] s. farce, f.

fare [fèeʳ] s. prix du voyage, de la course; tarif, m.; nourriture, f.; v. voyager; avoir tel ou tel sort; se porter [health]; bill of fare, menu, carte; round trip fare, prix d'un aller et retour. ‖ **farewell** [-wèl] s. adieu, m.

farina [feraⁱne] s. farine, f.; amidon, m.

farm [fàrm] s. ferme; métairie, f.; v. affermer; exploiter; farm products, produits agricoles; to farm out, donner à ferme. ‖ **farmer** [-eʳ] s. fermier; cultivateur, Fr. Can. habitant, m. ‖

farming [-ing] s. agriculture; exploitation agricole, f.; adj. agricole; de la terre.

farrier [farieʳ] s. maréchal-ferrant, m.

farsightedness [fàrsaⁱtidnis] s. clairvoyance; presbytie (med.), f.

farther [fàrzheʳ] adv. plus loin; audelà; en outre; davantage, de plus; adj. ultérieur; plus éloigné. ‖ **farthest** [fàrzhist] adv. le plus loin; adj. le plus éloigné.

farthing [fàrzhing] s. liard, sou, m.

fascinate [fas'néⁱt] v. fasciner, séduire. ‖ **fascination** [fas'néⁱsheⁿ] s. fascination, f.

fascism [fashiz'm] s. fascisme, m. ‖ **fascist** [-ist] s. fasciste, m.

fashion [fasheⁿ] s. façon; forme, mode, f.; usage; style, m.; v. façonner; former; to go out of fashion, passer de mode; to bring into fashion, mettre à la mode; after a fashion, tant bien que mal, en quelque sorte; fashion-show, présentation de collection; fashion-writer, chroniqueur de mode. ‖ **fashionable** [-eb'l] adj. élégant, à la mode, chic.

fast [fast] adj. rapide; dissipé [life]; en avance [clock]; adv. vite, rapidement; to live fast, mener la vie à grandes guides.

fast [fast] s. jeûne, m.; v. jeûner; breakfast, déjeuner; fast day, jour maigre.

fast [fast] adj. ferme; solide; fixe; amarré (naut.); bon teint [dye]; serré [tie]; fidèle [friend]; profond [sleep]; adv. solidement; profondément; fermement.

fasten [fas'n] v. fixer; attacher; fermer [door]; agrafer; cramponner; to fasten on, imputer à. ‖ **fastener** [-eʳ] s. agrafe, f.; fermoir, m.; paper fastener, trombone; zip-fastener, fermeture à glissière, fermeture Éclair.

fastidious [fastidies] adj. difficile, délicat, chipoteur.

fastness [fastnis] s. fermeté; forteresse; promptitude; dissipation, licence, f.

fat [fat] adj. gros; gras; s. graisse, f.; gras, m.; v. engraisser; fat profits, profits substantiels.

fatal [féⁱt'l] adj. fatal; mortel [disease]. ‖ **fatalism** [-téliz'm] s. fatalisme, m. ‖ **fatalist** [-tᵉlist] s. fataliste, m. f. ‖ **fatality** [fetalᵉti] s.* fatalité, f. ‖ **fate** [féⁱt] s. destin; sort, m. ‖ **fated** [-id] adj. inéluctable; marqué par le destin. ‖ **fateful** [-foul] adj. décisif; fatal.

father [fàzheʳ] s. père, m. ‖ **fatherhood** [-houd] s. paternité, f. ‖ **fatherin-law** [-ìnlau] s. beau-père, m. ‖

fatherland [-land] *s.* patrie, f. || *fatherless* [-lis] *adj.* orphelin de père. || *fatherly* [-li] *adj.* paternel; *adv.* paternellement.

fathom [fazhⁿm] *s.* brasse, f.; *v.* sonder; approfondir; pénétrer. || *fathomable* [-ⁿb'l] *adj.* sondable. || *fathomless* [-lis] *adj.* insondable; impénétrable.

fatigue [fⁿtîg] *s.* fatigue; corvée (mil.); usure [material], f.; *v.* fatiguer.

fatness [fatnis] *s.* embonpoint, m.; fertilité [land], f. || *fatten* [-'n] *v.* engraisser. || *fatty* [-i] *adj.* graisseux.

fatuity [fⁿtyouiti] *s.* sottise, f. || *fatuous* [fatshou·s] *adj.* sot, vain.

fauces [fausîz] *s. pl.* gosier, m.

faucet [fausit] *s.* robinet; fausset, m.; douille, f.

fault [fault] *s.* défaut, m.; faute; faille (geol.), f.; *to be at fault*, être en défaut; *faultfinder*, critiqueur; *faultiness*, imperfection; *faultless*, parfait. || *faulty* [-i] *adj.* fautif; en faute; défectueux, imparfait.

favo(u)r [fé·v·r] *s.* faveur, f.; *v.* favoriser; gratifier; préférer; *to have everything in one's favo(u)r*, avoir tout pour soi; *to find favo(u)r with*, se faire bien voir de. || *favo(u)rable* [-ⁿb'l] *adj.* favorable. || *favo(u)red* [-d] *adj.* favorisé; *well-favo(u)red*, de bonne mine. || *favo(u)rite* [-rit] *adj. s.* favori. || *favo(u)ritism* [fé·vritiz·m] *s.* favoritisme, m.

fawn [faun] *s.* faon, m.; *adj.* fauve.

fawn [faun] *v.* ramper, se coucher [dog]; s'aplatir, flagorner [man]. || *fawning* [-ing] *s.* servilité, flatterie, f.

fealty [fié·lti] *s.* loyauté, f.

fear [fiⁿr] *s.* crainte; peur, f.; *v.* craindre; redouter. || *fearful* [-f·l] *adj.* craintif; timide; redoutable. || *fearless* [-lis] *adj.* intrépide; sans peur. || *fearlessness* [-lisnis] *s.* intrépidité; bravoure, f.

feasible [fîz·b'l] *adj.* faisable; réalisable, praticable.

feast [fîst] *s.* fête, f.; festin, m.; *v.* fêter; régaler; *to feast one's eyes with*, se repaître les yeux de.

feat [fît] *s.* exploit, m.; *feat of arms*, fait d'armes.

feather [fezh·r] *s.* plume, f.; sillage d'un sous-marin (naut.), m.; *v.* emplumer; empenner; *to feather one's nest*, s'enrichir; *to show the white feather*, laisser voir qu'on a peur; *featherless*, déplumé; *feather-weight*, poids plume; *feathery*, couvert de plumes; duveteux; léger; doux.

feature [fîtsh·r] *s.* trait, m.; caractéristique, f.; gros titre; clou; grand

film, m.; *v.* donner la vedette à; représenter; dépeindre; imaginer; *featureless*, terne, peu caractéristique.

February [fèbrouèri] *s.* février, m.

feculent [fèkyoul·nt] *s.* féculent, m.

fecund [fèk·nd] *adj.* fécond. || *fecundate* [-é·t] *v.* féconder. || *fecundation* [fékœndé·sh·n] *s.* fécondation, f. || *fecundity* [fikœnditi] *s.* fécondité, f.

federal [fèd·r·l] *adj.* fédéral. || *federate* [fèd·rit] *adj., s.* fédéré. || *federation* [fèd·ré·sh·n] *s.* fédération; confédération, f.

fee [fî] *s.* fief; honoraires, m.; propriété héréditaire (jur.), f.; *admission fee*, droit d'entrée; *retaining fee*, provisions à un avocat.

feeble [fîb'l] *adj.* faible, débile; *feebleness*, faiblesse; *feebly*, faiblement.

feed [fîd] *v.** nourrir; faire paître [cattle]; *s.* nourriture; alimentation; pâture, f.; *fuel feed*, alimentation en combustible ou en essence; *feeding-bottle*, biberon, f. || *feeder* [-·r] *s.* mangeur; pourvoyeur; éleveur [cattle]; alimentateur (mech.), m.; mangeoire, f.

feel [fîl] *v.** sentir; se sentir; toucher; éprouver; *s.* toucher, tact, m.; sensation, f.; *to feel one's way*, avancer à tâtons; *to feel strongly on*, avoir à cœur; *to feel for*, partager la douleur de; *to feel like*, avoir envie de. || *feeler* [-·r] *s.* antenne [insect]; moustache [cat], f.; ballon d'essai, m. || *feeling* [-ing] *s.* toucher [sense]; sentiment, m.; sensation; sensibilité, f.; *adj.* sensible, ému; *feelingly*, d'une manière émue.

feet [fît] *pl. of foot*.

feign [fé·n] *v.* feindre; simuler. || *feint* [fé·nt] *s.* feinte, f.

felicitate [fèlis·té·t] *v.* féliciter. || *felicitous* [fèlisit·s] *adj.* heureux. || *felicity* [-ti] *s.** félicité, f.

fell [fèl] *v.* abattre [tree], *Fr. Can.* bûcher; rabattre [seam]; *pret. of to fall.*

fellow [fèloou] *s.* camarade, compagnon; individu; membre [society]; universitaire; pendant [thing], m.; *fellow citizen*, concitoyen; *fellow student*, condisciple. || *fellowship* [-ship] *s.* association; camaraderie; situation universitaire; bourse à un étudiant gradué, f.

felon [fèl·n] *s.* criminel; panaris (med.), m.; *adj.* perfide, scélérat. || *felony* [-i] *s.** crime, m.

felt [fèlt] *pret. of to feel.*

felt [fèlt] *s.* feutre, m.; *adj.* en feutre; *v.* (se) feutrer.

female [fîmé·l] *adj.* féminin; femelle; *s.* femme; femelle, f.; *female friend*, amie.

feminine [fèmᵉnĭn] *adj.* féminin;
efféminé. ‖ **femininity** [fèminĭnĭti] *s.*
féminité; gent féminine, f. ‖ **feminism**
[fèminĭz'm] *s.* féminisme, m. ‖ **feminist** [-ĭst] *adj., s.* féministe.

fen [fèn] *s.* marécage, m.

fence [fèns] *s.* clôture; enceinte;
escrime, f.; receleur, m.; *v.* enclore;
faire de l'escrime; *to be on the fence,*
être indécis. ‖ **fencing** [-ĭng] *s.*
escrime, f.; **fencing school,** salle
d'armes.

fend [fènd] *v.* parer; détourner. ‖
fender [-ᵉr] *s.* pare-feu; *Am.* garde-
boue; pare-choc [auto] m.; *Am.*
chasse-pierres, m.

fennel [fèn'l] *s.* fenouil, m.

ferment [fë˝rmᵉnt] *s.* ferment, m.;
agitation, f.; [fᵉrmènt] *v.* fermenter.
‖ **fermentation** [fë˝rmᵉntéⁱshᵉn] *s.* fermentation, f.

fern [fë˝rn] *s.* fougère, f.

ferocious [fᵉroᵘshᵉs] *adj.* féroce. ‖
ferocity [fᵉràsᵉti] *s.* férocité, f.

ferret [fèrĭt] *s.* furet, m.; *v.* fureter;
dénicher; *to ferret out,* dépister.

ferrous [fèrᵉs] *adj.* ferreux.

ferrule [fèrᵉl] *s.* virole, f.; bout
ferré; manchon, m.

ferry [fèri] *s.°* bac; passage de rivière, m.; *v.* passer en bac; transporter par mer ou air; *aerial ferry,*
pont transbordeur; *ferry-boat,* bac
transbordeur, *Fr. Can.* traversier;
ferryman, passeur, **ferry-pilot,** con-
voyeur.

fertile [fë˝rt'l] *adj.* fertile. ‖ **fertility**
[fë˝rtĭlᵉti] *s.°* fertilité; fécondation, f.
‖ **fertilize** [fë˝rtĭlaⁱz] *v.* fertiliser;
féconder. ‖ **fertilizer** [fë˝rtĭlaⁱzᵉr] *s.*
engrais, m.

fervent [fë˝rvᵉnt] *adj.* fervent. ‖
fervid [-vĭd] *adj.* bouillant, ardent. ‖
fervo(u)r [fë˝rvᵉr] *s.* ferveur; ardeur, f.

fester [fèstᵉr] *v.* (s')envenimer; *s.*
pustule, f.

festival [fèstᵉv'l] *s.* fête, f. ‖ **festi-
vity** [fèstĭvᵉti] *s.°* festivité; fête, f.

festoon [fèstoᵘn] *s.* guirlande, f.;
feston, m.; *v.* festonner.

fetch [fètsh] *v.* aller chercher; amener; apporter; pousser [sigh]; atteindre
[price].

fetid [fètĭd] *adj.* fétide.

fetish [fétĭsh] *s.* fétiche, m.

fetter [fètᵉr] *s.* entraves, f. pl.; fers,
m. pl.; *v.* entraver; enchaîner.

feud [fyoud] *s.* brouille à mort;
haine; vendetta, f.

feud [fyoud] *s.* fief, m.; **feudal,** féodal; **feudality,** féodalité, f.

fever [fīvᵉr] *s.* fièvre, f.; *scarlet
fever,* scarlatine; *swamp fever,* paludisme, malaria. ‖ **feverish** [-rĭsh] *adj.*
fiévreux; fébrile. ‖ **feverishness** [-rĭsh-
nĭs] *s.* fièvre, fébrilité, f.

few [fyou] *adj., pron.* peu; *a few,*
quelques.

fiancé(e) [fĭenséⁱ] *s.* fiancé, m.; fiancée, f.

fib [fĭb] *s.* petit mensonge, m.; blague,
f.; *v.* mentir, blaguer. ‖ **fibber** [-ᵉr] *s.*
menteur, blagueur, m.

fiber [faⁱbᵉr] *s.* fibre, f.; filament, m.

fibroma [faⁱbroᵘmᵉ] *s.* fibrome, m.

fibrous [faⁱbrᵉs] *adj.* fibreux.

fickle [fĭk'l] *adj.* inconstant; volage.
‖ **fickleness** [-nĭs] *s.* inconstance, f.

fiction [fĭkshᵉn] *s.* fiction, f. ‖ **fictitious** [fĭktĭshᵉs] *adj.* fictif.

fiddle [fĭd'l] *s.* violon, m.; *v.* jouer du
violon; gesticuler; **fiddle stick,** archet; **fiddlesticks,** sornettes, balivernes.

fidelity [faⁱdèlᵉti] *s.* fidélité, f.

fidget [fĭdjĭt] *v.* s'agiter; *s.* sursaut,
m.; agitation, f.; agité, m. ‖ **fidgety**
[-ĭ] *adj.* remuant; fébrile.

field [fīld] *s.* champ; champ de bataille; terrain; espace, m.; campagne,
f.; *in the field,* aux armées; *field of
study,* spécialité; *landing field,* terrain d'atterrissage.

fiend [fīnd] *s.* diable, démon; *Am.* fanatique, mordu, m.; **fiendish,** diabolique, démoniaque.

fierce [fĭᵉrs] *adj.* féroce; furieux; farouche. ‖ **fierceness** [-nĭs] *s.* férocité;
fureur; violence, f.

fiery [faⁱri] *adj.* embrasé, flamboyant; fougueux, ardent.

fifteen [fĭftīn] *adj., m.* quinze. ‖ **fifteenth** [-th] *adj., s.* quinzième. ‖ **fifth**
[fĭfth] *adj., s.* cinquième. ‖ **fiftieth**
[fĭftĭith] *adj., s.* cinquantième. ‖ **fifty**
[fĭfti] *adj.* cinquante.

fig [fĭg] *s.* figue, f.; **fig-tree,** figuier.

fight [faⁱt] *s.* combat, m.; lutte; rixe;
action (mil.), f.; *v.°* combattre; se
battre; *air fight,* combat aérien; *dog
fight,* mêlée générale; *hand-to-hand
fight,* corps-à-corps. ‖ **fighter** [-ᵉr] *s.*
combattant; lutteur; avion de combat
ou de chasse, m. ‖ **fighting** [-ĭng] *s.*
combat, m.; lutte, f.

figuration [fĭgyouréⁱshᵉn] *s.* figuration; forme, f. ‖ **figurative** [fĭgyou-
rᵉtĭv] *adj.* figuré. ‖ **figure** [fĭgyᵉr] *s.*
figure; silhouette; forme; taille; tournure, f.; dessin; chiffre, m.; *v.* figurer; calculer; *to figure on,* compter
sur; se trouver sur [list].

filament [fĭlᵉmᵉnt] *s.* filament, m.

file [faⁱl] *s.* lime, f.; *v.* limer.

file [fa¹l] *s.* file, f.; classeur; *pl.* dossier, m.; *v.* défiler; classer; *file card,* fiche; *file closer,* serre-file; *card index file,* fichier.

filial [fíli•l] *adj.* filial. ‖ *filiation* [filié¹sh•n] *s.* filiation, f.

filing [fa¹ling] *s.* limaille, f.

fill [fil] *s.* suffisance, f.; content; remblai [road], m.; *v.* remplir; tenir [part]; combler; rassasier [food]; plomber [tooth]; occuper [post]; exécuter [order]; *to fill out a blank,* remplir une formule; *to fill in,* insérer. ‖ *filler* [-•ʳ] *s.* compte-gouttes, m.; recharge, f.

fillet [filé¹] *s.* filet [meat], m.; [fílit] *s.* bande, f.; ruban; bandeau; bloc de remplissage (aviat.); collet (mech.), f.

filling [fíling] *s.* remplissage; plombage, m.; *filling-station,* poste d'essence; *gold filling,* aurification, f.

filly [fíli] *s.*° pouliche, f.

film [film] *s.* pellicule; taie; bande [cinema]; couche, f.; film, m.; *v.* couvrir d'une pellicule; filmer.

filter [fílt•ʳ] *s.* filtre, m.; *v.* filtrer; *filter-tip,* bout filtre.

filth [filth] *s.* ordure, f.; immondice, m.; *filthy,* sale, immonde.

fin [fin] *s.* nageoire [fish]; ailette [auto]; aileron (aviat.); *Am.* billet de cinq dollars (slang), m.

final [fa¹n'l] *adj.* final; définitif; *finally,* finalement, définitivement.

finance [f•nàns] *s.* finance, f.; *pl.* finances, f.; fonds, m.; *v.* financer; commanditer. ‖ *financial* [f•nànsh•l] *adj.* financier, pécuniaire. ‖ *financier* [fin•nsí•ʳ] *s.* financier, m. ‖ *financing* [f•nànsing] *s.* financement, m.

finch [fintsh] *s.* pinson, m.

find [fa¹nd] *v.*° trouver; découvrir; constater; *to find guilty,* déclarer coupable. ‖ *finder* [-•ʳ] *s.* trouveur [person]; chercheur; viseur (phot.), m.; lunette de repère [telescope], f.; *altitude finder,* altimètre. ‖ *finding* [-ing] *s.* découverte; constatation; trouvaille, f.; *pl.* conclusions (jur.), f.

fine [fa¹n] *s.* amende, f.; *v.* mettre à l'amende.

fine [fa¹n] *adj.* fin; menu; subtil; joli; raffiné; excellent; *I am fine, je vais bien; fine arts,* beaux-arts; *v.* affiner; amincir; clarifier [wine]. ‖ *fineness* [-nis] *s.* finesse; délicatesse; élégance; excellence, f. ‖ *finery* [-•ri] *s.* parure, f. ‖ *finesse* [fínès] *s.* ruse; habileté; impasse, f.; *v.* finasser.

finger [fíng•ʳ] *s.* doigt, m.; *little finger,* auriculaire; *middle finger,*

médius; *ring finger,* annulaire; *fingerprint,* empreinte digitale; *finger tip,* bout du doigt; *v.* toucher, palper.

finicky [fíniki] *adj.* difficile, délicat, chipoteur; soigné, fignolé.

finish [fínish] *v.* finir; terminer; compléter; *s.* fin; conclusion, f.; fini; finissage, m.; *he's finished,* c'en est fait de lui; *to finish up,* mettre la dernière main.

Finn [fin] *s.* Finnois, m.

fir [fëʳ] *s.* sapin, m.

fire [fa¹r] *s.* feu; incendie; tir, m.; flamme, ardeur, f.; *v.* allumer; enflammer; incendier; faire feu; congédier; *belt of fire,* zone de feu; *drum fire,* feu roulant; *firearm,* arme à feu; *firebrand,* tison; *firecracker,* pétard; *fire extinguisher,* extincteur; *fire insurance,* assurance-incendie; *firewood,* bois de chauffage; *fireworks,* feu d'artifice. ‖ *firehouse* [-ha⁰us] *s.* poste des pompiers, m. ‖ *fireman* [-m•n] *s.* (*pl. firemen*) *s.* pompier; chauffeur (mech.), m. ‖ *fireplace* [-plé¹s] *s.* cheminée, f.; âtre, foyer, m. ‖ *fireproof* [-pruuf] *adj.* incombustible; ignifuge. ‖ *fireside* [-sa¹d] *s.* coin du feu, m.; *adj.* intime. ‖ *firewater* [-waut•ʳ] *s.* eau-de-vie, f.; alcool, m.

firm [fëʳm] *s.* firme, maison de commerce, f.

firm [fëʳm] *adj.* ferme; résolu; stable [price]; *firmly,* fermement; solidement.

firmament [fëʳm•m•nt] *s.* firmament, m.

firmness [fëʳmnis] *s.* fermeté, f.

first [fëʳst] *adj.*, *s.* premier; *adv.* premièrement; *s.* commencement, début, m.; *at first,* d'abord; *first aid kit,* pansement individuel; *first born,* aîné; *first class,* de qualité supérieure; *first hand,* de première main; *first rate,* de premier ordre; *first sergeant,* sergent-chef.

fisc [fisk] *s.* fisc, m. ‖ *fiscal* [-'l] *adj.* fiscal; *fiscal year,* année budgétaire.

fish [fish] (*pl. fishes*) *s.* poisson, m.; *v.* pêcher; *fish bone,* arête; *fish story,* histoire à dormir debout. ‖ *fisher* [-•ʳ], *fisherman* [-•ʳm•n] *s.* pêcheur, m. ‖ *fishing* [-ing], *fishery* [-•ri] *s.*° pêche, f. ‖ *fishhook* [-houk] *s.* hameçon, m. ‖ *fishmonger* [-moeng•ʳ] *s.* marchand de poisson, m. ‖ *fishwife* [-wa¹f] *s.* marchande (f.) de poisson; harangère, f. ‖ *fishy* [-¹] *adj.* poissonneux; de poisson; vitreux; louche.

fission [fish•n] *s.* fission, f.

fissure [fish•ʳ] *s.* fissure; fente, f.

fist [fist] *s.* poing, m.; *to clench one's fist,* serrer les poings.

fistula [fístshoule] *s.* fistule (med.), f.

fit [fít] *s.* attaque; crise (med.), f.; accès, m.; *by fits and starts*, par accès; *to throw into fits*, donner des convulsions à. ‖ **fitful** [-fᵉl] *adj.* agité; capricieux; variable; quinteux (med.).

fit [fít] *adj.* propre, convenable; opportun; en bonne santé; *s.* ajustement; ajustage (mech.), m.; *v.* convenir à; ajuster; adapter; *to think fit*, juger bon; *to fit in with*, s'harmoniser avec; *to fit out*, équiper; *to fit up a shop*, monter une boutique; *a coat that fits you*, un habit qui vous va bien. ‖ **fitness** [-nis] *s.* aptitude; bienséance; justesse, f. ‖ **fitted** [-id] *adj.* ajusté, monté. ‖ **fitter** [-ᵉr] *s.* ajusteur; monteur (mech.); installateur (electr.); essayeur [tailor], m. ‖ **fitting** [-ing] *adj.* convenable, opportun; *s.* garniture, fournitures, f.; agencement; montage, m.

five [faïv] *adj.* cinq.

fix [fíks] *v.* fixer; établir; régler; repérer [radio]; *s.ᵉ* embarras, m.; difficulté, f.; point observé (naut.), m. ‖ **fixed** [-t] *adj.* fixe; ferme; *to be fixed for*, disposer de. ‖ **fixity** [-iti] *s.* fixité, f. ‖ **fixture** [-tshᵉr] *s.* meuble, m.

fizz [fiz] *v.* siffler; pétiller; *s.* pétillement, m.; *fizz-water*, eau gazeuse.

flabbergasted [flabᵉrgâstid] *adj.* éberlué, ébahi; épaté.

flabby [flabi] *adj.* flasque, mou.

flaccid [flaksid] *adj.* mou, flasque.

flag [flag] *s.* glaïeul, m.

flag [flag] *s.* dalle [stone], f.; *v.* daller.

flag [flag] *s.* drapeau; pavillon, m.; *v.* pavoiser; faire des signaux; *flag at half-mast*, drapeau en berne; *flagship*, vaisseau amiral; *flagstaff*, hampe.

flag [flag] *v.* faiblir, languir.

flagrant [fléígrᵉnt] *adj.* flagrant; énorme, scandaleux.

flail [fléíl] *s.* fléau, m.; *v.* battre au fléau [corn].

flair [flèᵉr] *s.* flair, instinct, m.

flake [fléík] *s.* flocon [snow], m.; écaille, f.; *v.* floconner; s'écailler; *corn flakes*, flocons de maïs.

flame [fléím] *s.* flamme, f.; feu; zèle, m.; *v.* flamber, flamboyer; s'enflammer; *to flame up*, s'emporter; *flame thrower*, lance-flammes; *flaming*, flamboyant; passionné.

flamingo [flᵉminggoᵘ] *s.* flamant, m.

flange [flàndj] *s.* rebord; collet (mech.); patin [rail], m.

flank [flàngk] *s.* flanc, m.; *v.* flanquer; prendre de flanc.

flannel [flàn'l] *s.* flanelle, f.

flap [flap] *s.* tape, f.; claquement; coup, m.; pan [coat]; bord [hat]; battant [table]; rabat [envelope]; lobe [ear]; lambeau [flesh]; volet (aviat.); affolement (colloq.), m.; patte [pocket]; trappe [cellar], f.; *v.* taper; battre; pendre.

flare [flèᵉr] *s.* flamme vacillante; fusée éclairante, f.; feu signalisateur, m.; *v.* flamber; s'enflammer; *ground flare*, feu d'atterrissage (aviat.); *to flare up*, s'emporter.

flash [flash] *s.ᵉ* éclair; éclat; trait; clin d'œil, instant, m.; *v.* jeter des lueurs; étinceler; jaillir; darder; *a flash of hope*, un rayon d'espoir; *a flash of lightning*, un éclair d'orage; *a flash of wit*, un trait d'esprit; *it flashed upon me*, soudain l'idée me vint; *news flash*, dernières nouvelles; *flashlight*, lampe de poche. ‖ **flashy** [flashi] *adj.* voyant, tapageur, criard.

flask [flask] *s.* flacon, m.; bouteille, f.; fiasque (artill.), m.

flat [flat] *adj.* plat; uni; épaté [nose]; éventé [drink]; dégonflé [tire]; monotone, terne; bémol [music]; *s.* plaine, f.; appartement; bas-fond (naut.), m.; paume [hand], f.; *to fall flat*, tomber à plat; *flat rate*, à prix fixe; *flat car*, wagon-plate-forme; *flat iron*, fer à repasser; *to sing flat*, chanter faux. ‖ **flatten** [-'n] *v.* aplanir; laminer; (s')aplatir; *flattening mill*, laminoir.

flatter [flatᵉr] *v.* flatter. ‖ **flatterer** [-rᵉr] *s.* flatteur, m. ‖ **flattering** [-ring] *adj.* flatteur; *flattery*, flatterie.

flaunt [flaunt] *v.* se pavaner; étaler; *s.* étalage, m.; parade, ostentation, f.

flavo(u)r [fléívᵉr] *s.* saveur, f.; goût; arôme; bouquet [wine], m.; *v.* donner du goût; assaisonner; aromatiser. ‖ **flavo(u)rless** [-lis] *adj.* insipide; fade.

flaw [flau] *s.* défaut; vice (jur.), m.; imperfection; paille [metal]; fêlure [glass], f.; *v.* rendre défectueux; fêler [glass]. ‖ **flawless**, impeccable.

flax [flaks] *s.* lin, m.; *flaxseed*, graine de lin; *flaxen*, de lin; blond.

flay [fléí] *v.* écorcher; s'acharner sur.

flea [flî] *s.* puce, f.; *fleabite*, piqûre de puce.

fleck [flèk] *s.* tache; moucheture, f.; *v.* moucheter.

fled [flèd] *pret.*, *p. p. of* **to flee**.

flee [flî] *v.ᵉ* fuir; s'enfuir; échapper.

fleece [flîs] *s.* toison, f.; *v.* tondre; dépouiller.

fleet [flît] *s.* flotte, f.; *home fleet*, flotte britannique.

fleet [flît] *adj.* prompt, rapide. ‖ **fleeting** [-ing] *adj.* fugace; éphémère.

Flemish [flèmish] *adj.*, *s.* flamand.

flesh [flèsh] s. chair; viande; pulpe [fruit], f.; v. assouvir; acharner [dogs]; **flesh-broth**, bouillon de viande; **flesh-eater**, carnassier; **fleshless**, décharné; **fleshliness**, désirs charnels; **flesh-worm**, asticot; **fleshy**, charnel; charnu.

flew [flou] pret. of to fly.

flex [flèks] v. fléchir. ‖ **flexibility** [flèks•bi•lѐti] s. flexibilité, f. ‖ **flexible** [flèks•b'l] adj. flexible, souple; influençable. ‖ **flexor** [flѐks•ʳ] s. fléchisseur, m. ‖ **flexure** [flѐks•ʳ] s. flexion; courbure, f.; fléchissement, m.

flick [flik] s. chiquenaude, f.; claquement; sursaut, m.; v. donner une chiquenaude à.

flicker [flik•ʳ] s. vacillement; battement [wing], m.; lueur [interest], f.; v. vaciller; clignoter; battre [wing]; trembler; papilloter.

flier [flaⁱ•ʳ] s. avion; aviateur, m.

flight [flaⁱt] s. vol; essor, m.; volée; fuite, f.; Am. unité de trois à six avions, f.; **flight of stairs**, escalier; **to put to flight**, mettre en fuite; **soaring flight**, vol à voile.

flimsy [flìmzi] adj. fragile; sans valeur; sans force; s. papier pelure, m.

flinch [flìntsh] v. fléchir; défaillir; broncher.

fling [fling] v.* jeter, lancer; désarçonner; s. coup; trait; sarcasme, m.; joyeuse vie, f.; **to fling out**, tuer; **to fling at**, viser.

flint [flìnt] s. silex, m.; pierre à briquet, à fusil, f.

flip [flìp] v. chiquenaude, f.; v. voleter; caresser ou épousseter d'une chiquenaude.

flippancy [flìp•nsi] s. désinvolture; pétulance, f. ‖ **flippant** [flìp•nt] adj. étourdi; désinvolte.

flirt [flë•ʳt] s. flirteur, m.; flirteuse, f.; v. flirter. ‖ **flirtation** [flë•ʳtéⁱsh•n] s. flirt, m.

flit [flìt] v. voltiger, voleter; s. déménagement, m.

float [floⁱt] s. flotteur (mech.); ballonnet (aviat.); radeau, train de bois, m.; v. flotter, Fr. Can. draver; surnager; renflouer (naut.); faire la planche [swimming]; lancer (comm.); **wood-floater**, Fr. Can. draveur, m. ‖ **floating** [-ing] adj. flottant; s. lancement, m.; **floating capital**, fonds de roulement.

flock [flåk] s. troupeau, m.; troupe, f.; **to flock together**, s'attrouper.

flock [flok] s. flocon, m.

floe [floⁱ] s. banquise, f.

flog [flåg] v. fouetter, flageller. ‖ **flogging** [-ing] s. flagellation, f.

flood [flœd] s. flot; flux; déluge, m.; inondation; marée [sea]; crue [river], f.; v. inonder; submerger; **floodgate**, vanne; **floodlight**, phare, projecteur; **to floodlight**, illuminer par projecteurs.

floor [floⁱ•ʳ] s. plancher; parquet; étage; sol, m.; aire; varangue (naut.), f.; **first floor**, Br. premier étage; Am. rez-de-chaussée; v. planchéier, parqueter; jeter à terre; **to take the floor**, prendre la parole.

flop [flåp] s. floc, bruit mat, m.; four (colloq.), m.; v. laisser tomber; jeter; faire floc; **to flop down**, s'affaler.

florid [flaurid] adj. fleuri; haut en couleur.

florist [floⁱrist] s. fleuriste, m. f.

floss [flaus] s. bourre de soie, f.

flotilla [floⁱtíl•] s. flottille, f.

flotsam [flaⁱts•m] s. épave, f.

flounce [flaⁱóⁿs] s. volant, m.

flounder [flaⁱóⁿd•ʳ] v. se débattre; **to flounder about**, patauger.

flounder [flaⁱóⁿd•ʳ] s. carrelet, m.

flour [flaⁱóⁿʳ] s. farine, f.; **floury**, enfariné.

flourish [flë•ʳish] s.* fioriture [music]; fanfare [trumpet]; arabesque, f.; parafe [pen]; moulinet [sword], m.; v. fleurir; faire des fioritures; brandir [sword]; prospérer.

flout [flaⁱóⁿt] v. se moquer de; s. raillerie. moquerie, f.

flow [floⁱóⁿ] s. écoulement; flux; courant, flot [music]; passage [air], m.; v. couler; s'écouler; monter; passer [air]; affluer; **to be flowing with riches** nager dans l'opulence.

flower [flaⁱóⁿ•ʳ] s. fleur, f.; v. fleurir; **flower bed**, parterre; **flower leaf**, pétale; **flower-pot**, pot à fleurs; **flower show**, exposition de fleurs. ‖ **flowered** [-d] adj. fleuri; épanoui; à fleurs. ‖ **flowery** [-i] adj. à fleurs; fleuri [style].

flowing [floⁱóⁿing] adj. coulant; fluide, facile [style].

flown [floⁱóⁿn] p. p. of to fly.

flu [flou] s. grippe, f.

fluctuate [flœktshouéⁱt] v. ondoyer; fluctuer; ballotter; osciller. ‖ **fluctuation** [flœktshouéⁱsh•n] s. fluctuation, f.

flue [flou] s. tuyau de cheminée; tuyau d'échappement, m.

fluency [flou•nsi] s. facilité [speech], f. ‖ **fluent** [flou•nt] adj. coulant; disert; **to speak fluently**, parler couramment.

fluff [flœf] s. duvet; mouton, m.; v. rendre pelucheux; pelucher; louper (theatr.); **fluffy**, duveteux; pelucheux; flou [hair].

fluid [fioui̯d] *adj.*, *s.* fluide; liquide, m.; *de-icing fluid*, liquide antigivre; *fire-extinguishing fluid*, liquide extincteur.

fluke [flouk] *s.* patte d'ancre, f.; coup de chance, m.

flung [flœng] *prep.*, *p. p. of* to fling.

flunk [flœngk] *s.* échec [exam.], m.; *v.* échouer; être recalé.

flunky [flœngki] *s.** laquais; larbin, m.

fluorescence [fiou°rès'ns] *s.* fluorescence, f. ‖ **fluorescent** [-n't] *adj.* fluorescent; à incandescence (electr.).

flurry [flë̈ˡi] *s.** agitation; commotion, f.; coup de vent, m.; *v.* agiter; troubler, émouvoir.

flush [flœsh] *s.** flux, m.; rougeur; ecchymose (med.); chasse d'eau, f.; *hot flush*, bouffée de chaleur; *adj.* éclatant; frais, fraîche; riche (*with*, de); à fleur (*with*, de); *v.* faire rougir; s'empourprer; **exalter**; laver à grande eau; *flushed*, empourpré, rouge.

fluster [flœstᵉˡ] *v.* agiter; *s.* agitation, f.; trouble, énervement, m.; *to become flustered*, se troubler, se démonter.

flute [flout] *s.* flûte; cannelure, f.; *v.* jouer de la flûte; canneler.

flutter [flœtᵉˡ] *s.* battement d'ailes; voltigement, m.; agitation; palpitation (med.), f.; *v.* voltiger; flotter au vent; palpiter [heart]; frémir; osciller (mech.); agiter; *to flutter its wings*, battre des ailes.

flux [flœks] *s.* flux; décapant, m.; *v.* purger; décaper.

fly [fla¹] *s.* mouche, f.; *fly-paper*, papier tue-mouches.

fly [fla¹] *s.** volée [baseball]; braguette, f.; couvre-bouton, m.; *v.** voler [bird, airplane]; fuir, s'enfuir; battre [flag]; *to fly at*, s'élancer sur; *to fly open*, s'ouvrir brusquement; *to fly away*, s'envoler; *to fly off the handle*, sortir de ses gonds, lâcher les pédales. ‖ **flying** [-ing] *s.* vol, m.; aviation, f.; *blind flying*, vol sans visibilité; *glider flying*, vol par planeur; *flying boat*, hydravion.

foal [fo°l] *s.* poulain, m.; pouliche, f.; ânon, m.; *v.* pouliner.

foam [fo°m] *s.* écume, mousse, f.; *v.* écumer; mousser; moutonner.

focal [fo°k'l] *adj.* focal. ‖ **focus** [fo°kᵉˢ] *s.* foyer, m.; *v.* mettre au point (phot.); concentrer; faire converger.

fodder [fâdᵉˡ] *s.* fourrage, m.

foe [fo°] *s.* ennemi, m.

foetus [fîtᵉˢ] *s.** fœtus, m.

fog [fâg] *s.* brouillard, m.; brume, f.; voile (phot.), m.; *v.* assombrir; embrumer; enbrouiller; voiler; *pea-soup fog*, purée de pois; *fog-horn*, corne de brume; *fog-light*, phare antibrouillard; *foggy*, brumeux.

foil [fo¹l] *s.* feuille [metal], f.; tain [mirror]; repoussoir, m.

foil [fo¹l] *s.* fleuret, m.

foil [fo¹l] *v.* déjouer; dépister.

fold [fo°ld] *s.* pli; repli, m.; *v.* plisser; plier; envelopper; croiser [arms]. ‖ **folder** [-ᵉˡ] *s.* plieur; plioir (compl.); dossier, m.; chemise (comm.), f. ‖ **folding** [-ing] *adj.* pliant; *folding bed*, lit pliant; *folding machine*, plieuse; *folding ruler*, mètre pliant, *Fr. Can.* pied-de-roi; *folding screen*, paravent; *folding stool*, pliant.

fold [fo°ld] *s.* bergerie, f.; parc à moutons, m.; *v.* parquer [sheep].

foliage [fo°lidij] *s.* feuillage, m.

folio [fo°lio°] *s.* folio [page]; in-folio, m.; *v.* paginer.

folk [fo°k] *s.* gens; peuple, m.; *pl.* parents, amis, m.; *adj.* du peuple, populaire; *folklore*, folklore.

follow [fâlo°] *v.* suivre; poursuivre; s'ensuivre; exercer [profession]. ‖ **follower** [-ᵉˡ] *s.* suivant; compagnon; partisan; imitateur; satellite, m. ‖ **following** [-ing] *s.* suite, f.; partisan, adepte, m.; *adj.* suivant.

folly [fâli] *s.** sottise, bêtise, absurdité, folie [purchase], f.

foment [fo°mᵉnt] *v.* fomenter.

fond [fând] *adj.* affectueux, aimant; *to be fond of*, aimer. ‖ **fondle** [-'l] *v.* caresser. ‖ **fondly** [-li] *adv.* affectueusement. ‖ **fondness** [-nis] *s.* affection, f.; attrait, m.; faiblesse, f.

font [fânt] *s.* fonts baptismaux, m. pl.; source, origine, f.

food [foud] *s.* aliment, m.; nourriture, f.; *Food Minister*, ministre du Ravitaillement; *food rations*, rations de vivres; *foodstuff*, produits comestibles, denrée alimentaire.

fool [foul] *s.* sot, imbécile; fou, bouffon, m.; *to play the fool*, faire l'idiot; *v.* faire l'imbécile; duper; *to fool away time*, perdre son temps en niaiseries. ‖ **foolish** [-ish] *adj.* sot, sotte; imbécile, *Fr. Can.* sans dessein; insensé. ‖ **foolishly** [-ishli] *adv.* sottement. ‖ **foolishness** [-ishnis] *s.* sottise, bêtise, imbécillité, f.

foot [fout] (*pl.* **feet** [fît]) *s.* pied [man]; bas [page]; fond [sail], m.; patte [animal]; base [pillar]; jambe [compasses], f.; *v.* aller à pied; fouler [ground]; faire le total de [numbers]; *footbindings*, attaches de skis; *foot-bridge*, passerelle; *footnote*, note en bas de page; **footprint**, empreinte de pas; **footrace**, course à pied; **footsoldier**, fantassin; **footstool**, tabouret; **footwarmer**, bouillotte, chaufferette. ‖ **football** [-baul] *s.* football, m. ‖ **footing** [-ing] *s.* marche; position ferme, f.; point d'appui, m. ‖ **footlights** [-la¹ts] *s. pl.* rampe (theat.), f. ‖ **footpath** [-path] *s.* bas-côté [road]; trottoir, m.; piste (f.) pour piétons. ‖ **footstep** [-stèp] *s.* pas, m. ‖ **footwear** [-wè⁰r] *s.* chaussures, f. pl.

fop [fâp] *s.* dandy, gommeux, m. ‖ **foppery** [fâp⁰ri] *s.* fatuité, f. ‖ **foppish** [-ish] *adj.* fat; d'une élégance prétentieuse.

for [faur] *prep.* pour; de; par; pendant; depuis; *conj.* car; *as for me*, quant à moi; *for the whole day*, pendant tout le jour; *to send for someone*, envoyer chercher quelqu'un; *he has been here for two months*, il est ici depuis deux mois; *to wait for*, attendre.

forage [fauridj] *s.* fourrage, m.; *v.* fourrager; aller au fourrage; **forager**, *s.* fourrageur, m.

foray [faurè¹] *s.* incursion, f.; *v.* faire une incursion; piller.

forbade [fo⁰rbad] *pret. of to forbid.*

forbear [faurbè¹r] *s.* ancêtre, m.

forbear [faurbèr] *v.*° cesser; s'abstenir de; supporter. ‖ **forbearance** [-⁰ns] *s.* abstention; patience, f.

forbid [f⁰rbid] *v.*° interdire; empêcher de. ‖ **forbidden** [-'n] *adj.* interdit, prohibé; *p. p. of to forbid.* ‖ **forbidding** [-ing] *adj.* rébarbatif, repoussant; sombre, menaçant.

forbore [faurbo⁰r] *pret. of to forbear.* ‖ **forborn** [faurbo⁰rn] *p. p. of to forbear.*

force [fo⁰rs] *s.* force; vigueur; violence; contrainte; troupe, f.; corps (mil.), m.; *armed force*, force armée (mil.), m.; *armed force*, force armée, covering forces, troupes de couverture; *landing force*, troupe de débarquement; *v.* forcer; contraindre; *to force a smile*, sourire d'une manière forcée; *to force back*, faire reculer. ‖ **forceful** [-f⁰l] *adj.* vigoureux, énergique; violent. ‖ **forcible** [-⁰b'l] *adj.* fort; énergique; violent; forcé.

forceps [faurs⁰ps] (*pl.* **forceps**) *s.* forceps, m.; *dental forceps*, davier.

ford [fo⁰rd] *s.* gué, m.; *v.* guéer.

fore [fo⁰r] *adj.* antérieur; de l'avant.

forearm [fo⁰rârm] *s.* avant-bras, m.

forebode [fo⁰rbo⁰d] *v.* pressentir; présager, annoncer.

forecast [fo⁰rkast] *s.* pronostic, m.; prévision, f.; [fo⁰rkast] *v.* pronostiquer; prédire; *prep.*, *p. p. of to forecast*; *weather forecast*, prévision météorologique.

forefather [fo⁰rfâzh⁰r] *s.* ancêtre, aïeul, m.

forefinger [fo⁰rfingg⁰r] *s.* index, m.

forefoot [fo⁰rfout] (*pl.* **forefeet** [-fît]) *s.* patte de devant, f.

forego [fo⁰rgo⁰u], *see* forgo. ‖ **foregone** [fo⁰rgaun] *p. p. of to forego*; *adj.* passé; inévitable; prévu, escompté.

foreground [fo⁰rgra⁰und] *s.* premier plan, m.

forehead [faurid] *s.* front, m.

foreign [faurin] *adj.* étranger; extérieur; *foreign office*, ministère des Affaires étrangères; *foreign service*, service diplomatique; *foreign trade*, commerce extérieur. ‖ **foreigner** [-⁰r] *s.* étranger, m.

forelock [fo⁰rlâk] *s.* mèche sur le front [hair], f.; toupet, m.

foreman [fo⁰rm⁰n] (*pl.* **foremen**) *s.* contremaître; chef (m.) de fabrication; premier juré, m.

foremast [fo⁰rmast] *s.* mât de misaine, m.

foremost [fo⁰rmo⁰ust] *adj.* premier; principal; de tête; *adv.* en avant, en premier.

forenoon [fo⁰rnoun] *s.* matinée, f.; *Fr. Can.* avant-midi, m.

forerunner [fo⁰rræn⁰r] *s.* précurseur; signe avant-coureur, m.

foresaw [fo⁰rsau] *pret. of to foresee.* ‖ **foresee** [fo⁰rsî] *v.* prévoir. ‖ **foreseen** [fo⁰rsîn] *p. p. of to foresee.*

foresight [fo⁰rsa¹t] *s.* prévision; prévoyance; mire [gun]; visée directe [survey], f.

forest [faurist] *s.* forêt, f.; *v.* boiser; **forester**, forestier, *s.*; **forestry**, sylviculture.

forestall [fo⁰rstaul] *v.* anticiper; devancer; accaparer (comm.).

foretaste [faurtè¹st] *s.* avant-goût, m.; [fautè¹st] *v.* avoir un avant-goût de.

foretell [fo⁰rtèl] *v.* prédire.

foretoken [fo⁰rto⁰uk'n] *s.* présage; [fau⁰to⁰uk'n] *v.* présager, annoncer.

foretold [fo⁰rto⁰uld] *pret.*, *p. p. of to foretell.*

forever [f⁰rèv⁰r] *adv.* pour jamais.

forewarn [fo⁰rwaurn] *v.* prévenir; avertir; prémunir, mettre en garde contre.

foreword [fo⁰rwè⁰rd] *s.* avant-propos, m.

forfeit [faurfît] *s.* amende; pénalité; déchéance, f.; *v.* être déchu de, perdre; forfaire à. ‖ **forfeiture** [faurfitsh⁰r] *s.* perte; confiscation; déchéance; forfaiture, f.

forgave [fᵉrgéⁱv] *pret. of* to forgive.

forge [faurdj] *s.* forge, f.; *v.* forger; contrefaire; falsifier. || **forgery** [-ᵉri] *s.** falsification; contrefaçon, f.; faux, m.

forget [fᵉrgèt] *v.** oublier; *to forget oneself*, s'oublier, se laisser aller. || **forgetful** [-fᵉl] *adj.* oublieux; distrait; négligent. || **forgetfulness** [-fᵉlnis] *s.* oubli, m.; inattention; négligence, f. || **forget-me-not** [-minât] *s.* myosotis, m.

forgive [fᵉrgiv] *v.** pardonner; absoudre; faire grâce. || **forgiven** [-ᵉn] *p. p. of* to forgive. || **forgiveness** [-nis] *s.* pardon, m.; grâce, f. || **forgiving** [-ing] *adj.* clément; sans rancune.

forgo [faurgoᵘ] *v.* renoncer à; se passer de.

forgot [fᵉrgât] *pret., p. p. of* to forget. || **forgotten** [fᵉrgât'n] *p. p. of* to forget.

fork [faurk] *s.* fourche; fourchette; bifurcation [road], f.; zigzag, m. [lightning]; *v.* prendre à la fourche; fourcher; bifurquer; *tuning fork*, diapason [music]; *forked*, fourchu, bifurqué; *to fork out*, abouler, casquer (colloq.).

forlorn [fᵉrlaurn] *adj.* abandonné; désespéré; misérable.

form [faurm] *s.* forme; formule; formalité; classe (educ.), f.; formulaire, banc, m.; *v.* former; façonner; arranger; se former. || **formal** [-'l] *adj.* régulier; conventionnel; cérémonieux; de pure forme. || **formality** [faurmaᵉ-eti] *s.** formalité; cérémonie, f. || **formally** [-'li] *adv.* dans les formes; cérémonieusement; solennellement. || **formation** [faurméⁱshᵉn] *s.* formation; structure, f.; ordre; dispositif, m. || **formative** [fauᵉmᵉtiv] *adj.* formatif; plastique; de formation.

former [faurmᵉr] *adj.* premier; antérieur; précédent; ancien. || **formerly** [-li] *adv.* autrefois; jadis; auparavant.

formidable [faurmidᵉb'l] *adj.* formidable; terrifiant.

formless [fauᵉmlis] *adj.* informe.

formula [faurmyᵉlᵉ] *s.* formule, f. || **formulate** [-léit] *v.* formuler.

forsake [fᵉrséⁱk] *v.** abandonner; délaisser. || **forsaken** [fᵉrséⁱkᵉn] *adj.* abandonné; *p. p. of* to forsake. || **forsook** [fᵉrsouk] *pret. of* to forsake.

forswear [faurswèr] *v.* abjurer; se parjurer; nier avec serment.

fort [foᵘrt] *s.* fort, m.

forth [foᵘrth] *adv.* en avant; (au) dehors; au loin; *to go forth*, sortir; *and so forth*, et cætera; et ainsi de suite. || **forthcoming** [-kœming] *adj.* prochain; sur le point de paraître [book]; à venir. || **forthwith** [-with] *adv.* sur-le-champ; immédiatement.

fortieth [faurtiith] *adj., s.* quarantième.

fortification [faurtᵉféⁱshᵉn] *s.* fortification, f.; *coastal fortifications*, fortifications côtières. || **fortify** [faurtᵉfaⁱ] *v.* fortifier.

fortitude [faurtᵉtyoud] *s.* force d'âme, f.

fortnight [faurtnaⁱt] *s.* quinzaine, f.; quinze jours, m.

fortress [faurtris] *s.** forteresse; place forte, f.; *flying fortress*, forteresse volante (aviat.).

fortuitous [faurtyouᵉtᵉs] *adj.* fortuit, inopiné.

fortunate [faurtshᵉnit] *adj.* fortuné. || **fortunately** [-li] *adv.* heureusement, par bonheur. || **fortune** [faurtshᵉn] *s.* fortune, f.; destin, m.; *fortune-hunter*, coureur de dot; *fortune-teller*, diseuse de bonne aventure.

forty [faurti] *adj.* quarante.

forward [faurwᵉrd] *adj.* avancé; précoce; prompt; empressé; hardi; effronté; *adv.* en avant; *s.* avant [football], m.; *v.* avancer; hâter; expédier; acheminer; faire suivre [letter]; promouvoir [plan]. || **forwarder** [-ᵉr] *s.* expéditeur, m.; expéditrice, f.; transitaire, m.; promoteur, m. (fig.).

fossil [fâs'l] *adj., s.* fossile.

foster [faustᵉr] *v.* nourrir; élever encourager [art]; *adj.* adoptif; putatif nourricier; *foster-child*, nourrisson *foster-father*, père nourricier.

fought [faut] *pret., p. p. of* to fight.

foul [faᵘl] *adj.* immonde; souillé odieux; infâme; bourbeux [water] malsain [air]; malhonnête [behavior] mauvais [weather]; grossier [language]; *foul word*, gros mot; *s.* coup irrégulier [boxing], m.; faute [sport] collision (naut.), f.; *v.* salir; souiller (s')encrasser [gun]; entrer en collision (naut.); violer la règle [sport].

found [faᵘnd] *pret., p. p. of* to find

found [faᵘnd] *v.* fonder; instituer || **foundation** [faᵘndéⁱshᵉn] *s.* fondement, m.; fondation; base; dotation, f

founder [faᵘndᵉr] *s.* fondateur; bienfaiteur, m.

founder [faᵘndᵉr] *s.* fondeur (metall.), m.

founder [faᵘndᵉr] *v.* bronche [horse]; sombrer [ship]; échouer.

foundling [faᵘndling] *s.* enfan trouvé, m.

foundry [faᵘndri] *s.** fonderie, f.

fountain [fa^{ou}nt'n] *s.* fontaine; source, f.; *fountain pen*, stylo.

four [fo^{ou}r] *adj.* quatre; *on all fours*, à quatre pattes; *fourfooted*, quadrupède; *fourscore*, quatre-vingts. ‖ **fourteen** [fo^{ou}rtîn] *adj.* quatorze. ‖ **fourteenth** [fo^{ou}rtînth] *adj., s.* quatorzième. ‖ **fourth** [fo^{ou}rth] *adj., s.* quatrième; quatre (kings, title); *s.* quart, m.

fowl [fa^{ou}l] *s.* volaille; poule, f.; oiseau, m.

fox [fâks] *s.* renard, m.; *fox-glove*, digitale; *fox-tail*, queue de renard; *foxy*, rusé, astucieux.

fraction [fraksh^en] *s.* fraction, f.; fragment, m.; *representative fraction*, échelle cartographique. ‖ *fracture* [fraktsh^er] *s.* fracture (med.); rupture, f.; *v.* fracturer (med.); rompre; se fracturer.

fragile [fradj^el] *adj.* fragile. ‖ *fragility* [fradjîliti] *s.* fragilité, f.

fragment [fragm^ent] *s.* fragment, m.

fragrance [fréⁱgr^ens] *s.* parfum, m. ‖ *fragrant* [fréⁱgr^ent] *adj.* parfumé, embaumé.

frail [fréⁱl] *adj.* fragile, frêle. ‖ *frailty* [-ti] *s.* fragilité; faiblesse, f.

frame [fréⁱm] *s.* charpente; membrure (ship), f.; châssis (window); chambranle (door); cadre (picture); bâti; couple (naut., aviat.); métier (embroidery), m.; *v.* former; construire; charpenter; encadrer (picture); inventer; *frame-work*, charpente; ossature, f.; *to frame someone*, conspirer contre quelqu'un.

franc [fràngk] *s.* franc, m.

France [fràns] *s.* France, f.

franchise [fràntshaⁱz] *s.* franchise; immunité, f.; droit constitutionnel, m.

frank [fràngk] *adj.* franc, sincère; *s.* franchise postale, f.; *v.* envoyer en franchise postale.

frankfurter [frangkf^ert^er] *s.* saucisse fumée, f.

frantic [fràntik] *adj.* frénétique; forcené.

fraternal [frat^er'n'l] *adj.* fraternel. ‖ *fraternity* [frat^er'nti] *s.* fraternité; confrérie, f.; club, m. ‖ *fraternize* [frat^er'naⁱz] *v.* fraterniser.

fraud [fraud] *s.* fraude; tromperie, f. ‖ *fraudulent* [-j^el^ent] *adj.* frauduleux; *fraudulent conversion*, détournement de fonds.

fray [fréⁱ] *s.* bagarre; mêlée, f.

fray [fréⁱ] *v.* (s')effranger, (s')effilocher; *s.* effilochure, f.

freak [frîk] *s.* caprice, m.; frasque, f.; phénomène, m.

freckle [frèk'l] *s.* tache de rousseur, f.; *freckled*, tavelé.

free [frî] *adj.* libre; exempt; aisé; gratuit; généreux; *v.* délivrer; débarrasser; affranchir; dégager (techn.); exempter (taxes); *adv.* gratis; franco; *free and easy*, sans gêne; *to make free with*, prendre des libertés avec; *delivered free*, franco à domicile; *free goods*, marchandises en franchise; *freemason*, franc-maçon; *freemasonry*, franc-maçonnerie; *free port*, franco de port; *free thinker*, libre-penseur; *Am. freeway*, autoroute; *free-wheel*, roue libre. ‖ *freedom* [-d^em] *s.* liberté; exemption, f.; sans-gêne, m.

freeze [frîz] *v.* geler; glacer; figer; (se) congeler. ‖ *freezer* [-^er] *s.* sorbetière; glacière, f. ‖ *freezing* [-ing] *adj.* glacial; réfrigérant; *freezing point*, point de congélation; *freezing up*, givrage.

freight [fréⁱt] *s.* fret; chargement, m.; cargaison, f.; *pl.* prix du fret; *v.* fréter; affréter; *freight plane*, avion de transport; *freight train*, train de marchandises.

French [frèntsh] *adj., s.* français. ‖ *Frenchman* [-m^en] (pl. Frenchmen) *s.* Français, m. ‖ *Frenchwoman* [-woum^en] (pl. Frenchwomen) *s.* Française, f.

frenzy [frènzi] *s.* frénésie, f.; transport; délire, m.; *v.* rendre fou.

frequency [frîkw^ensi] *s.* fréquence, f. ‖ *frequent* [frîkw^ent] *adj.* fréquent; [frikwènt] *v.* fréquenter. ‖ *frequentation* [frìkw^entéⁱsh^en] *s.* fréquentation, f. ‖ *frequently* [frikwèntli] *adv.* fréquemment.

fresh [frèsh] *adj.* frais, fraîche; nouveau, nouvelle; novice; *Am.* impertinent; sans gêne; *fresh water*, eau douce. ‖ *freshen* [-^en] *v.* rafraîchir; raviver; fraîchir. ‖ *freshening* [-^ening] *s.* rafraîchissement, m. ‖ *freshly* [-li] *adv.* fraîchement; nouvellement. ‖ *freshman* [-m^en] *s.* novice; « bizuth », m. ‖ *freshness* [-nis] *s.* fraîcheur; nouveauté, f.

fret [frèt] *v.* frotter; user; (s')irriter; (se) ronger; *s.* irritation; éraillure; érosion; agitation; préoccupation, f.

fret [frèt] *s.* entrelacs, m.; grecque, f.; *v.* orner.

fretful [frètfoul] *adj.* maussade; agacé, irritable.

friar [fraⁱer] *s.* frère, moine, m.

friction [frîksh^en] *s.* frottement, m.; friction, f.

Friday [fraⁱdi] *s.* vendredi, m.; *Good Friday*, vendredi saint.

fried [fraⁱd] *p. p. of* to fry.

friend [frènd] *s.* ami, amie. ‖ **friendliness** [-linis] *s.* amitié, affabilité, f. ‖ **friendly** [-li] *adj.* amical, affable ; **friendly society**, amicale. ‖ **friendship** [-ship] *s.* amitié, f.

frigate [frígit] *s.* frégate, f.

fright [fra¹t] *s.* effroi, m. ; frayeur ; horreur, f. ‖ **frighten** [-'n] *v.* épouvanter ; terrifier ‖ **frightful** [-f°l] *adj.* effroyable, terrifiant. ‖ **frightfulness** [-f°lnis] *s* horreur, f. ; terrorisme, m.

frigid [frídjid] *adj.* froid ; glacial ; frigide. ‖ **frigidity** [fridjíditi] *s.* froideur ; frigidité, f.

fringe [frìndj] *s.* frange ; bordure, f. ; *v.* franger.

frippery [fríp°ri] *s.** pacotille, camelote, f. ; *pl.* colifichets, m. pl.

frisk [frisk] *s* gambade, f. ; *v.* gambader, folâtrer ; palper, fouiller (slang). ‖ **frisky** [-i] *adj.* folâtre ; frétillant [dog] ; fringant [horse] ; sémillant.

fritter [frít°r] *s.* beignet, m. ; *v. to fritter away*, gaspiller, éparpiller [time].

frivolity [frivǽl°ti] *s.** frivolité, f. ‖ **frivolous** [frív°l°s] *adj.* frivole ; sans valeur ; injustifié ; futile.

frizzle [fríz'l] *v.* friser ; griller ; grésiller ; faire frire ; *s.* frisure, friture, f. ; **frizzy**, frisé, crêpu.

fro [fro°n], *see* to and fro.

frock [frâk] *s.* robe ; blouse, f. ; froc, m. ; **frock-coat**, redingote.

frog [frâg] *s.* grenouille ; fourchette [horse's foot], f. ; chat dans la gorge, m. ; **bullfrog**, grenouille d'Amérique, Fr. Can. ouaouaron ; **frogman**, homme-grenouille.

frolic [frâlik] *s.* ébats, m. pl. ; *v.* folâtrer, gambader ; batifoler.

from [frâm, frœm] *prep.* de ; à ; avec ; contre ; pàr ; d'après ; dès ; *the train from London*, le train de Londres ; *to borrow from*, emprunter à ; *from that point of view*, à ce point de vue ; *made from butter*, fait avec du beurre ; *to shelter from*, abriter contre ; *from spite*, par dépit *from what you say*, d'après ce que vous dites ; *from the beginning*, dès le commencement.

front [frœnt] *s* front (anat., mil.) ; devant, plastron [shirt], m. ; face ; façade [house], f. ; *v* faire face à ; donner sur ; affronter ; braver ; *to come to the front* avancer au premier rang ; *in front of*, en face de. ‖ **frontage** [-ldj] *s.* façade, largeur du front (mil.), f. ‖ **frontier** [frœnti°r] *s.* frontière, f.

frost [frâust] *s.* gelée, f. ; gel, m. ; *v.* glacer ; givrer, **glazed frost**, verglas ; **frostbitten foot**, pied gelé ; **hoar frost**, givre, gelée blanche. ‖ **frosty** [-i] *adj.* glacé ; glacial ; givré.

froth [frauth] *s.* écume ; mousse ; futilités [speech], f. ; *v.* écumer ; mousser ; *to froth at the mouth*, écumer de rage. ‖ **frothy** [-i] *adj.* écumeux ; écumant ; mousseux ; creux (fig.).

frown [fra°ºn] *s.* froncement de sourcils ; regard furieux, m. ; *v.* froncer le sourcil ; *to frown at*, regarder d'un mauvais œil.

froze [fro°ºz] *pret. of to* freeze. ‖ **frozen** [-'n] *p. p. of to* freeze.

fructify [frœkt°fa¹] *v.* fructifier.

frugal [froug'l] *adj.* frugal ; sobre ; économe.

fruit [frout] (*pl.* fruit) *s.* fruit, m. ; *v.* porter des fruits, **dried fruit**, fruits secs ; **stewed fruit**, fruits en compote ; **fruit tree**, arbre fruitier. ‖ **fruiterer** [-°r] *s.* fruitier, m. ‖ **fruitful** [-f°l] *adj.* fécond ; fructueux ; productif ; **fruitless** [-lis] *adj.* stérile ; infructueux ; improductif.

frustrate [frœstré¹t] *v.* frustrer ; faire échouer ; contrecarrer. ‖ **frustration** [frœstré¹sh°n] *s.* anéantissement, m. ; déception ; frustration, f.

fry [fra¹] *s.** friture, f. ; fretin, m. ; *v.* frire ; faire frire ; *Am.* French fries, pommes de terre frites ; **frying-pan**, poêle à frire ; **small fry**, menu fretin.

fuchsia [fyoush°] *s.* fuchsia, m.

fudge [fœdj] *s.* baliverne ; blague, f. ; fondant, m.

fuel [fyou°l] *s.* combustible ; carburant ; propergol ; aliment, m. (fig.) ; *v.* (s')alimenter en combustible ; **alcohol-blended fuel**, carburant à base d'alcool ; **coal-oil fuel**, mazout ; **fuel pump**, distributeur d'essence ; **fuel-saving**, économique ; **fuel station**, poste à essence ; **wood fuel**, bois de chauffage

fugacious [fyougé¹sh°s] *adj.* fugace. ‖ **fugacity** [fyougásiti] *s.* fugacité, f. ‖ **fugitive** [fyoudj°tiv] *adj.*, *s.* fugitif.

fulfil(l) [foulfíl] *v.* accomplir ; combler [wish] ; exaucer [prayer]. ‖ **fulfil(l)-ment** [-m°nt] *s* accomplissement, m.

full [foul] *adj.* plein ; entier ; rempli ; repu ; complet *adv* complètement ; totalement pleinement, tout à fait ; *I am full* je suis rassasié ; *in full*, complètement *two full hours*, deux bonnes heures **full dress**, grande tenue ; **full session**, assemblée plénière ; **full size** grandeur nature ; **full stop**, un point **full text**, texte intégral ; **full weight**, poids juste. ‖ **fullness** [-nis] *s* plénitude ; ampleur, abondance, f.

fuller [foul°r] *s.* foulon, m.

fumble [fœmbl] *v.* tâtonner ; hésiter ; *s.* tâtonnement, m.

fume [fyoum] *v.* fumer ; rager ; *s.* fumée, vapeur, émanation, f.

fumigate [fyoum°gé¹t] *v.* fumiger; désinfecter par fumigation.

fun [fœn] *s.* amusement, m.; plaisanterie, f.; *v.* plaisanter; *for fun,* pour rire; *to make fun of,* se moquer de; *to have fun,* s'amuser beaucoup.

function [fœngksh°n] *s.* fonction; charge; cérémonie officielle, f.; *v.* fonctionner; opérer. ‖ *functionary* [-èri] *s.°* fonctionnaire, m. f. ‖ *functionate* [-é¹t] *v.* fonctionner.

fund [fœnd] *s.* fonds, m.; caisse, f.; *v.* consolider [debts]; *fund-holder,* rentier; *sinking-fund,* caisse d'amortissement. ‖ *fundamental* [fœnd°mènt'l] *adj.* fondamental; *s.* fondement, m.

funeral [fyoun°r'l] *s.* funérailles, f. pl.; *adj.* funèbre; *funeral home,* Fr. Can. salon mortuaire. ‖ *funereal* [fyoun¹ri°l] *adj.* triste et solennel.

funicular [fyoun/kyoul°r] *s.*, *adj.* funiculaire, m.

funnel [fœn'l] *s.* entonnoir; tuyau [air], m., cheminée (naut.), f.

funny [fœni] *adj.* amusant; comique; ridicule, *the funnies,* la page comique [magazine].

fur [fër] *s.* fourrure, f.; tartre, m.; *v.* fourrer; s'entartrer; *fur trade,* pelleterie; *furrier,* fourreur.

furious [fyouri°s] *adj.* furieux.

furl [fër'l] *v.* ferler; ployer; replier.

furlough [fërlo⁰u] *s.* permission (mil.), f.; congé, m.

furnace [fër¹nis] *s.* four; foyer; fourneau, m., fournaise, f.; *blast furnace,* haut fourneau.

furnish [fër¹nish] *v.* fournir; produire; équiper; meubler [room]. ‖

furniture [fër¹nitsh°r] *s.* meubles; ameublement, m.; *Am.* équipement, m.; garniture, f.; *furniture-warehouse,* garde-meuble.

furrow [fëro⁰u] *s.* sillon; cassis, m.; ride, f.; *v.* sillonner; canneler; rider.

further [fër¹zh°r] *adj.* ultérieur; plus éloigné; additionnel; autre; *adv.* plus loin; plus tard, ultérieurement; *v.* promouvoir. ‖ *furthermore* [-mo⁰ur] *adv.* de plus. ‖ *furthest* [fër¹zhist] *adj.* le plus éloigné; *adv.* au plus tard, au plus loin.

furtive [fër¹tiv] *adj.* furtif.

furuncle [fyou°rœngk'l] *s.* furoncle, m.

fury [fyouri] *s.°* furie, m.

furze [fërz] *s.* ajonc, m.

fuse [fyouz] *v.* fondre; liquéfier; étoupiller [charge]; *see fuze.*

fuselage [fyouz'lidj] *s.* fuselage, m.

fusible [fyouzⁱb'l] *adj.*, *s.* fusible.

fusion [fyouj°n] *s.* fusion; fonte, f.; fusionnement; fondage (metall.), m.

fuss [fœs] *s.°* vacarme; embarras, m.; dispute, f.; *v.* tatillonner; faire des histoires, *fussy,* faiseur d'embarras; affairé; voyant.

futile [fyout'l] *adj.* futile; frivole.

future [fyoutsh°r] *adj.* futur; *s.* avenir, m., *futurist,* futuriste.

fuze [fyouz] *s.* fusée; mèche; amorce, f.; *electric fuze,* plomb, fusible; *see fuse.*

fuzz [fœz] *s.* duvet, m.; peluche, f. ‖ *fuzzy* [-i] *adj.* duveteux; flou (phot.); bouffant [hair]; incertain; *to be fuzzy about,* ne pas se rappeler clairement.

G

gab [gab] *v.* bavarder; *s.* faconde; loquacité, f.; *gift of the gab,* bagout.

gabardine [gab°rdîn] *s.* gabardine, f.

gabble [gab'l] *v.* babiller; *s.* babil, bavardage, m.

gable [gé¹b'l] *s.* pignon, m.

gad [gad] *v. to gad about,* vagabonder; courir la pretantaine.

gadfly [gadfla¹] *s.°* taon, m.

gadget [gadjit] *s.* dispositif; bidule (colloq.), m.

gage, *see gauge.*

gaiety [gé¹eti] *s.°* gaieté, f. ‖ *gaily* [gé¹li] *adv.* gaiement, allègrement.

gain [gé¹n] *s.* gain; profit, m.; *v.* gagner avancer [clock]. ‖ *gainer* [-°r] *s.* gagnant, gagneur, m.

gait [gé¹t] *s.* démarche; allure; cadence f., pas (mil.), m.

gale [gé¹l] *s.* coup de vent; grain; éclat [laughter], m.

gall [gaul] *s.* fiel, m.; bile; *Am.* impudence, f.; *gall bladder,* vésicule biliaire.

gall [gaul] *s.* écorchure; irritation, f.; *v.* écorcher fâcher blesser.

gallant [gal°nt] *adj* vaillant, noble; [g°lænt] *adj.* galant, courtois, *s.* galant, amoureux, *m.* ‖ *gallantry* [gal°ntri] *s.* vaillance; élégance; galanterie; intrigue amoureuse, f.

gallery [gal°ri] *s.°* galerie, f.; balcon, m.

galley [gali] *s.* galère ; cuisine (naut.), f.; *galley proof*, placard (typogr.); *galley slave*, galérien.

gallon [gal⁰n] *s* gallon, m.

gallop [gal⁰p] *s.* galop, m.; *v.* gáloper ; faire galoper.

gallows [galoᵘz] *s. pl.* potence, f.; gibet, m . *gallows bird*, gibier de potence

galosh [g⁰lǎsh] *s.* galoche, f.; caoutchouc [shoe]. m.

galvanize [galv⁰na¹z] *v.* galvaniser; stimuler

gamble [gàmb'l] *v.* jouer; risquer; *to gamble away*, perdre au jeu ; *s.* spéculation de hasard, f.; *gambling-house*, maison de jeu, *Fr. Can.* barbote.

gambol [gàmb⁰l] *v.* gambader; *s.* gambade cabriole, f.

game [gé¹m] *s.* jeu, amusement, match, m., *Fr Can.* joute, f.; gibier, m.; intrigue f.; *adj* courageux, résolu, crâne *Am* boiteux (fam.); *game-bird*, gibier a plumes *game-preserves*, chasses gardées, *small game*, men⁰ gibier, *to play a game*, faire une partie

gamut [gam⁰t] *s* gamme, f.

gander [gand⁰r] *s* jars, m.

gang [gang] *s* bande ; équipe, f.

ganglion [gangli⁰n] *s* ganglion, m.

gangrene [gànggrin] *s.* gangrène, f.; *v.* gangrene

gangster [gàngst⁰r] *s.* bandit, gangster, m

gangway [gàngwé¹] *s.* passerelle (naut.), coupée (naut.), f.; passage, couloir allée f

gap [gap] *s* brèche ; trouée ; ouverture ; lacune f interstice , col de montagne m ; ébrécher ; échancrer.

gape [gé¹p] *s* bâillement m.; *v.* bâille bayer au corneilles.

garage [g⁰rǎj] *s* garage, m.

garb [gàrb] *s* vêtement, m.; apparence allure f vêtir, habiller

garbage [gàrbidj] *s* rebuts, déchets, détritus n pl ordures, f. pl.; *garbage can* poubelle

garden [gàd'n] *s* jardin, m.; *v.* jardiner, *gardener*, jardinier *gardening*, jardinage *garden party*, garden-party

gargle [gàng'l] *s* gargarisme, m.; *v.* se gargarise

garish [gé⁰rish] *adj* cru; criard.

garland [gàrl⁰nd] *s* guirlande, f.

garlic [gàɔ lik] *s* ail m. (*pl* aulx).

garment [gàrm⁰nt] *s.* habit, m.

garner [gàrn⁰r] *v.* stocker, engranger, amasser; *s.* grenier, m.

garnish [gàrnish] *v.* garnir; *s.* garniture, f.

garret [garit] *s.* mansarde, f.

garrison [gares'n] *s.* garnison, f.; *v.* être en garnison

garrulous [gàrel⁰s] *adj.* bavard; volubile verbeux

garter [gàrt⁰r] *s.* jarretière, f.; *v.* attacher avec une jarretière ; *Br.* décorer de l'ordre de la Jarretière ; *Am. garter belt*, porte-jarretelles.

gas [gas] *s* * gaz, m., *Am.* essence, f.; *v* gazer asphyxier, *mustard gas*, ypérite *poison gas*, gaz toxique, *tear gas*, gaz lacrymogène *gas-burner*, bec de gaz *gas-meter*, compteur à gaz. ‖ *gaseous* [-¹⁰s] *adj* gazeux.

gash [gash] *s.* * balafre, f.; *v.* balafrer; entailler

gasify [gasifa¹] *v.* gazéifier.

gasoline [gaslin] *s. Am.* essence, f.

gasp [gasp] *s.* halètement; souffle, m.; *v.* haleter

gastronomy [gastrân⁰mi] *s.* gastronomie, f.

gate [gé¹t] *s* porte; grille, f.; *gateway*, passage, portail.

gather [gazh⁰r] *v* assembler; amasser; recueillir prendre [speed]; cueillir [fruit] froncer percevoir [taxes]; rassemble [strength], *s* froncis m. ‖ *gathering* [-ring] *s* assemblée, réunion, récolte cueillette, fronces, perception [taxes] f.; rassemblement; attroupement m

gaudy [gaudi] *adj.* voyant; fastueux.

gauge [gé¹dj] *s* jauge; mesure, f.; calibre gabarit indicateur, écartement [wheels] m capacité, f (fig.); *v.* jauger estimer mesurer; calibrer; étalonne peser

gaunt [gaunt] *adj.* émacié, décharné [face] creux [cheek]; lugubre; féroce (fig.).

gauntlet [gauntlit] *s.* gantelet, m.; *to throw down the gauntlet*, défier, provoque

gauze [gauz] *s* gaze, f.

gave [gé¹v] *pret. of* to give.

gawky [gauki] *adj.* maladroit, lourdaud gauche

gay [gé] *adj* gai, allègre; pimpant.

gaze [gé z] *s* fixer [eye], contempler; *s.* regard fixe ou attentif m

gazette [g⁰zé¹t] *s* gazette, f.; journal officiel m. *v* mettre à l'officiel.

gean [gîn] *s* merise, f.; *gean-tree*, merisier

gear [gi⁰r] *s* accoutrement; attirail; outillage mécanisme dispositif; appareil; engrenage, embrayage, m.; vitesse; transmission, commande (mech.), f.; v. démultiplier; (s')engrener (with, avec); to throw into gear. embrayer; to throw out of gear débrayer; gearbox, boîte de vitesses, gear-case, carter; gearshift, changement de vitesse; dérailleur

geese [gîs] pl. of goose.

gelatin [djèl•t'n] s. gélatine, f.

gem [djèm] s pierre précieuse, f.; fleuron. m., v. gemmer.

gender [djènd•r] s. genre (gramm.), m.

genealogy [djìnìalâdji] s. généalogie, f.

general [djèn•r'l] adj général, commun; universel public • général, m.; **general headquarters** grand quartier général **generality** [djèn•ral•ti] s. généralité, f **generalize** [djèn•r•la'z] v. généraliser (from. à partir de).

generate [djèn•ré¹t] v engendrer; produire **generation** [djènèré¹shen] s. génération, production, f. ‖ **generator** [djèn•ré¹t•r] s. génératrice, f. dynamo, f

generosity [djèn•raus•ti] s.* générosité; libéralité, f. ‖ **generous** [djèn•r•s] adj généreux; abondant; magnanime.

genial [djnì•l] adj. affable; sympathique cordial [person]; clément [climate] réconfortant [warmth].

genius [djîny•s] s * génie, m.

genteel [djèntîl] adj. distingué; élégant; courtois

gentian [djènshen] s. gentiane, f.

gentile [djènta¹l] adj., s. gentil (eccles.)

gentle [djènt'l] adj. aimable; bien né; honorable doux **gentleman** [-m•n] (pl. **gentlemen**) s galant homme gentilhomme: m he is a gentleman c'est un Monsieu **gentleness** [-nis] s. douceu amabilité f **gently** [-li] adv. doucement poliment calmement

gentry [djèntri] s haute bourgeoisie, élite, f.

genuflexion [djènyouflékshen] s. génuflexion f

genuine [djènyouin] adj. sincère; authentique véritable.

geographical [djì•grafik'l] adj. géographiqu **geography** [djiâgr•fi] s. géographie f

geology [djiâl•dji] s géologie, f.

geometric [djì•mètrik] adj. géométrique **geometry** [djiâmetri] s.* géométrie. f

geranium [djèré¹ni•m] s. géranium, m

geriatrics [djèri•triks] s. Am. gérontologie, f.

germ [djë⁰m] s. germe; microbe, m.; origine, f.

German [djë⁰m•n] adj., s. allemand. ‖ **Germany** [-i] s Allemagne, f.

germicide [djë⁰m•sa¹d] s. microbicide bactéricide m.

germinate [djë⁰m•né¹t] v. germer.

gerund [djèr•nd] s gérondif; substantif verbal (gramm) m.

gestation [djèsté¹shen] s. gestation, f.

gesticulate [djèstìky•lé¹t] v. gesticuler. ‖ **gesture** [djèstsh•r] s. geste; signe, m. v gesticuler, a mere gesture, une pure formalité

get [gèt] v.* obtenir; acquérir; se procurer devenir; to get in, entrer; to get over franchir to get a cold, prendre froid, to get angry, se mettre en colère to get ill tomber malade; to get at, atteindre, to get married, se marier, to get ready (se) préparer; to get rid of, se débarrasser de; to get up, monter. organiser se lever.

gewgaw [gyougau] s babiole, f.

geyser [gé¹z•r] s geyser; chauffebain, m soupe-au-lait, f. (colloq.).

ghastly [gastli] adj. horrible; macabre; livide.

gherkin [gë⁰kin] s. cornichon, m.

ghost [go⁰st] s spectre. fantôme, revenant nègre [writer]. m. âme; ombre [notion] f the Holy Ghost, le Saint-Esprit **ghostly**, spectral; fantomatique spirituel

giant [dja¹ent] s. géant, m.

gibberish [djib•rish] s.* baragouin, m

giblets [djiblits] s. pl. abattis, m.

giddy [gidi] adj. étourdi; vertigineux; frivole léger

gift [gift] s don, cadeau; talent, m.; donation f **gifted**, doué.

gigantic [dja¹gantik] adj. gigantesque.

giggle [gig'l] s gloussement, m.; v. glousse risoter

gild [gild] v dorer. ‖ **gilding** [-ing] s. dorure f

gill [gil] s oules [fish], f. pl

gillyflower [djiliflaou•r] s. giroflée, f.

gilt [gilt adj doré, s dorure, f.; **gilt-edged**, doré sur tranches.

gimlet [gimlit] s vrille [tool], f.

gin [djin] s gin. genièvre, m.

ginger [djindj•r] s gingembre, m.; **ginger-bread**, pain d'épices.

gingerly [djindj•rli] adv. délicatement ave précaution.

gipsy, see gypsy.

giraffe [djeraf] s. girafe, f.

gird [gërd] *v.* ceindre; attacher; entourer; *to gird oneself for*, se préparer pour. || *girdle* [-'l] *s.* ceinture; gaine; enceinte; limite, f.; *v.* ceinturer, entourer.

girl [gërl] *s.* (jeune) fille, f. || *girl·hood* [-houd] *s.* jeunesse, enfance d'une femme, f. || *girlish* [-ish] *adj.* puéril; de fillette, de jeune fille.

girt [gërt] *pret., p. p. of to gird.*

girth [gërth] *s.* sangle; circonférence, f.; tour de taille, m.

gist [djist] *s.* substance, f.; fond, essentiel, m.

give [giv] *v.°* donner; livrer; céder; accorder; remettre; rendre [verdict]; pousser [cry]; *s.* élasticité, f.; *to give in*, céder; se rendre; *to give out*, divulguer; *to give off*, émettre; *to give up*, renoncer; *to give way*, fléchir, céder du terrain. || *given* [-'n] *p.p. of give; adj.* donné; offert; adonné (*to*, à); *given time*, heure déterminée; *given that*, étant donné que; *given the circumstances*, vu les circonstances. || *giver* [-ºr] *s.* donateur, m.; donatrice, f.

glacial [glé¹sh°l] *adj.* glacial. || *glacier* [glé¹shºr] *s.* glacier, m.

glad [glad] *adj.* content; heureux. || *gladden* [-'n] *v.* (se) réjouir (*at*, de).

glade [glé¹d] *s.* clairière; éclaircie, f.

gladiolus [gladioºl°s] *s.° glaïeul; iris, m.

gladly [gladli] *adv.* joyeusement; de bon cœur. || *gladness* [gladnis] *s.* joie, f.; contentement, m.

glamo(u)r [glamºr] *s.* charme, m.; grâce, f. || *glamo(u)rous* [-rºs] *adj.* fascinant, ravissant; prestigieux.

glance [glàns] *s.* coup d'œil, regard, m.; œillade, f.; *v.* jeter un regard; lancer; dévier; briller par éclats.

gland [glànd] *s.* glande, f.

glare [glèºr] *s.* lueur, f.; éclat; regard farouche, m.; *v.* briller; jeter un regard étincelant; *to glare at*, foudroyer du regard.

glass [glas] *s.° verre, m.; vitre; lentille [optics], f.; *field glass*, jumelles; *magnifying glass*, loupe, *shatter-proof glass*, verre incassable ∈ Sécurit ›; *glass-blower*, verrier *glass-case*, vitrine *glass-ware*, verrerie, f. || *glasses* [-iz] *s. pl.* lorgnon, m.; lunettes, f. pl. *snow-glasses*, lunettes d'alpiniste; *smoked glasses*, verres fumés. || *glassy* [-i] *adj.* vitreux.

glaze [glé¹z] *s.* lustre, vernis, m.; *v.* vernir; lustrer; glacer [pastry]; vitrer. || *glazier* [glé¹jºr] *s.* vitrier, m.

gleam [glïm] *s.* rayon, m.; lueur, f.; *v.* scintiller, luire.

glean [glïn] *v.* glaner.

glee [glï] *s.* allégresse; chanson à reprises, f.; *glee club*, chorale; *glee-man*, ménestrel.

glib [glib] *adj.* délié; facile [excuse]; bien pendue [tongue].

glide [gla¹d] *s.* glissement; vol plané, m.; *v.* glisser; s'insinuer; planer. || *glider* [-ºr] *s.* planeur; hydroglisseur, m.

glimmer [glimºr] *v.* luire faiblement; *s.* lueur, f.; miroitement, m.

glimpse [glimps] *s.* coup d'œil, aperçu, m.; *v.* jeter un coup d'œil; entrevoir.

glint [glint] *s.* lueur, f.; rayon, m.

glisten [glis'n] *v.* reluire, miroiter.

glitter [glitºr] *v.* briller, scintiller; *s.* scintillement, m.

gloat [gloºut] *v. to gloat over*, couver d'un regard avide, se repaître la vue de; faire des gorges chaudes de.

global [gloºub°l] *adj.* global; sphérique, mondial. || *globe* [gloºub] *s.* globe, m.; terre, f.

globule [gláb̆youl] *s.* globule, m.

gloom [gloum] *s.* obscurité, ténèbres; tristesse, f.; *v.* (s')assombrir. || *gloomy* [-i] *adj.* sombre; ténébreux; triste.

glorification [gloºurºfºké¹sh°n] *s.* glorification, f. || *glorify* [gloºurºfa¹] *v.* glorifier. || *glorious* [gloºuri°s] *adj.* glorieux, splendide; resplendissant; illustre. || *glory* [gloºuri] *s.° gloire; célébrité, splendeur, f.; *v.* (se) glorifier; s'enorgueillir [*in*, de].

gloss [glaus] *s.* lustre, luisant, apprêt, m.; *v.* lustrer; polir; *glossy*, lustré, luisant.

gloss [glaus] *s.° glose, f.; *v.* gloser. || *glossary* [glâs°ri] *s.° glossaire, m.

glottis [glâtis] *s.* glotte, f.

glove [glœv] *s.* gant, m.; *v.* ganter; *driving gloves*, gants de chauffeur; *rubber gloves*, gants en caoutchouc.

glow [gloºu] *s.* incandescence; ardeur, f.; rougeoiement, m.; *v.* rougir, s'embraser irradier. || *glowing* [-ing] *adj.* incandescent, ardent; rouge [embers]. || *glowworm* [-wêrm] *s.* ver luisant, m.

glucose [gloukoºus] *s.* glucose, m.

glue [glou] *s.* colle; glu, f.; *v.* coller, engluer.

glum [gloum] *adj.* triste, renfrogné.

glut [glœt] *s.* rassasiement; engorgement, m.; satiété; pléthore, surabondance, f.; *v.* gorger; rassasier; inonder, engorger [market].

glutton [glœt'n] *s.* glouton, *Fr. Can.* carcajou [animal], m. || *gluttonous* [-°s] *adj.* glouton, goulu. || *gluttony* [-i] *s.* gloutonnerie; goinfrerie, f.

glycerin [glísrin] *s.* glycérine, f.

gnarled [nârld] *adj.* noueux [wood].

gnash [nash] *v.* grincer [teeth].

gnat [nat] *s.* moustique; moucheron, *Fr. Can.* maringouin, m.

gnaw [nau] *v.* ronger.

go [goou] *v.** aller; s'en aller; devenir; fonctionner; s'écouler [time]; *to go for,* aller chercher; *to go without,* se passer de ; *to let go,* lâcher; *to go about,* circuler. se mettre à; s'en prendre à, *to go after,* briguer; *to go on,* continuer; *to go by,* passer; *to go off,* partir, *to go between,* s'entremettre; *no go!,* rien à faire! ; *s.* affaire; mode, façon, f.; mouvement, m.

goad [goou d] *s.* aiguillon, m.; *v.* aiguillonner, stimuler.

goal [goou l] *s.* but; objectif, m.; **goalkeeper**, gardien de but, goal.

goat [goout] *s.* chèvre, f.; bouc émissaire, m., *male goat,* bouc; **goatherd**, chevrier. ‖ **goatee** [goou tî] *s.* bouc [beard], m.

gobble [gáb'l] *v.* gober; glouglouter; *to gobble up,* engloutir; s'empiffrer. ‖ **gobbler** [-ᵉr] *s.* dindon; glouton, m.

go-between [goou bᵉtwîn] *s.* intermédiaire, entremetteur, m.

goblet [gáblit] *s.* gobelet, m.

goblin [gáblin] *s.* lutin, m.

God [gâd] *s.* Dieu, m.; *pl.* dieux. ‖ **godchild** [-tshaⁱld] *s.* filleul, m.; filleule, f. ‖ **goddess** [-is] *s.** déesse, f. ‖ **godfather** [-fâzhᵉr] *s.* parrain, m. ‖ **godhead** [-hêd] *s.* divinité, f. ‖ **godless** [-lis] *adj.* athée. ‖ **godlike** [-laⁱk] *adj.* divin. ‖ **godly** [-li] *adj.* pieux, dévot, divin. ‖ **godmother** [-mœzhᵉr] *s.* marraine, f. ‖ **godsend** [-sènd] *s* aubaine providentielle, f. ‖ **godson** [-sœn] *s.* filleul, m.

goggle [gâg'l] *v* rouler de gros yeux; *s. pl.* lunettes protectrices, f.; *flying goggles,* lunettes d'aviateur.

going [goou ing] *pr. p. of* to go; *adj.* allant, en vie; *s.* allure; marche; conduite, f.; *comings and goings,* allées et venues.

goiter [goⁱtᵉr] *s.* goitre (med.), m.

gold [goou ld] *s.* or, m.; *dead gold,* or mat; *gold standard,* étalon or.

goldbrick [goou ldbrik] *v. Am.* tirer au flanc. se défiler

golden [goou ldᵉn] *adj.* d'or; doré; précieux, prospère, *golden mean,* juste milieu ‖ **goldfinch** [-fintsh] *s.** chardonneret, m. ‖ **goldfish** [-fish] *s.** poisson rouge, m. ‖ **goldsmith** [-smith] *s.* orfèvre, m.

golf [gâlf] *s.* golf, m.

gondola [gândᵉlᵉ] *s.* gondole; nacelle, f.; **gondola car,** wagon plate-forme.

gone [gaun] *p. p. of* to go; *adj.* parti; disparu; passé; *gone west,* mort; **goner**, homme fichu.

gong [gaung] *s.* gong, m.

good [goud] *adj.* bon; avantageux; satisfaisant, vertueux; valide; *s.* bien; profit, m.; *pl* biens, m.; marchandises, f.; *adv* bien bon, **good-bye**, adieu, au revoir, **good day,** bonjour; **good evening,** bonsoir **good night,** bonne nuit; **good-looking,** de bonne mine, beau; *be so good as to,* veuillez avoir la bonté de, *to make good,* exécuter [contract]. compenser [loss]; *what's the good of ?,* à quoi bon ?; *to have a good time.* passer un bon moment. ‖ **goodness** [-nis] *s.* bonté; probité; bienveillance; qualité, f. ‖ **goodwill** [-wil] *s.* bonne volonté; bienveillance, f.; clientèle, f. (comm.). ‖ **goody** [-i] *s.** friandise, sucrerie, f.

goose [gous] (*pl.* **geese** [gîs]) *s.* oie, f.; dinde. sotte, f (colloq.); *Canada goose, Fr Can.* outarde, f.; *pl.* carreau [tailor's iron], m., *goose step,* pas de l'oie. ‖ **gooseberry** [-bèri] *s.** groseille à maquereau, f. ‖ **goose-flesh** [-flèsh] *s.* chair de poule, f. ‖ **gooseherd** [-hᵉrd] *s.* gardeuse d'oies, f.

gore [goou r] *s.* sang coagulé, m. ‖ **gory** [-i] *adj.* sanglant, ensanglanté.

gore [goou r] *s.* panneau (aviat.); fuseau [parachute], m.; langue, pointe de terre, f.

gore [goou r] *v.* percer; donner un coup de corne à.

gorge [gaurdj] *adj., s.* gorge, f.; couloir; repas, m.; *v.* gorger; s'empiffrer.

gorgeous [gaurdjᵉs] *adj.* magnifique, fastueux

gorilla [gᵉrílᵉ] *s.* gorille, m.

gosling [gázling] *s.* oison, m.

gospel [gausp'l] *s.* évangile, m.

gossip [gásip] *s.* commère, f.; bavard; commérage potin, m.; *v.* bavarder, *Fr. Can.* bavasser; *gossip-writer,* échotier.

got [gât] *pret., p. p. of* to get.

Gothic [gâthik] *adj.* gothique; *s.* gotique [language]; gothique [style].

gotten [gât'n] *p. p. of* to get.

gouge [gaudj] *s.* gouge, f.; *v.* faire un trou dans; *Am.* duper, rouler.

gourd [goou rd] *s.* gourde, f.

gout [gaout] *s.* goutte (med.), f.

govern [gœvᵉrn] *v.* gouverner; diriger. ‖ **governess** [-is] *s.** gouvernante, institutrice, f. ‖ **government** [-mᵉnt] *s.* gouvernement; conseil municipal;

conseil d'administration, m.; **government funds,** fonds d'Etat. || **governmental** [gœvᵉrnmᵉnt'l] adj. gouvernemental. || **governor** [gœvᵉrnᵉr] s. gouverneur; gouvernant; patron; régulateur (mech.), m.

gown [gaᵒᵘn] s. robe; toge, f.; **dressing gown,** peignoir; **night-gown,** chemise de nuit.

grab [grab] v. empoigner, saisir; s. prise, f.; grappin, m.; **grabber,** accapareur.

grace [gré¹s] s. grâce; faveur, f.; pardon, m.; **to say grace,** dire les grâces. || **graceful** [-fᵉl] adj. gracieux; élégant. || **gracefulness** [-fᵉlnis] s. grâce, élégance, f. || **gracious** [gré¹shᵉs] adj. gracieux; courtois.

gradation [gré¹dé¹shᵉn] s. gradation, f.; degré, échelon, m. || **grade** [gré¹d] s. grade; degré; rang, m.; rampe; *Am.* pente (railw.); inclinaison, f.; v. classer; graduer; qualifier; **grade crossing,** passage à niveau. || **gradual** [gradjouᵉl] adj. graduel; progressif. || **gradually** [-i] adv. peu à peu, progressivement. || **graduate** [gradjouit] adj. gradué, diplômé; [gradjoué¹t] v. graduer; prendre ses diplômes. || **graduation** [gradjoué¹shᵉn] s. graduation; gradation; remise (or) réception (f.) d'un grade.

graft [graft] s. greffe; concussion, f.; v. greffer; tripoter. || **grafter** [-ᵉr] s. concussionnaire, m.

grain [gré¹n] s. céréales, f. pl.; grain [corn, weight, wood, marble]; brin, m.; **against the grain,** à rebours, à rebrousse-poil.

gram [gram] s. gramme, m.

grammar [gramᵉr] s. grammaire, f.; **grammar school,** *Am.* école primaire; *Br.* lycée. || **grammatical** [grᵉmatik'l] adj. grammatical.

gramophone [gram°foᵒᵘn] s. gramophone, phonographe, m.

granary [granᵉri] s.° grenier, m.

grand [grànd] adj. grand; grandiose. || **grandchild** [-tshaild] (pl. **grandchildren** [-tshildrᵉn]) s. petit-enfant, m. || **granddaughter** [-dautᵉr] s. petite-fille, f. || **grandeur** [gràndjᵉr] s. grandeur, majesté, f. || **grandfather** [-fàzhᵉr] s. grand-père, m. || **grandiose** [-ioᵒᵘs] adj. grandiose. || **grandma** [-mâ] s. grand-maman, mémé, f. || **grandmother** [-mœzhᵉr] s. grand-mère, f. || **grandness** [-nis] s. grandeur, magnificence, f. || **grandpa** [-pâ] s. grand-papa, pépé, m. || **grandparent** [-pèrᵉnt] s. grand-parent, aïeul, m. || **grandson** [-sœn] s. petit-fils, m.

grange [gré¹ndj] s. manoir, m.; *Am.* fédération agricole, f.

granite [granit] s. granit, m.

granny [grani] s.° bonne-maman, f.

grant [grànt] v. accorder; octroyer; allouer; transférer; s. concession; allocation; cession, f.; octroi, m.; **grantee,** donataire; **grantor,** donateur.

granulate [grany°lé¹t] v. granuler. || **granulation** [grany°lé¹shᵉn] s. granulation, f.; grenaillement, m. || **granule** [granyoul] s. granule, m. || **granulous** [-°s] adj. granuleux.

grape [gré¹p] s. grain de raisin; pl. raisin, m. || **grapefruit** [-frout] s. pamplemousse, m. || **grapestone** [-stoun] s. pépin de raisin, m.

graph [graf] s. graphique; diagramme, m.; courbe, f.; v. tracer un graphique; faire un diagramme. || **graphic** [-ik] adj. graphique.

graphite [grafa¹t] s. graphite, m.; mine de plomb; plombagine, f.

grapnel [grapnᵉl] s. grappin, m.

grapple [grap'l] v. **to grapple with,** accrocher; agripper; prendre au corps; aborder [subject].

grasp [grasp] v. empoigner; serrer; saisir; étreindre; comprendre; s. étreinte; prise; poigne; poignée [arms]; compréhension, f.; **within one's grasp,** à portée de la main; **to have a good grasp of a subject,** bien connaître une question; **grasping,** avare; avide.

grass [gras] s. herbe, f.; gazon, m. || **grasshopper** [grashâpᵉr] s. sauterelle, f. || **grassplot** [-plât] s. pelouse, f. || **grassy** [-i] adj. herbeux, herbu.

grate [gré¹t] s. grille, f.; v. griller [window].

grate [gré¹t] v. râper; frotter; grincer [teeth]; irriter; froisser; être désagréable (on, à).

grateful [gré¹tfᵉl] adj. reconnaissant (for, de; to, à). || **gratefulness** [-nis] s. reconnaissance, gratitude, f.; réconfort, agrément, m.

grater [gré¹tᵉr] s. râpe, f.

gratification [gratᵉfᵉké¹shᵉn] s. gratification, f.; plaisir, m. || **gratify** [gratᵉfa¹] v. satisfaire; obliger, faire plaisir à; contenter.

grating [gré¹ting] s. grincement [sound], m.; adj. grinçant, discordant, désagréable.

gratitude [gratᵉtyoud] s. gratitude, f.

gratuitous [grᵉtyouᵉtᵉs] adj. gratuit; arbitraire. || **gratuity** [grᵉtyouᵉti] s.° pourboire, m.; gratification, f.

grave [gré¹v] adj. grave; important; solennel.

grave [gré¹v] s. tombe; fosse, f.; tombeau, m.; **gravedigger,** fossoyeur; **gravestone,** pierre tombale; **graveyard,** cimetière.

gravel [grav'l] *s.* gravier, m.; gravelle, f.; *v.* graveler.

graven [gré¹v°n] *adj.* gravé.

gravity [grav°ti] *s.* gravité; importance; pesanteur, f.

gravy [gré¹vi] *s.* sauce, f.; jus, m.; *gravy-boat*, saucière; *gravy-train*, *Am.* assiette au beurre.

gray [gré¹] *adj., s.* gris; *graybeard*, vieillard. ‖ *grayish* [-ish] *adj.* grisâtre. ‖ *grayness* [-nis] *s.* teinte grise; pénombre, f.

graze [gré¹z] *v.* brouter; faire paître; pâturer; effleurer; raser (mil.); écorcher [skin]; *s* action de paître; éraflure, f.; effleurement; écrêtement, m.

grease [grīs] *s* graisse, f.; *v.* graisser; lubrifier; *grease remover*, dégraisseur; *greasy*, gras; graisseux; huileux.

great [gré¹t] *adj.* grand; éminent; excellent; magnifique; *a great deal*, beaucoup, *great-aunt*, grand-tante; *great-grand-daughter*, arrière-petite-fille; *great-grand-father*, arrière-grand-père *great-grand-mother*, arrière-grand mère *great-grand-son*, arrière-petit-fils *great-nephew*, petit-neveu; *great-niece*, petite-nièce; *great-uncle*, grand-oncle. ‖ *greatly* [-li] *adv.* grandement, beaucoup, considérablement; avec grandeur. ‖ *greatness* [-nis] *s.* grandeur, f.

greaves [grīvz] *s. pl.* fritons, rillons, m. pl.; *Fr Can.* cretons, m. pl.

Grecian [grīsh°n] *adj., s.* grec, grecque. ‖ *Greece* [grīs] *s.* Grèce, f

greed [grīd] *s.* avidité; convoitise; gloutonnerie, f. ‖ *greediness* [-inis] *s.* voracité, avidité, f. ‖ *greedy* [-i] *adj.* avide; cupide; glouton, vorace.

Greek [grīk] *adj., s.* grec, grecque.

green [grīn] *adj.* vert; inexpérimenté; naïf; novice; *to grow green*, verdoyer; *s.* vert; gazon, m.; verdure; pelouse, f.; *pl.* légumes verts, m.; *greengrocer*, fruitier, *greenish*, verdâtre. ‖ *greenhouse* [-haºus] *s.* serre, f. ‖ *greenness* [-nis] *s.* vert, m.; verdure; verdeur inexpérience, f.

greet [grīt] *v* saluer. ‖ *greeting* [-ing] *s.* salutation f.; accueil; salut, m.; *pl.* compliments, m. pl.

grenade [grin°é¹d] *s.* grenade (mil.), f. ‖ *grenadier* [gr°n°di°r] *s.* grenadier, m.

grew [grou] *pret.* of *to grow*.

grey, *see* gray.

greyhound [gré¹haºund] *s.* lévrier, m.

grid [grid] *s.* quadrillage [survey]; gril; grillage, m.

griddle [grid'l] *s.* gril, m.; *griddle-cake*, crêpe.

gridiron [grida¹°rn] *s.* gril; *Am.* terrain de football, m.

grief [grīf] *s.* chagrin, m.; peine, f.; *to come to grief*, finir mal; *grief-stricken*, accablé de chagrin. ‖ *grievance* [grīv°ns] *s.* grief, tort, m.; offense, f. ‖ *grieve* [grīv] *v.* chagriner, peiner; regretter; s'affliger. ‖ *grievous* [grīv°s] *adj.* douloureux; attristant; grave; atroce, cruel.

grill [gril] *s.* gril, m.; grillade, f.; *men's grill*, restaurant pour hommes; *v.* griller; interroger (jur.); cuisiner [police]; être sur le gril (fig.); *grill-room*, rôtisserie.

grim [grim] *adj.* farouche; sinistre; menaçant; sardonique [smile]; rébarbatif; impitoyable.

grimace [grimé¹s] *s.* grimace, f.; *v.* grimacer.

grime [gra¹m] *s.* crasse, saleté, f.; *v.* salir, noircir; *grimy*, sale, barbouillé.

grin [grin] *s.* sourire moqueur, grimaçant, malin; ricanement, m.; *v.* sourire.

grind [gra¹nd] *v.* moudre; broyer; aiguiser [knife]; bûcher [lesson]; jouer [hand organ]; grincer [teeth]; *s.* broyage grincement; boulot, travail acharné *Am* bûcheur, m.; routine, f.; *grindstone*, meule. ‖ *grinder* [-°r] *s.* meule, f.; broyeur; moulin [coffee], m.

grip [grip] *s.* prise; étreinte; poigne; poignée; *Am.* valise, trousse, f.; emprise, f. (fig.); *v.* étreindre; serrer; *to come to grips*, en venir aux mains.

gripe [gra¹p] *s.* colique (med.); *Am.* récrimination, f.; *v.* se plaindre.

grippe [grip] *s.* grippe (med.), f.

grisly [grisli] *adj.* terrifiant; macabre; horrible.

gristle [gris'l] *s.* cartilage, m.

grit [grit] *s.* gruau; gravier; grès; courage, m.; endurance, f.; *v.* grincer; *gritty*, caillouteux.

grizzly [grizli] *adj.* grisâtre; *s.* ours gris d'Amérique, m.

groan [graun] *s.* gémissement, m.; *v.* gémir murmurer.

groats [groºuts] *s. pl.* gruau, m.

grocer [groºus°r] *s.* épicier, m. ‖ *grocery* [-ri] *s.* épicerie, f.; *pl.* denrées comestibles, f. pl.

grog [graug] *s.* grog, m. ‖ *groggy* [-i] *adj.* ivre; chancelant; hébété.

groin [gro¹n] *s.* aîne (med.); arête (arch.), f.

groom [groum] *s.* palefrenier; marié, m.; *v.* panser [horse]; soigner, astiquer (colloq.); *groomsman*, garçon d'honneur.

groove [grouv] *s.* rainure; cannelure; rayure; coulisse, f.; *v.* évider; strier; faire une rainure dans.

grope [grou°p] *v.* tâtonner; *to grope for*, chercher à tâtons.

gross [grou°s] *adj.* gros, grosse; rude; grossier; brut [weight]; épais [ignorance]; *s.°* grosse [measure], f.; *Am.* recette brute, f.

grotesque [grou°tĕsk] *adj.*, *s.* grotesque.

grotto [grauto°u] *s.* grotte, f.

grouch [grao°utsh] *s.°* mauvaise humeur, f.; ronchon, m.; *v.* ronchonner. ‖ **grouchy** [-i] *adj.* grognon; acariâtre.

ground [grao°und] *s.* terrain; sol; fond; fondement, motif; chef d'accusation; point de vue, m.; terre; masse (electr.); cause; base, f.; *v.* mettre à terre; fonder; enseigner les principes de; atterrir (aviat.); masser (electr.); *to gain ground*, gagner du terrain; *to stand one's ground*, tenir bon; *to break ground*, creuser une tranchée; *to be well grounded in*, avoir une connaissance solide de; *ground - floor*, rez - de - chaussée; *groundnut*, arachide; *coffee-grounds*, marc de café.

ground [grao°und] *pret.*, *p. p. of to grind*.

group [group] *s.* groupe, m.; escouade, f.; *v.* grouper; *blood group*, groupe sanguin.

grouse [grao°us] *s.* coq de bruyère, grouse, m.; *v.* ronchonner.

grove [grou°v] *s.* bosquet, m.

grovel [grăv'l] *v.* se vautrer; ramper; flagorner; *groveller*, chien couchant (fig.); *grovelling*, rampant.

grow [grou°] *v.°* pousser, croître; grandir; devenir; avancer; augmenter; faire pousser; *to grow old*, se faire vieux; *to grow better*, s'améliorer. ‖ **grower** [-°r] *s.* cultivateur, producteur, m.

growl [grao°ul] *s.* grognement, m.; *v.* grogner.

grown [grou°n] *p. p. of to grow*; *adj.* développé, cultivé; *full-grown*, adulte; *grown-ups*, grandes personnes. ‖ **growth** [grou°th] *s.* croissance; crue; excroissance (med.), f.; accroissement; produit, m.

grub [grŏb] *v.* creuser, défricher; trimer; *s.* asticot, m.; larve; mangeaille, boustifaille (pop.), f.

grudge [grŏdj] *s.* rancune, f.; *v.* donner à contrecœur; *to bear a grudge against*, garder une dent contre.

gruesome [grou°s°m] *adj.* terrifiant; horrible; lugubre.

gruff [grŏf] *adj.* bourru, brusque.

grumble [grŏmb'l] *s.* murmure, grognement, m.; *v.* grogner, murmurer; *grumbler*, grognon, m.

grumpy [grŏmpi] *adj.* maussade, grognon, grincheux.

grunt [grŏnt] *s.* grognement [hog], m.; *v.* grogner.

guarantee [gar°ntī] *s.* garantie; caution, f.; garant, m.; *v.* garantir; se porter garant. ‖ **guarantor** [gar°nt°r] *s.* garant; répondant, m.

guard [gârd] *s.* garde, protection, f.; garde, m.; *v.* garder; protéger; défendre, *guardhouse*, corps de garde; *guardrail*, garde-fou, main-courante; *on guard*, de garde, sur le qui-vive. ‖ **guardian** [gârdi°n] *s.* gardien; administrateur; tuteur, m. ‖ **guardianship** [-ship] *s.* garde; tutelle, f.

gudgeon [gœdj°n] *s.* goujon; tourillon (mech.), m.; jobard, m. (colloq.).

guerilla [gĕrĭl°] *s.* guérilla, f.; guérillero, m.

guess [gĕs] *s.°* conjecture, supposition, f.; *v.* deviner; conjecturer; penser; *at a guess*, au jugé.

guest [gĕst] *s.* convive; hôte; visiteur; invité, m.; *guest room*, chambre d'amis.

guffaw [gĕfau] *s.* gros rire bruyant, m.

guggle [gŏg'l] *v.* glousser.

guidance [ga°ïd°ns] *s.* conduite; direction, f. ‖ **guide** [ga°ïd] *s.* guide; conducteur, m.; *v.* guider; conduire; gouverner; *guidebook*, guide; *guidepost*, poteau indicateur.

guild [gild] *s.* corporation, association, guilde, f.

guile [ga°ïl] *s.* astuce; ruse, f.; *guileful*, rusé, fourbe, astucieux; *guileless*, candide, loyal.

guilt [gĭlt] *s.* culpabilité; faute, f.; crime, m. ‖ **guiltless** [-lis] *adj.* innocent. ‖ **guilty** [-i] *adj.* coupable.

guinea-fowl [gĭnĭfa°ul] *s.* pintade, f.

guinea-pig [gĭnipĭg] *s.* cobaye, m.

guise [ga°ïz] *s.* façon; guise; mode, f.; aspect; déguisement, m.

guitar [gĭtâr] *s.* guitare, f.; *guitarist*, guitariste.

gulch [gœltsh] *s.°* ravin, m.

gulf [gœlf] *s.* golfe; gouffre, m.

gull [gœl] *s.* mouette, f.; goéland, m.

gull [gœl] *s.* dupe, f.; *v.* duper.

gullet [gœlit] *s.* œsophage; goulet; gosier, m.

gullible [gœl°b'l] *s.* jobard, m.

gully [gœli] *s.°* ravin, m.; ravine, f.

gulp [gœlp] *s.* gorgée; goulée, f.; *v.* avaler; gober; *at a gulp*, d'un trait, d'une bouchée.

gum [gœm] *s.* gomme; gencive [teeth], f.; *gum arabic*, gomme arabique; *gum-tree*, gommier; *v.* gommer. ‖ *gummy* *adj.* collant; chassieux [eyes].

gun [gœn] *s.* fusil; canon, m.; arme à feu, f.; *v.* mettre les gaz; *assault gun*, canon de 75; *automatic gun*, fusil automatique, *camera gun*, cinémitrailleuse; *machine gun*, mitrailleuse; *submachine gun*, mitraillette; *gunboat*, canonnière, *gun carriage*, affût de canon; *gunfire*, canonnade; *gunshot*, coup de canon. ‖ *gunner* [-ᵉʳ] *s.* pointeur; mitrailleur; artilleur, m.

gurgle [gᵉʳg'l] *s.* glouglou; gargouillement, m.; *v.* gargouiller.

gush [gœsh] *s.ᵉ* jaillissement, m.; effusion, f.; *v.* jaillir; couler à flots; se répandre en effusions.

gust [gœst] *s.* jet [flame], m.; bouffée [smoke]; rafale [wind], f.; accès [rage], m.; *gusty*, de grand vent.

gut [gœt] *s.* boyau; intestin, m.;

tripe, f.; *v.* vider, déboyauter; *to have guts*, avoir du cran.

gutter [gœtᵉʳ] *s.* gouttière, rigole, f.; ruisseau [street], m.

guttural [gœtᵉrᵉl] *adj.* guttural.

guy [gaⁱ] *s.* hauban; étai, m.

guy [gaⁱ] *s.* type, individu; épouvantail, m.

guzzle [gœz'l] *v.* ingurgiter; lamper, pomper; bâfrer.

gymnasium [djimnéⁱziᵉm] *s.* gymnase, m. ‖ *gymnastics* [djimnastiks] *s.* gymnastique, f.

gynecology [djaⁱnikᵉlâdji] *s.* gynécologie, f.

gyp [djip] *v.* refaire, carotter (colloq.).

gypsy [djipsi] *s.ᵉ* gitan, m.; gitane, f.

gyrate [djaⁱréⁱt] *v.* tournoyer. ‖ *gyration* [djaⁱréⁱshᵉn] *s.* giration, f. ‖ *gyroplane* [djaⁱrᵉplèn] *s.* hélicoptère, m.

H

haberdasher [habᵉrdashᵉr] *s.* mercier; chemisier, m. ‖ *haberdashery* [-ri] *s.ᵉ* mercerie; *Am.* chemiserie, f.

habit [habit] *s.* habitude, coutume, f.; habillement; costume, m.; *drug habit*, toxicomanie.

habitual [hᵉbitshouᵉl] *adj.* habituel. ‖ *habituate* [hᵉbitshouéⁱt] *v.* habituer; accoutumer.

hack [hak] *s.* fiacre; cheval de louage; mercenaire, m.; rosse, f.; *hack-writer*, nègre, écrivain à gages.

hack [hak] *s.* pioche; entaille, coche, f.; *v.* hachurer, ébrécher; toussoter.

hackneyed [haknid] *adj.* rebattu; commun, banal.

had [had] *pret., p. p. of to have.*

haft [haft] *s.* manche [knife], m.; poignée [sword], f.; *v.* emmancher.

hag [hag] *s.* sorcière, f.

haggard [hagᵉrd] *adj.* hagard; farouche; livide.

haggle [hag'l] *v.* marchander; disputer, débattre.

hail [héⁱl] *s.* salut; appel, m.; *v.* saluer; héler; *Hail Mary*, Ave Maria.

hail [héⁱl] *s.* grêle, f.; grésil, m.; *v.* grêler; *hailstone*, grêlon, m.

hair [hèᵉr] *s.* cheveu; poil, m.; chevelure, f.; crin; filament, m.; *hairbrush*, brosse à cheveux; *haircut*, coupe de cheveux; *hair net*, filet à cheveux; *hair-setting*, mise en plis; *hair-splitting*, ergotage. ‖ *hairdo* [hèᵉrdou] *s.* coiffure, f. ‖ *hairdresser*

[hèᵉrdrèsᵉr] *s.* coiffeur, m. ‖ *hairless* [hèᵉrlis] *adj.* chauve; sans poil. ‖ *hairpin* [hèᵉrpin] *s.* épingle à cheveux, f. ‖ *hairy* [hèᵉri] *adj.* chevelu; poilu; hirsute.

hale [héⁱl] *adj.* robuste; sain; en bon état; vigoureux; valide.

half [haf] (*pl.* *halves* [havz]) *s.* moitié; demie, f.; *adj.* demi; *half-breed*, métis, *half-brother*, demi-frère; *half-hearted*, peu généreux, peu enthousiaste; *half-hour*, demi-heure; *half-open*, entrebâillé; *half-sister*, demi-sœur; *halfway*, à mi-chemin; *one hour and a half*, une heure et demie; *too short by half*, moitié trop court.

halibut [halᵉbᵉt] *s.* flétan, m.

hall [haul] *s.* salle, f.; hall; vestibule; édifice public, m.; *town hall*, hôtel de ville; *hallmark*, estampille, poinçon de garantie.

hallo, see hello.

hallow [halouᵉ] *v.* sanctifier; consacrer; *s.* saint, m.; *All-Hallows*, Toussaint; *Hallowe'en*, vigile de la Toussaint.

hallucination [hᵉlyousᵉnéⁱshᵉn] *s.* hallucination, f. ‖ *hallucinatory* [hᵉlyᵉusinᵉtᵉri] *adj.* hallucinatoire.

halo [héⁱlouᵉ] *s.* halo, m.; auréole, f.

halt [hault] *s.* halte; station, f.; arrêt, m.; *v.* faire halte; arrêter.

halt [hault] *s.* boitement, m.; *v.* boiter; *adj.* boiteux; *halting*, claudicant, éclopé; ânonnant.

halter [hault^er] *s.* licou, m.; hart, f.

halve [hav] *v.* partager en deux. ‖ **halves** [-z] *pl. of* **half**.

ham [ham] *s.* jambon; jarret; cabotin (colloq.), m.

hamlet [hamlit] *s.* hameau, m.

hammer [ham^er] *s.* marteau; percuteur; chien de fusil, m.; *v.* marteler; forger; enfoncer; *drop hammer,* marteau-pilon; *sledge hammer,* marteau de forgeron; *hammer-drill,* marteau pneumatique. ‖ *hammering* [hamring] *s.* martèlement; pilonnage, m.; rossée, f. ‖ *hammerless* [ham^erlis] *adj.* sans chien [gun].

hammock [ham^ek] *s.* hamac, m.

hamper [hàmp^er] *s.* panier, m.; manne, bourriche, f.

hamper [hàmp^er] *v.* gêner, entraver; brouiller [lock].

hand [hànd] *s.* main; écriture; signature; part, aiguille [watch], f.; ouvrier; jeu [cards]; côté [side], m.; *v.* passer, donner; *to hand in,* remettre; *to hand on,* transmettre; *at hand,* sous la main; *hands up!,* haut les mains!; *on the one hand,* d'une part; *on the right hand side,* à droite; *to hand about,* faire passer; *handbag,* sac à main; *handsel,* étrenne, denier à Dieu. ‖ *handball* [-baul] *s.* handball, m. ‖ *handbill* [-bil] *s.* prospectus, m. ‖ *handcuff* [-kœf] *v.* mettre les menottes; *s. pl.* menottes, f. pl. ‖ *handful* [-f^el] *s.* poignée, f. ‖ *handicap* [-ikap] *s.* handicap, obstacle, m.; *v.* handicaper. ‖ *handiwork* [-w^erk] *s.* ouvrage manuel, m. ‖ *handkerchief* [hàng-k^ertshif] *s.* mouchoir, m. ‖ *handle* [hànd'l] *s.* manche; bouton [door]; bras [wheelbarrow], m.; poignée [sword]; brimbale [pump]; queue [pan]; anse [basket]; manivelle; manette (mech.), f.; *v.* manier; traiter; palper; manipuler; faire commerce de. ‖ *handmade* [hànméⁱd] *adj.* fait à la main. ‖ *hand-rail* [-réⁱl] *s.* rampe, f.; garde-fou, m. ‖ *handshake* [-shéⁱk] *s.* poignée de main, f.

handsome [hàns^em] *adj.* beau, m.; belle, f. ‖ *handsomeness* [-nis] *s.* beauté, f.

handwriting [hàndraⁱting] *s.* écriture, f.

handy [hàndi] *adj.* proche, sous la main; adroit; commode; maniable.

hang [hàng] *v.* pendre, suspendre; accrocher; tapisser; baisser [head]; être pendu, suspendu; *s.* chute, inclinaison; tendance, f.; *to hang back,* hésiter; *to hang on,* tenir bon; *to hang over,* surplomber.

hangar [hàng^er] *s.* hangar, m.

hanger [hàng^er] *s.* crochet; croc; portemanteau; bourreau; coutelas;

paper-hanger, tapissier. ‖ **hanging** [hàngⁱng] *s.* pendaison; tenture; tapisserie; pose de papiers; suspension, f.; montage, m.; *adj.* pendant; suspendu. ‖ **hangman** [hàngm^en] (*pl.* **hangmen**) *s.* bourreau, m. ‖ **hangnail** [-néⁱl] *s.* envie (med.), f. ‖ **hangover** [-o^uv^er] *s.* gueule (f.) de bois (colloq.).

hank [hàngk] *s.* écheveau, m.

hanker [hàngk^er] *v.* désirer, aspirer (*for,* à).

haphazard [haphaz^erd] *adv.* au hasard, à l'aventure; *adj.* accidentel, fortuit.

hapless [haplis] *adj.* infortuné; malchanceux. ‖ *haply* [-li] *adv.* par hasard.

happen [hap^en] *v.* arriver; advenir; survenir; *to happen upon,* trouver par hasard; *if you happen to go,* s'il vous arrive d'y aller. ‖ *happening* [-ing] *s.* événement, m.

happily [hap'li] *adv.* heureusement. ‖ *happiness* [hapinis] *s.* bonheur, m.; félicité, f. ‖ *happy* [hapi] *adj.* heureux; fortuné; *happy-go-lucky,* sans souci; à la va-comme-je-te-pousse.

harangue [h^eràng] *s.* harangue, f.; *v.* haranguer.

harass [har^es] *v.* harasser; harceler (mil.): épuiser.

harbo(u)r [hàrb^er] *s.* port; havre; asile; refuge; abri, m.; *v.* héberger; abriter. ‖ *harbo(u)rage* [-ridj] *s.* hospitalité, f.; refuge, m.

hard [hàrd] *adj.* dur; difficile; pénible rude; ferme; ardu; *adv.* durement. fermement; péniblement; violemment *hard drink,* boisson alcoolique *hard labo(u)r,* travaux forcés; *hard luck,* mauvais sort; *hard-working,* laborieux; *hard of hearing,* dur d'oreille; *hard up,* gêné; *hard by,* tout près. ‖ *harden* [-'n] *v.* durcir; endurcir; indurer; scléroser (med.); tremper [steel]; se raidir. ‖ *hardening* [-'ning] *s.* durcissement; endurcissement, m.; sclérose (med.); trempe [metal], f. ‖ *hardly* [-li] *adv.* difficilement; avec peine, à peine; guère. ‖ *hardness* [-nis] *s.* dureté; fermeté; solidité; rigueur. difficulté, f. ‖ *hardship* [-ship] *s.* fatigue; épreuve; privation; souffrance, f. ‖ *hardtack* [-tak] *s. Am.* biscuit de mer, m. ‖ *hardware* [-wèe^r] *s.* quincaillerie, f.; *hardwareman,* quincaillier.

hardy [hàrdi] *adj.* robuste; hardi, audacieux; vivace [plant].

hare [hèe^r] *s.* lièvre, m.; *harebell,* campanule; *hare-brained,* écervelé; *harelip,* bec-de-lièvre.

harem [hèr^em] *s.* harem, m.

haricot [hariko^u] *s.* navarin, m.; *haricot-bean,* haricot blanc.

harlot [hârlet] *s.* prostituée, f.

harm [hârm] *s.* tort, dommage ; mal, m. ; *v.* faire du mal à ; faire tort à. ‖ **harmful** [-fel] *adj.* malfaisant ; nuisible ; préjudiciable. ‖ **harmless** [-lis] *adj.* innocent ; inoffensif. ‖ **harmlessness** [-lisnis] *s.* innocence ; innocuité, f. : caractère inoffensif, m.

harmonic [hârmânik] *adj., s.* harmonique. ‖ **harmonica** [-e] *s.* harmonica, m. ‖ **harmonious** [hârmoouni•s] *adj.* harmonieux. ‖ **harmonize** [hârme-na¹z] *v.* (s')harmoniser ; concorder. ‖ **harmony** [hârme•ni] *s.*° harmonie, f.

harness [hârnis] *s.*° harnais ; harnachement, m. ; *v.* harnacher ; *parachute harness*, ceinture de parachute ; *to get back into harness*, reprendre le collier ; *harness maker*, sellier.

harp [hârp] *s.* harpe, f. ; *v.* jouer de la harpe ; *to harp on one string*, rabâcher toujours la même chose.

harpoon [hârpoun] *s.* harpon ; obus de baleinier, m. ; *v.* harponner.

harpy [hâr¹pi] *s.*° harpie, f.

harrow [haroou] *s.* herse, f. ; *v.* herser ; tourmenter. ‖ **harrowing** [-ing] *adj.* déchirant ; horripilant.

harry [hari] *v.* harceler ; molester ; ravager, dévaster, piller.

harsh [hârsh] *adj.* âpre ; rude ; rigoureux ; discordant [sound]. ‖ **harshness** [-nis] *s.* rudesse ; âpreté ; rigueur ; dureté ; discordance, f.

harvest [hârvist] *s.* récolte ; moisson, f. ; *v.* moissonner ; récolter.

hash [hash] *s.* hachis, m. ; *v.* hacher.

hasp [hasp] *s.* fermoir ; loquet, m. ; *v.* cadenasser.

hassock [hasek] *s.* coussin-agenouilloir, m.

haste [hé¹st] *s.* hâte ; précipitation, f. ; *to make haste*, *v.* (se) dépêcher. ‖ **hasten** [hé¹s'n] *v.* (se) hâter ; accélérer. ‖ **hastily** [hé¹stli] *adv.* à la hâte. ‖ **hasty** [hé¹sti] *adj.* hâtif ; improvisé ; ébauché ; inconsidéré ; violent ; précipité : prompt, rapide.

hat [hat] *s.* chapeau, m. ; *hat-maker*, chapelier ; *hat-peg*, patère.

hatch [hatsh] *s.*° éclosion ; couvée, f. ; *v.* éclore ; couver ; machiner.

hatch [hatsh] *s.*° porte coupée ; vanne d'écluse, f. ‖ **hatchway** [-wé¹] *s.* écoutille (naut.), f.

hatchet [hatshit] *s.* hachette, f.

hate [hé¹t] *s.* haine ; aversion, f. ; *v.* haïr, détester. ‖ **hateful** [-fel] *adj.* haïssable, exécrable ; détestable. ‖ **hatred** [-rid] *s.* haine, f.

haughtily [haut'li] *adv.* avec hauteur. ‖ **haughtiness** [hautinis] *s.*

hauteur, arrogance, f. ‖ **haughty** [hauti] *adj.* hautain ; altier ; arrogant.

haul [haul] *v.* haler ; remorquer ; traîner ; transporter ; *s.* traction ; aubaine, f. ; transport, m.

haunch [hauntsh] *s.*° hanche, f. ; arrière-train ; cuissot (m.) de venaison.

haunt [haunt] *v.* hanter ; fréquenter ; *s.* rendez-vous ; repaire, m. ; *haunted house*, maison hantée.

have [hav] *v.*° avoir ; posséder ; prendre : tenir ; contenir ; *to have a suit made*, faire faire un complet ; *I have come*, je suis venu ; *I had better*, je ferais mieux ; *you have been had*, on vous a eu ; *have him down*, faites-le descendre ; *to have it over*, en finir.

haven [hé¹ven] *s.* havre ; port ; refuge, asile, m.

havoc [havek] *s.* ravage ; dégât, m.

hawk [hauk] *s.* faucon, m. ; *v.* chasser au faucon ; *hawker*, fauconnier.

hawk [hauk] *v.* colporter ; *hawker*, colporteur.

hawser [hauzer] *s.* haussière, f.

hawthorn [hauthaurn] *s.* aubépine, f.

hay [hé¹] *s.* foin, m. ; herbe sèche, f. ; *haycock*, meulon de foin ; *hay-fever*, rhume des foins ; *hayloft*, fenil ; *hay-making*, fenaison ; *haystack*, meule de foin.

hazard [hazerd] *s.* hasard ; risque ; obstacle ; danger, m. ; *v.* hasarder, risquer. ‖ **hazardous** [-•s] *adj.* hasardeux ; périlleux.

haze [hé¹z] *s.* brume, f. ; *hazy*, brumeux ; confus ; *v.* embrumer.

hazel [hé¹z'l] *s.* noisetier, m. ; *adj.* couleur de noisette ; *hazel nut*, noisette.

he [hi] *pers. pron.* il ; lui ; *he who*, celui qui ; *it is he*, c'est lui ; *there he is*, le voilà.

head [hèd] *s.* tête, f. ; bon sens ; bout [table] ; chevet [bed] ; fond [cask] ; titre ; chapitre, m. ; proue (naut.) ; source, f. ; *v.* conduire ; diriger ; *adj.* principal, premier ; de tête ; *heads or tails*, pile ou face ; *Am. to be out of one's head*, avoir perdu la tête ; *to keep one's head*, conserver son sang-froid ; *to head off*, barrer la route à ; *headache*, mal de tête ; *headdress*, coiffure ; *headland*, promontoire, cap (geogr.) ; *headline*, manchette [newspaper] ; *head-office*, bureau central ; *head-on*, de front ; *headwork*, travail intellectuel. ‖ **heading** [-ing] *s.* en-tête, f. ; titre, m. ‖ **headlamp** [-lamp] *s.* phare ; projecteur, m. ‖ **headlight** [-la¹t] *s.* fanal (railw.) ; phare, m. ‖ **headlong** [-laung] *adv.* précipitamment, témérairement. ‖ **headphone**

[-fo^un] s. casque téléphonique, m. ‖
headquarters [-kwaurt^erz] s. quartier
général; poste de commande, m. ‖
headrope [-ro^up] s. longe, f. ‖ **head-**
strong [-straung] adj. têtu; obstiné. ‖
headway [-wé^1] s. progrès, m.; avance,
f.; to make headway, progresser. ‖
heady [-i] adj. capiteux; impétueux.

heal [hîl] v. guérir; cicatriser. ‖ **heal-**
ing [-ing] s. guérison, f. ‖ **health**
[hèlth] s. santé, f. ‖ **healthful** [-f^el]
adj. salubre; sain. ‖ **healthy** [-i] adj.
sain; en bonne santé; hygiénique.

heap [hîp] s. tas; monceau, m.; v.
amasser; entasser; charger; combler
[with, de].

hear [hî^er] v.* entendre; écouter;
apprendre; entendre parler (of, de); to
hear from, recevoir des nouvelles de. ‖
heard [hë^rd] pret., p. p. of to hear. ‖
hearer [hîr^er] s. auditeur, m.; audi-
trice, f. ‖ **hearing** [hîring] s. audition;
audience; ouïe; chose entendue; portée de voix, f.; to get a hearing, obtenir audience. ‖ **hearsay** [hîrsé^1] s. ouï-
dire, m.; rumeur, f.

hearse [hë^rs] s. corbillard, m.

heart [hârt] s. cœur; courage; centre;
pl. cœur [cards], m.; to one's heart's
content, à cœur joie; to take to heart,
prendre à cœur. ‖ **heartache** [-é^1k] s.
chagrin, m.; angoisse, f.; douleur au
cœur, f. ‖ **heartbeat** [-bît] s. battement de cœur, m. ‖ **heartbroken**
[-bro^uk^en] adj. au cœur brisé; navré. ‖
hearten [-'n] v. encourager. ‖ **heart-**
felt [-fèlt] adj. cordial, sincère, senti.

hearth [hârth] s. foyer; âtre, m.

heartily [hârt'li] adv. cordialement;
de bon cœur. ‖ **heartless** [-lis] adj. sans
cœur; insensible; dur. ‖ **heart-rending**
[-rènding] adj. navrant, déchirant. ‖
hearty [-i] adj. sincère, cordial; sain;
nutritif [food]; substantiel [meal]; sonore [laugh]; s. gars de la Marine, m.

heat [hît] s. chaleur; colère; surexcitation; période d'activité intense;
épreuve éliminatoire [race], f.; v.
chauffer; réchauffer; s'échauffer; **heat-**
insulating, calorifuge; **heat-insula-**
tion, calorifugeage; **heat-wave**, vague
de chaleur. ‖ **heater** [-^er] s. appareil
de chauffage, m.

heathen [hîth^en] adj., s. païen; hea-
thendom, heathenism, paganisme.

heather [hézh^er] s. bruyère, f.

heating [hîting] s. chauffage, m.;
central heating plant, installation de
chauffage central; **heating-apparatus**,
calorifère; **heating power**, pouvoir
calorifique.

heave [hîv] v. lever; pousser [sigh];
hisser; palpiter [heart]; (se) soulever;
virer (naut.); avoir des nausées; s.
soulèvement; effort, m.

heaven [hèv^en] s. ciel, m.; **heavenly**,
céleste.

heavily [hèv'li] adv. pesamment;
tristement; fortement. ‖ **heaviness**
[hèvinis] s. pesanteur; lourdeur; tristesse, f.; accablement, m. ‖ **heavy**
[hèvi] adj. pesant; lourd; massif [me-
tal]; accablant; abattu [heart]; mauvais [road]; sévère [blame]; **heavy-**
handed, maladroit.

hecatomb [hèk^etoumb] s. hécatombe, f.

hectic [hèktik] adj. fiévreux; tuberculeux; trépidant (fam.).

hedge [hèdj] s. haie, f.; v. entourer
d'une haie; user de subterfuges;
hedge-hopping, rase-mottes; **natural**
hedge, haie vive.

hedgehog [hèdjhaug] s. hérisson, m.

heed [hîd] v. faire attention; prendre
garde; s. attention, f.; **heedful**, vigilant; **heedless**, étourdi; **heedlessness**,
étourderie.

heel [hîl] s. talon, m.; quignon
[bread]; Am. salaud, m.; v. mettre
des talons à; down at the heel, éculé
[shoe]; dans la dèche; to heel over,
donner de la bande (naut.).

heft [hèft] s. poids, m.; majeure partie, f.; v. soulever; soupeser.

heifer [hèf^er] s. génisse, f.

height [ha^it] s. hauteur; élévation;
altitude, f. ‖ **heighten** [ha^it'n] v. augmenter; accroître; intensifier; rehausser, relever.

heinous [hé^in^es] adj. atroce; odieux;
infâme.

heir [è^er] s. héritier, m. ‖ **heiress**
[è^eris] s.* héritière, f.; **heirloom**, souvenir de famille.

held [hèld] pret., p. p. of to hold.

helicopter [hèlikâpt^er] s. hélicoptère, m.; helicopter-borne, héliporté.

helix [hîliks] (pl. helices [hîlisìz]) s.
spirale; hélice, f.

hell [hèl] s. enfer, m.; **hellish**, infernal, diabolique.

hello! [hèlo^u] interj. holà!; allô!

helm [hèlm] s. gouvernail, m.; **helms-**
man, timonier.

helmet [hèlmit] s. casque, m.

help [hèlp] s. aide; secours; personnel assistant, m.; assistance, f.; v.
aider; secourir; he cannot help it,
n'y peut rien; I cannot help laughing,
je ne peux m'empêcher de rire; help
yourself, servez-vous [food]. ‖ **helper**
[-^er] s. aide; assistant, m. ‖ **helpful**
[-f^el] adj. utile; serviable; **helping**
[-ing] s. portion [food]; aide, f. ‖
helpless [-lis] adj. impuissant; désemparé; faible; perplexe; inextricabl

[situation]. || **helplessness** [-lisnis] s. faiblesse ; impuissance ; invalidité ; incapacité, f.

hem [hèm] s. ourlet ; bord, m.; v. ourler, border ; to hem in, cerner ; Am. hem binding, extra-fort.

hem [hèm] v. toussoter ; faire hum ; interj. hem ! hum ! ; to hem and haw, ânonner.

hemiplegia [hèmiplîdji] s. hémiplégie, f.

hemisphere [hèmᵉsfiᵉʳ] s. hémisphère, m.

hemlock [hèmlâk] s. ciguë, f. || hemlock fir, Fr. Can. pruche, f.

hemoptysis [hèmauptisis] s. hémoptysie, f.

hemorrhage [hèmᵉridj] s. hémorragie, f.

hemp [hèmp] s. chanvre, m.

hemstitch* [hèmstitsh] s. point d'ourlet ; ourlet à jour, m.; v. ourler à jour.

hen [hèn] s. poule ; femelle d'oiseau, f.; hen-coop, cage à poules ; henhouse, poulailler ; henpecked husband, mari que sa femme mène par le bout du nez; henroost, juchoir.

hence [hèns] adv. d'ici, de là ; par suite ; en conséquence. || henceforth [-foᵘrth] adv. dorénavant ; désormais.

henna [hénᵉ] s. henné, m.; v. teindre au henné.

hep [hèp] adj. averti, affranchi ; à la page.

hepatic [hipatik] adj. hépatique.

her [hëʳ] pron. elle ; la ; lui ; adj. son, sa, ses ; à elle ; d'elle ; I saw her, je la vis ; I speak to her, je lui parle ; she loves her father, elle aime son père ; she lost her senses, elle a perdu connaissance ; she has cut her finger, elle s'est coupé le doigt.

herald [hèrᵉld] s. héraut ; messager ; précurseur, m.; v. proclamer ; introduire, annoncer.

heraldry [hèrᵉldri] s. science héraldique ; armoiries, f. pl.

herb [ë°b] s. herbe, f.; herb-shop, herboristerie. || herbalist [ë°bᵉlist] s. botaniste ; herboriste, m. f. || herby [-i] adj. herbeux.

herd [hë°d] s. troupeau, m.; foule, cohue, f. ; the common herd, le « vulgum pecus » ; v. réunir ; s'attrouper. || herdsman [-zmᵉn] s. bouvier, berger, m.

here [hiᵉʳ] adv. ici ; here and there, çà et là ; here's to you, à votre santé ; here we are, nous voici arrivés. || hereabout(s) [-ᵉbaᵘt(s)] adv. près d'ici, dans ces parages. || hereafter [hiᵉʳaftᵉʳ] adv. ci-après, ci-dessous ;

désormais ; à l'avenir ; s. la vie future, f. || hereby [hiᵉʳbaⁱ] adv. par là, par ce moyen ; près d'ici, par la présente (comm.).

hereditary [hᵉrèdᵉtèri] adj. héréditaire ; transmissible. || heredity [hᵉrèdᵉti] s. hérédité, f.

herein [hiᵉrin] adv. en ceci, sur ce point ; ci-inclus.

heresy [hèrᵉsi] s.* hérésie, f. || heretic [hèrᵉtik] adj., s. hérétique.

heretofore [hiᵉrᵗtofoᵘr] adv. auparavant, jusqu'ici. || hereupon [hiᵉrᵉpᵊn] adv. là-dessus. || herewith [hiᵉrwith] adv. ci-joint ; avec ceci ; inclus.

heritage [hèrᵉtidj] s. héritage, m.

hermetic [hᵉrmètik] adj. hermétique.

hermit [hëʳmit] s. ermite, m.

hernia [hëʳniᵉ] s. hernie, f.

hero [hiroᵘ] s.* héros, m. || heroic [hiroᵘik] adj. héroïque. || heroine [hèroᵘin] héroïne, f. || heroism [hèroᵘizᵉm] s. héroïsme, m.

heron [hèrᵉn] s. héron, m.

herring [hèring] s. hareng, m.; red herring, hareng saur.

hers [hëʳz] poss. pron. le sien, la sienne, les siens, les siennes ; à elle ; s. ses parents à elle ; les siens ; are these books hers?, ces livres sont-ils à elle ? ; it is no business of hers, cela ne la regarde pas. || herself [hᵉrsèlf] pron. elle-même ; soi-même ; she cut herself, elle s'est coupée ; she saw herself in the mirror, elle se vit dans le miroir ; she was sitting by herself, elle était assise seule.

hesitate [hèzᵉtéⁱt] v. hésiter ; balbutier. || hesitating [-ing] adj. hésitant ; indécis ; irrésolu. || hesitatingly [-ingli] adv. avec hésitation. || hesitation [hèzᵉtéⁱshᵉn] s. hésitation ; indécision, f.

heterogeneous [hétᵉrodjînîᵉs] adj. hétérogène.

hew [hyou] v.* tailler, couper ; abattre [tree]. || hewn [hyoun] p. p. of to hew ; rough-hewn, taillé à coups de serpe.

hexagon [hèksᵉgân] s. hexagone, m.

hey! [héⁱ] interj. hé ! hein !

heyday [héⁱdéⁱ] s. beaux jours, m. pl.; période florissante ; fleur [youth], f.; éclat [glory], m.; faîte [prosperity], m.

hibernate [haⁱbᵉrnéⁱt] v. hiberner ; hiverner ; somnoler, paresser.

hiccup [hík°p], **hiccough** [híkauf] s. hoquet, m.; v. avoir le hoquet ; hoqueter.

hickory [híkᵉri] s.* hickory ; noyer d'Amérique, m.

hid [hid] *pret.*, *p. p. of* to hide. ‖ **hidden** [hid'n] *p. p. of* to hide; *adj.* caché; secret; mystérieux. ‖ **hide** [ha¹d] *v.** (se) cacher; enfouir; masquer; couvrir; *to hide from*, se cacher de; *to play hide and seek*, jouer à cache-cache; *hiding-place*, cachette.

hide [ha¹d] *s.* peau, f.; cuir, m.; *v.* rosser; *hidebound*, à l'esprit étroit.

hideous [hídi•s] *adj.* hideux.

hierarchical [ha¹e•rákik•l] *adj.* hiérarchique. ‖ **hierarchy** [ha¹e•rár'ki] *s.** hiérarchie, f.

high [ha¹] *adj.* haut; élevé; hautain, fier; faisandé [game]; lointain [antiquity]; puissant [explosive]; violent [wind]; *Am.* ivre (fam.); *adv.* haut, hautement; grandement; fortement; *it is high time that*, il est grand temps que; *to play high*, jouer gros jeu, *high altar*, maître-autel; *high-born*, de haute extraction; *high-handed*, despotique; *high-heeled*, à hauts talons; *high-priced*, coûteux; *high-road*, grand-route; *high-sounding*, sonore, ronflant; ‖ **highland** [-l•nd] *s.* terre haute, f.; *the Highlands*, les Highlands d'Écosse. ‖ **highly** [-li] *adv.* beaucoup; très; supérieurement; hautement; *highly paid*, très bien payé. ‖ **highness** [-nis] *s.* hauteur; élévation; Altesse [title], f. ‖ **highway** [-wé¹] grand-route; voie publique; chaussée, f.; *express highway*, autoroute; *highwayman*, voleur de grand chemin.

hike [ha¹k] *s.* marche; excursion à pied, f.; *v.* faire un trajet à pied; trimer (slang). ‖ **hiker** [-e^r] *s.* excursionniste, m. f.

hilarious [hilè•ri•s] *adj.* hilare. ‖ **hilarity** [hilar•ti] *s.* hilarité, f.

hill [hil] *s.* colline; butte; montée, f.; monticule; coteau, m.; *up hill and down dale*, par monts et par vaux; *hillock*, mamelon, *hillside*, flanc de coteau; *hilltop*, éminence, cime; *hilly*, accidenté, montagneux, vallonné.

hilt [hilt] *s.* poignée [sword], f.

him [him] *pron.* le; lui; celui; *I see him*, je le vois; *I speak to him*, je lui parle; *to him who speaks*, à celui qui parle. ‖ **himself** [himsèlf] *pron.* lui-même; soi-même; se; *he came himself*, il vint lui-même; *he avenged himself*, il s'est vengé.

hind [ha¹nd], **hinder** [ha¹nde^r] *adj.* postérieur; de derrière; *hindmost*, dernier, ultime.

hind [ha¹nd] *s.* biche, f.

hinder [hinde^r] *v.* empêcher; gêner; retarder. ‖ **hindrance** [-re^ns] *s.* empêchement; obstacle (*to*, à), m.

hinge [hindj] *s.* gond, m.; charnière, f.; principe essentiel, m.; *v.* tourner sur des gonds, sur une charnière;

off one's hinges, déboussolé; *to hinge on*, dépendre de, être axé sur.

hint [hint] *s.* allusion; insinuation, f.; aperçu; mode d'emploi, m.; *v.* insinuer; faire allusion; suggérer; *to take the hint*, comprendre à demi-mot.

hip [hip] *s.* hanche, f.; *hip-joint disease*, coxalgie; *hip-bath*, bain de siège; *hipbone*, os iliaque.

hippodrome [hip•dro°um] *s.* hippodrome, m.

hippopotamus [hip•pât•m•s] *s.** hippopotame, m.

hire [ha¹e^r] *s.* louage; gages, m.; location, f.; *v.* louer; engager; soudoyer; *hireling*, mercenaire.

hirsute [he^rsyout] *adj.* hirsute.

his [hiz] *poss. pron.* son, sa, ses; le sien, la sienne, les siens, les siennes; à lui; *it is his*, c'est le sien, c'est à lui; *he has broken his leg*, il s'est cassé la jambe.

hiss [his] *s.** sifflement; sifflet, m.; *v.* siffler.

historian [histo°uri•n] *s.* historien, m. ‖ **historic(al)** [histaurik'l] *adj.* historique. ‖ **history** [histri] *s.** histoire, f.

hit [hit] *v.** frapper; heurter; toucher [target]; atteindre [mark]; convenir (*with*, à); *s.* coup, choc, m.; trouvaille; touche, réussite, f.; *to hit back*, rendre coup pour coup; *to hit the mark*, toucher juste; *to hit upon*, tomber sur; *direct hit*, coup au but; *great hit*, succès fou, *hit-and-run driver*, chauffard, *hit-the-baby*, *Am.* jeu de massacre.

hitch [hitsh] *s.** accroc; obstacle; incident; contretemps; nœud, m.; anicroche, f.; *v.* (s')accrocher; amarrer; empêtrer; sautiller, boiter; *hitch hike*, faire de l'auto-stop, *hitch hiker*, auto-stoppeur. *hitch hiking*, auto-stop.

hither [hizhe^r] *adv.* ici; *hitherto* jusqu'ici.

hive [ha¹v] *s.* ruche, f.

hives [ha¹vz] *s. pl.* urticaire (med.), m.

hoar [ho°ur] *adj.* blanchi, chenu; *s.* givre, m.; *hoar-frost*, gelée blanche.

hoard [ho°urd] *s.* tas; trésor, magot, m.; *v.* accumuler; thésauriser.

hoarse [ho°urs] *adj.* enroué, rauque ‖ **hoarsen** [-e^n] *v.* (s') enrouer. *hoarseness* [-nis] *s.* enrouement, m.

hoax [ho°uks] *s.** mystification attrape, f.; *v.* mystifier.

hob [hâb] *s.* plaque; matrice (mech.) f.; clou [shoe], m.

hobble [hâb'l] *v.* clopiner; entraver *s.* clopinement, m.; entrave, f.

hobby [hâbi] *s.** dada, m.; marotte, f

hobo [ho^{o}ubo^{o}u] *s.* vagabond; clochard, m.

hock [hâk] *s.* jarret, m.; *v.* couper le jarret [horse].

hockey [hâki] *s.* hockey, m.

hocus-pocus [ho^{o}uk^{e}s-po^{o}uk^{e}s] *s.* tour de passe-passe, m.

hod [hâd] *s.* auge, augette, f.; oiseau [tool], m.

hodgepodge [hâdjpâdj] *s.* méli-mélo, salmigondis, m.

hoe [ho^{o}u] *s.* houe, binette, f.; *v.* sarcler.

hog [hâg] *s.* cochon, porc; dos de chat (aviat.); goret (naut.), m.; *v.* manger gloutonnement; **hoggish**, sale, glouton; **hogherd**, porcher; **hog-pen**, étable à cochons; **hogshead**, barrique.

hoist [ho^{i}st] *s.* grue, f.; *v.* hisser; arborer [flag].

hold [ho^{o}uld] *v.** tenir; contenir; détenir, retenir; se maintenir; durer; endurer; être d'avis; demeurer; *s.* prise; garde; place forte; cale (naut.), f.; appui, soutien, m.; *to hold down*, empêcher de monter; *to hold fast*, tenir bon; *to hold off*, tenir à distance; *to hold good*, demeurer valable; *to hold out*, tenir jusqu'au bout; *to hold with*, être du parti de; *to hold on*, s'accrocher; *to catch hold of*, s'emparer de; *to let go one's hold*, lâcher prise. ‖ **holder** [-^{e}r] *s.* teneur; détenteur; support; tenancier; porteur (comm.); titulaire, m.; **pen-holder**, porte-plume. ‖ **holding** [-ing] *s.* possession; terre affermée, f. ‖ **hold-up** [-$_e$p] *s.* attaque à main armée, f.; embarras, m.; entrave, f.

hole [ho^{o}ul] *s.* trou; creux, m.; cavité, f.; *v.* trouer; *air hole*, trou d'air; *to be in a hole*, être dans le pétrin.

holiday [hâl^{e}dé^i] *s.* jour de fête; jour férié; congé, m.; vacances, f. pl.

holiness [ho^{o}ulinis] *s.* sainteté, f.

Holland [hâl^{e}nd] *s.* Hollande, f.

hollow [hâlo^{o}u] *adj.* creux; vide; trompeur; *s.* creux; vallon, m.; *v.* creuser; excaver.

holly [hâli] *s.* houx, m.

hollyhock [hâlihâk] *s.* rose trémière, f.

holster [ho^{o}ulst^{e}r] *s.* étui [revolver], m.; fonte, f.

holy [ho^{o}uli] *adj.* saint; sacré; bénit [water].

home [ho^{o}um] *s.* logis; pays; foyer, m.; demeure; habitation; patrie, f.; *at home*, chez soi; *to come home*, rentrer chez soi; *make yourself at home*, faites comme chez vous; *to hit home*, frapper juste; **homeland**, terre natale; **homeless**, sans-abri; apatride; **homelike**, familial, intime, commode; **homely**, simple, terne; sans beauté; **home-made bread**, pain de ménage; **home office**, bureau central; **home run**, *Fr. Can.* coup de circuit; **home-sick**, nostalgique; **homesickness**, mal du pays; **homespun**, étoffe de fabrication domestique; **homestead**, château, propriété, f.; **homeward**, vers la maison; vers le pays; **homeward voyage**, voyage de retour.

homicide [hâm^{e}sa^{i}d] *s.* homicide; assassin, meurtrier, m.

homily [hâmili] *s.** homélie, f.

homing [ho^{o}uming] *s.* vol de rentrée (aviat.), m.; **homing mechanism**, radiogoniomètre; **homing pigeon**, pigeon voyageur.

homogeneous [ho^{o}um$_e$djini^{e}s] *adj.* homogène.

homologate [hemâlgé^{i}t] *v.* homologuer. ‖ **homologous** [-g^{e}s] *adj.* homologue.

homonym [hâm^{e}nim] *s.* homonyme, m.

hone [ho^{o}un] *s.* pierre à aiguiser, f.; *v.* repasser [razor]; affiler; affûter.

honest [ânist] *adj.* honnête; probe; sincère; loyal et marchand [goods]. ‖ **honestly** [-li] *adv.* honnêtement; loyalement; sans fraude. ‖ **honesty** [-i] *s.* honnêteté; loyauté; probité, f.

honey [hâni] *s.* miel, m.; *v.* sucrer; flatter; *honey !*, chéri(e) ! ‖ **honeycomb** [-ko^{o}um] *s.* rayon de miel; filtre à alvéoles, m.; **honeycombed**, criblé; gaufré. ‖ **honeyed** [-id] *adj.* mielleux; doux. ‖ **honeymoon** [-moun] *s.* lune de miel, f.; *v.* passer sa lune de miel. ‖ **honeysuckle** [-sœk'l] *s.* chèvrefeuille, m.

honk [haungk] *s.* coup de Klaxon, m.; *v.* klaxonner.

hono(u)r [ân^{e}r] *s.* honneur, m.; *v.* honorer. ‖ **hono(u)rable** [ân^{e}r^{e}b'l] *adj.* honorable. ‖ **honorary** [ân^{e}r^{e}ri] *adj.* honoraire; d'honneur; bénévole; honorifique. ‖ **honorific** [ân^{e}rifik] *adj.* honorifique.

hood [houd] *s.* coiffe; capote, f.; capot [auto]; chapeau (mech.), m.; *v.* encapuchonner; **hoodwink**, bander les yeux; jeter de la poudre aux yeux à; aveugler.

hoof [houf] *s.* sabot [horse], m.; **hoofed**, ongulé.

hook [houk] *s.* croc; crochet; crampon; hameçon, m.; agrafe, f.; *v.* accrocher; agrafer; attraper [fish]; *by hook and by crook*, par tous les moyens; *to hook it*, décamper; *on his own hook*, pour son propre compte. ‖ **hooky** [-i] *adj.* crochu; *Am.* to play hooky, faire l'école buissonnière.

hoop [houp] *s.* cerceau; cercle; arceau [croquet], m.; jante [wheel]; frette (techn.), f.; *v.* cercler; fretter; *hoop-skirt,* crinoline.

hoot [hout] *v.* huer; hululer; *s.* huée, f.; hululement, m.; *hooter,* Klaxon; sirène; sifflet; *hooting,* huée.

hop [hâp] *s.* saut, sautillement, m.; *v.* sauter à cloche-pied.

hop [hâp] *s.* houblon, m.

hope [hooup] *s.* espérance, f.; espoir, m.; *v.* espérer; *to hope for,* s'attendre à; *hopeful,* optimiste, prometteur; *hopeless,* sans espoir, irrémédiable, incurable; *hopelessness,* désespérance; état désespéré.

hopscotch [hâpskâtsh] *s.* marelle, f.

horde [hoourd] *s.* horde, f.; *v.* vivre en horde.

horizon [h*e*ra¹z*e*n] *s.* horizon, m. ‖ *horizontal* [haur*e*zânt'l] *adj.* horizontal.

hormone [hau*r*moo*u*n] *s.* hormone, f.

horn [haurn] *s.* corne, f.; Klaxon; cor [music], m.; *v.* corner; klaxonner, avertir [car].

hornet [haurnit] *s.* frelon, m.

horologe [hâr*e*lâdj] *s.* horloge, f.

horrible [haur*e*b'l] *adj.* horrible; horribly, horriblement.

horrid [haurid] *adj.* horrible; hideux; affreux.

horrific [h*e*rifik] *adj.* horrible. ‖ *horrify* [haur*e*fa¹] *v.* horrifier; épouvanter. ‖ *horror* [haur*e*r] *s.* horreur, f.

horse [haurs] *s.* cheval; chevalet, m.; cavalerie, f.; *adj.* de cheval; à chevaux; hippique; *blooded horse,* pursang; *pack horse,* cheval de bât; *saddle-horse,* cheval de selle; *horseflesh,* viande de cheval; *horse-fly,* taon; *horse-hair,* crin; *horse race,* course de chevaux; *horse sense,* gros bon sens; *horse shoe,* fer à cheval; *horse-show,* concours hippique; *horsewhip,* cravache, fouet. ‖ *horseman* [-m*e*n] (*pl. horsemen*) *s.* cavalier; écuyer, m.; *horsemanship,* équitation. ‖ *horsepower* [-paou*e*r] *s.* cheval-vapeur, m.; puissance en chevaux, f. ‖ *horse radish* [-radish] *s.* raifort, m.

hose [hoouz] *s.* bas [stockings]; tuyau, m.; canalisation, f.; *men's hose,* chaussettes d'homme. ‖ *hosiery* [hoou jri] *s.** bonneterie, f.

hospitable [hâspit*e*b'l] *adj.* hospitalier. ‖ *hospital* [hâspit'l] *s.* hôpital, m.; infirmerie, f.; *surgical hospital,* ambulance militaire; *hospital train,* train sanitaire. ‖ *hospitality* [hâspital*e*ti] *s.* hospitalité, f. ‖ *hospitalization* [hâspit*e*lizé¹sh*e*n] *s.* hospitalisation, f. ‖ *hospitalize* [hâspitla¹z] *v.* hospitaliser.

host [hooust] *s.* armée; multitude, f.

host [hooust] *s.* hôte; hôtelier, m.

host [hooust] *s.* hostie, f.; *sacred host,* hostie consacrée.

hostage [hâstidj] *s.* otage; gage, m.

hostel [hâst*e*l] *s.* maison universitaire, f.; *youth hostel,* auberge de jeunesse.

hostess [hâstis] *s.** hôtesse, f.

hostile [hâst'l] *adj.* hostile; ennemi. ‖ *hostility* [hastil*e*ti] *s.** hostilité, inimitié, f.

hot [hât] *adj.* chaud; brûlant; ardent; coléreux. épicé; *it is hot,* il fait très chaud; *white hot,* chauffé à blanc; *hotbed,* couche (hort.); foyer (fig.); *hothouse,* serre chaude; *hot-plate,* chauffe-plat.

hotel [hoout*e*l] *s.* hôtel, m.; *hotelkeeper,* hôtelier.

hotly [hâtli] *adv.* chaudement; ardemment; violemment; avec véhémence.

hound [haound] *s.* chien courant, m.; *v.* chasser; poursuivre; pister; *pack of hounds,* meute; *hound's-tooth check,* Am. pied-de-poule.

hour [aou*r*] *s.* heure, f.; *office hours,* heures de présence, heures de bureau; *hour hand,* aiguille des heures; *hourly* [-li] *adv.* d'heure en heure; fréquemment; *adj.* horaire; fréquent.

house [haous] *s.* maison; demeure; habitation; salle (theat.); assemblée politique, f.; [haouz] *v.* loger; héberger; donner l'hospitalité à; garer [auto]; *country house,* maison de campagne; *housebreaking,* cambriolage; *Br the House of Commons,* la Chambre des communes. *Am. the House of Representatives,* la Chambre des représentants. ‖ *household* [haousho*u*ld] *s.* maisonnée, famille, f.; *adj.* domestique, de ménage. ‖ *housekeeper* [haouskip*e*r] *s.* femme de charge; gouvernante, ménagère, f. ‖ *housekeeping* [-kip*i*ng] *s.* ménage, m. ‖ *housetop* [-tâp] *s.* toit, m. ‖ *housewife* [-wa¹f] (*pl housewives* [-wa¹vz]) *s.* maîtresse de maison; ménagère [hæzif] trousse de couture, f. ‖ *housework* [-wërk] *s.* travaux domestiques, m. pl.

hove [hoouv] *pret., p. p. of to heave.*

hovel [hæv'l] *s.* appentis, m.; baraque, cahute, f.

hover [hæv*e*r] *v.* planer; se balancer; voltiger; rôder (*around,* autour).

how [haou] *adv.* comment; comme à quel degré; *how much* (sing.), *how many* (plur.), combien?; *how far is it?,* à quelle distance est-ce?; *how old are you?,* quel âge avez-vous? *how long have you been in France?*

depuis quand êtes-vous en France?;
any how, n'importe comment, quoi
qu'il en soit; *anyhow,* de toute façon. ‖ **however** [ha⁰uèvᵉr] *adv., conj.*
de toute façon; cependant; néanmoins; du reste; quelque ... que; si ...
que; *however difficult it may be,*
quelque difficile que ce soit; *however
much,* si fort que.

howitzer [ha⁰uitsᵉr] *s.* obusier, m.

howl [ha⁰ul] *s.* hurlement [dog, wolf],
m.; *v.* hurler; se lamenter.

hub [hœb] *s.* moyeu, m.

hubbub [hœbœb] *s.* tintamarre; boucan; brouhaha, m.

huckster [hœkstᵉr] *s.* revendeur, m.;
Am. marchand (m.) des quatre-saisons; agent (m.) de publicité; trafiquant, m.; *v.* colporter; trafiquer;
marchander.

huddle [hœd'l] *s.* confusion, f.; pêle-
mêle, m.; *v.* brouiller; jeter en vrac;
fourrer; *to huddle together,* se serrer
les uns contre les autres.

hue [hyou] *s.* teinte, nuance, f.

huff [hœf] *s.* accès de colère, m.; *v.*
s'emporter; malmener; *huffish,* susceptible, irritable.

hug [hœg] *v.* étreindre; serrer; *to hug
the wind,* serrer le vent (naut.); *s.*
étreinte, f.; embrassement, m.

huge [hyoudj] *adj.* énorme; immense.

hull [hœl] *s.* coque, carène (naut.;
aviat.); cosse, gousse, balle, f.; *v.*
écosser, décortiquer.

hum [hœm] *v.* bourdonner; fredonner; murmurer; *s.* bourdonnement;
fredon, m.; *interj.* hum!

human [hyoumᵉn] *adj., s.* humain. ‖
humane [hyoumé¹n] *adj.* humain,
humanitaire. ‖ *humanism* [-iz'm] *s.*
humanisme, m. ‖ *humanitarian* [hyou-
manⁱtèrⁱᵉn] *adj.* humanitaire, *s.* phi-
lanthrope, m. f. ‖ *humanity* [hyou-
mᵃnⁱti] *s.⁰* humanité, f.

humble [hœmb'l] *adj.* humble; modeste; *v* humilier, abaisser; *to humble
oneself,* s'humilier, **humbly,** humblement. ‖ *humbleness* [-nis] *s.* humilité;
modestie, f.

humbug [hœmbœg] *s.* sornette; tromperie, f.; farceur, m.

humid [hyoumid] *adj.* humide. ‖
humidify [hyoumidⁱfa¹] *v.* humidifier.
‖ *humidity* [-dᵉti] *s.* humidité, f.

humiliate [hyoumⁱlié¹t] *v.* humilier.
‖ *humiliation* [hyoumⁱlié¹shᵉn] *s.* humiliation, f. ‖ *humility* [hyoumⁱlⁱti] *s.*
humilité, f.

hummingbird [hœmingbërd] *s.* oiseau-mouche, m.

hummock [hœmᵉk] *s.* monticule, m.

humo(u)r [hyoumᵉr] *s.* humeur; disposition, f.; caprice; humour, m.; *out
of humo(u)r,* de mauvaise humeur;
v. complaire à; flatter; se prêter à;
suivre l'humeur de. ‖ *humorist* [hyou-
mᵉrist] *s.* humoriste, m. ‖ *humoristic*
[hyoumᵉrⁱstik] *adj.* humoristique. ‖
humorous [hyoumᵉrᵉs] *adj.* humoristique, plein d'humour; comique.

hump [hœmp] *s.* bosse, f.; dos-d'âne
[road]; dos de chat (aviat.), m.; *v.*
courber, arquer; cambrer.

hunch [hœntsh] *s.⁰* bosse, f.; gros
morceau; chanteau [bread]; *Am.* pressentiment, m.; *v.* arrondir, voûter. ‖
hunchback [-bak] *s.* bossu, m.

hundred [hœndrᵉd] *adj.* cent; *s.* centaine, f. ‖ *hundredth* [-th] *adj.* centième.

hung [hœng] *pret., p. p. of* **to hang.**

Hungarian [hœnggèⁱrⁱᵉn] *adj., s.*
hongrois. ‖ *Hungary* [hœngᵉri] *s.* Hon-
grie, f.

hunger [hœnggᵉr] *s.* faim, f.; *v.* avoir
faim, affamer; désirer ardemment. ‖
hungrily [-grⁱli] *adv.* avidement; vo-
racement. ‖ *hungry* [-gri] *adj.* affamé;
famélique; *to be hungry,* avoir faim.

hunk [hœngk] *s.* gros morceau; quignon [bread], m.

hunt [hœnt] *s.* chasse; poursuite;
meute, f.; *v.* chasser; poursuivre;
chercher; *to hunt down,* traquer. ‖
hunter [-ᵉr] *s.* chasseur; cheval de
chasse, m. ‖ *huntsman* [-smᵉn] (*pl.*
huntsmen) *s.* chasseur, m.

hurdle [hërd'l] *s.* claie; clôture, f.;
obstacle, m.; *v.* clôturer; sauter un
obstacle.

hurl [hërl] *v.* jeter, lancer.

hurly-burly [hërlibèⁱli] *s.* tumulte,
tohu-bohu, m.

hurrah! [hᵉra] *interj.* hourra!; *v.*
pousser des vivas.

hurricane [hërⁱké¹n] *s.* ouragan, m.

hurried [hèrⁱd] *adj.* précipité; hâtif;
hurriedly, précipitamment. ‖ *hurry*
[hëri] *s* hâte, précipitation, f.; *v.* presser; (se) hâter, *to be in a hurry,* être
pressé, *there is no hurry,* ça ne presse
pas; *to hurry on,* activer, faire presser.

hurst [hërst] *s.* tertre; banc de sable,
m.; colline boisée, f.

hurt [hërt] *v.⁰* faire mal à; nuire à;
offenser; endommager; *s.* mal; préjudice, dommage, m.; blessure, f.; *my
tooth hurts me,* j'ai mal à une dent;
pret., p. p. of **to hurt.** ‖ *hurter* [-ᵉr]
s. heurtoir, m.

husband [hœzbᵉnd] *s.* mari; époux,
m.; *v.* économiser; marier. ‖ *hus-
bandman* [-mᵉn] (*pl.* *husbandmen*) *s.*
fermier, m. ‖ *husbandry* [-ri] *s.* économie; agriculture, f.

hush [hœsh] v. se taire; faire taire; s. silence, m.; interj. chut!; to hush up a scandal étouffer un scandale; hush-money, argent obtenu par chantage, prix du silence.

husk [hœsk] s cosse; gousse; écale; pelure, peau, f.; brou [nut], m.; v. éplucher [corn], monder [barley]; écosser, écaler.

husky [hœski] adj. enroué; robuste, solide; s chien esquimau, m.

hustle [hœs'l] v bousculer; presser; précipiter se presser Am s'activer; s. activité, hâte, presse; énergie; vigueur, f.; Am. allant; esprit (m.) d'entreprise.

hut [hœt] s. hutte; cabane, f.; baraquement, m.; forester's hut, maison forestière

hutch [hœtsh] s.* huche, f.; clapier, m.

hyacinth [ha¹ɛsinth] s. jacinthe, f.

hydrant [ha¹drɛnt] s. bouche à incendie, prise d'eau, f **hydrate** [-e¹t] v. hydrater s **hydrate** m.

hydraulic [ha¹draulik] adj. hydraulique.

hydrogen [ha¹drɛdjɛn] s. hydrogène, m.

hydroplane [ha¹drɛplé¹n] s. hydravion, m.

hyena [ha¹inɛ] s. hyène, f.

hygiene [ha¹djin] s. hygiène, f.

hymn [him] s. hymne, m.

hyphen [ha¹fɛn] s. trait d'union, m.

hypnosis [hipnoᵘsis] (pl hypnoses [-iz]) s hypnose || **hypnotic** [-nâtik] adj. hypnotique, s. hypnotique, m.; personne (f.) en état d'hypnose. || **hypnotism** [hipnâtizᵉm] s. hypnotisme, m

hypocrisy [hipâkrᵉsi] s.* hypocrisie, f. || **hypocrite** [hipâkrit] s. hypocrite, m f

hypothecate [ha¹pâthᵉké¹t] v. hypothéquer

hypothesis [ha¹pâthᵉsis] (pl. hypotheses) s. hypothèse, f.

hysteria [histiri⁶] s hystérie, f. || **hysterical** [histèrik'l] adj hystérique; nerveux frénétique convulsif, Am. désopilant. || **hysterics** [histèriks] s. pl. crise de nerfs, f.

I

I [a¹] pron. je; moi.

ice [a¹s] s. glace; crème glacée, f.; v. glacer frappé [wine] congeler; ice bag, vessie à glace iceberg, iceberg; ice box, glacière ice-cream, glace, Fr Can crème à la glace, icefloe, banquise iced fruits, Am fruits confits, ice-pail, seau à glace ice-pick, piolet icicle [a¹sik'l] s glaçon n || icy [a¹si] adj. glacé; congelé glacial

idea [a¹di⁶] s idée. f.

ideal [a¹di⁶l] adj s idéal. || idealism [a¹di⁶liz⁶m] idéalisme m. || idealist [-di⁶list] idéaliste m. f. || idealistic [a¹di⁶listik] adj idéaliste. || idealize [¹ di⁶la¹z] idéaliser

identical [a¹dentik'l] adj identique || identification [a¹dèntᵉf⁶ké¹sh⁶n] s identification identité f identify [a¹dèntᵉfa¹] identifier || identity [a¹dèntᵉti] s * identité, f.

idiom [idi⁶m] s idiome, idiotisme, m.

idiot [idi⁶t] s idiot, m. || **idiotic** [idiâtik] adj idiot

idle [a¹d'l] adj oisif; désœuvré; futile; paresseux s ralenti m., v. paresser flâner tourner au ralenti, à vide (mech.) || **idleness** [-nis] s oisiveté; paresse futilité f désœuvrement, m. || idler [-ᵉr] s fainéant; flâneur; oisif, m.; roue folle (mech.), f.

idol [a¹d'l] s. idole, f. || **idolatry** [a¹dâlᵉtri] s. idolâtrie, f. || **idolize** [a¹d'la¹z] v idolâtrer.

idyl [aid'l] s idylle, f.

i. e. [a¹ì] abbrev. c'est-à-dire.

if [if] conj. si; as if, comme si; if not, sinon.

igloo [iglou] s. igloo, m.

ignite [igna¹t] v allumer; mettre le feu à prendre feu **igniter** [-ᵉr] s. allumeur moyen d'allumage m. || **ignition** [igni sh⁶n] allumage m.; ignition ignition plug, bougie.

ignoble [ignoᵘb'l] adj. ignoble; abject vi bas

ignominy [ignâmini] s ignominie, f.

ignorance [ign ns] s ignorance, f. || **ignorant** [ign rᵉnt] adj ignorant. || **ignore** [ignoᵘr] ne pas admettre; prétendre ignore dédaigner, ne pas tenir compte de s ignore a bill, prononcer un non-lieu (jur)

ill [il] adj malade mauvais; impropre adv mal s mal malheur, m., **ill-advised** malavisé **ill-bred**, mal élevé **ill-clad**, mal vêtu **ill-humo(u)red**, mal luné **ill-mannered**, sans-gêne discourtois

illegal [ilⁱg'l] adj. illégal; illicite. || **illegality** [ilⁱgaliti] s.* illégalité, f.

illegible [ilèdj•b'l] *adj.* illisible.

illegitimate [ilidjít•mit] *adj.* illégitime ; bâtard , naturel [son].

illicit [ilisit] *adj.* illicite.

illimitable [ilimit•b'l] *adj.* illimité.

illiterate [ilit•rit] *adj., s.* illettré ; analphabète

illness [ilnis] *s.* maladie, f.

illogical [ilâdjik'l] *adj.* illogique.

illuminate [iloum•né¹t] *v.* illuminer ; éclaircir enluminer colorier ‖ *illumination* [iloum•né¹sh•n] *s.* illumination , enluminure, f ., éclairage, m.

illusion [ilou•n] *s* illusion, f. ‖ *illusive* [ilousiv] *adj* illusoire, fallacieux. ‖ *illusory* [ilous•ri] *adj* illusoire.

illustrate [il•stré¹t] *v.* illustrer ; démontrer , embellir ‖ *illustration* [il•stré¹sh•n] *s* illustration, gravure, explication. f ‖ *illustrative* ['il•stré¹tiv] *adj* explicatif, illustrant **s** *illustrator* [il•stré¹t•r] *s* illustrateur ; exemple (fig.), m ‖ *illustrious* [il•stri•s] *adj* illustre , glorieux , brillant.

image [imidj] *s* image , ressemblance, f.; symbole. m ‖ *imagery* [-ri] *s* images, imaginations, f pl. ‖ *imaginable* [imadjin•b'l] *adj* imaginable. ‖ *imaginary* [imadj•nèri] *adj* imaginaire. ‖ *imagination* [imadj•né¹sh•n] *s.* imagination f ‖ *imaginative* [imadj•né¹tiv] *adj* imaginatif ‖ *imagine* [imadjin] • (s')imaginer , supposer.

imbecile [imbisa¹l] *adj., s.* débile ; imbécile n ‖ *Imbecility* [imbisiliti] *s.* débilité imbécillité f

imbibe [imba¹b] • absorber ; s'imbiber ; se pénétrer de

imbricate [imbriké¹t] *v.* imbriquer.

imbue [imbyou] *v.* imprégner ; pénétrer (*with* de)

imitate [im•té¹t] *v* imiter. ‖ *imitation* [im•té¹sh•n] *s* imitation ; copie, f. ‖ *imitator* [im•té¹t•r] *s* imitateur, m.

immaculate [imaky•lit] *adj.* immaculé, san tache

immanent [im•n•nt] *adj.* immanent

immaterial [im•tiri•l] *adj* immatériel, spirituel sans importance, *it is immaterial t• m•* cela m'est égal, cela m'est indifférent

immature [im•tour] *adj.* prématuré ; pas mûr

immediacy [imidy•si] *s* imminence f. ‖ *immediate* [-diit] *adj* immédiat, proche direc *immediately*, immédiatement directement

immense [imèns] *adj* immense. ‖ *immensity* [-ti] *s* • immensité, f.

immerse [imèrs] • immerger ‖ *immersion* [imèr•sh•n] *s* immersion, f.

immigrant [im•gr•nt] *adj., s.* immigrant ; immigré. ‖ *immigrate* [-gré¹t]

v. immigrer. ‖ *immigration* [im•gré¹sh•n] *s.* immigration, f.

imminent [im•n•nt] *adj.* imminent.

immobile [imoou•b'l] *adj* immobile. ‖ *immobility* [imoou•bîl•ti] *s* immobilité, f. ‖ *immobilization* [imoou•b'l•zé¹sh•n] *s.* immobilisation, f. ‖ *immobilize* [imoou•b'la¹z] • immobiliser

immoderate [imâd•rit] *adj.* immodéré ; déréglé démesuré.

immodest [imaudist] *adj.* immodeste, indécent

immoral [imaur•l] *adj.* immoral ; licencieux ‖ *immorality* [im•ral•ti] *s.* immoralité. f

immortal [imaurt'l] *adj., s.* immortel. ‖ *immortality* [imaurtal•ti] *s.* immortalité, f ‖ *immortalize* [imaurt•la¹z] • immortaliser

immovable [imouv•b'l] *adj.* immobile, inébranlable insensible ; inamovible, immeuble (jur.).

immune [imyoun] *adj.* exempt ; dispensé. ‖ *immunity* [-ti] *s.* immunité ; exemption dispense, f.

immunize [imy•na¹z] *v.* immuniser.

imp [imp] *s* lutin, m.

impact [impakt] *s* choc ; impact, m. ; collision, f [impakt] *v.* serrer ; presser ; enfoncer [*into* dans] ; se heurter [*against* contre] *impacted*, encastré.

impair [impèr] • endommager ; altérer ; diminuer s'affaiblir, se détériorer. • *impairment* [-m•nt] *s.* diminution, détérioration f

impalpable [impalp•b'l] *adj.* impalpable imperceptible

impart [impart] • faire participer à ; faire par de annoncer [news].

impartial [impârsh•l] *adj.* impartial. ‖ *impartiality* [impârshal•ti] *s.* impartialité f

impassable [impas•b'l] *adj.* infranchissable impraticable

impasse [in pâs *s* impasse, f.

impassibility [impâsibiliti] *s.* impassibilité ‖ *Impassible* [impas•b'l] *adj.* impassible

impassioned [impash•nd] *adj.* passionné véhément

impassive [impasiv] *adj.* impassible, insensible

impatience [impé¹sh•ns] *s.* impatience f ‖ *impatient* [-•nt] *adj.* impatient.

impeach [impitsh] *v.* accuser ; blâmer ; contester ‖ *impeachment* [-m•nt] *s* accusation contestation, f.

impede [impîd] • empêcher, entraver ; retarder. ‖ *impediment* [impèd•m•nt] *s.* empêchement ; obstacle ; embarras, m.

impel [impĕl] v. pousser; forcer; obliger; activer.

impend [impĕnd] v. être imminent; menacer. ‖ **impendent** [-ˤnt] adj. imminent.

imperative [impĕrˤtiv] adj. impératif; impérieux; urgent; s. impératif, m.

imperceptible [impĕrsĕptˤb'l] adj. imperceptible.

imperfect [impĕrfikt] adj. imparfait; incomplet; s. imparfait, m.

imperial [impiriˤl] adj. impérial. ‖ **Imperialism** [-iz'm] s. impérialisme, m.

imperil [impĕrˤl] v. mettre en danger.

imperious [impiriˤs] adj. impérieux.

imperishable [impĕrishˤb'l] adj. impérissable.

impermeable [impĕrmiˤb'l] adj. imperméable; étanche.

impersonal [impĕrsn'l] adj. impersonnel. ‖ **Impersonate** [impĕrsˤnéˤt] v. personnifier; jouer le rôle de.

impertinent [impĕrtˤnˤnt] adj. impertinent; inopportun. ‖ **Impertinence** [-t'nˤns] s. impertinence; inconvenance, f.; manque d'à-propos (or) de rapport, m.

imperturbable [impĕrtĕrbˤb'l] adj. imperturbable.

impervious [impĕrviˤs] adj. impénétrable, insensible; étanche.

impetuous [impĕtshouˤs] adj. impétueux. ‖ **Impetus** [impĕtˤs] s. impulsion, f.; entrain; élan, m.

impinge [impĭnj] v. entrer en collision; empiéter.

impious [impiˤs] adj. impie.

impish [impish] adj. espiègle.

implacable [implékˤb'l] adj. implacable.

implant [implànt] v. implanter.

implement [implˤmˤnt] s. outil; ustensile; pl. attirail, m.

implicate [implikéˤt] v. impliquer; sous-entendre, entraîner.

implore [implouˤr] v. implorer.

imply [impla¹] v. impliquer; sous-entendre; insinuer.

impolite [impˤla¹t] adj. impoli; **impoliteness**, impolitesse.

imponderable [impàndˤrˤb'l] adj. impondérable.

import [impouˤrt] s. importation (comm.), importance; signification, f.; [impouˤrt] v. importer; signifier. ‖ **Importance** [impauˤrt'ns] s. importance, f. ‖ **important** [-t'nt] adj. important. ‖ **importer** [-ˤr] s. importateur, m.

importunate [impauˤrtshˤnit] adj. importun; [-néˤt] v. importuner.

impose [impoouᶻ] v. imposer; en imposer (upon, à); to impose upon, duper, abuser de; **imposing**, imposant, impressionnant. ‖ **Imposition** [impⁱzishˤn] s. imposition; charge; imposture, f.; abus de confiance, m.

impossibility [impàsˤbilˤti] s.ᵉ impossibilité, f. ‖ **Impossible** [impàsˤb'l] adj. impossible.

impostor [impàstˤr] s. imposteur, m. ‖ **Imposture** [impàstshˤr] s. imposture, f.

impotence [impˤtˤns] s. impotence, f. ‖ **Impotent** [impˤtˤnt] adj. impotent; impuissant.

impoverish [impàvˤrish] v. appauvrir, s'appauvrir.

impracticable [impraktikˤb'l] adj. impraticable; irréalisable; impossible; insociable.

impregnate [imprĕgnéˤt] v. imprégner, féconder; Am. fertiliser.

impress [imprĕs] s.ᵉ empreinte; impression, f.; [imprĕs] v. imprimer; impressionner; empreindre; racoler (mil.). ‖ **impression** [imprĕshˤn] s. impression, conviction, f. ‖ **Impressionable** [imprĕshˤnˤb'l] adj. impressionnable, sensible. ‖ **impressive** [imprĕsiv] adj. impressionnant. ‖ **Impressment** [imprĕsmˤnt] s. enrôlement forcé, m.; presse (mil.), f.

imprint [imprint] s. empreinte; marque de l'éditeur, f.; [imprint] v. imprimer; estampiller; appliquer une empreinte.

imprison [impriz'n] v. emprisonner. ‖ **Imprisonment** [impriz'nmˤnt] s. emprisonnement, m., incarcération, f.

improbable [impràbˤb'l] adj. improbable ‖ **improbably**, sans probabilité.

improper [impràpˤr] adj. impropre; malséant inconvenant. ‖ **Impropriety** [improprai¹ˤti] s.ᵉ impropriété, inexactitude incorrection, inconvenance, f.

improve [improuv] v améliorer; embellir faire valoir [land]; (se) perfectionner ‖ **Improvement** [-mˤnt] s. progrès perfectionnement, m.; amélioration culture, f.

improvisation [imprˤva¹zéˤshˤn] s. improvisation, f. ‖ **Improvise** [imprˤva¹z] improviser.

imprudence [improudˤns] s. imprudence f ‖ **imprudent** [-d'nt] adj. imprudent **Imprudently**, imprudemment.

impudence [impyˤdˤns] s. impudence, f. ‖ **Impudent** [-dˤnt] adj. impudent, insolent.

impulse [impœls] s. impulsion; poussée, f., instinct, m.; on impulse, impulsivement. ‖ **impulsion** [impœlshˤn] s. impulsion, f.

impunity [impyouˤti] s. impunité, f.

impure [impy*our*] *adj.* impur; impudique; souillé. ‖ **impurity** [-°ti] *s.**
impureté, f.

impute [impy*out*] *v.* imputer (*to*, à); attribuer (*to*, à).

in [in] *prep.* dans, en; à; de; *adv.* dedans; *Am.* in-pupil, pensionnaire; *in time*, à temps; *in the morning*, le matin; *to succeed in*, réussir à; *in this way*, de cette manière; *dressed in white*, vêtu de blanc; *one in ten*, un sur dix; *is he in?*, est-il chez lui, est-il rentré?; *the train is in*, le train est arrivé.

inability [in*°bí*l°ti] *s.* incapacité, f.

inaccessible [in°kses°b'l] *adj.* inaccessible.

inaccurate [in*a*ky°rit] *adj.* inexact.

inactive [in*a*ktiv] *adj.* inactif; inerte. ‖ **inactivity** [in*a*ktiv°ti] *s.* inactivité, f.; inertie, f.

inadequate [in*a*d°kwit] *adj.* inadéquat; insuffisant; inadapté.

inadvertent [in°dvë̈r't'nt] *adj.* étourdi; involontaire; *inadvertently*, par inadvertance, par mégarde.

inane [in*é*¹n] *adj.* vide; vain; inepte; *s.* vide, m.

inanimate [in*a*n°mit] *adj.* inanimé.

inanition [in°ní*sh*°n] *s.* inanition, f.

inanity [in*a*niti] *s.** inanité; ineptie, f.

inappropriate [in°pro*ou*priit] *adj.* non indiqué; impropre.

inapt [in*a*pt] *adj.* inapte; inapproprié. ‖ **inaptitude** [-l*t*youd] *s.* inaptitude, f.

inasmuch [in°zm*æ*tsh] *conj.* dans la mesure où; tant, vu (*as*, que).

inattentive [in°tèntiv] *adj.* inattentif; distrait; peu attentionné.

inaugurate [in*au*gy°ré¹t] *v.* inaugurer; ouvrir; *inauguration*, inauguration.

inborn [in*ba*urn] *adj.* inné; congénital.

incandescent [ink°ndès'nt] *adj.* incandescent.

incapable [ink*é*¹p°b'l] *adj.* incapable; inapte. ‖ **incapacitate** [ink°pas°té¹t] *v.* rendre incapable; mettre hors d'état.

incarcerate [ink*á*s°re¹t] *v.* incarcérer.

incarnate [ink*á*ne¹t] *v.* incarner; [-nit] *adj.* incarné; *incarnation*, incarnation.

incendiary [insèndi°ri] *adj.*, *s.** incendiaire.

incense [insèns] *s.* encens, m.; [insèns] *v.* encenser.

incense [insèns] *v.* irriter; courroucer; exciter.

incentive [insèntiv] *s.* stimulant, m.

incessant [insès'nt] *adj.* incessant.

inch [intsh] *s.** pouce (2,54 cm), m.; *v.* avancer pas à pas; *to be within an inch of*, être à deux doigts de.

incident [ins°d'nt] *s.* incident, m. ‖ **incidental** [-'l] *adj.* fortuit; accidentel; accessoire; *incidental expenses*, faux frais.

incinerate [insin°ré¹t] *v.* incinérer.

incision [insíj°n] *s.* incision, f.

incitation [insité¹sh°n] *s.* incitation, f. ‖ **incite** [insa¹t] *v.* inciter. ‖ *incitement* [-m°nt] *s.* incitation, f.; mobile; stimulant, m.

inclination [inkl°né¹sh°n] *s.* inclination; inclinaison, f. ‖ *incline* [inkla¹n] *s.* inclinaison; pente; oblique, f. [inkla¹n] *v.* (s')incliner; pencher; obliquer.

include [inkloud] *v.* renfermer; inclure; *the tip is included*, le service est compris. ‖ *inclusive* [inklousiv] *adj. v.* compris; inclus.

incoherence [inko*ou*hí°r*ens] *s.* incohérence, f. ‖ *incoherent* [inko*ou*hir°nt] *adj.* incohérent; hétéroclite.

income [ink*œ*m] *s.* revenu, m.; rente, f.; *income tax*, impôt sur le revenu.

incomparable [ink*a*mp°r°b'l] *adj.* incomparable.

incompatible [ink°mp*a*t°b'l] *adj.* incompatible.

incompetent [ink*a*mp°t°nt] *adj.* incompétent, inhabile (jur.).

incomplete [ink°mpl*í*t] *adj.* incomplet; inachevé ‖ *incompletion* [-pl*í*sh°n] *s.* inachèvement, m.

incomprehensible [ink°mprihèns°b'l] *adj.* incompréhensible.

incongruous [ink*a*ngrou°s] *adj.* disparate; inharmonieux; inapproprié; inconvenant. incongru.

inconsiderate [ink°nsid°rit] *adj.* inconsidéré irréfléchi.

inconsistent [ink°ns*í*st°nt] *adj.* inconsistant, inconséquent; incongru.

inconspicuous [ink°nsp*í*kyou°s] *adj.* inapparent peu en vue; banal.

inconstant [ink*a*nst°nt] *adj.* inconstant; versatile.

inconvenience [ink°nv*í*ny°ns] *s.* inconvénient dérangement, m.; incommodité, f.; *v* incommoder; déranger. ‖ *inconvenient* [-°nt] *adj.* incommode gênant; inopportun; importun.

incorporate [ink*a*urp°rit] *adj.* incorporé; associé; [-ré¹t] *v.* (s')incorporer; former une société (comm.); incarner.

incorrect [ink°rèkt] *adj.* incorrect; inexact.

increase [inkrîs] *s.* augmentation, f.; accroissement; gain, m.; [inkrîs] *v.* augmenter; grandir; accroître. ‖ *increasingly* [-ingli] *adv.* de plus en plus.

incredible [inkrèd•b'l] *adj.* incroyable; inadmissible.

incredulity [inkr•dyoul•ti] *s.* incrédulité, f. ‖ *incredulous* [inkrèdj•l•s] *adj.* incrédule.

incriminate [inkrîm•né¹t] *v.* incriminer.

incubate [inky•bé¹t] *v.* couver; incuber; *incubation,* incubation; *incubator,* couveuse.

inculcate [inkœlké¹t] *v.* inculquer.

inculpate [inkœlpé¹t] *v.* inculper. ‖ *inculpation* [inkœlpé¹she•n] *s.* inculpation, f.

incur [inkёr] *v.* encourir; s'exposer à; contracter [debts].

incurable [inkyour•b'l] *adj., s.* incurable.

incursion [inkёrsh•n] *s.* incursion, f.

incurve [inkёrv] *v.* incurver.

indebted [indètid] *adj.* endetté; redevable (*for,* de).

indecent [indîs•nt] *adj.* indécent; grossier, inconvenant, déplacé.

indeed [indîd] *adv.* en effet; en vérité; réellement, vraiment.

indefinable [indifa¹n•b'l] *adj.* indéfinissable.

indefinite [indèfinit] *adj.* indéfini.

indelible [indèl•b'l] *adj.* indélébile.

indelicate [indèl•ké¹t] *adj.* indélicat; grossier.

indemnify [indèmn•fa¹] *v.* indemniser. ‖ *indemnity* [indèmn•ti] *s.°* indemnité, f.; dédommagement, m.

indent [indènt] *v.* denteler; échancrer; commander (comm.); *Am.* aller à la ligne; passer un contrat; *s.* commande (comm.), f.; bon; ordre de réquisition (mil.), m.

independence [indipènd•ns] *s.* indépendance, f. ‖ *independent* [-d•nt] *adj.* indépendant.

indescribable [indiskra¹b•b'l] *adj.* indescriptible.

index [indèks] *s.°* indice, signe; index; exposant (math.), m.; *v.* répertorier; faire l'index; *index-card,* fiche.

India [indi•] *s.* Inde, f. ‖ *Indian* [-n] *adj., s.* indien; hindou; *Indian ink,* encre de Chine.

indicate [ind•ké¹t] *v.* indiquer; montrer; marquer. ‖ *indication* [ind•ké¹sh•n] *s.* indication; marque, f.; renseignement, m. ‖ *indicative* [indìk•tiv] *adj., s.* indicatif. ‖ *indicator* [ind•ké¹tёr] *s.* indicateur; signalisateur, m.

indict [inda¹t] *v.* inculper. ‖ *indictment* [-m•nt] *s.* inculpation, f.

indifference [indifr•ns] *s.* indifférence; apathie, f. ‖ *indifferent* [-r•nt] *adj.* indifférent; apathique.

indigenous [indidj•n•s] *adj.* indigène.

indigent [ind•dj•nt] *adj.* indigent.

indigestion [ind•djèstsh•n] *s.* indigestion, f.

indignant [indign•nt] *adj.* indigné. ‖ *indignation* [indigné¹sh•n] *s.* indignation, f. ‖ *indignity* [indign•ti] *s.°* indignité; insulte, f.; affront, m.

indirect [ind•rèkt] *adj.* indirect; oblique.

indiscipline [indisiplin] *s.* indiscipline, f.

indiscreet [indiskrît] *adj.* indiscret. ‖ *indiscretion* [indiskré¹sh•n] *s.* indiscrétion, f.

indiscriminate [indiskriminit] *adj.* sans discrimination; fait au hasard; aveugle.

indispensable [indispèns•b'l] *adj.* indispensable.

indispose [indispoᵒuz] *v.* indisposer. ‖ *indisposition* [indisp•zish•n] *s.* indisposition, f.

indistinct [indistìnkt] *adj.* indistinct; *indistinctness,* vague, manque de netteté; imprécision, f.

indite [inda¹t] *v.* composer, rédiger.

individual [ind•v¹djouᵉl] *adj.* individuel; *s.* individu, m. ‖ *individualism* [-iz'm] *m.* individualisme, m. ‖ *individualist* [-ist] *s.* individualiste, m. ‖ *individuality* [ind•v¹djouᵃl•ti] *s.* individualité, f. ‖ *individualize* [indiv¹djou•la¹z] *v.* individualiser.

indivisible [ind•viz•b'l] *adj.* indivisible.

indoctrinate [indáktriné¹t] *v.* endoctriner; *indoctrination,* endoctrinement.

indolent [ind•l•nt] *adj.* indolent; apathique; nonchalant.

indomitable [indámit•b'l] *adj.* indomptable, intraitable.

indoor [indoᵒᵘr] *adj.* intérieur, domestique. ‖ *indoors* [-z] *adv.* à l'intérieur; à la maison.

indorse [indaurs] *v.* endosser; adopter; confirmer; garantir. ‖ *indorsement* [-m•nt] *s.* endossement [check]; endos, m.; souscription; adhésion; garantie, f. ‖ *indorser* [-ёr] *s.* endosseur, m.

induce [indyous] *v.* induire; persuader; amorcer (mech.). ‖ *inducement* [-m•nt] *s.* attrait; motif, mobile, m. ‖ *inducer* [-er] *s.* provocateur, m.; provocatrice, f.

induct [indækt] *v.* introduire; installer; initier. || **induction** [indæksh⁰n] *s.* installation; initiation (mil.); induction (electr.), f.

indulge [indœldj] *v.* céder à; être indulgent (*to*, pour); s'adonner (*in*, à). || **indulgence** [-⁰ns] *s.* indulgence; complaisance, f.; plaisir, m. || **indulgent** [-⁰nt] *adj.* indulgent; accommodant; complaisant; patient.

indurate [indyouré¹t] *v.* durcir; indurer; endurcir.

industrial [indœstri⁰l] *adj.* industriel. || **industrialist** [-ist] *s.* industriel, m. || **industrious** [indœstri⁰s] *adj.* industrieux; laborieux. || **Industry** [indœstri] *s.* industrie; diligence; activité, f.

inebriate [in⁰brīit] *s.* ivrogne, m.; [in⁰brié¹t] *v.* enivrer; **inebriation**, enivrement; ébriété.

inedible [inédib'l] *adj.* immangeable; non comestible.

ineffective [in⁰féktiv] *adj.* inefficace. || **inefficiency** [in⁰físh⁰nsi] *s.* inefficacité; incompétence, f. || **inefficient** [in⁰físh⁰nt] *adj.* inefficace, inefficient, incapable.

ineligible [inélidjib'l] *adj.* sans attrait; inacceptable; inéligible; impropre.

inept [inépt] *adj.* inepte; inapproprié; balourd; vain.

inequality [inikwal⁰ti] *s.* inégalité, f.

inert [in⁰rt] *adj.* inerte. || **inertia** [in⁰rsh⁰] *s.* inertie, f.

inestimable [inèstim⁰b'l] *adj.* inestimable, inappréciable.

inevitable [inévit⁰b'l] *adj.* inévitable; inéluctable; fatal.

inexcusable [inikskjous⁰b'l] *adj.* inexcusable.

inexhaustible [inigzaust⁰b'l] *adj.* inépuisable.

inexpensive [inikspènsiv] *adj.* économique; bon marché.

inexperience [înikspiri⁰ns] *s.* inexpérience, f. || **inexperienced** [-t] *adj.* inexpérimenté.

inexplicable [inèksplik⁰b'l] *adj.* inexplicable.

inexpressible [iniksprès⁰b'l] *adj.* inexprimable, indicible.

infallible [infal⁰b'l] *adj.* infaillible.

infamous [inf⁰m⁰s] *adj.* infâme, ignoble; infâmant.

infancy [inf⁰nsi] *s.* bas âge, m. || **infant** [inf⁰nt] *s.* petit enfant; bébé; mineur (jur.). || **infantile** [-ta¹l] *adj.* infantile. || **infantine** [inf⁰ntin] *adj.* enfantin.

infantry [inf⁰ntri] *s.* infanterie, f.

infarct [infâᵏkt] *s.* infarctus, m.

infatuate [infatyoué¹t] *v.* affoler; enticher; *to become infatuated with*, se toquer de, avoir un béguin pour.

infect [infèkt] *v.* infecter; contaminer; corrompre. || **infection** [infèksh⁰n] *s.* infection; contamination, f. || **infectious** [-sh⁰s] *adj.* infectieux; contagieux.

infer [inf⁰r] *v.* déduire, inférer. || **inference** [inf⁰r⁰ns] *s.* déduction, f.

inferior [infrī⁰r] *adj.*, *s.* inférieur. || **inferiority** [infirlaur⁰ti] *s.* infériorité, f.

infernal [inf⁰r'n'l] *adj.* infernal.

infest [infèst] *v.* infester.

infiltrate [infiltre¹t] *v.* imprégner; noyauter; (s') infiltrer; faire pénétrer; **infiltration**, infiltration; noyautage.

infinite [inf⁰nit] *adj.*, *s.* infini.

infinitive [infin⁰tiv] *adj.*, *s.* infinitif.

infinity [infin⁰ti] *s.* infinité, f.; *to infinity*, à l'infini.

infirm [inf⁰rm] *adj.* infirme; faible. || **infirmary** [-⁰ri] *s.* infirmerie, f. || **infirmity** [-⁰ti] *s.* infirmité, f.

inflame [inflé¹m] *v.* enflammer; incendier; irriter; échauffer. || **inflammation** [infl⁰mé¹sh⁰n] *s.* inflammation, f.

inflate [inflé¹t] *v.* gonfler; enfler. || **inflation** [inflé¹sh⁰n] *s.* inflation, f.; gonflement, m. || **inflator** [-t⁰r] *s.* pompe à bicyclette, f.; gonfleur, m.

inflection [inflèksh⁰n] *s.* inflexion, f.

inflict [inflīkt] *v.* infliger.

inflow [infloᵒᵘ] *s.* affluence; rentrée [money], f.; afflux, m.

influence [infloᵘ⁰ns] *s.* influence, f.; *v.* influencer; influer. || **influential** [infloᵘènsh⁰l] *adj.* influent.

influenza [infloᵘènz⁰] *s.* grippe, f.

influx [inflœks] *s.* affluence; invasion, f.; afflux, m.

infold [infoᵒᵘld] *v.* envelopper; embrasser.

inform [infaurm] *v.* informer; aviser; renseigner; *to inform against*, dénoncer; **informer**, indicateur [police]. || **informal** [-'l] *adj.* sans cérémonie. || **information** [inf⁰rmé¹sh⁰n] *s.* information; nouvelles; dénonciation, f.; renseignement, m. || **informer** [infaurm⁰r] *s.* dénonciateur; indicateur (m.) de police.

infringe [infrindj] *v.* enfreindre; transgresser; empiéter.

infuriate [infyouré¹t] *v.* exaspérer.

infuse [infyouz] *v.* infuser; inculquer; remplir (*with*, de). || **infusion** [-j⁰n] *s.* infusion, f.

ingathering [*i*ngaxh*e*ring] *s.* récolte, f.

ingenious [indj*í*ny*e*s] *adj.* ingénieux. ‖ **ingenuity** [indj*e*n*ou*ti] *s.* ingéniosité; habileté, f.

ingenuous [indj*è*ny*ou*s] *adj.* ingénu, naïf; sincère, franc.

ingest [indj*è*st] *v.* ingérer.

ingot [*i*ngg*e*t] *s.* lingot, m.

ingratiate [ingr*é*i*shi*é*i*t] *v. to ingratiate oneself with*, se faire bien voir de.

ingratitude [ingrat*e*tyoud] *s.* ingratitude, f.

ingredient [ingríd*i*nt] *s.* ingrédient, m.

ingrown [*i*ngro*ou*n] *adj.* incarné [nail]; invétéré [habit].

ingurgitate [ing*ë*rdjite*i*t] *v.* ingurgiter.

inhabit [inhabit] *v.* habiter. ‖ **inhabitant** [-*e*nt] *s.* habitant, m.

inhale [inhé*i*l] *v.* inhaler; respirer.

inherent [inhír*e*nt] *adj.* inhérent; propre.

inherit [inhérit] *v.* hériter. ‖ **inheritance** [-t*e*ns] *s.* héritage, m.

inhibit [inhíbit] *v.* prohiber; interdire; réprimer, refréner. ‖ **inhibition** [inibísh*e*n] *s.* interdiction; inhibition, f.

inhospitable [inh*â*spit*e*b'l] *adj.* inhospitalier.

inhuman [inhyoum*e*n] *adj.* inhumain.

inhumation [inhjoume*i*sh*e*n] *s.* inhumation, f.; **inhume**, inhumer.

inimical [in*í*mik*e*l] *adj.* inamical; hostile; défavorable; contraire.

inimitable [in*í*met*e*b'l] *adj.* inimitable.

iniquity [in*í*kweti] *s.** iniquité, injustice, f.

initial [in*í*sh*e*l] *adj.* initial, s. initiale, f.; *v.* parafer; marquer d'initiales, émarger.

initiate [in*í*shié*i*t] *v.* initier; instituer; commencer. ‖ **initiation** [in*í*shié*i*sh*e*n] *s.* inauguration, f.; début, m.; initiation, f. ‖ **initiative** [in*í*shié*i*tiv] *s.* initiative, f.

inject [indj*è*kt] *v.* injecter. ‖ **injection** [indj*è*ksh*e*n] *s.* injection, piqûre, f.

injunction [indj*æ*ngksh*e*n] *s.* injonction, f.; commandement (jur.), m.

injure [*i*ndj*ë*r] *v.* nuire à; léser; blesser; faire mal à; endommager; avarier [goods]. ‖ **injurious** [indjouri*e*s] *adj.* nuisible, préjudiciable. ‖ **injury** [*i*ndj*e*ri] *s.** préjudice; tort; dégât, m.; blessure; avarie, f.

injustice [indj*æ*stis] *s.* injustice, f.

ink [*i*ngk] *s.* encre, f.; *v.* encrer; **inking ribbon**, ruban à machine. ‖ **inkling** [-ling] *s.* indication; idée; notion, f. ‖ **inkstand**, **inkwell**, encrier.

in-law [*i*nlau] *s.* parent par mariage, m.

inlay [inlé*i*] *v.* incruster; marqueter; [inlé*i*] *s.* incrustation; marqueterie, f.

inmate [*i*nmé*i*t] *s.* habitant; pensionnaire; *Am.* prisonnier, m.

inmost [*i*nmo*ou*st] *adj.* le plus profond, secret, intime.

inn [in] *s.* auberge, f.

innate [iné*i*t] *adj.* inné.

inner [in*e*r] *adj.* intérieur; intime; interne; **innermost**, *see* inmost.

inning [ining] *s.* rentrée, f.

innkeeper [inkâp*e*r] *s.* aubergiste; hôtelier, m.

innocence [in*e*s'ns] *s.* innocence, f. ‖ **innocent** [in*e*s'nt] *adj.* innocent (*of*, de); simple, niais.

innocuous [in*â*kyou*e*s] *adj.* inoffensif; **innocuousness**, innocuité.

innovation [in*e*vé*i*sh*e*n] *s.* innovation, f.

innoxious [in*â*ksh*e*s] *adj.* inoffensif. ‖ **innoxiousness** [-nis] *s.* innocuité, f.

innuendo [inyouèndo*ou*] *s.** insinuation malveillante, f.

innumerable [inyoum*e*r*e*b'l] *adj.* innombrable.

inobservance [in*e*bzër*v*ns] *s.* inattention; inobservation; inobservance, f.

inoculate [in*â*ky*e*lé*i*t] *v.* inoculer. ‖ **inoculation** [in*â*ky*e*lé*i*sh*e*n] *s.* inoculation; vaccination, f.

inodorous [ino*ou*d*e*r*e*s] *adj.* inodore.

inoffensive [in*e*fènsiv] *adj.* inoffensif, anodin; acceptable; non offensant.

inopportune [in*â*p*e*rtyoun] *adj.* inopportun, fâcheux; **inopportuneness**, inopportunité.

inordinate [inau*r*dinit] *adj.* désordonné; immodéré; indu [hour].

inquest [*i*nkwest] *s.* enquête, f.; jury, m.

inquire [inkwa*í*r] *v.* demander; s'enquérir (*about*, de). ‖ **inquiring** [-ing] *adj.* curieux, investigateur, interrogateur. ‖ **inquiry** [-i] *s.** question; investigation; enquête, f.; interrogatoire, m. ‖ **inquisition** [inkw*e*zísh*e*n] *s.* inquisition; enquête, f. ‖ **inquisitive** [inkwís*e*tiv] *adj.* curieux; investigateur.

inroad [*i*nro*ou*d] *s.* incursion, f.; empiètement, m.

inrush [*i*nr*œ*sh] *s.** irruption, f.

insalubrious [ins⁰loubri⁰s] *adj.* insalubre.

insane [insé¹n] *adj.* fou; insensé. ‖ *insanity* [ins⁰ⁿti] *s.* ⁰ démence, f.

insatiable [insé¹shie'b'l] *adj.* insatiable.

inscribe [inskra¹b] *v.* inscrire. ‖ *inscription* [inskripsh⁰n] *s.* inscription, f.

insect [ïnsèkt] *s.* insecte, m.; *Fr. Can.* bibite, f. ‖ *insecticide* [insèkt⁰sa¹d] *s.* insecticide, m.

insecure [insikyour] *adj.* incertain; dangereux.

insemination [insemine¹sh⁰n] *s.* insémination, f.

insensible [insèns⁰b'l] *adj.* insensible; sans connaissance.

insensitive [insèns⁰tiv] *adj.* insensible.

inseparable [insèp⁰r⁰b'l] *adj.* inséparable.

insert [ïnsèrt] *s.* insertion, f.; [ïnsèrt] *v.* insérer; intercaler. ‖ *insertion* [insêr'sh⁰n] *s.* insertion, f.; intercalage; ajout, m.

inside [insa¹d] *s.* intérieur, m.; [ïnsa¹d] *adj.* intérieur; interne; [insa¹d] *adv.* dedans, à l'intérieur; [insa¹d] *prep.* en dedans de.

insight [ïnsa¹t] *s.* perspicacité; intuition, f.; discernement, m.

insignia [insigni⁰] *s. pl.* insignes; emblèmes, m.; *Am.* **collar insignia,** écussons.

insignificant [insignif⁰k⁰nt] *adj.* insignifiant.

insincere [insinsi⁰r] *adj.* peu sincère, faux.

insinuate [insinyoué¹t] *v.* insinuer; sous-entendre.

insipid [insipid] *adj.* insipide.

insist [insïst] *v.* insister; persister. ‖ *insistence* [-⁰ns] *s.* insistance, f. ‖ *insistent* [-⁰nt] *adj.* persistant; obstiné; pressant.

insobriety [insobra¹eti] *s.* intempérance, f.

insolation [insoºulé¹sh⁰n] *s.* insolation, f.; coup de soleil, m.

insolence [ïns⁰l⁰ns] *s.* insolence, f. ‖ *insolent* [-l⁰nt] *adj.* insolent.

insoluble [insâlyoub'l] *adj.* insoluble.

insolvent [insâlv⁰nt] *adj.* insolvable.

inspect [inspèkt] *v.* inspecter; vérifier. ‖ *inspection* [inspèksh⁰n] *s.* inspection, f.; contrôle, m. ‖ *inspector* [inspèkt⁰r] *s.* inspecteur; contrôleur, m.

inspiration [insp⁰ré¹sh⁰n] *s.* inspiration; impulsion; aspiration, f. ‖ *inspire* [inspa¹r] *v.* inspirer; animer; suggérer; susciter.

inspiriting [inspïriting] *adj.* vivifiant; égayant; stimulant.

instable [insté¹b'l] *adj.* instable; inconstant.

install [instaul] *v.* installer. ‖ *installation* [insté¹sh⁰n] *s.* installation, f. ‖ *instal(l)ment* [instaulm⁰nt] *s.* acompte, m.; livraison (en partie); portion, f.; **instalment plan,** facilités de paiement.

instance [ïnst⁰ns] *s.* occasion, circonstance; instance, f.; exemple, m.; **for instance,** par exemple. ‖ *instancy* [-i] *s.* imminence; urgence; instance, f.

instant [ïnst⁰nt] *s.* instant; moment, m.; *adj.* urgent; immédiat; **the 1st instant,** le premier courant. ‖ *instantaneous* [inst⁰nté¹ni⁰s] *adj.* instantané.

instauration [instauré¹sh⁰n] *s.* Restauration, f.

instead [instèd] *adv.* au lieu de; à la place (of, de).

instep [instèp] *s.* cou-de-pied, m.

instigate [inst⁰gé¹t] *v.* pousser; provoquer. ‖ *instigation* [inst⁰gé¹sh⁰n] *s.* instigation, f.

instill [instïl] *v.* instiller; inspirer.

instinct [ïnstingkt] *s.* instinct, m.; *instinctive,* instinctif.

institute [inst⁰tyout] *s.* institut, m.; institution, f.; *v.* instituer; engager; constituer; intenter; investir (eccles.). *institution,* institution; introduction (jur.); investiture (eccles.).

instruct [instrækt] *v.* instruire; enseigner. ‖ *instruction* [-sh⁰n] *s.* instruction, f.; enseignement, m.; *pl.* instructions, f.; ordres, m. ‖ *instructive* [-tiv] *adj.* instructif. ‖ *instructor* [-t⁰r] *s.* instructeur, m.

instrument [ïnstr⁰m⁰nt] *s.* instrument; appareil, m.; **instrument board,** tableau de bord. ‖ *instrumental* [instroumént'l] *adj.* contributif; utile; instrumental.

insubordination [ins⁰baurd'né¹sh⁰n] *s.* insubordination; indiscipline, f.

insufferable [ins⁰fr⁰b'l] *adj.* intolérable, insupportable.

insufficient [ins⁰fïsh⁰nt] *adj.* insuffisant; incapable.

insular [insyoul⁰r] *adj.* insulaire; en plaques (sclerosis); isolé; borné (fig.).

insulate [ins⁰lé¹t] *v.* isoler; *insulator,* isolant; isolateur.

insult [insœlt] *s.* insulte, f.; [insœlt] *v.* insulter.

insuppressible [insᵉprésib'l] *adj.* irrépressible.

insurance [inshourᵉns] *s.* assurance, f. ‖ *insurant* [-ᵉnt] *s.* assuré, m. ‖ *insure* [inshour] *v.* assurer; garantir. ‖ *insurer* [-ᵉʳ] *s.* assureur, m.

insurgent [insëʳdjᵉnt] *adj.*, *s.* insurgé; rebelle.

insurmountable [insᵉrmaᵒᵘntᵉb'l] *adj.* insurmontable; infranchissable.

insurrection [insᵉréⁱkshᵉn] *s.* insurrection, f.

intact [intakt] *adj.* intact; indemne.

intake [intéⁱk] *s.* appel, m. [air]; prise, f. [water]; ration, f. [food]; recrues, f. pl. (milit.); diminution, f. [knitting].

integer [intdjᵉʳ] *s.* nombre entier, m. ‖ *integral* [intᵉgrᵉl] *adj.* intégral; s. intégrale, f. ‖ *integration* [intigréⁱshᵉn] *s.* intégration, f. ‖ *integrity* [intégrᵉti] *s.* intégrité; droiture, f.

intellectual [int'lèktshouᵉl] *adj.*, *s.* intellectuel. ‖ *intelligence* [intèlidjᵉns] *s.* intelligence; police secrète, f.; service de renseignements, m. ‖ *intelligent* [-jᵉnt] *adj.* intelligent.

intemperance [intèmpᵉrᵉns] *s.* intempérance, f.

intend [intènd] *v.* avoir l'intention (*to*, de); destiner (*for*, à). ‖ *intended* [-id] *adj.* intentionnel; projeté; futur; *s.* fiancé, m.

intense [intèns] *adj.* intense; acharné. ‖ *intensity* [-ᵉti] *s.*° intensité; force, f. ‖ *intensive* [-iv] *adj.* intensif.

intent [intènt] *s.* intention, f.; but, m.; *adj.* appliqué; déterminé; acharné (*on*, à); *to all intents and purposes*, sous tous les rapports; en réalité. ‖ *intention* [intènshᵉn] *s.* intention, f.; but, m.; *intentional*, intentionnel.

inter [intᵉʳ] *adv.* entre; *inter-war period*, l'entre-deux-guerres.

inter [intëʳ] *v.* enterrer.

intercalate [intèrkᵉleⁱt] *v.* intercaler.

intercede [intᵉrsîd] *v.* intercéder.

intercept [intᵉrsèpt] *v.* intercepter.

intercession [intᵉrsèshᵉn] *s.* intercession, f.

interchange [intᵉrtshéⁱndj] *s.* échange, m.; [intertshéⁱndj] *v.* échanger; permuter.

intercom [intᵉrkâm] *s.* interphone, m.

intercourse [intᵉrkoᵒᵘrs] *s.* fréquentation, f.; relations, f. pl.; rapports, m. pl.

interdiction [intᵉrdîkshᵉn] *s.* interdiction, f.

interest [intᵉrist] *s.* intérêt; bénéfice. m.; influence, f.; *v.* intéresser; *interesting*, intéressant.

interfere [intᵉrfjᵉʳ] *v.* intervenir; s'entremettre; *to interfere with*, contrarier. gêner. ‖ *interference* [-rᵉns] *s.* intervention; interférence, f.; obstacle brouillage [radio], m.

interim [intᵉrim] *s.* intérim, m.

interior [intîriᵉʳ] *adj.*, *s.* intérieur.

interjection [intᵉrdjèkshᵉn] *s.* intercalation; interjection, f.

interlace [intᵉrléⁱs] *v.* entrelacer.

interlock [intᵉrlâk] *v.* (s')entrelacer; (s')engrener.

interlude [intᵉrlyoud] *s.* intermède; interlude; intervalle, m.

intermediate [intᵉrmîdiit] *adj.* intermédiaire; *v.* s'entremettre.

interminable [intëʳminᵉb'l] *adj.* interminable.

intermingle [intᵉrmingg'l] *v.* entremêler: se mêler.

intermission [intᵉrmîshᵉn] *s.* interruption, f.; intermède; *Am.* entracte, m. ‖ *intermittent* [-mit'nt] *adj.* intermittent.

intern [intëʳn] *s.* interne, m.; [intëʳn] *v.* interner; incarcérer. ‖ *internal* [intëʳn'l] *adj.* interne.

international [intᵉrnashᵉn'l] *adj.* international.

internecine [intᵉrnîsin] *adj.* meurtrier; ravageur; *internecine war*, guerre d'extermination.

internee [intᵉrnî] *s.* interné, m. ‖ *internment* [intᵉrnmᵉnt] *s.* internement, m.

interpellate [intëʳpèlⁱt] *v.* interpeller; *interpellation*, interpellation.

interplanetary [intᵉrplanᵉtᵉri] *adj.* interplanétaire.

interpolate [intëʳpᵉléⁱt] *v.* interpoler; intercaler.

interpose [intᵉrpoᵒᵘz] *v.* (s')interposer.

interpret [intëʳprit] *v.* interpréter. ‖ *interpretation* [intëʳpritéⁱshᵉn] *s.* interprétation, f. ‖ *interpreter* [intëʳpritᵉʳ] *s.* interprète, m. f.

interrogate [intèʳgéⁱt] *v.* interroger. ‖ *interrogation* [intèrᵉgéⁱshᵉn] *s.* interrogation, f.; interrogatoire, m. ‖ *interrogative* [intᵉrâgᵉtiv] *adj.* interrogatif; *s.* interrogation, m. ‖ *interrogatory* [intᵉrâgᵉtoᵒᵘri] *s.*° interrogatoire, m.

interrupt [intᵉræpt] *v.* interrompre. ‖ *interrupter* [-tᵉʳ] *s.* interrupteur; rupteur (electr.), m. ‖ *interruption* [-shᵉn] *s.* interruption, f.

intersect [int**e**rsèkt] v. (s')entrecouper. ‖ **intersection** [int**e**rsèksh**e**n] s. intersection, f.; croisement [street], m.

intersperse [int**e**rspë̀rs] v. parsemer; entremêler.

intertwine [int**e**rtwaïn] v. entrelacer, s'enlacer.

interurban [int**e**rerben] adj. Am. de banlieue [train].

interval [int**e**rv'l] s. intervalle, m.; récréation [at school], f.; entracte (theatr.), m.; mi-temps, f. [game]; distance, f. (fig.).

intervene [int**e**rvîn] v. intervenir; survenir; s'écouler [time]. ‖ **intervention** [int**e**rvénsh**e**n] s. intervention, f.

interview [int**e**ryou] s. entrevue; interview, f.; v. interviewer.

intestine [intèstin] s. intestin; boyau, m.; adj. intérieur; **intestine war**, guerre intestine.

intimacy [int**e**mes**ï**] s. intimité, f. ‖ **intimate** [int**e**mit] adj., s. intime; [int**e**mé**ï**t] v. insinuer. ‖ **intimation** [int**e**mé**ï**sh**e**n] s. conseil, m.; insinuation, f.

intimidate [intimedé**ï**t] v. intimider.

into [ïntou, int**e**] prep. dans, en.

intolerable [int**á**lereb'l] adj. intolérable. ‖ **intolerance** [-rens] s. intolérance, f. ‖ **intolerant** [-rent] adj. intolérant.

intonation [intoou**ï**né**ï**sh**e**n] s. intonation, f.

intoxicants [int**á**ks**e**k**e**nts] s. pl. boissons alcooliques, f. ‖ **intoxicate** [-ké**ï**t] v. enivrer; intoxiquer (med.); **intoxicated**, ivre. ‖ **intoxication** [int**á**ks**e**ké**ï**sh**e**n] s. ivresse; intoxication (med.), f.

intractable [intrakteb'l] adj. invétéré (med.); indocile; insoluble.

intransigency [intransidj**e**nsi] s. intransigeance, f.; **intransigent**, intransigeant.

intravenous [intrev**ï**n**e**s] adj. intraveineux.

intrench [intré**ï**ntsh] v. (se) retrancher.

intrepid [intrèpid] adj. intrépide.

intricacy [ïntrik**e**si] s.* imbroglio; dédale, m.; complications, f. pl.; complexité, f. ‖ **intricate** [ïntr**e**kit] adj. embrouillé; compliqué.

intrigant [ïntrigent] s. intrigant, m. ‖ **intrigue** [intrîg] s. intrigue, f.; v. intriguer; tramer; intéresser; avoir une liaison.

intrinsic [intrïnsik] adj. intrinsèque.

introduce [intr**e**dyous] v. introduire; présenter. ‖ **introduction** [intr**e**dæksh**e**n] s. introduction; présentation, f.

introspection [introspéksh**e**n] s. introspection, f.

intrude [introud] v. pénétrer; se faufiler: s'infiltrer; abuser; déranger; **intruder**, intrus. ‖ **intrusion** [introuj**e**n] s intrusion, f. ‖ **intrusive** [introusiv] adj. intrus.

intuition [intou**ï**sh**e**n] s. intuition, f.

inundate [inœndé**ï**t] v. inonder. ‖ **inundation** [inœndé**ï**sh**e**n] s. inondation, f.

inured [inyourd] adj. endurci.

inusable [injouzeb'l] adj. non utilisable.

inutility [injout**ï**liti] s. inutilité, f.

invade [invé**ï**d] v. envahir. ‖ **invader** [-**e**r] s. envahisseur, m.

invalid [ïnvélid] adj., s. invalide, infirme; malade; v. réformer (mil.).

invalid [invalid] adj. non valable; invalide (jur.). ‖ **invalidate** [-é**ï**t] v. invalider. ‖ **invalidity** [invel**ï**diti] s. invalidité; déficience, maladie, f.

invaluable [invaly**e**b'l] adj. inappréciable; inestimable.

invariable [invérieb'l] adj. invariable.

invasion [invé**ï**j**e**n] s. invasion, f.

invent [invènt] v. inventer; imaginer. ‖ **invention** [-sh**e**n] s. invention, f. ‖ **inventive** [-tiv] adj. inventif. ‖ **inventor** [-t**e**r] s. inventeur, m. ‖ **inventory** [ïnvèntou**ï**ri] s.* inventaire, m.; v. inventorier.

inverse [invë̀rs] adj. inverse. ‖ **invert** [invë̀rt] v. intervertir; [ïnvë̀rt] s. inverti, m.

invest [invèst] v. investir; cerner (mil.); placer (comm.); vêtir [dress]; revêtir [honor].

investigate [invèst**e**gé**ï**t] v. rechercher faire une enquête. ‖ **investigation** [invèstigé**ï**sh**e**n] s. examen, m.; enquête, investigation, f. ‖ **investigator** [-**e**r] adj., s. investigateur, investigatrice.

investment [invèstm**e**nt] s. investissement (mil.); placement (comm.), m. ‖ **investor** [-t**e**r] s. actionnaire; bailleur de fonds, m.

inveterate [invèt**e**rit] adj. invétéré; obstiné; chronique.

invigorate [invig**e**ré**ï**t] v. fortifier.

invincible [invïnseb'l] adj. invincible.

invisible [invïzeb'l] adj. invisible.

invitation [invèté**ï**sh**e**n] s. invitation, f. ‖ **invite** [inva**ï**t] v. inviter. ‖ **inviting** [-ing] adj. attrayant; appétissant.

invoice [ïnvo**ï**s] s. facture; expédition de marchandises facturées, f.; v. facturer.

invoke [invo^uk] v. invoquer.

involuntary [invál^entèri] adj. involontaire; irréfléchi.

involve [inválv] v. impliquer; entraîner [consequence]; envelopper; entortiller (*in*, dans).

inwall [inwaul] v. Am. clore de murs.

inward(s) [inw^erd(z)] adj. intérieur; interne; adv. à l'intérieur.

iodine [a¹eda¹n] s. iode, f.

ipecac [ipikak] s. ipéca, m.

irascible [a¹ras^eb'l] adj. irascible.

Iraq [irâk] s. Irak, m.; *Iraqi*, Irakien.

Ireland [a¹rl^end] s. Irlande, f.

iridescent [ir^edès'nt] adj. irisé.

iris [a¹ris] s. iris [eye, flower], m.

Irish [a¹rish] adj., s. irlandais.

irksome [ërks^em] adj. ennuyeux.

iron [a¹e^rn] s. fer, m.; adj. en fer, de fer; v. ferrer; charger de chaînes; mettre aux fers; repasser [garment]; *scrap iron*, ferraille; *wrought iron*, fer forgé; *iron ore*, mineral de fer.

ironical [a¹rânik'l] adj. ironique.

ironing [a¹r^ening] s. repassage, m.

ironmaster [a¹e^rnmast^er] s. métallurgiste, m.; *ironmonger*, quincaillier; *ironmongery*, quincaillerie; *ironwork*, ferrure; *ironworks*, forge, hauts fourneaux.

irony [a¹r^eni] s.* ironie, f.

irradiant [iré¹di^ent] adj. irradiant; rayonnant.

irrational [irashn'l] adj. irraisonnable; déraisonnable; irrationnel.

irrecoverable [irikæv^er^eb'l] adj. non récupérable; irrécouvrable; irréparable, irrémédiable.

irregular [irègy^el^er] adj. irrégulier. ‖ *irregularity* [irègy^elar^eti] s.* irrégularité; dissymétrie, f.; vice de forme (jur.), m.

irrelevant [irèl^ev^ent] adj. inopportun; inapplicable; hors de propos.

irreligious [irili^dj^es] adj. irréligieux; impie.

irremediable [irimîdi^eb'l] adj. irrémédiable.

irreparable [irèp^er^eb'l] adj. irréparable.

irreplaceable [iriplé¹s^eb'l] adj. irremplaçable.

irreproachable [iripro^{ou}tsh^eb'l] adj. irréprochable.

irresolute [irèz^elout] adj. irrésolu.

irresponsible [irispâns^eb'l] adj. irresponsable.

irresponsive [irispânsiv] adj. fermé; insensible, indifférent.

irretrievable [iritrîv^eb'l] adj. irréparable, irrécouvrable.

irreversible [irivë^rs^eb'l] adj. irrévocable; irréversible.

irrevocable [irév^ek^eb'l] adj. irrévocable.

irrigate [irigé¹t] v. irriguer. ‖ *irrigation* [irigé¹sh^en] s. irrigation, f.; arrosage, m.

irritable [ir^et^eb'l] adj. irritable. ‖ *irritant* [-t^ent] adj., s. irritant. ‖ *irritate* [-té¹t] v. irriter. ‖ *irritating* [-té¹ting] adj. irritant. ‖ *irritation* [irité¹sh^en] s. irritation, f.

Islam [izlâm] s. Islam, m.; *islamism*, islamisme.

island [a¹l^end] s. île, f.; *islander*, insulaire.

isle [a¹l] s. île, f.

isolate [a¹s¹lé¹t] v. isoler. ‖ *isolation* [a¹s¹lé¹sh^en] s. isolement, m.

Israel [izre¹l] s. Israël, m.; *Israeli*, Israélien; *Israelite*, Israélite.

issue [ishou] s. issue; émission [money]; question (jur.); sortie (mil.); publication; progéniture, f.; événement; numéro [newspaper]; écoulement [liquid], m.; v. expédier; sortir; publier [books]; émettre (Stock Exchange); lancer (jur.); faire paraître [order]; déboucher (mil.); provenir; *issue par*, prix d'émission.

isthmus [ism^es] s.* isthme, m.

it [it] pron. il, elle; le, la, lui; ce; *is it vous?*, est-ce vous?; *it is said*, on dit; *don't think of it*, n'y pensez pas; *to brave it*, avoir du cran.

Italian [italy^en] adj., s. italien.

italic [italik] adj. italique.

Italy [it^eli] s. Italie, f.

itch [itsh] s.* démangeaison; gale, f.; v. démanger; *to be itching to*, avoir grande envie de; *itchy*, galeux.

item [a¹t^em] s. article; écho, entrefilet [newspaper]; détail; item, m.; *usable items*, articles de consommation courante.

iterate [it^eré¹t] v. réitérer; répéter.

itinerary [a¹tin^er^eri] s.* itinéraire, m. ‖ *itinerate* [-é¹t] v. se déplacer constamment.

its [its] poss. adj. son, sa, ses. ‖ *itself* [itsélf] pers. pron. lui-même, elle-même, se; *by itself*, tout seul; *in itself*, en soi.

ivory [a¹vri] s.* ivoire, m.

ivy [a¹vi] s.* lierre, m.; *poison-ivy*, sumac vénéneux, *Fr. Can.* herbe à puces.

J

jab [djab] *v.* piquer; *s.* coup de canif, de coude; direct [boxing], m.

jack [djak] *s.* valet [cards]; cric [auto]; pavillon de beaupré (naut.); vérin (techn.); chevalet [saw-horse]; tire-bottes; tourne-broche; brochet [fish], m.; *v.* mettre sur cric; *jack of all trades*, factotum; *to jack up*, hausser brusquement [price]; *jack-in-the-box*, diable-surprise; *jackass*, âne, sot, imbécile.

jackal [djakaul] *s.* chacal, m.

jacket [djakit] *s.* tunique (mil.); veste; vareuse; enveloppe (mech.); jaquette [book], f.

jade [djé¹d] *s.* rosse; coquine, f.; *v.* harasser; s'éreinter.

jagged [djagid] *adj.* dentelé; ébréché, découpé.

jail [djé¹l] *s.* prison, f.; *v.* emprisonner; *jailer*, geôlier.

jalopy [djₐlâpi] *s.** *Am.* bagnole (fam.).

jam [djam] *s.* confiture, f.

jam [djam] *s.* embouteillage [traffic]; enrayage [weapon]; brouillage [radio], m.; *v.* coincer; obstruer; bloquer; *to jam up*, tasser; *to jam on the brakes*, caler les freins; *to be in a jam*, être dans le pétrin.

James [djé¹mz] *s.* Jacques, m.

janitor [djanₑtₑr] *s.* concierge, portier, m.

January [djₐnyouₑri] *s.* janvier, m.

Japan [djₑpan] *s.* Japon, m.; laque, f.; *v.* laquer.

Japanese [djapₑnîz] *adj., s.* japonais.

jar [djâr] *s.* discordance; querelle, f.; *v.* grincer; vibrer; secouer; ébranler; se quereller.

jar [djâr] *s.* jarre, f.; pot, bocal, m.

jargon [djârgₑn] *s.* jargon, m.

jasmine [djazmìn] *s.* jasmin, m.

jasper [djaspₑr] *s.* jaspe, m.

jaundice [djaundis] *s.* jaunisse, f.

jaunt [djaunt] *s.* excursion, f.; *v.* faire un tour.

jaunty [djaunti] *adj.* vif, insouciant; désinvolte, cavalier; prétentieux.

jaw [djau] *s.* mâchoire; gueule, f.; laïus, m.; *v.* bavarder; caqueter; engueuler (slang); *jawbone*, maxillaire.

jay [djé¹] *s.* geai, m.

jazz [djaz] *s.* jazz; entrain, m.; *v.* arranger (ou) jouer en jazz; animer.

jealous [djèlₑs] *adj.* jaloux; *jealousy*, jalousie.

Jeep [djîp] *s.* Jeep, f.

jeer [djîₑr] *s.* raillerie, f.; *v.* railler; se moquer (*at*, de).

jelly [djèli] *s.** gelée, f.; *v.* mettre en marmelade; *jellyfish*, méduse.

jeopardize [djépₑda¹z] *v.* risquer, mettre en péril. ‖ *jeopardy* [-di] *s.* danger, risque, m.

jerk [djèrk] *s.* saccade; secousse, f.; réflexe (med.), m.; *v.* secouer; tirer brusquement; se mouvoir par saccades; se crisper.

jerk [djèrk] *v.* boucaner.

jersey [djèrzi] *s.* jersey, maillot, m.

jest [djèst] *s.* plaisanterie, f.; *v.* plaisanter; *jester*, bouffon, railleur, plaisantin.

jet [djèt] *s.* jet; gicleur [auto], m.; *jet plane*, avion à réaction; *v.* jeter, lancer.

jet [djèt] *s.* jais, m.; *adj.* de jais.

jetsam [djètsₑm] *s.* épave; marchandise jetée à la mer (jur.), f.

jettison [djètₑs'n] *v.* délester; jeter à la mer.

Jew [djou] *s.* Juif; Israélite, m.

jewel [djouₑl] *s.* joyau; bijou, m. ‖ *jeweler* [-lₑr] *s.* bijoutier, m. ‖ *jewelry* [-ri] *s.** bijouterie, f.

Jewish [djouish] *adj.* juif.

jiffy [djifi] *s.** instant, m.; *in a jiffy*, en un clin d'œil.

jig [djig] *s.* gigue, f.; appareil de montage, m.; *v.* danser la gigue; *jig-saw*, scie mécanique.

jiggle [djig'l] *v.* sautiller; gigoter.

jilt [djilt] *v.* repousser un amoureux, lâcher (fam.); *s.* inconstante, lâcheuse, f.

jingle [djing'l] *s.* tintement, cliquetis; grelot, m.; *v.* tinter.

jingo [djingoou] *s., adj.* chauvin.

jitters [djitₑrs] *s. pl.* frousse, f. (colloq.).

job [djâb] *s.* travail; emploi, m.; place; besogne, f.; *Br. cushy job*, *Am. soft job*, filon, « fromage » (slang); *v.* donner à l'entreprise; spéculer; traiter en sous-main; *job lot*, articles dépareillés d'occasion; *job work*, travail à la pièce.

jockey [djaki] *s.* jockey, m.; *v.* maquignonner, intriguer.

jocular [djắkyoul^{er}] *adj.* facétieux, plaisant.

jog [djắg] *v.* secouer, cahoter; pousser; rafraîchir [memory]; *s.* saccade, secousse, f.; cahot; petit trot; coup de coude, m.; *to jog along*, aller son petit train.

John [djăn] *s.* Jean. ‖ *Johnny* [-i] *s.* Jeannot; type, m.

join [djo¹n] *v.* joindre; unir; s'associer; rejoindre. ‖ *joiner* [-^{er}] *s.* menuisier, m. ‖ *joinery* [-ri] *s.* menuiserie, f.

joint [djo¹nt] *s.* joint; raccord; assemblage; gond, m.; articulation; jointure; jonction; pièce de viande; charnière, f.; *adj.* solidaire; joint; concerté; combiné; *v.* joindre; rapporter; découper [meat]; (s')ajuster; *out of joint*, disjoint; *joint tenants*, copropriétaires; *rail joint*, éclisse.

joist [djo¹st] *s.* solive, f.; madrier, m.

joke [djo⁰⁰k] *s.* plaisanterie, f.; bon mot, m.; *v.* plaisanter. ‖ *joker* [-^{er}] *s.* plaisantin; farceur; joker [cards], m. ‖ *jokingly* [-ingli] *adv.* en plaisantant, pour rire.

jolly [djắli] *adj.* jovial, enjoué; éméché; plaisant; formidable.

jolt [djo⁰⁰lt] *s.* choc; cahot, m.; *v.* secouer, cahoter.

jostle [djắs'l] *v.* coudoyer, bousculer; *s.* cohue, bousculade, f.

jot [djắt] *s.* iota; brin, m.

jot [djặt] *v.* noter, pointer.

journal [djë'r'n'l] *s.* journal [newspaper, diary, daybook, register]; tourillon (mech.), m. ‖ *journalism* [-iz^em] *s.* journalisme, m. ‖ *journalist* [-ist] *s.* journaliste, m. f.

journey [djë'rni] *s.* voyage; trajet; parcours, m.; *v.* voyager; *to take a journey*, faire un voyage.

journeyman [djë'nim^en] (*pl.* journeymen) *s.* ouvrier, journalier, m.

jovial [djo⁰⁰vi^el] *adj.* jovial.

joy [djo¹] *s.* joie, f.; *joyful, joyous*, joyeux; *joyless*, triste.

jubilant [djoub'l^ent] *adj.* joyeux, triomphant; *jubilate*, jubiler; *jubilation*, jubilation. ‖ *jubilee* [djoub'lî] *s.* jubilé, m.

judge [djœdj] *s.* juge; arbitre, m.; *v.* juger; décider; apprécier [distances]. ‖ *judgment* [-m^ent] *s.* jugement; arrêt, m.; opinion, f.

judicial [djoudish^el] *adj.* judiciaire; juridique. ‖ *judicious* [djoudish^es] *adj.* judicieux.

jug [djœg] *s.* broc; *Am.* « violon » (fam.), m.

juggle [djœg'l] *v.* jongler; escamoter; *s.* jonglerie, f.; tour de passe-passe, m.; *juggler*, jongleur, prestidigitateur.

juice [djous] *s.* jus; suc, m. ‖ *juiciness* [-inis] *s.* succulence, f. ‖ *juicy* [-i] *adj.* juteux; succulent; osé [story].

jukebox [djoukbằks] *s.* Am.* pick-up électrique à sous, m.

July [djoula¹] *s.* juillet, m.

jumble [djœmb'l] *v.* jeter pêle-mêle; (s')embrouiller; *s.* embrouillamini, m.; *jumble-sale*, déballage.

jump [djœmp] *s.* saut, m.; *v.* sauter; bondir; se précipiter; sauter; *to jump at the chance*, sauter sur l'occasion; *to jump over*, laisser de côté, passer; *parachute jump*, saut en parachute. ‖ *jumper* [-^{er}] *s.* sauteur; jumper, m.; *Am.* barboteuse, f.

junction [djœngksh^en] *s.* jonction; bifurcation [road], f.; nœud [rail], m. ‖ *juncture* [-tsh^{er}] *s.* jointure; conjoncture, f.

June [djoun] *s.* juin, m.

jungle [djœngg'l] *s.* jungle, f.

junior [djouny^{er}] *s.* cadet; plus jeune; subalterne; *s.* cadet; *Am.* étudiant de troisième année (univ.), m.

junk [djœngk] *s.* jonque, f.

junk [djœngk] *s.* vieux cordages; rebut, m.; *v.* mettre au rebut; *junkman, Am.* chiffonnier.

juridical [djouridik^el] *adj.* juridique.

jurisdiction [djourisdĭksh^en] *s.* juridiction; compétence, f.

jurisprudence [djourisproud'ns] *s.* jurisprudence, f.

jurist [djou^erist] *s.* juriste; étudiant en droit, m.

juror [djour^{er}] *s.* juré, m. ‖ *jury* [djouri] *s.* jury, m.; *juryman*, juré; *jurywoman*, femme juré.

just [djœst] *adj.* juste; équitable; impartial; exact; *adv.* exactement; justement; seulement; *I have just seen him*, je viens de le voir; *just as*, à l'instant où; tout comme; *just out*, vient de paraître; *just before*, immédiatement avant; *he had just finished*, c'est à peine s'il a fini. ‖ *justice* [-is] *s.* justice, f.; juge, magistrat, m. ‖ *justification* [djœst^ef^eké¹sh^en] *s.* justification, f. ‖ *justificative* [djœstifiké¹tiv] *adj.* justificatif. ‖ *justificatory* [-eri] *adj.* justificateur. ‖ *justify* [-t^efa¹] *v.* justifier; autoriser.

jut [djœt] *v.* faire saillie.

jute [djout] *s.* jute, m.

juvenile [djouv'na¹l] *adj.* juvénile.

juxtaposition [djœkst^epĕzish^en] *s.* juxtaposition, f.

K

kangaroo [kàng°rou] *s.* kangourou, m.

kapok [kâpâk] *s.* kapok, m.

keck [kék] *v.* avoir des nausées; être soulevé.

keel [kîl] *s.* quille, f.; *v.* faire chavirer; *to keel over*, chavirer.

keelson [kèls'n] *s.* carlingue, f.

keen [kîn] *adj.* affilé; aigu; perçant [noise]; vif [cold]; pénétrant [mind]; perspicace. ‖ **keenness** [-nis] *s.* acuité; perspicacité; finesse; ardeur, f.

keep [kîp] *v.** garder; tenir; retenir; maintenir; entretenir; célébrer [feast]; protéger; nourrir; *s.* entretien [food]; donjon, m.; *to keep at it*, travailler sans relâche; *to keep from*, s'abstenir de; empêcher de; *to keep in*, rester chez soi; *to keep up*, soutenir; *to keep going*, continuer à aller. ‖ **keeper** [-°r] *s.* gardien; garde; surveillant, m. ‖ **keeping** [-ing] *s.* surveillance; garde; conservation, f.; entretien; maintien, m.; *in keeping with*, en harmonie avec. ‖ **keepsake** [-sé¹k] *s.* souvenir, m.

keg [kèg] *s.* baril, m.

kennel [kèn'l] *s.* niche, f.; *pl.* chenil, m.

kept [kèpt] *pret., p. p. of* to keep.

kerb [kë²b] *s.* bord du trottoir, m.; margelle, f.

kerchief [kë²tshif] *s.* fichu, foulard, carré, m.

kernel [kë²n'l] *s.* grain; noyau, m.; amande, f.; cœur, m. (fig.).

kerosene [kè²esin] *s.* pétrole, m.

kettle [kèt'l] *s.* marmite, f.; coquemar, m.; bouilloire, f.; gâchis, m.; *kettle-drum*, timbale [music].

key [kî] *s.* clef; clavette; touche [piano]; fiche (electr.), f.; *v.* caler; harmoniser; *to key up*, surexcité, nerveux; *key of F*, clef de fa; *under lock and key*, sous clef; *master key*, passepartout; *keyboard*, clavier; *keyhole*, trou de la serrure; *keyman*, cheville ouvrière; *keynote*, note tonique [music]; *keystone*, clef de voûte, base; *key-word*, mot d'ordre, mot clef.

khaki [kâki] *s.* kaki, m.

kick [kik] *s.* coup de pied; recul [gun], m.; ruade [horse], f.; *v.* donner des coups de pied; reculer [gun]; ruer [horse]; regimber; *to kick about*, gigoter; *to kick the bucket*, passer l'arme à gauche, « claquer » (pop.).

kid [kid] *s.* chevreau [flesh, fur, skin]; *Am.* gosse, gamin, m.; *adj.* en chevreau; *v. Am.* se moquer de; chevreter, mettre bas [goats]; *kidding*, blague.

kidnap [kidnap] *v.* enlever; kidnapper; *kidnapper*, ravisseur, kidnappeur; *kidnapping*, rapt.

kidney [kidni] *s.* rognon; rein, m.

kill [kil] *v.* tuer; détruire; *kill-joy*, rabat-joie. ‖ **killer** [-°r] *s.* meurtrier, tueur; tombeur de cœurs, m. (colloq.). ‖ **killing** [-ing] *adj.* meurtrier; mortel; exténuant; désopilant; conquérant; *s.* tuerie, f.

kiln [kiln] *s.* four; séchoir, m.; étuve, f.

kilogram [kil°gram] *s.* kilogramme, m.

kilometer [kil°mit°r] *s.* kilomètre, m.

kilowatt [kil°wât] *s.* kilowatt, m.

kimono [k°mo°un°] *s.* kimono, m.

kin [kin] *s.* parenté, f.; parent; allié, m.

kind [ka¹nd] *s.* genre, m.; espèce, f.; *adj.* bon, aimable; affable; bienveillant; *kindest regards*, bien vifs compliments; *to pay in kind*, payer en nature.

kindergarten [kind°rgârt'n] *s.* jardin d'enfants, m.

kindle [kind'l] *v.* (s')allumer; enflammer; inciter.

kindly [ka¹ndli] *adj.* bon, bienveillant; aimable; *adv.* aimablement; gracieusement. ‖ **kindness** [ka¹ndnis] *s.* bonté; amabilité; bienveillance, f.

kindred [kindrid] *adj.* apparenté; en relations; *s.* parenté, f.

king [king] *s.* roi, m.; dame [draughts], f. ‖ **kingdom** [-d°m] *s.* royaume, m. ‖ **kingly** [-li] *adj.* royal; *adv.* royalement.

kink [kingk] *s.* nœud; torticolis, m.; coque; déviation, déformation; lubie, f.; *v.* (s')entortiller. ‖ **kinky** [kingki] *adj.* noué; crépu.

kinship [kinship] *s.* parenté, f. ‖ **kinsman** [kinzm°n] (*pl.* kinsmen) *s.* parent, m.; **kinswoman** (*pl.* kinswomen), parente, f.

kiss [kis] *s.** baiser, m.; embrassade, f.; *v.* embrasser; *to kiss the hand*, baiser la main.

kit [kit] *s.* équipement; sac; nécessaire, m.; musette (mil.); trousse, f.; *medicine kit*, trousse de médecin; *mess kit*, cantine (mil.).

kitchen [kitshin] *s.* cuisine, f.; *kitchen garden*, jardin potager; *kitchen maid*, fille de cuisine; *kitchenwares*, ustensiles de cuisine.

kite [ka¹t] *s.* cerf-volant; milan [bird], m.; *kite balloon*, ballon captif.

kitten [kit'n] *s.* petit chat, m.

kittle [kít'l] *adj.* épineux, délicat; chatouilleux.

knack [nak] *s.* adresse; habileté, f.; talent, m.; *to have a knack for*, avoir la bosse de.

knapsack [nápsak] *s.* havresac, m.

knave [né¹v] *s.* coquin; valet [cards], m.

knead [nîd] *v.* pétrir.

knee [nî] *s.* genou; coude (techn.), m.; *v.* pousser du genou, faire du genou à; faire des poches à [trousers]; *kneecap*, rotule.

kneel [nîl] *v.** s'agenouiller.

knell [nèl] *s.* glas, m.; *v.* sonner le glas.

knelt [nèlt] *pret.*, *p. p. of* **to knell**.

knew [nyou] *pret. of* **to know**.

knickknack [níknak] *s.* babiole, f.; bibelot, m.

knife [na¹f] (*pl.* **knives** [na¹vz]) *s.* couteau, m.; *v.* donner un coup de couteau; poignarder; *clasp knife*, couteau de poche; *paper-knife*, coupe-papier; *pocket knife*, canif; *knife grinder*, rémouleur.

knight [na¹t] *s.* chevalier; cavalier [chess], m.; *v.* armer chevalier; *knighthood*, chevalerie; *knightliness*, conduite chevaleresque, courtoisie.

knit [nít] *v.** tricoter; joindre; nouer; froncer [brows]; *pret.*, *p. p. of* **to knit**. || *knitting* [-ing] *s.* tricotage; tricot, m.

knives [na¹vz] *pl. of* **knife**.

knob [nâb] *s.* bosse [swelling], f.; bouton [door], m.

knock [nâk] *v.* cogner; frapper; *Am.* dénigrer; *s.* coup; cognement (mech.), m.; *to knock down*, abattre, renverser; *to knock out*, mettre hors de combat; *to knock off*, cesser le travail; *to knock up*, éreinter; *knock-kneed*, cagneux. || *knockabout* [nák⁰ba⁰ut] *s. Am.* rixe, f. || *knocker* [-ᵉʳ] *s.* marteau [door], m.

knoll [no⁰ul] *s.* monticule, tertre, m.

knot [nât] *s.* nœud; petit groupe, m.; *v.* lier; (se) nouer; *sword knot*, dragonne. || *knotty* [-i] *adj.* noueux; embrouillé; peu clair.

know [no⁰u] *v.** connaître; savoir; reconnaître; *to know how to swim*, savoir nager; *to know about*, être informé de; *to know of*, avoir connaissance de; *he ought to know better*, il devrait être plus raisonnable; *let me know*, faites-moi savoir; *know-how*, technique, manière de s'y prendre. || *knowing* [-ing] *adj.* au courant, informé, instruit, malin, entendu; délibéré; déniaisé, dessalé (colloq.). || *knowingly* [-ingli] *adv.* sciemment; à bon escient, habilement. || *knowledge* [nâlidj] *s.* connaissance, science, f.; savoir, m.; *not to my knowledge*, pas que je sache. || *known* [no⁰un] *p. p. of* **to know**.

knuckle [nœk'l] *s.* jointure, articulation, f.; nœud [finger]; osselet, m.; *knuckle of veal*, jarret de veau.

kohlrabi [ko⁰ulrâbi] (*pl.* **kohlrabies**) *s.* chou-rave, m.

L

label [lé¹b'l] *s.* étiquette; marque, f.; écriteau, m.; *v.* étiqueter; enregistrer.

labo(u)r [lé¹ber] *s.* travail; labeur, m.; main-d'œuvre, f.; *v.* travailler; s'appliquer (à); *hard labo(u)r*, travaux forcés; *to labo(u)r under*, être victime de, lutter contre; *Br. labo(u)r exchange*, bureau de placement; *Br. Labour Party*, parti travailliste; *Am. Department of Labor*, ministère du Travail.

laboratory [labreto⁰uri] *s.** laboratoire, m.

labo(u)rer [lé¹berᵉʳ] *s.* travailleur; homme de peine; ouvrier, m. || *labo(u)rious* [lᵉbo⁰uri⁰es] *adj.* laborieux.

labyrinth [labᵉrìnth] *s.* labyrinthe, m.

lace [lé¹s] *s.* galon; ruban; lacet, m.; dentelle, — f.; *Am.* goutte, f. (colloq.); *v.* galonner; orner de dentelle; (se) lacer.

lacerate [lasᵉré¹t] *v.* lacérer.

lack [lak] *s.* manque; défaut, m.; pénurie, f.; *v.* manquer; faire défaut; être dénué de; *he lacks courage*, le courage lui manque.

laconic [lᵉkânik] *adj.* laconique. || *laconism* [lak⁰niz'm] *s.* laconisme, f.

lacquer [lakᵉʳ] *s.* laque, f.; *v.* laquer.

lacrosse [làkros] *s. Fr. Can.* crosse [sport], f.

lacuna [lᵉkyoun⁰] *s.* lacune, f.

lad [lad] *s.* garçon; jeune homme, m.

ladder [ladᵉʳ] *s.* échelle, f.; fil tiré, démaillage, m.; *ladder-mender*, remmailleuse; *ladder-proof*, indémaillable.

laden [lé¹d'n] *adj.* chargé.

ladies [lé¹diz] *s. pl. of* **lady**.

ladle [lé¹d'l] *s.* louche, f.

lady [lé¹di] (*pl.* **ladies**) *s.* dame; madame, f.; *young lady*, jeune femme, demoiselle; **lady-bird**, coccinelle; **Lady day**, Annonciation.

lag [làg] *s.* retard; ralentissement; décalage, m.; *v.* rester en arrière; (se) traîner. ‖ **laggard** [-°d] *s.* lambin; retardataire, m.; *adj.* lent; en retard.

lagoon [l°goun] *s.* lagune, f.

laic [lé¹ik] *adj.* laïque.

laid [lé¹d] *pret., p. p. of* **to lay**; *laid up,* malade, alité; *laid paper,* papier vergé.

lain [lé¹n] *p. p. of* **to lie**.

lair [lè°r] *s.* tanière; bauge, f.; antre, repaire, m.

lake [lé¹k] *s.* lac, m.

lamb [làm] *s.* agneau, m. ‖ **lambkin** [-kin] *s.* agnelet, m.

lame [lé¹m] *adj.* boiteux; estropié; défectueux; *v.* estropier; *lame duck,* failli; *Am.* battu aux élections.

lament [l°mènt] *s.* lamentation, f.; *v.* se lamenter; déplorer. ‖ **lamentable** [lam°nt°b°l] *adj.* lamentable. ‖ **lamentation** [lâménté¹sh°n] *s.* lamentation, f.

laminate [lam°né¹t] *v.* laminer; feuilleter; plaquer.

lamp [làmp] *s.* lampe; lanterne, f.; *kerosene lamp,* lampe à pétrole; *lamp-post,* réverbère; *lamp shade,* abat-jour; *pocket lamp,* lampe de poche; *trouble lamp,* baladeuse (electr.).

lampion [lampi°n] *s.* lampion, m.

lampoon [làmpoun] *s.* libelle, m.

lance [làns] *s.* lance, f.; *v.* percer d'un coup de lance; percer [abscess].

lancet [lànsit] *s.* lancette (med.), f.

lancination [lânsiné¹sh°n] *s.* élancement, m.

land [lànd] *s.* terre, f.; terrain; pays; domaine, m.; *v.* débarquer; aborder (naut.); atterrir (aviat.); poser à terre; obtenir [situation]; *fallow land,* terre en friche. ‖ **landholder** [-hoould°r] *s.* propriétaire foncier, m. ‖ **landing** [-ing] *s.* débarquement; atterrissage; débarcadère; palier, m.; *emergency landing,* atterrissage forcé. ‖ **landlady** [-lé¹di] (*pl.* landladies) *s.* propriétaire; logeuse; hôtelière, f. ‖ **landlord** [-lourd] *s.* propriétaire; logeur; hôtelier, m. ‖ **landmark** [-mârk] *s.* borne, limite, f.; point de repère; point saillant, m. ‖ **landowner** [-o°un°r] *s.* propriétaire foncier, m. ‖ **landscape** [-ské¹p] *s.* paysage, panorama, m. ‖ **landslide** [-sla¹d] *s.* éboulement, m.

lane [lé¹n] *s.* ruelle, f.; chemin, m.; route (naut.), f.; *Am. pedestrian lane,* passage clouté.

language [lànggwidj] *s.* langue, f.; langage, m.

languid [làngguid] *adj.* languide, languissant. ‖ **languish** [-gwish] *v.* languir. ‖ **languor** [-g°r] *s.* langueur, f.

lank [làngk] *adj.* efflanqué.

lantern [lànt°rn] *s.* lanterne, f.; phare, m.

lap [làp] *s.* giron, m.; genoux, m. pl.; lobe [ear]; isolant [electr.], m.; *to sit in s.o.'s lap,* s'asseoir sur les genoux de qqn; *lap robe, Am.* plaid.

lap [làp] *v.* laper; *s.* gorgée; étape [journey], f.

lap [làp] *s.* recouvrement (mech.), m.; *v.* envelopper; s'étendre; recouvrir; roder (mech.); boucler [course]; s'enrouler.

lapel [l°pèl] *s.* revers d'habit, m.

lapse [làps] *s.* cours; laps; manquement, m.; chute de température (aviat.); erreur, f.; *v.* s'écouler [time]; tomber; périmer (jur.); faillir.

larboard [lârb°rd] *s.* bâbord, m.

larceny [lârs'ni] *s.°* larcin, m.

lard [lârd] *s.* saindoux, m.; *v.* larder; *larder,* garde-manger.

large [lârdj] *adj.* grand; gros; vaste. ‖ **largely** [-li] *adv.* abondamment; amplement; beaucoup.

lark [lârk] *s.* alouette, f.; joyeuse équipée; farce, f.; *v.* s'amuser; chahuter.

larva [lârv°] *s.* larve, f.

larynx [laringks] *s.°* larynx, m.

lascivious [l°sivi°s] *adj.* lascif.

lash [làsh] *s.°* coup de fouet; cil [eye], m.; mèche [whip], f.; *v.* cingler; fouetter.

lash [làsh] *v.* attacher; amarrer (naut.); jouer (mech.).

lass [làs] *s.°* fille, f.

lassitude [las°tyoud] *s.* lassitude, f.

lasso [laso°u] *s.* lasso, m.; *v.* prendre au lasso.

last [làst] *adj.* dernier; ultime; passé; *v.* durer; *last night,* hier soir; *at last,* enfin, à la fin; *lastly,* enfin, en dernier lieu. ‖ **lasting** [-ing] *adj.* durable; permanent.

latch [làtsh] *s.°* loquet; verrou, m.; *Am. to latch on to,* s'emparer de.

late [lé¹t] *adj.* tard; en retard; ancien; défunt; avancé [hour]; *adv.* tard; *to be late,* être en retard; *of late, lately,* récemment; dernièrement; *until lately,* jusqu'à ces derniers temps.

later [lé¹t°r] *comp. of* **late**.

lateral [lat°r°l] *adj.* latéral.

latest [léʰtist] *sup. of late; latest news*, dernières nouvelles; *at latest*, au plus tard.

lath [lath] *s.* latte, f.

lathe [léʰzh] *s.* tour (techn.), m.

lather [lazhᵉr] *s.* mousse; écume, f.; *v.* mousser. écumer; savonner.

Latin [lat'n] *adj., s.* latin.

latitude [latᵉtyoud] *s.* latitude; liberté, f.

latter [latᵉr] *adj.* dernier; récent; moderne

lattice [latis] *s.* treillis, m.

laud [loud] *s* louange, f.; *v.* louer. ‖ **laudative** [-ᵉtiv] *adj.* laudatif. ‖ **laudatory** [-ᵉtri] *adj.* louangeur.

laugh [laf] *s* rire, m.; risée, f.; *v.* rire; *to laugh at*. se moquer de; *to burst out laughing*. éclater de rire; *to laugh up one's sleeve*, rire sous cape; *to laugh on the wrong side of one's mouth*. rire jaune *it is no laughing matter* il n'y a pas de quoi rire; **laughable**, risible. dérisoire; **laugher**, rieur, **laughing** riant, rieur, risible; hilarant ‖ **laughter** [-tᵉr] *s.* rire, m.; **laughter-provoking**, désopilant.

launch [launtsh] *s* * chaloupe, f.; *v.* mettre à l'eau. lancer (naut.; comm.); déclencher (mil.). ‖ **launching** [-ing] *s.* lancement m., **launching-ramp**, rampe de lancement

launder [laundᵉr] *v* blanchir, laver; **laundress**, blanchisseuse; **laundry**, blanchissage buanderie, blanchisserie; **laundryman**, blanchisseur.

laureate [lauriit] *s.* lauréat, m. ‖ **laurel** [-ᵉl] *s* laurier, m.; gloire, f.

lava [lavᵉ] *s* lave, f.

lavatory [lavᵉtooⁱri] *s.* * lavoir; *Br.* cabinets *Am* lavabos publics, m. pl.

lavender [lavᵉndᵉr] *s* lavande, f.

lavish [lavish] *adj.* prodigue; copieux, abondant, *v.* gaspiller, dilapider, prodiguer; **lavishness**, prodigalité.

law [lau] *s* loi, f., droit, m.; **commercial law**, droit commercial **law court**, tribunal **law department**, service de contentieux **law student**, étudiant en droit. ‖ **lawful** [-ᵉl] *adj.* légal; légitime; licite ‖ **lawless** [-lis] *adj.* illégal effréné déréglé **lawmaker** [-méⁱkᵉr] *s* législateur, m.

lawn [laun] *s* pelouse, f.; **lawn mower**, tondeuse

lawn [laun] *s* linon, m.

lawsuit [lausout] *s* procès; litige, m. ‖ **lawyer** [lauyᵉr] *s* homme de loi; avocat, jurisconsulte avoué, m.

lax [laks] *adj.* lâche; distendu; négligent; relâché. ‖ **laxative** [-ᵉtiv] *s.*

laxatif, m. ‖ **laxity** [-ᵉti] *s.* relâchement, m.; mollesse, f.; **moral laxity**, légéreté de mœurs.

lay [léⁱ] *pret. of to lie.*

lay [léⁱ] *v.* * poser; mettre; coucher; étendre, pondre [eggs]; abattre [dust]; tendre [snare] rejeter [blame]; *to lay aside* mettre de côté, *to lay bare*, mettre à nu révéler. *to lay down arms*, déposer les armes. *to lay a gun*, pointer un canon. *to lay off*, congédier, *to lay out*, disposer placer [money]; *to lay waste*, dévaster. ‖ **layer** [-ᵉr] *s.* couche, assise, marcotte [shoot]; pondeuse [hen], f.; pointeur [gunner], m.

layman [léⁱmᵉn] (*pl. laymen*) *s.* laïc, m.

lazily [léⁱzili] *adv.* paresseusement. ‖ **laziness** [léⁱzinis] *s.* paresse, f. ‖ **lazy** [léⁱzi] *adj* paresseux; indolent, mou.

lead [lèd] *s* plomb, m.; mine de plomb, sonde, f.; *v.* plomber; **leaden**, de plomb, plombé; **lead-work**, plomberie.

lead [lîd] *v.* * conduire; mener; diriger [orchestra] introduire; dominer; avoir la main [cards]; *s.* conduite; direction préséance. f., commandement, m *Am* **lead article**, leader, article de fond [newspaper]. **leading lady**, vedette **leading part**, premier rôle; *to lead astray* égarer, dissiper; *to lead the way* montrer le chemin.

leader [lîdᵉr] *s* chef; conducteur; meneur dirigeant *Br* article de fond [newspaper] m. ‖ **leadership** [-ship] *s* direction autorité, f.; commandement m | **leading** [lîding] *adj.* principal de tête en chef.

leaf [lîf] (*pl leaves* [lîvz]) *s.* feuille, f.; feuille [book] battant [door], m.; rallonge [table]. *v* se couvrir de feuilles **leafless**, dénudé, effeuillé; **leafy**, feuillu. touffu ‖ **leaflet** [-lit] *s.* feuillet dépliant, imprimé; prospectus, tract m

league [lîg] *s.* ligue; union, f.; *v.* (se) liguer

league [lîg] *s* lieue, f.

leak [lîk] *s* fuite. voie d'eau, f.; *v.* fuir. faire eau (naut.) *to leak out*, sourdre se faire jour, transpirer (fig.). ‖ **leakage** [-idj] · perte, fuite, f.; coulage, m **leaky**, qui fuit, qui prend l'eau; défaillant [memory].

lean [lîn] *v* * s'incliner se pencher; s'appuyer, *s* pente. inclinaison, f.

lean [lîn] *adj* maigre. émacié.

leant [lènt] : **leaned**, see **lean**.

leap [lîp] *v* * sauter bondir; s'élancer; franchir, *s* saut; bond, m.; **leap year**, année bissextile. ‖ **leapt** [lèpt] *pret., p. p. of to leap.*

learn [lë°n] v.* apprendre; étudier. **learned** [-id] adj. érudit, instruit, lettré. || **learner** [-°r] s. élève; débutant; apprenti, m. || **learning** [-ing] s. savoir, m.; science; érudition, f. || **learnt** [-t] pret., p. p. of to learn.

lease [lîs] v louer; affermer; s. bail, m.; ferme, f

leash [lîsh] s. laisse, f.; v. attacher; mener en laisse; to hold in leash, tenir en lisière

least [lîst] adj. le moindre; le plus petit; adv le moins; at least, au moins, du moins leastwise, du moins.

leather [lèzh°r] s cuir, m.; peau, f.; leather-dresser, mégissier.

leave [lîv] v laisser; s'en aller; partir; quitter abandonner. s. permission; liberté f, congé m. sick leave, congé de convalescence, to leave about, laisser traîner, to leave off, renoncer. to leave out, omettre.

leaven [lèv°n] s levain, m.; v. lever.

leaves [lîvz] pl. of leaf.

lecherous [lètsh°r°s] adj. débauché; sensuel

lectern [lèkt°rn] s. lutrin, pupitre, m.

lecture [lèktsh°r] s. conférence; réprimande f, v. faire des conférences; sermonner || **lecturer** [-r°r] s. conférencier, maître de conférences (univ.), m.

led [lèd] pret., p. p. of to lead.

ledge [lèdj] s. rebord, m.; saillie, f.

ledger [lèdj°r] s. grand-livre; registre, m

leech [lîtsh] s.* sangsue, f.

leek [lîk] s poireau, m.

leer [lî°r] s œillade, f.; regard de côté, m.; v regarder de coin.

left [lèft] pret., p p. of to leave; I have two books left, il me reste deux livres

left [lèft] adj gauche; s. main gauche f left-handed, gaucher; on the left à gauche leftist [lèftist] s homme (m) de gauche leftovers [lèftoºv°rz] s pl restes m pl (culin.) || **lefty** [lèfti] s Am gaucher, m.

leg [lèg] s jambe patte tige [boots]; cuisse [hen branche [compasses], f. pied [furniture, gigo [mutton], m. on one leg .. the-pied one-legged, unijambist leg-up, coup de main, dépannage ir (colloq.).

legacy [lèg°ıı] s legs, m.

legal [lîg'l] adj légal licite. || **legalize** [-a'z] légalise autoriser

legate [lègit] s léga délégué, m. || **legatee** [lèg°tî] s légataire, m || **legation** [lîgê'sh°n] s. légation, f.

legend [lèdj°nd] s. légende; inscription, f.; **legendary**, légendaire.

legging [lèging] s. guêtre; molletière, f

legible [lèdj°b'l] adj. lisible.

legion [lîdj°n] s légion, f.

legislate [lèdjislê't] v légiférer. || **legislation** [lèdjislê'sh°n] s. législation, f. || **legislator** [lèdjislê't°r] s. législateur, m **legislature** [lèdjislê'tsh°r] s. législature f

legitimate [lidjît°mit] adj. légitime.

leisure [lij°r] s. loisir, m.; **leisurely**, à loisir

lemon [lèm°n] s. citron, m. || **lemonade** [lèm°nê'd] s. limonade, f.; citron pressé, m.

lend [lènd] v.* prêter; lender, prêteur.

length [lèngkth] s. longueur; étendue; durée distance; quantité (gramm.) f. the whole length, jusqu'au bout, lengthwise, en longueur, lengthy, long, prolixe || **lengthen** [-°n] v allonger; prolonger; (s')étendre.

lenient [lînient] adj. indulgent; adoucissant lénitif.

lens [lènz] s.* lentille, f.; objectif (phot.), verre, ménisque, m.

lent [lènt] pret., p. p. of to lend.

Lent [lènt] s carême, m.

leopard [lèp°rd] s léopard, m.

leprosy [lèpr°sı] s. lèpre, f. || **leprous** [lèpr°s] adj lépreux.

lesion [lîz°n] s lésion, f.

less [lès] adj moindre; adv. moins.

lessee [lèsî] s locataire, preneur, m.

lessen [lès°n] v diminuer, amoindrir; atténuer **lesser** [lès°r] adj. plus petit, moindre inférieur

lesson [lès°n] s leçon, f.

lest [lèst] conj de peur que.

let [lèt] v * laisser, permettre; louer; imper aux let him come qu'il vienne house to let maison à louer; to let know, faire savoir to be let off with, en être quitte pour to let out, laisser échapper libérer to let alone, laisser tranquille pret p p. of to let.

lethargy [lèth°rdjı] s. léthargie, f.

letter [lèt°r] s lettre f caractère, m.; capital letter, majuscule letter box, boîte aux lettres letter-carrier, facteur letter-head, en-tête.

lettuce [lètis] s laitue, f.

letup [lètœp] s détente, f.; ralentissement m

level [lèv'l] adj. horizontal; de niveau; s. niveau, m.; v. niveler; équilibrer; plafonner (aviat.); pointer

[arm]; *to level out*, égaliser; *adv.* de niveau; à ras; *Am. on the level*, honnête, droit; *level-crossing*, passage à niveau; *level-headed*, bien équilibré, rassis, d'aplomb; *leveller*, niveleur; *levelling*, nivellement.

lever [lèv°r] *s.* levier, m.; manette, f.; *control lever*, levier de commande; *to lever up*, soulever avec un levier.

levity [léviti] *s.* légèreté, f.

levy [lèvi] *s.°* levée; réquisition; imposition, f.; embargo, m.; *v.* lever; percevoir; imposer; mettre l'embargo.

lewd [loud] *adj.* lascif; impudique. ‖ **lewdness** [-nis] *s.* lubricité, f.

lexicography [lèksikogr°fi] *s.* lexicographie, f.; *lexicology*, lexicologie, f.

lexicon [lèksik°n] *s.* lexique, m.

liability [la¹°bfl°ti] *s.°* responsabilité, f.; engagement, m. ‖ *liable* [la¹°b'l] *adj.* responsable; passible (*to*, de); soumis, sujet (*to*, à).

liaison [lié¹zaun] *s.* liaison, f.

liar [la¹°r] *s.* menteur, m.

libel [la¹b'l] *s.* libelle, m.; diffamation, f.; *v.* diffamer. ‖ *libellous* [-°s] *adj.* diffamatoire.

liberal [lïbèr°l] *adj.*, *s.* libéral, m. ‖ *liberality* [lïbèral°ti] *s.°* libéralité, f. ‖ *liberate* [lïb°ré¹t] *v.* libérer. ‖ *liberation* [lïb°ré¹sh°n] *s.* libération, f. ‖ *liberator* [lïb°ré¹t°r] *s.* libérateur, m. ‖ *libertine* [lïb°rtïn] *adj.*, *s.* libertin. ‖ *liberty* [lïb°rti] *s.°* liberté, f.

librarian [la¹brèri°n] *s.* bibliothécaire, m. ‖ *library* [la¹brèri] *s.°* bibliothèque, f.

lice [la¹s] *pl. of louse.*

licence [la¹s°ns] *s.* permission; licence; patente, f.; brevet; permis, m. ‖ *license* [la¹s°ns] *v.* autoriser (*to*, à); permettre (*to*, de); breveter; patenter; *operator's license*, *driving license*, permis de conduire. ‖ *licentious* [la¹sènsh°a] *adj.* licencieux, dissolu.

lichen [la¹kin] *s.* lichen, m.

lick [lik] *v.* lécher; laper; rosser; *not to do a lick of work*, ne pas faire un brin de travail; *licking*, raclée.

lid [lid] *s.* couvercle, m.; *eye-lid*, paupière.

lie [la¹] *s.* mensonge, m.; *v.* mentir; *to give the lie to*, donner un démenti à.

lie [la¹] *s. Br.* position; configuration, f.; gisement (geol.), m.; *v.°* être couché; reposer; être situé; stationner; *to lie low*, se tapir, se taire; *to lie about*, traîner.

lief [lif] *adv.*; *I had as lief*, j'aimerais autant.

lieutenant [loutèn°nt] *s.* lieutenant, m.; *lieutenant-colonel*, lieutenant-colonel; *lieutenant-commander*, capitaine de corvette; *lieutenant-general*, général de division.

life [la¹f] (*pl. lives* [la¹vz]) *s.* vie; vivacité; durée (techn.), f.; *life-belt*, ceinture de sauvetage; *live insurance*, assurance sur la vie; *lifeless*, sans vie, inanimé; *lifelike*, vivant, naturel; *lifelong*, perpétuel, de toute la vie; *life pension*, pension alimentaire; *life-size*, grandeur nature.

lift [lift] *v.* lever; soulever; *Am.* voler (slang); *s.* haussement; *Br.* ascenseur, m.; poussée; force ascensionnelle; levée; balancine (naut.); portance (aviat.), f.

ligament [lïg°m°nt] *s.* ligament, m.

light [la¹t] *s.* lumière; clarté; lueur, f.; phare; jour; éclairage, m.; *v.* allumer; éclairer; *to come to light*, se révéler; *give me a light*, donnez-moi du feu; *to put out the light*, éteindre la lumière; *beacon light*, balisage (aviat.); *driving lights*, éclairage-code [auto]; *night light*, veilleuse; *northern lights*, aurore boréale.

light [la¹t] *adj.* léger; *light-headed*, frivole; *light-hearted*, allègre; *light-minded*, frivole, volage; *v.* descendre, retomber.

lighten [la¹t'n] *v.* éclairer; illuminer; éclaircir.

lighten [la¹t'n] *v.* alléger, soulager.

lighter [la¹t°r] *s.* allumeur; briquet; chaland (naut.), m. ‖ *lighthouse* [la¹tha°s] *s.* phare, m. ‖ *lighting* [la¹ting] *s.* éclairage; allumage, m.; illumination, f.

lightly [la¹tli] *adv.* légèrement; superficiellement; étourdiment. ‖ *lightness* [la¹tnis] *s.* légèreté; frivolité; inconstance, f.

lightness [la¹tnis] *s.* clarté, lumière, f. ‖ *lightning* [-ning] *s.* éclair, m.; foudre, f., *lightning conductor*, *lightning rod*, paratonnerre; *lightning war*, guerre-éclair.

lights [la¹ts] *s. pl.* mou (of veal), m.

lightsome [la¹ts°m] *adj.* lumineux; agile, léger, leste; gracieux; gai.

likable [la¹k°b'l] *adj.* agréable; aimable sympathique.

like [la¹k] *v.* aimer; trouver à son goût, vouloir bien; *do whatever you like*, faites ce que vous voulez.

like [la¹k] *adj.* ressemblant; tel; pareil; semblable; *prep.* comme; *what is he like?*, à quoi ressemble-t-il?; *something like*, à peu près, plus ou moins; *to look like*, ressembler. ‖ *likelihood* [-lihoud] *s.* vraisemblance, probabilité, f. ‖ *likely* [-li] *adj.* plausible, probable; *adv.* probablement. ‖ *liken*

[-ᵉn] v. comparer. ‖ **likeness** [-nis] s. apparence ; ressemblance, f. ; air ; portrait, m. ‖ **likewise** [-wa¹z] adv. de même ; pareillement.

liking [la¹king] s. goût ; penchant ; gré, m. ; sympathie, inclination, f.

lilac [la¹lᵉk] adj., s. lilas.

lily [lili] s.* lis, m. ; *lily of the valley*, muguet.

limb [lim] s. membre, m. ; grosse branche, f.

limber [limbᵉʳ] adj. souple ; v. assouplir.

limber [limbᵉʳ] s. caisson ; avant-train (mil.), m.

lime [la¹m] s. chaux ; glu, f. ; v. chauler ; prendre à la glu.

lime [la¹m] s. citron, m. ; lime, f.

lime [la¹m] s. tilleul, m. ; *lime-tree*, tilleul.

limelight [la¹mla¹t] s. lumière oxhydrique ; gloire ; célébrité, f.

limestone [la¹msto⁰ᵘn] s. calcaire, m.

limit [limit] s. limite ; frontière ; tolérance (techn.), f. ; v. limiter, borner. ‖ **limitation** [limité¹shᵉn] s. limitation ; restriction, f. ‖ **limited** [limitid] adj. limité ; restreint ; anonyme ; à responsabilité limitée [company] ; rapide, de luxe (train).

limp [limp] s. claudication, f. ; v. boiter, clocher.

limp [limp] adj. flasque ; flexible ; amorphe.

limpid [limpid] adj. limpide.

linden [lindᵉn] s. tilleul, m.

line [la¹n] s. ligne ; corde ; lignée ; voie, f. ; contour ; cordeau ; trait ; vers [poetry] ; Am. métier, m. ; v. aligner ; border ; sillonner ; doubler ; *line shooting*, galéjade, tartarinade ; *plumb line*, fil à plomb ; *to line up*, s'aligner, faire queue ; *to fall in line with*, se conformer à.

line [la¹n] v. doubler [clothes] ; revêtir [masonry] ; remplir [one's pocket].

lineage [linidj] s. lignée, f.

linear [liniᵉʳ] adj. linéaire. ‖ **lined** [la¹nd] adj. rayé.

linen [linin] s. toile de lin, f. ; linge, m.

liner [la¹nᵉʳ] s. transatlantique, m. ; *air liner*, avion de transport.

linger [linggᵉʳ] v. s'attarder ; traîner ; se prolonger. ‖ **lingerer** [-rᵉʳ] s. retardataire ; lambin, m.

lingerie [lànjᵉri] s. lingerie, f.

linguist [linggwist] s. linguiste, m. ‖ **linguistic** [linggwistik] adj. linguistique. ‖ **linguistics** [-iks] s. linguistique, f.

lining [la¹ning] s. doublure, f. ; doublage ; revêtement, m.

link [lingk] s. anneau ; maillon ; chaînon, m. ; articulation, f. ; v. lier ; unir ; enchaîner ; (s')articuler ; se raccorder ‖ **links** [-s] s. pl. terrain de golf, m.

linnet [linit] s. linotte, f.

linoleum [lino⁰ᵘliᵉm] s. linoléum, m.

linseed [linsîd] s. graine de lin, f. ; *linseed oil*, huile de lin.

lint [lint] s. charpie, f.

lintel [lint'l] s. linteau, m.

lion [la¹ᵉn] s. lion, m. ; *lioness*, lionne.

lip [lip] s. lèvre, f. ; *lipsalve*, pommade dermophile pour les lèvres ; *lipstick*, rouge à lèvres.

liquefy [likwᵉfa¹] v. liquéfier ; fluidifier. ‖ **liqueur** [likiou⁰ᵉʳ] s. liqueur, f. ‖ **liquid** [likwid] adj., s. liquide. ‖ **liquidate** [-é¹t] v. liquider ; amortir ; solder [accounts]. ‖ **liquidation** [likwidé¹shᵉn] s. liquidation, f. ; solde des comptes, m. ‖ **liquor** [likᵉʳ] s. liqueur, f. ; spiritueux ; liquide, m.

lisp [lisp] v. zézayer ; s. zézaiement, m.

list [list] s. liste ; bande (naut.), f. ; registre ; tableau, m. ; v. inscrire ; *army list*, annuaire de l'armée ; *wine list*, carte des vins ; *list price*, tarif, prix du catalogue.

list [list] s. lisière [cloth], f.

listen [lis'n] v. écouter ; prêter attention ; *to listen in*, écouter à la radio ; *listener*, auditeur.

listless [listlis] adj. insouciant ; inattentif ; indolent. ‖ **listlessness** [-nis] s. indifférence ; insouciance ; nonchalance, f.

lit [lit] pret., p. p. of **to light**.

literal [litᵉrᵉl] adj. littéral ; mot à mot ; s. coquille (typogr.), f. ‖ **literary** [-rèri] adj. littéraire. ‖ **literate** [-it] adj. sachant lire et écrire, alphabète. ‖ **literature** [-rᵉtshᵉʳ] s. littérature, f.

lithe [la¹zh], **lithesome** [-sᵉm] adj. souple, flexible.

litigate [litigé¹t] v. plaider ; contester. ‖ **litigation** [litigé¹shᵉn] s. litige ; procès, m. ‖ **litigious** [litidjᵉs] adj. litigieux ; procédurier.

litter [litᵉʳ] s. litière ; civière ; portée [animals], f. ; brancard ; désordre, m. ; v. faire une litière ; mettre en désordre ; salir, joncher ; mettre bas [animals] ; *litter bearer*, brancardier.

little [lit'l] adj. petit ; mesquin ; adv. peu ; *a little*, un peu ; *for a little*, pendant quelque temps ; *little by little*, peu à peu ; *ever so little*, tant soit peu. ‖ **littleness** [-nis] s. petitesse, f.

littoral [litᵉrᵉl] s. littoral, m.

livable [líveb'l] *adj.* logeable, habitable; supportable. ‖ **live** [liv] *v.* vivre; habiter; [laᶦv] *adj.* vif, vivant; actif; palpitant [question]; ardent [coal]; sous tension (electr.); *to live down*, faire oublier; *live rail*, rail conducteur. ‖ **livelihood** [laᶦvlihoud] *s.* subsistance, f.; moyen d'existence, m. ‖ **liveliness** [-linis] *s.* vivacité, f. ‖ **lively** [-li] *adj.* vif; animé; gai; *adv.* vivement; avec gaieté.

liver [líver] *s.* viveur, m.; *good liver*, bon vivant.

liver [líver] *s.* foie, m.

livery [líveri] *s.*° livrée; pension pour chevaux, f.

lives [laᶦvz] *pl. of life.*

livestock [laᶦvstâk] *s.* bétail, cheptel, m.

livid [lívid] *adj.* livide.

living [líving] *adj.* vivant; vif; *s.* vie, subsistance, f.; *living-room*, salle de séjour, Fr. Can. vivoir; *living wage*, minimum vital; *the living*, les vivants; *to earn a living*, gagner sa vie; *good living*, bonne chère.

lizard [lizerd] *s.* lézard, m.

load [loᵒud] *s.* charge, f.; fardeau; chargement, m.; *v.* charger; plomber [stick]; accabler (fig.); piper [dice]; *dead load*, poids mort; *loader*, chargeur.

loadstar [loᵒudstar] *s.* étoile Polaire, f.; *loadstone*, magnétite.

loaf [loᵒuf] (*pl.* **loaves** [loᵒuvz]) *s.* miche de pain, f.; *sugar loaf*, pain de sucre.

loaf [loᵒuf] *v.* flâner; *loafer*, fainéant, flâneur.

loam [loᵒum] *s.* glaise, f.

loan [loᵒun] *s.* prêt; emprunt, m.; *v.* prêter; *loan shark*, usurier; *loan society*, société de crédit.

loath [loᵒuth] *adj.* peu enclin, répugnant [to, à]; *nothing loath*, volontiers; *to be loath to*, faire à contrecœur. ‖ **loathe** [loᵒuzh] *v.* abhorrer; répugner à. ‖ **loathsome** [loᵒuzhsem] *adj.* dégoûtant; odieux.

loaves [loᵒuvz] *pl. of loaf.*

lobby [lábi] *s.*° couloir, vestibule, m.; *v.* « faire les couloirs » (polit.).

lobe [loᵒub] *s.* lobe, m.

lobster [lábster] *s.* homard, m.; *spiny lobster*, langouste.

local [loᵒuk'l] *adj.* local; localisé [pain]; externe [remedy]; de lieu [adverb.]; *s.* journal (ou) train (ou) équipe (ou) agent local; *local* [loᵒukal] *s.*° localité, f. ‖ **locality** [lokaliti] *s.*° localisation; région; résidence; localité, f. ‖ **localization** [loᵒukelazéᶦshen] *s.* localisation, f. ‖ **localize**

locate [loᵒuklaᶦz] *v.* localiser. ‖ **locate** [loᵒukéᶦt] *v.* situer; établir; repérer; poser. ‖ **location** [loᵒukéᶦshen] *s.* emplacement; site; repérage, m.; situation, f.

lock [lâk] *s.* mèche [hair], f.

lock [lâk] *s.* serrure; fermeture; écluse [river]; platine [firearm], f.; blocage (mech.); verrou, m.; *v.* fermer à clef; verrouiller, Fr. Can. barrer; bloquer; *to double-lock*, fermer à double tour; *safety lock*, verrou de sûreté. ‖ **locker** [-er] *s.* coffre, m. ‖ **locket** [-it] *s.* médaillon, m. ‖ **locksmith** [-smith] *s.* serrurier, m.

locomotion [loᵒukemoᵒushen] *s.* locomotion, f. ‖ **locomotive** [loᵒukemoᵒutiv] *s.* locomotive, f.

locust [loᵒukœst] *s.* sauterelle, f.; caroube, f.; *locust-tree*, caroubier, m.

locution [loᵒukyoushen] *s.* locution; expression, f.

lode [loᵒud] *s.* filon, m.

lodestone [loᵒudstoᵒun] *s.* aimant naturel, m.

lodge [lâdj] *s.* loge; maisonnette, f.; *v.* loger; abriter; présenter [complaint]. ‖ **lodger** [-er] *s.* locataire, m. ‖ **lodging** [-ing] *s.* logement; abri, m.; *furnished lodging*, garni; *lodging-house*, hôtel meublé.

loft [lauft] *s.* grenier; réduit, m.; soupente, f.; *choir loft*, tribune du chœur. ‖ **lofty** [-i] *adj.* élevé; noble; altier; pompeux.

log [laug] *s.* bûche; bille; souche, f.; *v.* couper; tronçonner; *log house*, Fr. Can. maison en bois rond.

log [laug] *s.* loch (naut.), m.; journal de bord (naut.), m.; *v.* porter au journal de bord; filer des nœuds (naut.); *air log*, carnet de route (aviat.).

logic [lâdjik] *s.* logique, f. ‖ **logical** [-'l] *adj.* logique; *logician*, logicien; *logistics*, logistique.

loin [loᶦn] *s.* rein, m.; lombe; longe, f.

loiter [loᶦter] *v.* flâner; rôder. ‖ **loiterer** [-rer] *s.* flâneur; traînard; rôdeur, m.

loll [lâl] *v.* se prélasser; pendre, tirer [tongue].

lollipop [lâlipâp] *s.* sucette, f.

London [lænden] *s.* Londres, m.; *adj.* londonien; *Londoner*, Londonien.

lone [loᵒun] *adj.* seul; solitaire. ‖ **loneliness** [-linis] *s.* isolement, m. ‖ **lonely** [-li] *adj.* isolé; désemparé. ‖ **lonesome** [-sem] *adj.* solitaire; nostalgique; esseulé; désert.

long [laung] *adj.* long; allongé; prolongé; *adv.* longtemps; *a long time*, longtemps; *in the long run*, à la longue; *long ago*, autrefois; *to be long* *in coming*, tarder à venir; **long-sighted**, presbyte; prévoyant; **long-suffering**, résigné, tolérant; **long-winded**, prolixe.

long [laung] *v.* aspirer; désirer; soupirer; *I long to know*, il me tarde de savoir; *to long for peace*, aspirer à la paix.

longer [laung°r] *comp. adj. of* long.

longevity [lândjèv°ti] *s.* longévité, f.

longing [launging] *s.* aspiration, f.; grand désir, m.; *adj.* désireux; nostalgique.

longitude [lândj°tyoud] *s.* longitude, f.

longshoreman [laungshoo°urm°n] *s.* débardeur, m.

longsome [lângs°m] *adj.* long, ennuyeux. || **longways** [-wè¹z] *adv.* en long.

look [louk] *v.* regarder; sembler, paraître; donner [to face]; *s.* regard; air, m.; apparence, f.; *it looks well on you*, cela vous va bien; *to look about*, ouvrir l'œil; *to look after*, surveiller; s'occuper de; *to look away*, détourner les yeux; *to look back*, regarder en arrière; *to look for*, chercher; espérer; *to look into*, examiner, regarder dans; *to look on*, être spectateur; *to look out*, prendre garde; *to look over*, parcourir du regard; *to look to*, veiller à; *he looks ill*, il a l'air malade; **looker-on**, spectateur; **looking-glass**, miroir; **lookout**, vigie; surveillance.

loom [loum] *s.* métier à tisser, m.

loom [loum] *v.* apparaître; se distinguer au loin; s'estomper; **looming**, mirage.

loon [loun] *s.* plongeon (zool.), Fr. Can. huard, m.

loony [louni] *adj.* toqué.

loop [loup] *s.* boucle; bride; maille; ganse [rope], f.; **looping** (aviat.), m.; *v.* boucler; faire un looping (aviat.).

loophole [louphoo°l] *s.* meurtrière, f.; échappatoire, f.

loose [lous] *adj.* lâche; délié; détendu, relâché [morals]; ample [garments]; dévissé (mech.); libre (mech.); *v.* lâcher; détacher; déchaîner; défaire; larguer (naut.); **loose cash**, menue monnaie; *to get loose*, se détacher; *to give loose to*, donner libre cours à; *to work loose*, prendre du jeu. || **loosen** [-'n] *v.* lâcher; desserrer; dénouer; dévisser. || **looseness** [-nis] *s.* relâchement; jeu (mech.); dérèglement, m.; ampleur, f.

loot [lout] *s.* pillage; butin, m.; *v.* piller.

lop [lâp] *v.* élaguer; tomber mollement; clapoter; **lop-eared**, aux oreilles pendantes.

loquacious [loo°ukwé¹sh°s] *adj.* loquace, disert. || **loquacity** [loo°ukwasiti] *s.* loquacité, f.

lord [laurd] *s.* seigneur; maître; lord, m.; *v.* dominer; *Lord's Prayer*, Pater; *Our Lord*, Notre Seigneur. || **lordly** [-li] *adj.* seigneurial; noble; despotique; hautain; *adv.* avec noblesse; avec hauteur; impérieusement. || **lordship** [-ship] *s.* seigneurie, f.

lore [loo°r] *s.* savoir, m.

lorry [lauri] *s.*° Br. camion, m.

lose [louz] *v.*° perdre; égarer; retarder [clock]; *to lose sight of*, perdre de vue; *to lose one's temper*, perdre patience, perdre son sang-froid. || **loss** [laus] *s.*° perte; déperdition, f.; sinistre (naut.), m.; *to be at a loss*, être perplexe; *to sell at a loss*, vendre à perte. || **lost** [-t] *pret., p. p. of* to lose; *adj.* perdu; égaré; sinistré (naut.); plongé [thoughts]; gaspillé [time]; *lost and found*, objets trouvés.

lot [lât] *s.* lot; sort; tirage; paquet (fin.), m.; *to draw lots*, tirer au sort; *a lot of, lots of*, beaucoup de, un tas de.

lotion [loo°sh°n] *s.* lotion, f.

lottery [lât°ri] *s.*° loterie, f.

loud [lao°d] *adj.* fort; haut; sonore; bruyant; éclatant [color]; tapageur; **loud-mouth**, braillard; **loud-speaker**, haut-parleur; **loudly**, bruyamment. || **loudness** [lao°dnis] *s.* force, nature bruyante, f.; clinquant, m.

lounge [lao°ndj] *s.* flânerie; chaise-longue, f.; divan; promenoir; foyer; salon de repos, m.; *v.* flâner; se prélasser.

louse [lao°s] (*pl.* **lice** [la¹s]) *s.* pou, m.; **lousy**, pouilleux, vil, « moche » (fam.).

lout [lao°t] *s.* rustre; lourdaud, m.

lovable [lœv°b'l] *adj.* aimable. || **love** [lœv] *s.* amour, m.; affection; amitié, f.; zéro [tennis], m.; *v.* aimer; *love at first sight*, coup de foudre; *to make love to*, faire la cour à; *to be in love*, être amoureux; *to fall in love with*, s'éprendre de. || **loveliness** [-linis] *s.* charme, m.; grâce; amabilité, f. || **lovelock** [-lâk] *s.* accroche-cœur, m. || **lovely** [-li] *adj.* aimable; charmant; beau. || **lover** [-°r] *s.* amoureux; amant; amateur, ami, m.; *music lover*, mélomane. || **loving** [-ing] *adj.* aimant; tendre, affectueux. || **lovingly** [-ingli] *adv.* tendrement; aimablement; affectueusement; amoureusement.

low [loo°] *adj.* bas; faible; vil; débile, déficient; **low comedy**, farce; **low gear**, première vitesse; **lowland**, plaine; **low mass**, messe basse; **low-necked**, décolleté; *adv.* bas; à bas prix; bassement; *in low spirits*, **low spirited**, abattu, déprimé, découragé.

low [lo⁰u] *s.* beuglement, m.; *v.* beu-gler, meugler.

lower [la⁰uer] *v.* se renfrogner, regar-der de travers; s'assombrir; *s.* visage renfrogné, m.

lower [lo⁰uer] *adj.* plus bas; infé-rieur; d'en bas; *v.* baisser; abaisser; diminuer; humilier; rabattre.

lowering [la⁰uerïng] *adj.* menaçant.

lowliness [lo⁰ulinis] *s.* humilité, f. ‖ **lowly** [lo⁰uli] *adj.* humble, modeste; peu élevé; *adv.* humblement. ‖ **low-ness** [lo⁰unis] *s.* infériorité; bassesse; humilité; gravité [sound], f.; faible altitude, f.; abattement, m.

lox [lâks] *s.* Am. saumon fumé, m.

loyal [lo¹el] *adj.* loyal; fidèle. ‖ **loyalty** [-ti] *s.* fidélité; solidarité; loyauté, f.

lubber [lœber] *s.* lourdaud, m.

lubricant [loubrikent] *adj., s.* lubri-fiant. ‖ **lubricate** [-ké¹t] *v.* lubrifier; graisser. ‖ **lubrication** [loubriké¹shen] *s.* lubrification, f.; graissage, m. ‖ **lubricity** [loubrisiti] *s.* onctuosité; lubricité, f.

lucid [lousid] *adj.* lucide; limpide. ‖ **lucidity** [lousiditi] *s.* luminosité; luci-dité, f.

Lucifer ['lousifer] *s.* Lucifer, m.; Vé-nus, f. [star]; allumette-tison, f.

luck [lœk] *s.* hasard; bonheur, m.; chance; fortune; f.; *ill-luck,* mau-vaise fortune. ‖ **luckily** [-'li] *adv.* heu-reusement; par bonheur. ‖ **lucky** [-i] *adj.* heureux; chanceux; fortuné; favo-rable.

lucrative [loukretiv] *adj.* lucratif.

ludicrous [loudikres] *adj.* risible, comique, grotesque.

luff [lœf] *s.* lof, m.; *v.* lofer (naut.).

lug [lœg] *v.* tirer; traîner; entraîner.

luge [lyoudj] *s.* luge, f.; *v.* luger.

luggage [lœgidj] *s.* bagage, m.; *lug-gage-carrier,* porte-bagages; *luggage-rail,* galerie (auto).

lukewarm [loukwaurm] *adj.* tiède; tempéré. ‖ **lukewarmness** [-nis] *s.* tié-deur, f.

lull [lœl] *v.* se calmer; bercer; endormir; *s.* accalmie; embellie (naut.), f.

lullaby [lœlebaı] *s.* berceuse, f.

lumber [lœmber] *s.* Am. bois de charpente; bric-à-brac, m; *v.* entas-ser; encombrer; se mouvoir pesam-ment; Am. exploiter le bois; *lumber camp, Fr. Can.* chantier; *lumberman,* bûcheron; *lumber-room,* débarras, fourre-tout.

luminous [loumenes] *adj.* lumineux.

lump [lœmp] *s.* motte; masse, f.; bloc; morceau; lourdaud, m.; *v.* mettre en tas; prendre en bloc; *lump-sugar,* sucre en morceaux.

lumpish [lœmpish] *adj.* balourd; lour-daud. ‖ **lumpishness** [-nis] *s.* gauche-rie, f.; lourdeur (f.) d'esprit.

lunar [louner] *adj.* lunaire.

lunatic [lounetik] *adj., s.* aliéné; fou.

lunch [lœntsh] *s.*,* *v.* déjeuner. ‖ **luncheon** [-] *s.* lunch, m.; collation, f.; *luncheon-basket,* panier-repas.

lung [lœng] *s.* poumon; mou, m.

lunge [lœndj] *s.* coup porté, m.; botte [fencing], f.; *v.* porter une botte [fencing]; allonger un coup (at, à).

lurch [lërtsh] *s.*,* embardée, f.; *v.* faire une embardée; tituber; *to leave in the lurch,* planter là.

lurch [lërtsh] *s.*,* panne (fam.), f.; *to be left in the lurch,* rester en carafe.

lure [lour] *s.* leurre; appât; attrait, m.; *v.* leurrer; amorcer; attirer.

lurid [lourid] *adj.* mélodramatique; exagéré; livide.

lurk [lërk] *v.* se tapir; être aux aguets.

luscious [lœshes] *adj.* succulent, exquis, délicieux.

lust [lœst] *s.* convoitise; luxure; concupiscence, f.; *v.* convoiter.

luster [lœster] *s.* lustre; éclat, m.

lustful [lœstfel] *adj.* luxurieux; lascif; lubrique. ‖ **lustfulness** [-nis] *s.* désir, m.; lasciveté, f.

lusty [lœsti] *adj.* fort, vigoureux.

lute [lout] *s.* luth, m.

luxation [lœksé¹shen] *s.* luxation, f.

luxe [louks] *s.* luxe, m.

luxuriant [lœgjourient] *adj.* luxu-riant; abondant; exubérant.

luxurious [lœgjouries] *adj.* luxueux, somptueux. ‖ **luxury** [lœksheri] *s.*,* luxe, m.; volupté, f.

lustrous [lœstres] *adj.* brillant; lustré.

lyceum [la¹sïem] *s.* auditorium, m.; salle f.) de conférences.

lye [la¹] *s.* lessive, f.

lying [la¹ing] *s.* lieu pour se coucher; *lying down,* action de se coucher; *adj.* couché.

lying [la¹ing] *adj.* menteur; *s.* men-songe, m.

lymph [lïmf] *s.* lymphe, f.

lynch [lïntsh] *v.* lyncher.

lynx [lïngks] *s.*,* lynx, m.

lyre [la¹r] *s.* lyre, f. ‖ **lyric** [lirik] *adj.* lyrique; *s.* poème lyrique; *lyrical,* lyrique. ‖ **lyricism** [lirisizem] *s.* ly-risme, m.

M

mac [mak] *s.* imperméable, imper, m.; gabardine, f.

macadam [m^ekad^em] *s.* macadam, m.

macaroni [mak^ero^{ou}ni] *s.* macaroni, m.

macaroon [mak^eroun] *s.* macaron, m.

machine [m^eshîn] *s.* machine, f.; appareil, instrument, dispositif, m.; *v.* usiner; façonner; *machine-gun*, mitrailleuse; *machine-gunner*, mitrailleur; *mincing-machine*, hache-viande; *sewing-machine*, machine à coudre. ‖ **machinery** [-^eri] *s.* mécanisme, m.; mécanique, f. ‖ **machinist** [-ist] *s.* machiniste; mécanicien, m.

mackerel [mak^er^el] *s.* maquereau, m.; *adj.* moutonné [sky].

mackintosh [makintâsh] *s.* imperméable, imper, m.; gabardine, f.

maculate [makiouleⁱt] *v.* maculer.

mad [mad] *adj.* fou; furieux; enragé [dog]; *madly*, follement, furieusement.

madam [mad^em] *s.* madame, f.

madcap [madkap] *adj.* écervelé; téméraire. ‖ **madden** [mad'n] *v.* devenir fou; rendre furieux.

made [méⁱd] *pret., p. p. of to make;* *self-made man,* fils de ses œuvres; *made-to-order,* fait sur mesure; *made-up,* factice; maquillé.

madman [madm^en] (*pl.* **madmen**) *s.* fou, m. ‖ **madness** [madnis] *s.* folie, démence; rage, f. ‖ **madwoman** [-woum^en] (*pl.* **madwomen**) *s.* folle, démente, f.

magazine [mag^ezîn] *s.* magasin, dépôt, m.; soute, f.

magazine [mag^ezîn] *s.* revue, magazine, f.; périodique, m.

magic [madjik] *s.* magie, f.; *adj.* magique. ‖ **magician** [m^edjish^en] *s.* magicien, prestidigitateur, m.

magistracy [madjistr^esi] *s.* magistrature, f. ‖ **magistrate** [madjistréⁱt] *s.* magistrat, m.

magnanimous [magnan^em^es] *adj.* magnanime.

magnet [magnit] *s.* aimant, m. ‖ **magnetic** [magnètik] *adj.* magnétique; aimanté; attirant. ‖ **magnetize** [magnitaⁱz] *v.* aimanter; magnétiser; attirer. ‖ **magneto** [magnitou] *s.* magnéto, f.

magnificence [magnif^es'ns] *s.* magnificence, f. ‖ **magnificent** [-s'nt] *adj.* magnifique.

magnify [magn^efai] *v.* grandir; agrandir; grossir; amplifier [sound];

magnifying glass, loupe. ‖ **magnitude** [magn^etyoud] *s.* grandeur, importance, f.

magpie [magpaⁱ] *s.* pie, f.

mahogany [m^ehâg^eni] *s.* acajou, m.

mahout [m^eha^{ou}t] *s.* cornac, m.

maid [méⁱd] *s.* fille; vierge; servante, bonne, f.; *maid of hono(u)r*, demoiselle d'honneur. ‖ **maiden** [-'n] *s.* jeune fille, f.; *adj.* virginal; inaugural. ‖ **maidenhead** [-hèd] *s.* virginité, f. ‖ **maidenhood** [-houd] *s.* célibat, m.

mail [méⁱl] *s.* courrier, m.; poste; correspondance, f.; *v.* expédier; mettre à la poste; *air mail,* poste aérienne; *mailbox,* boîte aux lettres; *Am. mailman, mail carrier,* facteur.

mail [méⁱl] *s.* cotte de mailles, f.

maim [méⁱm] *v.* mutiler; tronquer.

main [méⁱn] *adj.* principal; essentiel; gros; *s.* haute mer, f.; force; canalisation principale, f.; secteur; grand collecteur, m.; *in the main,* en général; *main-traveled, Am.* à large circulation [road]; *mainland,* continent. ‖ **mainly** [-li] *adv.* principalement.

maintain [méⁱntéⁱn] *v.* maintenir; conserver; entretenir; prétendre; soutenir. ‖ **maintenance** [méⁱnten^ens] *s.* soutien; entretien; maintien; service de dépannage et de ravitaillement; moyens d'existence, m.; *separate maintenance,* séparation de biens.

maintop [méⁱntâp] *s.* grand-hune, f.

maize [méⁱz] *s.* maïs, m.

majestic [m^edjèstik] *adj.* majestueux. ‖ **majesty** [madjisti] *s.* majesté, f.

major [méⁱdj^er] *s.* major; commandant, m.; *adj.* plus grand; majeur; *major key,* ton majeur [music]. ‖ **majority** [m^edjâr^eti] *s.* majorité, f.

make [méⁱk] *v.* faire; fabriquer; façonner; rendre; atteindre; former; prononcer; forcer; *s.* façon; forme; fabrication; marque, f.; modèle [car], m.; *to make away with,* se défaire de, gaspiller; *to make fast,* amarrer (naut.); *to make for,* se diriger vers; *to make land,* atterrir, aborder; *to make it,* réussir; *to make off,* filer; *to make over,* transférer, refaire; *to make out,* établir; discerner; dresser; *to make over to,* céder à; *to make up for,* compenser, réparer; *to make up,* se maquiller; inventer; se réconcilier; *make-believe,* feinte; *make-do,* de fortune; *makeshift,* pis-aller, expédient; *make-up,* arrangement, maquillage. ‖ **maker** [-^er] *s.* auteur; faiseur; fabricant; créateur, m.

maladjusted [mal•djœstid] *adj.* mal ajusté, mal réglé.

malady [mal•di] *s.** maladie, f.

malapropism [mal•prâpiz'm] *s.* impropriété d'expression, f.

malaria [mᵉlèriᵉ] *s.* malaria, f.; paludisme, m.

malcontent [malk•ntènt] *adj.* mécontent.

male [méᶦl] *adj.* mâle; masculin; *s.* mâle, m.

malediction [malidíksh•n] *s.* malédiction, f.

malefactor [malifakt•r] *s.* malfaiteur, m.

malevolence [mᵉlévᵉlᵉns] *s.* malveillance, f. || *malevolent* [-ᵉnt] *adj.* malveillant.

malice [malis] *s.* malice; méchanceté; malveillance; rancune, f. || *malicious* [mᵉlishᵉs] *adj.* méchant, malveillant; délictueux; volontairement coupable (jur.).

malign [mᵉlaᶦn] *adj.* méchant; pernicieux; *v.* calomnier; diffamer. || *malignant* [mᵉlignᵉnt] *adj.* méchant, venimeux, pernicieux; *malignity*, malignité.

malinger [mᵉlìngᵍᵉʳ] *v.* simuler la maladie, tirer au flanc.

malleable [maliᵉb'l] *adj.* malléable.

mallet [malit] *s.* maillet, m.; mailloche, f.

malnutrition [malnyoutrish•n] *s.* sous-alimentation; mauvaise hygiène alimentaire, f.

malpractice [malpraktis] *s.* malfaçon; incurie, f.

malt [mault] *s.* malt, m.

maltreat [maltrît] *v.* maltraiter.

mammal [mam'l] *s.* mammifère, m.

mammoth [mamᵉth] *s.* mammouth, m.; *adj.* énorme, gigantesque.

mammy [mami] *s.** maman; nounou, f.

man [màn] *(pl.* **men** [mèn]) *s.* homme; pion [draughts]; soldat; employé, m.; pièce [chess], f.; *v.* armer; équiper; *man and wife*, mari et femme; *to a man*, tous, unanimement; *man-of-war*, navire de guerre; *man-power*, main-d'œuvre; *single man*, célibataire.

manage [manidj] *v.* diriger; gérer; administrer; (s')arranger; manier; maîtriser; trouver moyen; *I shall manage it*, je m'en tirerai. || *manageable* [-ᵉb'l] *adj.* maniable; docile. || *management* [-mᵉnt] *s.* administration; gestion; gérance, f.; maniement, m. || *manager* [-ᵉr] *s.* administrateur; gérant; régisseur; impresario; manager,

m.; *advertising manager*, chef de publicité. || *managing* [-ing] *adj.* directeur, gérant, principal; actif, entendu; *Am.* managing editor, rédacteur en chef.

mandarin [mandᵉrin] *s.* mandarin, m.; mandarine, f.

mandate [mᵉnoᵘvᵉʳ] *s.* mandat; ordre, m.; *v.* mandater.

mandolin(e) [mandolin] *s.* mandoline, f.

mane [méᶦn] *s.* crinière, f.

maneuver [mᵉnoᵘvᵉʳ] *s.* manœuvre, tactique, f.; *v.* manœuvrer.

manful [manfᵉl] *adj.* viril; vaillant.

mange [méᶦndj] *s.* gale, f.

manger [méᶦndjᵉʳ] *s.* mangeoire; crèche, f.

mangle [mànggᶦl] *v.* déchiqueter; déchirer; mutiler.

mangle [mànggᶦl] *s.* calandre, f.; *v.* calandrer.

mangy [méᶦndji] *adj.* galeux.

manhandle [mànhàndᶦl] *v.* malmener; manutentionner.

manhole [mànhoᵘl] *s.* trou d'homme, m.; bouche d'égout, f.

manhood [mànhoud] *s.* virilité, f.

mania [méᶦniᵉ] *s.* folie; manie, f. || *maniac* [-niak] *adj.* fou furieux (med.); maniaque, enragé, mordu.

manicure [manikyour] *s.* manucure, f.

manifest [mànᵉfèst] *adj.* manifeste; évident, notoire; *s.* manifeste, m.; déclaration d'expédition (naut.), f.; *v.* manifester; témoigner; déclarer. || *manifestation* [manᵉfèstéᶦshᵉn] *s.* manifestation, f. || *manifesto* [manifèstoᵘ] *s.* manifeste, m.; proclamation, f.

manifold [mànᵉfoᵘld] *adj.* multiple; divers; nombreux; *manifold writer*, machine à polycopier; *s.* tuyauterie; tubulure; polycopie, f.; *v.* polycopier.

manikin [mànᵉkin] *s.* mannequin, m.; petit bout d'homme, m.

manioc [maniàk] *s.* manioc, m.

manipulate [mᵉnípyᵉléᶦt] *v.* manipuler; manier. || *manipulation* [mᵉnipyᵉléᶦshᵉn] *s.* manipulation, f.

manitou [mànᵉtou] *s.* manitou, m.

mankind [mànkaᶦnd] *s.* humanité, f.; genre humain, m. || *manliness* [mànlinis] *s.* virilité, f. || *manly* [mànli] *adj.* viril; *adv.* virilement.

manner [manᵉʳ] *s.* manière; mœurs; coutume; méthode, f.; *after the manner of*, à la manière de; *he has no manners*, il n'a pas de savoir-vivre; *all manners of*, toutes sortes de; *the* *manner* how, la façon dont. ‖ *mannerless* [-lis] *adj.* sans éducation. ‖ *mannerliness* [-linis] *s.* savoir-vivre, m. ; courtoisie, f. ‖ *mannerly* [-li] *adj.* courtois, bien élevé.

mannish [mǎnish] *adj.* hommasse.

manœuvre, *see* maneuver.

manometer [mₑnǎmₑtₑʳ] *s.* mano-mètre, m.

manor [manₑʳ] *s.* manoir, m.

mansion [mǎnshₑn] *s.* château ; hôtel ; palais, m.

manslaughter [mǎnslautₑʳ] *s.* homi-cide involontaire, m. ‖ *manslayer* [-sléiₑʳ] *s.* meurtrier, m.

mantel [mǎnt'l], *mantelpiece* [-pis] *s.* manteau de cheminée, m.

mantle [mǎnt'l] *s.* manteau ; man-chon [gas], m. ; *v.* couvrir ; s'épan-dre ; cacher, voiler ; mousser [liquid] ; affluer [blood] ; rougir [face]. ‖ *mant-let* [-lit] *s.* mantelet, m.

manual [manyouₑl] *adj.* manuel ; *s.* manuel ; clavier, m.

manufactory [manyₑfaktₑri] *s.* Br. usine, fabrique, f.

manufacture [manyₑfaktshₑʳ] *s.* ma-nufacture, industrie, f. ; produit ma-nufacturé, m. ; *v.* manufacturer ; fabri-quer. ‖ *manufacturer* [-rₑʳ] *s.* fabricant, industriel, m. ‖ *manufac-turing* [-ring] *s.* fabrication, f. ; *adj.* industriel, manufacturier.

manure [mₑnyour] *s.* fumier ; engrais, m. ; *v.* fumer.

manuscript [manyₑskript] *adj.,* *s.* manuscrit.

Manx [mangks] *adj.* de l'île de Man ; *s.* manx, mannois, m. ; *Manxman,* Mannois.

many [mèni] *adj.* beaucoup de ; maint ; bien des ; *pron.* beaucoup ; *how many?,* combien ? ; *as many as,* autant que ; *not so many,* pas tant ; *so many,* tant ; *too many,* trop ; a *great many,* un grand nombre.

map [map] *s.* carte (topogr.), f. ; *v.* faire une carte ; *astronomical map,* carte du ciel ; *large-scale map,* carte à grande échelle ; *road map,* carte rou-tière ; *map of the world,* mappemonde.

maple [mé¹p'l] *s.* érable, m. ; *sugar maple,* érable à sucre ; *maple bush,* Fr. Can. sucrerie ; *maple grove,* éra-blière ; *maple sap,* eau d'érable ; *maple sugar,* sucre d'érable.

maquis [maki] *s.* maquis ; maqui-sard, m.

mar [mâr] *v.* endommager ; défigu-rer, gâter.

marble [mârb'l] *s.* marbre, m. ; bille, f. ; *adj.* de marbre ; *v.* marbrer ; *to play marbles,* jouer aux billes.

march [mârtsh] *s.** marche ; avance, f. ; progrès, m. ; *v.* marcher ; avancer ; être en marche ; *to march past,* défiler ; *day march,* étape journalière.

march [mârtsh] *s.** frontière, mar-che, f.

March [mârtsh] *s.* mars [month], m.

marchioness [mâʳshⁿnis] *s.** mar-quise, f.

mare [mèₑʳ] *s.* jument, f.

margin [mârdjin] *s.* marge, f. ; bord, m. ; *v.* marginer ; annoter en marge ; *marginal,* marginal.

marigold [marₑgoould] *s.* souci, m.

marinade [mariné¹d] *s.* marinade, f. ; *v.* faire mariner.

marine [mₑrîn] *adj.* marin ; mari-time ; *s.* soldat de l'infanterie de marine, m. ; *marines,* fusiliers marins. ‖ *mariner* [marⁿeʳ] *s.* marinier ; ma-rin, m. ‖ *maritime* [marₑta¹m] *adj.* maritime.

mark [mârk] *s.* marque ; empreinte, cible, f. ; signe ; but ; jalon ; repère, m. ; note [school], f. ; *v.* marquer ; repérer ; *question mark,* point d'in-terrogation ; *marksman,* tireur d'élite ; *to hit the mark,* atteindre le but ; *to make one's mark,* se distinguer ; *to mark out,* délimiter ; *to mark up,* haus-ser [price] ; *mark my words,* écoutez-moi bien. ‖ *marker* [-ₑʳ] *s.* pointeur ; indicateur ; repère ; avertisseur, m.

market [mârkit] *s.* marché, m. ; *v.* faire son marché ; faire un marché ; vendre, mettre sur le marché ; *black market,* marché noir ; *market price,* prix courant.

marmalade [mârm'lé¹d] *s.* confiture d'orange, de citron, f.

marmot [mâmaut] *s.* marmotte, f.

maroon [mₑroun] *adj.,* *s.* marron.

maroon [mₑroun] *s.* nègre marron ; homme abandonné dans une île dé-serte, m.

marquetry [mâʳkitri] *s.** marquete-rie, f.

marquis [mârkwis] *s.** marquis, m. ‖ *marquise* [mâʳkiz] *s.* marquise, f.

marriage [maridj] *s.* mariage, m. ‖ *married* [marid] *adj.* marié ; conjugal.

marrow [marouᵘ] *s.* moelle ; quintes-sence ; vigueur, f.

marry [mari] *v.* (se) marier ; épou-ser ; s'allier (*with,* à).

marsh [mârsh] *s.** marais ; maré-cage, m. ; *marsh-fever,* paludisme.

marshal [mârshₑl] *s.* maréchal ; *Am.* prévôt [police], m. ; *v.* disposer ; régler une cérémonie ; *marshalling station,* gare de triage.

marshmallow [mârshmaloºu] *s.* gui-mauve, f.

marshy [mârshi] *adj.* marécageux.

mart [mârt] *s.* marché [place], m.; salle de vente, f.

martial [mârshºl] *adj.* martial.

martin [mârtin] *s.* martinet [bird], m. ‖ **martinet** [mâˈtinét] *s.* gendarme, m. (colloq.).

martingal [mârtˈngéˈl] *s.* martin-gale, f.

martyr [mârtºr] *s.* martyr, m.; *v.* martyriser. ‖ **martyrdom** [-dºm] *s.* martyre, m. ‖ **martyrize** [-raˈz] *v.* mar-tyriser.

marvel [mârvˈl] *s.* merveille, f.; *v.* s'émerveiller; s'étonner; se demander; **marvel(l)ous**, merveilleux; surprenant.

mascot [maskºt] *s.* mascotte, f.

masculine [maskyºlin] *adj.* mascu-lin; viril; mâle; *s.* masculin, m.; **masculinity**, masculinité.

mash [mash] *v.* triturer; brasser [beer]; réduire en pâtée, en bouillie; **mashed potatoes**, purée de pommes de terre.

mask [mask] *s.* masque; loup, m.; mascarade, f.; *v.* (se) masquer; ca-cher; (se) déguiser.

mason [méˈsˈn] *s.* maçon, m.; *v.* maçonner; construire. ‖ **masonry** [-ri] *s.* maçonnerie; franc-maçonnerie, f.

masquerade [maskˈréˈd] *s.* masca-rade, f.; *v.* faire partie d'une masca-rade; se masquer; se faire passer (*as*, pour).

mass [mas] *s.*² messe, f.

mass [mas] *s.*² masse; foule; multi-tude; majorité, f.; *v.* (se) masser; en-tasser; s'accumuler; **mass meeting**, rassemblement populaire; **mass pro-duction**, production en série.

massacre [masˈkºr] *s.* massacre, m.; *v.* massacrer.

massage [mˈsâj] *s.* massage, m.; *v.* masser.

massing [masing] *s.* agglomération, f.; attroupement, rassemblement; amoncellement, m.

massive [masiv] *adj.* massif.

mast [mast] *s.* mât, m.; **radio mast**, mât de T.S.F.; **topgallant mast**, mât de perroquet.

master [mastºr] *s.* maître; patron; jeune garçon, m.; *v.* maîtriser; dompt-er; connaître à fond [language]; diri-ger, gouverner; *adj.* principal; maître; directeur; dominant; **Master of Arts**, licencié ès lettres; **masterful**, auto-ritaire, magistral; **master key**, passe-partout; **masterly**, magistral; **master-piece**, chef-d'œuvre. ‖ **mastery** [-ri] *s.* maîtrise; supériorité, f.; empire, m.

mastic [mastik] *s.* mastic, m.; len-tisque, m.

masticate [mastikéˈt] *v.* mastiquer. ‖ **mastication** [mastikéˈshºn] *s.* mastica-tion, f.

mastiff [mastif] *s.* mâtin, m.

mat [mat] *s.* natte, f.; paillasson; napperon; dessous-de-plat, -d'assiette, m.; *v.* natter; enchevêtrer; tresser.

mat [mat] *adj.* mat, terne.

match [matsh] *s.*² allumette; mèche, f.

match [matsh] *s.*² égal, pair; assorti-ment; mariage; match, m.; *Fr. Can.* joute, f.; *v.* assortir; appareiller; ac-coupler; tenir tête à; rivaliser; *he has no match*, il est sans égal; *she is a good match*, c'est un bon parti; *and a hat to match*, et un chapeau à l'avenant; *these colo(u)rs do not match*, ces couleurs ne s'assortissent pas; **match-mark**, point de repère. ‖ **match-ing** [-ing] *s.* assortiment, m. ‖ **match-less**, sans rival, inégalable.

mate [méˈt] *s.* camarade; conjoint; officier (naut.), m.; *first mate*, second (naut.); *second mate*, lieutenant (naut.); *v.* unir, marier; épouser; s'accoupler.

mate [méˈt] *s.* mat [chess], m.; *v.* ma-ter; subjuguer; faire échec et mat.

material [mˈtriˈl] *adj.* matériel; essentiel; important; *s.* matière, f.; tissu; matériel, m.; **raw material**, ma-tière première. ‖ **materialism** [-iz'm] *s.* matérialisme, m. ‖ **materialist** [-ist] *s.* matérialiste, m. ‖ **materialization** [mˈtiºriˈlaˈzéˈshºn] *s.* matérialisation, f. ‖ **materialize** [mˈtiºriˈlaˈz] *v.* (se) matérialiser.

maternal [mˈtëˈnˈl] *adj.* maternel. ‖ **maternity** [mˈtëˈnˈti] *s.* maternité, f.

mathematical [mathˈmatikˈl] *adj.* mathématique. ‖ **mathematician** [ma-thˈmˈtishˈn] *s.* mathématicien, m. ‖ **mathematics** [mathˈmatiks] *s. pl.* ma-thématiques, f. pl.

matriculate [mˈtriˈkyˈléˈt] *v.* imma-triculer. ‖ **matriculation** [mˈtrikyˈ-léˈshˈn] *s.* immatriculation, f.

matrimony [matrˈmoºnˈi] *s.*² ma-riage, m.; vie conjugale, f.

matrix [méˈtriks] *s.*² matrice; gan-gue, f.; moule, m.

matron [méˈtrˈn] *s.* matrone; infir-mière major; surveillante, f. [hospi-tal]; intendante; dame âgée, f.

matter [matºr] *s.* matière; affaire; chose, f.; sujet; fait; pus (med.), m.; *v.* importer; *it is of no matter*, cela n'a pas d'importance; *it does not matter*, peu importe; *no matter how*, de n'importe quelle manière; *as a matter of fact*, à vrai dire; *a matter-of-fact man*, un homme positif; *a* *matter of law,* une question de droit ; *a matter of course,* une chose qui va de soi ; *what's the matter with you ?,* qu'avez-vous ? ; *printed matters,* imprimés.

mattress [matris] *s.* matelas, m. ; *spring mattress,* sommier.

mature [mᵉtyouʳ] *adj.* mûr ; *v.* mûrir ; venir à échéance (comm.). || **maturity** [mᵉtyouʳᵉti] *s.* maturité ; date d'échéance (comm.), f.

maul [maul] *v.* marteler ; maltraiter ; meurtrir.

mausoleum [mausᵉliᵉm] *s.* mausolée, m.

maxim [maksim] *s.* maxime, f.

maximum [maksᵉmᵉm] *adj., s.* maximum, m.

may [méⁱ] *defect. v.* pouvoir ; avoir le droit, l'autorisation, la possibilité de ; *may I sit down ?,* puis-je m'asseoir ? ; *may you live happily !* puissiez-vous vivre heureux ! ; *it may rain,* il se peut qu'il pleuve ; *maybe,* peut-être.

May [méⁱ] *s.* mai, m. ; *May Day,* premier mai ; *May-beetle,* hanneton ; *May-bush,* aubépine.

mayday [méⁱdéⁱ] *s.* S.O.S., signal de détresse, m.

maypole [méⁱpoᵘl] *s.* mai, m.

mayor [méⁱeʳ] *s.* maire, m.

maze [méⁱz] *s.* labyrinthe, dédale, m. ; perplexité, f.

me [mî, mi] *pers. pron.* moi ; me.

meadow [mèdoᵘ] *s.* pré, m. ; prairie, f.

meager [mîgeʳ] *adj.* maigre ; insuffisant, pauvre.

meal [mîl] *s.* repas, m. ; *meal-time,* heure du repas.

meal [mîl] *s.* farine, f. ; *mealy,* farineux ; *mealy-mouthed,* patelin ; doucereux, cauteleux.

mean [mîn] *adj.* médiocre ; mesquin ; vil ; avare ; *mean trick,* vilain tour.

mean [mîn] *adj.* moyen ; *s.* milieu ; moyen ; procédé, m. ; moyenne (math.), f. ; *pl.* ressources, f. ; moyens, m. ; *by no means,* nullement ; *by means of,* au moyen de ; *private means,* fortune personnelle ; *come by all means,* venez sans faute ; *golden mean,* juste milieu.

mean [mîn] *v.* signifier ; avoir l'intention de ; *I didn't mean it,* je ne l'ai pas fait exprès ; *to mean well,* avoir de bonnes intentions ; *what do you mean ?,* que voulez-vous dire ?

meander [miandeʳ] *s.* méandre, m. ; *v.* serpenter ; errer. || **meandrous** [-ᵉs] *adj.* sinueux.

meaning [mîning] *s.* intention ; signification, f. ; sens, m. ; *adj.* intentionné ; *meaningful,* plein de sens, significatif ; *meaningless,* dénué de sens.

meanness [mînnis] *s.* mesquinerie ; médiocrité ; abjection, f.

meant [mènt] *pret., p. p. of* to mean.

meantime [mîntaⁱm], **meanwhile** [-hwaⁱl] *adv.* en attendant ; sur ces entrefaites ; d'ici là ; *s.* intérim ; intervalle, m.

measles [mîz'lz] *s. pl.* rougeole, f.

measurable [mèjrᵉb'l] *adj.* mesurable. || **measure** [mèjᵉʳ] *s.* mesure ; quantité ; disposition ; proposition [law] ; démarche, f. ; *v.* mesurer ; *to measure,* sur mesure ; *to bring forward a measure,* déposer un projet de loi. || **measured** [-ᵉd] *adj.* mesuré ; modéré ; circonspect. || **measurement** [-mᵉnt] *s.* mesurage ; arpentage ; jaugeage, m. ; dimension, f.

meat [mît] *s.* viande ; nourriture, f. ; aliment, m. ; *meat ball,* boulette ; *meat-chopper,* hache-viande ; *meat-safe,* garde-manger.

mechanic [mᵉkanik] *adj.* mécanique. || **mechanics** [-s] *s. pl.* mécanique, f. ; mécanicien, m. || **mechanism** [mèkᵉnizᵉm] *s.* mécanisme ; machinisme ; système, m. || **mechanization** [mèkᵉnaⁱzeⁱshᵉn] *s.* mécanisation, f. || **mechanize** [mèkᵉnaⁱz] *v.* mécaniser.

medal [mèd'l] *s.* médaille ; décoration, f. ; *life-saving medal,* médaille de sauvetage. || **medallion** [-ⁱᵉn] *s.* médaillon, m.

meddle [mèd'l] *v.* se mêler (*with,* de) ; s'immiscer (*with,* dans) ; *meddler,* intrigant ; *meddlesome,* indiscret, importun, intrigant ; *meddling,* immixtion, ingérance.

median [midiᵉn] *adj.* médian ; moyen.

mediate [midiéⁱt] *v.* s'entremettre ; servir d'intermédiaire ; intervenir. || **mediation** [midiéⁱshᵉn] *s.* intervention ; médiation, f. || **mediator** [midiétᵉʳ] *s.* médiateur ; intercesseur, m.

medical [mèdik'l] *adj.* médical ; *medical equipment,* matériel sanitaire. || **medicament** [médîkᵉmᵉnt] *s.* médicament, m. || **medicated** [médîkᵉⁱtid] *adj.* hydrophile [cotton]. || **medicine** [mèdᵉs'n] *s.* médecine, f. ; médicament, remède, m. ; *medicine man,* sorcier.

medieval [mîdîîv'l] *adj.* médiéval.

mediocre [mîdioᵘkᵉʳ] *adj.* médiocre. || **mediocrity** [mîdiâkrᵉti] *s.* médiocrité, f.

meditate [mèdᵉtéⁱt] *v.* méditer ; projeter. || **meditation** [mèdᵉtéⁱshᵉn] *s.* méditation, f. || **meditative** [médîtèⁱtiv] *adj.* méditatif.

medium [mídiᵉm] *s.* moyen; milieu; intermédiaire; médium, m.; *adj.* moyen; *advertising medium,* organe de publicité. *circulating medium,* monnaie en circulation; *culture medium,* bouillon de culture; *medium distance,* demi-fond (sports). ‖ *mediumistic* [mìdiᵉmìstik] *adj.* médiumnique.

medley [médli] *s.* mélange; pot-pourri, m.; *adj.* hétéroclite, mêlé; *v.* mêler, mélanger.

meek [mîk] *adj.* doux; docile. ‖ *meekness* [-nis] *s.* docilité; soumission; douceur, f.

meet [mît] *v.* rencontrer; aller à la rencontre de; faire connaissance avec; faire face à; satisfaire [requirements]; se réunir; se rencontrer (*with*, avec); faire honneur à [debts]; répondre à [views]. ‖ *meeting* [-ing] *s.* assemblée; réunion; rencontre, f.; meeting, m.

megaphone [mégᵉfoᵘn] *s.* mégaphone; porte-voix, m.

melancholy [mélᵉnkâli] *s.* mélancolie, f.; *adj.* mélancolique.

mellifluous [mélíflouᵉs] *adj.* mielleux, doucereux.

mellow [méloᵘ] *adj.* moelleux; fondant; fondu [color]; mûr [fruit]; *v.* mûrir; adoucir; devenir moelleux; ameublir.

melodic [milâdik] *adj.* mélodique. ‖ *melodious* [mᵉloᵘdiᵉs] *adj.* mélodieux ‖ *melodrama* [mélodrâmᵉ] *s.* mélodrame, m. ‖ *melody* [mélᵉdi] *s.* mélodie, f. ‖ *melomaniac* [mélomé¹niak] *adj.* mélomane.

melon [mélᵉn] *s.* melon, m.

melt [mèlt] *v.* fondre; couler; se dissoudre; s'attendrir (fig.).

member [mémbᵉʳ] *s.* membre; député [Parliament]; associé; sociétaire, m. ‖ *membership* [-ship] *s.* sociétariat, ensemble des membres, m.; qualité de membre; adhésion, f.

membrane [mèmbré¹n] *s.* membrane, f.

memento [miméntoᵘ] *s.* mémento; souvenir, m.

memoir [mémwâr] *s.* mémoire, m.; mémoires, f. pl. ‖ *memorable* [mémᵉrᵇl] *adj.* mémorable. ‖ *memorandum* [mèmᵉrandᵉm] *s* mémorandum, mémoire; bordereau (comm.), m.; *memorandum pad,* bloc-notes. ‖ *memorial* [mᵉmoᵘriᵉl] *s* mémorial, monument, m.; plaque commémorative, f.; *adj.* commémoratif. ‖ *memorize* [mémᵉra¹z] *v.* apprendre par cœur. ‖ *memory* [mémᵉri] *s.* mémoire, f.

men [mèn] *pl. of man.*

menace [mènis] *s.* menace, f.; *v.* menacer.

mend [mènd] *v.* raccommoder; réparer; améliorer; *to mend one's ways,* changer de conduite; *s.* amélioration, f.; *to be on the mend,* être en voie de guérison.

mendacious [méndé¹shᵉs] *adj.* mensonger.

mendicant [mèndíkᵉnt] *s.* mendiant, m. ‖ *mendicity* [-siti] *s.* mendicité, f.

menial [mìniᵉl] *adj.* domestique; servile; *s.* subalterne; valet, m.

meninges [mᵉníndjiz] *s. pl.* méninges, f. pl. ‖ *meningitis* [méníndja¹tis] *s.* méningite, f.

menopause [mènopauz] *s.* ménopause, f. ‖ *menses* [ménsìz] *s. pl.* menstrues, règles, f.

mensuration [mènshᵉré¹shᵉn] *s.* mensuration, f.; mesurage, m.

mental [mènt'l] *adj.* mental; psychiatrique, intellectuel; toqué (colloq.). ‖ *mentality* [mèntᵉl¹ti] *s.* mentalité, f.

mention [mènshᵉn] *s.* mention, f.; *v.* citer; mentionner; *don't mention it,* il n'y a pas de quoi.

menu [mènyou] *s.* menu, m.

mercantile [mᵉʳkᵉntíl] *adj.* mercantile; commercial; marchand; *mercantile agency,* agence commerciale.

mercenary [mᵉʳs'nèri] *s.* mercenaire, m.

mercerize [mᵉʳsera¹z] *v.* merceriser.

merchandise [mᵉʳtshᵉnda¹z] *s.* marchandise, f.; *v.* faire du commerce. ‖ *merchant* [mᵉʳtshᵉnt] *s.* négociant; commerçant; marchand, m.; *adj.* marchand; *merchantman,* navire marchand.

merciful [mᵉʳsifᵉl] *adj.* miséricordieux. ‖ *merciless* [-lis] *adj.* impitoyable; sans merci.

mercurial [mᵉʳkyouᵉri¹l] *adj.* éloquent, rusé, commerçant; éveillé, prompt, inconstant; mercuriel. ‖ *mercury* [mᵉʳky°r¹] *s.* mercure [metal], m.

mercy [mᵉʳsi] *s.* miséricorde; pitié, f.; *mercy stroke,* coup de grâce; *to be at the mercy of,* être à la merci de.

mere [miᵉʳ] *adj.* simple; seul; *a mere formality,* une pure formalité; *the mere sight of him,* sa seule vue; *merely,* purement, simplement.

merge [mᵉrdj] *v.* fusionner; (se) fondre; s'amalgamer.

meridian [mᵉr¹di¹n] *adj., s.* méridien.

merit [mèrit] *s.* mérite, m.; *v.* mériter. ‖ *meritorious* [mèr°toᵘri°s] *adj.* méritoire, méritant.

mermaid [mᵉʳmé¹d] *s.* sirène, f. ‖ *merman* [-mᵉn] *s.* triton, m.

merrily [mèrᵉli] *adv.* joyeusement. ‖
merriment [-mᵉnt] *s.* gaieté, f. ‖
merry [mèri] *adj.* gai, joyeux; plaisant; *to make merry*, se réjouir, se divertir; **merry-go-round**, carrousel, manège de chevaux de bois; **merrymaker**, noceur; **merrymaking**, réjouissance, partie de plaisir.

mesh [mèsh] *s.°* maille, f.; filet; engrenage, m.; *v.* s'engager; s'engrener.

mess [mès] *s.°* plat; mess; ordinaire, m.; ration; popote; pâtée, f.; brouet, m.; *v.* manger au mess.

mess [mès] *s.°* gâchis; désordre, m.; *v.* gâcher; salir; *to make a mess*, faire du gâchis; *to be in a mess*, être dans le pétrin.

message [mèsidj] *s.* message; télégramme, m.; communication, f.; *telephone message*, message téléphonique. ‖ **messenger** [mès'ndjᵉr] *s.* messager, m.

Messiah [misaiᵉ] *s.* Messie, m.; **Messianic**, messianique.

met [mèt] *pret.*, *p. p. of to meet*.

metal [mèt'l] *s.* métal, m.; *adj.* métallique; en métal; *coarse metal*, métal brut; *sheet metal*, tôle. ‖ **metallic** [mᵉtalik] *adj.* métallique. ‖ **metallurgy** [mèt'lᵉrdji] *s.* métallurgie, f.

metamorphosis [mèt°maurf°sis] (*pl.* **metamorphoses**) *s.* métamorphose, f.

metaphor [mètᵉfᵉr] *s.* métaphore, f.

metaphysics [métᵉfiziks] *s. pl.* métaphysique, f.

meteor [mîtiᵉr] *s.* météore, m. ‖ **meteorological** [mîtiᵉrᵉlâdjik'l] *adj.* météorologique. ‖ **meteorology** [mîtiᵉrâl°dji] *s.* météorologie, f.

meter, metre [mîtᵉr] *s.* mètre; compteur; jaugeur [gasoline], m.

method [mèth°d] *s.* méthode, technique, f.; procédé, m. ‖ **methodical** [mᵉthâdik'l] *adj.* méthodique. ‖ **Methodist** [méth°dist] *s.* méthodiste. m. f.

metric [mètrik] *adj.* métrique. ‖ **metrics** [-s] *s. pl.* métrique, f.

metropolis [mᵉtrâp'lis] *s.°* métropole; capitale, f. ‖ **metropolitan** [mètr°pâl°t'n] *adj.* métropolitain.

mettle [mèt'l] *s.* courage, enthousiasme, m.; fougue; étoffe, f. (fig.).

mew [myou] *s.* mouette, f.

mew [myou] *s.* miaulement, m.; *v.* miauler.

mew [myou] *v.* muer, changer de.

mew [myou] *s.* mue, cage; *pl.* étable, f.; *v.* encager; enfermer.

Mexican [mèksik°n] *adj.*, *s.* mexicain; *Mexico*, Mexique [country]; *Mexico* [town].

mezzanine [mèz°nîn] *s.* entresol, m.

mica [maikᵉ] *s.* mica, m.

mice [mais] *pl. of mouse*.

microbe [maikrooᵇb] *s.* microbe, m.

microgroove [maikrᵉgrouv] *s.* microsillon, m. ‖ **microphone** [-fo°un] *s.* microphone, m.

microscope [maikrᵉsko°up] *s.* microscope, m. ‖ **microscopic** [maikrᵉskâpik] *adj.* microscopique.

mid [mid] *adj.* mi, moyen; intermédiaire; *s.* milieu, m.; *in mid air*, au milieu des airs. ‖ **midday** [-déi] *s.* midi, m. ‖ **middle** [-l'l] *adj.* moyen; intermédiaire; *s.* milieu; centre, m.; *middle size*, taille moyenne; *in the middle of*, au milieu de; **middleman**, intermédiaire. ‖ **middling** [-ling] *adj.* passable, moyen; *adv.* assez bien, pas mal. ‖ **middy** [-i] *s.°* aspirant de marine, m.

midge [midj] *s.* moucheron, m.

midget [midjit] *s.* nain, m.

midnight [midnait] *s.* minuit, m.; *adj.* de minuit.

midshipman [midshipmᵉn] (*pl.* **midshipmen**) *s.* aspirant de marine, m. ‖ **midships** [-s] *adv.* par le travers (naut.).

midst [midst] *s.* milieu, centre, m.; *adv.* au milieu; *prep.* au milieu de; *in our midst*, au milieu de nous. ‖ **midstream** [midstrîm] *s.* mi-courant, m. ‖ **midsummer** [midsæmᵉr] *s.* plein été; solstice d'été, m.; *midsummer day*, jour de la Saint-Jean. ‖ **midway** [-wéi] *adj.*, *adv.* à mi-chemin; *s.* milieu du chemin; moyen terme, m.

midwife [midwaif] (*pl.* **midwives**) *s.* sage-femme, f.

mien [mîn] *s.* mine, allure, f.

might [mait] *pret. of may*; *s.* force; puissance, f.; pouvoir, m. ‖ **mighty** [-i] *adj.* puissant, fort, vigoureux; *adv.* fort, extrêmement.

migrant [maigrᵉnt] *s.* émigrant, m.; *adj.* migrateur. ‖ **migrate** [-gréit] *v.* émigrer.

mike [maik], *see microphone*.

milch [miltsh] *adj.* laitière; à lait [cow].

mild [maild] *adj.* doux; paisible; affable; bénin. ‖ **mildness** [-nis] *s.* douceur; modération; affabilité, f.

mildew [mildyou] *s.* mildiou, m.

mile [mail] *s.* mille, m.; **mileage**, Fr. Can. millage; **milestone**, borne kilométrique ou milliaire.

militant [milᵉtᵉnt] *s.* militant, m.

militarism [milᵉtᵉriz°m] *s.* militarisme, m. ‖ **militarize** [milit°ra'z] *v.* militariser. ‖ **military** [milᵉtèri] *s.°* *adj.* militaire.

milk [milk] *s.* lait, m.; *v.* traire; *milk diet*, régime lacté; **milkmaid**, laitière; **milkman**, laitier; **milksop**, poule mouillée, empoté; **milky**, laiteux, lacté [way].

mill [mil] *s.* moulin; laminoir (mech.), m.; usine, f., *v* moudre, broyer; fraiser; fabriquer. *coffee mill*, moulin à café; *paper mill*, fabrique de papier; *saw mill*, scierie, *sugar mill*, sucrerie; *textile mill*, usine de textiles; *water mill*, moulin à eau. ‖ **miller** [-ᵉʳ] *s.* meunier; minotier, m.; fraiseuse, f.

milliner [milᵉnᵉʳ] *s.* modiste, f.; *Am.* chapelier, m. ‖ **millinery** [-ri] *s.** modes, f. pl.; *Am.* chapeaux; magasin, articles de mode, m.

million [milyᵉn] *s.* million, m. ‖ **millionaire** [milyᵉnèʳ] *s.* millionnaire, m. ‖ **millionth** [milyᵉnth] *adj., s.* millionième.

millstone [milstoᵒⁿn] *s.* meule de moulin, f.

mime [ma¹m] *s.* mime, m.; *v.* mimer. ‖ **mimic** [mimik] *adj.* imitatif; *s.* mime, m., imitation, f.; *v.* mimer, singer; **mimicry**, mimique.

mimosa [mimoᵒusᵉ] *s.* mimosa, m.

minaret [minᵉrèt] *s.* minaret, m.

mince [mins] *v.* hacher menu; émincer; minauder, *not to mince words*, ne pas mâcher ses mots; **mincemeat**, hachis, émincé.

mind [ma¹nd] *s.* esprit; penchant; avis, m.; intelligence; mémoire; opinion; conscience; intention, f.; *v.* faire attention, remarquer; observer; surveiller; obéir; *to bear in mind*, tenir compte de; *to have in mind*, avoir en vue; *to have a mind to*, avoir envie de; *to make up one's mind*, se décider; *to speak one's mind*, dire ce qu'on pense; *I don't mind*, cela m'est égal; *never mind*, peu importe; *mind your own business* occupez-vous de vos affaires ‖ **mindful** [-fᵉl] *adj.* attentif (*to*, à); soucieux, conscient (*of*, de). ‖ **mindless** [-lis] *adj.* inanimé; insouciant; indifférent (*of*, à).

mine [ma¹n] *pron.* le mien; la mienne; à moi.

mine [ma¹n] *s.* mine, f.; *v.* miner; exploiter, extraire; saper; *minesweeper*, dragueur de mines. ‖ **miner** [-ᵉʳ] *s.* mineur, m.

mineral [minᵉrᵉl] *adj., s.* minéral. ‖ **mineralize** [-a¹z] *v.* minéraliser.

mingle [miŋg'l] *v.* (se) mêler; mélanger; entremêler.

miniature [minitshᵉr] *s.* miniature, f.; *adj.* réduit; en miniature.

minimize [minᵉma¹z] *v.* minimiser. ‖ **minimum** [minᵉmᵉm] *adj., s.* minimum.

mining [ma¹niŋ] *s.* industrie minière; exploitation des mines, f.; *adj.* minier.

minister [ministᵉr] *s.* ministre; prêtre; pasteur; ecclésiastique, m.; *v.* servir; entretenir, officier. ‖ **ministry** [-tri] *s.** ministère, m.

minium [miniᵉm] *s.* minium, m.

mink [miŋk] *s.* vison, m.

minnow [minoᵒu] *s.* vairon, m.

minor [ma¹nᵉr] *s.* mineur, m.; mineure, f.; *adj.* mineur, moindre; secondaire, *minor key*, ton mineur [music]. ‖ **minority** [mᵉnaurᵉti] *s.** minorité, f.

minster [minstᵉr] *s.* abbatiale; cathédrale, f.

minstrel [minstrᵉl] *s.* musicien; ménestrel, acteur comique, m.

mint [mint] *s.* menthe, f.

mint [mint] *s.* hôtel de la Monnaie, m.; *v.* monnayer, frapper; fabriquer, forger.

minuet [minyouèt] *s.* menuet, m.

minus [ma¹nᵉs] *adj.* négatif; en moins; *s* moins (math.), m.

minute [minit] *s.* minute, f.; *pl.* procès-verbaux, comptes rendus, m. pl.; *v.* minuter, *to minute down*, prendre note, inscrire.

minute [mᵉnyout] *adj.* menu; minuscule; de peu d'importance; minutieux; détaillé.

minx [miŋgks] *s.** espiègle, chipie, coquine, f.

miracle [mirᵉk'l] *s.* miracle, m. ‖ **miraculous** [mᵉrakyᵉlᵉs] *adj.* miraculeux.

mirage [mᵉrâj] *s.* mirage, m.

mire [ma¹r] *s.* boue; vase, fange, f.; bourbier. m.; *v.* (s')embourber.

mirror [mirᵉr] *s.* miroir, m.; glace, f.; *v.* refléter. miroiter.

mirth [mērth] *v.* joie, gaieté, f.; **mirthful**, joyeux, gai.

miry [ma¹r¹] *adj.* fangeux, bourbeux, boueux; souillé; infect (fig.).

misappropriate [mis'proᵒuprié¹t] *v.* détourner, faire un mauvais emploi de. ‖ **misappropriation** [mis'proᵒuprié¹shᵉn] *s.* détournement, abus de confiance, m.

misbehave [misbihé¹v] *v.* se conduire mal.

miscarriage [miskaridj] *s.* échec; accident, m.; inconduite; fausse couche, f.; *miscarriage of justice*, erreur judiciaire. ‖ **miscarry** [miskari] *v.* échouer; avorter; se perdre [letter].

miscellaneous [mis'lé¹ni'es] *adj.* divers; varié; éclectique.

mischief [místshif] *s.* mal; tort;
dommage, m.; méchanceté; frasque, f.
‖ **mischievous** [-tshivᵉs] *adj.* malicieux; méchant; nuisible; espiègle.

misconduct [miskándœkt] *s.* mauvaise conduite; mauvaise administration, f.; [miskᵉndækt] *v.* diriger mal;
gérer mal; *to misconduct oneself*, se
mal conduire.

misdeed [misdíd] *s.* méfait, m.

misdemeanor [misdimínᵉr] *s.* délit,
m.; inconduite, f.

miser [ma¹zᵉr] *s.* avare, m.

miserable [mízrᵉb'l] *adj.* misérable;
pitoyable.

miserly [ma¹zᵉrli] *adj.* avare; mesquin; chiche.

misery [mízri] *s.ᵉ* misère; indigence,
f.; tourment, m.

misfire [misfa¹r] *s.* raté, m.; *v.* rater;
avoir des ratés.

misfit [misfit] *s.* laissé-pour-compte
(comm.); inadapté (colloq.), m.

misfortune [misfaurtshᵉn] *s.* malheur, m.; adversité, f.

misgiving [misgiving] *v.* appréhension, f.; soupçon; pressentiment, m.

misgotten [misgátᵉn] *adj.* mal acquis.

mishap [mis'háp] *s.* malheur; accident; contretemps, m.

misinform [misinfaurm] *v.* renseigner mal.

mislaid [mislé¹d] *pret., p. p. of to
mislay.* ‖ **mislay** [mislé¹] *v.* égarer,
perdre.

mislead [mislíd] *v.* fourvoyer; égarer. ‖ **misled** [mislèd] *pret., p. p. of
to mislead.*

misogynist [misádjinist] *s.* miso-
gyne, m.

misplace [misplé¹s] *v.* mal placer,
mal classer; déplacer.

misprint [misprint] *s.* faute d'impression, f.; *v.* imprimer avec une
coquille.

mispronounce [misprᵉnaᵒᵘns] *v.* mal
prononcer, écorcher.

misquotation [miskwoᵘté¹shᵉn] *s.*
fausse citation, f.

misrepresent [misrèprizènt] *v.* représenter mal; déformer; dénaturer;
calomnier.

miss [mis] *v.* manquer; omettre; souffrir de l'absence, du manque de; *s.*
manque; raté, m.; perte; faute;
erreur; déficience, f.; *to miss one's way*,
se tromper de route; *he just missed
falling*, il a failli tomber; *I miss you*,
vous me manquez.

miss [mis] *s.ᵉ* mademoiselle, f.

missal [misᵉl] *s.* missel, m.

missile [mís'l] *s.* projectile, m.; *adj.*
de jet; qu'on peut lancer.

missing [mising] *adj.* absent; manquant; disparu (milit.).

mission [míshᵉn] *s.* mission, f. ‖
missionary [-èri] *adj., s.ᵉ* missionnaire.

misspell [misspèl] *v.* mal orthographier; mal épeler.

mist [mist] *s.* brume; bruine; buée,
f.; brouillard, m.; *v.* bruiner; envelopper d'un brouillard.

mistake [mᵉsté¹k] *s.* erreur; faute;
méprise; gaffe, f.; mécompte (comm.),
m.; *v.ᵉ* se tromper; se méprendre; *to
make a mistake*, se tromper, commettre une bévue. ‖ **mistaken** [-ᵉn]
p. p. of to mistake; adj. erroné; fait
par erreur.

mister [místᵉr] *s.* monsieur, m.

mistify [mistifa¹] *v.* vaporiser, pulvériser, atomiser.

mistletoe [mísltoᵒᵘ] *s.* gui, m.

mistook [mistouk] *pret. of to mistake.*

mistreat [mistrít] *v.* maltraiter.

mistress [místris] *s.ᵉ* madame; maîtresse; patronne, f.; *school mistress*,
institutrice.

mistrust [mistræst] *s.* méfiance, f.;
v. se méfier de. ‖ **mistrustful** [-fᵉl]
adj. méfiant; soupçonneux.

misty [misti] *adj.* brumeux; vague,
indécis.

misunderstand [misœndᵉrstánd] *v.*
mal comprendre; se méprendre; mal
interpréter. ‖ **misunderstanding** [-ing]
s. mésintelligence, mauvaise interprétation; équivoque, f.; malentendu, m. ‖
misunderstood [misœndᵉrstoud] *pret.,
p. p. of to misunderstand.*

misuse [misyoᵘs] *s.* abus; mauvais
usage; mauvais traitements, m.; malversation, f.; [misyouz] *v.* mésuser;
abuser; maltraiter; détourner; employer mal à propos.

mite [ma¹t] *s.* mite; obole, f.; denier, m.; (colloq.) brin; mioche, m.

miter [ma¹tᵉr] *s.* mitre; dignité
épiscopale, f.

mitigate [mítᵉgé¹t] *v.* mitiger; atténuer, modérer; apaiser.

mitten [mít'n] *s.* mitaine; moufle, f.

mix [miks] *v.* (se) mêler; (se) mélanger; s'associer; *s.ᵉ* mélange, gâchis,
m.; *mix-up*, cohue, pagaille, mêlée;
to mix up, bien mélanger; embrouiller.
‖ **mixed** [-t] *adj.* mélangé; mixte;
panaché (culin.); fractionnaire (math.);
perplexe (fig.). ‖ **mixture** [míkstshᵉr]
s. mélange; amalgame, m.; mixture, f.

mizzen [miz'n] *s.* artimon, m.

moan [mo°ⁿ] *s.* gémissement, m.; plainte f.; *v.* gémir; se lamenter; pleurer, déplorer.

moat [mo°ᵘt] *s.* fossé, m.; douve, f.

mob [mâb] *s* foule; populace, cohue, f.; attroupement, rassemblement, m.; *v.* se ruer en foule sur; s'attrouper.

mobile [mo°ᵘb'l] *adj.* mobile.

mobilization [mo°ᵘb'lezé¹shen] *s.* mobilisation, f. || *mobilize* [mo°ᵘb'la¹z] *v.* mobiliser

moccasin [mâk°s'n] *s.* mocassin, m.

mocha [mo°ᵘk°] *s.* moka, m.; *adj.* au café.

mock [mâk] *v.* se moquer; singer; rire de. *s.* moquerie, f.; *adj.* faux; imité; fictif. *mock-up*, maquette. || *mockery* [-ri] *s* • moquerie; dérision; parodie, f simulacre, m.

modality [modaliti] *s.*• modalité, f. || *mode* [mo°ᵘd] *s* mode; façon; méthode, f. système mode [music], m.

model [mâd'l] *s* modèle; patron; mannequin. m copie, f.; *adj.* modèle; en miniature, réduit; *v.* modeler; prendre modèle; faire le mannequin; poser.

moderate [mâd°rit] *adj.* modéré; modique. médiocre [-ré¹t] *v.* modérer; (se) calmer || *moderation* [mâd°ré¹sh°n] *s* modération; retenue; tempérance. f

modern [mâd°ᵣn] *adj.* moderne. || *modernism* [-is'm] *s* modernisme, m.; nouveauté f || *modernize* [-a¹z] *v.* moderniser

modest [mâd¹st] *adj.* modeste. || *modesty* [-i] *s* modestie pudeur, f.

modification [mâd°f°ké¹sh°n] *s.* modification f || *modify* [mâd°fa¹] *v.* modifier

modiste [mo°ᵘdist] *s.* couturière, f.

modulate [mâd°lé¹t] *v.* moduler. || *modulus* [mâd°l°s] *s.* module, coefficient m

Mohammedan [mo°ᵘham°d°n] *adj.*, *s.* mahométan

moil [m° ¹l] *v* trimer.

moist [m°¹st] *adj* humide; moite. || *moisten* [mo¹s'n] humecter; humidifier. *moisture* [mo¹stsh°r] *s.* humidité, f

molar [mo°ᵘl°ʳ] *adj.*, *s.* molaire.

molasses [m°lasiz] *s.* mélasse, f.; *molasses candy*, bonbon, *Fr. Can.* tire.

mo(u)ld [mo°ᵘld] *s.* moisi, m.; *v.* moisir *mo(u)ldy*, moisi.

mo(u)ld [mo°ᵘld] *s.* terre, f.; terreau, m. || *mo(u)lder* [-°ʳ] *v.* s'émietter; s'effriter.

mo(u)ld [mo°ᵘld] *s.* moule, m.; *v.* mouler; modeler; *mo(u)lding*, moulage, moulure.

mole [mo°ᵘl] *s.* môle, m.

mole [mo°ᵘl] *s.* tache, f.; grain de beauté, m.

mole [mo°ᵘl] *s.* taupe, f.; *mole-hill*, taupinière

molecule [mâl°kyoul] *s.* molécule, f.

molest [m°lèst] *v* molester; tourmenter *molestation*, molestation.

mollify [mâl°fa¹] *v.* amollir; pacifier; adoucir calmer.

mollusc [mâul°sk] *s.* mollusque, m.

molten [mo°ᵘlt'n] *adj* fondu.

moment [mo°ᵘm°nt] *s* moment, instant, m importance f || *momentary* [-èri] *adj* momentané; imminent || *momentous* [mo°ᵘmènt°s] *adj.* important, considérable || *momentum* [mo°ᵘmènt°m] *s* force d'impulsion, f.

monarch [mân°ʳk] *s* monarque, m. || *monarchy* [-i] *s* • monarchie, f.

monastery [mân°stèri] *s.*• monastère, m. *monastic*, monastique. monacal. *monasticism*, monachisme, vie monastique

Monday [mændi] *s.* lundi, m.

monetary [mæn°tèri] *adj.* monétaire. || *money* [mœni] *s* argent, m.; monnaie espèce f., *money-bag*, sacoche richard *money-box*, tronc tirelire *money dealer*, changeur *money-minded*, intéressé *money order*, mandat-poste *money-making*, lucratif *counterfeit money*, fausse monnaie *moneyed* [-d] *adj.* possédant; fortuné pécuniaire.

mongrel [mænggr°l] *adj.*, *s.* bâtard; métis. m

monitor [mânit°ʳ] *s* moniteur; contrôleur d'enregistrement, m.; *monitorroom*, cabine (radio)

monk [mœngk] *s* moine, m.

monkey [mængki] *s* singe m.; guenon, f singer se mêler à, *monkeyshine*, tour farce. *monkey wrench*, clef anglaise

monogamy [m°nâg°mi] *s.* monogamie f

monogram [mân°gram] *s.* monogramme m

monologue [mân'laug] *s.* monologue m

monopolize [m°nâp'la¹z] *v.* monopoliser accaparer *monopoly* [-li] *s.*• monopole accaparement, m.

monosyllable [mân°sil°b'l] *s.* monosyllabe m

monotonous [m°nât'n°s] *adj.* monotone. || *monotony* [-ni] *s* monotonie, f.

monsoon [mânsou̯n] *s.* mousson, f.

monster [mânstᵉr] *s.* monstre, m.; *adj.* énorme. || **monstrosity** [mânstrâs-ᵉti] *s.* monstruosité, f. || **monstrous** [mânstrᵉs] *adj.* monstrueux.

month [mænth] *s.* mois, m. || **monthly** [-li] *adj.* mensuel; *adv.* mensuellement; *s.* publication mensuelle, f

monument [mânyᵉmᵉnt] *s.* monument, m. || **monumental** [mânyᵉmènt'l] *adj.* monumental, colossal, grandiose.

moo [mou] *s.* mugissement, m.; *v.* mugir; meugler.

mood [moud] *s.* humeur, f.; état d'esprit, m.; *to be in a good mood,* être de bonne humeur; *to be in the mood to* être d'humeur à, disposé à.

mood [moud] *s* mode (gramm.), m.

moody [moudi] *adj.* maussade; capricieux, quinteux

moon [moun] *s.* lune, f.; *moonlight,* clair de lune; *moonstruck,* lunatique, toqué, sidéré.

moor [mouᵉr] *v.* amarrer; mouiller.

moor [mouᵉr] *s.* lande, f.; terrain inculte, m.

Moor [mouᵉr] *s.* Maure, m.; *Moorish,* mauresque.

moose [mous] *s.* élan (zool.), *Fr. Can.* orignal, m.

mop [mâp] *s.* balai; faubert (naut.), m.; *Am* tignasse, f.; *v.* éponger, balayer, *dish mop,* lavette.

mope [mou̯p] *v.* faire grise mine.

moral [maurᵉl] *adj.* moral; *s.* morale; moralité f , pl. mœurs, f pl. || **morale** [mᵉral] *s* moral, m. || **moralist** [maurᵉlist] *s* moraliste, m. | **morality** [mᵉralᵉti] *s* ° moralité, f. || **moralize** [maurᵉla¹z] *v* moraliser.

morbid [maurbid] *adj.* morbide; maladif; malsain

mordacious [mârdéᵊshᵉs] *adj.* mordant, caustique

more [mouᵉr] *adj.* plus de; *adv.* plus; davantage, *some more,* encore un peu; *the more,* The more plus. plus; *once more,* encore une fois, *never more,* jamais plus; *more and more,* de plus en plus *more or less,* plus ou moins, *all the more,* à plus forte raison, d'autant plus.

morel [mârèl] *s.* morille, f.

moreover [mouᵉrou̯vᵉr] *adv.* de plus; en outre; d'ailleurs.

moribund [mauribænd] *adj.* moribond.

morning [maurning] *s.* matin, *Fr. Can.* avant-midi, m.; *adj.* du matin.

Moroccan [mᵉrâkᵉn] *adj., s.* marocain. || **Morocco** [mᵉrâkou̯] *s.* Maroc, m.

morrow [mourou̯] *s.* lendemain, m.

morsel [maurs'l] *s.* morceau; brin, m.; bouchée, f.

mortal [maurt'l] *adj., s.* mortel. || **mortality** [maurtalᵉti] *s.*° mortalité, f.

mortar [maurtᵉr] *s.* mortier, m.; *knee-mortar,* lance-grenades.

mortgage [maurgidj] *s.* hypothèque, f.; *v.* hypothéquer

mortification [mârtifiké¹shᵉn] *s.* mortification; gangrène, f. || **mortify** [maurtᵉfa¹] *v.* mortifier, gangrener (méd.).

mortise [maurtis] *s.* mortaise, f.; *v.* mortaiser

mortuary [mârtyouᵉri] *adj.* mortuaire; *s.* morgue, f.

mosaic [mou̯zé¹ik] *s.* mosaïque, f.; relevé photographique aérien; *v.* mosaïquer

mosquito [mᵉskîtou̯] *s.* moustique, m. *Fr. Can* maringouin, m.; *mosquito net,* moustiquaire.

moss [maus] *s.* mousse, f.; tourbe, f.; *mossy,* moussu

most [mou̯st] *adj.* le plus, la plus, les plus, *adv.* on ne peut plus; *most people,* la plupart des gens; *most likely,* très probablement, *at most,* au plus; *most of all* surtout *to make the most of* tirer le meilleur parti de. || **mostly** [-li] *adv* pour la plupart; le plus souvent, surtout; *s.* la plupart de.

mote [mou̯t] *s.* grain de poussière, m.; paille, f. (fig.).

motel [mou̯tel] *s.* motel, m.

motet [mou̯tèt] *s* motet, m.

moth [mauth] *s* phalène; mite; teigne, f || *moth ball,* boule de naphtaline; *moth-eaten,* mité

mother [mæzhᵉr] *s* mère, f.; *adj.* de mère maternel *v* servir de mère à; dorloter donner naissance à (fig.); *mother tongue,* langue maternelle, *motherhood,* maternité *mother-in-law,* belle-mère *motherly,* maternel; *mother-of-pearl,* nacre.

motif [mou̯tîf] *s.* motif, thème (music) m.

motion [mou̯shᵉn] *s.* mouvement; déplacement m., motion, f., *v.* faire signe de *to second a motion* appuyer une proposition *motionless,* immobile, *motion picture,* cinéma; film cinématographique

motive [mou̯tiv] *s.* motif, m.; *adj.* moteur, motrice; cinétique; *v.* motiver; *motive power,* force motrice.

motley [mátli] *adj.* bigarré, multicolore; varié, hétérogène; *s.* bigarrure, f.; salmigondis, m.

motor [moouter] *s.* moteur, m.; auto, f.; *v.* aller en auto; *motor-school,* auto-école. ‖ *motorboat* [-boout] *s.* canot automobile, m. ‖ *motorcar* [-kâr] *s.* automobile, f. ‖ *motorcoach* [-kooutsh] *s.°* autobus, m. ‖ *motorcycle* [-sa¹k¹l] *s.* motocyclette, f. ‖ *motorist* [-rist] *s.* automobiliste, m. ‖ *motorize* [-ra¹z] *v.* motoriser. ‖ *motorman* [-m°n] (*pl.* motormen) *s.* wattman; machiniste, m.

mottled [mât'ld] *adj.* moucheté, bigarré; pommelé; chiné; brouillé [complexion].

motto [mátoou] *s.* devise, f.

mould, see mold.

mound [maound] *s.* tertre, monticule, m.

mount [maount] *s.* mont, m.

mount [maount] *s.* monture, f.; *v.* chevaucher; gravir; monter, installer; sertir; encadrer.

mountain [maount'n] *s.* montagne, f.; *adj.* de montagne; *mountain lion,* puma; *mountaineer,* alpiniste; montagnard; *mountainous,* montagneux.

mountebank [maountibangk] *s.* saltimbanque; charlatan, m.

mounting [maounting] *s.* affût; support, m.

mourn [moourn] *v.* se lamenter; pleurer; regretter; porter le deuil (*for,* de); *mournful,* funèbre, lugubre, triste. ‖ *mourning* [-ing] *s.* deuil, m.; affliction, f.; *adj.* de deuil; *mourning-band,* crêpe.

mouse [maous] (*pl.* mice [ma¹s]) *s.* souris, f.; *mouse-trap,* souricière, f.

moustache, see mustache.

mouth [maouth] *s.* bouche; gueule; embouchure, f.; orifice; goulot, m.; *with open mouth,* bouche bée; *mouth-organ,* harmonica, f. ‖ *mouthful* [-f°l] *s.* bouchée, f. ‖ *mouthing* [-ing] *s.* déclamation, f.; verbiage, m. ‖ *mouth-piece* [-pîs] *s.* embouchure (mus.), f.; porte-parole (fig.), m. ‖ *mouthy* [-i] *adj.* déclamatoire; hâbleur; braillard.

movable [moouv°b'l] *adj.* mobile; mobilier; *s. pl.* (biens) meubles, m. pl. ‖ *move* [moouv] *v.* mouvoir; remuer; transporter; déménager [furniture]; proposer [motion]; émouvoir; *s.* mouvement; coup [chess], m.; *to move away,* s'éloigner; *to move back* (faire) reculer; *to move forward,* avancer; *to move in,* emménager; *it is your move,* c'est à vous de jouer [game]. ‖ *movement* [-m°nt] *s.* mouvement; déplacement; mécanisme, m.; manœuvre; opération, f. ‖ *movie* [-i] *s.* cinéma;

film, m. ‖ *moving* [-ing] *adj.* mouvant; émouvant; touchant.

mow [moou] *v.°* faucher. ‖ *mower* [-°r] *s.* faucheur, m.; faucheuse [machine]; tondeuse, f. ‖ *mown* [-n] *adj.,* *p. p.* fauché.

much [mœtsh] *adj.* beaucoup de; *adv.* beaucoup; *as much as,* autant que; *much as,* pour autant que; *how much?,* combien?; *so much,* tant; *ever so much,* tellement; *too much,* trop; *very much,* beaucoup; *to think much of,* faire grand cas de; *so much the better,* tant mieux; *not much of a book,* un livre sans grande valeur.

muck [mœk] *s.* fumier, m.; fange, f.; *v.* fumer; souiller; salir.

mucosity [myoukâsiti] *s.°* mucosité, f. ‖ *mucous* [myouk°s] *adj.* muqueux; *mucous membrane,* muqueuse.

mud [mœd] *s.* boue, fange, f.; *mudguard,* garde-boue. ‖ *muddle* [-'l] *v.* barboter, patauger; troubler; salir; embrouiller; gaspiller; *s.* gâchis, trouble, désordre, m.; confusion, f. ‖ *muddy* [-i] *adj.* boueux; confus; *v.* couvrir de boue; troubler; rendre confus.

muff [mœf] *s.* manchon, m.

muff [mœf] *v.* bousiller, saboter; gâcher; louper; rater.

muffin [mœfin] *s.* brioche; galette, f.; *Am.* pain moufflet, m.

muffle [mœf'l] *v.* emmitoufler; assourdir [sound]. ‖ *muffler* [-°r] *s.* cache-nez; amortisseur de son; pot d'échappement, m.

mufti [mœfti] *s.* costume civil, m.

mug [mœg] *s.* pot, gobelet, m.

muggy [mœgi] *adj.* mou, chaud et humide.

mulatto [m°latoou] *s.* mulâtre, m.; *mulatress,* mulâtresse, f.

mulberry [mœlbèri] *s.°* mûre, f.

mulct [mœlkt] *s.* amende, f.; *v.* frapper d'une amende.

mule [myoul] *s.* mulet, m.; mule, f. ‖ *muleteer* [myoul°tîr] *s.* muletier, m.

mull [mœl] *v.* réfléchir (*over,* à); chauffer et épicer une boisson.

multiple [mœlt°p'l] *adj.,* *s.* multiple. ‖ *multiplication* [mœlt°pl°ké¹sh°n] *s.* multiplication, f. ‖ *multiply* [mœlt°pla¹] *v.* (se) multiplier. ‖ *multitude* [mœlt°tyoud] *s.* multitude, f.

mum [mœm] *adj.* muet, silencieux; *interj.* chut!; *to keep mum,* se taire.

mum [mœm] *s.* maman, f. (pop.).

mumble [mœmb'l] *v.* marmonner; *s.* grognement, murmure, m.; *to talk in a mumble,* marmotter entre ses dents.

mummy [mæmi] *s.** momie, f.; maman, f. (pop.); *v.* momifier; *mummify*, (se) momifier.

mumpish [mæmpish] *adj.* renfrogné, boudeur.

mumps [mæmps] *s. pl.* oreillons, m. pl.

munch [mœntsh] *v.* croquer, mâcher.

mundane [mænde¹n] *adj.* du monde, mondain; terrestre.

municipal [myounis⁰p'l] *adj.* municipal. || *municipality* [myounis⁰pal⁰ti] *s.** municipalité, f.

munificence [myounifis'ns] *s.* munificence, f. || *munificent* [-'nt] *adj.* munificent.

munition [myounish⁰n] *s.* munition, f.; *munition plant*, arsenal.

mural [myour⁰l] *adj., s.* mural.

murder [mœr̄d⁰r] *s.* meurtre, m.; *v.* assassiner, écorcher [language]. || *murderer* [-r⁰r] *s.* meurtrier, assassin, m. || *murderous* [-r⁰s] *adj.* meurtrier; homicide.

murky [mœrki] *adj.* sombre, obscur; *murky past*, passé obscur.

murmur [mœr̄m⁰r] *s.* murmure, m.; *v.* murmurer.

muscle [mœs'l] *s.* muscle, m. || *muscular* [mæskyel⁰r] *adj.* musculaire; musculeux. || *musculature* [mæskyoul⁰tsh⁰r] *s.* musculature, f.

muse [myouz] *v.* rêver, méditer; *s.* méditation. rêverie; Muse, f.

museum [myouzi⁰m] *s.* musée, m.

mush [mœsh] *s.** bouillie de farine de maïs; gaude; niaiserie, f.; brouillage, m.

mushroom [mæshroum] *s.* champignon, m.; *v.* foisonner; pousser vite; s'aplatir, s'écraser.

music [myouzik] *s.* musique, f.; *music stand*, pupitre; *music stool*, tabouret de piano. || *musical* [-⁰l] *adj.* musical; musicien; mélodieux, *s.* opérette, f. || *musicality* [myouzikaliti] *s.* musicalité, f. || *musicalness* [-nis] *s.* harmonie, mélodie, f. || *musician* [myouzish⁰n] *s.* musicien, m.

muskrat [mæskrat] *s.* rat musqué, m.

muslin [mæzlin] *s.* mousseline, f.

muss [mœs] *s.* désordre, m.; confusion, f.; *v.* déranger; froisser.

mussel [mœs'l] *s.* moule, f.

Mussulman [mæs'lm⁰n] (*pl.* Mussulmans [-z], Mussulmen [-m⁰n]) *adj., s.* musulman.

must [mœst] *s.* moût, m.

must [mœst] *defect. v.* devoir, falloir; *I must say*, il faut que je dise, je ne peux pas m'empêcher de dire.

mustache [mæstash] *s.* moustache, f.

mustard [mæst⁰rd] *s.* moutarde, f.; *mustard gas*, ypérite; *mustard plaster*, sinapisme.

muster [mæst⁰r] *s.* appel; rassemblement, m.; revue, f.; *v.* faire l'appel de; passer en revue; rassembler; *mustering-in, Am.* enrôlement; *mustering-out*, démobilisation.

musty [mæsti] *adj.* moisi.

mutable [myout⁰b'l] *adj.* variable; changeant. || *mutation* [myouté¹sh⁰n] *s.* altération, f.; changement, m.

mute [myout] *adj.* muet; *s.* muet, m.; muette (gramm.), f.; sourdine [music], f.; *v.* amortir, assourdir. || *muteness* [-nis] *s.* mutisme, m.

mutilate [myout'lé¹t] *v.* mutiler; tronquer. || *mutilation* [myout'lé¹sh⁰n] *s.* mutilation, f.

mutineer [myoutini⁰r] *s.* mutin, m. || *mutiny* [myout'ni] *s.** mutinerie, f.; *v.* se mutiner, se révolter.

mutter [mæt⁰r] *v.* marmotter; grommeler; gronder [thunder]; *s.* marmottement, m.

mutton [mæt'n] *s.* mouton [flesh], m.; *mutton chop*, côtelette de mouton; *leg of mutton*, gigot.

mutual [myoutshou⁰l] *adj.* mutuel; réciproque; commun [friend]; *mutualism*, mutualisme; *mutuality*, mutualité, f.

muzzle [mœz'l] *s.* museau [animal], m.; muselière; bouche, gueule [firearm], f.; *v.* museler.

muzzy [mœzi] *adj.* flou [ideas]; abruti, hébété.

my [ma¹] *adj.* mon, ma, mes.

myope [ma¹o⁰p] *s.* myope, m. f. || *myopia* [ma¹o⁰upi⁰] *s.* myopie, f.

myosotis [ma¹oso⁰utis] *s.* myosotis, m.

myriad [miriad] *s.* myriade, f.

myrrh [mœr] *s.* myrrhe, f.

myrtle [mœr't'l] *s.* myrte, m.; *Am.* pervenche, f.

myself [ma¹sèlf] *pron.* moi-même; moi; me; *I have hurt myself*, je me suis blessé.

mysterious [mistiri⁰s] *adj.* mystérieux, *mysteriously*, mystérieusement. || *mystery* [mistri] *s.** mystère, m.

mystic [mistik] *adj., s.* mystique; *mystical*, mystique. || *mysticism* [mist⁰siz⁰m] *s.* mysticisme, m.

mystification [mistifiké¹sh⁰n] *s.* mystification, complexité; perplexité, f.; mystère; tour, m. || *mystify* [mistifa¹] *v.* mystifier; obscurcir; intriguer.

myth [mith] *s.* mythe, m.; *mythical*, mythique. || *mythology* [mithâl⁰dji] *s.** mythologie, f.

N

nab [nab] *v.* saisir; happer; appréhender, arrêter.

nag [nag] *s.* bidet, petit cheval, m.

nag [nag] *v.* gronder, grogner; importuner; critiquer; criailler; harceler; *s.* querelle, f.

nail [né¹l] *s.* clou; ongle, m.; *v.* clouer; *nail file*, lime à ongles; *to hit the nail on the head*, mettre le doigt dessus, tomber juste; *nail maker*, cloutier; *nail polish*, vernis à ongles.

naive [naiv] *adj.* naïf, ingénu.

naked [né¹kid] *adj.* nu. ‖ *nakedness* [-nis] *s.* nudité, f.

name [né¹m] *s.* nom; renom, m.; réputation, f.; *v.* nommer; appeler; fixer; mentionner; désigner; *what is your name?*, comment vous appelez-vous?; *Christian name*, nom de baptême; *to know by name*, connaître de nom; *assumed name*, pseudonyme; *nickname*, sobriquet, surnom; *nameless*, sans nom, anonyme, inconnu; *namely*, à savoir, nommément. ‖ *namesake* [-sé¹k] *s.* homonyme, m.

nap [nap] *s.* duvet, poil, m.

nap [nap] *s.* somme [sleep], m.; sieste, f.; *v.* sommeiller; faire la sieste.

nape [né¹p] *s.* nuque, f.

naphtha [napth°] *s.* naphte, m.

napkin [napkin] *s.* serviette; couche, f.

narcissus [nârsis°s] *s.°* narcisse, m.

narcosis [nârko°sis] *s.* narcose, f.

narcotic [nârkâtik] *adj., s.* narcotique.

narrate [naré¹t] *v.* raconter, narrer. ‖ *narration* [naré¹sh°n] *s.* narration, f. ‖ *narrative* [nar°tiv] *adj.* narratif; *s.* récit; exposé, m.; relation, f.

narrow [naro°u] *adj.* étroit; rétréci; borné; intolérant; *s. pl.* détroit; défilé, m.; *v.* (se) rétrécir; *narrow circumstances*, gêne, f. ‖ *narrowness* [-nis] *s.* étroitesse, f.; rétrécissement, m.

nasal [né¹z'l] *adj.* nasal.

nastiness [nastinis] *s.* saleté, malpropreté; grossièreté, f.

nasturtium [nastër°sh°m] *s.* capucine, f.

nasty [nasti] *adj.* sale; grossier; obscène; odieux; *a nasty customer*, un mauvais coucheur; *a nasty trick*, un sale tour; *to smell nasty*, sentir mauvais.

natality [n°taliti] *s.* natalité, f.

natation [nété¹sh°n] *s.* natation, f.

nation [né¹sh°n] *s.* nation, f. ‖ *national* [-'l] *adj.* national. ‖ *nationalism* [nash°n°liz'm] *s.* nationalisme, m. ‖ *nationalist* [-ist] *s.* nationaliste; étatiste, m. ‖ *nationalistic* [nash°n°listik] *adj.* nationaliste. ‖ *nationality* [nash°naleti] *s.°* nationalité, f. ‖ *nationalization* [nash°n°la¹zé¹sh°n] *s.* nationalisation, f. ‖ *nationalize* [nash°n'la¹z] *v.* nationaliser; naturaliser; être naturalisé.

native [né¹tiv] *adj.* natif; originaire; natal; *s.* indigène, naturel, m. ‖ *nativity* [né¹tive¹ti] *s.°* naissance; nativité, f.

natty [nati] *adj.* pimpant, coquet; habile; commode.

natural [natsh°r°l] *adj.* naturel; normal; simple; réel; bécarre [music]. ‖ *naturalism* [-iz°m] *s.* naturalisme, m. ‖ *naturalist* [-ist] *s.* naturaliste, m. ‖ *naturalization* [natshr°l°zé¹sh°n] *s.* naturalisation, f. ‖ *naturalize* [natsh°r°la¹z] *v.* naturaliser. ‖ *naturally* [-li] *adv.* naturellement. ‖ *naturalness* [-nis] *s.* naturel, m. ‖ *nature* [né¹tsh°r] *s.* nature, f.; naturel; caractère, m.; simplicité, f.

naught [naut] *s.* rien, zéro; *to come to naught*, n'aboutir à rien, échouer. ‖ *naughty* [-i] *adj.* malicieux, polisson, indocile; mauvais, pervers.

nausea [nauj°] *s.* nausée, f. ‖ *nauseate* [-jié¹t] *v.* avoir des nausées; dégoûter. ‖ *nauseous* [-j°s] *adj.* nauséabond; écœurant.

nautical [nautik°l] *adj.* nautique; marin; naval; de marine.

naval [né¹v'l] *adj.* naval; *Am. naval academy*, école navale; *naval officer*, officier de marine.

nave [né¹v] *s.* nef [church], f.

nave [né¹v] *s.* moyeu, m.

navel [né¹v'l] *s.* nombril, ombilic, m.

navigable [nav°g°b'l] *adj.* navigable. ‖ *navigate* [-gé¹t] *v.* naviguer; gouverner; piloter. ‖ *navigation* [nav°gé¹sh°n] *s.* navigation, f.; *radio navigation*, radio-goniométrie. ‖ *navigator* [nav°gé¹t°r] *s.* navigateur, m. ‖ *navy* [né¹vi] *s.°* marine; flotte, f.; *navy blue*, bleu marine.

nay [né¹] *adv.* non; *interj.* vraiment! voyons!; *s.* vote négatif, m.

Nazi [nâtsi] *s.* nazi, m.; *Nazism*, nazisme.

near [nĭᵉʳ] *adv*, près; *prep*. près de; *adj*. proche; rapproché; voisin; in-time; *v*. approcher de; *near at hand*, sous la main; *to be near to laughter*, être sur le point de rire; *a near trans-lation*, une traduction près du texte; *to come near*, s'approcher; *near-by*, proche, près; *near-sighted*, myope; *near silk*, rayonne. ‖ **nearly** [-li] *adv*. de près; presque; à peu près; *he nearly killed me*, il a failli me tuer. ‖ **nearness** [-nis] *s*. proximité; immi-nence [danger]; intimité, f.

neat [nît] *adj*. propre; net; pur [drink]; habile. ‖ **neatly** [-li] *adv*. net-tement, proprement, coquettement; habilement. ‖ **neatness** [-nis] *s*. pro-preté, netteté, élégance; habileté, f.

nebulous [nébyoul³s] *adj*. nébuleux.

necessarily [nès³sèr³li] *adv*. néces-sairement. ‖ **necessary** [nès³sèri] *adj*. cessaire. ‖ **necessaries** [-z] *s. pl*. né-cessaire; équipement individuel, m. ‖ **necessitate** [n³sès³té¹t] *v*. nécessiter. ‖ **necessitous** [n³sès³t³s] *adj*. nécessi-teux. ‖ **necessity** [n³sès³ti] *s*.* néces-sité; indigence, f.; besoin, m.

neck [nèk] *s*. cou; col; goulot, m.; encolure, f.; *neck of land*, isthme; *neck and neck*, côte à côte; *low necked*, décolleté; *stiff neck*, tortico-lis; *neck beef*, collet de bœuf; **neckerchief**, foulard; **necklace**, col-lier; **necktie**, cravate.

need [nîd] *s*. besoin, m.; nécessité; indigence; circonstance critique, f.; *v*. avoir besoin de; nécessiter; *I need a pen*, il me faut un stylo; *for need of*, faute de; *if need be*, en cas de be-soin. ‖ **needful** [-f³l] *adj*. nécessaire; **needfully**, nécessairement. ‖ **neediness** [-inis] *s*. gêne, indigence, f.; be-soin, m.

needle [nîd'l] *s*. aiguille, f.

needless [nîdlis] *adj*. inutile.

needlework [nîd'lwĕ³k] *s*. travaux (m. pl.) d'aiguille; ouvrage, m.; cou-ture, f.

needy [nîdi] *adj*. nécessiteux, beso-gneux.

nefarious [nifèri³s] *adj*. abominable.

negation [nigé¹sh³n] *s*. négation, f. ‖ **negative** [nèg³tiv] *adj*. négatif; *s*. (cliché) négatif, m.; *v*. repousser, rejeter.

neglect [niglèkt] *s*. négligence, f.; oubli, m.; *v*. négliger; omettre (*to*, de). ‖ **neglectful** [-f³l] *adj*. négligent; insouciant; oublieux. ‖ **negligence** [nèg³dj³ns] *s*. négligence, f. ‖ **negli-gent** [nèg³dj³nt] *adj*. négligent; ou-blieux. ‖ **negligible** [nèg³dj³b'l] *adj*. négligeable.

negotiate [nigo⁰ushié¹t] *v*. négo-cier; traiter; surmonter [difficulty]. ‖

negotiation [nigo⁰ushié¹sh³n] *s*. négo-ciation, f.; pourparlers, m. pl. ‖ **negotiator** [nigo⁰ushié¹t³r] *s*. négocia-teur, m.

negress [nîgris] *s*.* négresse, f. ‖ **ne-gro** [nîgro⁰u] *adj*., *s*.* nègre, Noir, m.

neigh [né¹] *s*. hennissement, m.; *v*. hennir.

neighbo(u)r [né¹b³r] *adj*. voisin, proche, *s*. voisin; prochain, m.; *v*. avoisiner. ‖ **neighbo(u)rhood** [-houd] *s*. voisinage; alentours, m.; *in our neighbo(u)rhood*, dans notre quartier. ‖ **neighbo(u)ring** [-ring] *adj*. voisin, contigu.

neither [nîzh³r] *pron*. aucune, ni l'un ni l'autre; *adv*. ni, ni... non plus; *neither of the two*, aucun des deux; *neither... nor*, ni... ni.

neon [nî³n] *s*. néon, m.

nephew [néfyou] *s*. neveu, m.

nerve [nĕrv] *s*. nerf; courage, m.; nervure, f., *pl*. nervosité, f.; *Am*. au-dace, sans-gêne; *v* donner du nerf, du courage *optical nerve*, nerf optique. ‖ **nervous** [-³s] *adj*. nerveux; inquiet, timide ‖ **nervousness** [-³snis] *s*. nervo-sité; agitation, inquiétude, f.; trac, m. ‖ **nervy** [-i] *adj*. énervé; nerveux; culotté (colloq.).

ness [nès] *s*. cap, promontoire, m.

nest [nèst] *s*. nid, m.; nichée, f.; *v*. nicher; *nest-egg*, nichet. ‖ **nestle** [nès'l] *v* nicher; se blottir; cajoler. ‖ **nestling** [-ling] *s* oisillon, m.

net [nèt] *s* filet; rets; réseau, m.; *v*. prendre au filet, tendre des filets; faire du filet; *road net*, réseau rou-tier; *trawl-net*, chalut.

net [nèt] *adj*. net; pur; *v*. gagner net; *net profit*, bénéfice net.

Netherlander [nézh³rl³nd³r] *s*. Néerlandais Hollandais, m.; *Ne-therlandish*, néerlandais, hollandais; *Netherlands*, Pays-Bas, Hollande.

nethermost [nèzh³rmo⁰ust] *adj*. le plus bas.

nettle [nèt'l] *s*. ortie, f.; *v*. piquer, irriter.

network [nètwĕrk] *s*. réseau, m.; *radio network*, réseau radiophonique.

neuralgia [nyouráldj³] *s*. névralgie, f. ‖ **neurasthenia** [nyourᵃsthîniᵉ] *s*. neu-rasthénie, f ‖ **neurasthenic** [-ik] *adj*. neurasthénique. ‖ **neurologist** [nyouᵉ-rál³djist] *s* neurologue, m. ‖ **neurol-ogy** [-dji] *s*. neurologie, f. ‖ **neuropath** [nyouᵉropath] *s* névropathe, m. f. ‖ **neurosis** [nyouᵉroᵒᵘsis] *s*. névrose, f. ‖ **neurotic** [-rátik] *adj*., *s*. névrosé, m. f.

neuter [nyout³r] *adj*. neutre (gramm.). ‖ **neutral** [nyoutr³l] *adj*. neutre [country]. ‖ **neutrality** [nyoutral⁻eti] *s.* neutralité, f. ‖ **neutralize** [nyoutre-la⁻iz] *v.* neutraliser.

never [nèv⁻er] *adv.* jamais; *never mind*, peu importe, cela ne fait rien; *never more*, jamais plus; *never-ending*, incessant, interminable; *never-never*, achat à tempérament; *never-never land*, pays de légende. ‖ **nevertheless** [nèverzh⁻elès] *adv.*, *conj.* néanmoins; cependant; nonobstant.

new [nyou] *adj.* neuf; nouveau; récent; frais; *adv.* nouvellement, récemment; à nouveau; *new-born baby*, nouveau-né; *newcomer*, nouveau venu; *newfangled*, très moderne; *New-foundland*, Terre-Neuve; *brand-new*, flambant neuf. ‖ **newly** [-li] *adv.* nouvellement; récemment; *newly wed*, nouveau marié. ‖ **newness** [-nis] *s.* nouveauté, f. ‖ **news** [-z] *s. pl.* nouvelles, f. pl.; *newscast*, les informations; *newsreel*, les actualités; *a piece of news*, une nouvelle; *news boy*, *newsy*, vendeur de journaux; *news stand*, kiosque à journaux. ‖ **news-monger** [-mœngg⁻er] *s.* cancanier, potinier, m. ‖ **newspaper** [-pé¹p⁻er] *s.* journal, m.

next [nèkst] *adj.* le plus proche; contigu; suivant; prochain; *adv.* ensuite; *next to*, à côté de; *the next two days*, les deux jours suivants; *the morning after next*, après-demain matin; *next to nothing*, pour ainsi dire rien.

nib [nib] *s.* pointe, f.; bec [pen], m.

nibble [nib⁻l] *v.* mordiller; grignoter; chicaner; *s.* grignotement, m.

nice [na¹s] *adj.* agréable; sympathique; aimable; charmant; gentil; délicat; difficile. ‖ **nicely** [-li] *adv.* bien; agréablement; délicatement; minutieusement. ‖ **nicety** [-ti] *s.*⁰ délicatesse; exactitude; minutie; friandise, f.

niche [nitsh] *s.* niche, f.

nick [nik] *s.* encoche; entaille, f.; *v.* encocher, entailler; ébrécher.

nick [nik] *s.* moment précis, m.; *in the nick of time*, à point; *v.* tomber à pic.

nickel [nik⁻l] *s.* nickel, m.; *nickel-in-the-slot machine*, appareil à sous. ‖ **nickel-plate**, *v.* nickeler.

nickname [nik⁻né¹m] *s.* surnom, sobriquet, diminutif, m.; *v.* surnommer.

niece [nîs] *s.* nièce, f.

niggard [nig⁻erd] *adj.*, *s.* ladre. ‖ **niggardly** [-li] *adj.* avare; *adv.* avec avarice; chichement.

nigger [nig⁻er] *s.* noir, nègre (pop.), m.; noire, négresse, f.; *v.* noircir.

niggle [nig⁻l] *v.* tatillonner.

night [na¹t] *s.* nuit, f.; soir, m.; *adj.* du soir, nocturne; *last night*, hier soir; *to-night*, ce soir; *night bird*, oiseau de nuit; *nightfall*, tombée de la nuit, *Fr. Can.* brunante; *night-gown*, chemise de nuit; *night watch-man*, veilleur de nuit. ‖ **nightingale** [-ingé¹l] *s.* rossignol, m. ‖ **nightly** [-li] *adj.* nocturne; *adv.* de nuit. ‖ **night-man** [-m⁻en] (*pl.* nightmen) *s.* vidangeur, m. ‖ **nightmare** [-mèⁱr] *s.* cauchemar, m.

nimble [nimb⁻l] *adj.* agile, leste; léger; vif.

nine [na¹n] *adj.*, *s.* neuf; *ninepins*, quilles. ‖ **nineteen** [-tîn] *adj.*, *s.* dix-neuf. ‖ **nineteenth** [-tînth] *adj.*, *s.* dix-neuvième. ‖ **ninetieth** [na¹ntiith] *adj.*, *s.* quatre-vingt-dixième. ‖ **ninety** [na¹nti] *adj.*, *s.* quatre-vingt-dix.

ninny [nini] *adj.* niais, sot.

ninth [na¹nth] *adj.*, *s.* neuvième.

nip [nip] *v.* pincer; couper; mordre; siroter; *s.* pincement, m.; morsure; goutte, f. [drink].

nippers [nip⁻ers] *s.* pinces; tenailles, f. pl.

nipple [nip⁻l] *s.* bout de sein, mamelon, m.

nippy [nipi] *adj.* preste, vif; mordant.

nitrate [na¹tré¹t] *s.* nitrate, m.

nitrogen [na¹tr⁻edjen] *s.* azote, m.

no [noᵘ] *adv.* non; pas; *adj.* aucun; pas de; ne... pas de; *no doubt*, sans doute; *no more*, pas davantage; *no longer*, pas plus longtemps; *no smoking*, défense de fumer; *no one*, nul, personne; *of no use*, inutile.

nobility [noᵘbil⁻eti] *s.* noblesse, f. ‖ **noble** [noᵘb⁻l] *s. adj.* noble. ‖ **nobleman** [-m⁻en] (*pl.* noblemen) *s.* noble, aristocrate, m. ‖ **nobleness** [-nis] *s.* noblesse, f. ‖ **nobly** [-i] *adv.* noblement.

nobody [noᵘbâdi] *pron.* personne, nul, aucun.

nocuous [nâkyouⁱs] *adj.* nocif.

nod [nâd] *v.* faire signe de la tête; opiner; hocher la tête; sommeiller; dodeliner; *s.* signe de tête, hochement, m.

nodosity [nodoᵘsiti] *s.*⁰ nodosité, f.

noise [no¹z] *s.* bruit; tapage, m.; *v.* publier; répandre; *to make a noise*, faire du bruit; *it is being noised about that*, le bruit court que; *noiseless*, silencieux, sans bruit; *noiselessly*, silencieusement; *noisily*, bruyamment; *noisiness*, tintamarre; turbulence.

noisome [no¹s⁻em] *adj.* puant, fétide; nuisible.

noisy [no¹zi] *adj.* bruyant, tapageur.

nomad [noᵒumad] *adj., s.* nomade,
m. f.

nominal [nâm°n'l] *adj.* nominal. ||
nominate [nâm°né¹t] *v.* nommer; dési-
gner. || **nomination** [nâm°né¹sh°n] *s.*
nomination; désignation, f. || **nomi-
native** [nâm°né¹tiv] *adj.* nominatif.

nonage [nânidj] *s.* minorité, f.

none [nœn] *pron.* aucun; nul; *adj.*
ne... aucun; *none of that,* pas de ça;
none the less, pas de moins.

nonentity [nânènt°ti] *s.* néant; bon
à rien, m.; futilité; nullité, f.

nonplus [nânplœs] *v.* déconcerter;
désemparer.

nonsense [nânsèns] *s.* absurdité, sottise, baliverne, f.

noodle [noud'l] *s.* nigaud, m.

noodles [noud'lz] *s. pl.* nouilles, f. pl.

nook [nouk] *s.* coin, recoin, m.

noon [noun] *s.* midi, m. || **noonday**
[-dé¹] *s.* milieu de la journée; midi, m.

noose [nous] *s.* nœud coulant; lacet,
m.; *v.* prendre au lacet; nouer.

nor [naur, n°r] *conj.* ni; *neither... nor,*
ni... ni; *nor he either,* ni lui non plus.

norm [naurm] *s.* norme, f. || **normal**
[-'l] *adj.* normal; *s.* normale, f.;
normalcy, normality, normalité; **nor-
malization,** normalisation. || **nor-
malize** [-la¹z] *v.* normaliser.

Norman [naum°n] *adj., s.* normand;
Normandy, Normandie, f.

north [naurth] *s.* nord, m.; *north
star,* étoile Polaire; *north pole,* pôle
Nord; *north wind,* aquilon, f.; *north-
east* [-ïst] *adj., s.* nord-est; *adv.* direc-
tion nord-est. || **northern** [naurzhe°rn]
adj. du nord, septentrional; *northern
lights,* aurore boréale. || **northerner**
[-°r] *s.* nordique, habitant du Nord, m.
|| **northward** [naurthw°rd] *adv.* vers le
nord. || **northwest** [-wèst] *adj., s.* nord-
ouest; **northwestern** [-wèst°rn] *adj.*
du nord-ouest.

Norway [naurwé¹] *s.* Norvège, f. ||
Norwegian [naurwidj°n] *adj., s.* nor-
végien.

nose [noᵒuz] *s.* nez; museau; bec
(techn.), m.; *nose dive,* piqué (aviat.);
to nose down, piquer du nez (aviat.);
to nose around, fouiner.

nosegay [noᵒuzgé¹] *s.* bouquet, m.

nostalgia [nâstaldji°] *s.* nostalgie, f.
|| **nostalgic** [-djik] *adj.* nostalgique.

nostril [nâstr°l] *s.* narine, f.; naseau, m.

nosy [noᵒuzi] *adj.* fouinard.

not [nât] *adv.* ne... pas; non; pas;
point; *not at all,* pas du tout; *if not,*
sinon; *not but that,* non pas que.

notable [noᵒut°b'l] *adj.* notable;
considérable; remarquable; *s.* notable, m.; **notableness,** notabilité.

notary [noᵒut°ri] *s.* notaire, m.

notation [noᵒuté¹sh°n] *s.* notation, f.

notch [nâtsh] *s.* entaille; coche;
dent [wheel]; brèche, f.; cran, m.;
v. entailler; denteler; créneler; cocher.

note [noᵒut] *s.* note; lettre; remarque; annotation; marque, facture, f.;
bulletin; billet; ton (mus.), m.; *v.*
noter; remarquer; indiquer; *bank-
note,* billet de banque; *promissory
note,* billet à ordre; *to take note of,*
prendre note de, acte de; *notebook,*
carnet, calepin, *note paper,* papier à
lettres, **noteworthiness,** importance;
noteworthy, notable. || **noted** [-id]
adj. remarquable; distingué, renommé.

nothing [nœthing] *s.* rien, m.; *pron.*
rien, rien de; *adv.* en rien, rien, pas
du tout; *to do nothing but,* ne faire
que; *to come to nothing,* n'aboutir à
rien.

notice [noᵒutis] *s.* notice; notification;
affiche; observation; mention, f.; avis;
avertissement; congé, m.; *v.* prêter
attention à; remarquer; observer;
mentionner; prendre connaissance de;
to come into notice, se faire connaître;
to give notice, informer; donner congé;
at a day's notice, du jour au lendemain; *to attract notice,* se faire
remarquer; *without notice,* sans avertissement; *notice-board,* tableau d'affi-
chage, *Fr. Can.* babillard. || **noticeable**
[-°b'l] *adj.* remarquable; perceptible.
|| **notification** [noᵒutifiké¹sh°n] *s.* no-
tification, f.; avis, m. || **notify** [noᵒu-
t°fa¹] *v.* notifier; aviser; informer.

notion [noᵒush°n] *s.* notion; idée;
opinion; fantaisie, f.; *pl. Am.* mercerie; bimbeloterie, f.; *Am. notions
shop,* mercerie. || **notional** [-'l] *adj.*
imaginaire; spéculatif; *Am.* capricieux.

notoriety [noᵒut°ra¹eti] *s.* notoriété,
f. || **notorious** [noᵒutoᵒuri°s] *adj.*
notoire; insigne.

notwithstanding [nâtwithstânding]
prep. nonobstant; malgré; *conj.* bien
que; en dépit de; quoique; *adv.*
cependant, néanmoins.

nougat [nougâ] *s.* nougat, m.

nought, *see* **naught.**

noun [naᵒun] *s.* nom, substantif, m.

nourish [në¹ish] *v.* nourrir; alimen-
ter; fomenter; entretenir. || **nourishing**
[-ing] *adj.* nourrissant, nutritif. || **nou-
rishment** [-m°nt] *s.* nourriture; alimentation; nutrition, f.

novel [nâv'l] *s.* roman, m.; *adj.* nou-
veau; récent; original. || **novelette**
[-'t] *s.* nouvelle, f. || **novelist** [-ist]

s. romancier, m. ‖ **novelty** [-ti] s.*
nouveauté ; innovation, f.

November [noᵒᵘvèmbᵉʳ] s. novembre, m.

novena [novinᵉ] s. neuvaine, f.

novice [nâvis] s. novice, m. f. ‖ **novi-
ciate** [noᵒᵘvìshiit] s. noviciat, m.

now [naᵒᵘ] adv. maintenant ; actuellement ; or ; now... now, tantôt... tantôt ; right now, tout de suite ; between
now and then, d'ici là ; till now, jusqu'ici ; he left just now, il vient de
partir ; nowadays, de nos jours.

nowhere [noᵒᵘhwèᵉʳ] adv. nulle part.

nowise [noᵒᵘwa¹z] adv. nullement.

noxious [nâkshᵉs] adj. nuisible ;
nocif ; malsain ; malfaisant. ‖ **noxious-
ness** [-nis] s. nocivité, f.

nozzle [nâz'l] s. lance, f. ; nez, bec
(techn.) ; embout (mech.) ; gicleur, m.

nubile [nyoubil] adj. nubile.

nuclear [nyoukliᵉʳ] adj. nucléaire ;
atomique. ‖ **nucleus** [-kliᵉs] (pl. nu-
clei [-a¹]) s. nucléus ; noyau, m.

nude [nyoud] adj., s. nu.

nudge [nᵉdj] s. coup de coude, m. ;
v. pousser du coude.

nudism [nyoudiz'm] s. nudisme, m. ‖
nudist [-ist] s. nudiste, m. f. ‖ **nudity**
[-ti] s. nudité, f.

nugatory [nyougᵉtoᵒᵘri] adj. frivole,
futile ; vain, inefficace.

nugget [nᵉgit] s. pépite, f.

nuisance [nyoᵘs'ns] s. désagrément ;
ennui ; fléau ; dommage (jur.), m. ;
contravention (jur.), f.

null [nᵉl] adj. nul, nulle ; nul and
void, nul et non avenu. ‖ **nullify**
[-efa¹] v. annuler. ‖ **nullity** [-eti] s.*
nullité, f.

numb [nᵉm] adj. engourdi ; v. engourdir. ‖ **numbness** [-nis] s. engourdissement, m.

number [nᵉmbᵉʳ] s. nombre ; chiffre ; numéro ; v. numéroter ; compter ;
six in number, au nombre de six ;
number-card, dossard. ‖ **numbering**

[-ring] s. calcul ; numérotage, m. ‖
numberless [-lis] adj. innombrable.

numeral [nyoumrᵉl] s. chiffre ; nom
de nombre, m. ; adj. numéral. ‖ **numerary** [-ᵉri] adj. numéraire. ‖ **numer-
ation** [nyoumᵉreᵉshᵉn] s. numération,
f. ‖ **numerical** [nyoumèrik'l] adj.
numérique. ‖ **numerous** [nyoumrᵉs]
adj. nombreux.

numskull [nᵉmskœl] s. imbécile,
crétin, m.

nun [nᵉn] s. nonne, religieuse, f.

nuncio [nᵉnshioᵒᵘ] s. nonce, m.

nunnery [nᵉnᵉri] s.* couvent, m.

nuptial [nᵉpshᵉl] adj. nuptial ; s. pl.
noce, f.

nurse [nëʳs] s. garde-malade ; infir-
mière ; bonne d'enfant ; nourrice, f. ;
v. soigner ; allaiter ; dorloter ; se bercer de [illusion] ; **nurse-child**, nourrisson ; **nursemaid**, bonne d'enfant ;
male nurse, infirmier. ‖ **nursery** [-ri]
s.* nursery ; pépinière, f. ; **nursery-
school**, école maternelle. ‖ **nursling**
[-ling] s. nourrisson, m.

nurture [nëʳtshᵉʳ] s. nourriture ; alimentation ; éducation, f. ; v. nourrir ;
élever.

nut [nᵉt] s. noix ; noisette, f. ; écrou ;
Am. toqué (fam.), m. ; **chestnut**, châtaigne ; **doughnut**, beignet ; **nut-
cracker**, casse-noisettes ; **nutmeg**, muscade ; **nut-oil**, huile de noix ; **union-
nut**, écrou-raccord.

nutria [nyoutriᵉ] s. ragondin, castor
du Chili, m.

nutriment [nyoutrᵉmᵉnt] s. nourriture, f. ‖ **nutrition** [nyoutrìshᵉn] s.
nutrition, f. ‖ **nutritious** [-trìshᵉs] adj.
nourrissant. ‖ **nutritive** [nyoutritiv]
adj. nutritif.

nutshell [nᵉtshᵉl] s. coquille de noix ;
in a nutshell, en un mot.

nuzzle [nᵉz'l] v. frotter ; fouiner ;
fouiller avec le groin ; renifler, flairer ;
se blottir.

nylon [na¹lân] s. Nylon, m.

nymph [nìmf] s. nymphe, f.

O

oak [oᵒᵘk] s. chêne, rouvre, m. ; holm
oak, yeuse ; **oaken**, en chêne ; **oakling**,
jeune chêne.

oakum [oᵒᵘkᵉm] s. étoupe ; filasse, f.

oar [oᵒᵘr] s. rame, f. ; aviron, m. ; v.
ramer ; **oarlock**, porte-rame ; **oarsman**,
rameur.

oasis [oᵒᵘé¹sis] (pl. oases) s. oasis, f.

oat, oats [oᵒᵘt, oᵒᵘts] s. avoine, f.

oath [oᵒᵘth] s. serment ; juron ;
Fr. Can. blasphème, sacre, m. ; to
administer oath, faire prêter serment.

oatmeal [oᵒᵘtmîl] s. farine d'avoine, f.

obedience [ᵉbìdiᵉns] s. obéissance ;
soumission, f. ‖ **obedient** [-diᵉnt] adj.
obéissant.

obelisk [âb'lisk] s. obélisque, m.

obesity [oᵒᵘbìsᵉti] s. obésité, f.

obey [ebé¹] v. obéir (à).

object [ábdjikt] s. objet; but; complément (gramm.), m.; chose, f.; [ebdjèkt] v. objecter; désapprouver. ‖ **objection** [-shen] s. objection; opposition; aversion, f.; inconvénient, m. ‖ **objective** [-tiv] adj. objectif; s. objectif; but, m. ‖ **objectivity** [-tiviti] s. objectivité, f. ‖ **objector** [ebdjèkter] s. objecteur; protestataire; contradicteur, m.

obligate [ábleg⁶é¹t] v. obliger. ‖ **obligation** [áblegé¹shen] s. obligation, f.; devoir; engagement, m. ‖ **obligatory** [aublige¹tri] adj. obligatoire. ‖ **oblige** [ebla¹dj] v. obliger; forcer; rendre service; *much obliged!*, merci beaucoup! ‖ **obliging** [-ing] adj. obligeant, serviable; *obligingness*, obligeance.

oblique [eblîk] adj. oblique; en biais; de côté.

obliterate [eblit⁶ré¹t] v. rayer; oblitérer. ‖ **obliteration** [eblit⁶ré¹shen] s. rature; oblitération, f.

oblivion [eblîvien] s. oubli, m. ‖ **oblivious** [-vies] adj. oublieux; ignorant (*of*, de).

obnoxious [ebnákshes] adj. odieux; détestable; antipathique.

oboe [o⁰ubo⁰u] s. hautbois, m.

obscene [ebsîn] adj. osé, grossier; obscène. ‖ **obscenity** [ebsèneti] s.° obscénité; grossièreté, f.

obscuration [ábskyouré¹shen] s. obscurcissement, m. ‖ **obscure** [ebskyour] adj. obscur; sombre; caché; v. obscurcir. ‖ **obscurity** [-ti] s.° obscurité, f.

obsequies [ábsikwiz] s. pl. obsèques, funérailles, f. pl. ‖ **obsequious** [ebsîkwies] adj. obséquieux.

observable [ebzĕrveb'l] adj. observable. ‖ **observance** [-vens] s. observance; pratique; conformité, f. ‖ **observant** [-vent] adj. attentif; observateur; fidèle. ‖ **observation** [aubzĕrvé¹shen] s. observation; surveillance; remarque, f. ‖ **observatory** [ebzĕrveto⁰uri] s.° observatoire, m. ‖ **observe** [ebzĕrv] v. observer; noter; apercevoir; célébrer [feast]. ‖ **observer** [-er] s. observateur, m.; observatrice, f.

obsess [ebsès] v. obséder. ‖ **obsession** [ebsèshen] s. obsession, f.; *obsessionist*, obsédé; *obsessive*, obsessif.

obsolete [ábselît] adj. vieilli; inusité; hors d'usage.

obstacle [ábstek'l] s. obstacle; empêchement, m.; difficulté, f.

obstinacy [ábsten⁶si] s. obstination, f. ‖ **obstinate** [ábstenit] adj. obstiné, opiniâtre.

obstruct [ebstrækt] v. obstruer; barrer; encombrer; empêcher. ‖

obstruction [ebstrækshen] s. obstruction, f.; obstacle; encombrement; empêchement, m.; *obstructionism*, obstructionnisme.

obtain [ebté¹n] v. obtenir; réussir; gagner; se procurer; être le cas (*with*, pour); *obtainable*, disponible; trouvable.

obtrude [obtroud] v. mettre en avant; *to obtrude on*, s'imposer auprès de.

obtrusive [ebtro⁰usiv] adj. importun.

obturate [ábtyouré¹t] v. obturer; *obturation*, obturation; *obturator*, obturateur.

obtuse [ebtous] adj. obtus.

obviate [ábvié¹t] v. obvier à.

obvious [ábvies] adj. évident, manifeste; visible, palpable; *obviousness*, évidence.

ocarina [ák⁶rîn⁶] s. ocarina, m.

occasion [eké¹jen] s. occasion; cause, raison, f.; besoin; sujet, m.; v. occasionner; déterminer; provoquer. ‖ **occasional** [-'l] adj. occasionnel; fortuit; peu fréquent; intermittent. ‖ **occasionally** [-'li] adv. à l'occasion; de temps en temps; parfois.

occident [áksidént] s. occident, m. ‖ **occidental** [áksedènt'l] adj., s. occidental.

occlude [okloud] v. fermer; **occlusion**, occlusion.

occult [ekælt] adj. occulte; *occultism*, occultisme; *occultist*, occultiste.

occupant [ákyepent] s. occupant, m. ‖ **occupation** [ákyepé¹shen] s. occupation; profession, f. ‖ **occupy** [ákyepa¹] v. occuper; employer; habiter; posséder.

occur [ekĕr] v. arriver; survenir; avoir lieu. ‖ **occurrence** [-ens] s. occurrence, f.; fait, événement, m.

ocean [o⁰ushen] s. océan, m.; adj. océanique; au long cours; *Am.* par mer; *oceanic*, océanique.

ochre [o⁰uke] s. ocre, f.

octave [ákté¹v] s. octave, f.

October [ákto⁰ub⁶r] s. octobre, m.

octopus [auktopes] s. pieuvre, f.

ocular [ákyouler] adj., s. oculaire. ‖ **oculist** [ákye¹list] s. oculiste, m.

odd [ád] adj. dépareillé; étrange; drôle; original; impair [number]; irrégulier, divers; s. pl. inégalité, disparité, chances, f.; *twenty odd*, vingt et quelques; *odd moments*, moments perdus; *the odds are that*, il y a gros à parier que; *to be at odds with*, être brouillé avec. ‖ **oddity** [ád⁶ti] s.° bizarrerie, f.

ode [o⁰ud] s. ode, f.

odious [o°udi°s] adj. odieux.

odo(u)r [o°ud°r] s. odeur, f.; **odorous**, odorant, parfumé; **odourless**, inodore.

of [ăv, °v] prep. de; du; de la; des; à; sur; en; parmi; *what do you do of an evening?*, que faites-vous le soir?; *of necessity*, nécessairement; *to have the advantage of*, avoir l'avantage sur; *Am. a quarter of three*, trois heures moins le quart.

off [auf] adv. au loin; à distance; adj. enlevé; parti; interj. oust!; hors d'ici!; *hats off!*, chapeaux bas!; *off with!*, enlevez, ôtez; *off and on*, de temps à autre; *I'm off*, je me sauve; *two miles off*, à deux milles de là; *to be well off*, être à l'aise; *a day off*, un jour de congé; **offcenter**, décalé, décentré; **off-shore**, au large, du côté de la terre.

offend [°fĕnd] v. offenser; froisser; enfreindre. ‖ **offender** [-°r] s. délinquant; malfaiteur; coupable, m.; *joint offender*, complice. ‖ **offense** [°fĕns] s. offense; infraction; contravention; offensive (mil.); délit, m.; *to take offense*, s'offenser; *continuing offense*, récidive. ‖ **offensive** [-iv] adj. offensant, choquant; offensif; s. offensive, f.

offer [auf°r] v. (s')offrir; (se) présenter; s. offre; proposition, f. ‖ **offering** [-ring] s. offrande, f. ‖ **offertory** [auf°rtoouri] s.* offertoire, m.

offhand [aufhănd] adv. au premier abord; sur-le-champ; adj. improvisé; dégagé; cavalier.

office [aufis] s. fonction; charge, f.; bureau; office; emploi; service, m.; *to take office*, entrer en fonctions; prendre le pouvoir; *booking office*, guichet des billets; *doctor's office*, cabinet médical; *lawyer's office*, étude d'avocat; *main office*, siège social (comm.). ‖ **officer** [auf°s°r] s. officier; fonctionnaire, employé, m.; *sanitation officer*, officier de santé; v. commander; encadrer d'officiers; **officering**, encadrement; commandement. ‖ **official** [°fish°l] adj. officiel; titulaire; s. fonctionnaire, employé, m.; **officialdom**, bureaucratie, fonctionnarisme. ‖ **officiate** [°fishi°it] v. officier. ‖ **officious** [-sh°s] adj. officieux; importun, trop empressé.

offing [aufing] s. large, m.; *in the offing*, en perspective.

offish [aufish] adj. distant.

offset [aufsĕt] v. compenser; [aufsĕt] s. compensation (comm.); offset (impr.); rejeton, m.

offspring [aufspring] s. progéniture; conséquence, f.; descendant; résultat; produit (fig.), m.

offtake [auftè¹k] s. écoulement, m.

oft, often [auft, auf°n] adv. souvent; fréquemment; *how often?*, combien de fois?

ogive [o°udja¹v] s. ogive, f.

ogle [o°ug'l] s. œillade, f.; v. lorgner.

ogre [o°ug°r] s. ogre, m.

oil [o¹l] s. huile, f.; pétrole brut, m.; v. huiler; graisser; lubrifier; oindre; *fuel oil*, mazout; *linseed oil*, huile de lin; **oil-cloth**, toile cirée; **oil-painting**, peinture à l'huile; *oil of turpentine*, essence de térébenthine. ‖ **oily** [-i] adj. huileux; graisseux; onctueux.

ointment [o¹ntm°nt] s. onguent, m.; pommade, f.

O. K. [o°ukĕ¹] interj. d'accord, parfait, très bien.

old [o°uld] adj. vieux, vieil, vieille; âgé; *old man*, vieillard; *of old*, jadis; *how old are you?*, quel âge avez-vous?; *to grow old*, vieillir; **old-fashioned**, démodé; **old-time**, d'autrefois; **old-timer**, vieux routier. ‖ **oldness** [-nis] s. vieillesse; vétusté, f.

oleander [o°uliănd°r] s. laurier-rose, m.

olive [ăliv] s., adj. olive; *olive oil*, huile d'olive; *olive drab*, drap gris olive réglementaire pour uniforme; **olive-tree**, olivier.

omelet [ămlit] s. omelette, f.

omen [o°umin] s. signe, présage, augure, m.; **ominous**, sinistre, menaçant, inquiétant.

omission [o°umish°n] s. omission; négligence, f.; oubli; manquement, m. ‖ **omit** [o°umit] v. omettre; oublier; négliger.

omnibus [ămnib°s] s. autobus; car, m.; adj. omnibus.

omnipotent [ămnip°t°nt] adj. omnipotent, tout-puissant.

omniscient [ămnisj°nt] adj. omniscient.

omoplate [o°umoplè¹t] s. omoplate, f.

on [ăn] prep. sur; à; en; de; contre; avec; pour; dès; adv. dessus; *on horseback*, à cheval; *on leave*, en congé; *on this account*, pour cette raison; *on her opening the door*, dès qu'elle ouvrit la porte; *and so on*, ainsi de suite; *the light is on*, la lumière est allumée.

once [wŏns] adv. une fois; jadis; *at once*, tout de suite, à la fois; *all at once*, tout d'un coup; *when once*, une fois que; *once in a while*, une fois en passant; *Am. to give the once over*, jeter un coup d'œil scrutateur.

one [wŏn] adj., pron. un, une; *one day*, un certain jour; *someone*, quelqu'un; *anyone*, n'importe qui; *everyone*, tout le monde; *one and all*, tous sans exception; *one by one*, un à un; *one another*, l'un l'autre; *the one who*, celui qui; *this one*, celui-ci; *one-armed*, manchot; *one-eyed*, borgne; *one-price*, à prix unique; *one-way*, à sens unique.

onerous [ǎn°r°s] *adj.* onéreux; lourd.

oneself [wœnsèlf] *pron.* soi, soi-même; *by oneself*, seul.

onion [œny°n] *s.* oignon, m.

onlooker [ǎnlouk°r] *s.* spectateur, assistant; participant, m.

only [o°unli] *adj.* seul, unique; *adv.* seulement, uniquement; *she is only five*, elle n'a que cinq ans; *he only laughs*, il ne fait que rire; *only yesterday*, hier encore.

onset [ǎnsèt] *s.* assaut, m.; attaque; impulsion, f.; *at the onset*, au premier abord.

onslaught [ǎnslaut] *s.* attaque furieuse, f.

onward [ǎnw°rd] *adv.* en avant.

onyx [ǎniks] *s.* onyx, m.

ooze [ouz] *s.* vase, boue, f.; suintement, m.; *v.* suinter; transpirer [news].

opal [o°up'l] *s.* opale, f.; *opalin*, opalin, opaline.

opaque [o°upé¹k] *adj.* opaque.

open [o°up°n] *v.* (s')ouvrir; exposer; révéler; *adj.* ouvert; découvert; exposé; franc; *wide open*, grand ouvert; *an open truth*, une vérité évidente; *open market*, marché public; *to open up*, ouvrir, dévoiler; *the door opens into the garden*, la porte donne sur le jardin; *half-open*, entrouvert; *open secret*, secret de Polichinelle; *open-handed*, libéral, généreux; *open-minded*, libéral, réceptif; *open-mouthed*, bouche bée; *in the open*, en rase campagne; *to lay oneself open to*, s'exposer à. ‖ **opening** [-ing] *s.* ouverture; embouchure; inauguration; percée, f.; débouché; orifice; déclenchement; vernissage; début, m.; *adj.* naissant; débutant; premier; *opening statement*, discours d'ouverture. ‖ **openly** [-li] *adv.* ouvertement; publiquement; carrément.

opera [ǎp°r°] *s.* opéra, m.; *opera-glass*, jumelles; *comic opera*, opéra-comique.

operate [ǎp°ré¹t] *v.* opérer; spéculer; manœuvrer; commander (mech.). ‖ **operation** [ǎp°ré¹sh°n] *s.* opération; exécution, f.; fonctionnement, m.; *to be in operation*, fonctionner; *in full operation*, en pleine activité. ‖ **operative** [ǎp°ré¹tiv] *adj.* actif; efficace; opératoire; *s.* ouvrier, m. ‖ **operator** [ǎp°ré¹t°r] *s.* opérateur, m.

operetta [ǎp°rèt°] *s.* opérette, f.

ophtalmic [ǎfthalmík] *adj.* ophtalmique. ‖ **ophtalmologist** [-mǎl°djist] *s.* ophtalmologiste, m. f.

opine [opa¹n] *v.* opiner; penser. ‖ **opinion** [°píny°n] *s.* opinion, f.; avis, m.; décision motivée (jur.), f.; **opinionated**, opiniâtre.

opiomaniac [o°upiomé¹ni°k] *s.* opiomane, m. f. ‖ **opium** [o°upi°m] *s.* opium, m.

opponent [°po°un°nt] *s.* adversaire; opposant; antagoniste, m.

opportune [ǎp°rtyoun] *adj.* opportun; à propos. ‖ **opportuneness** [-nis] *s.* opportunité, f.; **opportunism**, opportunisme; **opportunist**, opportuniste. ‖ **opportunity** [-°ti] *s.°* occasion, f.

oppose [°po°uz] *v.* (s')opposer; combattre; arrêter, empêcher. ‖ **opposing** [-ing] *adj.* opposé, contraire. ‖ **opposite** [ǎp°zit] *adj.* opposé; contraire; vis-à-vis; de front; *s.* contraire, adversaire, m.; *opposite to*, en face de. ‖ **opposition** [ǎp°zish°n] *s.* opposition; résistance; concurrence; hostilité, f.; parti adverse, m.

oppress [°près] *v.* opprimer; oppresser. ‖ **oppression** [°prèsh°n] *s.* oppression, f. ‖ **oppressive** [°prèsiv] *adj.* opprimant; accablant, étouffant, angoissant; tyrannique. ‖ **oppressor** [°près°r] *s.* oppresseur, m.

opprobrious [°pro°ubri°s] *adj.* infamant, injurieux. ‖ **opprobrium** [-bri°m] *s.* opprobre, m.

opt [ǎpt] *v.* opter.

optical [ǎptik'l] *adj.* optique. ‖ **optician** [ǎptish°n] *s.* opticien, m. ‖ **optics** [ǎptiks] *s. pl.* optique.

optimism [ǎpt°miz°m] *s.* optimisme m. ‖ **optimist** [-mist] *s.* optimiste, m. ‖ **optimistic** [ǎpt°místik] *adj.* optimiste.

option [ǎpsh°n] *s.* option; alternative, f.; choix, m. ‖ **optional** [-'l] *adj.* facultatif.

opulence [ǎpy°l°ns] *s.* opulence; abondance, f. ‖ **opulent** [-l°nt] *adj.* opulent; riche; abondant.

opuscule [ǎpæskyoul] *s.* opuscule, m.

or [aur, °r] *conj.* ou, ou bien; soit; *or else*, ou bien; autrement; sinon.

oracle [aur°k'l] *s.* oracle, m.

oral [o°ur°l] *adj.* oral.

orange [aurindj] *s.* orange, f.; *orange blossom*, fleur d'oranger; *orange-tree*, oranger; *adj.* orangé [color]; *orangeade*, orangeade.

oration [o°uré¹sh°n] *s.* discours, m.; harangue, f. ‖ **orator** [aur°t°r] *s.* orateur, m. ‖ **oratory** [aur°too°uri] *s.°* éloquence, f.; oratoire, m.

orb [aurb] *s.* globe; cercle, m.; orbe, f. ‖ **orbit** [aurbit] *s.* orbite, orbe, f.; *v.* tourner autour de; *orbital,* orbital; orbitaire; de ceinture.

orchard [aurtsherd] *s.* verger, m.

orchestra [aurkistr*] *s.* orchestre, m. ‖ **orchestrate** [-tré¹t] *v.* orchestrer. ‖ **orchestration** [ârkestré¹shen] *s.* orchestration, f.

orchid [aurkid] *s.* orchidée, f.

ordain [aurdé¹n] *v.* ordonner; décréter; déterminer, fixer. ‖ **ordainer** [-er] *s.* ordonnateur; ordinant (eccles.), m.

ordeal [aurdîl] *s.* épreuve, f.; jugement de Dieu, m.

order [aurder] *s.* ordre; mandat (fin.), m.; consigne; ordonnance; commande; décoration, f.; *v.* ordonner; commander; diriger; régler; arranger; *to break an order,* manquer à la consigne; *citation in orders,* citation à l'ordre du jour; *counter-order,* contrordre; *executive order,* décretloi; *full marching order,* tenue de campagne; *holy orders,* ordres sacrés; *order-blank,* bon de commande; *made to order,* fait sur commande, fait à mesure [suit]; *in order that,* afin que; *to be out of order,* être détraqué, en panne. ‖ **orderly** [-li] *adj.* ordonné; discipliné; *s.* ordonnance (mil.), f.; planton, m.; infirmier, m. ‖ **ordinance** [aurd'n•ns] *s.* ordonnance (jur.), f.; décret, m. ‖ **ordinarily** [-'nèr•li] *adv.* ordinairement. ‖ **ordinary** [-'nèri] *adj.* ordinaire, commun, habituel. ‖ **ordnance** [-n•ns] *s.* artillerie, f.; matériel de guerre, m.

ore [o°ur] *s.* minerai, m.

organ [aurg•n] *s.* orgue; organe, m.; *hand organ,* orgue de Barbarie. ‖ **organic** [aurganik] *adj.* organique; fondamental. ‖ **organism** [aurg•niz•m] *s.* organisme, m. ‖ **organist** [-nist] *s.* organiste, m. ‖ **organization** [aurg•nzé¹shen] *s.* organisation, f.; agencement, aménagement; organisme, m. ‖ **organize** [aurg•na¹z] *v.* (s')organiser. ‖ **organizer** [-er] *s.* organisateur, m.; organisatrice, f.

orgy [aurdji] *s.* orgie, f.

orient [o°uriènt] *s.* orient, m.; *v.* orienter. ‖ **oriental** [o°urièntl] *adj., s.* oriental. ‖ **orientate** [o°urièntê¹t] *v.* orienter. ‖ **orientation** [o°urièntê¹shen] *s.* orientation, f.

orifice [aurefis] *s.* orifice, m.; ouverture, f.

origin [aur•djin] *s.* origine; provenance, f. ‖ **original** [•ridj•n'l] *adj., s.* original. ‖ **originality** [•ridj•nal•ti] *s.** originalité, f. ‖ **originally** [•ridj•n'li] *adv.* primitivement; originalement. ‖ **originate** [•ridj•né¹t] *v.* faire naître;

produire; inventer; provenir; dériver. ‖ **originator** [-er] *s.* créateur, promoteur; point de départ, m.

orison [áriz•n] *s.* oraison, f.

ornament [aurn•m•nt] *s.* ornement, m.; parure, f.; [aurn•mènt] *v.* ornementer, décorer. ‖ **ornamental** [aurn•mènt'l] *adj.* ornemental, décoratif. ‖ **ornamentation** [ârn•mènté¹shen] *s.* ornementation, f.; embellissement, m. ‖ **ornament** [â•n•mènt•r] *s.* décorateur, m. ‖ **ornate** [aurné¹t] *adj.* paré, ornementé; fleuri [style].

ornithology [aunithaul•dji] *s.* ornithologie, f.

orphan [aurf•n] *adj., s.* orphelin, m.; *v.* rendre orphelin; *orphan asylum, orphanage,* orphelinat.

orris [auris] *s.* iris, m.

orthography [aurthâgr•fi] *s.** orthographe, f.

orthopaedics [â•thopîdiks] *s.* orthopédie, f.

ortolan [â•t•l•n] *s.* ortolan, m.

oscillate [âs'lé¹t] *v.* osciller; balancer; s'affoler [compass]. ‖ **oscillation** [âs'lé¹sh•n] *s.* oscillation, f.

osier [ouj•r] *s.* osier, m.; *osiery,* oseraie; vannerie.

ossify [âs•fa¹] *v.* ossifier.

ostensible [âstèns•b'l] *adj.* ostensible. ‖ **ostentation** [âst•nté¹shen] *s.* ostentation, f. ‖ **ostentatious** [-shes] *adj.* ostentatoire; vaniteux.

ostracism [âstr•siz'm] *s.* ostracisme, m. ‖ **ostracize** [-sa¹z] *v.* frapper d'ostracisme.

ostrich [austritsh] *s.** autruche, f.

otary [o°ut•ri] *s.* otarie, f.

other [œzh•r] *adj., pron.* autre; *s.* autrui; *every other day,* tous les deux jours; *the two others,* les deux autres; *other than,* autre que. ‖ **otherwise** [-wa¹z] *adv.* autrement; par ailleurs; à part cela; sous d'autres rapports; sinon.

otter [ât•r] *s.* loutre, f.

ought [aut] *defect. v.* devoir; *he ought to say,* il devrait dire.

ounce [a°uns] *s.* once, f.

our [a°ur] *adj.* notre, nos. ‖ **ours** [-z] *pron.* le nôtre, la nôtre, les nôtres. ‖ **ourselves** [-sèlvz] *pron.* nous-mêmes; nous.

oust [a°ust] *v.* expulser, chasser.

out [a°ut] *adv.* hors; dehors; *adj.* découvert; disparu; exposé; éteint; *prep.* hors de; *out of fear,* par crainte; *out of money,* sans argent; *out of print,* épuisé [book]; *out with it!,* expliquez-vous!; *to speak out,* parler clairement; *out of breath,* à bout de souffle ; *out and out*, absolu, avéré; *the week is out*, la semaine est achevée ; *the secret is out*, le secret est divulgué ; *he is out*, il est sorti ; *he is out five dollars*, cela lui a coûté cinq dollars, il a fait une erreur de cinq dollars.

outbreak [aᵒutbréⁱk] *s.* éruption, f.; soulèvement, tumulte, m.

outburst [aᵒutbërst] *s.* explosion; éruption, f.

outcast [aᵒutkast] *adj.* exclus; *s.* proscrit, paria, m.

outcome [aᵒutkœm] *s.* résultat; dénouement, m.

outcry [aᵒutkraⁱ] *s.*˙ clameur, f.

outdoor [aᵒutdoᵒur] *adj.* extérieur; externe ; de plein air [game]. ǁ *outdoors* [-z] *adv.* en plein air ; au-dehors.

outer [aᵒutᵉr] *adj.* extérieur; externe; du dehors; *outermost*, extrême.

outfit [aᵒutfit] *s.* équipement; attirail; outillage; trousseau, m.; *v.* équiper.

outing [aᵒuting] *s.* excursion, sortie, promenade, f.

outlaw [aᵒutlau] *s.* bandit; proscrit; fugitif, m.; *v.* proscrire.

outlay [aᵒutléⁱ] *s.* débours, m.; dépense, f.; [aᵒutléⁱ] *v.* dépenser, débourser.

outlet [aᵒutlèt] *s.* sortie; issue, f.; débouché, m.

outline [aᵒutlaⁱn] *s.* contour; sommaire ; tracé, m.; esquisse, f.; *v.* esquisser, ébaucher; tracer.

outlive [aᵒutlív] *v.* survivre à.

outlook [aᵒutlouk] *s.*˙ guet, m.; perspective, f.

outlying [aᵒutlaⁱing] *adj.* détaché, isolé; écarté.

outmaneuver [aᵒutmᵉnoᵘvᵉr] *v.* déjouer; tromper; rouler (fam.).

outnumber [aᵒutnœmbᵉr] *v.* surpasser en nombre.

outpost [aᵒutpoᵒust] *s.* avantposte, m.

output [aᵒutpout] *s.* rendement, m.; production, puissance, f.

outrage [aᵒutréⁱdj] *s.* outrage; attentat, m.; *v.* outrager; violenter. ǁ *outrageous* [aᵒutréⁱdjᵉs] *adj.* outrageux; outrageant; atroce; exorbitant.

outran [aᵒutræn] *pret. of to* outrun. ǁ *outrun* [aᵒutrœn] *v.* gagner de vitesse; dépasser à la course; *outrunner*, avant-coureur.

outset [aᵒutsèt] *s.* début, commencement, m.; ouverture, f.; *from the outset*, dès le premier abord.

outshine [aᵒutshaⁱn] *v.* éclipser en éclat. ǁ *outshone* [aᵒutshoᵒun] *pret., p. p. of to* outshine.

outside [aᵒutsaⁱd] *adj.* extérieur; externe; *adv.* dehors, à l'extérieur; *prep.* à l'extérieur de, au-dehors de; *s.* extérieur, m. ǁ *outsider* [-ᵉr] *s.* étranger; profane; outsider [sport]; ailier; coulissier (fin.), m.

outskirts [aᵒutskërts] *s. pl.* lisière, f.

outspoken [aᵒutspoᵒukᵉn] *adj.* franc, direct; explicite.

outspread [aᵒutsprèd] *adj.* déployé; *s.* déploiement, m.

outstanding [aᵒutstanding] *adj.* notable; saillant; non payé (comm.).

outstretched [aᵒutstrètsht] *adj.* étendu; tendu [arm]; ouvert [hand].

outward(s) [aᵒutwᵉrd(z)] *adj.* extérieur; externe; apparent; superficiel; *adv.* au-dehors; extérieurement; vers le dehors.

outweigh [aᵒutwéⁱ] *v.* excéder en poids, en valeur.

oval [oᵒuv'l] *adj., s.* ovale, m.

ovary [oᵒuvᵉri] *s.*˙ ovaire, m.

ovation [oᵒuvéⁱshᵉn] *s.* ovation, f.

oven [œven] *s.* four, m.

over [oᵒuvᵉr] *prep.* sur; plus de; au-dessus de; *adv.* par-dessus; en plus; *adj.* de dessus; de l'autre côté; *s.* excès, m.; *all over the country*, dans tout le pays; *my life is over*, ma vie est finie; *over there*, là-bas; *overalls*, salopette; *overboard*, par-dessus bord; *overcoat*, pardessus; capote; *overdone*, trop cuit; surmené; épuisé; outré, exagéré; *overdose*, trop forte dose; *overdue*, échu, en souffrance; *overindulgence*, indulgence excessive.

overcame [oᵒuvᵉrkéⁱm] *pret. of to* overcome.

overcast [oᵒuvᵉrkast] *adj.* couvert, nuageux; trop élevé [sum]; [oᵒuvᵉrkast] *v.* assombrir; couvrir de nuages.

overcharge [oᵒuvᵉrtshärdj] *v.* faire payer trop cher; écorcher; saler.

overcome [oᵒuvᵉrkœm] *v.* surmonter; vaincre; conquérir; dominer; accabler; venir à bout de.

overcrowd [oᵒuvᵉrkraᵒud] *v.* remplir excessivement; *overcrowded*, bondé; surpeuplé; *overcrowding*, encombrement; surpeuplement.

overdo [oᵒuvᵉrdou] *v.* exagérer; charger; faire trop cuire; se surmener.

overdraw [oᵒuvᵉrdrau] *v.* mettre à découvert (comm.); tirer un chèque sans provision; trop enjoliver.

overdrive [oᵒuvᵉrdraⁱv] *s.* vitesse surmultipliée, f.; [oᵒuvᵉrdraⁱv] *v.* surmener.

overexcite [oᵒuvᵉriksaⁱt] *v.* surexciter; *overexcitement*, surexcitation, effervescence.

overexert [o⁰uvᵉrigzët] *v.* tendre à l'excès; se surmener; **overexertion,** surmenage.

overflow [o⁰uvᵉrfloᵒu] *s.* inondation, f.; trop-plein, débordement, m.; [o⁰uvᵉrfloᵒu] *v.* inonder, déborder.

overgrown [o⁰uvᵉrgroᵒun] *adj.* énorme; trop grand; dense [leafs]; dégingandé [boy].

overhang [o⁰uvᵉrhang] *v.* surplomber; faire saillie.

overhead [o⁰uvᵉrhèd] *s. pl.* frais généraux (comm.), m. pl.; *adj.* au-dessus, en haut; élevé; [-hèd] *adv.* en haut, au-dessus de la tête.

overhear [o⁰uvᵉrhîᵉr] *v.* surprendre, entendre par hasard. ‖ **overheard** [o⁰uvᵉrhërd] *pret., p. p. of* to overhear.

overheat [o⁰uvᵉrhît] *v.* surchauffer.

overhung [o⁰uvᵉrhœng] *pret., p. p. of* to overhang.

overladen [o⁰uvᵉrlé¹dᵉn] *adj.* surchargé.

overland [o⁰uvᵉrlᵃnd] *adj.* voyageant par terre; de terre; [o⁰uvᵉrlᵃnd] *adv.* par terre.

overlap [o⁰uvᵉrlap] *s.* recouvrement; empiètement, m.; [o⁰uvᵉrlap] *v.* recouvrer; empiéter; chevaucher; dépasser.

overload [o⁰uvᵉrloᵒud] *v.* surcharger; [o⁰uvᵉrloᵒud] *s.* surcharge, f.

overlook [o⁰uvᵉrlouk] *v.* oublier, laisser passer; fermer les yeux sur; parcourir des yeux; donner sur; surveiller.

overman [o⁰uvᵉrmᵉn] *(pl.* overmen) *s.* contremaître, m.

overmatch [o⁰uvᵉrmatsh] *v.* surclasser; avoir l'avantage sur.

overmuch [o⁰uvᵉrmœtsh] *adj.* trop de; *adv.* trop.

overnight [o⁰uvᵉrna¹t] *adv.* (pendant) la nuit; *adj.* de nuit; de la veille au soir.

overpower [o⁰uvᵉrpaᵒuᵉr] *v.* subjuguer; maîtriser; vaincre; accabler.

overprint [o⁰uvᵉrprĭnt] *s.* surimpression; surcharge, f.; *v.* surimprimer; surcharger.

overran [o⁰uvᵉrran] *pret. of* to overrun. ‖ **overrun** [o⁰uvᵉrrœn] *v.** parcourir; se répandre; envahir; inonder.

oversea [o⁰uvᵉrsî] *adj.* d'outre-mer, de l'autre côté de la mer; *pl. adv.* outre-mer.

oversee [o⁰uvᵉrsî] *v.* surveiller. ‖ **overseer** [o⁰uvᵉrsîᵉr] *s.* surveillant, inspecteur, m.

oversensitive [o⁰uvᵉrsènsitiv] *adj.* hypersensible.

oversight [o⁰uvᵉrsa¹t] *s.* négligence, inadvertance; surveillance, f.

overstate [o⁰uvᵉrsté¹t] *v.* exagérer; **overstatement,** exagération.

overstep [o⁰uvᵉrstèp] *v.* dépasser, franchir.

overt [o⁰uvᵉt] *adj.* évident, non déguisé; public.

overtake [o⁰uvᵉrté¹k] *v.* rattraper, rejoindre; doubler [auto]. ‖ **overtaken** [o⁰uvᵉrté¹kᵉn] *p. p. of* to overtake. ‖ **overtaking** [-ing] *s.* dépassement, m.

overthrew [o⁰uvᵉrthrou] *pret. of* to overthrow. ‖ **overthrow** [o⁰uvᵉrthroᵒu] *s.* renversement, m.; ruine, f.; *v.* renverser, culbuter; mettre en déroute. ‖ **overthrown,** *p. p. of* to overthrow.

overtime [o⁰uvᵉrta¹m] *s.* heures supplémentaires, f. pl.

overtook [o⁰uvᵉrtouk] *pret. of* to overtake.

overture [o⁰uvᵉrtshᵉr] *s.* ouverture; proposition, f.; prélude, m.

overturn [o⁰uvᵉrtën] *v.* renverser; verser, capoter [auto]; chavirer (naut.); bouleverser.

overweening [o⁰uvᵉrwîning] *adj.* outrecuidant; insensé [pride].

overweight [o⁰uvᵉrwé¹t] *s.* excédent de poids, de bagages, m.; [o⁰uvᵉrwé¹t] *v.* surcharger.

overwhelm [o⁰uvᵉrhwèlm] *v.* écraser, opprimer; surcharger; submerger. ‖ **overwhelming** [-ing] *adj.* accablant, écrasant; submergeant; irrésistible.

overwork [o⁰uvᵉrwёrk] *v.* (se) surmener; *s.* surmenage, m.

owe [oᵒu] *v.* devoir; être redevable; *to be owing to,* être dû à; *owing to,* à cause de; grâce à.

owl [aᵒul] *s.* chouette, f.; hibou, m.; *screech-owl,* chat-huant.

own [oᵒun] *adj.* propre, à soi; *v.* posséder; avoir en propre; avoir la propriété de; *a house of his own,* une maison à lui; *to hold one's own,* tenir bon.

own [oᵒun] *v.* reconnaître; convenir de, avouer.

owner [oᵒunᵉr] *s.* propriétaire; possesseur, m. ‖ **ownership** [-ship] *s.* propriété; possession, f.

ox [âks] *(pl.* oxen [-n]) *s.* bœuf, m.; *ox-fly,* taon.

oxide [âksa¹d] *s.* oxyde, m. ‖ **oxidize** [âksᵉda¹z] *v.* oxyder.

Oxonian [auksoᵒuniᵉn] *adj.* Oxonien; d'Oxford.

oxygen [âksᵉdjᵉn] *s.* oxygène, m.

oyster [o¹stᵉr] *s.* huître, f.; *oyster-bed,* banc d'huîtres; *oyster-plant,* salsifis.

ozone [ozoᵒun] *s.* ozone, m.; *Am.* air pur, plein air, m.

P

pace [péᵢs] s. pas, m.; allure, f.; v. marcher au pas; arpenter; suivre; *to mend one's pace,* presser le pas.

pacific [pɛsífik] adj., s. pacifique. ‖ *pacification* [pasᵉfeké¹shᵉn] s. pacification, f.; apaisement, m. ‖ *pacify* [pasefa¹] v. pacifier; calmer.

pack [pak] s. paquet, ballot; paquetage; sac, m.; troupe, bande, meute, f.; jeu [cards], m.; v emballer empaqueter; bâter *pack-animal,* bête de somme *pack saddle,* bât; *to pack off,* plier bagages *to send packing,* envoyer promener. ‖ *package* [-idj] s. paquet, colis, m. ‖ *packer* [-ᵉr] s. emballeur, m. ‖ *packet* [-it] s. paquet, m. ‖ *packing* [-ing] s. emballage, empaquetage; bourrage (mech.), m. ‖ *packthread* [-thrèd] s. ficelle, f.

pact [pakt] s. pacte; accord; contrat, m.; convention, f.

pad [pad] s tampon; bourrelet; coussinet, bloc [paper]; plastron [fencing], m.; v rembourrer. ouater, matelasser; *writing-pad,* sous-main, f. ‖ *padding* [-ing] s rembourrage; remplissage, m.

paddle [pad'l] s. pagaie, f., *Fr. Can.* aviron, m.; palette, f.; v. pagayer, ramer, *Fr. Can.* avironner; patauger; *Am.* fesser (fam.); *paddle wheel,* roue à aubes.

paddock [padᵉk] s. paddock, pesage; enclos, m.

padlock [padlâk] s. cadenas, m.; v. cadenasser.

pagan [pé¹gᵉn] adj., s. païen, m. ‖ *paganism* [-izᵉm] s. paganisme, m.

page [pé¹dj] s. page, f.; v. paginer.

page [péidj] s chasseur [boy], m.; v. envoyer chercher par un chasseur (ou) un groom.

pageant [padjᵉnt] s. parade; manifestation, représentation en plein air; revue, f.; spectacle, m.

paid [pé¹d] pret., p. p. of *to pay.*

pail [pé¹l] s. seau, m.

pain [pé¹n] s. douleur; peine; souffrance, f.; v. faire souffrir; affliger; *on pain of,* sous peine de; *to have a pain in,* avoir mal à; *to take pains,* se donner du mal; *pain-killer,* antalgique. ‖ *painful* (-fᵉl] adj. pénible, douloureux, laborieux. ‖ *painless* [-lis] adj. indolore. ‖ *painstaking* [-zté¹king] adj. laborieux, appliqué; s. effort, m.

paint [pé¹nt] s. couleur; peinture, f.; v. peindre, *Fr. Can.* peinturer; *paint-brush,* pinceau; *wet paint,* attention à la peinture. ‖ *painter* [-ᵉr] s. peintre, m. ‖ *painting* [-ing] s. peinture, f.

pair [pèᵉr] s. paire, f.; couple, m.; v. (s')apparier; (s')accoupler; assortir; marier.

pajamas [pᵉdjamᵉz] s. pl. *Am.* pyjama, m.

pal [pal] s. copain, m.

palace [palis] s. palais, m.

palate [palit] s. palais (anat.); goût, m.; *palatable,* savoureux.

palaver [pᵉlâvᵉr] s. palabre, f.; v. palabrer flagorner.

pale [pé¹l] adj. pâle, blême; v. pâlir. ‖ *paleness* [-nis] s. pâleur, f.

palette [palit] s. palette, f.

palisade [palᵉsé¹d] s. palissade; falaise escarpée, f.; v. palissader.

pall [paul] s. vêtement de cérémonie; poêle mortuaire, m.; v. recouvrir, revêtir.

pall [paul] v. s'affadir; s'éventer; s'affaiblir; décourager; blaser; rassasier.

palliate [paliᵉ¹t] v. pallier; atténuer. ‖ *palliative* [paliᵉtiv] adj., s. palliatif.

pallid [palid] adj. pâle, blême. ‖ *pallor* [palᵉr] s pâleur, f.

palm [pâm] s palme, f.; palmier, m.; *Palm Sunday,* dimanche des Rameaux.

palm [pâm] s paume [hand], f.; v. empaumer, tromper; *to palm something off on someone* faire avaler quelque chose à quelqu'un; *palmist,* chiromancien, *palmistry,* chiromancie.

palpable [palpᵉb'l] adj. palpable, tangible.

palpitate [palpᵉté¹t] v. palpiter. ‖ *palpitation* [palpᵉté¹shᵉn] s. palpitation, f.

palsy [paulzi] s.* paralysie, f.

palter [paultᵉr] v. biaiser; marchander; badiner.

paltry [paultri] adj. mesquin; insignifiant chétif.

pamper [pampᵉr] v. choyer, gâter.

pamphlet [pamflit] s. brochure, plaquette, f.; pamphlet; dépliant, m.

pan [pàn] s. casserole; cuvette, f.; bassinet (mech.); carter, m.; *a flash in the pan,* un raté; *to pan out well,* donner de bons résultats; *frying-pan,* poêle.

pancake [pànké¹k] s. crêpe, f.; v. descendre à plat (aviat.).

pancreas [pangkriᵉs] s.* pancréas, m.

pander [pandᵉr] s. entremetteur, m.; v. s'entremettre.

pane [pé¹n] s. carreau, panneau, m.; vitre, f.

panegyric [panidjírik] *s.* panégyrique, m.; *adj.* élogieux.

panel [pan'l] *s.* panneau, lambris, m.; *v.* diviser en panneaux; lambrisser; *code panels*, panneaux de signalisation; *jury panel*, liste des jurés, jury.

pang [pàng] *s.* angoisse, douleur aiguë, f.; affres, f. pl.

panic [panik] *adj.*, *s.* panique, f.; *v.* semer la panique; être pris de panique; *panicky*, alarmiste; paniquard (colloq.).

pansy [pànzi] *s.* pensée [flower], f.

pant [pànt] *v.* haleter, panteler; *to pant for*, aspirer à.

panther [pànth°r] *s.* panthère, f.

panting [pànting] *s.* palpitation, f.; essoufflement, m.; *adj.* pantelant; palpitant.

pantomime [pant°ma¹m] *s.* mime, m.; revue-féerie, f.; *v.* mimer; s'exprimer en pantomime.

pantry [pàntri] *s.* office, m.; dépense, f.

pants [pànts] *s.* pl. *Am.* pantalon; *Br.* caleçon, m.

papa [pâp°] *s.* papa, m.

papacy [pé¹p°si] *s.* papauté, f. ‖ *papal* [-'l] *adj* papal.

paper [pé¹p°r] *s.* papier; document; article; journal, m.; *v.* garnir de papier; tapisser; *paper-currency*, papier monnaie; *paper-hangings*, papiers peints; *paper-knife*, coupe-papier; *paper-mill*, papeterie; *paper-weight*, presse-papiers; *on paper* par écrit.

par [pâr] *s* pair (fin.), m.; égalité, f.; *par value*, valeur au pair; *on a par with*, à égalité avec, *to feel below par*, ne pas être dans son assiette.

parable [par°b'l] *s.* parabole, f.

parabola [p°rab°l°] *s.* parabole (geom.), f.

parachute [par°shout] *s.* parachute, m.; *v.* sauter descendre en parachute; parachuter; *parachute jump*, saut en parachute; ‖ *parachutist* [-ist] *s.* parachutiste, m.

parade [p°ré¹d] *s.* parade; prise d'armes; procession, f.; défilé; cortège, m.; *v.* parader, faire parade de; défiler; se promener de long en large.

paradise [par°da¹s] *s.* paradis, m.; *paradisiac*, paradisiaque.

paradox [par°dàks] *s.* paradoxe, m.

paraffin [par°fin] *s.* paraffine, f.

paragraph [par°graf] *s.* paragraphe, m.; *v.* diviser en paragraphes.

parallel [par°lèl] *adj.*, *s.* parallèle; *v.* comparer à.

paralysis [p°ral°sis] (*pl. paralyses*) *s.* paralysie, f. ‖ *paralytic* [par°litik] *adj.*, *s.* paralytique.

paramount [par°ma°unt] *adj.* souverain; dominant; suprême.

parapet [par°pit] *s.* parapet, m.

paraph [par°f] *s.* paraphe, m.

paraphrase [par°fré¹z] *v.* paraphraser; *s.* paraphrase, f.

parasite [par°sa¹t] *s.* parasite, m.

parasol [par°saul] *s.* parasol, m.; ombrelle, f.

parcel [pàrs'l] *s.* paquet; colis; lot, m.; parcelle; partie; portion, f.; *v.* morceler; diviser en portions; répartir; *parcel post*, service des colis postaux.

parch [pârtsh] *v.* brûler; (se) dessécher; se griller.

parchment [pàrtshm°nt] *s.* parchemin, m.

pardon [pârd'n] *s.* pardon, m.; grâce, f.; pardonner, gracier.

pare [pè°r] *v.* peler [fruit]; tailler [nails]; ébarber [paper]; rogner, réduire [expenditures].

parent [pèr°nt] *s.* père, m.; mère, f.; *pl.* parents, m. pl. ‖ *parentage* [-idj] *s.* extraction; origine; naissance; famille, f.

parenthesis [p°rènth°sis] (*pl. parentheses*) *s.* parenthèse, f.

paring [pè°ring] *s.* épluchure, f.

parish [parish] *s.* paroisse; commune, f. ‖ *parishioner* [p°rish°n°r] *s.* paroissien; habitant de la commune, m.

parity [pariti] *s.* égalité; parité, f.

park [pârk] *s.* parc, m.; *v.* parquer; enclore; garer, stationner; *no parking*, défense de stationner; *free parking*, stationnement libre et gratuit; *parkway*, autoroute.

parley [pârli] *s.* négociation, f.; pourparlers, m. pl.; *v.* négocier; parlementer, discuter.

parliament [pârl°m°nt] *s.* parlement, m. ‖ *parliamentary* [pârl°mèntèri] *adj.* parlementaire.

parlo(u)r [pârl°r] *s.* (petit) salon; *Am. beauty parlor*, salon de coiffure; *Am. parlor car*, wagon-salon.

parochial [p°rou°ki°l] *adj.* paroissial; communal.

parody [paredi] *s.* parodie, f.; *v.* parodier.

parole [p°rou°l] *s.* parole, f.; mot d'ordre, m.; *v.* libérer sur parole.

paroxysm [par°ksiz°m] *s.* paroxysme, accès, m.; crise, f.

parquet [pârké¹] *s.* parquet, m.

parricide [parisa¹d] *s.* parricide, m.

parrot [par°t] *s.* perroquet, m.; *v.* répéter, rabâcher.

parry [pari] *v.* parer [fencing]; esquiver; *s.*ᵃ parade. f.

parsimonious [pârsimoᵒuni°s] *adj.* parcimonieux, *parsimony,* parsimonie.

parsley [pârsli] *s.* persil, m.

parsnip [pârsn°p] *s.* panais, m.

parson [pârs°n] *s.* curé; pasteur, m.

part [pârt] *s.* part, partie, pièce; raie [hair]; région. f., élément /organe, rôle (theat.), parti. m., *pl* dons. talents, m. pl. *v* partager diviser; (se) séparer (*with de*). *part-owner,* copropriétaire; **spare parts,** pièces détachées; *to act a part,* jouer un rôle *for the most part* pour la plupart. *to part company* se séparer *to part with money* se démunir d'argent. *part... part.* moitié moitié *partake* [p°rté¹k] *v* participer, partager; *to partake of (a meal),* goûter, manger. *partaken* [p°rté¹k°n] *p. p. of to partake*

partial [pârsh°l] *adj* partiel; partial; aimant ‖ **partiality** [pârshal°ti] *s.* partialité; prédilection f ‖ **partially** [-li] *adv.* partialement partiellement

participant [p°rtis°p°nt] *adj., s.* participant ‖ **participate** [p°rtis°pé¹t] *v.* participer ‖ **participation** [p°rtis°pé¹sh°n] *s* participation f. *participle* [pârt°°p'l] *s* participe, m.

particle [pârtik'l] *s.* particule; parcelle, f. atome brin, m.

particoloured [pârtik°el°d] *adj.* bigarré, panaché

particular [p°rtíky°l°r] *adj.* particulier spécial exigeant méticuleux. difficile pointilleux , *pl* détail. m. circonstance particularité f ‖ **particularize** [pârtiky°ul°raiz] *v* particulariser détailler spécifier préciser ‖ **particularly** [p°rtiky°l°rli] *adj* particulièrement surtout spécialement.

parting [pârting] *s* séparation; raie [hair], f départ, m. *adj.* du départ.

partisan [pârt°z'n] *adj., s.* partisan, m.

partition [p°rtish°n] *s.* répartition; cloison, f.. morcellement; partage, m.; *v.* partager diviser; cloisonner; répartir partager, partitif.

partly [pârtli] *adv.* partiellement, en partie.

partner [pârtn°r] *s.* associé; partenaire; collègue cavalier, danseur, m. ‖ **partnership** [-ship] *s.* association; société (comm.), f.

partook [p°rtouk] *pret. of to partake.*

partridge [pârtridj] *s.* perdrix, f.

party [pârti] *s.*ᵃ parti; groupe; détachement (mil.); individu. tiers, m.; réception. partie de plaisir partie (jur.), f.; **firing party,** peloton d'exécution; **hunting party,** partie de chasse. **political party,** parti politique. **working party,** équipe d'ouvriers; **party wall,** mur mitoyen.

parvis [pavis] *s.* parvis, m.

pasque-flower [pâskflaᵒuer] *s.* anémone, f.

pass [pas] *v.* passer, dépasser; doubler [auto], s'écouler voter [law]; adopter [bill] approuver [account]; recevoir [candidate] être reçu à [exam], *s* passage, laissez-passer, permis; billet de faveur (theat), col (geogr.). m.. gorge (geogr.). passe; difficile crise, carte de circulation; botte [fencing] f., *to pass round,* faire circuler *to pass over* sauter; survoler; passer sous silence *to pass off,* se passer (*as* pour). *to pass out,* sortir s'évanouir ‖ **passable** [-°b'l] *adj.* passable praticable franchissable; carrossable *passage* [-°b'l] *s* passage couloir trajet m traversée adoption [bill]. f ‖ **passenger** [-'ndj°r] *s.* passager voyageur m. ‖ **passer-by** [-°rba¹] *s* passant. m. ‖ **passing** [-ing] *adj.* passager fortuit. *s* passage, trépas; dépassement [auto] écoulement [time]. m.. *adv* extrêmement. très.

passion [pash°n] *s* passion. f.; emportement m *to fly into a passion,* se mettre en colère **Passion week,** semaine sainte ‖ **passionate** [-it] *adj.* passionné emporté

passive [pasiv] *adj., s.* passif; **passiveness, passivity,** passivité

passport [paspoᵒurt] *s.* passeport, m.

password [paswë̃rd] *s.* mot de passe, m.; consigne f.

past [past] *adj.* passé; écoulé; fini; *s.* passé. m *prep.* après au-delà de; plus loin que *ten past six* six heures dix; *he is past sixty* il a dépassé la soixantaine **past-master** qui est passé maître qui excelle dans . the past presidens l'ex-président. *past tense* temps passé (gramm.); *to go past,* passer *past bearing,* intolérable ; *past hope,* désespéré

paste [pé¹st] *s* pâte. colle, f.; strass, m.; *v* coller à la colle de pâte.

pasteboard [pé¹stboᵒurd] *s.* carton, m.

pastel [past°l] *s* pastel, m.

pasteurize [past°ra¹z] *v.* pasteuriser.

pastille [pastîl] *s* pastille, f.

pastime [pasta¹m] *s.* passe-temps, m.

pastor [past°r] *s* pasteur, ecclésiastique, m. ‖ **pastoral** [-r°l] *adj.* pastoral; *s.* pastorale, f.

pastry [pé¹stri] *s.* pâtisserie, f.; *pastry cook*, pâtissier; *pastry shop*, pâtisserie.

pasture [pastsh°r] *s.* pâturage, m.; *v.* pâturer; (faire) paître.

pasty [pasti] *adj.* pâteux; *s.* pâté, m.

pat [pat] *adj.* à point, opportun; *adv.* à propos, juste; *s.* petite tape, f.; *v.* tapoter.

pat [pat] *s.* coquille [butter], f.

patch [patsh] *s.* pièce, plaque, tache; mouche [cosmetics]; petite portion, f.; emplâtre, écusson, m.; *v.* rapiécer; arranger; *Am. tire-repair patch*, rustine.

pate [pé¹t] *s.* tête, caboche, f.; *bald pate*, chauve (fam.).

patent [pat'nt] *adj.* patent, évident; *s.* patente, f.; brevet d'invention, m.; *v.* breveter. *patent leather*, cuir verni; *patent medicine*, spécialité pharmaceutique, *patently*, clairement, manifestement.

paternal [p°të°rn'l] *adj.* paternel. ‖ **paternity** [p°të°rn°ti] *s.* paternité, f.

path [path] *s.* sentier, chemin; circuit (electr.), m.; trajectoire; piste, f.

pathetic [p°thetik] *adj.* pathétique; lamentable; pitoyable.

pathology [path°l°dji] *s.* pathologie, f.

pathos [pé¹thâs] *s.* pathétique, m.; émotion, f.

pathway [pathwé¹] *s.* sentier, voie (fig.), f.

patience [pé¹sh°ns] *s.* patience, f. ‖ *patient* [-sh°nt] *adj., s.* patient.

patriarch [pé¹triärk] *s.* patriarche, m.

patrimony [patr°mo°¹ni] *s.* patrimoine, m.

patriot [pé¹tri°t] *s.* patriote, m. ‖ *patriotic* [pé¹triätik] *adj.* patriotique. ‖ **patriotism** [pé¹tri°tiz°m] *s.* patriotisme, m.

patrol [p°tro°ul] *s.* patrouille; ronde, f.; *v.* patrouiller.

patron [pé¹tr°n] *s.* patron; protecteur; client, m. ‖ *patronage* [-idj] *s.* patronage, m.; protection, f. ‖ *patroness* [-is] *s.* patronne; protectrice, f. ‖ *patronize* [-a¹z] *v.* patronner, protéger; traiter avec condescendance.

patter [pat°r] *v.* tapoter; trottiner; *s.* bruit sec; crépitement; fouettement [rain]; grésillement [snow], m.

patter [pat°r] *v.* marmotter, murmurer; *s.* bavardage; boniment, m.

pattern [pat°rn] *s.* modèle; dessin; patron; exemple; échantillon, m.; *v.* modeler; suivre l'exemple de, copier.

paucity [pausiti] *s.* rareté, pénurie, f.; manque, m.

paunch [pauntsh] *s.* panse, f.

pauper [paup°r] *s.* indigent, m.

pause [pauz] *s.* pause, f.; silence; point d'orgue, m.; *v.* faire une pause.

pave [pé¹v] *v.* paver; *to pave the way for*, préparer les voies pour, aplanir les difficultés de; *to pave with bricks*, carreler. ‖ **pavement** [-m°nt] *s.* pavé; dallage; trottoir, m.; *cobble pavement*, pavé en cailloutis; *wood-block pavement*, pavé en bois.

pavilion [p°vily°n] *s.* pavillon, m.

paw [pau] *s.* patte, f.; *v.* piaffer; caresser [dog].

pawky [pauki] *adj.* rusé.

pawl [paul] *s.* linguet, cliquet (mech.), m.

pawn [paun] *s.* gage; pion [chess]; nantissement, m.; *v.* mettre en gage; *pawnbroker*, prêteur sur gages; *pawnshop*, mont-de-piété.

pay [pé¹] *v.* payer; acquitter [bill]; rétribuer; rendre; rapporter; faire [visit, compliment]; *s.* paye; solde, f.; appointements, salaire, gages, m.; *to pay attention*, faire attention; *to pay back*, restituer; *to pay down*, payer comptant; *to pay one's respects*, présenter ses respects; *it does not pay*, ça ne rapporte rien; *to pay out*, débourser *pay card*, feuille de paye; *travel pay*, frais de déplacement; *paymaster*, trésorier payeur; *pay-roll*, état de paiements. ‖ *payable* [-b'l] *adj.* payable; dû. ‖ *payee* [pé¹¹] *s.* bénéficiaire, m. f. ‖ *paying* [pé¹ing] *s.* paiement; règlement, m.; *adj.* payant; rémunérateur. ‖ *payment* [-m°nt] *s.* paiement, versement, m.; *payment in full*, paiement global.

pea [pî] *s.* pois, m.; *green peas*, petits pois; *sweet peas*, pois de senteur; *chick-peas*, pois chiches; *pea-shooter*, sarbacane; *pea-pod*, cosse de pois.

peace [pîs] *s.* paix; tranquillité, f. ‖ *peaceful* [-f°l] *adj.* paisible; tranquille pacifique. ‖ *peacemaker* [-mé¹k°r] *s.* pacificateur, conciliateur, m.

peach [pîtsh] *s.* pêche [fruit], f.; *peach-tree*, pêcher.

peacock [pîkâk] *s.* paon, m.; *peahen*, paonne.

peak [pîk] *s.* pic; sommet, m.; cime; pointe [beard]; visière [cap], f.

peal [pîl] *s.* carillon; bruit retentissant; fracas [thunder]; éclat [laughter], m.; *v.* résonner; carillonner; (faire) retentir.

peanut [pînœt] *s.* cacahuète; arachide, f.; *peanut butter*, *Fr. Can.*

beurre d'arachide; **peanut oil,** huile d'arachide.

pear [pè•r] *s.* poire, f.; **pear-tree,** poirier.

pearl [pë•l] *s.* perle, f.; **pearl neck-lace,** collier de perles; **mother-of-pearl,** nacre, **pearl oyster,** huître per-lière; **pearly,** perlé, nacré; perlier.

peasant [pèz'nt] *adj., s,* paysan; **peasantry,** paysannerie.

pease [pîz] *s.* pois, m. pl.

peat [pît] *s.* tourbe, f.

pebble [pèb'l] *s.* caillou; galet, m.

peck [pèk] *v.* becqueter; picoter; pi-corer; *s.* coup de bec, m.

peck [pèk] *s.* picotin; tas, m.; grande quantité, f

peculate [pékyoulé•t] *v.* détourner des fonds **peculator,** concussionnaire.

peculiar [pikyou•ly•r] *adj.* parti-culier; propre, singulier; bizarre. ‖ **peculiarity** [pikyouliar•ti] *s.** parti-cularité; individualité; singularité; bizarrerie, f.

pedagogue [pèd•gåg] *s.* pédagogue, m. f.; **pedagogics, pedagogy,** péda-gogie.

pedal [pèd'l] *s.* pédale, f.; *v.* pédaler.

pedant [pèd'nt] *s* pédant, m. ‖ **pe-dantic** [pidantik] *adj.* pédantesque; *s.* pédant, m. ‖ **pedantry** [pèd•ntri] *s.* pédantisme, m.

peddle [pèd'l] *v.* colporter. ‖ **peddler** [-•r] *s.* colporteur, m.

pedestal [pèdist'l] *s.* piédestal, m.

pedestrian [p•dèstri•n] *s.* piéton, m.; *adj.* pédestre, **pedestrian crossing,** passage clouté.

pedigree [pèd•grî] *s.* pedigree; cer-tificat d'origine, m.; généalogie, f.

peek [pîk] *v.* épier.

peel [pîl] *s.* pelure, peau, f.; zeste, m.; *v.* peler, éplucher, décortiquer; **orange-peel,** écorce d'orange; **peel-ing,** épluchure; décortiquage; desqua-mation.

peep [pîp] *v.* jeter un coup d'œil; re-garder furtivement; poindre [day]; *s.* coup d'œil; point du jour, m.

peep [pîp] *v.* piauler, pépier; pousser des petits cris aigus; *s.* piaulement, pépiement; petit cri aigu, m.

peer [pi•r] *s.* pair, noble, égal, m.; **peerless,** incomparable.

peer [pi•r] *v.* regarder avec attention, scruter; pointer.

peeve [pîv] *v* irriter; agacer; **peev-ish,** maussade, acariâtre.

peg [pèg] *s.* cheville; patère, f.; faus-set [cask], m.; *v.* cheviller; **to take down a peg,** rabattre le caquet à.

pellet [pèlit] *s.* boulette [paper], f.

pell-mell [pèl-mèl] *adj.* pêle-mêle; confus; *adv.* sans précaution, im-pétueusement.

pelt [pèlt] *s.* peau, f.

pelt [pèlt] *v.* assaillir; *to pelt with stones,* lapider; **pelting rain,** pluie battante.

pen [pèn] *s.* plume, f.; *v.* écrire; **penholder,** porte-plume; **pen-name,** pseudonyme; **fountain pen,** stylo; **ball-point pen,** pointe-bille.

pen [pèn] *s* enclos; parc [sheep]; poulailler, m.; soue [pig]; *Am.* prison, f.; *v.* parquer

penal [pîn'l] *adj.* pénal. ‖ **penalty** [-ti] *s.** pénalité, sanction, f.; **death penalty,** peine de mort. ‖ **penance** [pèn•ns] *s* pénitence, f.

pence [pèns] *pl. of* penny.

pencil [pèns'l] *s.* crayon; pinceau, m.; *v.* marquer au crayon; **pencil shar-pener,** taille-crayon; **automatic pen-cil,** porte-mine.

pendant [pènd•nt] *s.* pendant, m.; pendeloque; suspension [lamp]; pan-toire (naut.), f *adj* pendant; penché. ‖ **pending** [pènding] *adj* pendant; en cours; *prep* pendant, durant; en attendant.

pendulum [pèndy•l•m] *s.* pendule; balancier, m

penetrability [pèn•trabil•ti] *s.* péné-trabilité, f ‖ **penetrable** [pèn•tréb'l] *adj.* pénétrable

penetrate [pèn•tré•t] *v.* pénétrer. ‖ **penetrating** [-ing] *adj* pénétrant. ‖ **penetration** [pèn•tré•sh•n] *s* pénétra-tion, f.; **penetrative,** pénétrant.

penguin [pènggwin] *s.* manchot (zool.), m.

penholder [pènhoould•r] *s.* porte-plume, m.

peninsula [p•nins•l•] *s.* péninsule, f.

penitent [pèn•t•nt] *adj* repentant; *s.* pénitent, m. ‖ **penitentiary** [pèn•tènsh•rl] *adj.* pénitentiaire; *s.** péni-tencier, m.

penknife [pènna•f] (*pl.* penknives [-na•vz]) *s.* canif, m.

penmanship [pènm•nship] *s.* calli-graphie, f.

pennant [pèn•nt] *s.* banderole; flamme (naut.), f.; fanion (mil.), m.

penniless [pènilis] *adj.* sans le sou. ‖ **penny** [pèni] (*pl* **pennies** [-z] *or* **pence** [pèns] *s.* sou, m.

pension [pènsh•n] *s.* pension, re-traite, f.; *v.* pensionner; mettre à la retraite; **pensioner,** retraité, pen-sionné; invalide.

pensive [pènsiv] *adj.* pensif.

pent [pènt] *adj.* enfermé, enclos; *pent-up emotions*, sentiments réprimés.

pentagon [pènt⁰g⁰n] *s.* pentagone, m.

Pentecost [péntikaust] *s.* Pentecôte, f.

penthouse [pèntha⁰us] *s.* appentis; hangar; auvent, m.

penumbra [pénœmbr⁰] *s.* pénombre, f.

penury [pèny⁰ri] *s.* pénurie, disette, f.

peony [pi⁰ni] *s.*ᵉ pivoine, f.

people [pîp'l] *s.* peuple; gens, m.; parents, m. pl.; *v.* peupler.

pep [pép] *s.* allant, m.; vitalité, f.; *v. to pep up*, animer.

pepper [pèp⁰ʳ] *s.* poivre, m.; *v.* poivrer; *to pepper with bullets*, cribler de balles; *pepper-shaker*, poivrière; *red, green peppers*, piments rouges, verts; *peppermint*, menthe poivrée; *peppery*, poivré; irascible.

per [p⁰ʳ] *prep.* pour; *per cent*, pour cent; *per year*, par an.

perambulator [p⁰rambioulé¹t⁰ʳ] *s.* voiture d'enfant, f.

percale [p⁰ʳké¹l] *s.* percale, f.

perceive [p⁰ʳsìv] *v.* (s')apercevoir; percevoir.

percentage [p⁰ʳsèntidj] *s.* pourcentage, m.

perceptible [p⁰ʳsèpt⁰b'l] *adj.* perceptible. ‖ *perception* [p⁰ʳsèpsh⁰n] *s.* perception, f.; discernement, m.

perch [p⁰ʳtsh] *s.*ᵉ perche [fish], f.; *yellow perch, Fr. Can.* perchaude, f.

perch [p⁰ʳtsh] *s.*ᵉ perche [rod], f.; perchoir, m.

perchance [p⁰ʳtshɑns] *adv.* par hasard.

percolate [p⁰ʳk⁰lé¹t] *v.* filtrer.

percuss [p⁰ʳkœs] *v.* percuter.

perdition [p⁰ʳdìsh⁰n] *s.* perdition, f.

peremptory [p⁰rèmpt⁰ri] *adj.* péremptoire; décisif; absolu.

perennial [pèrèni⁰l] *adj.* durable; vivace (bot.); perpétuel.

perfect [p⁰ʳfikt] *adj.* parfait; achevé; accompli, *s.* parfait (gramm.); [p⁰ʳfèkt] *v.* perfectionner; parfaire; améliorer; *pluperfect*, plus-que-parfait, m. ‖ *perfection* [p⁰ʳfèksh⁰n], *s.* perfection, f.

perfidious [p⁰ʳfìdi⁰s] *adj.* perfide. ‖ *perfidy* [p⁰ʳfⁱdi] *s.*ᵉ perfidie, f.

perforate [p⁰ʳf⁰ré¹t] *v.* perforer; percer; *perforation*, perforation, f.

perform [p⁰ʳfaurm] *v.* représenter (theat.); accomplir; remplir [task]. ‖ *performance* [-⁰ns] *s.* accomplissement; fonctionnement; rendement, m.; représentation (theat.); performance, f. ‖ *performer* [-⁰ʳ] *s.* artiste, m. f.; exécutant, m.

perfume [p⁰ʳfyoum] *s.* parfum, m.; [p⁰ʳfyoum] *v.* parfumer. ‖ *perfumery* [p⁰ʳfyoum⁰ri] *s.*ᵉ parfumerie, f.

perfunctory [p⁰fœngkt⁰ri] *adj.* négligent; superficiel; de pure forme.

perhaps [p⁰ʳhaps] *adv.* peut-être.

peril [pèr⁰l] *s.* péril, m.; *v.* exposer au danger; *perilous*, périlleux; dangereux.

perimeter [p⁰rim⁰t⁰ʳ] *s.* périmètre, m.

period [pⁱri⁰d] *s.* période; durée, f.; délai, cycle, m.; *Am.* point (gramm.); *running-in period*, période de rodage. ‖ *periodic* [pⁱriâdik] *adj.* périodique. ‖ *periodical* [-'l] *s.* périodique, m.; revue, f.; *adj.* périodique.

perish [pèrish] *v.* périr; mourir; se gâter; *perishable*, périssable.

periwinkle [pèriwink'l] *s.* pervenche, f.

perjure [p⁰ʳdj⁰ʳ] *v.* se parjurer. ‖ *perjury* [-ri] *s.*ᵉ parjure, m.

perky [p⁰ʳki] *adj.* éveillé.

perm [p⁰ʳm] *s.* permanente, f.; *v.* onduler.

permanence [p⁰ʳm⁰n⁰ns] *s.* permanence; stabilité, f. ‖ *permanent* [-n⁰nt] *adj.* permanent; durable; stable.

permeate [p⁰ʳmié¹t] *v.* pénétrer; imprégner; s'insinuer.

permissible [p⁰ʳmìs⁰b'l] *adj.* permis; admissible. ‖ *permission* [-sh⁰n] *s.* permission; autorisation, f.; permis, m. ‖ *permit* [p⁰ʳmit] *s.* permis; congé; laissez-passer, m.; autorisation, f.; [p⁰ʳmít] *v.* permettre, autoriser; *permit of residence*, permis de séjour.

permute [p⁰myout] *v.* permuter.

pernicious [p⁰ʳnish⁰s] *adj.* pernicieux.

pernickety [p⁰nⁱkiti] *adj.* délicat; méticuleux.

perorate [pér⁰ré¹t] *v.* pérorer; *peroration*, péroraison, f.

perpendicular [p⁰ʳp⁰ndⁱky⁰l⁰ʳ] *adj., s.* perpendiculaire.

perpetrate [p⁰ʳp⁰tré¹t] *v.* perpétrer; commettre.

perpetual [p⁰ʳpètshou⁰l] *adj.* perpétuel. ‖ *perpetuate* [-shou⁰¹t] *v.* perpétuer. ‖ *perpetuity* [p⁰ʳpityouiti] *s.* perpétuité, f.

perplex [p⁰ʳplèks] *v.* confondre, embarrasser; embrouiller. ‖ *perplexed* [-t] *adj.* perplexe, embarrassé; embrouillé, confus. ‖ *perplexity* [-⁰ti] *s.*ᵉ perplexité; confusion, f.; enchevêtrement, m.

persecute [p⁰ʳsikyout] *v.* persécuter. ‖ *persecution* [p⁰ʳsikyoush⁰n] *s.* persécution, f.

perseverance [përsevírens] *s.* persévérance, f. ‖ **persevere** [përsevíer] *v.*
persévérer; persister (*in*, à, dans).

persist [perzíst] *v.* persister (*in*, à,
dans); affirmer; s'obstiner. ‖ **persistence** [-ens] *s.* persistance, f. ‖ **persistent** [-ent] *adj.* persistant.

person [përs'n] *s.* personne, f.; individu, type, m. ‖ **personage** [-idj] *s.*
personnage. m. ‖ **personal** [-'l] *adj.*
personnel; en personne. ‖ **personality**
[përs'nal•ti] *s.*ª personnalité, f.; personnage, m ‖ **personification** [përsân-
ifiké¹sh•n] *s.* personnification, f. ‖
personify [përsânifa¹] *v* personnifier.
‖ **personnel** [përs'nél] *s.* personnel, f.

perspective [perspèktiv] *s.* perspective, f.

perspicacious [përspiké¹sh•s] *adj.*
perspicace, **perspicacity**, perspicacité.

perspiration [përsp·ré¹sh•n] *s.* transpiration; sueur, f. ‖ **perspire** [për-
spa¹r] *v.* transpirer.

persuade [pers·wé¹d] *v.* persuader;
déterminer. ‖ **persuasion** [përswé¹jen]
s. persuasion; croyance, f. ‖ **persuasive** [-siv] *adj* persuasif, convaincant.

pert [përt] *adj.* effronté, insolent.

pertain [perté¹n] *v.* appartenir.

pertinacity [përtinasiti] *s.* entêtement, m.

pertinent [përt'n•nt] *adj.* pertinent;
opportun, **pertinently**, pertinemment,
avec à-propos.

perturb [pertërb] *v.* perturber, troubler. ‖ **perturbation** [përterbé¹sh•n] *s.*
perturbation, f.

perusal [p•rouz•l] *s.* examen, m.; lecture, f. ‖ **peruse** [p•rouz] *v.* examiner,
lire avec attention, consulter.

pervade [pervé¹d] *v.* traverser, se
répandre, pénétrer.

perverse [pervërs] *adj.* pervers;
entêté; revêche. ‖ **pervert** [-vërt] *v.*
pervertir; fausser; détourner de;
[përvërt] *s* pervers, vicieux, m.

pessimism [pès·miz•m] *s.* pessimisme, m. ‖ **pessimist** [-mist] *s.* pessimiste, m. ‖ **pessimistic** [-mistik] *adj.*
pessimiste.

pest [pèst] *s.* peste, f.; fléau, m.

pester [pèst•r] *v.* importuner.

pestilence [pèst'l•ns] *s.* peste, f.

pestle [pés'l] *s* pilou, m.

pet [pèt] *s* animal favori; enfant
gâté; objet préféré, m.; *v.* caresser,
choyer, gâter **pet name,** nom d'amitié, diminutif

petal [pèt'l] *s.* pétale, m.

petition [p•t¹sh•n] *s.* pétition; requête, f.; *v.* pétitionner; présenter une
requête.

petrify [pétrifa¹] *v.* (se) pétrifier.

petrol [pètr•l] *s.* Br. essence, f.

petroleum [p•troo·li•m] *s.* pétrole, m.

petticoat [pètikoout] *s.* jupon, m.;
combinaison, f.; cotillon, m.

petty [pèti] *adj* insignifiant; mesquin; menu (jur.). **petty cash,** menue
monnaie; **petty officer,** officier marinier, quartier-maître.

pew [pyou] *s.* banc d'église, m.

phantom [fant•m] *s.* fantôme, m.

pharmacist [fârm•sist] *s.*- pharmacien, m. ‖ **pharmacy** [-si] *s.*ª pharmacie, f.

phase [fé¹z] *s.* phase, f.; *out of phase,*
décalé [motor].

pheasant [fèz'nt] *s.* faisan, m.

phenomenon [fen•m•nân] (*pl.* phe-
nomena [fen•m•n•]) *s.* phénomène, m.

phial [fa¹l] *s* fiole, f.; flacon, m.

philosopher [f•lâs•f•r] *s.* philosophe,
m. ‖ **philosophical** [f•s•âfik¹l] *adj.*
philosophique ‖ **philosophy** [f•lâs•fi]
*s.*ª philosophie, f.

phlegmatic [flègmatik] *adj.* flegmatique.

phone [fooun] *s.* téléphone, m.; *v.*
téléphoner.

phonetics [foounètiks] *s. pl.* phonétique, f.

phonograph [fooun•graf] *s.* phonographe. m.

phosphate [fâsfé¹t] *s.* phosphate, m.

phosphorus [fâsf•r•s] *s.* phosphore, m.

photo [foouto⁰u] *s.* photo, f.; *photo-
electric,* photo-électrique; *photograph,* photographie; prise de vue; *v.*
photographier *photographer,* photographe *photography,* photographie;
photogravure, photogravure; *photoprint,* photocopie.

phrase [fré¹z] *s.* phrase (mus.); locution; expression, f.; *v.* exprimer, formuler.

phthisis [tha¹sis] *s.* phtisie, f.

physic [fizik] *s.* médecine; purge, f.;
médicament, m.; *v* (pop.) médiciner;
purger. droguer ‖ *physical* [-'l] *adj.*
physique ‖ *physician* [fezish•n] *s.* médecin, m ‖ *physicist* [fiz·sist] *s.* physicien, m. ‖ *physics* [fiziks] *s. pl.* physique. f

physiological [fizi•lâdjik'l] *adj.* physi-
ologique ‖ *physiology* [fizi•lâdji] *s.*
physiologie. f.

physique [fizík] *s.* physique, m.

pianist [pi•nist] *s.* pianiste, m. f. ‖
piano [pianoou] *s* piano, m.; *piano
stool,* tabouret de piano; *grand piano,*
piano à queue; *baby-grand-piano,*

demi-queue; **upright-piano,** piano droit.

piccolo [pík*e*lo*ou*] *s.* octavin, piccolo [music], m.

pick [pik] *s.* pic, m.; pioche, f.; choix, m.; *v.* percer, trouer; becqueter; crocheter [lock]; plumer [fowl]; curer [teeth]; ronger [bone]; cueillir; choisir; extraire; piocher (techn.); *to pick flaws,* critiquer; *to pick up,* ramasser; gagner; (se) reprendre; **pickaxe,** pioche; **pickpocket,** voleur à la tire; **tooth-pick,** cure-dents.

picket [píkit] *s.* piquet; pieu; jalon; piquet militaire, m.; *v.* entourer de piquets; former un piquet (mil.); monter la garde; **outlying picket,** poste avancé.

pickle [pík'l] *s.* marinade; saumure, f.; *pl.* conserves au vinaigre; *v.* mariner; conserver dans du vinaigre; décaper (techn.); **pickled cucumbers,** cornichons; **picklefish,** poisson mariné; *to be in a pickle,* être dans de beaux draps.

picnic [píknik] *s.* pique-nique, m.; *v.* pique-niquer.

pictorial [piktâri*e*l] *adj.* pittoresque; illustré.

picture [píktsh*e*r] *s.* tableau; portrait, m.; peinture; gravure; image cinématographique, f.; *v.* peindre, représenter; décrire; (s')imaginer; *picture gallery,* musée de peinture; **picturesque,** pittoresque; *motion picture,* film.

pie [pa*i*] *s.* pâté, m.; tourte; tarte; tartelette, f.

piece [pîs] *s.* pièce, f.; morceau, fragment, m.; *piece of advice,* conseil; *piece of land,* parcelle de terrain; *piece of news,* nouvelle; *to piece on to,* ajouter à; *to piece together,* réunir les morceaux de, se faire une idée d'ensemble de; **piecemeal,** fragmentaire.

pier [pi*e*r] *s.* jetée; pile de pont, f.; appontement; pilastre, pilier, m.

pierce [pi*e*rs] *v.* percer; pénétrer; *to pierce through,* transpercer.

piety [pa*i*ti] *s.* piété, f.

pig [pig] *s.* porc, cochon, pourceau, m.; *pig-headed,* cabochard; *pig iron,* fonte brute, gueuse.

pigeon [pídj*e*n] *s.* pigeon, m. ‖ **pigeonhole** [-ho*ou*l] *s.* case, f.; casier, m.; *v.* classer; *pigeon house,* colombier.

piglet [píglit] *s.* porcelet, m.

pigment [pígm*e*nt] *s.* pigment, m.

pigskin [pígskin] *s.* peau (f.) de porc.

pike [pa*i*k] *s.* pique; pointe, f.; pic, m.

pike [pa*i*k] *s.* brochet, *Fr. Can.* doré, m.

pile [pa*i*l] *s.* pieu, pilot, m.; *v.* piloter, soutenir avec des pilots; *pile-work,* pilotis.

pile [pa*i*l] *s.* pile (electr.), f.; tas, monceau; faisceau (mil.), m.; *v.* empiler; entasser; accumuler; *to pile arms,* former les faisceaux.

pilfer [pílf*e*r] *v.* chiper, chaparder.

pilgrim [pílgrim] *s.* pèlerin, m. ‖ **pilgrimage** [-idj] *s.* pèlerinage, m.

pill [pil] *s.* pilule; *Am.* personne désagréable (fam.), f.

pillage [pílidj] *v.* piller; *s.* pillage, m. ‖ **pillager** [-*e*r] *s.* pillard, saccageur, m.

pillar [píl*e*r] *s.* pilier, m.; colonne, f.; *from pillar to post,* de-ci de-là; *pillar-box,* borne postale [letters].

pillow [pílo*ou*] *s.* oreiller; coussin, m.; *pillowcase,* taie d'oreiller.

pilot [pa*i*l*e*t] *s.* pilote; guide, m.; *v.* piloter, guider; conduire; *pilot balloon,* ballon d'essai; *robot pilot,* pilote automatique.

pimple [pímp'l] *s.* bouton (med.), m.

pin [pin] *s.* épingle; cheville; clavette; goupille, f.; boulon, m.; *v.* épingler; clouer, goupiller; *to pin up,* engager formellement, lier; *to pin up,* trousser, retrousser; *pin-up,* jolie fille, pin-up; *breast pin,* broche; *rolling-pin,* rouleau à pâtisserie; *pin money,* argent de poche; *pinworm,* oxyure.

pincers [píns*e*rz] *s. pl.* pinces; pincettes, f. pl.

pinch [pìntsh] *v.* pincer; serrer; être serré, gêné; *s.** pincée; prise [tobacco]; gêne, f.; pincement, m.; *pinchbar,* levier; *pinch-penny,* grippe-sou.

pine [pa*i*n] *s.* pin, m.; *pine cone,* pomme de pin.

pine [pa*i*n] *v.* languir; déplorer; *to pine for,* soupirer après; *to pine away,* dépérir.

pineapple [pa*i*nap'l] *s.* ananas, m.

pink [pingk] *s.* œillet, m.; *in the pink of condition,* en parfaite santé; *adj.* rose.

pinnacle [pín*e*k'l] *s.* faîte; pinacle, m.; tourelle, f.

pint [pa*i*nt] *s.* pinte, *Fr. Can.* chopine, f.

pioneer [pa*i*eni*e*r] *s.* pionnier; précurseur, m.; *v.* explorer; promouvoir; faire office de pionnier.

pious [pa*i*es] *adj.* pieux.

pipe [pa*i*p] *s.* pipe [smoking]; canule (med.), f.; tuyau; tube; conduit; pipeau; sifflet, m. ; v. canaliser, capter ; siffler ; jouer du pipeau, du fifre ; *to pipe down*, baisser la voix ; *pipe-line*, pipe-line ; *pipe down !*, la barbe ! ; *pipe organ*, grand orgue ; *pipe-stem*, tuyau de pipe. ‖ *piper* [-ᵉʳ] *s.* flûtiste ; joueur de cornemuse, m. ‖ *piping* [-ing] *s.* tubulure, f. ; tuyautage, m. ; son ou jeu du fifre, m. ; *adj.* flûté ; *piping hot*, bouillant.

pippin [pípìn] *s.* pomme de reinette, f.

pique [pîk] *s.* pique, brouillerie, f. ; ressentiment, m. ; v. vexer ; irriter ; *to pique oneself on*, se piquer de.

piracy [pa¹rᵉsi] *s.* piraterie, f. ; plagiat, m. ‖ *pirate* [pa¹rᵉt] *s.* pirate ; plagiaire, m. ; v. pirater ; plagier.

pirogue [piroᵘg] *s.* pirogue, f.

pirouette [pirouét] *s.* pirouette, f. ; v. pirouetter.

pistil [pistil] *s.* pistil, m.

pistol [píst'l] *s.* pistolet, m.

piston [píst'n] *s.* piston, m. ; *piston rod, ring*, tige, segment de piston.

pit [pit] *s.* trou ; puits [mining], m. ; fosse, f.

pitch [pitsh] *s.* poix, f. ; bitume, m. ; v. bitumer.

pitch [pitsh] *s.* degré, niveau, point ; diapason [music] ; tangage (naut.) ; pas [screw], m. ; pente, f. ; v. dresser [tent] ; fixer ; jeter, lancer ; tanguer (naut.) ; donner le ton [music] ; *to pitch in*, se mettre à la besogne ; *to pitch into*, attaquer.

pitcher [pítshᵉr] *s.* cruche, f. ; pichet ; lanceur [baseball], m.

pitchfork [pítshfaurk] *s.* fourche, f.

pitching [pítshing] *s.* lancement ; tangage, m.

piteous [pitiᵉs] *adj.* piteux ; pitoyable ; compatissant ; lamentable.

pitfall [pitfâl] *s.* piège, m. ; trappe, f.

pith [pith] *s.* moelle ; substance ; quintessence, f. ; essentiel, m. ‖ *pithy* [-i] *adj.* plein de moelle ; vigoureux, substantiel ; savoureux, plein de suc.

pitiful [pitifᵉl] *adj.* compatissant ; pitoyable ; lamentable. ‖ *pitiless* [-lis] *adj.* impitoyable. ‖ *pity* [pití] *s.* pitié ; compassion, f. ; dommage, m. ; v. plaindre ; avoir pitié ; *what a pity !*, quel dommage !

pivot [pívᵉt] *s.* pivot, axe, m. ; v. pivoter ; faire pivoter.

placard [plakârd] *s.* placard ; écriteau, m. ; affiche, pancarte, f. ; v. placarder, afficher.

placate [plᵉké¹t] *v.* apaiser, calmer.

place [plé¹s] *s.* place ; situation ; demeure ; localité, f. ; lieu ; endroit ; poste ; établissement, m. ; v. placer ; mettre ; *place of worship*, église, temple ; *in place of*, au lieu de ; *to take place*, avoir lieu ; *hiding place*, cachette ; *market place*, place du marché.

placid [plasid] *adj.* placide ; *placidity*, placidité, calme.

plagiarism [plé¹djᵉriz'm] *s.* plagiat, m. ‖ *plagiarist* [-ist] *s.* plagiaire, m. ‖ *plagiarize* [-a¹₃] *v.* plagier. ‖ *plagiary* [-i] *s.* plagiat, m.

plague [plé¹g] *s.* peste, bête noire, f. ; fléau, m. ; v. tourmenter ; harceler ; frapper de la peste.

plaid [plad] *s.* plaid, m. ; tissu écossais, m.

plain [plé¹n] *adj.* uni, plat ; égal ; commun ; facile ; évident ; franc ; *s.* plaine, f. ; *adv.* franchement ; simplement ; clairement ; *plain cooking*, cuisine bourgeoise ; *plain-spoken*, sincère, carré ; *in plain clothes*, en civil ; *she is plain*, elle est sans attraits. ‖ *plainsong* [plé¹nsaung] *s.* plain-chant, m.

plaintiff [plé¹ntif] *s.* plaignant ; demandeur (jur.), m. ‖ *plaintive* [-tiv] *adj.* plaintif, plaintive.

plan [plàn] *s.* plan ; projet ; dessein ; système, procédé, m. ; v. projeter ; tracer ; dessiner ; décider.

plane [plé¹n] *s.* rabot, m. ; v. raboter.

plane [plé¹n] *s.* platane, m.

plane [plé¹n] *s.* surface plane, f. ; plan ; avion, m. ; v. aplanir ; planer (aviat.) ; *plane detector*, détecteur d'avions.

planet [plànit] *s.* planète, f. ‖ *planetary* [-ᵉri] *adj.* planétaire.

plank [plàngk] *s.* planche, f. ; bordage (naut.) ; madrier, m. ; *Am.* programme électoral, m. ; v. planchéier ; border (naut.) ; déposer de force [money] ; servir [on a board].

plant [plànt] *s.* plante, f. ; plant ; matériel, outillage, m. ; usine ; machinerie, f. ; v. planter ; ensemencer ; implanter ; fonder, introduire ; *electric-light plant*, génératrice électrique ; *printing plant*, imprimerie. ‖ *plantation* [plànté¹shᵉn] *s.* plantation, f. ‖ *planter* [plàntᵉr] *s.* planteur, m.

plaque [plak] *s.* plaque, f.

plasma [plazmᵃ] *s.* plasma, m.

plaster [plastᵉr] *s.* emplâtre ; plâtre ; mortier, m. ; v. plâtrer ; mettre un emplâtre ; *court plaster*, sparadrap ; *mustard plaster*, sinapisme.

plastic [plastik] *adj., s.* plastique.

plasticity [plastisiti] *s.* plasticité, f.

plate [plé¹t] *s.* assiette; vaisselle; planche (typogr.); plaque [metal], f.; *v.* plaquer; blinder; argenter; étamer; *dental plate*, dentier.

plateau [platoᵘ] *s.* plateau (geogr.), m.

plateful [plé¹tfoul] *s.* assiettée, f.

platform [platfaurm] *s.* plateforme; estrade, f.; quai; programme politique, m.; *arrival platform*, quai d'arrivée (railw.), débarcadère (naut.).

platinum [plat'n⁰m] *s.* platine, m.

platitude [plat⁰tyoud] *s.* platitude; banalité, f.

platonic [plⁱt⁰nik] *adj.* platonique; platonicien.

platter [plat⁰r] *s.* gamelle, écuelle, f.

plausible [plauzib'l] *adj.* plausible; spécieux; enjôleur.

play [plé¹] *s.* jeu; fonctionnement, m.; pièce de théâtre, f.; *v.* jouer, avoir du jeu (mech.); représenter (theat.); *to play high*, jouer gros jeu; *to play cards*, jouer aux cartes; *to play the piano*, jouer du piano; *to play the fool*, faire l'imbécile; *play on words*, calembour, jeu de mots. ‖ *player* [-⁰r] *s.* joueur; musicien; acteur, m.; *player piano*, piano mécanique; *piano player*, pianiste. ‖ *playful* [-f⁰l] *adj.* enjoué, folâtre. ‖ *playground* [-graºund] *s.* terrain de jeux. ‖ *plaything* [-thing] *s.* jouet, m. ‖ *playtime* [-ta¹m] *s.* récréation, f. ‖ *playwright* [-ra¹t] *s.* auteur dramatique, dramaturge, m.

plea [pli] *s.* défense; excuse; allégation, f.; argument, m.; *on the plea of*, sous prétexte de.

plead [plid] *v.* plaider; alléguer; *pleader*, plaideur. ‖ *pleading* [plǐding] *s.* plaidoirie, f.; *adj.* implorant.

pleasant [plèz'nt] *adj.* agréable; plaisant; gracieux; sympathique. ‖ *pleasantry* [-ri] *s.* plaisanterie, f. ‖ *please* [plíz] *v.* plaire à; contenter; faire plaisir à; *(if you) please*, s'il vous plaît; *to be pleased with*, être satisfait de; *please be seated*, veuillez vous asseoir; *to do as one pleases*, faire à sa guise; *if you will be pleased to*, si vous vouliez prendre la peine de. ‖ *pleasing* [-ing] *adj.* agréable, charmant. ‖ *pleasure* [plèj⁰r] *s.* plaisir; gré, m.; volonté, f.; *at your pleasure*, à votre gré; *pleasure trip*, voyage d'agrément.

pleat [plít] *s.* plissé, m.; *v.* plisser.

plebiscite [plèb⁰sa¹t] *s.* plébiscite, m.

pledge [plèdj] *s.* gage; engagement; vœu; nantissement, m.; promesse; garantie, f.; *v.* (s')engager; promettre; mettre en gage; *to take the pledge*, faire vœu de tempérance.

plenipotentiary [plèn⁰p⁰tènsh⁰ri] *s.* plénipotentiaire, m.

plentiful [plèntif⁰l] *adj.* abondant, copieux. ‖ *plenty* [plènti] *s.* abondance; plénitude; profusion, f.

pliable [pla¹eb'l] *adj.* flexible; souple. ‖ *pliant* [pla¹ent] *adj.* docile, pliant.

pliers [pla¹ᵉrz] *s. pl.* pinces, f. pl.

plight [pla¹t] *s.* état, m.; condition; situation difficile, f.

plinth [plinth] *s.* plinthe, f.

plod [plâd] *v.* marcher péniblement; trimer, piocher.

plot [plât] *s.* complot; coin de terre; plan, m.; intrigue; conspiration, f.; *v.* comploter; machiner; relever le plan; *to plot a curve*, tracer une courbe. ‖ *plotter* [-⁰r] *s.* conspirateur; conjuré; traceur de route, m.

plough, plow [plaºu] *s.* charrue, f.; *v.* labourer; sillonner (naut.); *ploughman*, laboureur; *plough-share*, soc.

pluck [plœk] *v.* arracher; cueillir; plumer [fowl]; coller [exam]; pincer de la guitare; *s.* courage; cran, m.; *to pluck one's eyebrows*, s'épiler les sourcils; *to pluck up*, reprendre courage. ‖ *plucky* [-i] *adj.* courageux; *to be plucky*, avoir du cran.

plug [plœg] *s.* tampon; bouchon; robinet; plombage [tooth]; fausset; gibus [hat], m.; prise de courant (electr.), f.; *v.* boucher; *drain plug*, bouchon de vidange; *plug of tobacco*, carotte de tabac; *to plug up*, obstruer; *to plug in*, brancher (electr.).

plum [plœm] *s.* prune, f.; *dried plum*, pruneau; *plum-tree*, prunier; *sugar plum*, dragée.

plumage [ploumidj] *s.* plumage, m.

plumb [plœm] *s.* plomb, m.; *v.* plomber; *adv.* d'aplomb; *out of plumb*, oblique; déplombé; *adj.* perpendiculaire, vertical; *Am.* juste; *plumb bob*, fil à plomb; *plumb crazy*, tout à fait toqué. ‖ *plumber* [-⁰r] *s.* plombier, m. ‖ *plumbing* [-ing] *s.* plomberie; tuyauterie, f.

plume [ploum] *s.* panache; plumet, m.; plume, f.; *v.* empanacher; garnir d'une aigrette; plumer [fowl]; lisser ses plumes [bird]; se vanter (*on*, de), faire la roue.

plump [plœmp] *adj.* dodu, potelé; *v.* engraisser; gonfler.

plump [plœmp] *v.* tomber lourdement; *adv.* subitement; tout droit; en plein.

plunder [plœnd⁰r] *s.* butin; pillage, m.; *v.* piller; dépouiller; saccager.

plunge [plœndj] *v.* (se) plonger; s'enfoncer; *s.* plongeon, m.; *plunger*, plongeur; *Am.* spéculateur; *plunging*, embarras financier.

pluperfect [ploupë⁻fikt] *adj.*, *s.* plus-que-parfait, m.

plural [plourᵉl] *s.* pluriel, m.; *adj.* pluriel; plural. ‖ *pluralism* [-iz'm] *s.* cumul, m. ‖ *pluralist* [-ist] *s.* cumulard, m. ‖ *plurality* [plouᵉraliti] *s.** cumul, m.; majorité, f.

plus [plœs] *s.* plus (math.; print.), m.; *plus sign*, signe de l'addition.

plush [plœsh] *s.* peluche, f.

ply [pla¹] *v.* manier avec vigueur; exercer [trade]; presser, solliciter; plier; courber; louvoyer (naut.); faire le service (naut.); *to ply the needle*, tirer l'aiguille; *to ply the oars*, faire force de rames, *plywood*, contre-plaqué, m.

pneumatic [nyoumatik] *adj.* pneumatique.

pneumonia [nyoumoᵒⁿnyᵉ] *s.* pneumonie, f.

poach [poᵒⁿtsh] *v.* pocher.

poach [poᵒⁿtsh] *v.* braconner. ‖ *poacher* [-ᵉʳ] *s.* braconnier, m.; *poaching*, braconnage.

pocket [pâkit] *s.* poche; cavité, f.; blouse [billiards]; *v.* empocher; avaler [insult]; *air pocket*, trou d'air (aviat.).

pocketbook [pâkitbouk] *s.* portefeuille; porte-billets; carnet, livre de poche; *Am.* sac à main, m.

pocketknife [pâkitna¹f] (*pl.* pocketknives [-na¹vz]) *s.* couteau de poche; canif, m.

pod [pâd] *s.* cosse, f.

podgy [pâdji] *adj.* rondelet.

poem [poᵒⁿim] *s.* poème, m.; poésie, f. ‖ *poet* [poᵒⁿit] *s.* poète, m. ‖ *poetess* [-is] *s.** poétesse, f. ‖ *poetic* [poᵒⁿtik] *adj.* poétique; *s. pl.* art poétique, m. ‖ *poetical* [-'l] poétique. ‖ *poetry* [poᵒⁿitri] *s.* poésie, f.

poignant [po¹nᵉnt] *adj.* mordant; piquant; *Am.* émouvant.

point [po¹nt] *s.* point; essentiel, m.; pointe; extrémité; aiguille [steeple]; question, f.; *v.* pointer; signaler; montrer; ponctuer; viser; aiguiser; *it is not the point*, ce n'est pas la question; *to come to the point*, en venir au fait; *datum point, reference point*, point de repère; *dead point*, point mort [auto]; *starting point*, point de départ; *point-blank*, à bout portant; *pointsman*, aiguilleur (railw.). ‖ *pointed* [-id] *adj.* pointu; piquant; mordant; ogival (arch.). ‖ *pointer* [-ᵉʳ] *s.* pointeur; index; chien d'arrêt, m.

poise [po¹z] *s.* poids; aplomb, m.; *v.* balancer, tenir en équilibre.

poison [po¹z'n] *s.* poison; toxique, m.; *v.* empoisonner; intoxiquer. ‖

poisoner [-ᵉʳ] *s.* empoisonneur, m. ‖ *poisoning* [-ing] *s.* empoisonnement, m. ‖ *poisonous* [-ᵉs] *adj.* empoisonné; toxique; vénéneux; venimeux.

poke [poᵒⁿk] *v.* tisonner; fourrer, pousser; *s.* coup de coude, coup de poing, m.; *to poke fun at someone*, se moquer de; *to poke about*, fouiller, fourgonner; *poker*, tisonnier; poker.

Poland [poᵒⁿlᵉnd] *s.* Pologne, f.

polar [poᵒⁿlᵉʳ] *adj.* polaire. ‖ *polarity*, polarité; *polarization*, polarisation, f.; *polarize*, (se) polariser.

pole [poᵒⁿl] *s.* pôle (geogr.), m.

pole [poᵒⁿl] *s.* mât; poteau; timon, m.; gaule; poutre, f.; *telegraph pole*, poteau télégraphique.

Pole [poᵒⁿl] *s.* Polonais, m.

polecat [poᵒⁿlkat] *s.* putois, m.; *Am.* mouffette, f.

polemics [pᵉlémiks] *s. pl.* polémique, f.

police [pᵉlís] *s.* police, f.; *v.* faire la police; maintenir l'ordre; surveiller; *police department*, préfecture de police; *police headquarters*, commissariat de police; *police station*, poste de police. ‖ *policeman* [-mᵉn] (*pl.* policemen) *s.* agent de police; gardien de la paix, m.

policy [pâlᵉsi] *s.** politique; ligne de conduite, f.

policy [pâlᵉsi] *s.** police d'assurance, f.

poliomyelitis [poᵒⁿlioᵒⁿma¹ᵉla¹tis] *s.* poliomyélite, f.

Polish [poᵒⁿlish] *adj.*, *s.* polonais.

polish [pâlish] *s.* poli; vernis, m.; *v.* polir; vernir; cirer; astiquer.

polite [pᵉla¹t] *adj.* courtois, poli. ‖ *politeness* [-nis] *s.* politesse, f.

politic [pâlᵉtik] *adj.* politique; prudent; rusé. ‖ *political* [pᵉlitik'l] *adj.* politique. ‖ *politician* [pâlᵉtishᵉn] *s.* politicien, m. ‖ *politics* [pâlᵉtiks] *s. pl.* politique, f.

poll [poᵒⁿl] *s.* vote; scrutin, m.; tête; urne électorale, f.; *v.* (faire) voter; tenir le scrutin; obtenir des votes; *polling booth*, isoloir, m.

pollen [pâlᵉn] *s.* pollen, m.

pollute [pᵉlout] *v.* polluer, contaminer, souiller.

polo [poᵒⁿloᵒⁿ] *s.* polo, m.

poltroon [pâltroun] *s.* poltron, m.

polygamist [poligᵉmist] *s.* polygame, m; *polygamy*, polygamie.

polygon [pâligᵉn] *s.* polygone, m.

polyvalent [pâlive¹lᵉnt] *adj.* polyvalent.

pomade [poᵒⁿmé¹d] *s.* pommade. f.

pomegranate [pɒmgranit] *s.* grenade (bot.), f.; grenadier, m.

pommel [pɒm'l] *s.* pommeau, m.

pomp [pɒmp] *s.* pompe; ostentation, f.; faste, m. ‖ **pompous** [-ᵉs] *adj.* pompeux; fastueux.

pond [pɒnd] *s.* étang, m.; mare, f.; **fishpond**, vivier.

ponder [pɒndᵉʳ] *v.* peser; considérer; méditer (*over*, sur). ‖ **ponderous** [-rᵉs] *adj.* pesant.

pontiff [pɒntif] *s.* pontife, m. ‖ **pontify** [-aⁱ] *v.* pontifier.

pontoon [pɒntouⁿ] *s.* flotteur d'hydravion; ponton; bac, m.

pony [pouⁿni] *s.*ᵃ poney, m.

poodle [poud'l] *s.* caniche, m.

pool [poul] *s.* étang; bassin, m.; **swimming-pool**, piscine.

pool [poul] *s.* pool, fonds commun, m.; poule [sport], f.; *v.* faire un pool.

poop [poup] *s.* poupe (naut.), f.

poor [pouᵉʳ] *adj.* pauvre; piètre; indigent; *the poor*, les pauvres; **poorly**, pauvrement, tristement, mal; **poorhouse**, hospice.

pop [pɒp] *s.* explosion, détonation, f.; saut [cork], m.; *v.* éclater, détoner; sauter [cork]; tirer [gun]; poser à brûle-pourpoint [question]; *to pop in*, entrer à l'improviste; *to pop corn*, faire griller et éclater des épis de maïs; *to pop one's head out*, sortir brusquement la tête; *soda pop*, boisson gazeuse; **popeyed**, aux yeux exorbités.

pope [poup] *s.* pape; pope, m.

poplar [pɒplᵉʳ] *s.* peuplier, m.

poppy [pɒpi] *s.*ᵃ pavot; coquelicot, m.

populace [pɒpyᵘlis] *s.* populace, f. ‖ **popular** [pɒpyᵘlᵉʳ] *adj.* populaire. ‖ **popularity** [pɒpyᵘlᵃʳᵉti] *s.* popularité, f. ‖ **popularize** [pɒpyᵘlᵉʳaiz] *v.* populariser. ‖ **populate** [pɒpyᵘléⁱt] *v.* peupler. ‖ **population** [pɒpyᵘléⁱshᵉn] *s.* population, f. ‖ **populous** [pɒpyᵘlᵉs] *adj.* populeux.

porcelain [pouᵉrslin] *s.* porcelaine, f.

porch [pouᵉrtsh] *s.*ᵃ porche, m.

porcupine [pɔurkyᵉpaⁱn] *s.* porcépic, m.

pore [pouᵉr] *s.* pore, m.

pork [pɔurk] *s.* viande de porc, f.; *salt pork*, petit salé, *Fr. Can.* lard salé; *pork and beans*, *Fr. Can.* fèves au lard; **porker**, porc à l'engrais, goret.

porous [pouᵉrᵉs] *adj.* poreux, perméable.

porpoise [pɔurpᵉs] *s.* marsouin, m.

porridge [pɔuridj] *s.* bouillie, f.; porridge, m.

porringer [pɔrindjᵉʳ] *s.* écuelle, f.

port [pouᵉrt] *s.* port, havre, m.; *free port*, port franc; *sea port*, port de mer; *port of call*, escale.

port [pouᵉrt] *s.* sabord (naut.); bâbord (naut.), m.; **porthole**, hublot.

port [pouᵉrt] *s.* porto [wine], m.

portable [pouᵉrtᵉb'l] *adj.* portatif.

portage [pouᵉrtidj] *s.* portage, m.; *v. Fr. Can.* portager.

portal [pouᵉrt'l] *s.* portail, m.

portcullis [pouᵉrtkœlis] *s.* sarrasine, herse, f.

portent [pouᵉrtènt] *s.* mauvais présage, m.; **portentous**, de mauvais augure; prodigieux.

porter [pouᵉrtᵉʳ] *s.* portier, concierge, m.

porter [pouᵉrtᵉʳ] *s.* portefaix; commissionnaire, m.

portfolio [pouᵉrtfoᵘlioᵘ] *s.* portefeuille, m.; serviette, f.

portico [pauᵉrtikoᵘ] *s.* portique, m.

portion [pouᵉrshᵉn] *s.* portion, part; dot, f.; *v.* partager; doter.

portly [pauᵉrtli] *adj.* corpulent.

portmanteau [pauᵉrtmantoᵘ] *s.* valise, f.

portrait [pouᵉrtréⁱt] *s.* portrait, m.; **portraitist**, portraitiste. ‖ **portray** [pouᵉrtréⁱ] *v.* peindre; décrire. ‖ **portrayal** [-ᵉl] *s.* peinture, description, représentation, f.

Portuguese [pouᵉrtshᵉgîz] *adj., s.* portugais.

pose [pouᵉz] *s.* pose; attitude; affectation, f.; *v.* poser; disposer; prendre la pose; affecter une attitude; *to pose as*, se faire passer pour.

position [pᵉzishᵉn] *s.* position, place; situation; attitude, f.; rang; état, m.; *in a position to*, à même de.

positive [pɒzᵉtiv] *adj.* positif; affirmatif; certain; catégorique, formel; **positiveness**, certitude, assurance.

possess [pᵉzès] *v.* posséder. ‖ **possession** [pᵉzèshᵉn] *s.* possession, f. ‖ **possessor** [pᵉzèsᵉʳ] *s.* possesseur, m.

possibility [pâsᵉbîlᵉti] *s.*ᵃ possibilité, f. ‖ **possible** [pâsᵉb'l] *adj.* possible. ‖ **possibly** [-li] *adv.* peut-être; possiblement.

post [pouᵉst] *s.* poteau; pieu; pilier, m.; colonne [bed], f.; *v.* afficher, placarder.

post [pouᵉst] *s.* poste, emploi, m.; poste, f.; *v.* poster, placer; mettre à la poste; *army post*, garnison; **postcard**, carte postale; *post office*, bureau de poste; *post-paid*, affranchi, port payé ; **post marked at,** timbré de ; *by return of post,* par retour du courrier. ‖ **postage** [-idj] *s.* affranchissement ; port, m. ; **postage stamp,** timbre-poste. ‖ **postal** [-'l] *adj.* postal ; **postal money order,** mandat-poste.

poster [po^ust^er] *s.* afficheur, m. ; affiche, f.

posterior [pâstiri^er] *adj.* postérieur. ‖ **posterity** [pâstèr^eti] *s.* postérité, f.

posthumous [po^usthyoum^es] *adj.* posthume.

postman [po^ustm^en] *(pl.* **postmen**) *s.* facteur, m. ‖ **postmaster** [-mast^er] *s.* receveur des postes, m.

postpone [po^ustpo^un] *v.* remettre ; différer. ‖ **postponement** [-m^ent] *s.* ajournement, m.

postscript [po^ustskript] *s.* post-scriptum, m.

postulate [pâstshelé¹t] *v.* postuler.

posture [pâstsh^er] *s.* posture, attitude ; condition ; situation, f. ; *v.* adopter une posture.

posy [po^uzi] *s.** bouquet, m.

pot [pât] *s.* pot, vase, m. ; marmite ; mitre [chimney], f. ; *pot-bellied,* ventru, pansu.

potable [po^ut^eb'l] *adj.* potable.

potassium [p^etasi^em] *s.* potassium, m.

potash [pâtash] *s.* potasse, f.

potato [p^eté¹to^u] *s.** pomme de terre, f. ; *sweet potato,* patate.

potency [po^ut'nsi] *s.** puissance ; capacité ; efficacité, f. ‖ **potent** [-t'nt] *adj.* puissant, fort ; efficace. ‖ **potential** [p^etènsh^el] *adj., s.* potentiel.

potion [po^ush^en] *s.* dose, f. ; breuvage, m.

pottage [pâtidj] *s.* brouet, m.

potter [pât^er] *s.* potier, m. ‖ **pottery** [-ri] *s.** poterie, f.

pouch [pa^{ou}tsh] *s.** poche ; blague [tobacco] ; musette, f. ; sac, m. ; *mail pouch,* sac du courrier ; *cartridge pouch,* cartouchière.

poulp [pou¹p] *s.* poulpe, m.

poultice [po^{ou}ltis] *s.* cataplasme, m.

poultry [po^{ou}ltri] *s.* volaille, f. ; *poultry yard,* basse-cour.

pounce [pa^{ou}ns] *v.* saisir ; foncer ; fondre *(on,* sur).

pound [pa^{ou}nd] *s.* livre, f.

pound [pa^{ou}nd] *v.* broyer ; piler ; concasser.

pound [pa^{ou}nd] *s.* fourrière, f.

pour [po^{ou}r] *v.* verser, répandre ; se déverser ; pleuvoir à verse.

pout [pa^{ou}t] *v.* faire la moue ; bouder ; *s.* moue, f.

poverty [pâv^erti] *s.* pauvreté ; misère ; pénurie ; disette, f. ; *poverty-stricken,* indigent.

powder [pa^{ou}d^er] *s.* poudre, f. ; *v.* pulvériser ; poudrer ; *powder magazine,* poudrerie ; *powder-puff,* houppe à poudre ; *powder train,* traînée de poudre ; *to powder one's face,* se poudrer ; *Am. to take a powder,* prendre la poudre d'escampette.

power [pa^{ou}er] *s.* pouvoir, m. ; puissance ; force ; autorité, f. ; *man power,* effectifs (mil.) ; *power breakdown,* panne (electr.) ; *power-house, Am.* centrale électrique ; foyer d'énergie (fig.) ; *power-plant,* groupe électrogène ; *water power,* énergie hydraulique ; *high-powered,* de haute puissance ; *powerful,* puissant ; *powerless,* impuissant ; *exceeding one's power,* abus de pouvoir ; *Am. balance of power,* équilibre européen ; *six horse-power,* six chevaux(-vapeur).

pox [pâks] *s.* variole, f.

practicable [praktik^eb'l] *adj.* praticable ; carrossable ; faisable.

practical [praktik'l] *adj.* pratique ; réel, positif ; *a practical joke,* un mauvais tour, une farce. ‖ **practice** [praktis] *s.* pratique ; habitude ; clientèle, f. ; exercice, art, m. ; *v.* pratiquer ; exercer ; étudier ; **practiced,** expert, versé *(in,* dans).

prairie [prèri] *s.* savane, prairie, f.

praise [pré¹z] *s.* louange, f. ; éloge, m. ; *v.* louer ; *praiseworthy,* louable.

pram [pram] *s.* voiture d'enfant, f.

prance [prâns] *v.* caracoler ; se cabrer.

prank [pràngk] *s.* escapade, espièglerie, f. ; *to play pranks,* faire des niches.

prate [pré¹t] *v.* bavarder, babiller ; *s.* babillage, m.

prattle [prat'l] *v.* bavarder, jaser ; *s.* bavardage, babil, m.

prawn [praun] *s.* bouquet (zool.), m. ; crevette, f.

pray [pré¹] *v.* prier ; *pray, take a chair,* asseyez-vous, je vous prie. ‖ **prayer** [prè^er] *s.* prière ; supplication, f. ; *Prayer Book,* rituel.

preach [prîtsh] *v.* prêcher. ‖ **preacher** [-^er] *s.* prédicateur, m. ‖ **preaching** [-ing] *s.* prédication, f. ; sermon, m.

preamble [prîàmb'l] *s.* préambule, m.

prearranged [prî^eré¹ndjd] *adj.* arrangé d'avance.

precarious [prikèri^es] *adj.* précaire.

precast [prîkâst] *adj.* précontraint ; préfabriqué.

precaution [prikaush^en] *s.* précaution, f.

precede [prîsîd] *v.* précéder; devancer. ‖ **precedence** [-'ns] *s.* préséance; priorité, f. ‖ **precedent** [près'd^ent] *s.* précédent, m. ‖ **preceding** [prîsîding] *adj.* précédent.

precept [prîsèpt] *s.* précepte, m.

precinct [prîsingkt] *s.* enceinte; limite, f.; *pl.* pourtour, m; *Am.* circonscription électorale, f.

precious [prèsh^es] *adj.* précieux.

precipice [près^epis] *s.* précipice, m. ‖ **precipitate** [prisip't^eéⁱt] *v.* hâter; (se) précipiter; *adj.*, *s.* précipité. ‖ **precipitation** [prisip^etéⁱsh^en] *s.* précipitation, f. ‖ **precipitous** [prisip^et^es] *adj.* escarpé, à pic.

precise [prisaⁱs] *adj.* précis, exact. ‖ **preciseness** [-nis] *s.* précision; méticulosité, f. ‖ **precision** [prisij^en] *s.* précision, exactitude, f.

preclude [prikloud] *v.* exclure; empêcher (de).

precocious [priko^{ou}sh^es] *adj.* précoce; **precociousness,** précocité.

precursor [prikö^es^er] *s.* précurseur, m.

predacious [prédeⁱsh^es] *adj.* rapace; **predacity,** rapacité.

predecessor [pridisès^er] *s.* prédécesseur, m.

predestinate [pridéstinéⁱt] *v.* prédestiner; [-nit] *adj.*, *s.* prédestiné. ‖ **predestine** [pridéstin] *v.* prédestiner.

predicament [pridîk^em^ent] *s.* catégorie; classe; situation, f.

predicate [prèdikit] *adj.*, *s.* attribut.

predict [pridikt] *v.* prédire. ‖ **prediction** [pridîksh^en] *s.* prédiction, prévision, f.

predilection [prîd'lèksh^en] *s.* prédilection, préférence, f.

predispose [prîdispo^{ou}z] *v.* prédisposer.

predominance [pridám^en^ens] *s.* prédominance, f. ‖ **predominant** [-n^ent] *adj.* prédominant. ‖ **predominate** [-néⁱt] *v.* prédominer, prévaloir.

prefab [prifab] *adj.* préfabriqué. ‖ **prefabricate** [-fabrikéⁱt] *v.* préfabriquer.

preface [préf^es] *s.* préface, f; exorde, m.; *v.* préfacer; servir de prélude; faire précéder.

prefect [prîfèkt] *s.* préfet, m.; **prefecture,** préfecture.

prefer [prifö^er] *v.* préférer; intenter; présenter [claim]; déposer [charge]; promouvoir. ‖ **preferable** [préf^erb'l] *adj.* préférable. ‖ **preferably** [-i] *adv.* de préférence. ‖ **preference** [préfr^ens]

s. préférence, f. ‖ **preferential** [préfèr-énsh^el] *adj.* préférentiel. ‖ **preferment** [prifö^em^ent] *s.* promotion, f.; avancement, m.

prefix [prifiks] *s.** préfixe, m.; [prifiks] *v.* préfixer.

pregnancy [prègn^ensi] *s.** grossesse, f. ‖ **pregnant** [-n^ent] *adj.* enceinte; gros (fig.).

prehistory [prîhist^eri] *s.* préhistoire, f.

prejudice [prèdj^edis] *s.* préjugé; parti pris; préjudice (jur.), m.; prévention, f.; *v.* inspirer des préventions; porter préjudice à; **prejudicial,** préjudiciable.

prelate [prèlit] *s.* prélat, m.

preliminary [prilim^enèri] *adj.*, *s.** préliminaire.

prelude [prèlyoud] *s.* prélude, m.; [prilyoud] *v.* préluder.

premature [prim^etyour] *adj.* prématuré; avant terme.

premeditate [priméditéⁱt] *v.* préméditer; **premeditation,** préméditation.

premier [prîmi^er] *s.* Premier ministre, m.; *adj.* premier, principal.

premise [prèmis] *s.* prémisse, f.; *pl.* locaux; immeubles, m. pl.; *on the premises,* sur place.

premium [prîmi^em] *s.* prime; récompense, f.; **premium bond,** obligation à lots; *to be at a premium,* faire prime.

premonition [prim^enîsh^en] *s.* prémonition, f.; pressentiment; indice, m.; **premonitory,** prémonitoire.

preoccupation [priaky^epéⁱsh^en] *s.* préoccupation, f. ‖ **preoccupy** [priáky^epaⁱ] *v.* préoccuper; prévenir.

prepaid [prîpéⁱd] *adj.* affranchi; franco.

preparation [prèp^eréⁱsh^en] *s.* préparation, f.; préparatif, m. ‖ **preparatory** [pripar^eto^{ou}ri] *adj.* préparatoire. ‖ **prepare** [pripè^er] *v.* (se) préparer; apprêter. ‖ **preparedness** [-ridnis] *s.* état de préparation, équipement, m.

preponderance [pripánd^er^ens] *s.* prépondérance, f. ‖ **preponderant** [-n^ent] *adj.* prépondérant. ‖ **preponderate** [-éⁱt] *v.* l'emporter; être prépondérant.

preposition [prèp^ezish^en] *s.* préposition, f.

prepossessing [pripozésing] *adj.* attirant.

preposterous [pripástr^es] *adj.* absurde, déraisonnable.

prerequisite [prirèkw^ezit] *adj.* requis; *s.* nécessité préalable, f.

prerogative [prirág^etiv] *s.* prérogative, f.

presage [prèsidj] *s.* présage, m.; [priséⁱdj] *v.* présager.

presbyopic [prezbio⁰upik] *adj.* presbyte.

prescience [préshiens] *s.* prescience, f.

prescribe [priskra¹b] *v.* prescrire; légiférer. || **prescription** [priskripshen] *s.* prescription; ordonnance, f.

presence [prèz'ns] *s.* présence, f.; *presence of mind,* présence d'esprit. || **present** [prèz'nt] *adj.* présent; prompt; actuel; *s.* présent, m.; heure actuelle, f.; *for the present,* pour le moment; *present participle,* participe présent. || **present** [prizènt] *v.* (se) présenter; s'offrir; faire cadeau; *s.* présent, cadeau, m. || **presentation** [prèzn'té¹shen] *s.* présentation, f.; cadeau, m.; *presentation copy,* hommage de l'auteur [book].

presentiment [prizèntement] *s.* pressentiment, m.

presently [prèz'ntli] *adv.* tout à l'heure; sous peu.

preservation [prèzervé¹shen] *s.* préservation; conservation, f. || **preserve** [prizèrv] *v.* préserver; protéger; conserver; faire des conserves; *s.* conserves; confiture; chasse réservée, f.

preside [priza¹d] *v.* présider. || **presidency** [prèzedensi] *s.* présidence, f. || **president** [prèzedent] *s.* président, m. || **presidential** [prèzedènshel] *adj.* présidentiel.

press [près] *v.* presser; étreindre; satiner [paper]; repasser [clothes]; repousser; inciter; insister; *to press one's point,* insister sur ses arguments; *to press down upon,* peser sur, accabler; *to be hard pressed,* être aux abois; *s.* presse; foule; pression; urgence, f.; *printing press,* machine à imprimer. || **pressing** [-ing] *adj.* pressant; urgent; *s.* repassage, m. || **pressure** [prèsher] *s.* pression; poussée (mech.); urgence, f.; *blood pressure,* tension artérielle; *pressure-cooker,* autocuiseur, Cocotte Minute (trademark); *pressure gauge,* manomètre.

prestidigitation [prèstidididjité¹shen] *s.* prestidigitation, f.; **prestidigitator,** prestidigitateur.

prestige [prèstidj] *s.* prestige, m.

presumable [prizoumeb'l] *adj.* présumable; probable. || **presume** [prizoum] *v.* présumer; supposer; *to presume on,* abuser de. || **presumption** [prizæmpshen] *s.* présomption; prétention; supposition, f. || **presumptuous** [-ptshou⁰s] *adj.* présomptueux; prétentieux.

presuppose [prìse-po⁰uz] *v.* présupposer.

pretend [pritènd] *v.* prétendre; prétexter; faire semblant. || **pretense** [-tèns] *s.* prétexte; faux-semblant, m.;

excuse; feinte, f.; *under pretense of,* sous prétexte de. || **pretension** [pritènshen] *s.* prétention; ostentation, f. || **pretentious** [-shes] *adj.* prétentieux.

pretext [pritèkst] *s.* prétexte, m.

prettily [pritili] *adv.* joliment. || **prettiness** [pritinis] *s.* charme, m.; gentillesse, joliesse, f. || **pretty** [priti] *adj.* joli; gentil; *adv.* assez; à peu près; passablement; *pretty nearly,* à peu de chose près; *pretty well,* presque, assez bien.

prevail [privé¹l] *v.* prévaloir; dominer; l'emporter sur; *to prevail upon oneself,* se résoudre. || **prevailing** [-ing] *adj.* dominant; courant; répandu. || **prevalent** [-ent], *see prevailing.*

prevaricate [privariké¹t] *v.* biaiser; mentir; **prevarication,** équivoque, faux-fuyant, mensonge.

prevent [privènt] *v.* prévenir; empêcher; détourner. || **prevention** [privènshen] *s.* empêchement, m.; précautions; mesure préventive, f. || **preventive** [-tiv] *adj.* préventif. || **preview** [prívyou] *s.* projection en avant-première, première vision, f.; *v.* visionner.

previous [privies] *adj.* antérieur; précédent; préalable.

prey [pré¹] *s.* proie, f.; *v.* faire sa proie (*on, de*); *it preys upon my mind,* cela me mine.

price [pra¹s] *s.* prix; coût, m.; *v.* tarifer; coter; *at a reduced price,* au rabais; *priceless,* inestimable; *price-list,* prix courant, catalogue.

prick [prik] *v.* piquer; aiguillonner; pointer; *s.* pointe, piqûre, f.; piquant; remords, m.; *to prick up one's ears,* dresser les oreilles. || **prickly** [-li] *adj.* épineux; piquant.

pride [pra¹d] *s.* orgueil, m.; fierté, f.; *v. to pride oneself,* s'enorgueillir (*on, upon, de*).

priest [prist] *s.* prêtre, m. || **priesthood** [-houd] *s.* prêtrise, f.; sacerdoce, m.

priggish [prigish] *adj.* poseur, pédant; collet monté.

prim [prim] *adj.* affecté; coquet; tiré à quatre épingles.

primarily [pra¹mereli] *adv.* primitivement; à l'origine; surtout. || **primary** [pra¹mèri] *adj.* primaire; élémentaire; premier; primordial; primitif. || **primate** [-it] *s.* primat (eccles.), m. || **prime** [pra¹m] *adj.* premier, principal; excellent; *s.* origine; première heure, f.; commencement; printemps; nombre premier, m.; *v.* amorcer; instruire, styler; *Prime Minister,* Premier ministre; *to be in one's prime,* être dans la fleur de l'âge.

primer [prĭmᵉr] *s.* traité élémentaire, m.

primer [praɪmᵉr] *s.* amorce, f.

primitive [prĭmitiv] *adj.* primitif.

primness [prĭmnis] *s.* afféterie, préciosité, f.

primordial [praɪmauʳdiᵉl] *adj.* primordial; originel.

primp [prĭmp] *v.* se parer; s'attifer.

primrose [prĭmrouᶻz] *s.* primevère, f.

prince [prĭns] *s.* prince, m. ‖ **princely** [-li] *adj.* princier; somptueux. ‖ **princess** [-is] *s.* princesse, f.

principal [prĭnsᵉp'l] *adj.* principal; premier; *s.* principal; proviseur; mandant; commettant, m.

principle [prĭnsᵉp'l] *s.* principe; fondement, m.; base, f.

print [prĭnt] *s.* impression; empreinte; épreuve (phot.); estampe, gravure; cotonnade imprimée, indienne, f.; *v.* imprimer; *printed matter,* imprimés; *out of print,* épuisé. ‖ **printer** [-ᵉr] *s.* imprimeur, m. ‖ **printing** [-ing] *s.* impression, imprimerie, f.

prior [praɪᵉr] *adj.* antérieur; préalable; *s.* prieur, m.; *prior to,* antérieur à. ‖ **priority** [praɪauʳeti] *s.* priorité; antériorité, f. ‖ **priory** [praɪᵉri] *s.* prieuré, m.

prism [prĭzᵉm] *s.* prisme, m.

prison [prĭz'n] *s.* prison, f.; *v.* emprisonner. ‖ **prisoner** [-ᵉr] *s.* prisonnier; captif, m.

privacy [praɪvᵉsi] *s.* retraite; solitude; intimité, f. ‖ **private** [praɪvit] *adj.* privé; personnel, particulier; confidentiel; *s.* soldat, m.; *private citizen,* simple particulier. ‖ **privation** [praɪvéⁱshᵉn] *s.* privation, f.

privilege [prĭvilidj] *s.* privilège, m.; *privileged,* privilégié.

prize [praɪz] *s.* prix, lot, m.; récompense; prise (naut.); capture, f.; *prize book,* livre de prix; *prize-packet,* pochette-surprise; *prize-list,* palmarès.

prize [praɪz] *v.* priser; estimer; évaluer; tenir à.

probability [prâbᵉbĭleti] *s.* probabilité, f. ‖ **probable** [prâbᵉb'l] *adj.* probable; *probably,* probablement.

probation [prouᵒbéⁱshᵉn] *s.* probation; épreuve, f.; stage; noviciat, m.; *Probation Act,* loi de sursis; *on probation,* à l'essai.

probe [prouᵒb] *v.* sonder; approfondir; *s.* sonde (med.); enquête; investigation, f.; *probity,* probité.

problem [prâblᵉm] *s.* problème, m.

procedure [prᵉsĭdjᵉr] *s.* procédure; méthode, f.; procédé; fonctionnement, m. ‖ **proceed** [prᵉsĭd] *v.* procéder;

avancer; continuer; aller, se rendre; *to proceed against,* intenter un procès à; *to proceed with,* continuer; *to proceed from,* provenir de. ‖ **proceeding** [-ing] *s.* procédé, m.; marche à suivre, f.; relèvement (naut.), m.; *pl.* procédure; délibérations; poursuites; démarches, f. ‖ **proceeds** [prouᵒsîdz] *s. pl.* produit; montant, m.

process [prâsès] *s.* procédé; processus; procès, m.; marche; méthode; opération, f.; *v.* soumettre à un procédé; *due process of law,* procédure légale. ‖ **processing** [-ing] *s.* traitement, m.; transformation, f.; *food-processing industry,* industrie alimentaire.

procession [prᵉsèshᵉn] *s.* procession, f.; cortège, m.; *v.* défiler.

proclaim [prouᵒkléⁱm] *v.* proclamer; annoncer. ‖ **proclamation** [prâklᵉméⁱshᵉn] *s.* proclamation; déclaration, f.

procrastinate [prokrâstinéⁱt] *v.* atermoyer, remettre au lendemain; *procrastination,* remise au lendemain.

procreate [prouᵒkriéⁱt] *v.* procréer; *procreation,* procréation, f.; *procreative,* procréateur.

procuration [praukiouréⁱshᵉn] *s.* procuration; proxénétisme; acquisition, f.

procure [prouᵒkyour] *v.* (se) procurer; faire obtenir. ‖ **procurement** [-mᵉnt] *s.* obtention, acquisition, f.; *Am.* approvisionnement, m.; *procurer,* proxénète; *procuress,* entremetteuse.

prod [prâd] *v.* piquer; aiguillonner.

prodigal [prâdig'l] *adj.,* *s.* prodigue.

prodigious [prᵉdidjᵉs] *adj.* prodigieux. ‖ **prodigy** [prâdᵉdji] *s.* prodige, m.

produce [prâdyous] *s.* produit; rendement, m.; [prᵉdyous] *v.* produire; exhiber; fabriquer. ‖ **producer** [-ᵉr] *s.* producteur, impresario, m. ‖ **product** [prâdᵉkt] *s.* produit, m.; denrée, f.; *farm product,* produit agricole. ‖ **production** [prᵉdækshᵉn] *s.* production; fabrication; représentation (theat.); œuvre [book], f. ‖ **productive** [-tiv] *adj.* productif; *productiveness,* productivité.

profanation [prâfᵉnéⁱshᵉn] *s.* profanation, f. ‖ **profane** [prᵉféⁱn] *adj.* profane; *v.* profaner; *profaner,* profanateur; *profanity,* caractère profane; impiété; juron.

profess [prᵉfès] *v.* professer, prétendre. ‖ **profession** [prᵉfèshᵉn] *s.* profession, f.; métier; état; emploi, m. ‖ **professional** [-'l] *adj.,* *s.* professionnel. ‖ **professor** [-ᵉr] *s.* professeur, m.; *professorship,* professorat; chaire.

proffer [prâfᵉr] *s.* offre, f.; *v.* offrir, proposer.

proficiency [prᵉfíshᵉnsĭ] *s.* compétence; capacité, f.; talent; progrès, m. || **proficient** [-shᵉnt] *adj.* compétent; habile; calé.

profile [proᵘfaⁱl] *s.* profil; contour, m.; silhouette, f.; *v.* profiler.

profit [práfĭt] *s.* profit; bénéfice; avantage; rapport, m.; *v.* profiter; bénéficier; mettre à profit. || **profitable** [-eb'l] *adj.* profitable; avantageux; lucratif. || **profiteer** [práfᵉtĭr] *s.* profiteur; mercanti, m.; *v.* exploiter.

profligacy [práfĭigᵉsĭ] *s.* débauche, f.; *profligate,* débauché.

profound [prᵉfaᵘnd] *adj.* profond; *profoundness* [-nĭs], *profundity* [prᵉfǽndĭti] *s.* profondeur, f.

profuse [prᵉfyoᵘs] *adj.* profus; prodigue; abondant; *profusion,* profusion.

progeny [prádjᵉnĭ] *s.* progéniture; descendance; postérité, f.

prognostic [prǎgnástĭk] *s.* pronostic; symptôme, m.; *prognosticate,* pronostiquer.

program(me) [proᵘugram] *s.* programme; plan, m.

progress [prágrĕs] *s.* progrès; cours [events]; voyage; avancement, m.; [prᵉgrĕs] *v.* progresser; avancer; faire des progrès. || *progression* [-shᵉn] *s.* progression, f. || *progressive* [prᵉgrĕsĭv] *adj.* progressif; *s.* progressiste, m.

prohibit [proᵘhĭbĭt] *v.* prohiber; interdire. || *prohibition* [proᵘᵉbĭshᵉn] *s.* prohibition; interdiction, f. || *prohibitive* [proᵘhĭbĭtĭv] *adj.* prohibitif.

project [prádjĕkt] *s.* projet; dessein, m.; intention, f.; [prᵉdjĕkt] *v.* projeter; lancer; faire saillie; s'avancer.

projectile [prᵉdjĕkt'l] *s.* projectile, m. || *projection* [-djĕkshᵉn] *s.* projection; saillie, f. || *projector* [prodjĕktᵉr] *s.* projecteur, m.

proletarian [proᵘulĕtĭrĭᵉn] *adj.*, *s.* prolétaire. || *proletariat* [-rĭᵉt] *s.* prolétariat, m.

proliferate [prolĭfᵉréⁱt] *v.* proliférer; *proliferation,* prolifération.

prolific [proᵘlĭfĭk] *adj.* prolifique; *prolification,* prolifération; procréation; fécondité.

prolixe [proᵘlĭks] *adj.* prolixe; *prolixity,* prolixité.

prologue [proᵘulaug] *s.* prologue, m.

prolong [prᵉlaung] *v.* prolonger. || *prolongation* [proᵘulaunggéⁱshᵉn] *s.* prolongation, f.; prolongement, m.

promenade [prámᵉnéⁱd] *s.* promenade, f.; *v.* se promener.

prominent [prámĭnᵉnt] *adj.* proéminent; éminent; saillant.

promiscuity [proᵘmĭskyoᵘᵉtĭ] *s.* promiscuité, f. || *promiscuous* [prᵉmĭskyoᵘᵉs] *adj.* confus; pêle-mêle; débauché.

promise [prámĭs] *s.* promesse, f.; *v.* promettre. || *promising* [-ĭng] *adj.* prometteur; d'avenir. || *promissory* [prǎmᵉsoᵘurĭ] *adj.* à ordre; *promissory note,* billet à ordre.

promontory [prámᵉntoᵘurĭ] *s.* promontoire, m.

promote [prᵉmoᵘut] *v.* faire avancer; promouvoir; encourager; contribuer à. || *promoter* [-ᵉr] *s.* promoteur, m. || *promotion* [prᵉmoᵘushᵉn] *s.* promotion, f.; avancement, m. || *promotive* [prᵉmoᵘutĭv] *adj.* favorable, favorisant.

prompt [prámpt] *adj.* prompt; rapide; empressé; immédiat; ponctuel; *v.* inciter; suggérer; souffler (theat.). || *promptly* [-lĭ] *adv.* promptement; immédiatement; ponctuellement. || *promptness* [-nĭs] *s.* promptitude; ponctualité, f; empressement, m.

promulgate [prᵉmǽlgéⁱt] *v.* promulguer. || *promulgation* [proᵘmǽlgéⁱshᵉn] *s.* promulgation, f.

prone [proᵘun] *adj.* incliné; en pente; enclin (to, à); couché à plat ventre.

prong [praung] *s.* dent, f. [fork]; *v.* enfourcher.

pronoun [proᵘunaᵘun] *s.* pronom, m.

pronounce [prᵉnaᵘuns] *v.* prononcer; déclarer. || *pronounced* [-t] *adj.* prononcé, marqué. || *pronunciation* [prᵉnœnsĭéⁱshᵉn] *s.* prononciation, f.

proof [prouf] *s.* preuve; justification; épreuve (phot.), f.; *adj.* à l'épreuve de, résistant; étanche; imperméable; *proof-sheet,* épreuve (typogr.).

prop [práp] *s.* étai; tuteur; support; soutien, m.; *v.* étayer; soutenir.

propaganda [prápᵉgandᵉ] *s.* propagande, f.; *propagandize,* faire de la propagande.

propagate [prápᵉgéⁱt] *v.* (se) propager. *propagation* [prápᵉgéⁱshᵉn] *s.* propagation, f.; *propagative,* propagateur.

propel [prᵉpĕl] *v.* propulser. || *propellant* [-ᵉnt] *s.* propulseur; propergol, m. || *propeller* [-ᵉr] *s.* propulseur, m.; hélice, f.

propense [propĕns] *adj.* porté (to, à); *propensity,* propension.

proper [prápᵉr] *adj.* propre; convenable, exact; à propos; régulier juste, *proper noun,* nom propre. || *properly* [-lĭ] *adv.* régulièrement; convenablement; en propre. || *property* [prápᵉrtĭ] *s.* propriété; possession; qualité, f.; biens; matériel, m.; *property-man,* accessoiriste.

prophecy [práfesi] *s.* prophétie, f. ‖ **prophesy** [práf•sa¹] *v.* prophétiser; pronostiquer. ‖ **prophet** [práfit] *s.* prophète, m. ‖ **prophetic** [prefètik] *adj.* prophétique.

propinquity [proºupínkwiti] *s.* proximité; affinité, ressemblance; proche parenté, f.

propitiate [prepíshié¹t] *v.* rendre propice; **propitiation**, propitiation; **propitiatory**, propitiatoire; **propitious**, propice.

proportion [prepoºurshen] *s.* proportion, f.; *v.* proportionner; *out of proportion*, disproportionné, hors de proportion (*to*, avec). **proportional**, proportionnel; **proportionate**, proportionné; **proportionately**, proportionnellement.

proposal [prepoºuz'l] *s.* proposition; demande en mariage; déclaration d'amour, f.; projet, m. ‖ **propose** [prepoºuz] *s.* proposer, offrir; demander en mariage. ‖ **proposition** [prápezíshen] *s.* proposition; offre; affaire, f.

propound [prepaºund] *v.* proposer; émettre [idea], poser [problem].

proprietor [prepra¹•ter] *s.* propriétaire, m. f. ‖ **propriety** [-ti] *s.* propriété; opportunité, bienséance, f.

propulsion [propœlshen] *s.* propulsion, f.

prorate [proºuré¹t] *v.* taxer proportionnellement.

prorogation [proºuregé¹shen] *s.* prorogation, f. ‖ **prorogue** [proroºug] *v.* (se) proroger

prosaic [proºuzé¹ik] *adj.* prosaïque.

proscribe [proskra¹b] *v.* proscrire; **proscription**, proscription.

prose [proºuz] *s.* prose, f.; *prose writer*, prosateur

prosecute [prásikyout] *v.* poursuivre; traduire en justice; revendiquer [right] intente; une action ‖ **prosecution** [prásikyoushen] *s.* poursuites judiciaires; accusation, continuation [studies], f. *witness for the prosecution*, témoin à charge. ‖ **prosecutor** [prásikyout•r] *s.* procureur; plaignant, m.

proselyte [prásila¹t] *s.* prosélyte, m. f.; *v. Am* faire du prosélytisme.

prosody [práse•di] *s.* prosodie, f.

prospect [práspèkt] *s.* perspective; vue; espérances f., avenir, panorama, m. *prospecter* explorer. ‖ **prospective** [pre•spèktiv] *adj* prospective présumé prévoyant, *s* perspective, f. ‖ **prospector** [pre•spèkt•r] *s.* prospecteur; chercheur d'or, m.

prosper [práspe•r] *v.* réussir; (faire) prospérer ‖ **prosperity** [práspèr•ti] *s.* prospérité, f. ‖ **prosperous** [práspe•r•s] *adj.* prospère, florissant.

prostitute [prást•tyout] *s* prostituée, f.; *v.* prostituer ‖ **prostitution** [prástityoushen] *s.* prostitution, f.

prostrate [prástré¹t] *adj.* prosterné; prostré; [prástré¹t] *v.* abattre; prosterner. ‖ **prostration** [-tré¹shen] *s.* prostration, prosternation, f.

protagonist [protag•nist] *s.* protagoniste, m. f.

protect [pretèkt] *v.* protéger; défendre. ‖ **protection** [-shen] *s.* protection; défense; sauvegarde, f. ‖ **protective** [-tiv] *adj.* protecteur; de protection. ‖ **protector** [-t•r] *s.* protecteur, m ‖ **protectorate** [-trit] *s.* protectorat, m. ‖ **protectress** [-tris] *s.* protectrice, f.

protégé [proºutejé¹] *s.* protégé, m.

protein [proºutíin] *s* protéine, f.

protest [proºutèst] *s* protestation, f.; protêt, m [prºtèst] • protester, faire protester (comm.) ‖ **protestant** [prátistºnt] *adj. s* protestant. ‖ **protestation** [prát•sté¹shen] *s.* protestation, f.; **protester**, protestataire

protocole [proºutokál] *s.* protocole, m.

protoplasm [proºut•plazºm] *s.* protoplasme, m

protract [proºutrakt] *v.* prolonger; traîner en longueur.

protrude [proºutroud] *v.* (faire) sortir; faire saillie

protuberance [proºutyoub•r•ns] *s.* protubérance, f.; **protuberant**, protubérant.

proud [praºud] *adj.* orgueilleux; fier; arrogant; fougueux [horse].

prove [prouv] *v* prouver; démontrer; vérifier éprouver; homologuer; se montrer

proverb [práv•rb] *s.* proverbe, m.; maxime, f.. **proverbial**, proverbial.

provide [preva¹d] *v* pourvoir, fournir; munir (*with* de); stipuler [article], pourvoir (*for* à). *to be well provided for* être à l'abri du besoin. ‖ **provided** [-id] *conj.* pourvu, à condition (*that* que)

providence [práv•dºns] *s.* providence; prévoyance, f. ‖ **providential** [práv•dènshºl] *adj.* providentiel.

provider [preva¹d•r] *s.* pourvoyeur; fournisseur, m.

province [právins] *s.* province; juridiction, f.. ressort, m.; *it is not within my province* ce n'est pas de mon rayon. ‖ **provincial** [pre•vínshºl] *adj., s.* provincial.

provision [prəvíjən] *s.* stipulation; mesure; clause; somme d'argent; provisions, f.; acte de pourvoir aux besoins de quelqu'un, m.; *v.* s'approvisionner; *provisional*, provisoire; provisionnel (jur.).

provisory [prəváizəri] *adj.* conditionnel; provisoire.

provocation [prâvəkéishən] *s.* provocation; irritation, f.; stimulant, m. ‖ **provoke** [prəvóuk] *v.* provoquer; irriter; fâcher; susciter. ‖ *provoking* [-ing] *adj.* contrariant; fâcheux.

provost [prâvəst] *s.* prévôt, m.

prow [praou] *s.* proue, f.

prowess [praouis] *s.** prouesse, f.

prowl [praoul] *v.* rôder.

proximity [prâksiməti] *s.* proximité, f.; voisinage, m.

proxy [prâksi] *s.** procuration, f.; mandataire, m.

prude [proud] *s.* prude, f.

prudence [proud'ns] *s.* prudence, f. ‖ *prudent* [-d'nt] *adj.* prudent.

prudery [proudəri] *s.* pruderie, f. ‖ *prudish* [-dish] *adj.* prude.

prune [proun] *s.* pruneau, m.

prune [proun] *v.* élaguer; émonder.

Prussia [præshə] *s.* Prusse, f.; **Prussian**, Prussien.

pry [prai] *v.* fouiller; fureter; se mêler de; fourrer le nez dans.

pry [prai] *s.** levier, m.; *v.* soulever avec un levier.

psalm [sâm] *s.* psaume, m. ‖ *psalmodize* [-oda¹z] *v.* psalmodier.

pseudonym [syoud'nim] *s.* pseudonyme, m.

psychiatrist [sa¹ka¹trist] *s.* psychiatre, m. ‖ *psychiatry* [-tri] *s.* psychiatrie, f. ‖ *psychic* [sa¹kik] *adj.* psychique; *s.* médium. m. **psychics**, métapsychique; *psychism*, psychisme.

psychological [sa¹kəlâddjik'l] *adj.* psychologique. ‖ *psychologist* [-djist] *s.* psychologue, m. ‖ *psychology* [-dji] *s.* psychologie, f.

psychosis [sa¹koousis] (*pl.* **psychoses**) *s.* psychose, f.

public [pæblik] *adj.* public; *s.* public; peuple, m.; *public authorities*, pouvoirs publics; *public officers*, fonctionnaires; *public spirited*, dévoué au bien public ‖ *publication* [pæbliké¹shən] *s.* publication promulgation, f. ‖ *publicity* [pæblísəti] *s* publicité; réclame, f. ‖ *publicize* [-sa¹z] *v* faire de la publicité. ‖ *publish* [pæblish] *v.* publier; éditer. ‖ *publisher* [-ər] *s.* éditeur, m.

puck [pæk] *s.* palet, m.; *Fr. Can.* rondelle (hockey), f.

pucker [pækər] *v.* plisser, froncer, rider; se froncer.

pudding [pouding] *s.* boudin; pudding, m.; saucisse, f.

puddle [pæd'l] *s.* flaque; mare, f.; *v.* patauger.

puerile [pyouəra¹l] *adj.* puéril. ‖ *puerility* [pyouəríliti] *s.* puérilité, f.

puff [pœf] *s.* souffle, m.; bouffée; houppe; vantardise, réclame, louange exagérée, f.; *v.* souffler, tirer des bouffées; gonfler; prôner. *puff-box*, boîte à houppe; *puff-paste*, pâte feuilletée; *puffed up with pride*, bouffi d'orgueil.

pug [pœg] *s.* singe; renard; carlin, m.; *pug-nose*, nez camus.

pugilism [pioudjiliz'm] *s.* pugilat, m; *pugilist*, pugiliste.

pugnacious [pœgné¹shəs] *adj.* batailleur.

pule [pyoul] *v.* pépier; vagir.

pull [poul] *v.* tirer; arracher; faire aller à la rame; *s.* traction; secousse; promenade en bateau; *s.* coup de collier; tirage; avantage, m.; *to pull about*, tirailler; *to pull away*, arracher; *to pull down*, abattre, démolir; *to pull through*, se tirer d'affaire; *to pull to pieces*, mettre en pièces; *to pull oneself together*, se ressaisir; *to pull someone's leg*, faire marcher quelqu'un.

pullet [poulit] *s.* poulette, f.

pulley [pouli] *s.* poulie, f.

pulmonary [pælmənəri] *adj.* pulmonaire; tuberculeux.

pulp [pœlp] *s.* pulpe; pâte [paper], f.; *v.* réduire en pâte.

pulpit [poulpit] *s.* chaire, f.

pulsate [pœlsé¹t] *v* battre, palpiter (med.). ‖ *pulsation* [pœlsé¹shən] *s.* pulsation, f. ‖ *pulse* [pœls] *s.* pouls, m.

pulverize [pælvəra¹z] *v.* pulvériser.

pumice [pœmis] *s* ponce, f.; *v.* poncer; *pumice stone*, pierre ponce.

pump [pœmp] *s* pompe, f.; *v.* pomper; gonfler [pneu]; débiter (mech.); *gasoline pump*, pompe à essence; *hand pump*, pompe à main; *tire pump*, pompe à pneus; *to pump someone*, tirer les vers du nez à quelqu'un.

pumpkin [pæmpkìn] *s.* citrouille, courge, f.; potiron, m.

pun [pœn] *s.* calembour; jeu de mots, m.; *v.* faire des jeux de mots.

punch [pœntsh] *s.** poinçon; perçoir; découpoir (techn.); emporte-pièce, m.; *v.* percer; perforer.

punch [pœntsh] *s.* punch, m.; vitalité, énergie, f.; *v.* battre, frapper.

punch [pœntsh] *s.* punch [drink], m.

punctilious [pœngti̇̃li•s] *adj.* pointilleux.

punctual [pœngktshou•l] *adj.* ponctuel; exact. ‖ **punctuality** [pœngktshoual•ti] *s.* ponctualité, f.; *v.* ponctuer. ‖ **punctuation** [-ktshoué̇̃sh•n] *s.* ponctuation, f. ‖ **puncture** [pœngkshe̊r] *v.* piquer, faire une piqûre; crever [tire]; *s.* ponction; piqûre; perforation, crevaison [tire], f.

pungent [pœndj•nt] *adj.* piquant; aigu; mordant; poignant.

puniness [pyouninis] *s.* débilité, chétivité, f.

punish [pœnish] *v.* punir, châtier. ‖ **punishment** [-m•nt] *s.* punition; sanction; peine, f.; châtiment, m.; *capital punishment*, peine capitale, *mitigation of punishment*, réduction de peine.

punk [pœngk] *s.* amadou, m.; insanité, ineptie, f. (fam.); *adj. Am.* pourri [wood]; mal fichu (pop.).

puny [pyouni] *adj.* chétif; débile.

pup [pœp] *s.* chiot; morveux, m.

pupil [pyoup'l] *s.* élève, m. f.

pupil [pyoup'l] *s.* pupille; prunelle [eye], f.

puppet [pœpit] *s.* marionnette; poupée, f.; pantin, m. (colloq.).

puppy [pœpi] *s.*° chiot; morveux, m.

purchase [pë̊rtshe̊s] *s.* achat, m.; acquisition; emplette, f.; *v.* acheter, acquérir.

pure [pyou•r] *adj.* pur.

purée [pyouré̇̃] *s.* purée, f.

purgative [pë̊rg•tiv] *adj., s.* purgatif. ‖ **purgatory** [-too•ri] *s.*° purgatoire, m. ‖ **purge** [pë̊rdj] *s.* purge; purgation, épuration, f.; *v.* purger; purifier, nettoyer, épurer.

purify [pyou•rfȧ̃] *v.* purifier; dépurer. ‖ **Puritan** [pyourit•n] *s., adj.* puritain; *puritanism*, puritanisme, m. ‖ **purity** [pyou•rti] *s.* pureté; propreté, f.

purple [pë̊rp'l] *adj., s.* pourpre; violet; rouge violacé.

purport [pë̊rpoou̇̃rt] *s.* teneur; portée, f.; [p•rpoou̇̃rt] *v.* signifier; impliquer.

purpose [pë̊rp•s] *s.* but; objet, m.; intention, f.; *v.* se proposer; *with the purpose of*, dans l'intention de; *for no purpose*, sans but, inutilement, en vain; *on purpose*, à dessein, *purposeful*, réfléchi; avisé; pondéré; entêté, tenace; *purposely*, exprès.

purr [pë̊r] *s.* ronron, m.; *v.* ronronner; faire ronron.

purse [pë̊rs] *s.* bourse; ressources, f.; porte-monnaie, m.; *v.* plisser, froncer; *to purse one's lips*, pincer les lèvres.

pursue [p•rsou̇̃] *v.* poursuivre; exercer [profession]. ‖ **pursuit** [-t] *s.* poursuite; occupation; recherches, f.; *pursuit plane*, avion de chasse.

purulent [pyouroul•nt] *adj.* purulent. ‖ **pus** [pœs] *s.* pus (med.), m.

purvey [p•vé̇̃] *v.* fournir; *purveyance*, approvisionnement; *purveyor*, fournisseur.

purview [pë̊rvyou] *s.* portée (f.) du regard.

push [poush] *v.* pousser; presser; inciter, *to push aside*, écarter; *to push down*, renverser; *to push a reform through*, faire aboutir une réforme; *to push off*, se mettre en route; *push button*, poussoir; presse - bouton; *pushcart*, voiture à bras; *pusher*, propulseur; arriviste, m.; *pushfulness*, arrivisme.

pusillanimity [pyousil•ni̇̃miti] *s.* pusillanimité, f.; *pusillanimous*, pusillanime.

pussy [pousi] *s.*° minet, chat, m.

pussyfoot [pousifout] *s.* prohibition, f.; *v.* faire patte de velours.

pustule [pœstyoul] *s.* pustule, f.

put [pout] *v.*° mettre; poser; placer; *to be put out*, être déconcerté, contrarié; *to put back*, retarder, *to put down*, noter; *to put on a dress*, mettre une robe; *to put off*, renvoyer, ajourner; ôter, déposer; *to put on airs*, se donner des airs; *to put out* [fire], éteindre [le feu]; *to put up with*, supporter, tolérer; *a put-up job*, une affaire montée, *pret.*, p. p. of *to put*.

putrefaction [pyoutr•faksh•n] *s.* putréfaction, f. ‖ **putrefy** [pyoutr•fȧ̃] *v.* pourrir; (se) putréfier, *putrescible*, putrescible.

putrid [pyoutrid] *adj.* putride.

puttee [pœti] *s.* bande molletière, f.

putter [pœte̊r] *v.* bricoler.

putter [poute̊r] *s.* metteur; instigateur; poteur, m.

putting [pouting] *s.* mise, pose, f.; *putting away*, rangement; économie; *putting down*, inscription, mouillage [boat], *putting to sea*, appareillage; *putting the shot* (or) *weight*, lancement du poids.

putty [pœti] *s.* mastic, m.; *v.* mastiquer.

puzzle [pœz'l] *s.* énigme, f.; jeu de patience, m.; *v.* intriguer; embarrasser; embrouiller; se creuser la tête; *crossword puzzle*, mots croisés; *to puzzle out*, déchiffrer, découvrir; *to be puzzled*, être perplexe.

pyjamas [pidjâm•z] *s. pl.* pyjama, m.

pylon [pȧ̃lân] *s.* pylône, m.

pyramid [pir•mid] *s.* pyramide, f.

pyx [piks] *s.* ciboire; contrôle (fin.), m.

Q

quack [kwak] *s.* charlatan; médicastre; couin-couin; couac, m.; *adj.* charlatanesque; *v.* crier comme un canard; faire des couacs; agir en charlatan.

quadrant [kwâdr•nt] *s.* quart; quart de cercle; quadrant, m.

quadrilateral [kwâdr•lat•r•l] *s.* quadrilatère, m.

quadruped [kwâdroupéd] *s.*, *adj.* quadrupède, m. ‖ **quadruple** [-p'l] *adj.*, *s.* quadruple; *v.* (se) quadrupler; **quadruplet**, quadruplé.

quagmire [kwagma¹•r] *s.* fondrière, f.; marécage, m.

quail [kwé¹l] *s.* caille, f.

quaint [kwé¹nt] *adj.* curieux; original; ingénieux, pittoresque.

quake [kwé¹k] *v.* trembler; frémir; *s.* tremblement, m. ‖ **Quaker** [-•r] *s.* Quaker, m.

qualification [kwâl•f•ké¹sh•n] *s.* qualification; aptitude; compétence, f. ‖ **qualify** [kwâl•fa¹] *v.* (se) qualifier; rendre, être capable; être reçu; obtenir les titres (*for*, pour). ‖ **qualitative** [kwâl•té¹tiv] *adj.* qualitatif. ‖ **quality** [kwâl•ti] *s.*° qualité, f.

qualm [kwâm] *s.* nausée, f.; scrupule; remords, m.

quantitative [kwânt•té¹tiv] *adj.* quantitatif. ‖ **quantity** [kwânt•ti] *s.*° quantité; abondance; somme, f.; **unknown quantity**, inconnue (math.).

quarantine [kwaur•ntîn] *s.* quarantaine, f.; *v.* mettre en quarantaine.

quarrel [kwaur•l] *s.* querelle; brouille, f.; *v.* se quereller; se disputer; se brouiller. ‖ **quarrelsome** [-s•m] *adj.* querelleur; irascible; grincheux.

quarry [kwauri] *s.*° carrière [pit], f.; *v.* exploiter une carrière; **slate quarry**, ardoisière; **quarrystone**, moellon.

quart [kwaurt] *s.* quarte, f.; *Fr. Can.*, pinte [milk], f.

quarter [kwaurt•r] *s.* quart; quartier (mil.; topogr.); terme [rent]; trimestre, m.; *Am.* pièce de 25 cents, f.; *v.* diviser en quatre; écarteler; cantonner (mil.). ‖ **quartered** [-d] *adj.* divisé en quatre; cantonné; caserné; logé. ‖ **quarterly** [-li] *adv.* par trimestre; *adj.* trimestriel. ‖ **quartet** [kwaurtèt] *s.* quatuor, m.

quartz [kwaurts] *s.* quartz; cristal de roche, m.

quatrain [kwautr•n] *s.* quatrain, m.

quaver [kwé¹v•r] *s.* tremblement; trémolo; trille, m.; *v.* trembler; trembloter; faire des trilles.

quay [kî] *s.* quai; appontement, m.

queasy [kwîzi] *adj.* nauséeux.

queen [kwîn] *s.* reine; dame [cards], f.; **queenly**, royal.

queer [kwi•r] *adj.* bizarre, étrange; excentrique; mal à l'aise; inverti (colloq.); *v.* gâcher; déranger; rendre malade; **queerness**, bizarrerie; malaise.

quell [kwèl] *v.* réprimer; calmer; étouffer [rebellion].

quench [kwèntsh] *v.* éteindre [fire]; étancher [thirst]; étouffer [revolt]; *to quench one's thirst*, se désaltérer.

quern [kwërn] *s.* moulin, m.

querulous [kwèr•l•s] *adj.* ronchon; rouspéteur (colloq.).

query [kwi•ri] *s.*° question; interrogation, f.; *v.* questionner; révoquer en doute; contester.

quest [kwèst] *s.* enquête, f.; *in quest of*, en quête de.

question [kwèstsh•n] *s.* question; demande; interpellation, f.; problème, m.; *v.* interroger, questionner; douter; se demander; *to ask a question*, poser une question; *leading question*, question tendancieuse (jur.); **question mark**, point d'interrogation. ‖ **questionable** [-•b'l] *adj.* douteux; contestable. ‖ **questioner** [-•r] *s.* interrogateur, m. ‖ **questioning** [-ing] *s.* interrogatoire, m.; *adj.* interrogateur. ‖ **questionless** [-lis] *adj.* indiscutable. ‖ **questionnaire** [kwèstsh•nèr] *s.* questionnaire, m.

queue [kyou] *s.* queue; file, f.; *v.* faire la queue.

quibble [kwib'l] *v.* argutie, chicane, f.; *v.* ergoter.

quick [kwik] *adj.* prompt; rapide; preste; fin; *adv.* vite; *s.* vif, vivant, m.; **quick edge**, haie vive; **quick fire**, tir rapide; **quicklime**, chaux vive; **quicksand**, sable mouvant; **quicksilver**, mercure; **quickstep**, pas accéléré (mil.). **quick wit**, esprit vif; *to cut to the quick*, tailler dans le vif. ‖ **quicken** [-•n] *v.* vivifier; (s')animer; accélérer; stimuler. ‖ **quickly** [-li] *adv.* vite; rapidement; bientôt; tôt. ‖ **quickness** [-nis] *s.* rapidité; promptitude; vitesse; vivacité; acuité, f.

quid [kwid] *s.* chique, f.; (fam.). livre, f.

quiescence [kwa¹ès•ns] *s.* calme, repos, m.

quiet [kwa¹t] *adj.* tranquille; calme; paisible; serein; *s.* tranquillité; quiétude; accalmie, f.; *v.* calmer; apaiser;

tranquilliser; faire taire, faire tenir tranquille; *on the quiet*, en douce; *to be quiet*, se taire, rester tranquille; *quietly*, tranquillement, en silence. ‖ *quietness* [-nis] *s.* tranquillité, f.; calme; silence; repos; recueillement, m.

quietus [kwa¹îtⁱs] *s.* quitus, m.; quittance; mort, f.

quill [kwil] *s.* plume [bird], f.; curedent; piquant, m.

quilt [kwilt] *s.* couvre-pieds, m.; couverture piquée, f.; *v.* rembourrer, piquer.

quince [kwins] *s.* coing, m.; *quince-tree*, cognassier.

quincunx [kwinkœngks] *s.* quinconce, m.

quinine [kwa¹na¹n] *s.* quinine, f.

quinquina [kwingkinⁿ] *s.* quinquina, m.

quinsy [kwinsi] *s.* angine, f.

quintet [kwintèt] *s.* quintette, m. ‖ *quintuple* [kwintyoup'l] *adj.*, *s.* quintuple; *v.* quintupler. ‖ *quintuplet* [kwintyouplit] *s.* quintuplé, m.

quip [kwip] *s.* raillerie; repartie; argutie; pointe, f.; sarcasme; bon mot, m.; *v.* railler.

quit [kwit] *v.* quitter; laisser; abandonner; démissionner; acquitter; *adj.* quitte, libéré; *pret., p. p. of to quit*; *notice to quit*, congé.

quite [kwa¹t] *adv.* tout à fait; entièrement; parfaitement; bien; *in quite another tone*, sur un tout autre ton; *she is quite a beauty*, c'est une vraie beauté.

quitter [kwitⁿ] *s. Am.* défaitiste, déserteur, lâcheur; javart (vet.).

quiver [kwivⁿ] *v.* trembler; frissonner; vibrer, palpiter; *s.* tremblement, frisson; carquois, m.

quixotic [kwiksâtik] *adj.* exalté, donquichottesque.

quiz [kwiz] *(pl. quizzes) s.* examen; questionnaire, m.; colle (fam.); moquerie, f.; *v. Am.* poser des colles à; railler, persifler; lorgner; *quizzing-glass*, lorgnon.

quorum [kwoᵒurⁿm] *s.* quorum, m.

quota [kwoᵒutⁿ] *s.* quote-part; cotisation, f.; contingent, m.; *quota system*, contingentement.

quotation [kwoᵒutⁿshⁿn] *s.* citation; cote; cotation, f.; cours, m.; *quotation mark*, guillemet. ‖ *quote* [kwoᵒut] *v.* citer; coter [price]; mettre des guillemets; *in quotes*, entre guillemets.

quotient [kwoᵒushⁿn] *s.* quotient, m.

R

rabbi [raba¹] *s.* rabbin, m.

rabbit [rabit] *s.* lapin, m.

rabble [rab'l] *s.* racaille; canaille; populace; cohue, f.

rabid [rabid] *adj.* furieux; féroce; enragé. ‖ *rabies* [ré¹bîz] *s.* rage, f.

raccoon [rakoun] *s.* raton laveur, m.

race [ré¹s] *s.* course; carrière, f.; cours, courant; affolement [motor], m.; *v.* courir, s'emballer; s'affoler (techn.); *hurdle race*, course de haies; *tide race*, raz de marée; *race track*, champ de courses, piste.

race [ré¹s] *s.* race, lignée, f.

racer [ré¹sⁿr] *s.* coureur; cheval, bateau, avion de course, m.

racial [ré¹shⁿl] *adj.* racial; *racialism*, *Am. racism*, racisme; *racialist*, *Am. racist*, raciste.

rack [rak] *s.* chevalet [torture]; râtelier [arms]; casier [bottles]; filet, porte-bagages [train], m.; crémaillère, f.; *v.* torturer, distendre; extorquer; *bomb rack*, lance-bombes; *hat rack*, porte-chapeau; *towel rack*, porte-serviettes; *to rack one's brains*, se creuser la tête.

rack [rak] *s.* ruine, f.; *to go to rack and ruin*, s'en aller à vau-l'eau.

racket [rakit] *s.* raquette; *Am.* palette, f.; battoir, m.

racket [rakit] *s.* vacarme, tapage, m.; métier louche, racket, m.; *v.* faire du boucan; faire la sarabande. ‖ *racketeer* [rakitîⁿr] *s.* tapageur; noceur; escroc; gangster, m.; *v.* escroquer; extorquer; combiner.

radar [ré¹daʳ] *s.* radar, m.

radiance [ré¹diⁿns] *s.* rayonnement, m. ‖ *radiant* [-diⁿnt] *adj.* rayonnant; radieux; irradiant. ‖ *radiate* [-dié¹t] *v.* irradier; rayonner. ‖ *radiation* [ré¹dié¹shⁿn] *s.* radiation, f.; rayonnement, m. ‖ *radiator* [ré¹dié¹tⁿr] *s.* radiateur, m.; *radiator-cap*, bouchon de radiateur.

radical [radik'l] *adj.*, *s.* radical, m.; fondamental; foncier.

radio [ré¹dioᵒu] *s.* radio; T. S. F., f.; *v.* émettre; radiodiffuser; radiotélégraphier; *radioactivity*, radioactivité; *radiobroadcast*, radiodiffusion; *radiologist*, radiologue; *radiology*, radiologie; *radio set*, poste de T. S. F.; *radiotherapy*, radiothérapie.

radish [radish] *s.** radis, m.; *radish-dish*, ravier.

radium [ré¹diᵉm] *s.* radium, m.

radius [ré¹diᵉs] *s.** rayon, m.

raffia [rafia] *s.* raphia, m.

raffle [raf'l] *s.* loterie, tombola, f.; *v.* mettre en loterie.

raft [raft] *s.* radeau, train de bois, m.; *air raft*, radeau pneumatique.

raft [raft] *s. Am.* tas, amas, m.

rafter [raftᵉʳ] *s.* chevron, m.; *under the rafters*, sous les combles.

raftsman [raftsmᵉn] (*pl.* **raftsmen**) *s.* flotteur, *Fr. Can.* draveur, m.

rag [rag] *s.* haillon; chiffon, m.; guenille, f.; *rag doll*, poupée en chiffon; *rag-and-bone-man, rag-picker, ragman*, chiffonnier.

ragamuffin [ragᵉmœfin] *s.* gueux, vagabond, m.

rage [ré¹dj] *s.* rage, fureur, f.; *v.* être déchaîné; divaguer; dérailler; enrager (*with*, de); *to be all the rage*, faire fureur, être du dernier cri, être du dernier chic.

ragged [ragid] *adj.* déguenillé; déchiqueté; en haillons; rocailleux.

raid [ré¹d] *s.* raid; coup de main, m.; incursion; razzia; descente de police, f.; *v.* conduire un raid; faire un coup de force; razzier; *police raid*, rafle; *raider*, maraudeur; croiseur, corsaire (naut.); commando (milit.); avion ennemi.

rail [ré¹l] *s.* barre; rampe [staircase]; balustrade; barrière, f.; barreau; rail; étrésillon, m.; *by rail*, par fer; *rail car*, autorail; *to go off the rails*, dérailler. ‖ *railing* [-ing] *s.* palissade, grille, balustrade, f. ‖ *railroad* [-roᵒud] *s. Am.* voie ferrée, f.; chemin de fer, m.; *railroad station*, gare; *railroader*, *Am.* cheminot. ‖ *railway* [-wé¹] *s.* chemin de fer, m.; *Am. railway crossing*, passage à niveau; *railway system*, réseau de chemin de fer; *railwayman*, cheminot.

rain [ré¹n] *s.* pluie, f.; *v.* pleuvoir; *rain water*, eau de pluie; *to rain down*, faire pleuvoir. ‖ *rainbow* [-boᵒu] *s.* arc-en-ciel, m. ‖ *raincoat* [-koᵒut] *s.* imperméable, m. ‖ *raindrop* [-dråp] *s.* goutte d'eau, f. ‖ *rainfall* [-faul] *s.* averse; pluviosité, f. ‖ *raingauge* [-gé¹dj] *s.* pluviomètre, m. ‖ *rainy* [-i] *adj.* pluvieux; humide.

raise [ré¹z] *v.* lever; élever; soulever [question]; hausser; pousser [cry]; évoquer [spirit]; ressusciter [dead]; se procurer [money]; émettre [loan]; augmenter; produire; *to raise a laugh*, faire rire; *s.* augmentation, hausse [price], f.

raisin [ré¹z'n] *s.* raisin sec, m.

rake [ré¹k] *s.* rateau; dégagement (techn.); viveur, m.; ratissoire, f.; *v.* ratisser, râcler; *rake-off*, ristourne, « gratte » (pop.).

rally [rali] *s.* ralliement [mast], f.; rallier; reprendre ses forces.

ram [ràm] *s.* bélier; éperon (naut.); coulisseau, m.; *v.* heurter; tamponner; enfoncer; bourrer; éperonner.

ramble [ràmb'l] *s.* randonnée; promenade; divagation, f.; *v.* errer; rôder; se promener; divaguer.

ramify [ramifa¹] *v.* (se) ramifier.

rampant [rampᵉnt] *adj.* déchaîné; luxuriant.

rampart [ràmpârt] *s.* rempart, m.

ran [ràn] *pret. of* **to run**.

ranch [ràntsh] *s.** ranch, m.

rancid [rànsid] *adj.* rance.

ranco(u)r [ràngkᵉʳ] *s.* rancune, f.; ressentiment, m.

random [ràndᵉm] *adj.* fortuit; à tort et à travers; *s.* hasard; *at random*, au hasard.

rang [ràng] *pret. of* **to ring**.

range [ré¹ndj] *s.* rangée; chaîne [mountains]; étendue; portée; distance; direction, f.; domaine, champ d'activité; champ de tir; alignement; fourneau de cuisine, m.; *v.* (se) ranger; parcourir; s'étendre; aligner; s'échelonner; *adjusted range*, tir ajusté; *gas-range*, fourneau à gaz; *long range*, longue portée; *within range of*, à portée de; *range of vision*, champ visuel.

rank [ràngk] *s.* rang; ordre; grade, m.; classe, f.; *v.* (se) ranger; classer; disposer; *Am.* avoir un rang supérieur à; *Br.* occuper un rang; *rank and file*, les hommes de troupe; *to rank with*, être à égalité de rang, de grade, avec; être au niveau de; *promoted from the ranks*, sorti du rang.

rank [ràngk] *adj.* fort [odor]; complet, absolu, éclatant; répugnant; fétide; dru; luxuriant.

ransack [rànsak] *v.* saccager; piller; fouiller.

ransom [rànsᵉm] *s.* rançon, f.; *v.* rançonner; racheter.

rant [rànt] *v.* déclamer; divaguer; *s.* divagation; rodomontade, f.

ranunculus [rᵉnᵉngkyoulᵉs] *s.** renoncule, f.

rap [rap] *s.* tape, f.; *v.* frapper; heurter; donner des petits coups secs; *to rap out*, débiter vite.

rap [rap] *s.* fausse pièce de monnaie [halfpenny], f.; *not to care a rap*, s'en soucier comme d'une guigne, s'en moquer.

rapacious [rᵊpéⁱshᵊs] *adj.* rapace; *rapaciousness, rapacity*, rapacité.

rape [réⁱp] *s.* viol; rapt, m.; *v.* violer; enlever.

rapid [rapid] *adj.* rapide; accéléré; prompt; *s. pl.* rapides, m. pl. || *rapidity* [rᵊpidᵉti] *s.* rapidité, f.

rapier [réⁱpiᵉr] *s.* rapière, f.

rapine [rapaⁱn] *s.* rapine, f.

rapport [rapauᵊʳ] *s.* rapport, m.

rapt [rapt] *adj.* ravi, extasié, transporté. || *rapture* [raptshᵉr] *s.* ravissement; transport, enthousiasme, m.; extase, f.

rare [rèᵉr] *adj. Am.* à demi cru, mal cuit, saignant.

rare [rèᵉr] *adj.* rare; précieux; extraordinaire; excellent. || *rarefy* [-faⁱ] *v.* (se) raréfier; affiner (fig.). || *rarely* [-li] *adv.* rarement; parfaitement, admirablement.

rarity [rèrᵉti] *s.*⁰ rareté; curiosité, f.

rascal [rask'] *s.* gredin, polisson, m.

rash [rash] *s.* éruption (med.), f.

rash [rash] *adj.* téméraire; irréfléchi; impétueux; imprudent. || *rashness* [-nis] *s.* impétuosité; témérité; imprudence, f.

rasp [rasp] *s.* râpe, f.; *v.* râper.

raspberry [razbèri] *s.*⁰ framboise, f.; *raspberry bush*, framboisier.

raspy [raspi] *adj.* rugueux, râpeux, âpre.

rat [rat] *s.* rat; lâcheur; jaune [workman]; renégat, m,; *v.* dératiser; trahir; tourner casaque.

rate [réⁱt] *s.* taux; pourcentage; prix; cours [exchange]; régime, débit; impôt, m.; catégorie; cadence; vitesse, f.; *v.* évaluer; taxer; tarifer; imposer; coter; étalonner; classer; tancer; *at any rate*, de toute façon; *at the rate of*, à raison de; *he rates high*, on le tient en haute estime; *first rate*, de premier ordre; épatant (fam.); *rate-office*, recette municipale.

rather [razhᵉr] *adv.* plutôt; assez, passablement; de préférence; *rather than*, plutôt que; *I had rather stay*, j'aimerais mieux rester.

ratification [ratᵊfikéⁱshᵉn] *s.* ratification, f. || *ratify* [ratᵊfaⁱ] *v.* ratifier.

rating [réⁱting] *s.* estimation, évaluation; répartition [taxes]; capacité, puissance, valeur, f.; rang; classement, m.; semonce, f.

ratio [réⁱshoᵘ] *s.* rapport, m.; proportion, f.; *in indirect ratio*, en raison inverse.

ration [réⁱshᵉn] *s.* ration, f.; *v.* rationner; ravitailler.

rational [rashᵉn'l] *adj.* rationnel; raisonnable; raisonné; logique; *rationalism*, rationalisme; *rationalist*, rationaliste; *rationalize*, rationaliser.

rationing [réⁱshᵉning] *s.* rationnement, m.

rattan [ratan] *s.* rotin, m.

rattle [rat'l] *s.* cliquetis; bruit de ferraille, m.; crécelle, f.; *v.* cliqueter; *to rattle off*, débiter rapidement; *deathrattle*, râle; *rattle-snake*, serpent à sonnette, crotale.

raucous [raukᵉs] *adj.* rauque.

ravage [ravidj] *s.* ravage; pillage, m.; ruine, f.; *v.* ravager; piller.

rave [réⁱv] *v.* délirer; divaguer; déraisonner; s'extasier (*over, sur*).

ravel [rav'l] *v.* emmêler; s'embrouiller; *to ravel out*, démêler; s'effilocher.

raven [réⁱvᵉn] *s.* corbeau, m.; *adj.* noir luisant.

ravenous [ravᵉnᵉs] *adj.* vorace, dévorant; affamé.

ravine [rᵊvîn] *s.* ravin, m.; ravine, f.

ravish [ravish] *v.* ravir; enlever; violer; enchanter, transporter; *ravishment*, rapt; viol; ravissement, m.

raw [rau] *adj.* cru; brut; aigre [weather]; grège [silk]; vif [air]; inexpérimenté; novice; *s.* point sensible, m.; *rawhide*, cuir vert; *raw material*, matière première; *raw sugar*, cassonade; *raw wound*, plaie à vif.

ray [réⁱ] *s.* rayon, m.; radiation, f.

rayon [réⁱân] *s.* rayonne, soie artificielle, f.

raze [réⁱz] *v.* raser; effacer; rayer. || *razor* [-ᵉr] *s.* rasoir, m.; *razor blade*, lame de rasoir.

reach [rîtsh] *v.* atteindre; rejoindre; (s')étendre; aboutir à; arriver à; *to reach for*, s'efforcer d'atteindre; *to reach into*, mettre la main dans; *reach me over my hat*, passez-moi mon chapeau; *reach-me-down*, décrochez-moi-ça; *s.* portée, étendue, f.; *beyond the reach of*, hors d'atteinte de; *within the reach of*, à portée de.

react [riakt] *v.* réagir; jouer de nouveau. || *reaction* [riakshᵉn] *s.* réaction; résistance, f.; processus, m. || *reactionary* [-èri] *adj.*, *s.*⁰ réactionnaire; conservateur. || *reactor* [riaktᵉr] *s.* réacteur, m.

read [rîd] *v.*⁰ (se) lire; *to read up*, étudier; *to read out*, lire tout haut; *to read over*, parcourir; *readable*, lisible; [rèd] *pret., p. p. of to read*. || *reader* [-ᵉr] *s.* lecteur, m.; lectrice, f.

readily [rèd'li] *adv.* promptement; volontiers, de bon cœur. || *readiness* [rèdinis] *s.* promptitude; facilité; vivacité; bonne volonté, f.

reading [rìding] *s.* lecture; indication; cote, f.; relevé, m.; *reading-desk*, pupitre; lutrin.

readjust [rì·djœst] *v.* rajuster; réorganiser. ‖ *readjustment* [-mᵉnt] *s.* rajustement, m.; réorganisation, f.

ready [rèdi] *adj.* prêt; vif; disposé; comptant [money]; *ready-made,* tout fait; *ready-to-wear*, prêt à porter.

real [rìᵉl] *adj.* réel; véritable; matériel; *real estate*, propriété immobilière. ‖ *realism* [-izᵉm] *s.* réalisme, m. ‖ *realist* [-ist] *s.* réaliste, m. ‖ *realistic* [-istik] *adj.* réaliste. ‖ *reality* [rìalti] *s.*ᵃ réalité, f. ‖ *realizable* [rìᵉla¹zᵉb'l] *adj.* concevable; imaginable; réalisable. ‖ *realization* [rìᵉlᵉzé¹shᵉn] *s.* réalisation, f.; conception nette, f. ‖ *realize* [rìᵉla¹z] *v.* réaliser; effectuer; comprendre, saisir; se rendre compte de. ‖ *really* [rìᵉli] *adv.* réellement; véritablement; vraiment, en vérité.

realm [rèlm] *s.* royaume; domaine, m.

reanimate [rìanimé¹t] *v.* réanimer; ranimer; *reanimation*, réanimation; reprise.

reap [rìp] *v.* moissonner; recueillir. ‖ *reaper* [-ᵉr] *s.* moissonneur, m.

reappear [rìᵉpìᵉr] *v.* reparaître; *reappearance*, réapparition; rentrée (theatr.).

rear [rìᵉr] *adj.* arrière; d'arrière; *s.* arrière; derrière, m.; file, queue, f.; *rear admiral*, contre-amiral; *rear guard*, arrière-garde.

rear [rìᵉr] *v.* lever, soulever; élever; redresser; se cabrer [horse].

reason [rìz'n] *s.* raison; cause, f.; motif, m.; *v.* raisonner; *by reason of*, à cause de; *to stand to reason*, être raisonnable; *to reason upon*, argumenter sur. ‖ *reasonable* [-ᵉb'l] *adj.* raisonnable; juste; rationnel; modéré; justifié [doubt]. ‖ *reasonably* [-ᵉbli] *adv.* raisonnablement; modérément; passablement. ‖ *reasoning* [-ing] *s.* raisonnement, m.

reassure [rìᵉshour] *v.* rassurer; réassurer.

rebate [rìbé¹t] *s.* escompte; rabais, m; remise, f.; *v.* diminuer; rabattre; escompter.

rebel [rèb'l] *adj., s.* rebelle; [ribèl] *v.* se révolter; se rebeller. ‖ *rebellion* [-yᵉn] *s.* rébellion, f. ‖ *rebellious* [-yᵉs] *adj.* rebelle, mutin, révolté.

rebirth [rìbᵉrth] *s.* renaissance; réincarnation, f.; *reborn*, réincarné; né de nouveau.

rebound [ribaᵒund] *v.* (faire) rebondir; [ribaᵒund] *s.* rebondissement, ricochet, m.

rebuff [ribœf] *s.* rebuffade, f.; échec, m.; *v.* repousser; rebuter.

rebuild [ribìld] *v.* reconstruire; rééditifier. ‖ *rebuilt* [-bìlt] *pret., p. p. of* **to rebuild**.

rebuke [ribyouk] *s.* reproche, blâme, m.; *v.* réprimander.

rebus [rìbᵉs] *s.* rébus, m.

rebut [ribœt] *v.* réfuter; rejeter.

recalcitrant [rikalsitrᵉnt] *adj.* récalcitrant.

recalcitrate [rikalsitré¹t] *v.* regimber.

recall [rìkaul] *s.* rappel, m.; rétractation; annulation, f.; [rikaul] *v.* (se) rappeler; se souvenir de; retirer, annuler.

recant [rikant] *v.* (se) rétracter.

recapitulate [rikᵉpìtyoulé¹t] *v.* récapituler; *recapitulation*, récapitulation.

recede [risìd] *v.* se retirer; s'éloigner; renoncer (*from*, à).

receipt [risìt] *s.* quittance; facture; réception [letter], f.; récépissé [parcel], m.; *pl.* recette; rentrées, f.; *v.* donner un reçu; acquitter.

receive [risìv] *v.* recevoir; accepter. ‖ *receiver* [-ᵉr] *s.* destinataire [letter]; receveur; récepteur, réceptionnaire; *Am.* recéleur, m.

recent [rìs'nt] *adj.* récent, nouveau, de fraîche date.

receptacle [risèptᵉk'l] *s.* réceptacle; récipient, m.

reception [risèpshᵉn] *s.* réception, f.; *receptionist*, réceptionniste; *receptive*, réceptif; *receptivity*, réceptivité.

recess [risès] *s.*ᵃ repli; coin solitaire; évidement; renfoncement; creux, m.; alcôve; niche; gorge; cavité; vacances; récréation, f.; *v.* enfoncer; encastrer; évider; prendre des vacances; suspendre les séances; *recession*, récession.

recipe [rèsᵉpi] *s.* recette; ordonnance, f.

recipient [risìpiᵉnt] *s.* récipient; destinataire, bénéficiaire, m.; *adj.* réceptif; qui reçoit.

reciprocal [risìprᵉk'l] *adj.* réciproque, mutuel; inverse. ‖ *reciprocate* [risìprᵉké¹t] *v.* échanger; payer de retour; répondre à. ‖ *reciprocity* [rèsᵉprᵉsti] *s.* réciprocité, f.

recital [risa¹t'l] *s.* récit; exposé; récital [music], m. ‖ *recitation* [rèsᵉté¹shᵉn] *s.* récitation, f. ‖ *recite* [risa¹t] *v.* réciter; raconter; relater, exposer.

reckless [rèklis] *adj.* téméraire; imprudent; insouciant. ‖ *recklessness* [-nis] *s.* insouciance; témérité, f.

reckon [rèkⁿn] v. compter (*on*, sur); calculer; *Am.* supputer, croire. ‖ *reckoning* [-ing] s. compte; calcul, m.

reclaim [riklé¹m] v. réclamer; récupérer; réformer; défricher; *reclamation*, réclamation; récupération; amendement.

recline [rikla¹n] v. incliner; reposer; (s')appuyer; s'étendre.

recluse [riklous] adj. reclus. ‖ *reclusion* [riklouⱼⁿn] s. réclusion, f.

recognition [rèkⁿgníshⁿn] s. reconnaissance; identification, f. ‖ *recognize* [rèkⁿgna¹z] v. reconnaître; identifier; admettre.

recoil [rⁿko¹l] v. reculer; hésiter; rebondir; s. recul [gun]; contrecoup; dégoût, m.

recollect [rèkⁿlèkt] v. se souvenir, se rappeler. ‖ *recollection* [rèkⁿlèkshⁿn] s. souvenir, m.; mémoire, f.; recueillement, m.

recommend [rèkⁿmènd] v. recommander; conseiller. ‖ *recommendation* [rékⁿmèndé¹shⁿn] s. recommandation, f.

recompense [rèkⁿmpèns] s. récompense, f.; dédommagement, m.; v. récompenser; dédommager.

reconcile [rèkⁿnsa¹l] v. réconcilier; faire accepter; arranger; *to become reconciled to*, se résigner à. ‖ *reconciliation* [rèkⁿnsilié¹shⁿn] s. réconciliation; conciliation; résignation, f.

recondite [rèkⁿnda¹t] adj. abstrus; profond.

reconnoissance [rikânisⁿns] s. reconnaissance (mil.), f. ‖ *reconnoiter* [rîkⁿno¹tⁿr] v. *Am.* reconnaître, explorer (mil.).

reconsider [rîkⁿnsídⁿr] v. reconsidérer; réviser (jur.).

reconstitute [rîkⁿnstityout] v. reconstituer; *reconstitution*, reconstitution.

reconstruct [rîkⁿnstrækt] v. reconstruire; réédifier. ‖ *reconstruction* [rîkⁿnstrækshⁿn] s. reconstruction, f.

record [rèkⁿrd] s. attestation; note; mention, f.; procès-verbal; dossier; registre; disque [gramophone]; record [sport]; casier judiciaire, m.; adj. notable, marquant; [rikⁿurd] v. enregistrer; consigner; attester; graver; imprimer (fig.); faire un disque; *record-player*, pick-up; *public records*, archives nationales; *service record*, état de service; *to break the speed record*, battre le record de vitesse; *off-the-record*, à titre confidentiel. ‖ *recorder* [-ⁿr] s. enregistreur; indicateur; greffier (jur.), m.

recount [rîkaⁿunt] s. recomptage, état, m.; [rikaⁿunt] v. raconter; énumérer; recompter.

recoup [rikoup] v. dédommager; récupérer; défalquer (jur.).

recourse [rîkoⁿurs] s. recours, m.

recover [rikævⁿr] v. recouvrer; récupérer; guérir.

recover [rikævⁿr] v. recouvrir.

recovery [rikævri] s.* recouvrement; rétablissement (med.); redressement, m.; reprise (comm.); récupération [industry], f.

recreate [rèkrié¹t] v. (se) distraire. ‖ *recreation* [rèkrié¹shⁿn] s. récréation; distraction, f.; divertissement, m.; *recreative*, récréatif.

recriminate [rikrimⁿné¹t] v. récriminer; *recrimination*, récrimination.

recrudescence [rikroudés¹ns] s. recrudescence, f.

recruit [rikrout] v. recruter; s. recrue, f.; *recruiting*, recrutement.

rectangle [rèktàngg'l] s. rectangle, m; *rectangular*, rectangulaire.

rectify [rèktⁿfa¹] v. rectifier.

rector [rèktⁿr] s. recteur, m.

rectum [rèktⁿm] s. rectum, m.

recuperate [rikyoupⁿré¹t] v. récupérer; recouvrer; *Am.* se rétablir (med.). ‖ *recuperator* [-ⁿr] s. récupérateur; régénérateur, m.

recur [rikⁿr] v. revenir; se reproduire; se renouveler. ‖ *recurrence* [-ⁿns] s. retour, m.; récidive, f.

red [rèd] adj., s. rouge; roux; *redbreast*, rouge-gorge; *red-haired*, roux; *red-hot*, chauffé au rouge.

redaction [ridakshⁿn] s. rédaction, f.; *redactor*, rédacteur.

redden [rèd'n] v. rougir; *reddish*, rougeâtre.

redeem [ridîm] v. racheter, sauver; compenser; exécuter [promise]; rembourser; défricher [land]. ‖ *redeemer* [-ⁿr] s. libérateur, sauveur, Rédempteur, m. ‖ *redemption* [ridèmpshⁿn] s. rédemption; délivrance, f.; remboursement; paiement; rachat; amortissement, m.

redness [rèdnis] s. rougeur; inflammation, f.

redouble [rîdœb'l] v. redoubler.

redoubt [ridaⁿut] s. redoute, f.

redoubtable [ridaⁿutⁿb'l] adj. redoutable.

redress [rîdrès] s. redressement; remède, m.; réparation, réforme; revanche, f.; [ridrès] v. redresser; réparer; remédier.

reduce [ridyous] v. réduire; diminuer; amoindrir; maigrir; rétrograder; subjuguer. ‖ *reduction* [ridækshⁿn] s. réduction; diminution, f.

redwood [rèdwoud] *s.* séquoïa, m.

reed [rîd] *s.* roseau; chalumeau; peigne [weaving], m.; anche, f.

reef [rîf] *s.* récif; écueil; atoll; ris (naut.), m.; *v.* prendre les ris dans.

reek [rîk] *v.* fumée; vapeur; mauvaise odeur, f.; *v.* fumer; enfumer; puer; *to reek of*, empester.

reel [rîl] *s.* bobine; titubation, f.; rouleau; dévidoir; moulinet, m.; *v.* bobiner, dévider; tournoyer; avoir le vertige; (faire) tituber; *to reel off*, débiter, dégoiser (fam.).

re-establish [rîestablish] *v.* rétablir; réinstaller; restaurer.

refection [rifékshen] *s.* collation, f. || **refectory** [-teri] *s.* réfectoire, m.

refer [rifër] *v.* renvoyer; référer; transmettre; s'adresser, s'en remettre (*to*, à); *referring to*, comme suite à. || **referee** [rèfferî] *s.* arbitre, m.; *v.* arbitrer. || **reference** [rèfrens] *s.* référence; mention; recommandation; allusion; f.; rapport; répondant; renvoi, m.; *referendum*, référendum.

refill [rîfill] *v.* remplir; réapprovisionner; [rîfill] *s.* mine de rechange [pencil], cartouche [fountain pen], f.

refine [rifaïn] *v.* raffiner; renchérir (*upon*, sur); polir [manners]; affiner [metal]; s'épurer. || **refined** [-d] *adj.* raffiné; délicat; distingué; cultivé. || **refinement** [-ment] *s.* raffinage; raffinement; affinage, m.; épuration, f. || **refiner** [-er] *s.* raffineur, m. || **refinery** [-eri] *s.** raffinerie, f.

reflect [riflèkt] *v.* réfléchir; refléter; méditer. || **reflection** [riflèkshen] *s.* réflexion; critique, f.; reflet, m.; *on reflexion*, réflexion faite. || **reflector** [riflèkter] *s.* réflecteur, m.

reflex [rîflèks] *adj.*, *s.** réflexe.

reflexive [riflèksiv] *adj.*, *s.* réfléchi.

reflux [rîflœks] *s.* reflux; jusant, m.

reform [rifaurm] *s.* réforme, f.; *v.* réformer. || **reformation** [rèfermé-shen] *s.* réforme, f.; amendement, m. || **reformer** [rifaurmer] *s.* réformateur, m.; réformiste, m. f.

refract [rifrakt] *v.* réfracter; *refraction*, réfraction; *refractivity*, réfringence.

refractory [rifrakteri] *adj.* réfractaire; récalcitrant; indiscipliné.

refrain [rifréin] *v.* s'abstenir, se garder; s'empêcher (*from*, de); refréner; contenir.

refresh [rifrèsh] *v.* rafraîchir; délasser; rénover; se restaurer; se reposer. || **refreshing** [-ing] *adj.* rafraîchissant; délassant; réparateur. || **refreshment** [-ment] *s.* rafraîchissement; casse-croûte, m.

refrigeration [rifridjeréishen] *s.* réfrigération, f.; refroidissement, m. || **refrigerate** [-réit] *v.* réfrigérer; frigorifier; frapper [wine]. || **refrigerator** [rifridjeréiter] *s.* réfrigérateur, m.; glacière, f.

refuge [rèfyoudj] *s.* refuge; asile, m. || **refugee** [rèfyoudjî] *s.* réfugié, m.

refund [rîfœnd] *s.* remboursement, m.; [rifœnd] *v.* rembourser, restituer; [rîfœnd] *v.* consolider.

refusal [rifyouz'l] *s.* refus; déni, m. (jur.). || **refuse** [rifyouz] *v.* refuser; repousser; rejeter; se refuser (*to*, à).

refuse [rèfyous] *s.* détritus; déchets, m. pl.; ordures, f. pl.

refutal, refutation [rifyout'l, rifyou-téishen] *s.* réfutation, f. || **refute** [rifyout] *v.* réfuter.

regain [rigéin] *v.* regagner; récupérer; recouvrer.

regal [rîg'l] *adj.* royal.

regale [rigéil] *v.* (se) régaler; *to regale oneself on*, savourer.

regalia [rigéilie] *s. pl.* insignes, m. pl.

regard [rigârd] *v.* regarder; faire attention à; considérer; concerner; estimer, juger; *s.* égard; respect, m.; considération, estime, f.; pl. compliments, m.; *as regards*, quant à; *with regard to*, relativement à; *best regards*, meilleurs souvenirs; *regardful*, attentif, soigneux, respectueux; *regardless*, négligent, inattentif. || **regarding** [-ing] *prep.* concernant, relativement à.

regatta [rigate] *s.* régate, f.

regenerate [ridjénéreit] *v.* régénérer. || **regeneration** [ridjeneréishen] *s.* régénération, f.; *regenerative*, régénérateur.

regent [rîdjent] *s.* régent, m.

regime [rijîm] *s.* régime, m.

regiment [rèdjement] *s.* régiment, m.

region [rîdjen] *s.* région, f.; *regionalism*, régionalisme.

register [rèdjister] *s.* registre; compteur; repérage (mil.), m.; *v.* enregistrer; inscrire; repérer (mil.); recommander [mail]; déposer [trademark]; immatriculer. || **registrar** [-trâr] *s.* greffier; secrétaire (univ.); archiviste, m. || **registration** [rèdjistréishen] *s.* inscription; immatriculation; recommandation [post], f.; enregistrement; repérage (mil.), m. || **registry** [rèdjistri] *s.** acte (ou) bureau d'enregistrement, m.

regress [rigrès] *v.* retourner en arrière; rétrograder; *s.* régression, f.

regret [rigrèt] *s.* regret, m.; *v.* regretter; *to send regrets*, envoyer ses excuses; *regrettable*, regrettable; fâcheux.

regular [règyᵉlᵉr] *adj.* régulier; courant [price]; méthodique; permanent [army]; *a regular fool*, un vrai sot. ‖ **regularity** [règyᵉlarᵉti] *s.* régularité; assiduité, f. ‖ **regularize** [règyoulᵉra¹z] *v.* régulariser. ‖ **regulate** [règyᵉlé¹t] *v.* régler; réglementer; ajuster; déterminer. ‖ **regulation** [règyᵉlé¹shᵉn] *s.* règlement; réglage, m.; réglementation, f.; *regulative, regulator*, régulateur.

rehearsal [rihᵉrs'l] *s.* répétition (theat.), f.; énumération, f. ‖ **rehearse** [-hᵉrs] *v.* répéter.

reign [ré¹n] *s.* règne, m.; *v.* régner.

reimburse [rîimbᵉrs] *v.* rembourser. ‖ **reimbursement** [-mᵉnt] *s.* remboursement, m.

rein [ré¹n] *s.* rêne, guide, f.; *v.* guider, conduire; *bridoon rein*, bride; *to give free rein to*, lâcher la bride à.

reincarnate [rîinkânᵉ¹t] *v.* réincarner; *reincarnation*, réincarnation.

reindeer [ré¹ndiᵉr] *s.* renne, m.

reinforce [rîinfaurs] *v.* renforcer. ‖ **reinforcement** [-mᵉnt] *s.* renfort, m.

reiterate [rîitéré¹t] *v.* réitérer.

reject [ridjèkt] *v.* rejeter; repousser; refuser.

rejoice [ridjo¹s] *v.* réjouir; égayer. ‖ **rejoicing** [-ing] *s.* réjouissance; allégresse, f.

rejoin [rîdjo¹n] *v.* rejoindre; réunir; [ridjo¹n] *v.* répliquer; *rejoinder*, riposte, réplique.

rejuvenate [ridjouvᵉné¹t] *v.* rajeunir; rénover.

relapse [rilaps] *s.* rechute, f.; *v.* retomber; rechuter; récidiver (jur.).

relate [rilé¹t] *v.* relater; raconter; (se) rapporter (*to*, à). ‖ **related** [-id] *adj.* apparenté; allié; ayant rapport à; en relation avec. ‖ **relation** [rilé¹shᵉn] *s.* rapport; récit, m.; parenté, f.; *pl.* parents, m.; *with relation to*, par rapport à. ‖ **relationship** [-ship] *s.* parenté, f. ‖ **relative** [rèlᵉtiv] *adj.* relatif; *s.* parent, m.; *relative to*, relativement à; *relativism*, relativisme; *relativity*, relativité.

relax [rilaks] *v.* relâcher; (se) détendre; faire de la relaxation. ‖ **relaxation** [rîlaksé¹shᵉn] *s.* relâchement; délassement, m.; détente; relaxation, f.

relay [rîlé¹] *s.* relais, m.; relève, f.; [rîlé¹] *v.* relayer; transmettre par relais.

release [rilîs] *v.* relâcher; délivrer; libérer [prisoner]; rendre public [news]; décharger (*from*, de); dégager (jur.); élargissement; déclenchement (techn.), m.; libération, délivrance, f.; *release on bail*, mise en liberté sous caution.

relegate [rèlᵉgé¹t] *v.* reléguer; renvoyer; bannir.

relent [rilènt] *v.* se laisser fléchir; revenir sur une décision; *relentless*, implacable, inflexible.

relevant [rèlᵉvᵉnt] *adj.* pertinent, à propos; applicable (*to*, à).

reliability [rila¹ᵉbîlᵉti] *s.* sûreté; solidité; crédibilité, f. ‖ **reliable** [rila¹ᵉb'l] *adj.* sûr, digne de confiance. ‖ **reliance** [rila¹ᵉns] *s.* confiance, f.; *self-reliance*, confiance en soi.

relic [rèlik] *s.* relique, f.

relief [rilîf] *s.* soulagement; secours; allégement; relief, m.; réparation; relève (mil.), f.; *relief association*, société de secours. ‖ **relieve** [rilîv] *v.* soulager; secourir; délivrer; dégager; redresser (jur.); relever (mil.); mettre en relief.

religion [rilidjᵉn] *s.* religion, f. ‖ *religious* [-djᵉs] *adj.* religieux.

relinquish [rilingkwish] *v.* abandonner; abdiquer; *relinquishment*, abandon, renonciation.

reliquary [rèlikwᵉri] *s.* reliquaire, m.

relish [rèlish] *s.* saveur, f.; *v.* savourer, goûter; avoir goût de.

reluctance [rilᵉktᵉns] *s.* répugnance; aversion, f. ‖ *reluctant* [-tᵉnt] *adj.* peu disposé; qui agit à contrecœur; réfractaire; *reluctantly*, à contrecœur, à regret.

rely [rila¹] *v.* se fier; s'appuyer; compter (*on*, sur).

remain [rimé¹n] *v.* rester; demeurer. ‖ *remainder* [-dᵉr] *s.* reste; restant; reliquat, m.; *remainder sale*, solde. ‖ *remains* [-z] *s. pl.* restes, vestiges, m. pl.

remake [rîmé¹k] *v.* refaire.

remanence [rèmᵉnᵉns] *s.* rémanence, f.

remark [rimârk] *s.* remarque; observation; note, f.; *v.* remarquer; noter; observer. ‖ *remarkable* [-ᵉb'l] *adj.* remarquable, notable.

remarriage [rîmaridj] *s.* remariage, m. ‖ *remarry* [-ri] *v.* se remarier (avec).

remediable [rimîdiᵉb'l] *adj.* remédiable. ‖ *remedy* [rèmᵉdi] *s.* remède; recours (jur.), m.; *v.* remédier à; soigner.

remember [rimèmbᵉr] *v.* se rappeler; se souvenir de. ‖ *remembrance* [-brᵉns] *s.* souvenir, m.; mémoire, f.; *pl.* souvenirs, compliments, m. pl.

remind [rima¹nd] *v.* rappeler; remémorer. ‖ *reminder* [-ᵉr] *s.* aide-mémoire; mémento; rappel, m.

reminiscence [rèmᵉnis'ns] *s.* réminiscence, f.; souvenir, m.; *reminiscent*, ayant souvenance; évocateur.

remiss [rim*i*s] *adj.* négligent; relâché; insouciant. ‖ **remission** [rimish*e*n] *s.* rémission; remise (jur.); atténuation, f.

remit [rim*i*t] *v.* remettre; livrer; relâcher; pardonner. ‖ **remittance** [-'ns] *s.* remise, f.; versement, envoi de fonds, m.

remnant [rèmn*e*nt] *s.* reste; résidu; vestige, m.; *pl.* soldes, m. pl.

remodel [rîm*â*d'l] *v.* réorganiser; refondre; remodeler; remanier.

remonstrance [rim*â*nstr*e*ns] *s.* remontrance; protestation, f. ‖ **remonstrant** [-*e*nt] *adj.* protestataire; de remontrance; *s.* protestataire; sermonneur, m. ‖ **remonstrate** [-*é*¹t] *v.* faire des remontrances; protester; faire observer.

remorse [rim*au*rs] *s.* remords, m.; **remorseless**, impitoyable; sans remords.

remote [rim*o*out] *adj.* éloigné; reculé; écarté; distant (fig.); **remote control**, commande à distance; **remoteness**, éloignement; réserve.

removal [rim*ou*v'l] *s.* déménagement; déplacement; enlèvement, m.; révocation; suppression; levée; élimination, f. ‖ **remove** [rim*ou*v] *v.* enlever; transférer; éliminer; révoquer; assassiner; déménager; (se) déplacer. ‖ **removed** [-d] *adj.* éloigné; différent. ‖ **remover** [-*e*r] *s.* déménageur; dissolvant, m.

remunerate [rimy*ou*n*e*ré¹t] *v.* rémunérer; **remuneration**, rémunération; **remunerative**, rémunérateur.

renaissance [rèn*e*z*â*ns], **renascence** [rin*a*s'ns] *s.* renaissance, f.

rend [rènd] *v.** déchirer; fendre; arracher.

render [rènd*e*r] *v.* rendre; remettre; interpréter [music]; traduire.

renew [riny*ou*] *v.* rénover; renouveler; rajeunir; prolonger. ‖ **renewal** [-*e*l] *s.* renouvellement, m.

renounce [rin*a*ouns] *v.* renoncer à; **renouncement**, renoncement; désaveu.

renovate [rèn*e*vé¹t] *v.* rénover.

renown [rin*a*oun] *s.* renom, m.; **renowned**, renommé, réputé.

rent [rènt] *s.* déchirure; crevasse, fissure; rupture, f.; *pret., p. p. of* **to rend**.

rent [rènt] *s.* loyer; fermage, m.; redevance, f.; *v.* louer; affermer; **rental**, loyer; **renter**, locataire, loueur.

renunciation [rin*œ*nsié¹sh*e*n] *s.* renonciation; reniement.

reopen [ri*ou*p*e*n] *v.* rouvrir; recommencer. ‖ **reopening** [ing] *s.* réouverture; reprise, f.

repair [rip*è*ʳr] *v.* réparer; radouber (naut.); restaurer; raccommoder; *s.* réparation, f.; raccommodage; radoub, m.; *under repair*, en réparation; *out of repair*, en mauvais état; *beyond repair*, irréparable; *in good repair*, en bon état.

reparation [rèpéré¹sh*e*n] *s.* réparation, f.; dédommagement, m.

repatriate [rip*a*trié¹t] *v.* rapatrier; **repatriation**, rapatriement, m.

repay [ripé¹] *v.* rembourser; payer; récompenser, dédommager. ‖ **repayment** [-m*e*nt] *s.* restitution, f.; remboursement; dédommagement.

repeal [rip*î*l] *v.* abroger; annuler; *s.* abrogation, annulation, f.

repeat [rip*î*t] *v.* répéter; réitérer; *s.* répétition, f.; **repeater**, récidiviste.

repel [rip*è*l] *v.* repousser; rebuter; **repellent**, répulsif, repoussant.

repent [rip*è*nt] *v.* se repentir de; regretter. ‖ **repentance** [-*e*ns] *s.* repentir, m. ‖ **repentant** [-*e*nt] *adj.* repentant.

repercussion [r*i*p*e*rk*œ*sh*e*n] *s.* répercussion, f.

repertoire [rèp*e*tw*â*r], **repertory** [-t*e*ri] *s.* répertoire, m.

repetition [rèp*i*tish*e*n] *s.* répétition; récidive; reprise, f.

replace [riplé¹s] *v.* remplacer; replacer; déplacer. ‖ **replaceable** [-*e*b'l] *adj.* remplaçable. ‖ **replacement** [-m*e*nt] *s.* remplacement, m.; substitution, f.

replenish [riplènish] *v.* remplir; recompléter; refaire le plein. ‖ **replenishment** [-m*e*nt] *s.* remplissage, m.

replete [ripl*î*t] *adj.* rempli; repu; **repletion**, satiété.

replica [rèplik*e*] *s.* réplique, reproduction, f.; fac-similé, m.

reply [ripla¹] *v.* répondre; répliquer; *s.** réponse; réplique, f.

report [rip*o*ourt] *v.* rapporter; rendre compte; relater; signaler; dénoncer; *s.* rapport; compte rendu; procès-verbal; exposé; bulletin, m.; nouvelle; rumeur; détonation (gun), f.; *to report oneself*, se présenter; **news report**, reportage. ‖ **reporter** [-*e*r] *s.* reporter; rapporteur, m.

repose [rip*o*ouz] *v.* (se) reposer; *s.* repos, m; **repository**, dépôt; dépositaire.

reprehensible [réprihénsib'l] *adj.* répréhensible.

represent [rèprizènt] *v.* représenter. ‖ **representation** [rèbrizènté¹sh*e*n] *s.* représentation, f. ‖ **representative** [rèprizènt*e*tiv] *adj.* représentatif; typique; *s.* représentant, m.

repress [riprès] v. refréner; contenir. ‖ **repression** [ripré¹shen] s. répression, f.

reprieve [riprív] v. surseoir à; accorder un délai à; s. délai; sursis, m.

reprimand [rèpremand] v. réprimander; s. réprimande, f.

reprisals [ripra¹z'ls] s. pl. représailles, f. pl.

reproach [ripro⁰utsh] v. reprocher; blâmer; s.* reproche, blâme, m.; **reproachful,** réprobateur.

reprobate [rèprobé¹t] v. réprouver; adj., s. réprouvé, m. f.; **reprobation,** réprobation

reproduce [rîpredyous] v. reproduire. ‖ **reproduction** [rîpredæskshen] s. reproduction. réplique, f.

reproof [riprouf] s. reproche, m. ‖ **reprove** [riprouv] v. réprimander, blâmer.

reptile [rèpt'l] s. reptile, m.

republic [ripæblik] s. république, f.; **republican,** républicain.

repudiate [ripyoudié¹t] v. répudier.

repugnance [ripægnens] s. répugnance aversion, f. ‖ **repugnant** [-nent] adj. répugnant; repoussant; antipathique

repulse [ripœls] v. repousser; rejeter; refouler; s. échec; refus, m.; rebuffade, f.; to sustain a repulse, essuyer un échec. ‖ **repulsive** [-iv] adj. repoussant; écœurant. distant.

reputable [rèpyete⁴b'l] adj. honorable. ‖ **reputation** [rèpyeté¹shen] s. réputation; renommée, f. ‖ **repute** [ripyout] v. réputer; considérer; estimer; s. réputation, f.; **reputed,** supposé, prétendu.

request [rikwèst] s. requête, demande; pétition, f.; v. demander; solliciter; prier; inviter à; at the request of, sur les instances de; request stop, arrêt facultatif; « faire signe au machiniste ». ‖ **require** [rikwa¹er] v. exiger, requérir, avoir besoin de. ‖ **requirement** [-ment] s. exigence; condition requise, nécessité, f.; besoin, m. ‖ **requisite** [rèkwezit] adj. requis, indispensable; s requis, m., condition requise, f. ‖ **requisition** [rèkwezishen] s. réquisition; requête, f.; v. réquisitionner.

requital [rikwa¹tel] s. vengeance, f.; représailles, f. pl.; récompense, f. ‖ **requite** [rikwa¹t] v. récompenser; venger.

rescind [risînd] v. annuler; abroger; **rescission,** annulation, abrogation.

rescue [rèskyou] v. délivrance; rescousse, f.; secours; sauvetage, m.; v. sauver; secourir; délivrer; rescue service, service de sauvetage.

research [rîsë²rtsh] s.* recherche; investigation, f.; [rîsë²rtsh] v. rechercher; enquêter; **researcher,** chercheur.

resemblance [rizèmblens] s. ressemblance, f. ‖ **resemble** [-b'l] v. ressembler à.

resent [rizènt] v. se fâcher de, tenir rigueur à. ‖ **resentful** [-fel] adj. rancunier, irascible. vindicatif. ‖ **resentment** [-ment] s ressentiment, m.

reservation [rèzervé¹shen] s. réserve; restriction, arrière-pensée; réservation (jur.), f., Am terrain réservé, m.; mental reservation, restriction mentale. ‖ **reserve** [rizë²v] v. réserver, louer; s. réserve discrétion; restriction, f. ‖ **reservist** [-ist] s. réserviste, m. ‖ **reservoir** [rèzë²vaur] s. réservoir, m.

reside [riza¹d] v. résider; habiter. ‖ **residence** [rèzedens] s. résidence; habitation, f. ‖ **resident** [-dent] s. résident, m.; adj. résidant; **residential,** résidentiel.

residue [rèzedyou] s. résidu; reliquat, reste, m.

resign [riza¹n] v. résigner, renoncer à; démissionner; to resign oneself, se résigner à ‖ **resignation** [rèzigné¹shen] s. démission, résignation, f.

resilient [rizil¹ent] adj. élastique; énergique. plein de ressort.

resin [rèz'n] s. résine, f.

resist [rizíst] v résister à; s'opposer à; combattre ‖ **resistance** [-ens] s. résistance opposition. f., electric resistance, résistance électrique. ‖ **resistant** [-ent] adj résistant.

resolute [rèzelout] adj. résolu; déterminé. ‖ **resolution** [rèzeloushen] s. résolution détermination solution; délibération f. ‖ **resolve** [rizôlv] v. (se) résoudre. (se) décider, déterminer; dissoudre, fondre, dissiper. ‖ **resolvent** [-ent] s résolvant, résolutif, m.

resonance [rèz'nens] s. résonance, f. ‖ **resonant** [-nent] adj. résonnant, sonore, **resonator,** résonateur.

resort [rizaurt] v. recourir à; fréquenter; s recours, rendez-vous; ressort (jur.), m., ressource, f.; as a last resort, en dernier ressort; summer resort, villégiature d'été.

resound [riza⁰und] v. résonner; retentir; répercuter.

resource [riso⁰urs] s. ressource, f.; **resourceful,** avisé, débrouillard.

respect [rispèkt] v. respect; égard, m.; estime, considération, f.; pl. hommages, m. with respect to, relativement à; in all respects, à tous égards. ‖ **respectable** [-eb'l] adj. respectable. ‖ **respectful** [-fel] adj. respectueux. ‖ **respecting** [-ing] prep. relativement à, touching à, quant à. ‖ **respective** [-iv] *adj.* respectif; relatif.

respiration [rèspᵉréⁱshᵉn] *s.* respiration, f.; **respiratory,** respiratoire; **respire,** respirer.

respite [rèspit] *s.* répit; sursis (jur.); délai, m.; trêve, f.

resplendent [risplèndᵉnt] *adj.* resplendissant, éblouissant.

respond [rispánd] *v.* répondre; payer de retour; convenir (*to,* à). ‖ **response** [rispáns] *s.* réponse; réaction, f.; répons, m.

responsibility [rispânsᵉbíᶥᵗi] *s.** responsabilité, f. ‖ **responsible** [rispánsᵉb'l] *adj.* responsable; solidaire (jur.); digne de confiance; lourd de responsabilité. ‖ **responsive** [-siv] *adj.* sensible; vibrant; nerveux [motor].

rest [rèst] *s.* repos; calme; appui, support, m.; pause [music], f.; *v.* (se) reposer; s'appuyer (*on,* sur); *to rest with,* incomber à.

rest [rèst] *v.* rester; *s.* reste; restant, m.; *to rest there,* en rester là.

restaurant [rèstᵉrᵉnt] *s.* restaurant, m.

restful [rèstfᵉl] *adj.* reposant; paisible, calme, tranquille.

restitute [rèstityout] *v.* restituer. ‖ **restitution** [rèstᵉtyoushᵉn] *s.* restitution, f.

restless [rèstlis] *adj.* agité; inquiet; turbulent; infatigable. ‖ **restlessness** [-nis] *s.* agitation; inquiétude; turbulence; insomnie, f.

restoration [rèstᵉréⁱshᵉn] *s.* restauration; réintégration; restitution; reconstitution, f.; rétablissement, m. ‖ **restorative** [ristoᵘᵣᵉtiv] *s.* reconstituant; fortifiant, m. ‖ **restore** [ristoᵘᵣ] *v.* restaurer; rénover; réparer; restituer; reconstituer; rétablir; réintégrer; *to restore to oneself,* ranimer, faire revenir à soi; **restorer,** restaurateur; fortifiant.

restrain [ristréⁱn] *v.* restreindre; retenir; contenir; réprimer; entraver, limiter. ‖ **restraint** [ristréⁱnt] *s.* restriction; circonspection; contrainte, f.; empêchement, m.

restrict [ristríkt] *v.* restreindre; réduire; limiter. ‖ **restriction** [-triksʰᵉn] *s.* restriction, limitation, f.; **restrictive,** restrictif.

result [rizǽlt] *v.* résulter (*from,* de); aboutir (*in,* à); *s.* résultat, m.; **resultful,** fructueux.

resume [rizoum] *v.* reprendre; réassumer; se remettre à; récapituler.

résumé [rèzoumᵉⁱ] *s.* résumé, m.

resurgence [rizᵉᵣdjᵉns] *s.* résurrection, f. ‖ **resurrect** [rèzᵉrèkt] *v.* ressusciter; **resurrection,** résurrection.

resuscitate [risǽsᵉtéⁱt] *v.* ressusciter; **resuscitation,** résurrection.

retail [rítéⁱl] *s.* détail, m.; vente au détail, f.; *v.* détailler, débiter; **retail merchant, retailer,** détaillant.

retain [rítéⁱn] *v.* retenir; garder; conserver; **retainer,** détenteur; suivant; provisions (jur.).

retaliate [ritaliéⁱt] *v.* rendre coup pour coup; contre-attaquer; user de représailles. ‖ **retaliation** [ritaliéⁱsʰᵉn] *s.* représailles; contre-attaque; revanche, f.; talion, m.

retard [ritárd] *v.* retarder; différer; *s.* retard, délai, m.

reticence [rétisᵉns] *s.* réticence, f.; **reticent,** réticent.

retina [rétinᵉ] *s.* rétine, f.

retinue [rètnyou] *s.* suite, escorte, f.

retire [ritaⁱᵣ] *v.* (se) retirer; se replier; prendre sa retraite. ‖ **retirement** [-mᵉnt] *s.* retraite, f.; repli; retrait, m.

retort [ritauᵣt] *v.* riposter; rétorquer; *s.* riposte, réplique, f.

retouch [ritǽtsh] *s.** retouche, f.; *v.* retoucher.

retrace [ritréⁱs] *v.* revenir sur; remonter à la source de; *to retrace one's steps,* rebrousser chemin.

retract [ritrakt] *v.* (se) rétracter; revenir sur; **retractation,** rétractation; **retractile,** rétractile; **retraction,** rétraction.

retransmission [ritransmisʰᵉn] *s.* retransmission, f. ‖ **retransmit** [ritrànsmit] *v.* retransmettre.

retreat [ritrît] *s.* retraite, f.; refuge, asile, m.; *v.* se retirer; rétrocéder; battre en retraite.

retrench [ritrèntsh] *v.* (se) retrancher; économiser. ‖ **retrenchment** [-mᵉnt] *s.* retranchement, m.

retribution [rètribyousʰᵉn] *s.* rétribution, récompense, f.; châtiment, m.

retrieve [ritrîv] *v.* réparer; recouvrer, regagner; récupérer.

retroactive [rètroᵘaktiv] *adj.* rétroactif.

retrograde [rétrogreⁱd] *v.* rétrograder; *adj.* rétrograde.

retrogression [rètrᵉgrèsʰᵉn] *s.* recul, m.; dégénérescence, f.

retrospect [rètrospèkt] *s.* rétrospective, f.; **retrospection,** rétrospection; **retrospective,** rétrospectif.

return [ritèrn] *v.* retourner; revenir; répliquer; rapporter; renvoyer; rendre; rembourser; restituer; *s.* retour; renvoi; relevé; compte rendu, m.; rentrée; ristourne; restitution; compensation; revanche; réciprocité; réponse, f.; *pl.* profit, rendement, m.;

return address, adresse de l'expéditeur ; **return profit,** rendement ; **return ticket,** billet d'aller et retour ; **election returns,** compte rendu des élections.

reunion [rîyo͞uny⁽ᵉ⁾n] *s.* réunion ; assemblée, f. ‖ **reunite** [rîyo͞una¹t] *v.* (se) réunir ; réconcilier.

reveal [rivî͞l] *v.* révéler ; dévoiler.

reveille [révéli] *s.* diane (mil.), f.

revel [rèv'l] *s.* orgie, fête, f. ; *v.* faire la fête ; faire bombance ; se délecter (*in,* à).

revelation [rèv'lé¹sh⁽ᵉ⁾n] *s.* révélation ; Apocalypse, f.

revelry [rèv'lri] *s.* * orgie ; réjouissance, f ; divertissement, m.

revendication [rivèndiké¹sh⁽ᵉ⁾n] *s.* revendication, f.

revenge [rivèndj] *s.* revanche ; vengeance, f. ; *v.* (se) venger (*for something,* de quelque chose, *on somebody,* de quelqu'un) ; *to take revenge for,* se venger de, **revengeful,** vindicatif ; vengeur, vengeresse ; **revenger,** vengeur.

revenue [rèv⁽ᵉ⁾nyou] *s.* revenu ; trésor public, fisc, m. ; recette budgétaire ; administration des impôts, f.

reverberate [rivë͞rb⁽ᵉ⁾ré¹t] *v.* renvoyer, réfléchir ; reverberation, réverbération.

revere [rivi⁽ᵉ⁾r] *v.* révérer, vénérer. ‖ **reverence** [rèv'r⁽ᵉ⁾ns] *s* vénération, f. ; respect, m. ; ‖ **reverend** [-r⁽ᵉ⁾nd] *adj.* révérend, vénérable. ‖ **reverent** [-r⁽ᵉ⁾nt] *adj.* respectueux, révérencieux ; **reverential,** révérenciel.

reverie [rèv⁽ᵉ⁾ri] *s.* rêverie, musardise, f.

reversal [rivë͞rs'l] *s.* revirement ; renversement, m.

reverse [rivë͞rs] *adj.* contraire, opposé ; *s.* revers ; verso [leaf] ; contraire, m. ; marche arrière [auto], f. ; *v.* renverser ; inverser ; intervertir ; révoquer [decision] ; faire marche arrière. ‖ **reversement** [-m⁽ᵉ⁾nt] *s.* renversement, m. ‖ **reversible** [-⁽ᵉ⁾b'l] *adj.* réversible. ‖ **reversion** [rivë͞rj⁽ᵉ⁾n] *s.* réversion, f. ‖ **revert** [rivë͞rt] *v.* revenir, retourner (*to,* à).

review [rivyou] *v.* revoir ; reviser ; rendre compte, critiquer [book] ; passer en revue (mil.) ; *s.* revue ; revision ; critique [book], f. ; compte rendu ; examen ; contrôle, m. ; *board of review,* conseil de révision ; **reviewer,** critique.

revile [riva¹l] *v.* insulter, injurier.

revise [riva¹z] *v.* reviser ; revoir ; relire ; corriger, modifier. ‖ **revision** [rivij⁽ᵉ⁾n] *s.* révision, f.

revival [riva¹v'l] *s.* renaissance ; remise en vigueur ; reprise [play], f. ; renouveau ; réveil, m. ‖ **revive** [riva¹v]

v. (se) ranimer ; réveiller ; revigorer ; faire revivre.

revocation [rèv⁽ᵉ⁾ké¹sh⁽ᵉ⁾n] *s.* révocation ; abrogation, f. ‖ **revoke** [rivo͞ᵘk] *v.* révoquer ; abroger ; retirer ; rétracter.

revolt [rivo͞ᵘlt] *s.* révolte ; rébellion, f. ; soulèvement, m. ; *v.* (se) révolter ; s'indigner ‖ **revolution** [rèv⁽ᵉ⁾lo͞ush⁽ᵉ⁾n] *s.* révolution . rotation, f. ; circuit, tour, m. ‖ **revolutionary** [-èri] *adj.*, *s.* révolutionnaire **revolutionist** [-ist] *s.* révolutionnaire, m. ‖ **revolutionize** [-a¹z] *v.* révolutionner.

revolve [rivâlv] *v.* tourner, girer ; retourner, pivoter ; *to revolve in one's mind,* retourner dans son esprit, réfléchir à.

revolver [rivâlv⁽ᵉ⁾r] *s.* revolver, m.

revulsion [rivœlsh⁽ᵉ⁾n] *s.* révulsion, f. ; revirement m., **revulsive,** révulsif.

reward [riwaurd] *s.* récompense ; gratification, f . dédommagement, m. ; *v.* récompenser

rewrite [rira¹t] *v.* récrire, remanier.

rhetoric [rèt⁽ᵉ⁾rik] *s.* rhétorique, f.

rheum [ro͞um] *s.* chassie, f. ; mucosités, f. pl.

rheumatism [ro͞umᵉtiz⁽ᵉ⁾m] *s.* rhumatisme, m.

rhinoceros [ra¹nâs⁽ᵉ⁾r⁽ᵉ⁾s] *s.* * rhinocéros, m.

rhubarb [ro͞ubârb] *s.* rhubarbe, f.

rhyme [ra¹m] *s.* rime, f. ; *v.* rimer.

rhythm [rizhᵉm] *s.* rythme, m. ‖ **rhythmical** [rizhmik'l] *adj.* rythmique, cadencé.

rib [rib] *s.* côte ; nervure ; baleine [umbrella] ; éclisse [violin] ; armature, f.

ribbon [ribᵉn] *s.* ruban, m. ; bande, f.

rice [ra¹s] *s.* riz, m. ; *rice-field,* rizière ; *rice wine,* saké.

rich [ritsh] *adj.* riche ; succulent ; fertile, fécond . généreux [wine] ; épicé ; luxuriant [vegetation], gras [food] ; vif [color] ; **riches** [-iz] *s. pl.* richesse ; fortune, f ‖ **richness** [-nis] *s.* richesse ; fécondité ; opulence, abondance ; chaleur [color] ; fertilité, f.

rickety [rikiti] *adj.* rachitique ; délabré ; boiteux [chair].

ricochet [rikâshé¹] *s.* ricochet, m. ; *v.* ricocher.

rictus [riktᵉs] *s.* * rictus, m.

rid [rid] *v.* libérer ; délivrer, débarrasser ; *to get rid of,* se débarrasser de ; *pret., p. p. of* rid.

ridden [rid'n] *p. p. of* to ride.

riddle [rid'l] *s.* énigme ; devinette, f. ; *v.* expliquer ; interpréter ; embarrasser.

riddle [rid'l] *s.* crible, tamis, m.; *v.* cribler (*with*, de).

ride [ra¹d] *v.** chevaucher; aller en voiture; rouler; *s.* promenade; randonnée; course, f.; voyage; parcours, m.; *to ride a bicycle,* aller à bicyclette; *to ride horseback,* monter à cheval; *to ride at anchor,* être à l'ancre. ‖ *rider* [-ᵉʳ] *s.* cavalier; codicille, m.; annexe (jur.), f.

ridge [ridj] *s.* crête; arête; échine; croupe, f.; faîte; billon, m.

ridicule [ridikyoul] *s.* dérision; moquerie, f.; *v.* ridiculiser. ‖ *ridiculous* [ridíky•lᵉs] *adj.* ridicule.

riff-raff [rifraf] *s.* racaille, pègre, canaille, f.

rifle [ra¹f'l] *s.* fusil, m.; carabine, f.; *v.* fusiller; rayer; *automatic rifle,* fusil mitrailleur; *rifleman,* fusilier, carabinier.

rifle [ra¹f'l] *v.* rafler, piller; détrousser, dévaliser.

rig [rig] *v.* gréer, équiper; accoutrer; échafauder; *s.* gréement; équipement; accoutrement; échafaudage, m. ‖ *rigging* [-ing] *s.* agrès; gréement (naut.); montage (mech.), m.

right [ra¹t] *adj.* droit; exact; juste; vrai; direct; régulier; *adv.* droit; directement; comme il faut; tout à fait; *s.* droit, m.; équité; droite, f.; *v.* rectifier; corriger; faire justice à; (se) redresser; *right away,* tout de suite; *he is right,* il a raison; *keep to the right,* tenez votre droite; *to set right,* mettre en ordre, régler; *all right,* très bien, ça va; *right now,* immédiatement; *by right of,* en raison de; *is that the right street?,* est-ce bien la rue? ‖ *righteous* [-ᵉs] *adj.* juste; droit. ‖ *righteousness* [-ᵉsnis] *s.* droiture; rectitude; équité, f. ‖ *rightful* [-fᵉl] *adj.* juste; légitime. ‖ *right-hand* [-hànd] *adj.* de droite; à main droite; *right-hand man,* bras droit, alter ego. ‖ *rightly* [-li] *adv.* à juste titre; avec raison; correctement.

rigid [ridjid] *adj.* rigide, raide. ‖ *rigidity* [ridjid•ti] *s.* rigidité; raideur; rigueur, f.

rigo(u)r [rig•r] *s.* rigueur; rigidité, f. ‖ *rigorism,* rigorisme; *rigorous,* rigoureux.

rim [rim] *s.* bord, m.; *wheel rim,* jante.

rime [ra¹m] *s.* givre, m.; gelée blanche, f.; *v.* givrer.

rind [ra¹nd] *s.* écorce [tree]; pelure [fruit]; couenne; croûte [cheese], f.

ring [ring] *s.* anneau; cercle, m.; bague; boucle [ear]; couronne (geom.); arène, piste, f.; *ring* [box], m.; *v.* entourer, encercler; cerner;

anneler; baguer; *ring-finger,* annulaire.

ring [ring] *v.** sonner, tinter; résonner; faire sonner; *s.* son métallique; son de clochette; coup de sonnette, m.; *to ring up on the phone,* appeler au téléphone; *to ring for the maid,* sonner la bonne.

ringlet [ringlit] *s.* anneau, m.; boucle [hair], f.

rink [ringk] *s.* patinoire, f.

rinse [rins] *v.* rincer; *s.* rinçage, m.

riot [ra¹et] *s.* émeute; sédition, f.; tumulte, m.; *v.* faire une émeute; faire du vacarme; *riot of colo(u)rs,* débauche de couleurs; *rioter,* émeutier; noceur, *riotous,* séditieux; tapageur; débauché.

rip [rip] *v.* fendre; déchirer; éventrer; *s.* fente; déchirure, f.; *to rip off,* arracher.

ripe [ra¹p] *adj.* mûr; parfait; à point. ‖ *ripen* [-ᵉn] *v.* mûrir; faire mûrir. ‖ *ripeness* [-nis] *s.* maturité, f.

ripple [rip'l] *s.* ride; ondulation, f.; murmure [water]; rire perlé, m.; *v.* se rider; onduler; murmurer.

rise [ra¹z] *v.** se lever; s'élever; monter; renchérir; augmenter; naître, prendre sa source; grandir; faire des progrès; *s.* ascension; montée; crue; hausse; élévation; augmentation; croissance, f.; lever; avancement, m.; *to rise up in rebellion,* se soulever. ‖ *risen* [riz'n] *p. p. of* to rise.

risk [risk] *s.* risque; danger; hasard, m.; *v.* risquer; aventurer; hasarder; *to risk defeat,* s'exposer à l'échec. ‖ *risky* [-i] *adj.* risqué; hasardeux; hardi, audacieux; *risqué* [-é¹] *adj.* osé, scabreux.

rite [ra¹t] *s.* rite, m.; cérémonie, f. ‖ *ritual* [ritshou•l] *adj., s.* rituel. ‖ *ritualism* [rityou•liz'm] *s.* ritualisme, m. ‖ *ritualist* [-ist] *s.* ritualiste m. f. ‖ *ritualistic* [rityou•listik] *adj.* ritualiste.

rival [ra¹v'l] *s.* rival; concurrent; compétiteur, m.; *v.* rivaliser avec; *adj.* adverse, opposé. ‖ *rivalry* [-ri] *s.** rivalité, concurrence, f.

river [riv•r] *s.* fleuve, m.; rivière, f.

rivet [rivit] *s.* rivet, m.; *v.* riveter, river; *riveting,* rivure, rivetage; *riveting-machine,* riveuse.

rivulet [rivy•lit] *s.* ruisselet, m.

road [ro•d] *s.* route; voie; chaussée; rade (naut.), f.; *branch road,* embranchement; *convex road,* route bombée; *high road,* grand-route; *military road,* route stratégique; *unimproved road,* route en mauvais état; *winding road,* route en lacets; *roadside,* accotement; *roadway,* chaussée, voie carrossable.

roam [roᵒum] *v.* errer; rôder.

roar [roᵒur] *v* rugir; mugir [sea]; gronder [thunder]; éclater [laughter]; *s.* rugissement. mugissement; grondement; éclat, m

roast [roᵒust] *v.* rôtir; torréfier; griller; *s.* rôti, m.. **roast beef**, rosbif; **roaster**, rôtissoire; rôtisseur; brûloir; volaille à rôtir

rob [râb] *v.* voler, dérober; cambrioler; *to rob someone of something.* voler quelque chose à quelqu'un. ‖ **robber** [-ᵉr] *s* voleur, brigand, m.; **sea-robber**, pirate ‖ **robbery** [-ri] *s.* vol; cambriolage m.

robe [roᵒub] *s* robe, toge, f.; *Am.* **automobile robe**, plaid, m.

robin [râbin] *s* rouge-gorge, m.; *Am.* grive migratrice, f.

robot [roᵒubât] *s.* robot, m.; *adj.* automatique

robust [roᵒubæst] *adj.* robuste; solide; vigoureux.

rock [râk] *s* roc, rocher; *Am.* moellon, m.. roche, f.. **rock garden**, rocaille. **rock salt**, sel gemme

rock [râk] *v* (faire) balancer, bercer; se balancer chanceler, *to rock to sleep*, bercer ‖ **rocker** [-ᵉr] *s.* culbuteur, m. bascule, f.

rocket [râkit] *s.* fusée, f.; savon [colloq.], m.. *v* monter en flèche; passer en éclair

rocking [râking] *s.* balancement; bercement m ‖ **rocking-chair**, chaise à bascule. *Fr Can* berceuse.

rocky [râki] *adj.* rocailleux; rocheux.

rocky [râki] *adj.* instable; branlant, chancelant

rod [râd] *s* baguette; tringle [curtain], tige canne [fishing] bielle [piston]. verge f.. **tie-rod**, barre d'accouplement (mech.); **divining-rod**, baguette de sourcier

rode [roᵒud] *pret of to ride.*

rodent [roᵒudᵉnt] *s* rongeur, m.

roe [roᵒu] *s* chevreuil; œufs (ou) laitance de poisson

rogue [roᵒug] *s* fripon; espiègle, vagabond drôle. gredin; rustre, m. ‖ **roguish** [roᵒugish] *adj.* malhonnête, coquin. espiègle

roister [rôistᵉr] *v* faire du chahut; **roistering**, tapage. tapageur.

rôle [roᵒul] *s* rôle, m.

roll [roᵒul] *v* rouler passer au rouleau; laminer [metal] cylindrer. faire le tonneau (aviat.). *s* liste f rôle rouleau, roulement rouli̇ (naut.) petit pain m. *to call the roll* faire l'appel ‖ **roller** [-ᵉr] *s* rouleau cylindre laminoi̇ galet tambour (mech.) m ‖ **roller coaster**, montagnes russes; **roller skate**, patin à roulettes.

rollick [rolik] *v.* folâtrer.

Roman [roᵒumᵉn] *adj.*, *s.* romain; **Roman nose**, nez aquilin.

romance [roᵒumâns] *s* roman, m.; romance. f. *adj* roman, *v* faire un récit romancé être romanesque. ‖ **romanesque** [roᵒumᵉnèsk] *adj* romanesque roman [style] ‖ **romantic** [roᵒumantik] *adj* romantique. romanesque ‖ **romanticism** [-tᵉsizᵉm] *s.* romantisme m ‖ **romanticist** [-tᵉsist] *s.* romantique. m

romp [râmp] *v* jouer bruyamment; être turbulent gambader; *s.* enfant turbulent garçon manqué, m.

rood [roud] *s.* croix, f.; quart d'arpent, m.

roof [rouf] *s* toit; palais [mouth]; comble [house], plafond (aviat.). m.; voûte. f. *v* couvrir, mettre un toit; abriter. **flat roof**, terrasse; **roofless**, sans abri

room [roum] *s.* chambre; pièce; salle; place, f lieu; espace, m.. *v.* loger, habiter en garni; *there is no room for* il n'y a pas lieu de. il n'y a pas de place pour. **dressing room**, cabinet de toilette **roommate**, compagnon de chambre « cothurne ». ‖ **roomer** [-ᵉr] *s* locataire. m. ‖ **roominess** [-inis] *s* grande étendue, grande dimension, f ‖ **roomy** [-i] *adj.* spacieux vaste

roost [roust] *s.* perchoir, m.; *v.* se percher [bird, fowl]. ‖ **rooster** [-ᵉr] *s.* coq, m

root [rout] *s.* racine; base; origine; souche, f. fondement principe, m.; *v.* s'enraciner prendre racine; *to root out*, déraciner extirper déterrer; *to root out*, déraciner extirper dénicher

rope [roᵒup] *s.* corde f.; cordage; câble. m *v* corder, encorder, lier; prendre au lasso *to be at the end of one's rope* être au bout de son rouleau; *to know the ropes*, connaître son affaire

rosary [roᵒuzᵉri] *s.* rosaire, m.

rose [roᵒuz] *pret of to rise.*

rose [roᵒuz] *v* rose rosace. pomme d'arrosoir f *Brazilian rosewood*, palissandre **rosebud**, bouton de rose, **rose bush** rosier **rosette**, rosette; **rose-window**, rosace **rosin**, colophane.

rostrum [râstrᵉm] *s* tribune, f.

rosy [roᵒuzi] *adj* rose, rosé; riant.

rot [rât] *v* pourrir, se gâter; se carier [tooth], *s* pourriture; putréfaction; carie; clavelée f

rotary [roᵒutᵉri] *adj.* rotatif; tournant, rotatoire **rotate** [roᵒutéit] *v.* tourner gire̍r pivoter ‖ **rotation** [roᵒutéishᵉn] *s* rotation révolution, f.; roulement tour, m.. *in rotation*, par roulement, **rotation of crops**, assolement.

rote [roᵒut] *s.* routine, f.; *by rote*, par cœur, machinalement.

rotten [rât'n] *adj.* corrompu; pourri; putréfié; gâté.

rotundity [rotœnditi] *s.* rondeur; redondance, f.; embonpoint, m.

roué [roué¹] *s.* débauché, m.

rouge [rouj] *s.* rouge, fard, m.; *v.* farder; se mettre du rouge.

rough [rœf] *adj.* rude, brut; non poli [glass], âpre; orageux [weather]; raboteux, hérissé, accidenté; *rough draft*, ébauche, brouillon; *rough estimate*, calcul approximatif; *to rough it*, faire du camping, vivre primitivement ‖ **roughen** [-ən] *v.* endurcir, devenir rude. ‖ **roughly** [-li] *adv.* rudement, grossièrement; en gros; à peu près; âprement ‖ **roughness** [-nis] *s.* rudesse; rugosité, grossièreté, aspérité; âpreté, rigueur [weather], f.

round [raound] *adj.* rond, circulaire; *s.* rond, cercle; round [boxing], tour, m.; sphère, tournée, ronde, cartouche, f.; *v.* arrondir, contourner; entourer, faire une ronde; *adv.* tout autour, autour de, à la ronde; du premier au dernier, d'un bout à l'autre; *round of applause*, salve d'applaudissements; *round of pleasures*, succession de plaisirs; *to pay for the round*, payer la tournée; *to go the round*, circuler, faire le tour; *to round off*, arrondir; *to round*, compléter; *to hand round*, faire passer; *roundabout* détourné [way]; sens giratoire; détour, manège, rond-point; circonlocution; *round-shouldered*, voûté; *round-trip ticket*, billet circulaire; *roundup*, conclusion, rassemblement; rodéo, rafle.

rouse [raouz] *v.* réveiller, exciter; soulever, ranimer; provoquer.

rout [raout] *s.* cohue, foule, réunion; déroute (mil.), f.; *v.* mettre en déroute; *to rout out*, chasser de.

route [rout] *s.* route, voie, f.; itinéraire, m.; *v.* acheminer, diriger; *route-map*, carte routière.

routine [routïn] *s.* routine, f.; cours habituel des événements; service courant, m.; *adj.* routinier, courant habituel; *routine-bound*, enrouliné; *routine-minded*, routinier; *routinist*, routinier.

rove [rοουv] *v.* rôder; errer, vagabonder; divaguer; *rover*, vagabond, rôdeur, éclaireur, routier, pirate.

row [rau] *s.* tapage, vacarme, boucan, m.; dispute, f.; *v.* se quereller; *rowdy*, tapageur, batailleur, voyou.

row [rοου] *s.* rang, m.; rangée, ligne, file; colonne [figures], f.

row [rοου] *v.* ramer, canoter, nager (naut.), *s.* promenade en bateau; *rowboat*, bateau à rame, canot, barque, *Fr. Can.* chaloupe; *rower* [-ər] *s.* rameur, m. ‖ **rowing** [-ing] *s.* canotage, m.

royal [ro¹el] *adj.* royal. ‖ **royalist** [-ist] *s.* royaliste, m. ‖ **royalty** [-ti] *s.* royauté; redevance, f.; droit d'auteur ou d'inventeur, m.

rub [rœb] *v.* frotter, frictionner; astiquer; *s.* frottement, astiquage, m.; friction, difficulté, f.; *there is the rub*, voilà le hic; *to rub out*, effacer; *to rub someone the wrong way*, prendre quelqu'un à rebrousse-poil; *to rub up*, fourbir; *rub-down*, friction. ‖ **rubber** [-ər] *s.* frotteur, frottoir; caoutchouc, m.; gomme, f.; *Fr. Can.* claque, f.; rob [bridge], m.; *hard rubber*, ébonite.

rubbish [rœbish] *s.* détritus, débris; résidu, déblais, m.; décombres, m. pl; ordures, f. pl.; camelote, f., absurdités, f. pl.; *rubbish-shoot*, vide-ordures.

rubella [rou'bèlæ] *s.* rubéole, f.

rubicund [roubikænd] *adj.* rubicond.

ruby [roubi] *s.* rubis, m.

rudder [rœdər] *s.* gouvernail, m.; *rudder tiller*, barre du gouvernail.

ruddy [rœdi] *adj.* vermeil, rouge.

rude [roud] *adj.* grossier, rude; impoli, rébarbatif, rigoureux. ‖ **rudeness** [-nis] *s.* rudesse; grossièreté; impolitesse; rigueur [weather], f.

rudiment [roudəmənt] *s.* rudiment; élément, m ‖ **rudimentary** [roudə-mènt'ri] *adj.* rudimentaire.

rueful [rou'fəl] *adj.* pitoyable; navrant, triste, morne.

ruff [rœf] *s.* fraise, f.; collier, m.

ruffian [rœfiən] *s.* bandit, ruffian, m.

ruffle [rœf'l] *v.* froisser, froncer; ébouriffer [hair]; chiffonner, troubler; irriter, *s.* fronce, ruche, agitation, irritation, ride [water], f.

rug [rœg] *s.* tapis, m.; couverture, f.

rugged [rœgid] *adj.* rude, âpre; rugueux, raboteux dentelé [hills]; tempétueux, *Am* fort, robuste; peu commode ‖ **ruggedness** [-nis] *s.* aspérité; anfractuosité; rudesse, f.

ruin [rouin] *s.* ruine, perte, destruction, f.; *v.* ruiner, démolir, détruire. ‖ **ruinous** [-əs] *adj.* ruineux; désastreux, coûteux.

rule [roul] *s.* règle; autorité, f.; règlement, ordre, pouvoir, m.; *v.* régler; réglementer, gouverner, juger (jur.); conseiller, persuader; *rule of three*, règle de trois; *as a rule*, en général, ordinairement; *to be ruled by*, être sous la domination de, se laisser guider par; ‖ **ruler** [-ər] *s.* règle, f.; régleur, chef, gouvernant, m. ‖ **ruling** [-ing] *s.* décision, f.; gouvernement, m.; *adj.* gouvernant, dirigeant; principal, prédominant.

rum [rœm] *s.* rhum, m.

rumble [rœmb'l] *s.* grondement; roulement; grouillement; coffre [auto], m.; v. gronder; rouler [thunder]; ré-sonner.

ruminant [roumin°nt] s., adj. rumi-nant, m. ‖ **ruminate** [roum°né¹t] v. ruminer; méditer (on, sur); **rumina-tion**, rumination; **ruminative**, médi-tatif.

rummage [ræmidj] v. fouiller; remuer; bouleverser; s. remue-mé-nage; bouleversement, m.; fouilles, recherches, f. pl.; **rummage sale**, déballage.

rumo(u)r [roum°r] s. rumeur; opi-nion, f.; on-dit, m.; v. faire courir le bruit.

rump [ræmp] s. croupe, f.; posté-rieur, derrière; croupion, m.; culotte [meat], f.

rumpish [ræmpish] adj. bruyant.

rumple [ræmp'l] v. chiffonner; fri-per; s. ride, f.

rumpus [ræmp°s] s. chahut, boucan, potin, m.; prise (f.) de bec.

run [ræn] v.* courir; fuir, perdre; fonctionner; diriger [business]; couler [water]; passer [time]; se répandre [rumor], être candidat, se présenter (for, à); se démailler [stockings]; to run away, s'enfuir, to run across, ren-contrer par hasard; traverser en cou-rant; to run ashore, s'échouer, to run into debts, s'endetter, to run into, tam-ponner; to run down, écraser [auto]; to run through a book, parcourir un livre; s. course; suite; série; maille [stockings], f., in the long run, à la longue, run of performances, série de représentations, to run for something, courir chercher quelque chose; to get run in, se faire coffrer, to have the run of, avoir le libre usage de; run-away, fugitif, fuyard, déserteur; run-down, épuisé, déchargé [accumulator]; pret., p. p. of to run.

rung [ræng] s. tige, barre, f.; bâton; échelon, m.

rung [ræng] p. p. of to ring.

runner [ræn°r] s. coureur; courrier; agent de transmission; patin de trai-neau, m. ‖ **running** [ræning] s. course;

marche; suppuration, f.; cours; fonc-tionnement; écoulement, m.; adj. cou-rant; consécutif; continu; **running board**, marchepied; **running commen-tary**, reportage en direct (radio); **running down**, éreintement; **running fire**, feu roulant; **running in**, en ro-dage. **running water**, eau courante.

runt [rænt] s. nabot, avorton; animal (m.) de petite race.

runway [rænwé¹] s. piste (aviat.), f.

rupee [roûpî] s. roupie, f.

rupture [ræptsh°r] s. rupture; her-nie; brouille, f.; v. (se) rompre; don-ner une hernie à.

rural [rour°l] adj. rural; champêtre; rustique.

ruse [rouz] s. ruse de guerre, f.; stra-tagème, m.

rush [ræsh] v. s'élancer; se précipiter se ruer; prendre d'assaut; s'empres-ser; bousculer; s.° élan; bond; rush, m.; ruée; affluence, foule, masse; presse, f.; rush hours, heures d'af-fluence; to make a rush at, for, se précipiter sur.

rush [ræsh] s.° jonc, m.; rush-bot-tomed, à fond de jonc, paillé.

rusk [ræsk] s. biscotte, f.

Russian [ræsh°n] adj., s. russe. ‖ **Russia** [ræsh°] s. Russie, f.

russet [ræsit] adj. roux, mordoré.

rust [ræst] s. rouille, f.; v. (se) rouil-ler; s'oxyder; **rustproof**, inoxydable.

rustic [ræstik] adj. rustique; s. paysan, rustre, m.; **rusticate**, se reti-rer à la campagne.

rustle [ræst'l] v. bruire; froufrouter; s. bruissement; frou-frou, m.

rusty [ræsti] adj. rouillé; oxydé; rauque [voice].

rut [ræt] s. ornière, f.; v. sillonner; to get into a rut, s'encroûter.

ruthless [routhlis] adj. impitoyable; implacable, cruel. ‖ **ruthlessness** [-nis] s. cruauté; brutalité, f.

rye [ra¹] s. seigle, m.; rye bread, pain de seigle.

S

sabbath [sabeth] s. sabbat, m.

saber, sabre [sé¹b°r] s. sabre, m.

sable [sé¹b'l] s. zibeline, f.; pl. vête-ments (m. pl.) de deuil; adj. noir.

sabotage [sab°tâj] s. sabotage, m.; v. saboter.

saccharin [sak°rin] s. saccharine, f.

sacerdotal [sas°do°ut'l] adj. sacer-dotal.

sack [sak] s. sac; pillage, m.; v. piller; ensacher; saquer, renvoyer.

sacrament [sakr°m°nt] s. sacre-ment, m.; sacramental, sacramentel.

sacred [sé¹krid] adj. sacré. ‖ **sacred-ness** [-nis] s. sainteté; inviolabilité, f.; caractère sacré, m.

sacrifice [sakr°fa¹s] s. sacrifice, m.;

v. sacrifier; *to sell at a sacrifice*, vendre au rabais.

sacrilege [sakrᵉlidj] *s.* sacrilège, m. ‖ **sacrilegious** [sakrilidjᵉs] *adj.* sacrilège.

sacristan [sakristᵉn] *s.* sacristain, m. ‖ **sacristy** [-ti] *s.*⃰ sacristie, f.

sad [sad] *adj.* triste; mélancolique; cruel [loss]; sombre [color]. ‖ **sadden** [-'n] *v.* (s')attrister.

saddle [sad'l] *s.* selle; sellette, f.; *v.* seller; bâter; charger; *flat saddle*, selle anglaise; *pack saddle*, bât; *saddle-bag*, sacoche; *to saddle someone with responsibilities*, accabler quelqu'un de responsabilités. ‖ **saddler** [sadlᵉr] *s.* sellier, m.

sadism [sé¹diz'm] *s.* sadisme, m. ‖ **sadist** [-ist] *s.* sadique, m. f. ‖ **sadistic** [sadistik] *adj.* sadique.

sadness [sadnis] *s.* tristesse, f.

safe [sé¹f] *adj.* sauf; sûr; hors de danger, intact; *s.* coffre-fort, m.; *safe and sound*, sain et sauf; *safe conduct*, sauf-conduit; *safely*, en sûreté, sans encombre; *safe from*, à l'abri de. ‖ **safeguard** [-gârd] *s.* sauvegarde; escorte, f.; *v.* sauvegarder, protéger. ‖ **safety** [-ti] *s.*⃰ sécurité; protection; sauvegarde, f.; cran de sûreté, m.; *in safety*, en lieu sûr; *safety deposit box*, coffre, *Fr. Can.* coffret de sûreté; *safety-device*, mécanisme de sécurité; *safety pin*, épingle de sûreté; *safety razor*, rasoir mécanique; *safety valve*, soupape de sûreté.

saffron [safrᵉn] *s., adj.* safran, m.

sag [sag] *v.* ployer; fléchir; s'affaisser; *s.* fléchissement; affaissement, m.; courbure [shoulders], f.

sagacious [sᵉgé¹shᵉs] *adj.* sagace; subtil; avisé. ‖ **sagacity** [sᵉgasᵉti] *s.* sagacité; perspicacité, f.

sage [sé¹dj] *adj.* sage; avisé; modéré; instruit; *s.* sage, m.

sage [sé¹dj] *s.* sauge, f.

said [sé¹d] *pret., p. p. of* **to say.**

sail [sé¹l] *s.* voile; aile [mill]; promenade en bateau à voiles, f.; *v.* faire voile, voguer; *under full sail*, toutes voiles dehors; *to take in sail*, carguer la voile (naut.); *to set sail*, prendre la mer; *sailboat*, voilier; *sailplane*, planeur de vol à voile (aviat.), *foresail*, misaine. ‖ **sailing** [-ing] *s.* navigation, f.; départ, m. ‖ **sailor** [-ᵉr] *s.* marin; matelot, m.; *to be a good sailor*, avoir le pied marin; *deep-sea sailor*, navire long courrier.

saint [sé¹nt] *s.* saint, m.; *All Saints' Day*, la Toussaint; *Saint Vitus's dance*, danse de Saint-Guy; *v.* canoniser; faire le saint. ‖ **saintly** [-li] *adj.* saint; pieux; *adv.* saintement.

sake [sé¹k] *s.* cause, f.; but, égard, amour, intérêt, m.; *for the sake of*, à cause de; *do it for my sake*, faites-le pour moi; *for God's sake*, pour l'amour de Dieu; *for the sake of appearances*, pour sauver les apparences.

salad [salᵉd] *s.* salade, f.; *salad bowl*, saladier.

salamander [salᵉmàndᵉr] *s.* salamandre, f.

salary [salᵉri] *s.*⃰ salaire, m.; appointements, m. pl.; *v.* salarier; appointer.

sale [sé¹l] *s.* vente, f.; débit; solde, m.; *private sale*, vente à l'amiable; *for sale*, à vendre; *on sale*, en vente; *charity sale*, kermesse, *Fr. Can.* bazar; *wholesale*, vente en gros. ‖ **salesman** [-zmᵉn] (*pl.* **salesmen**) *s.* vendeur; marchand, m.; *Am. traveling salesman*, voyageur de commerce, commis voyageur. ‖ **saleswoman** [-zwoumᵉn] (*pl.* **saleswomen**) *s.* vendeuse, f.

salient [sé¹liᵉnt] *adj.* saillant; remarquable; proéminent.

saline [sé¹la¹n] *adj.* salin; salé; *s.* saline, f.; sel purgatif, m.

saliva [sᵉla¹vᵉ] *s.* salive, f. ‖ **salivate** [salivé¹t] *v.* (faire) saliver.

sallow [saloᵘ] *adj.* blême, jaune.

sally [sali] *s.*⃰ sortie; saillie; boutade, f.; *v.* saillir; faire une sortie.

salmon [samᵉn] *s.* saumon, m.; *salmon-trout*, truite saumonée; *land-locked salmon*, *Fr. Can.* ouananiche.

salon [saloⁿ] *s.* salon, m.; *Am. beauty salon*, institut de beauté.

saloon [sᵉloun] *s.* salon; bar; *Am.* bistrot; *saloon-car*, wagon-salon.

salsify [salsᵉfi] *s.* salsifis, m.

salt [sault] *s.* sel, m.; *adj.* salé; *v.* saler; *salt cellar*, salière; *salt mine*, mine de sel; *salt provisions*, salaisons; *old salt*, loup de mer; *smelling salts*, sels volatils.

saltpeter [saultpitᵉr] *s.* salpêtre, m.

salty [saulti] *adj.* salé; saumâtre.

salubrity [sᵉloubrᵉti] *s.* salubrité, f.

salutary [salyᵉtèri] *adj.* salutaire.

salutation [salyᵉté¹shᵉn] *s.* salutation, f.; salut, m. ‖ **salute** [sᵉlout] *s.* salut, m.; salve, f.; *v.* saluer.

salvage [salvidj] *s.* sauvetage; objet récupéré, m.; récupération, f.

salvation [salvé¹shᵉn] *s.* salut, m.; salvation, f.; *Salvation Army*, Armée du Salut.

salve [sav] *s.* onguent; baume, m.; pommade, f.; *v.* oindre; appliquer un onguent à; adoucir.

salvo [salvoᵘ] *s.* salve (mil.), f.

same [séᵢm] *adj.* même; semblable; *it is all the same to me,* cela m'est égal; *it is all the same,* c'est tout comme; *the same to you,* pareillement; *to do the same,* en faire autant.

sample [sàmp'l] *s.* échantillon; exemple; prélèvement (méd.), m.; *v.* échantillonner; déguster; *sampler,* modèle; échantillonneur.

sanatorium [sanᵉtoᵒuᵣᵢem] *s.* sanatorium, m.

sanctification [sàngktᵉkéᵢshᵉn] *s.* sanctification, f. ‖ **sanctify** [sàngktefaᵢ] *v.* sanctifier. ‖ **sanctimonious** [sangktimoᵒuniᵉs] *adj.* papelard, cagot, bigot.

sanction [sàngkshᵉn] *s.* sanction; approbation, f.; *v.* sanctionner; ratifier; autoriser.

sanctity [sàngktᵉti] *s.* sainteté, f.

sanctuary [sàngktshouèri] *s.** sanctuaire, m.

sand [sànd] *s.* sable, m.; *pl.* grève, f.; *v.* sabler; ensabler; *sandbank,* banc de sable; *Am. sand glass,* sablier; *sandpaper,* papier de verre; *sandstone,* grès.

sandwich [sàndwitsh] *s.** sandwich, m.; *v.* intercaler; *sandwich-loaf,* pain de mie.

sandy [sàndi] *adj.* sableux; sablonneux; blond roux [hair].

sane [séᵢn] *adj.* sain; sensé; raisonnable.

sang [sàng] *pret. of* to sing.

sanguinary [sànggwinèri] *adj.* sanguinaire, f. ‖ **sanguine** [sàngwin] *adj.* de sang; rubicond; sanguin; optimiste; *v.* ensanglanter.

sanitarium [sanᵉtârᵢem] *s.* sanatorium, m. ‖ **sanitary** [sanᵉtèri] *adj.* sanitaire; hygiénique. ‖ **sanitation** [sanᵉtéᵢshᵉn] *s.* hygiène; salubrité, f.; assainissement, m. ‖ **sanity** [sanᵉti] *s.* santé; raison, f.; équilibre mental, m.

sank [sàngk] *pret. of* to sink.

sap [sap] *s.* sève, f.; aubier, m.; *saphouse,* *Fr. Can.* cabane à sucre.

sap [sap] *s.* sape, f.; *Am.* crétin, m.; *v.* saper.

sapling [sapling] *s.* arbrisseau, m.

sapper [sapᵉr] *s.* sapeur, m.

sapphire [safaᵢr] *s.* saphir, m.

sappy [sapi] *adj.* plein de sève; naïf, niais.

saraband [sarᵉband] *s.* sarabande, f.

sarcasm [sâᵣkaz'm] *s.* sarcasme; esprit sarcastique, m. ‖ **sarcastic** [sᵉrkastik] *adj.* sarcastique.

sarcophagus [sâkaufᵉgᵉs] *s.* sarcophage, m.

sardine [sârdîn] *s.* sardine, f.

sardonic [sardânik] *adj.* sardonique.

sarsaparilla [sârspᵉrîlᵉ] *s.* salsepareille, f.

sash [sash] *s.** ceinture; écharpe; *Fr. Can.* ceinture fléchée, f.; *v.* ceinturer; orner d'une écharpe.

sash [sash] *s.** châssis de fenêtre, m.; *sash window,* fenêtre à guillotine.

Satan [séᵢtᵉn] *s.* Satan, m.; *satanic,* satanique.

satchel [satshᵉl] *s.* cartable, m.; gibecière; sacoche, f.

sate [séᵢt] *v.* rassasier; assouvir, satisfaire.

sateen [satîn] *s.* satinette, f.

satellite [satlaᵢt] *s.* satellite, m.

satiate [séᵢshiéᵢt] *v.* rassasier; assouvir. ‖ **satiety** [sᵉtaᵢeti] *s.* satiété, f.

satin [satin] *s.* satin, m.; *adj.* de satin; *v.* satiner.

satire [sataᵢr] *s.* satire, f. ‖ **satirical** [sᵉtirik'l] *adj.* satirique. ‖ **satirize** [satᵉraᵢz] *v.* satiriser.

satisfaction [satisfakshᵉn] *s.* satisfaction, f.; contentement, m. ‖ **satisfactory** [satisfaktri] *adj.* satisfaisant; satisfactoire (theol.). ‖ **satisfy** [satisfaᵢ] *v.* satisfaire; contenter; donner satisfaction; *to satisfy oneself that,* s'assurer que.

saturate [satshᵉréᵢt] *v.* saturer; imprégner; imbiber. ‖ **saturation** [satyouréᵢshᵉn] *s.* saturation; imprégnation, f.

Saturday [satᵉrdi] *s.* samedi, m.

satyr [satᵉ] *s.* satyre, m.

sauce [saus] *s.* sauce; *Br.* impertinence, f.; assaisonnement, m.; *v.* assaisonner; être insolent avec. ‖ *saucepan* [sauspàn] *s.* casserole, f. ‖ *saucer* [sausᵉr] *s.* soucoupe, f. ‖ *sauciness* [sausinis] *s.* effronterie; insolence, f. ‖ *saucy* [sausi] *adj.* impertinent; effronté.

sauerkraut [saᵒuᵉrkraᵒut] *s.* choucroute, f.

saunter [sauntᵉr] *v.* flâner; musarder; déambuler; *s.* flânerie, f.

sausage [sausidj] *s.* saucisse, f.; saucisson, m.; *sausage balloon,* saucisse (aviat.).

savage [savidj] *adj.* sauvage; farouche; brutal; désert, inculte; *s.* sauvage, m. f. ‖ **savagery** [-ri] *s.** sauvagerie; brutalité; fureur, f.

savanna [sᵉvànᵉ] *s.* savane, f.

save [séᵢv] *v.* sauver; épargner; économiser; ménager; *prep.* sauf; excepté; *to save from,* préserver de, sauver de; *save for,* à l'exception de; *save* *that*, si ce n'est que. ‖ **saver** [-ᵉʳ] *s.* sauveur, libérateur, m.; personne économe, f.; économiseur (mech.), m. ‖ **saving** [-ing] *s.* sauvetage, m.; économie, f.; *adj.* économe; **savings bank**, caisse d'épargne; *prep.* sauf; à l'exception de. ‖ **savio(u)r** [sé¹vyᵉʳ] *s.* sauveur, m.

savo(u)r [sé¹vᵉʳ] *s.* saveur, f.; goût; parfum, m.; *v.* savourer; avoir goût (*of*, de); *it savo(u)rs of treason*, cela sent la trahison; **savourless**, insipide, fade; **savo(u)ry**, savoureux; épicé, relevé.

saw [sau] *pret. of* **to see**.

saw [sau] *s.* scie, f.; *v.** scier; *fret saw*, scie à découper; *hand saw*, égoïne; *lumberman's saw*, scie passe-partout; *power saw*, scie mécanique; *sawdust*, sciure de bois; *sawmill*, scierie.

sawn [saun] *p. p. of* **to saw**.

saxophone [sᴀksᵉfoᵒun] *s.* saxophone, m.

say [sé¹] *v.** dire; réciter; raconter; s'exprimer; *as they say*, comme on dit; *that is to say*, c'est-à-dire; *say what I would*, j'avais beau dire; *to say nothing of*, sans parler de; *the final say*, le dernier mot; *to have one's say*, donner son avis. ‖ **saying** [-ing] *s.* dicton; adage, m.; *as the saying goes*, comme dit le proverbe.

scab [skab] *s.* croûte (med.); gale; escarre, f.; *Am.* « jaune » [blackleg]; *v.* faire croûte; se cicatriser.

scabbard [skabᵉrd] *s.* fourreau; étui, m.; gaine, f.

scabby [skabi] *adj.* galeux; couvert de croûtes; teigneux. ‖ **scabies** [ské¹-biïz] *s.* gale, f.

scabrous [ské¹brᵉs] *adj.* rugueux, raboteux; scabreux, risqué.

scaffold [skaf'ld] *s.* échafaud, m.; **scaffolding**, échafaudage, m.

scald [skauld] *s.* brûlure, f.; *v.* échauder; brûler; ébouillanter.

scale [ské¹l] *s.* échelle; proportion, f.; *v.* escalader; *on a limited scale*, sur une petite échelle; *scale model*, maquette; *wage scale*, barème des salaires.

scale [ské¹l] *s.* plateau de balance, m.; balance, f.; *v.* peser; *to turn the scale*, faire pencher la balance; *platform scale*, bascule.

scale [ské¹l] *s.* écale; écaille; squame, f.; tartre, m.; *v.* écaler; écailler; s'exfolier; s'entartrer.

scallion [skᴀly°n] *s.* ciboule, f.

scallop [skaul°p] *s.* coquillage; mollusque; feston, m.; *v.* festonner; faire cuire en coquilles; faire gratiner.

scalp [skalp] *s.* cuir chevelu; scalp, m.; *v.* scalper; écorcher; *Am.* vendre au-dessus du prix; **scalpel**, scalpel, m.

scaly [ské¹li] *adj.* écailleux; *scaly with rust*, rouillé.

scamp [skàmp] *s.* chenapan; vagabond, m.; *v.* bâcler; bousiller [colloq.].

scamper [skàmpᵉr] *v.* courir allègrement; *to scamper away*, décamper; *s.* fuite rapide, f.

scampi [skampi] *s.* langoustine, f.

scan [skàn] *v.* scander; scruter.

scandal [skànd'l] *s.* calomnie; honte; médisance; diffamation, f.; scandale, m. ‖ **scandalize** [-a¹z] *v.* scandaliser; médire; *to be scandalized at*, se scandaliser de. ‖ **scandalous** [-ᵉs] *adj.* scandaleux; honteux; diffamatoire.

Scandinavia [skandiné¹vi°] *s.* Scandinavie, f. ‖ **Scandinavian** [-ᵉn] *adj.*, *s.* scandinave.

scant [skànt] *adj.* rare; épars; insuffisant; exigu; *v.* limiter; réduire; rogner. ‖ **scantiness** [-inis] *s.* rareté; insuffisance, f. ‖ **scanty** [-i] *adj.* rare; insuffisant, maigre.

scapegoat [ské¹pgoᵒut] *s.* bouc émissaire; « lampiste », m.

scapegrace [ské¹pgré¹s] *s.* vaurien; garnement, m.

scapula [skapyoul°] *s.* omoplate, f.

scar [skâr] *s.* cicatrice; balafre; f.; *v.* cicatriser; balafrer; couturer.

scarab [skarᵉb] *s.* scarabée, m.

scarce [skèᵉrs] *adj.* rare; peu commun; mal pourvu; pauvre (*of*, de); **scarcely**, à peine; ne...; guère; *scarcely anything*, presque rien.

scare [skèᵉr] *s.* panique, f.; *v.* effrayer; épouvanter; effarer; *scarecrow*, épouvantail; *scary*, peureux, alarmé.

scarf [skârf] *s.* écharpe; cravate; étole, f.; fichu, m.; *Am.* chemin (m.) de table.

scarf [skârf] *s.* assemblage (mech.), m.

scarify [skarᵉfa¹] *v.* scarifier.

scarlet [skârlit] *adj.*, *s.* écarlate; *scarlet fever*, scarlatine.

scathe [ské¹zh] *s.* dommage, m.; *v.* endommager; détruire; *scathing*, acerbe, mordant; *scatheless*, indemne.

scatter [skatᵉr] *v.* répandre; éparpiller; (se) disperser; *scatterbrained*, étourdi; écervelé.

scavenger [skavindjᵉr] *s.* boueur, balayeur; égoutier, m.

scenario [sinârioᵒu] *s.* scénario, m.; *scenario-writer*, scénariste. ‖ **scene**

[sîn] *s.* scène, vue, f.; décor, m.; **scene-shifter**, machiniste. ‖ **scenery** [-ri] *s.* scène; vue; perspective; mise en scène, f.; décors, m. pl. ‖ **scenic** [-ik] *adj.* scénique; théâtral.

scent [sènt] *s.* senteur, f.; parfum; flair; odorat, m.; *v.* parfumer; flairer; *my dog has a keen scent*, mon chien a du nez; *to be on the scent*, être sur la piste; *to get scent of*, avoir vent de; **scentless**, inodore.

scepter [sèpt**e**r] *s.* sceptre, m.

sceptic [skèptik] *adj.* sceptique. ‖ **scepticism** [skèpt**e**sizem] *s.* scepticisme, m.

schedule [skèdyoul] *s.* horaire; tarif [price]; bilan (comm.); plan [work]; bordereau; inventaire; barème, m.; nomenclature; liste; cédule; annexe, f.; *v.* établir un horaire, un plan, un programme; **training schedule**, programme d'études.

schematic [skîmatik] *adj.* schématique. ‖ **schematize** [skîm**e**ta¹z] *v.* schématiser. ‖ **scheme** [skîm] *s.* plan; projet; schéma, m.; *v.* projeter; arranger; ourdir; **colo(u)r scheme**, combinaison de couleurs; **metrical scheme**, système de versification. ‖ **schemer** [-er] *s.* intrigant; faiseur de projets, m. ‖ **scheming** [-ing] *adj.* intrigant; spéculateur; *s.* machination, intrigue, f.

schism [sizem] *s.* schisme, m. ‖ **schismatic** [sizmatik] *adj.*, *s.* schismatique.

schist [shist] *s.* schiste, m.

scholar [skål**e**r] *s.* écolier; élève; savant; érudit, m.; *a Greek scholar*, un helléniste. ‖ **scholarly** [-li] *adj.* érudit; savant. ‖ **scholarship** [-ship] *s.* instruction; érudition; science; bourse (univ.), f.

scholastic [sko**ou**lastik] *adj.* scolaire; scolastique; pédant.

school [skoul] *s.* école, f.; banc [fish], m.; *v.* instruire; enseigner; faire la leçon à; discipliner; *adj.* d'école, scolaire; **boarding school**, pensionnat; **trade school**, école professionnelle; **school book**, livre de classe; **schoolboy**, écolier, lycéen; **schoolhouse**, bâtiment scolaire; **schoolmaster**, professeur; **schoolmate**, condisciple; **schoolmistress**, maîtresse d'école, institutrice; **schoolroom**, classe; **schoolteacher**, maître, instituteur; institutrice. ‖ **schooling** [-ing] *s.* enseignement, m.; instruction, f.

schooner [skoun**e**r] *s.* goélette, f.; *Am.* chope, f.

sciatica [sa¹atik**e**] *s.* sciatique, f.

science [sa¹**e**ns] *s.* science, f. ‖ **scientific** [sa¹**e**ntifik] *adj.* scientifique; de précision. ‖ **scientifically** [-'li] *adv.*

scientifiquement. ‖ **scientist** [sa¹**e**ntist] *s.* savant, homme de science, m.

scintillate [sintilé¹t] *v.* scintiller.

scion [sa¹**e**n] *s.* scion; descendant, m.

scission [síshen] *s.* coupage, m.; scission, division, f.

scissors [siz**e**rz] *s. pl.* ciseaux, m. pl.

scoff [skauf] *s.* moquerie; raillerie, f.; *v.* railler; se moquer (*at*, de); **scoffer**, moqueur.

scold [sko**ou**ld] *v.* gronder; réprimander; *s.* grondeur, m.; mégère; grondeuse, f. ‖ **scolding** [-ing] *s.* réprimande; semonce, f.; savon, m.; *adj.* grondeur, criard; plein de reproches.

sconce [skåns] *s.* bougeoir; flambeau, m.; bobèche, applique, f.

scone [sko**ou**n] *s.* galette (f.) au lait.

scoop [skoup] *s.* épuisette; écope; louche; nouvelle sensationnelle, exclusivité, f.; godet, m.; *v.* écoper; vider; creuser; **scoopful**, grande cuillerée, pleine louche; **scoop-net**, épuisette, drague.

scoot [skout] *v.* filer, déguerpir.

scooter [skout**e**r] *s.* trottinette, f.; scooter, m.

scope [sko**ou**p] *s.* champ d'action, m.; portée, f.; *within the scope of*, dans les limites de.

scorch [skaurtsh] *v.* brûler; roussir; *s.** brûlure; roussissure, f.; **scorching**, brûlant.

score [sko**ou**r] *s.* entaille, coche; marque; dette; cause, raison; partition [music]; point; compte; vingt; sujet, m.; *v.* entailler; marquer; compter; inscrire; orchestrer; marquer des points [game]; *on that score*, à ce sujet; *on the score of*, à propos de, à cause de; *to score a point*, marquer un point; **eightscore**, cent soixante.

scorn [skaurn] *s.* dédain; mépris, m.; *v.* mépriser, dédaigner; **scornful**, méprisant, dédaigneux; **scornfully**, avec dédain.

scorpion [skaurpi**e**n] *s.* scorpion, m.

scot [skåt] *s.* écot, m.; **scot-free**, gratis; indemne.

Scot [skåt] *s.* Ecossais, m. ‖ **Scotch** [skåtsh] *adj.*, *s.* écossais; *s.* whisky, m.

scotch [skåtsh] *s.** entaille, éraflure, f.; *v.* érafler; égratigner.

Scotland [skåtl**e**nd] *s.* Ecosse, f.; **Scots**, Ecossais; **Scottish**, écossais.

scoundrel [ska**ou**ndr**e**l] *s.* coquin; gredin, m.; canaille, f.

scour [ska**ou**r] *v.* récurer; dégraisser; décaper; fourbir; curer; purger.

scour [ska**ou**r] *v.* parcourir; *to scour the country*, battre la campagne.

scourge [skë^rdj] *s.* fouet; fléau, m.; discipline, f.; *v.* fouetter; opprimer.

scout [ska^{ou}t] *s.* éclaireur; scout, m.; vedette, f.; *v.* partir en éclaireur; reconnaître (mil.); *air scout*, avion de reconnaissance; *submarine scout*, patrouilleur anti-sous-marin; *scout-master*, chef scout; *scout-mistress*, cheftaine. || *scouting* [-ing] *s.* exploration, reconnaissance, f.

scowl [ska^{ou}l] *s.* froncement de sourcils; air renfrogné, m.; *v.* froncer le sourcil; prendre un air renfrogné.

scraggy [skragi] *adj.* décharné, maigre; noueux; anfractueux (geol.).

scramble [skrāmb'l] *v.* jouer des pieds et des mains; se bousculer; mettre pêle-mêle; avancer difficilement; brouiller (radio); *s.* marche difficile; mêlée, confusion, f.; *scrambled eggs*, œufs brouillés; *to scramble up*, grimper.

scrap [skrap] *s.* fragment; morceau; chiffon; lambeau, m.; bribe, f.; *pl.* restes, m.; *v.* envoyer au rebut; mettre hors de service; *scrap book*, album de découpures; *scrap iron*, ferraille.

scrape [skrē¹p] *v.* gratter; racler; décrotter; *s.* raclement, m.; situation embarrassante, f.; *to scrape up a hundred pounds*, réussir à rassembler cent livres. || *scraper* [-^er] *s.* racloir; grattoir; décrottoir; grippe-sou, m.

scratch [skratsh] *v.* égratigner; (se) gratter; effacer; abandonner; griffonner; *adj.* disparate; improvisé; sommaire; *s.*[*] égratignure; rayure, raie, f.; coup de griffe; griffonnage, m.; *to scratch out*, rayer, biffer.

scrawl [skraul] *s.* griffonnage, m.; pattes de mouches, f. pl.; *v.* griffonner.

scream [skrīm] *s.* cri perçant, m.; *v.* pousser un cri aigu; *he is a scream*, il est « rigolo », « marrant ».

screech [skrītsh] *s.*[*] cri aigu, m.; *v.* crier; *screech owl*, chat-huant.

screen [skrīn] *s.* écran; rideau; paravent; crible, tamis; pare-brise, m.; *v.* masquer; protéger; porter à l'écran; *smoke screen*, rideau de fumée; *motion-picture screen*, écran de cinéma.

screw [skrou] *s.* vis; hélice, f.; écrou, m.; *v.* visser; contracter; pressurer; exploiter; extorquer, arracher; *screw-bolt*, boulon; *screw-driver*, tournevis; *screw propeller*, propulseur à hélice; *Br. screw-wrench*, clef anglaise; *to put the screws on*, forcer la main à; *to screw up one's courage*, prendre son courage à deux mains.

scribble [skrib'l] *v.* griffonner; *s.* griffonnage, m. || *scribbler* [-^er] *s.* gribouilleur; gratte-papier, m.

scrimp [skrimp] *v.* lésiner; saboter. || *scrimpy* [-i] *adj.* étriqué; chiche.

script [skript] *s.* écriture, main, f.; manuscrit; scénario, m.; *script-writer*, scénariste. || *Scripture* [skriptsh^er] *s.* Écriture sainte, f.

scrivener [skrivn^er] *s.* plumitif, m.

scroll [skro^{ou}l] *s.* rouleau de parchemin, de papier; ornement en volute, en spirale, m.

scrub [skrœb] *v.* récurer, frotter, briquer; faire de gros travaux; *s.* arbuste rabougri, m.; brosse usée, f.; poils drus, m. pl.; récurage (m.) à la brosse; avorton, m.; *adj. Am.* malingre, chétif; *Am. scrub woman*, laveuse, femme de journée; *scrubby*, rabougri; chétif; dru; broussailleux.

scruff [skrœf] *s.* nuque, f.

scruple [skroup'l] *s.* scrupule, m.; *v.* avoir des scrupules; hésiter à. || *scrupulous* [-l^es] *adj.* scrupuleux; méticuleux.

scrutinize [skroutina¹z] *v.* scruter; dévisager; faire une enquête sévère. || *scrutiny* [-ni] *s.*[*] examen rigoureux, m.; enquête minutieuse, f.

scuffle [skœf'l] *s.* mêlée; rixe; échauffourée, f.; *v.* se bousculer, se battre; marcher en traînant les pieds.

scull [skœl] *s.* rame, f.; *v.* ramer, godiller.

scullery [skœl^eri] *s.*[*] arrière-cuisine, f.; *scullery-boy*, plongeur; *scullion*, marmiton; plongeur.

sculptor [skœlpt^er] *s.* sculpteur, m. || *sculpture* [-tsh^er] *s.* sculpture, f.; *v.* sculpter; ciseler.

scum [skœm] *s.* écume; scorie; lie (fig.), f.; *v.* écumer; *scummer*, écumeur, écumoire; *scummy*, écumeux.

scurf [skë^rf] *s.* pellicules, f. pl.; teigne, f.; tartre, m. || *scurfy* [-i] *adj.* pelliculeux; dartreux; squameux.

scurrilous [skë^ril^es] *adj.* grossier; indécent; ignoble, méprisable.

scurry [skë^ri] *v.* courir vite; *to scurry away*, détaler.

scurvy [skë^rvi] *s.* scorbut, m.; *adj.* bas, vil, indigne.

scutcheon [skœtsh^en] *s.* écusson, m.

scuttle [skœt'l] *s.* écoutillon; hublot (naut.), m.; *v.* saborder (naut.).

scuttle [skœt'l] *s.* seau à charbon, m.

scythe [sa¹zh] *s.* faux, f.

sea [sī] *s.* mer, f.; *adj.* de mer, marin; *to go to sea*, prendre la mer; *to put to sea*, prendre le large; *high sea*, haute mer; *inland sea*, mer intérieure; *open sea*, pleine mer; *seaboard*, côtes; *seacoast*, littoral; *sea fight*, combat naval; *sea-green*, vert de mer; *sea-gull*, mouette; *sea lion*, otarie; *seaman*, marin; *seashore*, bord de la mer; **seasickness,** mal de mer; **sea-side,** bord de la mer; **sea wall,** digue; **seawards,** en direction de la mer; **seaweed,** algue marine; **seaworthy,** en état de naviguer.

seal [sîl] *s.* sceau; cachet, m.; *v.* sceller; cacheter, plomber; authentifier; approuver; **sealing wax,** cire à cacheter.

seal [sîl] *s.* phoque, m.; **sealskin,** phoque (comm.).

seam [sîm] *s.* couture; suture (med.); veine (geol.), f.; *v.* faire une couture; suturer; **soldered seam,** soudure; **seamstress,** couturière, lingère.

seaplane [sîplé¹n] *s.* hydravion, m.

sear [si⁰ʳ] *v.* cautériser; brûler; saisir (culin.); *adj.* séché, flétri, sec; *s.* gâchette, f.

search [së⁰tsh] *v.* chercher; scruter; fouiller; perquisitionner dans; visiter (customs); *s.** recherche; perquisition (jur.); visite (customs); descente (police); investigation, f.; *to search after,* aller à la recherche de; *to search for,* essayer de découvrir; *to search into,* chercher à pénétrer; **searcher,** chercheur; perquisitionneur; sonde; **searching,** scrutateur; **searchlight,** projecteur, phare; *Am.* lampe de poche, f.; **search warrant,** mandat de perquisition.

season [sîz'n] *s.* saison; époque, f.; *v.* assaisonner; acclimater; sécher; tempérer; aguerrir; **seasonable,** opportun; **season ticket,** carte d'abonnement; *in good season,* au bon moment; *seasoned troops,* troupes aguerries. ‖ **seasoning [-ing]** *s.* assaisonnement; séchage [wood], m.

seat [sît] *s.* siège, m.; place assise; assiette [horseman]; résidence, f.; *v.* asseoir; faire asseoir; placer; mettre un fond [trousers]; *to seat oneself,* s'asseoir; *this room seats three hundred,* cette salle contient trois cents places; **folding seat,** pliant; **seating capacity,** nombre de places assises.

sebaceous [sibé¹sh⁰s] *adj.* sébacé.

secant [sîk⁰nt] *s.* sécante, f.

secede [sisîd] *v.* se séparer. ‖ **secession** [sisèsh⁰n] *s.* sécession; scission; dissidence, f. ‖ **secessionist** [-ist] *s.* *Am.* sécessionniste.

seclude [sikloud] *v.* séparer; écarter; éloigner; *to seclude oneself from,* se tenir à l'écart de; **secluded,** retiré, écarté; solitaire. ‖ **seclusion** [siklouj⁰n] *s.* éloignement; isolement, m.; retraite, f.

second [sèk⁰nd] *adj.* second, deuxième; secondaire; *s.* second; inférieur, m.; seconde, f.; *v.* seconder; appuyer [motion]; **second-hand,** d'occasion; **second hand of the clock,** grande aiguille

d'horloge; **second lieutenant,** sous-lieutenant; **second-rate,** de deuxième qualité; **second-sighted,** doué de seconde vue. ‖ **secondary** [-èri] *adj.* secondaire; accessoire; subordonné. ‖ **secondly** [-li] *adv.* deuxièmement.

secrecy [sîkr⁰si] *s.* discrétion; réserve, f.; secret, m. ‖ **secret** [sîkrit] *adj., s.* secret; **open secret,** secret de Polichinelle; **secretly,** secrètement, dans la clandestinité.

secretary [sèkr⁰tèri] *s.** secrétaire; ministre, m.; *Secretary of State,* secrétaire d'Etat; **secretaryship,** secrétariat.

secrete [sikrît] *s.* sécréter (med.); dissimuler; recéler. ‖ **secretion** [sikrîsh⁰n] *s.* sécrétion, f. ‖ **secretive** [-tiv] *adj.* qui sécrète ou favorise la sécrétion; réservé; peu communicatif.

sect [sèkt] *s.* secte, f. ‖ **sectarian** [sèktè⁰ri⁰n] *adj., s.* sectaire. ‖ **sectarianism** [-iz'm] *s.* sectarisme, m. ‖ **sectary** [sèkt⁰ri] *adj.* schismatique.

section [sèksh⁰n] *s.* section; coupe (techn.); tranche, f.; *v.* sectionner; diviser en sections. ‖ **sector** [-t⁰ʳ] *s.* secteur, m.

secular [sèky⁰l⁰ʳ] *adj.* séculaire; séculier; profane; *s.* laïc, m.; prêtre séculier, m. ‖ **secularize** [-ra¹z] *v.* séculariser.

secure [sikyour] *adj.* sûr; en sûreté; *v.* mettre en sûreté; assurer; s'emparer de; acquérir; retenir; **securely,** sans crainte, en sécurité, comme il faut. ‖ **security** [-⁰ti] *s.** sécurité; sûreté; protection; garantie, f.; nantissement, m.; *pl.* titres, m. pl.; valeurs, f. pl.

sedan [sidan] *s.* chaise à porteur; *Am.* conduite intérieure [car], f.

sedate [sidé¹t] *adj.* posé, sérieux. ‖ **sedative** [sèd⁰tiv] *adj.* sédatif, calmant.

sedentary [sèd⁰ntèri] *adj.* sédentaire.

sedge [sèdj] *s.* laîche, f.; jonc, m.

sediment [sèd⁰m⁰nt] *s.* sédiment, m.

sedition [sidish⁰n] *s.* sédition, f. ‖ **seditious** [-sh⁰s] *adj.* séditieux.

seduce [sidyous] *v.* séduire; détourner. ‖ **seducer** [-⁰ʳ] *s.* séducteur, m. ‖ **seduction** [sidœksh⁰n] *s.* séduction, f. ‖ **seductive** [-tiv] *adj.* séduisant.

sedulous [sèdyoul⁰s] *adj.* assidu, diligent, empressé.

see [sî] *v.** voir; apercevoir; veiller à; accompagner; *to see somebody out,* reconduire quelqu'un; *to see about,* s'occuper de; *to see through,* voir ce qui se cache derrière, voir à travers; *to see something through,* mener quelque chose à bien; *to see a person through a difficulty,* aider quelqu'un à sortir d'une difficulté; *to see to one's affairs,* veiller à ses affaires.

see [sî] *s.* siège, m.; *Holy See,* Saint-Siège.

seed [sîd] *s.* graine, f.; grain; pépin; germe; principe; sperme; frai, m.; semence; cause, f.; *v.* ensemencer; grener; parsemer (*with,* de); *to run to seed,* monter en graine; *canary seed,* millet; *seed bed,* semis; *seed-drill,* semoir; *seedling,* jeune plant; *élève;* semis; *seedless,* sans graine, sans pépin; *seedsman,* grainetier; *seedtime,* semaison, temps des semailles; *seedy,* grenu; patraque (fam.).

seek [sîk] *v.** chercher; rechercher; poursuivre; solliciter; *to seek out,* essayer de découvrir; *to seek for fame,* chercher la gloire; *to go and seek one's fortune,* aller chercher fortune; *seeker,* chercheur.

seem [sîm] *v.* sembler; paraître; *it seemed as though,* on aurait dit que; *seemingly,* apparemment, en apparence. ‖ *seemliness* [-linis] *s.* grâce, beauté; bienséance, f. ‖ *seemly* [-li] *adj.* convenable; décent; bienséant.

seen [sîn] *p. p. of* to see.

seep [sîp] *v.* suinter; filtrer.

seer [sier] *s.* prophète, voyant, devin; visionnaire, m. f.

seesaw [sîsau] *s.* balançoire, bascule, f.; *v.* basculer; balancer.

seethe [sîzh] *v.* bouillonner; foisonner.

segment [sègment] *s.* segment, m.; division, portion, f.

segregate [sègrigé¹t] *v.* séparer; isoler; [-git] *adj.* séparé, isolé. ‖ *segregation* [ségregé¹shen] *s.* ségrégation, f.

seism [sa¹z'm] *s.* séisme, m.

seize [sîz] *v.* saisir; prendre; capturer; confisquer; empoigner; coincer (mech.); *to seize upon,* s'emparer de. ‖ *seizure* [sîjer] *s.* saisie; prise; capture; mainmise; attaque [illness]; appréhension, f.; grippement (mech.), m.

seldom [sèldem] *adv.* rarement.

select [sèlèkt] *v.* choisir; *adj.* choisi. ‖ *selection* [-shen] *s.* sélection, f.; choix, m. ‖ *selective* [-tiv] *adj.* sélectif; électeur.

self [sèlf] (*pl. selves* [sèlvz]) *pron.* même; *s.* moi; individu, m.; *self-centered,* égocentriste; *self-confident,* sûr de soi; *self-conscious,* conscient; contraint, timide; *self-contained,* autonome, indépendant; *self-control,* sang-froid, empire sur soi-même; *self-defense,* légitime défense; *self-denial,* abnégation; *self-evident,* flagrant; manifeste; *self-government,* autonomie, gouvernement démocratique; *self-interest,* intérêt personnel; *selfish,* égoïste; *selfishness,* égoïsme; *self-essness,* désintéressement; *self-love,*

amour-propre; égoïsme; *self-reliance,* confiance en soi; *self-respect,* respect de soi-même; *self-starter,* autodémarreur; *self-supporting,* qui vit de son travail; *self-taught,* autodidacte.

sell [sèl] *v.** vendre; *to sell out,* liquider; *seller,* vendeur, vendeuse; *selling,* vente.

selves [sèlvz] *pl. of* self.

semaphore [sémefaur] *s.* sémaphore, m.

semblance [sèmblens] *s.* ressemblance; apparence, f.

semiannual [sèmianyouel] *adj.* semestriel.

semicircle [sèmeserk'l] *s.* demi-cercle, m.

semicolon [sèmekoºulen] *s.* point et virgule, m.

semimonthly [sèmemânthli] *adj.* bi-mensuel; semi-mensuel.

seminar(y) [sèminer, sèmenèri] *s.** séminaire, m. ‖ *seminarist* [sèmenèrist] *s.* séminariste.

semiweekly [sèmewîkli] *adj.* bi-hebdomadaire; semi-hebdomadaire.

senate [sènit] *s.* sénat, m.; *senator,* sénateur; *senatorial,* sénatorial.

send [sènd] *v.* envoyer; expédier; lancer; *to send for,* envoyer chercher; *to send away,* renvoyer, expédier; *to send forth,* exhaler, émettre, produire; *to send word of,* faire prévenir de; *to send on,* faire suivre, transmettre; *sender,* expéditeur; expéditionnaire; transmetteur.

senile [sîna¹l] *adj.* sénile. ‖ *senility* [senîleti] *s.* sénilité, f.

senior [sînyer] *adj., s.* aîné; supérieur; *to be someone's senior by three years,* avoir trois ans de plus que quelqu'un. ‖ *seniority* [sinyaureti] *s.* aînesse; ancienneté; doyenneté, f.

sensation [sènsé¹shen] *s.* sensation; impression; émotion, f.; *sensational,* sensationnel; émouvant.

sense [sèns] *s.* sens; sentiment, m.; impression; sensibilité; direction, f.; *v.* percevoir; sentir; *common sense,* sens commun; *good sense,* bon sens; *to be out of one's senses,* avoir perdu la tête; *to make sense,* comprendre, avoir un sens; *sense of duty,* sentiment du devoir. ‖ *senseless* [-lis] *adj.* insensible; inanimé; insensé; stupide. ‖ *sensibility* [sènsebîleti] *s.** sensibilité, f. ‖ *sensible* [sènseb'l] *adj.* sensible; conscient; sensé; *sensibly,* sensiblement; avec bon sens; raisonnablement; perceptiblement. ‖ *sensitive* [sènsetiv] *adj.* sensible; sensitif; susceptible. ‖ *sensitivity* [sènsetiveti] *s.* sensitivité; sensibilité, f. ‖ *sensorial* [sénsauri°l] *adj.* sensoriel. ‖ **sensual** [sénshou°l] *adj.* sensuel; voluptueux. ‖ **sensuality** [sènshoual°ti] *s.* sensualité, f. ‖ **sensuous** [sènshyou°s] *adj.* capiteux; voluptueux; sensuel; matérialiste.

sent [sènt] *pret., p. p. of to send.*

sentence [sént°ns] *s.* sentence; maxime; phrase, f.; jugement, m.; *v.* condamner; rendre un jugement contre; *death sentence,* condamnation à mort; *reconsideration of sentence,* révision de jugement; *suspended sentence,* sursis; *a well-turned sentence,* une phrase bien tournée; *sententious,* sentencieux.

sentient [sènsh°nt] *adj.* sensible.

sentiment [sènt°m°nt] *s.* sentiment, m.; opinion, f. ‖ **sentimental** [sènt°mènt°l] *adj.* sentimental. ‖ **sentimentality** [sènt°m°ntal°ti] *s.* sentimentalité, f.; sentimentalisme, m. ‖ **sentimentalize** [sènt°mènt°la¹z] *v.* faire du sentiment.

sentinel, sentry [sènt°n°l], [sèntri] *s.*⁎ sentinelle, f.; factionnaire; guetteur, m.; *sentry box,* guérite, f.

separable [sèp°r°b°l] *adj.* séparable (*from,* de). ‖ **separate** [sèprit] *adj.* séparé; distinct; isolé; à l'écart; *separate interests,* intérêts privés; *separately,* séparément, à part; [-ré¹t] *v.* (se) séparer; désunir; disjoindre. ‖ **separation** [sèp°ré¹sh°n] *s.* séparation; scission, f. ‖ **separatism** [sèp°r°tiz°m] *s.* séparatisme, m. ‖ **separatist** [-tist] *s.* séparatiste, m. f.

September [sèptèmb°r] *s.* septembre, m.

septic [sèptik] *adj.* septique (med.).

sepulcher [sèp'lk°r] *s.* sépulcre, m. ‖ **sepulchral** [sipœlkr°l] *adj.* sépulcral.

sepulture [sèp'ltsh°r] *s.* sépulture, f.

sequel [sîkw°l] *s.* suite; conséquence, f.

sequela [sikwîl] *s.* séquelle, f.

sequence [sîkw°ns] *s.* suite; série; conséquence; séquence; concordance, f.; enchaînement, m.; *sequent, sequential,* conséquent; consécutif.

sequester [sikwèst°r] *v.* séquestrer; confisquer. ‖ **sequestration** [sikwèstré¹sh°n] *s.* séquestration; confiscation, f.; séquestre, m.

seraglio [sérâlio°u] *s.* sérail; harem, m.

seraph [sér°f] (*pl.* **seraphim** [-fim] *s.* séraphin, m.

serenade [sèr°nèd] *s.* sérénade, f.; *v.* donner une sérénade.

serene [s°rîn] *adj.* serein; paisible; *keep serene,* gardez le sourire. ‖ **serenity** [s°rèn°ti] *s.*⁎ sérénité, f.

serf [së̀rf] *s.* serf, m.; serve, f. ‖ **serfdom** [së̀rfd°m] *s.* servage, m.

sergeant [sârdj°nt] *s.* sergent; maréchal des logis, m.; *sergeant-at-arms,* sergent d'armes.

serial [sîri°l] *adj.* en série; périodique; consécutif; *serial novel,* roman feuilleton; *serial number,* numéro matricule; *series,* série; succession, f.

serin [sérin] *s.* serin, m.

serious [sîri°s] *adj.* sérieux; grave; *seriously,* sérieusement. ‖ **seriousness** [-nis] *s.* sérieux, m.; gravité, f.

sermon [së̀rm°n] *s.* sermon, m.

serpent [së̀rp°nt] *s.* serpent, m.

serrate [sèrit] *adj.* dentelé; en dents de scie.

serum [sîr°m] *s.* sérum, m.

servant [së̀rv°nt] *s.* serviteur; domestique; servant, m.; servante, f.; *Br. civil servant,* fonctionnaire. ‖ **serve** [së̀rv] *v.* servir; suffire; faire le service militaire; desservir [transportation]; signifier (jur.); *it serves him right,* c'est bien fait pour lui; *he serves me with wine,* il me fournit de vin; *to serve as,* servir de; *to serve notice on,* notifier, aviser, signifier. ‖ **service** [-is] *s.* service; emploi; entretien des voitures, m.; distribution [gas, electricity], f.; *v.* entretenir, réparer (mech.); desservir; *to service and repair,* dépanner [car]; *detached service,* mission spéciale; *divine service,* office divin; *funeral service,* service funèbre; *mail service,* service des postes; *table service,* service de table; *service-station,* poste d'essence. ‖ **serviceable** [-is°b'l] *adj.* utile; utilisable. ‖ **servicing** [-ising] *s.* entretien m.; réparation, f. ‖ **servile** [-'l] *adj.* servile, obséquieux. ‖ **servitude** [-ityoud] *s.* servitude, f.; asservissement, esclavage, m.

session [sèsh°n] *s.* session; séance f.; *Am.* trimestre universitaire, m.

set [sèt] *v.*⁎ poser; placer; mettre; désigner; arranger; ajuster; établir, [rule]; donner [example]; repasser [knife]; affûter [saw]; sertir [gem]; tendre [trap]; régler [watch]; se fixer; se coucher [sun]; se serrer [teeth]; se nouer [fruit]; *s.* ensemble, assortiment; groupe; service [for tea]; équipage; coucher [sun]; jeu, m.; série; garniture; partie [game]; tranche (math.), f.; *adj.* placé, situé; fixe; serré; immuable, arrêté; résolu; obstiné; *to set aside,* affecter; mettre à part; *to set out,* se mettre en route; *to set up,* installer, apprêter; *to set oneself about,* se mettre à; *to set right,* redresser; *to set to music,* mettre en musique; *the smart set,* le monde élégant; *of set purpose,* de propos délibéré; *set of furniture,* ameublement

set of teeth, denture; **radio set**, poste de T.S.F.; **tea set**, service à thé; **telephone set**, poste téléphonique; **setback**, échec, recul; **settee**, canapé; **set-up**, dispositif. ‖ **setting** [-ing] *s.* pose; position; monture; composition (typogr.); mise en scène, f.; montage; réglage; affûtage [knife]; coucher [sun], m.

settle [sèt'l] *v.* établir; déterminer; arranger; organiser; régler [account]; résoudre; coloniser; assigner [property]; s'établir; se calmer [sea]; se poser [liquid]; se remettre [weather]; se tasser [building]; se liquider [debts]; *to settle down*, s'installer; *to settle down to*, s'atteler à. ‖ **settlement** [-m'nt] *s.* établissement; arrangement; règlement; accord, m.; installation colonisation; liquidation (comm.); pension, f.; **penal settlement**, colonie pénitentiaire; **settler**, colon; arbitre.

seven [sèv'n] *adj.* sept. ‖ **seventeen** [sèv'ntîn] *adj.* dix-sept. ‖ **seventeenth** [-tînth] *adj.* dix-septième; se [sèv'nth] *adj.* septième. ‖ **seventieth** [sèv'ntiith] *adj.* soixante-dixième. ‖ **seventy** [sèv'nti] *adj.* soixante-dix.

sever [sèv'r] *v.* (se) séparer; diviser; trancher; (se) disjoindre.

several [sèv'rl] *adj.* divers; plusieurs; quelques; respectif; individuel; séparé, **severally**, séparément; respectivement.

severe [sevi'r] *adj.* sévère; austère; rigoureux; **severely**, sévèrement. ‖ **severity** [sevèr'ti] *s.* sévérité; dureté; rigueur, f.

sew [sou] *v.* coudre; brocher.

sewer [syou'r] *s.* égout; collecteur, m.

sewing [souing] *s.* couture, f.; **sewing-machine**, machine à coudre. ‖ **sewn** [soun] *p. p.* of **to sew**.

sex [sèks] *s.** sexe, m.

sextant [sèkst'nt] *s.* sextant, m.

sexton [sèkst'n] *s.* sacristain; fossoyeur, m.

sexual [sèkshou'l] *adj.* sexuel. ‖ **sexuality** [sèksyoualiti] *s.* sexualité, f. ‖ **sexy** [sèksi] *adj.* capiteuse, troublante [woman].

shabby [shabi] *adj.* râpé; fripé; minable; mesquin; miteux.

shack [shak] *s.* hutte, cabane, f.

shackle [shak'l] *v.* enchaîner; entraver; maniller (naut.); accoupler (railw.); *s.* maillon, m.; manille, f.; *pl.* fers, m. pl.; entraves, f. pl.

shad [shad] *s.* alose, f.

shade [shé'd] *s.* ombre; visière [cap]; nuance, f.; store [window], m.; *v.* ombrager; ombrer; obscurcir; abriter; nuancer; **shadeless**, sans ombre;

lamp shade, abat-jour. ‖ **shadow** [shadou] *s.* ombre; obscurité; trace, f.; fantôme, m.; *v.* ombrager; obscurcir; ombrer; suivre comme une ombre; **shadowy**, ombreux; indécis; **shady**, ombragé; louche [transaction]; douteux [character].

shaft [shaft] *s.* flèche; hampe [flag], f.; trait; fût [column]; timon [pole]; manche [tool]; arbre (mech.); rayon [light]; brancard [vehicle]; puits [mine], m.; **drive shaft**, arbre de transmission.

shaggy [shagi] *adj.* poilu; hirsute; raboteux, hérissé (*with*, de).

shagreen [shegrîn] *s.* chagrin, m.

shake [shé'k] *v.** secouer; branler; agiter; bouleverser; trembler; ébranler; chanceler; *s.* secousse; agitation, f.; serrement; tremblement; trille [music]; hochement, m.; *to shake hands with*, serrer la main à; *to shake one's head*, hocher la tête; *to shake off*, se débarrasser de; *to shake with laughter*, se tordre de rire; **shakedown**, lit improvisé. ‖ **shaken** [-'n] *p. p.* of **to shake**. ‖ **shaker** [-'r] *s.* mixeur, secoueur, m. ‖ **shaky** [-i] *adj.* branlant, chancelant.

shall [shal] *defect. aux.; I shall go to London*, j'irai à Londres; *shall I open the window?*, voulez-vous que j'ouvre la fenêtre?; *you shall be our umpire*, vous allez être notre arbitre.

shallop [shal'p] *s.* chaloupe, f.

shallot [shel'ât] *s.* échalote, f.

shallow [shalou] *adj.* peu profond; superficiel; frivole; *s.* haut-fond, basfond, m. ‖ **shallowness** [-nis] *s.* manque de profondeur, m.; frivolité, futilité, f.

sham [sham] *s.* feinte; frime, f.; chiqué, m.; *adj.* feint, truqué; **sham battle**, petite guerre; *v.* feindre; contrefaire.

shamble [shamb'l] *v.* marcher en traînant les pieds; *s. pl.* décombres, m. pl.; ruines, f. pl.

shame [shé'm] *s.* honte; pudeur, f.; *v.* faire honte, faire affront à; déshonorer : *to bring shame upon*, jeter le discrédit sur; **shamefaced**, timide, honteux. ‖ **shameful** [-f'l] *adj.* honteux; indécent; déshonorant. ‖ **shameless** [-lis] *adj.* impudent, éhonté. ‖ **shamelessness** [-lisnis] *s.* impudence, impudeur, f.; dévergondage, m.

shammer [sham'r] *s.* imposteur; simulateur.

shampoo [shàmpou] *s.* shampooing, m.; *v.* faire un shampooing.

shamrock [shàmrâk] *s.* trèfle, m.

shank [shàngk] *s.* tibia; canon [horse], m.; partie inférieure de la jambe; tige (mech.); queue [flower], f.

shanty [shànti] *s.** bicoque, masure, cabane, f.

shape [shé¹p] *s.* forme; tournure; configuration; façon, coupe, f.; contour, galbe, m.; *v.* former; façonner; modeler, *in a bad shape*, mal en point; *to get out of shape*, se déformer; *to shape up well*, prendre bonne tournure; **shapeless**, informe; **shapeliness**, beauté de forme, belles proportions, galbe, **shapely**, bien tourné.

share [shéⁱʳ] *s.* part, portion; action, valeur, f.; titre, m.; *v.* partager; participer (*in*, à; *with*, avec); *in half shares*, de compte à demi. ‖ **share-cropper** [-kràpⁱʳ] *s. Am.* métayer, m. ‖ **shareholder** [-hoᵘldⁱʳ] *s.* actionnaire; sociétaire, m. ‖ **sharer** [-rⁱʳ] *s.* participant, m.

share [shèⁱʳ] *s.* soc [plow], m.

shark [shârk] *s.* requin; filou, m.; *loan shark*, usurier.

sharp [shârp] *adj.* aigu; acéré; violent [struggle]; âcre [taste]; mordant; brusque [curve]; saillant; fin [ear]; accusé [features]; perçant; acide; rusé; dièse [music]; *adv.* exactement; attentivement, *at six o'clock sharp*, à six heures précises; **sharper**, chevalier d'industrie ‖ **sharpen** [-ⁿn] *v.* aiguiser; tailler [pencil]; diéser [music]; exciter; **sharpener**, affûteuse. ‖ **sharply** [-li] *adv.* vivement; rudement; nettement; attentivement; *to arrive sharply*, tomber à pic. ‖ **sharpness** [-nis] *s.* acuité, finesse, netteté; rigueur, âpreté; acidité, f.

shatter [shatⁱʳ] *v.* briser; mettre en pièces; délabrer; fracasser; se briser en miettes; se disperser; *s. pl.* morceaux, débris, m. pl.

shave [shé¹v] *v.* (se) raser; « tondre », duper; effleurer, frôler; *to have a close shave*, l'échapper belle; **clean-shaven**, rasé de frais, glabre. ‖ **shaven**, *p. p.* of *to shave*. ‖ **shaving** [-ing] *s.* action de (se) raser; planure (techn.), f.; copeau, m.; **shaving brush**, blaireau; **shaving soap**, savon à barbe.

shawl [shaul] *s.* châle; fichu, m.

she [shî] *pron.* elle; *she who*, celle qui; *she is a good woman*, c'est une brave femme; **she-bear**, ourse; **she-goat**, chèvre.

sheaf [shîf] (*pl.* **sheaves** [shîvz]) *s.* gerbe; liasse; botte, f.; faisceau, m.; *v.* mettre en gerbes.

shear [shîⁱʳ] *v.** tondre; cisailler; corroyer; *s.* tonte, f.; cisaillement, m.; *pl.* cisailles, f. pl.; cisailleuse (mech.), f.; **shearer**, tondeur; **shearing-machine**, tondeuse.

sheath [shîth] *s.* fourreau; étui; élytre, m.; gaine, f. ‖ **sheathe** [shîzh] *v.* rengainer; recouvrir; revêtir.

sheave [shîv] *s.* réa, m.; poulie, f.

sheaves [shîvz] *pl. of* **sheaf**.

shed [shèd] *s.* hangar; appentis; abri, m.; remise, f.

shed [shèd] *v.** répandre; verser; perdre, laisser fuir; déverser; *to shed leaves*, s'effeuiller.

sheen [shîn] *s.* éclat; lustre; miroitement, m.

sheep [shîp] *s.* mouton, m.; **black sheep**, brebis galeuse; **sheep dog**, chien de berger; **sheep-fold**, bercail, bergerie **sheepish**, niais, moutonnier, gauche, **sheepskin**, peau de mouton, basane; peau d'âne (diploma).

sheer [shîⁱʳ] *adj.* pur; escarpé; transparent; *by sheer force*, de vive force; *adv.* tout à fait; à pic; *v.* descendre (ou) monter à pic.

sheet [shît] *s.* drap, m.; feuille; nappe [water]; tôle [metal]; épreuve (typogr.), f.; **sheet iron**, tôle; **sheet lightning**, éclair de chaleur; **asbestos sheet**, plaque d'amiante.

sheik [shé¹k] *s.* cheik, m.

shelf [shèlf] (*pl.* **shelves** [shèlvz]) *s.* rayon; casier; plateau; écueil; récif; bas-fond, m.; planche, f.

shell [shèl] *s.* coquille; cosse; écaille; carapace; enveloppe (mech.), f.; obus, m.; *v.* écosser, écaler, bombarder; **shell hole**, trou d'obus, entonnoir.

shellac [shⁱlak] *s.* gomme laque, f.

shellfish [shèlfish] *s.** coquillage, m.

shelter [shèltⁱʳ] *s.* abri; refuge, m.; *v.* abriter, protéger; *to take shelter*, s'abriter; **shelter trench**, tranchée-abri.

shelve [shèlv] *v.* mettre de côté; garnir de rayons; classer, remiser.

shelve [shèlv] *v.* pencher; être en pente.

shelves [shèlvz] *pl. of* **shelf**.

shepherd [shèpⁱʳd] *s.* berger, m.; *the Good Shepherd*, le Bon Pasteur; **shepherdess**, bergère.

sherbet [shèⁱbit] *s.* sorbet, m.

sheriff [shèrif] *s.* shérif, m.

sherry [shèri] *s.** xérès, m.

shew [shoᵘ], *see* **show**.

shield [shîld] *s.* bouclier; pare-éclats, m.; *v.* défendre, protéger; blinder; **shield-bearer**, écuyer.

shift [shift] *v.* changer; changer de linge, de vitesse, de place; transférer; dévier; décaler, finasser, biaiser; *s.* changement; relais; expédient; subterfuge, m.; équipe; journée de travail, f.; *to shift about*, tourner casaque; **gear shift**, changement de vitesse; **wind shift**, saute de vent; *to shift for*

oneself, se débrouiller tout seul. ||
shifting [shĭftĭng] *adj.* changeant; mouvant; instable; rusé. || **shiftless** [-lĭs] *adj.* incapable; empoté; mou.

shilling [shĭlĭng] *s.* shilling, m.

shilly-shally [shĭlĭshali] *v.* tergiverser.

shimmer [shĭmᵉʳ] *v.* chatoyer; *s.* lueur, f.

shin [shĭn] *s.* tibia; jarret; bas de la jambe; *to shin up a tree,* grimper à un arbre.

shindy [shĭndi] *s.* tapage, m.; bagarre, f.; *Am.* sauterie, f.

shine [shaⁱn] *v.*⁎ briller; luire; cirer [shoes]; *s.* éclat, brillant; lustre, m.; *rain and shine,* la pluie et le beau temps; *to shine on,* éclairer.

shingle [shĭng'l] *s.* bardeau (techn.), m.; échandole, f.; enseigne, plaque, f.

shingles [shĭng'lz] *s. pl.* zona, m.

shining [shaⁱnĭng] *adj.* brillant; resplendissant; illustre; *s.* éclat; lustre, m. || *shiny* [shaini] *adj.* luisant; bien ciré [shoe].

ship [shĭp] *s.* bateau; vaisseau; navire, m.; *v.* embarquer; expédier par bateau; enrôler comme marin; *merchant ship,* navire marchand; *shipload,* cargaison, fret; *shipmate,* compagnon d'équipage; *ship-owner,* armateur, fréteur; *shipyard,* chantier de construction navale. || *shipment* [-mᵉnt] *s.* embarquement; chargement; transport, m.; expédition, f. || *shipper* [-ᵉʳ] *s.* expéditeur, chargeur, m. || *shipping* [-ĭng] *s.* marine; navigation; expédition, f.; transport maritime; tonnage, m.; *shipping charges,* frais d'embarquement; *shipping company,* compagnie de messageries maritimes, compagnie de navigation. || *shipwreck* [-rèk] *s.* naufrage, m.; *v.* faire naufrage; détruire.

shire [shaⁱᵉʳ] *s. Br.* comté, m.

shirk [shë⁎rk] *v.* éviter; esquiver; tirer au flanc; *shirker,* lâcheur, flanchard; tireur au flanc.

shirt [shë⁎t] *s.* chemise d'homme, f.; *shirt-maker,* chemisier [person]; *shirtwaist,* chemisier [dress].

shiver [shĭvᵉʳ] *v.* frissonner; grelotter; *s.* tremblement, frisson, m.

shiver [shĭvᵉʳ] *s.* morceau, éclat, m.; *v.* fracasser; briser en miettes; ralinguer (naut.).

shoal [shoᵘl] *s.* banc; haut-fond; traquenard, m.

shock [shăk] *s.* choc; impact; coup, m.; commotion, secousse, f.; *v.* choquer; heurter; commotionner; offenser; *shock absorber,* amortisseur;

shock troops, troupes de choc; *return shock,* choc en retour. || *shocking* [-ĭng] *adj.* choquant; révoltant; scandaleux; affreux.

shod [shăd] *pret., p. p. of* **to shoe.**

shoddy [shădi] *adj.* de camelote; *s.* camelote, pacotille.

shoe [shou] *s.* soulier; chaussure; fer [horse]; sabot; patin (mech.), m.; *v.*⁎ chausser; ferrer; saboter (mech.); *calked shoe,* fer à glace; *shoeblack,* décrotteur, cireur; *shoe blacking,* cirage noir; *shoehorn,* chausse-pied; *shoelace,* lacet de soulier; *shoemaker,* cordonnier; *shoe polish,* crème à chaussure; *shoe repairs,* cordonnerie; *shoe store,* magasin de chaussures; *shoe tree,* embauchoir.

shone [shoᵘn] *pret., p. p. of* **to shine.**

shook [shouk] *pret. of* **to shake.**

shoot [shout] *v.*⁎ tirer; décocher; décharger; faire feu; toucher; fusiller; chasser au fusil; *Fr. Can.* lancer [hockey]; pousser [plant]; photographier, filmer; filer [star]; *v.* pousse; chute d'eau, f.; coup de fusil; *Fr. Can.* lancer [hockey]; jet, m.; *to shoot a film,* tourner un film; *to shoot by,* passer en trombe; *to shoot forth,* germer, bourgeonner; *to shoot down,* abattre. || *shooter* [-ᵉʳ] *s.* tireur, m. || *shooting* [-ĭng] *s.* tir; élancement [pain], m.; pousse; chasse; décharge; prise de vue, f.; tournage, m. [film]; *shooting-script,* découpage; *shooting star,* étoile filante.

shop [shăp] *s.* magasin; atelier, m.; boutique; officine, f.; *v.* faire des emplettes, courir les magasins; *beauty shop,* institut de beauté; *shopgirl,* employée de magasin; *shop-lifting,* vol à l'étalage; *shop window,* devanture. || *shopkeeper* [-kĭpᵉʳ] *s.* boutiquier, marchand, m. || *shopper* [-ᵉʳ] *s.* acheteur, client, m. || *shopping* [-ĭng] *s.* achat, *Fr. Can.* magasinage, m.; *to go shopping,* aller faire des courses, *Fr. Can.* magasiner.

shore [shaᵘᵉʳ] *s.* côte; plage, f.; rivage; littoral, m.; *off shore,* au large; *on shore,* à terre.

shore [shaᵘᵉʳ] *s.* étai; étançon, m.; *v.* étayer; accorer (naut.); *shoring,* étaiement.

shorn [shoᵘʳn] *p. p. of* **to shear.**

short [shaᵘʳt] *adj.* court; bref; passager, brusque; insuffisant; *adv.* court, brièvement, brusquement; *to be short of,* être à court de; *in short,* bref; *short circuit,* court-circuit; *shortcut,* raccourci; *short story,* conte; *short syllable,* syllabe brève; *for short,* pour abréger; *to stop short,* s'arrêter net. || *shortage* [-ĭdj] *s.* manque; déficit, m.; pénurie, f. || *shortcoming* [-kœmĭng] *s.* insuffisance, f.; manquement, m. ‖ **shorten** [-'n] *v.* raccourcir; abréger. ‖ **shortening** [-ning] *s.* abréviation; graisse à pâtisserie, f.; saindoux, m. ‖ **shorthand** [-hand] *s.* sténographie, f.; **shorthand-typist**, sténo-dactylo. ‖ **shortly** [-li] *adv.* sous peu, brièvement; sèchement, vivement ‖ **shortness** [-nis] *s.* brièveté, courte durée, concision; petitesse; insuffisance, f. ‖ **shorts** [-s] *s. pl.* caleçon; slip; short, m.

shot [shât] *pret.*, *p. p. of to shoot*; *s.* coup de feu; boulet; grain de plomb; tireur, m. piqûre (med.), f.; *adj.* changeant; saillant *an expert pistol shot*, un bon tireur au pistolet; *like a shot*, comme un trait **shotgun**, fusil de chasse. *Am big shot*, « grosse légume »; *buck-shot*, chevrotine.

should [shoud] *defect aux.*; *you should be more attentive*, vous devriez être plus attentif, *I said that I should go*, j'ai dit que j'irais, *if it should rain*. s'il pleuvait, *how should I know?*, comment voulez-vous que je le sache?; *I should have gone*, j'aurais dû aller.

shoulder [shoᵒuldᵉr] *s.* épaule, f.; épaulement (mech.), m.; *v.* mettre sur les épaules pousser de l'épaule; **shoulder-belt, -sash, -strap**, bandoulière; **shoulder blade**, omoplate; **shoulder braid**, fourragère; *to turn a cold shoulder to*, battre froid à.

shout [shaᵒut] *v.* crier; s'écrier; *s.* clameur, acclamation, f.

shove [shœv] *v* pousser, bousculer; *s.* poussée, f.; *to shove off*, pousser au large; *shove off!*, fiche le camp!

shovel [shœv'l] *s* pelle; pelletée, f.; *v.* pelleter, remuer, jeter à la pelle; **intrenching shovel**, pelle-bêche.

show [shoᵒu] *v.* montrer; indiquer; faire voir, exposer, *s.* apparence; parade; exposition, f., étalage, spectacle; concours, m **advance show**, vernissage; **autoshow**, salon de l'automobile; **showdown**, étalement du jeu [cards]; *show him to his seat*, conduisez-le à sa place; *to show in*. introduire; *to show out*, reconduire, *to show off*, faire étalage. *to go to the show*, aller au spectacle, *to make a show of oneself*, s'exhiber.

shower [shoᵒuᵉr] *s.* exposeur; exposant; démonstrateur, m.

shower [shaᵒuᵉr] *s.* averse; ondée; douche, f.; *v.* faire pleuvoir, arroser; tomber à verse; combler; *April shower*, giboulée. ‖ **shower-bath**, *s.* douche, f.

shown [shoᵒun] *p. p. of to show*.

showy [shoᵒui] *adj.* voyant; éclatant; tapageur.

shrank [shràngk] *pret. of to shrink*.

shrapnel [shrápnᵉl] *s.* shrapnel, m.

shred [shrèd] *s.* lambeau; fragment; filament, m.; *v.* déchiqueter; effilocher; mettre en lambeaux; *to be in shreds*, être en loques; **shreddy**, déchiqueté, en lambeaux.

shrew [shrou] *s.* mégère, f.; **shrewmouse**, musaraigne ‖ **shrewd** [-d] *adj.* rusé, malin acéré, perspicace; subtil. ‖ **shrewdly** [-dli] *adv* avec sagacité. ‖ **shrewdness** [-dnis] *s* sagacité; perspicacité; finesse, f. ‖ **shrewish** [-ish] *adj.* acariâtre, querelleur, criard.

shriek [shrīk] *s* cri perçant, m.; *v.* pousser des cris aigus.

shrike [shraik] *s.* pie-grièche, f.

shrill [shril] *adj.* aigu, perçant; *v.* rendre un son aigu.

shrimp [shrimp] *s.* crevette, f.; gringalet, avorton, m. [colloq.].

shrine [shrain] *s.* châsse, f.; sanctuaire; tombeau, m.

shrink [shringk] *v.* rétrécir; rapetisser; diminuer, se ratatiner; se resserrer; *to shrink back*, reculer. ‖ **shrinkage** [-idj] *s* rétrécissement, m.; diminution, réduction; contraction, f.

shrive [shraiv] *v.* confesser et absoudre.

shrivel [shriv'l] *v.* (se) ratatiner; se recroqueviller.

shroud [shraᵒud] *s.* linceul; suaire; blindage (mech.), m.; *v.* ensevelir; envelopper. voiler

Shrovetide [shroᵒuvtaid] *s.* les jours gras, m. **Shrove Tuesday**, Mardi gras.

shrub [shrœb] *s* arbuste; arbrisseau, m.; **shrubbery**, bosquet.

shrug [shrœg] *v* hausser les épaules; *s.* haussement d'épaules, m.

shrunk [shrœngk], **shrunken** [-ᵉn] *p. p. of to shrink*.

shuck [shœk] *s. Am.* bogue; cosse; écale, f.; *v.* écosser, décortiquer, écailler. *interj.* zut!

shudder [shœdᵉr] *s.* frisson, m.; vibration, f.; *v.* frissonner; vibrer.

shuffle [shœf'l] *v.* mêler, battre [cards], traîner [feet], ruser, biaiser; danser une danse glissée; *s.* confusion; allure traînante, f., acte de battre les cartes; pas glissé, m.

shun [shœn] *v.* éviter, esquiver.

shunt [shœnt] *v* (se) garer; changer de voie, manœuvrer (railw.); dériver; *s.* détour, changement, m.; dérivation (electr.); aiguille (railw.), f.; **shunter**, aiguilleur.

shut [shœt] *v.* fermer; *to shut out*, empêcher d'entrer; exclure; *to shut* *off*, couper (electr.); *to shut up*, enfermer; emprisonner; se taire; *pret.*, *p. p. of* **to shut**; *adj.* fermé, clos. ‖ **shutter** [shæt°r] *s.* volet; contrevent; obturateur (phot.), m.; persienne, f.

shuttle [shæt'l] *s.* navette, f.; *v.* faire la navette; **shuttlecock**, volant; **shuttle-service**, navette.

shy [sha¹] *adj.* timide; ombrageux; *v.* faire un écart [horse]; se jeter de côté; **shyly**, timidement; *to be shy of*, être intimidé par; *to look shy at*, regarder d'un air défiant; ‖ **shyness** [-nis] *s.* timidité; réserve, f. ‖ **shyster** [-st°r] *s.* canaille, f.; *adj.* véreux.

si [si] *s.* si, m. (mus.).

sibyl [sibil] *s.* sibylle; devineresse, f.; **sibylline**, sibyllin.

sick [sik] *adj.* malade; souffrant; nauséeux; écœuré; las; nostalgique; *s.* les malades, m. pl.; *to report sick*, se faire porter malade; *to be sick for*, soupirer après; *to be sick of*, être dégoûté de; *to be sick*, avoir mal au cœur (ou) des nausées; **sick-brained**, malade du cerveau; **sick leave**, congé de maladie; **seasick**, qui a le mal de mer. ‖ **sicken** [-en] *v.* tomber malade; rendre malade; écœurer. ‖ **sickening** [-ning] *adj.* écœurant; navrant; répugnant.

sickle [sik'l] *s.* faucille, f.

sickly [sikli] *adj.* maladif; chétif; malsain. ‖ **sickness** [siknis] *s.* maladie; nausée, f.; **seasickness**, mal de mer; **air sickness**, mal de l'air.

side [sa¹d] *s.* côté; bord; versant [hill]; camp [game]; parti; effet [billiards], m.; *v.* prendre parti (*with*, pour; *against*, contre); *side by side*, côte à côte; *by his side*, à côté de lui; *to sidestep*, esquiver; **side-car**, sidecar; **side glance**, regard de côté; **side issue**, à-côté, question secondaire; **sideslip**, glissade sur l'aile (aviat.), dérapage [auto]; **wrong side**, envers. ‖ **sideboard** [-bo°rd] *s.* buffet, m. ‖ **sidetrack** [-trak] *v.* garer; reléguer; dévier; dépister. ‖ **sidewalk** [-wauk] *s.* Am. trottoir, m. ‖ **sideways** [-wé¹z] *adv.* de côté; latéralement; *adj.* latéral; par le flanc. ‖ **siding** [sa¹ding] *s.* voie de garage; voie secondaire, f. ‖ **sidle** [sa¹d'l] *v.* marcher de côté.

siege [sidj] *s.* siège, m.; *to lay siege to*, assiéger; *to lift the siege*, lever le siège.

sierra [sér°] *s.* sierra, f.

siesta [siést°] *s.* sieste, f.

sieve [sîv] *s.* tamis; crible, m.; *v.* tamiser; passer au crible.

sift [sift] *v.* tamiser; passer au crible.

sigh [sa¹] *s.* soupir, m.; *v.* soupirer; se lamenter.

sight [sa¹t] *s.* vue; vision; inspection; mire; hausse (milit.), f.; spectacle; guidon, m.; *v.* apercevoir; viser; *by sight*. de vue; *within sight*, en vue; **dial sight**, goniomètre, m.; *Am.* **far sighted**, presbyte. ‖ **sightless**, aveugle; **sightly**, plaisant; *to catch sight of*, apercevoir; *to lose sight of*, perdre de vue; *a sight of*, un tas de; *to see the sights* faire le tour des curiosités. ‖ **sightseeing** [-sîing] *s.* tourisme, m.; **sightseeing tour**, circuit touristique; **sightseer**, touriste, curieux, excursionniste.

sign [sa¹n] *s.* signe; symbole; indice, m.; trace; enseigne, f.; *v.* signer; faire un signe, un signal; **sign board**, panneau d'affichage; **call sign**, indicatif d'appel [radio]; **street sign**, plaque de rue; **signer**, signataire, endosseur; *to sign up for a job*, signer un contrat de travail.

signal [sign'l] *s.* signal; signe; indicatif; avertisseur; indicateur; insigne; sémaphore, m.; *v.* signaler; donner le signal; faire des signaux; *adj.* signalé; **distress signal**, S. O. S., **stop signal**, signal d'arrêt; **signal communications**, transmissions, **signalman**, signaleur. ‖ **signal(l)ing** [-ing] *s.* signalisation, f. ‖ **signalize** [sign°la¹z] *v.* signaler; faire des signaux.

signatory [sign°t°ri] *adj.*, *s.* signataire, m. f. ‖ **signature** [-tsh°r] *s.* signature; clef [music], f.; **signature tune**, indicatif musical [radio], m.

signet [sign°t] *s.* sceau, signet, m.; **signet-ring**, chevalière.

significance [signif°k°ns] *s.* sens, m.; signification importance, f. ‖ **significant** [k°nt] *adj.* significatif. ‖ **signification** [sign°fiké¹sh°n] *s.* signification, f. ‖ **significative** [signifik°tiv] *adj.* significatif. ‖ **signify** [signifa¹] *v.* signifier; vouloir dire; faire savoir, déclarer.

signpost [sa¹npo°st] *s.* poteau indicateur; signal routier, m.

silence [sa¹l°ns] *s.* silence, m.; *v.* faire le silence; faire taire. ‖ **silencer** [-°r] silencieux, amortisseur de bruit, m. ‖ **silent** [sa¹l°nt] *adj.* silencieux; taciturne; muet, **silent partner**, commanditaire. ‖ **silently** [-li] *adv.* silencieusement, sans bruit.

silhouette [silouèt] *s.* silhouette, f.; *v. to be silhouetted*, se profiler.

silicon [siliko°n] *s.* silicone, m.

silk [silk] *s.* soie, f.; *silken*, de soie; **silkworm**, ver à soie; **silky**, soyeux.

sill [sil] *s.* seuil [door]; rebord [window], m.; longrine; culée, f.

silly [sili] *adj.* sot; niais; absurde; ridicule.

silo [sa¹lo⁰u] *s.* silo, m.; *v.* ensiler.

silt [silt] *s.* vase; fange, f.; limon, m.; *v. to silt up,* (s') envaser.

silver [silv°r] *s* argent, m.; *v.* argenter étamer [mirror]; *adj.* argent; gris argent. **argenté** *silver fox,* renard argenté *silver wedding,* noces d'argent. ‖ **silversmith** [-smith] *s* orfèvre, m. ‖ **silverware** [-wè°r] *s.* argenterie, f. ‖ **silvery** [-ri] *adj.* argenté; argentin [sound]

similar [sim°l°r] *s.* similaire; analogue, **similarly,** de la même manière ‖ **similarity** [sim°lar°ti] *s.* similarité, ressemblance analogie, f. ‖ **simile** [sim°li] *s* comparaison, f. ‖ **similitude** [semil°tyoud] *s* similitude, f.

simmer [sim°r] *v* mijoter, cuire à petit feu frémir, fermenter (fig).

simper [simp°r] *s.* sourire niais, m.; *v.* minauder

simple [simp'l] *adj.* simple; naturel; candide sincère ingénu; *s* simple, m.; simple [plant] f. *simple-minded,* simplet. **simpleton** [simp'lt°n] *s* simplet, niais m **simplicity** [simplis°ti] *s.* simplicité naïveté candeur. f. ‖ **simplification** [simplef°ké¹sh°n] *s.* simplification. f ‖ **simplify** [simpl°fa¹] *v.* simplifier

simulate [simy°lé¹t] *v.* feindre; simuler; affecter ‖ **simulation** [simyoulé¹sh°n] *s* simulation. f

simultaneity [sim°lt°né¹iti] *s.* simultanéité, f ‖ **simultaneous** [sa¹m°lté¹ni°s] *adj* simultané

sin [sin] *s* péché. m.; faute, f.; *v.* pécher; commettre une faute.

sinapism [sin°piz'm] *s* sinapisme, m.

since [sins] *conj* depuis que; puisque; *prep.* depuis si: years since. il y a six ans; *ever since* depuis (ce moment-là); *since when?* depuis quand?

sincere [sinsi°r] *adj.* sincère; franc; de bonne foi ‖ **sincerity** [sinsèr°ti] *s.* sincérité. f.

sinecure [sinikyour] *s.* sinécure, f.

sinew [sinvou] *s* tendon; nerf, m.; énergie f **sinewless,** sans force; amorphe **sinewy,** tendineux; musculeux; nerveux muscle.

sinful [sinfoul] *adj.* coupable.

sing [sing] *v.* chanter, célébrer en vers; *to sing small.* déchanter; *to sing to sleep* endormir en chantant *to sing out of tune* détonner **singer,** chanteur; cantatrice chanteuse.

singe [sindj] *v* roussir; brûler [hair]; flambe [poultry] se roussir.

single [singg'l] *adj.* seul; unique; simple, célibataire; franc, sincère; *v.* sélectionner; séparer; *to single out,*

remarquer, singulariser; *to remain single,* rester célibataire; **single-breasted,** droit [jacket] **single-handed,** sans aide. **single-seater,** monoplace. ‖ **singleness** [singg'lnis] probité; sincérité; unicité f célibat, m.

singsong [singsaung] *s* rengaine, f.; *adj.* monotone chantant.

singular [singgv°l°r] *adj.* singulier; étrange. insolite curieux. rare; *s.* singulier. m ‖ **singularity** [singgyoula-riti] *s.* singularité particularité; bizarrerie rareté. f ‖ **singularize** [singgyoul°ra¹z] *v* singulariser.

sinister [sinist°r] *adj.* sinistre; funeste; menaçant.

sink [singk] *v* couler; sombrer (naut.) décliner s'enfoncer; s'embourber rabaisser [value]; se coucher [sun]; amortir [debts] placer à fonds perdus [money]. *s.* évier, égout; cloaque m.. *to sink under,* succomber à. **sinking-fund,** caisse d'amortissement ‖ **sinker** [-°r] *s.* plomb (m.) de ligne [fishing].

sinless [sinlès] *adj.* sans péché, innocent. ‖ **sinner** [sin°r] *s.* pécheur, m.; pécheresse, f.

sinuosity [sinyouâsiti] *s.* sinuosité, f. ‖ **sinuous** [sinyou°s] *adj.* sinueux; tortueux, souple.

sinus [sa¹n°s] *s.* sinus (med.), m.; **sinusitis,** sinusite.

sip [sip] *v.* siroter, déguster; *s.* petite gorgée, f

siphon [sa¹f°n] *s.* siphon, m.; *v.* tirer au siphon, siphonner.

sir [sër] *s* monsieur, m.

sire [sa¹°r] *s.* sire; père; mâle [animal], m.; *v.* engendrer.

siren [sa¹r°n] *s.* sirène, f.

sirloin [së¹lo¹n] *s.* aloyau; fauxfilet, m.

sirocco [siroko⁰u] *s.* sirocco, m.

sirup [sir°p] *s.* sirop, m.

sister [sist°r] *s.* sœur; religieuse, f.; *sister-in-law,* belle-sœur; *sister ship,* navire jumeau.

sit [sit] *v.* s'asseoir; être assis; siéger (jur.): tenir une séance; poser [portrait]. couver [hen] *to sit down,* s'asseoir *to sit still* se tenir tranquille. *to sit up all night* veiller toute la nuit, *to sit astride* être assis à califourchon *to sit well* aller bien. convenir (on, à).

site [sa¹t] *s.* site, emplacement, m.

sitter [sit°r] *s* personne assise; couveuse, f modèle qui pose m . *sitter-up,* personne qu veille tard ‖ **sitting** [-ing] *s* séance session, f. *adj.* couveuse; assis; *sitting-room,* salon; *sitting up,* veillée.

situated [sĭtshoué¹tĭd] *adj.* situé, sis. ‖ **situation** [sĭtshoué¹shᵉn] *s.* situation; position circonstance, f.; emploi; emplacement, m.

sitz-bath [sĭtsbâth] *s.* bain de siège, m

six [sĭks] *adj. s.* six. ‖ **sixteen** [-tîn] *adj., s.* seize ‖ **sixteenth** [-tînth] *adj. s.* seizième *April sixteenth* le 16 avril ‖ **sixth** [-th] *adj. s.* sixième **sixthly** [sĭksthlĭ] *adv* sixièmement **sixty** [-tĭ] *adj., s.* soixante ‖ **sixtieth** [-tiith] *adj., s.* soixantième

size [sa¹z] *s.* grandeur; dimension; pointure, taille encolure, capacité. étendue. f. calibre volume format. m.; *v* calibrer, classifier *full size,* grandeur naturelle *large size,* grande taille; *to size up,* estimer, se faire une idée de

sizzle [sĭz'l] *v.* frire; pétiller; grésiller; *s.* grésillement, m.

skate [ské¹t] *s* raie, f.

skate [ské¹t] *s* patin, m.; *v.* patiner; *ice skate,* patin à glace; *roller skate,* patin à roulettes **skater,** patineur; **skating,** patinage

skein [ské¹n] *s* écheveau, m.

skeleton [skèl*e*'t*n] *s* squelette, m.; ossature carcasse, charpente, f.; **skeletal,** squelettique

skeptic, *see* **sceptic.**

sketch [skètsh] *s.* croquis; relevé, m.; esquisse ébauche étude f.; *v* esquisser faire un croquis *rough sketch,* brouillon **sketching,** dessin à main levée, **sketchy,** sommaire, ébauché imprécis rudimentaire.

skewer [skyou*e*r] *s* brochette, f.

ski [skî] *s* ski, m.; *v.* skier; *ski-lift,* remonte-pente

skid [skĭd] *s* sabot-frein; patin (aviat.) traîneau dérapage. m.; *v.* glisser patiner déraper, chasser [wheels] **skidding,** dérapage.

skiff [skĭf] *s* esquif, m.

skilful [skĭlf'l] *adj* adroit, habile; **skilfully,** avec adresse avec dextérité

skill [skĭl] *s* habileté dextérité, f. art, talent, m. **skilled** [-d] *adj.* habile; expérimenté, fort (*in*, en).

skillet [skĭlĭt] *s* poêlon, m.; poêle, f.

skim [skĭm] *v* écumer, écrémer; effleurer **skim milk,** lait écrémé; **skimmer,** écumoire

skimp [skĭmp] *v.* lésiner; bâcler.

skin [skĭn] *s* peau; pellicule, f.; *v.* peler, écorcher éplucher, se cicatriser; *drenched to the skin* trempé jusqu'aux os, *to skin someone out of his money,* « plumer » quelqu'un, lui

soutirer de l'argent; *skin-deep,* superficiel; à fleur de peau; *skinflint,* grippe-sou **skinner,** peaussier, pelletier; *skinny,* décharné, osseux, parcheminé.

skip [skĭp] *v.* sauter; bondir; omettre, négliger. *Am. to skip rope,* sauter à la corde. *skipping rope,* corde à sauter.

skipper [skĭpᵉr] *s.* capitaine; patron d'un petit navire, m.

skirmish [skĕr'mĭsh] *s* escarmouche, échauffourée f., *v* escarmoucher; **skirmisher,** tirailleur

skirt [skĕrt] *s* jupe, basque; lisière, f.; quartier de selle, m.; *v* côtoyer, longer border contourner; **skirting-board,** plinthe

skit [skĭt] *s* sketch comique et satirique, m. pasquinade, f.

skittish [skĭtĭsh] *adj* capricieux; frivole, ombrageux [horse].

skittle [skĭt'l] *s.* quille, f.; jeu (m.) de quilles

skulk [skŏlk] *v.* se cacher; se défiler, tirer au flanc, rôder.

skull [skŏl] *s.* crâne, m.; *skullcap,* calotte

skunk [skœngk] *s.* sconse; putois (m.) d'Amérique moufette; *Fr. Can.* bête puante f. mufle [man], m.

sky [ska¹] *s.* ciel. m.; *skylark,* alouette *to skylark* faire des farces, *skylight,* lucarne *sky-line,* ligne d'horizon *skyrocket,* fusée volante, *skyscraper* gratte ciel *skyward,* vers le ciel, *skyway,* route aérienne *mackerel sky,* ciel moutonné cirro-cumulus

slab [slab] *s* dalle plaque, tablette [chocolate] planche f pavé [gingerbread] marbre (typogr.), m

slack [slak] *adj* négligent inactif; flasque distendu *s* flottement relâchement jeu m *pl* pantalon m., *business is slack* les affaires ne vont pas; *slack season.* morte-saison, *v.* = **slacken** **slacken** [-'n] *v* (se) relâcher détendre ralentir mitiger, diminuer **slacker** [-ᵉr] *s* tire-au-flanc flemmard embusqué (slang).

slag [slag] *s* scorie, f.

slain [slé¹n] *p p. of* to **slay.**

slake [slé¹k] *v* étancher [thirst]; éteindre [lime] assouvir (fig.).

slam [slam] *v.* claquer [door].

slam [slam] *s* chelem [bridge], m.

slander [slàndᵉr] *s* calomnie, diffamation f *v* calomnier diffamer; **slanderer,** calomniateur **slanderous,** calomnieux, diffamatoire

slang [slang] *s* argot, m.; *adj.* argotique; *v.* enguirlander (colloq.).

slant [slànt] *s.* pente; inclinaison, f.; plan oblique, m.; *adj.* incliné; oblique; *v.* être en pente; (s') incliner; *slanting*, en pente, en biais, oblique.

slap [slap] *s.* gifle; tape, f.; *v.* souffleter; gifler; *slap-dash*, impétueux; bâclé; *slap-happy*, cinglé (colloq.).

slash [slash] *s.** entaille; coupure, f.; *v.* taillader; balafrer.

slat [slat] *s.* lamelle; latte; traverse [bed], f.

slate [slé¹t] *s.* ardoise, f.; *Am.* liste des candidats d'un parti politique, f.; *v.* couvrir en ardoises; *Am.* inscrire sur la liste.

slattern [slatɛʳn] *s.* souillon, f.

slaughter [slautɛʳ] *s.* carnage; massacre, m.; *v.* massacrer, tuer; *slaughter house*, abattoir.

Slav [slâv] *s.* Slave, m. f.

slave [slé¹v] *s.* esclave, m. f.; *v.* trimer; *slave dealer*, marchand d'esclaves; *slave-holder*, propriétaire d'esclaves.

slaver [slavɛʳ] *s.* bave, f.; *v.* baver.

slaver [slé¹vɛʳ] *s.* négrier, m. ‖ *slavery* [-i] *s.* esclavage, m. ‖ *slavish* [slé¹vish] *adj.* servile, d'esclave.

slaw [slau] *s.* chou au vinaigre, m.

slay [slé¹] *v.** tuer; massacrer; *slayer*, tueur, meurtrier.

sleazy [slé¹zi] *adj.* léger, de camelote.

sled [slèd], **sledge** [slèdj] *s.* traîneau, m.

sledge [slèdj] *s.* marteau de forgeron, m.

sleek [slîk] *adj.* lisse; luisant; mielleux, doucereux; *v.* polir, lisser.

sleep [slîp] *s.* sommeil, m.; *v.** dormir; sommeiller; *to sleep off*, cuver [wine]; *to sleep off a headache*, guérir sa migraine en dormant; *to go to sleep*, s'endormir; *to sleep out*, découcher; *broken sleep*, sommeil entrecoupé, interrompu; ‖ *sleeper* [-ɛʳ] *s.* dormeur; voiture-lit, f.; traverse (railw.), f. ‖ *sleepiness* [-inis] *s.* assoupissement, sommeil, m.; somnolence, f. ‖ *sleeping* [-ing] *adj.* endormi, sommeillant; *sleeping bag*, sac de couchage; *sleeping-berth*, couchette; *sleeping car*, voiture-lit; *sleeping pills*, somnifère; *sleeping-room*, chambre à coucher, dortoir; *sleeping sickness*, encéphalite léthargique. ‖ *sleepless* [-lis] *adj.* sans sommeil, d'insomnie, blanche [night]. ‖ *sleeplessness* [-lisnis] *s.* insomnie, f. ‖ *sleepy* [-i] *adj.* somnolent; assoupi; soporifique; *to be sleepy*, avoir sommeil.

sleet [slît] *s.* grésil, m.; *v.* grésiller.

sleeve [slîv] *s.* manche; chemise; douille (mech.), f.; manchon (mech.), m.; *sleeveless*, sans manche; *sleeveboard*, jeannette.

sleigh [slé¹] *s.* traîneau, m.; *v.* aller en traîneau.

sleight [slé¹t] *s.* adresse, f.; *sleight of hand*, prestidigitation.

slender [slèndɛʳ] *adj.* mince; svelte; fragile; faible; insuffisant; maigre. ‖ *slenderness* [-nis] *s.* minceur, sveltesse, modicité; faiblesse, f.

slept [slèpt] *pret., p. p. of to sleep.*

sleuth [slouth] *s.* détective, m.

slew [slou] *pret. of to slay.*

slice [sla¹s] *s.* tranche, f.; *v.* couper en tranches; *slice of bread and butter*, tartine beurrée.

slick [slik] *adj.* glissant; lisse, luisant; gracieux; doucereux; matois, rusé, adroit.

slicker [slikɛʳ] *s. Am.* imperméable; (fam.) roublard, m.

slid [slid] *pret., p. p. of to slide.* ‖ *slidden* [-ʼn] *p. p. of to slide.* ‖ *slide* [sla¹d] *v.** glisser; coulisser; *s.* glissement; coulant; chariot, curseur (mech.), m.; glissade; glissière; glissoire; platine [microscope]; coulisse, f.; *slide rule*, règle à calcul; *slide-trombone*, trombone à coulisse; *to slide in*, entrer furtivement; *to let slide*, ne pas s'occuper de, laisser tomber. ‖ *sliding* [-ing] *adj.* glissant; à coulisse [door]; amovible [seat]; mobile [panel].

slight [sla¹t] *adj.* léger; insignifiant; fragile; maigre; rare; *v.* mépriser; dédaigner, manquer d'égards envers; *slightly*, légèrement; fort peu; avec dédain.

slim [slim] *adj.* mince, élancé, délié; rare; faible.

slime [sla¹m] *s.* boue, vase; bave [snails], f.; limon, m.; *slimy*, visqueux, baveux, limoneux.

sling [sling] *s.* fronde; bretelle [gun]; écharpe (med.), f.; *v.** lancer avec une fronde; porter en bandoulière.

slink [slingk] *v.* s'esquiver; *to slink in*, se faufiler dans; *to slink away*, se débiner.

slip [slip] *v.* (se) glisser; s'échapper; se détacher; diminuer [prices]; patiner (mech.), faire un faux pas; filer [cable]; *s.* glissade, gaffe; erreur; bande [land]; cale de construction (naut.); combinaison [garment]; laisse [leash], bouture [plant], f.; glissement; bout [paper]; placard (typogr.), m.; *to slip on*, enfiler [dress]; *to slip away*, se dérober; *a slip of the tongue*, un lapsus ; *to slip out of joint*, se disloquer ; *it slipped my mind*, cela m'est sorti de l'esprit **slip cover**, housse ; **slip knot**, nœud coulant **deposit slip**, fiche de dépôt. **slipper** [-ᵉʳ] *s*. pantoufle, f. ; **rope slipper**, sandale. ‖ **slippery** [-ri] *adj* glissant ; incertain ; scabreux ; rusé.

slit [slit] *s* fente, fissure ; déchirure ; incision, f., ajour, m. ; *v*.* (se) fendre ; (se) déchirer ; éclater ; inciser ; *to slit into strips*, déchiqueter ; *pret., p. p. of to slit*.

slither [slithᵉʳ] *v*. glisser ; onduler.

sliver [slivᵉʳ] *s*. éclat de bois, m. ; tranche mince, f. ; *v*. (se) fendre ; couper en tranches

slobber [slâbᵉʳ] *s*. bave, f. ; *v*. baver ; **slobbering**, baveux.

sloe [sloᵘ] *s*. prunelle, f.

slogan [sloᵘgᵉn] *s*. slogan, m. ; devise, f.

sloop [sloup] *s*. sloop, aviso (naut.), m.

slop [slâp] *v* répandre ; renverser, faire déborder inonder ; *s. pl.* mare ; lavasse, eaux sales, f. ; sentimentalisme, f. ; **slop pail**, seau à toilette.

slope [sloᵘp] *v*. pencher ; aller en pente ; *s*. pente, inclinaison ; rampe, f. ; talus ; versant, m.

sloppy [slâpi] *adj*. bourbeux ; négligé ; flasque ; larmoyant, fade.

slot [slât] *s* fente ; rainure ; mortaise, f. ; *v*. fendre, entailler ; **slot machine**, appareil à jetons, distributeur automatique.

sloth [slauth] *s*. paresse, indolence, f. ; paresseux [animal], m. ; **slothful**, paresseux, indolent.

slouch [slaᵘtsh] *s*.* maladroit, lourdaud, m. ; *Am* fainéant ; bord rabattu d'un chapeau mou avachi, m. ; démarche mal assurée, f. ; *v*. marcher lourdement ; s'avachir ; s'affaisser.

slough [slaᵘ] *s*. fondrière ; mare, f. ; bourbier, m.

slough [slœf] *s*. mue, dépouille [snake] ; escarre (med.), f.

sloven [slœvᵉn] *s*. négligent ; souillon, m. ‖ **slovenliness** [-linis] *s* malpropreté ; négligence, f. ‖ **slovenly** [-li] *adj*. malpropre ; négligent ; bâclé.

slow [sloᵘ] *adj*. lent ; borné ; en retard ; terne, sans vie ; *v*. ralentir ; *to slow down*, diminuer la vitesse ; *to be slow to*, tarder à ; *ten minutes too slow*, en retard de dix minutes. **slowacting**, à action lente, **slowly**, lentement, tardivement. ‖ **slow-motion**, ralenti (ciném.). ‖ **slowness** [-nis] *s*. lenteur ; lourdeur d'esprit, f. ; retard ; manque d'empressement, m.

sludge [slœdj] *s*. boue ; neige fondue, f. ; cambouis, m.

slug [slœg] *s*. limace, f. ‖ **sluggard** [slœgᵉrd] *s* paresseux, m. ‖ **sluggish** [-ish] *adj*. lambin, traînard ; stagnant ; mou, lent, paresseux, **sluggish engine**, moteur qui ne tire pas. ‖ **sluggishness** [-ishnis] *s*. paresse ; mollesse ; lenteur, f.

sluice [slous] *s*. écluse, f. ; **sluice gate**, vanne.

slum [slœm] *s*. zone, f. ; taudis, m. ; *v*. visiter les taudis.

slumber [slœmbᵉr] *s*. assoupissement, sommeil, m. ; *v* s'assoupir, sommeiller ; **slumberous**, somnolent, assoupi ; endormant, endormi (fig.).

slump [slœmp] *s* effondrement, m. ; dépression, crise, chute [prices], f. ; *v*. s'enfoncer brusquement ; s'affaisser ; s'effondrer [prices].

slung [slœng] *pret., p. p. of to sling*.

slunk [slœngk] *pret., p. p. of to slink*.

slur [slër] *s*. tache ; insinuation malveillante ; flétrissure, f. ; affront, m. ; *v*. flétrir, salir ; calomnier.

slur [slër] *v*. glisser, faire peu de cas (*over*, de) ; déprécier ; bredouiller, mal prononcer ; lier [music] ; *s*. liaison [music], f.

slush [slœsh] *s*. neige fondue ; boue ; sentimentalité larmoyante, f. ; *v*. patauger ; éclabousser.

slut [slœt] *s*. souillon ; coureuse, f.

sly [slaᵢ] *adj*. rusé ; madré ; retors ; fourbe ; *on the sly*, à la dérobée. ‖ **slyness** [-nis] *s*. ruse, f.

smack [smak] *v*. claquer ; faire claquer un baiser . *s*. claquement, m. ; claque, f., baiser bruyant, m. ; **smacking**, sonore ; *to smack one's lips*, se lécher les babines.

small [smaul] *adj*. petit ; peu nombreux ; exigu ; mesquin, sans importance ; médiocre, bref, **small letters**, (lettres) minuscules **small mind**, esprit étroit ; **small talk**, commérages ; **small voice**, voix fluette ; *a small matter*, peu de chose , *to feel small*, se sentir tout petit ‖ **smallness** [-nis] *s*. petitesse, insignifiance, f. ‖ **smallpox** [-pâks] *s* petite vérole, variole, f.

smart [smârt] *adj*. vif ; éveillé ; pimpant ; élégant, chic, intelligent ; cuisant ; *v* picoter, cuire ; **smartly**, avec élégance vivement, d'une manière cuisante. ‖ **smartness** [-nis] *s*. élégance ; finesse, vivacité, f.

smash [smash] *s*.* débâcle ; faillite (fin.) ; collision (auto), f. ; fracassement ; smash [tennis], m. ; *v*. fracasser ; anéantir ; faire faillite ; écraser, ruiner; pulvériser; *to smash into*, entrer en collision avec; *smash-up*, collision. ‖ *smasher* [-ᵉʳ] *s.* écraseur; fracas; coup (m.) de massue; argument (m.) massue.

smattering [smatᵉring] *s.* teinture, connaissance rudimentaire, f.

smear [smiᵉʳ] *v.* barbouiller; maculer; brouiller [radio]; *s.* tache, f.; barbouillage, m.; calomnie, f.

smell [smèl] *v.** sentir; flairer; *s.* odeur, f.; parfum; odorat, m.; *to smell out*, découvrir par le flair; *to smell close*, sentir le renfermé. ‖ *smelly* [-i] *adj.* odorant.

smelt [smèlt] *pret., p. p. of* to smell.

smelt [smèlt] *v.* fondre [metal]; *smelting works*, fonderie; *smelter*, fondeur.

smelt [smèlt] *s.* éperlan, m.; *Fr. Can.* petits poissons des chenaux, m. pl.

smile [smaïl] *s.* sourire, m.; *v.* sourire. ‖ *smiling* [-ing] *adj.* souriant, agréable; *smilingly*, en souriant, avec le sourire.

smirch [smᵉrtsh] *v.* salir; noircir; *s.** souillure; noircissure, f.

smirk [smᵉrk] *v.* sourire avec affectation; minauder.

smite [smaït] *v.** frapper; affliger.

smith [smith] *s.* forgeron, m. ‖ *smithy* [-i] *s.** forge, f.

smitten [smit'n] *p. p. of* to smite; *adj.* épris, féru, atteint (with, de).

smock [smâk] *s.* blouse, f.

smoke [smoᵘk] *s.* fumée, f.; *v.* fumer; enfumer; *I will have a smoke*, je vais en griller une; *smoke black*, noir de fumée; *smokeless*, sans fumée. ‖ *smoker* [-ᵉʳ] *s.* fumeur, m.; compartiment pour fumeurs, m. ‖ *smokestack* [-stak] *s.* cheminée, f. ‖ *smoking* [-ing] *adj.* de fumeur; fumant; à fumer; *s.* action de fumer, f.; *no smoking*, défense de fumer; *smoking car*, wagon de fumeurs; *smoking room*, fumoir, m. ‖ *smoky* [-i] *adj.* fumeux; enfumé.

smo(u)lder [smoᵘldᵉʳ] *v.* couver [fire].

smooth [smouzh] *adj.* uni; lisse; glabre; calme [sea]; coulant [style]; *v.* polir; lisser; aplanir; adoucir; dérider; caresser [animal]; *smooth disposition*, caractère égal; *smooth talker*, beau parleur insinuant et doucereux; *smooth-faced*, imberbe; glabre; *smoothly*, doucement; sans heurt. ‖ *smoothness* [-nis] *s.* surface plane, lisse et unie; tranquillité, harmonie; absence de heurt, f.; calme, m. [sea]; douceur, onction, f.

smote [smoᵘt] *pret. of* to smite.

smother [smᵃthᵉʳ] *v.* étouffer, suffoquer; supprimer.

smoulder [smoᵘldᵉʳ] *v.* couver; *s.* feu (m.) qui couve; combustion lente, f.

smudge [smœdj] *s.* fumée suffocante; tache, f.; *v.* noircir, maculer, tacher, salir.

smug [smœg] *adj.* pimpant, frais; vaniteux, suffisant.

smuggle [smœg'l] *v.* faire de la contrebande; *smuggler*, contrebandier; *smuggling*, contrebande.

smut [smœt] *s.* tache noire; nielle, f.; noir de suie; langage indécent, m.; *v.* noircir; nieller; se barbouiller. ‖ *smutty* [-i] *adj.* barbouillé de noir; taché de suie; niellé; grivois, grossier.

snack [snak] *s.* casse-croûte, m.; *v.* casser la croûte, manger sur le pouce.

snag [snag] *s.* chicot, m.; fil tiré [stocking]; écueil, hic, m.; difficulté, f.; *v.* heurter; accrocher; *to snag a stocking*, accrocher un bas.

snail [snéïl] *s.* colimaçon, escargot, m.

snake [snéïk] *s.* serpent (prop.; fig.), m.; *coral snake*, vipère aspic; *garter snake*, couleuvre; *rattlesnake*, serpent à sonnette. ‖ *snaky* [-ki] *adj.* sinueux; vipérin; perfide; plein de serpents.

snap [snap] *v.* briser; (se) casser net; claquer; faire claquer [whip]; happer [dog]; *s.* claquement; bruit sec; ordre bref; gâteau sec; bouton pression, m.; période de froid vif; vivacité; photo (pop.); chose facile, f.; *adj.* brusque, instantané; *to snap one's fingers at*, faire la nique à; *to snap off*, casser net; *to snap up*, happer; *to snap at*, essayer de mordre; rembarrer; *to snap shut*, fermer d'un coup sec. ‖ *snappy* [-i] *adj.* hargneux [dog]; acariâtre; *Am.* chic, élégant; preste, vif; *snappy cheese*, fromage piquant. ‖ *snapshot* [-shât] *s.* instantané (phot.), m.; *v.* faire un instantané.

snare [snèᵉʳ] *s.* piège; collet, lacet, m.; *v.* prendre au piège.

snarl [snârl] *v.* gronder; montrer les dents; parler d'un ton hargneux; *s.* grognement, m.

snarl [snârl] *v.* embrouiller; (s')enchevêtrer; (s')emmêler.

snatch [snatsh] *v.* empoigner; enlever, arracher; *s.** tentative pour saisir; courte période; bribe, f.; morceau; *Am.* enlèvement, m.; *to snatch up*, ramasser vivement.

sneak [snïk] *v.* se glisser furtivement; flagorner; ramper; chaparder, chiper; *s.* sournois, fureteur; chapardeur; rapporteur, mouchard, m. ‖ *sneakers* [-ᵉrz] *s. pl. Am.* espadrilles, chaussures de tennis, f. pl.

sneer [sni^{er}] v. ricaner; persifler; s. ricanement; persiflage, m.; to sneer at, se moquer de, dénigrer.

sneeze [sníz] v. éternuer; s. éternuement, m.

sniff [snif] v. renifler; s. reniflement, m.; to sniff at, dédaigner.

sniffle [snif'l], see snuffle.

snigger [snig^{er}] s. ricanement, m.; v. ricaner.

snip [snip] s. coup de ciseaux; petit morceau, m.; v. couper; enlever d'un coup de ciseaux.

snipe [snai^p] s. bécassine, f.; v. canarder; critiquer; sniper, canardeur, tireur d'élite.

snippy [snipi] adj. morcelé; fragmentaire; insignifiant; dédaigneux.

snitch [snitsh] v. chiper; escamoter.

snivel [sniv'l] s. morve, f.; v. pleurnicher; renifler.

snob [snâb] s. snob, m.; snobbishness, snobisme, m.

snoop [snoup] v. rôder; s. curieux, rôdeur, m.

snooze [snouz] v. faire un somme; s'assoupir; s. somme, m., sieste, f.

snore [sno^{ou}r] v. ronfler; s. ronflement, m.

snort [snaurt] v. renâcler; s'ébrouer; ronfler; s. ébrouement, m.; grognement; ronflement; reniflement, m.

snot [snât] s. morve, f.; morveux, m. || snotty [-i] adj. morveux.

snout [sna^{ou}t] s. museau; groin, m.

snow [sno^{ou}] s. neige, f.; v. neiger; snow ball, boule de neige. snowblower, Fr Can. souffleuse snowbound, bloqué par la neige. snowdrift, congère Fr. Can. banc de neige; snowdrop, perce-neige snowfall, chute de neige. Fr. Can bordée de neige; snowflake, flocon de neige; snow - man, bonhomme de neige; snowplow, chasse-neige. snow-shoe, raquette. snowshoer, Fr Can raquetteur; snowslip, avalanche. snowstorm, blizzard drifting snow, Fr. Can. poudrerie powdered snow, poudreuse. || snowy [-i] adj. neigeux.

snub [snœb] s. rebuffade; v.; adj. camus [nose]; v. mépriser; rabrouer; encombrer.

snuff [snœf] v. moucher [candle]; détruire, éteindre [hope].

snuff [snœf] v priser; s. tabac à priser, m. a pinch of snuff, une prise de tabac; snuff-box, tabatière; snufftaker, snuffer, priseur.

snuffle [snœf'l] v. nasiller; renifler; s. nasillement; reniflement, m.

snug [snœg] adj. douillet; abrité; confortable; commode; gentil, coquet. || **snuggle** [snœg'l] v. dorloter; se pelotonner. || **snugness** [-nis] s. confort; bien-être, m.

so [so^{ou}] adv. ainsi; aussi; si, tellement; alors; donc; as... so, de même que... de même; and so on, and so forth, et ainsi de suite, so be it, ainsi soit-il; so lazy that, si paresseux que; so as to, de manière à; so much the better, tant mieux; I think so, je le crois; so that, de sorte que; five minutes or so, cinq minutes environ; so-and-so, un tel; is that so?, vraiment? so-called, soi-disant, prétendu.

soak [so^{ou}k] v. tremper; imbiber; s'infiltrer (in, dans); Am. estamper; s. Am. ivrogne, m., to be soaked through, être trempé jusqu'aux os; to soak up, absorber; boire comme un trou.

soap [so^{ou}p] s. savon, m.; v. savonner; soap bubble, bulle de savon; Am. soap opera, mélo radiodiffusé; soap-suds, eau de savon; soapwort, saponaire. || soapy [-i] adj. savonneux; doucereux.

soar [so^{ou}r] s. essor, m.; v. prendre son essor, s'élever; planer; soaring, vol plané (aviat.).

sob [sâb] s sanglot, m.; v. sangloter.

sober [so^{ou}b^{er}] adj. de sang-froid; qui n'a pas bu, modéré, pondéré; v. dégriser; calmer, to sleep oneself sober, cuver son vin en dormant, to be sober, ne pas être ivre to sober down, (se) calmer. s'apaiser || soberly [-li] adv. avec sobriété. pondération. || soberness [-nis]. sobriety [so^{ou}brai'ti] s. sobriété; modération, gravité, f.

soccer [sâk^{er}] s. football association, m.

sociable [so^{ou}sheb'l] adj. sociable; affable

social [so^{ou}shel] adj. social; mondain; de société; s. réunion, soirée, f. || socialism [-iz^em] s socialisme, m. || socialist [-ist] s socialiste, m.

society [s^esai^et'i] s.* société; association, compagnie, f. a society woman, une femme du monde.

sociologist [so^{ou}siâl^edjist] s. sociologue, m. f. || sociology [-dji] s. sociologie, f.

sock [sâk] s. chaussette, f.

sock [sâk] v. frapper, corriger.

socket [sâkit] s. emboîture; alvéole; orbite, douille; bobèche, f.; manchon (mech.), m.

socle [sâk'l] s. socle, m.

sod [sâd] s. gazon, m.; v. couvrir de gazon.

soda [so°u°de] *s.* soude, f.; *soda water*, soda; *baking soda*, bicarbonate de soude.

sodium [so°u°di°m] *s.* sodium, m.

sofa [so°u°fe] *s.* divan, m.; *sofa-bed*, canapé-lit.

soft [sauft] *adj.* doux; tendre; faible; efféminé; non alcoolique [drink]; malléable [metal]; *soft-boiled egg*, œuf mollet; *soft-hearted*, tendre; compatissant; *soft-soap*, savon noir; pommade, lèche [colloq.]; flatter; *soft water*, eau douce. || **soften** [sauf°n] *v.* adoucir; assouplir; atténuer; efféminer; (s')amollir; (s')attendrir; baisser [voice]. || **softness** [sauftnis] *s.* douceur; tendresse; mollesse; faiblesse, f.

soggy [sági] *adj.* saturé, détrempé; lourd; pâteux.

soil [so°l] *s.* saleté; tache, f.; *v.* salir, tacher; fumer [field].

soil [so°l] *s.* sol; terrain; pays, m.

sojourn [so°u°djë°n] *s.* séjour, m.; [so°u°djë°n] *v.* séjourner.

solace [sális] *s.* consolation, f.; soulagement, m.; *v.* consoler; soulager; réconforter.

solar [so°u°le°r] *adj.* solaire; *solarium*, solarium.

sold [so°u°ld] *pret., p. p. of* **to sell**; *Am.* to be sold on an idea, être persuadé, très attaché à une idée.

solder [sâde°r] *s.* soudure, f.; *v.* souder.

soldier [so°u°ldje°r] *s.* soldat, m.; *v.* être soldat; tirer au flanc (slang); *fellow soldier*, frère d'armes; *foot soldier*, fantassin; *private soldier*, simple soldat; *soldierly*, martial, militaire.

sole [so°u°l] *adj.* seul; unique; exclusif; *solely*, uniquement, seulement.

sole [so°u°l] *s.* semelle; plante [foot], f.; *v.* ressemeler.

sole [so°u°l] *s.* sole, f.

solecism [sál°siz°m] *s.* solécisme, m.; infraction à l'étiquette, f.

solemn [sál°m] *adj.* solennel; grave; sérieux. || **solemnity** [s°lèm°nti] *s.* solennité; gravité; majesté, f. || **solemnize** [sál°mna°z] *v.* solenniser, célébrer.

solicit [s°lísit] *v.* solliciter; briguer; tenter. || **solicitation** [s°lisété°shen] *s.* sollicitation; tentation; tentative de corruption (jur.), f.; racolage, m. || **solicitor** [s°lísite°r] *s.* avoué; *Am.* démarcheur, m.; *solicitor general*, avocat général. || **solicitous** [s°lísit°s] *adj.* inquiet; préoccupé de; désireux. || **solicitude** [s°lísi°tyoud] *s.* sollicitude; inquiétude, f.

solid [sálid] *s.* solide, m.; *adj.* solide; massif [gold]; uni [color]; digne de confiance; sérieux; *to be solid for*, se déclarer énergiquement pour. || **solidarity** [sâl°dar°ti] *s.* solidarité, f. || **solidify** [s°líd°fa°] *v.* (se) solidifier. **solidity** [s°líd°ti] *s.* solidité, f.

soliloquy [s°líl°kwi] *s.** soliloque; monologue, m.

solitary [sál°tèri] *adj.* solitaire; retiré; isolé; *s.** solitaire, m. || **solitude** [sál°tyoud] *s.* solitude, f.; isolement; lieu isolé, m.

solo [so°u°lo°u] *s.* solo, m.; action exécutée par une seule personne, f.; *adj.* solo; exécuté en solo; *soloist*, soliste.

solstice [sálstis] *s.* solstice, m.

solubility [sály°bfl°ti] *s.* solubilité; résolubilité, f. || **soluble** [sály°b'l] *adj.* soluble; résoluble.

solution [s°loush°n] *s.* solution; mixture, f.

solvable [sálv°b'l] *adj.* soluble; résoluble. || **solve** [sálv] *v.* résoudre.

solvency [sálv°nsi] *s.* solvabilité, f. || **solvent** [-v°nt] *adj.* dissolvant; solvable; *s.* solvant, m.

somatic [so°u°matik] *adj.* somatique.

somber [sâmbe°r] *adj.* sombre; *somberly*, sombrement.

some [sæm] *adj.* quelque; certain; du, de la, de l', des; *pron.* quelques-uns, quelques-unes; *some milk*, un peu de lait; *of some importance*, d'une certaine importance; *for some five months*, pour cinq mois environ; *some say that*, d'aucuns disent que; *some... some*, les uns... les autres. || **somebody** [-bádi] *pron.*, *s.** quelqu'un. || **somehow** [-ho°u] *adv.* d'une manière ou d'une autre. || **someone** [-wœn] *pron.* quelqu'un.

somersault [sæm°rsault] *s.* saut périlleux; capotage, m.; culbute, f.; *v.* faire le saut périlleux, la culbute; capoter.

something [sæmthing] *pron.* quelque chose; *adv.* un peu, quelque peu.

sometime [sæmta°m] *adv.* autrefois; une fois ou l'autre. || **sometimes** [-s] *adv.* quelquefois; parfois; tantôt.

somewhat [sæmhwàt] *adv.* un peu; tant soit peu; *s.* un peu de; un brin.

somewhere [sæmhwèr] *adv.* quelque part; *somewhere before midday*, un peu avant midi.

somnambulism [sâmnæmbyouliz°m] *s.* somnambulisme, m. || **somnambulist** [-ist] *s.* somnambule, m., f. || **somniferous** [sâmníf°r°s] *adj.* somnifère, f. || **somnolence** [-n°l°ns] *s.* somnolence, f. || **somnolent** [sâmn°l°nt] *adj.* somnolent.

son [sœn] s. fils, *Fr. Can.* garçon, m.;
son-in-law, gendre; **step-son**, beau-
fils.

sonata [sᵉnât⁰] s. sonate, f.

song [saung] s. chanson, f.; chant;
cantique, m.; **song bird**, oiseau chanteur; **song-writer**, chansonnier; **to buy
something for a song**, acheter quelque
chose pour un morceau de pain. ||
songster [saungstᵉʳ] s. chanteur;
oiseau chanteur, m. || **songstress**
[-stris] s. chanteuse, cantatrice, f.

sonnet [sᵃnit] s. sonnet, m.

sonority [sᵉnoᵒuriti] s. sonorité, f. ||
sonorous [-rᵉs] adj. sonore; timbré
[voice].

soon [soun] adv. bientôt; sous peu;
as soon as, aussitôt que; **too soon**,
trop tôt; **so soon**, si tôt; **how soon?**,
quand?; **soon after**, peu après; **no
sooner**, pas plus tôt, à peine.

soot [sout] s. suie, f.

soothe [souzh] v. apaiser; soulager;
flatter; **soothing**, calmant.

soothsayer [southséᶦeʳ] s. devin, m.

sooty [souti] adj. de suie; couvert de
suie; charbonneux.

sop [sâp] v. tremper; imbiber; s.
trempette; soupe, f.; appât, dérivatif, m.

sophism [sâfizᵉm] s. sophisme, m.;
sophist, sophiste; **sophistic**, sophis-
tique. || **sophisticated** [sᵉfístiké¹tid]
adj. blasé; frelaté [wine]; falsifié [do-
cument]; **a sophisticated novel**, un
roman pour lecteurs avertis. || **sophis-
tication** [sᵉfistiké¹shᵉn] s. sophistica-
tion; falsification, f. || **sophistry** [sâ-
fistri] s. sophisme, m.; sophistique, f.

sophomore [sâf'moᵒuʳ] s. *Am.* étudiant de seconde année, m.

soporific [soᵒupᵉrifik] adj. soporifique; s. somnifère, m.

soprano [sᵉpranoᵒu] s. soprano, m.

sorcerer [saursᵉrᵉʳ] s. sorcier, m.;
sorceress, sorcière; **sorcery**, sorcellerie.

sordid [saurdid] adj. sordide; **sor-
didly**, d'une manière sordide ou mes-
quine.

sore [soᵒuʳ] adj. douloureux; endolori; fâché; cruel [loss]; dur [trial];
sore eyes, mal d'yeux; **to have a sore
throat**, avoir mal à la gorge; **to make
sore**, irriter, enflammer; s. plaie; écorchure, f.; **sorely**, douloureusement,
extrêmement; **to be sorely in need of**,
avoir un urgent besoin de.

sorghum [saurgᵉm] s. sorgho, m.

sorrel [saurᵉl] adj., s. alezan.

sorrel [saurᵉl] s. oseille, f., *Fr. Can.*
surette, f.

sorrow [sârooᵘ] s. chagrin, m.; affliction, f.; v. s'affliger; avoir de la peine.
|| **sorrowful** [-fᵉl] adj. triste; affligeant;
pénible; peiné. || **sorry** [sauri] adj.
fâché, chagriné; pitoyable, lamentable;
désolé; **I am sorry**, je regrette.

sort [saurt] s. espèce; sorte; manière,
f.; v. assortir; classer; distribuer;
s'entendre; **all sorts of**, toute sorte de;
a wine of sorts, un vin médiocre; **out
of sorts**, de mauvaise humeur, mal en
train.

sortie [saurti] s. sortie (mil.), f.

sot [sât] s. ivrogne, m.; **sottish**, abruti
par l'alcool; ivre.

soufflé [souflé¹] s. soufflé, m.

sough [saoᵘ] s. murmure, soupir, m.;
v. soupirer, murmurer.

sought [saut] pret., p. p. of **to seek**.

soul [soᵒul] s. âme, f.; **not a soul**, pas
un chat, personne; **a simple soul**, une
bonne âme; **All Souls' Day**, le jour
des Morts; **soulful**, expressif; sentimental.

sound [saoᵘnd] adj. sain; solide; bien
fondé; en bon état; profond [sleep];
robuste [constitution]; légal [title]; **to
sleep soundly**, dormir profondément.

sound [saoᵘnd] s. son; bruit, m.; v.
résonner; faire résonner; exprimer;
sound-damping ou **-proofing**, insonorisation; **sound-effects**, bruitage;
sound-proof, v. insonoriser; adj. inso-
norisé; insonore; isolant.

sound [saoᵘnd] v. sonder; s. sonde, f.

soundness [saoᵘndnis] s. santé; vigueur; justesse; légitimité, f.

soup [soup] s. consommé, potage, m.;
soup-tureen, soupière, f.

sour [saoᵘʳ] adj. aigre; acide; acariâtre; tourné [milk]; v. (s')aigrir;
fermenter; devenir morose.

source [soᵒuʳs] s. source; origine, f.;
début, m.

sourish [saoᵘrish] adj. aigrelet; su-
ret. || **sourness** [saoᵘrnis] s. acidité;
acrimonie, f.

souse [saoᵘs] s. marinade; douche, f.
[colloq.]; v. mariner; tremper.

south [saoᵘth] s. sud; midi, m.; adj.
du sud, méridional; adv. vers le sud;
South American, sud-américain; **south
pole**, pôle Sud. || **southeast** [-îst] s.,
adj., sud-est; adv. vers le sud-est. ||
southeastern [-îstᵉrn] adj. du sud-est.
|| **southern** [sæzhᵉrn] adj. méridional,
du sud. || **southerner** [sæzhᵉrneʳ] s.
méridional, m. || **southward** [saoᵘth-
wᵉrd] adj. vers le sud. || **southwest**
[saoᵘthwèst] s., adj. sud-ouest; adv.
vers le sud-ouest. || **southwestern**
[saoᵘthwèstᵉrn] adj. du sud-ouest.

souvenir [souv°nîr] *s.* objet-souve-nir, m.

sovereign [såvrìn] *adj.*, *s.* souverain. ‖ *sovereignty* [såvrìnti] *s.* souverai-neté, f.

Soviet [soºuviit] *s.* soviet, m.; *adj.* soviétique.

sow [saºu] *s.* truie; gueuse [iron], f.

sow [soºu] *v.** semer; ensemencer; répandre; *sower*, semeur; *sowing*, se-mailles; *sowing-machine*, semeuse. ‖ *sown* [-n] *p. p. of* to sow.

soy(a) [sâi(°)] *s.* soya, m.

spa [spâ] *s.* ville d'eau, f.

space [spé¹s] *s.* espace; intervalle; espacement, m.; étendue, surface, f.; *v.* espacer; échelonner; écarter; *air space*, cubage d'air; *occupied space*, encombrement, place occupée [vehi-cle]. ‖ *spacious* [spé¹sh°s] *adj.* spa-cieux; ample.

spade [spé¹d] *s.* bêche, f.; *pl.* pique [cards], m.; *v.* bêcher; *spadeful*, pelle-tée, pleine bêche.

Spain [spé¹n] *s.* Espagne, f.

span [spàn] *s.* empan; écartement; pont; moment, m.; envergure [wings]; ouverture (arch.); paire [horses]; tra-vée; portée; largeur, f.; *v.* embrasser; mesurer; traverser; enjamber; *span of life*, longévité.

spangle [spàngg'l] *s.* paillette, f.; *v.* pailleter; *star-spangled*, étoilé.

Spaniard [spany°rd] *s.* Espagnol, m.

spaniel [spany°l] *s.* épagneul, m.

Spanish [spanish] *adj.*, *s.* espagnol; *Spanish American*, hispano-américain.

spank [spàngk] *v.* donner une fessée à; *s.* fessée, f.

spanking [spàngking] *adj.* vif; ra-pide; *spanking new*, flambant neuf.

spanner [span°r] *s.* clef anglaise, f.

spar [spâr] *s.* espar (naut.); poteau; longeron (aviat.), m.

spare [spè°r] *v.* épargner; ménager; se passer de; *s.* pièce de rechange, f.; *adj.* disponible; de réserve; rare, maigre, frugal; *to spare no expense*, ne pas lésiner sur la dépense; *spare cash*, argent disponible; *spare time*, loisirs; *spare tire*, pneu de secours; *sparing*, économe; *sparingness*, épargne, frugalité, parcimonie.

spark [spârk] *s.* étincelle; lueur, f.; *v.* faire des étincelles; *spark advance*, avance à l'allumage [motor]; *spark arrester*, pare-étincelles; *spark coil*, bobine d'induction (electr.); *spark condensor*, condensateur (electr.); *Am.* spark plug, bougie [motor]; *Br.* spark-ing plug, bougie. ‖ *sparkle* [-'l] *s.*

étincellement, m.; *v.* étinceler; scin-tiller; chatoyer; mousser [wine]; *sparkling*, étincelant, effervescent; mousseux [wine].

sparrow [sparoºu] *s.* moineau, m.

sparse [spârs] *adj.* épars; clairsemé; rare [hair].

spasm [spaz°m] *s.* spasme, m. ‖ *spas-modic* [spazmâdik] *adj.* spasmodique; convulsif; fait par à-coups. ‖ *spastic* [spastik] *adj.* spasmodique; *s.* para-plégique, m. f.

spat [spat] *pret., p. p. of* to spit.

spat [spat] *v. Am.* taper; se quereller; *s.* prise de bec, f.

spatial [spé¹sh°l] *adj.* spatial.

spats [spats] *s. pl.* guêtres, f. pl.

spatter [spat°r] *v.* éclabousser; *s.* éclaboussure, f.

spatula [spatyoul°] *s.* spatule, f.

spawn [spaun] *s.* frai; fretin, m.; engeance, f.; *v.* frayer, naître [fish].

speak [spîk] *v.** parler; causer; pro-noncer [word]; exprimer; *so to speak*, pour ainsi dire; *to speak one's mind*, dire ce qu'on pense; *speak to the point*, venez-en au fait; *to speak up*, parler sans réserve. ‖ *speaker* [-°r] *s.* ora-teur; interlocuteur; speaker; président de la Chambre (*Br.* des Communes, *Am.* des Représentants), m.; *loud speaker*, haut-parleur.

spear [spi°r] *s.* lance, f.; épieu, m.; pousse [grass], f.; *v.* percer de la lance; harponner; poindre; *spear-head*, fer de lance; pointe; *spearman*, lancier; *spearmint*, menthe verte.

special [spèsh°l] *adj.* spécial; parti-culier; exprès; *s.* train, autobus spé-cial, m.; entrée spéciale, f.; *specially*, spécialement; particulièrement; sur-tout. ‖ *specialist* [-ist] *s.* spécialiste, technicien, m. ‖ *speciality* [-ti] *s.** spécialité, f. ‖ *specialize* [-a¹z] *v.* se spécialiser.

species [spîshiz] (*pl.* species) *s.* es-pèce, f.; genre, m.; *a species of*, une sorte de.

specific [spisìfik] *adj.* spécifique; ca-ractéristique; *s.* remède spécifique, m.; spécialité médicale, f.; *specific grav-ity*, poids spécifique; *specifically*, spé-cifiquement; particulièrement; *speci-fication*, caractéristique, condition; *specificity*, spécificité. ‖ *specify* [spè-s°fa¹] *v.* spécifier; stipuler; désigner; énoncer; préciser.

specimen [spès°m°n] *s.* spécimen; échantillon; exemplaire, m.

specious [spîsh°s] *adj.* spécieux.

speck [spèk] *s.* tache, f.; point; grain, brin, m.; *v.* tacheter, moucheter.

speckle [spèk(l)] *s.* petite tache; moucheture, f.; *v.* tacheter, moucheter.

spectacle [spèktⁱkˈl] *s.* spectacle, m.; *pl.* lunettes, f. pl.; *colo(u)red spectacles*, lunettes de soleil; *to make a spectacle of oneself*, se donner en spectacle. ‖ **spectacular** [spèktakyᵉlᵉʳ] *adj.* spectaculaire; ostentatoire; théâtral. ‖ **spectator** [spèktᵉtᵉʳ] *s.* spectateur; témoin, m. ‖ **spectatress** [-tris] *s.* spectatrice, f.

specter [spèktᵉʳ] *s.* spectre, fantôme, m.

spectrum [spèktrᵉm] *s.* spectre solaire, m.

speculate [spèkyᵉléⁱt] *v.* spéculer; réfléchir. ‖ **speculation** [spèkyᵉléⁱshᵉn] *s.* spéculation; conjecture; réflexion, f. ‖ **speculative** [spèkyᵉléⁱtiv] *adj.* spéculatif; théorique. ‖ **speculator** [-tᵉʳ] *s.* spéculateur; penseur, m.

sped [spèd] *pret., p. p. of* **to speed**.

speech [spîtsh] *s.** parole; allocution, f.; discours, m.; *speech defect*, défaut d'élocution; **speechify**, discourir, pérorer; **speechless**, sans parole; muet; stupéfié.

speed [spîd] *s.* vitesse; allure, f.; succès, m.; *v.** (se) hâter; faire de la vitesse; prospérer; favoriser; *at full speed*, à toute allure; **speedometer**, **speed counter**, compteur de vitesse; **speed limit**, vitesse limite autorisée; **speedway**, piste, autostrade. ‖ **speedily** [-'li] *adv.* promptement, vite. ‖ **speedy** [-i] *adj.* rapide; expéditif; vite.

speleologist [spilᵋâlᵋdjist] *s.* spéléologue, m. f. ‖ **speleology** [-dji] *s.* spéléologie, f.

spell [spèl] *s.* relais; temps, m.; période, f.; *cold spell*, coup de froid; *dry spell*, période de sécheresse; *spell of duty*, tour de service; *to work by spells*, travailler d'une façon intermittente; *v. Am.* relever, relayer.

spell [spèl] *s.* sortilège, m.; **spellbound**, fasciné, ensorcelé.

spell [spèl] *v.* épeler; orthographier; signifier; exprimer; **spelling**, orthographe; épellation; **spelling-book**, abécédaire, m. ‖ **spelt** [-t] *pret., p. p. of* **to spell**.

spend [spènd] *v.** dépenser; consumer; épuiser; passer [time]; **spendthrift**, prodigue. ‖ **spent** [spènt] *pret., p. p. of* **to spend**.

spew [spyou] *v.* vomir; cracher.

sphere [sfiᵉʳ] *s.* sphère, f.; rayon, domaine, m. ‖ **spherical** [sfèrikˈl] *adj.* sphérique.

sphinx [sfingks] *s.* sphinx, m.

spice [spaⁱs] *s.* épice, f.; condiment, m.; *v.* épicer; assaisonner; **spicy**, épicé, aromatisé; leste, grivois.

spider [spaⁱdᵉʳ] *s.* araignée; *Am.* sauteuse (f.) sur trépied; *spider's web*, toile d'araignée.

spigot [spiɡᵉt] *s.* cannelle, f.; fausset [barrel], m.

spike [spaⁱk] *s.* clou; épi; spic, m.; *v.* clouer; armer de pointes; **spiky**, pointu, plein de piquants.

spill [spil] *v.** répandre; renverser; divulguer; *s.* chute de cheval, de voiture, f.; *to have a spill*, ramasser une bûche. ‖ **spilt** [-t] *pret., p. p. of* **to spill**.

spin [spin] *v.** tourner; tournoyer; descendre en vrille (aviat.); chasser [wheel]; filer [thread]; débiter [story]; *s.* tournoiement, m.; rotation; vrille (aviat.), f.; *to spin out*, faire traîner en longueur; *to spin yarns*, conter des histoires.

spinach [spinitsh] *s.* épinards, m. pl.

spinal [spaⁱnˈl] *adj.* spinal; *spinal column*, épine dorsale; *spinal cord*, cordon médullaire.

spindle [spindlˈ] *s.* fuseau; arbre; axe; pivot, m.; *v.* monter (ou) rouler en fuseau.

spindrift [spindrift] *s.* embruns, m. pl.

spinner [spinᵉʳ] *s.* fileur; filateur; métier à filer, m.; araignée; cuiller [fishing], f. ‖ **spinning** [-ing] *s.* filage; tournoiement; repoussage (mech.), m.; *spinning mill*, filature; *spinning-wheel*, rouet.

spinster [spinstᵉʳ] *s.* femme célibataire; vieille fille (colloq.), f.

spiny [spaⁱni] *adj.* épineux; *spiny lobster*, langouste.

spiral [spaⁱrˈl] *s.* spirale, f.; *adj.* en colimaçon [staircase]; *v.* descendre (ou) monter en spirale (aviat.).

spire [spaⁱʳ] *s.* spire; pointe; flèche [steeple], f.; brin [grass], m.

spirit [spirit] *s.* esprit; caractère; courage; entrain; *pl.* spiritueux, m.; fougue, f.; *a man of spirit*, un homme de cœur; *in low spirits*, déprimé; *to spirit away*, enlever comme par enchantement; *spirit of wine*, esprit de vin; *spirit of turpentine*, essence de térébenthine; *fighting spirit*, humeur belliqueuse; *methylated spirit*, alcool dénaturé, alcool à brûler; *spirit level*, niveau à bulle d'air. ‖ **spirited** [-id] *adj.* vif, animé. ‖ **spiritless** [-lis] *adj.* abattu, sans force; éteint. ‖ **spiritual** [-shouèl] *adj.* spirituel; *s.* chant religieux des Noirs du sud des Etats-Unis, m. ‖ **spiritualism** [-shoulizᵉm] *s.* spiritualisme; spiritisme, m. ‖ **spirituality** [spiritshouâlᵉti] *s.* spiritualité, f. ‖ **spirituous** [spiritshouᵉs] *adj.* spiritueux.

spit [spit] v.* cracher; s. crachat, m.; salive, f.; pret., p. p. of to spit.

spit [spit] s. broche, f.

spite [spa¹t] s. dépit, m.; rancune, f.; v. dépiter; détester; in spite of, malgré; **spiteful**, rancunier, malveillant, venimeux; **spitefulness**, rancœur; rancune; malveillance; caractère rancunier.

spitting [spiting] s. expectoration, f.; **blood spitting**, hémoptysie.

spittle [spit'l] s. salive, f.; crachat, m.

spittoon [spitoun] s. crachoir, m.

splash [splash] v. éclabousser; barboter; clapoter; s.* éclaboussure, f.; clapotement [water]; bariolage [colors]; écrasement [bullet], m.; **splashboard**, garde-boue.

spleen [splîn] s. rate; bile; mauvaise humeur; hypocondrie, f.

splendid [splèndid] adj. splendide; éclatant; somptueux; épatant (colloq.). ‖ **splendo(u)r** [-dᵉr] s. splendeur, f.; faste, éclat, m.

splice [spla¹s] s. épissure; ligature; soudure, f.; v. épisser; joindre; raccorder; **splice bar**, éclisse.

splint [splint] s. éclisse; attelle, f.; suros [horse], m.; v. éclisser. ‖ **splinter** [-ᵉr] v. voler en éclats; (faire) éclater; s. éclat, m.; éclat; écharde; esquille, f.

split [split] s. fente; crevasse; scission, f.; v.* fendre; morceler; mettre la division; to split hairs, couper les cheveux en quatre; to split one's sides with laughter, se tordre de rire; to split the difference, partager le différend; to split the atom, désintégrer l'atome; split pin, goupille fendue.

splurge [splẽrdj] s. épate (colloq.), f.; v. Am. faire de l'épate.

splutter [splœtᵉr] v. bredouiller.

spoil [spo¹l] v.* gâter; gâcher; endommager; dépouiller, spolier; s. butin, m.; dépouilles, f. pl.; **spoil-sport**, rabat-joie.

spoke [spoᵘk] s. échelon; rayon [wheel], m.

spoke [spoᵘk] pret. of to speak.

spoken [spoᵘkᵉn] p. p. of to speak.

spokesman [spoᵘksmᵉn] (pl. spokesmen) s. porte-parole, m.

spoliate [spoᵘlié¹t] v. spolier. ‖ **spoliation** [spoᵘlié¹shᵉn] s. spoliation, f.; pillage, m.

sponge [spœndj] s. éponge, f.; écouvillon; écornifleur, m.; v. éponger; écouvillonner; écornifler; to throw in the sponge, s'avouer vaincu; **sponge-cake**, biscuit de Savoie; **sponger**, pêcheur d'éponges; épongeur; écornifleur; **spongy**, spongieux.

sponsor [spânsᵉr] s. parrain, m.; marraine, f.; répondant, m.; v. parrainer; répondre pour; être le garant de.

spontaneity [spântᵉnᵉ¹ti] s. spontanéité, f. ‖ **spontaneous** [spânté¹niᵉs] adj. spontané.

spoof [spouf] v. filouter; faire marcher; s. attrape, filouterie, f.

spook [spouk] s. revenant, spectre, fantôme, m.

spool [spoul] s. bobine; canette, f.; v. bobiner.

spoon [spoun] s. cuiller, f.; v. prendre à la cuiller; **spoonful**, cuillerée; **teaspoon**, cuiller à café.

sport [spoᵘrt] s. jeu; amusement; sport, m.; v. jouer; divertir; faire du sport; in sport, pour rire; to make sport of, se moquer de; **sport(s) clothes**, vêtement de sport; **sportive**, gai, badin, folâtre; **sportiveness**, enjouement. ‖ **sportsman** [-smᵉn] (pl. **sportsmen**) s. sportif; beau joueur, m. ‖ **sportswoman** [-woumᵉn] (pl. sportswomen) s. sportive, f.

spot [spât] s. tache, souillure, f.; endroit, coin, m.; v. tacher; marquer; repérer; détecter; on the spot, sur-le-champ, sur le coup; to pay spot cash, payer comptant; **spotless**, immaculé; **spotlight**, feu de projecteur, rampe; **weak spot**, point faible. ‖ **spotted** [-id] adj. tacheté; moucheté; tigré; **spotted fever**, méningite cérébro-spinale; **spotted tie**, cravate à pois.

spouse [spaᵒuz] s. époux, m.; épouse, f.; conjoint, m.; conjointe, f.

spout [spaᵒut] v. jaillir, gicler; déclamer; s. jet; dégorgeoir, goulot; bec d'écoulement, m.; trombe, f.; **spouter**, péroreur; **spout-hole**, évent.

sprain [spré¹n] s. foulure; entorse, f.; v. fouler.

sprang [sprâng] pret. of to spring.

sprat [sprat] s. sprat; gringalet, m.

sprawl [spraul] v. s'étaler; se vautrer; s. attitude affalée, f.; **sprawling**, les quatre fers en l'air.

spray [spré¹] s. branche; brindille, f.

spray [spré¹] s. jet, m.; éclaboussure; poussière d'eau, f.; vaporisateur, pulvérisateur, m.; v. vaporiser; pulvériser; arroser; sea spray, embrun; **sprayer**, vaporisateur; pulvérisateur; arroseuse; **tar-sprayer**, goudronneuse.

spread [sprèd] v.* étendre; dresser [tent]; tendre [sail]; déployer; (se) répandre; (se) propager; (s') étaler; s.

étendue; envergure; ouverture; diffusion; dispersion, f.; dessus-de-lit, m.; *to spread butter on*, beurrer; *a well-spread table*, une table bien servie; *to spread to*, gagner; *pret., p. p. of to spread.*

spree [sprî] *s.* orgie, noce; cuite (colloq.), *Fr. Can.* brosse, f.; *Am. to go on a spree*, aller faire la bombe.

sprig [sprig] *s.* brindille, f.

sprightly [spra¹tli] *adj.* vif; enjoué.

spring [spring] *s.* bond, saut; ressort; printemps, m.; élasticité; origine; source, f.; *pl.* suspension [auto], f.; *v.** sauter; bondir; s'élancer, pousser [plant]; jaillir [water]; faire sauter [mine]; surgir; se détendre, *adj.* à ressort; printanier; *to spring back*, faire un bond en arrière, faire ressort; *to spring a leak*, faire eau [naut.]; *to spring to one's feet*, se lever d'un bond; *springboard*, tremplin *spring mattress*, sommier élastique *springtime*, printemps; *spring water*, eau de source; *springy*, souple; élastique; à ressort; agile.

sprinkle [spriŋk'l] *v.* asperger; saupoudrer; répandre; *s.* pincée [salt]; petite pluie de, f.; *sprinkled*, moucheté, jaspé; *sprinkler*, appareil d'arrosage; goupillon.

sprint [sprint] *v.* sprinter; *s.* sprint, m.; *sprinter*, sprinter.

sprout [spra^{ou}t] *v.* pousser; germer; *s.* pousse, f.; *Brussels sprouts*, choux de Bruxelles.

spruce [sprous] *s.* épicéa, m.; *Fr. Can.* épinette, f.

spruce [sprous] *adj.* élégant, pimpant; *v. to spruce up*, s'habiller coquettement.

sprung [sproeng] *p. p. of to spring.*

spume [spioum] *s.* écume, f.; *v.* écumer.

spun [spoen] *pret., p. p. of to spin.*

spur [spë͏r] *s.* éperon; stimulant; contrefort; ergot [cock]; aiguillon; embranchement [railw.], m.; *v.* éperonner; aiguillonner; stimuler; *on the spur of the moment*, impromptu; *spur-gear*, engrenage; *spur-wheel*, roue dentée.

spurious [spyouri^es] *adj.* contrefait, falsifié.

spurn [spë͏rn] *v.* mépriser; dédaigner; écarter.

spurt [spë͏rt] *v.* (faire) jaillir; cracher; *s.* jet; effort, coup de collier, m.; explosion [anger], f.

sputter [spæt^er] *v.* crachoter; bredouiller; *s.* bredouillement; crachotis, m. ‖ *sputum* [spyout^em] *s.* crachat, m.

spy [spa¹] *s.** espion, m.; *v.* espionner; épier; apercevoir; *to spy out*, explorer, reconnaître; *spyglass*, lunette d'approche; *spying*, espionnage.

squabble [skwáb'l] *s.* querelle, f.; *v.* se chamailler; se quereller.

squad [skwâd] *s.* escouade; équipe, f.

squadron [skwâdr^en] *s.* escadron, m.; escadre (naut.); escadrille (aviat.), f.

squalid [skwâlid] *adj.* crasseux, sordide; répugnant; miséreux.

squall [skwaul] *s.* grain, m.; bourrasque, rafale, f.; *v.* souffler en rafale.

squall [skwaul] *s.* braillement, m.; *v.* crier; brailler.

squander [skwând^er] *v.* gaspiller; dilapider; *squanderer*, dissipateur, gaspilleur; *squandering*, gaspillage.

square [skwè͏r] *s.* carré; carreau [glass]; square [garden]; *Am.* pâté de maisons, m.; équerre; case [chess-board], f.; *adj.* carré; vrai; exact; équitable; net; franc; *v.* carrer (math. mil.); équarrir; ajuster; cadrer; mesurer; balancer [accounts]; *square-built*, trapu, aux épaules carrées, *square root*, racine carrée; *to square oneself with*, se mettre en règle avec; *to be square with someone*, être quitte avec quelqu'un; *he is on the square*, il est honnête et de bonne foi; *squarely*, carrément; honnêtement; nettement.

squash [skwâsh] *s.** bruit mou, m.; chute lourde, f.; *v.* (s')écraser; *lemon squash*, citron pressé.

squash [skwâsh] *s.** courge, f.

squat [skwât] *v.* s'accroupir; s'établir sans titre; occuper les lieux abusivement; *squatter*, squatter.

squawk [skwauk] *s.* cri rauque, m.; crier d'une voix rauque; protester.

squeak [skwîk] *v.* pousser un cri aigu; glapir; grincer; *s.* cri aigu; grincement, m.

squeal [skwîl] *v.* crier; dénoncer; *s.* cri aigu, m.; *squealer*, dénonciateur, mouchard, m.

squeamish [skwîmish] *adj.* difficile; chipoteur; pudibond; nauséeux.

squeeze [skwîz] *v.* presser; comprimer; pressurer; pousser; *s.* cohue, f.; *to squeeze out the juice*, exprimer le jus; *to squeeze money*, extorquer de l'argent; *to squeeze through a crowd*, se frayer un chemin dans la foule; *lemon-squeezer*, presse-citron; *squeezing*, pressurage; compression; oppression.

squelch [skwèltsh] *v.* (s')écraser; déconcerter; étouffer [revolt].

squib [skwĭb] *s.* pétard; brocard, m.; *v.* brocarder.

squint [skwĭnt] *v.* loucher; regarder de côté, *s.* strabisme; coup d'œil furtif, m.; *squint-eyed*, bigle.

squire [skwa¹e⁰r] *s.* écuyer; titre anglais; châtelain; gros propriétaire, m.; *v.* escorter; être le cavalier de.

squirm [skwër̃m] *v.* se tortiller.

squirrel [skwër̃el] *s.* écureuil, m.

squirt [skwër̃t] *v.* faire gicler; jaillir; *s.* seringue, f.; jet, m.

squish [skwĭsh] *v.* gicler.

stab [stab] *v.* poignarder; donner un coup de couteau à; *s.* coup de couteau, de poignard, m.

stability [ste⁰bĭl⁰ti] *s.* stabilité, f. *stabilize* [sté¹b'la¹z] *v.* stabiliser. || *stable* [sté¹b'l] *adj.* stable; constant; solide.

stable [sté¹b'l] *s.* écurie, f.; *stable-boy*, palefrenier.

stack [stăk] *s.* meule; pile; souche; cheminée, f.; faisceau [arms], m.; *v.* mettre en meule; empiler; mettre en faisceaux (mil.); *library stacks*, rayons de bibliothèque.

stadium [sté¹di⁰m] *s.* stade, m.

staff [staf] *s.* bâton; mât; soutien, tuteur; état-major; personnel (comm.), m.; gaule; hampe [flag]; mire [levelling]; portée [music], f.; *bishop's staff*, crosse épiscopale; *clerical staff*, personnel de bureau; *editorial staff*, rédaction d'un journal; *general staff*, état-major général; *pilgrim's staff*, bâton de pèlerin; *teaching staff*, corps enseignant.

stag [stag] *s.* cerf; cervidé mâle, m.; coulissier [Stock Exchange], m.; *stag dinner*, *stag party*, dîner, réunion d'hommes.

stage [sté¹dj] *s.* estrade; scène (theat.); étape (fig.); plate-forme; phase (techn.); platine [microscope], f.; tréteau; échafaudage; relais [horses], m.; *v.* mettre à la scène, monter; progresser par étapes; *stage (-coach)*, diligence; *stage door*, entrée des artistes; *stage fright*, trac; *stage hand*, machiniste; *stage manager*, régisseur; *stage player*, comédien; *stage-struck*, entiché de théâtre.

stagger [stag⁰r] *v.* chanceler; hésiter; décaler (aviat.); échelonner [working hours]; (faire) tituber; disposer en zigzag; confondre; consterner; *s.* chancellement; étourdissement; décalage (aviat.); échelonnage; *pl.* vertige, vertigo, m.

stagnancy [stagn⁰nsi] *s.* stagnation, f.; marasme, m. || *stagnant* [-⁰nt] *adj.*

stagnant; inactif, mort. || *stagnate* [-é¹t] *v.* stagner. || *stagnation* [stagné¹sh⁰n] *s.* stagnation, f.

staid [sté¹d] *adj.* sérieux; posé.

stain [sté¹n] *s.* tache; souillure; couleur, f.; *v.* tacher, souiller; teindre, colorier; *stained-glass window*, fenêtre aux vitres de couleur, vitrail; *stainless*, immaculé; inoxydable [metal].

stair [stè⁰r] *s.* marche, f.; *pl.* escalier, m.; *staircase*, *stairway*, escalier.

stake [sté¹k] *s.* pieu; poteau; bûcher; jalon; enjeu [gambling], m.; *v.* garnir de pieux; jalonner; parier; hasarder; *Am.* subvenir aux besoins de; tuteurer [plants]; *to be at stake*, être en jeu; *to have much at stake*, avoir pris beaucoup de risques; *to have a stake in*, avoir des intérêts dans; *to stake one's reputation*, jouer sa réputation.

stalactite [stal⁰kta¹t] *s.* stalactite, f. || *stalagmite* [-gma¹t] *s.* stalagmite, f.

stale [sté¹l] *adj.* rassis [bread]; renfermé; vicié [air]; éventé [liquor]; vieilli; périmé; défraîchi; rebattu [joke]; *v.* éventer; défraîchir; rendre insipide; déflorer.

stalk [stauk] *s.* tige; queue [flower], f.; pied [shoot]; tuyau [quill]; trognon [cabbage]; manche [whip], m.

stalk [stauk] *v.* marcher dignement; suivre furtivement à la chasse.

stall [staul] *s.* stalle [church]; étable; écurie; boutique; perte de vitesse (aviat.), f.; étalage; étal; blocage (mech.), m.; *v.* mettre à l'étable; caler [motor]; *stalled in the mud*, embourbé.

stallion [staly⁰n] *s.* étalon, m.

stalwart [staulwër̃t] *adj.* vigoureux; vaillant; fort, solide.

stamen [sté¹m⁰n] *s.* étamine, f.

stamina [stam⁰n⁰] *s.* résistance, vigueur, force vitale, f.

stammer [stam⁰r] *v.* bégayer; bredouiller; *s.* bégaiement, m.; *stammerer*, bègue; *stammering*, bégaiement, balbutiement.

stamp [stàmp] *v.* trépigner; imprimer, marquer, estampiller; contrôler [gold]; poinçonner; timbrer; plomber [customs]; estamper [metal]; emboutir (techn.); *s.* trépignement; poinçon; timbre; cachet, m.; estampille; marque; empreinte, f.; *postage stamp*, timbre-poste; *rubber stamp*, timbre en caoutchouc; *stamp duty*, droit de timbre.

stampede [stàmpîd] *s.* débandade; panique, f.; *v.* se débander; fuir en désordre.

stance [stans] *s.* position, f.

stanch [stântsh] *adj.* ferme, sûr.

stand [stànd] *v.* se tenir debout; (se) mettre, (se) placer; être situé; rester; durer; exister; stationner; supporter; *s.* position; station; situation, béquille [motorcycle]; estrade; résistance (mil.), f.; stand; support; socle; chevalet; banc, pied; affût [telescope], m.; *to let tea stand*, laisser infuser le thé; *to stand by*, appuyer, défendre, être près de; *to stand fast*, tenir bon, *to stand for*, tolérer, supporter, tenir la place de, signifier; *to stand in need*, avoir besoin de; *to stand in the way* encombrer; *to stand out*, faire saillie, se détacher; tenir ferme; *to stand to*, s'en tenir à; *to stand up for*, soutenir; *to stand one's ground*, se maintenir sur ses positions; *to make a stand*, offrir de la résistance (mil.); *to stand up*, se lever; *Am.* poser un lapin; *music stand*, lutrin; *test stand*, banc d'essai; *umbrella stand*, porte-parapluie; *stand-by*, soutien, partisan, ressource; *standpoint*, point de vue; *standstill*, immobilisation.

standard [stànderd] *s.* étendard; étalon, titre [gold]; degré; programme; standard, m.; norme, f., *adj.* réglementaire; classique [book]. définitive [edition]; courant, normal *standard-bearer*, porte-drapeau; *standard price*, prix homologué; *standard time*, heure légale. || *standardization* [stànderdezéshen] *s.* normalisation, standardisation, f.; étalonnage, titrage, m. || *standardize* [stànderdaiz] *v.* standardiser; normaliser; étalonner.

standing [stànding] *s.* station debout; durée; place, pose, f.; rang, m.; *adj.* debout; stationnant; sur pied; stagnant; permanent [army]; fixe; traditionnel; *standing-room*, place(s) debout.

standstill [stàndstil] *s.* stagnation; accalmie; panne, f.; marasme, m.

stank [stàngk] *pret. of* stink.

stanza [stànze] *s.* stance, strophe, f.

staple [stéipl] *adj.* principal; commercial; indispensable; *s.* produit principal; produit brut, m.; matière première; fibre, soie, f.; *pl.* articles de première nécessité, m. pl.

staple [stéipl] *s.* crampon, m.; gâche; broche [bookbinding], f.; *v.* brocher; fixer, attacher; *stapler*, agrafeuse.

star [stâr] *s.* étoile; vedette, f.; astérisque; astre, m.; *v.* étoiler; marquer d'un astérisque; être (ou) mettre en vedette; *shooting star*, étoile filante; *stars and stripes*, bannière étoilée, drapeau des Etats-Unis; *star fish*, astérie, étoile de mer; *star-spangled*, étoilé.

starboard [stârbooerd] *s.* tribord, m.

starch [stârtsh] *s.* amidon; empois, m.; fécule, f.; *v.* amidonner; empeser; *starchy*, amidonné; féculent [foods]; guindé, compassé (fig.).

stare [stèer] *v.* regarder fixement; *s.* regard fixe, m.; *to outstare*, faire baisser les yeux. || *staring* [-ring] *adj.* fixe, grand ouvert.

stark [stârk] *adj.* raide, rigide; rigoureux, désolé, désert; absolu, véritable; *stark naked*, nu comme un ver; *adv.* complètement, tout à fait.

starling [stârling] *s.* sansonnet, étourneau, m.

starry [stâri] *adj.* étoilé, étincelant, constellé.

start [stârt] *v.* partir; démarrer; commencer; entamer; sursauter; sauter; se détacher; lever [game]; réveiller, exciter; ouvrir [subscription]; *s.* tressaillement; commencement; départ; saut; écart [horse]; démarrage; élan; haut-le-corps, m.; *to start off*, démarrer; *to start out*, se mettre en route; *to start up from one's sleep*, se réveiller en sursaut; *by starts*, par accès, par saccades. || *starter* [-er] *s.* démarreur, m.; *self-starter*, démarreur automatique. || *starting* [-ing] *s.* démarrage; départ; début, m.; mise en marche, f.; *starting point*, point de départ.

startle [stârtl] *v.* faire frémir; réveiller en sursaut; sursauter. || *startling* [-ling] *adj.* saisissant; sensationnel.

starvation [stârvéishen] *s.* inanition, famine, f. || *starve* [stârv] *v.* mourir d'inanition; réduire à la famine; *starveling*, meurt-de-faim, famélique.

state [stéit] *s.* état; rang; degré; apparat, m.; condition; situation, f.; *v.* déclarer; spécifier; préciser; affirmer; *in (great) state*, en grande pompe; *buffer state*, Etat tampon; *state of emergency*, état d'exception. || *stately* [-li] *adj.* majestueux, imposant; *adv.* majestueusement, d'un air noble. || *statement* [-ment] *s.* déclaration, f.; exposé; rapport; état; bilan; compte rendu, m.; *statement of account*, relevé de compte, f. || *state-room* [-roum] *s.* cabine (naut.), f. || *statesman* [-smen] (pl. *statesmen*) *s.* homme d'Etat; homme politique, m.

static [statik] *adj.* statique; *s.* perturbation atmosphérique [radio]; *pl.* statique, f.

station [stéishen] *s.* station; gare; position sociale; place de stationnement, f.; poste, m.; *v.* placer; ranger; poster; *broadcasting station*, poste émetteur [radio]; *first aid station*, poste de secours; *police station*, poste de police; *regulating station*, gare régulatrice; *station-master*, chef de gare. ‖ **stationary** [-èri] *adj.* stationnaire, immobile.

stationery [sté¹sh•nèri] *s.* papeterie, f.; papier à lettres, m.

statistician [statistish•n] *s.* statisticien, m. ‖ **statistics** [st•tistiks] *s. pl.* statistique, f.

statuary [statshouèri] *s.* statuaire, f. ‖ **statue** [statshou] *s.* statue, f.

stature [statsh•r] *s.* stature; taille, f.

status [sté¹t•s] *s.* statut; état; rang; standing, m.; condition, f.

statute [statshout] *s.* statut, m.; ordonnance, f.; code, m.; *statutory*, statutaire, réglementaire.

staunch [stauntsh] *v.* étancher; *adj.* étanche; ferme; solide; sûr.

stave [sté¹v] *s.* douve [cask]; portée [music]; strophe, stance, f.; *v.* défoncer; *to stave off*, maintenir à distance.

stay [sté¹] *s.* support; soutien; séjour, m.; suspension (jur.), f.; *v.*° (s')arrêter; séjourner; demeurer; étayer; différer [execution]; *to stay up all night*, veiller toute la nuit; *to stay away*, s'absenter; *to stay for*, attendre.

stead [stèd] *s.* place, f.; *in his stead*, à sa place. ‖ **steadfast** [-fast] *adj.* constant; ferme; stable. ‖ **steadily** [-'li] *adv.* avec fermeté ou constance; résolument; fixement. ‖ **steadiness** [-inis] *s.* fermeté; stabilité; assiduité, f. ‖ **steady** [-i] *adj.* ferme; rangé, sérieux; constant; sûr; *v.* fixer; affermir; assujettir; calmer; *to keep steady*, ne pas bouger, ne pas broncher.

steak [sté¹k] *s.* bifteck, m.; tranche; entrecôte, f.

steal [stîl] *v.*° voler; aller à la dérobée; *to steal away*, subtiliser; s'esquiver; *to steal a glance*, jeter un regard furtif; *stealer*, voleur. ‖ **stealth** [stèlth] *s.* dérobée, f.; *by stealth*, furtivement, en tapinois; *stealthily*, à la dérobée; *stealthiness*, nature furtive; *stealthy*, furtif, secret.

steam [stîm] *s.* vapeur; buée, f.; *adj.* à vapeur; par la vapeur; *v.* fumer; jeter de la vapeur; passer, cuire à la vapeur; s'évaporer; *steam engine*, machine à vapeur. ‖ **steamboat** [-bo°t], *steamer* [-•r], *steamship* [-ship] *s.* bateau à vapeur, steamer, m.; *cargo steamer*, cargo.

steed [stîd] *s.* coursier; cheval de combat, destrier, m.

steel [stîl] *s.* acier; fusil [sharpening]; fer [sword], m.; *v.* aciérer; endurcir; aguerrir (*against*, contre); *stainless steel*, acier inoxydable; *steelworks*, aciérie.

steep [stîp] *adj.* escarpé; à pic; exorbitant [price]; *s.* escarpement, m.; pente rapide, f.

steep [stîp] *v.* tremper; infuser; macérer; saturer.

steeple [stîp'l] *s.* clocher, m.; *steeple-chase*, course d'obstacles.

steer [stî•r] *s.* bouvillon, m.

steer [stî•r] *v.* piloter; tenir la barre (naut.); conduire; *to steer the course*, faire route; *the car steers easily*, la voiture se conduit facilement; *steering gear*, gouvernail; *steering wheel*, volant [auto]; *steerage*, entrepont; *steersman*, timonier.

stellar [stél•r] *adj.* stellaire.

stem [stèm] *s.* tige, queue; pied [glass]; étrave (naut.), f.; tuyau [pipe], m.

stem [stèm] *v.* arrêter; endiguer; refouler; remonter [tide]; s'opposer à; *to stem from*, descendre de, provenir de.

stench [stènsh] *s.*° puanteur, f.

stencil [stèns'l] *s.* pochoir; stencil, m.

stenographer [st•nàgr•f•r] *s.* sténographe, m. f. ‖ **stenography** [-fi] *s.* sténographie, f. ‖ **stenotypist** [sténo-ta¹pist] *s.* sténotypiste, m. f. ‖ **stenotypy** [sténota¹pi] *s.* sténotypie, f.

step [stèp] *s.* pas, m.; marche [stairs]; démarche; emplanture [mast], f.; échelon; marchepied [vehicle], m.; *pl.* échelle, f.; perron, m.; *v.* marcher; avancer; faire un pas; *to step aside*, s'écarter; *to step out*, allonger le pas; *to take a step*, faire une démarche, prendre un parti; *to take steps*, prendre des mesures; *to step back*, rebrousser chemin; *to step on the gas*, appuyer sur l'accélérateur, mettre les gaz; *to be in step with*, marcher au pas avec, être d'accord avec; *stepladder*, échelle double.

stepchild [stèptsha¹ld] (*pl. stepchildren*) [-tshildr•n] *s.* beau-fils, m.; belle-fille, f. ‖ **stepdaughter** [-daut•r] *s.* belle-fille, f. ‖ **stepfather** [-fâzh•r] *s.* beau-père, m. ‖ **stepmother** [-mœzh•r] *s.* belle-mère, f.

steppe [stèp] *s.* steppe, f.

stepsister [stèpsist•r] *s.* demi-sœur, f. ‖ **stepson** [-scen] *s.* beau-fils, m.

stereotype [stèri•ta¹p] *s.* cliché; stéréotype, m.

sterile [stèr•l] *adj.* stérile; aseptique. ‖ **sterility** [st•ril•ti] *s.* stérilité, f. ‖ **sterilize** [stèr•la¹z] *v.* stériliser.

sterling [stër'ling] *s.* sterling, m.; monnaie de bon aloi, f.; *adj.* qui a cours légal; vrai, authentique; *pound sterling*, livre sterling.

stern [stër̈n] *adj.* austère; sévère; rigoureux; rébarbatif.

stern [stër̈n] *s.* arrière, m.; poupe, f.; **sternlight**, feu de poupe; **sternpost**, étambot.

sternutation [stër̈nyouté¹shen] *s.* éternuement, m.

stethoscope [stèthesko°°p] *s.* stéthoscope, m.

stevedore [stīvedo°°r] *s.* débardeur; déchargeur, m.

stew [styou] *v* faire un ragoût; mettre en ragoût ou en civet fricasser, cuire à l'étouffée; *s* ragoût civet, m., fricassée; étuvée, f.; *to be in a stew*, être dans la panade, être très agité; **stewed fruit**, compote de fruits; **stewpan**, cocotte.

steward [styouwerd] *s.* intendant; régisseur, économe, maître d'hôtel; commis aux vivres steward, m.; **stewardess**, femme de chambre.

stick [stìk] *s* baguette tige; canne, f.; **cleft stick**, piquet fourchu; **control stick**, manche à balai (aviat.).

stick [stìk] *v* piquer percer; enfoncer adhérer (se) coller s'embourber; s'empêtrer (se) cramponner; *to stick out*, faire saillie *stick to it!*, tenez bon! *to stick to one's friends*, cramponner ses amis, être collant; *to stick one's hands up* lever les mains; **sticking-plaster**, taffetas gommé, sparadrap **stickiness** [-nis] viscosité; viscosité, f **stickler** [-er] *s.* farouche partisan, m. (*for*, de). **sticky** [-i] *adj.* collant; adhésif; visqueux, tatillon.

stiff [stif] *adj.* raide, rigide; ankylosé; inflexible obstiné opiniâtre guindé; difficile (exam.). **stiffen** [n] *v.* (se) raidir durcir se zuinder obstiner **stiffness** [-nis] rigidité raideur, consistance, opiniâtreté difficulté, f.

stifle [sta¹f°l] *v* étouffer, suffoquer; amortir réprimer, éteindre.

stigma [stigme] *s.* stigmate, m.; marque, f., **stigmatist**, stigmatisé; **stigmatize**, stigmatiser.

stiletto [stilèto°°] *s.* stylet; poinçon, m.; *stiletto heel*, talon aiguille.

still [stil] *adj* calme silencieux; tranquille, *s* calme silence, m. *v.* calmer; apaiser tranquilliser faire taire *adv.* toujours encore instamment cependant, néanmoins *but still*, mais enfin, tout de même **still born**, mortné; *still life*, nature morte.

still [stil] *s.* alambic, m.; distillerie, f.; *v.* distiller; faire tomber goutte à goutte.

stillness [stìlnis] *s.* calme, silence, m.; tranquillité, f.

stilt [stilt] *s.* échasse, f.; **stilted**, compassé, gourmé, guindé.

stimulant [stìmyel¹nt] *adj.. s.* stimulant. tonique. ¶ **stimulate** [-lé¹t] *v.* stimuler; encourager exciter aiguillonner ‖ **stimulation** [stìmv*lé¹shen] *s.* stimulation excitation, f encouragement, m. ‖ **stimulus** [stìmv*lés] (*pl.* **stimuli** [-i]) *s.* stimulant; aiguillon; stimulus (med.), m.

sting [stìng] *s.* aiguillon; dard, m.; pointe piqûre, f.; *v.** piquer, picoter; cuire blesser mortifier *stung to the quick* piqué au vif; **stingless**, sans dard, sans épine.

stinginess [stìndjinis] *s.* avarice; mesquinerie, f. ‖ **stingy** [stìndji] *adj.* avare maigre, rare.

stink [stìngk] *v.* puer, empester; *s.* puanteur, pestilence, f **stinker**, salaud, **stinking**, puant, fétide.

stint [stìnt] *v.* limiter rationner; lésiner sur; *s.* tâche journalière besogne convenue, restriction, réserve, f.

stipend [sta¹pènd] *s.* salaire, traitement, appointements, m.; **stipendiary**, salarié.

stipulate [stìpyelé¹t] *v.* stipuler; arrêter, préciser. ‖ **stipulation** [stìpyelé¹shen] *s.* stipulation, clause, convention, f.

stir [stër̈] *v.* remuer; agiter, bouger; irriter attiser, émouvoir; troubler; *s.* mouvement, m. agitation activité; émotion, f. *Am* prison slang) *to stir up a revolt* susciter une révolte *to stir up to* pousser à, encourager **stirring** [-ing] *adj* émouvant stimulant, mouvementé, entraînant, intéressant; sensationnel.

stirrup [stìrep] *s.* étrier; collier (mech.), m.; **stirrup-strap**, étrivière, f.

stitch [stìtsh] *s.** point, point de suture. m. maille, f.; *v.* coudre, piquer; faire des points de suture; brocher (books).

stoat [sto°°t] *s.* hermine, f.

stock [stâk] *s.* souche lignée; bûche; monture giroflée [flower] ente [grafting], f provisions munitions rentes, valeurs, f. pl. approvisionnement, stock [stores]; fonds état tronc [tree], billot [wood], *pl* chantier, tins de cale (naut.) consommé [broth], m.; *v.* approvisionner, monter. stocker; outiller peupler [game or fish] *to have on the stocks* avoir en chantier; *to take stock of*, faire l'inventaire de; *to take stock in*, prendre les actions de; *Am* accorder créance à; *to stock a farm*, monter le bétail d'une ferme; **live stock**, bétail; **rolling stock**, matériel roulant (railw.); **stock-broker**, agent de change; *Am.* **stock car**, wagon à bestiaux; *Stock Exchange*, Bourse des valeurs; *stock-holder*, actionnaire; *stock market*, marché des valeurs. *stock-piling*, stockage. *stock raising*, élevage du bétail; *stock-room*, magasin. *stock-yards*, parc à bétail.

stockade [stăkéᵉld] *s.* palissade, f.

stocking [stăking] *s.* bas, m.

stocky [stăki] *adj.* trapu.

stodgy [stădji] *adj.* pâteux; bourratif; indigeste.

stoic [stoᵒuik] *adj.*, *s.* stoïque. ‖ **stoicism** [stoᵒuisizᵉm] *s.* stoïcisme, m.

stoke [stoᵒuk] *v.* chauffer, entretenir un feu, *stokehold*, chaufferie; *stoker*, chauffeur (naut.).

stole [stoᵒul] *pret. of to steal.* ‖ *stolen* [staulⁿ] *p. p. of to steal.*

stole [stoᵒul] *s.* étole, f.

stolid [stălid] *adj.* lourd; passif; flegmatique; *stolidness*, flegme, m.

stomach [stœmᵉk] *s.* estomac, m.; *v.* digérer, supporter; *stomach-ache*, douleur d'estomac, mal de ventre; *stomachal*, stomacal.

stone [stoᵒun] *s.* pierre, f.; noyau [fruit]; calcul (med.), m.; *adj.* de pierre; complètement; *v.* lapider; passer à la pierre (techn.); dénoyauter; *altar stone*, pierre d'autel. *building stone*, moellon. *cut stone*, pierre de taille; *grindstone*, meule. *hail-stone*, grêlon; *stone-deaf*, sourd comme un pot; *stoneware*, grès, poterie; *stonework*, maçonnerie. ‖ *stony* [-i] *adj.* pierreux; de pierre; endurci, insensible; *stony-broke*, dans la dèche.

stood [stoud] *pret., p. p. of to stand.*

stooge [stoudj] *s.* comparse, m. f.

stool [stoul] *s.* tabouret; escabeau; petit banc, m.; *to go to stool*, aller à la selle. *camp-stool*, pliant; *stool pigeon*, appeau; *Am.* mouchard.

stoop [stoup] *v.* (se) pencher; (s')incliner; s'abaisser, humilier; *s.* dos rond, m.; attitude voûtée, f.; inclinaison, f.; *stoop-shouldered*, voûté.

stop [stăp] *v.* arrêter; cesser; empêcher; obstruer, boucher; *Br.* plomber [teeth]; stopper, parer (naut.); *s.* arrêt; obstacle, empêchement; dispositif de blocage. butoir (mech.); jeu [organ], m.; interruption; obstruction; station (railw.); escale (naut.), f.; *to stop at a hotel*, descendre à l'hôtel; *to stop from*, cesser de; *to stop over at*, faire escale à. *stop consonant*, consonne explosive; *stopblock*, butoir; *Am. stop-over*, arrêt, escale. *stopwatch*, chronomètre compte-secondes; *full-stop*, point [punctuation]. ‖ *stoppage* [-idj] *s.* arrêt; enrayage (mil.); obstacle; *Br.* plombage [teeth], m.;

halte; pause; interruption; retenue [pay], f. ‖ *stopper* [-ᵉr] *s.* bouchon; obturateur, m.

storage [stoᵒuridj] *s.* emmagasinage; entreposage. frais d'entrepôt, m.; *storage battery*, accumulateur; *storage cell*, élément d'accu. ‖ *store* [stoᵒur, stauᵉr] *s.* provisions; fourniture; boutique, f.; approvisionnement; entrepôt; magasin, m.; *pl.* vivres; matériel, m.; munitions, f. pl.; *v.* fournir; approvisionner, emmagasiner; mettre en dépôt; *book store*, librairie; *department store*, grand magasin; *fruit store*, fruiterie. *shoe store*, magasin de chaussures; *to hold in store*, garder en réserve; *to store up*, accumuler. ‖ *storehouse* [-haᵒus] *s.* magasin; entrepôt; dépôt, m. ‖ *storekeeper* [-kîpᵉr] *s.* garde-magasin; magasinier; *Am.* boutiquier, m.

stork [staurk] *s.* cigogne, f.

storm [staurm] *s.* tempête, f.; orage; assaut (mil.), m.; *v.* tempêter; faire de l'orage; se déchaîner; monter à l'assaut; prendre d'assaut; *storm troops*, troupes d'assaut; *in a storm of*, dans un accès de. ‖ *stormy* [-i] *adj.* orageux; tempétueux; turbulent.

story [stoᵒuri] *s.* histoire, f.; récit; conte; mensonge, m.; *story teller*, conteur, mythomane.

story [stoᵒuri] *s.* étage, m.; *Am. second story*, premier étage; *upper story*, étage supérieur.

stout [staᵒut] *s.* stout, m.; bière anglaise, f.; *adj.* fort; corpulent; vigoureux; substantiel; énergique; *stout-hearted*, vaillant, intrépide. ‖ *stoutness* [stoᵒutnis] *s.* vigueur, force; corpulence, f.; embonpoint, m.

stove [stoᵒuv] *s.* poêle, fourneau, m.; étuve, f.; *stovepipe*, tuyau de poêle.

stove [stoᵒuv] *pret., p. p. of to stave.*

stow [stoᵒu] *v.* mettre en place; installer; entasser; arrimer (naut.); *to stow away on a ship*, embarquer clandestinement; *stowage*, arrimage (naut.); *stowaway*, passager clandestin.

strabismus [strᵉbizmᵉs] *s.* strabisme, m.

straddle [stradᵊl] *v.* enfourcher; être à cheval sur; encadrer (mil.); se tenir à califourchon; biaiser (fig).

strafe [stréᶦf] *v.* bombarder; *strafing*, marmitage.

straggle [stragᵊl] *v.* traîner; rôder; s'écarter; rester en arrière; *straggler*, traînard, rôdeur.

straight [stréᶦt] *adj.* droit; direct; en bon état, en ordre; loyal; *adv.* directement, tout droit; immédiatement; loyalement; *to keep a straight* *face*, garder son sérieux ; *for two hours straight*, deux heures de suite ; *to keep somebody straight*, maintenir quelqu'un dans le devoir ; *keep straight on*. allez tout droit ; *straight away*, immédiatement ; *straight off*, d'emblée. ‖ **straighten** [-'n] v. redresser ; ranger. ‖ **straightforward** [-faurwᵉrd] *adj.* direct, droit ; sans détours ; *adv* directement ; tout droit, f. ‖ **straightness** [-nis] *s.* rectitude, f. ‖ **straightway** [-wéⁱ] *adv.* aussitôt, sur-le-champ, tout de suite.

strain [stréⁱn] v. tendre ; fouler (med.) ; forcer ; contraindre ; faire un effort ; suinter [liquid] ; *s.* effort, m. ; tension ; entorse, foulure ; fatigue excessive, f. ; *to strain oneself*, se surmener. ‖ **strainer** [-ᵉr] *s.* tamis, filtre, m. ; passoire, f.

strait [stréⁱt] *adj.* étroit ; *s.* détroit, m. ; *strait jacket*, camisole de force ; *the Straits of Dover*, le pas de Calais. ‖ **straiten** [-'n] v. resserrer ; mettre dans la gêne.

strand [strǎnd] v. (s')échouer (naut.) ; *s.* plage, grève, *Fr. Can.* batture, f. ; *stranded*, échoué [ship] ; en panne ; en plan ; décavé.

strand [strǎnd] *s.* toron [rope], m. ; v. toronner ; *strand of pearls*, collier de perles.

strange [stréⁱndj] *adj.* étrange ; bizarre ; inhabituel ; inconnu. ‖ **strangeness** [-nis] *s* étrangeté ; réserve, froideur, f. ‖ **stranger** [-ᵉr] *s.* étranger ; inconnu, m. ; *you are quite a stranger*, on ne vous voit plus.

strangle [strǎngg'l] v. étrangler ; étouffer. **strangulate** [strǎnggylêⁱt] v. étrangler (med.). ‖ **strangulation** [strǎnggylêⁱshᵉn] *s.* strangulation, f. ; étranglement, m.

strap [strap] *s.* courroie ; sangle ; lanière ; bande ; bride ; chape (mech.) ; étrivière, f. ; v. sangler ; ceinturer ; *breast strap*, bricole ; *chin strap*, jugulaire.

strapping [straping] *adj.* bien découplé.

stratagem [stratᵉdjᵉm] *s.* stratagème, m. ; ruse, f.

strategic [strᵉtîdjik] *adj.* stratégique. ‖ **strategist** [stratîdjist] *s.* stratège, m. ‖ **strategy** [stratᵉdji] *s.* stratégie, f.

stratification [stratifikêⁱshᵉn] *s.* stratification, f. ‖ **stratify** [stratifaⁱ] v. stratifier.

stratosphere [stratᵉsfîᵉr] *s.* stratosphère, f.

straw [straụ] *s.* paille, f. ; chalumeau, m. ; *adj.* de paille ; en paille ; *truss of straw*, botte de paille ; *it is the last straw !*, c'est le bouquet ! ; *straw hat*,

chapeau de paille ; *straw mattress*, paillasse. ‖ **strawberry** [-bèri] *s.* fraise, f. ; **strawberry-tree**, arbousier.

stray [stréⁱ] v. s'égarer ; s'éloigner ; *adj.* égaré ; fortuit ; accidentel ; *s.* animal errant ; vagabond, m. ; dispersion (electr.), f. ; *stray bullet*, balle perdue.

streak [strîk] *s.* rayure ; raie ; bande, f. ; v. rayer ; strier ; barioler ; *streak of lightning*, éclair.

stream [strîm] *s.* ruisseau ; flot ; courant ; fleuve, m. ; rivière, f. ; v. couler ; ruisseler, flotter [flag] ; *mountain stream*, torrent ; *a stream of cars*, un flot de voitures ; *to stream out*, sortir à flots. ‖ **streamer** [-ᵉr] *s.* banderole, f. ‖ **streamlined** [-laⁱnd] *adj.* fuselé ; profilé ; aérodynamique ; *Am.* abrégé, plus rapide.

street [strît] *s.* rue, f. ; *back street*, rue détournée, *main street*, artère principale ; *street door*, porte d'entrée. ‖ **streetcar** [-kâr] *s. Am.* tramway, m.

strength [strength] *s.* force ; intensité, f. ; effectif (mil.), m. ‖ **strengthen** [-ᵉn] v. fortifier ; affermir ; renforcer, consolider ; **strengthener**, fortifiant.

strenuous [strènyouᵉs] *adj.* énergique ; vif ; acharné ; actif.

streptomycin [streptomaⁱsin] *s.* streptomycine, f.

stress [strès] *s.* force ; violence [weather] ; tension ; pression ; insistance ; charge (mech.) ; contrainte, f. ; accent tonique ; effort, m. ; v. charger (mech.) ; insister ; accentuer ; *to lay the stress on*, mettre l'accent sur.

stretch [strètsh] v. tendre ; (s')étirer ; (s')étendre ; (se) déployer ; *s.* étendue ; extension ; portée ; élasticité ; section [roads], f. ; allongement ; étirage (mech.), m. ; *to stretch one's legs*, se dégourdir les jambes ; *at a stretch*, d'un trait. ‖ **stretcher** [-ᵉr] *s.* brancard ; tendeur [shoes] ; traversin [rowboat], m. ; civière, f. ; **stretcher-bearer**, brancardier.

strew [strou] v. semer ; joncher ; répandre. ‖ **strewn** [-n] *p. p. of* **to strew**.

stria [straⁱe] *s.* strie, f. ; **striate**, strié ; strier.

stricken [strikᵉn] *p. p. of* **to strike**, *adj.* frappé, atteint.

strict [strikt] *adj.* strict ; précis ; exact ; rigide ; sévère ; *in strict confidence*, sous le sceau du secret ; sous toute réserve. ‖ **strictness** [-nis] *s.* rigueur ; sévérité ; exactitude ; précision, f.

stridden [strid'n] *p. p. of* **to stride**.

stride [straⁱd] v. aller à grands pas ; enjamber ; enfourcher [horse] ; *s.* enjambée, f. ; grand pas, m.

strident [stra¹d'nt] *adj.* strident.

strife [stra¹f] *s.* lutte, f.; *at strife with*, en guerre avec.

strike [stra¹k] *v.* frapper; assener; cogner; sonner [clock]; saisir; tamponner; frotter [match]; conclure [bargain]; baisser [flag]; arrêter [account]; *v.* faire grève; *s* grève; matrice [printing]; frappe [coins], f.; coup, m.; *to strike off*, rayer, biffer, abattre; *to strike a balance*, établir un bilan; *how does he strike you?*, quelle impression vous fait-il?; *sit-down strike*, grève sur le tas; *slow-down strike*, grève perlée; *strike-breaker*, briseur de grève. ‖ **striker** [-ᵉʳ] *s.* gréviste; percuteur [firearm]; brosseur (mil.), m. ‖ **striking** [-ing] *adj.* frappant; remarquable; saisissant; en grève.

string [string] *s.* corde; ficelle; file; enfilade; kyrielle, f.; fil; cordon; lacet [shoes]; ruban; chapelet [onions], m.; *v.* garnir de cordes; tendre accorder [music]; enfiler [beads]; aligner; mettre, aller à la file; enlever les fils de; *to string together*, faire un chapelet de; *string of boats*, train de bateaux; *string of cars*, file de voitures; *to string up*, pendre **fiddle string**, corde de violon; **stringbean**, haricot vert; **stringy**, filandreux; visqueux.

strip [strip] *v.* dépouiller, déshabiller; (se) mettre à nu; écorcer [tree]; *to strip off*, ôter [dress]; **strip-tease**, déshabillage, strip-tease.

strip [strip] *s.* bande; bandelette; lanière; piste (aviat.), f.; lambeau; ruban, m.; **weather strip**, bourrelet [window].

stripe [stra¹p] *s.* raie, rayure; bande, f.; chevron; galon, m.; *v.* rayer; **striped**, à rayures, rayé.

stripling [stripling] *s.* adolescent, m.

strive [stra¹v] *v.* lutter; s'efforcer; tenter de; se démener; rivaliser (*with*, avec); *to strive to*, s'efforcer de. ‖ **striven** [striven] *p. p. of* to strive.

strode [strooᵘd] *pret. of* to stride.

stroke [strooᵘk] *s.* coup; choc; trait, m.; attaque; apoplexie, f.; *to row a long stroke*, allonger la nage (naut.); *stroke of a bell*, coup de cloche; **sunstroke**, coup de soleil.

stroke [strooᵘk] *v.* caresser; *s.* caresse, f.

stroll [strooᵘl] *v.* errer; se promener; *s.* promenade, flânerie, f.; *to stroll the streets*, flâner dans les rues; **stroller**, flâneur, vagabond.

strong [straung] *adj.* fort; solide; vigoureux, énergique; marqué, prononcé; *adv.* fort, fortement; *strong market*, marché ferme; **strong-willed**, décidé, volontaire. ‖ **stronghold** [-hooᵘld] *s.* place forte, f.; fort, m. ‖ **strongly** [-li] *adv.* fortement; énergiquement; fermement; vigoureusement; solidement; avec netteté.

strop [strâp] *s.* cuir à rasoir, m.; *v.* repasser, aiguiser.

strove [strooᵘv] *pret. of* to strive.

struck [strœk] *pret.*, *p. p. of* to **strike**; *adj.* frappé (*with*, de).

structural [strœktsher³l] *adj.* structural; morphologique. ‖ **structure?** [-shᵉʳ] *s.* structure, f.; bâtiment, immeuble, m.

struggle [strœg'l] *s.* lutte, f.; effort, m.; *v.* lutter, combattre; se démener; *to struggle on*, avancer péniblement; **struggler**, lutteur.

strum [strœm] *v.* jouailler (mus.).

strung [strœng] *pret.*, *p. p. of* to **string**.

strut [strœt] *v.* se pavaner; *s.* démarche orgueilleuse; entretoise, f.

stub [stœb] *s.* souche, f.; tronc; talon [check]; chicot [tooth]; mégot, m.; *v.* déraciner; buter contre; **stub pen**, plume à pointe émoussée.

stubble [stœb'l] *s.* chaume, m.; éteule barbe rude, f.; **stubbly hair**, cheveux en brosse.

stubborn [stœbᵉʳn] *adj.* têtu, entêté; opiniâtre; réfractaire; rétif [horse]; acharné [work]. ‖ **stubbornness** [-nis] *s.* entêtement, m.; obstination, f.

stubby [stœbi] *adj.* hérissé, hirsute [beard].

stucco [stœkooᵘ] *s.* stuc, m.; *v.* enduire de stuc.

stuck [stœk] *pret.*, *p. p. of* to **stick**; *adj.* **stuck-up**, affecté, poseur.

stud [stœd] *s.* poteau, montant; support; étai (naut.); contact (electr.); clou [nail]; bouton de chemise; tenon [bayonet], m.; *v.* clouter; parsemer.

stud [stœd] *s.* haras; étalon; chenil d'élevage, m.; **stud-farm**, haras.

student [styoudᵉnt] *s.* étudiant; élève, m.; **senior student**, Fr. Can. finissant. ‖ **studied** [stœdid] *adj.* étudié; apprêté, prémédité; versé (*in*, dans). ‖ **studio** [styoudiooᵘ] *s.* atelier; studio [radio], m. ‖ **studious** [styoudiᵉs] *adj.* studieux; appliqué; soigné. ‖ **study** [stœdi] *s.* étude; attention; préoccupation; méditation, f.; cabinet de travail, m.; *v.* étudier; faire ses études; réfléchir, chercher; *to study for an examination*, préparer un examen.

stuff [stœf] *s.* matière; étoffe, f.; tissu, m.; *v.* rembourrer; obstruer; calfater; empailler; farcir; *what stuff!*, quelle sottise! ; *stuffer*, empailleur. ‖ *stuffing* [-ing] *s.* bourre, étoupe, f.; rembourrage; empaillage, m.; farce, f. (culin.). ‖ *stuffy* [-i] *adj.* étouffant; qui sent le renfermé; calfeutré; collet monté.

stumble [stœmb'l] *v.* trébucher; broncher; faire un faux pas; *s.* faux pas, m.; *stumbling-block*, pierre d'achoppement.

stump [stœmp] *s.* tronçon; trognon [cabbage]; chicot [tooth]; moignon [limb]; bout [cigarette], m.; souche [tree]; *Am.* estrade de réunion publique, f.; *v.* dessoucher; faire une campagne électorale; marcher lourdement; embarrasser, coller; *to be up a stump*, être embarrassé; *to stump the country*, courir le pays pour une tournée électorale; *stumpy*, trapu.

stun [stœn] *v.* étourdir, assommer; *stunning*, épatant (fam.).

stung [stœng] *pret., p. p. of to sting.*

stunk [stœngk] *pret., p. p. of to stink.*

stunt [stœnt] *s.* acrobatie; nouvelle sensationnelle, f.; montage publicitaire; tour de force, m.; *v.* faire des acrobaties ou des tours.

stunt [stœnt] *v.* rabougrir; arrêter la croissance de.

stupefaction [styoupifaksh*e*n] *s.* stupéfaction, f. ‖ *stupefier* [styoupifa¹*e*r] *s.* stupéfiant, m. ‖ *stupefy* [styoup*e*fa¹] *v.* hébéter, abrutir; stupéfier (med.); frapper de stupeur.

stupendous [styoupœnd*e*s] *adj.* prodigieux, formidable.

stupid [styoupid] *adj.* stupide; sot; bête; *Fr. Can.* sans dessein. ‖ *stupidity* [styoupid*e*ti] *s.** stupidité; bêtise, f. ‖ *stupor* [styoup*e*r] *s.* stupeur, f.; engourdissement, m.

sturdiness [stē*r*dinis] *s.* robustesse; résolution, f. ‖ *sturdy* [stē*r*di] *adj.* robuste, vigoureux; *sturdy chap*, luron.

sturgeon [stē*r*dj*e*n] *s.* esturgeon, m.

stutter [stœt*e*r] *v.* bégayer; bredouiller; *stutterer* [-r*e*r] *s.* bègue, m. ‖ *stuttering* [-ring] *s.* bégaiement, m.; *adj.* bégayant.

sty [sta¹] *s.** porcherie, f.

sty [sta¹] *s.** orgelet (med.), m.

style [sta¹l] *s.* style; genre; type; modèle; cachet, chic, m.; manière, mode, f.; *v.* intituler, nommer, désigner; *stylish*, à la mode; chic; *stylist*, styliste; *stylistic*, stylistique; *stylus*, style.

subaltern [s*e*bault*e*rn] *s.* subalterne; subordonné, m.

subcommittee [sœbk*e*miti] *s.* sous-comité, m.; sous-commission, f.

subconscious [sœbkânsh*e*s] *s.* subconscient, m.

subdeacon [sœbdîk*e*n] *s.* sous-diacre, m.

subdivision [sœbd*e*vij*e*n] *s.* subdivision, f.; morcellement, m.

subdue [s*e*bdyou] *v.* subjuguer; réprimer; maîtriser; adoucir; assourdir; *subdued light*, demi-jour.

subject [sœbdjikt] *s.* sujet; individu, m.; matière question, f.; *adj.* assujetti; soumis, sujet, porté, subordonné (*to*, à); justiciable (*to*, de); [s*e*bdjèkt] *v.* assujettir, soumettre; exposer à; faire subir. ‖ *subjection* [-sh*e*n] *s.* sujétion; soumission, f. ‖ *subjective* [-tiv] *adj.* subjectif.

subjugate [sœbdj*e*gé¹t] *v.* subjuguer; asservir. *subjugation*, subjugation, asservissement.

subjunctive [s*e*bdjænktiv] *s.* subjonctif, m.

sublet [sœblèt] *v.* sous-louer.

sublimate [sœblimit] *adj.*, *s.* sublimé, m.; [-mé¹t] *v* sublimer. ‖ *sublime* [s*e*bla¹m] *adj* sublime.

submachine gun [sœbm*e*shîng*æ*n] *s.* mitraillette, f.

submarine [sœbm*e*rîn] *adj.* sous-marin; [sœbm*e*rîn] *s.* sous-marin, m.

submerge [s*e*bmē*r*dj] *v.* submerger; inonder, plonger. ‖ *submersible* [-sib'l] *adj.*, *s.* submersible, m.

submission [s*e*bmish*e*n] *s.* soumission; résignation, f. ‖ *submissive* [s*e*bmísiv] *adj.* soumis, résigné. ‖ *submit* [s*e*bmit] *v.* (se) soumettre; se résigner (*to*, à).

subordinate [s*e*baurd'nit] *adj.* subordonné, secondaire; *s.* subordonné; sous-ordre, m.; [-né¹t] *v.* subordonner (*to*, à); *subordination*, subordination.

suborn [sœbau*r*n] *v.* suborner; *suborner*, suborneur.

subpoena [s*e*bpîn*e*] *s.* citation de témoin; assignation, f.; *v.* citer; assigner.

subscribe [s*e*bskra¹b] *v.* souscrire; s'abonner (*for*, à); adhérer (*to*, à). ‖ *subscriber* [-*e*r] *s.* souscripteur; abonné, signataire; contractant, m. ‖ *subscription* [s*e*bskripsh*e*n] *s.* souscription; cotisation, f.; abonnement, m.

subsequent [sœbsikwènt] *adj.* subséquent; ultérieur; consécutif.

subservient [s*e*bsē*r*vi*e*nt] *adj.* utile; subordonné; servile.

subside [s*e*bsa¹d] *v.* s'apaiser; s'effondrer; tomber, laisser, diminuer.

subsidiary [s*e*bsidi*e*ri] *adj.* subsidiaire; mercenaire; *s.** auxiliaire, m. f.

subsidize [sᵆbsᵉdaɪz] v. subventionner; primer. ‖ **subsidy** [sᵆbsᵉdi] s.º subvention, f.; subside, m.

subsist [sᵉbsíst] v. subsister; exister; vivre; **subsistence**, subsistance.

substance [sᵆbstᵉns] s. substance; matière; ressources, f.; fond; essentiel, m. ‖ **substantial** [sᵉbstánshᵉl] adj. substantiel; réel; considérable; résistant, solide.

substantive [sᵆbstᵉntiv] s. substantif, m.; adj. explicite, effectif.

substitute [sᵆbstᵉtyout] v. substituer; remplacer; subroger (jur.); s. substitut; suppléant; remplaçant; succédané, m. ‖ **substitution** [sᵆbstᵉtyoushᵉn] s. substitution; suppléance; subrogation (jur.), f.; remplacement, m.

substructure [sᵆbstrᵆktshᵉʳ] s. infrastructure; base, f.; soubassement, m.

subtenancy [sᵆbténᵉnsi] s. sous-location, f. ‖ **subtenant** [-ᵉnt] s. sous-locataire, m.

subterfuge [sᵆbtᵉʳfyoudj] s. subterfuge, m.; échappatoire, f.

subterranean [sᵆbtᵉréⁱniᵉn] adj. souterrain.

subtilize [sᵆbtilaⁱz] v. sublimer; raffiner; alambiquer; ergoter.

subtle [sᵆtˡl] adj. subtil; ingénieux; habile; pénétrant. ‖ **subtlety** [-ti] s.º subtilité, f.

subtract [sᵉbtrakt] v. retrancher; soustraire. ‖ **subtraction** [sᵉbtrakshᵉn] s. soustraction; défalcation, f.

suburb [sᵆbᵉʳb] s. faubourg, m.; banlieue, f. ‖ **suburban** [sᵉbᵉʳbᵉn] adj. suburbain; de banlieue.

subvention [sᵉbvénshᵉn] s. subvention, f.

subversion [sᵉbvᵉʳshᵉn] s. subversion, f. ‖ **subversive** [-siv] adj. subversif. ‖ **subvert** [-ᵉt] v. renverser.

subway [sᵆbwéⁱ] s. Am. métropolitain; Br. passage souterrain, m.

succedaneous [sᵆksidéⁱniᵉs] adj. succédané.

succeed [sᵉksíd] v. succéder; remplacer; suivre; réussir (in, à). ‖ **success** [sᵉksès] s. succès, m. ‖ **successful** [-fᵉl] adj. heureux; prospère; réussi. ‖ **succession** [sᵉksèshᵉn] s. succession; suite; série; accession, f. ‖ **successive** [sᵉksésiv] adj. consécutif; successif. ‖ **successor** [sᵉksèsᵉʳ] s. successeur, m.

succinct [sᵉksíngkt] adj. succinct; **succinctness**, concision.

succo(u)r [sᵆkᵉʳ] s. secours, m.; v. secourir; **succo(u)rer**, secouriste.

succulence [sᵆkyᵉlᵉns] s. succulence, f. ‖ **succulent** [-nt] adj. succulent.

succumb [sᵉkœm] v. succomber; céder.

such [sœtsh] adj. tel; pareil; semblable; pron. tel; such as, tel que; such a friend, un tel ami; such patience, une telle patience; in such a way that, de telle sorte que; on such occasions, en pareils cas; such as it is, tel quel; such a one, un tel; suchlike, de ce genre.

suck [sœk] v. sucer; absorber; téter; to give suck to, allaiter; Am. sucker, poire, gobeur. ‖ **suckle** [-ˡl] v. allaiter; **suckling**, nourrisson. ‖ **suction** [sœkshᵉn] s. succion; aspiration, f.

sudden [sœdˡn] adj. soudain; imprévu; prompt; all of a sudden, tout à coup; suddenly, brusquement, subitement. ‖ **suddenness** [-nis] s. soudaineté; promptitude; précipitation, f.

suds [sœdz] s. pl. eau de savon, f.; to be in the suds, être dans l'ennui.

sue [sou] v. traduire en justice; plaider; solliciter; to sue for damages, intenter un procès en dommages-intérêts; to sue for counsel, solliciter un conseil.

suede [swéⁱd] s. suède; daim, m.

suet [souit] s. graisse de bœuf, f.; suif, m.

suffer [sᵆfᵉʳ] v. souffrir; supporter; subir; tolérer; essuyer [losses]; sufferer, patient, malade. ‖ **suffering** [-ring] s. souffrance; douleur, f.; adj. souffrant; dolent.

suffice [sᵉfaⁱs] v. suffire (à). ‖ **sufficiency** [sᵉfíshᵉnsi] s.º suffisance; capacité; aisance, f. ‖ **sufficient** [sᵉfíshᵉnt] adj. suffisant; compétent. ‖ **sufficiently** [-li] adv. suffisamment.

suffix [sᵆfiks] s. suffixe, m.

suffocate [sᵆfᵉkéⁱt] v. suffoquer; étouffer; asphyxier (med.). ‖ **suffocation** [sᵆfᵉkéⁱshᵉn] s. suffocation; asphyxie, f.

suffrage [sᵆfridj] s. suffrage, m.

suffuse [sᵉfyouz] v. inonder.

sugar [shougᵉʳ] s. sucre, m.; v. sucrer; granulated sugar, sucre semoule; lump sugar, sucre en morceaux; maple sugar, sucre d'érable; powdered sugar, sucre en poudre; sugar bowl, sucrier; sugar bush, Fr. Can. sucrerie; sugaring party, Fr. Can. partie de sucre; lump of sugar, morceau de sucre.

suggest [sᵉdjèst] v. suggérer; proposer. ‖ **suggestion** [-shᵉn] s. suggestion, f. ‖ **suggestive** [-iv] adj. suggestif.

suicide [souˢsaⁱd] s. suicide, m.; to commit suicide, se suicider.

suit [sout, syout] *s.* costume, complet; procès, m.; requête; poursuite (jur.); couleurs [cards], f.; *v.* adapter; assortir; accommoder; convenir à; plaire à; s'accorder; *that suits me,* ça me va; *to follow suit,* jouer de la même couleur, suivre le mouvement; *to bring suit,* intenter un procès; *suit yourself,* faites à votre gré. ‖ **suitable** [-ᵉb'l] *adj.* convenable; adapté; apte; *suitably,* convenablement; conformément (to, à). ‖ **suitcase** [-kéⁱs] *s.* valise, mallette, f.

suite [swît] *s.* suite; escorte; série, f.; *suite of rooms,* appartement; *suite of furniture,* ameublement.

suitor [soutᵉʳ, syoutᵉʳ] *s.* prétendant, amoureux; solliciteur; plaideur, m.

sulk [sœlk] *v.* bouder; *s.* bouderie, f.; *sulkiness,* bouderie, *sulky,* boudeur, maussade.

sullen [sœlin] *adj.* morose; renfrogné; taciturne.

sully [sœli] *v.* souiller; ternir.

sulphate [sœlféⁱt] *s.* sulfate, m. ‖ **sulphide** [-faⁱd] *s.* sulfure, m. ‖ **sulphur** [-fᵉʳ] *s.* soufre, m.; **sulphuric,** sulfurique; **sulphurous,** sulfureux.

sultan [sœlt'n] *s.* sultan, m. ‖ **sultana** [sœltânᵉ] *s.* sultane, f.; raisin (m.) de Smyrne.

sultry [sœltri] *adj.* étouffant; orageux; suffocant [heat].

sum [sœm] *s.* somme, f.; total; calcul; sommaire; summum, m.; *to sum up,* additionner; récapituler; *to work out a sum,* faire un calcul; *sum total,* total. ‖ **summarize** [sœmᵉraⁱz] *v.* résumer. ‖ **summary** [sœmᵉri] *s.** sommaire; abrégé; aperçu; relevé, m.; *adj.* sommaire; bref; résumé; expéditif.

summation [sᵉmeⁱshᵉn] *s.* addition, f.

summer [sœmᵉr] *s.* été, m.; *Indian summer,* été de la Saint-Martin, *Fr. Can.* été des sauvages; *adj.* estival; *v.* estiver.

summit [sœmit] *s.* sommet; faîte; comble, m.

summon [sœmᵉn] *v.* convoquer; sommer; assigner; poursuivre (jur.). ‖ **summons** [-z] *s. pl.* sommation; convocation; assignation; citation (jur.), f.

sump [sœmp] *s.* carter; puisard, m.

sumptuary [sœmptshouèri] *adj.* somptuaire. ‖ **sumptuous** [-shouᵉs] *adj.* somptueux, fastueux; *sumptuousness,* somptuosité.

sun [sœn] *s.* soleil, m.; *v.* exposer au soleil; (se) chauffer au soleil; *sunbeam,* rayon de soleil; *sunburn,* coup de soleil, hâle; *Sunday,* dimanche; *sun-dial,* cadran solaire.

sunder [sœndᵉr] *v.* séparer.

sundown [sœndaᵒun] *s.* coucher de soleil, m.

sundries [sœndriz] *s. pl.* articles divers; faux frais, m. pl. ‖ **sundry** [-i] *adj.* divers, varié.

sunfish [sœnfish] *s.** poisson-lune; *Fr. Can.* crapet-soleil, m.; **sunflower,** tournesol; **sunlight,** lumière du soleil; **sunlight;** **sunny,** ensoleillé, radieux, rayonnant, *sunny side,* bon côté; **sunproof,** inaltérable au soleil; **sunrise,** lever du soleil; **sunset,** coucher du soleil; **sunshine,** clarté du soleil; **sunspot,** tache solaire; **sunstroke,** insolation.

super [soupᵉr] *s.* figurant, m.

superabundance [soupᵉrᵉbœndᵉns] *s.* surabondance, f.; **superabundant,** surabondant.

superannuated [soupᵉrᵉnyoué¹tid] *adj.* démodé.

superb [soupᵉrb] *adj.* superbe; majestueux; somptueux.

supercargo [soupᵉrkârgoᵒu] *s.* subrécargue, m.

supercharger [soupᵉrtshârdjᵉr] *s.* supercompresseur, m.

supercilious [soupᵉrsíliᵉs] *adj.* sourcilleux; hautain.

superficial [soupᵉrfishᵉl] *adj.* superficiel. ‖ **superficies** [-shìz] (*pl.* **superficies**) *s.* superficie, f.

superfluity [soupᵉrflouᵉti] *s.* superfluité, f.; superflu, m. ‖ **superfluous** [-flouᵉs] *adj.* superflu.

superhuman [soupᵉrhyoumᵉn] *adj.* surhumain.

superintend [souprintènd] *v.* diriger; surveiller. ‖ **superintendence** [-ᵉns] *s.* surveillance; surintendance, f.; contrôle, m. ‖ **superintendent** [-ᵉnt] *s.* surintendant; chef, m.

superior [sᵉpiriᵉr] *adj.,* *s.* supérieur. ‖ **superiority** [sᵉpiriaurᵉti] *s.* supériorité, f.

superlative [sᵉpᵉʳlᵉtiv] *adj.,* *s.* superlatif.

superman [soupᵉrmᵉn] (*pl.* **supermen**) *s.* surhomme, m.

supernatural [soupᵉrnatshrᵉl] *adj.* surnaturel; **supernaturalness,** surnaturel.

supernumerary [soupᵉrnyoumᵉrèri] *s.** surnuméraire; excédent, m.

superposable [syoupᵉrpoᵒuzeb'l] *adj.* superposable; **superpose,** superposer; **superposition,** superposition.

supersede [soupᵉrsîd] *v.* supplanter; remplacer; surseoir à (jur.).

supersonic [soupᵉrsoᵒᵘnik] *adj.* supersonique.

superstition [soupᵉrstíshᵉn] *s.* superstition, f. ‖ **superstitious** [-shᵉs] *adj.* superstitieux.

superstructure [soupᵉrstrœktshᵉr] *s.* superstructure, f.; accastillage (naut.), m.

supervise [soupᵉrva�¹z] *v.* surveiller; diriger. ‖ **supervisor** [-pᵉrvaᵢzᵉr] surveillant; contrôleur; directeur, m. ‖ **supervision** [soupᵉrvíjᵉn] *s.* surveillance; inspection; direction, f.; contrôle, m.

supine [soupaᵢn] *s.* supin, m.; [soupaᵢn] *adj.* couché sur le dos; en pente; indolent.

supper [sœpᵉr] *s.* souper, m.; *the Lord's Supper*, la Cène.

supplant [sᵉplánt] *v.* supplanter.

supple [sœp'l] *adj.* souple; flexible; docile, soumis.

supplement [sœplᵉmᵉnt] *s.* supplément; appendice, m.; annexe, f.; [-mᵉnt] *v.* suppléer; compléter; **supplementary**, supplémentaire.

suppliant [sœplíᵉnt] *adj., s.* suppliant. ‖ **supplicate** [sœpliké¹t] *v.* supplier; implorer; **supplication**, supplication.

supplier [sᵉplaᵢᵉr] *s.* fournisseur, m. ‖ **supplies** [sᵉplaᵢz] *s. pl.* approvisionnements, m. pl.; fournitures, f. pl.; *food supplies*, vivres; *medical supplies*, matériel sanitaire. ‖ **supply** [sᵉplaᵢ] *s.* ravitaillement, m.; alimentation; fourniture, f.; *v.* approvisionner; ravitailler; *supply base*, centre de ravitaillement; *supply and demand*, l'offre et la demande.

support [sᵉpoᵒᵘrt] *v.* soutenir; appuyer; entretenir; *s.* appui; entretien; support (techn.), m.; adhésion, f.; *to support oneself*, gagner sa vie. ‖ **supporter** [-ᵉr] *s.* partisan; soutien; supporter; adhérent, m.; jarretière, f.

suppose [sᵉpoᵒᵘz] *v.* supposer; s'imaginer; prendre pour. ‖ **supposed** [-d] *adj.* supposé; présumé; imaginaire. ‖ **supposition** [sœpᵉzíshᵉn] *s.* supposition; hypothèse, f.

suppository [sᵉpâzᵉtoᵒᵘri] *s.* suppositoire, m.

suppress [sᵉprès] *v.* supprimer; réprimer [revolt]; étouffer [voice]. ‖ **suppression** [sᵉprèshᵉn] *s.* suppression; répression, f.

suppurate [sœpyouré¹t] *v.* suppurer; *suppuration*, suppuration.

supremacy [sᵉprèmᵉsi] *s.* suprématie, f.; *air supremacy*, maîtrise de l'air. ‖ **supreme** [sᵉprîm] *adj.* suprême; souverain.

surcharge [sᵉrshâdj] *s.* surcharge; surtaxe; majoration, f.

sure [shouᵉr] *adj.* sûr; assuré; certain; solide, stable; *adv.* sûrement; *sure enough*, en effet, sans doute; *be sure and come*, ne manquez pas de venir. ‖ **surely** [-li] *adv.* assurément; certainement; sans faute. ‖ **surety** [-ti] *s.** sûreté; certitude; caution (jur.), f.; garant (jur.), m.

surf [sᵉrf] *s.* ressac; brisants, m.

surface [sᵉrfis] *s.* surface; superficie, f.; extérieur, dehors, m.; *v.* apprêter; revêtir; aplanir; remonter à la surface (naut.).

surfeit [sᵉrfit] *s.* excès, m.; satiété, f.; *v.* rassasier; écœurer; dégoûter; se gorger.

surge [sᵉrdj] *s.* lame; vague; houle, f.; *v.* être houleux [sea]; se soulever [waters]; monter sur la vague (naut.); surgir.

surgeon [sᵉrdjᵉn] *s.* chirurgien; médecin (mil.; naut.), m. ‖ **surgery** [-djᵉri] *s.* chirurgie; clinique, f.; cabinet; dispensaire, m.; *surgery-hours*, heures de consultation. ‖ **surgical** [-djik'l] *adj.* chirurgical.

surly [sᵉrli] *adj.* maussade; renfrogné; hargneux.

surmise [sᵉrmaᵢz] *v.* soupçonner; supposer; *s.* supposition; conjecture, f.

surmount [sᵉrmaᵒᵘnt] *v.* surmonter; franchir; dépasser; vaincre.

surname [sᵉrné¹m] *s.* nom de famille, m.

surpass [sᵉrpás] *v.* surpasser; excéder; franchir; *surpassing*, excellent; éminent.

surplice [sᵉrplis] *s.* surplis, m.

surplus [sᵉrplœs] *s.** surplus; excédent, m.; plus-value, f.; *adj.* excédentaire; *surplus property*, matériel en excédent; *surplus stock*, stock soldé.

surprise [sᵉrpraᵢz] *s.* surprise, f.; étonnement, m.; *v.* surprendre; prendre en flagrant délit; *surprising*, surprenant.

surrender [sᵉrèndᵉr] *s.* capitulation; reddition; abdication (jur.); restitution; concession, f.; abandon, m.; *v.* rendre; céder; (se) livrer; capituler; renoncer à; s'abandonner.

surreptitious [sœrᵉptíshᵉs] *adj.* subreptice.

surround [sᵉraᵒᵘnd] *v.* entourer; environner; cerner; *surrounding*, environnant. ‖ **surroundings** [-ingz] *s. pl.* alentours, m. pl.; entourage, m.

surtax [sᵉrtaks] *s.* surtaxe, f.; *v.* surtaxer.

survey [sĕrvé¹] *s.* examen; arpentage [land], m.; vue; inspection; étude; expertise; levée de plans, f.; [sĕ'vé¹] *v.* examiner; arpenter; lever le plan de; hydrographier; cadastre. || **surveying** [-ing] *s.* relevé de plans, m.; expertise, f.; *land surveying*, arpentage, géodésie; *naval surveying*, hydrographie. || **surveyor** [sĕrvé¹ᵉr] *s.* arpenteur géomètre; ingénieur topographe, m.

survival [sᵉrva¹v'l] *s.* survivance; survie, f. || **survive** [sᵉrva¹v] *v.* survivre. || **survivor** [-ᵉr] *s.* survivant; rescapé, m.

susceptibility [sᵉsèptᵉbíl'ti] *s.*° susceptibilité, f. || **susceptible** [sᵉsèptᵉb'l] *adj.* susceptible; sensible (*to*, à); capable; accessible (*of*, à).

suspect [sœspèkt] *s.* suspect, m.; [sᵉspèkt] *v.* soupçonner; suspecter; s'imaginer.

suspend [sᵉspènd] *v.* suspendre; interrompre; surseoir (jur.). || **suspenders** [-ᵉrz] *s. pl.* bretelles; jarretelles, f. pl.; fixe-chaussettes, m.

suspense [sᵉspèns] *s.* suspens; doute; suspense [cinema], m.; indécision, f. || **suspension** [sᵉspènshᵉn] *s.* suspension; surséance (jur.), f.; *suspension-bridge*, pont suspendu.

suspicion [sᵉspíshᵉn] *s.* soupçon; doute, m.; suspicion, f. || **suspicious** [-shᵉs] *adj.* soupçonneux; suspect.

sustain [sᵉsté¹n] *v.* soutenir; éprouver [loss]; subir [injury]; *to sustain oneself by*, se donner du courage en; *sustaining*, soutènement (arch.); fortifiant (med.). || **sustenance** [sœstᵉnᵉns] *s.* subsistance, f.; aliments, m. pl.

sutler [sœtlᵉr] *s.* cantinier, m.; vivandière, f.

suture [soutshᵉr] *s.* suture, f.

suzerain [souzᵉre¹n] *s.* suzerain, m.; *suzerainty*, suzeraineté.

swab [swâb] *s.* torchon; écouvillon (naut.); tampon d'ouate, m.; *v.* écouvillonner.

swaddle [swâd'l] *v.* emmailloter; *swaddling-clothes*, maillot, langes.

swagger [swagᵉr] *v.* crâner; fanfaronner; se pavaner.

swain [swé¹n] *s.* galant, prétendant, m.; berger, m. (obsolete).

swallow [swâloᵘ] *s.* hirondelle, f.; *swallow-tail coat*, queue-de-pie.

swallow [swâloᵘ] *v.* avaler; ingurgiter; endurer; *s.* gorgée, f.

swam [swam] *pret. of* **to swim**.

swamp [swâmp] *s.* marécage; marais, m.; *v.* submerger; faire chavirer; embourber; *swamped with work*, débordé de travail; *swampy*, marécageux.

swan [swân] *s.* cygne, m.

swap [swâp] *v.* troquer; échanger; *s.* troc, m.

swarm [swaurm] *s.* essaim, m.; nuée, f.; *v.* fourmiller; essaimer.

swarthy [swaurzhi] *adj.* basané.

swash [swâsh] *s.*° clapotis, m.; *v.* clapoter; *swashbuckler*, fanfaron.

swastika [swâstikᵉ] *s.* croix gammée, f.; svastika, m.

swat [swât] *v.* écraser; taper; *s.* coup, m.

swathe [swé¹zh] *s.* maillot, m.; *v. Br.* emmailloter.

sway [swé¹] *v.* osciller; ballotter; se balancer; gouverner; régir; influencer; *s.* balancement; empire, m.; influence; autorité, f.

swear [swèᵉr] *v.*° jurer, *Fr. Can.* sacrer, blasphémer; (faire) prêter serment; *to swear at*, maudire; *to swear in*, assermenter; *to swear to*, attester sous serment; *to swear by*, jurer par; se fier à; *swear word*, juron, *Fr. Can.* sacre, blasphème.

sweat [swèt] *s.* sueur; transpiration, f.; suintement; ressuage, m.; *v.* suer; transpirer; suinter. || **sweater** [swètᵉr] *s.* sudorifique; exploiteur; chandail, m. || **sweatiness** [-inis] moiteur, f.; *sweating*, sudation, suée; suintement; exploitation (fam.). || *sweaty*, en sueur, suant; moite; pénible.

Swede [swîd] *s.* Suédois. || **Sweden** [swîd'n] *s.* Suède, f. || **Swedish** [swîdish] *adj.* suédois.

sweep [swîp] *v.*° balayer; ramoner; draguer; *s.* balayage; balayeur; ramoneur, m.; courbe; étendue, f.; *to sweep by*, glisser, passer rapidement. || **sweeper** [-ᵉr] *s.* balayeur; ramoneur, m.; *carpet sweeper*, balai mécanique. || *sweeping* [-ing] *s.* balayage; ramonage; dragage, m.; *pl.* balayures, f.; *adj.* rapide; complet [victory].

sweet [swît] *adj.* doux; sucré; parfumé; mélodieux; suave; gentil; délicieux; frais [milk]; sans sel [butter]; *s.* mets sucré; entremets; dessert; bonbon, m.; *sweetbread*, ris de veau; *sweetbrier*, églantier; *sweet pea*, pois de senteur; *sweet potato*, patate; *sweet-shop*, confiserie; *to have a sweet tooth*, aimer les douceurs. || **sweeten** [-'n] *v.* sucrer; adoucir; parfumer; assainir. || **sweetheart** [-hârt] *s.* amoureux, m.; petite amie, *Fr. Can.* blonde, f. || **sweetness** [-nis] *s.* douceur; gentillesse, f.

swell [swèl] v.* enfler; gonfler; (se) tuméfier; se pavaner; s. houle [sea], f.; gonflement, m.; adj. Am. remarquable; épatant; chic; to have a swelled head, se donner des airs. ‖ swelling [-ing] s. enflure; boursouflure; protubérance; crue [river], f.

swelter [swèlter] v. être étouffant [air]; étouffer de chaleur; être en nage; s. chaleur étouffante, f.

swept [swèpt] pret., p. p. of to sweep.

swerve [swër̄v] v. faire un écart, une embardée; se dérober [horse]; s. écart, m.; embardée; incartade [horse]; dérive, f.

swift [swift] adj. rapide; prompt. ‖ swiftness [-nis] s. rapidité; vélocité; promptitude, f.

swig [swig] v. lamper; s. lampée, f.

swill [swil] v. laver à grande eau; lamper, entonner (colloq.); s. lavage, m.; eaux grasses, f. pl.; ordure, f. (fig.); lampée, f. (colloq.).

swim [swim] v.* nager; s. nage, f.; to swim across, traverser à la nage; my head swims, la tête me tourne; swim suit, maillot. ‖ swimmer [-er] s. nageur, m.; nageuse, f. ‖ swimming [-ing] s. natation, nage, f.; swimming pool, piscine.

swindle [swind'l] s. escroquerie, f.; v. escroquer; swindler, escroc.

swine [swaïn] s. porc, cochon, m.; swineherd, porcher.

swing [swing] v.* se balancer; pivoter; être suspendu; brandir; branler; lancer [propeller] (aviat.); Am. donner un coup de poing à; s. balancement; tour; évitage (naut.); libre cours, libre essor; entrain, m.; oscillation; amplitude; escarpolette, balançoire, f.; to swing at anchor éviter sur l'ancre (naut.); to swing back, se rabattre; to be in full swing, battre son plein; swing-back, revirement; swing-gate, tourniquet, barrière pivotante; swing-round, tête-à-queue.

swinish [swaïnish] adj. grossier, bestial; immonde; de pourceau; swinishly, salement.

swipe [swaïp] v.* cogner; chaparder (pop.); s. coup violent, m.

swirl [swër̄l] s. remous, tourbillon, m.; v. (faire) tourbillonner.

swish [swish] v. cingler; siffler [whip]; susurrer; s. bruit cinglant; susurrement, m.

Swiss [swis] adj., s. suisse.

switch [switsh] s.* badine; aiguille (railw.), f.; commutateur (electr.), m.; v. cingler; aiguiller (railw.); to switch off, couper le courant (electr.); to switch on, mettre le contact (electr.);

switchback, montagnes russes; **switchboard**, tableau de distribution (electr.), standard (teleph.); switchboard operator, standardiste; **switchman**, aiguilleur (railw.).

Switzerland [switserlend] s. Suisse, f.

swivel [swiv'l] s. tourniquet, pivot; tourillon, m.; v. pivoter; swivelseat, siège tournant.

swizzle [swiz'l] s. cocktail, m.; swizzle-stick, marteau à champagne.

swob [swâb], see swab.

swollen [swooulen] p. p. of to swell.

swoon [swoun] v. s'évanouir; s. évanouissement, m.; syncope; faiblesse, f.

swoop [swoup] v. fondre; foncer (on, sur); s. attaque, ruée; descente subite, brusque chute sur; at one swoop, d'un seul coup.

swop, see swap.

sword [saur̄d] s. épée, f.; sabre; glaive, m.; to draw the sword, dégainer; to put to the sword, passer au fil de l'épée; sword-belt, ceinturon; sword hilt, poignée de l'épée; swordplay, escrime.

swore [swoour̄] pret. of to swear. ‖ sworn [-n] p. p. of to swear.

swum [swœm] p. p. of to swim.

swung [swœng] pret., p. p. of to swing.

sycamore [sikemoour̄] s. sycomore, m.

syllable [sileb'l] s. syllabe, f.

syllogism [siledjizem] s. syllogisme, m.

sylph [silf] s. sylphe, m.; sylphide, f.

symbiosis [simbioousis] s. symbiose, f.

symbol [simbel] s. symbole; signe, m.; symbolic, symbolique; symbolize, symboliser.

symmetrical [simètrik'l] adj. symétrique.

sympathetic [simpethètik] adj. sympathique; compatissant. ‖ sympathize [simp'thaïz] v. sympathiser; compatir. ‖ sympathy [-thi] s.* sympathie; compassion, f.; condoléances, f. pl.

symphony [simfeni] s.* symphonie, f.

symptom [simtem] s. symptôme; indice, m. ‖ symptomatic [simptematik] adj. symptomatique.

synagogue [sinegaug] s. synagogue, f.

synchronize [singkrenaïz] v. synchroniser; être synchronique; synchronizer, synchroniseur; synchronous, synchronique.

syncope [sìngk°pi] *s.* syncope (med.), f.

syndicate [sìndikit] *s.* syndicat, m.; [-ké¹t] *v.* (se) syndiquer; vendre à un organisme de diffusion littéraire; *newspaper syndicate*, syndicat des périodiques, organisme de diffusion du livre.

synod [sìn°d] *s.* synode, m.

synonym [sìn°nim] *s.* synonyme, m. || **synonymous** [sìnán°m°s] *adj.* synonyme (*with*, de).

syntax [sìntaks] *s.* syntaxe, f.

synthesis [sìnth°sis] (pl. *syntheses*) *s.* synthèse, f.; **synthetic**, synthétique; **synthetics**, plastiques.

syphilis [sìfilis] *s.* syphilis, f.

Syria [sìri°] *s.* Syrie, f. || **Syrian** [-n] *adj.*, *s.* syrien.

syringe [sìrìndj] *s.* seringue, f.

system [sìst°m] *s.* système; réseau (railw.); dispositif, m.; méthode, f.; **communications system**, réseau de transmissions. || **systematic(al)** [sìst°matik('l)] *adj.* systématique, méthodique; **systematize**, systématiser.

T

tab [tab] *s.* écusson, m.; étiquette [baggage], f.; **index tab**, onglet; *Am.* **to keep tabs on**, ne pas perdre de vue.

tabernacle [tab°nak] *s.* tabernacle, m.

table [té¹b'l] *s.* table; tablette, f.; tableau; catalogue; plateau (mech.), m.; **billiard table**, billard; **card table**, table de jeu; **extension table**, table à rallonges; **operating table**, table d'opérations; **tablecloth**, nappe; **table land**, plateau (geogr.); **tablespoonful**, cuillerée à bouche; **tableware**, articles de table; **tablewater**, eau de table; **table of contents**, table des matières.

tablet [tàblit] *s.* tablette; plaque commémorative; pastille, f.; comprimé (med.); bloc-notes, m.

tabloid [tàblo¹d] *s.* **Br.** comprimé (med.); *Am.* journal à sensation, m.

taboo [t°bou] *adj.*, *s.* tabou, m.; *v.* proscrire.

tabular [tàby°l°r] *adj.* plat; tabulaire. || **tabulate** [tàby°lé¹t] *v.* disposer en tableaux; cataloguer; **tabulator**, tabulateur.

tachometer [t°kâm°t°r] *s.* tachymètre; compte-tours, m.

tacit [tàsit] *adj.* tacite.

taciturn [tàs°tër°n] *adj.* taciturne.

tack [tak] *s.* semence de tapissier; bordée (naut.); ligne de conduite, f.; *v.* clouer; bâtir, faufiler; louvoyer; unir; annexer.

tackle [tàk'l] *s.* attirail; palan; appareaux (naut.), m.; poulie, f.; *v.* accrocher; empoigner; aborder; s'attaquer (*to*, à); **fishing tackle**, articles de pêche.

tact [takt] *s.* tact; toucher, m.; **tactful**, délicat; plein de tact; **tactless**, sans tact, indiscret; **tactlessness**, manque de tact.

tactical [taktik'l] *adj.* tactique. || **tactics** [taktiks] *s.* tactique, f.

tactile [takt'l] *adj.* tactile; tangible.

tadpole [tadpo°ul] *s.* têtard, m.

taenia [tìni°] *s.* ténia; bandage, m.

taffeta [tàfit°] *s.* taffetas, m.

taffy [tàfi] *s.* * caramel, m.; *Fr. Can.* tire, f.; **maple taffy**, *Fr. Can.* tire d'érable.

tag [tag] *s.* ferret; tirant [boots], m.; étiquette [baggage], f.; *v.* attacher une fiche (or une étiquette) à; coller; marquer; **to tag after**, suivre comme une ombre.

tag [tag] *s.* chat [game], m.

tail [té¹l] *s.* queue; basque; pile [coin], f.; bout, manche [plow]; arrière [cart], m.; *v.* finir; *Am.* suivre; filer; **tail-piece**, cul-de-lampe; **tail-spin**, vrille (aviat.); **tail-wobble**, queue-de-poisson [autom.].

tailor [té¹l°r] *s.* tailleur; **ladies' tailor**, tailleur pour dames.

taint [té¹nt] *s.* tache, souillure; tare; corruption, f.; *v.* vicier; ternir; (se) gâter; (se) corrompre; **taintless**, pur, sans tache.

take [té¹k] *v.* * prendre, saisir; porter; ôter; conduire; accepter; amener, emmener; retrancher; considérer; contenir; faire [walk]; emprunter [passage]; suivre [road]; passer [examination]; souscrire [shares]; falloir [time]; *s.* prise; pêche, f.; **to take aim**, viser; **to take away**, emporter; **to take care**, prendre garde; **to take care of**, prendre soin de; **to take a chance**, courir un risque; **to take cover, to take shelter**, s'abriter; **to take effect**, entrer en vigueur; **to take hold of**, s'emparer de; **to take from**, ôter de; **to take heart**, reprendre courage; **to take in**, faire entrer, inclure, mettre dedans; **to take in water**, faire de l'eau; **to**

take into account, tenir compte; *to take leave*, prendre congé; *to take notice of*, prêter attention à; *to take off*, enlever, ôter; décoller (aviat.); *to take oneself off*, décamper; *to take on*, embaucher, conduire; *to take out*, (faire) sortir; *to take over*, prendre à sa charge; prendre possession de, prendre la succession de; *to take prisoner*, faire prisonnier; *to take stock*, faire l'inventaire; *to take the sun*, prendre un bain de soleil; *to take trouble*, se donner de la peine; *to take turns*, passer à tour de rôle; *to take unawares*, prendre au dépourvu; *take-off*, décollage (aviat.); caricature. ‖ *taken* [-ᵊn] *p. p. of to take*. ‖ *taking* [-ing] *s.* prise, f.; *taking-in*, diminution; *taking-off*, élan; décollage (aviat.); *taking-out*, extraction.

talcum [talkᵊm] *s.* talc, m.

tale [téᵉl] *s.* conte, récit; dénombrement, compte, m.; *to tell tales*, rapporter, dénoncer; *talebearer*, rapporteur.

talent [talᵉnt] *s.* talent, m.; *talented*, doué, de talent.

talesman [téᵉlîzmᵉn] (*pl.* talesmen) *s.* juré suppléant, m.

taleteller [téᵉltèlᵉr] *s.* conteur; rapporteur, m.

talisman [talizmᵉn] *s.* talisman, m.

talk [tauk] *v.* parler; causer; s'entretenir; *s.* conversation, f.; entretien; propos; bavardage; on-dit, m.; *to get talked about*, faire parler de soi; *small talk*, banalités; *to talk into*, persuader de; *to talk out of*, dissuader de; *to talk over*, discuter; *matter for talk*, sujet de conversation; *to be the talk of the town*, être la fable du pays; *table talk*, propos de table. ‖ *talkative* [-ᵉtiv] *adj.* bavard. ‖ *talker* [-ᵉr] *s.* bavard; fanfaron, m. ‖ *talking* [-ing] *s.* conversation, f.; bavardage, m.; *talking-to*, semonce.

tall [toul] *adj.* grand; haut; *how tall are you?* quelle taille avez-vous?; *tall tale*, conte à dormir debout. ‖ *tallboy* [-boᵉl] *s.* commode, f.; chiffonnier [furniture], m.

tallow [taloᵒu] *s.* suif, m.; *v.* suiffer; suager; *tallow candle*, chandelle.

tally [tali] *s.* taille; entaille; marque, étiquette, f.; pointage, m.; *v.* concorder; s'accorder; *Am.* compter, calculer; *tally shop*, magasin où l'on vend à crédit.

talon [talᵉn] *s.* serre; griffe, f.; talon, m. [check].

tambour [tambouʳ] *s.* tambour, m.; *tambourine*, tambourin.

tame [téᵉm] *adj.* apprivoisé; domestique; anodin; terne; *v.* apprivoiser; domestiquer; dompter; *to grow tame*,

s'apprivoiser; *tameless*, indomptable; *tameness*, docilité; pusillanimité; banalité, platitude; *tamer*, dompteur.

tam o' shanter [tamᵉshàntᵉr] *s.* béret, m.

tamper [tàmpᵉr] *v.* se mêler (*with*, de); tripoter, falsifier; toucher (*with*, à); essayer de suborner.

tan [tàn] *s.* tan; hâle, m.; *adj.* jaunebrun, hâlé, couleur feu; *v.* tanner; bronzer; rosser (fam.).

tandem [tàndᵉm] *adj.* en flèche; *tandem bicycle*, tandem.

tang [tàng] *s.* goût fort, m.

tangent [tàndjᵉnt] *adj.* tangent; *s.* tangente, f.

tangerine [tàndjᵉrîn] *s.* mandarine, f.

tangible [tàndjᵉb'l] *adj.* tangible.

Tangiers [tàndjiᵉr] *s.* Tanger, m.

tangle [tàng'l] *s.* enchevêtrement; fourré; fouillis, m.; affaire embrouillée, f.; *v.* embrouiller; (s')enchevêtrer.

tango [tangoᵒu] *s.* tango, m.

tank [tàngk] *s.* citerne, f.; réservoir; bidon; tank, char (mil.), m.; *auxiliary tank*, nourrice [motor]; *gasoline tank*, réservoir à essence, container, bac; *tank destroyer*, engin antichar. ‖ *tankard* [-ᵉd] *s.* chope, f. ‖ *tanker* [-ᵉr] *s.* bateau-citerne, m.; *oil-tanker*, pétrolier.

tanner [tanᵉr] *s.* tanneur, m. ‖ *tannery* [-ᵉri] *s.* tannerie, f. ‖ *tanning* [-ing] *s.* tannage, m.

tantalize [tànt'la'z] *v.* tenter; tourmenter.

tantamount [tantᵉmaᵒunt] *adj.* équivalent.

tantrum [tàntrᵉm] *s.* accès de colère, de mauvaise humeur, m.

tap [tap] *s.* tape, f.; *v.* taper, tapoter.

tap [tap] *s.* fausset; robinet; taraud, m.; *v.* mettre en perce; tarauder; faire une ponction (med.); capter (telegr.); *on tap*, en perce.

tape [téᵉp] *s.* ruban, lacet, m.; bande, f.; *v.* mettre un ruban à; ficeler; border; maroufler (aviat.); *insulating tape*, chatterton (electr.); *measuring tape*, mètre souple, *Fr. Can.* galon; *paper tape*, bande de papier gommé; *red tape*, paperasserie administrative; *tape-recorder*, magnétophone; *tapeworm*, ténia (med.).

taper [téᵉpᵉr] *s.* bougie; cire, f.; cierge; cône (techn.), m.; *v.* effiler; fuseler; *tapered*, *tapering*, conique; en pointe; effilé; *tapering trousers*, fuseaux.

tapestry [tapistri] *s.** tapisserie, f.; *v.* orner de tapisserie.

tapioca [tapio°uk°] *s.* tapioca, m.

tapir [té¹per] *s.* tapir, m.

tappet [tapit] *s.* taquet; butoir, m.

tar [târ] *s.* goudron, m.; *v.* goudronner; bitumer; *tar paper*, carton goudronné; *tarry*, goudronné.

tardy [târdi] *adj.* lent; tardif, traînard; nonchalant; en retard.

tare [tèer] *s.* tare (comm.), f.; *v.* tarer.

tare [tèer] *s.* ivraie, f.

target [târgit] *s.* cible, f.; objectif, but, m.

tariff [tarif] *s.* tarif, m.

tarmac [târmak] *s.* macadam, m.; piste (f.) d'envol.

tarnish [târnish] *v.* (se) ternir; *s.* ternissure, f.

tarpaulin [târpaulin] *s.* prélart, m.; bâche, f.

tarry [tari] *v.* s'attarder; demeurer; *to tarry for someone*, attendre quelqu'un.

tart [târt] *adj.* âcre, âpre; acide; piquant; acariâtre.

tart [târt] *s.* tarte, f.; grue (pop.), f.

tartar [târter] *s.* tartre, m.

tartlet [târtlit] *s.* tartelette, f.

task [task] *s.* tâche; besogne; mission (mil.), f.; ouvrage; devoir, m.; *v.* imposer une tâche à; charger.

tassel [tas'l] *s.* gland; tasseau, m.

taste [té¹st] *s.* goût; penchant, m.; *v.* goûter; sentir; *to taste of*, avoir goût de; *tasteful*, de bon goût; *tasteless*, insipide, fade; sans goût; *taster*, dégustateur; tâte-vin; *tasty*, savoureux.

tatter [tater] *s.* haillon, lambeau, m.; guenille, f.; *tattered*, déguenillé.

tatting [tating] *s.* frivolité, broderie, f.

tattle [tat'l] *v.* bavarder; *s.* cancan, m.; *tattle-tale*, rapporteur.

tattoo [t°tou] *s.* sonnerie de la retraite (mil.), f.

tattoo [t°tou] *s.* tatouage, m.; *v.* tatouer.

taught [taut] *pret., p. p. of* **to teach**.

taunt [taunt] *s.* insulte, invective, f.; reproche, m.; *v.* insulter; critiquer; blâmer; taquiner.

tavern [tavern] *s.* taverne, auberge, f.; bar, cabaret, m.; *tavern-haunter*, pilier de bistrot; *tavern-keeper*, cabaretier.

tawdry [taudri] *adj., s.* clinquant, m.

tawny [tauni] *adj.* fauve, feu [color]; hâlé, bronzé [skin].

tax [taks] *s.* impôt, m.; taxe; contribution, f.; droit, m.; *v.* imposer; taxer; accuser (*with*, de); sermonner, blâmer; mettre à contribution; *direct tax*, contribution directe; *excise tax*, droit de régie; *floor tax*, taxe sur la surface corrigée; *income tax*, impôt sur le revenu; *indirect tax*, contribution indirecte; *non-resident tax*, taxe de séjour; *stamp tax*, droit de timbre; *taxable*, imposable; *taxpayer*, contribuable.

taxi [taksi] *s.* taxi, m.; *v.* aller en taxi; rouler au sol (aviat.); *taxicab*, taxi; *taxi-girl*, entraîneuse; *taxi-rand*, (ou) *-stand*, station de taxis.

tea [tî] *s.* thé, m.; *tea cake*, gâteau pour le thé; *teacup*, tasse à thé; *tea-kettle*, bouilloire à thé; *tea party*, thé (reception); *teapot*, théière; *tea service*, service à thé; *tea spoon*, cuiller à café; *tea strainer*, passe-thé; *tea-urn*, samovar.

teach [tîtsh] *v.* enseigner; instruire; apprendre. ‖ *teacher* [-er] *s.* professeur; maître; instituteur, m.; institutrice, f. ‖ *teaching* [-ing] *s.* enseignement, m.; *pl.* préceptes, m. pl.; *practice teaching*, stage pédagogique.

teal [tîl] *s.* sarcelle, f.

team [tîm] *s.* attelage [horses], m.; équipe [workmen], f.; *v.* atteler; faire travailler en équipe; *to team up*, former une équipe; *teamster*, charretier; *Am.* camionneur; *teamwork*, travail d'équipe; bonne collaboration.

tear [tèer] *s.* accroc; déchirement, m.; déchirure, f.; *v.* (se) déchirer; arracher; se mouvoir très rapidement; *to tear along*, aller bride abattue; *to tear in(to)*, entrer en coup de vent; attaquer; *to tear out*, sortir en trombe; arracher; *to tear upstairs*, monter l'escalier quatre à quatre; *wear and tear*, usure, détérioration.

tear [tier] *s.* larme, f.; pleur, m.; *tearful*, éploré, en larmes; *tear-gas*, gaz lacrymogène; *tearless*, sans larmes, sec, insensible.

tease [tîz] *v.* taquiner; tracasser; carder [wool]; *s.* taquin, m.; *teaser*, taquin; *teasing*, taquinerie.

teat [tît] *s.* mamelon; pis, m.; tétine, f.

technical [tèknik'l] *adj.* technique. ‖ *technician* [tèknishen] *s.* technicien, m. ‖ *technics* [tèkniks] *s.* technologie, f. ‖ *technique* [tèknik] *s.* technique, f.

technocracy [tèknâkr°si] *s.* technocratie, f.; *technology*, technologie.

tedious [tidies] *adj.* ennuyeux; fastidieux; fatigant. ‖ *tediousness* [-nis] *s.* ennui, m.; fatigue, f.

teem [tîm] v. produire, engendrer; foisonner; regorger (with, de); Am. pleuvoir à verse; teeming, grouillant; bondé; torrentiel [rain].

teen-ager [tîné¹djᵉr] s. adolescent, m. ‖ **teens** [tînz] s. pl. âge de treize à dix-neuf ans; nombre de 13 à 19, m.

teeth [tîth] pl. of tooth. ‖ **teethe** [tîzh] v. faire ses dents.

teetotaller [tîtoᵘt'lᵉr] s. abstinent, m.

telegram [tèl⁰gram] s. télégramme, m.; dépêche, f.

telegraph [tèl⁰graph] s. télégraphe, m.; v. télégraphier; telegraph office, bureau du télégraphe; telegraph operator, télégraphiste. ‖ **telegraphy** [tᵉlègrᵉfi] s. télégraphie, f.; two-way telegraphy, duplex; wireless telegraphy, T.S.F., radio.

telemeter [tilémîtᵉr] s. télémètre, m.

telepathy [tilép⁰thi] s. télépathie, f.

telephone [tèl⁰foᵘn] s. téléphone, m.; v. téléphoner; telephone booth, cabine téléphonique; telephone exchange, central téléphonique; telephone number, numéro de téléphone; telephone operator, téléphoniste; telephonic, téléphonique; telephonist, téléphoniste.

telephotolens [tèlifoᵘt⁰lèns] s.* télé-objectif, m.

telescope [tèl⁰skoᵘp] s. télescope, m.; longue-vue, f.; v. télescoper. ‖ **telescopic** [-ik] adj. coulissant, rentrant; abrégé.

televiewer [tèlivyouᵉr] s. téléspectateur, m.; téléspectatrice, f.

televise [tèl⁰vaiz] v. téléviser. ‖ **television** [tèl⁰vij⁰n] s. télévision, f.; television set, televisor, téléviseur.

tell [tèl] v.* dire; raconter; déclarer; montrer; compter; avouer; distinguer (from, de); I am told, on me dit; to tell one's beads, dire son chapelet. ‖ **teller** [-ᵉr] s. narrateur, conteur; caissier; scrutateur [votes], m. ‖ **telling** [-ing] adj. fort, efficace; s. narration; divulgation, f. ‖ **telltale** [tèlté¹l] s. dénonciateur; compteur (mech.); axiomètre (naut.), m.; adj. révélateur.

temerity [t⁰mᵉr⁰ti] s. témérité, f.

temper [tèmp⁰r] s. tempérament; caractère, m.; humeur, trempe (techn.), f.; v. tempérer; détremper, délayer; tremper [metal]; to lose one's temper, s'emporter; to be in a temper, être en colère. ‖ **temperament** [tèmp⁰m⁰nt] s. tempérament, m.; constitution, f.; temperamental, capricieux, fantasque.

temperance [tèmpr⁰ns] s. tempérance; modération; retenue; sobriété, f.

temperate [tèmprit] adj. modéré; tempéré; sobre; sage. ‖ **temperature** [tèmpr⁰tshᵉr] s. température, f.; temperature chart, feuille de température; to have a temperature, avoir de la température.

tempest [tèmpist] s. tempête (naut.), f.; orage, m. ‖ **tempestuous** [tèmpèstshouᵉs] adj. tempétueux; orageux; turbulent.

temple [tèmp'l] s. temple, m.

temple [tèmp'l] s. tempe, f.

templet [tèmplé¹t] s. gabarit, m.

temporal [tèmpᵉr⁰l] adj. temporal.

temporal [tèmpᵉr⁰l] adj. temporel; séculier. ‖ **temporarily** [tèmpᵉrèr⁰li] adv. temporairement; provisoirement. ‖ **temporary** [tèmpᵉrèri] adj. temporaire; provisoire; intérimaire. ‖ **temporize** [tèmpᵉra¹z] v. temporiser.

tempt [tèmpt] v. tenter; inciter, pousser. ‖ **temptation** [tèmpté¹sh⁰n] s. tentation, f. ‖ **tempter** [tèmptᵉr] s. tentateur, m. ‖ **tempting** [-ting] adj. tentateur; séduisant.

ten [tèn] adj. dix; s. dix, m.; dizaine, f.

tenable [tèn⁰b'l] adj. soutenable.

tenacious [tiné¹shᵉs] adj. tenace; opiniâtre, attaché (of, à). ‖ **tenacity** [tinasᵉti] s. ténacité; obstination; persévérance, f.

tenancy [tèn⁰nsi] s.* location, f. ‖ **tenant** [tèn⁰nt] s. locataire, m. f.

tench [tèntsh] s.* tanche, f.

tend [tènd] v. tendre à; se diriger vers.

tend [tènd] v. garder; soigner; surveiller.

tendency [tènd⁰nsi] s.* tendance; inclination; orientation, f.; penchant, m. ‖ **tendential** [-shᵉl] adj. tendancieux.

tender [tèndᵉr] s. offre; soumission (comm.), f.; v. offrir; soumissionner; donner [resignation]; legal tender (currency), cours légal, monnaie légale.

tender [tèndᵉr] s. tender (techn.); transbordeur (naut.); ravitailleur (aviat.), m.

tender [tèndᵉr] adj. tendre; délicat; sensible susceptible; attentif (of, à); soucieux (of, de); tenderfoot, nouveau venu; novice; Am. louveteau (boyscout).

tenderloin [tèndᵉrlo¹n] s. filet, m.

tenderness [tèndᵉrnis] s. tendresse; sensibilité; délicatesse, f.

tendon [tènd⁰n] s. tendon, m.

tendril [tèndril] s. vrille, f.

tenement [tèn⁰m⁰nt] s. maison de rapport, f.; logement ouvrier, m.

tennis [tènis] s. tennis, m.

tenor [tèn⁰ʳ] s. ténor, m.; teneur; portée; échéance, f.

tenpins [tènpinz] s. Am. jeu (m.) de quilles.

tense [tèns] adj. tendu; raide; **tenseness**, tension.

tense [tèns] s. temps (gramm.), m.

tensile [tèns'l] adj. extensible; ductile. ‖ **tension** [tènsh⁰n] s. tension, f.

tent [tènt] s. tente, f.; v. camper; **tent peg**, piquet de tente.

tentacle [tént⁰k'l] s. tentacule, m.; filament, m.; **tentacular**, tentaculaire.

tentative [tènt⁰tiv] adj. expérimental; provisoire.

tenth [tènth] adj. dixième; s. dixième; dix [dates, titles], m.; dîme, f.

tenuity [t⁰nyouiti] s. ténuité; faiblesse, f. ‖ **tenuous** [tènyou⁰s] adj. ténu; effilé.

tepid [tèpid] adj. tiède.

tergiversate [tèʳdjv⁰ʳsé¹t] v. tergiverser; **tergiversation**, tergiversation.

term [tëʳm] s. terme; trimestre scolaire; énoncé [problem]; délai, m.; limite; durée; session (jur.), f.; pl. conditions, clauses; relations, f. pl.; termes, rapports, m. pl.; v. nommer; désigner; to come to terms, conclure un arrangement; on easy terms, avec facilités de paiement; the lowest term, la plus simple expression (math.); by the terms of, en vertu de. ‖ **terminal** [-⁰n'l] adj. terminal; ultime; s. terminus (railw.), m.; prise de courant (electr.); extrémité, f. ‖ **terminate** [-⁰né¹t] v. achever; (se) terminer; aboutir. ‖ **termination** [tëʳm⁰né¹sh⁰n] s. fin; terminaison; conclusion, f. ‖ **terminus** [tëʳm⁰n⁰s] s.* terminus, m.; tête de ligne, f.

termite [tëʳma¹t] s. termite, m.

terrace [tèris] s. terrasse, f.; terreplein, m.; v. disposer en terrasse.

terrain [téré¹n] s. terrain (mil.), m.

terrestrial [terèstri⁰l] adj. terrestre.

terrible [tèr⁰b'l] adj. terrible; épouvantable. ‖ **terribly** [-bli] adv. terriblement; affreusement; épouvantablement.

terrier [tèri⁰ʳ] s. terrier, m.

terrific [t⁰rífik] adj. terrible, effroyable; formidable. ‖ **terrify** [tèr⁰fa¹] v. terrifier; épouvanter; affoler.

territorial [térit⁰ri⁰l] adj. régional; territorial; terrien; **territoriality**, territorialité. ‖ **territory** [tèrit⁰ºri] s.* territoire, m.

terror [tèr⁰ʳ] s. terreur; frayeur, f.; effroi, m.; **terrorism**, terrorisme; **terrorist**, terroriste. ‖ **terrorize** [tèr⁰ra¹z] v. terroriser; épouvanter.

terse [tëʳs] adj. succinct, concis.

test [tèst] s. épreuve, f.; test; réactif (chem.), m.; v. éprouver; expérimenter; contrôler; blood test, prise de sang; test flight, vol d'essai; test tube, éprouvette.

testament [tèst⁰m⁰nt] s. testament, m. ‖ **testator** [tèsté¹t⁰ʳ] s. testateur, m. ‖ **testify** [tèstifai] v. témoigner; attester; déclarer; déposer (jur.). ‖ **testimonial** [tèstimoºuni⁰l] s. attestation, f.; certificat, m. ‖ **testimony** [-mouni] s.* témoignage, m.; déposition, f.

testy [tèsti] adj. susceptible; irritable.

tetanus [tèt⁰n⁰s] s. tétanos, m.

tether [tèzh⁰ʳ] s. longe; attache, f.; v. mettre à l'attache.

text [tèkst] s. texte, m.; **textbook**, manuel.

textile [tèkst'l] s. textile; tissu, m.; adj. textile.

textual [tèkstshou⁰l] adj. littéral; de texte; textuel.

texture [tèkstsh⁰ʳ] s. texture, contexture, f.; tissu, m.

Thames [témz] s. Tamise, f.

than [zhàn] conj. que; de [numbers]; more than he knows, plus qu'il ne sait; more than once, plus d'une fois.

thank [thàngk] v. remercier (for, de); s'en prendre (à); s. pl. remerciement; merci, m.; thank you, merci; to have oneself to thank for, être responsable de, s'en prendre à soi-même. ‖ **thankful** [-f⁰l] adj. reconnaissant. ‖ **thankfully** [-f⁰li] adv. avec gratitude. ‖ **thankfulness** [-f⁰lnis] s. reconnaissance; gratitude, f. ‖ **thankless** [-lis] adj. ingrat. ‖ **thanklessness** [-lisnis] s. ingratitude, f. ‖ **thanksgiving** [thàngksgiving] s. action de grâces; Am. fête d'action de grâces, f.

that [zhat] demonstr. adj. ce, cet; cette, ça; pron. cela, ce; qui; lequel; que; ce que; conj. que; that is, c'est-à-dire; that's all, voilà tout; all that I know, tout ce que je sais; that he may know, afin qu'il sache; in that, en ce que; that far, si loin; that will do, cela suffit; cela ira.

thatch [thatsh] s. chaume, m.; v. couvrir en chaume; thatched roof, toit de chaume.

thaw [thau] s. dégel, m.; v. dégeler; fondre.

the [zhᵉ] ([zhi] before a vowel) *def.
art.* le, la, les; *of the, from the,* du,
de la, des; *to the,* au, à la, aux; *adv.*
d'autant; *the sooner,* d'autant plus
tôt; *the less said the better,* moins on
en dit, mieux ça vaut.

theater [thíᵉtᵉr] *s.* théâtre, m. ‖
theatrical [thiatrik'l] *adj.* théâtral;
scénique; dramatique.

thee [zhî] *pron.* te, toi.

theft [thèft] *s.* vol; larcin, m.

their [zhèᵉr] *poss. adj.* leur; leurs.
‖ **theirs** [-z] *poss. pron.* le leur, la leur,
les leurs; à eux; à elles.

them [zhèm] *pron.* eux; elles; les;
leur; *take them,* prenez-les; *give them
a drink,* donnez-leur à boire; *for them,*
pour eux; *I see them,* je les vois.

theme [thîm] *s.* thème; sujet, m.;
composition, f.; *theme-song,* leitmo-
tiv; indicatif [radio].

themselves [zhèmsèlvz] *pron.* eux-
mêmes; elles-mêmes; se; eux; elles;
they flatter themselves, ils se flattent.

then [zhèn] *adv.* alors; puis; ensuite; donc; dans ce cas; *now and
then,* de temps en temps; *now... then,*
tantôt... tantôt; *even then,* déjà, à
cette époque. ‖ **thence** [-s] *adv.* de là;
dès lors; par conséquent; pour cette
raison; **thenceforth,** dès lors, désormais.

theology [thîálᵉdji] *s.* théologie, f.

theorem [thîᵉrᵉm] *s.* théorème
(math.), m.

theoretical [thîᵉrètik'l] *adj.* théorique; pur [chem.]; rationnel [mech.].
‖ **theory** [thîᵉri] *s.* théorie, f.

therapeutics [thèrᵉpyoutiks] *s.* thérapeutique, f.; **therapeutist,** théra-
peute; **therapist,** praticien.

there [zhèᵉr] *adv.* là; y; voilà; *there
is, there are,* il y a; *up there,* là-haut;
down there, là-bas; *there and then,*
sur-le-champ; *there he is,* le voilà. ‖
thereabouts [zhèrᵉbaᵒuts] *adv.* à peu
près; vers; dans les environs. ‖
thereafter [zhèraftᵉr] *adv.* ensuite;
par la suite; en conséquence. ‖ **thereby**
[zhèrba¹] *adv.* de cette manière; de ce
fait; par ce moyen. ‖ **therefore** [zhèr-
foᵒur] *adv.* donc; par conséquent;
pour cette raison. ‖ **therein** [zhèrín]
adv. là-dedans; en cela; y; ici. ‖
thereof [zhèráv] *adv.* de cela; en. ‖
thereon [zhèrán] *adv.* là-dessus; y.
‖ **thereupon** [zhèrᵉpân] *adv.* sur ce;
là-dessus; en conséquence. ‖ **therewith**
[zhèrwìth] *adv.* avec cela; ensuite.

thermal [thèrm'l] *adj.* thermique;
thermal. ‖ **thermometer** [thᵉrmámᵉ-
tᵉr] *s.* thermomètre, m. ‖ **thermonu-
clear** [thᵉrmᵉnyoukliᵉr] *adj.* thermo-

nucléaire. ‖ **Thermos** [thèrmᵉs] *s.*
Thermos [bottle], m. (trademark). ‖
thermostat [-tat] *s.* thermostat, m.

these [zhîz] *adj.* ces; *pron.* ceux-ci,
celles-ci; *these are yours,* voici les
vôtres.

thesis [thîsis] (*pl. theses*) *s.* thèse, f.

thews [thyouz] *s. pl.* nerfs; muscles,
m. pl., **thewy,** musclé, fort.

they [zhé¹] *pron.* ils; elles; *they who,*
ceux qui, celles qui; *they say,* on dit.

thick [thík] *adj.* épais; dense; inarti-
culé [voice]; consistant; intime; *s.*
gras, m.; *adv.* abondamment; rapidement; péniblement; gras [speech];
thick-skinned, à la peau dure, insensible; **thick-witted,** à l'esprit lourd. ‖
thicken [-ᵉn] *v* épaissir; s'obscurcir;
se compliquer [plot]. ‖ **thicket** [-it] *s.*
bosquet; fourré, hallier, m. ‖ **thickly**
[-li] *adv.* d'une façon drue; en foule;
abondamment; rapidement. ‖ **thickness** [-nis] *s.* épaisseur; grosseur; densité; consistance; dureté [ear]; difficulté d'élocution, f.

thief [thîf] (*pl. thieves* [thîvz]) *s.* voleur; larron, m. ‖ **thieve** [thîv] *v.* voler; dérober.

thigh [tha¹] *s.* cuisse, f.; **thighbone,**
fémur.

thimble [thìmb'l] *s.* dé à coudre,
m.; cosse (naut.), f.

thin [thìn] *adj.* mince; maigre; fin;
clairsemé [hair]; fluide [liquid]; léger
[clothing], raréfié [air]; *v.* amincir;
diluer, raréfier; allonger [sauce];
s'amincir, (s')éclaircir.

thine [zha¹n] *poss. pron.* le tien; la
tienne, les tiens; les tiennes; à toi.

thing [thìng] *s.* chose; affaire; créature, f., objet; *pl.* vêtements, m.; *the
very thing,* exactement ce qu'il faut;
how are things?, comment ça va?;
thingumajig, truc, machin.

think [thìngk] *v.* penser (*of*, à);
croire, réfléchir; imaginer; trouver;
s'aviser, *I will think it over,* j'y réflé-
chirai; *I thought better of it,* je me ra-
visai; *I think ill of,* j'ai mauvaise opinion de; *he thought much of,* il fit
grand cas de; *I think so,* je (le) crois;
je crois que oui. ‖ **thinkable** [-ᵉb'l]
adj. imaginable, concevable. ‖ **thinker**
[-ᵉr] *s.* penseur, m. ‖ **thinking** [-ing]
s. pensée; opinion, f.; avis, m.; *adj.*
pensant.

thinly [thìnli] *adv.* légèrement [clad];
à peine; en petit nombre; maigrement.
‖ **thinness** [-nis] *s.* minceur; maigreur; légèreté; faiblesse; rareté; ra-
réfaction, f.

third [thèrd] *adj., s.* troisième; trois
[month, king]; *s.* tiers, m. ‖ **thirdly**
[-li] *adv.* troisièmement.

thirst [thĕrst] *s.* soif, f.; *v.* avoir soif; être avide (*for*, de). ‖ **thirsty** [-i] *adj.* altéré; desséché [earth]; *to be thirsty*, avoir soif.

thirteen [thĕrtīn] *adj., s.* treize. ‖ **thirteenth** [-th] *adj., s.* treizième; treize [month, king]. ‖ **thirtieth** [thĕr-tiith] *adj.., s.* trentième trente [month, title]. ‖ **thirty** [thĕrti] *adj., s.* trente. **thirty-first**, trente et unième; trente et un [month].

this [zhis] *demonstr. adj.* ce; cet; cette; ce... ci; cet... ci; cette... ci; *pron.* ceci; *this one*, celui-ci, celle-ci; *this day*, aujourd'hui. *this way*, par ici; de cette façon; *upon this*, là-dessus; *this is London*, ici Londres [radio].

thistle [this'l] *s.* chardon, m.

thither [thizhᵉr] *adv.* là, y.

tho, *see* **though**.

thong [thaung] *s.* courroie; lanière; longe, f.

thorax [thauraks] *s.** thorax, m.

thorn [thaurn] *s.* épine, f.; buisson d'épines, m.; **thorny**, épineux; piquant.

thorough [thĕrouᵘ] *adj.* entier; complet; parfait; consciencieux. ‖ **thoroughbred** [-brĕd] *adj.* pur sang; de sang [horse]. ‖ **thoroughfare** [-fèᵉr] *s.* voie de communication, f.; *no thoroughfare*, passage interdit. ‖ **thoroughly** [-li] *adv.* entièrement; tout à fait; parfaitement, à fond.

those [thoᵘz] *demonstr. adj.* ces; *pron.* ceux-là, celles-là; *those who*, ceux qui, celles qui; *those which*, ceux qui, celles qui; *those of*, ceux de, celles de.

thou [thaᵘ] *pers. pron.* tu.

though [zhoᵘ] *conj.* quoique; bien que; encore que *as though*, comme si; *even though*, même si.

thought [thaut] *s.* pensée, idée; opinion; sollicitude, f.; *pret. of* **to think**; *to give it no thought* ne pas se préoccuper de **thought-transference**, télépathie. ‖ **thoughtful** [-fᵉl] *adj.* pensif réfléchi attentif soucieux **thoughtfulness** [-fᵉlnis] *s.* prévenance sollicitude, méditation, f ‖ **thoughtless** [-lis] *adj.* irréfléchi inconsidéré, insouciant étourdi, inattentif **thoughtlessness** [-lisnis] *s.* irréflexion; étourderie; insouciance, f.

thousand [thaᵘz'nd] *adj.* mille; *s.* millier, m.; *thousands of*, des milliers de. ‖ **thousandth** [-th] *adj.* millième.

thrash [thrash] *v.* rosser; battre le blé; *to thrash around*, se démener; *to thrash out a matter*, étudier une question à fond; **thrashing**, raclée; battage (agr.); **thrashing-floor**, aire; **thrashing-machine**, batteuse.

thread [thrĕd] *s.* fil filament; filet; filetage (mech.), m.; *v* enfiler fileter, tarauder (mech.).; *to thread one's way through the crowd* se faufiler dans la foule, **thread-like**, filiforme. ‖ **threadbare** [-bèᵉr] *adj.* usé jusqu'à la corde rebattu.

threat [thrĕt] *s.* menace, f. ‖ **threaten** [-'n] *v* menacer; **threatening**, menaçant.

three [thrī] *adj., s.* trois; *three-cornered hat*, tricorne; **threefold**, triple; **threephase**, triphasé (electr.).

thresh, *see* **thrash**.

threshold [thrĕshoᵘld] *s.* seuil, m.

threw [throu] *pret. of* **to throw**.

thrice [thraᵢs] *adv.* trois fois.

thrift [thrift] *s.* épargne, économie; frugalité, f.; **thrifty**, économe frugal.

thrill [thril] *v.* percer; faire vibrer; tressaillir, frémir; *s.* émotion vive, surexcitation, f; frisson, m. **thriller** [-ᵉr] *s* roman (ou) spectacle à sensation, m. ‖ **thrilling** [-ing] *adj.* émouvant, palpitant.

thrive [thraᵢv] *v.** prospérer; réussir. **thriven** [thrivᵉn] *p. p. of* **to thrive**. ‖ **thriving** [-ing] *adj.* vigoureux. florissant.

throat [throᵘt] *s.* gorge, f.; gosier; collet mech.), m.; *a sore throat*, un mal de gorge.

throb [thrâb] *v.* battre, palpiter [heart] vibrer; *s.* palpitation, pulsation. ' battement, m.

throe [throᵘ] *s.* agonie, angoisse, f.; douleurs de l'enfantement, f. pl.

thrombosis [thrambоᵘsis] *s.* thrombose, f.

throne [throᵘn] *s.* trône, m.

throng [thraung] *s.* foule; multitude, f., *v.* s'attrouper; accourir en foule (se) presser.

throstle [thrâs'l] *s.* grive, f.

throttle [thrât'l] *s.* obturateur, étrangleur mech.); gosier, m.; *v.* étouffer; étrangler; obstruer; *to open the throttle*, mettre les gaz; *to throttle down* ralentir réduire les gaz.

through [throu] *prep.* à travers; par; au moyen de, par de part en part *adj.* direct fait, achevé *adv* d'un bout à l'autre **through carriage**, voiture directe **through ticket**, billet direct; *wet through*, trempé jusqu'aux os; *to fall through*, échouer; *to see it through*, le mener à bonne fin; *let me through*, laissez-moi passer. ‖ **throughout** [-aᵒut] *adv.*, *prep.* partout; d'un bout à l'autre.

throve [throᵒᵘv] *pret. of* to **thrive.**

throw [throᵒᵘ] *v.*⁎ jeter; lancer; renverser, désarçonner; *s.* jet; coup; élan, m.; *to throw away*, rejeter, gaspiller; *to throw in gear*, engrener; *to throw off*, se débarrasser de; *to throw out*, expulser; *to throw up*, jeter en l'air; vomir; rejeter; *to throw out of work*, débaucher, mettre sur le pavé; *to throw in the clutch*, embrayer; *to throw out the clutch*, débrayer. ‖ **thrown** [throᵒᵘn] *p. p. of* to **throw.**

thrum [thrœm] *v.* tapoter; *s.* tapotement, m.

thrush [thrœsh] *s.*⁎ grive, f.

thrush [thrœsh] *s.*⁎ aphte (med.), f.

thrust [thrœst] *s.* coup de pointe, m.; estocade, poussée; butée, f.; *v.*⁎ pousser; enfoncer; porter une pointe; allonger une botte [fencing]; *propeller thrust*, traction de l'hélice (aviat.); *to thrust on*, faire avancer, inciter; *to thrust in*, fourrer, enfoncer.

thud [thœd] *v.* tomber avec un bruit sourd; *s.* floc, m.

thug [thœg] *s.* assassin, étrangleur, bandit, m.

thumb [thœmb] *s.* pouce m.; *v.* manier gauchement; feuilleter; *to thumb a lift*, faire de l'auto-stop; *under the thumb of*, sous la coupe de. ‖ **thumbtack** [-tak] *s.* Am. punaise, f.

thump [thœmp] *v.* bourrer de coups; sonner lourdement [footsteps]; *s.* coup violent, m. ‖ **thumping** [-ing] *adj.* (fam.), énorme.

thunder [thœndᵉʳ] *s.* tonnerre, m.; foudre, f.; *v.* tonner; gronder; retentir; fulminer. **thunderbolt**, coup de foudre, **thunderclap**, coup de tonnerre, **thundershower**, pluie d'orage; **thunderstorm**, orage. ‖ **thundering** [-ring] *adj* tonnant; tonitruant, foudroyant. ‖ **thunderous** [-rᵉs] *adj.* tonnant; redoutable, orageux [weather]. ‖ **thunderstruck** [-strœk] *adj.* foudroyé; pétrifié.

Thursday [thᵉʳzdi] *s.* jeudi, m.; *on Thursdays.* le jeudi, tous les jeudis.

thus [zhœs] *adv.* ainsi; donc; *thus far*, jusqu'ici.

t h u y a [thyouyᵉ] *s.* thuya, m.; *American thuya, Fr. Can.* cèdre.

thwart [thwaurt] *v.* contrarier; contrecarrer; déjouer.

thyme [taͥm] *s.* thym, m.

thy [zhaͥ] *poss. adj.* ton; ta; tes.

thyroid [thaͥroͥd] *adj.*, *s.* thyroïde.

thyself [zhaͥsèlf] *pron.* toi-même; te; toi.

tiara [taͥéͥrᵉ] *s.* tiare, f.

tibia [tíbiᵉ] *s.* tibia, m.

tic [tik] *s.* tic, m.

tick [tik] *s.* coutil, m.; toile à matelas, f.

tick [tik] *s.* tique, f.

tick [tik] *s.* tic-tac, m.; marque, f.; *v.* faire tic tac; *to tick off*, marquer, pointer.

tick [tik] *s.* crédit, m.; *on tick*, à crédit.

ticket [tíkit] *s.* billet; ticket; bulletin [luggage], m.; étiquette, f.; *v.* étiqueter; donner un billet; *ticket book*, carnet de tickets; *ticket office*, guichet.

tickle [tik'l] *v.* chatouiller; *s.* chatouillement, m.; **ticklish**, chatouilleux; scabreux, périlleux.

tidal [taͥd'l] *adj.* de marée; *tidal wave*, raz de marée. ‖ **tide** [taͥd] *s.* marée; saison, f.; courant, m.; *v.* aller avec la marée, *to go with the tide*, suivre le courant, *to tide over*, surmonter *ebb tide*, marée descendante, jusant, *flood tide*, marée montante; *high tide*, marée haute; *low tide*, marée basse, *tide-gate*, écluse; *tide race*, raz de marée.

tidily [taͥdili] *adv.* proprement, soigneusement. ‖ **tidiness** [taͥdinis] *s.* propreté, netteté, f.; ordre, m.

tidings [taͥdings] *s. pl.* nouvelles, f. pl.

tidy [taͥdi] *adj.* propre; net; en ordre; *v.* ranger; mettre en ordre; *a tidy sum*, une somme rondelette; *to tidy oneself up*, faire un brin de toilette.

tie [taͥ] *v.* attacher; nouer; (se) lier; *s.* lien; nœud; tirant (techn.); assujettissement ballottage. m.; attache; obligation cravate [neck-tie]; traverse [railw.) moise (techn.); partie nulle [sport]. f., *to tie down*, astreindre (*to*, à); *tie-up*, embouteillage [traffic]; arrêt de travail; impasse.

tier [tiᵉʳ] *s.* rangée; file, f.

tiff [tif] *s.* chamaillerie, f.; *v.* prendre la mouche.

tiger [taͥgᵉʳ] *s.* tigre, m.

tight [taͥt] *adj.* serré; raide, tendu; étroit [clothes]; hermétique; étanche; imperméable, ivre; *adv.* hermétiquement; fortement; *it fits tight*, c'est ajusté, collant, *tightwad*, grippe-sou. ‖ **tighten** [-'n] *v.* serrer, resserrer; tendre bloquer ‖ **tightness** [-nis] *s.* raideur, étroitesse, étanchéité; imperméabilité; tension; avarice, f.; resserrement, m.

tigress [taͥgris] *s.*⁎ tigresse, f.

tile [taͥl] *s.* tuile, f.; carreau de cheminée; tuyau de poêle, m.; *v.* couvrir de tuiles; carreler; *tiler*, couvreur.

till [til] *prep.* d'ici à, jusqu'à; *conj.* jusqu'à ce que; *not till,* pas avant.

till [til] *s.* tiroir-caisse, m.

till [til] *v.* cultiver, labourer. ‖ *tillage* [-ᵉdj] *s.* labourage, m.; agriculture, f.

tilt [tilt] *s.* bâche, f.; tendelet, m.; *v.* bâcher.

tilt [tilt] *s.* inclinaison; pente; bande (naut.), f.; *v.* incliner; donner de la bande; jouter avec; *at full tilt,* à bride abattue.

tilth [tilth] *s.* culture; couche arable, f.

timber [tìmbᵉʳ] *s.* bois de construction, m.; trempe (fig.), f.; *v.* charpenter.

time [taⁱm] *s.* temps, moment, m.; époque; saison; heure; occasion; fois; mesure [music], f.; *v.* régler; mettre à l'heure; calculer; chronométrer; ajuster; choisir le moment opportun; *at any time,* n'importe quand; *at times,* parfois; *two at a time,* deux à la fois; *to beat time,* battre la mesure; *by this time,* maintenant; *from this time,* dorénavant; *from that time,* dès lors; *in due time,* en temps voulu, *from time to time,* de temps en temps; *on time,* à l'heure; à temps; *in a short time,* sous peu; *next time,* la prochaine fois; *to lose time,* perdre du temps; retarder [clock]; *what time is it?,* quelle heure est-il?; *standard time, civil time,* heure légale; *timekeeper,* surveillant; pointeur; *timepiece,* chronomètre, pendule; *timetable,* horaire, indicateur (railw.). ‖ *timely* [-li] *adj.* opportun; à propos, *adv.* ‖ *timer* [-ᵉʳ] *s.* chronométreur, m.; minuterie, f.

timid [tìmid] *adj.* timide, craintif, peureux, ‖ *timidity* [timidᵉti] *s.* timidité, f.

timorous [timᵉrᵉs] *adj.* timoré.

tin [tìn] *s.* étain; fer-blanc; récipient en fer-blanc, m.; *v.* étamer; *adj.* d'étain; *tin can,* bidon en fer-blanc; *tin foil,* feuille d'étain; *tin hat,* casque; *tinsmith,* ferblantier, étameur; *tinware,* ferblanterie; *tinworks,* usine d'étain.

tincture [tìngktshᵉʳ] *s.* teinture, f.; *v.* teindre; *tincture of iodine,* teinture d'iode.

tinder [tìndᵉʳ] *s.* amadou, m.; *tindery,* inflammable.

tine [taⁱn] *s.* dent [fork], f.; andouiller, m.

tinge [tìndj] *s.* teinte; nuance, f.; *v.* nuancer, parfumer.

tingle [tìngg'l] *v.* tinter; vibrer; picoter, fourmiller; *s.* tintement; fourmillement, picotement, m.

tinker [tìngkᵉʳ] *s.* rétameur; bricoleur, m.; *v.* étamer; bricoler; rafistoler.

tinkle [tìngk'l] *v.* tinter; *s.* tintement, m.

tinned [tìnd] *adj.* étamé; conservé en boîte; *tinny,* d'étain; grêle.

tinsel [tìns'l] *s.* clinquant; oripeau, m.; *adj.* de clinquant.

tint [tìnt] *s.* teinte; nuance, f.; ton, m.; *v.* teinter.

tintinnabulate [tintinabᵉyoulé¹t] *v.* tintinnabuler. tinter.

tiny [taⁱni] *adj.* tout petit; menu.

tip [tip] *s* inclinaison, f.; pourboire; tuyau [horseracing], m.; *v.* donner un pourboire à; donner un tuyau à; basculer; *to tip over,* se renverser; chavirer.

tip [tip] *s.* bout, m.; extrémité; pointe, f.; *wing tip,* bout d'aile.

tippet [tìpit] *s.* collet [fur], m.

tipsy [tìpsi] *adj.* gris, éméché; *to get tipsy,* se griser.

tiptoe [tìptoᵒu] *s.* pointe du pied, f.; *v.* avancer sur la pointe des pieds.

tirade [taⁱré¹d] *s.* tirade, f.

tire, tyre [taⁱᵉʳ] *s.* pneu(matique); bandage de roue, m.; *v.* mettre un pneu; *balloon tire,* pneu ballon; *blown-out tire,* pneu éclaté; *flat tire,* pneu crevé. *nonskid tire,* pneu antidérapant; *retreaded tire,* pneu rechapé; *spare tire,* pneu de rechange.

tire [taⁱᵉʳ] *v.* (se) lasser; (se) fatiguer; épuiser. ‖ *tired* [-d] *adj.* fatigué; ennuyé; *tired out,* exténué; *to get tired,* se lasser. ‖ *tiredness* [-dnis] *s.* lassitude; fatigue, f. ‖ *tireless* [-lis] *adj.* infatigable. ‖ *tiresome* [-sᵉm] *adj.* lassant; fatigant; ennuyeux; fastidieux.

tisane [tizan] *s.* tisane, f.

tissue [tìshou] *s.* tissu, m.; *tissue-paper,* papier pelure; papier de soie.

tit [tit] *s.* mamelle, f.

tit [tit] *s.* mésange, f.

Titan [taⁱtᵉn] *s.* Titan, m.; *titanic,* titanesque.

titbit [tìtbit] *s.* friandise, f.

tithe [taⁱzh] *s.* dîme, f.

titillate [tìtilé¹t] *v.* titiller, chatouiller, émoustiller.

title [taⁱt'l] *s.* titre; droit (jur.), m.; *title to property,* titre de propriété; *title page,* page de titre.

titmouse [titmaᵒus] (*pl.* **titmice** [-maⁱs]) *s.* mésange, f.

titular [tìtshelᵉʳ] *adj., s.* titulaire.

to [tou] *prep.* à; vers; en; de; pour; jusque; jusqu'à; afin de; envers; *owing to,* grâce à; *in order to,* afin de; *to go to England,* aller en Angleterre; *to the last,* jusqu'au dernier; jusqu'au bout; *to all appearances,* selon toute apparence; *a quarter to five,* cinq heures moins le quart; *to and fro,* allée et venue, « navette ».

toad [tou°d] *s.* crapaud, m. ‖ *toady* [-i] *s.* flagorneur, m.

toast [tou°st] *s.* toast, m.; rôtie, f.; *v.* (faire) griller [bread]; porter un toast à.

tobacco [t°bako°] *s.* tabac, m.; *tobacconist,* débitant de tabac.

toboggan [t°bâg°n] *s.* toboggan, m.; *Indian toboggan, Fr Can.* traîne sauvage; faire du toboggan; *Am.* dégringoler [colloq.].

tocsin [tâksin] *s.* tocsin, m.

today [t°dé¹] *adv.* aujourd'hui.

toddle [tâd'l] *v.* trottiner; *s.* trottinement, m.

to-do [t°doû] *s.* remue-ménage, m.

toe [tou] *s.* orteil; bout [stocking], m.; *v. to toe in,* marcher les pieds en dedans; *to toe out,* marcher les pieds en dehors [angle d'orteil].

together [t°gezh°r] *adv.* ensemble; en même temps; à la fois; de suite.

toil [to¹l] *v.* travailler, trimer; *s.* labeur, m., peine, f.

toilet [to¹lit] *s.* toilette; ablutions, f.; costume cabinet, m. *toilet case,* nécessaire de toilette; *toilet paper,* papier hygiénique; *toilet water,* eau de Cologne.

toilsome [to¹ls°m] *adj.* ardu, laborieux.

token [tou°k°n] *s.* marque, f.; signe; gage, témoignage; jeton, m.

told [tou°ld] *pret. p. p. of* **to tell.**

tolerable [tâl°r°b'l] *adj.* tolérable; supportable passable. ‖ *tolerance* [-r°ns] *s.* tolérance, f *tolerant* [-r°nt] *adj.* tolérant, indulgent. ‖ *tolerate* [-ré¹t] *v.* tolérer, supporter. ‖ *toleration* [tâl°ré¹sh°n] *s.* tolérance, f.

toll [tou°l] *s.* octroi, péage; droit de passage, m., *toll-bridge,* pont payant; *toll gate,* barrière de péage, d'octroi.

toll [tou°l] *s.* tintement [bell], m.; *v.* tinter; sonner.

tomato [t°mé¹tou°] *s.*° tomate, f.

tomb [toum] *s.* tombe; sépulture, f., tombeau, m.; *tombstone,* pierre tombale.

tomboy [tâmbo¹] *s.* garçon manqué, m.

tomcat [tâmkat] *s.* matou, m.

tomorrow [t°mauro°u] *adv.* demain; *day after tomorrow,* après-demain.

tomtit [tâmtit] *s.* mésange, f.

ton [tœn] *s.* tonne, f.; tonneau (naut.), m.

tone [tou°n] *s.* ton; accent; son; tonus (med.), m.; *v.* débiter d'un ton monotone; accorder, régler; virer (phot.), tonifier (med.) *to tone in well with,* s'harmoniser avec; *to tone up,* revigorer; *toneless voice,* voix blanche.

tongs [taungz] *s. pl.* pincettes; pinces; tenailles, f. pl.

tongue [tœng] *s.* langue; languette, f.; ardillon [buckle], m.; *to hold one's tongue,* se taire; *tongue-tied,* bouche cousue *coated tongue,* langue chargée; *tonguelet,* languette.

tonic [tânik] *adj., s.* tonique; fortifiant *tonicity,* tonicité.

tonight [t°na¹t] *adv.* cette nuit; ce soir.

tonnage [tœnidj] *s.* tonnage, m.; jauge, f.

tonsil [tâns'l] *s.* amygdale, f. ‖ *tonsilitis* [tâns'la¹t¹s] *s.* amygdalite, f.

tonsure [tânsh°r] *s.* tonsure, f.; *v.* tonsurer.

too [tou] *adv.* trop; aussi, de même; *too much, too many,* trop, trop de.

took [touk] *pret. of* **to take.**

tool [toul] *s.* outil; instrument, m.; *tool bag,* trousse à outils; *tooling,* outillage; usinage; ciselage.

toot [tout] *v.* sonner de la trompette; donner un coup de klaxon; siffler; *s.* coup de klaxon; son du cor; sifflement, m.

tooth [touth] (*pl.* **teeth** [tîth]) *s.* dent, f.; *false tooth,* fausse dent *milk tooth,* dent de lait *wisdom tooth,* dent de sagesse *toothache,* mal de dents *toothbrush,* brosse à dents; *toothpaste,* pâte dentifrice *toothpick,* cure dent *toothpowder,* poudre dentifrice *toothsome,* savoureux.

top [tâp] *s.* sommet, faîte, haut; couvercle; dessus [table]; extrados (aviat.), ciel [furnace], comble (fig), m.; toupie, hune [naut.] surface [water], capote [car] impériale [bus], f.; *v* couronner surmonter surpasser; dominer piquer (naut.); *adj.* premier, de tête extrême principal; *at the top of one's voice,* à tue-tête; *from top to toe,* de la tête aux pieds; *on top of,* sur, par dessus, en plus de; *at top speed,* à toute vitesse *that tops everything* c'est le bouquet *to top off,* parfaire; *topcoat,* pardessus; *topmast,* mât de hune; *topmost,* le plus élevé, le plus haut.

topaz [to⁰upaz] s.* topaze, f.

toper [to⁰up⁰r] s. ivrogne, m.

topgallant [to⁰upgal⁰nt] s. perroquet, m. (naut.).

topic [tâpik] s. sujet, m.; matière, f.; *current topic,* actualité; *topical,* d'actualité; topique.

topography [to⁰upâgr⁰fi] s. topographie, f.

topper [tap⁰r] s. haut-de-forme; *Am.* surtout, m.

topple [tâp'l] v. dégringoler; (faire) culbuter; *to topple over,* renverser, faire choir; s'écrouler.

topsy-turvy [tâpsitë⁰vi] adj., adv. la tête en bas; à l'envers; sens dessus dessous; en désordre.

torch [taurtsh] s.* torche, f.; flambeau; chalumeau (techn.), m.; lampe de poche, f.

tore [to⁰ur] pret. of to tear.

toreador [târi•dâ⁰r] s. toréador, m.

torment [taurm⁰nt] s. tourment, m.; torture, f.; [taurmènt] v. tourmenter; torturer; harceler; *tormentor,* bourreau.

tormentor [taurm⁰nt⁰r] s. abat-son, panneau anti-sonore, m.

torn [to⁰urn] p. p. of to tear.

tornado [taurné¹do⁰u] s. tornade, f.; ouragan; cyclone, m.

torpedo [taurpî⁰do⁰u] s.* torpille, f.; v. torpiller; *torpedo boat,* torpilleur; *torpedo-tube,* lance-torpilles.

torpid [taurpid] adj. engourdi; inactif; *torpify,* engourdir; *torpor,* torpeur.

torrent [taur⁰nt] s. torrent; déluge; cours violent, m.; *torrential,* torrentiel; torrentueux.

torrid [taurid] adj. torride.

torsion [taursh⁰n] s. torsion, f.

torticollis [tau⁰tikâlis] s. torticolis, m.

tortoise [taurt⁰s] s. tortue, f.

tortuous [taurtshou⁰s] adj. tortueux; sinueux.

torture [taurtsh⁰r] s. torture, f.; supplice; tourment, m.; v. torturer, supplicier; tourmenter; *torturer,* bourreau, tourmenteur.

toss [taus] v. lancer, jeter en l'air; ballotter (naut.); secouer; sauter [cooking]; désarçonner; s.* secousse; chute de cheval, f.; ballottement, m.; *toss-up,* coup à pile ou face; affaire douteuse; *to toss up,* jouer à pile ou face.

tot [tât] s. petit enfant; gosse, m.

total [to⁰ut'l] adj., s. total; v. totaliser; s'élever à. || *totalitarian* [to⁰utal•l•tèri⁰n] adj. totalitaire. || *totality* [to⁰utal•ti] s.* totalité, f. || *totalizator* [to⁰ut'l•zé¹t⁰r] s. totalisateur, m. || *totalize* [to⁰ut'la¹z] v. totaliser. || *totally* [to⁰ut'li] adv. totalement; entièrement; tout à fait.

totem [to⁰ut⁰m] s. totem, m.

totter [tât⁰r] v. chanceler; vaciller.

touch [tœtsh] v. toucher; atteindre; faire escale (naut.); concerner; affecter; s.* toucher; tact; attouchement; contact, trait, aperçu, m.; touche; allusion, pointe, trace, f.; *touchstone,* pierre de touche; *touchwood,* amadou; *to get in touch,* se mettre en rapport; *to keep in touch,* garder le contact; *to make a touch,* taper, emprunter de l'argent; *to touch up,* retoucher; *to touch upon,* effleurer; *a touch of powder* un soupçon de poudre; *a touch of fever,* une pointe de fièvre. || *touching* [-ing] adj. touchant; émouvant; *touchy,* susceptible, pointilleux.

tough [tœf] adj. dur; coriace; résistant; tenace, ardu; *m.* voyou, apache, m. || *toughen* [-'n] v. durcir; s'endurcir; (se) raidir. || *toughness* [-nis] s. dureté; raideur; résistance; difficulté, f.

tour [tour] s. tour; voyage, m.; excursion; tournée, f.; v. voyager; visiter. || *tourism* [-riz'm] s. tourisme, f. || *tourist* [-ist] s. touriste, m.

tournament [të⁰n⁰m⁰nt] s. tournoi; concours; championnat, m.; compétition, f.

tourniquet [të⁰nikéi] s. garrot, m.

tousle [ta⁰uz'l] v. ébouriffer [hair]; chiffonner [dress]; bousculer.

tout [ta⁰ut] v. racoler; s. rabatteur; démarcheur, m.

tow [to⁰u] v. touer; remorquer; haler; dépanner; s. remorque, f.; touage, m.; *tow boat,* remorqueur; *tow path,* chemin de halage; *towing,* dépannage.

tow [to⁰u] s. étoupe; filasse, f.

toward(s) [to⁰urd(z)] prep. vers; envers; à l'égard de; du côté de.

towel [ta⁰u•l] s. serviette, f.; essuie-mains, m.

tower [ta⁰u•r] s. tour, f.; pylône, m.; v. dominer; planer; s'élever; *conning-tower,* tourelle de commandement (naut.); *towering,* gigantesque; dominant.

town [ta⁰un] s. ville; municipalité, f. || *town-hall,* mairie; *town-planning,* urbanification, urbanisme. || *township* [-ship] s. commune, f.

toxic [tŏksik] adj., s. toxique. ‖ **toxin** [tŏksĭn] s. toxine, f.

toy [to¹] s. jouet; colifichet, m.; v. jouer; manier; **toy trade**, bimbeloterie.

trace [tré¹s] s. trace; empreinte, f.; tracé, m.; v. calquer; tracer; pister; **tracer**, calqueur, traçoir; **tracing-paper**, papier-calque.

trace [tré¹s] s. trait [harness], m.

trachea [tré¹kie] s. trachée, f.; **tracheitis**, trachéite.

track [trak] s. piste; voie (railw.); route (naut.; aviat.); orbite (astron.), f.; sillage; chemin, m.; v. suivre à la trace; pister; tracer une voie; traquer; haler (naut.); **caterpillar track**, chenille tank; **race track**, piste de course; **to be off the track**, dérailler; **the beaten track**, les sentiers battus; **to track in mud**, faire des marques de pas.

tract [trakt] s. étendue; région; nappe [water], f.; tract; opuscule, m.; **digestive tract**, appareil digestif.

tractable [trakt°b'l] adj. traitable; docile; maniable.

traction [traksh°n] s. traction; tension; attraction, f. ‖ **tractor** [trakt°r] s. tracteur, m.; **farm tractor**, tracteur agricole.

trade [tré¹d] s. commerce; négoce; métier, m.; v. commercer; négocier; trafiquer; troquer; **trade-mark**, marque de fabrique; **trade name**, raison sociale; **trade school**, école professionnelle; **trade-union**, union ouvrière; **trade wind**, vent alizé. ‖ **trader** [-°r] s. commerçant; négociant; marchand; vaisseau marchand (naut.), m. ‖ **tradesman** [-zm°n] (pl. **tradesmen**) s. marchand, commerçant; boutiquier; fournisseur; artisan, m. ‖ **trading** [-ing] s. commerce; trafic, m.

tradition [tr°dish°n] s. tradition, f.

traduce [tr°dyous] v. diffamer; **traducer**, calomniateur, diffamateur.

traffic [trafik] s. trafic; négoce, commerce, m.; circulation, f.; v. trafiquer; faire du commerce; être en relation (with, avec); **traffic flow**, courant de circulation.

tragedian [tr°djĭdi°n] s. tragédien, tragique, m. ‖ **tragedy** [tradj°di] s.° tragédie, f. ‖ **tragic** [tradjik] adj. tragique.

trail [tré¹l] s. trace; piste; traînée; crosse d'affût (mil.), f.; v. traîner; suivre à la piste; **trail rope**, prolonge (artill.). ‖ **trailer** [-°r] s. remorque, f.; traînard, m.; **trailer-caravan**, caravane [autom.].

train [tré¹n] s. train; convoi; enchaînement [ideas], m.; traînée; traîne; escorte, f.; v. (s')entraîner; former, instruire; dresser [animals]; pointer (mil.); **express train**, express, rapide; **freight train**, train de marchandises; **local train**, omnibus; **passenger train**, train de voyageurs; Am. **subway train**, rame de métro. ‖ **trainer** [-°r] s. entraîneur; dompteur; avion-école (aviat.), m. ‖ **training** [-ing] s. entraînement; dressage; pointage (mil.), m.; instruction, éducation, f.; **basic training**, instruction élémentaire. ‖ **trainman** [-m°n] (pl. **trainmen**) s. cheminot, m.

trait [tré¹t] s. trait, m.; caractéristique, f.

traitor [tré¹t°r] s. traître, m.; **traitorous**, traître; **traitress**, traîtresse.

traject [tr°djèkt] v. projeter, jeter; s. trajet, m. ‖ **trajectory** [-°ri] s.° trajectoire, f.

tram [tram] s. tramway; wagonnet de houillère, m.

tramp [trămp] v. aller à pied; battre la semelle; marcher à pas rythmés; vagabonder; s. promenade à pied, marche, f.; piétinement; vagabond, chemineau, m. ‖ **trample** [-'l] v. piétiner; fouler aux pieds.

trance [trăns] s. extase; transe; catalepsie, f.

tranquil [trănkwil] adj. tranquille. ‖ **tranquillity** [trănkwĭl°ti] s. tranquillité, f. ‖ **tranquillizer** [trăngkwila¹z°r] s. tranquillisant, m.

transact [trănsakt] v. traiter; négocier avec. ‖ **transaction** [trănsaksh°n] s. transaction, affaire, f.; pl. compte rendu, m.; procès-verbaux, actes, m. pl. ‖ **transactor** [-°r] s. négociateur, m.

transalpine [trănsalpin] adj. transalpin.

transatlantic [trăns°tlàntik] adj. transatlantique.

transcend [trănsènd] v. outrepasser; dépasser; **transcendent**, transcendant.

transcribe [trănskra¹b] v. transcrire. ‖ **transcript** [trănskript] s. transcription; copie, f.; **transcription**, transcription; émission différée [radio].

transept [trănsèpt] s. transept, m.

transfer [trănsfër] s. transfert (jur.); déplacement; billet de correspondance (railw.); virement (fin.), m.; mutation; copie, f.; [trănsfër] v. transférer; permuter; transporter; transborder; transmettre; décalquer; virer; changer, correspondre (railw.); **transferable**, transportable; transmissible; transférable; négociable.

transfigure [trănsfigy°r] v. transfigurer.

transform [trànsfaurm] *v.* changer; (se) transformer. ‖ **transformation** [trànsfᵉrméⁱshᵉn] *s.* transformation, f. ‖ **transformer** [trànsfaurmᵉr] *s.* transformateur, m.

transfuse [trànsfyouz] *v.* transfuser; transvaser. ‖ **transfusion** [trànsfyou-jᵉn] *s.* transfusion, f.

transgress [trànsgrès] *v.* transgresser; pécher; dépasser [bounds]. ‖ **transgression** [trànsgréⁱshᵉn] *s.* transgression; infraction; violation, f. ‖ **transgressor** [trànsgrèsᵉr] *s.* transgresseur; délinquant; pécheur, m.

transient [trànshᵉnt] *adj.* transitoire; passager; fugitif; momentané. ‖ **transit** [trànsit] *s.* transit; passage; parcours; transport (comm.), m. ‖ **transition** [trànzishᵉn] *s.* transition, f. ‖ **transitive** [trànsᵉtiv] *adj.* transitif. ‖ **transitory** [trànstoⁿuri] *adj.* transitoire, éphémère.

translate [trànsléⁱt] *v.* traduire; transférer; retransmettre (telegr.). ‖ **translation** [trànsléⁱshᵉn] *s.* translation (eccles.); version, traduction, f. ‖ **translator** [trànsléⁱtᵉr] *s.* traducteur, m.; traductrice, f.

transliterate [trànslitᵉréⁱt] *v.* transcrire.

translucent [trànslousⁿnt] *adj.* translucide.

transmission [trànsmishᵉn] *s.* transmission; émission [radio]; transmission [auto], f. ‖ **transmit** [trànsmit] *v.* transmettre; émettre [radio]; transporter (electr.). ‖ **transmitter** [-ᵉr] *s.* transmetteur; émetteur [radio]; manipulateur (telegr.), m.

transmute [trànsmiout] *v.* transmuer.

transom [trànsᵉm] *s.* traverse, f.; *Am.* vasistas, m.

transparency [trànspèᵉrᵉnsi] *s.** transparence; diapositive, f. ‖ **transparent** [trànspèrᵉnt] *adj.* transparent; clair; diaphane.

transpierce [trànspiᵉrs] *v.* transpercer.

transpiration [trànspaⁱréⁱshᵉn] *s.* transpiration, f. ‖ **transpire** [trànspaⁱr] *v.* transpirer; s'ébruiter; avoir lieu.

transplant [trànsplànt] *v.* transplanter; greffer (med.).

transport [trànspoⁿurt] *s.* transport; enthousiasme, déporté, m.; [trànspoⁿurt] *v.* transporter; camionner; déporter; enthousiasmer; *transportable*, transportable. ‖ **transportation** [trànspᵉrtéⁱshᵉn] *s.* transport; enthousiasme, m.; déportation, f.; *air, motor, rail, water transportation*, transport par air, par camions, par fer, par eau. ‖ **transporter** [trànspoⁿurtᵉr] *s.* transporteur, m.

transpose [trànspoⁿuz] *v.* transposer. *transposition*, transposition.

transverse [trànsvë̀rs] *adj.* transversal; *s.* transverse, m.

trap [trap] *s.* trappe, f.; piège, m.; *v.* attraper; prendre au piège; *Fr. Can.* trapper; *trapdoor*, trappe; *trapper*, trappeur; *mouse trap*, souricière; *rattletrap*, guimbarde.

trapeze [trapîz] *s.* trapèze, m.

trappings [trapingz] *s. pl.* parures, f. pl.; ornements; atours, m. pl.

trash [trash] *s.** camelote; fadaise [talk], f.; déchets; rebuts, m. pl.

traumatism [traum•tiz•m] *s.* traumatisme, m.

travel [trav'l] *s.* voyage; trajet (mech.), m.; *v.* voyager; circuler; parcourir; tourner, rouler (mech.); *travel agency*, agence de voyage. ‖ **travel(l)er** [-ᵉr] *s.* voyageur; curseur; chariot (mech.), m. ‖ **travel(l)ing** [-ing] *adj.* mobile; ambulant; de voyage; s. travelling [cinema], m.

traverse [travë̀rs] *s.* traverse; traversée; entretoise (mech.); transversale (geom.), f.; obstacle, revers, m.; *v.* traverser.

travesty [travisti] *s.** travesti, parodie, f.; *v.* parodier; déguiser.

trawler [traulᵉr] *s.* chalutier, m.

tray [tréⁱ] *s.* plateau, m.; cuvette (phot.); auge, augette, f.

treacherous [trètsh•rᵉs] *adj.* traître; perfide. ‖ **treachery** [trètshᵉri] *s.** trahison; perfidie, f.

treacle [trîk'l] *s.* mélasse, f.

tread [trèd] *v.** fouler, écraser; piétiner; appuyer sur; *s.* (bruit de) pas; piétinement; écartement des roues [car], m.; marche; chape [tire]; semelle, f.; *treadle*, pédale.

treason [trîz'n] *s.* trahison, f.

treasure [trèjᵉr] *s.* trésor, m.; *v.* thésauriser; conserver précieusement. *treasurer* [-ᵉr] *s.* trésorier, m. ‖ **treasury** [-ri] *s.** trésor public, m.; trésorerie, f.

treat [trît] *v.* traiter; négocier; inviter; *s.* régal, m.; partie de plaisir; tournée [drink], f. ‖ **treater** [-ᵉr] *s.* négociateur; hôte, m. ‖ **treatise** [-is] *s.* traité, m. ‖ **treatment** [-mᵉnt] *s.* traitement, m.; cure, f. ‖ **treaty** [-i] *s.** traité; pacte, m.

treble [trèb'l] *adj.* triple; *s.* triple, m.; *v.* tripler; *treble clef*, clef de sol; *treble voice*, voix de soprano.

tree [trî] *s.* arbre, m.; *family tree*, arbre généalogique; *treeless*, sans arbre; *treetop*, cime d'un arbre.

trefoil [trifoⁱl] *s.* trèfle, m.

trellis [trèlis] *s.** treillis, m.; *v.* treillisser.

tremble [trèmb'l] *v.* trembler; trembloter; vibrer; *s.* tremblement, m.

tremendous [trimènd•s] *adj.* terrible; épouvantable; extraordinaire; formidable.

tremor [trèm•r] *s.* tremblement; frémissement, m.; trépidation, f. ‖ *tremulous* [trèmyoul•s] *adj.* tremblotant; frémissant.

trench [trèntsh] *s.** tranchée, f.; retranchement; fossé, m.; *trenchboard*, caillebotis; *trench-coat*, imperméable; *trench fever*, fièvre récurrente; *trench mortar*, mortier (mil.). ‖ *trenchant* [-•nt] *adj.* mordant, tranchant; vigoureux.

trend [trènd] *s.* tendance; direction, f.

trepan [tripàn] *s.* trépan, m.; *v.* trépaner.

trepidation [trèpidé¹sh•n] *s.* trépidation; agitation, f.; trac, m.

trespass [trèsp•s] *s.** violation; contravention, f.; délit, m.; *v.* enfreindre; violer; empiéter sur; pécher; *no trespassing*, défense d'entrer. ‖ *trespasser* [-•r] *s.* transgresseur; délinquant; maraudeur; intrus, m.

tress [très] *s.** tresse, f.

trestle [très'l] *s.* tréteau; support; chevalet, m.

trial [tra¹•l] *s.* épreuve, expérience, tentative, f.; essai; jugement, procès (jur.), m.; *to bring to trial*, mettre en jugement; *speed trial*, essai de vitesse.

triangle [tra¹àngg'l] *s.* triangle, m. ‖ *triangular* [-gy•l•r] *adj.* triangulaire.

tribe [tra¹b] *s.* tribu, f.

tribulation [triby¹lé¹sh•n] *s.* tribulation, f.

tribunal [tribyoun'l] *s.* tribunal, m.

tribune [tríbyoun] *s.* tribune, f.; [tribyoun] *s.* « tribune » [newspaper], f.

tributary [tríby•tèri] *adj.* tributaire; *s.** affluent, m. ‖ *tribute* [tríbyout] *s.* tribut; hommage, m.

trice [tra¹s] *s.* instant, m.

trick [trík] *s.* tour; truc, tic, m.; ruse; farce; levée [cards], f.; *v.* duper; escroquer; *trick-shot*, truquage [cinema]. ‖ *trickery* [-•ri] *s.** tromperie; tricherie; supercherie, f.

trickle [trík'l] *v.* couler; ruisseler; *s.* ruissellement; filet d'eau; ruisselet, m.

trickster [tríkst•r] *s.* escroc; fourbe, m. ‖ *tricky* [tríki] *adj.* rusé; astucieux; minutieux, compliqué, délicat.

tried [tra¹ed] *p. p. of to try; adj.* éprouvé.

trifle [tra¹f'l] *s.* bagatelle; vétille, f.; *v.* badiner; *to trifle away*, gaspiller; *to trifle with*, se jouer de; *trifling*, insignifiant.

trig [trig] *adj.* net; soigné; pimpant; bien tenu.

trigger [trig•r] *s.* détente; gâchette, f.; déclic, m.

trill [tril] *s.* trille, m.; *v.* triller; tinter; rouler les r.

trillion [trílli•n] *s.* trillion; *Am.* billion, m.

trim [trim] *v.* arranger; orner; ajuster; tailler; arrimer (aviat.; naut.); émonder [tree]; dégrossir [timber]; *s.* ornement; attirail; bon ordre; arrimage, m.; *adj.* ordonné; soigné; coquet. ‖ *trimming* [-ing] *s.* garniture, f.; arrimage; émondage; calibrage (phot.), m.; *pl.* passementerie, f.

trimonthly [tra¹mœnthli] *adj.* trimestriel.

trinket [trìngkit] *s.* colifichet, m.

trio [trio^ou] *s.* trio, m.

trip [trip] *s.* excursion; tournée, f.; tour; trajet, parcours; faux pas; déclenchement (mech.), m.; *v.* trébucher; broncher [horse]; déclencher (mech.); fourcher [tongue]; trottiner.

tripe [tra¹p] *s.* tripe; camelote, f.; *tripe-dealer*, *tripeman*, tripier; *tripe-shop*, triperie.

triple [trip'l] *adj.* triple; *v.* tripler; *triplet*, trio; triplet; tercet; triolet; *triplicate*, triplé, en triple exemplaire.

tripod [tra¹pâd] *s.* trépied, m.

triptych [triptik] *s.* triptyque, m.

trite [tra¹t] *adj.* banal; rebattu.

triturate [tritiouré¹t] *v.* triturer.

triumph [tra¹emf] *s.** triomphe, m.; *v.* triompher. ‖ *triumphal* [tra¹æmf'l] *adj.* triomphal. ‖ *triumphant* [tra¹æmf•nt] *adj.* triomphant; triomphateur. ‖ *triumphantly* [-li] *adv.* triomphalement. ‖ *triumpher* [-•r] *s.* triomphateur, m.; triomphatrice, f.

trivial [trívy•l] *adj.* trivial; insignifiant; banal; frivole.

trod [trâd] *pret., p. p. of to tread.* ‖ *trodden* [-'n] *p. p. of to tread.*

trolley [trâli] *s.* trolley; chariot; fardier; tramway, m.; *trolley car*, tramway; *trolley line*, ligne de tramways.

trollop [trâl•p] *s.* souillon; traînée, f.

trombone [trâmbo^oun] *s.* trombone, m.; *trombonist*, trombone [man].

troop [troup] *s.* troupe, f.; peloton; escadron, m. ‖ *trooper* [-•r] *s.* cavalier [soldier], m. ‖ *troops* [troups] *s. pl.* troupes, f. pl.; *covering troops*, troupes de couverture; *picked troops*, troupes d'élite.

trophy [tro°ufi] *s.** trophée, m.

tropic [tråpik] *s.* tropique, m. ‖ **tropical** [-'l] *adj.* tropical.

trot [tråt] *v.* trotter; *s.* trot, m.; *fast trot,* trot allongé.

trouble [træb'l] *s.* trouble; chagrin; ennui; souci; dérangement, m.; peine; affection (med.), f.; *v.* troubler; agiter; tracasser; affliger; préoccuper; ennuyer; déranger; gêner; *it is not worth the trouble,* cela n'en vaut pas la peine; *engine trouble,* panne de moteur; *trouble shooter,* dépanneur; *troublemaker,* agitateur, agent provocateur. ‖ **troublesome** [-s°m] *adj.* ennuyeux; fâcheux; gênant; incommode.

trough [trauf] *s.* auge, f.; pétrin; baquet; creuset (metall.); caniveau; creux des lames, m.; *drinking-trough,* abreuvoir.

trounce [tra°uns] *v.* rosser.

trousers [tra°uz°rz] *s. pl.* pantalon, m.

trousseau [trouso°u] *s.* trousseau, m.

trout [tra°ut] *s.* truite, f.

trowel [tra°u°l] *s.* truelle, f.; déplantoir (hort.), m.

truant [trou°nt] *s.* paresseux, m.; *adj.* paresseux; vagabond.

truce [trous] *s.* trêve, f.; *flag of truce,* drapeau de parlementaire.

truck [træk] *s.* camion; fourgon; wagon (railw.); chariot, diable, m.; *v.* camionner; *delivery truck,* camionnette; *truck garden,* jardin maraîcher.

truckle [træk'l] *v.* ramper, s'aplatir.

truculence [trækyoul°ns] *s.* férocité; violence, f.

trudge [trædj] *v.* cheminer péniblement; clopiner; se traîner; *s.* marche pénible, f.

true [trou] *adj.* vrai; exact; loyal, sincère; droit; juste; conforme; fidèle; centré (mech.); légitime; authentique; *to come true,* se réaliser.

truffle [træf'l] *s.* truffe, f.

truism [trouiz'm] *s.* truisme, m.

truly [trouli] *adv.* vraiment; réellement; sincèrement; franchement; *yours truly,* sincèrement vôtre.

trump [træmp] *s.* atout [cards], m.; *v.* jouer atout.

trump [træmp] *v.* inventer; *to trump up an excuse,* forger une excuse.

trumpet [træmpit] *s.* trompette, f.; *v.* jouer de la trompette; publier; *trumpeter,* trompettiste; *ear trumpet,* cornet acoustique.

truncate [trængké'it] *v.* tronquer; [-it] *adj.* tronqué.

truncheon [trænsh°n] *s.* matraque, f.; bâton, m.

trundle [trænd'l] *v.* (faire) rouler; pousser.

trunk [trœngk] *s.* tronc, m.; trompe [elephant]; malle [luggage]; ligne principale (railw.), f.; *pl.* caleçon court, m.

truss [trœs] *s.** bandage herniaire (med.); cintre (archit.), m.

trust [trœst] *s.* confiance; espérance; responsabilité, charge; garde; confidence, f.; trust; crédit (comm.), m.; *v.* se fier; (se) confier; faire crédit à; espérer. ‖ **trustee** [-i] *s.* dépositaire; administrateur, syndic, m.; *board of trustees,* conseil d'administration. ‖ **trustful** [-f°l] *adj.* confiant. ‖ **trustworthy** [-wë°zhi] *adj.* digne de confiance, honnête, sûr. ‖ **trusty** [trœsti] *adj.* sûr; fidèle; loyal; *s.** homme de confiance, m.

truth [trouth] *s.* vérité; sincérité; loyauté, f. ‖ **truthful** [-f°l] *adj.* véridique, vrai; sincère. ‖ **truthfulness** [-f°lnis] *s.* véracité, f.

try [tra¹] *v.* essayer; entreprendre; mettre à l'épreuve; juger (jur.); *s.** tentative, f.; essai [rugby], m.; *to try someone's patience,* éprouver la patience de quelqu'un; *to try on a suit,* essayer un costume. ‖ **trying** [-ing] *adj.* éprouvant; pénible; angoissant; vexant.

tub [tœb] *s.* cuve; baignoire, f.; baquet; tub, m.; *v.* prendre un tub.

tube [tyoub] *s.* tube; conduit; tuyau; *Br.* métro, m.; buse (techn.); lampe [radio], f.; *bronchial tube,* bronche; *inner tube,* chambre à air [tire]; *tube-station,* station de métro.

tubercle [tyoubë°k'l] *s.* tubercule, m. ‖ **tubercular** [tyoubë°kyel°r], **tuberculous** [-°s] *adj.* tuberculeux. ‖ **tuberculosis** [tyoubë°kyel°ou°sis] *s.* tuberculose, f.

tubing [tyoubing] *s.* tuyautage, m.; tuyauterie, f.; tubage, m. (med.).

tubular [tio°ubioul°r] *adj.* tubulaire.

tuck [tœk] *v.* retrousser; *s.* pli, plissé, m.; *to tuck in bed,* border le lit; *tuck-in,* gueuleton (colloq.).

Tuesday [tyouzdi] *s.* mardi, m.

tuft [tœft] *s.* touffe; huppe, f.; pompon, m.

tug [tœg] *v.* tirer, tirailler; remorquer; *s.* tiraillement; remorqueur [boat], m.; saccade, f.

tuition [tyouish°n] *s.* instruction; leçons, f.; enseignement, m.; *Am.* droits d'inscription, m. pl.

tulip [tyoul°p] *s.* tulipe, f.

tulle [tyoul] *s.* tulle, m.

tumble [tæmb'l] *v.* tomber, dégringoler; tourner et retourner; chiffonner; *to tumble to*, deviner; *to tumble over*, faire la culbute; *to tumble for*, se laisser prendre à. ‖ **tumbler** [-ᵉʳ] *s.* gobelet, grand verre, m.; timbale, f.; équilibriste, acrobate; pigeon culbutant, m.

tumefy [tyoumᵉfaⁱ] *v.* (se) tuméfier. ‖ **tumid** [tyoumid] *adj.* enflé; ampoulé (fig.).

tummy [tæmi] *s.* estomac, ventre, m. (colloq.).

tumo(u)r [tyoumᵉʳ] *s.* tumeur, f.

tumult [tyoumœlt] *s.* tumulte; vacarme; trouble, m. ‖ **tumultuous** [tyoumœltshouᵉs] *adj.* tumultueux.

tun [tœn] *s.* tonneau, fût, m.

tuna [tounᵉ] *s. Am.* thon, m.

tune [tyoun] *s.* air; ton; accord, m.; mélodie, f.; *v.* accorder; régler, syntoniser [radio]; *out of tune*, désaccordé; *in tune*, d'accord; accordé; juste; *tuneful*, harmonieux, mélodieux.

tunic [tyounik] *s.* tunique, f.

tuning [tyouning] *s.* accord; accordage, m.; mise au point (mech.); syntonisation [radio], f.; *tuning knob*, bouton de réglage [radio].

Tunisia [tyounishiᵉ] *s.* Tunisie, f.

tunnel [tæn'l] *s.* tunnel, m.; *v.* trouer, percer.

turbid [tëʳbid] *adj.* trouble; bourbeux; en désordre; embrouillé.

turbine [tëʳbaⁱn] *s.* turbine, f.

turbulent [tëʳbyᵉlᵉnt] *adj.* turbulent; tumultueux; tourbillonnant; séditieux.

tureen [tyourîn] *s.* saucière; soupière, f.

turf [tëʳf] *s.* gazon; terrain de course; turf, m.; tourbe, f. ‖ **turfite** [-aⁱt] *s.* turfiste, m. f.

turgid [tëʳdjid] *adj.* enflé, gonflé.

Turk [tëʳk] *s.* Turc, m.

turkey [tëʳki] *s.* dindon, m.; dinde, f.; *Am.* « four » (theat.).

Turkey [tëʳki] *s.* Turquie, f. ‖ **Turkish** [-sh] *adj., s.* turc.

turmoil [tëʳmoⁱl] *s.* tumulte; désordre; trouble, m.; agitation, f.

turn [tëʳn] *v.* (se) tourner; transformer; virer (aviat.); faire pencher [scale]; traduire; émousser; écœurer; se détourner; se changer, devenir; se diriger; *s.* tour; tournant; contour; virage; changement; penchant, m.; révolution (astron.); tournure; occasion, f.; *to turn back*, se retourner; renvoyer; rebrousser chemin; *to turn down an offer*, repousser une offre; *to turn about*, faire demi-tour; *to turn*

in, rendre, restituer; *Am.* se coucher; *to turn off*, fermer, couper [gas]; éteindre (electr.); *to turn on*, ouvrir, allumer (electr.); *to turn out*, expulser; *to turn over*, capoter [auto], se renverser; *to turn to*, avoir recours à; *to turn over and over*, tournoyer; *to turn sour*, aigrir; *turn of mind*, tournure d'esprit; *by turns*, alternativement; *in turn*, à tour de rôle.

turncoat [tëʳnkoᵘt] *s.* renégat, m.; girouette (fig.), f.

turnip [tëʳnip] *s.* navet, m.

turnkey [tëʳnki] *s.* geôlier, m.

turnover [tëʳnoᵘvᵉr] *s.* capotage; chiffre d'affaires [business]; chausson [apple], m.; *adj.* replié, rabattu; reversible; pliant [table].

turnpike [tëʳnpaⁱk] *s.* péage, m.; *Am.* autoroute, f.

turnsole [tëʳnsoᵘl] *s.* tournesol, m.

turntable [tëʳnté¹b'l] *s.* plaque tournante (railw.), f.; plateau [gramophone], m.

turpentine [tëʳpᵉntaⁱn] *s.* térébenthine, f.

turpitude [tëʳpᵉtyoud] *s.* turpitude; vilenie, f.

turquoise [tëʳkwoⁱz] *s.* turquoise, f.

turret [tëʳit] *s.* tourelle, f.

turtle [tëʳt'l] *s.* tortue, f.; *turtle-dove*, tourterelle; *to turn turtle*, capoter.

tusk [tœsk] *s.* défense, f.

tussle [tæs'l] *s.* bagarre, f.; *v.* se bagarrer.

tutelary [tyoutilᵉri] *adj.* tutélaire.

tutor [tyoutᵉr] *s.* précepteur; répétiteur; professeur adjoint; tuteur (jur.), m.; *v.* être le tuteur de; servir de tuteur à; enseigner; *tutorage*, tutelle; *tutoress*, monitrice; tutrice.

tuxedo [tœksidoᵘ] *s.* smoking, m.

twaddle [twåd'l] *s.* niaiseries, f. pl.; *v.* jacasser.

twang [twàng] *s.* nasillement; son métallique, m.; *v.* nasiller; (faire) vibrer; *twangy*, nasal, nasillant.

tweed [twîd] *s.* tweed, m.

tweet [twît] *v.* pépier.

tweezers [twîzᵉrz] *s. pl.* pince, f.

twelfth [twèlfth] *adj., s.* douzième; *Twelfth Night*, soir de l'Epiphanie. ‖ **twelve** [twèlv] *adj., s.* douze; *twelve o'clock*, midi, minuit. ‖ **twentieth** [twèntiith] *adj., s.* vingtième; vingt [month, title]. ‖ **twenty** [twènti] *adj., s.* vingt.

twice [twaⁱs] *adv.* deux fois.

twig [twig] *s.* brindille; ramille, f.

twilight [twa¹la¹t] *s.* crépuscule, m.; *adj.* crépusculaire.

twin [twìn] *adj.*, *s.* jumeau, m.; jumelle, f.; **twin-beds**, lits jumeaux.

twine [twa¹n] *s.* ficelle, f.; enroulement; entrelacement, m.; *v.* (s')enrouler.

twinge [twìndʒ] *s.* élancement, m.; *v.* pincer; élancer.

twining [twa¹ning] *adj.* sinueux; lancinant.

twinkle [twìngkl] *v.* scintiller; clignoter; *s.* scintillement; clignement, clin, m. || **twinkling** [-ing] *s.* clignement, clin, m.

twirl [twë¹rl] *v.* (faire) tournoyer; girer; *s.* tournoiement, m.; fioriture; volute; pirouette.

twist [twist] *s.* cordon; cordonnet; toron (naut.), m.; torsion; contorsion, f.; *v.* tordre; entortiller; enlacer; s'entrelacer, (s')enrouler; se tortiller; **twisted**, tordu, *Fr. Can.* croche.

twitch [twitsh] *s.** élancement; tic, m.; secousse; convulsion (med.), f.; chiendent, m. (bot.); *v.* se crisper; se contracter; se convulser; tirer vivement, arracher.

twitter [twi¹ter] *v.* gazouiller; palpiter; *s.* gazouillis; émoi, m.; palpitation, f.

two [tou] *adj.* deux; *by twos*, deux à deux; *two and two*, deux plus deux; **two-edged**, à deux tranchants. || **twofold** [-fo°uld] *adj.* double.

tycoon [ta¹ko°un] *s. Am.* magnat (m.) de la finance.

tympan [tìmpen] *s.* tympan, m.

type [ta¹p] *s.* type; individu; caractère (typogr.), m.; *v.* taper à la machine, dactylographier. || **typewrite** [-ra¹t] *v.* dactylographier, taper. || **typewriter** [-ra¹ter] *s.* machine à écrire, f., *Fr. Can.* dactylo, m. || **typewritten** [-rit'n] *adj.* dactylographié.

typhoid [ta¹fo¹d] *s.* typhoïde, f.

typhoon [ta¹foun] *s.* typhon, m.

typhus [ta¹fes] *s.* typhus, m.

typical [tipik'l] *adj.* typique. || **typify** [típifa¹] *v.* représenter, symboliser, figurer; être le type de.

typing [ta¹ping] *s.* dactylographie, f. || **typist** [ta¹pist] *s.* dactylo(graphe), m. f.

typographer [ta¹pâgrefer] *s.* typographe, m. || **typography** [-fi] *s.* typographie, f.

tyrannical [tiranik'l] *adj.* tyrannique. || **tyrannize** [tìrena¹z] *v.* tyranniser. || **tyranny** [tìreni] *s.** tyrannie, f. || **tyrant** [ta¹rent] *s.* tyran, m.

tyre [ta¹er] *s.* pneu, m.

tyro [ta¹ro] *s.* novice, m.

U

ubiquity [ioubíkwiti] *s.* ubiquité, f.

udder [æder] *s.* pis, m.

ugliness [æglinis] *s.* laideur, f. || **ugly** [ægli] *adj.* laid; vilain; mauvais [weather].

ulcer [ælser] *s.* ulcère, m.; plaie, f. || **ulcerate** [-ré¹t] *v.* (s')ulcérer. || **ulceration** [ælseré¹shen] *s.* ulcération, f.

ulterior [œltirier] *adj.* ultérieur.

ultimate [æltemit] *adj.* ultime. || **ultimately** [-li] *adv.* finalement; en définitive; définitivement.

ultra-sound [æltresa°und] *s.* ultrason, m. || **ultra-violet** [-va¹elit] *adj.* ultra-violet.

umbilicus [œmbílikes] (*pl.* **umbilici** [-a¹]) *s.* ombilic, m.

umbrage [œmbridj] *s.* ombrage, m.

umbrella [œmbrèle] *s.* parapluie, m.; ombrelle, f.

umpire [œmpa¹r] *s.* arbitre, m.; *v.* arbitrer.

un- [œn-] *prefix* in-; non-; dé-; mal; sans; peu.

unable [œné¹b'l] *adj.* incapable; empêché; impuissant; *to be unable to*, ne pouvoir.

unaccountable [œneka°unteb'l] *adj.* inexplicable; incompréhensible; irresponsable; indépendant.

unaccustomed [œnekæstemd] *adj.* inaccoutumé; insolite; peu usuel.

unacknowledged [œnekná:lidjd] *adj.* non reconnu; sans réponse [letter].

unaffected [œnefèktid] *adj.* simple, naturel; insensible.

unalloyed [œnelo¹d] *adj.* pur, sans mélange.

unambiguous [œnambígyoues] *adj.* non équivoque.

unamenable [œnemineb'l] *adj.* réfractaire, indocile.

unanimity [youneníme¹ti] *s.* unanimité, f.; *unanimous*, unanime.

unanswerable [œnânsereb'l] *adj.* sans réplique, incontestable.

unapproachable [œnepro°utsheb'l] *adj.* inaccessible; incomparable.

unarmed [œnârmd] *adj.* désarmé; sans armes.

unassailable [œnᵉsé¹leb'l] *adj.* inattaquable; irréfutable.

unassuming [œnᵉsyouming] *adj.* modeste, simple.

unattractive [œnᵉtraktiv] *adj.* sans attrait; peu séduisant.

unavailable [œnᵉvé¹leb'l] *adj.* indisponible; pas libre. || *unavailing* [œnᵉvé¹ling] *adj.* inutile; infructueux.

unavoidable [œnᵉvoideb'l] *adj.* inévitable; inéluctable.

unaware [œnᵉwèᵉr] *adj.* ignorant; non averti; non informé. || *unawares* [-z] *adv.* au dépourvu; à l'improviste; par mégarde.

unbalanced [œnbal⁼nst] *adj.* inéquilibré; déséquilibré (med.); non compensé (mech.).

unbearable [œnbèreb'l] *adj.* intolérable; intenable.

unbecoming [œnbikœming] *adj.* inconvenant; déplacé; peu seyant.

unbelief [œnbelîf] *s.* incrédulité, f. || *unbelievable* [-lîveb'l] *adj.* incroyable. || *unbeliever* [-lîvᵉr] *s.* incrédule; mécréant, m. || *unbelieving* [-lîving] *adj.* incrédule.

unbend [œnbènd] *v.* (se) redresser; (se) détendre. || *unbending* [-ing] *adj.* inflexible; intransigeant.

unbiased [œnba¹est] *adj.* sans préjugés; impartial.

unbosom [œnbouzᵉm] *v.* révéler.

unbounded [œnba⁰undid] *adj.* illimité; démesuré; effréné.

unbreakable [œnbré¹keb'l] *adj.* incassable. || *unbroken* [œnbro⁰ukᵉn] *adj.* intact; non brisé; non violé; ininterrompu; indompté [horse].

unburden [œnbᵉrd'n] *v.* alléger, soulager.

unbutton [œnbœt'n] *v.* déboutonner.

uncanny [œnkàni] *adj.* étrange; surnaturel; mystérieux.

unceasing [œnsîsing] *adj.* incessant, continuel.

uncertain [œnsërt'n] *adj.* incertain; irrésolu; indéterminé; douteux; aléatoire.

unchallenged [œntshalindjd] *adj.* incontesté; non contredit; non récusé.

unchangeable [œntshé¹ndjeb'l] *adj.* inaltérable; immuable; invariable. || *unchanged* [œntshé¹ndjd] *adj.* inchangé.

uncharted [œntshârtid] *adj.* qui ne figure pas sur la carte.

unclaimed [œnklé¹md] *adj.* non réclamé; de rebut [letter].

uncle [œngk'l] *s.* oncle, m.

unclean [œnklîn] *adj.* sale; impur.

unclear [œnklîᵉr] *adj.* peu clair.

uncomfortable [œnkœmfᵉrteb'l] *adj.* inconfortable; incommode; gêné; fâcheux, mal à l'aise.

uncommon [œnkâmᵉn] *adj.* peu commun; rare; insolite; *not uncommonly*, assez souvent.

uncommunicative [œnkᵉmyounikᵉtiv] *adj.* renfermé.

uncompleted [œnkᵉmplîtid] *adj.* inachevé.

uncomplimentary [œnkâmpliméntᵉri] *adj.* peu flatteur.

uncompromising [œnkâmprᵉma¹zing] *adj.* intransigeant.

unconcerned [œnkᵉnsërnd] *adj.* indifférent; insouciant.

unconditional [œnkᵉndíshᵉn'l] *adj.* absolu; inconditionnel.

uncongenial [œnkᵉndjinyᵉl] *adj.* antipathique; déplaisant; incompatible.

unconquerable [œnkângkᵉreb'l] *adj.* invincible; indomptable; insurmontable. || *unconquered* [œnkângkᵉrd] *adj.* invaincu; indompté.

unconscious [œnkânshᵉs] *adj.* inconscient; évanoui; *s.* inconscient, m. || *unconsciousness* [-nis] *s.* inconscience, f.; évanouissement, m.

unconsolable [œnkᵉnso⁰uleb'l] *adj.* inconsolable.

uncontrollable [œnkᵉntro⁰uleb'l] *adj.* incontrôlable; irrésistible; indomptable. || *uncontrolled* [œnkᵉntro⁰uld] *adj.* incontrôlé; sans frein; indépendant; irresponsable.

unconventional [œnkᵉnvènshᵉn'l] *adj.* peu conventionnel; original; affranchi, libre.

uncork [œnkaurk] *v.* déboucher.

uncouth [œnkouth] *adj.* étrange; gauche; grossier, malappris.

uncover [œnkœvᵉr] *v.* (se) découvrir.

unction [œngkshᵉn] *s.* onction, f. || *unctuous* [-shᵉs] *adj.* onctueux; *unctuousness*, onctuosité.

uncultivated [œnkœltᵉvé¹tid] *adj.* inculte. || *uncultured* [œnkœltshᵉrd] *adj.* inculte, sans culture, fruste.

undeceive [œndisîv] *v.* désabuser.

undecided [œndisa¹did] *adj.* indécis, irrésolu.

undeniable [œndina¹eb'l] *adj.* indéniable; incontestable.

undenominational [œndinᵉminé¹shᵉn'l] *adj.* laïque, non confessionnel.

under [œnd^er] *prep.* sous; au-dessous de; dans, en moins de; *adv.* dessous; *adj.* inférieur; *under the law*, en vertu de la loi.

underbrush [œnd^erbrœsh] *s.** taillis; sous-bois, m.; broussailles, f. pl.

undercarriage [œnd^erkaridj] *s.* train d'atterrissage (aviat.), m.

underclothes [œnd^erklou^{ou}z] *s.** pl. sous-vêtements, m. pl.; linge de corps, m.

underdone [œnd^erdœn] *adj.* pas assez cuit; saignant.

underestimate [œnd^erèst^emé¹t] *v.* sous-estimer; déprécier.

underfed [œnd^erfèd] *adj.* sous-alimenté.

undergo [œnd^ergo^{ou}] *v.* subir; supporter.

undergraduate [œnd^ergradyouit] *s.* étudiant non diplômé, m.

underground [œnd^ergra^{ou}nd] *adj.*, *s.* souterrain; *Br.* métro, m.; Résistance [war], f.; *adv.* en secret.

underhand [œnd^erhand] *adj.* clandestin; sournois.

underline [œnd^erla¹n] *v.* souligner.

underlying [œnd^erla¹ing] *adj.* sous-jacent; fondamental.

undermine [œnd^erma¹n] *v.* miner.

underneath [œnd^ernîth] *prep.* sous; au-dessous de; *adv.* dessous; en dessous; par-dessous.

underpass [œnd^erpâs] *s.** *Am.* passage souterrain (ou) sous un pont, m.

underpay [œnd^erpé¹] *v.* exploiter; payer au-dessous du tarif.

undersell [œnd^ersèl] *v.* vendre meilleur marché; solder.

undershirt [œnd^ershë^rt] *s.* chemisette, f.

undersigned [œnd^ersa¹nd] *adj.*, *s.* soussigné.

undersized [œnd^ersa¹zd] *adj.* de taille inférieure à la moyenne; sous-calibré (mech.); rabougri.

underskirt [œnd^erskë^rt] *s.* jupon, m.; sous-jupe, f.

understand [œnd^erstànd] *v.** entendre; comprendre; sous-entendre; apprendre; être habile à; *understandable*, compréhensible. ‖ *understanding* [-ing] *s.* compréhension; intelligence; harmonie; convention, f.; entendement; accord, m. ‖ *understood* [œnd^erstoud] *pret.*, *p. p. of to understand*.

understate [œnd^ersté¹t] *v.* amoindrir. ‖ *understatement* [-m^ent] *s.* atténuation (f.) des faits; euphémisme, m.

understructure [œnd^erstrœktsh^er] *s.* infrastructure, f.

understudy [œnd^erstœdi] *v.* doubler; *s.** doublure (theat.), f.

undertake [œnd^erté¹k] *v.* entreprendre; assumer; garantir. ‖ *undertaken* [-^en] *p. p. of to undertake*. ‖ *undertaker* [-^er] *s.* entrepreneur de pompes funèbres, m. ‖ *undertaking* [-ing] *s.* entreprise, f. ‖ *undertook* [-touk] *pret. of to undertake*.

undertow [œnd^erto^{ou}] *s.* ressac, m.

undervalue [œnd^ervalyou] *v.* sous-estimer; déprécier.

underwear [œnd^erwè^er] *s.* sous-vêtements, m. pl.

underwent [œnd^erwènt] *pret. of to undergo*.

underworld [œnd^erwë^rld] *s.* pègre, f.; enfers, m. pl.

underwrite [œnd^erra¹t] *v.* assurer; souscrire.

undeviating [undîvié¹ting] *adj.* droit; constant, rigide.

undid [œndid] *pret. of to undo*.

undiscoverable [œndiskœv^er^eb'l] *adj.* introuvable.

undiscriminating [œndiskrim^ené¹ting] *adj.* sans discernement; peu averti.

undistinguished [œndistinggwisht] *adj.* médiocre, banal.

undisturbed [œndistë^rbd] *adj.* serein; impassible; non dérangé; non troublé.

undo [œndou] *v.** défaire; détacher; délier; ruiner, perdre. ‖ *undone* [-dœn] *p. p. of to undo*; *adj.* non exécuté; défait; délié; perdu.

undress [œndrès] *v.* (se) déshabiller; [œndrès] *s.* petite tenue, f.

undrinkable [œndrink^eb'l] *adj.* imbuvable.

undue [œndyou] *adj.* non dû; non échu; excessif; irrégulier, indu.

undulate [œndyé lé¹t] *v.* onduler.

unduly [œndyouli] *adv.* indûment; à l'excès.

undying [œnda¹ing] *adj.* immortel.

unearned [œnë^rnd] *adj.* immérité.

unearth [œnë^rth] *v.* déterrer; exhumer; découvrir.

uneasily [œnîzli] *adv.* malaisément; difficilement; avec gêne ou inquiétude. ‖ *uneasy* [œnîzi] *adj.* mal à l'aise; préoccupé; gêné; pénible, difficile.

uneducated [œnèdj^eké¹tid] *adj.* ignorant; sans éducation.

unemployed [œnimplo¹d] *adj.* inoccupé; désœuvré; en chômage. ‖ **unemployment** [œnimplo¹mènt] *s.* chômage, m.

unending [œnènding] *adj.* interminable; sempiternel.

unequal [œn¹kwel] *adj.* inégal; non à la hauteur (*to*, de); insuffisant. ‖ **unequalled** [-d] *adj.* inégalé.

uneven [œni¹ven] *adj.* dénivelé; irrégulier; raboteux; impair [number]; accidenté. ‖ **unevenness** [-nis] *s.* inégalité; dénivellation; variabilité [temper], f.; accident du terrain, m.

unexpected [œnikspèktid] *adj.* inattendu; imprévu. ‖ **unexpectedly** [-li] *adv.* à l'improviste.

unfailing [œnfé¹ling] *adj.* inépuisable; infaillible; indéfectible.

unfair [œnfèeʳ] *adj.* injuste; déloyal; de mauvaise foi.

unfaithful [œnfé¹thfel] *adj.* infidèle; impie; inexact.

unfashionable [œnfashneb'l] *adj.* démodé.

unfasten [œnfas'n] *v.* détacher; délier; desserrer; déboutonner.

unfavo(u)rable [œnfé¹vreb'l] *adj.* défavorable; hostile.

unfeasible [œnfîzeb'l] *adj.* irréalisable, impraticable.

unfeeling [œnfîling] *adj.* insensible; inhumain; impitoyable.

unfinished [œnfinisht] *adj.* inachevé; incomplet; imparfait.

unfit [œnfit] *adj.* inapte; impropre; incapable; inopportun; *v.* rendre impropre à.

unflagging [œnflaging] *adj.* inlassable; soutenu [interest].

unfold [œnfoould] *v.* déplier; déployer; révéler; (se) dérouler.

unforeseen [œnfooʳsîn] *adj.* imprévu, inattendu.

unforgettable [œnfeʳgèteb'l] *adj.* inoubliable.

unforgivable [œnfeʳgiveb'l] *adj.* impardonnable. ‖ **unforgiving** [-ving] *adj.* implacable.

unfortunate [œnfaurtshenit] *adj.* infortuné; regrettable, fâcheux.

unfriendliness [œnfrèndlinis] *s.* inimitié, hostilité, f. ‖ **unfriendly** [-i] *adj.* peu amical; malveillant; *adv.* avec malveillance, avec inimitié.

unfurl [œnfëʳl] *v.* déployer; larguer [sail].

unfurnished [œnfëʳnisht] *adj.* non meublé.

ungainly [œngé¹nli] *adj.* gauche, dégingandé.

ungraceful [œngré¹sfoul] *adj.* disgracieux. ‖ **ungracious** [-gré¹shes] *adj.* peu aimable, déplaisant.

ungrateful [œngré¹tfel] *adj.* ingrat.

unhappy [œnhapi] *adj.* malheureux.

unharmed [œnhârmd] *adj.* indemne.

unhealthy [œnhèlthi] *adj.* malsain; insalubre; maladif.

unheard of [œnhëʳdâv] *adj.* inouï; inconnu, ignoré.

unhitch [œnhítsh] *v.* dételer.

unhook [œnhouk] *v.* décrocher; dégrafer.

unhurt [œnhëʳt] *adj.* indemne.

uniform [youn¹faurm] *s.* uniforme, m.; *v.* mettre en uniforme. ‖ **uniformity** [-èti] *s.* uniformité, f.

unify [youn¹fa¹] *v.* unifier.

unimpeachable [œnìmpîtsheb'l] *adj.* incontestable.

unimportant [œnimpauʳtent] *adj.* insignifiant, peu important.

uninjured [œnìndjëʳd] *adj.* intact, sain et sauf.

union [youny en] *s.* union, f.; syndicat, m.; *Union Jack*, pavillon britannique.

unique [younîk] *adj.* unique.

unison [younez'n] *s.* unisson, f.

unit [younit] *s.* unité, f.; élément; groupe; bloc, m.; *unitary*, unitaire.

unite [youna¹t] *v.* (s')unir; réunir; (se) joindre; se mêler. ‖ **unity** [youn-èti] *s.* unité; union; solidarité; concorde, f.

universal [younevèrsel] *adj.* universel; *universality*, universalité; *universalize*, universaliser. ‖ **universe** [younevèʳs] *s.* univers, m. ‖ **university** [younevèʳsèti] *s.* université, f.

unjust [œndjæst] *adj.* injuste; mal fondé. ‖ **unjustifiable** [-efa¹eb'l] *adj.* injustifiable. ‖ **unjustified** [-efa¹d] *adj.* injustifié.

unkempt [œnkèmpt] *adj.* mal peigné.

unkind [œnka¹nd] *adj.* méchant; malveillant, discourtois.

unknowingly [œnnoouingli] *adv.* inconsciemment.

unknown [œnnooun] *adj.* inconnu.

unlawful [œnlaufel] *adj.* illégal; frauduleux.

unleash [œnlîsh] *v.* lâcher [dogs].

unless [enlès] *conj.* à moins que; *prep.* excepté, sauf.

unlike [œnla¹k] *adj.* différent; dissemblable; *prep.* au contraire de; ne... pas comme. ‖ **unlikely** [-li] *adj.* improbable; invraisemblable.

unlimited [œnlímitid] *adj.* illimité.

unload [œnlo⁰ud] *v.* décharger; *unloaded*, déchargé, *Fr.· Can.* allège; soulagé (fig.).

unlock [œnlák] *v.* ouvrir; débloquer; révéler.

unlucky [œnlǽki] *adj.* malchanceux; malencontreux; néfaste.

unmanageable [œnmanidje⁶b'l] *adj.* indomptable, intraitable.

unmarried [œnmarid] *adj.* célibataire.

unmask [œnmask] *v.* démasquer.

unmatched [œnmatsht] *adj.* sans égal; incomparable; dépareillé.

unmerciful [œnmë⁶sif⁶l] *adj.* impitoyable; exorbitant.

unmindful [œnma¹ndf⁶l] *adj.* inattentif; négligent; indifférent.

unmistakable [œnmësté¹k⁶b'l] *adj.* évident, indubitable.

unmoved [œnmouvd] *adj.* immobile; impassible; indifférent.

unnatural [œnnatsh⁶r⁶l] *adj.* contre nature; dénaturé; artificiel.

unnerve [œnnë⁶v] *v.* faire perdre son courage à; démonter.

unnoticed [œnno⁰utist] *adj.* inaperçu; négligé; passé sous silence.

unobliging [œn⁶bla¹djing] *adj.* peu obligeant; sans courtoisie.

unobserved [œn⁶bzë⁶vd] *adj.* inaperçu; non remarqué; sans être vu.

unobtainable [œn⁶bté¹n⁶b'l] *adj.* inaccessible; inacquérable.

unobtrusive [œn⁶btrousiv] *adj.* discret, effacé.

unofficial [œn⁶fish⁶l] *adj.* non officiel; officieux; non confirmé.

unpack [œnpak] *v.* déballer.

unpaid [œnpé¹d] *adj.* impayé; non acquitté; non affranchi [letter].

unpalatable [œnpal⁶t⁶b'l] *adj.* d'un goût désagréable.

unpleasant [œnplèz'nt] *adj.* déplaisant; désagréable; fâcheux. || *pleasantness* [-nis] *s.* caractère désagréable; désagrément, m.; brouille légère, petite querelle, f.

unpopular [œnpâpyoul⁶ʳ] *adj.* impopulaire.

unprecedented [œnprès⁶dèntid] *adj.* sans précédent; sans exemple.

unprejudiced [œnprèdj⁶dist] *adj.* sans préjugé; impartial.

unprepared [œnpripèrd] *adj.* inapprêté; improvisé; impromptu.

unprofitable [œnprâft⁶b'l] *adj.* improfitable; inutile; peu lucratif.

unprovable [œnprouv⁶b'l] *adj.* indémontrable.

unpublished [œnpœblisht] *adj.* inédit.

unpunctual [œnpœngktshou⁶l] *adj.* inexact.

unqualified [œnquál⁶fa¹d] *adj.* non qualifié (*to*, pour); incompétent; non autorisé; catégorique [statement]; absolu; exprès.

unquenchable [œnkwèntsh⁶b'l] *adj.* inextinguible; inassouvissable.

unquestionable [œnkwèstsh⁶n⁶b'l] *adj.* indiscutable; incontestable.

unravel [œnrav'l] *v.* débrouiller, démêler.

unrehearsed [œnrihë⁶st] *adj.* inapprêté, non préparé.

unreal [œnrî⁶l] *adj.* irréel.

unreasonable [œnrîzn⁶b'l] *adj.* déraisonnable; irrationnel; excessif; *unreasoning*, irraisonné.

unrecognizable [œnrèk⁶gna¹z⁶b'l] *adj.* méconnaissable.

unrefined [œnrifa¹nd] *adj.* non raffiné; inculte; grossier.

unrelenting [œnrilènting] *adj.* implacable, acharné.

unreliable [œnrila¹⁶b'l] *adj.* peu sûr; douteux; instable.

unresponsive [œnrispânsiv] *adj.* froid, difficile à émouvoir; mou.

unrest [œnrèst] *s.* inquiétude; insomnie; agitation, émeute, f.

unrighteous [œnra¹ti⁶s] *adj.* inique, injuste; peu honnête.

unroll [œnro⁰ul] *v.* (se) dérouler; (se) déployer.

unruly [œnrouli] *adj.* indompté; insoumis; indocile.

unsafe [œnsé¹f] *adj.* peu sûr; dangereux; hasardeux.

unsal(e)able [œnsé¹l⁶b'l] *adj.* invendable; *unsal(e)able article*, rossignol.

unsatisfactory [œnsatisfaktri] *adj.* peu satisfaisant; défectueux; *unsatisfied*, peu satisfait; insatisfait; inassouvi; non convaincu.

unscathed [œnské¹xhd] *adj.* indemne.

unscrew [œnskrou] *v.* dévisser; déboulonner.

unseasonable [œnsîz⁶n⁶b'l] *adj.* inopportun; intempestif; hors de saison.

unseat [œnsît] *v.* supplanter; renverser; faire perdre son siège à [deputy]; désarçonner.

unseemly [œnsîmli] *adj.* inconvenant; incongru.

unseen [œnsîn] *adj.* inaperçu; invisible; occulte.

unselfish [œnsèlfish] *adj.* désintéressé, altruiste, sans égoïsme. ‖ *unselfishness* [-nis] *s.* désintéressement, m.; abnégation, f.

unserviceable [œnsër·vis·b'l] *adj.* inutilisable; hors de service.

unsettled [œnsètld] *adj.* non fixé; dérangé; non réglé; variable [weather]; instable; indécis; détraqué [health]; en suspens [question]; inquiet, agité; trouble [liquid].

unshaken [œnshé¹k·n] *adj.* inébranlable.

unshrinkable [œnshri·ngk·b'l] *adj.* irrétrécissable.

unsightly [œnsa¹tli] *adj.* laid; désagréable à voir.

unskilled [œnski·ld] *adj.* inexpérimenté; non spécialisé. ‖ *unskilful* [œnski·lf·l] *adj.* maladroit.

unsophisticated [œnsofi·stiké¹tid] *adj.* non frelaté; ingénu.

unsound [œnsa·o·u·nd] *adj.* malsain; corrompu; dépravé; taré [horse]; dérangé [mind].

unspeakable [œnspî·k·b'l] *adj.* indicible; ineffable; inexprimable; *unspoken*, non prononcé; sous-entendu; tacite.

unstable [œnsté¹b'l] *adj.* instable.

unsteady [œnstèdi] *adj.* peu solide; chancelant; incertain; irrésolu; inconstant; mal assuré; variable.

unstinted [œnsti·ntid] *adj.* abondant. ‖ *unstinting* [-ting] *adj.* généreux, prodigue.

unsuccessful [œns·ks·sf·l] *adj.* raté, manqué; infructueux.

unsuitable [œnsou·t·b'l] *adj.* inopportun; incongru; impropre.

unsuspected [œns·spèktid] *adj.* insoupçonné. ‖ *unsuspecting* [-ting] *adj.* confiant; sans défiance.

unsympathetic [œnsimp·thétik] *adj.* sec, peu compatissant.

unthinkable [œnthi·ngk·b'l] *adj.* inconcevable. ‖ *unthinking* [-king] *adj.* irréfléchi, étourdi.

untidiness [œnta¹dinis] *s.* malpropreté, f.; désordre, m. ‖ *untidy* [-di] *adj.* malpropre; débraillé; en désordre; sans soin, négligé.

untie [œnta¹] *v.* délier, dénouer.

until [œnti·l] *prep.* jusqu'à; *conj.* jusqu'à ce que; *until I am*, jusqu'à ce que je sois.

untimely [œnta¹mli] *adj.* prématuré; inopportun; *adv.* prématurément; inopportunément.

untiring [œnta¹ring] *adj.* inlassable, infatigable; assidu.

unto [œntou], *see* **to.**

untold [œnto·o·uld] *adj.* passé sous silence; indicible; incalculable, innombrable; inestimable.

untouched [œnt·tsht] *adj.* intact; sain et sauf; non traité; insensible.

untrained [œntré¹nd] *adj.* non entraîné; inexpérimenté; indiscipliné; non dressé.

untried [œntra¹d] *adj.* inéprouvé; inexpérimenté; non tenté; non ressenti; non jugé (jur.).

untroubled [œntr·b'ld] *adj.* paisible; sans souci; serein; limpide.

untrue [œntrou] *adj.* inexact; erroné; incorrect; déloyal; mensonger; infidèle (*to*, à). ‖ *untruth* [œntrouth] *s.* mensonge, m.; fausseté; inexactitude; déloyauté; perfidie, f.

unused [œnyouzd] *adj.* désaffecté [building], inusité; inaccoutumé (*to*, à). ‖ *unusual* [œnyoujou·l] *adj.* insolite, inusité; rare.

unvaried [œnvèrid] *adj.* uniforme, sans variété. ‖ *unvarying* [œnvèriing] *adj.* invariable, constant.

unveil [œnvé¹l] *v.* dévoiler; révéler; inaugurer [statue].

unwarranted [œnwaur·ntid] *adj.* inautorisé; injustifié; injustifiable; non garanti [quality].

unwary [œnwèri] *adj.* imprudent; irréfléchi.

unwashed [œnwâsht] *adj.* non lavé.

unwelcome [œnwèlk·m] *adj.* mal venu; importun; fâcheux.

unwell [œnwèl] *adj.* souffrant.

unwholesome [œnho·u·ls·m] *adj.* malsain; insalubre.

unwieldy [œnwi·ldi] *adj.* peu maniable, pesant, encombrant.

unwilling [œnwi·ling] *adj.* peu disposé; rétif; répugnant (*to*, à); involontaire, à contrecœur; *to be unwilling*, ne pas vouloir, refuser. ‖ *unwillingly* [-li] *adv.* à contrecœur; de mauvaise grâce. ‖ *unwillingness* [-nis] *s.* mauvaise volonté; répugnance (*to*, à), f.

unwind [œnwa¹nd] *v.* dérouler.

unwise [œnwa¹z] *adj.* malavisé; peu sage; imprudent.

unwittingly [œnwitingli] *adv.* involontairement, inconsciemment.

unworthy [œnwër·zhi] *adj.* indigne.

unwrap [œnrap] *v.* développer; révéler, découvrir.

unyielding [œnyî·lding] *adj.* inébranlable, inflexible.

up [œp] *adv.* en haut; en montant;
prep. au haut de; *adj., s.* haut; *the
ups and downs,* les hauts et les bas,
les vicissitudes; *to sweeten up,* sucrer
à point; *not yet up,* pas encore levé;
time is up, il est l'heure; *he is up
to something,* il manigance quelque
chose; *up to his task,* à la hauteur
de sa tâche; *up train,* train montant.

upbraid [œpbréⁱd] *v.* réprimander.

upgrade [œpgréⁱd] *s.* montée, côte, f.;
adj. montant; *adv.* en côte; *on the
upgrade,* en bonne voie d'amélioration.

upheaval [œphívˡl] *s.* soulèvement;
bouleversement, m.

upheld [œphèld] *pret., p. p. of* to
uphold.

uphill [œphíl] *adj.* montant, escarpé;
ardu.

uphold [œphoᵘld] *v.* soutenir; appuyer; étayer; épauler.

upholster [œphoᵘlstᵉʳ] *v.* tapisser,
capitonner, rembourrer. ‖ *upholsterer*
[-erᵉʳ] *s.* tapissier, *Fr. Can.* rembourreur, m. ‖ *upholstery* [-ri] *s.* tapisserie, f.

upkeep [œpkíp] *s.* entretien, m.

upland [œplànd] *s.* terrain élevé, m.;
région montagneuse, f.

uplift [œplíft] *s.* élévation, f.; [œplíft]
v. lever, élever.

upon [ᵉpân] *prep.* sur; *see on.*

upper [œpᵉʳ] *adj.* supérieur; d'en
haut; de dessus; *s.* dessus de chaussure, m.; tige de bottine, f.; *to get
the upper hand of,* l'emporter sur.

upright [œpraⁱt] *adj.* droit; vertical;
intègre; debout; *s.* montant de charpente; piano droit, m.; *adv.* tout droit;
verticalement; à pic. ‖ *uprightness*
[-nis] *s.* rectitude; droiture; position
verticale, f.

uprising [œpraⁱsing] *s.* soulèvement,
m.; insurrection, f.

uproar [œproᵒʳ] *s.* tumulte, tapage,
m.; *uproarious,* tumultueux.

uproot [œprout] *v.* déraciner.

upset [œpsèt] *v.** renverser; bouleverser; faire chavirer; déjouer [plan];
refouler [metal]; *adj.* renversé; bou-
leversé; navré; dérangé; chaviré;
[œpsèt] *s.* bouleversement, chambarde-
ment, m.; action de faire verser ou
chavirer, f.

upshot [œpshât] *s.* dénouement, m.

upside [œpsaⁱd] *s.* dessus, m.; *upside down,* la tête en bas, renversé;
biscornu, bizarre.

upstairs [œpstèrz] *adv.* en haut; aux
étages supérieurs; *adj.* d'en haut; *to
go upstairs,* monter.

upstart [œpstârt] *s.* parvenu, m.

up-to-date [œptᵉdéⁱt] *adj.* moderne;
dernier cri; à la page; mis à jour
[account].

upward [œpwᵉrd] *adj.* ascendant,
montant. ‖ *upwards* [-z] *adv.* vers le
haut; au-dessus; *upward(s) of,* plus de.

uranium [youréⁱniᵉm] *s.* uranium, m.

urban [ërbᵉn] *adj.* urbain. ‖ *urbane*
[ërbéⁱn] *adj.* courtois. ‖ *urbanity* [ër-
bàniti] *s.* urbanité, f. ‖ *urbanization*
[ërbᵉnaⁱzéⁱshᵉn] *s.* urbanisation, f.

urchin [ërtshin] *s.* hérisson; oursin;
gamin, m.

urea [youᵉriᵉ] *s.* urée, f.; *ur(a)emia,*
urémie; *uric,* urique.

urge [ërdj] *v.* pousser, presser; exhorter; alléguer [reason]; *s.* impulsion, f.
‖ *urgency* [-ᵉnsi] *s.** urgence, f. ‖
urgent [ërdjᵉnt] *adj.* urgent, pressant;
immédiat. ‖ *urgently* [-li] *adv.* d'urgence.

urinal [yourín'l] *s.* urinoir, m.; *street
urinal,* vespasienne; *urinary,* urinaire;
urinate, uriner; *urine,* urine.

urn [ërn] *s.* urne, f.; *tea-urn,* samovar.

urticaria [œrtikèᵉriᵉ] *s.* urticaire, f.

us [œs] *pron.* nous.

usage [yousidj] *s.* usage; traitement,
m.; coutume, f.; *hard usage,* mauvais
traitement. ‖ *use* [yous] *s.* usage;
emploi; service, m.; utilité; consommation, f.; [youz] *v.* employer; user;
consommer; utiliser; traiter; accoutumer; avoir coutume de; *of no use,*
inutile; *to make use of,* se servir de;
directions for use, mode d'emploi; *he
used to say,* il disait d'habitude; *to be
used to,* être accoutumé à; *to get used,*
s'habituer; *used car,* voiture d'occasion, *used up,* épuisé; entièrement
consommé. ‖ *useful* [yousfᵉl] *adj.* utile;
pratique. ‖ *usefulness* [-nis] *s.* utilité,
f. ‖ *useless* [youslis] *adj.* inutile; vain;
bon à rien. ‖ *uselessness* [-nis] *s.* inutilité, f.

usher [œshᵉʳ] *s.* huissier; appariteur;
placeur, m.; *v.* introduire; annoncer;
usherette, ouvreuse.

usual [youjoᵘᵉl] *adj.* usuel; habituel;
courant. ‖ *usually* [-i] *adv.* habituelle-
ment; en général.

usufruct [iouzioufrœkt] *s.* usufruit, m.

usurer [youjᵉrᵉʳ] *s.* usurier, m. ‖
usurious [youzouᵉriᵉs] *adj.* usuraire.

usurp [youzërp] *v.* usurper; *usurpation,* usurpation; *usurper,* usurpateur.

usury [youjᵉri] *s.* usure, f.

utensil [youtèns'l] *s.* ustensile, m.

utilitarian [youtilitéri∘n] *adj.* utilitaire ; **utilitarianism,** utilitarisme. ‖ **utility** [youtil∘ti] *s.* utilité, f. ‖ **utilizable** [youtila¹z∘b'l] *adj.* utilisable ; **utilization,** utilisation. ‖ **utilize** [youtila¹z] *v.* utiliser.

utmost [œtmo∘ust] *adj.* dernier ; extrême ; *s.* extrême ; comble, m. ; *to do one's utmost,* faire tout son possible ; *at the utmost,* tout au plus.

utopia [youto∘upi∘] *s.* utopie, f. ; *utopian,* utopique ; utopiste.

utter [œter] *adj.* complet ; total ; extrême ; absolu.

utter [œter] *v.* proférer ; prononcer ; émettre [coin] ; pousser [cry]. ‖ **utterance** [-r∘ns] *s.* prononciation ; articulation, expression ; émission, f. ; propos ; langage, m.

utterly [œter li] *adv.* complètement.

uttermost, *see* **utmost.**

uvula [youvy∘l∘] *s.* luette, f.

V

vacancy [vé¹k∘nsi] *s.* * vacance ; lacune ; distraction, f. ; vide ; poste vacant, m. ‖ **vacant** [vé¹k∘nt] *adj.* vacant, libre, vide, distrait. ‖ **vacate** [vé¹ké¹t] *v.* laisser libre ; vider ; rendre vacant. ‖ **vacation** [vé¹ké¹sh∘n] *s.* vacances, f. pl. ; *vacationist,* vacancier.

vaccinate [vaks'né¹t] *v.* vacciner ; inoculer. ‖ **vaccination** [vaks'né¹sh∘n] *s.* vaccination, f. ‖ **vaccine** [vaksìn] *s.* vaccin, m.

vacillate [vas'lé¹t] *v.* vaciller.

vacuous [vakyou∘s] *adj.* vide ; vague ; hébété. ‖ **vacuum** [vakyou∘m] *s* vide ; vacuum, m., *to get a vacuum* faire le vide ; *vacuum cleaner,* aspirateur.

vagabond [vag∘bând] *adj., s.* vagabond ; *vagabondage,* vagabondage ; *vagrant,* vagabond.

vague [vé¹g] *adj.* vague, imprécis.

vain [vé¹n] *adj.* vain ; vaniteux ; futile ; *vainglorious,* vaniteux, vain ; *vainglory,* gloriole.

valentine [val∘nta¹n] *s.* amoureux, m. ; amoureuse ; « valentine », f.

valet [valit] *s.* valet, m.

valiant [valy∘nt] *adj.* vaillant.

valid [valid] *adj.* valide ; valable. ‖ **validate** [validé¹t] *v.* valider. ‖ **validity** [v∘lid∘ti] *s.* validité, f.

valise [v∘lis] *s.* valise, f.

valley [vali] *s.* vallée, f. ; vallon, m.

valo(u)r [val∘r] *s.* valeur, vaillance, f. ‖ **valorous** [-r∘s] *adj.* valeureux.

valuable [valyou∘b'l] *adj.* de valeur ; précieux ; *s. pl.* objets de valeur, m. pl.

valuation [valyou∘¹sh∘n] *s.* estimation ; évaluation, expertise, appréciation, f. ‖ **value** [valyou] *s.* valeur, f. ; prix ; mérite, m. ; *v* évaluer, apprécier ; estimer, *food value,* valeur nutritive ; *market value,* valeur marchande ; *valuer,* expert.

valve [valv] *s.* valve ; soupape, f.

vamp [vamp] *s.* empeigne ; vamp, f. ; *v.* mettre une empeigne à ; provoquer.

vampire [vampa¹er] *s.* vampire, m.

van [vàn] *s.* voiture de déménagement ; fourgonnette, f. ; fourgon (railw.), m.

van [vàn] *s.* van, m.

van [vàn] *s.* avant, m.

vandalism [vand∘liz'm] *s.* vandalisme, m.

vane [vé¹n] *s.* girouette ; aile [windmill] ; aube [turbine] ; pinnule (techn.) ; palette (aviat.), f.

vanguard [vàngârd] *s.* avant-garde, f.

vanilla [v∘níl∘] *s.* vanille, f.

vanish [vanish] *v.* disparaître ; s'évanouir, se dissiper.

vanity [van∘ti] *s.* * vanité, f. ; *vanity case,* poudrier de sac.

vanquish [vànkwish] *v.* vaincre.

vantage [vàntidj] *s.* avantage, m.

vapid [vapid] *adj.* plat ; insipide.

vapo(u)r [vé¹p∘r] *s.* vapeur, buée, f. ‖ **vaporization** [vé¹p∘ra¹zé¹sh∘n] *s.* vaporisation, f. **vaporize** [vé¹p∘ra¹z] *v.* vaporiser gazéifier, carburer (mech.). **vaporizer,** vaporisateur. ‖ **vaporous** [-∘s] *adj.* vaporeux.

variable [vèri∘b'l] *adj.* variable ; inconstant ; *variance* [vèri∘ns] *s.* variation, divergence discorde, f. ‖ **variation** [vèrié¹sh∘n] *s.* variation ; différence, f., changement, m. ‖ *varied* [vèri∘d] *adj* varié, divers. ‖ *variegated* [vèrigé¹tid] *adj.* bigarré. ‖ **variety** [v∘ra¹∘ti] *s.* * variété ; diversité ; variation, f. ‖ **various** [vèri∘s] *adj.* divers, varié.

varnish [vârnish] *s.* * vernis, m. ; *v.* vernir, vernisser, *varnisher,* vernisseur ; *varnishing-day,* vernissage (art).

vary [vèri] *v.* varier ; diversifier.

vase [vé¹s] *s.* vase, m.

vaseline [vas'lìn] *s.* vaseline, f.

vast [vast] *adj.* vaste, étendu, immense. ‖ *vastness* [-nis] *s.* vaste étendue ; immensité, f.

vat [vat] *s.* cuve, f. ; cuveau, m.

vaudeville [voᵒᵘdᵉvil] *s.* vaudeville, m.

vault [vault] *s.* voûte ; cave ; chambre forte, f. ; *v.* voûter ; *family vault,* caveau de famille.

vault [vault] *s.* voltige, f. ; *v.* sauter, voltiger ; franchir d'un bond ; *pole vault,* saut à la perche.

vaunt [vaunt] *s.* jactance, f. ; *v.* (se) vanter ; faire étalage de.

veal [vîl] *s.* viande de veau, f.

veer [viᵉʳ] *v.* virer (naut.), obliquer ; tourner [wind] ; *s.* virage, m.

vegetable [vèdjtᵉb'l] *s.* légume, m. ; *adj.* végétal ; potager ; *dried vegetables,* légumes secs ; *vegetable man,* fruitier. ‖ *vegetal* [-it'l] *adj.*, *s.* végétal. ‖ *vegetarian* [vèdjitᵉʳiᵉn] *adj.*, *s.* végétarien.

vegetate [vèdjeté¹t] *v.* végéter. ‖ *vegetation* [vèdjeté¹shᵉn] *s.* végétation, f. ; *vegetative,* végétatif.

vehemence [vîᵉmᵉns] *s.* véhémence, f. ; *vehement,* véhément.

vehicle [vîik'l] *s.* véhicule ; moyen (fig.), m. ; voiture, f. ; *Am. combat vehicle,* engin blindé ; *half-track vehicle,* autochenille.

veil [vé¹l] *s.* voile, m. ; *v.* voiler ; dissimuler ; déguiser.

vein [vé¹n] *s.* veine, f. ; filon, m. ; *v.* veiner ; *in a talking vein,* en veine de bavardage ; *veined,* veiné, jaspé ; veineux.

velar [vîlᵉʳ] *adj.*, *s.* vélaire.

velocity [velàsᵉti] *s.* vélocité ; rapidité ; vitesse, f.

velvet [vèlvit] *s.* velours, m. ; *adj.* de velours ; velouté.

venal [vìnᵉl] *adj.* vénal ; *venality,* vénalité.

vendee [vèndî] *s.* acquéreur, acheteur.

vendor [vèndᵉʳ] *s.* vendeur, m. ; venderesse (jur.), f. ; *street vendor,* marchand des quatre-saisons.

veneer [venîᵉʳ] *s.* placage ; revêtement, m. ; vernis (fig.), m. ; *v.* plaquer.

venerable [vènᵉrᵉb'l] *adj.* vénérable. ‖ *venerate* [-ré¹t] *v.* vénérer. ‖ *veneration* [vènᵉré¹shᵉn] *s.* vénération, f.

venery [vénᵉri] *s.* vénerie, f.

vengeance [vèndjᵉns] *s.* vengeance, f. ; *with a vengeance,* furieusement ; *vengeful,* vindicatif ; vengeur.

venial [vìniᵉl] *adj.* véniel.

venison [vènᵉz'n] *s.* venaison, f.

venom [vènᵉm] *s.* venin, m. ‖ *venomous* [-ᵉs] *adj.* venimeux ; vénéneux [plant].

venous [vînᵉs] *adj.* veineux.

vent [vènt] *s.* orifice ; évent, m. ; lumière [gun] ; fente, f. ; *v.* éventer ; exhaler ; décharger.

ventilate [vènt'lé¹t] *v.* ventiler ; aérer ; oxygéner [blood] ; agiter [question]. ‖ *ventilation* [vènt'lé¹shᵉn] *s.* ventilation ; aération, f. ‖ *ventilator* [vènt'lé¹tᵉʳ] *s.* ventilateur ; volet d'aération, m.

ventricle [véntrik'l] *s.* ventricule, m. ‖ *ventriloquist* [véntrílᵉkwist] *s.* ventriloque, m.

venture [vèntshᵉʳ] *s.* aventure ; entreprise, f. ; risque, m. ; *v.* risquer ; hasarder, s'aventurer ; se permettre ; *business venture,* spéculation ; *venturesome,* aventuré ; aventureux ; *venturous,* aventureux ; osé.

venue [vènyou] *s.* juridiction, f. ; lieu du jugement (jur.), m.

veracious [vèré¹shᵉs] *adj.* véridique ; *veraciousness, veracity,* véracité.

veranda [vᵉràndᵉ] *s.* véranda, f.

verb [vᵉʳb] *s.* verbe, m. ‖ *verbal* [-'l] *adj.* verbal ; oral. ‖ *verbose* [vᵉʳboᵒᵘs] *adj.* verbeux, prolixe.

verdict [vᵉʳdikt] *s.* verdict (jur.), m.

verdigris [vᵉʳdigris] *s.* vert-de-gris, m.

verdure [vᵉʳdjᵉʳ] *s.* verdure, f.

verge [vᵉʳdj] *s.* bord ; confins, m. ; limite ; margelle, f. ; *v.* border, approcher (*to*, de) ; tendre (*towards*, à, vers) ; *on the verge of,* sur le point de.

verification [vèrifiké¹shᵉn] *s.* vérification, f. ; contrôle, m. ‖ *verify* [vèrᵉfa¹] *v.* vérifier, contrôler ; constater ; confirmer ; certifier.

verily [vèrᵉli] *adv.* en vérité ; vraiment.

verisimilitude [vèrisimílityoud] *s.* vraisemblance, f.

veritable [vèrᵉtᵉb'l] *adj.* véritable.

verjuice [vᵉʳdjous] *s.* verjus, m.

vermin [vᵉʳmìn] *s.* vermine, f.

vernacular [vᵉʳnakyᵉlᵉʳ] *adj.* vernaculaire ; vulgaire [language].

versatile [vᵉʳsᵉta¹l] *adj.* souple ; universel ; aux talents variés ; *versatility,* souplesse, faculté d'adaptation ; versatilité (bot.), f.

verse [vᵉʳs] *s.* vers ; verset, m. ; strophe, f.

versed [vᵉʳst] *adj.* versé, expert.

versifier [vĕʳsifaⁱeʳ] *s.* versificateur, m.; *versify*, versifier.

version [vĕʳjen] *s.* version, f.

vertebra [vĕʳtebrᵉ] *s.* vertèbre, f.

vertical [vĕʳtik'l] *adj.* vertical; *s.* verticale, f.

vertigo [vĕʳtegoᵘ] *s.* vertige (med.), m.

vervain [vĕʳveⁱn] *s.* verveine, f.

very [vĕri] *adv.* très; fort; bien; *adj.* vrai, véritable; *this very day*, aujourd'hui même; *the very best*, tout ce qu'il y a de mieux.

vesicle [vĕsik'l] *s.* vésicule; ampoule (med.), f.

vespers [vĕspeʳz] *s. pl.* vêpres, f. pl.

vessel [vĕs'l] *s.* vaisseau; navire; récipient, m.; *blood vessel*, vaisseau sanguin.

vest [vĕst] *s.* gilet, m.; *v.* vêtir; investir (*with*, de); attribuer.

vestal [vĕst'l] *s.* vestale, f.

vestibule [vĕstᵉbyoul] *s.* vestibule, couloir, m.; antichambre; entrée, f.

vestige [vĕstidj] *s.* vestige, m.

vestigial [vĕstidjiᵉl] *adj.* rudimentaire.

vestment [vĕstmᵉnt] *s.* vêtement, m.; chasuble [eccles.], f.

vestry [vĕstri] *s.* sacristie, f.; conseil paroissial; vestiaire, m.

veteran [vĕteren] *s.* vétéran; ancien combattant, m.

veterinarian [vĕtʳenèriᵉn] *s.* vétérinaire, m. || *veterinary* [vĕtʳnèri] *adj.*, *s.* vétérinaire.

veto [vītoᵘ] *s.* veto, m.; opposition, f.; *v.* opposer son veto; s'élever contre.

vex [vĕks] *v.* vexer, fâcher, molester; contrarier; incommoder déranger; importuner || *vexation* [vĕksᵉshᵉn] *s.* contrariété; vexation, f.; dépit; désagrément, m.; *vexatious*, vexatoire; irritant.

via [vaⁱe] *prep.* via, par.

viable [vaⁱeb'l] *adj.* viable.

viaduct [vaⁱedœkt] *s.* viaduc, m.

vial [vaⁱel] *s.* fiole, f.

viands [vaⁱendz] *s. pl.* victuailles, f. pl.; aliments, m. pl.

viaticum [vaⁱatikᵉm] *s.* viatique, m.

vibrate [vaⁱbréⁱt] *v.* vibrer, frémir. || *vibration* [vaⁱbréⁱshᵉn] *s.* vibration, f.; *vibratory*, vibratoire.

viburnum [vaⁱbĕʳnᵉm] *s.* viorne, f.

vicar [ˈvikeʳ] *s.* curé, m.; *vicar general*, vicaire général; *vicarious*, substitut; délégué; fait à la place d'autrui; *vicarship*, pastorat.

vice [vaⁱs] *s.* vice, m.; tare, f.

vice [vaⁱs] *pref.* vice-, suppléant, m.; *vice-chairman*, vice-président.

vice [yaⁱs] *s.* étau, m.

vicinity [vᵉsinᵉti] *s.* proximité, f.; voisinage, m.; abords, m. pl.

vicious [vishᵉs] *adj.* vicieux; dépravé; défectueux; ombrageux [horse]; méchant [dog].

vicissitude [vᵉsisᵉtyoud] *s.* vicissitude, f.

victim [viktim] *s.* victime; dupe, f.; sinistré, m.

victor [vikteʳ] *s.* vainqueur, m. || *victorious* [viktoᵘriᵉs] *adj.* victorieux, vainqueur. || *victory* [viktri] *s.* victoire, f.

victual(s) [vit'l(z)] *s.* vivres, m. pl.; victuailles, f. pl.

vie [vaⁱ] *v.* lutter, rivaliser.

view [vyou] *s.* vue; perspective; opinion; intention, f.; aperçu, m.; *v.* regarder; examiner; contempler; *bird's-eye view*, vue à vol d'oiseau; *side view*, vue de profil; *viewer*, spectateur, téléspectateur; visionneuse.

vigil [vidjᵉl] *s.* veille; veillée; vigile, f. || *vigilance* [-ᵉns] *s.* vigilance; circonspection, f. || *vigilant* [-ᵉnt] *adj.* vigilant; attentif.

vigo(u)r [vigeʳ] *s.* vigueur; vitalité; force, f.; *vigorous*, vigoureux, robuste.

vile [vaⁱl] *adj.* vil; abject. || *vilify* [-faⁱ] *v.* diffamer.

villa [vilᵉ] *s.* villa, f.

village [vilidj] *s.* village, m.; bourgade, f.; *villager*, villageois.

villain [vilᵉn] *s.* coquin; scélérat; traître (theat.); vilain, manant, m. || *villainous* [-ᵉs] *adj.* vil, bas; scélérat; exécrable. || *villainy* [-i] *s.* vilenie; infamie; scélératesse, f.

vim [vim] *s.* force, vigueur, f.

vinaigrette [vinᵉgrét] *s.* burette (f.) à vinaigre; flacon (m.) de sels; vinaigrette, f.

vindicate [vindᵉkéⁱt] *v.* défendre; disculper; revendiquer. || *vindication* [vindikéⁱshᵉn] *s.* justification, f.; *vindicative*, justificatif.

vindictive [vindiktiv] *adj.* vindicatif; vengeur.

vine [vaⁱn] *s.* vigne; plante grimpante, f.; sarment, cep, m.

vinegar [vinigeʳ] *s.* vinaigre, m.

vineyard [vinyârd] *s.* vignoble, m.; vigne, f.

vintage [vintidj] *s.* vendange, f.; cru, m.

viol [va¹e¹] s. viole, f. ‖ *viola* [vio°u¹e] s. alto, m.

violate [va¹é¹é¹t] v. violer; enfreindre; profaner. ‖ *violation* [va¹e¹é¹sh°n] s. violation; infraction; contravention, f. ‖ *violence* [va¹e¹ens] s. violence, f.; voies de fait (jur.), f. pl.; *to do violence to,* violenter. ‖ *violent* [va¹e¹ent] adj. violent.

violet [va¹e¹lit] s. violette, f.; adj. violet.

violin [va¹e¹lìn] s. violon, m.; *violinist,* violoniste; *violoncellist,* violoncelliste; *violoncello,* violoncelle.

viper [va¹per] s. vipère, f.

virgin [vër¹djn] adj., s. vierge; *virginal,* virginal. ‖ *virginity* [vër¹djn°ti] s. virginité, f.

virile [vìr¹l] adj. viril. ‖ *virility* [veríl°ti] s. virilité, f.

virtual [vër¹tshou°l] adj. virtuel; de fait; *virtuality,* virtualité.

virtue [vër¹tshou] s. vertu, qualité, f.; mérite, m.

virtuosity [vër¹tiou°siti] s. virtuosité, f.; *virtuoso,* virtuose; connaisseur, m.

virtuous [vër¹tshou°s] adj. vertueux.

virulence [vìry¹ens] s. virulence, f.; *virulent,* virulent. ‖ *virus* [va¹rˢs] s.* virus, m.

visa [viz°] s. visa, m.; v. viser [passport]; donner un visa.

visage [vizídj] s. visage, m.

viscera [vìsˢr] s. viscères, f. pl. ‖ *visceral,* viscéral.

viscid [vìsid] adj. visqueux.

viscosity [viskás°ti] s. viscosité, f.

viscount [va¹kaˢunt] s. vicomte, m.

viscous [vìskˢs] adj. visqueux, gluant.

vise [va¹s] s. étau, m.; *see vice.*

visibility [viz°bíl°ti] s. visibilité, f. ‖ *visible* [vìzˢb'l] adj. visible. ‖ *vision* [vìj°n] s. vision; vue, f. ‖ *visionary* [vìj°nèri] adj. visionnaire; chimérique; s.* visionnaire, m. f.

visit [vìzit] s. visite, f.; séjour; arraisonnement (naut.), m.; v. visiter; arraisonner (naut.). ‖ *visitation* [vìzˢté¹shˢn] s. visite, inspection; fouille; tournée; épreuve, f.; Visitation (relig.). ‖ *visitor* [vìzitˢr] s. visiteur, m.

visor [va¹zˢr] s. visière, f.; paresoleil, m.

vista [vistˢ] s. percée; perspective; échappée [view]; trouée [wood], f.

visual [vìjou°l] adj. visuel; optique. ‖ *visualize* [-a¹z] v. évoquer; se représenter; extérioriser.

vital [va¹t'l] adj. vital; essentiel; capital. ‖ *vitality* [va¹tal°ti] s. vitalité; vigueur, f.; *vitalize,* vitaliser.

vitamin [va¹tˢmln] s. vitamine, f.; *vitamin deficiency,* avitaminose.

vitiate [vìshlé¹t] v. vicier.

vitreous [vìtriˢs] adj. vitreux. ‖ *vitrify* [-trìfa¹] v. vitrifier.

vitriol [vìtriˢl] s. vitriol, m.; *copper vitriol,* sulfate de cuivre.

vituperate [va¹tyoupˢré¹t] v. vilipender; vitupérer.

vivacious [va¹vé¹shˢs] adj. vivace; enjoué, allègre. ‖ *vivacity* [va¹vas°ti] s. vivacité; verve, f.

vivid [vìvíd] adj. vif; animé. ‖ *vivify* [vìvìfa¹] v. vivifier. ‖ *vivisect* [-sèkt] v. pratiquer la vivisection.

vixen [vìksˢn] s. renarde; mégère, f.

vizier [vizjˢr] s. vizir, m.

vocabulary [vˢkaby¹èlèri] s.* vocabulaire, m.

vocal [vo°uk'l] adj. vocal; oral.

vocation [vo°ué¹shˢn] s. vocation; profession, f.; *vocational,* professionnel.

vociferate [vosifˢré¹t] v. vociférer.

vogue [vo°ug] s. vogue, mode, f.

voice [vo¹s] s. voix, f.; v. exprimer, énoncer; *with one voice,* à l'unanimité; *at the top of his voice,* à tue-tête; *voiced,* sonore [consonant]; *voiceless,* sans voix; muet; sourde [consonant].

void [vo¹d] adj. vide, vacant; dépourvu; nul (jur.); v. annuler; évacuer, vider.

volatile [vál°t'l] adj. volatil; volage. ‖ *volatilize* [vâlatila¹z] v. (se) volatiliser.

volcanic [vâlkˢnik] adj. volcanique. ‖ *volcano* [vâlké¹no] s. volcan, m.

volley [vâli] s. salve; rafale (mil.); bordée (naut.); volée, f.; v. tirer une salve; tomber en grêle.

volplane [vâlplé¹n] v. planer (aviat.).

volt [vo°ult] s. volt (electr.), m. ‖ *voltage* [-idj] s. voltage, m.; *high voltage,* haute tension.

voluble [vâlyoub'l] adj. volubile.

volume [vály°m] s. volume, m. ‖ *voluminous* [vˢlémínˢs] adj. volumineux.

voluntariness [vál°ntrinis] s. caractère volontaire, m.; spontanéité, f. ‖ *voluntary* [vál°ntèri] adj. volontaire; spontané; bénévole. ‖ *volunteer* [vâlˢntjˢr] s. volontaire, m.; adj. de volontaire; v. s'engager, agir comme volontaire.

voluptuous [vᵊlœptshou°s] *adj.* voluptueux; *voluptuousness,* sensualité.

vomit [vâmit] *v.* vomir. ‖ *vomiting* [-ing] *s.* vomissement, m. ‖ *vomitive* [-iv] *s.* vomitif, m.

voodoo [voûdou] *s.* vaudou, m.

voracious [voᵒuré¹shᵉs] *adj.* vorace.

voracity [voᵒurasiti] *s.* voracité, f.

vortex [vᵃurtèks] *s.** tourbillon, m.

vote [voᵒut] *s.* vote; scrutin, m.; voix; motion, f.; *v.* voter. ‖ *voter* [-er] *s.* électeur; votant, m. ‖ *voting* [-ing] *s.* scrutin; (mode de) suffrage, m.

vouch [vaᵒutsh] *v.* attester; garantir; *to vouch for,* répondre de. ‖ *voucher* [-er] *s.* garant, répondant; récépissé;

bon de garantie, m.; pièce justificative; pièce comptable, f. ‖ *vouchsafe* [vaᵒutshsé¹f] *v.* accorder; daigner.

vow [vaᵒu] *s.* vœu, m.; *v.* faire un vœu; jurer.

vowel [vaᵒuᵉl] *s.* voyelle, f.

voyage [vo¹idj] *s.* traversée; croisière, f.; *v.* naviguer, faire une croisière; *maiden voyage,* première traversée; *voyager,* passager; navigateur.

vulcanize [vœlkᵉna¹z] *v.* vulcaniser.

vulgar [vœlgᵉr] *adj.* vulgaire; trivial; populaire; commun. ‖ *vulgarity* [vœlgᵃreti] *s.** vulgarité, f. ‖ *vulgarize* [vœlgᵉra¹z] *v.* populariser.

vulnerable [vœlnᵉrᵉb'l] *adj.* vulnérable.

vulture [vœltshᵉr] *s.* vautour, m.

W

wad [wâd] *s.* bourre; liasse [banknotes], f.; rembourrage; tampon, m.; *v.* bourrer; ouater.

waddle [wâd'l] *v.* se dandiner; *s.* dandinement, m.

wade [wé¹d] *v.* passer à gué; patauger; avancer péniblement (fig.).

wafer [wé¹fᵉr] *s.* pain à cacheter; cachet, m.; hostie; gaufrette, f.

waffle [wâf'l] *s.* gaufre, f.

waft [waft] *v.* flotter; porter dans les airs; *s.* bouffée d'air, f.; coup d'aile, m.

wag [wag] *v.* branler; remuer, agiter; *s.* oscillation, f.; mouvement, m.; farceur, boute-en-train, m.

wage [wé¹dj] *s.* gage, m.; *pl.* salaire, m.; *v.* engager, entreprendre; *to wage war,* faire la guerre.

wager [wé¹djᵉr] *s.* pari, m.; gageure, f.; *v.* parier, gager.

waggish [wagish] *adj.* facétieux; badin.

wagon [wagᵉn] *s.* fourgon; chariot, m.; voiture, f.; *Br.* wagon, m.; *wagonload,* charretée.

waif [wé¹f] *s.* épave (jur.), f.; enfant abandonné, m.

wail [wé¹l] *v.* gémir; se lamenter; *s.* gémissement, m.; lamentation, f.

wain [wé¹n] *s.* chariot, m.

wainscot [wé¹nskᵉt] *s.* lambris, m.

waist [wé¹st] *s.* taille; ceinture; *Am.* blouse, chemisette, f.; *waistband,* ceinture du pantalon; *waistcoat,* gilet.

wait [wé¹t] *v.* attendre; *s.* attente; embuscade, f.; *wait for me,* attendez-moi; *to wait on,* être aux ordres de;

to wait at table, servir à table; *to lie in wait,* être aux aguets. ‖ *waiter* [-ᵉr] *s.* garçon de restaurant; serveur; domestique, m. ‖ *waiting* [-ing] *s.* attente, f.; *no waiting,* stationnement interdit; *waiting-room,* salle d'attente. ‖ *waitress* [-ris] *s.** serveuse; servante, bonne, f.; *waitress !,* mademoiselle !

waive [wé¹v] *v.* renoncer à; écarter; abandonner [right].

wake [wé¹k] *s.* sillon; sillage (naut.), m.

wake [wé¹k] *v.* éveiller; réveiller; veiller; *s.* veillée mortuaire, f.; *to wake up,* se réveiller. ‖ *wakeful* [-f¹l] *adj.* éveillé, vigilant; d'insomnie. ‖ *waken* [-ᵉn] *v.* éveiller; (se) réveiller.

walk [waul] *v.* marcher; se promener; aller à pied, au pas; mener en laisse [dog]; *s.* marche; promenade, f.; pas; tour; trottoir, m.; *to walk a horse,* conduire un cheval au pas; *walk of life,* carrière; position sociale; *walker,* marcheur, promeneur; *walker-on,* figurant; *walk-over,* victoire facile.

wall [waul] *s.* muraille; paroi, f.; mur; rempart; espalier, m.; *v.* murer; entourer de murs; *partition wall,* cloison, f.; *party wall,* mur mitoyen; *wallpaper,* papier peint. ‖ *walled* [-d] *adj.* muré; clos de murs; *walled in,* emprisonné.

wallet [wâlit] *s.* portefeuille, m.; sacoche, f.

wallflower [waulfiaᵒuᵉr] *s.* giroflée, ravenelle, f.; *to be a wallflower at a dance,* faire tapisserie.

wallop [wâlᵉp] *v.* rosser; galoper.

wallow [waloᵒu] *v.* se vautrer.

walnut [waulnᵉt] *s.* noix, f.; bois de noyer, m.; *walnut-tree,* noyer.

walrus [waulrᵉs] *s.* morse, m.

waltz [waults] *s.* valse, f.; *v.* valser.

wan [waun] *adj.* blême; livide.

wananish [wànanish] *s.* *Fr. Can.* ouananiche, f.

wand [wând] *s.* baguette, f.; bâton, m.; *Mercury's wand,* caducée.

wander [wândᵉr] *v.* errer; rôder; s'égarer; divaguer; *to wander from,* s'écarter de. ‖ *wanderer* [-rᵉr] *s.* errant; rôdeur; nomade, m.

wane [wéⁱn] *s.* déclin; décroît [moon], m.; *v.* être sur le déclin; décroître; décliner.

wangle [wang'l] *v.* se débrouiller, resquiller; *wangler,* resquilleur.

want [wânt] *v.* manquer de; avoir besoin de; désirer, souhaiter; demander; *s.* besoin; manque, défaut, m.; *for want of,* faute de; *he is wanted,* on le demande.

wanton [wântᵉn] *adj.* libre, libertin; licencieux; folâtre; inconsidéré.

war [waur] *s.* guerre, f.; *v.* guerroyer; faire la guerre; *war of attrition,* guerre d'usure; *warfare,* conduite de la guerre.

warble [waurb'l] *v.* gazouiller; *s.* gazouillis, m. ‖ *warbler* [-blᵉr] *s.* chanteur, m.; fauvette, f.

w a r d [waurd] *s.* garde; tutelle; pupille; salle [hospital], f.; quartier [prison], m.; *v.* se garder; *to ward off,* parer, détourner. ‖ *warden* [-'n] *s.* gardien, m. ‖ *warder* [-ᵉr] *s.* gardien de prison, m. ‖ *wardrobe* [-roᵒub] *s.* garde-robe; armoire, f.; vêtements, m. pl.

ware(s) [wèᵉr(z)] *s.* marchandises, f. pl.; produits manufacturés, m. pl.; faïence, f.; *China ware,* porcelaine.

warehouse [wèrhaᵒus] *s.* entrepôt, m.; *warehouseman,* magasinier, entreposeur; *furniture warehouse,* garde-meuble.

warlike [waurlaⁱk] *adj.* guerrier; belliqueux; martial.

warm [waurm] *adj.* chaud; tiède; chaleureux; *v.* chauffer; réchauffer; *to be warm,* avoir chaud; *it is warm,* il fait chaud. ‖ *warmth* [-th] *s.* chaleur; ardeur, f.; zèle, m.

warn [waurn] *v.* avertir, prévenir; mettre en garde (*against,* contre); *warner,* avertisseur. ‖ *warning* [-ing] *s.* avertissement; avis, m.; *to give warning,* donner l'éveil.

warp [waurp] *v.* ourdir; voiler [wood]; touer (naut.); colmater [land]; gauchir; dévier; *s.* chaîne de tissu, f.; gauchissement, m. ‖ *warped* [-t] *adj.* retiré [wood]; faussé [mind].

warrant [waurᵉnt] *s.* autorisation; garantie, f.; pouvoir; warrant (comm.); mandat (jur.), m.; *v.* garantir; autoriser; certifier.

warren [waurᵉn] *s.* garenne, f.

warrior [wauriᵉr] *s.* guerrier, m.

warship [waurship] *s.* navire de guerre, m.

wart [waurt] *s.* verrue, f.

wary [wèri] *adj.* avisé; vigilant.

was [wâz] *pret. of to be.*

wash [wâsh] *v.* (se) laver; blanchir; lotionner; *s.* blanchissage, m.; lessive; lotion; lavure, f.; lavis; remous (naut.), m.; *washable,* lavable; *washbowl,* cuvette; *washcloth,* lavette; *washed up,* lessivé; *wash-out,* fiasco; *washroom,* cabinet de toilette; *washstand,* lavabo; *washtub,* baquet à lessive, cuvier. ‖ *washer* [-ᵉr] *s.* machine à laver; rondelle (mech.), f. ‖ *washing* [-ing] *s.* lavage, m.; *washing-machine,* machine à laver.

wasp [wâsp] *s.* guêpe, f.

wastage [wéⁱstidj] *s.* gaspillage, coulage, m.; déperdition, f.

waste [wéⁱst] *s.* perte; usure, f.; déchets; gaspillage; dégâts (jur.); terrain inculte, m.; *v.* dévaster, gâcher; gaspiller; *to waste away,* dépérir; *wasteful,* prodigue, dissipateur; *wasteland,* terrain vague; *waste-paper basket,* corbeille à papier.

watch [wâtsh] *s.* garde; surveillance; veille; montre, f.; quart (naut.), m.; *v.* veiller; surveiller; faire attention; *by my watch,* à ma montre; *on the watch,* aux aguets; *watchdog,* chien de garde; *watchful,* vigilant; *watchman,* veilleur; *watchtower,* tour de guet; *watchword,* mot de passe.

water [wautᵉr] *s.* eau, f.; *v.* arroser [plants]; baptiser [wine]; abreuver [animals]; *watercolo(u)r,* aquarelle; *water power,* force hydraulique; *water sports,* jeux nautiques; *watering place,* abreuvoir; station thermale. ‖ *waterfall* [-faul] *s.* cascade; cataracte; chute d'eau, f. ‖ *waterproof* [-prouf] *adj., s.* imperméable. ‖ *waterspout* [-spaᵒut] *s.* gouttière; trombe d'eau, f. ‖ *watertight* [-taⁱt] *adj.* étanche; imperméable. ‖ *waterway* [-wéⁱ] *s.* voie d'eau; voie navigable, f.; canal, m. ‖ *watery* [-ri] *adj.* aqueux; humide.

wave [wéⁱv] v. onduler; (s')agiter; flotter; s. vague; lame; onde; ondulation [hair], f.; signe de la main, m.; *Am.* femme servant dans la Marine, f.; **cold wave**, vague de froid; **long waves**, grandes ondes [radio]; **permanent wave**, indéfrisable, permanente; **wave length**, longueur d'onde; **to wave good-by**, faire un signe d'adieu. ‖ **waver** [-ᵉʳ] v. osciller; hésiter. ‖ **wavy** [-i] adj. ondoyant; ondulé.

wax [waks] v. croître; devenir.

wax [waks] s. cire, f.; v. cirer; **wax-candle**, bougie; **waxen**, en cire; cireux; malléable.

way [wéⁱ] s. chemin; sens; moyen, m.; voie; direction; distance; manière, f.; **way in**, entrée; **way out**, sortie; **way through**, passage; **by the way**, en passant; **in no way**, en aucune façon; **half-way**, à mi-chemin; **to give way**, céder; **to make way for**, faire place à; **which way**, de quel côté, par où; **to feel one's way**, tâter le terrain; **to lose one's way**, s'égarer; **way-bill**, feuille de route, lettre de voiture; **wayside**, bord de la route. ‖ **waylay** [wéⁱléⁱ] v. dresser une embuscade à. ‖ **wayward** [wéⁱwᵉʳd] adj. volontaire, rebelle.

we [wî] pron. nous.

weak [wîk] adj. faible; débile; pauvre [fuel]; **weak-minded**, faible d'esprit. ‖ **weaken** [-ᵉn] v. affaiblir; (s')amollir; s'appauvrir; se débiliter. ‖ **weakly** [-li] adv. faiblement; adj. faible. ‖ **weakness** [-nis] s. faiblesse; débilité, f.; faible, m.

wealth [wélth] s. richesse; prospérité, opulence, f. ‖ **wealthy** [-i] adj. riche; opulent.

wean [wîn] v. sevrer. ‖ **weaning** [-ing] s. sevrage, m.

weapon [wépᵉn] s. arme, f.

wear [wèᵉr] v.* porter; user; lasser, épuiser; faire usage; s. usage, m.; usure; détérioration, f.; **to wear well**, faire bon usage; **worn out**, épuisé, complètement usé.

wearily [wîrili] adv. péniblement. ‖ **weariness** [wîrinis] s. fatigue; lassitude, f.; ennui; dégoût, m. ‖ **wearisome** [wîrisᵉm] adj. fatigant, ennuyeux. ‖ **weary** [wîri] adj. las; ennuyé; fatigué.

weasel [wîz'l] s. belette, f.

weather [wèzhᵉr] s. temps (meteor.), m.; v. résister; doubler [cape]; **changeable weather**, temps variable; **weather bureau**, office météorologique; **weathercock**, girouette; **weather conditions**, conditions atmosphériques.

weave [wîv] v.* tisser; tresser; ourdir; **to weave together**, entrelacer;

to weave into, entremêler à; s. texture, f.; tissage, m.; **weaver**, tisserand.

web [wèb] s. tissu, m.; trame; pièce d'étoffe; toile; membrane; palmure; taie (med.), f.; **spider's web**, toile d'araignée; **web-footed**, palmipède. ‖ **webbing** [-ing] s. sangles; toile à sangle, f.

wed [wèd] v. épouser; (se) marier; pret., p. p. of **to wed**. ‖ **wedded** [-id] adj. marié; conjugal; féru de. ‖ **wedding** [-ing] s. mariage, m.; noce, f.; **silver wedding**, noces d'argent; **wedding ring**, alliance, *Fr. Can.* jonc.

wedge [wèdj] s. coin, m.; cale, f.; v. coincer; caler; **to wedge into**, enfoncer, pénétrer comme un coin.

wedlock [wèdlâk] s. mariage, m.; vie conjugale, f.

Wednesday [wènzdi] s. mercredi, m.

wee [wî] adj. tout petit, minuscule.

weed [wîd] s. mauvaise herbe; herbe folle, f.; v. sarcler; désherber; **to weed out**, arracher, extirper. ‖ **weeds** [wîdz] s. pl. vêtements (m. pl.) de deuil. ‖ **weedy** [-i] adj. envahi par les herbes, en friche; malingre (pop.).

week [wîk] s. semaine, f.; **weekday**, jour ouvrable; jour de semaine; **week-end**, week-end, *Fr. Can.* fin de semaine; **a week from today**, d'aujourd'hui en huit. ‖ **weekly** [-li] adj. hebdomadaire; adv. tous les huit jours.

weep [wîp] v.* pleurer. ‖ **weeping** [-ing] adj. pleureur; s. pleurs, m. pl.

weevil [wîv'l] s. charançon, m.

weigh [wéⁱ] v. peser; avoir du poids; soupeser, estimer, évaluer; **to weigh anchor**, lever l'ancre; **to weigh down**, accabler. ‖ **weight** [-t] s. poids, m.; pesanteur; lourdeur; gravité, importance, f.; v. charger d'un poids; surcharger; **balance weight**, contrepoids; **gross weight**, poids brut; **net weight**, poids net. ‖ **weighty** [-ti] adj. pesant, lourd; grave, important.

welcome [wèlkᵉm] s. bienvenue, f.; adj. bienvenu; v. souhaiter la bienvenue à; faire bon accueil à.

weld [wèld] s. soudure, f.; v. souder.

welfare [wèlfèᵉr] s. bien-être, m.; prospérité, f.

well [wèl] s. source, fontaine, f.; puits; réservoir, m.; v. jaillir, sourdre; **artesian well**, puits artésien; **oil well**, puits de pétrole.

well [wèl] adv. bien; adj. bien portant; en bon état; heureux; avantageux; **I am well**, je vais bien; **to get well**, se rétablir; **as well as**, aussi bien que; **well-being**, bien-être; **well-bred**, bien élevé; **well-meaning**, bien intentionné; **well-nigh**, presque; **well-to-do**, aisé.

Welsh [wèlsh] *adj.*, *s.* gallois, m. [language]; *the Welsh*, les Gallois.

welt [wèlt] *s.* bordūre; trépointe, f.

welter [wèltᵉʳ] *adj.* lourd; *v.* se vautrer; bouillonner; *s.* désordre, m.; *welter-weight*, poids mi-moyen.

went [wènt] *pret. of* to go.

wept [wèpt] *pret.*, *p. p. of* to weep.

were [wĕr, wèᵉʳ] *pret. of* to be.

werewolf [wirwoulf] (*pl.* werewolves [-woulvz]) *s.* loup-garou, m.

west [wèst] *s.* ouest; occident, m.; *adj.* occidental; de l'ouest; *adv.* à l'ouest. ‖ **western** [-ᵉrn] *adj.* occidental; de l'ouest. ‖ **westerner** [-ᵉrnᵉʳ] *s.* habitant de l'ouest, m. ‖ **westward** [-wᵉrd] *adj.* à l'ouest; vers l'ouest. ‖ **westwards** [-wᵉrdz] *adv.* à l'ouest, vers l'ouest.

wet [wèt] *adj.* humide; mouillé; pluvieux; *v.* mouiller; humecter; arroser; imbiber; *wet blanket*, trouble-fête, rabat-joie; *pret.*, *p. p. of* to wet.

wether [wèzhᵉʳ] *s.* mouton, m.

wetness [wètnis] *s.* humidité, f.

whack [wak] *s.* coup bien appliqué, m.; *v.* frapper, cogner.

whale [hwèl] *s.* baleine, f.; *v.* chasser la baleine; *whale-boat*, baleinier; *whale-bone*, baleine.

wharf [hwaurf] *s.* quai; appontement; embarcadère; entrepôt, m.

what [hwàt] *pron.* ce qui, ce que; quoi; que; qu'est-ce que; *adj.* quel, quelle; quels, quelles; *what do you charge for?*, combien prenez-vous pour? ‖ **whatever** [hwàtᵉvᵉʳ] *pron.* tout ce qui, tout ce que; quoi (que ce soit) que; *adv.* quoi que ce soit; *adj.* quel que soit... qui; quelque... que ce soit; quelconque. ‖ **whatsoever** [-soᵘᵉvᵉʳ], *see* whatever.

wheat [hwît] *s.* froment; blé, m.

wheedle [hwid'l] *v.* cajoler; enjôler.

wheel [hwîl] *s.* roue, f.; volant; cercle, m.; *v.* rouler; tourner; faire rouler; pédaler; *to wheel the baby*, promener le bébé dans sa voiture; *wheel chair*, fauteuil roulant; *big wheel*, grosse légume; *front wheel*, roue avant; *rear wheel*, roue arrière; *spare wheel*, roue de rechange. ‖ **wheelbarrow** [-baroᵘ] *s.* brouette, f. ‖ **wheel-house** [-haᵒᵘs] *s.* timonerie, f. ‖ **wheelwright** [-raᶦt] *s.* charron, m.

wheezy [hwîzi] *adj.* asthmatique; poussif.

when [hwèn] *adv.*, *conj.* quand, lorsque; et alors que; où. ‖ **whence** [-s] *adv.* d'où. ‖ **whenever** [-èvᵉʳ] *adv.* toutes les fois que.

where [hwèᵉʳ] *adv.* où; *anywhere*, n'importe où; *elsewhere*, ailleurs; *nowhere*, nulle part. ‖ **whereabouts** [-ᵉbaᵒᵘts] *s.* lieu où l'on se trouve, m. ‖ **whereas** [hwèᵉʳas] *conj.* tandis que; vu que; puisque; attendu que; au lieu que. ‖ **whereby** [-baᶦ] *adv.* par lequel; par où; par quoi. ‖ **wherefore** [hwèᵉʳfoᵘʳ] *adv.* pourquoi; c'est pourquoi. ‖ **wherein** [hwèᵉʳîn] *adv.* en quoi, dans lequel; où [time]. ‖ **whereof** [-âv] *adv.* dont, duquel, de quoi. ‖ **whereupon** [-ᵉpân] *adv.* sur quoi; sur ce; là-dessus; après quoi. ‖ **wherever** [-èvᵉʳ] *adv.* n'importe où; partout où; en quelque lieu que ce soit. ‖ **wherewithal** [hwèᵉʳwizhᵉl] *s.* moyens, m. pl.

whet [hwèt] *v.* aiguiser, affûter; *s.* stimulant, m.

whether [hwèzhᵉʳ] *conj.* si que; soit que; si; *whether... or*, si... ou.

whetstone [hwètstoᵘn] *s.* affiloir, m.

whey [hwé¹] *s.* petit-lait, m.

which [hwitsh] *pron.* qui; que; lequel, laquelle, lesquels, lesquelles; ce qui, ce que; *adj.* quel, quelle, quels, quelles. ‖ **whichever** [-èvᵉʳ] *pron.*, *adj.* n'importe lequel; quelque.. que.

whiff [hwif] *s.* bouffée, f.; *v.* lancer des bouffées.

while [hwaᶦl] *s.* temps, moment, m.; *conj.* pendant que, tandis que; en même temps que; *in a little while*, sous peu; *it is not worth while*, cela n'en vaut pas la peine; *to while away the time*, tuer le temps.

whilst [hwaᶦlst] *conj.*, *see* while.

whim [hwim] *s.* caprice, m.; lubie, f.

whimper [hwimpᵉʳ] *v.* pleurnicher; *s.* pleurnicherie, f.

whimsical [hwimzik'l] *adj.* fantasque, capricieux.

whine [hwaᶦn] *v.* geindre, gémir; *s.* pleurnicherie, f.; gémissement, m. ‖ **whiner** [-ᵉʳ] *s.* pleurnicheur, m.

whip [hwip] *v.* fouetter, fustiger; battre [eggs]; *s.* cravache, f.; fouet; fouettement, m.; *to whip off*, décamper; *whipstock*, manche de fouet. ‖ **whipping** [-ing] *s.* fustigation, flagellation; raclée, f.; surjet [sewing], m.

whir [hwĕʳ] *v.* ronfler; bruisser; *s.* ronflement; bruissement, m.

whirl [hwĕʳl] *v.* faire tourner; tournoyer; pirouetter; *s.* tournoiement; tourbillon, m.; *my head whirls*, la tête me tourne; *whirlpool*, tourbillon d'eau; *whirlwind*, tourbillon, cyclone.

whisk [hwisk] *v.* épousseter; battre [eggs]; se mouvoir rapidement; *s.* mouvement rapide; fouet à œufs, m.; vergette, f.; *to whisk something out of sight*, escamoter quelque chose; *whisk-broom*, balayette.

whisker [hwĭskᵉʳ] *s.* moustache [cat, man], f.; *pl.* favoris, m. pl.

whisk(e)y [hwĭski] *s.*° whisky, m.

whisper [hwĭspᵉʳ] *v.* chuchoter; murmurer; parler bas; *s.* chuchotement; murmure, m.

whistle [hwĭs'l] *v.* siffler; siffloter; *s.* (coup de) sifflet; sifflement, m.

whit [hwĭt] *s.* brin, détail, rien.

white [hwaⁱt] *adj.* blanc; pur; loyal, honorable; *s.* blanc, m.; *whitecaps*, moutons [sea]; *white hot*, chauffé à blanc; *white lead*, blanc de céruse; *white lie*, petit mensonge; *white-livered*, poltron; *white slavery*, traite des blanches; *to show the white feather*, se montrer poltron. ‖ **whiten** [-'n] *v.* blanchir. ‖ **whiteness** [-nĭs] *s.* blancheur; pâleur, f. ‖ **white-wash** [-wâsh] *v.* blanchir à la chaux; badigeonner; couvrir (fig.); réhabiliter; *s.* blanc de chaux, m.

whither [hwĭzhᵉʳ] *adv.* où.

whiting [hwaⁱting] *s.* merlan, m.

whitish [hwaⁱtish] *adj.* blanchâtre.

whitlow [hwĭtloᵒᵘ] *s.* panaris, m.

Whitsuntide [hwĭtsœntaⁱd] *s.* Pentecôte, f.

whittle [hwĭt'l] *v.* amincir; aiguiser; réduire; couper; rogner.

whiz(z) [hwĭz] *v.* siffler [bullet]; *s.*° sifflement, m.

who [hou] *pron.* qui; qui est-ce qui; *he who*, celui qui. ‖ **whoever** [-ĕvᵉʳ] *pron.* quiconque; quel que soit; celui qui.

whole [hoᵒᵘl] *adj.* entier; complet; intégral; tout; sain; *s.* ensemble, m.; totalité; intégralité, f.; *in the whole*, au total; *on the whole*, somme toute, à tout prendre. ‖ **wholesale** [-séⁱl] *s.* vente en gros, f.; commerce de gros, m.; *adj.* en gros; en masse; en série; *v.* vendre en gros. ‖ **wholesome** [-sᵉm] *adj.* sain; salubre; salutaire. ‖ **wholesomeness** [-sᵉnnis] *s.* salubrité, f. ‖ **wholly** [-i] *adv.* entièrement, totalement; tout à fait.

whom [houm] *pron.* que; qui; lequel, laquelle, lesquels, lesquelles; qui est-ce qui. ‖ **whomsoever** [-soᵒᵘĕvᵉʳ] *pron.* quiconque; n'importe qui, que.

whoop [houp] *s.* quinte (med.), f.; cri; ululement, m.; huée, f.; *v.* crier; huer; ululer; *whooping cough*, coqueluche; *Am. to whoop it up*, pousser des cris; *whoopee*, hourra!, you!; *Am.* noce, f.

whopper [wâpᵉʳ] *s.* énormité, f.

whore [hoᵒᵘr] *s.* prostituée, f.

whortleberry [hwëᵘtⁱlbèri] *s.*° myrtille, f.; *Fr. Can.* bleuet, m.

whose [houz] *pron.* dont; de qui, duquel, de laquelle, desquels, desquelles; à qui.

why [hwaⁱ] *adv.* pourquoi; *interj.* eh bien!; voilà!; voyons!; tenez!; ma foi!; vraiment!

wick [wĭk] *s.* mèche, f.

wicked [wĭkid] *adj.* méchant; mauvais. ‖ **wickedness** [-nis] *s.* méchanceté; perversité, f.

wicker [wĭkᵉʳ] *s.* osier, m.

wicket [wĭkit] *s.* guichet, m.; barrière; barres [cricket], f.

wide [waⁱd] *adj.* large; vaste; étendu; ample; *adv.* largement; loin; grandement, bien; *a yard wide*, un mètre de large; *far and wide*, partout; *wide awake*, bien éveillé; *wide open*, grand ouvert. ‖ **widely** [-li] *adv.* amplement, largement; au loin. ‖ **widen** [-'n] *v.* (s')élargir; évaser; étendre; (s')aggraver. ‖ **widespread** [-sprĕd] *adj.* très répandu; général; bien diffusé.

widow [wĭdoᵒᵘ] *s.* veuve, f. ‖ **widower** [-ᵉʳ] *s.* veuf, m. ‖ **widowhood** [-houd] *s.* veuvage, m.

width [wĭdth] *s.* largeur; étendue; ampleur, f.; lé, m.

wield [wîld] *v.* manier; gouverner; exercer [power].

wife [waⁱf] (*pl.* **wives** [waⁱvz]) *s.* épouse, femme, f.

wig [wĭg] *s.* perruque, f.

wiggle [wĭg'l] *v.* se dandiner; *s.* dandinement, m.

wigwag [wĭgwâg] *s. Am.* signaux, m. pl.; *v.* osciller; faire des signaux.

wild [waⁱld] *adj.* sauvage; féroce; farouche; affolé; extravagant; bizarre; impétueux, effréné; *s.* lieu désert, m.; *wildcat*, chat sauvage; *wildcat scheme*, projet extravagant. ‖ **wilderness** [wĭldᵉʳnis] *s.* désert; lieu sauvage, m.; solitude, f. ‖ **wildness** [waⁱldnis] *s.* sauvagerie; férocité; étrangeté, f.

wile [waⁱl] *s.* ruse, astuce, f.

will(l)ful [wĭlfᵉl] *adj.* obstiné; volontaire; délibéré; intentionnel. ‖ **will** [wĭl] *s.* volonté; décision, f.; gré; testament, m.; *v.* vouloir; ordonner; léguer; sert d'auxiliaire à *defect. aux.*: *I will tell you*, je vais vous dire; je vous dirai; *she will knit for hours*, elle a l'habitude de tricoter pendant des heures; *the arena will hold a thousand*, l'arène peut contenir mille personnes; *he willed himself to sleep*, il s'est endormi à force de volonté; *free-will*, libre arbitre. ‖ **willing** [-ing] *adj.* bien disposé; enclin à; prêt à;

he is willing to, il veut bien. || **willingly** [-ingli] *adv.* volontiers; de bon cœur. || **willingness** [-ingnis] *s.* bonne volonté, f.; empressement; consentement, m.

willow [wîlo^{ou}] *s.* saule, m.

willy-nilly [wîli-nîli] *adv.* bon gré mal gré.

wilt [wilt] *v.* se faner; dépérir.

wily [wa¹li] *adj.* rusé, astucieux.

wimple [wîmp'l] *s.* guimpe, f.

win [win] *v.** gagner; acquérir; obtenir; remporter [prize]; parvenir; fléchir; décider; *to win over,* persuader, endoctriner.

wince [wîns] *v.* broncher; défaillir.

winch [wîntsh] *s.** treuil, m.

wind [wînd] *s.* vent; air; souffle, m.; *v.* avoir vent de; essouffler; laisser souffler [horse]; flairer [game]; *to be winded about,* s'ébruiter.

wind [wa¹nd] *v.** tourner; enrouler; dévider; remonter [watch]; serpenter; *s.* détour; lacet, m.

windbag [wîndbag] *s.* baudruche, outre, f.; orateur verbeux, m. || **windfall** [-faul] *s.* bonne aubaine, f. || **winding** [-ing] *s.* sinuosité, f.; méandre; enroulement; remontage [watch], m.; *adj.* sinueux, en spirale; en colimaçon [staircase]. || **windmill** [-mil] *s.* moulin à vent, m.

window [wîndo^{ou}] *s.* fenêtre; vitrine; glace [auto], f.; vitrail, m.; *window display,* étalage; *window-pane,* vitre; *window-sill,* rebord de fenêtre; *Am. window-shade,* store.

windpipe [wîndpa¹p] *s.* trachée-artère, f. || **windshield** [-shîld] *s.* pare-brise, m. || **windy** [-i] *adj.* venteux; verbeux; froussard (pop.).

wine [wa¹n] *s.* vin, m.; *wine and water,* eau rougie; *wine cellar,* cave à vin; *wine glass,* verre à vin; *wine grower,* viticulteur; *wine waiter,* sommelier.

wing [wîng] *s.* aile; escadre aérienne; coulisse (theat.), f.; aileron, m.; *v.* donner des ailes; blesser à l'aile; voler; *to take wing,* prendre son vol; *winged,* ailé; *winglet,* aileron; *wing-spread,* envergure.

wink [wîngk] *v.* cligner de l'œil; clignoter; *s.* clin d'œil; *I didn't sleep a wink,* je n'ai pas fermé l'œil une seconde. || **winker** [-e^r] *s.* clignotant, m. || **winking** [-ing] *s.* clignement, m.; *adj.* clignotant.

winner [wîne^r] *s.* gagnant; vainqueur, m. || **winning** [wîning] *adj.* gagnant; engageant, attrayant; *s. pl.* gains, m. pl.

winnow [wîno^{ou}] *v.* vanner; trier; séparer; battre [air]; *winnowing-machine,* tarare, van.

winsome [wîns^em] *adj.* charmant.

winter [wînte^r] *s.* hiver, m.; *v.* hiverner; *adj.* d'hiver; hivernal; *winter-green,* thé du Canada, *Fr. Can.,* thé des bois. || **wintry** [-tri] *adj.* d'hiver; hivernal; glacial.

wipe [wa¹p] *v.* essuyer; *to wipe off,* effacer; essorer. || **wiper** [-e^r] *s.* torchon; tampon; essuyeur, m.; *Am. windshield wiper,* essuie-glace.

wire [wa¹e^r] *s.* fil de fer; fil métallique; télégramme, m.; dépêche, f.; *v.* attacher avec du fil de fer; télégraphier; poser des fils électriques; *barbed wire,* fil de fer barbelé; *fence wire,* ronce pour clôture; *piano wire,* corde à piano; *telegraph wire,* fil télégraphique; *to pull wires,* pistonner. || **wireless** [-lis] *adj.* sans fil; *s.* radio, T.S.F., f.; *wireless controlled,* radioguidé; *wireless operator,* radiotélégraphiste; *wireless set,* poste de radio. || **wiry** [-ri] *adj.* en fil de fer; sec et nerveux; raide [hair].

wisdom [wizd^em] *s.* sagesse; prudence, f.

wise [wa¹z] *adj.* sage; prudent; discret; sensé; *The Three Wise Men,* les trois rois mages; *to put wise,* donner un tuyau à; *v. Am. to wise up,* se mettre à la page; se dessaler; se détromper.

wise [wa¹z] *s.* façon, manière, f.

wiseacre [wa¹zé¹ke^r] *s.* benêt prétentieux, m. || **wisecrack** [-krak] *s.* plaisanterie, f.; *v.* faire de l'esprit.

wish [wish] *v.* désirer, souhaiter, vouloir; *s.** désir, souhait, vœu, m.; *best wishes,* meilleurs vœux; *I wish I were,* je voudrais être; *wishful,* désireux.

wisp [wisp] *s.* bouchon, tortillon, m. [straw]; ruban, m. [smoke].

wistaria [wistè^eri^e] *s.* glycine, f.

wistful [wistf^el] *adj.* pensif; sérieux; silencieux et attentif.

wit [wit] *s.* esprit, m.; *to live by one's wits,* vivre d'expédients; *to lose one's wits,* perdre la tête; *to wit,* à savoir; *a wit,* un bel esprit.

witch [witsh] *s.** sorcière, f.; *witchcraft,* sorcellerie; *witch hazel,* teinture d'hamamélis; *witching,* séduisant, ensorcelant.

with [wizh, with] *prep.* avec; de; par; à; chez; dans; parmi; *with his hat on,* le chapeau sur la tête; *with a view,* en vue de; *he was with us ten years,* il a été employé chez nous dix ans.

withdraw [wizhdrau] v.* (se) retirer; se replier; rétracter [statement]. ‖ **withdrawal** [-ᵉl] s. retrait; repli; rappel [order], m.; retraite; mainlevée (jur.), f. ‖ **withdrawn** [-n] p. p. of **to withdraw**. ‖ **withdrew** [wizhdrou] pret. of **to withdraw**.

wither [wizhᵉr] v. (se) faner, (se) flétrir; dépérir.

withers [wizhᵉrz] s. pl. garrot, m.

withheld [withhéld] pret., p. p. of **to withhold**. ‖ **withhold** [withhoᵒuld] v. retenir, arrêter; cacher.

within [wizhín] prep. dans; en dedans de; en moins de; adv. à l'intérieur; within the week, dans le courant de la semaine.

without [wizhaᵒut] prep. sans; hors de; en dehors de; adv. à l'extérieur, au-dehors; without my knowledge, à mon insu.

withstand [withstànd] v.* résister à; supporter. ‖ **withstood** [withstoud] pret., p. p. of **to withstand**.

witness [wítnis] s. témoin; déposant; témoignage, m.; v. déposer; témoigner; attester.

witticism [wítᵉsizᵉm] s. trait d'esprit, m.

wittingly [wítingli] adv. sciemment, de propos délibéré.

witty [wíti] adj. spirituel.

wives [waìvz] pl. of **wife**.

wizard [wizᵉrd] s. sorcier, m.

wobble [wàb'l] v. vaciller; tituber; branler; s. vacillement, m.

woe [woᵒu] s. douleur; misère, f.; malheur, m.; **woebegone**, navré.

woke [woᵒuk] pret. of **to wake**.

wolf [woulf] (pl. **wolves** [woulvz]) s. loup, m.; Am. don juan, coureur, m.

wolverine [woulvᵉraᶦn] s. glouton, Fr. Can., carcajou, m.

wolves [woulvz] pl. of **wolf**.

woman [woumᵉn] (pl. **women** [wimᵉn]) s. femme, f. ‖ **womanhood** [-houd] s. féminité, f. ‖ **womanize** [-aᶦz] v. efféminer; courir les jupons. ‖ **womankind** [-kaᶦnd] s. les femmes, f. pl. ‖ **womanly** [-li] adj. de femme; féminin; adv. en femme; de femme.

womb [woum] s. utérus, sein, m.; matrice, f.

women [wimin] pl. of **woman**.

won [wœn] pret., p. p. of **to win**.

wonder [wœndᵉr] s. étonnement; prodige, miracle, m.; surprise; merveille, f.; v. s'étonner (at, de); s'émerveiller; se demander (whether, si). ‖ **wonderful** [-fᵉl] adj. étonnant; prodigieux;

admirable. ‖ **wonderfully** [-fᵉli] adv. merveilleusement; extraordinairement. ‖ **wondrous** [wœndrᵉs] adj. merveilleux.

wont [woᵒunt] s. coutume; habitude, f.; adj. habitué, accoutumé; habituel; to be wont, avoir coutume.

won't = will not, see **will**.

woo [wou] v. courtiser.

wood [woud] s. bois, m.; soft wood, bois blanc; wood engraving, gravure sur bois; **woodcock**, bécasse; **woodcutter**, bûcheron; **wooded**, boisé; **wooden**, de bois, en bois. ‖ **woodland** [lànd] s. pays boisé, m. ‖ **wood(s)man** [-(z)mᵉn] (pl. **woodsmen**) s. homme des bois; trappeur; artisan du bois, m. ‖ **woodpecker** [-pèkᵉr] s. pic, pivert, Fr. Can., pique-bois, m. ‖ **woodwork** [-wᵉrk] s. boiserie; menuiserie; ébénisterie, f. ‖ **woodworker** [-wᵉrkᵉr] s. charpentier; menuisier; ébéniste; ouvrier du bois, m.

woof [wouf] s. trame, f.

wool [woul] s. laine, f.; adj. de laine; en laine. ‖ **wool(l)en** [-in] adj. de laine; en laine; s. lainage, m. ‖ **wool(l)y** [-i] adj. laineux; crépu; mou [style].

word [wᵉrd] s. mot; vocable; avis, m.; parole; nouvelle, f.; v. exprimer; rédiger; libeller; formuler; to have words with, se quereller avec; password, mot de passe. ‖ **wordy** [-i] adj. prolixe; verbeux.

wore [woᵒur] pret. of **to wear**.

work [wᵉrk] s. travail; ouvrage; emploi, m.; œuvre; besogne, f.; pl. usine, f.; mécanisme; mouvement, m.; v.* travailler; accomplir; fonctionner; fermenter; produire; exploiter; manœuvrer; se frayer; résoudre [problem]; to work away, travailler d'arrache-pied; to work out, produire, opérer; calculer; to be all worked up, être surexcité; workday, jour ouvrable. ‖ **worker** [-ᵉr] s. travailleur; ouvrier, m. ‖ **working** [-ing] s. travail, fonctionnement; tirage, m.; opération; manœuvre, f.; adj. travailleur; laborieux; working hours, heures de travail. ‖ **workingman** [-ingmᵉn], **workman** [-mᵉn] (pl. **workingmen**, **workmen**) s. ouvrier; travailleur; artisan, m. ‖ **workmanship** [-mᵉnship] s. ouvrage, m.; exécution du travail, f. ‖ **workshop** [-shàp] s. atelier, m.

world [wᵉrld] s. monde; univers, m.; a world of, une infinité de; for the world, pour tout au monde; World War, Grande Guerre, guerre mondiale. ‖ **worldly** [-li] adj. du monde; mondain; terrestre.

worm [wᵉrm] s. ver; serpentin [still]; tire-bourre (mech.), m.; vis sans fin, f.; v. se tortiller; se faufiler; ramper;

soutirer [secret]; *to worm oneself into,* s'insinuer dans; *worm-eaten,* vermoulu.

wormwood [wë*r*mwood] *s.* absinthe; amertume, f. (fig.).

worn [wo°*u*rn] *p. p. of to wear; worn out,* usé; éreinté.

worry [wë*r*i] *s.** tourment; tracas; ennui, m.; inquiétude, f.; *v.* ennuyer; importuner; (s')inquiéter; (se) tourmenter.

worse [wë*r*s] *adj.* pire; plus mauvais; *adv.* pis, plus mal; *worse and worse,* de mal en pis; *so much the worse,* tant pis; *he is none the worse for it,* il ne s'en trouve pas plus mal; *to change for the worse,* empirer, s'aggraver.

worship [wë*r*ship] *s.* culte; respect, m.; adoration; vénération, f.; *v.* adorer; rendre un culte à. ‖ **worship(p)er** [-er] *s.* adorateur, m.; adoratrice, f.

worst [wë*r*st] *adj.* le pire; le plus; le plus mauvais; *adv.* le pis; le plus mal; *v.* battre, vaincre, défaire; *to get the worst of it,* avoir le dessous.

worth [wë*r*th] *s.* valeur, f.; mérite; prix, m.; *adj.* valant; *to be worth,* valoir; *to have one's money's worth,* en avoir pour son argent. ‖ **worthless** [-lis] *adj.* sans valeur; sans mérite; inutile; indigne. ‖ **worthy** [wë*r*zhi] *adj.* digne; méritant; de valeur; estimable, honorable; bien fondé; *s.* sommité, célébrité, f.; grand homme, m.

would [woud] *pret. of will; she would come every day,* elle venait tous les jours (elle avait l'habitude de venir); *if you would do it,* si vous vouliez le faire; *she said she would go,* elle a dit qu'elle irait; *would-be,* soi-disant; prétendu.

wound [wound] *s.* blessure; plaie, f.; *v.* blesser.

wound [wa°*u*nd] *pret., p. p. of to wind.*

wove [wo°*u*v] *pret. of to weave.* ‖ **woven** [-°n] *p. p. of to weave.*

wrangle [ràng'l] *v.* se quereller; *s.* dispute, querelle, f.

wrap [rap] *v.* enrouler; rouler; envelopper; absorber (fig.); *s.* écharpe, f.; châle; manteau, m. ‖ **wrapper** [-er] *s.* emballeur; empaqueteur; couvre-livre, m.; toile d'emballage; robe de chambre; bande de journal, f. ‖ **wrapping** [-ing] *s.* emballage, m.; **wrapping-paper,** papier d'emballage.

wrath [rath] *s.* colère, f.; courroux, m.; **wrathful,** furieux.

wreath [rîth] *s.* guirlande; couronne, f.; *wreath of smoke,* tourbillon de fumée. ‖ **wreathe** [rîzh] *v.* tresser, entrelacer; enrouler; couronner (*with,* de).

wreck [rèk] *s.* naufrage; sinistre; accident; bris (naut.), m.; épave (naut.); ruine, f.; *v.* faire naufrager, couler; saborder; détruire; faire dérailler (railw.).

wren [rèn] *s.* roitelet, m. (zool.).

wrench [rèntsh] *s.** torsion; foulure, entorse; clef (mech.), f.; *v.* tordre; arracher; (se) fouler; *screw-wrench,* tournevis; *adjustable screw-wrench,* clef universelle.

wrest [rèst] *v.* arracher en tordant; tirer de force; forcer [text]. ‖ **wrestle** [rès'l] *v.* lutter; combattre (*with,* avec; *against,* contre); *s.* assaut de lutte, m.; **wrestler,** lutteur; **wrestling,** lutte.

wretch [rètsh] *s.** misérable; malheureux; scélérat, m.; *poor wretch,* pauvre diable. ‖ **wretched** [-id] *adj.* misérable; infortuné; piètre; méchant, méprisable.

wriggle [rig'l] *v.* se tortiller, frétiller; se faufiler (*into,* dans); s'insinuer (*in,* dans); *to wriggle out of a difficulty,* se tirer adroitement d'embarras.

wring [ring] *v.** tordre; arracher; presser, serrer; essorer; déchirer [heart]; extorquer [money]; forcer (fig.).

wrinkle [ringk'l] *s.* ride; rugosité du terrain, f.; faux pli [cloth], m.; *v.* rider; froisser; faire des faux plis.

wrist [rist] *s.* poignet, m.; **wrist-pin,** axe de piston; **wrist-watch,** montre-bracelet.

writ [rit] *s.* exploit, mandat, m.; assignation; ordonnance (jur.), f.; *Holy Writ,* l'Ecriture sainte. ‖ **write** [ra*i*t] *v.** écrire; tracer; *to write down,* coucher par écrit; *to write out,* transcrire; mettre au net; *to write up,* décrire; inscrire; *how is this word written?,* comment s'écrit ce mot? ‖ **writer** [-er] *s.* écrivain; auteur, m.

writhe [ra*i*zh] *s.* se tordre.

writing [ra*i*ting] *s.* écriture, f.; art d'écrire, m.; *pl.* écrits, m. pl.; *in writing,* par écrit; **writing-desk,** bureau, pupitre; **writing-paper,** papier à lettres. ‖ **written** [rit'n] *p. p. of to write.*

wrong [raung] *adj.* faux; erroné; mauvais; illégitime; qui a tort; *s.* mal; tort; préjudice; dommage, m.; injustice, f.; *adv.* mal; à tort; *v.* faire du tort; léser; *to be wrong,* avoir tort; se tromper; *my watch is wrong,* ma montre ne va pas; *the wrong side of a fabric,* l'envers d'un tissu; *he took the wrong train,* il s'est trompé de train; *to do wrong,* mal agir; *to do a wrong,* faire du tort; *wrong-doer,* méchant; délinquant; *wrong-doing,* iniquité; *wrongful,* injuste, injustifié; dommageable; illégal.

wrote [roᵒut] *pret. of* **to write**.

wrought [raut] *pret.*, *p. p. of* **to work**; *adj.* travaillé, façonné; **wrought iron**, fer forgé.

wrung [rœng] *pret.*, *p. p. of* **to wring**.

wry [ra¹] *adj.* tordu; de travers; *to make a wry face*, faire la grimace; **wryneck**, torticolis.

X - Y

X-ray [èks-ré¹] *s.* rayon X, m.; *v.* radiographier; **X-ray examination**, examen radioscopique; **X-ray photograph**, radiographie; **X-ray treatment**, radiothérapie.

xenophobia [zènᵉfoᵒubiᵉ] *s.* xénophobie, f.

xylography [za¹lᵉgrafi] *s.* xylographie, f.

xylophone [za¹lᵉfoᵒun] *s.* xylophone, m.

yacht [yât] *s.* yacht, m.; *v.* naviguer en yacht.

yam [yam] *s.* igname; *Am.* patate, f.

Yankee [yàngki] *adj.*, *s.* yankee.

yap [yap] *v.* japper; glapir; rouspéter; *s.* jappement, m.; rouspétance, f.

yard [yârd] *s.* yard [measure]; vergue (naut.), f.

yard [yârd] *s.* cour, f.; préau; chantier; dépôt, m.; **back yard**, arrière-cour; **churchyard**, cimetière; **classification yard**, gare de triage; **navy yard**, arsenal; **poultry yard**, basse-cour. ‖ **yardstick** [-stik] *s.* unité de mesure; aune, f.

yarn [yârn] *s.* fil [thread]; récit, m.; histoire, f.

yaw [yau] *s.* embardée (naut.), f.; *v.* embarder (naut.); gouverner (aviat.).

yawn [yaun] *s.* bâillement, m.; *v.* bâiller.

yea [yé¹] *adv.* oui.

year [yiᵉr] *s.* année, f.; an, m.; *he is six years old*, il a six ans; *by the year*, à l'année; *twice a year*, deux fois l'an; *New Year's Day*, jour de l'an; **half-year**, semestre; **leap year**, année bissextile; **year book**, annuaire; **yearling**, animal d'un an. ‖ **yearly** [-li] *adj.* annuel; *adv.* annuellement.

yearn [yᵉrn] *v.* désirer; soupirer (*for*, après). ‖ **yearning** [-ing] *s.* désir, m.; aspiration, f.

yeast [yîst] *s.* levure, f.; ferment, m.

yell [yèl] *v.* hurler; vociférer; *s.* hurlement, m.; vocifération, f.

yellow [yèloᵒu] *adj.*, *s.* jaune; **yellowish**, jaunâtre; **yellowness**, couleur jaune.

yelp [yèlp] *v.* japper; glapir; *s.* jappement, glapissement, m.

yeoman [yoᵒumᵉn] (*pl.* **yeomen**) *s.* petit propriétaire; *Br.* magasinier, *Am.* commis aux écritures (naut.), m.

yes [yès] *adv.* oui; si [after a negative].

yesterday [yèstᵉrdi] *adv.*, *s.* hier; *the day before yesterday*, avant-hier.

yet [yèt] *conj.* cependant; pourtant; néanmoins; toutefois; tout de même; *adv.* encore; toujours; déjà; malgré tout; jusqu'à maintenant; *as yet*, jusqu'ici; *not yet*, pas encore.

yield [yîld] *v.* céder; livrer; rendre; rapporter, produire; se soumettre; *s.* rendement; rapport; débit; produit; fléchissement, m.; récolte, f.; *to yield five per cent*, rapporter cinq pour cent; **yield capacity**, productivité; **yield point**, limite de résistance (mech.); **yielding**, doux; flexible; complaisant; accommodant.

yodel [yoᵒud'l] *v.* yodler, iouler; *s.* ioulement, m.; tyrolienne, f.

yoga [yoᵒugᵉ] *s.* yoga, m.; **yogi**, yogi.

yoke [yoᵒuk] *s.* joug, m.; *v.* atteler; enjuguer; **yoke-elm**, charme [tree].

yolk [yoᵒuk] *s.* jaune d'œuf, m.

yolk [yoᵒuk] *s.* suint, m.

yonder [yândᵉr] *adv.* là-bas.

yore [yoᵒur] *adv.* autrefois; *in days of yore*, au temps jadis.

you [you] *pron.* vous; *you never can tell*, on ne sait jamais.

young [yœng] *adj.* jeune; *s.* petit d'animal, m.; *to grow young again*, rajeunir; *young people*, la jeunesse; **youngster** [-stᵉr] *s.* gamin, mioche, gosse; jeune homme, blanc-bec, m.

your [your] *adj.* votre; vos; à vous. ‖ **yours** [-z] *pron.* le vôtre; la vôtre; les vôtres; à vous. ‖ **yourself** [yoursèlf] *pron.* vous-même; vous.

youth [youth] *s.* jeunesse; adolescence, f.; jeune homme, m. ‖ **youthful** [-foul] *adj.* jeune; juvénile. ‖ **youthfulness** [-foulnis] *s.* jeunesse, f.

yowl [yaᵒul] *v.* hurler; *s.* hurlement, m.

Yugoslav [yoûgoᵒuslâv] *adj.*, *s.* yougoslave, m.; **Yugoslavia**, Yougoslavie.

Yuletide [youlta¹d] *s.* fête de Noël, f.; temps de Noël, m.; **Yulelog**, bûche de Noël.

Z

zeal [zīl] *s.* zèle; enthousiasme, m.; ardeur, f. ‖ **zealot** [zèl^et] *s.* zélateur; fanatique, m. ‖ **zealotry** [zèl^etri] *s.* fanatisme, m. ‖ **zealous** [zèl^es] *adj.* zélé; ardent; enthousiaste; dévoué.

zebra [zībr^e] *s.* zèbre, m.

zebu [zībyou] *s.* zébu, m.

zenith [zīnith] *s.* zénith, m.

zephyr [zèf^er] *s.* zéphir, m.

zero [ziro^{ou}] *s.* zéro, m.; **zero hour,** heure H.

zest [zèst] *s.* saveur; verve, f.; piquant, m.

zigzag [zigzag] *s.* zigzag; lacet, m.; *v.* zigzaguer.

zinc [zìngk] *s.* zinc, m.

Zion [za¹en] *s.* Sion, f.; **Zionism,** sionisme; **Zionist,** sioniste.

zip [zip] *v.* aller à toute vitesse, brûler le pavé.

zip [zip] *s.* fermeture à crémaillère, f.; *Am.* allant, brio, m.; *v.* fermer avec une fermeture à crémaillère; **zip-fastener,** fermeture à crémaillère.

zipper [zip^er] *s.* fermeture à crémaillère, f.

zither [zith^er] *s.* cithare, f.

zodiac [zo^{ou}diak] *s.* zodiaque, m. ‖ **zodiacal** [zo^{ou}da¹ek'l] *adj.* zodiacal.

zona [zo^{ou}n^e] *s.* zona, m.

zone [zo^{ou}n] *s.* zone, f.; *v.* répartir en zones; *danger zone,* zone dangereuse; *prohibited zone,* zone interdite.

zoo [zou] *s.* zoo, jardin zoologique, m. ‖ **zoological** [zo^{ou}eLÂdjik'l] *adj.* zoologique. ‖ **zoology** [zo^{ou}âl^edji] *s.* zoologie, f.

zoom [zoum] *v.* monter en chandelle (aviat.); bourdonner, vrombir.

zyme [za¹m] *s.* enzyme, f.

founded in 1852.

THE LIBRAIRIE LAROUSSE

was established more than a century ago by Pierre Larousse and Augustin Boyer. The aim of the two associates was "to teach everything to everybody." In a short time the name of Larousse attained great fame, thanks especially to its encyclopedic dictionaries which put all human knowledge within the reach of the general public. Today the Librairie Larousse is among the leading publishing houses of the world and Larousse has become synonymous with dictionary for all Frenchmen and French-speaking people. There is no book in France more widely known and used than the *Nouveau Petit Larousse* in one volume. There is no book more important than the *Grand Larousse encyclopédique* in eleven large volumes, the equivalent of a 600-book library. Between these two famous works, a variety of other dictionaries are to be found, in one or several volumes, many of them specialized, as well as a whole series of bilingual dictionaries. The Librairie Larousse is well known also for its *Mementos* (Encyclopedias), *Quarto Collection, Grammars, "Nouveaux Classiques Larousse,"* etc.

For information about other Larousse publications:
LIBRAIRIE LAROUSSE U.S.A., 572 Fifth Avenue, NEW YORK; LES ÉDITIONS FRANÇAISES INC., 192, rue Dorchester, case postale 3459, St.-Roch, QUÉBEC 2, Canada; or: LIBRAIRIE LAROUSSE, 17, rue du Montparnasse, PARIS-6e.

● *THE* NOUVEAU PETIT LAROUSSE

is the only book in the world that can be used several times a day, for a lifetime, not only by Frenchmen but by everyone who has the advantage of knowing French. By its constant re-editions and revisions it assures the reader of the most modern and accurate definitions in existence.

● *THE* NOUVEAU PETIT LAROUSSE

is divided in two parts. The first covers over 50,000 French words, from A to Z, with pronunciations, spelling and definitions. The second section, from A to Z, deals with the arts, history, geography, science, etc. It has up-to-date maps of every country in the world. The whole 3-inch dictionary itself contains 70,500 entries, 1,800 pages, 5,535 illustrations in black and white, 56 color plates (of which 26 are maps), and a 8-page, 4-color atlas. The same dictionary is also available in a de luxe edition, with every page illustrated in full color, entitled NOUVEAU PETIT LAROUSSE EN COULEURS.

● *THE* NOUVEAU PETIT LAROUSSE

is edited by a group of scholars whose experience and knowledge make it today the last and authoritative word on the subject. It is one of the basic books in every public and private library. Not to have one is to be behind the times.